A New
& Other Great Features
from Frommer's!

In our continuing effort to publish the savviest, most up-to-date, and most appealing travel guides available, we've added some great new features.

Frommer's guides now include a new **star-rating system.** Every hotel, restaurant, and attraction is rated from 0 to 3 stars to help you set priorities and organize your time.

We've also added **seven brand-new features** that point you to the great deals, in-the-know advice, and unique experiences that separate travelers from tourists. Throughout the guide, look for:

Finds   Special finds—those places only insiders know about

Fun Fact Fun facts—details that make travelers more informed and their trips more fun

Kids   Best bets for kids—advice for the whole family

Moments   Special moments—those experiences that memories are made of

Overrated Places or experiences not worth your time or money

Tips   Insider tips—some great ways to save time and money

Value   Great values—where to get the best deals

We've also added a **"What's New"** section in every guide—a timely crash course in what's hot and what's not in every destination we cover.

Here's what the critics say about Frommer's:

"Amazingly easy to use. Very portable, very complete."
—Booklist

"Detailed, accurate, and easy-to-read information for all price ranges."
—Glamour Magazine

"Hotel information is close to encyclopedic."
—Des Moines Sunday Register

"Frommer's Guides have a way of giving you a real feel for a place."
—Knight Ridder Newspapers

Other Great Guides for Your Trip:

Frommer's Florida
Frommer's South Florida
Frommer's Portable Tampa Bay
Frommer's Walt Disney World® & Orlando
Frommer's Caribbean Cruises & Ports of Call
Frommer's Caribbean Ports of Call
The Unofficial Guide to Miami & the Keys
The Unofficial Guide to Walt Disney World®
Walt Disney World® For Dummies
Florida For Dummies

Frommer's

Florida
from $70 a Day

4th Edition

by Bill Goodwin, Lesley Abravanel
& Jim and Cynthia Tunstall

Wiley Publishing, Inc.

Published by:

Wiley Publishing, Inc.
909 Third Ave.
New York, NY 10022

Copyright © 2002 Wiley Publishing, Inc., New York, New York. All rights reserved. No part of this publication may be reproduced, stored in a retrieval system or transmitted in any form or by any means, electronic, mechanical, photocopying, recording, scanning or otherwise, except as permitted under Sections 107 or 108 of the 1976 United States Copyright Act, without either the prior written permission of the Publisher, or authorization through payment of the appropriate per-copy fee to the Copyright Clearance Center, 222 Rosewood Drive, Danvers, MA 01923, (978) 750-8400, fax (978) 750-4744. Requests to the Publisher for permission should be addressed to the Legal Department, Wiley Publishing, Inc., 10475 Crosspoint Blvd., Indianapolis, IN 46256, (317) 572-3447, fax (317) 572-4447, E-Mail: permcoordinator@wiley.com.

Wiley and the Wiley Publishing logo are trademarks or registered trademarks of Wiley Publishing, Inc. in the United States and other countries and may not be used without written permission. Frommer's is a trademark or registered trademark of Arthur Frommer. Used under license. All other trademarks are the property of their respective owners. Wiley Publishing, Inc. is not associated with any product or vendor mentioned in this book.

ISBN 0-7645-6663-6
ISSN 1092-5201

Editor: Kimberly Perdue
Production Editor: Ian Skinnari
Cartographer: John Decamillis
Photo Editor: Richard Fox
Production by Wiley Indianapolis Composition Services

For information on our other products and services or to obtain technical support, please contact our Customer Care Department within the U.S. at 800-762-2974, outside the U.S. at 317-572-3993 or fax 317-572-4002.

Wiley also publishes its books in a variety of electronic formats. Some content that appears in print may not be available in electronic formats.

Manufactured in the United States of America

5 4 3 2 1

Contents

List of Maps ix

What's New in Florida 1

1 The Best of Florida from $70 a Day 4

1 The Best Beaches 4
2 The Best Destinations for Low-Cost Vacations 6
3 The Best Experiences You Can Have for Free (or Almost) 7
4 The Best Adventure Trips 11
5 The Best Family Attractions 12
6 The Best Golf Courses with Greens Fees That Won't Break Your Budget 15
7 The Best of Natural Florida 17
8 The Best Affordable Accommodations 18
9 The Best Family Accommodations for Parents Who Don't Want to Blow the Kids' College Fund . . .22
10 The Best Places to Stay on a Shoestring 23
11 The Best Camping 25
12 The Best Affordable Restaurants 26
13 The Best Seafood Restaurants 29
14 The Best Deals for Serious Shoppers 31
15 The Best Bars & Nightspots 33

2 Planning an Affordable Trip to Florida 36

1 50 Money-Saving Tips 36
2 The Regions in Brief 44
3 Visitor Information 46
4 Money 47
5 When to Go 47
  Florida Calendar of Events 48
  The Boys of Spring 53
6 Insurance & Health 56
7 Tips for Travelers with Special Needs 58
8 Getting There 61
  What You Can Carry On— And What You Can't 63
  Travel Planning & Booking Sites 64
  All About E-Ticketing 65
9 Package & Escorted Tours 67
10 Getting Around 69
11 The Active Vacation Planner 70
12 Tips on Accommodations 76
  Fast Facts: Florida 79

3 For International Visitors 80

1 Preparing for Your Trip 80
2 Getting to the U.S. 85
3 Getting Around the U.S. 86
  Fast Facts: For the International Traveler 87

4 Miami 91

1. Orientation 91
   The Neighborhoods in Brief 94
2. Getting Around 97
   Fast Facts: Miami 100
3. Accommodations You Can Afford 102
4. Great Deals on Dining 119
   Cuban Coffee 132
   From Ceviche to Picadillo: Latin Cuisine at a Glance 135
5. Hitting the Beach 141
   Cheap Thrills: What to See & Do for Free (or Almost) in Miami 144
6. The Art Deco District 147
7. Miami Art & Museums 148
   Drive-by Art 150
8. Nature Preserves, Parks & Gardens 153
9. Animal Parks 155
10. Especially for Kids 157
11. Sightseeing Cruises & Organized Tours 157
12. Affordable Outdoor Pursuits ...160
    A Berry Good Time 161
13. Spectator Sports 164
14. A Bargain-Hunter's Shopping Guide 166
15. Affordable Fun After Dark 172
    Ground Rules: Stepping Out in Miami 174
    The Rhythm Is Gonna Get You 176

5 The Keys 186

1. The Upper & Middle Keys: Key Largo to Marathon 189
   Cheap Thrills: What to See & Do for Free (or Almost) in the Keys 192
2. The Lower Keys: Big Pine Key to Coppitt Key 204
3. Key West 210
   Going, Going, Gone: Where to Catch the Famous Key West Sunset 215
   Literary Key West 218

6 The Everglades & Biscayne National Park 231

1. Everglades National Park 231
   Florida's "Filet Mignon of the Ocean" 246
2. Biscayne National Park 248

7 The Gold Coast: Hallandale to the Palm Beaches 252

1. Broward County: Hallandale & Hollywood to Fort Lauderdale 253
   One if by Land Taxi if by Sea 259
   Where the Boys Are: Gay Fort Lauderdale 272
2. Boca Raton & Delray Beach ...272
3. Palm Beach & West Palm Beach 281
   The Sport of Kings 283
   Unreal Estate 286
4. Jupiter & Northern Palm Beach County 295
   Turtle-Watching in North Palm Beach 297

CONTENTS vii

8 The Treasure Coast: Stuart to Sebastian — 302

1 Stuart & Jensen Beach 304
  Wildlife Exploration: From Gators to Manatees to Turtles 306
2 Port St. Lucie & Fort Pierce 311
3 Vero Beach & Sebastian 316
4 A Side Trip Inland: Fishing at Lake Okeechobee 323
  Going After the Big One 325

9 Southwest Florida — 326

1 Fort Myers 328
  "Buggy" Rides Through a Mysterious Swamp 332
  Cheap Thrills: What to See & Do for Free (or Almost) in Southwest Florida 334
2 Fort Myers Beach 339
3 Sanibel & Captiva Islands 347
  Fishing with the Bushes in Boca Grande 364
4 Naples 366
5 Marco Island 379

10 The Tampa Bay Area — 384

1 Tampa 385
  How to See Busch Gardens ... 393
  Cheap Thrills: What to See & Do for Free (or Almost) in the Tampa Bay Area 394
2 St. Petersburg 409
  The Crystal River Area: Mermaids & Manatees 414
3 St. Pete & Clearwater Beaches 419
  The Sponge Capital of the World 433
4 Sarasota & Bradenton 434

11 Walt Disney World & Orlando — 456

1 Orientation 458
  Neighborhoods in Brief 461
  Fast Facts: Walt Disney World & Orlando 463
2 Accommodations You Can Afford, In & Around the Parks 465
  Enjoying the Parks Without Getting Fleeced 471
  So You Didn't Book a Room ... 476
3 Great Deals on Dining, In & Around the Parks 478
4 Tips for Visiting Walt Disney World Attractions 490
  Passes & Coupons That Save Your Orlan-Dough 492
5 The Magic Kingdom 493
  FASTPASS 493
6 Epcot 498
7 Disney–MGM Studios 502
8 Animal Kingdom 505
9 Other Walt Disney World Attractions 508
  Water Park Dos & Don'ts 509
  DisneyQuest 511
10 Universal Orlando 512
  Universal Cuisine 516
  Some Practical Advice for Island Adventurers 517
  Dining at Islands of Adventure 520

11 SeaWorld 522
12 Other Area Attractions 525
*Hot Links: Orlando's
Top Golf Courses* 530
13 Outdoor Activities
& Spectator Sports 530
14 Shopping 532
15 Walt Disney World
& Orlando After Dark 532

12 Northeast Florida   539

1 Cocoa Beach, Cape
Canaveral & the
Kennedy Space Center 539
*Cheap Thrills: What to See
& Do for Free (or Almost)
in Northeast Florida* 548
2 Daytona Beach 550
3 St. Augustine: America's
First City 564
Where Golf Is King 573
4 Jacksonville 581
5 Amelia Island 594

13 Northwest Florida: The Panhandle   602

1 Pensacola 604
Florida's Canoe Capital 607
Pensacola's Other Fort 611
2 Destin & Fort
Walton Beach 618
*Cheap Thrills: What to See
& Do for Free (or Almost)
in Northwest Florida* 622
3 Panama City Beach 636
4 Apalachicola 646
5 Tallahassee 651

Appendix: Useful Toll-Free Numbers & Websites   666

Index   669

List of Maps

Florida 38
Miami at a Glance 93
South Beach Accommodations & Dining 103
Miami Beach Accommodations & Dining 111
Key Biscayne, Downtown Miami, Coconut Grove & Coral Gables 115
Miami Attractions & Beaches 142
Attractions in Southern Miami-Dade County 147
The Florida Keys 187
Key West 211
Everglades & Biscayne National Parks 232
Broward County Attractions & Accommodations 255
Attractions from Boca Raton to Jupiter 273
The Treasure Coast 305
Southwest Florida 327
Fort Myers 329
Fort Myers Beach 341
Sanibel & Captiva Islands 349
Naples 367
Tampa & St. Petersburg 386
Tampa Attractions 390
Tampa Accommodations & Dining 402
Downtown St. Petersburg 411
St. Pete & Clearwater Beaches 421
Sarasota & Bradenton 435
Orlando/Walt Disney World Area 457
Walt Disney World 466
Universal Orlando 513
Northeast Florida 541
Cape Canaveral 543
Daytona Beach 551
St. Augustine 565
Jacksonville 583
Amelia Island 595
The Panhandle 603
Pensacola 605
Downtown Tallahassee 653

About the Authors

Bill Goodwin began his career as an award-winning newspaper reporter before becoming legal counsel and speechwriter for two U.S. senators. He is also the author of *Frommer's South Pacific* and *Frommer's Virginia*.

Lesley Abravanel is a freelance journalist and a graduate of the University of Miami School of Communication. When she isn't combing South Florida for the latest hotels, restaurants, and attractions, she is on the lookout for vacationing celebrities, about whom she writes in her weekly nightlife and gossip column, "Velvet Underground," for both the *Miami Herald* and its weekly entertainment newspaper, *Street*. She is a contributor to *Star Magazine* and the Miami correspondent for *Black Book Magazine* and is the author of *Frommer's South Florida*.

Jim and Cynthia Tunstall have been waiting impatiently in Walt Disney World lines since the Magic Kingdom's opening bell in 1971. In the 3 decades since, they've sampled just about every element of a great Orlando vacation. Those experiences are the credentials that allow these Florida insiders to separate the good from the bad and the ugly. Based close to the Disney epicenter, they have written three other Orlando-related books, including *Walt Disney World® For Dummies*.

An Invitation to the Reader

In researching this book, we discovered many wonderful places—hotels, restaurants, shops, and more. We're sure you'll find others. Please tell us about them, so we can share the information with your fellow travelers in upcoming editions. If you were disappointed with a recommendation, we'd love to know that, too. Please write to:

Frommer's Florida from $70 a Day, 4th Edition
Wiley Publishing, Inc. • 909 Third Ave. • New York, NY 10022

An Additional Note

Please be advised that travel information is subject to change at any time—and this is especially true of prices. We therefore suggest that you write or call ahead for confirmation when making your travel plans. The authors, editors, and publisher cannot be held responsible for the experiences of readers while traveling. Your safety is important to us, however, so we encourage you to stay alert and be aware of your surroundings. Keep a close eye on cameras, purses, and wallets, all favorite targets of thieves and pickpockets.

New! Frommer's Star Ratings & Icons

Every hotel, restaurant, and attraction listing in this guide has been ranked for quality, value, service, amenities, and special features using a star-rating scale. In country, state, and regional guides, we also rate towns and regions to help you narrow down your choices and budget your time accordingly. Hotels and restaurants are rated on a scale of zero (recommended) to two stars (very highly recommended); exceptional "worth a splurge" options may get three stars. Attractions, towns, and regions are rated according to the following scale: zero stars (recommended), one star (highly recommended), two stars (very highly recommended), and three stars (must-see).

In addition to the rating system, we also use seven icons to highlight insider information, useful tips, special bargains, hidden gems, memorable experiences, kid-friendly venues, places to avoid, and other useful information:

Finds   *Fun Fact*   *Kids*   *Moments*   *Overrated*   *Tips*   *Value*

The following abbreviations are used for credit cards:
- AE   American Express
- DISC   Discover
- DC   Diners Club
- MC   MasterCard
- V   Visa

FROMMERS.COM

Now that you have the guidebook to a great trip, visit our website at **www.frommers.com** for travel information on nearly 2,500 destinations. With features updated regularly, we give you instant access to the most current trip-planning information available. At Frommers.com, you'll also find the best prices on airfares, accommodations, and car rentals—and you can even book travel online through our travel booking partners. At Frommers.com, you'll also find the following:

- Online updates to our most popular guidebooks
- Vacation sweepstakes and contest giveaways
- Newsletter highlighting the hottest travel trends
- Online travel message boards with featured travel discussions

What's New in Florida

PLANNING YOUR TRIP TO FLORIDA Like most destinations, Florida saw its number of visitors plummet after the terrorist attacks on September 11, 2001. The industry has rebounded significantly, however, thanks in part to special discounts offered by **Visit Florida,** the state's official tourist information organization, on its website, www.flausa.com. You also can call ✆ **888/5-FLA-USA.**

Florida's state parks now have their own website at www.floridastateparks.org and a central camping reservations service (✆ **800/326-3521;** www.reserveamerica.com).

The no-frills carrier **AirTran** has discontinued service to Fort Walton Beach but is now flying to Pensacola and Tallahassee in northwest Florida.

Baseball **spring-training** fans should note that the Montreal Expos and Minnesota Twins may be disbanded before the start of the 2003 season.

MIAMI For complete information on Miami, see chapter 4.

Dining Proving its affection for things in the raw, Miami boasts a hot new sushi option. **Nobu,** a New York sushi import, opened (with Madonna's presence) at Shore Club (✆ **305/695-3100**). A slew of trendy restaurant/lounge combos has also opened. **Rumi** (✆ **305/672-4353**) serves haute cuisine in the early hours before giving way to the A-list scenesters.

Attractions About to open as a museum dedicated to Cuban Americans is downtown Miami's **Freedom Tower** (✆ **305/592-7768**), an old Spanish-style building purchased by the Cuban American National Foundation. Work still continues on the **Miami Beach Cultural Park** in South Beach, which includes the new Arquitectonica–design home of the **Miami City Ballet,** the **Miami Beach Regional Library,** the **Bass Museum of Art,** and a sculpture garden. The Bass (✆ **305/673-7530**) has expanded and received a dramatically new look by world-renowned Japanese architect Arata Isozaki. **The Vizcaya Museum & Gardens** has a new permanent orchid display garden.

After Dark Over the causeway from South Beach, a burgeoning nocturnal buzz is emanating from the once desolate area of **downtown Miami,** off Biscayne Boulevard, thanks to cheaper rents and 24-hour liquor licenses. Among them, the former South Beach hot spot, The Living Room, has opened on NE 11th Street as **The Living Room Downtown.** An old hot spot, **Liquid** (✆ **305/531-9411**), has reopened under different ownership in a space formerly known as Shadow Lounge. The cavernous **Billboard Live** music and dance club debuted, featuring several bars, restaurants, and a recording studio.

THE GOLD COAST For complete information on this region, see chapter 7.

Accommodations West Palm Beach gets hip to the idea of the boutique hotel with **Hotel Biba** (✆ **561/832-0094**), a very mod revamped motel turned hipster hangout.

WHAT'S NEW

Dining Boca Raton's new American restaurant **Zemi** (© 561/391-7177) is drawing rave reviews for its chili-crusted shrimp. For the West Palm Beach wine and cheese set, the Hotel Biba's **Biba Bar** (© 561/832-0094) serves sleek portions of cheese and various *charcuterie* (cold cuts of meat).

Shopping Fort Lauderdale's **Beach Place** (17 S. Fort Lauderdale Beach Blvd.) is receiving a face-lift, transforming itself from a Spring Break hangout into something more upscale.

SOUTHWEST FLORIDA For complete information on this region, see chapter 9.

Fort Myers Formerly a branch of Shooters Waterfront Cafe USA, the popular riverside restaurant at the Holiday Inn Riverwalk & Marina is now the **Seahorse Restaurant** (© 239/334-2727), with improved food and a curfew on its once boisterous weekend parties.

Sanibel & Captiva Islands The **Hungry Heron** (© 239/395-2300), Sanibel's best family restaurant, is now serving its popular weekend breakfast buffets year-round.

Marco Island The inexpensive **Kahuna Restaurant** (© 239/394-4300) is now serving breakfast during the busy winter months.

THE TAMPA BAY AREA For complete information on this region, see chapter 10.

Tampa Despite the drop in tourism after the September 11, 2001 terrorist attacks, both **Busch Gardens Tampa Bay** (© 888/800-5447) and **Adventure Island** (© 813/987-5600) raised their admission prices—and probably will again before you get there. Call for the latest.

Sarasota The city's famous Ringling Museums and Asolo Theatre are now officially part of the **FSU Ringling Center for the Cultural Arts** (© 941/359-5700), under the aegis of Florida State University.

WALT DISNEY WORLD & ORLANDO For complete information on this region, see chapter 11.

Accommodations Developers added about 4,000 new rooms to Orlando since spring 2001, which boosts the city's total over the 111,000-room mark. That's more than enough in most cases, but you'll still have trouble getting a room in some areas, including Disney, during holiday periods.

Speaking of Disney, **Animal Kingdom Lodge** (© 407/938-3000; www.disneyworld.com) came online in April 2001 with 1,293 rooms overlooking a mini-preserve inhabited by 130 kinds of animals.

Exploring Walt Disney World The economy has caused a lot of belt tightening around Mickeyville, but there have been a few new arrivals in the past year. The one with the most fanfare is the celebration honoring the 100th anniversary of Walt Disney's 1901 birth in Chicago. Uncle Walt's birthday bash is based at Disney–MGM Studios and includes new parades and special exhibits at all of the theme parks. It's set to end on December 31, 2002, but Disney has often hung on to parades from past celebrations, so things may still be going strong in 2003.

Here are some other new additions to Walt Disney World:

- **Journey Into Imagination** at Epcot reopened in June 2002 after a months-long refurbishment. The opening marked the return of an old and beloved favorite—Figment the dinosaur.
- Disney–MGM Studios continued upgrades with the addition of **Who Wants to Be a Millionaire—Play It!**, based on the Disney–ABC TV game show and

offering contestants a chance to win prizes—but no millions.
- Animal Kingdom debuted the new kids' ride **TriceraTop Spin**. **Primeval Whirl,** a carnival-style roller coaster, is set to debut in the summer of 2002.
- **SpectroMagic** in April 2001 returned for a second engagement at the Magic Kingdom, replacing the park's old favorite, the **Main Street Electrical Parade.**

Exploring Beyond Disney At Universal Studios Florida, Animal Actors Stage has been replaced by **Animal Planet Live!** The multimedia show stars a fox, a raccoon, and an Australian shepherd.

SeaWorld has added a twice-a-day **Clydesdale Parade** featuring Anheuser-Busch's renowned horses. And SeaWorld's sister park, **Discovery Cove,** has expanded its snorkeling and other areas. Despite the weakened economy and sagging attendance, SeaWorld hiked adult and kid ticket prices by $2 each in early 2002.

NORTHEAST FLORIDA For complete information on this region, see chapter 12.

Daytona Beach Already the city's largest hotel, the **Adams Mark Daytona Beach** (© 800/444-ADAM) has added 306 oceanfront rooms and a huge new ballroom to its inventory.

NORTHWEST FLORIDA: THE PANHANDLE For complete information on this region, see chapter 13.

Pensacola The **National Museum of Naval Aviation** (© 850/452-3604) has added a stomach-churning ride simulating the multi-G-force motion in the cockpit of a jet fighter.

With the state's new camping reservations system in place, **Blackwater River State Park** (© 850/983-5363) now accepts advance reservations for its campsites.

The Best of Florida from $70 a Day

Every year more than 40 million visitors escape bleak northern winters to bask in Florida's warmth, lured to the Sunshine State by the promise of clear skies and 800 miles of spectacular sandy beaches. A host of kid-pleasers, from Busch Gardens to Walt Disney World, make this state the country's most popular year-round family vacation destination.

Here you can choose from a wide array of accommodations, from deluxe resorts to mom-and-pop motels. You can visit remote little towns like Apalachicola or a megalopolis like Miami. Devour fresh seafood, from amberjack to oysters—and work off those calories in such outdoor pursuits as bicycling, golfing, or kayaking. Despite overdevelopment in many parts of the state, Floridians have maintained thousands of acres of wilderness areas, from the little respite of Clam Pass County Park in downtown Naples to the magnificent Everglades National Park, which stretches across the state's southern tip.

Choosing the "best" of all this is a daunting task, and the selections in this chapter are only a rundown on some of the affordable highlights. You'll find numerous other outstanding resorts, hotels, destinations, activities, and attractions—all described in the pages of this book. With a bit of serendipity you'll come up with some bests of your own.

And the real best of Florida: You can see it, do it, and eat it on a budget.

1 The Best Beaches

Many of Florida's best beaches are in its state parks and recreation areas. Admission to most of them is $3.25 per vehicle with up to eight occupants, $2 for a vehicle with one occupant, or $1 per pedestrian or bicyclist. Given the quality of what you'll see, that's one of Florida's best bargains.

- **Matheson Hammock Park Beach** (South Miami): This area features an enclosed man-made lagoon that is flushed naturally by the tidal action of the adjacent Biscayne Bay. The serene beach is surrounded by the bay's warm, calm waters and a backdrop of tropical hardwood forest. See "Hitting the Beach" in chapter 4.

- Miami's **Crandon Beach** (Key Biscayne): This beach is extremely popular for families with kids because of the shallow water created by a neighboring sandbar. Convenient parking, picnic areas, a winding boardwalk, and a multiethnic mix of families grilling, dancing, and relaxing are the benchmarks here. See "Hitting the Beach" in chapter 4.

- **Lummus Park Beach** (South Beach, Miami): World renowned, not necessarily for its pristine sands, but for its more common name of **South Beach,** seeing, being seen, and, at times, the obscene on this beach go hand in hand with the sunscreen and beach towels. See "Hitting the Beach" in chapter 4.

- **Sebastian Inlet** (North Hutchinson Island): At the tip of North Hutchinson Island, Sebastian Inlet is the beach where surfers find the biggest swells. Non-surfers will come for the flat, sandy beaches and miles of shaded walkways; facilities include kayak, paddleboat, and canoe rentals; picnic tables; and a snack shop. See "Vero Beach & Sebastian" in chapter 8.
- **Lover's Key State Park** (Fort Myers Beach): You'll have to walk or take a tram through a bird-filled forest of mangroves to this gorgeous, unspoiled beach just a few miles south of busy Fort Myers Beach. Although Sanibel Island gets all the accolades, the shelling here is just as good if not better. See "Fort Myers Beach" in chapter 9.
- **Cayo Costa State Park** (off Captiva Island): These days, deserted tropical islands with great beaches are scarce in Florida, but this 2,132-acre barrier strip of sand, pine forests, mangrove swamps, oak hammocks, and grasslands provides a genuine get-away-from-it-all experience. The only non-native residents are wild pigs and a lone park ranger; access is only by boat from nearby Gasparilla, Pine, and Captiva islands. See "Sanibel & Captiva Islands" in chapter 9.
- **Naples Beach** (Naples): Many Florida cities and towns have beaches, but few are as lovely as the gorgeous strip that runs in front of Naples's famous Millionaires' Row. You don't have to be rich to wander its length, peer at the mansions, and stroll on historic Naples Pier to catch a sunset over the gulf. See "Naples" in chapter 9.
- **Caladesi Island State Park** (Clearwater Beach): Even though it's in the heavily developed Tampa Bay area, 3½-mile Caladesi Island has a lovely, relatively secluded beach with soft sand edged in sea grass and palmettos. Dolphins cavort in offshore waters. In the park itself, there's a nature trail, and you might see one of the rattlesnakes, black racers, raccoons, armadillos, or rabbits that live here. The park is accessible only by ferry from Honeymoon Island State Recreation Area off Dunedin. See "St. Pete & Clearwater Beaches" in chapter 10.
- **Canaveral National Seashore** (Cape Canaveral): Midway between the crowded attractions at Daytona Beach and the Kennedy Space Center is a protected stretch of coastline 24 miles long, backed by cabbage palms, sea grapes, and palmettos. Their neighbor is the 140,000-acre Merritt Island National Wildlife Refuge, home to hundreds of Florida birds, reptiles, alligators, and mammals. Wooden boardwalks lead from a free parking lot to the huge expanse of soft brown sand and a few well-spaced picnic tables. See "Cocoa Beach, Cape Canaveral & the Kennedy Space Center" in chapter 12.
- **Gulf Islands National Seashore** (Pensacola): You could argue that all of Northwest Florida's gulf shore is one of America's great beaches, for here you will find an almost uninterrupted stretch of pure white sand that runs the entire length of the Panhandle, from Perdido Key to St. George Island. The Gulf Islands National Seashore preserves much of this natural wonder in its undeveloped state. Countless terns, snowy plovers, black skimmers, and other birds nest along the dunes topped with sea oats. East of the

national seashore and equally as beautiful are Grayton Beach State Recreation Area near Destin, and St. George Island State Park off Apalachicola. See chapter 13.

- **St. Andrews State Park** (Panama City Beach): With more than 1,000 acres of dazzling white sand and dunes, this preserved wilderness demonstrates what Panama City Beach looked like before motels and condominiums lined its shore. Lacy, golden sea oats sway in gulf breezes, and fragrant rosemary grows wild. The area is home to foxes, coyotes, and a herd of deer. See "Panama City Beach" in chapter 13.

2 The Best Destinations for Low-Cost Vacations

- **The Middle & Lower Keys:** With all the hype over Key West, the other keys are often neglected by tourists who race through en route to the wild tip of the continental United States. But that's a good thing. The string of islands that are far enough from Miami to dissuade day-trippers are a virtual treasure trove for active travelers who enjoy biking, boating, fishing, bird-watching, snorkeling, or just plain old relaxing. Areas like Conch Key, Grassy Key, Marathon, Big Pine Key, and Sugarloaf are dotted with lush parks, simple fish houses, and modest accommodations. There is the National Key Deer Refuge, home to hundreds of nearly extinct miniature golden deer, and Bahia Honda State Park, where Florida's unusual plant and animal life thrive for all to see. And of course, these keys are surrounded by some of the country's most incredible underwater attractions, including a living reef system that divers flock to from all over the world. See chapter 5.

- **Hollywood:** For about half what you'd spend in trendy South Beach, nearby Hollywood (whose most recent ad campaign strangely promoted itself as "Vintage South Florida") offers wide beaches, plenty of outdoor activities, a few funky nightspots, and some real bargain hotels. Plus, you can drive half an hour in either direction to visit Fort Lauderdale's elegant restaurants and tourist attractions, or head south to Miami Beach to partake in some of its outrageous activity. See "Broward County: Hallandale & Hollywood to Fort Lauderdale" in chapter 7.

- **Lake Okeechobee:** Head inland to Clewiston on Lake Okeechobee for a real feel of Old Florida. This is a popular spot for RVs and anglers. Everything from food to lodging is reasonably priced. You can stay in the nicest spot in town for about $40 a person. And while you're on the lake, why not catch your own dinner? See "A Side Trip Inland: Fishing at Lake Okeechobee" in chapter 8.

- **Fort Myers Beach:** Just a few miles from trendy Sanibel and Captiva islands and ritzy Naples, Fort Myers Beach offers just as much sun, sand, and shells—and at much less expensive prices—as its more affluent neighbors. Its busy "Times Square" and the rest of Estero Island offer some very comfortable accommodations at reasonable rates, even in the winter high season. And the gorgeous Lovers Key State Park is just across the bridge. See "Fort Myers Beach" in chapter 9.

- **Naples:** For a town with residents possessing industrial-strength money, charming and friendly Naples offers some surprisingly affordable accommodations and dining. And admission to Naples's great beach and historic pier is free. See "Naples" in chapter 9.

- **Anna Maria Island:** Although it sits next door to affluent Sarasota and expensive Longboat Key, Anna Maria Island is down-to-earth in both lifestyle and prices. It has fine beaches and a host of cost-conscious activities—and you only have to drive a few miles south to dine and shop on St. Armands Key, or to enjoy Sarasota's fine performing arts scene. See "Sarasota & Bradenton" in chapter 10.

- **The St. Pete & Clearwater Beaches:** The 20 miles of sand between St. Pete Beach and Clearwater Beach have been a vacation mecca for a century now, and they attract vacationers across the economic spectrum. Here is one of Florida's finest and most expensive grand old resorts, but you can also choose from many comfortable and inexpensive motels and condos, too. Granted, some four million guests a year can crowd this area at times, but there's a multitude of activities to keep them—and you—busy without breaking the bank. See "St. Pete & Clearwater Beaches" in chapter 10.

- **Daytona Beach:** Like the Panhandle, Daytona Beach attracts a working-class clientele—not to mention stock-car fans and bikers who make pilgrimages to this "World Center of Racing." Accordingly, you'll find many low-cost places to stay and dine here. In addition to its famous racetrack, the area sports a beach so hard-packed that you can drive on it. See "Daytona Beach" in chapter 12.

- **The Beaches of Northwest Florida:** Many visitors to Pensacola Beach, Fort Walton Beach, Destin, and Panama City Beach are working-class families, couples, and singles from Alabama and Georgia. They don't have all the money in the world to spend. As a result, the Panhandle has a multitude of inexpensive accommodations and restaurants. And there's plenty to keep everyone busy here, from touring historic Pensacola to trying your luck in Destin, "The World's Luckiest Fishing Village." The only problem: The Panhandle can get cold in winter. See chapter 13.

3 The Best Experiences You Can Have for Free (or Almost)

- **See the Boys of Spring** (Statewide): Although Florida has the big-league Florida Marlins in Miami and the Tampa Bay Devil Rays in St. Petersburg, the whole state goes baseball crazy during spring training from mid-February through March. Great seats close to the action are a bargain compared to what you'll pay when the Boys of Spring get home. See the box, "The Boys of Spring," in chapter 2.

- **Experience Pre- and Post-Castro Cuba on U.S. Soil** (Miami): Stroll down Little Havana's Calle Ocho, 8th Street, to get a flavor of Hispanic culture. Stop at Versailles, an iconoclastic, gaudy Cuban diner humming with old-timers reminiscing about pre-Castro Cuba, local politicos trying to appease them, and a slew of detached people only there for the fantastically cheap and authentic Cuban fare. Watch expert cigar rollers make handmade stogies at one of the many cigar factories. Overlook the purely American fast food joints in favor of a much more flavorful Little Havana bodega. See chapter 4.

- **Relish the View from Bill Baggs Cape Florida State Recreation Area:** You haven't truly seen South Florida until you've checked out the view from the southern point of Key Biscayne. Whether it's the turquoise water or the sight of Stiltsville—seven still-inhabited aquatic cabins dating back to the 1930s, perched smack in the middle of the Biscayne Channel—it may take a little coercing to get you to leave. See "Nature Preserves, Parks & Gardens" in chapter 4.

- **Drive along A1A:** This oceanfront route, which runs north up from Miami Beach, through Sunny Isles and Hollywood, and on along the entire eastern edge of Florida, embodies the essence of the state. Especially in South Florida, where you'll discover time-warped hotels steeped in Art Deco kitsch alongside multi-million-dollar modern high-rises, A1A is one of the most scenic, albeit heavily trafficked, roads in all of Florida.

- **Eye the Estates on Palm Beach:** The winter playground for the *Lifestyles of the Rich and Famous* set, Palm Beach is lined with jaw-dropping palatial estates. While many of them are hidden behind towering shrubbery, head south on South County Road, from Brazilian Avenue, where you will see some of the most opulent homes ever built. Make sure someone holds the steering wheel if you're driving, because you *will* do a double-take. See "Palm Beach & West Palm Beach" in chapter 7.

- **Catch the "Green Flash" at Sunset** (Key West & the Gulf Coast Beaches): Key West and the beaches of Southwest Florida and the Tampa Bay area face due west, thus providing glorious sunsets over the Gulf of Mexico and a chance to see the elusive "green flash"—a quick burst of green light just as the top of the sun dips below the horizon. It costs not a cent to wander down to the shore and keep a sharp eye peeled. Or for a few bucks, grab a drink from a beachside restaurant or gulf-front bar. See chapters 5, 9, and 10.

- **Walk or Ride Along Wildlife Drive** (Sanibel Island): The mangrove swamps, winding waterways, and uplands of Sanibel Island's **J. N. "Ding" Darling National Wildlife Refuge** (© **239/472-1100**) are great places to see alligators, raccoons, otters, and hundreds of species of birds. You can see many of the creatures from the 5-mile, one-way Wildlife Drive, which costs $5 per vehicle or $1 per pedestrian or biker. A naturalist will explain what you're seeing on a 2-hour narrated tram tour—a very good value at $8 for adults, $4 for children 12 and under. See "Sanibel & Captiva Islands" in chapter 9.

- **Stoop for Shells** (Sanibel Island): Okay, you'll have to pay a $3 toll to get here and a small fee to park your car (or lock your bike to a tree for nothing), but you can stroll Sanibel Island's world-famous shelling beaches as long as you want for free. After a few hours hunched over in the "Sanibel stoop," you're sure to go home with a prize find or two. See "Sanibel & Captiva Islands" in chapter 9.

- **Stroll Among the Millionaires** (Naples): Olde Naples residents love to stroll out on their ancient city pier to fish, catch a sunset, or look at Millionaires' Row, a string of magnificent mansions along the town's lovely beach. Now a state historic site, the pier is open 24 hours a day and is free, although it will cost you a few quarters to park in the nearby municipal lots. When you're done ogling the wealthy from the Naples Pier, you can walk among them while window-shopping in the ritzy 3rd Street district nearby. Naples is so Midwestern-friendly that nobody will care if you maxed out your credit cards just to get here. See "Naples" in chapter 9.

- **Walk, Jog, Bike, or Blade Along Bayshore Boulevard** (Tampa): A 7-mile promenade with an unmatched view across the bay to Tampa's downtown skyline, Bayshore Boulevard reputedly has the world's longest continuous sidewalk. It's a favorite for runners, joggers, walkers, and in-line skaters. The route passes stately old homes of Hyde Park, a few high-rise condos, retirement communities, and houses of worship before ending at Ballast Point Park. See "Tampa" in chapter 10.

- **Poke Through a Dusty Museum Dedicated to Sponges** (Tarpon Springs): The highlight of any stroll along the carnival-like Sponge Docks in Tarpon Springs is the rickety **Spongeorama** (© **727/943-9509**), a dusty museum dedicated to sponges and sponge divers. You can buy a wide variety of fresh-from-the-gulf sponges here and watch a 30-minute video about sponge-diving. Admission is free. The docks also have a host of inexpensive restaurants featuring authentic Greek cuisine brought here by the town's sponge-diving settlers. See the box, "The Sponge Capital of the World," in chapter 10.

- **See What Circus Money Bought** (Sarasota): Adults pay $9 or $10 to get in, but you'll have three "rings" to visit at the **FSU Ringling Center for the Cultural Arts** in Sarasota (© **941/359-5700**, or 941/351-1660 for recorded information), which houses the phenomenal collections of circus master John Ringling. A pink Italian Renaissance villa is filled with over 500 years of European and American art, including one of the world's most important collections of grand 17th-century baroque paintings. The Ringling's 30-room winter residence displays their personal mementos. And the Circus Galleries are devoted to memorabilia from The Greatest Show on Earth. See p. 441.

- **See Fine Art at a Free Museum** (Orlando): Admission is free to the **Cornell Fine Arts Museum** (© **407/646-2526**), a showplace with 6,000 works on display, making it one of Florida's most distinguished, comprehensive art collections. There also are lectures and gallery-talk walks. See p. 529.

- **Visit America's Oldest African-American Community** (Orlando): Established in 1887 just north of Orlando, Eatonville is the home of the **Zora Neale Hurston National Museum of Fine Arts** (© **407/647-3307**), which honors the town's too-little heralded African-American author. There's an annual festival in January honoring her work. A small gallery on the site has periodically changing exhibits of art and other work and there's a map for a walking tour of the community. Admission is free, with a donation suggested. See p. 529.

- **Take a Break on a Lake** (Orlando): With the city's skyline as a backdrop, **Lake Eola Park** (© **407/246-2827**) is a quiet hideaway in downtown Orlando. A cascading fountain features a 12-minute, lighted show at dark. The park has a .9-mile walking and jogging path, a playground, and paddleboats for rent ($7 per half hr.).

FunnyEola features comedy acts the second Tuesday of each month at 7:30pm, and there are a variety of other performances, most of them free. See p. 529.

- **Take a Giant Leap for Mankind** (Cape Canaveral): You'll have to pay to see a space shuttle launch at the **John F. Kennedy Space Center** in Cape Canaveral (© 321/452-2121), but you can watch a blastoff for free from the causeways leading to the center. Although it's not exactly inexpensive these days, admission to the center's visitors complex is well worth $26 for adults, $16 for kids 3 to 11, since it includes IMAX movies and a bus tour of the working launchpads and assembly buildings of the nation's premier space complex. See p. 541.

- **Imagine You're a Spanish Colonist** (St. Augustine): The nation's oldest town, St. Augustine's restored Spanish Quarter offers a look back to America's very beginnings. You'll have to pay a few dollars to enter sites such as the oldest store and the oldest jail, but you can freely stroll these narrow streets for hours. Poke your head into antiques shops, peer into lush yards surrounding ancient buildings, and watch the boats out on the Matanzas River. See "St. Augustine: America's First City" in chapter 12.

- **Visit a New Breed of National Park** (Jacksonville): The **Timucuan Ecological and Historic Preserve** isn't one chunk of land; instead, it's a vast, intriguing system of sites on both sides of the St. Johns River. The prime attraction is the Fort Carolina National Memorial (© 904/641-7155), the site of a 16th-century French Huguenot settlement. It's on the edge of the 600-acre Theodore Roosevelt Area, a beautiful, undisturbed wood- and marshland rich in history and wildlife. On the north side of the river, the Zephaniah Kingsley Plantation (© 904/251-3537) was an early 19th-century manse owned by Zephaniah Kingsley, a white man who married one of his slaves and then moved her and his family to Haiti to escape racism at home. Admission is free to all the park's attractions. See "Jacksonville" in chapter 12.

- **Walk the Streets of a Charming Victorian Town** (Fernandina Beach, Amelia Island): Amelia Island might be an exclusive, money-on-the-hoof kind of place, but you need not a penny to stroll around the gorgeous 50-block area of bayside **Fernandina Beach.** This charming small town is filled with so many Victorian and Queen Anne homes that it's listed in the National Register of Historic Places. See "Amelia Island" in chapter 12.

- **Hit a Talcum-Like Beach** (Northwest Florida): Admission is free to most of 100-plus miles of powdery, snow-white beaches that make the Panhandle special. And just a few bucks will let you into the Gulf Islands National Seashore at Pensacola, the Henderson Beach and Grayton Beach state recreation areas at Destin, the St. Andrews State Recreation Area at Panama City Beach, and St. George Island State Park near Apalachicola. You won't soon forget the time you spend on these protected sands and dunes, all consistently ranked among the nation's finest beaches. See chapter 13.

- **Imagine Yourself Under Five Flags** (Pensacola): You'll have to pay to go into its homes and museums, but there's no admission to walk the streets of **Historic Pensacola Village** (© 850/444-8905). The original part of

Pensacola resembles a shady English colonial community, but America's second oldest city saw the flags of five nations fly over its quaint streets. Some of Florida's oldest homes are here, along with charming boutiques and interesting restaurants. During summer, costumed characters go about their daily chores and demonstrate old crafts, and archaeologists unearth the old Spanish commanding officer's compound. See p. 609.

- **Visit the Blue Angels & Top Guns** (Pensacola and Fort Walton Beach): Next to the Smithsonian Institute's National Air and Space Museum in Washington, D.C., the next best places to see our nation's warplanes on display are at the **National Museum of Naval Aviation** in Pensacola (✆ **850/452-3604**) and at the **U.S. Air Force Armament Museum** in Fort Walton Beach (✆ **850/882-4062**). Admission to both is free. They cost a few dollars, but the naval museum's IMAX films will make you believe you're flying in a Blue Angel's cockpit. See p. 609 and 625.

- **See Where Johnny Weissmuller Played Tarzan** (Tallahassee): Wakulla Springs, 15 miles south of Tallahassee, is so jungly that some of the 1930s Tarzan movies starring Johnny Weissmuller were filmed here. Today they are within the 2,860 acres of **Edward Ball Wakulla Springs State Park** (✆ **850/922-3632**), which means you'll have to pay a few dollars to get in. You can also pay $4.50 for adults, half price for children, to take glass-bottom-boat sightseeing and wildlife-observation tours. You can swim in the lake formed by the springs, but watch for alligators! See "Tallahassee" in chapter 13.

4 The Best Adventure Trips

- **Discover your Inner Flipper** (Grassy Key/Marathon): At the highly regarded **Dolphin Research Center** (✆ **305/289-1121**) you'll learn to communicate with and touch, swim, or play with the mammals who may teach you a thing or two about human behavior. See p. 193.

- **Everglades National Park:** Unfettered by jet skis, cruise ships, and neon bikinis, the Everglades are Florida's outback, resplendent in its swampy nature, which is best explored via an airboat that can navigate its way through the most stubborn of sawgrass, providing you with an up-close and personal view of the land's inhabitants, from alligators and manatees to raccoons and Florida panthers. See "Everglades National Park" in chapter 6.

- **Jonathan Dickinson State Park** (Hobe Sound): Take a trip back in time to old, pre-Neon Florida. Rent a canoe and explore a scenic route that winds through a variety of botanical habitats. You may see a gator, a variety of reptiles, and even an occasional manatee. See "Stuart & Jensen Beach" in chapter 8.

- **Canoeing to Mound Key** (Fort Myers): An official Florida canoe trail, the slow-moving Estero River south of Fort Myers leads 3½ miles from U.S. 41 to Estero Bay, which is itself a state aquatic preserve. Near the mouth of the river lies Mound Key State Archeological Site, one of Florida's largest Calusa Indian shell middens (islets) dating back some 2,000 years. There's no park ranger on the key, but signs explain its history. Canoe rentals are available at Koreshan State Historical Site on the river (© **239/992-0311**) for $3 an hour, $15 per day. See "Fort Myers" in chapter 9.

- **Bird-Watching by Canoe or Kayak** (Sanibel Island): Naturalist, avid environmentalist, and former Sanibel mayor Mark "Bird" Westall (© **239/472-5218**) takes visitors on guided canoe trips through the J. N. "Ding" Darling National Wildlife Refuge and on the Sanibel River. They aren't cheap at $40 for adults, $20 for children under 18, but you won't soon forget this experience. See "Sanibel & Captiva Islands" in chapter 9.

- **Primitive Camping in Collier Seminole State Park** (Marco Island; © **239/394-3397**): This inviting, 6,423-acre preserve on the edge of Big Cypress Swamp, 12 miles east of Marco Island, offers a host of activities, including canoeing over a 13-mile loop with primitive camping. Canoes can be rented, but the park has only four campsites along the canoe trails, so book early. For the more civilized, narrated boat tours wander through these winding waterways daily. See "Marco Island" in chapter 9.

- **Canoeing in Blackwater River State Park** (Milton, near Pensacola; © **850/953-5363**): The little town of Milton is the official "Canoe Capital of Florida" (by act of the state legislature, no less). It's a well-earned title, for the nearby Blackwater River, Coldwater River, Sweetwater Creek, and Juniper Creek are all perfect for canoeing, kayaking, tubing, rafting, and paddleboating. The Blackwater is considered one of the world's purest sand-bottom rivers and has retained its primordial, backwoods beauty. See the box, "Florida's Canoe Capital," in chapter 13.

- **Trying Yours at the "World's Luckiest Fishing Village"** (Destin): Destin has Florida's largest charter-boat fleet, with more than 140 vessels. Rates for private charters range from about $360 to $900 per boat, depending on length of voyage, but a less expensive way to try your luck is on a larger, group-oriented party boat—about $25 to $35 per person, including gear, bait, and fishing license. See "Destin & Fort Walton Beach" in chapter 13.

- **Journeys of St. George Island** (Apalachicola; © **850/927-3259**): From her base in Apalachicola, Jeanni McMillan leads informative nature cruises to the offshore barrier islands, including mountain-bike excursions to the pristine St. Vincent National Wildlife Refuge, and on canoe trips in the creeks and streams of the Apalachicola River basin. Her very reasonable prices range from $15 to $70, including equipment. See "Apalachicola" in chapter 13.

5 The Best Family Attractions

- **Miami Seaquarium** (Key Biscayne; © **305/361-5705**): Kids seem to love the splashy and dramatic performances by killer whales and dolphins. Come early and get a very wet look at some of the biggest hams of marine life. See p. 156.

- **Miami Metrozoo** (Miami; © **305/251-0400**): This completely cageless (but safe!) zoo offers a horde of animals with much personality all ready for their close-ups. See p. 155.

- **Mel Fisher Maritime Heritage Museum** (Key West; ✆ **305/294-2633**): Because it's human nature to have somewhat of a morbid curiosity about disasters and wrecks, this museum full of doubloons, pieces of eight, emeralds, and solid-gold bars has fascinated visitors intrigued with shipwrecks. See p. 215.

- **Key West Aquarium** (Key West; ✆ **305/296-2051**): The oldest attraction on the island, this modest but fascinating exhibit is a great place for children who are accustomed to only animals of the animated kind. Touch tanks and feeding exhibitions get kids involved. See p. 214.

- **Playmobil Fun Park** (Palm Beach Gardens; ✆ **800/351-8697**): It's the only Playmobil park outside of Germany, it's free, and it's a ball. This indoor fantasy world offers more than 17,000 square feet filled with thousands of toys. *Warning:* All toys are also for sale. See p. 286.

- **Edison & Ford Winter Estates** (Fort Myers; ✆ **239/334-3614**): Inventor Thomas Alva Edison and his friend, automobile magnate Henry Ford, built side-by-side winter homes on the banks of the Caloosahatchee River in Fort Myers. Today these Victorian cottages serve as memorials to the two men, and especially to Edison. The museum will show the kids how we got the lightbulb, the phonograph, and hundreds of other Edison inventions. See p. 330.

- **Caribbean Gardens** (Naples; ✆ **239/262-5409**): Owned and operated by the family of noted animal trainer Larry Tetzlaff, this zoo features a variety of animals and birds, including a fascinating community of primates living free on their own island. Larry's son, David Tetzlaff, himself a talented trainer, puts lions and tigers through their paces in his Big Cat Show. For kids, there's a Petting Farm, elephant rides, and a playground. You can easily spend a day here. See p. 372.

- **Teddy Bear Museum** (Naples; ✆ **800/681-2327** or 239/598-2711): More than 3,000 examples of stuffed teddy bears from around the world are cleverly displayed at this enchanting museum. They descend from the rafters in hot-air balloons, attend board meetings, sip afternoon tea, celebrate a wedding, read in the "Li-bear-y," even do bear things like hibernate. Kids can buy their own bear to take home. See p. 372.

- **Busch Gardens Tampa Bay** (Tampa; ✆ **813/987-5283**): Although the thrill rides, live entertainment, shops, restaurants, and games get most of the ink at this 335-acre family theme park, Busch Gardens ranks among the top zoos in the country, with several thousand animals living in naturalistic environments. If you can get them off the roller coasters, the kids can find out what all those wild beasts they've seen on the Discovery Channel look like in person. You can save a few bucks off admission by buying your tickets outside the main gate. See p. 389.

- **Florida Aquarium** (Tampa; ✆ **813/273-4000**): This major aquarium will introduce you and the kids to more than 5,300 aquatic animals and plants that call Florida home. There's an Explore a Shore playground to educate the kids, a deep-water exhibit, and a tank housing moray eels. See p. 396.

- **MOSI (Museum of Science and Industry)** (Tampa; ⓒ 813/987-6300): One of the largest educational science centers in the Southeast, MOSI has more than 450 interactive exhibits in which the kids can experience hurricane-force winds, defy the laws of gravity, cruise the mysterious world of microbes, explore the human body, and much more. They can also watch stunning movies in MOSIMAX, Florida's first IMAX dome theater. Admission includes IMAX movies. See p. 397.
- **The Magic Kingdom & Disney–MGM Studios** (Orlando; ⓒ 407/824-4321): Of the four Disney parks, these two are the most fun for families. Young ones will be thrilled to meet and greet the famed characters, and rides will delight young and old alike. Yes, admission is expensive, but with a little know-how and a lot of planning, you can have a memorable Disney experience without breaking the bank. See chapter 11.
- **Universal Orlando** (Orlando; ⓒ 407/363-8000): Even with fast-paced, grown-up rides, Universal still is a ton of fun for kids (there's even a youngster-size roller coaster). And it's a working motion-picture and TV-production studio, so occasionally there's some live filming done in the park, especially at the Nickelodeon soundstage. The little ones can spend the whole day exploring the whimsical Seuss Landing and meeting MGM's cartoon characters such as Woody Woodpecker, Yogi, BooBoo, Scooby Doo, Fred, Barney, Fievel, and Elroy Jetson. See chapter 11.
- **SeaWorld** (Orlando; ⓒ 407/351-3600): Beautifully landscaped grounds, centering on a 17-acre lagoon, include flamingo and pelican ponds and a lush tropical rain forest. Shamu, a killer whale, is the star of the park along with his expanding family, which includes several baby whales. The newest addition is Journey to Atlantis, a flume coaster with plenty of twists and turns. See chapter 11.
- **Kennedy Space Center** (Cape Canaveral; ⓒ 321/452-2121): The nation's spaceport is a must-see. There is plenty to keep kids and parents busy for at least a full day, including interactive computer games, IMAX films, and dozens of informative displays on the space program. Try to schedule a trip during a real launch; there are more than a dozen each year. See p. 541.
- **Daytona USA** (Daytona Beach; ⓒ 386/947-6800): Opened in late 1996 on Daytona International Speedway grounds, this huge state-of-the-art interactive attraction is an exciting and fast-paced stop even for non-race fans. Kids can see real stock cars, go-carts, and motorcycles, and even participate in a pit stop on a NASCAR Winston Cup race car. See p. 553.
- **ZooWorld Zoological & Botanical Park** (Panama City Beach; ⓒ 850/230-1243): "Mr. Bubba," the largest captive alligator in Florida, lives in a re-created pine forest habitat at this educational and entertaining zoo, an active participant in the Species Survival Plan, which helps protect endangered species with specific breeding and housing programs. Other guests include rare and endangered animals as well as orangutans and other primates, big cats, and more reptiles. Also included are a walk-through aviary, a bat exhibit, and a petting zoo. See p. 639.

6 The Best Golf Courses with Greens Fees That Won't Break Your Budget

- **Crandon Park Golf Course** (Key Biscayne, Miami): Formerly known as the Links of Key Biscayne, this stunning and famous course was ranked the number-one municipal course in the state and one of the top five in the country. Located on a posh residential island, it's one of the few courses remaining in South Florida not surrounded by development. Golfers enjoy pristine vistas of hammocks and stretches of water, with a glimpse of Miami's dramatic skyline to the north. See "Affordable Outdoor Pursuits" in chapter 4.

- **Miami's Biltmore Golf Course, Biltmore Hotel** (Coral Gables): If it's good enough for former President Clinton, it's good enough for those of you who don't travel with a bevy of Secret Service agents. But the real question is: Are *you* good enough for the course? The sixth hole is notoriously difficult, with distracting water hazards among other difficulties. Nonetheless, it's an excellent course with a picture postcard setting. See "Affordable Outdoor Pursuits" in chapter 4.

- **Doral Golf Resort and Spa** (Miami): There are four championship courses here, including the famous Blue Monster, which is the site of the annual Doral-Ryder Open. The Gold Course, recently restored by golf great Raymond Floyd, has water on every hole. Look in the *Miami Herald* sports section for special discounts and coupons or call for twilight specials starting at $25 per person. See "Affordable Outdoor Pursuits" in chapter 4.

- **Haulover Park** (Miami): The longest hole on this par-27 course is 125 yards in a pretty bayside location. Golfers here are patient with beginners, and greens fees start at a remarkable $5 per person in winter. See "Affordable Outdoor Pursuits" in chapter 4.

- **The Boca Raton Municipal Golf Course** (Boca Raton): This 18-hole, par-72 course covers approximately 6,200 yards. With greens fees starting at $11 for nine holes, this is a superior deal. See "Boca Raton & Delray Beach" in chapter 7.

- **Emerald Dunes Golf Course** (West Palm Beach): This beautiful Tom Fazio championship course features 60 acres of water, including a waterfall, and great views of the Atlantic. Prime weekend times are pricey, but it is one of the only great courses open to the public in this area of ritzy resorts. Twilight prices from Monday through Thursday are a mere $35. See "Palm Beach & West Palm Beach" in chapter 7.

- **"Golf-A-Round"** (Gold Coast): From May to October or November, about a dozen private courses open their greens to visitors staying in Palm Beach County hotels. This "Golf-A-Round" program is free or severely discounted (carts are additional), and reservations can be made through most major hotels. Or contact the **Palm Beach County Convention and Visitors Bureau** (© **561/471-3995**). See chapter 7.

- **Orangebrook Golf Course** (Hollywood): Built in 1937, this 18-holer is one of the state's oldest courses and one of the area's best bargains. Morning and noon rates range from $17 to $32. After 3pm, prices go down to about $15. See "Broward County: Hallandale &

Hollywood to Fort Lauderdale" in chapter 7.

- **Fort Myers Country Club** (Fort Myers; © 239/936-2457): Designed in 1917 by Donald Ross, this municipal course is flat and uninteresting by today's standards, but it's right in town and looks like an exclusive private enclave. Fort Myers's other municipal course, Eastwood Golf Club (© 239/275-4848), is more challenging. Greens fees at both range from about $30 in summer to $55 during winter. See "Fort Myers" in chapter 9.

- **Babe Zaharias, Rocky Point, & Rogers Park Courses** (Tampa): With three fine municipal courses charging about $26 to $35, Tampa is a great place for affordable golf. The Babe Zaharias Municipal Golf Course (© 813/631-4374) is the shortest, but small greens and narrow fairways present ample challenges. Water presents obstacles on 12 of the 18 holes at Rocky Point Municipal Golf Course (© 813/673-4316). On the Hillsborough River, the Rogers Park Municipal Golf Course (© 813/673-4396) has a lighted driving and practice range. Lessons and club rentals are available. See "Tampa" in chapter 10.

- **Mangrove Bay Golf Course** (St. Petersburg; © 727/893-7797): One of the nation's top 50 municipal courses, these 18-hole, par-72 links hug the inlets of Old Tampa Bay. Facilities include a driving range; lessons and golf-club rental are also available. Fees are about $25, $35 including a cart in winter, slightly lower off-season. The city also operates the challenging, par-3 **Twin Brooks Golf Course**, 3800 22nd Ave. S. (© 727/893-7445), charging the same fees. See "St. Petersburg" in chapter 10.

- **Bobby Jones Golf Complex** (Sarasota; © 941/365-GOLF): Sarasota's municipal facility has two 18-hole championship layouts—the American (par 71) and British (par 72) courses—and a nine-hole executive course (par 30). Greens fees range from $25 to $35, including cart rental, a bargain in this affluent area. See "Sarasota & Bradenton" in chapter 10.

- **Buffalo Creek Golf Course** (Bradenton; © 941/776-2611): Locals love to play this 18-hole, par-72 municipal course on the north side of the Bradenton River. At well over 7,000 yards, it's the longest in the area, and lots of water and alligators will keep you entertained. Wintertime greens fees are about $35 with cart, $25 without. They drop to about $20 and $18, respectively, during summer. See "Sarasota & Bradenton" in chapter 10.

- **The Celebration Golf Club** (Orlando; © 407/566-4653): This club has an 18-hole regulation course (starting at $35) and a three-hole junior course for 5- to 9-year-olds. For more on golfing in Orlando, see the box, "Hot Links: Orlando's Top Golf Courses" in chapter 11.

- **Cocoa Beach Country Club** (Cocoa Beach; © 321/868-3351): This fine municipal course has 27 holes of championship golf and 10 lighted tennis courts set on acres of natural woodland, rivers, and lakes. Greens fees are about $40 in winter, dropping to about $35 in summer, including cart. Nearby, The Savannahs at Sykes Creek (© 321/455-1377) has 18 holes over 6,636 yards bordered by hardwood forests, lakes, and savannahs inhabited by a host of wildlife. You'll have to hit over a

lake to reach the seventh hole. Fees with cart are about $35 in winter, less in summer. See "Cocoa Beach, Cape Canaveral & the Kennedy Space Center" in chapter 12.
- **Pelican Bay Country Club** (Daytona Beach; © 386/788-6494): The South Course of this semi-private club is one of the area's favorites, with fast greens to test your putting skills. With-cart fees are about $40 in winter, less in summer (no walking allowed). See "Daytona Beach" in chapter 12.
- **The Moors** (Pensacola; © 800/727-1010 or 850/995-4653): Pot bunkers make you think you're playing in Scotland at this course, which has greeted the Nike Tour and is home to the Emerald Coast Classic, a PGA seniors' event. Greens fees here are about $30 without cart. The Moors also has a lodge with eight luxury rooms. See "Pensacola" in chapter 13.

7 The Best of Natural Florida

- **National Key Deer Refuge** (Big Pine Key): With patience and a bit of luck you may catch a glimpse of these delicate creatures in their natural habitat; with the country's largest herd (only about 300), the tiny, protected island of Big Pine Key is worth a stop. See "The Lower Keys: Big Pine Key to Coppitt Key" in chapter 5.
- **Exploring the Everglades:** The supermodel of swamps, the Everglades in all its marshy glory is absolutely stunning, full of lush greenery and beautiful wildlife. From egrets and orchids to gators and frogs, these quiet grounds are peaceful and intriguing. See "Everglades National Park" in chapter 6.
- **Lover's Key State Park** (Fort Myers Beach; © 239/463-4288): Just south of Fort Myers Beach, this gorgeous state preserve provides respite from the hustle and bustle of its busy neighbor. A highway runs the length of the island, but otherwise Lover's Key is totally undeveloped. Access through a mangrove forest to a truly fine beach is by foot or by a tractor-pulled tram driven by park rangers, who take a dim view of anyone leaving trash behind. See "Fort Myers Beach" in chapter 9.
- **J. N. "Ding" Darling National Wildlife Refuge** (Sanibel Island; © 239/472-1100): Preserving most of the mangrove forests and winding waterways on Sanibel Island's north side, this famous 5,000-acre refuge is rich in such barrier-island wildlife as roseate spoonbills, ospreys, shorebirds, white pelicans, ducks, loons, and mangrove cuckoos. Visitors can hike, bike, or canoe on their own or be escorted by experts such as former Sanibel Mayor Mark "Bird" Westall. See "Sanibel & Captiva Islands" in chapter 9.
- **Cayo Costa State Park** (off Captiva Island; © 941/964-0375): A huge variety of sea- and shorebirds congregate on this state preserve, which encompasses one of the northernmost of Southwest Florida's Ten Thousand Islands. This uninhabited island is only accessible via boat. See "Sanibel & Captiva Islands" in chapter 9.
- **Corkscrew Swamp Sanctuary** (Naples; © 239/348-9151): Maintained by the National Audubon Society, this 11,000-acre bald-cypress wilderness is a favorite wood-stork nesting ground. It's also home to herons, bald eagles, and a host of other birds and wildlife, plus ferns and

colorful orchids. Some of North America's oldest trees are here. See "Naples" in chapter 9.

- **Briggs Nature Center** (Marco Island; © **239/775-8569**): Operated by The Nature Conservancy and part of the Rookery Bay National Estuarine Research Reserve, this refuge is a pristine example of Florida's disappearing scrublands, home to the threatened scrub jays and gopher tortoises. There's a self-guided canoe trail and canoes for rent during winter. You can also canoe through The Conservancy's smaller Naples Nature Center in Naples. See "Marco Island" in chapter 9.

- **Harry P. Leu Gardens** (Orlando; © **407/246-2620**): This 50-acre botanical garden, on the shores of Lake Rowena near downtown Orlando, offers a serene respite from theme-park razzle-dazzle. Meandering paths lead through forests of giant camphors, moss-draped oaks, palms, and one of the world's largest collections of camellias (they bloom Oct–Mar). See p. 527.

- **Canaveral National Seashore/ Merritt Island National Wildlife Refuge** (Cape Canaveral; © **321/ 267-1110** or 321/861-0667): When the federal government set up the national space center at Cape Canaveral, it bought a lot more land than it needed to shoot rockets at the moon. The unneeded acres are now preserved in Canaveral National Seashore and the adjacent Merritt Island National Wildlife Refuge. The seashore's undeveloped Playalinda Beach is one of America's most beautiful stretches of sand. See "Cocoa Beach, Cape Canaveral & the Kennedy Space Center" in chapter 12.

- **St. Vincent National Wildlife Refuge** (Apalachicola; © **850/ 653-8808**): There are no facilities whatsoever on this 12,358-acre barrier island, which has been left in its natural state by the U.S. Fish and Wildlife Service. The local chamber of commerce will arrange a boat to get you here. Then you can walk through pine forests, marshlands, ponds, dunes, and beaches. In addition to native species like the bald eagle and alligators, the island is home to a small herd of sambar deer from Southeast Asia, and red wolves are bred here for reintroduction to other wildlife areas. See "Apalachicola" in chapter 13.

- **St. Marks National Wildlife Refuge** (Tallahassee; © **850/ 925-6121**): On the gulf, due south of Tallahassee, this 65,000-acre preserve is home to more species of birds than anyplace else in Florida except the Everglades. Built of limestone blocks 4 feet thick at the base, the 80-foot-tall St. Marks Lighthouse has marked the harbor entrance since 1842. The nearby Apalachicola National Forest is another good spot. See "Tallahassee" in chapter 13.

8 The Best Affordable Accommodations

- **Hotel Leon** (South Beach, Miami; © **305/673-3767**): This classy little hotel in the very hippest part of South Beach is beautifully maintained and fantastically practical. Although there are no fancy grounds or facilities, this has to be one of the best deals on the beach. See p. 108.
- **Aqua** (South Beach, Miami; © **305/538-4361**): The Jetsons meet the fabulous '50s at this

retro-hip 50-room motel that's very high-tech, very European and, most importantly, a real bargain. See p. 104.

- **Bay Harbor Inn and Suites** (Bay Harbor Island, Miami; ✆ **305/868-4141**): On an exclusive island in Miami Beach, this gem offers charm and value in an area that has precious little of either. See p. 112.
- **Indian Creek Hotel** (Miami Beach; ✆ **800/491-2772**): It's modest but full of character, and so close to South Beach. Rooms are brightly outfitted in period furnishings, and many overlook the pretty pool and garden. For the price, there's no competition. See p. 113.
- **Conch Key Cottages** (Marathon; ✆ **800/330-1577**): Right on the ocean, this little hideaway offers rustic but clean and well-outfitted cottages that are especially popular with families. Each has a hammock, barbecue grill, and kitchen. See p. 199.
- **The Grand** (Key West; ✆ **888/947-2630**): There's no better value than this little hotel that is slightly out of the way, but still within walking distance of Duval Street. All of the clean and quaint rooms have private bathrooms, air-conditioning, and private entrances for under $100. Suites are slightly more expensive but worth it if you want to save some money on food; the large two-room units come with kitchens. See p. 223.
- **Hotel Biba** (West Palm Beach; ✆ **561/832-0094**): West Palm Beach's first boutique hotel proves that it's hip to be square with this single-floor, 43-room property that has been renovated and redesigned in a remarkably retro-modern fashion. An enormous pool, Asian gardens, and requisite hipster bar make Biba a hot spot for those whose budgets aren't necessarily in the rock star category, even if their tastes are. See p. 288.
- **Beachcomber Apartment Motel** (Palm Beach; ✆ **800/833-7122**): This simple pink motel sits right on the ocean just a few miles from the super-high-priced accommodations that make Palm Beach, well, Palm Beach. No fancy frills here, but rooms are pleasant and clean. See p. 287.
- **Harborfront Inn Bed & Breakfast** (Stuart; ✆ **800/294-1703**): Located riverfront and within walking distance of the restaurants and shops of downtown Stuart, this handsome, highly recommended B&B offers private rooms with their own entrances. See p. 308.
- **Island House Motel** (Fort Myers Beach; ✆ **800/951-9975**): Sitting on stilts in the Old Florida fashion, but with modern furnishings, this clapboard-sided establishment enjoys a quiet location across the street from the beach and within walking distance of busy Times Square. You'll have screened porches, kitchens, ceiling fans, an open-air lounge with a small library, a small pool and sun-deck area, a guest laundry, beach chairs, and free local calls. See p. 343.
- **Palm Terrace Apartments** (Fort Myers Beach; ✆ **800/320-5783**): Many Europeans stay in these comfortable, well-maintained apartments about midway down Fort Myers Beach. The smaller, less expensive units are on the ground level, with sliding glass doors opening to a grassy yard, but even they have cooking facilities. There's beach access across Estero Boulevard, and Anthony's on the Gulf and the Junkanoo

Beach Bar are 3 short blocks away. See p. 343.

- **Cabbage Key Inn** (Cabbage Key, off Sanibel and Captiva islands; ℂ **239/283-2278**): You never know who's going to get off a boat on this 100-acre islet and walk unannounced into the funky, rustic house built in 1938 by the son and daughter-in-law of mystery novelist Mary Roberts Rinehart. Singer and avid yachtie Jimmy Buffett likes Cabbage Key so much that it inspired his hit song "Cheeseburger in Paradise." The inn has six rooms and six cottages, all with original 1920s furnishings, private bathrooms, and air-conditioners. Four of the cottages have kitchens, and one room reputedly has its own ghost. See "Sanibel & Captiva Islands" in chapter 9.

- **Boat House Motel** (Naples; ℂ **239/642-2400**): One of Southwest Florida's best bargains, this comfortable little motel sits beside the Marco River in historic Old Marco. There's a small heated swimming pool with lounge furniture, picnic tables, and barbecue grills beside the river. Bright paint, ceiling fans, and louvered doors add a tropical ambience throughout. See p. 381.

- **Best Western All Suites Hotel** (Tampa; ℂ **800/428-3438**): Whimsical signs lead you around a lush tropical courtyard with a heated pool, a hot tub, and a lively, sports-oriented tiki bar at this all-suites hotel, the most beach-like resort close to Busch Gardens Tampa Bay. Every unit is a suite and can accommodate up to four persons. See p. 401.

- **Beach Haven** (St. Pete Beach; ℂ **727/367-8642**): These low-slung, pink-with-white-trim structures were built in the 1950s but were gutted and completely rebuilt a few years ago. Today they have bright tile floors, vertical blinds, pastel tropical furniture, and many modern amenities, including TVs, VCRs, refrigerators, and coffeemakers. There's an outdoor heated pool surrounded by a white picket fence, plus a sunning deck with lounge furniture by the beach. It's in the heart of the hotel district, so lots of restaurants are just steps away. See p. 426.

- **Island's End Resort** (St. Pete Beach; ℂ **727/360-5023**): Owners Jone and Millard Gamble live at this little all-cottage hideaway on the southern tip of St. Pete Beach. Who can blame them: Theirs is a wonderful respite from the maddening crowd, and a great bargain to boot. You can step from the contemporary cottages right onto the beach. The cottages all have dining areas, living rooms, and kitchens. Worth a splurge, the largest unit even has its own private bayside pool. See p. 426.

- **Captiva Beach Resort** (Siesta Key, Sarasota; ℂ **800/349-4131** or 941/349-4131): Owners Robert and Jane Ispaso have done a terrific job updating this older motel about a half block from the beach on Siesta Key. Every one of their comfortable, sparkling-clean units has cooking facilities, and some have separate living rooms with sleeper sofas. Units go for $135 to $235 single or double in winter, but fall to $85 to $180 off-season. See p. 446.

- **Tropic Isle Inn** (Anna Maria Island; ℂ **800/883-4092**): Thanks to owners Bill and Heather Bomberger, this is another older motel that has come a long way from its humble beginnings. Most guest rooms, which have kitchens, open to a lushly landscaped courtyard sporting a tin-roof gazebo for lounging and a pool and brick patio for swimming and sunning. The beach is just across the road. See p. 448.

- **Hampton Inn Maingate West** (Orlando; © **800/426-7866**): The rooms aren't fancy, but they're clean and well kept. There's a free continental breakfast and a host of restaurants nearby on U.S. 192. See p. 475.

- **Disney's All-Star Resorts** (Orlando; © **407/934-7639**). There are three All-Star resorts in the Disney complex, with Movie, Sports, and Music themes. The rooms may be small, but at $77 to $124 a night, it's the least expensive way to take advantage of all the perks of being a Disney resort guest. Food courts serve pizza, pasta, sandwiches, and family dinner platters. There's also a full-size pool. See p. 470.

- **Shoreline All Suites Inn & Cabana Colony Cottages** (Daytona Beach; © **800/293-0653**): In a community with hundreds of inexpensive mom-and-pop motels, this one excels by offering 10 beachside cottages. Built in 1927, they have been completely modernized by owners Frank and Barbara Molnar. The little bungalows are about the size of motel rooms with kitchens, but they're light and airy, are attractively furnished with white wicker pieces, and have ceiling fans over their beds. The cottages share a heated beachside swimming pool with the adjacent Shoreline All Suites Inn, a motel built in 1954 but also substantially modernized. See p. 560.

- **Monterey Inn** (St. Augustine; © **904/824-4482**): A great choice for the price, this family-operated, wrought-iron-trimmed motel overlooks the Matanzas Bay from a location in St. Augustine's historic district. Three generations of the Six family have kept the 1960s building and grounds clean and comfortable. A small swimming pool, pleasant staff, and free coffee each morning are just some of the extras. See p. 576.

- **Kenwood Inn** (St. Augustine; © **904/824-2116**): Rooms in this Victorian wood-frame house with graceful verandas are larger and more private than most other accommodations in converted single-family homes. Everything from the carpeting to the linens to the china is first-class. There's an outdoor swimming pool, a lushly landscaped sun deck, and a secluded garden courtyard complete with a fish pond and neat flower bed under a sprawling pecan tree. See p. 576.

- **Beachside Motel Inn** (Amelia Island; © **904/261-4236**): The only motel beside the beach on this otherwise upscale island, this inexpensive property is clean and well-maintained by its resident owners. The rooms, many with ocean views, are spacious. Many long-term visitors return each season to stay in the efficiencies with fully equipped kitchens. An outdoor pool is surrounded by lounge chairs and a spacious deck overlooking the ocean. Rates include coffee and store-bought pastries each morning. See p. 598.

- **Florida House Inn** (Amelia Island; © **800/258-3301**): Built by a railroad in 1857, this clapboard Victorian building is Florida's oldest operating hotel. You can rock on the gingerbread-trimmed front veranda, from which President Ulysses S. Grant once made a speech. Although modernized, most rooms still have working fireplaces, and some have claw-foot tubs. Rates include breakfast in the boardinghouse-style dining room, which still provides family-style, all-you-can-eat Southern fare. See p. 598.

- **Five Flags Inn** (Pensacola Beach; ✆ 850/932-3586): This friendly motel looks like a jail from the road, but big picture windows look out to the swimming pool and gorgeous white-sand beach, which comes right up to the property. Although the accommodations are small, the rates are a bargain for well-furnished, gulf-front rooms. See p. 614.

- **Gibson Inn** (Apalachicola; ✆ 850/653-2191): Built in 1907 as a seaman's hotel, this brilliant, cupola-topped example of Victorian architecture is listed on the National Register of Historic Inns. No two guest rooms are alike—some still have the original sinks in the sleeping area—but all are richly furnished with period reproductions. Grab a drink from the oak bar and relax in one of the high-back rockers on the old-fashioned veranda. See p. 649.

9 The Best Family Accommodations for Parents Who Don't Want to Blow the Kids' College Fund

- **Riviera Court Motel** (Coral Gables; ✆ 800/368-8602): Built in 1954, this family-owned motel is a super-value option in this otherwise pricey area. There are no special facilities for children, but the pool and canal out back provide diversion. See p. 118.

- **Palm Beach Hotel** (Palm Beach; ✆ 800/536-7161): The best deal in town for those who want the convenience of a private apartment and don't need all the fancy extras of a full-service resort. A well-outfitted kitchenette means you don't have to rely on over-priced room service; you can always have milk, juice, and snacks on hand. A pool and sun deck, plus a coin laundry, all for less than the price of most Holiday Inns, make this a real steal. See "Palm Beach & West Palm Beach" in chapter 7.

- **Best Western Pink Shell Beach Resort** (Fort Myers Beach; ✆ 800/554-5454): This popular, family-oriented establishment's hotel rooms, suites, and one- and two-bedroom apartments can be affordable, especially if you opt for a package deal or weekly rate. The gulf-beach side of the property has water-sports equipment to rent, three heated swimming pools, a kiddie pool, and a thatch-roof bar. Sailboats and nature and sightseeing cruises pick up guests at the bayside marina, which rents boats. Facilities also include a coin laundry, a store for buying victuals, tennis courts, and rental bikes. Every unit has cooking facilities, but the Hungry Pelican Café, on a deck overlooking the channel, serves breakfast, lunch, and dinner. See p. 344.

- **Sundial Beach Resort** (Sanibel Island, ✆ 800/237-4184): A games area, kiddie pool, playground, small ecology center with touch tank, and fine children's recreation program make this large condo complex attractive to families. VCRs and movies can be rented, too. The one- to three-bedroom apartments have screened balconies overlooking the beach or tropically landscaped gardens. There are several dining options plus extensive recreational facilities. Winter rates starting at $290 per condo require a real splurge, but you can get in here for half that during off-season, even less on packages. See p. 355.

- **Best Western All Suites Hotel Near USF Behind Busch Gardens**

(Tampa; © **800/786-7446**): This hacienda-style building is the most beach-like vacation venue close to Busch Gardens Tampa Bay. Great for kids, "family suites" have over-and-under bunk beds in addition to a queen-size bed for parents. The three-story complex surrounds a courtyard with heated pool, hot tub, covered games area, and lively, sports-oriented tiki bar. You won't have kitchens in your suites (they do have microwave ovens), but you can graze a complimentary full-breakfast buffet, and the bar serves inexpensive char-grilled ribs, burgers, fish, and chicken for dinner. See p. 401.

- **Disney's Caribbean Beach Resort** (Orlando; © **407/934-7639**): Though the facilities aren't as extensive as at other Disney resorts, the Caribbean Beach offers good value for families. It's surrounded by 200 lush acres, and units are grouped into five distinct Caribbean "villages" around a large duck-filled lake. Children under 17 stay free in their parents' room. See p. 469.

- **Holiday Inn Family Suites** (Orlando; © **877/387-5437**): This modern, all-suite property does a wonderful job catering to a diverse clientele. Families appreciate the two-bedroom Kid Suites that feature a second semiprivate bedroom equipped with bunk beds and changing themes. Classic Suites have a semiprivate bedroom with a queen-size bed. Others are designed to accommodate romantics, fitness fanatics, and movie buffs. All suites have small kitchenettes. See p. 473.

- **Holiday Inn Nikki Bird Resort** (Orlando, © **800/206-2747**): Nikki Bird, the resident strolling mascot, is just one of the family-friendly perks at this property. The hotel has recently renovated its lobby, pool area, and rooms. Free transportation is provided to WDW parks. See p. 477.

- **Larson Inn Family Suites** (Lake Buena Vista, near Orlando; © **800/327-9074**): With a water park next door, an on-site playground, and poolside picnic tables, Larson's is an excellent family choice. All units have a microwave and refrigerator. Children under 18 stay free in their parents' room, and good package deals are available. See p. 475.

- **Victorian House** (St. Augustine; © **877/703-0432**): While most of St. Augustine's many bed-and-breakfasts won't accept children as guests, this one lets them stay in units occupying the Carriage House—actually an old store next door to the adults-only main house. The Carriage House units have TVs and private entrances, and one has a kitchen. See p. 577.

- **Sandestin Golf and Beach Resort** (Destin; © **800/277-0800** in the U.S., or 800/933-7846 in Canada): One of Florida's best sports-oriented resorts, this hotel/condo complex sprawls over 2,300 acres complete with a spectacular beach. While the adults choose from 81 holes of championship golf, the kids can keep busy at three wading pools, a playground, a tennis camp, or a summer children's program. See p. 627.

10 The Best Places to Stay on a Shoestring

- **Banana Bungalow** (Miami Beach; © **800/7-HOSTEL**): This lively youth hostel-style hotel, where the MTV Spring Break set can be found basking poolside, is across the street from a popular beach and only 6 blocks from the best shops, clubs, and restaurants.

Rooms are fully equipped, and a cheap restaurant and bar operate in-season. See p. 106.

- **Clay Hotel & International Hostel** (South Beach, Miami; © 305/534-2988): Housed in a gorgeous Mediterranean building at the corner of bustling and historic Española Way, this is South Beach's best budget find. See p. 107.
- **Key West International Hostel** (Key West; © 800/51-HOSTEL): Whether you are renting a bed in one of the super-cheap dorm rooms or a pricier, private motel room, if you can get a spot at this well-run hostel you have found one of the best deals in Key West. Motel rooms come with cooking facilities, a real plus in a town where overpriced tourist restaurants dominate the scene. Cheap eats are prepared on the premises. See p. 225.
- **The Sea Downs (and the Bougainvillea)** (Hollywood; © 954/923-4968): On a relatively quiet but convenient stretch of Hollywood beach, these oceanside properties offer a heated pool, barbecue grills, a picnic area, laundry facilities, a sun deck, and many units with kitchens for very reasonable rates. See p. 264.
- **Stoney's Courtyard Inn** (Naples; © 800/432-3870): This locally owned and well-maintained motel offers rooms starting at $90 single or double in winter, but they drop to as little as $45 during the off-season. You'll pay even less if you can find a discount coupon at a visitor information center. A heated swimming pool sits in a tropical courtyard, and there's a fitness center and coin laundry. See p. 374.
- **Clearwater Beach International Hostel** (Clearwater Beach; © 727/433-1211): In a predominantly residential neighborhood a short walk north of Clearwater Beach's busy commercial area, this official youth hostel has a swimming pool, communal kitchen, TV lounge, canoes and other toys to borrow, and bicycles to rent. See "St. Pete & Clearwater Beaches" in chapter 10.
- **Pelican—East & West** (Indian Rocks Beach; © 727/595-9741): The furniture is simple and dated, and you won't get frills such as phones in your rooms or a swimming pool, but this clean, comfortable, and friendly motel has four suites with kitchens in a quiet residential neighborhood some 500 feet from the beach. They start at $45 year-round. Four more expensive apartments sit right beside the beach. See p. 428.
- **Econo Lodge Maingate East** (Orlando; © 800/365-6935): This property is set well back from the highway, and it comes with bargain rates ($30–$110) for those on a budget. The hotel provides free shuttles to WDW parks, and transportation is available to other attractions. See p. 474.
- **Days Inn Eastgate** (Kissimmee; © 800/423-3864): Families like the picnic tables and play area on the lawn. The rooms are nicely decorated and range from $39 to $89. There's a restaurant (kids eat free), a sports lounge, a video-game room, coin-op washers/dryers, and a gift shop. Guest services sells tickets to the surrounding theme parks and offers rides to and from them (free for Disney). See p. 474.
- **Beach House** (Daytona Beach; © 800/647-3448): It's right in the heart of Daytona Beach's busy Main Street area, but if you can stand the crowds, the Beach House is an excellent choice at $29 to $89 single or double room,

$70 to $120 for an oceanview suite. All accommodations have front lawns with umbrella tables overlooking the ocean, and all but two have full kitchens. There are barbecue grills and a heated swimming pool. See p. 559.
- **Pirate Haus Inn & Hostel** (St. Augustine; © **904/808-1999**): You won't find a more convenient base for seeing St. Augustine's sites than this youth hostel in the heart of the historic district. It has five private units (three with their own bathrooms), equipped with either a queen or double bed plus one or two bunk beds. Two other units have dormitory-style bunk beds. See "St. Augustine: America's First City" in chapter 12.
- **Sunset Inn** (Panama City Beach; © **850/234-7370**): Right on the beach but away from the crowds, this very well-maintained establishment offers one- and two-bedroom apartments with kitchens for as little as $65 single or double in summer, $50 off-season. The inn sports a large unheated swimming pool and a spacious sun deck with steps leading down to the beach. See p. 574.

11 The Best Camping

Florida's state parks offer a variety of camping facilities, from primitive sites without even running water to full hookups for RVs. The sites cost between $10 and $20 a night, depending on the season, and all state parks accept camping reservations up to 11 months in advance.

- **Everglades National Park:** Although the National Park Service recently instituted a $10 fee for backcountry permits, the Everglades still has some of the most affordable and scenic campsites around. Choose from beachfront sites, rough ground sites inland, or chickees, large wooden platforms built over water. The chickees, which have toilets, are the most civilized and unusual. Be prepared for the bugs! See "Everglades National Park" in chapter 6.
- **Boca Chita Key** (Biscayne National Park): After a thorough cleanup, Boca Chita, the former Gilligan's Island of the monied set, shines in its rustic glory, with somewhat primitive campsites accessible only by boat. Enjoy the calm and quiet with no noisy generators to drown out the gentle sound of waves lapping against the shore. See "Biscayne National Park" in chapter 6.
- **Koreshan State Historic Site** (Fort Myers; © **239/992-0311**): The shady sites here are near the gardens and some of the buildings erected by the Koreshan Unity Movement, a sect that believed that humans lived *inside* the earth and established a self-sufficient settlement on these 300 acres on the narrow Estero River in 1894. Nature and canoe trails (rentals available) wind downriver to Mound Key, an islet made of the shells discarded by the Calusa Indians. See p. 331.
- **Collier Seminole State Park** (Marco Island; © **239/394-3397**): You'll be on the edge of the Everglades in this state preserve 12 miles east of Marco Island. The shady sites are organized around screened-in activities buildings. RV and tent campers are segregated here. The park has a multitude of nature-oriented activities to keep you busy. See "Marco Island" in chapter 9.
- **Fort DeSoto Park** (St. Pete Beach; © **727/866-2662**): The 230 sites in this 900-acre bird,

animal, and plant sanctuary sit on an island by themselves, and all have water and electricity hookups. The bayside sites are some of Florida's best, but they're sold out, especially on weekends. There's one major drawback: Unless you get lucky and arrive when there's a vacancy, you must appear *in person* and pay for your site no more than 30 days in advance. See "St. Pete & Clearwater Beaches" in chapter 10.

- **Disney's Fort Wilderness Resort and Campground** (Orlando; ✆ 407/934-7639): This woodsy 780-acre camping resort offers fish-filled lakes and streams. It also has a lot of facilities to keep you busy, and you're close to the Magic Kingdom. Secluded campsites offer 110/220-volt outlets, barbecue grills, picnic tables, and children's play areas. See p. 470.
- **Anastasia State Park** (St. Augustine; ✆ 904/461-2033): You'll be near 4 miles of sandy beach bordered by picturesque dunes, as well as a lagoon flanked by tidal marshes, at this urban park. Anastasia is one of Florida's most popular state facilities for camping, with its 139 wooded sites in high demand all year. They have picnic tables, grills, and electricity. Campsite reservations are required. See "St. Augustine: America's First City" in chapter 12.
- **Fort Pickens Area, Gulf Islands National Seashore** (Pensacola; ✆ 800/365-2267): You'll be near one of Florida's finest beaches at these 200 sites (135 with electricity) in a pine forest beside Santa Rosa Sound. Nature trails lead from the camp through Blackbird Marsh and to the beach. A small store sells provisions. You can make reservations up to 5 months in advance here. See "Pensacola" in chapter 13.
- **St. Andrews State Park** (Panama City Beach; ✆ 850/233-5140): This preserve of dazzling white sand and dunes has RV and tent sites beautifully situated in a pine forest right on the shores of Grand Lagoon. See "Panama City Beach" in chapter 13.

12 The Best Affordable Restaurants

- **Shells** (Statewide): You'll see Shells restaurants all over Florida, and with good reason, for this casual, award-winning chain consistently provides excellent value, especially if you have a family to feed. Starting at under $7, main courses range from the usual fried-seafood platters to pastas and char-grilled shrimp, fish, steaks, and chicken. They all have the same prices and menu, including a children's menu.
- **Front Porch Café** (South Beach; ✆ 305/531-8300): An outdoor cafe on Ocean Drive that's affordable and delicious? Say it isn't so! But it is! Front Porch Café is a locals' favorite for friendly service and fantastic food at very un-South Beach prices. See p. 124.
- **Latin American Cafeteria** (Miami; ✆ 305/226-2393): Hands down, this place serves the best Cuban sandwich north of Havana. Not only cheap, it's so big, you'll have leftovers for a subsequent snack, meal, or craving. See p. 131.
- **Versailles** (Miami; ✆ 305/444-0240): This is the place where Miami's Cuban power brokers meet over *café con leche* and pastries. The homey food is plentiful and cheap, if not always gourmet quality. See p. 134.

- **El Toro Taco Family Restaurant** (Homestead, near Miami; ⓒ **305/245-8182**): It's worth the price in gas to schlep down to Homestead for the most fantastic, homemade Mexican food in Miami. See p. 141.
- **Thai Spice** (Fort Lauderdale; ⓒ **954/771-4535**): Worth trying just for the super-cheap lunch specials, this tiny storefront is a great find in Fort Lauderdale's often overpriced and uninspired dining scene. See p. 267.
- **Tom's Place** (Boca Raton; ⓒ **561/997-0920**): An institution in otherwise exorbitantly priced Boca Raton, this successful barbecue joint offers expertly grilled meats paired with well-spiced sauces. See p. 279.
- **Banana Café** (Key West; ⓒ **305/294-7227**): For fabulous French food, three meals a day, Banana Café is the place to indulge without breaking the bank. Their crepes are phenomenal. See p. 227.
- **Farmers Market Restaurant** (Fort Myers; ⓒ **239/334-1687**): The retail Farmers Market next door may be tiny, but the best of the cabbage, okra, green beans, and tomatoes end up here at this simple eatery, frequented by everyone from business executives to truck drivers. The specialties of the house are Southern favorites like smoked ham hocks with a bowl of black-eyed peas. See p. 338.
- **Francesco's Italian Deli & Pizzeria** (Fort Myers Beach; ⓒ **239/463-5634**): Wonderful aromas of baking pizzas, calzones, cannolis, breads, and cookies will lure you to this Italian deli, where you can take "heat-and-eat" meals of spaghetti, lasagne, eggplant parmigiana, manicotti, and ravioli back to your hotel or condo oven. See p. 346.
- **Hungry Heron** (Sanibel Island; ⓒ **239/395-2300**): There's something for everyone on the huge, tabloid-size menu at Sanibel's most popular family restaurant—from hot and cold "appiteezers" and overstuffed "seawiches" to pasta and steamed shellfish. And even though this is an affluent island, main courses start at just $9. To keep the kids occupied, video cartoons run all the time. An all-you-can-eat breakfast buffet on Saturday and Sunday is an excellent value. See p. 358.
- **Sanibel Cafe** (Sanibel Island; ⓒ **239/472-5323**): Be sure to call for preferred seating at Sanibel's most popular breakfast spot, whose tables are museum-like glass cases containing delicate fossilized specimens from the Miocene and Pliocene epochs. Fresh-squeezed orange and grapefruit juice, Danish Havarti omelets, and homemade muffins and biscuits highlight the breakfast menu, while lunch features specialty sandwiches; shrimp, Greek, and chicken-and-grape salads made with a very light, fat-free dressing; and a limited list of main courses such as grilled or blackened chicken breast. See p. 359.
- **R. C. Otter's Island Eats** (Captiva Island; ⓒ **239/395-1142**): You can spend a fortune at Captiva Island's haute-cuisine restaurants, but not at this friendly, Key West–style cottage a block from the beach. Bare feet and bathing suits are welcome. The wide-ranging menu includes the island's best breakfasts, from bacon-and-eggs to house-smoked salmon. Musicians perform out in the yard every day. See p. 361.
- **Old Naples Pub** (Naples; ⓒ **239/649-8200**): You would never guess that the person sitting next to you at the bar here is very, very

rich, so relaxed is this small, intimate pub. The fare is extraordinarily inexpensive, given the location in the center of Naples's high-end 3rd Street South shopping district. Best bets are the chicken salad with grapes and walnuts and the burgers, steaks, and fish from the grill. There's live entertainment nightly during winter, Wednesday to Saturday nights off-season. See p. 376.

- **First Watch** (Naples, © 239/434-0005; and Sarasota, © 941/954-1395): These little restaurants are everyone's favorite spots for breakfast, late brunch, or a midday meal in Naples and Sarasota. They are anything but diners: You get classical music and widely spaced tables topped with pitchers of lemon-tinged ice water. The identical menus lean heavily on healthy selections, but you can get your cholesterol from a sizzling skillet of fried eggs served over layers of potatoes, vegetables, and melted cheese. Lunch features large salads, sandwiches, and quesadillas. See p. 377 and "Sarasota & Bradenton" in chapter 10.

- **Mel's Hot Dogs** (Tampa; © 813/985-8000): Just outside Busch Gardens, Tampa Bay, this red-and-white cottage offers everything from "bagel-dogs" and corndogs to a bacon/cheddar Reuben. Even the decor is dedicated to wieners: The walls and windows are lined with hot-dog memorabilia. See p. 405.

- **Carmine's Restaurant & Bar** (Tampa; © 813/248-3834): A great variety of patrons gather at this noisy corner cafe, one of Ybor City's most popular—if not the cleanest—hangouts. For lunch or dinner, you can order a genuine Cuban sandwich—smoked ham, roast pork, Genoa salami, Swiss cheese, pickles, salad dressing, mustard, lettuce, and tomato on a crispy, submarine roll. There's a vegetarian version, too, and the combination half sandwich and bowl of Spanish soup made with sausages, potatoes, and garbanzo beans makes a hearty meal for just $6 at lunch, $7 at dinner. See p. 407.

- **Yoder's** (Sarasota; © 941/955-7771): It's worth driving about 3 miles east of downtown Sarasota to this award-winning, Amish restaurant evoking the Pennsylvania Dutch country. The simple dining room displays handcrafts, photos, and paintings celebrating the Amish way. You'll get plain, made-from-scratch meat loaf, baked and Southern fried chicken, country-smoked ham, and fried filet of flounder. Burgers, salads, soups, and sandwiches are also available. Leave room for traditional shoo-fly pie. See p. 449.

- **Gulf Drive Café** (Bradenton Beach; © 941/778-1919): The coral and green dining room of this inexpensive gem opens to a beachside patio with tables shaded by a trellis. The breakfast fare is led by sweet Belgian waffles, which are available all day. You can also order salads, sandwiches, and burgers anytime here, with quiche du jour, Mediterranean seafood pasta, and regular seafood platters coming on line after 4pm. See p. 454.

- **Le Cellier Steakhouse** (Epcot; © 407/939-3463): Meet what is arguably one of the best menus in the theme parks' moderate class, featuring the usual cuts of beef in the $15 to $26 range and a good list of Canadian wine and Canadian beer. See p. 480.

- **Sunshine Season Food Fair** (Epcot; © 407/939-3463): Here's a great place where different tastes can dine under one roof. It's a six-in-one, counter-service restaurant that gives guests plenty of options, including sandwiches, barbecue, pasta, and more. Most items are $5 to $9. See p. 481.

- **Rainforest Cafés** (Lake Buena Vista; © 407/827-8500): Expect California fare with an island spin at these popular theme restaurants in Animal Kingdom and the Disney Marketplace. Main courses include chicken quesadillas, pot roast, turkey pitas, shrimp and pasta Alfredo, ribs, and chicken salad. See p. 481.

- **Pebbles** (Orlando, Lake Buena Vista; © 407/827-1111): Pebbles is one of Orlando's most popular restaurants, especially with yuppies. It offers the option of a casual meal, perhaps a cheddar burger on toasted brioche, honey-roasted spareribs, or a Caesar salad with grilled chicken. See p. 487.

- **Romano's Macaroni Grill** (Orlando; © 407/239-6676): Sure, it's a chain restaurant, but the ambience is warm and inviting, and the Northern Italian food is fresh and first rate. Especially scrumptious are the pizzas, fired in an oak-burning oven. A children's menu offers small-scale entrees for under $5. See p. 485.

- **Bahama Breeze** (Orlando; © 407/248-2499): Traditional Caribbean foods are used to create unusual items such as the moist and tasty "fish in a bag" (strips of mahimahi in a parchment pillow flavored with carrots, sweet peppers, mushrooms, celery, and spices) at this International Drive dining emporium. See p. 488.

- **The Bunnery Bakery & Café** (St. Augustine; © 904/829-6166): Alluring aromas waft from this bakery and cafe in the heart of St. Augustine's historic district. It's a great spot for breakfast before you start sightseeing, or for a fresh pastry and hot latte, cappuccino, or espresso any time you need a break. Lunch features soup, salads, burgers, panini, and croissants stuffed with walnut-and-pineapple chicken salad. See p. 578.

- **Biscottis** (Jacksonville; © 904/387-2060): This brick-walled little neighborhood gem might have come out of New York's East Village, San Francisco's downtown, or Washington's Georgetown. A young and hip wait staff is pleasant and well-informed. Daily specials, like pan-seared salmon or pork loin, are always fresh and beautifully presented, and huge and inventive salads are especially good. See p. 591.

13 The Best Seafood Restaurants

- **Fishbone Grille** (Miami; © 305/530-1915): It isn't scenic and it isn't where the tourists go, but this stellar little fish restaurant has some of the area's best seafood. In addition to an excellent ceviche, the stews, crab cakes, and starters are all superb. If you like Caribbean flavor, try the daily special with jerk seasoning. See p. 131.

- **Grillfish** (South Beach, Miami; © 305/538-2203): A limited menu of only the freshest and simplest seafood is served in a relaxed but upscale atmosphere. It's remained popular in an area where many others have failed because of its excellent food and trendy atmosphere but reasonable prices. See p. 121.

- **Sunfish Grill** (Pompano Beach in Broward County; © 954/788-2434): Chef Anthony Sindaco could be a star of Food Network proportions, but he prefers to have the spotlight shine on what some say (and we do, too) is the best seafood in South Florida. See p. 270.

- **Marker 88** (Islamorada; © 305/852-9315): A legend in the Keys, this dark, romantic restaurant has standard fare as well as a winning version of nouvelle cuisine. You'll find the area's largest selection of seafood, including lobster from the Keys, conch from the Bahamas, frogs' legs from the Everglades, stone crabs from the Florida Bay, and shrimp from the West Coast, among other dishes. See p. 203.

- **Monte's** (Summerland Key; © 305/745-3731): It's cash-only at this restaurant/fish market where plastic place settings rest on plastic-covered picnic-style tables in a screen-enclosed dining patio. Monte's has survived for more than 20 years because the food is very good and incredibly fresh. See p. 209.

- **Capt. Charlie's Reef Grill** (Juno Beach, in Northern Palm Beach County; © 561/624-9924): The cooking is imaginative and mouthwatering. A wide range of ever-changing selections include a Caribbean chili, a sizable tuna spring roll, and an enormous Cuban crab cake. Ask for suggestions, and enjoy this, one of the area's best-kept secrets, hidden behind a tiny strip mall. See p. 300.

- **Harbortown Fish House** (Fort Pierce; © 561/466-8732): This rustic, open-air fish house looks like a tourist trap, but last time we checked it was still serving the area's best seafood at reasonable prices. See p. 315.

- **Channel Mark** (Fort Myers Beach; © 239/463-9127): Every table looks out on a maze of channel markers on Hurricane Bay, and a dock with palms growing through it makes this a relaxing place for a waterside lunch. The atmosphere changes dramatically at night, when the relaxed tropical ambience is ideal for kindling romance. The delicately seasoned crab cakes are tops. See p. 345.

- **The Timbers Restaurant & Fish Market** (Sanibel Island; © 239/472-3128): This casual, upstairs restaurant, with bamboo railings, oversized canvas umbrellas, and paintings of tropical scenes through faux windows, is Sanibel's best place for the freshest fish available. The chef will charcoal-grill or blacken it to order. See p. 360.

- **Fourth Street Shrimp Store** (St. Petersburg; © 727/822-0325): The outside of this place looks like it's covered with graffiti, but it's actually a gigantic drawing of people eating. Inside, murals on two walls seem to look out on an early 19th-century seaport (one painted sailor permanently peers in to see what you're eating). This is the best and certainly the most interesting bargain in St. Petersburg. See p. 418.

- **Lobster Pot** (Redington Shores, near St. Pete Beach; © 727/391-8592): If you can afford a splurge, owner Eugen Fuhrmann supplies the finest seafood dishes on the St. Pete and Clearwater beaches. Among his amazing variety of lobster dishes is one flambéed in brandy with garlic, and the bouillabaisse is as authentic as any you'll find in the south of France. See p. 431.

- **Seafood & Sunsets at Julie's** (Clearwater Beach; © 727/441-2548): A Key West–style tradition takes over Julie Nichols's place at dusk as both locals and visitors gather to toast the sunset over the beach across the street. The best seats are in the tiny upstairs dining room. The menu features mahimahi charcoal-broiled with sour cream, fresh Florida grouper, and stuffed flounder. See p. 432.

- **Hemingway's** (St. Armands Circle, Sarasota; ✆ 239/388-3948): A laid-back, friendly Key West ambience prevails at this casual upstairs spot above ritzy St. Armands Circle. An eclectic "Floribbean" menu stars healthy mariner's shrimp: The crustaceans are perfectly chargrilled, basted with a light teriyaki sauce, and served over rice with fresh asparagus and baby carrots. See p. 452.
- **Down the Hatch** (Daytona Beach; ✆ 386/761-4831): This half-century-old fish camp on the Halifax River serves up fresh fish and seafood from its shrimp boat docked outside. You can start your day here with a country-style breakfast while taking in the scenic views of boats and shorebirds through the big picture windows—you might even see dolphins frolicking. In summer, light fare is served outside on an awninged wooden deck. Portions are large. See p. 562.
- **Singleton's Seafood Shack** (Mayport, near Jacksonville; ✆ 904/246-4442): This rustic restaurant has kept up with the times by offering fresh fish in more ways than just battered and fried. Yet, it has retained the charming casualness of a riverside fish camp. Even if you don't want seafood, this spot is worth stopping at just for a feel of Old Florida. See p. 592.
- **Back Porch** (Destin; ✆ 850/837-2022): The food isn't gourmet at this cedar-shingled shack, whose long porch offers glorious beach and gulf views, but this is where charcoal-grilled amberjack originated. Today, you'll see it on menus throughout Florida. Other fish and seafood, as well as chicken and juicy hamburgers, also come from the coals. See p. 630.
- **Staff's Seafood Restaurant** (Fort Walton Beach; ✆ 850/243-3526): Staff's started as a hotel in 1913 and moved to this barnlike building in 1931. Among the display of memorabilia are an old-fashioned phonograph lamp and a 1914 cash register. All main courses are served with heaping baskets of hot, home-baked wheat bread from a secret 70-year-old recipe. The tangy seafood gumbo also has gained fame for this casual, historic restaurant. See p. 633.
- **Chef Eddie's Magnolia Grill** (Apalachicola; ✆ 850/653-8000): Chef Eddie Cass's nightly specials emphasize fresh local seafood prepared in traditional French and New Orleans styles. Eddie sells gallons of his spicy seafood gumbo every November during the Florida Seafood Festival. See p. 649.
- **The Boss Oyster** (Apalachicola; ✆ 850/653-9364): This rustic, dockside eatery is a good place to see if what they say about the aphrodisiac properties of Apalachicola oysters is true. The bivalves are served raw, steamed, or under a dozen toppings ranging from capers to crabmeat. The chef will even steam three dozen of them and let you do the shucking. Dine inside or at picnic tables on a screened dockside porch. Everyone in town eats here, from bankers to watermen. See p. 649.

14 The Best Deals for Serious Shoppers

- **Prime Outlets at Florida City** (in the Upper Keys; ✆ 305/248-4727): This outlet mall has a manageable 60 or so stores including Nike Factory Store, Bass Co. Store, Levi's, OshKosh B'Gosh, and Izod. Although it is not well publicized, any customer at the mall is welcome to pick up a valuable "Come Back Pack" from the customer service desk. The square red packet contains dozens of coupons good for significant discounts. See "The Upper & Middle Keys: Key Largo to Marathon" in chapter 5.

- **Half Buck Freddie's** (Key West; © **305/294-2007**): Here, they stock out-of-season bargains and "rejected" clothing from the main store. See "Key West" in chapter 5.
- **Lord & Taylor Clearance Center** (Fort Lauderdale; © **954/720-1915**): The well-known department store operates this little-known clearance center, where discounts on new clothing for women, kids, and men can be as high as 75%. If you can handle open dressing rooms, overstuffed racks, and obnoxious sales help, it's a great find just west of Fort Lauderdale. See "Broward County: Hallandale & Hollywood to Fort Lauderdale" in chapter 7.
- **Sawgrass Mills** (Sunrise, Fort Lauderdale; © **800-FL-MILLS**): The monster of all outlet malls has more than 300 shops, kiosks, and restaurants in nearly 2.3 million square feet covering 50 acres. Look for discount coupon books at the information booth. They are good for substantial savings at dozens of mall stores. See "Broward County: Hallandale & Hollywood to Fort Lauderdale" in chapter 7.
- **The Shell Factory** (Fort Myers; © **239/995-2141**): Dating back more than half a century, this institution carries one of the world's largest collections of shells, shell jewelry, shell lamps, corals, sponges, and fossils. Many items here cost under $10, some under $1. There are plenty of amusement-park activities to keep the kids busy, too. See "Fort Myers" in chapter 9.
- **Fleamasters** (Fort Myers; © **239/334-7001**): This is one of the largest of Florida's numerous flea markets. The weekend Fleamasters has more than 800 busy booths offering bargains on antiques, crafts, fashions, and fresh produce. It has snack bars and entertainment, too. See "Fort Myers" in chapter 9.
- **Shells & Nature Toys** (Sanibel Island): If you have no luck scouring Sanibel Island's beaches for shells, head for **Sanibel Sea Shell Industries** (© **239/472-1603**), with more than 10,000 shells in stock; to one of the two locations of **She Sells Sea Shells** (© **239/472-6991** or 239/472-8080); or to **Neptune's Treasures Shell Shop** (© **239/472-3132**), which also has a good collection of fossils. Also on Sanibel, **Toys Ahoy!** (© **239/472-4800**) carries fascinating toys, games, and stuffed animals, and **The Cheshire Cat** (© **239/472-3545**) offers nature toys and other unique items for kids. See chapter 9.
- **Orlando Outlets** (Orlando): **Belz Factory Outlet World,** 5401 W. Oak Ridge Rd. (at the north end of International Dr.; © **407/354-0126**), and **Orlando Premium Outlets,** 8200 Vineland Ave. (© **407/238-7787**), are two of the better outlet malls in the area. See "Shopping" in chapter 11.
- **Ron Jon Surf Shop** (Cocoa Beach; © **321/799-8888**): Hundreds of billboards will lure you to this glaring, 24-hour surf shop, where you'll find a lot more than boards, wax, and everything else you need to look like a surfer. The shelves and racks hold souvenirs of

every description and a wide array of beachwear. See "Cocoa Beach, Cape Canaveral & the Kennedy Space Center" in chapter 12.
- **Silver Sands Factory Stores** (Destin; © **800/510-6255** or 850/864-9780): The third largest designer outlet center in the United States sports the upscale likes of Anne Klein, Donna Karan, J. Crew, Jones New York, Brooks Brothers, Hartman Luggage, Coach leathers, and Bose electronics. There are so many you'll have to drive from one end to the other to spot your favorite brands. See "Destin & Fort Walton" in chapter 13.

15 The Best Bars & Nightspots

- **Cafe Nostalgia** (Little Havana, Miami; © **305/541-2631**): They start with films from the old country and follow up with the hot sounds of Afro-Cuban jazz. It's become popular with a few non-Hispanics and lots of sentimental exiles. Plans are in the works to open a second Nostalgia in Miami Beach. See p. 177.
- **Fox's Sherron Inn** (South Miami; © **305/661-9201**): The spirit of Frank Sinatra is alive and well at this dark and smoky watering hole that dates back to 1946. Everything down to the vinyl booths and the red lights make Fox's a retro-fabulous dive bar. Cheap drinks, couples cozily huddling in booths, and a seasoned staff of bartenders and barflies make Fox's the perfect place to retreat from the trenches of trendiness. The food's actually good here, too. See p. 180.
- **Level** (South Beach; © **305/532-1525**): If you enter this cavernous, multi-leveled nocturnal playground slash dance club before midnight, you'll usually hit an open bar. Command central for countless events, parties and fashion shows, Level is above par when it comes to varying the program as far as dance clubs are concerned. See p. 174.
- **Mac's Club Deuce** (South Beach, Miami; © **305/673-9537**): Standing on its own amidst an oasis of trendiness, Mac's Club Deuce is the quintessential dive bar, with cheap drinks and a cast of characters ranging from your typical barfly to your atypical drag queen. It's got a well-stocked juke box, friendly bartenders, a pool table, and best of all, it's an insomniac's dream, open daily from 8am to 5am. See p. 181.
- **Tobacco Road** (Miami; © **305/374-1198**): Open every day of the year since 1912, Tobacco Road is a Miami institution. No matter who is playing, this two-story dive bar is worth a visit. From homegrown blues to nationally known jazz acts to poetry readings, you'll find the best live music and atmosphere at "The Road." Plus there are nightly dinner specials like complete lobster dinners on Tuesdays for $9.95 or a 14-ounce T-bone with all the fixings for $8 on Thursdays. Any night after midnight you can get a steak dinner for only $6. See p. 179.
- **Washington Avenue** (South Beach, Miami): On any Saturday night, you'll find the sidewalks packed from 6th Street to Española Way. There's no way to keep track of the many bars and clubs that go in and out as quickly as cars in a parking lot. See "Affordable Fun After Dark" in chapter 4.
- **Duval Street** (Key West): The partying-est strip this side of Bourbon Street is home to literally dozens of bars and dance spots.

Explore them for yourself. See "Key West" in chapter 5.

- **Epoch** (Key West; ⓒ **305/296-8521**): Formerly known as The Copa, this warehouse-style dance club made famous by its colorful gay patrons is right on Duval Street. It plays everything from techno to house to disco and welcomes anyone. See "Key West" in chapter 5.

- **Woody's Saloon and Restaurant** (Islamorada; ⓒ **305/664-4335**): This raunchy bar has live bands almost every night, but it is the house band you want to see. Big Dick and the Extenders is headed by a 300-pound Native American who does a lewd, rude, and crude routine of jokes and songs guaranteed to offend everyone in the house. Despite a small cover charge, drink specials, contests, and the legendary Big Dick keep this place packed until 4am almost every night. See "The Upper & Middle Keys: Key Largo to Marathon" in chapter 5.

- **Clematis Street** (West Palm Beach): This newly gentrified area has some of the area's best (and only) nightlife. Just over the bridge from stodgy Palm Beach, this 5-block area, from Flagler Drive to Rosemary Avenue, has everything from late-night bookshops and wine bars to dance clubs and outdoor cafes. See "Palm Beach & West Palm Beach" in chapter 7.

- **O'Hara's** (Hollywood/Fort Lauderdale; ⓒ **954/925-2555**): Kitty Ryan owns two of South Florida's best spots for live music. On Las Olas Boulevard in Fort Lauderdale, there is always a crowd enjoying smoking music. The newer Hollywood spot is swinging every night with live jazz and blues and good food, too. See p. 271.

- **Las Olas Boulevard** (Fort Lauderdale): This wide, scenic street, dotted with good clubs and late-night shopping, is especially popular with a more mature local crowd and European visitors. See "Broward County: Hallandale & Hollywood to Fort Lauderdale" in chapter 7.

- **The Leopard Lounge in the Chesterfield Hotel** (Palm Beach; ⓒ **561/659-5800**): This is a popular hangout, especially for older locals who come for live music, a great happy hour, and no cover charge. A generous spread of hot and cold appetizers, plus two-for-one drink specials, keep the blue-blazer crowd happy every evening starting at 5pm. See p. 294.

- **E. R. Bradley's Saloon** (Palm Beach; ⓒ **561/833-3520**): This big, old bar attracts a fun, loud crowd of young professionals and serious older drinkers. Come for the generous happy-hour buffets. See p. 294.

- **Junkanoo Beach Bar** (Fort Myers Beach; ⓒ **239/463-2600**): Away from the crowds of Fort Myers Beach's busy Times Square, the Junkanoo attracts a more affluent crowd for its constant Bohemian-style beach parties with live reggae and other island music. A concessionaire rents beach cabanas and water-sports toys, making it a good place for a lively day at the beach. See "Fort Myers Beach" in chapter 9.

- **Zoë's** (Naples; ⓒ **239/261-1221**): One of several excellent restaurants along Naples's trendy Fifth Avenue, Zoë's turns into a high-energy nightclub Friday and Saturday from 10:30pm to 2am. Nearby, **McCabe's Irish Pub** (ⓒ **239/403-7170**) features traditional Irish music nightly. See "Naples" in chapter 9.

THE BEST BARS & NIGHTSPOTS

- **The Dock at Crayton Cove** (Naples; © 239/263-9940): Right on the City Dock, this lively pub is a perfect place for an open-air meal or a libation while watching the action on Naples Bay. It's the best place in town to meet the locals; in fact, you're almost guaranteed to get into a conversation at the friendly bar. See p. 376.
- **Pleasure Island** (Lake Buena Vista; © 407/934-7781): Disney's after-dark headliner features clubs such as Mannequins (high-energy and techno), BET Soundstage (R&B, hip-hop, and more), Pleasure Island Jazz Club, Rock 'n' Roll Beach Club, and Comedy Warehouse. See p. 533.
- **Downtown Disney West Side** (Lake Buena Vista; © 407/824-4321): The happening hot spots here include Bongo's Cuban Café, House of Blues, and Planet Hollywood as part of a district that also includes shops and restaurants. See p. 534.
- **CityWalk** (Orlando; © 407/363-8000): Universal Orlando's nighttime entertainment district showcases several popular clubs, from the more laid-back pace of City-Jazz, Motown Café, and Bob Marley—A Tribute to Freedom to the giddy-up and go of the Latin Quarter, the groove, Pat O'Brien's, and a Hard Rock Live concert venue. See p. 534.
- **8 Seconds** (Orlando; © 407/839-4800): If you like country, it's hard to beat this place in O-Town, but the live riding during "Buckin' Bull Nights" help set this place apart from the others. See p. 536.
- **Sak Comedy Lab** (Orlando; © 407/648-0001): The head-to-head Duel of Fools and the improvisational play of Lab Rats keep the yuks coming at this downtown club. See p. 537.
- **Ocean Deck Restaurant & Beach Club** (Daytona Beach; © 386/253-5224): Generations of spring breakers, bikers, and other beach-goers know the Ocean Deck as Daytona's best "beach pub." Opening to the sand and surf, the sweaty, noisy downstairs bar is always packed, especially when the reggae bands crank up after 9:30pm nightly. The upstairs dining room can be noisy, too, but both you and the kids can come here for some very good chow, reasonable prices, and great views out the big window walls facing the ocean. See p. 562.
- **Seville Quarter** (Pensacola; © 850/434-6211): In Pensacola's Seville Historic District, this restored antique brick complex with New Orleans–style wrought-iron balconies contains pubs and restaurants whose names capture the ambience: Rosie O'Grady's Goodtime Emporium; Lili Marlene's Aviator's Pub; Apple Annie's Courtyard; End o' the Alley Bar; Phineas Phogg's Balloon Works (a dance hall, not a balloon shop); and Fast Eddie's Billiard Parlor (which has electronic games for kids, too). Live entertainment ranges from Dixieland jazz to country and western. See "Pensacola" in chapter 13.
- **Flora-Bama Lounge** (Perdido Key, near Pensacola; © 850/492-0611): Billing itself as the last great roadhouse, this slapped-together gulfside pub is almost a shrine to country music, with jam sessions from noon until way past midnight on Saturday and Sunday. Flora-Bama is the prime sponsor and a key venue for the Frank Brown International Songwriters' Festival during the first week of November. Take in the great gulf views from the Deck Bar. See "Pensacola" in chapter 13.

2

Planning an Affordable Trip to Florida

by Bill Goodwin

Most visitors go to Florida to see Orlando's theme parks or to relax on the beach. Choosing Walt Disney World as your destination is easy, but how do you pick a beach when Florida has some 800 miles of them?

Indeed, the Sunshine State has so much vying for your attention that planning a trip can seem overwhelming. But Florida's size and diversity also mean that it has bargains galore for the traveler who knows where to go, when to go, and how to mine for discounts.

We have scoured the state to come up with the great money-saving tips in this chapter, which will tell you where and how to look for the best deals. Also here is information and our advice about transportation, seasons and special events, taking care of your special needs, and picking among the myriad types of accommodations—always with an eye on saving you money.

Don't just rely on this chapter, however. We've captured Florida's many personalities, attractions, and specific bargains in the chapters that follow. Peruse each one to see which destinations offer the activities you're looking for and the prices that fit your budget. If you pick the right place and go at the right time of year, you can have a terrific trip to Florida without feeling forced into bankruptcy.

THE $70-A-DAY PREMISE

With careful planning, two people can travel in Florida from $70 a day, combining their money for accommodations and at least two meals a day. That is, we assume you have at least $140 a day between the two of you for room and board, less drinks and tip. The costs of sightseeing, outdoor activities, transportation, and entertainment are all extras, but don't worry: We'll provide tips on saving money in those areas as well.

1 50 Money-Saving Tips

IN GENERAL

1. Avoid traveling during the high seasons, especially in southern Florida where hotel rates can more than double from mid-December to April. Keep in mind also that many airlines have deep-discount promotional fares to Florida during the off-season. Central Florida sees less seasonal difference in prices, given its somewhat cooler winters and the year-round clientele visiting its theme parks. You can survive on $70 a day in northern Florida even during its high-summer season.

2. Always ask about discounts: corporate, students, military, auto club, senior citizen, and so on. Most airlines, car-rental firms, accommodations, attractions, and

even some restaurants offer such price breaks but don't necessarily volunteer the information. Be sure to bring identification or your group membership card with you. Most Florida activities and attractions offer discounts, but you'll need a valid ID to qualify for the bargain rates.

3. Use any coupons you can get your hands on. The ubiquitous give-away booklets (such as **Florida on the Go**) you'll see in racks at the tourist information offices and elsewhere may look like junk mail, but they're loaded with discount coupons you can use at hotels, motels, restaurants, and attractions throughout the state. Other, more comprehensive coupon books are for sale. In business since 1961, the **Entertainment** publications (☏ 800/374-4464) offer particularly well-stocked versions for Miami and the Keys and Orlando. Its books usually cost between $28 and $48, depending on the locale. Over at the St. Pete and Clearwater beaches, the **Gulf Beaches of Tampa Bay Chamber of Commerce** (☏ 800/944-1847 or 727/360-6957) sells a book with discounts at many area restaurants, attractions, and other establishments for about $30. You can recoup more than the cost of these books if you use them religiously. In Orlando, call the **Orlando/Orange County Convention & Visitors Bureau** (☏ 800-643-9492) and ask for a "Magicard" providing up to $500 in discounts on meals, some lodging, and at the smaller attractions. Also look for the free *Where Orlando* in restaurants and hotel lobbies; it contains discount coupons, and its website (www.travelfacts.com) has links to hot deals.

AIR TRAVEL

4. Ask for the cheapest airfare, not just the coach fare. As the tips below illustrate, there are many options.

5. Buy your ticket well in advance. Most airlines offer deep discounts on tickets purchased 7, 14, or 21 days before the departure date—and the cheap seats sell out first. Always ask about restrictions such as staying over a Saturday night. Tickets are usually nonrefundable if you must cancel your trip, but even if you have to pay an extra fee if you alter your plans later, you'll get substantial savings over the regular fare.

6. On the other hand, you can often benefit by buying at the last minute. You do run the risk of being stuck with a really expensive ticket—or no ticket at all—but when a flight is only half-sold, the airlines may offer deep, deep discounts to fill seats that aren't sold 72 hours before takeoff. This is a better strategy in the off-season, when flights are more likely to have empty seats.

7. Be flexible in your schedule. Flying on Tuesday, Wednesday, or Thursday can save you money with some airlines; the prime Friday, Sunday, and Monday flights are often priced higher. Also inquire about night flights; the red-eye may leave you bleary, but if it's substantially cheaper, it might be worth it—you can make up the sleep later.

8. Surf the Internet and save. There are lots of Web pages and online services designed to clue you in on discounted airfares, accommodations, and car rentals. And the airlines often sell last-minute unused seats on their websites.

9. If you don't have access to the Internet, consult a travel agent.

Florida

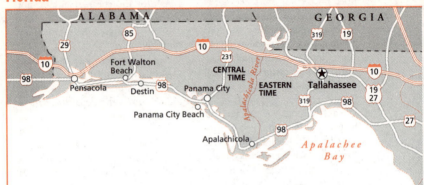

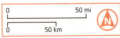

50 MONEY-SAVING TIPS

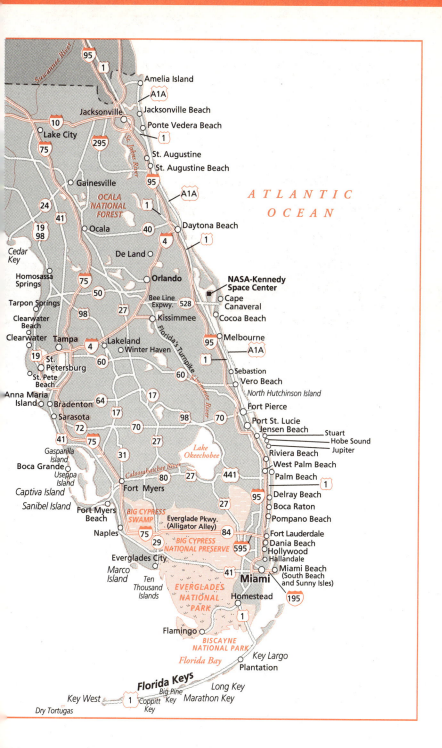

> **Tips** **Post 9/11 Discounts**
>
> In an effort to restore the state's tourism business in the wake of the September 11, 2001, terrorist attacks, **Visit Florida** is now offering special discounts on its website, www.flausa.com. Or you can call © 888/5-FLA-USA.

They can get on their machines and find you the cheapest airfares, room rates, package deals, and other travel bargains that you could never find. You're under no obligation to buy, although most agents now charge a fee for airline tickets, since most airlines have all but eliminated commissions in recent years. On the other hand, agents still work for commissions when selling hotels, car-rental companies, and tour operators.

10. Ask a travel agent about charter flights. Several airlines, such as the Canadian carrier Air Transat, have charter flights to Florida during winter. They can offer great savings over commercial airline fares, but make sure you book with a reputable firm and inquire about all restrictions before you pay.

11. Check out consolidators (also known as "bucket shops"). These wholesalers buy tickets directly from the airlines in bulk at heavy discounts, and then resell them. Many consolidators also book charter as well as commercial flights. The tickets are usually heavily restricted (ask about all the details), but you may save a bundle—usually 20% to 35%. See "Getting There," later in this chapter, for the names of reputable consolidators.

12. Check the travel ads in your local newspaper. Airlines, consolidators, and charter and tour companies love to advertise package deals and promotions in weekend travel sections around the country. Just remember: If you're dealing with a new company, or one that you're unfamiliar with, it's a good idea to check with the Better Business Bureau to make sure it's legit.

13. Take local shuttle services to and from the airports. Unless you're a family or group, they usually are less expensive than taxis. Some hotels will even pick you up at the airport for free, so be sure to ask if they have airport transportation when you book your room.

CAR RENTALS

14. Reserve your rental in advance, especially during the high seasons when cars, particularly the small, least expensive models, can be in heavy demand. Not only will you have a car waiting, you'll avoid paying top dollar for a vehicle that's larger than you need.

15. Call all the major car-rental firms, or check their websites, and compare rates (see "Getting Around," later in this chapter, for their toll-free numbers). Always ask for their cheapest rates. Even after you've made your reservations, call again and check rates a few days or weeks later—you may stumble upon a cheaper rate.

16. If you'll be visiting for a week or more, ask for a long-term rate. Most Florida firms offer substantial discounts for weekly rentals, especially during the off-season.

17. Be sure to ask for discounts if you belong to a national organization such as AAA, AARP, Costco Wholesale, or USAA, which negotiate special rates for their members. But be wary: Some of these

specials may be more expensive than the rental companies' weekly rates or promotional deals, so ask about all possibilities.

18. Keep in mind that Florida has a $2.05-per-day state highway fund surcharge, that state and local sales taxes will be added to your bill, and that many airports tack on another fee. The car-rental companies don't include these taxes when they quote rates, so before you hang up, be sure to ask how much your entire bill will be.
19. If there are only one or two of you traveling, reserve the least expensive subcompact or compact (sometimes called economy cars). You'll also save money on fuel and have an easier time parking. But be careful: Some reservations agents may tell you that all their least expensive cars are booked; this may be a ploy to get you to upgrade, so thank them and call another company. On the other hand, if you arrive with a valid reservation with a confirmation number, the agents are obligated to honor the rate you were quoted, even if they have to give you an upgrade. Make them stick to their original quote.
20. Never agree to buy gasoline from a car-rental company. It will always be less expensive at a station in town, so fill up just before returning the vehicle.
21. If you don't mind driving to Florida, ask about "drive out" programs that some firms use to reposition their fleets. Major companies like Avis, Budget, Hertz, and National sometimes move their cars from northern cities to southern Florida for the winter season, and you could get a ridiculously cheap rate if you'll drive the vehicles south (or back north in the warmer months).

ACCOMMODATIONS

22. Book early to get the least expensive room, and shop around. Use the toll-free numbers; at some chains, only the reservation clerks at the national number know about package deals that can save you money. Some major chains also post deals on their websites.
23. Don't just accept the "rack" or published rate—there's almost always a lower price available. Ask for the cheapest rate and about discounts for seniors, families, or any national organizations that you might belong to (especially AAA and AARP). Ask about special promotions and discounts for stays of a week or more.
24. Inquire about golf, tennis, and other packages. Many Florida establishments offer them, and you will pay less than if you ante up separately for the room and activities. Sometimes you can even get a rental car thrown in. We've mentioned the hotels and resorts that regularly offer package deals in the accommodations listings in this book. Their offers change frequently, however, so you'll have to ask.
25. Choose a hotel or motel that offers free continental breakfasts. The savings could enable you to afford better meals at lunch and dinner. The accommodations listings in this book indicate the properties that offer free breakfasts.
26. Stay a block or more from the beach, since hotels and motels not directly on the water usually are less expensive than those directly facing the sand. And in places where the prime resorts are on islands, mainland hotels and motels usually cost less than their offshore brethren (they also are more likely to offer discounted weekday or weekend rates). And

even if you elect a beachfront hotel, rooms with bay or garden views normally are less expensive than those directly facing the ocean or gulf.

27. If you're traveling with children, check to see if they can stay in your room for free. Or better yet, consider getting a one-bedroom suite with a pullout sofa in the living room; one suite is usually cheaper than two hotel rooms, and you'll still have privacy.

28. Get a room with cooking facilities. Many Florida establishments have units with at least kitchenettes. They cost a bit more than regular rooms, but preparing your own breakfast and lunch could slash your food costs in half. And it makes life a lot easier, especially if you're traveling with kids.

29. If you're staying for a week or more, consider a condominium unit, apartment, or cottage, especially if you're traveling with children. Condos usually have a sleeper sofa as extra bedding, a kitchen that lets you prepare some of your own meals, and the complexes usually have a pool and often tennis courts and other recreational facilities. Most have weekly rates that are less than paying by the night at hotels. Do note, however, that you'll usually have to pay extra for daily maid service.

30. Choose a hotel or motel that lets you make local calls for free. Most charge 50¢ or more per local phone call, and some even hit you with a fee on credit-card calls. Use the pay phone down in the lobby instead. Many hotels also tack on hefty surcharges for laundry, dry cleaning, and other services. You can cut these costs by choosing one with a guest laundry and washing your own clothes, and you can easily find dry cleaners on your own.

31. If you show up without a reservation, bargain at the front desk. This usually won't work during the high seasons, when most hotels are nearly full, but you might be able to strike a very favorable off-season deal. If you try this, arrive in late afternoon or early evening, when the majority of the guests with reservations have already checked in, and rooms that aren't yet occupied are likely to stay empty for the night. If the front-desk clerk is unhelpful, ask to speak to the hotel manager, who may be the only employee who can discount rooms.

DINING

32. Take advantage of Florida's usually fine weather by planning daytime and romantic sunset picnics. Many towns and cities have shops purveying gourmet picnic fare, and most of the large supermarkets such as Publix, Albertson's, and Winn-Dixie have deli sections with good selections of meats, cheeses, breads, and salads.

33. Ask the staff at your hotel or motel which local restaurants and cocktail lounges have happy-hour specials. They signal reduced prices on drinks, and sometimes appetizers.

34. If you don't mind dining before 6pm, take advantage of the early-bird specials offered by many restaurants. The selections may be limited, but they are a less-expensive way to sample the fine fare at otherwise expensive establishments. We've pointed out many of them in the dining listings in this book.

35. If you're traveling with the kids, inquire about children's menus or discounts. Most restaurants in Florida offer them—and at

resort-restaurant prices, they can be a real boon to your budget.

36. Look for fixed-price menus at the pricier restaurants, or splurge on a special meal at lunch rather than dinner. In general, you'll pay half (and sometimes even less than that) as much for a lunchtime main course as you will at dinner. You may not get the attentive service, but you'll be surprised at the quality, even at some of the pricier restaurants.

37. The Friday Calendar section of *The Orlando Sentinel* sometimes includes two-for-one dinner special coupons and other discounts on entertainment. It also lists cultural events and concerts throughout Central Florida, some of them free or for a small admission.

GOLF

38. Bring your own golf clubs, tennis rackets, snorkeling and scuba gear, and other equipment. In addition to saving the rental costs, your gear will fit correctly and be in top condition.

39. Before booking a tee-time, check with the agencies that represent many Florida golf courses (see "The Active Vacation Planner," later in this chapter). Some of them offer discounted fees and golf-travel packages. The best way to find a good deal for Orlando's many golf courses is to look in the sports section of the local newspaper, *The Orlando Sentinel,* for discount coupons and otherwise unadvertised specials.

THE MAJOR THEME PARKS

40. Stick with the Value Pass over the Park Hopper when buying multi-day tickets to the Walt Disney parks in Orlando. Both options permit visits to multiple parks over 4 days, but the Park Hopper pass allows you to visit more than one park during a single day. This can take considerable effort and time, so it's better to stick to the Value Pass, especially if you are traveling with children. And the 4-day Value Pass will save you about $17 per person.

41. Buy a combined pass to Universal Studios Florida, SeaWorld, Wet 'n Wild in Orlando, and Busch Gardens Tampa. You pay one price to get into all three over either a 7- or a 10-day period. The combined passes cost more up front, but you'll save in the long run. You can also save 10% if you purchase tickets on the Internet at Universal's site (www.uescape.com).

42. Look for discount tickets to SeaWorld and Universal Studios Florida on 2-liter bottles of Pepsi products. These discounts are usually available during Halloween Horror Night at Universal.

43. You can save 10% by purchasing your SeaWorld tickets through its website (www.SeaWorld.com).

44. Take food and drink with you into the parks. Grocery stores and discount drugstores tend to be a little more expensive in tourist areas, but filling coolers or backpacks with snacks, lunch basics, sodas, bottled water, juices, and other drinks will save you a bundle over the cost inside the parks.

45. Invest in inexpensive plastic rain ponchos for the entire family before you leave home. Many major parks include water rides, and it's miserable to walk around wet all day, even in the summer. Plus, they will come in handy during summer storms, which can come up quickly. In the parks, they cost twice what you'll pay at home.

46. If you have young children, bring lightweight, easy-to-carry strollers, since rentals inside the parks can add up. Don't bring your Cadillac

of kiddie carriers: It could be stolen.
47. Think twice about items such as souvenir cups or fanny packs that some hotels leave in your room. These are not complimentary: If you use them, you will be charged.
48. The Disney parks have outdoor carts selling things such as turkey legs, baked potatoes, and fresh fruit. These can easily make a simple meal and are cheaper than any restaurant food.
49. Buy your tickets to Busch Gardens Tampa Bay at Tampa Bay Visitor Information Center, across the street from the main entrance (© **813/985-3601**). You'll save a few dollars, and the staff is expert at advising you on how to maximize your time in the park. Many area hotels and motels have packages that include free or discounted admission.

NIGHTLIFE

50. Check out the local newspapers for free concerts and other entertainment in municipal parks. The Friday newspapers usually have entertainment sections listing activities for the upcoming weekend. And be sure to pick up copies of the local "alternative" tabloid newspapers; they're free and are packed with entertainment ideas.

2 The Regions in Brief

After you've figured out how much you have to spend, the next decision you'll have to make is where to go in Florida. You'll find ample sun, sea, and sand all along the 800 miles of shoreline here, but not every place in the Sunshine State is warm all the time. Many Florida beaches are lined with towering hotels and condominiums, whereas others are pristinely preserved in their natural states. You can spend your days in busy cosmopolitan cities or while them away in picturesque small towns steeped in history. You can take the kids to see Mickey Mouse, or you can find a romantic retreat far from the madding crowds.

Here is a brief rundown of the state's regions to help get you started.

MIAMI & MIAMI BEACH Sprawling across the southeastern corner of the state, metropolitan Miami is a city with many distinct personalities and a vibrant, international flair. Here you will hear Spanish and many other languages, not to mention accents, spoken all around you, for this cosmopolitan area is a melting pot of immigrants from Latin America, the Caribbean, and, undeniably, the northeastern United States in particular. Cross the causeways and you'll come to the sands of Miami Beach, long a resort mecca and home to the hypertrendy South Beach, famous for its Art Deco architecture, electric nightlife, and celebrity sightings. See chapter 4.

THE KEYS From the southern tip of Florida, U.S. 1 travels through a 100-mile-long string of islands stretching from Key Largo to the famous, laid-back "Conch Republic" of Key West, only 90 miles from Cuba and the southernmost point in the continental United States (it's always warm down here). While some of the islands are crammed with strip malls and tourist traps, most are dense with unusual species of tropical flora and fauna. The Keys don't have the best beaches in Florida, but the waters here—all in a vast marine preserve—offer the state's best scuba diving and snorkeling and some of its best deep-sea fishing. See chapter 5.

THE EVERGLADES Encompassing more than 2,000 square miles and 1.5 million acres, Everglades National Park covers the entire southern tip of Florida. The park, along with nearby Big Cypress National Preserve, protects a unique and fragile "River of Grass" ecosystem teeming with wildlife that is best seen by canoe, by boat, or on long or short hikes. To the east of the Everglades is Biscayne National Park, preserving the northernmost living-coral reefs in the continental United States. See chapter 6.

THE GOLD COAST North of Miami, the Gold Coast is aptly named, for here are booming Hollywood, Fort Lauderdale, ritzy Boca Raton, and Palm Beach—sun-kissed, sandy playgrounds of the rich and famous. Beyond its dozens of gorgeous beaches, the area offers fantastic shopping, entertainment, dining, boating, golfing, tennis, and just plain relaxing. With some of the country's most famous golf courses and even more tennis courts, this area attracts big-name tournaments. See chapter 7.

THE TREASURE COAST Despite gaining unprecedented numbers of new residents in recent years, the beach communities running from Hobe Sound north to Sebastian Inlet retain their small-town feel. In addition to a vast array of wildlife, the area has a rich and colorful history. Its name stems from a violent 1715 hurricane that sank an entire fleet of treasure-laden Spanish ships. Excavators turned up hundreds of ancient coins in the 1950s and 1960s, and you'll still see treasure hunters prowling the beaches with metal detectors. The sea around Sebastian Inlet draws surfers to the largest swells in the state. See chapter 8.

SOUTHWEST FLORIDA Ever since inventor Thomas Alva Edison built a home here in 1885, some of America's wealthiest families have spent their winters along Florida's southwest coast. They are attracted by the area's subtropical climate, shell-strewn beaches, and intricate waterways winding among 10,000-plus islands. Many charming remnants of old Florida coexist with modern resorts in the sophisticated riverfront towns of Fort Myers and Naples and on islands like Gasparilla, Useppa, Sanibel, Captiva, and Marco. And thanks to some timely preservation, the area has many wildlife refuges, including the "backdoor" entrance to Everglades National Park. See chapter 9.

THE TAMPA BAY AREA Halfway down the west coast of Florida lies Tampa Bay, one of the state's most densely populated areas. A busy seaport and commercial center, the city of Tampa is home to Busch Gardens Tampa Bay, which is both a major theme park and one of the country's largest zoos. Boasting a unique pier and fine museums, St. Petersburg's waterfront downtown is one of Florida's most pleasant. Most visitors elect to stay near the beaches skirting the narrow barrier islands running some 25 miles between St. Pete Beach and Clearwater Beach. Across the bay to the south lie Sarasota, one of Florida's prime performing-arts venues; the riverfront town of Bradenton; and another string of barrier islands with great beaches and resorts spanning every price range. See chapter 10.

WALT DISNEY WORLD & ORLANDO Walt Disney announced plans to build the Magic Kingdom in 1965, a year before his death and 6 years before the theme park opened, changing forever what was then a sleepy Southern town. In fact, Walt created a whole new world—if not universe—in central Florida. Today, at the dawn of the millennium, it seems that at least one full-scale theme park opens every year. Walt Disney World claims four distinct parks, two entertainment districts, enough hotels and restaurants to fill a small city, and several smaller attractions including water parks and miniature-golf courses. And then there are the rapidly expanding Universal Orlando, SeaWorld, and many more non-Disney attractions. Orlando is Florida's most popular tourist destination, and its visitors have never had more options. See chapter 11.

NORTHEAST FLORIDA The northeast section of the state contains the oldest permanent settlement in America—St. Augustine, where Spanish colonists arrived and settled more than 4 centuries ago. Today, its history comes to life in a quaint historic district. St. Augustine is bordered to the north by Jacksonville, an up-and-coming sunbelt metropolis with miles of oceanfront beach and beautiful marine views along the St. Johns River. Up on the Georgia border, Amelia Island has two of Florida's finest resorts and its own historic town of Fernandina Beach. To the south of St. Augustine, Daytona Beach is home of the Daytona International Speedway and is a spring-break mecca for the college crowd. Another brand of excitement is offered down at Cape Canaveral, where the Kennedy Space Center launches all manned U.S. space missions. See chapter 12.

NORTHWEST FLORIDA: THE PANHANDLE Historical roots run deep in Florida's narrow northwest extremity; and Pensacola's historic district, which blends Spanish, French, and British cultures, is a highlight of any visit to today's Panhandle. So, too, are the powdery, dazzlingly white beaches that stretch for more than 80 miles past the resorts of Pensacola Beach, Fort Walton Beach, Destin, and Panama City Beach. The Gulf Islands National Seashore has preserved much of this beach and its wildlife, and inland are state parks that offer some of the state's best canoeing adventures. All this makes the area a favorite summertime vacation destination for residents of neighboring Georgia and Alabama, with whom Northwest Floridians share many Deep South traditions. Sitting in a pine and oak forest just 30 miles from the Georgia line, the state capital of Tallahassee has a moss-draped, football-loving charm all its own. See chapter 13.

3 Visitor Information

Your best sources for detailed information about a specific destination in Florida are the **local visitor information offices.** They're listed under "Orientation" or "Essentials" in the following chapters.

Contact **Visit Florida,** P.O. Box 1100, Tallahassee, FL 32302-1100 (© **888/7-FLA-USA;** www.flausa. com), the state's official tourism marketing agent, for a free comprehensive guide to the state.

Visit Florida also operates **welcome centers** 16 miles west of Pensacola on I-10, 4 miles north of Jennings on I-75, 7 miles north of Yulee on I-95, and 3 miles north of Campbellton on U.S. 231. There's also a walk-in information office in the west foyer of the New Capitol Building in Tallahassee (see chapter 13).

Once you're here, you can call Visit Florida's 24-hour **tourist assistance hot line** (© **800/656-8777**) if you need help with lost travel documents, directions, emergencies, or references to attractions, restaurants, and shopping anywhere in the state. Hot-line operators speak several languages, including Spanish, French, German, Portuguese, Japanese, and Korean.

4 Money

The best way to get cash while you're traveling in Florida is to use your debit or credit cards at **ATMs**. Of the big national banks, **First Union Bank** and **Bank of America** have offices with ATMs throughout Florida.

Most ATMs are linked to a national network that most likely includes your bank at home. **Cirrus** (© 800/424-7787; www.mastercard.com/atm/) and **PLUS** (© 800/843-7587; www.visa.com/atms) are the two most popular networks; check the back of your ATM card to see which network your bank belongs to. Use the toll-free numbers to locate ATMs in your destination.

THEFT Almost every credit-card company has an emergency toll-free number you can call if your wallet or purse is stolen. Your own bank's customer service number is on the back of your credit card; write it down and put it someplace where it isn't likely to be lost or stolen. If you do lose it, the toll-free information directory (© 800/555-1212) will provide the number. Citicorp Visa's U.S. emergency number is © 800/336-8472. American Express cardholders and traveler's check holders should call © 800/221-7282 for all money emergencies. MasterCard holders should call © 800/307-7309.

The credit-card companies may be able to wire you a cash advance off your credit card immediately; in many places, they can deliver an emergency credit card in a day or two.

Odds are that if your wallet is gone, the police won't be able to recover it for you. However, after you realize that it's gone and you cancel your credit cards, it is still worth informing the police. Your credit-card company or insurer may require a police report number.

5 When to Go

To a large extent, the timing of your visit will determine how much you'll spend—and how much company you'll have—once you get to Florida. That's because room rates can more than double during the high seasons, when countless visitors migrate to the Florida sunshine.

The weather determines the more costly high seasons (see "Climate," below). In subtropical Southern Florida, it's during the winter, from mid-December to mid-April. On the other hand, you'll be rewarded with incredible bargains if you can stand the heat and humidity of a South Florida summer between June and early September. In North Florida, the reverse is true: Tourists flock here during the summer, from Memorial Day to Labor Day.

Presidents' Day weekend in February, Easter week, Memorial Day weekend at the end of May, the Fourth of July, Labor Day weekend at the start of September, Thanksgiving, Christmas, and New Year's are busy throughout the state, and especially at Walt Disney World and the other Orlando area attractions, which can be packed any time school's out (see chapter 11).

Northern and Southern Florida share the same "shoulder seasons": April and May and from September to November, when the weather is pleasant throughout Florida and hotel rates are considerably lower than during the high seasons. If price is a consideration, then these months of pleasant temperatures and fewer tourists are the best times to visit.

CLIMATE

Northern Florida has a temperate climate, and even in the warmer southern third of the state, it's subtropical, not tropical. Accordingly, Florida sees more extremes of temperatures than, say, the Caribbean islands.

Spring sees warm temperatures throughout Florida, but it also brings tropical showers.

Summer runs from May to September in Florida, when it's hot and very humid throughout the state. If you're in an inland city during these months, you may not want to do anything too taxing when the sun is at its peak. Coastal areas, however, reap the benefits of sea breezes. Severe afternoon thunderstorms are prevalent during the summer heat (there aren't professional sports teams here named *Lightning* and *Thunder* for nothing), so schedule your activities for earlier in the day, and take precautions to avoid being hit by lightning during the storms.

Autumn is a great time to visit—the really hottest days are gone, and the crowds have thinned out. Unless a hurricane blows through, November usually is Florida's driest month. August through November is hurricane season here, but even if one threatens, the National Weather Service closely tracks the storms and gives ample warning if there's need to evacuate coastal areas.

Winter can get a bit nippy throughout the state, and sometimes downright cold in Northern Florida. Although snow is rare, a flake or two has been known to fall as far south as Miami. The "cold snaps" usually last only a few days in the southern half of the state, however, and daytime temperatures quickly return to the 70s.

Average Temperatures in Selected Florida Cities (°F)

	Jan	Feb	Mar	Apr	May	June	July	Aug	Sept	Oct	Nov	Dec
Key West	69	72	74	77	80	82	85	85	84	80	74	72
Miami	69	70	71	74	78	81	82	84	81	78	73	70
Tampa	60	61	66	72	77	81	82	82	81	75	67	62
Orlando	60	63	66	71	78	82	82	82	81	75	67	61
Tallahassee	53	56	63	68	72	78	81	81	77	74	66	59

FLORIDA CALENDAR OF EVENTS

January

Toyota Gator Bowl, Jacksonville. Yet two more of the country's better college football teams battle it out in Alltel Stadium. Call ☎ **904/798-1700** or go to www.gatorbowl.com. Usually January 1.

Outback Bowl, Tampa. Two top college teams kick off at Houlihan's Stadium, preceded by weeklong series events. Call ☎ **813/874-2695;** www.outbackbowl.com. Usually January 1.

FedEx Orange Bowl Classic, Miami. Football fanatics flock down to the big Orange Bowl game at Pro Player Stadium on New Year's Day, featuring two of the year's best college football teams. Tickets are available from March 1 of the previous year through the Orange Bowl Committee (☎ 305/371-4600), but call early as they sell out quickly. January 1.

Epiphany Celebration, Tarpon Springs. After morning services at St. Nicholas Cathedral, young folks dive for the Epiphany cross in Spring Bayou. Call ☎ 727/937-3540. First Saturday in January.

Key West Literary Seminar. This 3-day festival attracts the biggest names in literature. Some past participants include Frank McCourt, Joyce Carol Oates, Amy Tan, and Jamaica Kincaid. This event sells out months in advance. Call ⓒ **888/293-9291** for details or check out the website at www.keywestliteraryseminar.org. Early to mid-January.

Art Miami, Miami. This annual fine-arts fair attracts more than a hundred galleries from all over the world. International, modern, and contemporary works are featured here, attracting thousands of visitors and buyers. For information call ⓒ **312/553-8924** or visit www.art-miami.com. Early January.

Art Deco Weekend, South Beach, Miami. Gain a newfound appreciation for the Necco-wafered Art Deco buildings, furniture, history, and fashion at this weekend-long festival of street fairs, films, lectures, and other events. Held along the Beach between 5th and 15th streets. Call ⓒ **305/672-2014** for details. Usually held Martin Luther King, Jr. weekend.

Goodland Mullet Festival, Marco Island. Stan Gober's Idle Hour Seafood Restaurant in Goodland is mobbed during a massive party featuring the Buzzard Lope dance and the Best Men's Legs Contest. Call ⓒ **239/394-3041;** www.stansidlehour.com. Mid-January.

Royal Caribbean Golf Classic, Key Biscayne, Miami. Watch as pro golfers such as Lee Trevino tee off for over $1 million at this tournament played on the scenic Crandon Park Golf Course. Call ⓒ **305/374-6180.** Late January.

Zora Neale Hurston Festival of the Arts and Humanities, Eatonville. This 4-day celebration of the author's life and works is held in the nation's first African-American municipality. Call ⓒ **800/352-3865** or 407/647-3307 for details. Usually last week in January.

February

Edison Pageant of Light, Fort Myers. The spectacular Parade of Lights tops off arts-and-crafts shows, pageants, and a 5K race. Call ⓒ **239/489-9314;** www.edisonfestival.org. First 2 weeks in February.

Gasparilla Pirate Fest, Tampa. Hundreds of boats and rowdy "pirates" invade the city, then parade along Bayshore Boulevard, showering crowds with beads and coins. Call ⓒ **813/353-8108;** www.gasparillapiratefest.com. Early February.

Everglades Seafood Festival, Florida City. Fish lovers flock to Florida City for a 2-day feeding frenzy, in which delicacies from stone crabs to gator tails are served from shacks and booths on the outskirts of this quaint old Florida town. Call ⓒ **239/695-4100.** First full weekend in February.

Miami Film Festival, Miami. Not exactly Cannes, but the Miami Film Festival, sponsored by the Film Society of America, is an impressive 10-day celluloid celebration, featuring world premieres of Latin American, domestic, and other foreign and independent films. Actors, producers, and directors plug their films and participate in Q & A sessions with the audiences. Call ⓒ **305/377-FILM.** Early to mid-February.

Speedweeks, Daytona. Nineteen days of events, with a series of races that draw the top names in NASCAR stock-car racing, all culminate in the Daytona 500. All events take place at the Daytona International Speedway. Especially for the **Daytona 500,** tickets must be purchased even a year in advance. They go on sale January 1 of the prior year. Call ⓒ **904/253-7223;** www.daytonaintlspeedway.com. First 3 weeks of February.

Miami International Boat Show, Miami. This show draws almost a quarter of a million boat enthusiasts to the Miami Beach Convention Center and the surrounding locations to see the megayachts, sailboats, dinghies, and accessories. It's the biggest anywhere. Call ⓒ **305/531-8410** for more information and ticket prices. Mid-February.

Florida State Fair, Tampa. Despite all its development, Florida still is a major agricultural state, which status it celebrates at this huge annual exposition. See judged competitions, botanical gardens, crafts buildings, carny rides, and nationally known entertainers. Call ⓒ **800/345-FAIR;** www.floridastatefair.com. Early to mid-February.

Mardi Gras at Universal Studios, Orlando. Authentic parade floats from New Orleans, stilt walkers, and traditional doubloons and beads thrown to the crowd add to the fun of this event, and all are included in the regular park admission. Call ⓒ **800/837-2273** or 407/363-8000; www.universalorlando.com. Mid-February.

Coconut Grove Arts Festival, Coconut Grove, Miami. Florida's largest art festival features over 300 artists who are selected from thousands of entries to exhibit their work. Possibly one of the most crowded street fairs in South Florida, the festival attracts art lovers, artists, and lots of college students who seem to think this event is the Mardi Gras of art fairs. Call ⓒ **305/447-0401.** Presidents' Day weekend.

March

Bike Week, Daytona Beach. An international gathering of motorcycle enthusiasts draws a crowd of more than 200,000. In addition to major races held at Daytona International Speedway (featuring the world's best road racers, motocrossers, and dirt trackers), there are motorcycle shows, beach parties, and the Annual Motorcycle Parade, with thousands of riders. Call ⓒ **800/854-1234** or 904/255-0981;www.officialbikeweek.com. First week in March.

Sanibel Shell Fair, Sanibel and Captiva Islands. Featured are a show of shells from around the world and the sale of unusual shell art. Call ⓒ **239/472-2155;** www.sanibel-captiva.org. Begins first Thursday in March.

Spring Break, Daytona Beach, Miami Beach, Panama City Beach, Key West, and other beaches. College students from all over the United States and Canada flock to Florida for endless partying, wet T-shirt and bikini contests, free concerts, volleyball tournaments, and more. Tune into MTV if you can't be here. Call the local visitor information offices. Three weeks in March.

Winter Party, Miami Beach. Gays and lesbians from around the world book trips to Miami as far as a year in advance to attend this weekend-long series of parties and events benefiting the Dade Human Rights Foundation. Travel arrangements can be made through Different Roads Travel, the event's official travel company, by calling ⓒ **888/ROADS-55, ext. 510.** For information on specific events and prices, call ⓒ **305/538-5908** or visit www.winterparty.com. Early March.

Calle Ocho Festival, Miami. What Carnivale is to Rio, the Calle Ocho Festival is to Miami—a 10-day extravaganza, also known as Carnival Miami, featuring a lengthy block party spanning 23 blocks, live salsa music, parades and, of course, tons of savory Cuban delicacies. Those afraid of mob scenes should avoid this party at all costs. Southwest 8th Street between Fourth and 27th avenues. Call © **305/644-8888.** Early to mid-March.

Grand Prix of Miami, Homestead. A little bit of Daytona in Miami, the Grand Prix is a premier racing event, attracting celebrities, Indy car drivers, and curious spectators who get a buzz from the smell of gasoline. Get tickets early; this event sells out quickly. Call © **305/250-5200.** Sometime in March.

Bay Hill Invitational, Orlando. Hosted by Arnold Palmer and featuring Orlando-based golfers like Tiger Woods, this PGA Tour event is held at the Bay Hill Club, 9000 Bay Hill Blvd. Call © **407/876-2429** or 407/876-2888 for details. Mid-March.

April

Springtime Tallahassee, Tallahassee. The state capital welcomes abundant azaleas, camellias, and other blossoms. A don't-miss event for garden lovers. Call © **850/224-5012;** www.springtimetallahassee.com. Runs 4 weeks from late March.

Festival of States, St. Petersburg. Since 1921, one of the South's largest civic celebrations offers national band competition, three parades, concerts, sports, and more. Call © **727/898-3654;** festivalofstates@aol.com. First full week in April.

Black College Reunion, Daytona Beach. Some 75,000 students from 115 predominantly African-American universities bring a sometimes-rowdy end to the spring-break season. Call © **800/854-1234** or 904/255-0415; www.daytonabeach.com. Mid-April.

PGA Seniors Golf Championship, Palm Beach Gardens. Held at the PGA National Resort & Spa, it's the oldest and most prestigious of the senior tournaments. Call © **561/624-8400** for the lineup. Mid-April.

Epcot International Flower & Garden Festival, Orlando. This event showcases gardens, topiary characters, floral displays, speakers, and seminars. Call © **407/824-4321** or visit www.disneyworld.com. Six weeks, beginning in mid-April.

Sunfest, West Palm Beach. A huge party happens on Flagler Drive in the downtown area with four stages of continuous music, a crafts marketplace, a juried art show, a youth park, and fireworks. Call © **561/659-5992** for details. Late April to early May.

Orlando International Fringe Festival, Orlando. From sword swallowing to a 7-minute version of *Hamlet,* this 10-day festival presents over 100 acts. See drama, comedy, political satire, and experimental theater at various outdoor stages in downtown Orlando. Call © **407-648-0077** for ticket information. Late April to early May.

May

Isle of Eight Flags Shrimp Festival, Amelia Island. Blessing of the fleet, best-decorated shrimp boat contest, and tons of shrimp to eat are part of what make this festival so much fun. Call © **800/2-AMELIA;** www.shrimpfestival.com. First weekend in May.

The Shell Air & Sea Show, Fort Lauderdale. It's a tough call as far as what's more crowded—the air, the sea, or the ground, which attracts over two million onlookers craning their necks for a view of big-name airwolves such as the Blue Angels and the Thunderbirds. Call ✆ **954/467-3555.** Early May.

Florida Springfest, Pensacola. National rock, country, jazz, reggae, and pop musicians perform over 4 days, plus there are children's activities and more. Call ✆ **850/469-1069;** www.springfest.net. Mid-May.

Mayfest, Destin. This upscale arts-and-crafts festival attracts more than 20,000 people to look, buy, and sample fine cuisine at the Panhandle's ritziest resort. Call ✆ **850/837-6241;** www.destinchamber.com. Third full weekend in May.

Coconuts Dolphin Tournament, Key Largo. This is the largest fishing tournament in the Keys, offering $5,000 and a Dodge Ram pickup truck to the person who breaks the record for the largest fish caught. The competition is fierce! Call ✆ **305/451-4107** for details. Mid-May, usually the weekend before Memorial Day.

June

Fiesta of Five Flags, Pensacola. This extravaganza commemorates the Spanish conquistador Tristan de Luna's arrival in 1559. Call ✆ **850/433-6512;** www.fiestaoffiveflags.org. First week in June.

Gay Weekend, Orlando. This weekend, grown out of the "Gay Day" that has been unofficially held at Walt Disney World since the early 1990s, attracts tens of thousands of gay and lesbian travelers to central Florida. Special events at other attractions, including Universal and SeaWorld, also cater to gay and lesbian travelers. You can get information at **www.gayday.com.** First weekend in June.

Billy Bowlegs Festival, Fort Walton Beach. A fleet of modern-day pirates captures the Emerald Coast in a rollicking, weeklong bash honoring notorious buccaneer William Augustus Bowles. A treasure hunt, parade, and carnival are also featured. Call ✆ **800/322-3319;** www.destin-fwb.com. First week of June.

Coconut Grove Goombay Festival, Miami. They may say it's better in the Bahamas, but you may disagree after attending Miami's own Bahamian bash, featuring lots of dancing in the streets, marching bands, scorching Caribbean temperatures, and the ever buzz-worthy and refreshing Goombay punch. Call ✆ **305/372-9966** for festival details. Early June.

Spanish Night Watch Ceremony, St. Augustine. Actors in period dress lead a torchlight procession through historic St. Augustine and reenact the closing of the city gates with music and pageantry. Call ✆ **800/OLD-CITY;** www.visitoldcity.com. Third Saturday in June.

July

Pepsi 400, Daytona. This race marks the halfway point in the NASCAR Winston Cup Series for stock cars. Held at the Daytona International Speedway at 11am. Call ✆ **904/253-7223;** www.daytonaintlspeedway.com. July 4.

World's Richest Tarpon Tournament, Boca Grande. Some $175,000 is at stake in the great tarpon waters off Southwest Florida. Call ✆ **941/964-0568;** www.bocagrandechamber.com. Second Wednesday and Thursday in July.

Lower Keys Underwater Music Fest, Looe Key. At this outrageous celebration, boaters go out to the

The Boys of Spring

Major-league baseball fans can watch the Florida Marlins in Miami and the Tampa Bay Devil Rays in St. Petersburg throughout their seasons from April through September, but the entire state is a baseball hotbed from late February through March, when many other teams tune up for the regular season with "Grapefruit League" exhibition games.

Most of Florida's spring-training stadiums are relatively small, so fans can see their favorite players up close, maybe even get a handshake or an autograph. Also, tickets are priced from $5 to $12, a bargain when compared with admission for regular-season games. Many games sell out by early March, so don't wait until you're in Florida to buy tickets.

The teams can move from year to year, so contact the **Florida Sports Foundation,** 2390 Kerry Forest Pkwy., Suite 101, Tallahassee, FL 32309 (**850/488-8347;** fax 850/922-0482; www.flasports.com), which usually posts the Grapefruit League schedules on its website late in January. The main office of **Major League Baseball,** 350 Park Ave., New York, NY 10022 (**212/339-7800;** www.mlb.com), is another place to find out where your favorite teams will be playing.

Here's where they played in 2002 (except for the Florida Marlins, who had announced plans to relocate to Jupiter in 2003). See the outdoor activities sections in subsequent chapters for specifics.

Atlanta Braves, Lake Buena Vista, near Orlando (**407/939-GAME;** www.braves.mlb.com); **Baltimore Orioles,** Fort Lauderdale (**954/776-1921;** www.orioles.mlb.com); **Boston Red Sox,** Fort Myers (**877/733-7699;** www.redsox.mlb.com); **Cincinnati Reds,** Sarasota (**941/954-4464;** www.reds.mlb.com); **Cleveland Indians,** Winter Haven (**863/293-3900;** www.indians.mlb.com); **Detroit Tigers,** Lakeland (**813/287-8844** or 407/839-3900; www.tigers.mlb.com); **Florida Marlins,** Jupiter (**305/930-HITS;** www.marlins.mlb.com); **Houston Astros,** Kissimmee, near Orlando (**407/933-2520;** www.astros.mlb.com); **Kansas City Royals,** Davenport (**868/424-2500;** www.royals.mlb.com); **Los Angeles Dodgers,** Vero Beach (**561/569-4900;** www.dodgers.mlb.com); **Minnesota Twins,** Fort Myers (**800/338-9467;** www.twins.mlb.com); **Montreal Expos,** Jupiter (**561/775-1818;** www.expos.mlb.com); **New York Mets,** Port St. Lucie (**561/871-2115;** www.mets.mlb.com); **New York Yankees,** Tampa (**813/879-2244;** www.yankees.mlb.com); **Philadelphia Phillies,** Clearwater (**727/442-8496;** www.phillies.mlb.com); **Pittsburgh Pirates,** Bradenton (**941/748-4610;** www.pirates.mlb.com); **St. Louis Cardinals,** Jupiter (**561/775-1818,** ext. 7; www.cardinals.mlb.com); **Tampa Bay Devil Rays,** St. Petersburg (**888/FAN-RAYS** or 727/825-3250; www.devilrays.mlb.com); **Texas Rangers,** Port Charlotte (**941/625-9500;** www.rangers.mlb.com); **Toronto Blue Jays,** Dunedin (**800/707-8269** or 813/733-0429; www.bluejays.mlb.com).

underwater reef of Looe Key Marine Sanctuary off Big Pine Key, drop speakers into the water, and pipe in music. A snorkeling Elvis can usually be spotted at this entertaining event. Call © **800/872-3722** for details. Usually second Saturday of July.

Blue Angels Air Show, Pensacola. World-famous navy pilots do their aerial acrobatics just 100 yards off Pensacola Beach. Call © **800/874-1234** or 850/434-1234; www.visitpensacola.com or www.blueangels.navy.mil. Early July.

August

Miami Reggae Festival, Miami. Jamaica's best dance-hall and reggae artists turn out for this 2-day festival. Burning Spear, Steel Pulse, Spragga Benz, and Jigsy King have participated recently. Call Jamaica Awareness at © **305/891-2944** for more details. Early August.

September

Labor Day Pro-Am Surfing Festival, Cocoa Beach. One of the largest surfing events on the East Coast draws pros and amateurs from around the country. Featured are rock-and-roll bands and swimsuit contests. Call © **800/927-9659;** www.space-coast.com. Labor Day weekend.

October

Destin Seafood Festival, Destin. The "World's Luckiest Fishing Village" cooks its bountiful catch in every style of cuisine imaginable. Also offered are arts, crafts, and music. This festival comes right after the Destin Fishing Rodeo, which has 450 angler awards and giant dock parties. Call © **850/837-6241;** www.destinchamber.com. First full weekend in October.

Biketoberfest, Daytona. Road-racing stars compete at the CCS Motorcycle Championship at Daytona International Speedway, plus there are parties, parades, concerts, and more. Call © **800/854-1235;** www.biketoberfest.org. Mid-October.

Clearwater Jazz Holiday, Clearwater. Top jazz musicians play for 4 days and nights at bayfront Coachman Park in this free musical extravaganza. Call © **727/461-5200;** www.clearwaterjazz.com. Mid-October.

Columbus Day Regatta, Miami. Find anything that can float—from an inner tube to a 100-foot yacht—and you'll fit right in. Yes, there actually is a race, but how can you keep track when you're partying with a bunch of semi-naked psychos in the middle of Biscayne Bay? It's free and it's wild. Rent a boat, jet ski, or sailboard to get up close. Be sure to secure a vessel early, though—everyone wants to be there. Check local newspapers for exact date and time. Columbus Day weekend.

Halloween Horror Nights, Orlando. Universal Studios transforms its grounds for 19 nights into haunted attractions with live bands, a psychopath's maze, special shows, and hundreds of ghouls and goblins roaming the streets. The studio closes at dusk, reopening in a new macabre form at 7pm. Full admission is charged for the event, which is geared toward adults. Call © **800/837-2273** or 407/363-8000; www.universalorlando.com. Mid-October through Halloween.

Mickey's Not-So-Scary Halloween Party, Orlando. At Walt Disney World, guests are invited to trick or treat in the Magic Kingdom, starting at 7pm. The party includes parades, storytelling, live music, and a bewitching fireworks display. Call © **407/934-7639** for information; www.disneyworld.com. End of October.

Guavaween, Tampa. Ybor City's Latin-style Halloween celebration begins with the "Mama Guava Stumble," a wacky costume parade. All-night concerts from rock to reggae are featured. Call © 877/934-3782 or 813/248-3712; www.ybor.org. October 31.

Fantasy Fest, Key West. Mardi Gras takes a Florida holiday as the streets of Key West are overtaken by wildly costumed revelers who have no shame and no parental guidance. Definitely leave the kids at home and join the parade! Call © 305/296-1817. Last week of October.

Epcot International Food & Wine Festival, Orlando. Sip and savor the food and wines of 30 cultures. Events include wine tastings, seminars, and celebrity-chef cooking demonstrations. Call © 407/827-7200 or 407/824-4321 for ticket information. Mid-October through early-November.

November

Frank Brown International Songwriters' Festival, Pensacola. Composers gather at the infamous Flora-Bama Lounge and other beach venues to perform their country-music hits. Call © 850/492-7664; www.fbisf.com. First week in November.

Florida Seafood Festival, Apalachicola. Book a room at the Gibson Inn 5 years in advance of this huge chow-down in Florida's oystering capital. Call © 888/653-8011; www.floridaseafoodfestival.com. First Saturday in November.

The Walt Disney World Festival of the Masters, Orlando. One of the largest art shows in the South takes place at Downtown Disney Marketplace over 3 days. The exhibition features top artists, photographers, and craftspeople, all winners of juried shows throughout the country. Free admission. Call © 407/824-4321; www.disneyworld.com. Second weekend in November.

Miami Bookfair International, downtown Miami. Bibliophiles, literati, and some of the world's most prolific authors descend upon downtown Miami for a weeklong homage to the written word in what happens to be the largest book fair in the U.S. The weekend street fair draws the biggest crowds: Regular folk mix with wordsmiths such as Tom Wolfe and Jane Smiley while indulging in snacks, antique books, and literary gossip. All lectures are free, but they fill up quickly, so get there early. Call © 305/237-3258 for lecture schedules. Mid-November.

Blue Angels Homecoming Air Show, Pensacola. World-famous navy pilots do their aerial acrobatics just 100 yards off the beach. Call © 850/452-2311; www.visitpensacola.com or www.blueangels.navy.mil. Second weekend in November.

American Sandsculpting Festival, Fort Myers Beach. Some 50,000 gather to sculpt or see the world's finest sand castles. Call © 800/782-9283 or 239/463-6451; www.fmbchamber.com. First weekend in November.

White Party Week, Miami. This weeklong series of parties to benefit AIDS research is built around the main event, the White Party, which takes place at Villa Vizcaya and sells out as early as a year in advance. Philanthropists and celebrities such as Calvin Klein and David Geffen join thousands of white-clad, mainly gay men (and some women) in what has become one of the world's hottest (and hardest-to-score) tickets. Call © 305/667-9296 or visit www.whitepartyweek.

com for a schedule of parties and events. Thanksgiving week.

December

Edison/Ford Winter Homes Holiday House, Fort Myers. Christmas music and thousands of lights hail the holiday season. At the same time, candles create a spectacular Luminary Trail along the full length of Sanibel Island's Periwinkle Way. Call © **239/334-7419;** www.edison-ford-estate.com. First week of December.

Captiva Sea Kayak Classic, Captiva Island. Sea kayaker and surf skiers from around the nation depart from the beach in front of 'Tween Waters Inn for a series of races. Call © **239/472-5161;** www.sanibel-captiva.org. First weekend in December.

Christmas at Walt Disney World, Orlando. As you would imagine, all of the Disney properties get into the holiday spirit. In the Magic Kingdom, Main Street is lavishly decked out with lights and holly and an 80-foot glistening tree. Attend Mickey's Very Merry Christmas Party in the Magic Kingdom, and Holidays Around the World and the Candlelight Procession at Epcot. Call © **407/824-4321** for holiday events, call © **407/934-7639** for special travel packages, or visit www.disney.com. Throughout December.

British Night Watch & Grand Illumination Ceremony, St. Augustine. A torchlight procession through the Spanish Quarter kicks off a month of Christmas festivities and the "Nights of Lights," in which 1.25 million twinkling bulbs bathe the Old City. Call © **800/OLD-CITY;** www.visitoldcity.com. First Saturday in December; Nights of Lights to January 31.

The Citrus Bowl Parade, Orlando. This parade features lavish floats and high school bands in a nationally televised event. Reserved seats are $12, but you can watch along the route in downtown Orlando free. Call © **800/297-2695** or 407/423-2476. Late December.

Winterfest Boat Parade, Fort Lauderdale. People who complain that the holiday season isn't as festive in South Florida as it is in colder parts of the world haven't been to this spectacular boat parade along the Intracoastal Waterways. Boats decked out in magnificent holiday regalia gracefully—and boastfully—glide up and down the water as if it were a sheet of ice. If you're not on a boat, the best views are from waterfront restaurants or anywhere you can squeeze in along the water. Call © **954/767-0686.** Late December.

6 Insurance & Health

TRAVEL INSURANCE

Check your existing insurance policies before you buy travel insurance to cover trip cancellation, lost luggage, medical expenses, or car rental. You're likely to have partial or complete coverage. But if you need some, ask your travel agent about a comprehensive package. The cost of travel insurance varies widely, depending on the cost and length of your trip, your age and overall health, and the type of trip you're taking. Insurance for extreme sports or adventure travel, for example, will cost more than coverage for a cruise. Some insurers provide packages for specialty vacations, such as skiing or backpacking. More dangerous activities may be excluded from basic policies.

For information, contact one of the following popular insurers:

- **Access America** (✆ 800/284-8300; www.accessamerica.com/)
- **Travel Guard International** (✆ 800/826-1300; www.travelguard.com)
- **Travel Insured International** (✆ 800/243-3174; www.travelinsured.com)
- **Travelex Insurance Services** (✆ 800/228-9792; www.travelex-insurance.com)

THE HEALTHY TRAVELER

Florida doesn't present any unusual health hazards for most people. Folks with certain medical conditions such as liver disease, diabetes, and stomach ailments, however, should avoid eating raw **oysters,** which can carry a natural bacterium linked to severe diarrhea, vomiting, and even fatal blood poisoning. Cooking kills the bacteria, so, if in doubt, order your oysters steamed, broiled, or fried.

Florida has millions of **mosquitoes** and invisible biting **sand flies** (known as "no-see-ums"), especially in the coastal and marshy areas. Fortunately, neither insect carries malaria or other diseases. Keep these pests at bay with a good insect repellent.

It's especially important to protect yourself against **sunburn.** Don't underestimate the strength of the sun's rays down here, even in the middle of winter. Remember that children need more protection than adults do.

WHAT TO DO IF YOU GET SICK AWAY FROM HOME

If you worry about getting sick away from home, consider purchasing **medical travel insurance** and carry your ID card in your purse or wallet. In most cases, your existing health plan will provide the coverage you need. If you require additional insurance, you might try **MEDEX International,** 9515 Deereco Rd., Timonium, MD 21093-5375 (✆ 888/MEDEX-00 or 410/453-6300; fax 410/453-6301; www.medexassist.com); or **Travel Assistance International** (✆ 800/821-2828 or 800/777-8710 for general information; www.travelassistance.com), 9200 Keystone Crossing, Suite 300, Indianapolis, IN 46240.

If you suffer from a chronic illness, consult your doctor before your departure. For conditions like epilepsy, diabetes, or heart problems, wear a **Medic Alert Identification Tag** (✆ 800/825-3785; www.medicalert.org), which will immediately alert doctors to your condition and give them access to your records through Medic Alert's 24-hour hot line.

Pack **prescription medications** in your carry-on luggage, and carry prescription medications in their original containers. Also bring along copies of your prescriptions in case you lose your pills or run out.

And don't forget sunglasses and an extra pair of contact lenses or prescription glasses.

Contact the **International Association for Medical Assistance to Travelers (IAMAT)** (✆ 716/754-4883 or 416/652-0137; www.sentex.net/~iamat) for tips on travel and health concerns in the countries you're visiting, and lists of local, English-speaking doctors. The United States **Centers for Disease Control and Prevention** (✆ 800/311-3435; www.cdc.gov) provides up-to-date information on necessary vaccines and health hazards by region or country (Their booklet, *Health Information for International Travel,* is $25 by mail; on the Internet, it's free). Any foreign consulate can provide a list of area doctors who speak English. If you get sick, consider asking your hotel concierge to recommend a local doctor—even his or her own. You can also try the emergency room at a local hospital;

many have walk-in clinics for emergency cases that are not life-threatening. You may not get immediate attention, but you won't pay the high price of an emergency room visit (usually a minimum of $300 just for signing your name).

7 Tips for Travelers with Special Needs

FOR TRAVELERS WITH DISABILITIES

Most disabilities shouldn't stop anyone from traveling. There are more resources out there than ever before. Here in Florida, for example, **Walt Disney World** and **Universal Studios** both assist guests with disabilities. Disney's many services are detailed in their *Guidebook for Guests with Disabilities*. Disney no longer mails copies prior to visits, but you can pick one up at Guest Services near the front entrance to the parks. Also, you can call © **407/824-4321** if you have any questions. For information about Universal Studios, CityWalk, and Islands of Adventure, contact Universal Studios Escape, 1000 Universal Studios Dr., Orlando, FL 32816 (© **407/393-8080**).

AGENCIES/OPERATORS

- **Flying Wheels Travel** (© **800/535-6790**; www.flyingwheelstravel.com) offers escorted tours and cruises that emphasize sports and private tours in minivans with lifts.
- **Access Adventures** (© **716/889-9096**), a Rochester, New York–based agency, offers customized itineraries for a variety of travelers with disabilities.
- **Accessible Journeys** (© **800/TINGLES** or 610/521-0339; www.disabilitytravel.com) caters specifically to slow walkers and wheelchair travelers and their families and friends.

ORGANIZATIONS

- **The Moss Rehab Hospital** (© **215/456-9603**; www.mossresourcenet.org) provides friendly, helpful phone assistance through its **Travel Information Service.**
- **The Society for Accessible Travel and Hospitality** (© **212/447-7284**; fax 212/725-8253; www.sath.org) offers a wealth of travel resources for all types of disabilities and informed recommendations on destinations, access guides, travel agents, tour operators, vehicle rentals, and companion services. Annual membership costs $45 for adults; $30 for seniors and students.
- **The American Foundation for the Blind** (© **800/232-5463**; www.afb.org) provides information on traveling with Seeing Eye dogs.

PUBLICATIONS

- **Mobility International USA** (© **541/343-1284**; www.miusa.org) publishes *A World of Options*, a 658-page book of resources, covering everything from biking trips to scuba outfitters, and a biannual newsletter, *Over the Rainbow*. Annual membership is $35.
- **Twin Peaks Press** (© **360/694-2462**) publishes travel-related books for travelers with special needs.
- ***Open World for Disability and Mature Travel*** magazine, published by the Society for Accessible Travel and Hospitality (see above), is full of good resources and information. A year's subscription is $13 ($21 outside the U.S.).

FOR GAY & LESBIAN TRAVELERS

Florida is not without its intolerant contingent, but there are active gay and lesbian groups in most cities here. In fact, the editors of *Out and About,* a gay and lesbian newsletter, have described Miami's **South Beach** as the "hippest, hottest, most happening gay travel destination in the world." For many years that could also be said of **Key West,** which still is one of the country's most popular destinations for gays. **Fort Lauderdale**—where gays own more than 20 motels, 40 bars, and numerous other businesses—is definitely on the gay-friendly map.

The popularity of **Orlando** with gay and lesbian travelers is highlighted with Gay Weekend in early June, which draws as many as 40,000 participants and includes events at Disney World, Universal Studios, and SeaWorld. You can get information on the event at **www.gayday.com**. **Universal City Travel (© 800/224-3838)** offers a "Gay Weekend" tour package including tickets to Universal Studios, SeaWorld, and Church Street Station. For information about events for that weekend, or throughout the year, contact the **Gay, Lesbian & Bisexual Community Services of Central Florida,** 934 N. Mills Ave., Orlando, FL 32803 (© **407/425-4527** or 407/843-4297; www.glbcc.org). Welcome packets usually include the latest issue of the *Triangle,* a quarterly newsletter (© **407/849-0099**) dedicated to gay and lesbian issues, and a calendar of events pertaining to the gay and lesbian community. Although not a tourist-specific packet, it includes information and ads for the area's gay and lesbian clubs.

Watermark, P.O. Box 533655, Orlando, FL 32853 (© **407/481-2243;** fax 407/481-2246; www.watermarkonline.com), is a biweekly tabloid newspaper covering the gay and lesbian scene, including dining and entertainment options, in Orlando, the Tampa Bay area, and Daytona Beach.

Nationally, **The International Gay & Lesbian Travel Association** (IGLTA) (© **800/448-8550** or 954/776-2626; fax 954/776-3303; www.iglta.org) links travelers with gay-friendly hoteliers, tour operators, and airline and cruise-line representatives. It offers monthly newsletters, marketing mailings, and a membership directory that's updated once a year. Membership is $150 yearly, plus a $100 administration fee for new members.

AGENCIES/OPERATORS

- **Above and Beyond Tours** (© **800/397-2681;** www.abovebeyondtours.com) offers gay and lesbian tours worldwide and is the exclusive gay and lesbian tour operator for United Airlines.
- **Now, Voyager** (© **800/255-6951;** www.nowvoyager.com) is a San Francisco–based gay-owned and operated travel service.
- **Olivia Cruises & Resorts** (© **800/631-6277** or 510/655-0364; http://oliviatravel.com) charters entire resorts and ships for exclusive lesbian vacations all over the world.

PUBLICATIONS

- *Out and About* (© **800/929-2268** or 415/644-8044; www.outandabout.com) offers guidebooks and a newsletter 10 times a year packed with solid information on the global gay and lesbian scene.
- *Spartacus International Gay Guide* and *Odysseus* are good, annual English-language guidebooks focused on gay men, with some information for lesbians. You can get them from most gay and lesbian bookstores, or order them from **Giovanni's Room** bookstore, 1145 Pine St., Philadelphia, PA 19107 (© **215/923-2960;** www.giovannisroom.com).

- *Gay Travel A to Z: The World of Gay & Lesbian Travel Options at Your Fingertips,* by Marianne Ferrari (Ferrari Publications), is a very good gay and lesbian guidebook series.

FOR SENIORS

With one of the largest retired populations of any state, Florida offers a wide array of activities and benefits for seniors. Don't be shy about asking for discounts, but always carry some kind of identification, such as a driver's license, that shows your date of birth.

Major airlines offer coupons for domestic travel for seniors over 60. Typically, a book of four coupons costs less than $700, which means you can fly anywhere in the continental U.S. for under $350 round-trip. In most cities, people over the age of 60 qualify for reduced admission to theaters, museums, and other attractions, as well as discounted fares on public transportation.

Members of **AARP** (formerly known as the American Association of Retired Persons), 601 E St. NW, Washington, DC 20049 (© **800/424-3410** or 202/434-2277; www.aarp.org), get discounts on hotels, airfares, and car rentals. AARP offers members a wide range of benefits, including *Modern Maturity* magazine and a monthly newsletter. Anyone over 50 can join.

The Alliance for Retired Americans, 8403 Colesville Rd., Suite 1200, Silver Spring, MD 20910 (© **301/578-8422;** www.retiredamericans.org), offers a newsletter six times a year and discounts on hotel and auto rentals; annual dues are $13 per person or couple. *Note:* Members of the former National Council of Senior Citizens receive automatic membership in the Alliance.

The **U.S. National Park Service** offers a **Golden Age Passport** that gives seniors 62 years or older lifetime entrance to Florida's many U.S. national park facilities for a one-time processing fee of $10, which must be purchased in person at any NPS facility that charges an entrance fee. Besides free entry, a Golden Age Passport also offers a 50% discount on federal-use fees charged for such facilities as camping, swimming, parking, boat launching, and tours. For more information, visit www.nps.gov/fees_passes.htm or call © **888/GO-PARKS.**

AGENCIES/OPERATORS

- **Grand Circle Travel** (© **800/221-2610** or 617/350-7500; www.gct.com) offers package deals for the 50-plus market, mostly of the tour-bus variety, with free trips thrown in for those who organize groups of 10 or more.
- **Elderhostel** (© **877/426-8056;** www.elderhostel.org) arranges study programs for those ages 55 and over (and a spouse or companion of any age) in the U.S. and in more than 80 countries around the world. Most courses last 5 to 7 days in the U.S. (2–4 weeks abroad), and many include airfare, accommodations in university dormitories or modest inns, meals, and tuition.
- **Interhostel** (© **800/733-9753;** www.learn.unh.edu/interhostel), organized by the University of New Hampshire, also offers educational travel for seniors. On these escorted tours, the days are packed with seminars, lectures, and field trips, with sightseeing led by academic experts. **Interhostel** takes travelers 50 and over (with companions over 40), and offers 1- and 2-week trips, mostly international.

PUBLICATIONS

- *The Book of Deals* is a collection of more than 1,000 senior discounts on airlines, lodging, tours,

and attractions around the country; it's available for $9.95 by calling ⓒ 800/460-6676.
- *101 Tips for the Mature Traveler* is available from Grand Circle Travel (ⓒ 800/221-2610 or 617/350-7500; fax 617/346-6700).
- *The 50+ Traveler's Guidebook* (St. Martin's Press).
- *Unbelievably Good Deals and Great Adventures That You Absolutely Can't Get Unless You're Over 50* (Contemporary Publishing Co.).

FOR FAMILIES

Florida is a great family destination, with Walt Disney World leading the list of theme parks geared to young and old alike. Consequently, most Florida hotels and restaurants are willing if not eager to cater to families traveling with children. Many hotels and motels let children 17 and under stay free in their parents' room (be sure to ask when you reserve).

At the beaches, it's the exception rather than the rule for a resort not to have a children's activities program (some will even mind the youngsters while the parents enjoy a night off!). Even if they don't have a children's program of their own, most will arrange babysitting services.

If you call ahead before dining out, you'll see that most restaurants have some facilities for children, such as booster chairs and low-priced kids' menus.

PUBLICATIONS

For a host of invaluable tips and other information, pick up copies of *Frommer's Unofficial Guide to Florida with Kids* and *Frommer's Unofficial Guide to Walt Disney World with Kids*.

WEBSITES

- **Family Travel Network** (www.familytravelnetwork.com) offers travel tips and reviews of family-friendly destinations, vacation deals, and thoughtful features such as "What to Do When Your Kids Are Afraid to Travel" and "Kid-Style Camping."
- **Travel with Your Children** (www.travelwithyourkids.com) is a comprehensive site offering sound advice for traveling with children.
- The Busy Person's Guide to Travel with Children (http://wz.com/travel/TravelingWithChildren.html) offers a "45-second newsletter" in which experts weigh in on the best websites and resources for tips on traveling with children.

8 Getting There

BY PLANE

Most major domestic airlines fly to and from many Florida cities. Choose from **American** (ⓒ 800/433-7300; www.aa.com), **Continental** (ⓒ 800/525-0280; www.continental.com), **Delta** (ⓒ 800/221-1212; www.delta.com), **Northwest/KLM** (ⓒ 800/225-2525; www.nwa.com), **TWA** (ⓒ 800/221-2000; www.twa.com), **United** (ⓒ 800/241-6522; www.united.com), and **US Airways** (ⓒ 800/428-4322; www.usairways.com).

Of these, Delta and US Airways have the most extensive network of commuter connections within Florida (see "Getting Around," later in this chapter).

Several so-called no-frills airlines—low fares but few if any amenities—fly to Florida. The biggest and best is **Southwest Airlines** (ⓒ 800/435-9792; www.southwest.com), which has flights from many U.S. cities to Fort Lauderdale, Jacksonville, Orlando, and Tampa.

Others flying to Florida include **AirTran** (✆ **800/AIR-TRAN;** www.airtran); **American Trans Air** (✆ **800/435-9282;** www.ata.com); **Carnival Air** (✆ **800/824-7386**), an arm of the popular cruise line; **JetBlue** (✆ **800/538-2583;** www.jetblue.com); **MetroJet,** an arm of US Airways (✆ **800/888-638-7653;** www.flymetrojet.com); **Midway** (✆ **800/44-MIDWAY;** www.midwayair.com); **Midwest Express** (✆ **800/452-2022;** www.midwestexpress.com); **PanAm** (✆ **800/FLY-PANAM;** www.flypanam.com); **Spirit** (✆ **800/722-7117;** www.spiritair.com); and **Vanguard** (✆ **800/826-4827;** www.flyvanguard.com).

Internet resources such as **Travelocity** (www.travelocity.com) and **Microsoft Expedia** (www.expedia.com) make it relatively easy to compare prices, and even purchase tickets.

NEW AIR TRAVEL SECURITY MEASURES

In the wake of the terrorist attacks of September 11, 2001, the airline industry began implementing sweeping security measures in airports. This is especially true at Washington Reagan National Airport, whose approach patterns take planes within a few seconds of the White House, the U.S. Capitol, the Pentagon, and other important federal buildings. You cannot get out of your seat for any reason whatsoever during the last 30 minutes of your plane's approach to Reagan National (we shouldn't have to tell you to take care of any pressing needs beforehand).

Whatever the airport, expect a lengthy check-in process and extensive delays. Although regulations vary from airline to airline, you can expedite the process by taking the following steps:

- **Arrive early.** Arrive at the airport at least 2 hours before your scheduled flight.
- **Try not to drive your car to the airport.** Parking and curbside access to the terminal may be limited. Call ahead and check.
- **Don't count on curbside check-in.** Some airlines and airports have stopped curbside check-in altogether, whereas others offer it on a limited basis. For up-to-date information on specific regulations and implementations, check with the individual airline.
- **Be sure to carry plenty of documentation.** A government-issued photo ID (federal, state, or local) is now required. You may need to show this at various checkpoints. With an E-ticket, you may be required to have with you printed confirmation of purchase, and

---

Frommers.com: The Complete Travel Resource

For an excellent travel-planning resource, we highly recommend **Frommers.com** (www.frommers.com). We're a little biased, of course, but we guarantee that you'll find the travel tips, reviews, monthly vacation giveaways, and online-booking capabilities thoroughly indispensable. Among the special features are our popular **Message Boards,** where Frommer's readers post queries and share advice (sometimes even our authors show up to answer questions); **Frommers.com Newsletter,** for the latest travel bargains and inside travel secrets; and Frommer's **Destinations Section,** where you'll get expert travel tips, hotel and dining recommendations, and advice on the sights to see for more than 2,500 destinations around the globe. When your research is done, the **Online Reservation System** (www.frommers.com/booktravelnow) takes you to Frommer's favorite sites for booking your vacation at affordable prices.

> **Tips** **What You Can Carry On—And What You Can't**
>
> The Transportation Security Administration (TSA), the government agency that now handles all aspects of airport security, has devised new restrictions for carry-on baggage, not only to expedite the screening process but to prevent potential weapons from passing through airport security. Passengers are now limited to bringing just one carry-on bag and one personal item onto the aircraft (previous regulations allowed two carry-on bags and one personal item, like a briefcase or a purse). For more information, go to the TSA's web site www.tsa.gov. The agency has released an updated list of items passengers are not allowed to carry onto an aircraft:
>
> **Not permitted:** knives and box cutters, corkscrews, straight razors, metal scissors, golf clubs, baseball bats, pool cues, hockey sticks, ski poles, ice picks.
>
> **Permitted:** nail clippers, nail files, tweezers, eyelash curlers, safety razors (including disposable razors), syringes (with documented proof of medical need), walking canes and umbrellas (must be inspected first).
>
> The airline you fly may have **additional restrictions** on items you can and cannot carry on board. Call ahead to avoid problems.

perhaps even the credit card with which you bought your ticket (see "All about E-Ticketing," below). This varies from airline to airline, so call ahead to make sure you have the proper documentation. And be sure that your ID is **up-to-date:** An expired driver's license, for example, may keep you from boarding the plane altogether.

- **Know what you can carry on–and what you can't.** Travelers in the United States are now limited to one carry-on bag, plus one personal bag (such as a purse or a briefcase). The Transportation Security Administration (TSA) has also issued a list of newly restricted carry-on items; see the box "What You Can Carry On– And What You Can't."
- **Prepare to be searched.** Expect spot-checks. Electronic items, such as a laptop or cell phone, should be readied for additional screening. Limit the metal items you wear on your person.
- **It's no joke.** When a check-in agent asks if someone other than you packed your bag, don't decide that this is the time to be funny. The agents will not hesitate to call an alarm.
- **No ticket, no gate access.** Only ticketed passengers will be allowed beyond the screener checkpoints, except for those people with specific medical or parental needs.

FLYING FOR LESS: TIPS FOR GETTING THE BEST AIRFARE

There's no shortage of **discounted and promotional fares** to Florida. November, December, and January often see fare wars that can result in savings of 50% or more. Watch for advertisements in your local newspaper and on TV, call the airlines, or check out their websites.

If you call the airlines or a travel agent, ask for the lowest fares, and ask

Tips: Travel Planning & Booking Sites

Keep in mind that because several airlines are no longer willing to pay commissions on tickets sold by online travel agencies, these agencies may either add a $10 surcharge to your bill if you book on that carrier—or neglect to offer those carriers' schedules.

The list of sites below is selective, not comprehensive. Some sites will have evolved or disappeared by the time you read this.

- **Travelocity** (www.travelocity.com or www.frommers.travelocity.com) and **Expedia** (www.expedia.com) are among the most popular sites, each offering an excellent range of options. Travelers search by destination, dates, and cost.
- **Orbitz** (www.orbitz.com) is a popular site launched by United, Delta, Northwest, American, and Continental airlines. (Stay tuned: At press time, travel-agency associations were waging an antitrust battle against this site.)
- **Qixo** (www.qixo.com) is another powerful search engine that allows you to search for flights and accommodations from some 20 airline and travel-planning sites (such as Travelocity) at once. Qixo sorts results by price.
- **Priceline** (www.priceline.com) lets you "name your price" for airline tickets, hotel rooms, and rental cars. For airline tickets, you can't say what time you want to fly—you have to accept any flight between 6am and 10pm on the dates you've selected, and you may have to make one or more stopovers. Tickets are nonrefundable, and no frequent-flier miles are awarded.

whether it's cheaper to book in advance, fly in midweek, or stay over a Saturday night. Don't stop at the 7-day advance purchase; ask how much the 14- and 30-day plans cost. Decide when you want to go before you call, since many of the best deals are nonrefundable.

Passengers within the same airplane cabin are rarely paying the same fare. Business travelers who need to purchase tickets at the last minute, change their itinerary at a moment's notice, or get home for the weekend pay the premium rate. Passengers who can book their ticket long in advance, who can stay over Saturday night, or who are willing to travel on a Tuesday, Wednesday, or Thursday after 7pm, will pay a fraction of the full fare. On many flights, even the shortest hops, the full fare is close to $1,000 or more, while a 7- or 14-day advance purchase ticket may cost less than half that amount. Here are a few other easy ways to save.

- Airlines periodically lower prices on their most popular routes. Check the travel section of your Sunday newspaper for advertised discounts or call the airlines directly and ask if any **promotional rates** or special fares are available. You'll almost never see a sale during the peak summer vacation months of July and August, or during the Thanksgiving or Christmas seasons; but in periods of low-volume travel, you should pay no more than $400 for a domestic cross-country flight. If your schedule is flexible, say so, and ask if you can secure a cheaper fare by staying an extra day, by flying midweek, or by flying at less-trafficked hours. If you already hold a ticket when a sale breaks, it may even pay to exchange your ticket, which usually incurs a $100 to $150 charge.

Note: The lowest-priced fares are often nonrefundable, require advance purchase of 1 to 3 weeks and a certain length of stay, and carry penalties for changing dates of travel.

- **Consolidators,** also known as bucket shops, are a good place to find low fares. Consolidators buy seats in bulk from the airlines and then sell them back to the public at prices usually below even the airlines' discounted rates. Their small ads usually run in Sunday newspaper travel sections. And before you pay, request a confirmation number from the consolidator and then call the airline to confirm your seat. Be aware that bucket shop tickets are usually nonrefundable or rigged with stiff cancellation penalties, often as high as 50% to 75% of the ticket price. Protect yourself by paying with a credit card rather than cash. Keep in mind that if there's an airline sale going on, or if it's high season, you can often get the same or better rates by contacting the airlines directly, so do some comparison shopping before you buy. Also check out the name of the airline; you may not want to fly on some obscure Third World airline, even if you're saving $10. And check whether you're flying on a charter or a scheduled airline; the latter is more expensive but more reliable.

  Council Travel (© 800/226-8624; www.counciltravel.com) and **STA Travel** (© 800/781-4040; www.statravel.com) cater especially to young travelers, but their bargain-basement prices are available to people of all ages. **The TravelHub** (© 888/AIR-FARE; www.travelhub.com) represents nearly 1,000 travel agencies, many of whom offer consolidator and discount fares. Other reliable consolidators include **1-800-FLY-CHEAP** (www.1800flycheap.com); **TFI Tours International**

> **Tips All About E-Ticketing**
>
> Only yesterday **electronic tickets (E-tickets)** were the fast and easy ticket-free alternative to paper tickets. E-tickets allowed passengers to avoid long lines at airport check-in, all the while saving the airlines money on postage and labor. With the increased security measures in airports, however, an E-ticket no longer guarantees an accelerated check-in. You often can't go straight to the boarding gate, even if you have no bags to check. You'll probably need to show your printed E-ticket receipt or confirmation of purchase, as well as a photo ID, and sometimes even the credit card with which you purchased your E-ticket. That said, buying an E-ticket is still a fast, convenient way to book a flight; instead of having to wait for a paper ticket to come through the mail, you can book your fare by phone or on the computer, and the airline will immediately confirm by fax or e-mail. In addition, airlines often offer frequent flier miles as incentive for electronic bookings.

(⌒ **800/745-8000** or 212/736-1140; www.lowestprice.com), which serves as a clearinghouse for unused seats; or "rebators" such as **Travel Avenue** (⌒ **800/333-3335;**www.travelavenue.com) and the **Smart Traveller** (⌒ **800/448-3338** in the U.S. or 305/448-3338), which rebate part of their commissions to you.

- Search **the Internet** for cheap fares. Great last-minute deals are available through free weekly e-mail services provided directly by the airlines.
- Join a travel club such as **Moment's Notice** (⌒ **718/234-6295;** www.momentsnotice.com) or **Sears Discount Travel Club** (⌒ **800/433-9383,** or 800/255-1487 to join; www.travelersadvantage.com), which supply unsold tickets at discounted prices. You pay an annual membership fee to get the club's hot-line number. Of course, you're limited to what's available, so you have to be flexible.
- Join **frequent-flier clubs.** It's best to accrue miles on one program, so you can rack up free flights and achieve elite status faster. But it makes sense to open as many accounts as possible, no matter how seldom you fly a particular airline. It's free, and you'll get the best choice of seats, faster response to phone inquiries, and prompter service if your luggage is stolen, your flight is canceled or delayed, or you want to change your seat.

BY CAR

Florida is reached by **I-95** along the East Coast, **I-75** from the central states, and **I-10** from the west. **The Florida Turnpike,** a toll road, links Orlando, West Palm Beach, Fort Lauderdale, and Miami (it's a shortcut from Wildwood on I-75 north of Orlando to Miami). **I-4** cuts across the state from Cape Canaveral through Orlando to Tampa.

See "Getting Around," below, for more information about driving in Florida and the car-rental firms operating here.

If you're a member, your local branch of the **American Automobile Association (AAA)** will provide a free trip-routing plan. AAA also has nationwide emergency road service for its members (⌒ **800/AAA-HELP;** www.aaa.com).

BY TRAIN

Amtrak (⌒ **800/USA-RAIL;** www.amtrak.com) offers train service to Florida from both the East and West Coasts. It takes some 26 hours from New York to Miami, 68 hours from Los Angeles to Miami, and Amtrak's fares aren't much less—if not more—than many of the airlines' lowest fares.

Amtrak's *Silver Meteor* and *Silver Star* both run twice daily between New York and either Miami or Tampa, with intermediate stops along the East Coast and in Florida. Amtrak's Thruway Bus Connections are available from the Fort Lauderdale Amtrak station and Miami International Airport to Key West; from Tampa to St. Petersburg, Treasure Island, Clearwater, Sarasota, Bradenton, and Fort Myers; and from Deland to Daytona Beach. From the West Coast, the *Sunset Limited* runs three times weekly between Los Angeles and Orlando. It stops in Pensacola, Crestview (north of Fort Walton Beach and Destin), Chipley (north of Panama City Beach), and Tallahassee. Sleeping accommodations are available for an extra charge.

If you intend to stop off along the way, you can save money with Amtrak's **Explore America** (or All Aboard America) fares, which are based on three regions of the country.

Amtrak's **Auto Train** runs daily from Lorton, Virginia (12 miles south of Washington, DC), to Sanford, Florida (just northeast of Orlando). You ride in a coach while your car is secured in an enclosed vehicle carrier. You should make your train reservations as far in advance as possible.

9 Package & Escorted Tours

More than 120 travel companies offer hundreds of package tour options to the Sunshine State, particularly to Orlando and Miami. Quite often these deals will result in savings not just on airfares but on hotels and other activities as well. You pay one price for a package that varies from one tour operator to the next. Airfare, transfers, and accommodations are always covered, and sometimes meals and specific activities are thrown in.

Before you start your search for the lowest airfare, therefore, you may want to consider booking your flight as part of a travel package, such as an escorted tour or a package tour. What you lose in adventure, you could gain in time and money saved when you book accommodations, and maybe even food and entertainment, along with your flight—but not necessarily.

PACKAGE TOURS FOR INDEPENDENT TRAVELERS

Package tours are not the same thing as escorted tours. With a package tour, you travel independently but pay a group rate. Packages usually include airfare, a choice of hotels, and car rentals, and packagers often offer several options at different prices. In many cases, a package that includes airfare, hotel, and transportation to and from the airport will cost you less than just the hotel alone would have, had you booked it yourself. That's because packages are sold in bulk to tour operators—who resell them to the public at a cost that drastically undercuts standard rates.

RECOMMENDED PACKAGE TOUR OPERATORS

One good source of package deals is the airlines themselves. Most major airlines offer air/land packages, including **American Airlines Vacations** (© 800/321-2121; http://aav1.aavacations.com), **Delta Vacations** (© 800/221-6666; www.deltavacations.com), **US Airways Vacations** (© 800/455-0123 or 800/422-3861; www.usairwaysvacations.com),

---

Tips Saving with Golf & Tennis Packages

Many Florida hotels and resorts and even some motels offer **golf and tennis packages,** which bundle the cost of room, greens and court fees, and sometimes equipment into one price. These deals usually don't include airfare, but they do represent savings over paying for the room and golf or tennis separately. See the accommodations sections in the following chapters for hostelries offering special packages to their guests.

Summer, early fall, and the first 3 weeks of December are good times to search for discounted deals in Southern Florida. For example, the Naples Beach Hotel & Golf Club in Naples (see section 4 in chapter 9, "Southwest Florida") recently offered a bed-and-breakfast special for about $125 a night per room, including a full breakfast buffet, during September and December. Regular autumn rooms are more than twice that amount, without breakfast.

Continental Airlines Vacations (© 800/301-3800; www.coolvacations.com), and **United Vacations** (© 888/854-3899; www.unitedvacations.com/).

Online Vacation Mall (© 800/839-9851; www.onlinevacationmall.com) allows you to search for and book packages offered by a number of tour operators and airlines. The **United States Tour Operators Association's** website (www.ustoa.com) has a search engine that allows you to look for operators that offer packages to a specific destination. Travel packages are also listed in the travel section of your local Sunday newspaper. **Liberty Travel** (© 888/271-1584; www.libertytravel.com), one of the biggest packagers in the Northeast, often runs full-page ads in Sunday papers. Or check ads in the national travel magazines such as *Arthur Frommer's Budget Travel Magazine*, *Travel & Leisure*, *National Geographic Traveler*, and *Condé Nast Traveler*.

THE PROS & CONS OF PACKAGE TOURS

Packages can save you money because they are sold in bulk to tour operators, who sell them to the public. They offer group prices but allow for independent travel. The disadvantages are that you're usually required to make a large payment up front; you may end up on a charter flight; and you have to deal with your own luggage and with transfers between your hotel and the airport, if transfers are not included in the package price. Packages often don't allow for complete flexibility or a wide range of choices. For instance, you may prefer a quiet inn but have to settle for a popular chain hotel instead. Your choice of travel days may be limited as well.

ESCORTED TOURS (TRIPS WITH GUIDES)

Some people love escorted tours. They let you relax and take in the sights while a bus driver fights traffic for you and a guide explains what you're seeing. They spell out your costs up front, and they take you to the maximum number of sights in the minimum amount of time with the least amount of hassle.

For example, the very reputable **Tauck Tours** (© 800/468-2825; fax 203/221-6828; www.tauck.com) recently offered an 11-day, 10-night escorted tour of southern Florida beginning in Tampa and ending at Walt Disney World in Orlando. It included accommodations, most meals, bus transportation between the cities, most activities, and a guide, but not your airfare to join the tour in Tampa or to return home from Orlando. These "land" costs were about $2,750 to $3,000 per person, double occupancy ($3,750–$4,200 if you traveled alone). The hotels were all top-end, so this was a good deal, especially during the high winter season in South Florida.

THE PROS & CONS OF ESCORTED TOURS

If you book an escorted tour, most everything is paid for up front, so you deal with fewer money issues. They allow you to enjoy the maximum number of sites in the shortest time, with the least amount of hassle, as all the details are arranged by others. Escorted tours give you the security of traveling in a group and are convenient for people with limited mobility. Many escorted tours are theme tours, putting people together who share the same interest or activity (such as cooking or sailing).

On the downside, if you book an escorted tour you often have to pay a lot of money up front, and your lodging and dining choices are predetermined. Escorted tours can be jam-packed with activities, leaving little room for individual sightseeing, whim, or adventure. They also often focus only on the heavily touristed sites, so you miss out on the lesser-known gems. Plus, you may not always be happy rubbing suitcases with strangers.

10 Getting Around

Having a car is the best and easiest way to see Florida's sights, or just to get to and from the beach. Public transportation is available only in the cities and larger towns, and even there it may provide infrequent or even inadequate service. When it comes to getting from one city to another, cars and planes are the ways to go.

BY PLANE

The commuter arms of **Continental** (© **800/525-0280;** www.flycontinental.com), **Delta** (© **800/221-1212;** www.delta.com), and **US Airways** (© **800/428-4322;** www.usair.com) provide extensive service between Florida's major cities and towns. Fares for these short hops tend to be reasonable.

Cape Air (© **800/352-0714;** www.flycapeair.com) flies between Key West, Fort Myers, and Naples, which means you can avoid backtracking to Miami from Key West if you're touring the state. (You can also take a boat between Key West and Fort Myers Beach, Naples, or Marco Island during the winter months; see the introduction to chapter 9, "Southwest Florida.")

Two new small airlines are now providing in-state connections to the Keys. **Discover Air** (© **888/596-9247;** www.discoverair.com) flies between Orlando and Key West and Marathon, and **Paradise Aviation** (© **305/743-4222**) connects Fort Lauderdale with Marathon.

BY CAR

Jacksonville is about 350 miles north of Miami and 500 miles north of Key West, so don't underestimate how long it will take you to drive all the way down the state. The speed limit is either 65 miles per hour or 70 miles per hour on the rural interstate highways, so you can make good time between cities. Not so on U.S. 1, U.S. 17, U.S. 19, U.S. 41, and U.S. 301; although most have four lanes, these older highways tend to be heavily congested, especially in built-up areas.

Every major car-rental company is represented here, including **Alamo** (© 800/327-9633; www.goalamo.com), **Avis** (© 800/331-1212; www.avis.com), **Budget** (© 800/527-0700; www.budgetrentacar.com), **Dollar** (© 800/800-4000; www.dollarcar.com), **Enterprise** (© 800/325-8007; pickenterprise.com), **Hertz** (© 800/654-3131; www.hertz.com), **National** (© 800/227-7368; www.nationalcar.com), and **Thrifty** (© 800/367-2277; www.thrifty.com).

If you decide to rent a car, shop around and ask a lot of questions. Reservations clerks are used to being asked for the lowest rate available, and most will find it in order to get your business. You may have to try different dates, different pickup and drop-off points, and different discount offers to find the best deal. Also, if you're a member of any organization (AARP or AAA, for example), be sure to ask if you're entitled to discounts. It's not widely known, but members of **Costco Wholesale** stores get hefty discounts at Alamo, Avis, and Dollar.

Check the rental firms' websites. Most will automatically bring up the lowest available rate, and there are boxes to click if you are an association member or have a discount coupon or ID number.

State and local **taxes** will add as much as 20% to your final bill. You'll pay an additional $2.05 per day in statewide use tax, and local sales taxes will tack on at least 6% to the total, including the statewide use tax (the state is being sued over this tax-on-a-tax practice). Some airports add another 35¢ per day and as much as 10% in "recovery" fees. You can avoid the recovery fee by picking up your car in town rather than at the airport. Budget and Enterprise both have numerous rental locations away from the airports. But be sure to weigh the cost of transportation to and from your hotel against the amount of the fee.

Most of the companies pad their profits by selling **Loss/Damage Waiver** (LDW) insurance at $15 or more per day. Your automobile insurance carrier and credit-card companies may already provide coverage, so check with them before wasting your money on something you don't need.

Also, the rental companies will offer to refill your **gas** tank at "competitive" prices per gallon when you return. Regular gas is always less expensive in town, so fill up your vehicle on the way back to the airport.

Competition is so fierce among Florida rental firms that most have now stopped charging **drop-off fees** if you pick up a car at one place and leave it at another, rather than making a round-trip.

You must have a **valid credit card** (not a debit or check card) in your name, and most companies require you to be at least 25 years old to rent a car. Some also set maximum ages and may deny cars to anyone with a bad driving record. Ask about rental requirements and restrictions when you book in order to avoid problems later.

BY TRAIN

You'll find that train travel isn't terribly feasible within Florida, and it's not much less expensive than flying, if at all. See "Getting There," earlier in this chapter, for Florida towns served by **Amtrak** (© **800/USA-RAIL;** www.amtrak.com).

11 The Active Vacation Planner

Bird-watching, boating and sailing, camping, canoeing and kayaking, fishing, golfing, tennis—you name it, the Sunshine State has it. In fact, you'll find these activities almost everywhere you go. Of course, beach lovers and water-sports enthusiasts can indulge their passions almost anywhere along the state's lengthy coastlines. Merely head east or west, and you'll easily find plenty to do—or viewed another way, Florida's multitudinous water-sports operators will find you.

These and other activities are described in the outdoor activities sections of the following chapters, but here's a brief overview of some of the best places to move your muscles, with tips on how to get more detailed information.

The **Florida Sports Foundation,** 2390 Kerry Forest Pkwy., Suite 101, Tallahassee, FL 32309 (© **850/488-8347;** fax 850/922-0482; www.flasports.com), publishes free brochures, calendars, schedules, and guides to outdoor pursuits and spectator sports throughout Florida. Some of its specific publications are noted in the sections below.

For excellent color maps of state parks, campgrounds, canoe trails, aquatic preserves, caverns, and more, contact the **Florida Department of Environmental Protection,** Office of Communications, 3900 Commonwealth Blvd., Tallahassee, FL 32399 (© **850/488-2960;** www.dep.state.fl.us). Some of the department's publications are mentioned below.

ACTIVITIES A TO Z
BIKING & IN-LINE SKATING

Florida's relatively flat terrain makes it

ideal for riding bikes and in-line skating. You can bike right into the **Everglades National Park** along the 38-mile-long Main Park Road, for example, and bike or skate from St. Petersburg to Tarpon Springs on the 47-mile-long converted railroad bed known as the **Pinellas Trail.** Many towns and cities have designated routes for cyclists, skaters, joggers, and walkers, such as the paved pathways running the length of Sanibel Island, the lovely Bayshore Boulevard in **Tampa,** and the bike lanes from downtown **Sarasota** out to St. Armands, Lido, and Longboat Keys. We've detailed all the many options in the following chapters.

BIRD-WATCHING With hundreds of both land- and sea-based species, Florida is one of America's best places for bird-watching—if you're not careful, pelicans will even steal your picnic lunch on the historic **Naples Pier.** The **J. N. "Ding" Darling National Wildlife Refuge** is great for watching, and it shares Sanibel Island with luxury resorts and fine restaurants.

With its northeast Florida section now open, the **Great Florida Birding Trail** will eventually cover some 2,000 miles throughout the state. Fort Clinch State Park on Amelia Island and Merritt Island National Wildlife Refuge in Cape Canaveral are gateways to the northeast trail. Information is available from the Birding Trail Coordinator, Florida Fish & Wildlife Conservation Commission, 620 S. Meridian St., Tallahassee, FL 32399-1600 (ⓒ **850/922-0664;** fax 850/488-1961; www.floridabirdingtrail.com). You can download trail maps from the website.

Many of the state's wildlife preserves have gift shops that carry books about Florida's birds, including the *Florida Wildlife Viewing Guide,* in which authors Susan Cerulean and Ann Morrow profile 96 great parks, refuges, and preserves throughout the state. The guide is also available directly from the publisher, Falcon Press, at ⓒ **800/582-2665;** www.falconbooks.com.

BOATING & SAILING With some 1,350 miles of shoreline, it's not surprising that Florida is a boating and sailing mecca. In fact, you won't be anyplace near the water very long before you see flyers and other advertisements for rental boats and for cruises on sailboats. Many of them are mentioned in the following chapters.

The Moorings, the worldwide sailboat charter company, has its headquarters in Clearwater and its Florida yacht base nearby in St. Petersburg (ⓒ **800/437-7880** or 813/530-5424; www.moorings.com). From St. Pete, experienced sailors can take its bareboats as far as the Keys and the Dry Tortugas, out in the Gulf of Mexico.

Key West keeps gaining prominence as a world sailing capital. *Yachting* magazine sponsors the largest winter regatta in America here each January, and smaller events take place regularly.

Even if you've never hauled on a halyard, you can learn the art of sailing at **Steve and Doris Colgate's Offshore Sailing School,** headquartered at the South Seas Plantation Resort & Yacht Harbour on Captiva Island, with an outpost in St. Petersburg (www.offshsore-sailing.com). The prestigious **Annapolis Sailing** has bases in St. Petersburg and on Marathon in the Keys (http://annapolissailing.com).

The free *Florida Boating & Fishing* has tips about safe boating in the state, available from the **Florida Sports Foundation** (see the introduction to this section, above). It is a treasure trove of regulations; locations of marinas, hotels, and resorts; marine products and services; and more, in magazine format.

CAMPING Florida is literally dotted with RV parks (if you own such a vehicle, it's the least-expensive way to spend your winters here). But for the best tent camping, look to Florida's national preserves and 110 state parks and recreation areas. Options range from luxury sites with hot-water showers and cable TV hookups to primitive island and beach camping with no facilities whatsoever.

Regular and primitive camping in **St. George Island State Park** near Apalachicola, in fact, is a birdwatcher's dream, and you'll be on one of the nation's most magnificent beaches. Equally great are the sands at **St. Andrews State Park** in Panama City Beach (with sites right beside the bay). Other top spots are **Fort DeSoto Park** in St. Pete Beach (more gorgeous bay-side sites), the remarkably preserved **Cayo Costa Island State Park** between Boca Grande and Captiva Island in Southwest Florida, **Canaveral National Seashore** near the Kennedy Space Center, **Anastasia State Park** in St. Augustine, **Fort Clinch State Park** on Amelia Island, and **Bill Baggs Cape Florida State Park** on Key Biscayne in Miami. Down in the Keys, the oceanside sites in **Long Key State Park** are about as nice as it gets.

These are all popular campgrounds, so reservations are essential, especially in the high seasons. All of Florida's state parks take bookings up to 11 months in advance.

The **Florida Department of Environmental Protection,** Division of Recreation and Parks, Mail Station 535, 3900 Commonwealth Blvd., Tallahassee, FL 32399-3000 (© **850/488-2960;** www.dep.state.fl.us), publishes an annual guide of tent and RV sites in Florida's state parks and recreation areas.

Pet owners note: Pets are permitted at some—but not all—state park beaches, campgrounds, and food service areas. Before bringing your animal, check with the department or with the individual parks to see if your pet will be allowed. And bring your rabies certificate, which is required.

For private campgrounds, the **Florida Association of RV Parks & Campgrounds,** 1340 Vickers Dr., Tallahassee, FL 32303 (© **850/562-7151;** fax 850/562-7179; www.floridacamping.com), issues an annual *Camp Florida* directory with locator maps and details about its member establishments throughout the state.

CANOEING & KAYAKING Canoers and kayakers have almost limitless options here: picturesque rivers, sandy coastlines, marshes, mangroves, and gigantic Lake Okeechobee. Exceptional trails run through several parks and wildlife preserves, including **Everglades National Park,** the **J. N. "Ding" Darling National Wildlife Refuge** on Sanibel Island, and the **Briggs Nature Center,** both on the edge of the Everglades near Marco Island.

According to the Florida state legislature, however, the state's official "Canoe Capital" is the Panhandle town of **Milton,** on U.S. 90 near Pensacola. Up there, Blackwater River, Coldwater River, Sweetwater Creek, and Juniper Creek are perfect for tubing, rafting, and paddleboating, as well as canoeing and kayaking.

Another good venue: the waterways winding through the marshes between **Amelia Island** and the mainland.

Many conservation groups throughout the state offer half-day, full-day, and overnight canoe trips. For example, **The Conservancy of Naples** (© **239/262-0304;** www.conservancy.org) has a popular series of moonlight canoe trips through the mangroves, among other programs.

Based during the winter at Everglades City, on the park's western border, **North American Canoe Tours, Inc.** (© **239/695-4666** Nov–Apr, or

860/739-0791 May–Oct; www.evergladesadventures.com) offers weeklong guided canoe expeditions through the Everglades.

Thirty-six creek and river trails, covering 950 miles altogether, are itemized in the excellent free **Canoe Trails** booklet published by the **Florida Department of Environmental Protection,** Office of Communications, 3900 Commonwealth Blvd., Tallahassee, FL 32399 (© **850/488-2960;** www.dep.state.fl.us).

Specialized guidebooks include *A Canoeing and Kayaking Guide to the Streams of Florida:* Volume 1, *North Central Florida and Panhandle,* by Elizabeth F. Carter, Liz Carter, and John Pearce; and Volume 2, *Central and Southern Peninsula,* by Elizabeth F. Carter, Lou Glaros and Doug Sphar. Both are published by Menasha Ridge Press (www.menasharidge.com).

ECO-ADVENTURES If you don't want to do it yourself, you can observe Florida's flora and fauna on guided field expeditions—and contribute to conservation efforts while you're at it.

The **Sierra Club,** America's oldest and largest grassroots environmental organization, offers eco-adventures through its Florida chapters. Recent outings have included canoeing or kayaking through the Everglades, hiking the Florida Trail in America's southernmost national forest, camping on a barrier island, and exploring the sinkhole phenomenon in North Central Florida. You do have to be a Sierra Club member, but you can join at the time of the trip. Contact the club's national outings office at 85 2nd St., 2nd Floor, San Francisco, CA 94105-3441 (© **415/977-5500;** www.sierraclub.org).

The Florida chapter of **The Nature Conservancy** has protected 578,000 acres of natural lands in Florida and presently owns and manages 36 preserves. For a small fee, you can join one of its field trips or work parties that take place periodically throughout the year; fees vary from year to year, event to event, so call for more information. Participants get a chance to learn about and even participate in the preservation of the ecosystem. For details of all the preserves and adventures, contact The Nature Conservancy, Florida Chapter, 222 S. Westmonte Dr., Suite 300, Altamonte Springs, FL 32714 (© **407/682-3664;** fax 407/682-3077; http://nature.org).

A nonprofit organization dedicated to environmental research, the **Earthwatch Institute,** 3 Clocktower Place, Suite 100 (P.O. Box 75), Maynard, MA 01754 (© **800/776-0188** or 617/926-8200; fax 617/926-8532; www.earthwatch.org), has excursions to survey dolphins and manatees around Sarasota and to monitor the well-being of the captivity-raised whooping cranes that have been released in the wilds of Central Florida. Another research group, the **Oceanic Society,** Fort Mason Center, Building E, San Francisco, CA 94123 (© **800/326-7491** or 415/441-1106; fax 415/474-3395; www.oceanicsociety.org), also has Florida trips among its expeditions, including manatee monitoring in the Crystal River area north of Tampa.

FISHING In addition to the amberjack, bonito, grouper, mackerel, mahimahi, marlin, pompano, redfish, sailfish, snapper, snook, tarpon, tuna, and wahoo running offshore and in its inlets, Florida has countless miles of rivers and streams, plus about 30,000 lakes and springs stocked with more than 100 species of freshwater fish. Indeed, Floridians seem to fish everywhere: off canal banks and old bridges, from fishing piers and fishing fleets. You'll even see them standing alongside the Tamiami Trail (U.S. 41) that cuts across the Everglades—one eye on their line, the other watching for alligators.

We listed our favorite places to fish in chapter 1, but nearly every marina in Florida harbors charter boats. You don't have to pay them a small fortune to try your luck, for most ports also have party boats that take groups out to sea. You'll have lots of company, but their rates are reasonable, they provide the gear and bait, and you won't need a fishing license.

Anglers age 16 and older need fishing licenses for any other kind of saltwater or freshwater fishing, including lobstering and spearfishing. Licenses are sold at bait and tackle shops.

The **Florida Department of Environmental Protection,** 3900 Commonwealth Blvd., Tallahassee, FL 32399-3000 (© **850/488-2960;** www.dep.state.fl.us), publishes the annual *Fishing Lines,* a free magazine with a wealth of information about fishing in Florida, including regulations and licensing requirements. It also distributes free brochures with annual freshwater and saltwater limits. And the **Florida Sports Foundation** (see the introduction to this section, above) publishes *Florida Fishing & Boating,* another treasure trove of information.

HIKING Although you won't be climbing any mountains in this relatively flat state, there are thousands of beautiful hiking trails in Florida. The ideal hiking months are October through April, when the weather is cool and dry and mosquitoes are less prominent. Like anywhere else, you'll find trails that are gentle and short and others that are challenging—some trails in the Everglades require you to wade waist-deep in water!

If you're venturing into the backcountry, watch out for gators, and don't ever try to feed them (or any wild animal). You risk getting bitten (they can't tell the difference between the food and your hand). You're also upsetting the balance of nature, since animals fed by humans lose their ability to find their own food. Most Florida snakes are harmless, but a few have deadly bites, so it's a good idea to avoid them all.

The **Florida Trail Association,** 5415 SW 13th St., Gainesville, FL 32608 (© **800/343-1882** or 352/378-8823; www.floridatrail.org), maintains a large percentage of the public trails in the state and puts out an excellent book packed with maps, details, and color photos.

For a copy of *Florida Trails,* which outlines the many options, contact Visit Florida (see "Visitor Information," earlier in this chapter). Another resource is *A Guide to Your National Scenic Trails,* Office of Greenways and Trails, Department of Environmental Protection, 3900 Commonwealth Blvd., Tallahassee, FL 32399 (© **850/488-2960;** www.dep.state.fl.us/gwt). You can also contact the office of **National Forests in Florida,** Woodcrest Office Park, 325 John Knox Rd., Suite F-100, Tallahassee, FL 32303 (© **850/942-9300;** www.southernregion.fs.fed.us/florida) . And *Hiking Florida,* by M. Timothy O'Keefe (Falcon Press; www.falconbooks.com), details 132 hikes throughout the state, with maps and photos.

GOLF Florida is the unofficial golf capital of the United States—some would say the world—since the **World Golf Hall of Fame** is located near St. Augustine. This state-of-the-art museum and shrine is worth a brief visit even if you're not in love with the game.

One thing's for certain: Florida has more golf courses than any other state—more than 1,150 at last count and growing. We picked the best in chapter 1, but suffice it to say that you can tee off almost any time there's daylight. The highest concentrations of excellent courses are in Southwest

Florida around Naples and Fort Myers (more than 1,000 holes!), in the Orlando area (Disney alone has 99 holes open to the public), and in the Panhandle around Destin and Panama City Beach. And it's a rare town in Florida that doesn't have a municipal golf course—even Key West has 18 great holes.

Greens fees are usually much lower at the municipal courses than at privately owned clubs. Whether public or private, greens fees tend to vary greatly depending on the time of year. You could pay $150 or more at a private course during the high season, but less than half that when the tourists are gone. The fee structures vary so much that it's best to call ahead and ask, and always reserve a tee time as far in advance as possible.

You can learn the game or hone your strokes at one of several excellent golf schools in the state. David Ledbetter has teaching facilities in Orlando and Naples, Fred Griffin is in charge of the Grand Cypress Academy of Golf at Grand Cypress Resort in Orlando, and you'll find Jimmy Ballard's school at the Ocean Reef Club on Key Largo. The Westin Innisbrook Resort at Tarpon Springs has its Innisbrook Golf Institute. Amelia Island (near Jacksonville) is home to Amelia Island Plantation Golf School.

You can get information about most Florida courses, including current greens fees, and reserve tee times through **Tee Times USA,** P.O. Box 641, Flagler Beach, FL 32136 (© **800/374-8633,** 888/465-3567, or 904/439-0001; fax 904/439-0099; www.teetimesusa.com). This company also publishes a vacation guide that includes many stay-and-play golf packages.

Florida Golf, published by the **Florida Sports Foundation** (see the introduction to this section), lists every course in Florida. It's the state's official golf guide and is available from Visit Florida (see "Visitor Information," earlier in this chapter).

Golfer's Guide magazine publishes monthly editions covering most regions of Florida; it is available free at all the local visitor centers and hotel lobbies, or you can contact the magazine at P.O. Box 5926, Hilton Head, SC 29938 (© **800/864-6101** or 843/842-7878; fax 843/842-5743; www.golfersguide.com). Northwest Florida is covered by *Gulf Coast Tee Time,* published by Tee Time LLC, 3 W. Garden St., Pensacola, FL 32501 (© **888/520-4300** or 850/435-4858; fax 850/435-7383; www.teetimeweb.com).

You also can get more information from the **Professional Golfers' Association (PGA),** 100 Avenue of the Champions, Palm Beach Gardens, FL 33418 (© **561/624-8400;** www.pga.com), or the **Ladies Professional Golf Association (LPGA),** 2570 Volusia Ave., Suite B, Daytona Beach, FL 32114 (© **904/254-6200;** www.lpga.com).

More than 700 courses are profiled in *Florida Golf Guide* by Jimmy Shacky (Open Roads Publishing; $19.95), available at bookstores.

SCUBA DIVING & SNORKELING

Divers love the Keys, where you can see magnificent formations of tree-sized elkhorn coral and giant brain coral, as well as colorful sea fans and dozens of other varieties, sharing space with 300 or more species of rainbow-hued fish. Reef diving is good all the way from Key Largo to Key West, with plenty of tour operators, outfitters, and dive shops along the way. Particularly worthy are **John Pennekamp Coral Reef State Park** in Key Largo and **Looe Key National Marine Sanctuary** off Big Pine Key. *Skin Diver* magazine picked Looe Key as the number-one dive spot in North America. Also, the clearest waters in which to view some of the 4,000 sunken ships along Florida's coast are in the Middle Keys and the waters between Key West and the Dry Tortugas. Snorkeling in the Keys is particularly fine between Islamorada and Marathon.

In Northwest Florida, the 100-fathom curve draws closer to the white, sandy Panhandle beaches than to any other spot on the Gulf of Mexico. It's too far north here for coral, but you can see brilliantly colored sponges and fish and, in Timber Hole, discover an undersea "petrified forest" of sunken planes, ships, and even a railroad car. And the battleship USS *Massachusetts* lies in 30 feet of water just 3 miles off Pensacola. Every beach town in Northwest Florida has dive shops to outfit, tour, or certify visitors.

In the Crystal River area, north of the St. Petersburg and Clearwater beaches, you can snorkel with the manatees as they bask in the warm spring waters of Kings Bay.

If you want to keep up with what's going on statewide, you can subscribe to *Florida Scuba News,* a monthly magazine published in Jacksonville (© **904/783-1610;** www.scubanews.com). You might also want to pick up a specialized guidebook. Some good ones include *Coral Reefs of Florida,* by Gilbert L. Voss (Pineapple Press; www.pineapplepress.com), and *The Diver's Guide to Florida and the Florida Keys,* by Jim Stachowicz (Windward Publishing).

TENNIS Year-round sunshine makes Florida great for tennis. There are some 7,700 places to play, from municipal courts to exclusive resorts. Even some of the municipal facilities—Cambier Park Tennis Center in Naples leaps to mind—are equal to those at expensive resorts, and they're either free or close to it.

If you can afford it, you can learn from the best in Florida. **Nick Bollettieri** has sports academies in Bradenton. Safety Harbor Resort and Spa near St. Petersburg hosts the **Phil Green Tennis Program.** Amateurs can hobnob with the superstars at **ATP Tour International Headquarters** in Ponte Vedra Beach, near Jacksonville. **Mary Jo Fernandez** is affiliated with the **Arthur Ashe Tennis Center** at the Doral Golf Resort & Spa in Miami. And **Chris Evert, Robert Seguso,** and **Carling Basset** have their own center in Boca Raton.

Other top places to learn and play are **Amelia Island Plantation** on Amelia Island; **Colony Beach and Tennis Resort** on Longboat Key off Sarasota (which *Tennis* magazine picked as the number-two tennis resort in the nation); **Sanibel Harbour Resort & Spa** in Fort Myers, whose 5,500-seat stadium has hosted Davis Cup matches; **South Seas Plantation Resort & Yacht Harbour** on Captiva Island; and **The Registry Resort** in Naples.

12 Tips on Accommodations

Florida has such a vast array of accommodations—from rock-bottom roadside motels to some of the nation's finest resorts—that we can cover only the tip of the iceberg in this book. Whether you'll spend a pittance or a bundle depends on your budget and your tastes. But, to repeat a well-worn phrase, you can enjoy "champagne on a beer budget"—if you plan carefully.

The annual trip-planning guide published by the state's tourism promotion agency, *Visit Florida* (see "Visitor Information," earlier in this chapter), lists most hotels and motels in the state. It's particularly handy if you're taking your animal along, since it tells whether they accept pets.

Another excellent source is **Superior Small Lodgings** ⭐, a national organization of quality hotels, motels, and inns. None of these properties has more than 75 rooms, and all have been inspected for cleanliness, quality, comfort, privacy, and safety. Contact the local tourist information offices for lists of members in their areas, or the **Florida Superior Small Lodging Association,** 1809 Silver Valley Court, Apokpa, FL 32712 (© **407/ 880-1707;** fax 407/884-1301; www.SuperiorSmallLodging.com). Many hotels and motels recommended in this book are members.

Inn Route, P.O. Box 6187, Palm Harbor, FL 34684 (© **800/524-1880;** fax 281/403-9335; www.florida-inns.com), publishes the *Inns of Florida,* which lists inns and bed-and-breakfasts throughout the state. Inn Route also inspects each property, thus ensuring the quality and cleanliness of its members.

At the inexpensive end, **Hostelling International/American Youth Hostels,** 735 15th St. NW, Suite 840, Washington, DC 20005 (© **202/783-6161;** www.hiayh.org), offers low-cost accommodations in Miami Beach, Key West, Florida City, Orlando, St. Augustine, and Clearwater Beach.

UNDERSTANDING HOTEL ROOM RATES

The rates quoted in this book are "rack" or "published" rates; that is, the highest regular rates charged by a hotel or motel at the time we researched this edition. Not long ago the rack rate was what you paid, unless you were part of a tour group or had purchased a vacation package. Today most hotels give discounts to corporate travelers, government employees, seniors, automobile club members, active duty military personnel, and others. Most hotels don't advertise these discounted rates or even volunteer them at the front desk.

Computerized reservations systems also have permitted many larger properties to adjust their rates on an almost daily—if not hourly—basis, depending on how much business they anticipate having.

Most hotels have free self-parking, but fees can run up the cost at some downtown and beachfront hotels. We've indicated in the listings if a hotel or resort charges for parking; if no charge is given, parking is free.

TIPS FOR SAVING ON YOUR HOTEL ROOM

- **Don't be afraid to bargain.** Most rack rates include commissions of 10% to 25% for travel agents, which some hotels may be willing to reduce if you make your own reservations and haggle a bit. Always ask whether a room less expensive than the first one quoted is available, or whether any special rates apply to you. You may qualify for corporate, student, military, senior citizen, or other discounts. Be sure to mention membership in AAA, AARP, frequent-flier programs, or trade unions, which may entitle you to special deals as well. Find out the hotel policy on children—do kids stay free in the room or is there a special rate?
- **Rely on a qualified professional.** Certain hotels give travel agents discounts in exchange for steering business their way, so if you're shy about bargaining, an agent may be better equipped to negotiate discounts for you.
- **Dial direct.** When booking a room in a chain hotel, compare the rates offered by the hotel's local line with that of the toll-free number. Also check with an agent and online. A hotel makes nothing on a room that stays empty, so the local hotel reservation desk

may be willing to offer a special rate unavailable elsewhere.
- **Remember the law of supply and demand.** Resort hotels are most crowded and therefore most expensive on weekends, so discounts are usually available for midweek stays. Business hotels in downtown locations such as Tampa are busiest during the week, so you can expect discounts over the weekend. Avoid high-season stays whenever you can: planning your vacation just a week before or after official peak season can mean big savings.
- **Look into group or long-stay discounts.** If you come as part of a large group, you should be able to negotiate a bargain rate, since the hotel can then guarantee occupancy in a number of rooms. Likewise, if you're planning a long stay (at least 5 days), you might qualify for a discount. As a general rule, expect 1 night free after a 7-night stay.
- **Book an efficiency.** A room with a kitchenette allows you to shop for groceries and cook your own meals. This is a big money saver, especially for families on long stays.
- Join hotel **frequent-visitor clubs,** even if you don't use them much. You'll be more likely to get upgrades and other perks.
- Many hotels offer **frequent-flier points.** Don't forget to ask for yours when you check in.

CONDOMINIUMS, HOMES & COTTAGES

It may seem at first impression that many Florida beaches are lined with great walls of high-rise condominium buildings. That's not much of an overstatement, for the state literally has thousands upon thousands of condominium units. People actually live in many of them year-round, but others are for rent on a daily, weekly, or monthly basis. In addition, many private homes and cottages are for rent throughout Florida.

Be aware, however, that in Florida real estate and resort parlance, the word *villa* does not mean a luxurious house standing all by itself. Down here, "villa" means an apartment.

Some of the resorts listed in this book actually are condominium complexes operated as full-service hotels, but usually you'll have to do without such hotel amenities as on-site restaurants, room service, and even daily maid service. On the other hand, almost every condominium, home, and cottage has a fully equipped kitchen, and many have washers, dryers, and other such niceties of home, which means they can represent significant savings, especially if you're traveling with children or are sharing with another couple or family.

We have pointed out a few of the best condominium complexes in the "Accommodations You Can Afford" sections of the following chapters, and we have named some of the **reputable real estate agencies** that have inventories of condominiums, private homes, and cottages to rent.

If you think a condominium will meet your needs, your best bet is to contact the rental agencies well in advance and request a brochure describing all the properties they represent, and their rates.

If You're Under 25

Some Florida hotels and motels refuse to rent units to persons under 25 years of age, especially during Spring Break. Be sure to ask if there are age restrictions when you make your reservations.

FAST FACTS: Florida

American Express There are a number of American Express offices in Florida. Call Cardmember Services (© **800/528-4800**; www.americanexpress.com) for the location nearest you.

Banks Banks are usually open Monday to Friday from 9am to 3 or 4pm, and most have automated teller machines (ATMs) for 24-hour banking. You won't have a problem finding a Cirrus or PLUS machine. See "Money," earlier in this chapter.

Car Rentals See "Getting Around," earlier in this chapter.

Climate See "When to Go," earlier in this chapter.

Currency Exchange See "Money," in section 1, "Preparing for Your Trip," in chapter 3, "For International Visitors."

Emergencies Call © **911** anywhere in the state to summon the police, the fire department, or an ambulance.

Liquor Laws You must be 21 to purchase or consume alcohol in Florida. This law is strictly enforced, so if you look young, carry some photo identification that gives your date of birth. Minors can usually enter bars where food is served.

Newspapers/Magazines Most cities of any size have a local daily paper. The well-respected *Miami Herald* is generally available all over the state, with regional editions available in many areas. In the major cities, you can also find coin-operated boxes for *USA Today,* the *Wall Street Journal,* and the *New York Times.*

Safety Whenever you're traveling in an unfamiliar city, stay alert. Be aware of your immediate surroundings. Always lock your car doors and the trunk when your vehicle is unattended, and don't leave any valuables in sight. See "Safety" in section 1 of chapter 3 for more information.

Taxes The Florida state sales tax is 6%. Many municipalities add 1% or more to that, and most levy a special tax on hotel and restaurant bills. In general, expect at least 9% to be added to your final hotel bill. There also are hefty taxes on rental cars here (see "Getting Around," earlier in this chapter).

Time The Florida peninsula observes eastern standard time, but most of the Panhandle west of the Apalachicola River is on central standard time, 1 hour behind the rest of the state.

3

For International Visitors

Whether it's your first visit or your tenth, a trip to the United States may require an additional degree of planning. This chapter will provide you with essential information, helpful tips, and advice for the more common problems that some visitors encounter.

1 Preparing for Your Trip

ENTRY REQUIREMENTS

Immigration laws have been a hot political issue in the United States in recent years, and especially since the terrorist attacks of September 11, 2001, so it's wise to check at any U.S. embassy or consulate for current information and requirements. You can also plug into the U.S. State Department's Internet site at **www.state.gov**.

VISAS & PASSPORTS Canadians may enter the United States without passports or visas; you need only proof of residence.

As we went to press, the "Visa Waiver Program" allowed citizens of Andorra, Argentina, Australia, Austria, Belgium, Brunei, Denmark, Finland, France, Germany, Iceland, Ireland, Italy, Japan, Liechtenstein, Luxembourg, Monaco, the Netherlands, New Zealand, Norway, San Marino, Slovenia, Spain, Sweden, Switzerland, and the United Kingdom to enter the U.S. with a valid passport and a round-trip air or cruise ticket in their possession upon arrival in order to stay in the U.S. for up to 90 days. Once here, you may then visit Mexico, Canada, Bermuda, and/or the Caribbean islands and return to the United States without needing a visa. But note that system may change, so check with the nearest U.S. embassy or consulate, or visit the U.S. State Department's Internet site at www.state.gov, to see if your country is still included in the Visa Waiver Program.

If you're from any other country, you must have (1) a valid **passport** with an expiration date at least 6 months later than the scheduled end of your visit to the United States; and (2) a **tourist visa,** which may be obtained without charge from the nearest U.S. consulate.

Obtaining a Visa & Passport To obtain a tourist visa, submit a completed application form with a 1½-inch-square photo and demonstrate binding ties to your residence abroad. If you cannot go in person, contact the nearest U.S. embassy or consulate for directions on applying by mail. Your travel agent or airline office may also be able to provide you with the visa application forms and instructions. The U.S. embassy or consulate where you apply will determine whether you receive a multiple- or single-entry visa and any restrictions regarding the length of your stay. This may take a few days or even weeks, so apply well in advance.

British subjects can obtain up-to-date visa information by calling the **U.S. Embassy Visa Information Line** (© 0891/200-290) or the **London**

Passport Office (✆ 0990/210-410 for recorded information).

Irish citizens can obtain up-to-date passport and visa information through the **Embassy of USA Dublin,** 42 Elgin Rd., Dublin 4, Ireland (✆ **353/1-668-8777**; or check the visa website at www.usembassy.ie/consulate/applications.html).

Australian citizens can obtain up-to-date passport and visa information by calling the **U.S. Embassy Canberra,** Moonah Place, Yarralumla, ACT 2600 (✆ **02/6214-5600**) or check the website's visa page at www.usis-australia.gov/consular/niv.html.

Citizens of **New Zealand** can obtain up-to-date passport and visa information by calling the **U.S. Embassy New Zealand,** 29 Fitzherbert Terrace, Thorndon, Wellington, New Zealand, (✆ **644/472-2068**; or get the information directly from the website http://usembassy.org.nz).

DRIVER'S LICENSES Foreign driver's licenses are generally recognized in the U.S., although you may want to get an international driver's license if your home license is not written in English.

MEDICAL REQUIREMENTS Unless you're arriving from an area known to be suffering from an epidemic (particularly cholera or yellow fever), inoculations or vaccinations are not required for entry into the United States. If you have a disease that requires treatment with narcotics or syringe-administered medications, carry a valid signed prescription from your physician to allay any suspicions that you may be smuggling narcotics (a serious offense that carries severe penalties in the U.S.).

For **HIV-positive visitors,** requirements for entering the United States are somewhat vague and change frequently. According to the latest publication of *HIV and Immigrants: A Manual for AIDS Service Providers,* the Immigration and Naturalization Service (INS) doesn't require a medical exam for entry into the United States, but INS officials may stop individuals because they look sick or because they are carrying AIDS/HIV medicine.

If an HIV-positive noncitizen applies for a non-immigrant visa, the question on the application regarding communicable diseases is tricky no matter which way it's answered. If the applicant checks "no," INS may deny the visa on the grounds that the applicant committed fraud. If the applicant checks "yes" or if INS suspects the person is HIV-positive, it will deny the visa unless the applicant asks for a special waiver for visitors. This waiver is for people visiting the United States for a short time, to attend a conference, for instance, to visit close relatives, or to receive medical treatment. It can be a confusing situation. For further up-to-the-minute information, contact the Centers for Disease Control's **National Center for HIV** (✆ **404/332-4559**; www.hivatis.org) or the **Gay Men's Health Crisis** (✆ **212/367-1000**; www.gmhc.org).

CUSTOMS
WHAT YOU CAN BRING IN
Every visitor more than 21 years of age may bring in, free of duty, the following: (1) 1 liter of wine or hard liquor; (2) 200 cigarettes, 100 cigars (but not from Cuba), or 3 pounds of smoking tobacco; and (3) $100 worth of gifts. These exemptions are offered to travelers who spend at least 72 hours in the United States and who have not claimed them within the preceding 6 months. It is altogether forbidden to bring into the country foodstuffs (particularly fruit, cooked meats, and canned goods) and plants (vegetables, seeds, tropical plants, and the like). Foreign tourists may bring in or take out up to $10,000 in U.S. or foreign currency with no formalities; larger

sums must be declared to U.S. Customs on entering or leaving, which includes filing form CM 4790. For more specific information regarding U.S. Customs, call your nearest U.S. embassy or consulate, or the **U.S. Customs** office at ✆ 202/927-1770; or visit www.customs.ustreas.gov.

WHAT YOU CAN TAKE HOME
U.K. citizens returning from a non-EC country have a Customs allowance of: 200 cigarettes; 50 cigars; 250 grams of smoking tobacco; 2 liters of still table wine; 1 liter of spirits or strong liqueurs (over 22% volume); 2 liters of fortified wine, sparkling wine, or other liqueurs; 60cc (ml) perfume; 250cc (ml) of toilet water; and £145 worth of all other goods, including gifts and souvenirs. People under 17 cannot have the tobacco or alcohol allowance. For more information, contact HM Customs & Excise, Passenger Enquiry Point, 2nd Floor Wayfarer House, Great South West Road, Feltham, Middlesex, TW14 8NP (✆ **0181/910-3744;** from outside the U.K. 44/181-910-3744), or consult their website at www.open.gov.uk.

For a clear summary of **Canadian** rules, write for the booklet *I Declare,* issued by **Revenue Canada,** 2265 St. Laurent Blvd., Ottawa K1G 4KE (✆ **506/636-5064**). Canada allows its citizens a C$750 exemption, and you're allowed to bring back duty-free one carton of cigarettes, one can of tobacco, 40 imperial ounces of liquor, and 50 cigars. In addition, you're allowed to mail gifts to Canada valued at less than C$60 a day, provided they're unsolicited and don't contain alcohol or tobacco (write on the package "Unsolicited gift, under C$60 value"). All valuables should be declared on the Y-38 form before departure from Canada, including serial numbers of valuables you already own, such as expensive foreign cameras. ***Note:*** The $750 exemption can only be used once a year and only after an absence of 7 days.

The duty-free allowance in **Australia** is A$400 or, for those under 18, A$200. Personal property mailed back from the U.S. should be marked "Australian goods returned" to avoid payment of duty. Upon returning to Australia, citizens can bring in 250 cigarettes or 250 grams of loose tobacco, and 1,125ml of alcohol. If you're returning with valuable goods you already own, such as foreign-made cameras, you should file form B263. A helpful brochure, available from Australian consulates or Customs offices, is *Know Before You Go.* For more information, contact **Australian Customs Services,** GPO Box 8, Sydney NSW 2001 (✆ **02/9213-2000**).

The duty-free allowance for **New Zealand** is NZ$700. Citizens over 17 can bring in 200 cigarettes, or 50 cigars, or 250 grams of tobacco (or a mixture of all three if their combined weight doesn't exceed 250g); plus 4.5 liters of wine and beer, or 1.125 liters of liquor. New Zealand currency does not carry import or export restrictions. Fill out a certificate of export, listing the valuables you are taking out of the country; that way, you can bring them back without paying duty. Most questions are answered in a free pamphlet available at New Zealand consulates and Customs offices: *New Zealand Customs Guide for Travellers, Notice no. 4.* For more information, contact New Zealand Customs, 50 Anzac Ave., P.O. Box 29, Auckland (✆ **09/359-6655**).

HEALTH INSURANCE

Although it's not required of travelers, health insurance is highly recommended. Unlike many European countries, the United States does not usually offer free or low-cost medical care to its citizens or visitors. Doctors and hospitals are expensive, and in most cases will require advance payment or proof of coverage before they render their services. Policies can cover everything from the loss or theft of your baggage and trip cancellation to the guarantee of bail in case you're arrested. Good policies will also cover the costs of an accident, repatriation, or death. See "Insurance & Health" in chapter 2, "Planning An Affordable Trip to Florida," for more information. Packages such as **Europ Assistance** in Europe are sold by automobile clubs and travel agencies at attractive rates. **Worldwide Assistance Services,** Inc. (© 800/821-2828; www.worldwideassistance.com) is the agent for Europ Assistance in the United States.

Though lack of health insurance may prevent you from being admitted to a hospital in nonemergencies, don't worry about being left on a street corner to die: the American way is to fix you now and bill the living daylights out of you later.

INSURANCE FOR BRITISH TRAVELERS Most big travel agents offer their own insurance, and will probably try to sell you their package when you book a holiday. Think before you sign. **Britain's Consumers' Association** recommends that you insist on seeing the policy and reading the fine print before buying travel insurance. **The Association of British Insurers** (© 0171/600-3333; www.abi.org.uk/) gives advice by phone and publishes *Holiday Insurance,* a free guide to policy provisions and prices. You might also shop around for better deals: Try **Columbus Direct** (© 0171/375-0011; www.columbusdirect.net/).

INSURANCE FOR CANADIAN TRAVELERS Canadians should check with their provincial health plan offices or call **Health Canada** (© 613/957-2991; www.hc-sc.gc.ca/) to find out the extent of their coverage and what documentation and receipts they must take home in case they are treated in the United States.

MONEY

The U.S. monetary system has a decimal base: 1 American dollar ($1) = 100 cents (100¢). Notes come in $1 (sometimes called a "buck"), $5, $10, $20, $50, and $100 denominations (the last two are not welcome when paying for small purchases and are not accepted in taxis or at subway ticket booths). There are also $2 bills, but you are unlikely to see any because they are no longer made. There are six denominations of coins: 1¢ (one cent, known here as "a penny"), 5¢ (five cents, or "a nickel"), 10¢ (ten cents, or "a dime"), 25¢ (twenty-five cents, or "a quarter"), 50¢ (fifty cents, or "a half dollar"), and the rare $1 piece.

Changing foreign currency in the United States is a hassle, so leave any currency other than U.S. dollars at home—it will prove more of a nuisance than it's worth. Even banks here may not want to change your home currency into U.S. dollars. The exceptions are the currency exchange desks in the Miami, Orlando, Tampa, and Fort Myers airports, and **Thomas Cook Foreign Exchange,** which changes foreign currency and sells commission-free foreign and U.S. traveler's checks, drafts, and wire transfers. Thomas Cook's Florida office is in Fort Lauderdale (© 800/287-7362; www.us.thomascook.com).

Traveler's checks denominated in U.S. dollars are readily accepted at most hotels, motels, restaurants, and large stores. Do not bring traveler's checks denominated in other currencies. Sometimes a passport or other photo identification is necessary. The three types of traveler's checks that are most widely recognized—and least likely to be denied—are **Visa, American Express,** and **Thomas Cook.** Be sure to record the numbers of the checks, and keep that information in a safe place (not in your wallet or purse) in case they get lost or stolen.

> **Tips** **Speaking Your Language**
>
> You can call Visit Florida's 24-hour **tourist assistance hotline** (✆ 800/656-8777) if you need help with lost travel documents, directions, emergencies, or information about attractions, restaurants, and shopping anywhere in the state. Hotline operators speak several languages, including Spanish, French, German, and Portuguese. The phone call is free.
>
> In Orlando, **Walt Disney World** (✆ 407/2-DISNEY) has numerous services designed to meet the needs of foreign visitors, including personal translators and a special phone number (✆ 407/824-7900) to speak to someone in French, Spanish, German, and other languages.

American Express, Diners Club, Discover, MasterCard (EuroCard in Europe, Access in Britain, Chargex in Canada), and Visa (BarclayCard in Britain) **credit and charge cards** are the most widely used form of payment in the United States. You should bring at least one with you—if for no other reason than to rent a car, since all rental companies require them.

Most **automated teller machines (ATMs),** located throughout Florida, will allow you to draw U.S. currency against your bank and credit cards. When available, this is the easiest way to get U.S. dollars, and you get the bank's rate of exchange, normally better than you will receive at hotels and other businesses. Check with your bank before leaving home, and remember that you will need your personal identification number (PIN) to do so. See "Money" in chapter 2 for more information.

SAFETY

GENERAL While tourist areas are generally safe and crime rates have been decreasing in the U.S., urban areas here tend to be less safe than those in Europe or Japan. You should always stay alert. This is particularly true of large U.S. cities. It is wise to ask your hotel's front-desk staff or the city's or area's tourist office if you're in doubt about which neighborhoods are safe.

Remember also that hotels are open to the public, and in a large hotel, security may not be able to screen everyone entering. Always lock your room door. Don't assume that once inside your hotel you are automatically safe and no longer need to be aware of your surroundings.

DRIVING SAFETY Driving safety is important too, and carjacking is not unprecedented. Question your rental agency about personal safety and ask for a traveler-safety brochure when you pick up your car. Obtain written directions—or a map with the route clearly marked—from the agency showing how to get to your destination. (Many agencies now offer the option of renting a cellular phone for the duration of your car rental; check with the rental agent when you pick up the car.) And, if possible, arrive and depart during daylight hours.

If you drive off a highway and end up in a dodgy-looking neighborhood, leave the area as quickly as possible. If you have an accident, even on the highway, stay in your car with the doors locked until you assess the situation or until the police arrive. If you're bumped from behind on the street or are involved in a minor accident with no injuries, and the situation appears to be suspicious, motion to the other driver to follow you. Never get out of your car in such situations. Go directly to the nearest police precinct, well-lit service station, or 24-hour store. You may want to look into renting a cellphone

GETTING TO THE U.S.

on a short-term basis. One recommended wireless rental company is **InTouch USA** (© 800/872-7626; www.intouchusa.com).

Park in well-lit and well-traveled areas whenever possible. Always keep your car doors locked, whether the vehicle is attended or unattended. Never leave any packages or valuables in sight. If someone attempts to rob you or steal your car, don't try to resist the thief/carjacker. Report the incident to the police department immediately by calling © **911**.

2 Getting to the U.S.

A number of U.S. airlines offer service from Europe and Latin America to Florida, including American, Delta, Northwest, and United (see "Getting There," in chapter 2). Many of the major international airlines, such as **British Airways** (www.british-airways.com), **KLM Royal Dutch Airlines** (www.klm.com), and **Lufthansa** (www.lufthansa.com) also have direct flights from Europe to various Florida cities, either in their own planes or in conjunction with an American "partner" airline (Northwest–KLM, to name one such partnership). You can get here from Australia and New Zealand via **Air New Zealand** (www.airnz.com), **Qantas** (www.qantas.com), **American** (www.aa.com), and **United** (www.ual.com), with a change of planes in Los Angeles. Call the airlines' local offices or contact your travel agent, and be sure to ask about promotional fares and discounts.

From Great Britain, **Virgin Atlantic Airways** (© 800/662-8621 in the U.S., or 01/293-74-77-47 in the U.K.; www.virgin-atlantic.com) has attractive deals on its flights from London and Manchester to Miami and Orlando. From Germany, **LTU International Airways** (© 800/888-0200 in the U.S., 11/948-8466 in Germany; www.ltu.com) frequently has reduced fares to Miami, Orlando, and Fort Myers from Frankfurt, Munich, and Düsseldorf. From Johannesburg and Cape Town, **South African Airways** and **Delta Airlines** (www.delta.com) fly to Fort Lauderdale.

Canadians should check with **Air Canada** (© 800/776-3000; www.aircanada.ca), which offers service from Toronto and Montréal to Miami, Tampa, West Palm Beach, Fort Lauderdale, and Fort Myers. Also ask your travel agent about **Air Transat** (© 800/470-1011; www.airtransat.com), which has wintertime charter flights to several Florida destinations.

AIRFARES Whichever airline you choose, always ask about **advance purchase excursion (APEX)** fares, which represent substantial savings over regular fares. Most require tickets to be bought 21 days prior to departure.

On the Web, the European Travel Network (ETN) operates a site at **www.discount-tickets.com**, which offers cut-rate prices on international airfares to the United States, accommodations, car rentals, and tours. Another site to check for current discount fares worldwide is **www.etn.nl/discount.htm#disco**.

See "Getting There" in chapter 2 for more ideas of how to save on airfares.

IMMIGRATION & CUSTOMS CLEARANCE When you arrive in the U.S., getting through immigration control may take as long as 2 hours on some days, especially summer weekends. Accordingly, you should make very generous allowances for delay in planning connections between international and domestic flights.

In contrast, travelers arriving by car or by rail from Canada will find border-crossing formalities to be more streamlined. And air travelers from Canada, Bermuda, and some places in the Caribbean can sometimes go through Customs and Immigration at the point of departure.

For further information, see "Getting There" in chapter 2.

3 Getting Around the U.S.

The United States is one of the world's largest countries, with vast distances separating many of its key sights. If you fly from Europe to New York, for example, you still have a trip of more than 1,350 miles (2,173km) to Miami. Accordingly, flying is the quickest and most comfortable way to get around the country.

BY PLANE Some large airlines (for example, Northwest and Delta) offer travelers on their transatlantic or transpacific flights special discount tickets under the name **Visit USA**, allowing mostly one-way travel from one U.S. destination to another at very low prices. These discount tickets are not on sale in the United States and must be purchased abroad in conjunction with your international ticket. This system is the best, easiest, and fastest way to see the United States at low cost. You should obtain information well in advance from your travel agent or the office of the airline concerned, since the conditions attached to these discount tickets can be changed without advance notice.

BY TRAIN International visitors (excluding Canada) can also buy a **USA Railpass,** good for 15 or 30 days of unlimited travel on Amtrak (© **800/USA-RAIL;** www.amtrak.com). The pass is available through many foreign travel agents. Prices in 2002 for a 15-day pass were $295 off-peak, $440 peak; a 30-day pass costs $385 off-peak, $550 peak. With a foreign passport, you can also buy passes at some Amtrak offices in the United States, including locations in San Francisco, Los Angeles, Chicago, New York, Miami, Boston, and Washington, D.C. Reservations are generally required and should be made for each part of your trip as early as possible. Regional rail passes are also available.

BY BUS Although bus travel is often the most economical form of public transit for short hops between U.S. cities, it can also be slow and uncomfortable—certainly not an option for everyone (particularly when Amtrak, which is far more luxurious, offers similar rates). **Greyhound/Trailways** (© 800/231-2222), the sole nationwide bus line, offers an **International Ameripass** that must be purchased before coming to the United States, or by phone through the Greyhound International Office at the Port Authority Bus Terminal in New York City (© **212/971-0492**). The pass can be obtained from foreign travel agents and costs less than the domestic version. Passes for 2002 cost from $135 for 4 days to $494 for 60 days. You can get more info on the pass at www.greyhound.com, or by calling © **212/971-0492** (14:00–21:00 GMT) and © **402/330-8552** (all other times). In addition, special rates are available for seniors and students.

> **Important Note**
>
> In the United States we drive on the **right side of the road** as in Europe, not on the left side as in the United Kingdom, Australia, New Zealand, and South Africa.

BY CAR Unless you plan to spend the bulk of your vacation time in New York City or New Orleans, the most cost-effective, convenient, and comfortable way to travel around the United States is by car. The interstate highway system connects cities and towns all over the country; in addition to these high-speed, limited-access roadways, there's an extensive network of federal, state, and local highways and roads. For car-rental agencies, see "Getting Around" in chapter 2.

FAST FACTS: For the International Traveler

Automobile Organizations Auto clubs will supply maps, suggested routes, guidebooks, accident and bail-bond insurance, and emergency road service. The **American Automobile Association (AAA)** is the major auto club in the United States. If you belong to an auto club in your home country, inquire about AAA reciprocity before you leave. You may be able to join AAA even if you're not a member of a reciprocal club; to inquire, call AAA (© 800/222-4357; www.aaa.com). AAA is actually an organization of regional auto clubs; in Florida, look under "AAA Automobile Club South" in the White Pages of the telephone directory. AAA has a nationwide emergency road-service telephone number (© **800/AAA-HELP**).

Automobile Rentals See "Getting Around," in chapter 2.

Currency & Currency Exchange See "Money," under "Preparing for Your Trip," above.

Electricity Like Canada, the United States uses 110 to 120 volts AC (60 cycles), compared with 220 to 240 volts AC (50 cycles) in most of Europe, Australia, and New Zealand. If your small appliances use 220 to 240 volts, you'll need a 110-volt transformer and a plug adapter with two flat parallel pins to operate them here. Downward converters that change 220 to 240 volts to 110 to 120 volts are difficult to find in the United States, so bring one with you.

Embassies & Consulates All embassies are located in the national capital, Washington, D.C. Some consulates are located in major U.S. cities, and most nations have a mission to the United Nations in New York City. Some key embassies are listed here:

Australia: 1601 Massachusetts Ave. NW, Washington, DC 20036 (© 202/797-3000; www.austemb.org). There are Australian consulates in New York City, Honolulu, Houston, Los Angeles, and San Francisco.

Canada: 501 Pennsylvania Ave. NW, Washington, DC 20001 (© 202/682-1740; www.canadianembassy.org). In Florida, there's a Canadian consulate at 200 S. Biscayne Blvd., Suite 1600, Miami, FL 33131 (© **305/579-1600**). Other Canadian consulates are in Buffalo (NY), Chicago, Detroit, Los Angeles, New York, and Seattle.

Republic of Ireland: 2234 Massachusetts Ave. NW, Washington, DC 20008 (© 202/462-3939). Irish consulates are in Boston, Chicago, New York City, and San Francisco.

New Zealand: 37 Observatory Circle NW, Washington, DC 20008 (© 202/328-4800; www.emb.com/nzemb). New Zealand consulates are in Los Angeles, Salt Lake City, San Francisco, and Seattle.

United Kingdom: 3100 Massachusetts Ave. NW, Washington, DC 20008 (© **202/462-1340**). In Florida, there's a full-service British consulate in Miami at Suite 2800, Brickell Bay Dr. (© **305/374-1522**), and a vice consulate for emergency situations in Orlando at the Sun Bank Tower, Suite 2110, 200 S. Orange Ave. (© **407/426-7855**). Other British consulates are in Atlanta, Boston, Chicago, Cleveland, Dallas, Houston, Los Angeles, and New York City.

Emergencies Call © **911** to report a fire, contact the police, or get an ambulance anywhere in the United States. This is a toll-free call (no coins are required at public telephones).

Visit Florida, the state's tourist information agency, operates a 24-hour, multilanguage **tourist assistance hotline** (© **800/656-8777**), which will give advice and information in case of an emergency.

If you encounter traveler's problems, check the local telephone directory to find an office of the **Traveler's Aid Society** (www.travelersaid.org), a nationwide, not-for-profit social-service organization geared to helping travelers in difficult straits. Their services might include reuniting families separated while traveling, providing food and/or shelter to people stranded without cash, or even offering emotional counseling. If you're in trouble, seek them out.

Gasoline (Petrol) Petrol is known as gasoline (or simply "gas") in the United States, and petrol stations are known as both gas stations and service stations. Gasoline costs about half as much (about $1.13 per gallon or more) here as it does in Europe. One U.S. gallon equals 3.8 liters, or .85 Imperial gallon. A majority of gas stations in Florida are now actually convenience grocery stores with gas pumps outside. They do not service your automobile for you; all but a very few stations have self-service gas pumps.

Holidays Banks, government offices, post offices, and many stores, restaurants, and museums are closed on the following legal national holidays: January 1 (New Year's Day), the third Monday in January (Martin Luther King, Jr. Day), the third Monday in February (Presidents' Day, Washington's Birthday), the last Monday in May (Memorial Day), July 4 (Independence Day), the first Monday in September (Labor Day), the second Monday in October (Columbus Day), November 11 (Veterans' Day/Armistice Day), the last Thursday in November (Thanksgiving Day), and December 25 (Christmas). The Tuesday following the first Monday in November is Election Day and is a federal government holiday in presidential-election years (the next is in 2004).

Legal Aid The foreign tourist will probably never become involved with the American legal system. If you are "pulled over" for a minor driving infraction (for example, of the highway code, such as speeding), never attempt to pay the fine directly to a police officer; this could be construed as attempted bribery, a much more serious crime. Pay fines by mail, or directly into the hands of the clerk of the court. If accused of a more serious offense, say and do nothing before consulting a lawyer or your embassy or consulate. Here the government must prove a person's guilt beyond a reasonable doubt, and everyone has the right to remain silent, whether he or she is suspected of a crime or actually arrested. If arrested, a person can make one telephone call to a party of his or her choice, and foreigners have a right to call their embassies or consulates.

Mail If you aren't sure what your address will be in the United States, mail can be sent to you, in your name, **c/o General Delivery** at the main post office of the city or region where you expect to be. You must pick up your mail in person and must produce proof of identity (driver's license, passport, and so on).

Generally to be found at intersections, **mailboxes** are blue with a red-and-white stripe and carry the inscription U.S. MAIL. If your mail is addressed to a U.S. destination, don't forget to add the five-digit postal code, or ZIP code, after the two-letter abbreviation of the state to which the mail is addressed (FL for Florida).

At press time, **domestic postage rates** were 23¢ for a postcard and 37¢ for a letter. For international mail, a first-class letter of up to one-half ounce costs 80¢ (60¢ to Canada and Mexico) and a first-class postcard costs 70¢ (50¢ to Canada and Mexico).

Newspapers/Magazines All over Florida, you'll be able to purchase *USA Today,* the national daily, and the *Miami Herald,* one of the most highly respected dailies in the country. Every city has its own daily paper.

Taxes In the United States there is no value-added tax (VAT) or other indirect tax at the national level. However, every state, county, and city has the right to levy its own local tax on all purchases, including hotel and restaurant bills, airline tickets, and so on. For Florida's sales taxes, see "Fast Facts: Florida" in chapter 2.

Telephone & Telegraph The telephone system in the United States is run by private corporations, so rates, especially for long-distance service and operator-assisted calls, can vary widely. Generally, hotel surcharges on long-distance and local calls are astronomical, so you're usually better off using a **public pay telephone,** which you'll find clearly marked in most public buildings and private establishments as well as on the street. Convenience grocery stores and gas stations always have them. Many convenience groceries and packaging services sell **prepaid calling cards** in denominations up to $50; these can be the least expensive way to call home. Many public phones at airports now accept American Express, MasterCard, and Visa credit cards. Local calls made from public pay phones in Florida cost 35¢.

Most **long-distance and international calls** can be dialed directly from any phone. For calls within the United States and to Canada, dial **1** followed by the area code and the seven-digit number. For other international calls, dial **011** followed by the country code, city code, and telephone number of the person you are calling.

Calls to area codes 800, 888, and 877 are toll-free. However, calls to numbers in area codes 700 and 900 (chat lines, bulletin boards, "dating" services, and so on) can be very expensive—usually a charge of 95¢ to $3 or more per minute, and they sometimes have minimum charges that can run as high as $15 or more.

For **collect (reversed-charge) calls** and for **person-to-person calls,** dial 0 (zero, *not* the letter O) followed by the area code and number you want; an operator will then come on the line, and you should specify that you are calling collect, or person-to-person, or both. If your operator-assisted call is international, ask for the overseas operator.

For local **directory assistance** ("information"), dial 411; for long-distance information, dial 1, then the appropriate area code and 555-1212.

Telegraph and telex services are provided primarily by Western Union (www.westernunion.com). You can bring your telegram into the nearest Western Union office (there are hundreds across the country) or dictate it over the phone (© **800/325-6000**). You can also telegraph money, or have it telegraphed to you, very quickly over the Western Union system, but this service can cost as much as 15% to 25% of the amount sent.

There are two kinds of telephone directories in the United States. The so-called **White Pages** list private and business subscribers in alphabetical order. The inside front cover lists emergency numbers for police, fire, ambulance, the Coast Guard, poison-control center, crime-victims hotline, and so on. The first few pages will tell you how to make long-distance and international calls, complete with country codes and area codes. Government numbers are usually found on pages printed on blue paper. Printed on yellow paper, the so-called **Yellow Pages** list all local services, businesses, industries, and churches and synagogues by type of activity, with an index at the front or back. The Yellow Pages also include city plans or detailed area maps, often showing postal ZIP codes and public transportation routes.

Time The continental United States is divided into four **time zones:** eastern standard time (EST), central standard time (CST), mountain standard time (MST), and Pacific standard time (PST). Alaska and Hawaii have their own zones. For example, noon in New York City (EST) is 11am in Chicago (CST), 10am in Denver (MST), 9am in Los Angeles (PST), 8am in Anchorage (AST), and 7am in Honolulu (HST). Most of Florida observes eastern standard time, though the Panhandle west of the Apalachicola River is on central standard time (1 hour earlier than Tallahassee, Orlando, and Miami).

Daylight saving time is in effect from 2am on the first Sunday in April through 2am on the last Sunday in October. Daylight saving time moves the clock 1 hour ahead of standard time.

Tipping Tipping is so ingrained in the American way of life that the annual income tax of tip-earning service personnel is based on how much they should have received in light of their employers' gross revenues. Accordingly, they may have to pay tax on a tip you didn't actually give them.

Here are some rules of thumb: bartenders, 10% to 15% of the check; bellhops, at least 50¢ per bag, or $2 to $3 for a lot of luggage; cab drivers, 10% of the fare; chambermaids, $1 per day; checkroom attendants, $1 per garment; hairdressers and barbers, 15% to 20% of the bill; waiters and waitresses, 15% to 20% of the check; valet parking attendants, $1 per vehicle; rest-room attendants, 25¢. Do not tip theater ushers, gas station attendants, or the staff at cafeterias and fast-food restaurants.

Toilets You won't find public toilets (or "restrooms") on the streets in most U.S. cities, but they can be found in hotel lobbies, bars, restaurants, museums, libraries, department stores, railway and bus stations, and service stations. Note, however, that restaurants and bars in resorts or heavily visited areas may reserve their restrooms for the use of their patrons.

Miami

by Lesley Abravanel

If there's one thing Miami doesn't have, it's an identity crisis. In fact, it's the city's vibrant, multifaceted personality that attracts millions each year, from all over the world. South Beach may be on the top of many Miami to-do lists, but the rest of the city, a fascinating assemblage of multicultural neighborhoods, should not be overlooked or neglected. Once considered "God's Waiting Room," the Magic City now attracts an eclectic mix of old and young, celebs and plebes, American and international, and geek and chic with an equally varied roster of activities.

For starters, Miami boasts incredible natural beauty, with blinding blue waters, fine sandy beaches, and lush tropical parks that provide the perfect setting for relaxation and exploration. The city's human-made brilliance, in the form of Crayola-colored architecture, never seems to fade in Miami's unique Art Deco District. For cultural variation, the city offers the tastes, sounds, and rhythms of Cuba in Little Havana.

As in any metropolis, however, there are areas that have their drawbacks. Downtown Miami, for instance, is in the throes of a major, albeit slow, renaissance, in which the sketchier, warehouse sections of the city are being transformed into hubs of all things hip. In contrast to this development, however, are the still poverty-stricken areas of downtown such as Overtown, Liberty City, and Little Haiti. While it's obvious to advise you to exercise caution when exploring the less traveled parts of the city, we would also be remiss in telling you to bypass them completely.

Lose yourself in the city's nature and its neighborhoods, and, best of all, its people—a sassy collection of artists and intellectuals, beach bums and international transplants, dolled-up drag queens and bodies beautiful. No wonder celebrities love to vacation here—the spotlight is on the city and its residents. And unlike most stars, Miami is always ready for its close-up. With so much to do and see, Miami is a virtual amusement park that's bound to entertain all those who pass through its palm-lined gates.

1 Orientation

ARRIVING

BY PLANE **Miami International Airport (MIA)** has become second in the United States for international passenger traffic and 10th in the world for total passengers. Despite the heavy traffic, the airport is quite user-friendly and not as much of a hassle as you'd think. You can change money or use your ATM card at Nation's Bank of South Florida, located near the exit. Visitor information is available 24 hours a day at the **Miami International Airport Main Visitor Counter,** Concourse E, 2nd level (© **305/876-7000;** www.miami-airport.com). Because

MIA is the busiest airport in South Florida, travelers may want to consider flying into the less crowded, but expanding, **Fort Lauderdale–Hollywood International Airport (FLL)** (© 954/359-1200), which is closer to north Miami than MIA, or the **Palm Beach International Airport (PBI)** (© 561/471-7420), about 90 minutes away.

Miami International Airport is located about 6 miles west of downtown and about 10 miles from the beaches, so it's likely you can get from the plane to your hotel room in less than half an hour. All the major **car-rental** firms operate off-site branches reached via shuttles from the terminals. See "Getting Around," later in this chapter, for a list of major rental companies. **Taxis** line up outside the airport's arrivals terminals. Most cabs are metered, though some have flat rates to popular destinations. The fare should be about $20 to Coral Gables, $18 to downtown, and $24 to South Beach, plus tip, which should be at least 10% (add more for each bag the driver handles). Depending on traffic, the ride to Coral Gables or downtown takes about 15 to 20 minutes and 20 to 25 minutes to South Beach.

Group limousines (multi-passenger vans) circle the arrivals area looking for fares. Destinations are posted on the front of each van, and a flat rate is charged for door-to-door service to the area marked. **SuperShuttle** (© 305/871-2000; www.supershuttle.com) is one of the largest airport operators, charging between $10 and $20 per person for a ride within the county. This is a cheaper alternative to a cab (if you are traveling alone or with one other person), but be prepared to be in the van for quite a while, as you may have to make several stops to drop passengers off before you reach your own destination. SuperShuttle also began service from Palm Beach International Airport to the surrounding communities. The door-to-door, shared ride service operates from the airport to Stuart, Fort Pierce, Palm Beach, and Broward counties.

Public transportation in South Florida is a major hassle bordering on a nightmare. Painfully slow and unreliable, buses heading downtown leave the airport only once per hour (from the arrivals level), and connections are spotty at best. It could take about an hour and a half to get to South Beach. Journeys to downtown and Coral Gables are more direct. The fare is $1.25, plus an additional 25¢ for a transfer.

BY CAR No matter where you start your journey, chances are you'll reach Miami by way of I-95. This north-south interstate is the city's lifeline and an integral, albeit often frustrating, part of the region. Drivers here are notoriously bad, and many of Miami's road signs are completely confusing, if not absent. Be on the alert when behind the wheel here.

BY TRAIN Amtrak (© 800/USA RAIL; www.amtrak.com) has two trains daily between New York and Miami: the *Silver Meteor* and the *Silver Star*. You'll pull into Amtrak's Miami terminal at 8303 NW 37th Ave. None of the major car rental companies has an office at the train station (they're at the airport, 5 miles away), but taxis do meet each train. The 20-minute ride to downtown Miami costs about $22 and the ride to Miami Beach, which takes approximately 25 minutes, costs about $24.

BY BUS Greyhound (© 800/231-2222; www.greyhound.com) offers service into Miami from most major cities and smaller towns. Buses pull into a number of stations around the city, including 4111 NW 27th Ave. (near the airport), 700 Biscayne Blvd. (downtown), and 11650 NE Sixth Ave. (in North Miami Beach).

Miami at a Glance

VISITOR INFORMATION

The most up-to-date visitor information is provided by the **Greater Miami Convention and Visitor's Bureau,** 701 Brickell Ave., Suite 700, Miami, FL 33131 (© **800/933-8448** or 305/539-3000; fax 305/530-3113; www.miamiandbeaches.com). Several chambers of commerce in Greater Miami will send out information on their particular neighborhoods; for addresses and numbers, please see "Visitor Information," in chapter 2.

Always check local newspapers for special events during your visit. The city's only daily, the *Miami Herald,* is a good source for current events listings, particularly the "Weekend" section in Friday's edition and the paper's entertainment weekly offshoot, *The Street,* available free every Friday in freestanding boxes anchored to city streets. Even better is the free weekly alternative paper, the *Miami New Times,* found in bright red boxes throughout the city.

Information on everything from dining to entertainment in Miami is available on the Internet at **www.miami.citysearch.com**.

CITY LAYOUT

Miami may seem confusing at first, but it quickly becomes easy to negotiate. The small cluster of buildings that make up the downtown area is at the geographical heart of the city. In relation to downtown, the airport is northwest, the beaches are east, Coconut Grove is south, Coral Gables is west, and the rest of the city is north.

FINDING AN ADDRESS Miami is divided into dozens of areas with official and unofficial boundaries. Street numbering in the city of Miami is fairly straightforward, but you must first be familiar with the numbering system. The mainland is divided into four sections (NE, NW, SE, and SW) by the intersection of Flagler Street (north–south) and Miami Avenue (east–west). It's helpful to remember that avenues generally run north to south, while streets go east to west. Street numbers (1st St., 2nd St., and so forth) start from here and increase as you go further out from this intersection, as do numbers of avenues, places, courts, terraces, and lanes. Streets in Hialeah are the exceptions to this pattern; they are listed separately in map indexes.

Getting around the barrier islands that make up Miami Beach is somewhat easier than moving around the mainland. Street numbering starts with 1st Street, near Miami Beach's southern tip, and increases to 192nd Street, in the northern part of Sunny Isles. Collins Avenue makes the entire journey, from head to toe of the island. As in the city of Miami, some streets in Miami Beach have numbers as well as names. When they are part of listings in this book, both name and number are given.

The numbered streets in Miami Beach are not the geographical equivalents of those on the mainland, but they are close. For example, the 79th Street Causeway runs into 71st Street on Miami Beach.

STREET MAPS It's easy to get lost in sprawling Miami, so a reliable map is essential. The Trakker Map of Miami is a four-color accordion map that encompasses all of Dade County. The map is available at newsstands and shops throughout South Florida or online at www.trakkermaps.com.

Some maps of Miami list streets according to area, so you'll have to know which part of the city you are looking for before the street can be found. All the listings in this book include area information for this reason.

THE NEIGHBORHOODS IN BRIEF

South Beach—The Art Deco District Though there are many monikers used to describe Miami's publicity darling—Glitter Beach, SoBe, America's Riviera, Hollywood South, Manhattan South—South Beach is a uniquely surreal, Dalí-esque cocktail of cosmopolitan influences with a splash of saltwater thrown in to remind you that you're not in a concrete jungle anymore. South Beach's 10 miles of beach are alive with a frenetic, circus-like atmosphere and are center stage for a motley crew of characters, from eccentric locals, seniors, snowbirds, and college students to gender benders, celebrities, club kids, and curiosity-seekers: individuality is as widely accepted on South Beach as Visa and MasterCard.

Bolstered by a Caribbean-chic cafe society and a sexually charged, tragically hip nightlife, people-watching on South Beach (the portion of Miami Beach from 1st to 23rd sts.) is almost as good as a front row seat at a Milan fashion show. Sure, the beautiful people do flock here, but the models aren't the only sights worth drooling over. The thriving Art Deco District within South Beach contains the largest concentration of Art Deco architecture in the world. In 1979, much of South Beach was listed in the National Register of Historic Places. The pastel-hued structures are supermodels in their own right—only these models improve with age.

Miami Beach In the fabulous '50s, Miami Beach was America's true Riviera. The stomping ground of choice for the Rat Pack and notorious mobsters such as Al Capone, its huge self-contained resort hotels were vacations unto themselves, providing a full day's worth of meals, activities, and entertainment. Then, in the 1960s and 1970s, people who fell in love with Miami began to buy apartments rather than rent hotel rooms. Tourism declined, the Rat Pack fled to Vegas, Capone disappeared, and many area hotels fell into disrepair. However, since the late 1980s and South Beach's renaissance, Miami Beach (24th St. and up) has experienced a tide of revitalization. Huge beach hotels are finding their niche with new international tourist markets and are attracting large convention crowds. New generations of Americans are discovering the qualities that originally made Miami Beach so popular, and they are finding out that the sand and surf now come with a thriving international city.

Surfside, Bal Harbour, and **Sunny Isles** make up the north part of the beach (island). Hotels, motels, restaurants, and beaches line Collins Avenue and, with some outstanding exceptions, the farther north you go, the cheaper lodging becomes. All told, excellent prices, location, and facilities make Surfside and Sunny Isles attractive places to stay, although they are still a little rough around the edges. However, a revitalization is underway here, and beachfront properties continue to be at a premium; many of the area's moderately priced hotels have been converted to condominiums, and the number of affordable places to stay has begun to shrink.

In exclusive and ritzy Bal Harbour, where well-paid police officers are instructed to ticket drivers who go above the 30 mph speed limit, few hotels remain amid the many beachfront condominium towers. Instead, fancy homes, tucked away on the bay, hide behind gated communities, and the Rodeo Drive of Miami (known as the Bal Harbour Shops) attracts shoppers who don't flinch at four-, five-, and six-figure price tags.

Note that **North Miami Beach,** a residential area near the Dade–Broward County line (north of 163rd St.; part of North Dade County), is a misnomer. It is actually northwest of Miami Beach, on the mainland, and has no beaches, though it does have some of Miami's better restaurants and shops. Located within North Miami Beach is the posh residential community of **Aventura,** best known for its high-priced condos, the Turnberry Isle Resort, and the Aventura Mall.

Key Biscayne Miami's forested and secluded Key Biscayne is technically one of the first islands in the Florida Keys. However, this island is nothing like its southern neighbors. Located south of Miami Beach, off the shores of Coconut Grove, Key Biscayne is protected from the troubles of the mainland by the long Rickenbacker Causeway and its $1 toll.

Largely an exclusive residential community, with million-dollar homes and sweeping water views, Key Biscayne also offers visitors great public beaches, some top (read: pricey) resort hotels, and several good restaurants. Hobie Beach, adjacent to the causeway, is the city's premier spot for sailboarding and jet-skiing (see section 5 of this chapter, "Hitting the Beach"). On the island's southern tip, Bill Baggs State Park has great beaches, bike paths, and dense forests for picnicking and partying.

Downtown Miami's downtown boasts one of the world's most beautiful cityscapes. Unfortunately, that's about all it offers to visitors. Though during the day, a vibrant community of students, businesspeople, and merchants make their way through the bustling streets; at night, downtown is desolate and not a place in which you'd want to get lost. (NE 11th St. might be the only exception, with a burgeoning nightlife scene.) The downtown area does offer a few daytime attractions, including the Bayside Marketplace, where many cruise passengers come to browse; the Metro–Dade Cultural Center; and a few decent restaurants, as well as the new American Airlines Arena. A downtown revitalization project is in the works, in which a cultural arts center, among other things, is expected to bring downtown back to life.

Design District With restaurants springing up between galleries and furniture stores galore, the Design District is, as locals say, the new South Beach, adding a touch of New York's SoHo to an area formerly known as downtown Miami's "Don't Go." The district is loosely defined as the area bounded by NE Second Avenue, NE Fifth Avenue East and West, and NW 36th Street South. The district, which is a hotbed for furniture import companies, interior designers, and architects, has also become a player in Miami's ever-changing nightlife; with various nocturnal events from block parties and gallery openings to underground warehouse parties, it has become hipster central for South Beach expatriates and artsy bohemian types. In anticipation of its growing popularity, the district has also banded together to create a website, **www.designmiami.com**, which includes a calendar of events and is chock-full of information.

Biscayne Corridor From downtown near Bayside Marketplace to the 70s, where trendy curio shops and upscale restaurants are slowly opening, Biscayne Boulevard is aspiring to reclaim itself as a safe thoroughfare where tourists can wine, dine, and shop. Sketchy, dilapidated 1950s- and '60s-era hotels are giving way to a fresh look, as new residents fleeing the high prices of the beaches renovate Biscayne block by block. With the trendy Design District immediately west of 36th and Biscayne by 2 blocks, there is hope for the area.

Little Havana If you've never been to Cuba, just visit this small section of Miami and you'll come pretty close. The sounds, tastes, and rhythms are very reminiscent of Cuba's capital city. Some even jokingly say you don't have to speak a word of English to live an independent life here—even street signs are in Spanish and English.

Cuban coffee shops, tailor and furniture stores, and inexpensive restaurants line "Calle Ocho" (pronounced *Ka-yey O*-choh), SW 8th Street, the region's main thoroughfare. Salsa and merengue beats ring loudly from old record stores while old men in *guayaberas* (traditional Cuban shirts of loose-fitting cotton) smoke cigars over their daily game of dominoes. The spotlight focused on the neighborhood during the Elian Gonzalez situation in 2000, but the area was previously noted for the groups of artists and nocturnal types who have moved their galleries and performance spaces here, sparking a culturally charged neo-bohemian nightlife.

Coral Gables "The City Beautiful," created by George Merrick in the early 1920s, is one of Miami's first planned developments. This is not your typical cookie-cutter plot: The houses here were built in a Mediterranean style along lush tree-lined streets that open onto beautifully carved plazas, many with centerpiece fountains. The best architectural examples of the era have Spanish-style tiled roofs and are built from Miami oolite, native limestone commonly called "coral rock."

The Gables's European-style shopping and commerce center is home to many thriving corporations. Coral Gables also has landmark hotels, great golfing, upscale shopping, and some of the city's best restaurants, headed by world-renowned chefs.

Coconut Grove An arty, hippie hangout in the psychedelic '60s, Coconut Grove has given way from swirls of tie-dyes to the uniform color schemes of the Gap. Chain stores, theme restaurants, a megaplex, and bars galore make Coconut Grove a commercial success, but this gentrification has pushed most alternative types out.

The intersection of Grand Avenue, Main Highway, and McFarlane Road pierces the area's heart. Right in the center of it all is CocoWalk and the Shops at Mayfair, filled with boutiques, eateries, and bars. Sidewalks here are often crowded, especially at night, when University of Miami students come out to play.

Southern Miami–Dade County To locals, South Miami is both a specific area, southwest of Coral Gables, and a general region that encompasses all of southern Dade County and includes Kendall, Perrine, Cutler Ridge, and Homestead. For the purposes of clarity, this book has grouped all these southern suburbs under the rubric "Southern Miami–Dade County." Similar attributes unite the communities: They are heavily residential and packed with strip malls amidst a few remaining plots of farmland. Tourists don't usually stay in these parts, unless they are on their way to the Everglades or the Keys. However, Southern Miami–Dade County contains many of the city's top attractions, so you're likely to spend some time here.

2 Getting Around

Officially, Dade County has opted for a "unified, multimodal transportation network," which basically means you can get around the city by train, bus, and taxi. However, in practice, the network doesn't work very well. Things may improve when the city completes its transportation center in 2005, but until then, unless you are going from downtown Miami to a not-too-distant spot, you are better off in a rental car or taxi.

With the exception of downtown Coconut Grove and South Beach, Miami is not a walker's city. Because it is so spread out, most attractions are too far apart to make walking between them feasible.

BY PUBLIC TRANSPORTATION

BY RAIL Two rail lines, operated by the **Metro–Dade Transit Agency** (© **305/770-3131;** www.co.miami-dade.fl.us/mdta/), run in concert with each other:

Metrorail, the city's modern high-speed commuter train, is a 21-mile elevated line that travels north–south, between downtown Miami and the southern suburbs. Locals like to refer to this semi-useless rail system as Metro*fail.* If you are staying in Coral Gables or Coconut Grove, you can park your car at a nearby station and ride the rails downtown. However, that's about it. There are plans to extend the system to service Miami International Airport, but until those tracks are built, these trains don't go most places tourists go, with the exception of Vizcaya in Coconut Grove. Metrorail operates daily from about 6am to midnight. The fare is $1.25.

> **Moments   Joy Ride**
>
> Metromover offers a panoramic view of the city and skyline, making for a nice complement to your downtown tour.

Metromover, a 4.4-mile elevated line, circles the downtown area and connects with Metrorail at the Government Center stop. Riding on rubber tires, the single-car train winds past many of the area's most important attractions and shopping and business districts. You may not go very far, but you will get a beautiful perspective from the towering height of the suspended rails. System hours are daily from about 6am to midnight. The fare is 25¢.

BY BUS Miami's suburban layout is not conducive to getting around by bus. Lines operate and maps are available, but instead of getting to know the city, you'll find that relying on bus transportation will acquaint you only with how it feels to wait at bus stops. In short, a bus ride in Miami is grueling. You can get a bus map by mail, either from the Greater Miami Convention and Visitor's Bureau (see "Visitor Information," earlier in this chapter) or by writing the Metro-Dade Transit System, 3300 NW 32nd Ave., Miami, FL 33142. In Miami, call © **305/770-3131** for public-transit information. The fare is $1.25.

BY CAR

Tales circulate about vacationers who have visited Miami without a car, but they are very few indeed. If you are counting on exploring the city, even to a modest degree, a car is essential. Miami's restaurants, hotels, and attractions are far from one another, so any other form of transportation is relatively impractical. You won't need a car, however, if you are spending your entire vacation at a resort, are traveling directly to the Port of Miami for a cruise, or are here for a short stay centered in one area of the city, such as South Beach, where everything is within walking distance and parking is a costly nightmare.

When driving across a causeway or through downtown, allow extra time to reach your destination because of frequent drawbridge openings and slow boat crossings. Some bridges open about every half hour for large sailing vessels to make their way through the wide bays and canals that crisscross the city, stalling traffic for several minutes.

RENTALS It seems as though every car-rental company, big and small, has at least one office in Miami. Consequently, the city is one of the cheapest places in the world to rent a car. Many firms regularly advertise prices in the neighborhood of $140 per week for their economy cars. You should also check with the airline you have chosen to get to Miami: There are often special discounts when you book a flight and reserve your rental car simultaneously. A national car-rental broker, **Car Rental Referral Service** (© 800/404-4482), can often find companies willing to rent to drivers over the age of 21 and can also get discounts from major companies as well as some regional ones.

National car-rental companies with toll-free numbers include **Alamo** (© 800/327-9633), **Avis** (© 800/331-1212), **Budget** (© 800/527-0700), **Dollar** (© 800/800-4000 or 800/327-7607), **Hertz** (© 800/654-3131), **National** (© 800/328-4567), and **Thrifty** (© 800/367-2277). One excellent company that has offices in every conceivable part of town and offers extremely competitive rates is **Enterprise** (© 800/325-8007). Call around and comparison-shop—car-rental prices can fluctuate more than airfares. For information on car-rental insurance, see "Getting There," in chapter 2.

PARKING Always keep plenty of quarters on hand to feed hungry meters. Or, on Miami Beach, stop by the chamber of commerce at 1920 Meridian Ave. or any Publix grocery store to buy a magnetic **parking card** in denominations of $10, $20, or $25. Parking is usually plentiful (except on South Beach and Coconut Grove), but when it's not, be careful: Fines for illegal parking can be stiff, starting at a hefty $18.

In addition to parking garages, valet services are commonplace and often used. Expect to pay from $5 to $15 for parking in Coconut Grove and on South Beach's busy weekend nights.

LOCAL DRIVING RULES Florida law allows drivers to make a right turn on a red light after a complete stop, unless otherwise indicated. In addition, all passengers are required to wear seat belts, and children under 3 must be securely fastened in government-approved car seats.

BY TAXI

If you don't plan to travel much within the city, an occasional taxi is a good alternative to renting a car. If you plan to spend your vacation within the confines of South Beach's Art Deco District, you might also want to avoid the parking hassles that come with renting your own car. Taxi meters start at $1.50 for the first quarter-mile and add 25¢ for each additional one-eighth mile. There are standard flat-rate charges for frequently traveled routes—for example, Miami Beach's Convention Center to Coconut Grove will cost about $16.

Major cab companies include **Metro** (© 305/888-8888), **Yellow** (© 305/444-4444), and, on Miami Beach, **Central** (© 305/532-5555).

BY BIKE

Miami is a biker's paradise, especially on Miami Beach, where the hard-packed sand and boardwalks make it an easy and scenic route. However, unless you are a former New York City bike messenger, you won't want to use a bicycle as your main means of transportation.

For more information on bicycles, including where to rent the best ones, see section 12, "Affordable Outdoor Pursuits," later in this chapter.

Impressions

I figure marriage is kind of like Miami; it's hot and stormy, and occasionally a little dangerous . . . but if it's really so awful, why is there still so much traffic?

—Sarah Jessica Parker's character, Gwen Marcus, in *Miami Rhapsody*

FAST FACTS: Miami

Airport See "Orientation," earlier in this chapter.

American Express You'll find American Express offices in downtown Miami at 100 North Biscayne Blvd. (© **305/358-7350**); 9700 Collins Ave., Bal Harbour (© **305/865-5959**); and 32 Miracle Mile, Coral Gables (© **305/446-3381**). Offices are open weekdays from 9am to 5:30pm and Saturday from 9am to 5pm. To report lost or stolen traveler's checks, call © **800/221-7282**.

Area Code The original area code for Miami and all of Dade County was **305**. That is still the code for older phone numbers, but all phone numbers assigned since July 1998 have the area code **786**. For all local calls, even if you're just calling across the street, you must dial the area code first. Even though the Keys still share the Dade County area code of **305**, calls to there from Miami are considered long distance and must be preceded by a 1 plus the area code (within the Keys, simply dial the seven-digit number). The area code for Fort Lauderdale is **954**; for Palm Beach, Boca Raton, Vero Beach, and Port St. Lucie, it's **561**.

Business Hours Most banks are open weekdays from 9am to 3pm. Several stay open until 5pm or so at least 1 day during the week, and many banks feature automated teller machines (ATMs) for 24-hour banking. Most stores are open daily from 10am to 6pm. Shops in the Bayside Marketplace are usually open until 9 or 10pm, as are the boutiques in Coconut Grove. Boutiques on South Beach operate on their own time zone, and closing times range from 11 am to midnight, sometimes earlier, sometimes later. Stores in Bal Harbour and other malls are usually open an extra hour one night during the week (usually Thurs). As far as business offices are concerned, Miami is generally a 9-to-5 town.

Car Rentals See "Getting Around," earlier in this chapter.

Climate See "When to Go," in chapter 2.

Curfew Although not strictly enforced, there is an alleged curfew in effect for minors after 11pm on weeknights and midnight on weekends in all of Miami–Dade County. After those hours, children under 17 cannot be out on the streets or driving unless accompanied by a parent or on their way to work.

Dentists **A&E Dental,** 11400 N. Kendall Dr., Mega Bank Building (© **305/271-7777**), offers round-the-clock care and accepts MasterCard and Visa.

Doctors The Dade County Medical Association sponsors a **Physician Referral Service** (© **305/324-8717**) weekdays from 9am to 5pm. **Health South Doctors' Hospital,** 5000 University Dr., Coral Gables (© **305/666-2111**), is a 285-bed acute-care hospital with a 24-hour physician-staffed emergency department.

Driving Rules See "Getting Around," earlier in this chapter.

Emergencies To reach the police, ambulance, or fire department, dial © **911** from any phone. No coins are needed. Emergency hot lines include **Crisis Intervention** (© **305/358-HELP** or 305/358-4357) and the **Poison Information Center** (© **800/282-3171**).

Eyeglasses **Pearle Vision Center,** 7901 Biscayne Blvd. (© **305/754-5144**) can usually fill prescriptions in about an hour.

Hospitals See "Doctors," earlier in this section.

Information See "Visitor Information," earlier in this chapter.

Laundry/Dry Cleaning For dry-cleaning, self-service machines, and a wash-and-fold service by the pound, call **All Laundry Service,** 5701 NW 7th St. (© **305/261-8175**); it's open daily from 7am to 10pm. **Clean Machine Laundry,** 226 12th St., South Beach (© **305/534-9429**), is convenient to South Beach's Art Deco hotels and is open 24 hours a day. **Coral Gables Laundry & Dry Cleaning,** 250 Minorca Ave., Coral Gables (© **305/446-6458**), offers a lifesaving same-day service and is open weekdays from 7am to 7pm and Saturday from 8am to 3pm.

Liquor Laws Only adults 21 or older may legally purchase or consume alcohol in the state of Florida. Minors are usually permitted in bars, as long as they also serve food. Liquor laws are strictly enforced; if you look young, carry identification. Beer and wine are sold in most supermarkets and convenience stores. The city of Miami's liquor stores are closed on Sundays. Liquor stores in the city of Miami Beach are open all week.

Lost Property If you lost something at the airport, call the **Airport Lost and Found** office (© **305/876-7377**). If you lost something on the bus, Metrorail, or Metromover, call **Metro-Dade Transit Agency** (© **305/770-3131**). If you lost something anywhere else, phone the **Dade County Police Lost and Found** (© **305/375-3366**). You may also want to fill out a police report for insurance purposes.

Newspapers/Magazines For a large selection of foreign-language newspapers and magazines, check with any of the large bookstores (see section 14 of this chapter); or try **News Café** at 800 Ocean Dr., South Beach (© **305/538-6397**), or in Coconut Grove at 2901 Florida Ave. (© **305/774-6397**). Adjacent to the **Van Dyke Café,** 846 Lincoln Rd., South Beach (© **305/534-3600**), is a fantastic newsstand with magazines and newspapers from all over the world. Also check out **Eddie's Normandy,** 1096 Normandy Dr., Miami Beach (© **305/866-2026**), and **Worldwide News,** 1629 NE 163rd St., North Miami Beach (© **305/940-4090**).

Pharmacies **Walgreens Pharmacy** has dozens of locations all over town, including 8550 Coral Way (© **305/221-9271**), in Coral Gables; 1845 Alton Rd. (© **305/531-8868**), in South Beach; and 6700 Collins Ave. (© **305/861-6742**), in Miami Beach. The branch at 5731 Bird Rd. at SW 40th Street (© **305/666-0757**) is open 24 hours, as is **Eckerd Drugs,** 1825 Miami Gardens Dr. NE, at 185th Street, North Miami Beach (© **305/932-5740**).

Police For emergencies, dial © **911** from any phone. No coins are needed. For other matters, call © **305/595-6263.**

Post Office The **Main Post Office,** 2200 Milam Dairy Rd., Miami, FL 33152 (© **305/639-4280**), is located west of Miami International Airport. Conveniently located post offices include 1300 Washington Ave. in South Beach, and 3191 Grand Ave. in Coconut Grove. There is one central number for all post offices: © **800/275-8777.**

Radio On the AM dial, 610 (WIOD), 790 (WNWS), 1230 (WJNO), and 1340 (WPBR) are all talk. There is no all-news station in town, although 940 (WINZ) gives traffic updates and headline news in between its talk shows. WDBF (1420) is a good big-band station and WPBG (1290) features golden oldies. Switching to the FM dial, the two most popular R&B stations are WEDR/99 Jams (99.1) and Hot 105 (105.1). The best rock stations on the FM dial are WZTA (94.9), WBGG/Big 106 (105.9), and the progressive college station WVUM (90.5). WKIS (99.9) is the top country station. Top-40 music can be heard on WHYI (100.3) and classic disco on Mega 103 (103.5). WGTR (97.3) plays easy listening, WDNA (88.9) has the best Latin jazz and multiethnic sounds, and public radio can be heard either on WXEL (90.7) or WLRN (91.3).

Restrooms Stores rarely let customers use their restrooms, and many restaurants offer their facilities only for their patrons. However, most malls have bathrooms, as do many fast-food restaurants. Public beaches and large parks often provide toilets, though in some places you have to pay or tip an attendant. Most large hotels have clean restrooms in their lobbies.

Safety As always, use your common sense and be aware of your surroundings at all times. Don't walk alone at night, and be extra wary when walking or driving though downtown Miami and surrounding areas.

Taxes A 6% state sales tax (plus 0.5% local tax, for a total of 6.5% in Miami–Dade County [from Homestead to North Miami Beach]) is added on at the register for all goods and services purchased in Florida. In addition, most municipalities levy special taxes on restaurants and hotels. In Surfside, hotel taxes total 10.5%; in Bal Harbour, 9.5%; in Miami Beach (including South Beach), 11.5%; and in the rest of Dade County, a whopping 12.5%. In Miami Beach, Surfside, and Bal Harbour, the resort (hotel) tax also applies to hotel restaurants and restaurants with liquor licenses.

Taxis See "Getting Around," earlier in this chapter.

Time Zone Miami, like New York, is in the eastern standard time zone. Between April and October, daylight saving time is adopted, and clocks are set 1 hour ahead. America's eastern seaboard is 5 hours behind Greenwich mean time. To find out what time it is, call © 305/324-8811.

Transit Information For Metrorail or Metromover schedule information, phone © 305/770-3131 or surf over to www.co.miami-dade.fl.us/mdta/.

Weather For an up-to-date recording of current weather conditions and forecast reports, call © 305/229-4522.

3 Accommodations You Can Afford

While Miami is notorious for pricey hotels, with a little help you can still find a decent room at a fair cost. In the Art Deco District, for instance, many hotels are actually less Ritz-Carlton than they are Holiday Inn (unless, of course, they've been renovated). Many of these hotels were built in the 1930s for the middle class and are a wise choice for those who don't plan to spend much time in their room. Smart vacationers can almost name their price if they're willing to live without a few luxuries, such as an oceanfront view.

Below are our suggestions for some of the best values within Miami. If you happen to arrive without a reservation and run into trouble, check out South Beach's Collins Avenue, where there are also dozens of hotels and motels to choose from. If you do try the walk-in routine, don't forget to ask to see a room first. A few dollars extra could mean all the difference between flea and fabu.

Whenever booking your room, always ask how close your room will be to the center of the nightlife crowd; trying to sleep directly on Ocean Drive or Collins and Washington avenues, especially during the weekend, is next to impossible, unless your lullaby of choice happens to include throbbing salsa and bass beats.

SEASONS & RATES South Florida's tourist season is well defined, beginning in mid-November and lasting until Easter. Hotel prices escalate until about March, after which they begin to decline. During the off-season, hotel rates are typically 30% to 50% lower than their winter highs.

But timing isn't everything. In many cases, rates also depend on your hotel's proximity to the beach and how much ocean you can see from your window. Small motels a block or two from the water can be up to 40% cheaper than similar properties right on the sand.

Rates below have been broken down into two broad categories: winter (generally Thanksgiving–Easter) and off-season (about mid-May through Aug). The months in between, the shoulder season, should fall somewhere in between the highs and lows. Rates always go up on holidays. Remember, too, that state and city taxes can add as much as 12.5% to your bill in some parts of Miami. Some hotels, especially those in South Beach, also tack on additional service charges. And parking is pricey.

LONG-TERM STAYS If you plan to visit Miami for a month, a season, or more, think about renting a condominium apartment or a room in a long-term hotel. Long-term accommodations exist in every price category, from budget to deluxe, and in general are extremely reasonable, especially during the off-season. Check with the reservation services below, or write a short note to the chamber of commerce in the area where you plan to stay. In addition, many local real estate agents also handle short-term rentals (meaning less than a year).

RESERVATION SERVICES Central Reservation Service (© **800/950-0232** or 305/274-6832; www.reservation-services.com) works with many of Miami's hotels and can often secure discounts of up to 40%. It also gives advice on specific locales, especially in Miami Beach and downtown. During holiday time, there may be a minimum of a 3- to 5-day stay to use their services. Call for more information.

For bed-and-breakfast information throughout the state, contact **Florida Bed and Breakfast Inns** (© **800/524-1880;** www.florida-inns.com).

SOUTH BEACH

Choosing a hotel on South Beach is similar to deciding whether you'd rather pay $1.50 for french fries at Denny's or $8.50 for the same fries—but let's call them *pomme frites*—in a pricey haute cuisinerie. It's all about atmosphere. The rooms of some hotels may *look* ultrachic, but they can be as comfortable as sleeping on a concrete slab. Many Art Deco hotels, while pleasing to the eye, may be a bit run-down inside. Par for the course on South Beach, appearances are at times deceiving. Fortunately, for every chichi hotel in South Beach—and there are many—there are just as many moderately priced, more casual options.

Aqua *Value* It's been described as the Jetsons meets Jaws, but the Aqua isn't all Hollywood. Animated, yes, but with little emphasis on special effects and more on a friendly staff, Aqua is definitely a good catch for those looking to stay in style without compromising their budget. Rooms are ultra-modern in an Ikea or cheap chic sort of way. There are apartment-like junior suites, suites, and a really fabulous penthouse, but the standard deluxe rooms aren't too shabby either, with decent-size bathrooms and high-tech amenities. It's a favorite amongst Europeans and young hipsters on a budget. This '50s-style motel has definitely been spruced up, and its sun deck, courtyard garden, and small pool are popular hangouts for those who'd prefer to stay off the nearby sand. A small yet sleek lounge inside is a good place for a quick cocktail, breakfast, or snack.

1530 Collins Ave., Miami Beach, FL 33139. © 305/538-4361. Fax 305/673-8109. www.aquamiami.com. 50 units. Winter $125–$395 for deluxe rooms, junior suites, suites, and penthouse; off-season $95–$295 for deluxe rooms, junior suites, suites, and penthouse. Rates include European-style breakfast buffet. AE, DC, DISC, MC, V. Valet parking $18. **Amenities:** Lounge, bar; small pool. *In room:* A/C, TV, CD player, minibar.

Bayliss Guest House The Bayliss Guest House is the anti-budget budget hotel, with enormous, sparkling clean rooms, complete with sitting rooms and tubs. Built in 1939 in the tropical Art Deco style, rounded corners, glass blocks, neon, and a lobby floor of fancy terrazzo give the Bayliss a definite '40s feel. The property (offering hotel rooms, large efficiencies, and one-bedroom apartments) is a bit off the beaten path, but this quiet residential spot offers a break from the racket that defines Collins and Washington avenues.

504 14th St., South Beach, FL 33139. © 888/305-4863 or 305/538-5620. Fax 305/531-4440. Riviere1@aol.com. 20 units. Winter $75 double; $95 efficiency. Off-season $45 double; $60 efficiency. AE, DC, DISC, MC, V. **Amenities:** Room service (9am–7pm). *In room:* A/C, TV, kitchenette, coffeemaker, hair dryer.

Beachcomber Hotel The Beachcomber Hotel was built in 1937 and renovated in 1997. The rooms are decorated in a colorful Art Deco style and all have a private bathroom and shower, but they are a bit lackluster—blasé, in fact. Though nothing to rave about, they are clean and functional, serving the purpose of a place to crash after a day—or night—on South Beach. A Deco terrace on Collins Avenue provides the perfect place for sipping a cocktail. The hotel's restaurant serves breakfast, lunch, and dinner, but dine there only as a last resort. Check before arrival if a continental breakfast is included in your rate. The property's location couldn't be better, since it's away from the noise but near the action.

1340 Collins Ave., South Beach, FL 33139. © 888/305-4683 or 305/531-3755. Fax 305/673-8609. www.beachcombermiami.com. 29 units. Winter $90–$145 double; Off-season $70–$125 double. Continental breakfast included. AE, DC, DISC, MC, V. Municipal parking $7. **Amenities:** Restaurant, bar. *In room:* A/C, TV, fridge, hair dryer.

Brigham Gardens In a prime location, this funky place, consisting of two buildings (Art Deco and Mediterranean), is a homey and affordable oasis run by a mother-daughter team who will make sure you feel like a member of the family. Because most rooms have full kitchens—you can also barbecue in the garden—you'll find many people staying for longer than a weekend. Room no.12, in particular, is extremely charming and quiet, with cathedral ceilings, Art Deco decor, and views of the garden. When you enter the tropically landscaped garden, you'll hear macaws and parrots and see cats and lizards running through the bougainvillea. The tiny but lush grounds are framed by quaint Mediterranean buildings, which are pleasant, though in need of some improvements. A rooftop sun deck, with a view of the ocean, is the hotel's newest attraction, though the rooms are constantly being spruced up with funky artwork, furniture, and a colorful array of fresh paint.

1411 Collins Ave., South Beach, FL 33139. © **305/531-1331.** Fax 305/538-9898. www.brigham gardens.com. 23 units. Winter $100–$145 1-bedroom. Off-season $70–$110 1-bedroom. Additional person $10. 10% discount on stays of 7 days or longer. Pets accepted for $6 a night. AE, MC, V. **Amenities:** Concierge; coin-op laundry. *In room:* A/C, TV, dataport, kitchen, microwave, coffeemaker.

Mermaid Guesthouse ★★ There's something magical about this little hideaway tucked behind tropical gardens in the very heart of South Beach and less than 2 blocks from the ocean. You won't find the amenities of the larger hotels here, but the charm and hospitality at this one-story guesthouse keep people coming back. Owners Ana and Gonzalo Torres did a thorough clean-up, adding new brightly colored fretwork around the doors and windows and installing phones in each room. Also, the wood floors have been stripped or covered in straw matting, one of the many Caribbean touches that make this place so cheery. Rooms have four-poster beds with mosquito nets. There are no TVs, so guests tend to congregate in the lush garden in the evenings. The owners sometimes host free impromptu dinners for their guests and friends. Ask if they've scheduled any live Latin music during your stay; you won't want to miss it. What you also don't want to miss is a preview of your room before you put down a deposit, as some rooms tend not to be as tidy as the quaint garden.

909 Collins Ave., Miami Beach, FL 33140. © **305/538-5324.** Fax 305/538-2822. 8 units. Winter $115–$280 single or double. Off-season $95–$215 single or double. Additional person $10. Discounts available for longer stays. AE, MC, V. **Amenities:** Bar. *In room:* A/C, TV upon request.

Park Washington Hotel ★★ The Park Washington, designed in the 1930s by Henry Hohauser, is a large refurbished hotel, just 2 blocks from the ocean, that offers some of the best values in South Beach. Most of the rooms have original furnishings and well-kept interiors, and some have kitchenettes. Bathrooms are small but clean. Guests enjoy a decent-sized outdoor heated pool with a sun deck, as well as privacy, lush landscaping, consistent quality, and a value-oriented philosophy. This hotel attracts a large gay clientele.

1020 Washington Ave., South Beach, FL 33139. © **305/532-1930.** Fax 305/672-6706. www.park washingtonresort.com. 36 units. Winter $129–$159 double. Off-season $79–$109 double. Rates include self-serve coffee and Danish. Additional person $20. AE, MC, V. Off-site parking $6. **Amenities:** Pool; access to nearby health club; bike rentals. *In room:* A/C, TV, kitchenettes in some rooms, fridge.

Villa Paradiso ★★ *Finds* This guesthouse, like Brigham Gardens, is more like a cozy apartment house than a hotel. There's no elegant lobby or restaurant, but the amicable hosts, Lisa and Pascal Nicolle, are happy to give you a room key and advice on what to do. The recently renovated, spacious apartments are simple but elegant—hardwood floors, French doors, and stylish wrought-iron furniture—and are remarkably quiet considering their location, a few blocks from Lincoln Road and all of South Beach's best clubs. Most have full kitchens or at least a fridge, and Murphy beds or foldout couches for extra guests. Bathrooms have recently been renovated with marble tile. All rooms overlook the hotel's pretty courtyard garden.

1415 Collins Ave., Miami Beach, FL 33139. © **305/532-0516.** Fax 305/673-5874. www.villaparadiso hotel.com. 17 units. Winter $100–$165 apartment. Off-season $75–$129 apartment. Weekly rates are 10% cheaper. Additional person $10. AE, DC, MC, V. Parking nearby $12. Pets (including small "nonbarking" dogs) accepted for $10 with a $100 deposit. **Amenities:** Coin-op laundry. *In room:* A/C, TV, kitchen, fridge, coffeemaker.

SUPER-CHEAP SLEEPS

Banana Bungalow This hostel-like hotel is cheap, campy, and quintessentially Miami Beach. Popular with the MTV set, the Banana Bungalow is a redone 1950s two-story motel where it's always Spring Break. The hotel surrounds a pool and deck complete with shuffleboard, a small alfresco cafe serving cheap meals, and a tiki bar where young European travelers hang out. The best rooms face a narrow canal where motorboats and kayaks are available for a small charge. In general, rooms are clean and well kept, despite a few rusty faucets and chipped Formica furnishings. Guests in shared rooms need to bring their own towels. This is one of the only hotels in this price range with a private pool.

2360 Collins Ave., Miami Beach, FL 33139. ✆ **800/746-7835** or 305/538-1951. Fax 305/531-3217. www.bananabungalow.com. 90 units. Winter $18–$20 per person in shared units; $95–$104 double. Off-season $16–$18 per person in shared units; $50–$60 double. MC, V. Free parking. **Amenities:** Cafe, bar; large pool; access to nearby health club; game room; coin-op laundry. *In room:* A/C, TV, fridge.

Clay Hotel & International Hostel 🅕 A member of the International Youth Hostel Federation (IYHF), the Clay occupies a beautiful 1920s-style Spanish Mediterranean building at the corner of historic Española Way. Like other IYHF members, this hostel is open to all ages and is a great place to meet people. The usual smattering of Australians, Europeans, and other budget travelers makes it Miami's best clearinghouse of "insider" travel information. Even if you don't stay here, you might want to check out the ride board or mingle with fellow travelers over a beer at the sidewalk cafe.

Although a thorough renovation in 1996 made this hostel an incredible value and a step above any others in town, don't expect nightly turndown service or chocolates. But, for a hostel, it's full of extras. Ninety rooms have private bathrooms, and 12 "VIP" rooms have balconies overlooking quaint Española Way. You will find occasional movie nights, an outdoor weekend market, and a shared kitchen. Reservations for private rooms are essential in season and recommended year-round. Don't bother with a car in this congested area.

1438 Washington Ave. (at Española Way), South Beach, FL 33139. ✆ **800/379-2529** or 305/534-2988. Fax 305/673-0346. www.theclayhotel.com. 350 units. $45–75 double; $15–$17 dorm beds. During the off-season, pay for 6 nights in advance and get 7th night free. MC, V. Parking $10. **Amenities:** Cafe; access to nearby health club; bike rental; concierge; tour desk; car rental; coin-op laundry. *In room:* A/C, TV, dataport, fridge, hair dryer.

WORTH A SPLURGE

Abbey Hotel ★★ *Finds* This charming, off-the-beaten-path, '40s-revival boutique hotel is possibly the best deal on the entire beach. A haven for artists looking for quiet inspiration, the Abbey has recently undergone a $2.5 million renovation that restored its original Deco glory. Soft, white-covered chairs and candles grace the lobby, which doubles as a chic Mediterranean-style restaurant, the Abbey Dining Room. Rooms are furnished with oversized earth-toned chairs and chrome beds that are surprisingly comfortable. It's extremely quiet at this hotel, as it is located in the midst of a sleepy residential neighborhood, but it's only 1 block from the beach and within walking distance of the Jackie Gleason Theater, the Convention Center, the Bass Museum of Art, and the Miami City Ballet.

300 21st St., Miami Beach, FL 33139. ✆ **305/531-0031**. Fax 305/672-1663. www.abbeyhotel.com. 50 units. Winter $165–$210 double; $225 studio. Off-season $80–$165 double; $195 studio. AE, DC, DISC, MC, V. Off-site parking $17. Pets accepted with $500 deposit. **Amenities:** Restaurant, bar; exercise room; concierge; business services; room service; laundry and dry-cleaning service. *In room:* A/C, TV/VCR, dataport, hair dryer, iron. Studios also have stereo with CD player and a safe.

Chesterfield Hotel ★★ The Chesterfield Hotel is an oft-overlooked kitschy place, located in the heart of South Beach's Deco District, just a skip away from all the restaurants on Ocean Drive or the nightclubs on Washington Avenue. Its

Zimbabwe-meets-baroque lobby is a far cry from its original 1930s Art Deco beginnings, but it remains an attractive place for funk-loving hipsters. A recent renovation to the rooms added a luxe touch, with Frette linens and robes, down feather pillows, Judith Jackson spa amenities, and wood, chrome, and glass accents. Bathrooms are industrial, with free-floating showers with rainmaker shower heads, concrete sinks on aluminum stands, and mirrored walls. There's a happy hour at the hotel's Safari Bar/Café each evening from 4 to 8pm, with two-for-one cocktails. The hotel's proximity to area clubs and modeling agencies, and its ability to create its own eclectic nightlife, make the Chesterfield an award-worthy locale for people-watching.

855 Collins Ave., South Beach, FL 33139. © **800/244-6023** or 305/531-5831. Fax 305/672-4900. www.southbeachgroup.com. 50 units. Winter $175–$250 double. Off-season $135–$175 double. Rates include complimentary continental breakfast and complimentary cocktails 8–9pm nightly. AE, MC, DC, V. Valet parking $18. **Amenities:** Restaurant, bar; full service spa; concierge; free airport shuttle; in-room massage; dry cleaning. *In room:* A/C, TV, CD player, fax, minibar, coffeemaker, hair dryer, iron, safe.

Crest Hotel Suites ★★ *Finds* One of South Beach's best-kept secrets, the Crest Hotel is located next to the pricier, trendier Albion Hotel and features a quietly fashionable, relaxed atmosphere with fantastic service. Built in 1939, the Crest was restored to preserve its Art Deco architecture, but the interior of the hotel is thoroughly modern, with rooms resembling cosmopolitan apartments. All suites have a living room/dining room area, kitchenette, and executive workspace. An indoor/outdoor cafe with terrace and poolside dining isn't besieged with trendy locals, but it does attract a younger crowd. Crest Hotel Suites is conveniently located in the heart of the Art Deco Historic District, near all the major attractions. Around the corner from the hotel is Lincoln Road, with its sidewalk cafes, gourmet restaurants, theaters, and galleries. At press time, the Crest was about to open its second hotel, the South Beach Hotel, at 236 21st St.

1670 James Ave., Miami Beach, FL 33139. © **800/531-3880** or 305/531-0321. Fax 305/531-8180. www.cresthotel.com. Winter $155–$235 double. Off-season $115–$175 double. Packages available and 10% discount offered if booked on website. AE, MC, V. **Amenities:** Restaurant, cafe; pool; laundry/dry cleaning. *In room:* A/C, TV, dataport, kitchenette, fridge, coffeemaker.

Hotel Chelsea ★★ This recently restored Art Deco property is a boutique hotel with a bit of a twist, with accents and decor based on the Chinese practice of *feng shui*. Soft amber lighting, bamboo floors, full-slate baths, and Japanese-style furniture arranged in a way that's meant to refresh and relax you are what separate the Chelsea from just about any other so-called boutique hotel on South Beach. Complimentary breakfast, beach yoga classes, free sake at happy hour and, in case you've had enough relaxation, free passes to South Beach's hottest nightclubs are added bonuses.

944 Washington Ave. (at 9th St.), Miami Beach, FL 33139. © **305/534-4069**. Fax 305/672-6712. www.thehotelchelsea.com. 42 units. $95–$225 double. Rates include complimentary continental breakfast and complimentary cocktails 8pm–9pm daily. AE, MC, DC, V. Valet parking $18. **Amenities:** Bar; access to local gym; full-service spa; concierge; free pick-up from the airport; in-room massage; laundry. *In room:* A/C, TV, CD player, dataport, minibar, hair dryer, iron, safe.

Hotel Leon ★★ *Finds* A fabulous hotel without the fabulous attitude, the Hotel Leon is like a reasonably priced high-fashion garment found hidden on a rack full of overpriced threads. This charismatic sliver of a property has won the loyalty of fashion industrialists and romantics alike. Built in 1929 and restored in 1996, the hotel still retains many original details such as facades, woodwork, and even fireplaces (every room has one, not that you'll need to use it). The very central location 1 block from the ocean is a plus, especially since the Leon lacks a pool. Most of the spacious and stylish rooms are immaculate and reminiscent of a loft apartment; spacious bathrooms with large, deep tubs are especially enticing.

Gleaming wood floors and simple pale furnishings are appreciated in a neighborhood where many others overdo the Art Deco motif. However, some rooms have not seen such upgrades and are to be avoided; do not hesitate to ask to change rooms. Because its entrance is not directly on pedestrian-heavy Collins Avenue, the Hotel Leon remains one of South Beach's best-kept secrets.

841 Collins Ave., South Beach, FL 33139. © **305/673-3767.** Fax 305/673-5866. www.hotelleon.com. 18 units. Winter $145–$245 suite; $395 penthouse. Off-season $100–$195 suite; $335 penthouse. Additional person $10. AE, DC, MC, V. Valet parking $18. "Well-behaved" pets accepted for $20 per night. **Amenities:** Restaurant and lobby bar; reduced rates at local gym; concierge; business services; limited room service (breakfast); massage; babysitting; laundry/dry cleaning. *In room:* A/C, TV, CD player, hair dryer.

The Loft Hotel This boutique hotel along the lines of the Aqua Hotel (though less airy and whimsical) is a renovated apartment building and indeed gives you the feeling of staying in an apartment rather than a hotel. It offers 20 suites, all surrounding a tidy, tropically landscaped garden. Rooms are especially spacious, with queen-size beds, breakfast room, kitchen, conversation area, and hardwood or tile floors. Bathrooms are brand new and, for an old Art Deco building, pretty spacious. This hotel is popular with young, hip European types. Prices at The Loft are very reasonable, and the owners, who hail from Villa Paradiso, are extremely accommodating.

952 Collins Ave., Miami Beach, FL 33139. © **305/534-2244.** Fax 305/538-1509. 57 units. Winter $149–$179 double. Off-season $89–$129 double. AE, DC, MC, V. Valet parking $20. **Amenities:** Laundry. *In room:* A/C, TV/VCR, kitchen, hair dryer.

Nassau Suite Hotel ★★ Stylish and reasonably priced, this 1937 hotel feels more like a modern apartment building with its 22 suites (studios or one-bedrooms), featuring wood floors, rattan furniture, and fully equipped open kitchens. Beds are all king-size and rather plush, but the bed isn't the room's only place to rest: Each room also has a sitting area that's quite comfortable. Registered as a National Historic Landmark, the Nassau Suite Hotel may exist in an old building, but both rooms and lobby are fully modernized. The Nassau Suite caters to a young, hip crowd of both gay and straight guests. Continental breakfast is available for $5 per person.

1414 Collins Ave., South Beach, FL 33139. © **866/859-4177** or 305/532-0043. Fax 305/534-3133. www.nassausuite.com. 22 units. Winter $150 studio; $190 1-bedroom. Off-season $120 studio; $160 1-bedroom. AE, DC, DISC, MC, V. Parking $12. **Amenities:** Access to nearby health club; bike rental; concierge; secretarial services. *In room:* A/C, TV, dataport, fax, coffeemaker, hair dryer.

Royal Hotel ★★ *Finds* There are several words to describe this mod, hipster hotel located in the heart of South Beach. Jetsonian, funkadelic, and, as the hotel proudly and aptly declares, "Barbarella at bedtime." What it really is, however, is truly different, in that the rooms' curvy, white plastic beds (less comfortable than chic) have headboards that double as bars! Designer Jordan Mozer of Barneys New York fame has managed to transform this historic Art Deco hotel into a trippy, 21st-century state-of-the-art facility. Chaise lounges are "digital" with attached computer and television. Italian marble, pastel colors, and large, newly tiled bathrooms manage to successfully thwart a sterility that's all too common with many chic boutique hotels.

758 Washington Ave., Miami Beach, FL 33139. © **888/394-6835** or 305/673-9009. Fax 305/673-9244. www.royalhotelsouthbeach.com. Winter $130–$240 double. Off-season $120–$230 double. AE, DC, MC, V.

Valet parking $20. **Amenities:** Bar; small swimming pool; concierge. *In room:* A/C, TV/VCR, CD player, dataport, fridge, hair dryer, iron, safe.

MIAMI BEACH: SURFSIDE, BAL HARBOUR & SUNNY ISLES

Unrestricted by zoning codes throughout the 1950s, 1960s, and especially the 1970s, Miami Beach developers went crazy, building ever-bigger and more brazen structures, especially north of 41st Street, which is now known as "Condo Canyon." Consequently, there's now a glut of medium-quality condos, with a few scattered holdouts of older hotels and motels casting shadows over the beach by afternoon. Staying in the southern section, from 24th to 42nd streets, can be a good deal—it's still close to the South Beach scene, but the rates are more affordable.

The **Howard Johnson** (© **800/446-4656** or 305/532-4411) at 4000 Alton Rd., just off the Julia Tuttle Causeway (I-95), is a generic eight-story building, near a busy road, that is convenient to the beach by car or bike. Rooms, renovated in 1995, are clean and spacious, and some have pretty views of the city and the Intracoastal Waterway. Winter rates start at $100. The **Days Inn Oceanside** (© **800/356-3017** or 305/673-1513), at 4299 Collins Ave., is one of the most economical choices for travelers and great for families. Recently refurbished, the hotel welcomes children under 17 for free. Winter rates begin at $99.

Baymar Ocean Resort *Value*

Depending on what you're looking for, this hotel could be one of the beach's best buys. It's just south of Bal Harbour, in sleepy Surfside, right on the ocean, with a low-key beach that attracts few other tourists. In 2001, efficiencies were transformed into junior suites and all carpets were removed and replaced with terra-cotta tile. The location is close enough to walk to tennis courts and some shopping and dining; it's just a few minutes' drive to larger attractions. It may not be worth it to pay more for the oceanfront rooms, since they tend to be smaller than the others. Rooms overlooking the large pool and sun-deck area can get loud on busy days. The first-floor oceanview rooms have a nice shared balcony space.

9401 Collins Ave., Miami Beach, FL 33154. © **800/8-BAYMAR** or 305/866-5446. Fax 305/866-8053. 96 units. Winter $115–$125 double; $125–$235 suite. Off-season $75–$95 double; $95–$185 suite. Additional person $10. AE, DC, DISC, MC, V. Parking $5. **Amenities:** Restaurant, lounge, tiki bar; Olympic-size pool. *In room:* A/C, TV, kitchen.

Dezerland Beach Resort Hotel

Designed by car enthusiast Michael Dezer, the Dezerland is where *Happy Days* meets Miami Beach, with its visible homage to hot rods and antique cars. Visitors, many of them German tourists, are welcomed by a 1959 Cadillac stationed by the front door, one of a dozen mint-condition classics around the grounds and lobby. This kitschy beachfront hotel recently underwent a $2 million renovation of its guest rooms, lobby, and public areas. The rooms are still somewhat lackluster, despite the fact that the renovation added new drapes, bedspreads, furniture, and wall coverings. Though named for various fabulous cars, these, alas, are the Pintos of hotel rooms—nothing more than a typical motel room. The lovely pool, however, has its requisite Cadillac—a mosaic pink one, located at the bottom. For '50s kitsch and car fanatics, this is a fun place to stay; otherwise, you may think you were taken for a ride.

8701 Collins Ave., Miami Beach, FL 33154. © **800/331-9346** in the U.S., 800/331-9347 in Canada, or 305/865-6661. Fax 305/866-2630. www.dezerhotels.com. 227 units. Winter $99–$139 double. Off-season $69–$99 double. Additional person $10. Special packages and group rates available. AE, DC, DISC, MC, V. **Amenities:** Restaurant; pool; nearby tennis courts; small spa; Jacuzzi; water-sports rentals; game room; tour desk; car-rental desk; shuttle service to Aventura Mall and nearby antiques shop; coin-op laundry. *In room:* A/C, TV, kitchen in some rooms, fridge on request, hair dryer, iron, safe.

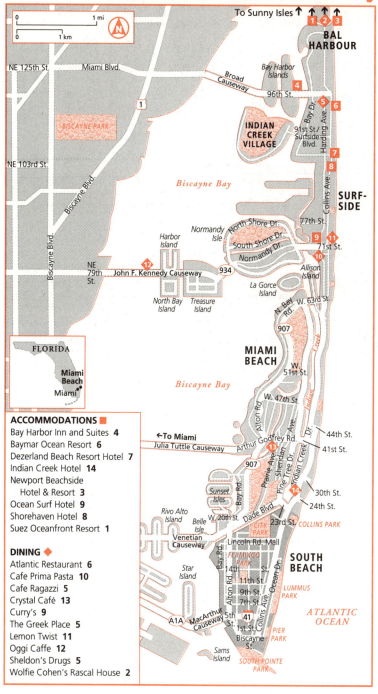

Ocean Surf Hotel 🌟 The Ocean Surf is a great find amid a little pocket of hotels just east of Collins Avenue. By far the most thorough renovation I have seen in the mid-beach area, this intimate, family-owned Deco jewel is worth a visit just to see the fine details that have been brought back to life by devoted second-generation owners Brian and Tamara Kraus. In the true spirit of Art Deco, the place resembles an ocean liner more than a hotel—wide porthole windows look directly out to sea, and the many wide balconies are edged with decorative railings. The sparkling clean rooms are larger than most in this era, and the decor is tasteful if a little stark. You'll be thankful for the complimentary cold sodas and juice upon your return from the large, under-populated beach just out the door. Travelers with disabilities will particularly appreciate the thoroughly accessible lobby, rooms, and common areas.

7436 Ocean Terrace (just east of Collins Ave.), Miami Beach, FL 33141. © **800/555-0411** or 305/866-1648. Fax 305/866-1649. www.oceansurf.com. 49 units. Year-round $69–$114 single or double; $89–$129 oceanfront. Rates include continental breakfast. AE, DC, DISC, MC, V. **Amenities:** Concierge; business services; laundry. *In room:* A/C, TV, fridge, hair dryer, safe.

Shorehaven Hotel 🌟🌟 The Shorehaven Hotel is a funky little haven for both couples and singles. Located in up-and-coming (but-not-there-yet) North Beach, this two-story 1950s beach motel was made over with style and earthy charm by Sabrina and Scott Barnett. The large rooms, outfitted in bright tropical prints, offer kitchens and spacious bathrooms. Each has its own theme, like the Lemon Twist room, which has huge murals of bright yellow lemons on the walls and wood floors painted a glossy royal blue. Other rooms have early Banana Republic decor with mosquito netting or other creative touches. There's also a holistic day spa providing everything from aromatherapy to Reiki treatment. Don't expect deluxe accommodations here, but it's a bargain, just 1 block from the beach, and a short drive to South Beach.

8505 Harding Ave. (1 block west of Collins Ave.), Miami Beach, FL 33141. © **888/775-0346** or 305/867-1906. Fax 305/867-1716. www.shorehaven.com. 15 units. Winter $89–$129 up to 3 people. Off-season $69–$79. Additional person $10. AE, DISC, MC, V. Free street parking. **Amenities:** Day spa; car-rental desk; room service (9am–2pm); in-room massage; laundry. *In room:* A/C, TV, kitchen, hair dryer, iron.

SUPER-CHEAP SLEEPS

Suez Oceanfront Resort The king of kitsch, the Las Vegas–like Suez is guarded by an undersized replica of Egypt's famed Sphinx—you can't miss it. Unfortunately, the Sphinx can't keep a quasi-seedy crowd from gathering here. The campy hotel does, however, offer newly renovated rooms on the beach, whereas most of the other old hotels have turned condo. Its location on Collins Avenue, in the middle of T-shirt shops, Denny's, and Walgreen's, isn't exactly ideal. If you stick to the back of the hotel, however, where the beach lies at your doorstep, you'll appreciate it more. For the price, it's a decent choice. There's also a restaurant on the premises, though we recommend trying elsewhere for meals.

18215 Collins Ave., Sunny Isles, FL 33160. © **800/327-2520** or 305/932-0661. Fax 305/937-0058. www.suezresort.com. 200 units. Winter $95–$105 double. Off-season $70–$85 double. Kitchenettes $10–$15 extra. AE, DC, MC, V. Free parking. **Amenities:** Restaurant; outdoor heated pool; tennis courts; exercise room; coin-op laundry. *In room:* A/C, TV, dataport, fridge, hair dryer, irons on request.

WORTH A SPLURGE

Bay Harbor Inn and Suites 🌟🌟 Under the management of Johnson & Wales University, this thoroughly renovated inn is just moments from the beach, fine restaurants, and the Bal Harbour Shops. The inn comes in two parts: The more modern section overlooks a swampy river, a heated outdoor pool, and a yacht named *Celeste,* where guests eat a complimentary breakfast buffet. On the other side of the street, "townside," is the cozier, antiques-filled portion, where glass-covered bookshelves hold good beach reading. The rooms have a hodgepodge of wood furnishings (mostly Victorian replicas), while suites boast an extra half-bathroom. You can often smell the aroma of cooking from the restaurant below, which is operated by students at Johnson & Wales Culinary Institute.

9660 E. Bay Harbor Dr., Bay Harbor Island, FL 33154. © **305/868-1156.** Fax 305/867-9094. www.bayharborinn.com. 45 units. Winter $149–$239 double; $159–$279 suite. Off-season $80–$159 double; $95–$179 suite. Additional person $35. Rates include continental breakfast. AE, MC, V. Free parking and dockage space. **Amenities:** Restaurant, brunch room, bar; exercise room; concierge; business center; limited room service. *In room:* A/C, TV, dataport, minibar, hair dryer.

Indian Creek Hotel ★★ *Finds*   Located off the beaten path, the Indian Creek Hotel is a meticulously restored 1936 building featuring one of the beach's first operating elevators. It's also the most charming hotel in the area, with impeccable service. Because of its location facing the Indian Creek waterway and its lush landscaping, this place feels more like an old-fashioned Key West bed-and-breakfast than your typical Miami Beach Art Deco hotel. The rooms are outfitted with Art Deco furnishings, such as an antique writing desk and pretty tropical prints, and contain small but spotless bathrooms. All the rooms have been completely renovated. Just 1 short block from a good stretch of sand, the hotel is also within walking distance of shops and restaurants and has a landscaped pool area that is a great place to lounge in the sun. If you're looking for peace and quiet, stay away from the South Beach hype and come here instead.

2727 Indian Creek Dr. (1 block west of Collins Ave. and the ocean), Miami Beach, FL 33140. © **800/491-2772** or 305/531-2727. Fax 305/531-5651. www.indiancreekhotel.com. 61 units. Winter $140–$240 double. Off-season $90–$150 double. Additional person $10. Group packages and summer specials available. AE, DC, DISC, MC, V. **Amenities:** Restaurant, bar; pool; concierge; car-rental desk; limited room service; laundry/dry cleaning. *In room:* A/C, TV/VCR, CD player, dataport, fridge in suites, hair dryer.

Newport Beachside Hotel & Resort *Value* *Kids*   This hotel is a great value, especially for young families who don't mind being away from the hustle and bustle of South Beach. The continental Newport Pub restaurant is very good and reasonably priced. The pool area is massive, which makes it great for kids. The hotel is situated directly on the beach, and for the aspiring angler, there is also a fishing pier out back. At night, by the poolside bar, a calypso band plays. Another plus is its location directly across the street from the R. K. Centres, a destination for both tourists and residents, with shopping and restaurants, from fine dining to fast food. Guest rooms are comfortable and spacious, and most have ocean views and balconies.

16701 Collins Ave., Sunny Isles, FL 33160. © **800/327-5476** or 305/949-1300. Fax 305/947-5873. www.newportbeachsideresort.com. 300 units. Winter $129–$299 double. Off-season $95–$250 double. AE, DC, MC, V. Valet parking $5. **Amenities:** Restaurant, sports bar; massive outdoor pool; concierge; business center; babysitting. *In room:* A/C, TV, minibar, fridge, microwave, coffeemaker, hair dryer, iron, safe.

KEY BISCAYNE
WORTH A SPLURGE

Silver Sands Beach Resort   Key Biscayne is not known for a wealth of budget options, but if this is where you'd like to base yourself, consider this quaint one-story motel. Everything is crisp and clean, and the pleasant staff will help with anything you may need, including babysitting. But despite the name, it's certainly no resort. Except for the beach and pool, you'll have to leave the premises for almost everything else, including food. The well-appointed rooms are very beachy, sporting a tropical motif and simple furnishings. Oceanfront suites have the added convenience of full kitchens, with stoves and pantries. You'll sit poolside with an unpretentious set of Latin-American families and Europeans who have come for a long and simple vacation—and get it.

301 Ocean Dr., Key Biscayne, FL 33149. © **305/361-5441.** Fax 305/361-5477. 56 units. Winter $149–$309 double. Off-season $129–$309 double. Additional person $30. Weekly rates available. AE, DC, MC, V. Free parking. **Amenities:** Medium-size pool; secretarial services; coin-op laundry. *In room:* A/C, TV, VCRs in some rooms, kitchenette, fridge, microwave, coffeemaker.

DOWNTOWN

If you've ever read Tom Wolfe's *Bonfire of the Vanities,* you may understand what downtown Miami is all about. If not, it's this simple: Take a wrong turn and you could find yourself in some serious trouble. Desolate and dangerous at night, downtown is trying to change its image, but it's a long, tedious process. Recently, however, part of the area has experienced a renaissance in terms of nightlife, with several popular dance clubs and bars opening up in the environs of NE 11th Street off Biscayne Boulevard.

Most downtown hotels cater primarily to business travelers and pre- and post-cruise passengers. Although business hotels are expensive, quality and service are of a high standard. Look for discounts and packages for the weekend, when offices are closed and rooms often go empty. If you're the kind of person who digs an urban setting, you may enjoy downtown, but if you're looking for shiny, happy Miami, you're in the wrong place (for now). As of press time, the developer of the Ritz-Carlton on South Beach was about to close a deal with downtown's shoddy DuPont Plaza, located on the sketchier side of the Miami River, in which millions of dollars would be invested to revamp the decrepit property, upgrading it into a classy lower-end hotel. Keep your eyes on this area.

Clarion Hotel & Suites ✯   This hotel is especially designed for the seasoned business traveler. Its location in downtown Miami (right on the river) provides excellent access to the commercial world of nearby Brickell Avenue and the legal precincts in downtown. Due to its position adjoining the Hyatt, a Metromover station, and some major parking lots, this hotel does, however, lack a room with a view, which may be disheartening for some guests. The spacious and elegantly appointed guest rooms and suites offer many amenities, and the two-room apartment suites are ideal for extended stays.

100 SE 4th St., Miami, FL 33131. © **800/838-6501** or 305/374-5100. Fax 305/381-9826. www.clarion miaconctr.com. 149 units. Year-round $99–$169 double. AE, DC, DISC, MC, V. Valet parking $15. **Amenities:** Restaurant, lounge; outdoor heated pool; exercise room; room service (7am–11:30pm); laundry. *In room:* A/C, TV, dataport, coffeemaker, hair dryer.

Miami River Inn ✯✯✯ *Finds*   The Miami River Inn, listed on the National Register of Historic Places, is a quaint country-style hideaway (Miami's *only* bed-and-breakfast!) consisting of four cottages smack in the middle of downtown Miami. In fact, it's so hidden that most locals don't even know it exists, which only adds to its panache. Every room has hardwood floors and is uniquely furnished with antiques dating from 1908. In one room, you might find a hand-painted bathtub, a Singer sewing machine, and an armoire from the turn of the 20th century, restored to perfection. In the foyer, you can peruse a library filled with books about old Miami, with histories of this land's former owners: Julia Tuttle, William Brickell, and Henry Flagler. It's close to public transportation, restaurants, and museums, and only 5 minutes from the business district.

Key Biscayne, Downtown Miami, Coconut Grove & Coral Gables

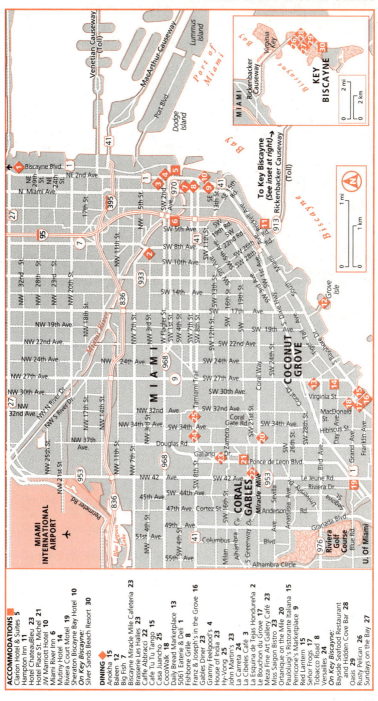

118 SW South River Dr., Miami, FL 33130. ✆ **800/468-3589** or 305/325-0045. Fax 305/325-9227. www.miamiriverinn.com. 40 units, 38 with private bathroom (some with tub or shower only). Winter $99–$229 double. Off-season $69–$109 double. Additional person $15. Rates include continental breakfast. AE, DC, DISC, MC, V. Free parking. Pets accepted for $25 per night. **Amenities:** Small, lushly landscaped swimming pool; access to nearby YMCA facilities; Jacuzzi; babysitting; coin-op washers and dryers, laundry/dry cleaning. *In room:* A/C, TV, hair dryer, iron.

WORTH A SPLURGE

JW Marriott Hotel ★★ Located smack in the middle of the business-oriented Brickell Avenue near downtown Miami, the JW Marriott is a *really* nice Marriott catering mostly to business travelers, but located conveniently enough between Coconut Grove and South Beach that it isn't a bad choice for vacationers, either. A small but elegant lobby features the classy, appropriately named Drake's Power Bar. The buzz of business deals being sealed amidst clouds of cigar smoke contributes to the smoky, but not staid, atmosphere here. Rooms are equipped with every amenity you might need. A lovely outdoor pool, fitness center, sauna, and hot tub should become everybody's business at this hotel. Next door is the area's bustling brewery, Gordon Biersch, which attracts well-heeled, young professional types who gather for postwork revelry.

1111 Brickell Ave., Miami, FL 33131. ✆ **800/228-9290** or 305/374-1224. Fax 305/374-4211. www.marriott.com. Winter $219 deluxe room; $319 concierge room; $450 junior suite. Off-season $149 deluxe room; $189 concierge room; $350 junior suite. AE, DC, DISC, MC, V. Valet parking $18; self-parking $16. **Amenities:** 2 restaurants, bar; outdoor pool; health club; spa; sauna; concierge; tour desk; business center; laundry. *In room:* A/C, TV, dataport, minibar, coffeemaker, hair dryer, iron, safe.

Sheraton Biscayne Bay Hotel ★ This downtown hotel's waterfront location is its greatest asset. Nestled between Brickell Park and Biscayne Bay, the Sheraton is set back from the main road and surrounded by a pleasant bay-front walkway. Since a recent $14 million renovation, this Sheraton is especially commendable. Its identical rooms are well furnished and comfortable. The hotel is popular with business travelers, but a fine choice for those who don't mind driving a few minutes to Miami's more populated areas.

495 Brickell Ave., Miami, FL 33131. ✆ **800/284-2000** or 305/373-6000. Fax 305/374-2279. www.sheraton.com. 598 units. Winter $199–$209 double; $225–$305 suite. Off-season $149–$175 double; $200–$250 suite. Additional person $10. Senior discounts and weekend and other packages available. AE, DC, DISC, MC, V. Self-parking $18. **Amenities:** Restaurant, bar; pool; exercise room. *In room:* AC, TV, dataport, fridges available on request, coffeemaker, hair dryer, iron.

COCONUT GROVE

This waterfront village hugs the shores of Biscayne Bay, just south of U.S. 1 and about 10 minutes from the beaches. Once a haven for hippies, head shops, and arty bohemian characters, the Grove succumbed to the inevitable temptations of commercialism and has become a Gap nation, featuring a host of fun themey restaurants, bars, a megaplex, and lots of stores. Outside of the main shopping area, however, you will find the beautiful remnants of old Miami in the form of flora, fauna, and, of course, water.

Hampton Inn This very standard chain hotel is a welcome reprieve in an area otherwise known for very pricey accommodations. The rooms are nothing exciting, but the freebies, like local phone calls, parking, in-room movies, breakfast buffet, and hot drinks around the clock make this a real steal. Although there is no restaurant or bar, it is close to lots of both—only about half a mile to the heart of the Grove's shopping and retail area and about as far from Coral Gables. Rooms are brand new, sparkling clean, and larger than that of a typical motel.

FREE TRIAL ISSUE

AWARD-WINNING MAGAZINE

☑ **YES!** Please send my **FREE** trial issue of *Arthur Frommer's Budget Travel* magazine. If I wish to continue, I'll pay my bill for just $12.00 for a one-year subscription (10 issues in all)—**a savings of 69% off the newsstand price.** If I choose not to subscribe, I'll simply return my invoice marked "Cancel" and owe nothing.

Name _____ (please print) _____

Address _____ Apt.# _____

City _____ State _____ Zip _____

E-mail (optional) _____

Please allow 4-6 weeks for delivery. Canadian orders add $12 per year for postage. Foreign orders add $18 per year. U.S. funds must accompany foreign orders. Residents of GA please add applicable sales tax.

C202A1

BUSINESS REPLY MAIL

FIRST-CLASS MAIL   PERMIT NO. 183   FLAGLER BEACH FL

POSTAGE WILL BE PAID BY ADDRESSEE

ARTHUR FROMMER'S
BudgetTravel™
vacations for real people

PO BOX 420772
PALM COAST FL 32142-8518

NO POSTAGE
NECESSARY
IF MAILED
IN THE
UNITED STATES

Located at the residential end of Brickell Avenue, it's a quiet, convenient location 15 minutes from South Beach and 5 minutes from Coconut Grove. If you'd rather save your money for dining and entertainment, this is a good bet.

2800 SW 28th Terrace (at U.S. 1 and SW 27th Ave.), Coconut Grove, FL 33133. © 888/287-3390 or 305/448-2800. Fax 305/442-8655. www.Hampton-inn.com. 137 units. Winter $134–$154 double. Off-season $104–$124 double. Rates include continental breakfast buffet and local calls. AE, DC, DISC, MC, V. Free parking. **Amenities:** Large outdoor pool; Jacuzzi; exercise room. *In room:* A/C, TV, microwave on request.

WORTH A SPLURGE

Mutiny Hotel ★★ En route to the center of the Grove, docked along Sailboat Bay and the marina, lies this revamped hotel best known as the hangout for the *Miami Vice* set—drug kingpins, undercover cops, and other shady characters—during the mid-'80s. Now it caters to a much more legitimate clientele. Service and style are bountiful at the Mutiny, which somehow has avoided the nouveau hotel hype and managed to stand on its own quiet merits without becoming part of the scene. The newly converted condos promise to be the best-kept secret in the Grove. The suites' British Colonial motif is warmed up with soft drapes, comfortable mattresses, and regal Old English furnishings. Each suite comes with a large bathroom (executive and two-bedroom suites have two bathrooms), full kitchen complete with china and complimentary coffee, and all the usual amenities associated with this class of hotel. The Mutiny is just a few blocks away from CocoWalk and the shops at Mayfair.

2951 S. Bayshore Dr., Miami, FL 33133. © 888/868-8469 or 305/441-2100. Fax 305/441-2822. www.mutinyhotel.com. 120 suites. Winter $229–$799 1- and 2-bedroom suites. Off-season $179–$599 1- and 2-bedroom suites. AE, DC, DISC, MC, V. Valet parking $16. **Amenities:** Restaurant; small outdoor heated pool with whirlpool; health club; spa; concierge; limited room service; babysitting; laundry/dry cleaning. *In room:* A/C, TV/VCR, dataport, kitchen, coffeemaker, hair dryer.

CORAL GABLES

Translated appropriately as "City Beautiful," the Gables, as it's affectionately known, was one of Miami's original planned communities and is still among the city's prettiest, pedestrian-friendly neighborhoods. Coral Gables has a number of wonderful luxury hotels, but fewer options for those on a smaller budget. Two popular and well-priced chain hotels in the area are a **Holiday Inn** (© **800/327-5476** or 305/667-5611) at 1350 S. Dixie Hwy., with rates between $75 and $125, and a **Howard Johnson** (© **800/446-4656** or 305/665-7501) at 1430 S. Dixie Hwy., with rates ranging from $65 to $95. Both are located directly across the street from the University of Miami and are popular with families and friends of students.

SUPER-CHEAP SLEEPS

Hotel ChateauBleau ★ Finding a bargain hotel in the heart of Coral Gables is like finding a pot of gold at the end of a rainbow. At last, the Hotel ChateauBleau is that accommodating pot of gold, a no-frills, albeit very clean hotel with spacious, recently renovated rooms, most with balconies overlooking Coral Gables. A nice pool as well as a very good Greek restaurant, Mylos, make this hotel an attractive choice in an area where the concept of value is pretty much a foreign one. A complimentary shuttle to and from the Miami International Airport is a bonus, too.

1111 Ponce de León Blvd., Coral Gables, FL 33134. © 305/448-2634. Fax 305/448-2017. www.hotelchateaubleau.com. 120 units. Winter $89 double. Off-season $69 double. AE, DC, DISC, MC, V. Free parking. **Amenities:** Restaurant, bar; small pool; free airport shuttle; room service (8am–10pm); self-service laundry. *In room:* A/C, TV.

Riviera Court Motel Besides the Holiday Inn down the road, this family-owned motel is the best discount option in the area. The comfortable and clean two-story property, dating from 1954, has a small pool and is set back from the road, so the rooms are all relatively quiet. Vending machines are the only choice for refreshments, but guests are near many great dining spots. You can also choose to stay in one of the efficiencies, which have fully stocked kitchens. For gossip mavens, this is the place where the pre-rehabilitated tennis star Jennifer Capriati was busted for drug possession many years ago.

5100 Riviera Dr. (on U.S. 1), Coral Gables, FL 33146. © 800/368-8602 or 305/665-3528. 30 units. Winter $75–$88 double. Off-season $68–$80 double. 10% discount for seniors and AAA members. AE, DC, DISC, MC, V. **Amenities:** Pool. *In room:* A/C, TV.

WORTH A SPLURGE

Hotel Place St. Michel ★★★ This European-style hotel in the heart of Coral Gables is one of the city's most romantic options. The accommodations and hospitality are straight out of Old World Europe, complete with dark wood-paneled walls, cozy beds, beautiful antiques, and a quiet elegance that seems startlingly out of place in trendy Miami. Everything here is charming—from the brass elevator and parquet floors to the paddle fans. One-of-a-kind furnishings make each room special. Bathrooms are on the smaller side but are hardly cramped. Guests are treated to fresh fruit baskets upon arrival and enjoy perfect service throughout their stay. The exceptional Restaurant St. Michel is a very romantic dining choice.

162 Alcazar Ave., Coral Gables, FL 33134. © 800/848-HOTEL or 305/444-1666. Fax 305/529-0074. www.hotelplacestmichel.com. 27 units. Winter $165 double; $200 suite. Off season $125 double; $160 suite. Additional person $10. Rates include continental breakfast and fruit basket upon arrival. AE, DC, MC, V. Self-parking $7. **Amenities:** Restaurant, lounge; access to nearby health club; concierge; room service (7am–10pm); laundry/dry cleaning. *In room:* A/C, TV, dataport, hair dryer, iron (available upon request).

NEAR THE AIRPORT/WEST MIAMI

As Miami continues to grow at a rapid pace, expansion has begun westward, where land is plentiful. Several resorts have taken advantage of the space to build world-class tennis and golf courses. While there's no sea to swim in, a plethora of facilities makes up for the lack of an ocean view.

Don Shula's Hotel and Golf Club Guests come to Shula's mostly for the golf, but there's plenty here to keep non-golfers busy, too. Opened in 1992 to much fanfare from the sports and business community, Shula's resort is an all-encompassing oasis in the middle of the planned residential neighborhood of Miami Lakes, complete with a Main Street and nearby shopping facilities—a good thing, since the site is more than a 20-minute drive from anything. The guest rooms, located in the main building or surrounding the golf course, are plain but pretty in typical, uninspiring Florida decor—pastels, wicker, and light wood. As expected, the hotel's Athletic Club features state-of-the-art equipment and classes, but costs hotel guests $10 per day or $35 per week. The award-winning Shula's Steak House and the more casual Steak House Two get high rankings nationwide. They serve huge Angus beef steaks and seafood, which can be worked off with a round of golf the next day.

Main St., Miami Lakes, FL 33014. © 800/24-SHULA or 305/821-1150. Fax 305/820-8190. 330 units. Winter $129–$289 suite. Off-season $99–$209 suite. Additional person $10. Business packages available. AE, DC, MC, V. **Amenities:** 6 restaurants, 2 bars; 2 pools; 2 golf courses and a driving range; 9 tennis courts; health club; sauna; sporting courts. *In room:* A/C, TV/VCR.

Miccosukee Resort and Convention Center ★ Located on the edge of the Everglades, about 30 to 40 minutes west of the airport, the Miccosukee

Resort is the closest thing South Florida's got to Las Vegas, but accommodations really are just a step above a Holiday Inn. The Miccosukee tribe was originally part of the lower Creek Nation, who lived in areas now known as Alabama and Georgia. Following the final Seminole War in 1858, the last of the Miccosukees settled in the Everglades. Following the lead set recently by many other Native American tribes, they built the resort to accumulate gambling revenue. Although many tourists go out to the resort solely to gamble, it also has spa services, great children's programs, entertainment, and excursions to the Florida Everglades. Guest rooms are standard, furnished with custom pieces made exclusively for the resort, but if you're here, you're not likely to spend that much time in your room.

500 SW 177th Ave. (at intersection with SW 8th St.), Miami, FL 33194. © **877/242-6464** or 305/221-8723. Fax 305/221-8309. www.miccosukee.com. 302 units. Year-round $99 double; $125 suite. All rooms sleep up to 4 people. AE, DC, DISC, MC, V. Free parking. **Amenities:** 3 restaurants, 24-hour deli; indoor heated pool; state-of-the-art health club & spa; game room; 24-hr. room service; dry cleaning/laundry. *In room:* A/C, TV, dataport, minibar, coffeemaker, hair dryer; some suites have whirlpool and wet bar.

4 Great Deals on Dining

Don't be fooled by the plethora of super-lean model types you're likely to see posing throughout Miami. Contrary to popular belief, dining in this city is as much a sport as in-line skating on Ocean Drive. With over 6,000 restaurants to choose from, dining out in Miami has become a passionate pastime for locals and visitors alike. In fact, Miami's star chefs have fused Californian–Asian with Caribbean and Latin elements to create a world-class flavor all its own: *Floribbean.* Think mango chutney splashed over fresh swordfish or a spicy sushi sauce served alongside Peruvian ceviche. Miami's new-wave cuisine, 10 years in the making, now rivals that of San Francisco or even New York. Indulging in this New World cuisine is not only high in calories; it's high in price. But if you can manage to splurge at least once, it's worth it.

Thanks to a thriving cafe society in both South Beach and Coconut Grove, you can also enjoy a reasonably priced meal and linger for hours without having a waiter hover over you, waiting to "turn" your table. In Little Havana, you can chow down on a meal that serves about six for less than $10. And since seafood is plentiful, it doesn't have to cost you an arm and a leg to enjoy the appendages of a crab or lobster. Don't be put off by the looks of our recommended seafood shacks in places such as Key Biscayne—oftentimes these spots get the best and freshest catches.

Many restaurants keep extended hours in season (roughly Dec–Apr), and may close for lunch and/or dinner on Monday, when the traffic is slower. Always call ahead, since schedules do change. Also, always look carefully at your bill—many Miami restaurants add a 15% gratuity to your total. Feel free to adjust it if you feel your server deserves more or less.

SOUTH BEACH

The renaissance of South Beach has spawned dozens of first-rate restaurants. The Lincoln Road area is packed with places offering good food and great atmosphere. Since it's impossible to list them all, I recommend strolling and browsing. Most restaurants post a copy of their menu outside. With very few exceptions, the places on Ocean Drive are crowded with tourists and priced accordingly. You'll do better to venture a little farther into the pedestrian-friendly streets just west of Ocean Drive.

Paninoteca, a gourmet Italian–style sandwich shop with delicious offerings such as grilled veggies and goat cheese on focaccia, is a great spot to purchase a picnic lunch. Locations are found in South Beach at 809 Lincoln Rd. (© **305/538-0058**), and in Coral Gables at 264 Miracle Mile, between Ponce de León Boulevard and Salzedo Street (© **305/443-8388**).

Like many cities in Europe and Latin America, it is fashionable to dine late in South Beach, preferably after 9, sometimes as late as midnight. Service on South Beach is for the most part notoriously slow and arrogant, but it comes with the turf.

Balan's MEDITERRANEAN Balan's provides undeniable evidence that the Brits actually do know a thing or two about cuisine. A direct import from London's hip Soho area, Balan's draws inspiration from various Mediterranean and Asian influences, labeling its cuisine "Mediterrasian." With a brightly colored interior straight out of a mod '60s flick, Balan's is a local favorite among the gay and arty crowds. The moderately priced food is rather good here—especially the sweet-potato soufflé with leeks and roasted garlic, fried goat cheese, and portobello mushrooms; and the Chilean sea bass with roasted tomato. When in doubt, the restaurant's signature lobster club sandwich is always a good choice. Adding to the ambience is the restaurant's people-watching vantage point on Lincoln Road.

1022 Lincoln Rd. (between Lenox and Michigan), South Beach. © **305/534-9191**. Reservations not accepted. Main courses $8–$18. AE, DISC, MC, V. Sun–Thurs 8am–midnight; Fri–Sat 8am–1am.

Big Pink *Kids* AMERICAN Real Food for Real People is the motto to which this restaurant strictly adheres. Scooters and motorcycles line the streets surrounding the place, which is a favorite among beach bums, club kids, and those craving Big Pink's comforting and hugely portioned pizzas, sandwiches, salads, and hamburgers. The fare is above average at best, and the menu is massive, but it comes with a good dose of kitsch, such as their "gourmet" spin on the classic TV dinner, which is done perfectly, right down to the compartmentalized dessert. Televisions line the bar area, and family-style table arrangement (there are several booths, too) promotes camaraderie among diners. Even picky kids will like the food here, and parents can enjoy the family-friendly atmosphere (not the norm for South Beach) without worrying if their kids are making too much noise.

157 Collins Ave., Miami Beach. © **305/532-4700**. Main courses $12.50–$19.95. AE, DC, MC, V. Sun, Thurs 8am–2am; Mon–Wed 8 am–midnight; Fri–Sat 8am–5am.

Dab Haus GERMAN This lively, often rowdy ale house/restaurant turns out good German fare. The honey-garlic Brie appetizer melted over hot French bread is irresistible and very pungent. A mug of one of the many German beers available here is the perfect accompaniment to the house specialties, which include veal bratwurst, *knodel mit pilzsauce* (bread dumplings served with a mushroom-wine sauce), and the ubiquitous Wiener schnitzel. Capped off with a dessert of apple strudel or crepes, a meal here is like taking a trip to Germany, minus the jet lag.

852 Alton Rd., South Beach. © **305/534-9557**. Main courses $7–$17. MC, V. Sun–Thurs 4–11pm; Fri–Sat 4pm–midnight.

David's Cafe II CUBAN From grilled sandwiches, roast pork, and rice and beans, to fried plantains and *cafecitos* (tiny cups of thick Cuban espresso), David's bright and airy cafe serves hearty, standard Cuban fare at good prices.

Though not as well-known as the now famous Puerto Sagua (see below), David's is typical of the cheap Cuban diners in the area and much better priced, especially for the lunch and brunch buffets. Daily specials might include *ropa vieja* (shredded beef stew), *arroz con pollo* (rice and chicken), or sautéed fish and vegetables. The homemade soups are always commendable (go for the black bean or the chicken noodle). An all-you-can-eat-buffet at $7.85, Monday through Friday from 11:30am to 3:30pm, is one of the best edible bargains in town. Waitresses struggle a bit with English, but they are used to gringos, so persevere.

1654 Meridian Ave. (north of Lincoln Rd.), South Beach. © 305/672-8707. Main courses $9.95–$13.95, sandwiches $4.95–$6.95, breakfast and lunch all-you-can-eat buffets from $5. AE, DC, DISC, MC, V. Daily 24 hr.

Grillfish SEAFOOD From the beautiful Byzantine-style mural and the gleaming oak bar, you'd think you were eating in a much more expensive restaurant, but Grillfish manages to pay the exorbitant South Beach rent with the help of a loyal local following who come for fresh, simple seafood in a relaxed but upscale atmosphere. The barroom seafood chowder is full of chunks of shellfish, as well as some fresh white fish filets in a tomato broth. The small ear of corn, included with each entree, is about as close as you'll get to any type of vegetable offering besides the pedestrian salad. Still, at these prices, it's worth a visit to try some local fare including mako shark, swordfish, tuna, marlin, and wahoo. For the surf and turf lovers, Grillfish has taken the plunge into a meaty venture right next door, at **Grillsteak** (1438 Collins Ave., same hours, credit cards, price range, and reservation policy).

1444 Collins Ave. (corner of Española Way), South Beach. © 305/538-9908. www.grillfish.com. Reservations for 6 or more only. Main courses $9–$26. AE, DC, DISC, MC, V. Sun–Thurs 6–11pm; Fri–Sat 6pm–midnight.

Jeffrey's *Finds* CONTINENTAL/BISTRO Some say this is the most romantic restaurant on the beach; South Beach's gay crowd certainly seems to agree. Old-fashioned lace curtains and candlelight are a welcome respite from the glitz and chrome of the rest of the island. You can choose a succulent three-quarter-pound burger or try a hearty chicken breast marinated in balsamic sauce and served with freshly mashed sweet potatoes over spinach, on white lace tablecloths. Some of the better seafood options include the conch fritters and the meaty crab cakes. Macadamia-encrusted tilapia is exceptional. Most desserts are tasty (there's an old-fashioned dessert cart to tempt you), but the homemade tarte tatin, a caramelly deep-dish apple tart, is delicious.

1629 Michigan Ave., South Beach. © 305/673-0690. Reservations highly recommended. Main courses $12–$24. AE, DC, MC, V. Tues–Sat 6–11pm; Sun 5–10pm. Closed Sept.

Lincoln Road Café *Value* CUBAN A local favorite, this down-to-earth Cuban-accented cafe is very popular for its cheap breakfasts. For $6, you can indulge in a hearty portion of eggs any style, with bacon, ham, sausage, Cuban toast, and coffee. Lunch and dinner specials are delicious and very cheap as well; try the ubiquitous black beans and rice or a chicken fricassee with plantains. The few tables inside are usually passed up in favor of the several outdoors, but in the evenings the house is full inside and out, as talented Latin musicians perform out front.

941 Lincoln Rd., South Beach. © 305/538-8066. Main courses $6–$11. AE, DC, MC, V. Daily 8am–midnight.

Macarena SPANISH/MEDITERRANEAN This Macarena has long outlived its passé line-dance namesake and is rather hip, actually, looked after by a young crew of Spanish imports whose families own several popular restaurants in Madrid. Show up before 10pm and you're sure to get a table. After that time, especially on weekends, it's standing room only. The gorgeous Euro crowd shows up for foot-stomping flamenco (every Wednesday and Friday—call for show times) and an outrageous selection of tapas, as well as Miami's very best paella (order a large portion and share it among at least four people). The garlic shrimp are tasty and aromatic and the yellow squash stuffed with seafood and cheese is especially delicious. All the seafood, such as mussels in marinara sauce and clams in green sauce, is worth sampling. With such reasonable prices, you can taste lots of dishes and leave satisfied. Try some of the terrific sangria made with slices of fresh fruit and a subtle tinge of sweet soda. Sidewalk seating is available on busy Washington Avenue, but the action is more entertaining inside.

1334 Washington Ave., South Beach. © 305/531-3440. Reservations recommended on weekends. Main courses $14–$22; tapas $7–$10. AE, DC, MC, V. Sun–Thurs 7pm–midnight; Fri–Sat 7pm–1:30am.

Mama Vieja ★ COLOMBIAN   This funky Colombian hangout looks like a total dive from the outside, but once inside you will want to dive right into the supremely fresh national specialties such as *pargo rojo estofado a la mama vieja* (red snapper stuffed with a super-creamy and delicate seafood sauce in a rice base). Brightly painted walls and elevated porches look out onto a large-screen TV showing music videos from the old country. The walls and ceilings are decorated with hundreds of hats that have been donated by customers and signed in exchange for a free meal. Bring in an interesting hat and mention it to the server before placing your order so that he or she can bring you to the attention of the owner. All the dishes here are worth trying and are so reasonably priced that it's easy to order a lot. Try to save room for the milky sweet desserts and a good strong coffee—you'll need it if you want to dance it off afterwards at Lola, the very popular, unpretentious hot spot next door. If not, there's live music here, too.

235 23rd St. (just west of Collins Ave.), South Beach. © 305/538-2400. Main courses $4.95–$14.95. AE, DC, DISC, MC, V. Wed–Mon noon–midnight. Closed Tues.

News Café ★ AMERICAN   In the late '80s, South Beach pioneer Mark Soyka opened this cafe on a depressed, decrepit Ocean Drive, sparking what some now call the South Beach renaissance. The thriving News has become part of Miami history and it still draws locals onto what has become the most tourist-ridden street in the area. Whether you come by foot, blade, Harley, or Ferrari, you should wait for an outside table, which is where you need to be to fully appreciate the experience. Service is notoriously slow and often arrogant (perhaps because the tip is included), but the menu, while not newsworthy, has some fairly good items, such as the Middle Eastern platter of hummus, tahini, tabouli, and grape leaves; hamburgers; and omelets. If it's not too busy, you can enjoy a leisurely cappuccino outside; creative types like to bring their laptops and sit here all day. There's also an extensive collection of national and international newspapers and magazines at the in-house newsstand. News Café also opened another clone, Café Cardozo, at the Cardozo Hotel at 1300 Ocean Dr. on South Beach in case 5 blocks is too much to walk to the original.

800 Ocean Dr., South Beach. © 305/538-6397. Main courses $5–$20. AE, DC, MC, V. Open 24 hr.

Piola ★★ PIZZA   This hip Italian import miraculously transforms pizza from an eat out of the box, stuff a slice into your mouth experience into a fun, sit-down meal that's hard to beat for the price, quality, and quantity. An unabridged menu of nearly 80 different kinds of pizzas-for-one that are really enough to share between two people is mind-numbing and mouthwatering. I suggest that you order several pizzas, depending on how many people you are dining with (two is more than enough for two, etc.). Start with the *quatro formaggio* pizza—brie, gorgonzola, parmesan, and mozzarella—and then consider a funkier version, say, smoked salmon and caviar. All pizzas are thin-crusted and full of flavor. Wait staff is extremely friendly, too, but be prepared for a lengthy wait, especially on weekend nights when the movie-going crowds next door spill over for a snack.

1625 Alton Rd., South Beach. © **305/674-1660.** Reservations accepted. Main courses $7–$15. AE, DC, MC, V. Daily 6pm–1am.

Puerto Sagua CUBAN/SPANISH   This brown-walled diner is one of the only old holdouts on South Beach. Its steady stream of regulars ranges from *abuelitos* (little old grandfathers) to hipsters who stop in after clubbing. It has endured because the food is good, if a little greasy. Some of the less heavy dishes are a super-chunky fish soup with pieces of whole flaky grouper, chicken, seafood paella, and marinated kingfish. Also good are most of the shrimp dishes, especially the shrimp in garlic sauce, which is served with white rice and salad. This is one of the most reasonably priced places left on the beach for simple, hearty fare.

700 Collins Ave., South Beach. © **305/673-1115.** Main courses $6–$24; sandwiches and salads $5–$10. AE, DC, MC, V. Daily 7:30am–2am.

Sport Café ITALIAN   When Sport Café first opened, way back when South Beach was still a fledgling in the trendoid business, it had a plain interior, wooden chairs, and a view of the parking lot. Televisions inside were tuned to soccer matches at all times—hence the name. The key to Sport's success was, and still is, its good, cheap, homemade Italian food—nothing fancy. Only now the cafe has moved up the block to a large corner space complete with private outdoor garden. The restaurant might have moved on to better digs, but one thing remains the same: The food is still great and the soccer matches continue to kick the crowd into a European-style frenzy. Try the nightly specials, especially when the owners' mother is cooking her secret lasagna.

560 Washington Ave., South Beach. © **305/674-9700.** Reservations accepted for 4 or more. Main courses $5–$18; sandwiches and pizzas $6–$9. AE, MC, V. Daily noon–1am.

Tap Tap HAITIAN   The whole place looks like an overgrown tap tap, a brightly painted jitney common in Haiti. Every inch is painted in vibrant neon hues (blue, pink, purple, and so on) and the atmosphere is always fun. It's where the Haiti-philes and Haitians, from journalists to politicians, hang out. The *lanbi nan citron,* a tart, marinated conch salad, is perfect with a tall tropical drink and maybe some lightly grilled goat tidbits, which are served in a savory brown sauce and are less stringy than a typical goat dish. Another super-satisfying choice is the pumpkin soup, a rich brick-colored puree of subtly seasoned pumpkin with a dash of pepper. An excellent salad of avocado, mango, and watercress is a great finish. Soda junkies should definitely try the watermelon soda.

819 5th St. (between Jefferson and Meridian aves., next to the Shell Station), South Beach. © **305/ 672-2898.** Reservations accepted. Main courses $6–$17. AE, DC, DISC, MC, V. Mon–Thurs 5–11pm; Fri–Sat 5pm–midnight; Sun 5–10pm. Closed in Aug.

Van Dyke Cafe AMERICAN   The younger, jazzier sibling of Ocean Drive's News Café, the Van Dyke is similar in spirit and cuisine but different in attitude. Unlike the much scenier and much more touristy News Café, Van

Dyke is a locals' favorite, at which people-watching is also premium, but attitude is practically nonexistent. Both cafes have nearly the same menu, with decent salads, sandwiches, and omelets, but the Van Dyke's warm wood-floored interior, upstairs jazz bar, accessible parking, and intense chocolate soufflé make it a less taxing alternative. Also, unlike News, Van Dyke turns into a sizzling nightspot, featuring live jazz nearly every night of the week (a $5 cover charge is added to your bill if you sit at a table; the bar's free). Outside there's a vast tree-lined seating area.

846 Lincoln Rd., South Beach. © 305/534-3600. Reservations recommended for dinner. Main courses $9–$17. AE, DC, MC, V. Daily 8am–2am.

SUPER-CHEAP EATS

Front Porch Café ★ AMERICAN Located in an unassuming, rather dreary-looking Art Deco hotel, the Front Porch Café is a relaxed local hangout known for cheap breakfasts. While some of the wait staff might be a bit sluggish (many are bartenders or club kids by night), it seems that nobody here is in a rush. If you are, this is *not* the place for you. Enjoy home-style French toast with bananas and walnuts, omelets, fresh fruit salads, pizzas, and classic breakfast pancakes that put IHOP to shame. Front Porch Café is also known for its daily dose of local gossip, which flows as freely as the syrup.

In the Penguin Hotel, 1418 Ocean Dr., South Beach. © 305/531-8300. Main courses $5[nd$16. AE, DC, DISC, MC, V. Daily 8:30am–10:30pm.

Mrs. Mendoza's Tacos al Carbon ★ MEXICAN Somehow this place manages to make Mexican food seem healthy with its flavorful, marinated char-broiled meats and fresh vegetarian selections. In addition to bountiful burritos, Mrs. Mendoza's is known for fabulous salsas, from mild to five-alarm spicy. Though lacking much atmosphere, Mrs. Mendoza's is also known for a low-frills clientele who know and want great Mexican food—not a scene. There's another location at 9739 NW 41st St. (the Doral Plaza) in West Miami (© **305/ 477-5119**).

1040 Alton Rd., South Beach. © 305/535-0808. Main courses $3–$5. No credit cards. Mon–Sat 11am–10pm, Sun noon–10pm.

Pizza Rustica ★ PIZZA Italians often scoff at the way Americans have mangled their recipe for pizza. But at Pizza Rustica, even the Italians marvel at these thin-crusted gourmet meals. This is the real deal—no thick, doughy, greasy concoctions here. Instead, Rustica features several delicious, huge slices of gourmet, authentically Tuscan-style pizza. Spinach and Gorgonzola cheese blend harmoniously with a brush of olive oil and garlic on a slate of the delicious, crispy dough. There's also a four-cheese, arugula, and rosemary potato slice, among others. Check out their new location at 1447 Washington Ave., South Beach (© **305/538-6009**).

863 Washington Ave., South Beach. © 305/674-8244. Slice $4. No credit cards. Daily 11am–6am.

WORTH A SPLURGE

Escopazzo ★★★ ITALIAN Escopazzo means "crazy" in Italian, but the only sign of insanity in this primo Northern Italian eatery is the fact that it only seats 70. The wine bottles have it better—the restaurant's cellar holds 1,000 bottles of various vintages. Should you be so lucky as to score a table at this romantic local favorite, you'll have trouble deciding between dishes that will have you swearing off the Olive Garden with your first bite. Among these are pappardelle with wild game and mushroom ragout, swordfish carpaccio, and braised leg of lamb with juniper berries, rosemary, and fennel. The hand-rolled pastas and risotto are near perfection. Eating here is like dining with a big Italian family—it's never boring (the menu changes five to six times a year), the service is excellent, and nobody's happy until you are blissfully full.

1311 Washington Ave., South Beach. © **305/674-9450.** Reservations required. Main courses $18–$28. AE, MC, V. Mon, Tues, and Thurs 6pm–midnight; Fri–Sat 6pm–1am; Sun 6–11pm.

Joe Allen ★★ *Finds* AMERICAN   It's hard to compete in a city with haute spots everywhere you look, but Joe Allen, a restaurant that has proven itself in both New York and London, has stood up to the challenge by establishing itself off the beaten path in possibly the only area of South Beach that has managed to remain impervious to trendiness and over-development. Located on the bay side of the beach, Joe Allen is nestled in an unassuming building conspicuously devoid of neon lights, valet parkers, and fashionable pedestrians. Inside, however, you discover a hidden jewel: a stark yet elegant interior and no-nonsense, fairly priced, ample-portioned dishes such as meat loaf, pizza, fresh fish, and salads. The scene has a homey feel favored by locals looking to escape the hype without compromising quality.

1787 Purdy Ave./Sunset Harbor Dr. (3 blocks west of Alton Rd.), South Beach. © **305/531-7007.** Reservations recommended, especially on weekends. Main courses $14.50–$25. MC, V. Mon–Fri 11:30am–11:45pm; Sat–Sun noon–11:45pm.

L'Entrecote de Paris ★★ FRENCH   New York's got the Statue of Liberty and Miami's got L'Entrecote de Paris. They don't complain. Everything in this little piece of Paris, a classy little bistro, is simple. For dinner, it's either steak, chicken, or seafood. We recommend sticking to the steaks, particularly the house special, L'Entrecote's French steak, with all-you-can-eat french fries (or *pommes frites,* rather). The salmon looks like spa cuisine, served with a pile of bald steamed potatoes and a salad with simple greens and an unmatchable vinaigrette. The steak, on the other hand, is the stuff cravings are made of, even if you're not a die-hard carnivore. Its salty sharp sauce is rich but not thick, and full of the beef's natural flavor. We love the *profiteroles au chocolat,* a perfect puff pastry filled with vanilla ice cream and topped with a dark bittersweet chocolate sauce. Servers are super-quick and professional, and almost friendly in a French kind of way.

413 Washington Ave., South Beach. © **305/673-1002.** Reservations recommended on weekends. Main courses $16–$24. DC, MC, V. Sun–Thurs 6:30pm–midnight; Fri–Sat 6pm–1am.

Macaluso's ★★★ ITALIAN   This restaurant epitomizes the Italians' love for—and mastery of—savory, plentiful, down-home Staten Island–style food. While the storefront restaurant is intimate and demure in nature, there's nothing delicate about the bold mix of flavors in every meat and pasta dish here. Catch the fantastic clam pie when in season—the portions are huge. Pricier

---

Tips **Free Snacks**

Hungry, but don't feel like spending money on an entire meal? **Joe Allen** (see above) is the place to go for a quick—and free—nosh. Always available at the bar are hard-boiled eggs—a retro-bar snack that is much more nourishing than peanuts and pretzels. On Friday happy hours, the restaurant's signature pizza bread, among other treats, are doled out for free to encourage patrons to quench their thirst at the bar.

items vary throughout the season, but will likely feature fresh fish handpicked by Chef (and owner) Michael, the Don of the kitchen, who is so accommodating he'll take special requests or even bring to your table a complimentary signature meatball. If he doesn't, don't hesitate to ask you waiter for one; he'll be glad to bring it to you. Everyone will recommend perennial favorites such as the rigatoni and broccoli rabe. Delicious desserts range from homemade anisette cookies to Patricia Scott's pastries. The wine list is also good. The George Duboeuf Beaujolais at $22 a bottle is a steal, when you consider it comes nicely chilled with slices of luscious Georgia peaches, which make a great and affordable dessert by themselves.

1747 Alton Rd., Miami Beach. © 305/604-1811. Main courses $14–$28; pizza $8–$13. AE, MC, V. Tues–Sat 6pm–midnight; Sun 6–11pm. After 10:30pm only pies are served. Closed Mon.

Mark's South Beach NEW WORLD/MEDITERRANEAN Named after owner and chef Mark Militello, this is one of the best restaurants in all of Miami. A cozy, contemporary restaurant nestled in the basement of the quietly chic Hotel Nash, Mark's New World and Mediterranean-influenced menu changes nightly. What doesn't change is the consistency and freshness of the restaurant's exquisite cuisine. The roasted rack of Colorado lamb with semolina gnocchi is exceptional and worth every bit of cholesterol it may have. Crispy-skinned yellowtail snapper with shrimp, tomato, black olives, oregano, and crumbled feta cheese is in a school of its own. Desserts, including an impressive cheese cart, are outrageous, especially the pistachio cake with chocolate sorbet. Unlike many South Beach eating establishments, the knowledgeable servers are here because of their experience in the restaurant—not modeling—business.

In the Hotel Nash, 1120 Collins Ave., South Beach. © 305/604-9050. Reservations recommended. Main courses $16–$38. AE, DC, DISC, MC, V. Sun–Thurs 7–11pm; Fri–Sat 7pm–midnight.

Nexxt Café AMERICAN Locals joke that this lively, always packed outdoor cafe should be called Nexxt Year to reflect the awfully slow service that has become its unfortunate trademark. Service aside, Nexxt has made quite a splash on South Beach, attracting an evening crowd looking for nighttime revelry and a morning crowd on the weekends for a standing-room-only brunch sensation. The fresh food comes in lavish portions that could easily feed two; the salads are an especially good bargain. Start your meal with the calamari fritti—they're a lot fresher here than at most other local restaurants—or the popcorn shrimp, which are larger than you might expect. The burgers and sandwiches are similarly big, and the steaks are well worth a taste. They have coffees in tall, grande, and "maxxi." There are also plenty of coffee cocktails, mixed drinks, frozen beverages, and wines, giving this place a nice bar life too.

700 Lincoln Rd. (off Euclid Ave.), South Beach. © 305/532-6643. Reservations accepted (no-shows will be charged $15 per seat). Main courses $12–$23. AE, MC, V. Daily 9am–1am.

Nobu SUSHI When Madonna ate here, no one really noticed. Not because they were purposely trying not to notice, but because the real star at Nobu is the sushi. The raw facts: Nobu has been hailed as one of the best sushi restaurants in the world, with always packed eateries in New York, London, and Los Angeles. The Omakase, or Chef's Choice—a multicourse menu entirely up to the chef for $70 per person and up—gets consistent raves. And although you won't wait long for your food to be cooked, you will wait forever to score a table here.

At the Shore Club Hotel, 1901 Collins Ave., South Beach. © 305/695-3100. Reservations for parties of 6 or more. Main courses $10–$30. AE, MC, V. Sun–Thurs 6pm–12am; Fri–Sat 6pm–1am.

Tambo ★★★ SUSHI/CEVICHE A hybrid of Japanese and Peruvian flavors, Tambo's Nikkei cuisine is exquisite. Skip the sushi here—there are too many other sushi restaurants in town to satisfy that craving—and go straight to the ceviches. When we read the offerings on this menu, our eyes zoomed in on the Ceviche Timbo: fresh scallops marinated in lime juice, with red onion, orange, mango, ginger, garlic, cilantro, scotch bonnet, and choclo salsa criolla. It is one of the best dishes your palate will experience; fresh and bursting with flavor, it will turn you into a ceviche convert. There's a total of 15 ceviches to choose from. We suggest the *Degustacion de Ceviches,* a variety pack, if you will, of three ceviches. The gorgeous, meticulous, food-as-art presentation is worthy of a photo shoot, but don't spend too much time gawking; it tastes as good, if not better, as it looks.

1801 Purdy Ave./Sunset Harbor Dr., South Beach. ⓒ 305/535-2414. Reservations accepted. Main courses $21–$30. AE, MC, V, DISC, DC. Mon–Sat 6:30pm–2:30am. (Kitchen open until 12:30am.)

MIAMI BEACH: SURFSIDE, BAL HARBOUR & SUNNY ISLES

The area north of the Art Deco District—from about 21st Street to 163rd Street—had its heyday in the 1950s, when huge hotels and gambling halls blocked the view of the ocean. Now, many of the old hotels have been converted into condos or budget lodgings, and the bay-front mansions have been renovated by and for wealthy entrepreneurs, families, and speculators. The area has many more residents, albeit seasonal, than visitors. On the culinary front, the result is a handful of super-expensive, traditional restaurants, as well as a number of value-oriented spots.

Cafe Prima Pasta ★★ ITALIAN Proving that good things do come in small packages, this tiny corner cafe's home cooking draws nightly hordes of carbo-craving diners who don't seem to mind waiting for a table for upward of an hour, maybe more on weekends. The scent of garlic wafting into the street is guaranteed to kill any vampire, and it makes the wait for a table a bit more torturous. Other choice ingredients include the ripest, freshest tomatoes, the finest olive oil, mozzarella that melts in your mouth, and fish that puts some seafood restaurants to shame. The spicy garlic and oil dip that comes with the bread is hard to resist and will likely linger with you for days, like the memory of this fine meal.

414 71st St. (half a block east of the Byron movie theater), Miami Beach. ⓒ 305/867-0106. Reservations not accepted. Main courses $9–$19; pastas $7–$9. No credit cards. Mon–Thurs noon–midnight; Fri noon–1am; Sat 1pm–1am; Sun 5pm–midnight.

Cafe Ragazzi ★★ ITALIAN This diminutive Italian cafe, with its rustic decor and a swift, knowledgeable wait staff, enjoys great success for its tasty simple pastas. The spicy puttanesca sauce with a subtle hint of fish is perfectly prepared. Also recommended is the salmon with radicchio. You can choose from many decent salads and carpacci, too. Lunch specials are a real steal at $7, including soup, salad, and daily pasta. Unlike Cafe Prima Pasta, Cafe Ragazzi isn't known as a scene—people come here for the food only. Expect to wait on weekend nights.

9500 Harding Ave. (on corner of 95th St.), Surfside. ⓒ 305/866-4495. Reservations accepted for 4 or more. Main courses $9–$18. MC, V. Mon–Fri 11:30am–3pm; daily 5:30–11pm.

Curry's *Value* AMERICAN Established in 1937, this large dining room on the ocean side of Collins Avenue is one of Miami Beach's oldest, and kitschiest, restaurants. Neither the restaurant's name nor the tacky Polynesian wall decorations are indicative of its offerings, which are straightforwardly American and reminiscent of the area's heyday. Broiled and fried fish dishes are available, but the best selections, including steak, chicken, and ribs, come off the open charcoal grill perched by the front window. Prices are incredibly reasonable here, and include an appetizer, soup, or salad, as well as a potato or vegetable, dessert, and coffee or tea.

7433 Collins Ave., Miami Beach. © **305/866-1571.** Reservations accepted. Main courses (including appetizer and dessert) $10–$20. MC, V. Tues–Sun 4–10pm.

Lemon Twist ★★ MEDITERRANEAN   In addition to great Mediterranean fare, there is a twist to this place in the form of a complimentary shot of the eponymous house spirit (a lemon vodka shot). But that comes after your meal. To start, you will receive a bowl of perfectly marinated olives, which can endanger your appetite, so go easy on them. A soothing, mellow interior makes for a romantic dining experience, or, if you prefer, outdoor tables are available (though the street is hardly as scenic). In between, expect friendly service and excellent meat and pasta dishes at terrific prices. Specialties such as spinach lasagna with smoked salmon and shank of lamb caramelized with whole garlic are savored by a savvy crowd that has likely escaped South Beach for this refreshing change of scenery.

908 71st St. (off the 79th St. Causeway), Miami Beach/Normandy Isle. © **305/868-2075.** Reservations recommended on weekends. Main courses $9–$18. AE, MC, V ($25 minimum). Tues–Sun 5:30pm–midnight. Closed July 4 weekend.

Oggi Caffe ★ ITALIAN   Tucked away in a tiny strip mall on the 79th Street Causeway, this neighborhood favorite makes fresh pastas daily. Each one, from the agnolotti stuffed with fresh spinach and ricotta to the wire-thin spaghettini, is tender and tasty. A hearty *pasta e fagiola* is filled with beans and vegetables and could almost be a meal. I also recommend the daily soups, especially the creamy spinach soup when it's on the menu. Though you could fill up on the starters, the entrees, especially the grilled dishes, are superb. The salmon is served on a bed of spinach with a light lemon-butter sauce. The place is small and a bit rushed, but it's worth the slight discomfort for this authentic, moderately priced food. Another Oggi Caffe opened at 7921 NW 2nd St. in downtown Miami. A sister restaurant, Caffe DaVinci, 1009 Kane Concourse in Bay Harbor Islands, just west of Bal Harbour, has been attracting a faithful following for several years.

1740 79th St. Causeway (in the White Star shopping center next to the Bagel Café), North Beach. © **305/866-1238.** Reservations recommended. Main courses $14–$25; pastas $9–$13. AE, DC, MC, V. Mon–Fri 11:30am–2:30pm; daily 6–11pm.

Wolfie Cohen's Rascal House ★ DELI   Open since 1954 and still going strong, this historic, nostalgic culinary extravaganza is one of Miami Beach's greatest traditions. Scooch into one of the ancient vinyl booths—which have hosted many a notorious bottom, from Frank Sinatra to mob boss Sam Giancana—and review the huge menu that's loaded with authentic Jewish staples. Consider the classic corned beef sandwich, stuffed cabbage, brisket, or potato pancakes. If you're lucky, the waitress will give you a wax-paper doggy bag to wrap up the leftover rolls and Danish from your breadbasket.

17190 Collins Ave. (at 163rd St.), Sunny Isles. © **305/947-4581.** Main courses $8–$30. AE, MC, V. Daily 7am–1am.

SUPER-CHEAP EATS

The Greek Place GREEK   This little hole-in-the-wall diner with sparkling white walls and about 10 wooden stools serves fantastic Greek and American diner-style food. Daily specials like pastitsio, chicken alcyone, and roast turkey with all the fixings are big lunchtime draws for locals working in the area. Typical Greek dishes like shish kebab, souvlaki, and gyro are cooked to perfection as you wait. Even the hamburger, prime ground beef delicately spiced and freshly grilled, is wonderful.

233 95th St. (between Collins and Harding aves.), Surfside. © 305/866-9628. Main courses $6–$7. No credit cards. Mon–Fri 10am–5pm; Sat 11am–3pm.

Sheldon's Drugs *Value* AMERICAN   This typical old-fashioned drugstore counter was a favorite breakfast spot of Isaac Bashevis Singer. Consider stopping into this historic site for a good piece of pie and a side of history. According to legend, the author was sitting at Sheldon's eating a bagel and eggs when his wife got the call in 1978 that he had won the Nobel Prize for Literature. The menu hasn't changed much since then. You can get eggs and oatmeal and a good tuna melt. A blue-plate special might be generic spaghetti and meatballs or grilled frankfurters. The food is pretty basic, but you can't beat the prices.

9501 Harding Ave., Surfside. © 305/866-6251. Main courses $4–$8; soups and sandwiches $2–$5. AE, DISC, MC, V. Mon–Sat 7am–9pm; Sun 7am–4pm.

WORTH A SPLURGE

Atlantic Restaurant AMERICAN   If you didn't know any better, you'd think you were in Nantucket at this comfortable blue and white beach-style restaurant designed to make you feel like you're eating in someone's guest house kitchen. The food, however, isn't your typical hamburger and hot dog on the grill fare. Sure, you can get all-American mac and cheese, but the Atlantic's version comes with truffles. Thanks to the Beach House Bal Harbour's owner, Jennifer Rubell, Atlantic gets delightfully kitschy with special themed-dinner nights such as the Clam Bake, in which a slew of fresh, all you can eat seafood is yours for the taking. Same goes for the Meat and Potatoes night. Brunches are particularly delicious here, too, as is the poolside and oceanfront seating.

In the Beach House Bal Harbour Hotel, 9449 Collins Ave., Bal Harbour. © 305/695-7930. Reservations recommended, required on weekends. Main courses $9.50–$22. AE, DC, MC, V. Daily 7am–11pm.

Crystal Café CONTINENTAL/NEW WORLD   The setting is sparse, with a bottle of wine and Lucite salt and pepper grinders as the only centerpiece on each of the 15 or so tables. Chef Klime, with the help of his affable wife and a superb wait staff, presides over this little-known hideaway, which attracts stars like Julio Iglesias and other in-the-know gourmands. Each of the entrees is beautifully presented and perfectly prepared. The shrimp cake appetizer, for example, is the size of a bread plate and rests on top of a small mound of lightly sautéed watercress and mushrooms. Surrounding the delicately breaded disc are concentric circles of beautiful sauces. The veal Marsala is served in a luscious brown sauce thickened not with heavy cream or flour but with delicate vegetable broth and a hearty mix of mushrooms. The osso buco is a masterpiece.

726 41st St., Miami Beach. © 305/673-8266. Reservations recommended on weekends. Main courses $11–$25. AE, DC, DISC, MC, V. Tues–Thurs 5–10pm; Fri–Sat 5–11pm.

NORTH MIAMI BEACH

Melting Pot FONDUE   Traditional fondue is supplemented by combination meat-and-fish dinners, which are served with one of almost a dozen different sauces. With its lace curtains and cozy booths, the Melting Pot can be quite romantic. To satisfy health-conscious diners, the owners have introduced a more wholesome version of fondue, in which you cook vegetables and meats in a low-fat broth. It tastes good, although this version is less fun than watching drippy cheese flow from the hot pot. Best of all, perhaps, is dessert: chunks of pineapple, bananas, apples, and cherries that you dip into a creamy chocolate fondue. No liquor is served here, but the wine list is extensive, and beer is available. A second Melting Pot is located at 11520 SW 72nd St. (Sunset Dr.) in Kendall (✆ **305/279-8816**).

In Sunny Isles Plaza shopping center, 3143 NE 163rd St. (between U.S. 1 and Collins Ave.), North Miami Beach. ✆ **305/947-2228**. www.meltingpot.net. Reservations recommended on weekends. Fondues $11–$18. AE, DC, DISC, MC, V. Sun–Thurs 5:30–11pm; Fri–Sat 5:30pm–midnight.

SUPER-CHEAP EATS

Here Comes the Sun ★ AMERICAN/HEALTH FOOD   One of Miami's first health-food spots, this bustling grocery-store-turned-diner serves hundreds of plates a night, mostly to blue-haired locals. It's noisy and hectic but worth it. In season, all types pack the place for a $7.95 special, served between 4 and 6:30pm, which includes one of more than 20 choices of entrees, soup or salad, coffee or tea, and a small frozen yogurt. Fresh grilled fish and chicken entrees are reliable and served with a nice array of vegetables. The miso burgers with "sun sauce" are a vegetarian's dream.

2188 NE 123rd St. (west of the Broad Causeway), North Miami Beach. ✆ **305/893-5711**. Reservations recommended in season. Main courses $8–$14; early-bird special $7.95; sandwiches and salads $5–$11. AE, DC, DISC, MC, V. Mon–Sat 11am–8:30pm.

WORTH A SPLURGE

Lagoon ★ SEAFOOD/CONTINENTAL   This old bay-front fish house has been around since 1936. Major road construction nearby should have guaranteed its doom years ago, but the excellent view and incredible specials make it a worthwhile stop. If you can disregard the somewhat disheveled bathrooms and nonchalant service, you'll find the best-priced juicy Maine lobsters around. Yes, it's true! Lobster lovers can get two 1½-pounders for $22.95. Try them broiled with a light buttery seasoned coating. This dish is not only inexpensive but incredibly succulent. Side dishes include fresh vegetables, like broccoli or asparagus, as well as a huge baked potato, stuffed or plain.

488 Sunny Isles Blvd. (163rd St.), North Miami Beach. ✆ **305/947-6661**. Reservations accepted. Main courses $12–$40. AE, MC, V. Daily 4:30–11pm. Happy hour daily 4:30–6pm.

DOWNTOWN

5061 Eaterie & Deli ★ AMERICAN/FRENCH/DELI   This two-story, 1949 building on the up and coming 50s block of Biscayne Boulevard features a mind-numbing selection of generously portioned, uncomplicated cuisine (think American diner meets French bistro) with a lively, hip atmosphere to match. The extensive menu and wine list are enhanced by an urban industrial decor, which showcases an open kitchen. The 5061 features everything from cheese plates to cheeseburgers, including quiche, fish, pasta, and salads. There's a large bar downstairs with an excellent wine list as well as a second floor bookstore slash cafe in which only travel, food, and wine books are sold.

For its On Tap Tuesdays, the restaurant offers its own 5061 Ale for 25¢ a glass to anyone ordering an appetizer and entree. You can also pick up the perfect picnic here any day of the week: The Homemade Deli Gourmet Menu for two includes a three-course meal and one complimentary bottle of wine for $29.95.

5061 Biscayne Blvd. (at 50th St.), Miami. ✆ **305/756-5051.** Main courses $9.95–$29.95. AE, DC, MC, V. Daily 10:30am–11:30pm; deli daily 6:30am–8:30pm.

Fishbone Grille ★★ SEAFOOD   Fish are flying in the open kitchen of this extremely popular, reasonably priced seafood joint. Whether you take yours grilled, blackened, or sautéed, the chefs here work wonders with super-fresh snapper, grouper, dolphin, tuna, sea bass, and shrimp, to name just a few. For the fish averse, there are delicious pizzas and an excellent New York strip steak. All meals come with salad and a fantastic slab of jalapeño cornbread. The interior is plain and simple; the only thing elaborate is the long list of daily specials.

650 S. Miami Ave., Miami. ✆ **305/530-1915.** Reservations recommended for 6 or more. Main courses $9–$20. AE, DC, DISC, MC, V. Mon–Thurs 11:30am–10pm; Fri 11:30am–11pm; Sat 5–11pm; Sun 5:30–9pm.

Granny Feelgood's AMERICAN/HEALTH FOOD   Owner Irving Fields has been in the business of serving healthful food for more than 28 years, and his flagship store's offerings are priced right. Due to its proximity to the courthouse, there's a lot of legal eagle traffic and networking going on here. Locals love Granny's for the fresh fish and poultry specials, a line of salads that define greenery and good health, and the always-impeccable service by a family-oriented staff who likes to get to know its clientele. Tourists swinging through downtown on the Metromover or just spinning by can munch healthily on anything from a brown rice and steamed vegetable plate to Granny's famous tuna salad platter. The chef's identity is a secret, but I happen to know he was trained under local chef extraordinaire Allen Susser and also did a stint at nearby Fisher Island's swanky members-only restaurant, so the cuisine here will most definitely please the palate. Granny Feelgood's sells its own line of vitamins and herbal products.

25 W. Flagler St., Miami. ✆ **305/377-9600.** Reservations not accepted. Main courses $9–$12. AE, MC, V. Mon–Fri 7am–5pm.

SUPER-CHEAP EATS

La Cibeles Café ★ *Value* CUBAN   This typical Latin diner serves some of the best food in town. Just by looking at the line that runs out the door every afternoon between noon and 2pm, you can see that you're not the first to discover it. For about $5, you can have a huge and filling meal. Pay attention to the daily lunch specials and go with them. A pounded, tender chicken breast *(pechuga)* is smothered in sautéed onions and served with rice and beans and a salad. The trout and the roast pork are both very good. When available, try the *ropa vieja*, a shredded beef dish delicately spiced and served with peas and rice.

105 NE Third Ave. (1 block west of Biscayne Blvd.), Miami. ✆ **305/577-3454.** Main courses $5–$9. No credit cards. Mon–Sat 7:30am–7:30pm.

Latin American Cafeteria ★★ CUBAN   The name may sound a bit generic, but this no-frills indoor-outdoor cafeteria has the best Cuban sandwiches in the entire city. They're big enough for lunch and a doggy-bagged dinner, too. Service is fast, prices are cheap, but be forewarned: English is truly a second language at this chain, so have patience. It's worth it.

9796 Coral Way, Miami. ✆ **305/226-2393.** Main courses $5–$9. AE, MC, V. Daily 7:30am–11pm.

Perricone's Marketplace ★ ITALIAN   A large selection of groceries and wine, plus an outdoor porch and patio for dining, make this one of the most welcoming spots downtown. Its rustic setting in the midst of downtown is a fantastic respite from city life. Sundays offer buffet brunches and all-you-can-eat

> **Cuban Coffee**
>
> Despite the fact that at least a dozen Starbucks have descended on Miami, locals still rely on the many Cuban cafeterias for their daily caffeine fix.
>
> Cuban coffee is a long-standing tradition in Miami. You'll find it served from the take-out windows of hundreds of *cafeterías* or *luncherías* around town, especially in Little Havana, downtown, Hialeah, and the beaches. Depending on where you are and what you want, you'll spend between 40¢ and $1.50 per cup.
>
> The best *café cubano* has a rich layer of foam on top formed when the hot espresso shoots from the machine into the sugar below. The result is the caramelly, sweet, potent concoction that's a favorite of locals of all nationalities.

dinners, too. But it's most popular weekdays at noon, when the suits show up for delectable sandwiches, quick and delicious pastas, and hearty salads.

15 SE 10th St. (corner of S. Miami Ave.), Miami. © 305/374-9693. Sandwiches $6.95–$8.25; pastas $11.50–$16.95. AE, MC, V. Sun–Mon 7:30am–10:30pm; Tues–Sat 7:30am–midnight.

Tobacco Road AMERICAN   Miami's oldest bar is a bluesy Route 66–inspired institution favored by barflies, professionals, and anyone else who wishes to indulge in good and greasy bar fare—chicken wings, nachos, and so on—for a reasonable price in a down-home, gritty-but-charming atmosphere. The burgers are also good—particularly the Death Burger, a deliciously unhealthy combo of choice sirloin topped with grilled onions, jalapeños, and pepper jack cheese—bring on the Tums! Also a live music venue, the Road, as it is known by locals, is well traveled, especially during Friday's happy hour and Tuesday's lobster night, when 100 1¼-pound lobsters go for only $10.99 apiece.

626 S. Miami Ave. © 305/374-1198. Main courses $7–$10. AE, DC, MC, V. Mon–Sat 11:30am–5am; Sun noon–5am. Cover charge $5 Fri–Sat night.

WORTH A SPLURGE

Big Fish ★★ Finds SEAFOOD/ITALIAN   This scenic seafood shack on the Miami River is a real catch—if you can find it. Hard to locate, but well worth the search, Big Fish's remote location keeps many people biting. In fact, Big Fish added some Italian options to its all-seafood menu in the hopes of luring more people, and that worked, too. Big Fish has a sweeping view of the Miami skyline and some of the freshest catch around; the pasta served with it is only a starchy diversion. But the spectacular setting may be the real draw, right there on the Miami River where freighters, fishing boats, dinghies, and sometimes yachts slink by to the amusement of the faithful diners who no longer have to fish around for a charming, serene seafood restaurant. Beware of Friday nights, when Big Fish turns into a big happy hour scene.

55 SW Miami Avenue Rd. © 305/373-1770. Main courses $15–$28. AE, DC, MC, V. Daily 11am–11pm. Cross the Brickell Ave. Bridge heading south and take the first right on SW 5th St. The road narrows under a bridge. The restaurant is just on the other side.

Porcao ★★ BRAZILIAN   The name sounds eerily like "pork out," which is what you'll be doing at this exceptional Brazilian *churrascaria* (Brazilian version of a steakhouse). For about $30, you can feast on salads and meats *after* you sample the unlimited gourmet buffet, which includes such fillers as pickled quail eggs, marinated onions, and an entire prosciutto. Do not stuff yourself here, as the next step is the meaty part: Choose as much lamb, filet mignon, chicken hearts, and steak as you like, grilled, skewered, and sliced right at your table. Side dishes also come with the meal, including beans and rice and fried yucca.

801 Brickell Bay Dr., Miami. © **305/373-2777**. Reservations accepted. Prix fixe $31.50 per person, all you can eat. AE, DC, MC, V. Daily noon–midnight.

LITTLE HAVANA

The main artery of Little Havana is a busy commercial strip called Southwest 8th Street, or Calle Ocho. Auto body shops, cigar factories, and furniture stores line this street, and on every corner there seems to be a pass-through window serving super-strong Cuban coffee and snacks. In addition, many of the Cuban, Dominican, Nicaraguan, Peruvian, and other Latin American immigrants have opened full-scale restaurants ranging from intimate candlelit establishments to bustling stand-up lunch counters.

Casa Juancho ★★ SPANISH   A generous taste of Spain comes to Miami in the form of the cavernous Casa Juancho, which looks like it escaped from a production of *Don Quixote*. The numerous dining rooms are decorated with traditional Spanish furnishings and enlivened nightly by strolling Spanish musicians (they expect tips when called over, but you can hear them loud and clear from other tables). Try not to be frustrated with the older staff that doesn't speak English or respond quickly to your subtle glance—the food's worth the frustration. Your best bet is to order lots of *tapas*, small dishes of Spanish finger food. Some of the best include mixed seafood vinaigrette, fresh shrimp in hot garlic sauce, and fried calamari rings. A few entrees stand out, like roast suckling pig, baby eels in garlic and olive oil, and Iberian-style snapper.

2436 SW 8th St. (just east of SW 27th Ave.), Little Havana. © **305/642-2452**. Reservations recommended but not accepted on Fri–Sat after 8pm. Main courses $15–$34; tapas $6–$8. AE, DC, DISC, MC, V. Sun–Thurs noon–midnight; Fri–Sat noon–1am.

Hy-Vong ★★ VIETNAMESE   A must in Little Havana, expect to wait hours for a table, and don't even think of mumbling a complaint. Despite the poor service, it's worth it. Vietnamese cuisine combines the best of Asian and French cooking with spectacular results. Food at Hy-Vong is elegantly simple and super-spicy. Appetizers include small, tightly packed Vietnamese spring rolls and *kim-chi*, a spicy, fermented cabbage. Star entrees include pastry-enclosed chicken with watercress cream-cheese sauce and fish in tangy mango sauce.

Enjoy the wait with a traditional Vietnamese beer and lots of company. Outside this tiny storefront restaurant, you'll meet interesting students, musicians, and foodies who come for the large, delicious portions.

3458 SW 8th St. (between 34th and 35th aves.), Little Havana. © **305/446-3674**. Reservations accepted for parties of 5 or more. Main courses $9–$19. AE, MC, DISC, V. Tues–Sun 6–11pm. Closed 2 weeks in Aug.

La Carreta ★ CUBAN   This cavernous family-style restaurant is filled with relics of an old farm, as well as college kids eating *medianoches* (midnight sandwiches with ham, cheese, and pickles) after partying all night. Waitresses are brusque but efficient and will help Anglos along who may not know the lingo. The menu is vast and very authentic, but is known for its sandwiches and smaller items. Try the *sopa de pollo*, a rich golden stock loaded with chunks of chicken and fresh vegetables, or the *ropa vieja*, a shredded beef stew in thick brown sauce. Because of its immense popularity and low prices, La Carreta has opened seven branches throughout Miami, including a counter in the Miami airport. Check the White Pages for other locations.

3632 SW 8th St., Little Havana. © 305/444-7501. Main courses $5–$22. AE, DC, DISC, MC, V. Daily 24 hr.

La Esquina de Tejas Hondureña ★★ *Value* CUBAN/HONDURAN Best known as the diner where Ronald Reagan ate during his 1983 campaign in Miami, La Esquina has gained a national reputation for its great food and low prices. Once known for Cuban food at its best, new owners have added a full Honduran menu as well. You must try the *arroz a la marinera*, the Cuban version of Spanish paella. It's filled with clams, oysters, mussels, lobster, shrimp, squid, snapper, stone crab, and scallops cooked in fresh seafood broth. If you're not in the mood for seafood, try the *vaca frita*, a grilled, shredded flank steak served with *moro* rice (black beans cooked with white rice) and *maduros* (sweet, fried plantains). Another house specialty is the *masas de puerco fritas*, a pork tenderloin cut in chunks, roasted, and then quickly deep-fried and served with mojo, grilled onions, garlic, olive oil, and bitter orange. You won't regret a trip here.

101 SW 12th Ave., Little Havana. © 305/545-0337. Daily specials $7–$15. AE, MC, V. Daily 8am–5pm.

Versailles ★★ CUBAN Versailles is the meeting place of Miami's Cuban power brokers, who meet daily over *cafe con leche* to discuss the future of the exiles' fate. A glorified diner, the place sparkles with glass, chandeliers, murals, and mirrors meant to evoke the French palace. There's nothing fancy here—nothing French, either—just straightforward food from the home country. The menu is a veritable survey of Cuban cooking and includes specialties such as Moors and Christians (flavorful black beans with white rice), ropa vieja, and fried whole fish. Whereas La Esquina de Tejas is known more for its food and Ronald Reagan than its atmosphere, Versailles is the place to come for *mucho* helpings of Cuban kitsch.

3555 SW 8th St., Little Havana. © 305/444-0240. Soup and salad $2–$10; main courses $5–$20. DC, DISC, MC, V. Mon–Thurs 8am–2am; Fri 8am–3:30am; Sat 8am–4:30am; Sun 9am–1am.

KEY BISCAYNE

Key Biscayne has some of the world's nicest beaches, hotels, and parks, yet it is not known for great food. Locals, or "Key rats" as they're known, tend to go off-island for meals or take-out, but here are some of the best choices on the island.

SUPER-CHEAP EATS

Bayside Seafood Restaurant and Hidden Cove Bar ★ *Finds* SEAFOOD Known by locals as "the Hut," this ramshackle restaurant and bar is a laid-back outdoor tiki hut and terrace that serves pretty good sandwiches and fish platters on paper plates. A blackboard lists the latest catches, which can be prepared blackened, fried, broiled, or in a garlic sauce. The fish dip is wonderfully smoky and moist, if a little heavy on mayonnaise. Local fishers and yachties share this rustic outpost with equal enthusiasm and loyalty. A completely new air-conditioned area for those who can't stand the heat is a welcome addition, as are the new deck and spruced-up decor. But behind it all, it's nothing fancier than a hut—if it was anything else, it wouldn't be nearly as appealing.

3501 Rickenbacker Causeway, Key Biscayne. © 305/361-0808. Reservations accepted for 15 or more. Appetizers, salads, and sandwiches $4.50–$8; platters $7–$13. AE, MC, V. Daily 11:30am until closing (which varies).

From Ceviche to Picadillo: Latin Cuisine at a Glance

In Little Havana and wondering what to eat? Many restaurants list menu items in English for the benefit of *norteamericano* diners. In case you're perplexed, though, here are translations and suggestions for filling and delicious meals:

Arroz con pollo Roast chicken served with saffron-seasoned yellow rice and diced vegetables.

Café cubano Very strong black coffee, served in thimble-size cups with lots of sugar. It's a real eye-opener.

Camarones Shrimp.

Ceviche Raw fish seasoned with spice and vegetables and marinated in vinegar and citrus to "cook" it.

Croquetas Golden-fried croquettes of ham, chicken, or fish.

Paella A Spanish dish of chicken, sausage, seafood, and pork mixed with saffron rice and peas.

Palomilla Thinly sliced beef, similar to American minute steak, usually served with onions, parsley, and a mountain of french fries.

Pan cubano Long, white crusty Cuban bread. Ask for it tostada, toasted and flattened on a grill with lots of butter.

Picadillo A rich stew of ground meat, brown gravy, peas, pimientos, raisins, and olives.

Plátano A deep-fried, soft, mildly sweet banana.

Pollo asado Roasted chicken with onions and a crispy skin.

Ropa vieja A delicious shredded beef stew, whose name literally means "old clothes."

Sopa de pollo Chicken soup, usually with noodles or rice.

Tapas A general name for Spanish-style hors d'oeuvres, served in grazing-size portions.

Jimbo's *Finds* SEAFOOD   Locals like to keep quiet about Jimbo's, a ramshackle seafood shack that started as a gathering spot for fishermen and has since become the quintessential South Florida watering hole, snack bar, and hangout for those in the know. If ever Miami had a backwoods, this was it, right down to the smoldering garbage can, stray dogs, and chickens. Do *not* get dressed up to come here—you will get dirty. Go to the bathroom before you get here, too, because the Porta Potties are absolutely rancid. Grab yourself a dollar can of beer (there's only beer, water, and soda, but you are allowed to bring your own choice of drink if you want) from the cooler and take in the view of the tropical lagoon where they shot *Flipper*. You may even see a manatee or two. Oddly enough, there's a bocce court here, and the owner, Jimbo, may challenge you to a game. Jimbo's smoked fish—marlin or salmon—is the best in town, but be forewarned: There are no utensils or napkins. When I asked for some, the woman said, "Lady, this is a place where you eat with your hands." I couldn't have said it better.

Off the Rickenbacker Causeway at Sewerline Rd., Virginia Key. © 305/361-7026. Fish $4; beer $2. No credit cards. Daily 6am–6:30pm. Head south on the main road towards Key Biscayne, make a left just after the MAST Academy (there will be a sign that says "Virginia Key"), tell the person in the toll booth you're going to Jimbo's, and he'll point you in the right direction.

Oasis *Value* CUBAN   Everyone, from the city's mayor to the local handymen, meet for delicious paella and Cuban sandwiches at this little shack. They gather outside, around the little take-out window, or inside at the few tables for super-powerful *cafesitos* and rich *croquetas*. It's slightly dingy, but the food is good and cheap.

19 Harbor Dr. (on corner of Crandon), Key Biscayne. © 305/361-5709. Main courses $4–$12; sandwiches $3–$4. No credit cards. Daily 6am–9pm.

WORTH A SPLURGE

Rusty Pelican ★ SEAFOOD   The Pelican's private tropical walkway leads over a lush waterfall into one of the most romantic dining rooms in the city, located right on beautiful blue-green Biscayne Bay. The restaurant's windows look out over the water onto the sparkling stalagmites of Miami's magnificent downtown. Inside, quiet wicker paddle fans whirl overhead and saltwater fish swim in pretty tableside aquariums. The restaurant's surf-and-turf menu features conservatively prepared prime steaks, veal, shrimp, and lobster. The food is good, but the atmosphere—the reason you're here—is even better, especially at sunset, when the view over the city is magical.

3201 Rickenbacker Causeway, Key Biscayne. © 305/361-3818. Reservations recommended. Main courses $16–$22. AE, DC, MC, V. Daily 11:30am–4pm; Sun–Thurs 5–11pm; Fri–Sat 5pm–midnight.

Sundays on the Bay ★ AMERICAN   Although its food is fine, Sundays is really a fun tropical bar that features an unbeatable view of downtown, Coconut Grove, and the Sundays' marina. The menu features local favorites—grouper, tuna, snapper, and good shellfish in season. Competent renditions of such classic dishes as oysters Rockefeller, shrimp scampi, and lobster fra diablo are commendable. Particularly popular is the Sunday brunch, when a buffet the size of Bimini attracts a lively, hungry crowd.

5420 Crandon Blvd., Key Biscayne. © 305/361-6777. Reservations recommended for Sun brunch. Main courses $15–$24; Sun brunch $18.95. AE, DC, MC, V. Daily 11:30am–11:45pm; Sun brunch 11am–4pm.

COCONUT GROVE

Coconut Grove was long known as the artists' haven of Miami, but the rush of developers trying to cash in on the laid-back charm of this old settlement has turned it into something of an overgrown mall. Still, there are several great dining spots both in and out of the confines of Mayfair or CocoWalk.

Cafe Tu Tu Tango ★ SPANISH/INTERNATIONAL   This restaurant in the bustling CocoWalk is designed to look like a disheveled artist's loft. Dozens of original paintings—some only half-finished—hang on the walls and on studio easels. Seating is either inside, among the clutter, or outdoors, overlooking the Grove's main drag. Flamenco and other Latin-inspired tunes complement a menu with a decidedly Spanish flair. Hummus spread on rosemary flat bread and baked goat cheese in marinara sauce are two good starters. Entrees include roast duck with dried cranberries, toasted pine nuts, and goat cheese, plus Cajun chicken egg rolls filled with corn, cheddar cheese, and tomato salsa. Pastas, ribs, fish, and pizzas round out the eclectic offerings, and several visits have proved each consistently good. Try the sweet, potent sangria and enjoy the warm, lively atmosphere from a seat with a view.

3015 Grand Ave. (on the second floor of CocoWalk), Coconut Grove. ✆ **305/529-2222.** Reservations not accepted. Tapas $3–$9.50. AE, MC, V. Sun–Wed 11:30am–midnight; Thurs 11:30am–1am; Fri–Sat 11:30am–2am.

Paulo Luigi's Ristorante Italiana ★ Kids ITALIAN
Paulo Luigi's serves rich dishes that include cold and hot appetizers, homemade soups and salads, pastas, and pizzas. Owners Paul and Lola Shalaj, restaurant entrepreneurs for the past 27 years, have gained and kept a large devoted clientele with their tasty light Italian cuisine, generous portions, and friendly environment that has served as the perfect fine-dining hideaway for both local and national customers alike. A favorite is the *jumbo rigatti rubino,* a chicken dish with a side of sausages, asparagus, and portobello mushrooms in light marinara sauce. There's also chicken Marsala, *linguine al fruitti di mare* (for poultry and seafood lovers), and a special children's menu.

3324 Virginia St., Coconut Grove. ✆ **305/445-9000.** Reservations recommended. Main courses $9–$17. AE, MC, V. Daily noon–4pm and 5–11pm; Fri–Sat 5pm–1am.

Red Lantern ★ CANTONESE
Miami is not known for having good Chinese food, but this popular Chinese spot is better than most. Specialties include shark's fin with chicken and steamed whole snapper with black-bean sauce. There's also an assortment of vegetarian dishes and some excellent soups. My favorite is the clay-pot stew of chicken in ginger broth. Although the atmosphere is nothing to speak of, the varied menu and interesting preparation keep locals happy and make a meal here worthwhile.

3176 Commodore Plaza (Grand Ave.), Coconut Grove. ✆ **305/529-9998.** Main courses $8–$20. AE, DC, DISC, MC, V. Mon–Thurs 11:30am–11pm; Fri 11:30am–midnight; Sat 4pm–midnight; Sun 5–11pm.

Señor Frogs ★ MEXICAN
Filled with a collegiate crowd, this restaurant is known for a raucous good time, a mariachi band, and powerful margaritas. The food at this rocking cantina is a bit too cheesy, but it's tasty, if not exactly authentic. The mole enchiladas, with 14 different kinds of mild chiles mixed with chocolate, is as flavorful as any I've tasted. Almost everything is served with rice and beans in quantities so large that few diners are able to finish.

3480 Main Hwy., Coconut Grove. ✆ **305/448-0999.** Reservations not accepted. Main courses $12–$17. AE, DC, MC, V. Mon–Sat 11:30am–2am; Sun 11:30am–1am.

WORTH A SPLURGE

Anokha ★★★ INDIAN
This is the best Indian restaurant in Miami. Anokha's motto is "a guest is equal to God and should be treated as such," and they do stick to it. The food here is from the gods, with fantastic tandooris, curries, and stews. The restaurant's location at the end of a quiet stretch of Coconut Grove is especially enticing because it prevents the throngs of pedestrians from overtaking what some people consider a diamond in the rough.

3195 Commodore Plaza (between Main Hwy. and Grand Ave.), Coconut Grove. ✆ **786/552-1030.** Main courses $10–$30. AE, DC, MC, V. Tues–Sun 11:30am–10:30pm.

Baleen ★★★ SEAFOOD/MEDITERRANEAN
While the prices aren't lean, the cuisine here is worth every pricey, precious penny. Oversized crab cakes, oak-smoked diver scallops, and steak house-quality meats are among Baleen's excellent offerings. The lobster bisque is the best on Biscayne Bay. Everything here is a la carte, so order wisely, as it tends to add up quicker than you can put your fork down. The restaurant's spectacular waterfront setting makes Baleen a true knockout. Brunch is particularly noteworthy as well.

4 Grove Isle Dr. (in the Grove Isle Hotel), Coconut Grove. ✆ **305/858-8300.** Reservations recommended. Main courses $18–$34. AE, DC, MC, V. Sun–Wed 7am–10pm; Thurs–Sat 7am–11pm.

Franz & Joseph's in the Grove ★★ CONTINENTAL/ITALIAN   This is a romantic restaurant, chock-full of old-world charm. Before you sit down to dine, enjoy a glass of wine at the intimate, atmospheric bar and begin to give in to the European ambience here. A few starters are recommended: The escargot in Roquefort butter with grilled herb bread is wonderful, as is the stuffed avocado with marinated sea scallops, mussels, and shrimp—a local favorite and absolutely fresh. Don't be afraid to order pasta, either. The penne with spicy grilled chicken, plum tomatoes, spinach, and feta cheese is wonderful. But if you've come to Florida for the seafood, you can't go wrong with the restaurant's filet of snapper, pan-seared with mango chutney and glazed banana over rice. Their delicious desserts are made on the premises. The kitchen is small, so the food is consistently fresh and cooked to order. The last thing the chef does each night before going home is to order for the next day's menu.

3145 Commodore Plaza, Coconut Grove. ✆ **305/448-2282.** Reservations highly recommended. Main courses $15–$20. AE, MC, V. Tues–Sun 11:30am–2:30pm and 6–10:30pm.

Le Bouchon du Grove ★★ FRENCH   This very authentic, exceptional bistro is French right down to the wait staff who may only speak French to you, forgetting that they are in the heart of Coconut Grove, U.S.A. But it matters not. The food, prepared by an animated French (what else) chef, is superb. An excellent starter is the wonderful *gratinée Lyonnaise* (traditional French onion soup). Fish is brought in fresh daily; try the Chilean sea bass when in season *(filet de loup poele)*. Though it is slightly heavy on the oil, it is delivered with succulent artichokes, tomato confit, and seasoned roasted garlic that is a gastronomic triumph. The *carre d'agneau roti* (roasted rack of lamb with Provence herbs) is served warm and tender, with an excellent amount of seasoning. There is also an excellent selection of pricey but do-able French and American red and white wines.

3430 Main Hwy., Coconut Grove. ✆ **305/448-6060.** Reservations recommended. Main courses $18–$25. AE, MC, V. Mon–Fri 10am–3pm; Mon–Thurs 5–11pm; Fri 5pm–midnight; Sat 8am–midnight; Sun 8am–11pm.

CORAL GABLES

Bargain meals are hard to come by in Coral Gables, Miami's Epicurean Epcot Center. However, we've searched for the best deals in town and actually found several. If ever you were to splurge on a meal, though, this is the place to do it.

Gables Diner ★ AMERICAN   This upscale diner serves an eclectic mix of comfort food and nouvelle health food. From meat loaf to Chinese chicken salad, there are moderately priced options for everyone. My favorite is the chicken pot pie, a flaky homemade crust filled with big chunks of white meat, pearl onions, peas, and mushrooms. Also good are the large burgers with every imaginable condiment. Vegetarians can find a few good choices, including pastas, bean soups, pizzas, vegetable stir-fry, and some hearty salads. All the ingredients are fresh and crisp. No need to dress up here, although the clean, almost romantic setting is as appropriate for first dates as it is for families.

2320 Galiano Dr. (between Ponce de León Blvd. and 37th Ave.), Coral Gables. ✆ **305/567-0330.** Main courses $9–$16; pastas $10–$12; burgers and sandwiches $7–$9; salads $8–$10. AE, DC, DISC, MC, V. Daily 8am–10pm; Fri–Sat 8am–10:30pm.

House of India ★ INDIAN   House of India's curries, kormas, and kabobs are very good, but the restaurant's well-priced all-you-can-eat lunch buffet is unsurpassed. All the favorites are on display, including tandoori chicken, naan, and various meat and vegetarian curries, as well as rice and *dal* (lentils). This place isn't fancy and could use a good scrub-down (in fact, I've heard it described as a "greasy spoon"), but the service is excellent and the food is good enough to keep you from staring at your surroundings.

22 Merrick Way (near Douglas and Coral Way, a block north of Miracle Mile), Coral Gables. © 305/444-2348. Reservations recommended. Main courses $8–$17. AE, DC, DISC, MC, V. Daily 11:30am–3pm; Sun–Thurs 5–10pm; Fri–Sat 5–11pm.

John Martin's ★ IRISH PUB   Forest green and dark wood give way to a very intimate, pub-like atmosphere in which local businesspeople and barflies alike come to hoist a pint or two. The menu offers some tasty British specialties (not necessarily an oxymoron!), such as bangers and mash and shepherd's pie as well as Irish lamb stew and corned beef and cabbage.

Of course, to wash it down, you'll want to try one of the ales on tap or one of the more than 20 single-malt scotches. The crowd is upscale and chatty, as is the young wait staff. Check out happy hour on weeknights, plus the Sunday brunch with loads of hand-carved meats and seafood.

253 Miracle Mile, Coral Gables. © 305/445-3777. Reservations recommended on weekends. Main courses $9–$20; sandwiches and salads $5–$16. AE, DC, DISC, MC, V. Mon–Thurs 11:30am–midnight; Fri–Sat 11:30am–1am; Sun noon–10pm.

Meza Fine Art Gallery Café ★★ ECLECTIC   This unique restaurant is located in a sleek, arty atmosphere featuring paintings, performance artists, and a multimedia array of talent—very Warhol. As eclectic as the art and artists who convene here, the menu is varied, with accents on Mediterranean and Italian, featuring well-priced, well-prepared dishes such as pan-seared tuna with sesame crust and balsamic vinegar reduction and a delicious grilled churrasco skirt steak with chimichurri. Over 500 wines by the bottle and 78 by the glass make Meza an oenophile's favorite. Live music nightly from jazz and Latin to electronica brings out a motley crew of youngsters who look as if they stepped out of a Gap ad. Earlier in the evenings, Meza caters to an older, more sophisticated dining crowd.

275 Giralda Ave., Coral Gables. © 305/461-2723. Reservations accepted. Main courses $6.95–$13.95. 3-course twilight dinner served Mon–Sat 6–8pm for $15.95 per person, including glass of wine. AE, DC, DISC, MC, V. Restaurant Mon–Fri noon–3pm; Mon–Sun 6–10:30pm. Bar Mon–Sun 5pm–2am.

Miss Saigon Bistro ★★ VIETNAMESE   Unlike Andrew Lloyd Webber's bombastic Broadway show, this Miss Saigon is small, quiet, and not at all flashy. Servers at this family-run restaurant—among them, Rick, the owners' son—will graciously recommend dishes or even custom-make something for you. The menu is varied and reasonably priced and the portions are huge—large enough to share. Noodle dishes and soup bowls are hearty and flavorful; caramelized prawns are fantastic, as is the whole snapper with lemongrass and ginger sauce. Despite the fact that there are few tables inside and a hungry crowd usually gathers outside in the street, they will never rush you through your meal, which is worth savoring.

Tips   A Free Buffet

Every day around 5pm, **John Martin's** breaks out the buffet table for its über-popular, daily happy hour, featuring sizeable sandwiches, mystery stews and, oddly enough for an Irish bar, fried rice. Best of all, it's free!

---

146 Giralda Ave. (at Ponce de León and 37th Ave.), Coral Gables. ⓒ **305/446-8006.** Main courses $4–$17. AE, DC, DISC, MC, V. Mon–Thurs 11am–3pm and 5:30–10pm; Fri–Sat 5:30–11pm; Sun 5:30–10pm.

SUPER-CHEAP EATS

Biscayne Miracle Mile Cafeteria ★ *Value* AMERICAN Here you'll find no bar, no music, and no flowers on the tables—just great Southern-style cooking at unbelievably low prices. The menu changes, but roast beef, baked fish, and barbecued ribs are typical entrees, few of which exceed $5. Food is picked up cafeteria style and brought to one of the many unadorned Formica tables. The restaurant is always busy. The kitschy 1950s decor is an asset in this last of the old-fashioned cafeterias, where the gold-clad staff is proud and attentive. Enjoy it while it lasts.

147 Miracle Mile, Coral Gables. ⓒ **305/444-9005.** Main courses $3.50–$4.50. MC, V. Daily 11am–8:30pm.

Daily Bread Marketplace GREEK This place is great for take-out food and homemade breads. The falafel and gyro sandwiches are large, fresh, and filling. The spinach pie for less than $1 is also recommended, though it's short on spinach and heavy on pastry. Salads, including luscious tabouli, hummus, and eggplant, are also worth a go. To take out or eat in, the Middle Eastern fare here is a real treat, especially in an area so filled with fancy French and Cuban fare. Plus, you can pick up hard-to-find groceries such as grape leaves, fresh olives, couscous, fresh nuts, and pita bread. A South Beach location has opened at 840 1st St. (at Alton Rd.), ⓒ **305/673-2252.**

2400 SW 27th St. (off U.S. 1 under the monorail), Coral Gables. ⓒ **305/856-0363** or 305/856-0366. Sandwiches and salads $3–$6. MC, V. Mon–Sat 8am–8pm; Sun 11am–5pm.

WORTH A SPLURGE

Brasserie Les Halles ★★ FRENCH Known especially for its fine steaks and delicious salads, this very welcome addition to the Coral Gables dining scene became popular as soon as it opened in 1997 and has since continued to do a brisk business. The moderately priced menu is particularly welcome in an area of overpriced, stuffy restaurants. For starters, try the mussels in white wine sauce and the escargot. For a main course, the duck confit is an unusual and rich choice. Pieces of duck meat wrapped in duck fat are slow-cooked and served on salad frissé with baby potatoes with garlic. Service by the young French staff is polite but a bit slow. The tables tend to be a little too close, although there is a lovely private balcony space overlooking the long, thin dining room where large groups can gather.

2415 Ponce de León Blvd. (at Miracle Mile), Coral Gables. ⓒ **305/461-1099.** Reservations recommended on weekends. Main courses $12.50–$22.50. AE, DC, DISC, MC, V. Daily 11:30am–midnight.

Caffe Abbracci ★★ ITALIAN You'll understand why this restaurant's name means "hugs" in Italian the moment you enter the dark romantic enclave: Your appetite will be embraced by the savory scents of fantastic Italian cuisine wafting through the restaurant. The homemade black and red ravioli filled with lobster in pink sauce, the risotto with porcini and portobello mushrooms, and the house specialty—grilled veal chop topped with tricolor salad—are irresistible and perhaps the culinary equivalent of a warm, embracing hug. A cozy bar and lounge were added recently to further encourage the warm and fuzzy feelings.

318 Aragon Ave. (1 block north of Miracle Mile, between Salzedo St. and Le Jeune Rd.), Coral Gables. ⓒ **305/441-0700.** Reservations recommended for dinner. Main courses $16–$26.50; pastas $15.50–$19.50. AE, DC, MC, V. Mon–Fri 11:30am–3pm; Sun–Thurs 6–11:30pm; Fri–Sat 6pm–12:30am.

Ortanique on the Mile ★★ NEW WORLD CARIBBEAN As you walk in, you'll be greeted by soft, spider-like lights and canopied mosquito netting that will make you wonder whether you're on a secluded island or inside one of King Tut's temples. Chef Cindy Hutson has truly perfected her tantalizing New World Caribbean menu. For starters, an absolute must is the pumpkin bisque with a hint of pepper sherry. Afterward, move on to the tropical mango salad with fresh marinated Sable hearts of palm, julienne mango, baby field greens, toasted Caribbean candied pecans, and passion fruit vinaigrette. For an entree, I recommend the pan-sautéed Bahamian black grouper marinated in teriyaki and sesame oil. It's served with an ortanique (an orange-like fruit) orange liqueur sauce and topped with steamed seasoned chayote, zucchini, and carrots on a lemon-orange boniato-sweet plantain mash. Entrees may not be cheap, but they're a lot less than airfare to the islands, from where most, if not all, the ingredients used here hail.

278 Miracle Mile (next to Actor's Playhouse), Coral Gables. © 305/446-7710. Reservations requested. Main courses $11–$29. AE, DC, MC, V. Mon–Tues 6–10pm; Wed–Sat 6–11pm; Sun 5:30–9:30pm.

SOUTH MIAMI & WEST MIAMI

Though mostly residential, these areas nonetheless have a couple eating establishments worth the drive.

El Toro Taco Family Restaurant ★★★ *Finds* MEXICAN You'd never know this Mexican oasis in the midst of South Florida farmland existed, but this 96-seat family-run restaurant is worth the trip. Fabulous, and we mean fabulous, Mexican fare, from the usual tacos, enchiladas, and burritos drenched with the freshest and zestiest salsa this side of Baja, is what you'll find here in abundance. Cheap and delicious, this place will have you coming back for more.

1 S. Krome Ave., Homestead. © 305/245-8182. Main courses $1.39–$8.75. DISC, MC, V. Tues–Sun 11am–9pm. Take 836 West (Dolphin Expressway) toward Miami International Airport. Take Florida Turnpike South Ramp toward Florida City/Key West. Take U.S. 41/SW 8th St. exit (no. 25) and turn left onto SW 8th St. Take SW 8th St. to Krome Ave. (.2 miles) and turn left onto Krome Ave.

Shorty's ★ BARBECUE A Miami tradition since 1951, this honky-tonk of a log cabin is still serving some of the best ribs and chicken in South Florida. People line up for the smoke-flavored, slow-cooked meat that's so tender it seems to fall off the bone. The secret, however, is to ask for your order with sweet sauce. The regular stuff tastes bland and bottled. All the side dishes, including the coleslaw, corn on the cob, and baked beans, look commercial, but are necessary to complete the experience. This is a jeans and T-shirt kind of place, but you may want to wear an elastic waistband, as overeating is not uncommon. A second Shorty's is located in Davie at 5989 S. University Dr. (© **305/944-0348**).

9200 S. Dixie Hwy. (between U.S. 1 and Dadeland Blvd.), South Miami. © 305/670-7732. Main courses $5–$9. DISC, MC, V. Mon–Thurs 11am–10pm; Fri–Sat 11am–11pm.

5 Hitting the Beach

Perhaps Miami's most popular attraction is its incredible 35-mile stretch of beachfront, which runs from the tip of South Beach north to Sunny Isles, and circles Key Biscayne and the numerous other pristine islands dotting the Atlantic.

Collins Avenue in **Miami Beach** fronts more than a dozen miles of white-sand beach and blue-green waters from 1st to 192nd streets. Although most of

Miami Attractions & Beaches

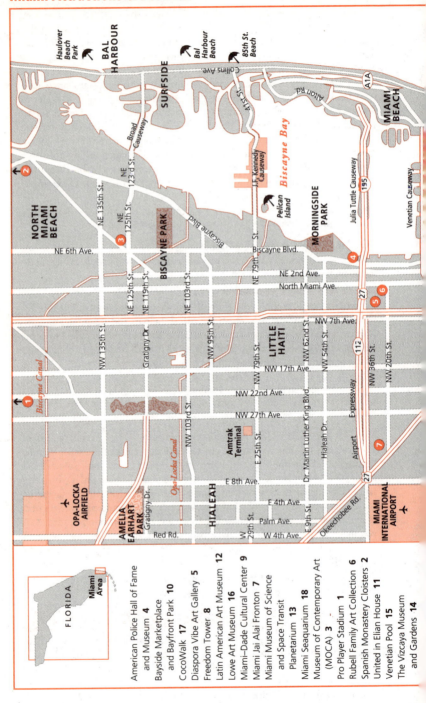

American Police Hall of Fame and Museum **4**
Bayside Marketplace and Bayfront Park **10**
CocoWalk **17**
Diaspora Vibe Art Gallery **5**
Freedom Tower **8**
Latin American Art Museum **12**
Lowe Art Museum **16**
Miami–Dade Cultural Center **9**
Miami Jai Alai Fronton **7**
Miami Museum of Science and Space Transit Planetarium **13**
Miami Seaquarium **18**
Museum of Contemporary Art (MOCA) **3**
Pro Player Stadium **1**
Rubell Family Art Collection **6**
Spanish Monastery Cloisters **2**
United in Elian House **11**
Venetian Pool **15**
The Vizcaya Museum and Gardens **14**

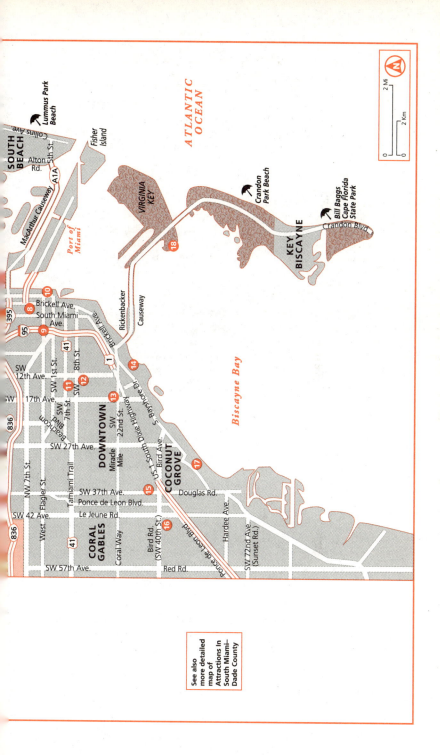

Cheap Thrills: What to See & Do for Free (or Almost) in Miami

- **Watch the sun set over downtown.** Driving west over the Julia Tuttle Causeway (Fla. 112), you can catch the best views in the city. Aqua, pink, and orange lights explode behind a cluster of skyscrapers, and the surrounding water reflects it all. Head back in the other direction, and catch the glow of neon decorating a cluster of towering palms.
- **Indulge in Ocean Drive's eye candy.** All along South Beach's Ocean Drive, the Champs Elysees of Miami, well-toned and tanned bodies abound. Scantily clad boys and girls, gender benders, leggy models, in-line skaters, and gawking tourists alike parade along the wide promenade, with a backdrop of cotton-candy–colored Art Deco buildings on one side and the glistening ocean on the other. If you're around in winter, you're almost guaranteed to find a preview fashion shoot in progress. Stake out a front row seat at any of the sidewalk cafes lining the strip where, for the price of a soda or a glass of wine, you'll be amused for hours.
- **Taste some Latin flavor in Little Havana.** To experience a little slice of Cuba on U.S. soil, stroll down Calle Ocho (8th St.) and stop into any of the shops catering to the huge exile population. Visit **Maximo Gomez Park,** 801 SW 15th Ave., where *viejitos* (old men) face off over chess boards from morning until sunset. Between 15th and 13th avenues is the street of *estrellas,* where stars like Celia Cruz have their names etched in the sidewalk, Hollywood-style. Visit a cigar factory, and then savor a *cafe con leche* at a local diner like Versailles (see "Great Deals on Dining," earlier in this chapter). There's no better way to get a feel for this city. (And if you don't *habla Español,* bring along a phrase book.)
- **Tour downtown from the Metro-Rail.** For 25¢, you can get a spectacular overview of Miami's bustling metropolis. The best part is, you can enjoy it all seated in the cool comfort of air-conditioned cars. It's like the monorail at Disney, but without the commentary.
- **Swim, stroll, and lounge on the beach.** Most of Miami's beaches are entirely free, though some in park areas do charge a fee for vehicles. You can enjoy miles of wide sandy beaches all along Miami Beach, where the water is calm and warm. South Beach between 5th and

this stretch is lined with a solid wall of hotels and condos, beach access is plentiful. There are lots of public beaches here, wide and well maintained, complete with lifeguards, bathroom facilities, concession stands, and metered parking (bring lots of quarters). Except for a thin strip close to the water, most of the sand is hard-packed—the result of a $10-million Army Corps of Engineers Beach Rebuilding Project meant to protect buildings from the effects of eroding sand.

In general, the beaches on this barrier island (all on the eastern, ocean side of the island) become less crowded the farther north you go. A wooden boardwalk runs along the hotel side of the beach from 21st to 46th streets—about 1½

20th streets has the most characters, from topless European women to super-buff body-builders.

- **Walk through the lobby of The Delano Hotel.** The **Delano**, 1685 Collins Ave., South Beach (© **305/672-2000**), is a tragically trendy outpost of seeing and being seen, with a gorgeous staff that competes for attention with the outlandish yet brilliantly minimalistic Philippe Starck decor. Check out the overflowing pool, out-of-proportion chess set, and funky (and pricey) gift shop. Splurge on a $10 drink poolside, and settle in for a few hours of celeb-spotting and people-watching. You won't be disappointed.

- **Sample the flavor of South Beach at its most venerated gourmet store.** A bunch of tomatoes might cost you $5 at **Epicure**, 1656 Alton Rd., Miami Beach (© **305/672-1861**), but if you can resist the temptation of buying the high-ticket items, this is a great place to browse and snack (for free—if you don't ask, you don't get!). On most days, a busy booth offers samples of anything from salsa to olive oils. Stop by the cheese department and taste a wedge of something exotic or familiar. The deli folks will happily share a forkful of chicken salad or a generous slice of nova to anyone who asks for a nibble, and the tough cookies at the bakery counter will soften up if you ask to sample a pastry or two.

- **Experience the real buzz of Coconut Grove at the Friday Night Wine Tasting Series.** For a mere $10, you can sample the fruits of the vine, get an earful from the gossipy local grapevine, and even down a few appetizers in the courtyard of the Mayfair House Hotel, 3000 Florida Ave., Coconut Grove (© **305/441-6409**) every Friday night. Who knows, you may even learn something about wine.

- **Rock out with headliners and legends at the Gulfstream Park Concert Series.** While some may consider acts like REO Speedwagon, Air Supply, and Cindy Lauper to be has-beens, devoted fans flock to see these groups and others live at this very popular concert series held at 21301 Biscayne Blvd., Hallandale. From January to April, the cost is free outside of the $5 charged for admission to the park. Call © **954/ 457-6940** for specific dates and times.

miles—offering you a terrific sun-and-surf experience without getting sand in your shoes. Aside from the beaches listed below, Miami's lifeguard-protected public beaches include 21st Street, at the beginning of the boardwalk; 35th Street, popular with an older crowd; 46th Street, next to the Fontainebleau Hilton; 53rd Street, a narrower, more sedate beach; 64th Street, one of the quietest strips around; and 72nd Street, a local old-timers' spot.

If Miami Beach doesn't provide the privacy you're looking for, try **Virginia Key** and **Key Biscayne**. Crossing the Rickenbacker Causeway ($1 toll), however, can be a lengthy process, especially on weekends, when beach bums and tan-o-rexics flock to the Key. The 5 miles of public beach there, however, are blessed with softer sand and are less developed and more laid-back than the hotel-laden strips to the north.

MIAMI'S BEST BEACHES

Crandon Park Beach ★ On Crandon Boulevard in Key Biscayne, you'll find this beach, National Lampoon's *Vacation* on the sand. It's got a diverse crowd consisting of dedicated beach bums and lots of leisure-seeking families, set to a soundtrack of salsa, disco, and reggae music blaring from a number of competing stereos. With 3 miles of oceanfront beach, bathrooms, changing facilities, 493 acres of park, 75 grills, three parking lots, several soccer and softball fields, and a public 18-hole championship golf course, Crandon is like a theme park on the sand. Admission is $2 per vehicle. It's open daily from 8am to sunset.

Lummus Park Beach ★★ Also called Glitter Beach, Lummus Park beach runs along Ocean Drive from about 6th to 14th streets on South Beach. It's the best place to go if you're seeking entertainment as well as a great tan. On any day of the week, you might spy models primping for a photo shoot, nearly naked (topless is legal on this beach) sun-worshippers avoiding tan lines, and an assembly line of washboard abs off which you could (but shouldn't) bounce your bottle of sunscreen. Restrooms and changing facilities are available on the beach, but don't expect to have a Cindy Crawford encounter in one of these. Most people tend to prefer using the somewhat drier, cleaner restrooms of the restaurants on Ocean Drive.

85th Street Beach ★ Along Collins Avenue, this beach is located away from the maddening crowds and is a great place to head for a swim. It's one of Miami's only stretches of sand with no condos or hotels looming over sunbathers. Lifeguards patrol the area throughout the day and restrooms are available, though they are not exactly the benchmark of cleanliness.

Hobie Beach ★★ On the side of the causeway leading to Key Biscayne, Hobie Beach is not really so much a beach as an inlet with predictable winds. This spot is perfect for windsurfing, and numerous rental spots dot the area in response. Restrooms are available.

Bal Harbour Beach ★ You'll find plenty of colorful shells at Bal Harbour Beach, Collins Avenue at 96th Street. There's also an exercise course and good shade—but no lifeguards, restrooms, or changing facilities.

Haulover Beach For that all-over tan, head here, just north of the Bal Harbour border, and join nudists from around the world in a top-to-bottom tanning session. Should you choose to keep your swimsuit on, however, there are changing rooms and restrooms. This area also gets some of Miami's biggest swells and is very popular with surfers.

Matheson Hammock Park Beach ★★★ Located at 9610 Old Cutler Rd. in South Miami (© **305/665-5475**), this beach is the epitome of tranquility, tucked away from the scene. It's a great beach for those seeking "alone time." It's also a great place to bring young children: Because of its man-made lagoon, which is fed naturally by the tidal movement of the adjacent Biscayne Bay, the waters are extremely calm, not to mention safe, and the area is secluded enough for families to keep an eye on the kids. Restrooms and changing facilities are available.

Attractions in Southern Miami–Dade County

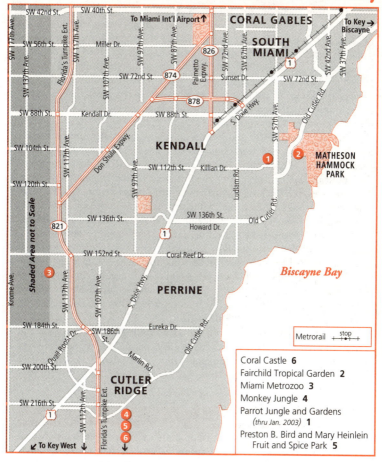

6 The Art Deco District

In South Beach, the Art Deco District is roughly bounded by the Atlantic Ocean on the east, Alton Road on the west, 6th Street to the south, and Dade Boulevard (along the Collins Canal) to the north. Simply put, Art Deco is a style of architecture that, in its heyday of the 1920s and '30s, used to be considered ultra modern. Today, fans of the style consider it retro-fabulous. According to the experts, Art Deco made its debut in 1925 in an exposition in Paris in which it set a stylistic tone, with buildings based on early neoclassical styles applied with exotic motifs like flora, fauna, and fountains based on geometric patterns. In Miami, Art Deco is marked by the pastel-hued buildings that line South and Miami Beach. But it's a lot more than just color. If you look carefully, you will see the intricacies and impressive craftsmanship that went into each building back in that day, which, in Miami's case was the '20s, '30s, and '40s, and now, thanks to intensive restoration, today.

Most of the finest examples of the whimsical Art Deco style are concentrated along three parallel streets—**Ocean Drive, Collins Avenue,** and **Washington**

Avenue—from about 6th to 23rd streets. If you're touring this unique neighborhood on your own, start at the **Art Deco Welcome Center,** 1001 Ocean Dr. (② **305/531-3484**), which is run by The Miami Design Preservation League. The only beachside building across from the Clevelander Hotel and bar, they give away lots of informational material including maps and pamphlets and run guided tours about the neighborhood. Art Deco books (including *The Art Deco Guide,* an informative compendium of all the buildings here), T-shirts, postcards, mugs, and other paraphernalia are for sale. It's open Monday to Saturday from 9am to 6pm, sometimes later.

Several tours of the Art Deco District are offered by **Miami Design Preservation League**. Each leaves from the Welcome Center. A self-guided **audio tour** (available 7 days a week, 10am–4pm) turns the streets into a virtual outdoor museum, taking you through the Art Deco District at your own leisure. The tours are offered in several languages for just $10 per person. **Guided tours** conducted by local historians and architects offer an in-depth look at the structures and their history. The 90-minute Ocean Drive and Beyond tour (offered every Sat at 10:30am) takes you through the district, pointing out the differences between Mediterranean Revival and Art Deco, for $15 per person. If you're not blinded by neon, the Thursday night Art Deco District Up-to-Date tour (leaving at 6:30pm) will whisk you around for 90 minutes, making note of how certain local hot spots were architecturally famous way before the likes of Madonna and Co. entered them. This tour costs $15. For more information on tours or reservations, call ② **305/672-2014.**

If you'd rather bike than walk, the **Art Deco Biking Tour** is a fun and interesting way to see the area, offered at 10am on the third Sunday of every month. The cost is $10 per person, plus $10 for a bike rental, and tours leave from the Miami Beach Bicycle Center, 601 5th St., South Beach. Call ② **305/674-0150** to reserve a spot.

7 Miami Art & Museums

Miami has never been known as a cultural mecca as far as museums are concerned. Though several exhibition spaces have made forays into collecting nationally acclaimed work, limited support and political infighting have made it a difficult proposition. Recently, however, things have changed as museums such as the Wolfsonian, the Museum of Contemporary Art, the Bass Museum of Art, and the Miami Art Museum have gotten on the bandwagon, boasting collections and exhibitions high on the lists of art aficionados.

Work continues to proceed on the **Miami Beach Cultural Park,** on Collins Park and Park Avenue (off Collins Ave.) and bounded by 21st to 23rd streets, which comprises a trio of arts buildings: the newly expanded Bass Museum of Art (see below), the new Arquitectonica-designed home of the Miami City Ballet, and the Miami Beach Regional Library, which broke ground in January 2001 and will have a special focus on the arts. The former site of the Miami Beach Library on Collins Park will return to its original incarnation as an open space extending to the Atlantic, but it will also be the site of large sculpture installations and cultural activities planned jointly by the organizations that share the space.

Listed below are Miami's most lauded museums, which have become a part of the city's cultural heritage, and as such, are as diverse as the city itself. For gallery lovers, see "Specialized Tours" under section 11, "Sightseeing Cruises & Organized Tours," of this chapter.

Bass Museum of Art ★★★
The Bass Museum of Art has expanded and received a dramatically new look, rendering it Miami's most progressive art museum. World-renowned Japanese architect Arata Isozaki designed the magnificent new facility, which has triple the former exhibition space, and added an outdoor sculpture terrace, a museum cafe and courtyard, and a museum shop, among other improvements. In addition to providing space in which to show the permanent collection, exhibitions of a scale and quality not previously seen in Miami will now be featured at the Bass. The museum's permanent collection includes European paintings from the 15th through the early 20th centuries with special emphasis on Northern European art of the Renaissance and baroque periods, including Dutch and Flemish masters such as Bol, Flinck, Rubens, and Jordaens. In 2001 an art lab opened, making it possible for all aspiring artists to create their own masterpieces on computers for free or a nominal charge.

2121 Park Ave. (1 block west of Collins Ave.), South Beach. © **305/673-7530.** www.bassmuseum.org. Admission $6 adults, $4 students and seniors; free for children 6 and under. Tues–Wed and Fri–Sat 10am–5pm; Thurs 10am–9pm; Sun 11am–5pm.

Holocaust Memorial ★★★
This heart-wrenching memorial is hard to miss and would be a shame to overlook. The powerful centerpiece, Kenneth Triester's *Sculpture of Love & Anguish,* depicts victims of the concentration camps crawling up a giant, yearning hand, stretching up to the sky, marked with an Auschwitz number tattoo. Along the reflecting pool is the story of the Holocaust, told in cut marble slabs. Inside the center of the memorial is a tableau that is one of the most solemn and moving tributes to the millions of Jews who lost their lives in the Holocaust I've seen. You can walk through an open hallway lined with photographs and the names of concentration camps and their victims. From the street, you'll see the outstretched arm, but do stop and tour the sculpture at ground level.

1933 Meridian Ave. (at Dade Blvd.), South Beach. © **305/538-1663.** www.holocaustmmb.com. Free admission. Daily 9am–9pm.

Wolfsonian–Florida International University ★★★ *Finds*
Mitchell Wolfson, Jr., heir to a family fortune built on movie theaters, was known as an eccentric, but I'd call him a pack rat. A premier collector of propaganda and advertising art, Wolfson was spending so much money storing his booty that he decided to buy the warehouse that was housing it. It ultimately held more than 70,000 of his items from controversial Nazi propaganda to the match collection of King Farouk of Egypt. Thrown into the eclectic mix are also zany works from great modernists such as Charles Eames and Marcel Duchamp. Wolfson then gave this incredibly diverse collection to Florida International University. The former 1927 storage facility has been transformed into a museum that is the envy of curators around the world. The museum is unquestionably fascinating and hosts lectures and rather swinging events surrounding particular exhibits.

1001 Washington Ave., South Beach. © **305/531-1001.** Admission $5 adults; $3.50 seniors, students with ID, and children 6–12; by donation Thurs 6–9pm. Mon–Tues and Fri–Sat 11am–6pm; Thurs 11am–9pm; Sun noon–5pm.

Diaspora Vibe Art Gallery ★★ *Value*
This art complex, housed in an old bakery, is a funky artist hangout and is home to some of the greatest artworks of Miami's diverse Caribbean, Latin American, and African-American cultures. On the last Friday of every month from May through October, the gallery holds its fabulous "Final Fridays," where the who's who of Miami's cognoscenti gather to recharge their cultural batteries. A new artist's work is spotlighted inside, while

Drive-by Art

You can see the following pieces of public art and prized architecture from the comfort of your car, if you like. Each is a free roadside attraction and a great photo opportunity if you're in the area.

- **Versace Mansion (Amsterdam Palace):** Morbid curiosity has led hordes of people to the only private home on Ocean Drive, better known as the Versace mansion. If you can get past the fact that the late designer was murdered on the steps of this palatial estate, you should definitely observe the intricate Italian architecture that makes this house stand out from its streamlined Deco neighbors. It was built in the 1930s as a replica of Christopher Columbus's son's palace in Santo Domingo. Today the house is owned by a private citizen from Texas. It's located at the northwest corner of Ocean Drive and 11th Street, South Beach.
- **Estefan Enterprises:** Miami's royal family—Gloria and Emilio Estefan—may reside on private Star Island, but the headquarters of their musical empire is located in a whimsical building designed by the world-famous Arquitectonica architecture company. Its facade is carved with color-lined waves and fanciful shapes. The address is 420 Jefferson Ave. (at 5th St.), Miami Beach.
- **Miami Beach Post Office:** Post offices are rarely considered a must-see, but this one's an exception. Built in 1937, this unusual and modern-looking Depression-era building features a fabulous rotunda. Utterly Floridian are the coral steps that lead to the entrance. Inside this magnificent building, an intricate sun motif on the ceiling surrounds a lantern, which illuminates an epic mural depicting some of South Florida's history. Find the post office at 1300 Washington Ave., Miami Beach.
- **Mermaid Sculpture:** A pop art masterpiece designed by Roy Lichtenstein, this sculpture captures the buoyant spirit of Miami Beach and its environs. It's in front of the Jackie Gleason Theater of the Performing Arts, 1700 Washington Ave., Miami Beach.
- **Morris Lapidus on Lincoln Road:** Famed designer/architect, the late Morris Lapidus—the "high priest of high kitsch"—who is best known for the Fountainebleau Hotel, created a series of sculptures that are angular, whimsical, and quirky. In addition to the sculptures on Lincoln Road (at Washington Ave.), which you can't miss, Lapidus also created the Colony Theater, 1040 Lincoln Rd., which was built by Paramount in 1943; the 1928 Sterling Building, 927 Lincoln Rd., whose glass blocks and blue neon are required evening viewing; and the Lincoln Theater, 555 Lincoln Rd., which features a remarkable tropical bas-relief.

outside in the courtyard are live music performances and readings of poetry and folk tales. Delicious Caribbean cuisine is also served, all for a $15 admission. 561 NW 32nd St., Studio 48 (Bakehouse Art Complex), Miami. © 305/759-1110. www.diasporavibe.com. Free admission; "Final Fridays" events $15. Mon–Fri by appointment; Sat–Sun 1–6pm. "Final Fridays" events May–Oct last Fri of the month 7–11pm.

Lowe Art Museum

Located on the University of Miami campus, the Lowe Art Museum has a dazzling collection of 8,000 works that include American paintings, Latin American art, Navajo and Pueblo Indian textiles, and Renaissance and baroque art. Traveling exhibits such as *Rolling Stone* magazine's photo collection also stop here. For the most part, the Lowe is known for its collection of Greek and Roman antiquities, and, as compared to the more modern MoCa, Bass, and Miami Art Museum, features mostly European and international art hailing back to ancient times.

University of Miami, 1301 Stanford Dr. (at Ponce de León Blvd.), Coral Gables. © 305/284-3603. Admission $5 adults, $3 seniors and students with ID. Donation day is first Tues of the month. Tues–Wed and Fri–Sat 10am–5pm; Thurs noon–7pm; Sun noon–5pm.

Miami Art Museum at the Miami–Dade Cultural Center

The Miami Art Museum (MAM) features an eclectic mix of modern and contemporary works by such artists as Eric Fischl, Max Beckmann, Jim Dine, and Stuart Davis. Rotating exhibitions span the ages and styles, and often focus on Latin American or Caribbean artists. There are also fantastic themed exhibits such as the Andy Warhol exhibit, which featured all-night films by the artist, make-your-own pop art, cocktail hours, and parties with local deejays. JAM at MAM is the museum's popular happy hour, which takes place the second Thursday of the month and is tied in to a particular exhibit.

The Miami–Dade Cultural Center, where the museum is housed, is a fortress-like complex designed by Phillip Johnson. In addition to the acclaimed Miami Art Museum, the center houses the main branch of the Miami–Dade Public Library, which sometimes features art and cultural exhibits, and the Historical Museum of Southern Florida, which highlights the fascinating history of the area.

101 W. Flagler St., Miami. © 305/375-3000. Admission $5 adults, $2.50 seniors and students; free for children under 12. Tues–Fri 10am–5pm; Sat–Sun noon–5pm. Third Thurs of each month 10am–9pm. Closed major holidays. From I-95 south, exit at Orange Bowl–NW 8th St. and continue south to NW 2nd St.; turn left at NW 2nd St. and go 1½ blocks to NW Second Ave.; turn right.

Miami Museum of Science and Space Transit Planetarium

The Museum of Science features more than 140 hands-on exhibits that explore the mysteries of the universe. Live demonstrations and collections of rare natural history specimens make a visit here fun and informative. Many of the demos involve audience participation, which can be lots of fun for willing and able kids and adults alike. There is also a Wildlife Center with more than 175 live reptiles and birds of prey. The adjacent Space Transit Planetarium projects astronomy and laser shows as well as interactive demonstrations of upcoming computer technology and cyberspace features.

AAA members receive a 25% discount here, and after 4:30pm, all ticket prices are half off. Tickets include entrance to all museum galleries, the planetarium, and the Wildlife Center.

Finds Checkmate

The World Chess Hall of Fame and Sidney Samole Chess Museum, 13755 SW 119th Ave. in South Miami (© **786/242-4255**), is eye-catching, housed in a 45-foot-tall chessboard-like structure. It features an interactive history of chess, an introduction to celebrity players, and computer-simulated, fully participatory games and challenges, among other attractions.

3280 S. Miami Ave. (just south of the Rickenbacker Causeway), Coconut Grove. © 305/646-4200 for general information or 305/854-2222 for planetarium show times. www.miamisci.org. $10 adults, $8 seniors and students, $6 children 3–12; free for children 2 and under. Laser shows $6 adults, $3 seniors and children 3–12. Museum of Science daily 10am–6pm; call for planetarium show times (last show at 4pm weekdays and 5pm weekends). Closed on Thanksgiving and Christmas Day.

Museum of Contemporary Art (MOCA) ★★★ MOCA boasts an impressive collection of internationally acclaimed art with a local flavor. It is also known for its forward thinking and ability to discover and highlight new artists. A high-tech screening facility allows for film presentations to complement the exhibitions. You can see works by Jasper Johns, Roy Lichtenstein, Larry Rivers, Duane Michaels, and Claes Oldenberg, plus there are special exhibitions by such artists as Yoko Ono, Sigmar Polke, John Baldessari, and Goya. Guided tours are offered in English, Spanish, French, Creole, Portuguese, German, and Italian.

770 NE 125th St., North Miami. © 305/893-6211. www.mocanomi.org. Admission $5 adults, $3 seniors and students with ID; free for children 12 and under. Tues by donation. Tues–Sat 11am–5pm; Sun noon–5pm. Closed major holidays and Mon.

Rubell Family Art Collection ★★★ *Finds* This impressive collection, owned by the Miami hotelier family, the Rubells, is housed in a former Drug Enforcement Agency warehouse in a sketchy area north of downtown Miami. The building looks like a fortress, which is fitting: Inside is a priceless collection of more than a thousand works of contemporary art, by the likes of Keith Haring, Damien Hirst, Julian Schnabel, Jean-Michel Basquiat, Paul McCarthy, Charles Ray, and Cindy Sherman. But be forewarned: Some of the art is extremely graphic and may be off-putting to some. The gallery changes exhibitions twice yearly, and there is a seasonal program of lectures and performances by prominent artists. As of press time, the gallery had plans to move to a larger space nearby toward the end of 2002; call ahead to confirm the location before your visit.

95 NW 29th St. (on the corner of NW First Ave. near the Design District), Miami. © 305/573-6090. Free admission. Thurs–Sat 9am–9pm and by appointment.

The Vizcaya Museum and Gardens ★★★ Sometimes referred to as the "Hearst Castle of the East," this magnificent villa is more Gatsby-esque than anything else you'll find in Miami. It was built in 1916 as a winter retreat for James Deering, co-founder and former vice president of International Harvester. The industrialist was fascinated by 16th-century art and architecture, and his

---

Fun Fact The Spanish Monastery Cloisters

Did you know that the alleged oldest building in the Western Hemisphere dates from 1133 and is located in Miami? The **Spanish Monastery Cloisters**, 16711 W. Dixie Hwy. (at NE 167th St.), North Miami Beach (© 305/945-1461; monastery@earthlink.net), were first erected in Segovia, Spain. Centuries later, newspaper magnate William Randolph Hearst purchased and brought them to America in pieces. The carefully numbered stones were quarantined for years until they were finally reassembled on the present site in 1954. Today it's often used as a backdrop for movies and commercials. Admission costs $5 for adults, $2.50 for seniors, and $2 children 3 to 12. The site is open Monday through Saturday 9am to 5pm and Sunday 1 to 5pm.

Freedom Tower

Driving north on Biscayne Boulevard in downtown Miami, you can't help but notice the dramatic **Freedom Tower,** 600 Biscayne Blvd. at NE 6th Street, built in 1925 and modeled after the Giralda Tower in Spain. The tower was bought by the U.S. General Services Administration in 1957 and used to process the over 500,000 Cubans fleeing their island following Castro's takeover. In 1997, the former Cuban American National Foundation chairman Jorge Mas Canosa bought and invested $30 million in the building, vowing to preserve it as Miami's version of the Statue of Liberty. He reopened it as the Cuban American National Foundation headquarters, envisioning it as the place in which a trade agreement with Cuba will be signed once the communist government falls. In the meantime, the building will also house a museum dedicated to the history of Cubans in the United States. For hours, directions, and more information, call © **305/592-7768.**

---

ornate mansion, which took 1,000 artisans 5 years to build, became a celebration of that period. The place is packed with European relics and works of art from the 16th to the 19th centuries. Most of the original furnishings, including dishes and paintings, are still intact. A free guided tour of the 34 furnished rooms on the first floor takes about 45 minutes, and the second floor is open to tour on your own. Outside the villa, lush formal gardens, accented with statuary, balustrades, and decorative urns, front an enormous swath of Biscayne Bay.

3251 S. Miami Ave. (just south of Rickenbacker Causeway), North Coconut Grove. © **305/250-9133.** www.vizcayamuseum.com. Admission $10 adults, $5 children 6–12; free for children 5 and under. Villa daily 9:30am–5pm (ticket booth closes at 4:30pm); gardens daily 9:30am–5:30pm.

8 Nature Preserves, Parks & Gardens

The Miami area is a great place for outdoors types, with beaches, parks, nature preserves, and gardens galore. For information on South Florida's two national parks, the Everglades and Biscayne National Park, see chapter 6.

The **Amelia Earhart Park**, 401 E. 65th St., Hialeah (© **305/685-8389**), has five lakes stocked with bass and bream for fishing; playgrounds; picnic facilities; and a big red barn that houses cows, sheep, and goats for petting and ponies for riding. Parking is free on weekdays and $3.50 per car on weekends. The park is open daily from 9am to sunset. To drive here, take I-95 north to the NW 103rd Street exit, go west to East Fourth Avenue, and then turn right. Parking is 1½ miles down the street. Hialeah is a half hour from downtown Miami.

At the historic **Bill Baggs Cape Florida State Recreation Area**, 1200 Crandon Blvd. (© **305/361-5811**), at the southern tip of Key Biscayne, about 20 minutes from downtown Miami, you can explore the unfettered wilds and enjoy some of the most secluded beaches in Miami. Bill Baggs has been consistently rated as one of the top 10 beaches in the U.S. for its 1¼ miles of wide, sandy beaches and its secluded, serene atmosphere. There's also a historic lighthouse built in 1825, which is the oldest building in South Florida. Bikes, hydro-bikes, kayaks, and many more water toys are rented here. It's a great place to picnic, and a newly constructed restaurant serves homemade Latin food. Admission is $4 per car with up to eight people, and the park is open daily from 8am to sunset. Tours of the lighthouse are available every Thursday through Monday at 10am and 1pm (arrive at least half an hour early to sign up, as only 10 people can join the tour at a time). Take I-95 to the Rickenbacker Causeway and take that all the way to the end.

The **Fairchild Tropical Garden** ★★★, 10901 Old Cutler Rd. in South Miami (© **305/667-1651;** www.ftg.org), contains a veritable rain forest of both rare and exotic plants, as well as 11 lakes and countless meadows, all spread across 83 acres. Palmettos, vine pergola, palm glades, and other unique species create a scenic, lush environment. More than 100 species of birds have been spotted at the garden, and it's home to a variety of animals. You should not miss the 30-minute narrated tram tour (tours leave on the hour 10am–3pm weekdays and 10am–4pm weekends) to learn about the various flowers and trees on the grounds. The 2-acre rain-forest exhibit, Windows to the Tropics, will save you a trip to the Amazon. Expect to spend a minimum of 2 hours here. Admission is $8 for adults, and free for children 12 and under. It's open daily, except December 25, from 9:30am to 4:30pm. Take I-95 south to U.S. 1, turn left onto Le Jeune Road, and follow it straight to the traffic circle; from there, take Old Cutler Road 2 miles to the park.

Located on Biscayne Bay in Coconut Grove, **The Kampong** ★★, 4013 Douglas Rd. (www.ntbg.org/kampong.html), is a must-see 7-acre botanical garden featuring a stunning array of flowering trees and tropical fruit trees including mango, avocado, and pomelo. The garden was first cultivated in the early 1900s by noted plant explorer David Fairchild, who traveled the world seeking rare plants of economic and aesthetic value for cultivation in the United States. In 1928, he and his wife, Marian, built a two-story residence here amid some of his collections, borrowing the Malaysian word *kampong* for his home in a garden. In the 1960s, the property was donated to the National Tropical Botanical Garden to promote and preserve this South Florida treasure. Tours are by appointment only, from Monday to Friday. Call © **305/442-7169.** Admission is $10. Take U.S. 1 to Douglas Road (SW 37th Ave.), and go east on Douglas Road for about a mile. The Kampong will be on your left.

Named after the late champion of the Everglades, the **Marjory Stoneman Douglas Biscayne Nature Center** ★, 6767 Crandon Blvd., Key Biscayne (© **305/361-6767;** www.biscaynenaturecenter.org), has just moved into a brand-new $4-million facility and offers hands-on marine exploration, hikes through coastal hammocks, bike trips, and beach walks. Local environmentalists and historians lead intriguing trips through the local habitat. Call to reserve a spot on a regularly scheduled weekend tour or program. About 25 minutes from downtown Miami, the area is open daily 10am to 7pm Memorial Day through Labor Day, and until 4pm the rest of year. Admission to the park is $4 per person; the nature center is free. To get there, take I-95 to the Rickenbacker Causeway Exit (no. 1), and take the Rickenbacker Causeway all the way until it

---

Finds Miami's Secret Garden

Because people are often so focused on the beach itself, the **Miami Beach Botanical Garden,** 2000 Convention Center Dr., Miami Beach (© **305/ 673-7256**), largely remains a secret. The lush, tropical 4½-acre garden is a fabulous, all-natural retreat from the hustle and bustle of the city. It's open Monday through Friday from 8:30am to 5pm, Saturday and Sunday from 9:30am to 5pm. Admission is free.

Kids The Venetian Pool

Miami's most beautiful and unusual swimming pool, dating from 1924, is honored with a listing in the National Register of Historic Places. Underground artesian wells feed the free-form lagoon, which is shaded by three-story Spanish porticos and features both fountains and waterfalls. During summer, the pool's 800,000 gallons of water are drained and refilled nightly thanks to an underground aquifer, ensuring a cool, *clean* swim. Visitors are free to swim and sunbathe here, and for a modest fee, you or your children can learn to swim during special summer programs. Visit the pool at 2701 DeSoto Blvd. (at Toledo St.), Coral Gables (© **305/460-5356**; www.venetianpool.com). Admission and hours vary seasonally, so call ahead. Children must be 38 inches tall to enter or provide proof of 3 years of age with birth certificate.

---

becomes Crandon Boulevard. The center is on the east side of the street. Driving time is about 25 minutes from downtown Miami.

The **Oleta River State Recreation Area**, 3400 NE 163rd St., North Miami (© **305/919-1846**), consists of 993 acres—the largest urban park in the state—on Biscayne Bay. With miles of bicycle and canoe trails, a sandy swimming beach, shaded picnic pavilions, and a fishing pier, Oleta River State Recreation Area offers visitors an outstanding outdoor recreational experience cloistered from the confines of the big city. Open daily 8am to sunset, admission for pedestrians and cyclists is $1 per person. Drivers are charged $2 when alone, or $4 for up to seven passengers (plus driver). A half-hour from downtown Miami, take 1-95 to Exit 17 (S.R. 826 East), and go all the way east until just before the causeway. The park entrance is on your right.

9 Animal Parks

Call the parks below to inquire about discount packages or coupons, which may be offered at area retail stores or in local papers.

Miami Metrozoo Kids   This 290-acre, sparsely landscaped complex (it was devastated by Hurricane Andrew) is quite a distance from Miami proper and the beaches—about 45 minutes—but worth the trip. The park is completely cageless—animals are kept at bay by cleverly designed moats. This is a fantastic spot to take younger kids; there's a wonderful petting zoo and play area, and the zoo offers several daily programs designed to educate and entertain. Residents include lions, two rare white Bengal tigers, a Komodo dragon, rare koala bears, a number of kangaroos, and an African meerkat. The air-conditioned Zoofari Monorail tour offers visitors a nice overview of the park. The zoo is always upgrading its facilities, including the impressive aviary. *Note:* The distance between animal habitats can be great, so you'll be doing a *lot* of walking here (there are many places to rest). Because the zoo can be miserably hot during summer months, plan these visits in the early morning or late afternoon. Expect to spend about 3 hours here.

12400 SW 152nd St., South Miami. © **305/251-0400**. www.zsf.org. Admission $8.95 adults, $4.75 children 3–12. Daily 9:30am–5:30pm (ticket booth closes at 4pm). Free parking. From U.S. 1 south, turn right on SW 152nd St. and follow signs about 3 miles to the entrance.

Miami Seaquarium ★ *Kids* *Overrated*   If you've been to Orlando's SeaWorld, you may be disappointed with Miami's version, which is considerably smaller and not as well maintained. You'll still need at least 2 hours to tour the 35-acre oceanarium and see the two most popular shows, the Flipper Show and Killer Whale Show. The highly regarded Water and Dolphin Exploration Program (WADE) allows visitors to touch and swim with dolphins in the Flipper Lagoon. The program costs $125 per person and is offered twice daily, Wednesday through Sunday. Call © 305/365-2501 in advance for reservations; children must be at least 52 inches tall to participate.

4400 Rickenbacker Causeway (south side), en route to Key Biscayne. © 305/361-5705. www.miami seaquarium.com. Admission $23.95 adults, $18.95 children 3–9; free for children under 3. Daily 9:30am–6pm (ticket booth closes at 4:30pm).

Monkey Jungle ★ *Overrated*   You have to love primates to get over the intense smell, flies, and humidity of the jungle here, but if they're your thing, you'll be in paradise. You'll see rare Brazilian golden lion tamarins and Asian macaques, plus there are no cages to restrain the antics of the monkeys as they swing and chatter around you. The Orangutans' Asiatic Ape Exhibit is especially amusing, and newer exhibits include the Cameroon Jungle and the Lemurs of Madagascar. Screened-in trails wind through acres of "jungle," and daily shows feature the talents of the park's most progressive pupils. Expect to spend about 2 hours exploring. The park's website sometimes offers downloadable discount coupons, so take a look before you visit.

14805 SW 216th St., South Miami. © 305/235-1611. www.monkeyjungle.com. Admission $15.95 adults, $12.95 seniors and active-duty military, $9.95 children 4–12. Daily 9:30am–5pm (tickets sold until 4pm). Take U.S. 1 south to SW 216th St., or from Florida Turnpike, take Exit 11 and follow the signs.

Parrot Jungle and Gardens ★★ *Kids*   This Miami institution will take flight from its current location in South Miami in the fall of 2002 and head north in the winter of 2003 to a new $46-million home on Watson Island, along the McArthur Causeway near Miami Beach. The island will double as a protected bird sanctuary, and the new 18.6-acre park will feature an Everglades exhibit, a petting zoo, and several theaters, jungle trails, and aviaries. Watch your head because flying above are hundreds of parrots, macaws, peacocks, cockatoos, and flamingos. Continuous shows star roller-skating cockatoos, card-playing macaws, and numerous stunt-happy parrots. There are also tortoises, iguanas, and a rare albino alligator on exhibit. The park's website sometimes offers downloadable discount coupons, so take a look before you visit.

Until the move: 11000 SW 57th Ave., Southern Miami–Dade County. © 305/666-7834. After the move: 1111 Parrot Jungle Trail, Watson Island (on the north side of MacArthur Causeway/I-395). © 305/372-3822. www.parrotjungle.com. Admission $15.95 adults, $13.95 seniors, $10.95 children 3–10. Daily 9:30am–6pm. Cafe opens at 8am. Take U.S. 1 south and turn left at SW 57th Ave., or exit Kendall Dr. from the Florida Turnpike and turn right on SW 57th Ave.

Sea Grass Adventures ★ *Value* *Kids*   Even better than the Seaquarium is Sea Grass Adventures, in which a naturalist from the Marjory Stoneman Douglas Biscayne Nature Center (see above) will introduce kids and adults to an amazing variety of creatures that live in the sea grass beds of the Bear Cut Nature Preserve near Crandon Beach on Key Biscayne. Not just a walking tour, you will be able to wade in the water with your guide and catch an assortment of sea life in nets provided by the guides. At the end of the program, participants gather on the beach while the guide explains what everyone's just caught, passing the creatures around in miniature viewing tanks. Call for available dates and reservations.

Marjory Stoneman Biscayne Nature Center, 6767 Crandon Blvd., Key Biscayne. ☏ **305/361-6767**. $10 per person. Daily 10am–4pm.

10 Especially for Kids

The following is a roundup of attractions that kids will especially enjoy. Details on each one can be found earlier in this chapter.

AMELIA EARHART PARK (p. 153)   This is the best park in Miami for kids. They'll like the petting zoos, pony rides, and a private island with hidden tunnels.

MARJORY STONEMAN DOUGLAS BISCAYNE NATURE CENTER (p. 154)   Kids seem to enjoy touching slimy marine animals and spotting unusual creatures out at sea. This brand-new exhibit and tour center offers lots of educational and fun programs.

MATHESON HAMMOCK PARK BEACH (p. 146)   With its man-made lagoon and calm waters, this is a great beach for small children.

MIAMI METROZOO (p. 155)   This completely cageless zoo offers such star attractions as a monorail "safari" and a petting zoo. Kids can take a ride on an elephant.

MIAMI MUSEUM OF SCIENCE AND SPACE TRANSIT PLANETARIUM (p. 151)   Kids can learn about space and science by trying the hands-on exhibits and watching entertaining cosmic shows. The space museum also offers child-friendly explanations for natural occurrences.

MIAMI SEAQUARIUM (p. 156)   Kids can touch, swim with, or kiss a dolphin and watch exciting performances.

PARROT JUNGLE AND GARDENS (p. 156)   Kids just love these well-trained feathered friends.

VENETIAN POOL (p. 155)   Kids can take a swimming lesson or just frolic in this fantasy lagoon with waterfalls and fountains.

11 Sightseeing Cruises & Organized Tours

BOAT & CRUISE-SHIP TOURS

You don't need a boating license or a zillion-dollar yacht to explore Miami by boat. Thanks to several enterprising companies, boat tours are easy to find, affordable, and an excellent way to see the city from a more liquid perspective.

Bay Escape ★ (☏ **305/373-7001**) is a 1-hour air-conditioned cruise which will take you past Millionaires' Row and the Venetian Islands, located just off Miami Beach, for just $10. There's also a food stand and cash bar. The tours are bilingual and leave from the Bayside Marketplace Marina, 401 Biscayne Blvd., downtown. Tickets cost $10 for adults; children 12 and under sail free. The Millionaires' Row tour leaves daily at 1, 3, 5, and 7pm. An evening party cruise (music and cash bar) leaves Friday and Saturday at 9pm and lasts 2 hours.

The ***Heritage Miami II*** **Topsail Schooner,** Bayside Marketplace Marina, 401 Biscayne Blvd., downtown (☏ **305/442-9697**), gives you a great feel of the water, as opposed to other tour company's cruising boats, and offers a relaxing ride and a fun way to see the city. The 2-hour cruise passes by Villa Vizcaya, Coconut Grove, and Key Biscayne, and puts you in sight of Miami's spectacular skyline and island homes. Call to make sure the ship is running on schedule, but tours generally leave September through May only, daily at 1:30, 4, and

> **Tips Go Ahead, Act Like a Tourist!**
>
> **The Miami Tourist Bus** may sound like a savvy traveler's worst nightmare, but if you want to see the city London-style on a double-decker diesel bus *and* get a tan, this is your best bet. Running daily from Aventura to Miami's Kendall suburb, the bus allows unlimited hop-on/hop-off service at popular stops such as Sunset Place, CocoWalk, and Bayside and has onboard commentary and history as you're being driven through the city. The bus also takes you through the Art Deco District and the tony Bal Harbour Shoppes, all for a $20 day pass. Weeklong passes are also available for $45. For more information, call © 305/573-8687 or log onto www.miamitouristbus.com.

6:30pm, and Friday through Sunday at 9, 10, and 11pm. The cost is $15 for adults, $10 for children 12 and under. On Friday, Saturday, and Sunday evenings, 1-hour tours priced at $10 per person are also offered if you want to see the lights of the city.

Not exactly a tour, per se, the **Water Taxi** ★★★ (© 305/467-6677; www.watertaxi.com) is a cheap and fantastic way to see the city via local waterways. There are two major routes, one running between Bayside Marketplace and the 5th Street Marina on South Beach; the second is basically a downtown water shuttle service between the various hotels downtown as well as the Port of Miami, the Hard Rock Cafe at Bayside, East Coast Fisheries, and Fisher Island. The cost is $7 one-way, $12 round-trip, and $15 for an all-day pass. The Bayside/South Beach trip is the best one to take because there aren't as many stops.

SIGHTSEEING TOURS

While there are several sightseeing tour operators in Miami, most, unfortunately, either don't speak English or are just plain shoddy. Out of all those available, **Miami Nice Excursion Travel and Service** ★, 18430 Collins Ave., Miami Beach (© 305/949-9180; miaminicetours.com), is the one we recommend. Pick your destination, and the Miami Nice tours will take you to the Everglades, Fort Lauderdale, South Beach, the Seaquarium, Key West, Cape Canaveral, or wherever else you desire. The best trip for first-timers is the City Tour, a comprehensive tour of the entire city and its various neighborhoods. Tours cost $29 to $55 for adults and $25 for children, depending on your destination, and are run daily between 7am and 10pm. Call ahead for directions to your pickup area.

SPECIALIZED TOURS

Dr. Paul George, a history teacher at Miami–Dade Community College and a historian at the Historical Museum of Southern Florida, leads knowledgeable and insightful tours through the Miami area. A set calendar of tours is available, all of them fascinating to South Florida buffs. Tours focus on neighborhoods, such as Little Havana, Brickell Avenue, or Key Biscayne, and on themes, such as Miami cemeteries and the Miami River. The often long-winded discussions can be a bit much for those who just want a quick look around, but Dr. George certainly knows his stuff. The cost is $15 to $25; reservations are required (© **305/375-1621**). Tours leave from the Historical Museum at 101 W. Flagler St., downtown.

The **Biltmore Hotel Tour** ★★★, 1200 Anastasia Ave., Coral Gables (© 305/445-1926; www.biltmorehotel.com), is a free Sunday walking tour of the hotel's beautiful grounds. The Biltmore is chock-full of history and mystery, including a few ghosts; go out there and see for yourself. Tours depart on Sundays at 1:30, 2:30, and 3:30pm. In addition, there are also free weekly fireside sessions that are open to the public and presented by Miami Storytellers. Learn about the hotel's early days and rich stories of the city's past. These wonderful sessions are held in the main lobby by the fireplace and are accompanied by a glass of champagne. Call ahead to confirm.

The **Coral Gables Art and Gallery Tour** ★★★ is a fabulous and *free* event that draws art aficionados and the generally curious to sip wine and analyze the various works of art displayed in the many galleries of Coral Gables. On the first Friday of every month, art lovers are shuttled to more than 20 galleries that participate in Gables Night. Gallery exhibits might include American folk, African, Native American, and Latin art, and photography. You can join the tour from outside any of the galleries in the area. Most galleries are on Ponce de León Boulevard, between SW 40th and SW 24th streets, and the vans run continuously from 7 to 10pm. For more information, call **Elite Fine Art** (© 305/448-3800), or stop by any of the galleries in the area.

Visit Miami–Dade's darker past from the 1800s to the present on the **Murder, Mystery, and Mayhem Bus Tour** ★★★. Explore the area's most celebrated crimes and criminals by video and bus, from the murder spree of the Ashley Gang to the most notorious murders and crimes of our century, including the murder of designer Gianni Versace. Historian Paul George conducts a most fascinating 3-hour tour of scandalous proportions. The tour leaves Saturdays at 10pm from the Dade Cultural Center, 101 W. Flagler St., Miami, and tickets cost $35. Advance reservations are required; call © 305/375-1621.

Less a tour than the artistic equivalent of a triathlon, the **Second Thursdays: Miami Beach Arts Night** ★★ is a free cultural open house in Miami Beach, held at various venues throughout the city. Hear a string quartet at an area church and then hop on the shuttle for a Haitian dance performance at the Miami Beach Recreation Center. A celebration of the arts, Second Thursdays are a wonderful way to explore the rich and diverse cultures that make the city such a fascinating melting pot. The event is held on the second Thursday of every month from 6 to 9pm. Call © 305/673-7600 (www.2ndthursdays.com) for venues.

Also see section 6, "The Art Deco District," for walking and bicycle tours of that area.

Eyeing the Storm

For Weather Channel fanatics and those who are just curious, the **National Hurricane Center,** Florida International University, 11691 SW 17th St., South Florida (© 305/229-4470), offers free tours before and after hurricane season. From January 15 through May 15, the tours explain everything from keeping track of storms to the history of some of the nation's most notorious and devastating hurricanes. Reservations are required.

12 Affordable Outdoor Pursuits

In addition to the outdoor options below, see section 5, "Hitting the Beach," and section 8, "Nature Preserves, Parks & Gardens," both earlier in this chapter.

BIKING The cement promenade on the southern tip of **South Beach** is a great place to ride, with views of sun, surf, and interesting people. Most of the big beach hotels rent bicycles, as does the **Miami Beach Bicycle Center,** 601 5th St., South Beach (© **305/674-0150**), which charges $5 per hour or $14 per day. Bikers can also enjoy more than 130 miles of paved paths throughout Miami, including the beautiful and quiet streets of **Coral Gables and Coconut Grove,** where old trees form canopies over wide, flat roads lined with grand homes and quaint street markers.

The terrain in Key Biscayne is perfect for biking, especially along the park and beach roads. If you don't mind the sound of cars whooshing by your bike lane, **Rickenbacker Causeway** is also fantastic, since it is one of the only bikeable inclines in Miami from which you get fantastic elevated views of the city and waterways. Be warned that this is a grueling ride, especially going up the causeway. **Key Biking,** 61 Harbor Dr., Key Biscayne (© **305/361-0061**), rents mountain bikes for $5 an hour or $15 a day.

If you want to avoid the traffic altogether, head out to **Shark Valley** in the Everglades National Park—one of South Florida's most scenic bicycle trails and a favorite haunt of city-weary locals. For more information, see chapter 6.

For a decent list of trail suggestions throughout South Florida, visit **www.geocities.com/floutdoorzone/bike.html**. *Biking note:* Children under the age of 16 are required by Florida law to wear a helmet, which can be purchased at any bike store or retail outlet selling biking supplies.

BOATING/JET-SKIING Private boat rental outfits include **Boat Rental Plus,** 2400 Collins Ave., Miami Beach (© **305/534-4307**), where 50-horsepower, 18-foot powerboats rent for some of the best prices on the beach. There's a 2-hour minimum and rates go from $99 to $449, including taxes and gas. They also have great specials on Sundays. Cruising is permitted only in and around Biscayne Bay; ocean access is prohibited. The rental office is at 23rd Street, on the inland waterway in Miami Beach. If you want a specific type of boat, call ahead to reserve.

Club Nautico of Coconut Grove, 2560 S. Bayshore Dr. (© **305/858-6258**), rents high-quality powerboats for fishing, water-skiing, diving, and cruising in the bay or ocean. All boats are Coast Guard–equipped, with VHF radios and safety gear. Rates range from $199 for 4 hours and $299 for 8 hours on weekdays, to as much as $419 for 8 hours on weekends. Another location is at the Crandon Park Marina, 4000 Crandon Blvd., Key Biscayne (© **305/361-9217**). For money-saving coupons, log onto .

Don't miss a chance to tour the islands on the back of your own powerful watercraft. Just watch out for the other speeding jet skiers and boaters who think they're in the Indy 500. Many beachfront concessionaires rent a variety of these popular (and loud) water scooters. Try **Tony's Jet Ski Rentals,** 3601 Rickenbacker Causeway, Key Biscayne (© **305/361-8280**), located on a private beach in the Miami Marine Stadium lagoon. Up to three people can ride their models, and rates range from $45 for a half hour to $80 for a full hour, depending on the number of riders.

FISHING Fishing licenses are required in Florida. If you go out with one of the fishing charter boats listed below, you are automatically accredited, but if

> **A Berry Good Time**
>
> South Florida's farming region has been steadily shrinking in the face of industrial expansion, but you'll still find several spots where you can get back to nature while indulging in a local gastronomic delight—picking your own produce at the "U-Pic-'Em" farms that dot South Dade's landscape. Depending on what's in season, you can get everything from fresh herbs and vegetables to a mélange of citrus fruits and berries. During berry season—January to April—it's not uncommon to see hardy pickers leaving the groves with hands and faces stained a telltale crimson and garnished with happy smiles. On your way through South Dade, keep an eye out for the bright red U-Pic signs.
>
> There are also a number of fantastic fruit stands in the region. **Burr's Berry Farms,** 12741 SW 216th St. (© **305/251-0145**), located in the township of Goulds about an hour from downtown Miami, has created a sensation with their fabulous strawberry milk shakes. To get there, go south on U.S. 1 and turn right on SW 216th Street. The fruit stand is about 1 mile west. It's open daily from 9am to 5:30pm.
>
> For fresh fruit in a tasty pastry or tart, head over to **Knaus Berry Farm** at 15980 SW 248th St. (© **305/247-0668**), in an area known as the Redlands. Some people erroneously call this farm an Amish farm, but in actuality it's run by a sect of German Baptists. The stand offers items ranging from fresh flowers to homemade ice cream, but be sure to indulge in one of their famous homemade cinnamon buns. Be prepared to wait in a long line to stock up—people flock here from as far away as Palm Beach. Head south on U.S. 1 and turn right on 248th Street. The stand is 2½ miles farther on the left-hand side. It's open Monday through Saturday from 8am to 5:30pm.

you go out on your own, you must have a Florida fishing license, which costs $16.50. Call © **888/FISH-FLORIDA** for more information.

Some of the best **surf casting** in the city can be had at **Haulover Beach Park** at Collins Avenue and 105th Street, where there's a bait-and-tackle shop right on the pier. **South Pointe Park,** at the southern tip of Miami Beach, is another popular fishing spot and features a long pier, comfortable benches, and a great view of the ships passing through Government Cut, the deep channel made when the port of Miami was dug.

You can also do some **deep-sea fishing** in the Miami area. One bargain outfitter, the **Kelley Fishing Fleet,** at the Haulover Marina, 10800 Collins Ave. (at 108th St.), Miami Beach (© **305/945-3801**), operates diesel-powered "party boats." The fleet emphasizes trolling and bottom fishing for snapper, sailfish, and mackerel. Half-day and night fishing trips are $29 for adults and $20 for children up to 10 years old; full-day trips are $40 for adults and $25 for children. Prices are $5 cheaper if you have your own rod. Daily departures are scheduled at 9am, 1:45pm, and 8pm; reservations are recommended.

Also at the Haulover Marina is the charter boat *Helen C* (10800 Collins Ave.; © **305/947-4081**). Captain Dawn Mergelsberg groups individuals together to get a full boat. Her *Helen* is a twin-engine 55-footer, equipped for big-game "monster" fish like marlin, tuna, dolphin fish, shark, and sailfish. The cost is $85 per person. Group rates and specials are also available. Sailings are scheduled for 8am to noon and 1 to 5pm daily; call for reservations. Children are welcome.

Bridge fishing in Biscayne Bay is also popular in Miami; you'll see people with poles over almost every waterway. But look carefully for signs telling you whether it's legal to do so wherever you are, since some bridges forbid fishing.

GOLF There are more than 50 private and public golf courses in the Miami area. Contact the **Greater Miami Convention and Visitors Bureau** (© **800/ 933-8448;** www.miamiandbeaches.com) for a list of courses and costs.

The **Biltmore Hotel** ★★, 1200 Anastasia Ave., Coral Gables (© **305/ 460-5364**), boasts modest greens fees and an 18-hole par-71 course located on the hotel's spectacular grounds. It must be good: Despite his penchant for privacy, former President Bill Clinton prefers teeing off at this course over any other in Miami! Green fees are $55 ($76 with cart) before 2pm and $27 ($48 with cart) after 2pm.

Crandon Park Golf Course, formerly known as the Links, 6700 Crandon Blvd., Key Biscayne (© **305/361-9129**), is ranked as the number one municipal course in the state and one of the top five in the country. The park is situated on 200 bay-front acres and offers a pro shop, rentals, lessons, carts, and a lighted driving range. The course is open daily from dawn to dusk; greens fees (including cart) are $86 per person during the winter and $45 per person during the summer. Special twilight rates are available.

One of the most popular courses among real enthusiasts is the **Doral Park Golf and Country Club,** 5001 NW 104th Ave., West Miami (© **305/ 591-8800**). Call to book in advance, since this challenging 18-holer is popular with locals and is one of the best in the country. The course is open from 6:30am to 6pm during the winter and until 7pm during the summer. Cart and greens fees vary, so call © **305/594-0954** for information.

Known as one of the best in the city, the **Golf Club of Miami,** 6801 Miami Gardens Dr., at NW 68th Avenue, North Miami (© **305/829-8456**), has three 18-hole courses of varying degrees of difficulty. You'll encounter lush fairways, rolling greens, and some history to boot. The west course, designed in 1961 by Robert Trent Jones and updated in the 1990s by the PGA, was where Jack Nicklaus played his first professional tournament and Lee Trevino won his first professional championship. The course is open daily from 6:30am to sunset. Cart and greens fees are $45 to $75 per person during the winter, and $20 to $34 per person during the summer. Special twilight rates are available.

Golfers looking for some cheap practice time will appreciate **Haulover Park Beach,** 10800 Collins Ave., Miami Beach (© **305/940-6719**), in a pretty bayside location. The longest hole on this par-27 course is 125 yards. It's open daily from 7:30am to 5:30pm during the winter, and until 7:30pm during the

---

Tips **Par for the Course**

You can get information about most Florida courses, including current greens fees and reserve tee times, through **Tee Times USA**, P.O. Box 641, Flagler Beach, FL 32136 (© **800/374-8633**, 888/465-3567, or 904/439-0001; fax 904/439-0099; www.teetimesusa.com). This company also publishes a vacation guide that includes many stay-and-play golf packages.

summer. Greens fees are $5 per person during the winter and $4 per person during the summer. Handcarts cost $1.40.

IN-LINE SKATING Miami's consistently flat terrain makes in-line skating a breeze. Lincoln Road, for example, is a virtual skating rink as bladers compete with bikers and walkers for a slab of slate. But the city's heavy traffic and construction do make it tough to find long routes suitable for blading. Because of the popularity of blading and skateboarding, the city has passed a law prohibiting skating on the west side (the cafe-lined strip) of Ocean Drive in the evenings as well as a law that all bladers must skate slowly and safely. Also, if you're going to partake in the sport, remember to keep a pair of sandals or sneakers with you, since many area shops won't allow you inside with skates on.

Despite all the rules, you can still have fun, and the following rental outfit can help chart an interesting course for you and supply you with all the necessary gear. In South Beach, **Fritz's Skate Shop,** 726 Lincoln Rd. Mall (© **305/ 532-1954**), rents top-quality skates, including safety pads, for $8 per hour, $24 per day, and $34 overnight. Skating lessons cost $25 an hour.

KAYAKING The laid-back **Urban Trails Kayak Company** rents boats at 10800 Collins Ave. in South Beach (© **305/947-1302**). The outfitters offer maps to solo paddlers, or you can join their very scenic 4-hour guided tours. The tours pass through rivers with mangroves and islands and cost $45 per person when less than 10 people are on the tour, or $35 per person when more than 10 people join. These must be booked in advance. Rates for solo rentals are $8 an hour, $20 for up to 4 hours, and $25 for over 4 hours. Tandems (for two people) are $12 an hour, $30 for up to 4 hours, and $35 for the day.

SAILING **Sailboats of Key Biscayne Rentals and Sailing School,** in the Crandon Marina (next to Sundays on the Bay), 4000 Crandon Blvd., Key Biscayne (© **305/361-0328** days, 305/279-7424 evenings), can get you out on the water. A 22-foot sailboat rents for $27 an hour or $81 for a half day. A Cat-25 or J24 is available for $35 an hour or $110 for a half day.

The Dezerland Beach Resort Hotel also rents sailboats through their beachfront concession desk (p. 110).

SCUBA DIVING & SNORKELING In 1981, the U.S. government began a wide-scale project to increase the number of habitats available to marine organisms. One of the program's major accomplishments has been the creation of artificial reefs in the Miami area, which have attracted all kinds of tropical plants, fish, and animals. In addition, Biscayne National Park (see chapter 6) offers a protected marine environment just south of downtown. **Diver's Paradise** of Key Biscayne, 4000 Crandon Blvd. (© **305/361-3483**), offers two dive expeditions daily to the more than 30 wrecks and artificial reefs off the coast of Miami Beach and Key Biscayne. You can take a 3-day certification course for $399, which includes all the dives and gear. If you already have your C-card, a dive trip costs about $90 if you need equipment and only $35 if you bring your own gear. Call ahead for times and locations of dives. For snorkeling, they will also set you up with equipment and maps on where to see the best underwater sights. Rental for mask, fins, and snorkel is $15.

South Beach Divers, 850 Washington Ave., Miami Beach (© **305/531-6110**), will also be happy to provide you with tips and rents a mask, fins, and snorkel for $30. They also offer dive trips to Key Largo three times a week and do dives off Miami on Sundays at $95 for a two-tank dive.

> **Finds** **Miami's Best Dive Bar**
>
> In May 2000, Jose Cuervo Tequila company celebrated Cinco de Mayo—or, as their clever marketing staff deemed it, Sinko de Mayo—by submerging an actual, $45,000 full-size margarita bar and six stools about 200 yards offshore from Ocean Drive and 3rd Street. Known as the **Jose Cuervo Underwater Bar,** the bar is 8 feet high and made of concrete and steel, lying 20 feet below the ocean's surface. Now an official artificial reef, it's one of South Beach's coolest—and most hidden—wreckreational watering holes.

SWIMMING There is no shortage of water in the Miami area. See the box "The Venetian Pool" in section 8, and "Hitting the Beach" in section 5, both earlier in this chapter, for descriptions of good swimming options.

TENNIS Hundreds of tennis courts in South Florida are open to the public for a minimal fee. Most courts operate on a first-come, first-served basis, and are open from sunrise to sunset. For information and directions, call the **City of Miami Beach Recreation, Culture, and Parks Department** (© 305/673-7730) or the **City of Miami Parks and Recreation Department** (© 305/575-5256).

Of the 590 public tennis courts throughout Miami, the three hard courts and seven clay courts at the **Key Biscayne Tennis Association,** 6702 Crandon Blvd. (© **305/361-5263**), are the best and most beautiful. Because of this, they often get crowded on weekends. You'll play on the same courts as Lendl, Graf, Evert, McEnroe, and other greats; this is also the venue for one of the world's biggest annual tennis events, the Nasdaq 100 Open. Only four courts are lit at night, but if you reserve at least 48 hours in advance, you can usually take your pick. They cost $6 per person per hour and are open daily from 8am to 9pm.

Other courts are pretty run of the mill and can be found in most neighborhoods. I do, however, recommend the **Miami Beach public courts at Flamingo Park,** 1001 12th St. in South Beach (© **305/673-7761**), where there are 19 clay courts that cost $2.50 per person an hour during the day and $3 per person an hour at night. It's first come, first serve.

WINDSURFING **Sailboards Miami,** Rickenbacker Causeway, Key Biscayne (© **305/361-SAIL**), operates out of big yellow trucks on Hobie Beach, the most popular windsurfing spot in the city. For those who've never ridden a board but want to try it, they offer a 2-hour lesson for $69 that's guaranteed to turn you into a wave warrior or you get your money back. After that, you can rent a board for $26 an hour or $38 for 2 hours. If you want to make a day of it, a 10-hour prepaid card costs $150. These cards require you to prepay, but they also reduce the price from $20 to $15 an hour. You can use the card all year, until the time on it runs out. Make your first right after the tollbooth to find the outfitters.

13 Spectator Sports

Check the *Miami Herald*'s sports section for a daily listing of local events and the paper's Friday "Weekend" section for comprehensive coverage and in-depth reports. For last-minute tickets, call the venue directly, since many season ticket holders sell singles and return unused tickets. Some tickets are also available through **Ticketmaster** (© **305/358-5885**).

BASEBALL The **Florida Marlins** shocked the sports world in 1997 when they became the youngest expansion team to win a World Series, but then floundered as their star players were sold off by former owner Wayne Huizenga. As long as the rebuilding process continues and the Marlins continue to struggle, tickets are easy to come by. If you're interested in catching a game, be warned: The summer heat in Miami can be unbearable, even in the evenings.

Home games are held at the **Pro Player Stadium,** 2267 NW 199th St., North Miami Beach (ⓒ 305/626-7426). Tickets are $4 to $30. Box office hours are Monday to Friday from 8:30am to 6pm, Saturday from 8:30am to 4pm, and before games; tickets are also available through Ticketmaster. The team currently holds spring training in Melbourne, Florida.

BASKETBALL The **Miami Heat** (ⓒ 305/577-HEAT or 305/835-7000), now led by celebrity coach Pat Riley, made its NBA debut in November 1988 and their games remain one of Miami's hottest tickets. Courtside seats are full of visiting celebrities from Puff Daddy to Madonna. The season lasts from October to April, with most games beginning at 7:30pm. They play in the brand-new waterfront **American Airlines Arena** located downtown on Biscayne Boulevard. Tickets are $14 to $50. Box office hours are Monday to Friday from 10am to 4pm (until 8pm on game nights); tickets are also available through Ticketmaster.

FOOTBALL Miami's golden boys are the **Miami Dolphins,** the city's most recognizable team, followed by thousands of "dolfans." The team plays at least eight home games during the season, between September and December, at **Pro Player Stadium,** 2267 NW 199th St., North Miami Beach (ⓒ 305/620-2578). Tickets cost between $20 and $40. The box office is open Monday to Friday from 8:30am to 5:30pm; tickets are also available through Ticketmaster.

HORSE RACING Located on the Dade–Broward County border in Hallandale (just north of North Miami Beach/Aventura) is **Gulfstream Park,** at U.S. 1 and Hallandale Beach Boulevard (ⓒ 305/931-7223; www.gulfstreampark.com), South Florida's very own version of the Kentucky Derby, albeit not nearly as scenery. This horse track is a haven for serious gamblers and voyeurs alike. Large purses and important races are commonplace at this sprawling suburban course, and the track is typically crowded, especially during its amusing and entertaining concert series from January to April featuring has-beens and one-hit wonders such as Cindy Lauper, REO Speedwagon, and Bryan Adams on the front lawn for just $5. Call for schedules. Admission is $3 to the grandstand and $5 to the clubhouse; parking is free. From January through March, post times are Wednesday to Monday at 1pm.

You might remember the pink flamingos at **Hialeah Park** ✪, 2200 E. Fourth Ave., Hialeah (ⓒ 305/885-8000; www.hialeahpark.com), from *Miami Vice.* This famous flamingo colony is the largest of its kind. The track, listed on the National Register of Historic Places, is one of the most beautiful in the world, featuring old-fashioned stands and acres of immaculately manicured grounds. Admission is $1 to the grandstand and $2 to the clubhouse on weekdays, and $2 and $4, respectively, on weekends. Children 17 and under enter free with an adult. Parking starts at $2. Races are held mid-March to mid-May. Call for post times. A free shuttle to the park leaves from the Marriott Miami Beach Hotel at 1st Street and Ocean Drive at 11am every Saturday and Sunday and departs the park at 5:30pm.

ICE HOCKEY The young **Florida Panthers** (ⓒ 954/835-7000) have already made history. In the 1994–95 season, they played in the Stanley Cup

> ### Jai Alai Explained
> Jai Alai originated in the Basque Country of Northern Spain, where players used to use church walls as their courts. The game looks very much like lacrosse, actually, with rules very similar to handball or tennis. The game is played on a court with numbered lines. What makes the game totally unique, however, is the requirement that the ball must be returned in one continuous motion. The server must bounce the ball behind the serving line and, with the basket, must hurl the ball to the front wall, with the aim being that, upon rebound, the ball will bounce between lines 4 and 7. If it doesn't, it is an under or over serve and the other team receives a point.

finals, and they have amassed a legion of fans who love them. Much to the disappointment of Miamians, they moved to a new venue in Sunrise, the next county north of Miami–Dade, more than an hour from downtown Miami. Call for directions and ticket information.

JAI ALAI Jai alai, sort of a Spanish-style indoor lacrosse, was introduced to Miami in 1924. Players use woven baskets, called *cestas*, to hurl balls, called *pelotas*, at speeds that sometimes exceed 170 miles per hour. Spectators, who are protected behind a wall of glass, place bets on the evening's players. The Florida Gaming Corporation owns the jai alai operations throughout the state, making betting on this sport as legal as buying a lottery ticket.

The **Miami Jai Alai Fronton,** 3500 NW 37th Ave., at NW 35th Street (© **305/633-6400**), is America's oldest fronton and Miami's main jai alai venue, dating from 1926. It schedules 13 games per night, which typically last 10 to 20 minutes but can occasionally go much longer. Admission is $1 to the grandstand, $5 to the clubhouse. There are year-round games on Monday and Wednesday to Saturday at 7pm and matinees on Monday, Wednesday, and Saturday at noon.

14 A Bargain-Hunter's Shopping Guide

Miami is one of the world's premier shopping cities; people come here from all over—from Latin America to Hong Kong—in search of all-American products. So if you're not into sunbathing and outdoor activities, or you just can't take the heat, you'll be in good company in one of Miami's many shops—and you are not likely to emerge empty-handed.

You may want to order the Greater Miami Convention and Visitors Bureau's "Shop Miami: A Guide to a Tropical Shopping Adventure." Although it is limited to details on the bureau's paying members, it provides some good advice and otherwise unpublished discount offers. Call © **800/283-2707** or 305/539-3034 for more information.

As a general rule, shop hours are Monday through Saturday from 10am to 6pm and Sunday from noon to 5pm. Many stores stay open late (until 9pm or so) one night of the week (usually Thurs). Shops in Coconut Grove are open until 9pm Sunday through Thursday and even later on Friday and Saturday nights. South Beach's stores also stay open later—as late as midnight. Department stores and shopping malls also keep longer hours, with most staying open from 10am to 9 or 10pm Monday through Saturday, and noon to 6pm on Sunday. With all these variations, call ahead to specific stores. The 6.5% state and local sales tax is added to the price of all purchases.

Most Miami stores can wrap your purchase and ship it anywhere in the world via United Parcel Service (UPS). If they can't, you can send it yourself, either through UPS (© 800/742-5877) or through the U.S. Postal Service (see "Fast Facts: Miami," earlier in this chapter).

SHOPPING AREAS

Most of Miami's shopping happens at the many megamalls scattered from one end of the county to the other; however, there is also some excellent boutique shopping and browsing to be done in the following areas:

AVENTURA   On Biscayne Boulevard between Miami Gardens Drive and the county line at Hallandale Beach Boulevard is a 2-mile stretch of major retail stores including Best Buy, Borders, Circuit City, Linens N' Things, Marshall's, Sports Authority, and more. Also here is the mammoth Aventura Mall, housing a fabulous collection of shops and restaurants.

CALLE OCHO   For a taste of "Little Havana," take a walk down 8th Street between SW 27th Avenue and SW 12th Avenue, where you'll find some lively street life and many shops selling cigars, baked goods, shoes, furniture, and record stores specializing in Latin music. For help, take your Spanish dictionary.

COCONUT GROVE   Downtown Coconut Grove, centered on Main Highway and Grand Avenue and branching onto the adjoining streets, is one of Miami's most pedestrian-friendly zones. The Grove's wide sidewalks, lined with cafes and boutiques, can provide hours of browsing pleasure. Coconut Grove is best known for its chain stores (Gap, Banana Republic, etc.) and some funky holdovers from the days when the Grove was a bit more bohemian, plus excellent sidewalk cafes centered around CocoWalk and the Streets of Mayfair.

MIRACLE MILE (CORAL GABLES)   Actually only a half-mile long, this central shopping street was an integral part of George Merrick's original city plan. Today, the strip still enjoys popularity, especially for its bridal stores, ladies' shops, haberdashers, and gift shops. Recently, newer chain stores, like Barnes & Noble, Old Navy, and Starbucks, have been appearing on the Mile.

DOWNTOWN MIAMI   If you're looking for discounts on all types of goods—especially watches, fabric, buttons, lace, shoes, luggage, and leather—Flagler Street, just west of Biscayne Boulevard, is the best place to start. I wouldn't necessarily recommend buying expensive items here, as many stores seem to be on the shady side and do not understand the word *warranty*. However, you can still have fun here as long as you are a savvy shopper and don't mind haggling with people who may not have the firmest grasp on the English language.

SOUTH BEACH   Slowly but surely South Beach has come into its own as far as shopping is concerned. While the requisite stores—Gap, Banana Republic, et al—have anchored here, several higher end stores have also opened on the southern blocks of Collins Avenue, which has become the Madison Avenue of Miami.

Impressions

Someday . . . Miami will become the great center of South American trade.

—Julia Tuttle, Miami's founder, 1896

For those who are interested in a little more fun with their shopping, consider South Beach's legendary Lincoln Road. This pedestrian mall, originally designed in 1957 by Morris Lapidus, recently underwent a multimillion-dollar renovation restoring it to its former glory. Here, shoppers find an array of clothing, books, tchotchkes, and art as well as a menagerie of sidewalk cafes flanked on one end by a multiplex movie theater and at the other by the Atlantic Ocean.

SHOPPING A TO Z

ANTIQUES/COLLECTIBLES Miami's antiques shops are scattered in small pockets around the city. Many that feature lower-priced furniture can be found in North Miami, in the 1600 block of NE 123rd Street, near West Dixie Highway. About a dozen shops sell china, silver, glass, furniture, and paintings. But you'll find the bulk of the better antiques in Coral Gables and in Southwest Miami along Bird Road between 64th and 66th avenues and between 72nd and 74th avenues. For international collections from Bali to France, check out the burgeoning scene in the Design District centered on NE 40th Street west of First Avenue.

Miami also hosts several large antiques shows each year. In October and November, the most prestigious one—the **Antique Show**—hits the Miami Beach Convention Center (© **305/754-4931**). Exhibitors from all over come to display their wares, including jewelry. There's also a decent monthly show at the **Coconut Grove Convention Center** (© **305/444-8554**). Miami's huge concentration of Deco buildings from the '20s and '30s makes this the place to find the best selections of Deco furnishings and decorations.

A word to the serious collectors: Dania Beach, up in Broward County (see chapter 7), about half an hour from downtown Miami, is the best place for antiques (it's known as the antiques capital of South Florida), so you may want to consider browsing in Miami and shopping up there.

BOOKS With half a dozen outlets in the area and more on the way, **Barnes & Noble** offers anything readers could ask for, including a comfortable cafe, a large children's section, and tons of magazines. Plus, the chain gives you a 10% discount on all best-sellers as well as incredible closeout specials. Though there are more than six locations in Miami. The branch at 152 Miracle Mile, Coral Gables (© **305/446-4152**), has an especially nice little scene, featuring local intellectuals, students, and professors from the nearby University of Miami.

A dedicated following turns out to browse **Books & Books,** a warm and wonderful little independent shop. Enjoy the upstairs antiquarian room at the 265 Aragon Ave. branch, Coral Gables (© **305/442-4408**), which specializes in art books and first editions; or attend one of the free lectures by noted authors, experts, and personalities almost nightly, from Monica Lewinsky to Martin Amis. The 933 Lincoln Rd. location in South Beach (© **305/532-3222**) stocks a large selection of gay literature and also features lectures.

At **Kafka's Cyberkafe,** 1464 Washington Ave., South Beach (© **305/673-9669**), check your e-mail and surf the Web while you sip a latte or snack on a sandwich or pastry with friendly neighborhood regulars. This popular used bookstore also stocks a wide range of foreign and domestic magazines and caters to an international youth hostel-type crowd.

CIGARS Although it is illegal to bring Cuban cigars into the United States, somehow, forbidden *Cohibas* show up at every dinner party and nightclub in town. Not that I condone it, but if you hang around the cigar smokers in town, no doubt one will be able to tell you where you can get some of the highly-prized contraband. Be careful, however, of counterfeits, which are typically Dominican cigars posing as Cubans. Cuban cigars are illegal and unless you go down a sketchy alley to buy one from a dealer (think of it as shady as a drug deal), you are going to be smoking Dominican ones.

The following stores sell excellent hand-rolled cigars made with domestic- and foreign-grown tobacco. Many of the *viejos* (old men) got their training in Cuba working for the government-owned factories in the heyday of Cuban cigars. **La Gloria Cubana,** 1106 SW 8th St., Little Havana (✆ **305/858-4162**), is a tiny storefront shop that employs about 45 veteran Cuban rollers, who sit all day rolling the very popular torpedoes and other critically acclaimed blends. They're usually back ordered, but it's worth stopping in. **Mike's Cigars,** 1030 Kane Concourse (at 96th St.), Bay Harbor Island (✆ **305/866-2277**), recently moved to this new location, but it's one of the oldest and best smoke shops in town. Since 1950, Mike's has been selling the best from Honduras, the Dominican Republic, and Jamaica, as well as the very hot local brand, La Gloria Cubana. Many say it has the best prices, too. Mike's has the biggest selection of cigars in town and the employees speak English.

FASHION Miami didn't become a fashion capital until—believe it or not— the pastel-hued, Armani-clad cops on *Miami Vice* had their close-ups on the tube. Before that, Miami was all about old men in white patent leather shoes and well-tanned women in bikinis. How things have changed! Miami is now a fashion mecca in its own right, with some of the same high-end stores you'd find on Rue de Faubourg St. Honore in Paris or Bond Street in London in Miami's South Beach and Bal Harbour. For more mainstream (and affordable) shopping, Miami boasts a plethora of malls and outdoor shopping and entertainment complexes. See "Malls" later in this section for a list of the best offerings.

FOOD There are dozens of ethnic markets in Miami, from Cuban bodegas to Jamaican import shops and Guyanese produce stands. Check the phone book under "Grocers" for listings. On Saturday mornings, vendors set up stands loaded with papayas, melons, tomatoes, and citrus fruits as well as cookies, ice creams, and sandwiches on South Beach's Lincoln Road.

At **Biga Bakery,** 305 Alcazar, Coral Gables (✆ **305/446-2111**), you'll be happy to pay upward of $6 a loaf when you sink your teeth into these inimitable old-world–style breads. Also, most of the locations have a to-die-for prepared food counter serving up everything from chicken curry salad to hummus and pot pies. Pastries and cakes are as gorgeous as they are delicious. Check the phone book for other locations. **Epicure,** 1656 Alton Rd., Miami Beach (✆ **305/672-1861**), is the closest thing Miami Beach has got to the famed Balducci's or Dean & DeLuca. Here, you'll find not only fine wines, cheeses, meats, fish, and juices, but some of the best produce, such as portobello mushrooms the size of a yarmulke. This neighborhood landmark is best known for supplying the Jewish residents of the beach with all their Jewish favorites, such as matzo ball soup, gefilte fish, and deli items. Prices are steep, but generally worth it. The cakes in particular are rich and decadent, and a rather large one doesn't cost more than $10.

Anything a gourmet or novice cook could desire can be found at **Gardner's Market,** at 7301 Red Rd., South Miami (✆ **305/667-9953**); 8287 SW 124th St., Pinecrest (✆ **305/255-2468**); or 651 Brickell Key Dr., downtown (✆ **305/371-3701**). One of the oldest and best grocery stores in Miami, all locations offer great take-out and the freshest produce. At **La Brioche Doree,** 4017 Prairie Ave., Miami Beach (✆ **305/538-4770**), you'll find luscious pastries and breads, plus soup and sandwiches at lunch. This tiny storefront off 41st Street is packed most mornings with French expatriates and visitors who crave the real thing. No one makes a better croissant.

Anything Italian you want—homemade ravioli, hand-cut imported Romano cheese, plus fresh fish and meats—can be found at **Laurenzo's Italian Supermarket and Farmer's Market,** 16385 and 16445 W. Dixie Hwy., North Miami Beach (© **305/945-6381** or 305/944-5052). Laurenzo's also offers one of the most comprehensive wine selections in the city. Be sure to see the neighboring store full of just-picked herbs, salad greens, and vegetables from around the world. A daily farmer's market is open from 7am to 6pm, and incredible daily specials lure thrifty shoppers from all over the city.

JEWELRY At least 50 reputable jewelers hustle their wares from individual counters at the **International Jeweler's Exchange,** one of the city's most active jewelry centers. Haggle your brains out for excellent prices on timeless antiques from Tiffany's, Cartier, or Bulgari, or on unique designs you can create yourself. You'll find the Exchange at 18861 Biscayne Blvd. (in the Fashion Island), North Miami Beach (© **305/931-7032**).

MALLS You can find any number of nationally known department stores among Miami's shopping centers, including Saks Fifth Avenue, Macy's, Lord & Taylor, Sears, and JC Penney, but Miami's own is **Burdines,** at 22 E. Flagler St., downtown (© **305/835-5151**), and 1675 Meridian Ave. (just off Lincoln Rd.) in South Beach (© **305/674-6311**). One of the oldest and largest department stores in Florida, Burdines specializes in good-quality home furnishings and fashions.

Aventura Mall, 19501 Biscayne Blvd. (at 197th St. near the Dade–Broward County line), Aventura (© **305/935-1110**), stands out among the plethora of Miami malls after a multimillion-dollar makeover. With more than 2.3 million square feet of space, this airy, Mediterranean-style mall has a 24-screen movie theater and more than 250 stores, including megastores JC Penney, Lord & Taylor, Macy's, Bloomingdale's, Sears, and Burdines. The mall offers moderate to high-priced merchandise and is extremely popular with families. A large indoor playground, Adventurer's Cove, is a great spot for kids, and the mall frequently offers activities and entertainment for children.

A popular stop for cruise-ship passengers, the touristy waterfront **Bayside Marketplace,** 401 Biscayne Blvd., downtown (© **305/577-3344**), is filled with the usual suspects of chain stores as well as a slew of tacky gift shops and carts. While we wouldn't recommend you necessarily drop big money at Bayside, you should go by just for the view of Biscayne Bay and the Miami skyline. In June you can watch the Opsail sailboat show, and in February, the Miami Sailboat Show, when sailboats dock in the area and make the view even nicer. Beware of the adjacent amphitheater known as Bayfront Park, which usually hosts large-scale concerts and festivals, causing major pedestrian and vehicle traffic jams.

CocoWalk, 3015 Grand Ave., Coconut Grove (© **305/444-0777**), is a lovely outdoor Mediterranean-style mall with the usual fare of Americana. Its open-air–style architecture is inviting not only for shoppers but also for friends or spouses of shoppers who'd prefer to sit at an outdoor cafe while said shopper is busy in the fitting room. A multiplex movie theater is also here, which comes in handy when there are big sales going on and the stores are mobbed. e **Streets of Mayfair,** 2911 Grand Ave. (just east of Commodore Plaza), Coconut Grove (© **305/448-1700**), was meant to compete with the CocoWalk shopping Complex (just across the street), but pales in comparison. This sleepy, labyrinthine neighbor contains a movie theater, several top-quality shops, a bookstore, restaurants, art galleries, bars, and nightclubs.

Traffic to the **Falls Shopping Center,** 8888 Howard Dr. (at the intersection of U.S. 1 and 136th St., about 3 miles south of Dadeland Mall), Kendall (✆ **305/255-4570**), borders on brutal, but once you get there, you'll feel a slight sense of serenity. Tropical waterfalls are the setting for this outdoor shopping center with dozens of moderately priced and slightly upscale shops. Miami's first Bloomingdale's is here, as are Polo, Ralph Lauren, Caswell-Massey, and more than 60 other specialty shops. A recent renovation added Macy's, Crate & Barrel, Brooks Brothers, and Pottery Barn, among others. If you are planning to visit any of the nearby attractions, which include Metro Zoo and Monkey Jungle, check with customer service for information on discount packages.

Completed in early 1999 at a cost of over $140 million, the sprawling outdoor **Shops at Sunset Place,** 5701 Sunset Dr. (at 57th Ave. and U.S. 1, near Red Rd.), South Miami (✆ **305/663-0482**), offers a calming setting as well. Visitors are blanketed by high-tech special effects, such as daily tropical storms (minus the rain) and the electronic chatter of birds and crickets, while they browse. In addition to a 24-screen movie complex and an IMAX theater, there's a GameWorks (Steven Spielberg's Disney-esque playground for kids and adults), a Virgin Records store, and a NikeTown, as well as mall standards.

Miami's **Sawgrass Mills,** 12801 W. Sunrise Blvd., Sunrise (west of Fort Lauderdale; ✆ **954/846-2300**), is the largest outlet mall in the country. Depending on what type of shopper you are, this experience can either be blissful or overwhelming. If you've got the patience, it is worth setting aside a day to do the entire place. Though it's located in Broward County, it is a phenomenon that attracts thousands of tourists and locals sniffing out bargains. From Miami, buses run three times daily; the trip takes just under an hour. Call **Coach USA** (✆ **305/887-6223**) for exact pick-up points at major hotels. The price is $10 for a round-trip ticket. If you are driving, take I-95 north to 595 west to Flamingo Road. Exit and turn right, driving 2 miles to Sunrise Boulevard. You can't miss this monster on the left. Parking is free, but don't forget where you parked your car or you might spend a day looking for it. **Dolphin Mall,** Florida Turnpike at S.R. 836, West Miami (✆ **305/365-7446**), rivals Sawgrass Mills with its 1.4-million-square-foot outlet mall. It features outlets such as Off Fifth, plus several discount shops, a 28-screen movie theater, and, not to be outdone by the Mall of the America in Minnesota, a roller coaster.

MUSIC **Blue Note Records,** 16401 NE 15th Ave., North Miami Beach (✆ **305/940-3394**), is music to the ears of music fanatics, with a good selection of hard-to-find progressive and underground music. There are new, used, and discounted CDs and old vinyl, too. Call to find out about performances; some great names show up occasionally. A second location features jazz and LPs only: 2299 NE 164th St., North Miami Beach (✆ **305/354-4563**). Also, at **Revolution Records and CDs,** 1620 Alton Rd., Miami Beach (✆ **305/673-6464**), you'll find a quaint and fairly well-organized collection of CDs, from hard-to-find jazz to original recordings of Buddy Rich. They'll search for anything and let you hear whatever you like.

Yesterday and Today Records, 7902 NW 36th St., Miami (✆ **305/468-0311**), is Miami's most unique and well-stocked store for vinyl—you know, the audio dinosaur that went out with the Victrola? Y & T, as it's known, is a collector's heaven, featuring every genre of music imaginable on every format. Chances are, you could find some eight-track tapes, too.

The young, hip salespeople at **Casino Records Inc.,** 1208 SW 8th St., Little Havana (C 305/856-6888), tend to be Latin music buffs and know their stuff. This store has the largest selection of Latin music in Miami, including pop icons such as Willy Chirino, Gloria Estefan, Albita, and local boy Nil Lara. Their slogan translates to "If we don't have it, forget it." Believe me, they've got it. According to the experts, **Esperanto Music,** 513 Lincoln Rd., Miami Beach (C 305/ 534-2003), might be an even better stop. An independently owned record store, Esperanto boasts an incredible collection of Cuban and Latin music.

THRIFT STORES/RESALE SHOPS Selling everything from layettes to overalls, the **Children's Exchange,** 1415 Sunset Dr., Coral Gables (C 305/ 666-6235), is a pleasant little shop chock-full of good Florida-style stuff for kids to wear to the beach and in the heat. **Red White & Blue,** 12640 NE Sixth Ave., North Miami (C 305/893-1104), offers especially good deals on children's clothes and housewares. Miami's best-kept secret, this mammoth thrift store is meticulously organized and well stocked.

Rags to Riches, 12577 Biscayne Blvd., North Miami (C 305/891-8981), is an old-time consignment shop where you might find some decent rags, and maybe even some riches. Though not as upscale as it used to be, this place is still a good spot for costume jewelry and shoes. At **Douglas Gardens Jewish Home and Hospital Thrift Shop,** 5713 NW 27th Ave., North Miami Beach (C 305/ 638-1900), prices are no longer the major bargain they once were, but for housewares and books, you can do all right. Call to see if they are offering any specials for seniors or students.

15 Affordable Fun After Dark

With all the hype, you'd expect Miami to have long outlived its 15 minutes of fame by now. But you'd be wrong: Miami's nightlife, especially in South Beach, is hotter than ever before, and getting still hotter. Though South Beach is certainly Miami's uncontested nocturnal nucleus, more and more diverse areas, such as the Design District, South Miami, and even Little Havana, are increasingly providing fun after-dark alternatives—without the ludicrous cover charges, "fashionably late" hours of operation (things don't typically get started on South Beach until after 11pm), lack of sufficient self-parking, or outrageous drink prices that come standard in South Beach.

Outside of Miami's raging bar and club scene, you can also find a variety of first-rate diversions in theater, music, and dance here, including a world-class ballet under the aegis of Edward Villella, a recognized symphony, and a talented opera company.

For up-to-date listing information, and to make sure time hasn't elapsed for the club of the moment, check the *Miami Herald*'s "Weekend" section, which runs on Friday, or the more comprehensive listings in *New Times,* Miami's free alternative weekly, available each Wednesday. You can also visit www.miami.city search.com online for the latest on nightlife activity around the city.

THE CLUB & MUSIC SCENE
DANCE CLUBS

Clubs are as much a cottage industry in Miami as is, say, cheese in Wisconsin. On any given night in Miami, there's something going on. Short of throwing a glammy event for the grand opening of a new gas station, Miami is very party hearty, celebrating everything from the fact that it's Tuesday night to the debut of a hot new DJ. Within this very bizarre after-dark community, a very colorful assortment of characters emerge, from your (a)typical nine-to-fivers to shady characters who have reinvented themselves as hot shots on the club circuit. While this scene of seeing and being seen may not be your cup of Absolut, it's certainly never boring.

Though things generally don't get started here before 11pm, you might consider arriving in the area earlier in the evening and killing some time by strolling around, having something to eat, or sipping a cocktail in a hotel bar. This diversion saves you from the likelihood of an absurd $20 valet charge for what's left of parking spaces later in the evening. Another advantage of arriving a bit earlier than the crowds is that some clubs don't charge a cover before 11pm or midnight, which could save you a wad of cash over time.

> **Impressions**
>
> Miami is where neon goes to die.
>
> —Lenny Bruce

Another way to avoid Miami clubs' ridiculous $20 cover charges is to make your way onto the guest list (see the box, "Ground Rules: Stepping Out in Miami," below). If your hotel lacks a concierge with connections, it's fairly easy to get on the guest list simply by calling the club ahead of time. Being on the list will often diminish or eliminate the cover charge.

Most dance clubs open at 10pm and close just before the sun rises, between 4am and 5am, though some in downtown Miami may stay open until after 8am. *Note:* Cover charges and days of operation are very haphazard here, so always call ahead.

Bermuda Bar and Grill This North Miami Beach spot is a sanctuary for those who'd rather not deal with the hustle, bustle, and hassle of driving and parking in South Beach or Coconut Grove. Bermuda Bar is a mega-dance club that is often frequented by young suburban professionals. Good pizzas and grilled foods are available, too. It's usually open until the sun comes up. Wednesday's ladies' nights are particularly popular, when women drink free and men are at their mercy. Open Wednesday to Saturday. 3509 NE 163rd St., North Miami Beach. © 305/945-0196. Cover $0–$10. No cover before 9pm.

Bongos Cuban Café Gloria Estefan's latest hit in the restaurant business pays homage to the sites, sounds, and cuisine of pre-Castro Cuba. Bongo's is a mammoth restaurant attached to the American Airlines Arena in downtown Miami. On Friday and Saturday after 11:30pm, it's transformed from a friendly family restaurant into the city's hottest 21-and-over salsa nightclub. Cover charge at that time is a hefty $20, but if you arrive earlier and grab some food, you won't be charged extra. Prepare yourself for standing room only. Open Wednesday to Sunday. At the American Airlines Arena, 601 Biscayne Blvd., downtown Miami. © 786/777-2100. Cover $20.

Club Space Clubland hits the mainland with this cavernous downtown warehouse of a club. With over 30,000 square feet of dance space, you can spin around a la Stevie Nicks (albeit to a techno beat) without having to worry about banging into someone. However, after hours (around 2am), Club Space packs them in. While Saturday caters to a more homogeneous and gay crowd, Friday is a free-for-all. Conveniently, the club often runs shuttles from the beach; call for more information, as it doesn't have a concrete schedule. Open Friday to Saturday in addition to special events. 142 NE 11th St., Miami. © 305/577-1007. Cover $0–$20 depending on the DJ.

crobar *Finds* Still haunted by the ghost of clubs past, the space formerly known as the Cameo Theatre is now possessed by the mod, millennial, industrial spirit that is crobar. With its intense, dance-heavy sound system, an industrially chic ambience, and crowds big enough to scare away any memories of a sadly abandoned Cameo, this Chicago import has raised the bar on South Beach nightlife with crazy theme nights (the monthly Sex night is particularly, uh, stimulating), top-name deejays, and the occasional celebrity appearance. On Sunday, the club hosts an extremely popular gay night known as Anthem. (See "The Gay & Lesbian Scene," later in this section.) Open daily. 1445 Washington Ave., South Beach. © 305/531-8225. www.crobarmiami.com. Cover $25.

Level Overdone and some say overhyped, Level takes the notion of South Beach excess even further with its outlet mall-size, 40,000-square-foot space featuring four dance floors, three levels, five rooms, and nine bars. Like a video game, your status here is determined by which level you can land on. If you befriend one of the club's owners, you may end up at the top. Leveling out the competition, this club has cornered the market on parties and events, throwing one nearly every night. Because it is the largest club on the beach, the velvet rope scene can be quite harassing, but if you call in advance, the accommodating staff will usually put you on the guest list, which means you don't have to pay the cover, though you will still have to wait in line. Friday night is a very popular gay night, while the rest of the week attracts a mixed crowd of straights, gays, and somewhere in betweens. Celebs love Level because it has so many VIP rooms. Open Monday and Thursday to Saturday. 1235 Washington Ave., South Beach. © 305/532-1525. www.levelnightclub.com. Cover $20–$30.

> **Tips — Ground Rules: Stepping Out in Miami**
>
> - Nightlife on South Beach doesn't really get going until after 11pm. As a result, you may want to consider taking what is known as a disco nap so that you'll be fully charged until the wee hours.
> - If you're unsure of what to wear out on South Beach, your safest bet will be anything black.
> - Do *not* try to tip the doormen manning the velvet ropes. That will only make you look desperate and you'll find yourself standing outside for what will seem like an ungodly amount of time. Instead, try to land your name on the ever-present guest lists by calling the club early in the day yourself, or, better yet, having the concierge at your hotel do it for you. Concierges have connections. If you don't have connections and you find yourself without a concierge, then act assertive, not surly, at the velvet rope, and your patience will usually be rewarded with admittance. If all else fails—for men, especially—surround yourself with a few leggy model types and you'll be noticed quicker.
> - Finally, have fun. It may look like serious business when you're on the outside, but once you're in, it's another story. Attacking clubland with a sense of humor is the best approach to a successful, memorable evening out.

Rock 'n' Bowl

Inspired by the alcohol-free rave dance parties of the '90s, Rave Bowling at **Cloverleaf Lanes,** 17601 NW Second Ave., North Dade (© **305/652-4197**), keeps teens off the streets, but in the gutters. Low lighting, glow-in-the-dark pins, and loud music keep things rolling every Friday and Saturday night from 8:30pm until 3am. Games are $4.50 each; shoes and balls are an extra $2.

Liquid Way back when, during South Beach's halcyon days and before Madonna became a mother and stopped her clubbing ways, Liquid was the Studio 54 of the south, and everyone who was anyone showed up here to show off. Then one of the club's owners was arrested for his alleged "family" connections and Liquid dried up. In late 2001, Liquid was resurrected by a completely new owner in a completely different space. Without Madonna, however, Liquid is just your generic dance club, just a ghost of a legend, which no one who experienced the original has any desire to visit. Open Tuesday to Saturday. 1532 Washington Ave., South Beach. © 305-531-9411. Cover $10–$20.

Living Room Downtown The downtown satellite of a now defunct South Beach club that was formerly the hautest of the hot (especially amongst European jet-setters), the Living Room Downtown is nearly as velvety chic as its original incarnation, only there's a twist: this one has a 24-hour liquor license. *Note:* This place is not for the weary. Open Wednesday and Friday to Saturday. 60 NE 11th St., downtown. © **305/342-7421**. Cover $10–$20.

Nikki Beach Club *(Finds* What the Playboy Mansion is to Hollywood, the Nikki Beach Club is to South Beach. This place is the product of local nightlife royalty Tommy Pooch and Eric Omores. Half-naked ladies and men actually venture into the daylight on Sundays for the legendary afternoon beach party (around 4pm, which is ungodly in this town) to see, be seen, and, at times, be obscene. It's worth a glimpse—that is, if you can get in. Egos are easily shattered, as surly doormen are known to reject those who don't drive up in a Ferrari. At night, it's very Brady Bunch goes to Hawaii, with a sexy tiki hut/Polynesian theme, albeit rated R. Also located within this bastion of hedonism is the super-hot **Pearl,** a mod, 380-seat, orange-hued restaurant and lounge that features a Continental menu created by Nikki chef Brian Rutherford. But you'd do better to forget the food and go for the eye candy. Open daily. 101 Ocean Dr., South Beach. © **305/538-1111**. Cover $10–$20.

Opium Garden Housed in the massive, open-air space formerly known as Amnesia, Opium Garden is a highly addictive nocturnal habit for those looking for a combination of sexy dance music, scantily clad dancers, and, for the masochists out there, an oppressive door policy in which two sets of velvet ropes are set up to keep those deemed unworthy out of this see and be sceney den of inequity. Open Friday to Sunday. 136 Collins Ave., South Beach. © **305/531-5535**. Cover $10–$30.

Rain A very minimalist dance club slash lounge, Rain is a great nightspot for many reasons. First and foremost, its location off the beachy path with ample parking is ideal for those who insist on clubbing and driving. Second, the music's great. Local DJ Mark Leventhal's Tuesday night funkfest known as Home Cookin' is particularly fun and comes complete with a free barbecue. If

The Rhythm Is Gonna Get You

Are you feeling shy about hitting a Latin club because you fear your two left feet will stand out? Then take a few lessons from one of the following dance companies or dance teachers. These folks have made it their mission to teach merengue and flamenco to non-Latinos and Latino left-foots and are among the most reliable, consistent, and popular ones in Miami, so what are you waiting for?

Thursday and Friday nights at **Bongo's Cuban Cafe,** American Airlines Arena, 601 Biscayne Blvd., downtown Miami (© 786/777-2100), are an amazing showcase of some of the city's best salsa dancers. Amateurs need not be intimidated thanks to the instructors at Latin Groove Dance Studios, who are on hand to help you with your two left feet.

At **Ballet Flamenco La Rosa,** 13126 W. Dixie Hwy., in the PAN building, North Miami (© 305/899-7730), you can learn to flamenco, salsa, or merengue. This is the only professional flamenco company in the area, charging $10 for a group lesson.

Nobody salsas like **Luz Pinto** (© 305/868-9418), and she also knows how to teach the basics with patience and humor. She charges $10 per person for a group lesson. A good introduction is her multilevel group class at 7pm Sunday evenings at the PAN (Performing Arts Network) building. Her specialty is Casino-style salsa, popularized in the 1950s in Cuba, Luz's homeland. A mix between disco and country square dancing, Casino-style salsa is all the rage in Latin clubs in town.

Angel Arroya has been teaching salsa to the clueless out of his home (at 16467 NE 27th Ave., North Miami Beach; © 305/949-7799) for the past 10 years. Just $10 will buy you an hour's time in his "school." He traditionally teaches Monday and Wednesday nights, but call ahead to check for any schedule changes.

you don't feel like dancing, outdoor and indoor lounging space is aplenty. Open Tuesday and Friday to Saturday. 323 23rd St., South Beach. © 786/295-9540. Cover $10–$30.

Rumi Named after a 13th-century Sufi mystic, South Beach's first upscale supper club is command central for hipsters hailing from all coasts. Designed by hot NYC designers Nancy Mah and Scott Kester, Rumi is an urbane oasis of reds, tans, and chocolates, reminiscent of the golden age of supper clubs of the '30s and '40s. This bi-level space features intimate lounge areas as well as private and public dining rooms, in which haute Florida-Caribbean cuisine is served until around 11pm, when the tables conspicuously disappear and give way to a neo-Zen-like stomping ground for South Beach's chic elite. Make sure to check out the queen-size Murphy bed that snaps down from the wall to make room for late-night lounging. As long as you can get past the velvet ropes (by either looking pretty, being on the guest list, or just getting the doorman on a good day), there is no cover to bask in this bastion of South Beach scenedom. Open daily. 330 Lincoln Rd., South Beach. © 305/672-4353. www.rumimiami.com. No cover.

LATIN CLUBS

Considering that Latin Americans make up a large part of Miami's population and that there's a huge influx of Spanish-speaking visitors, it's no surprise that there are some great Latin nightclubs in the city. Plus, with the meteoric rise of the international music scene based in Miami, many international stars come through the offices of MTV Latino, SONY International, and a multitude of Latin TV studios based in Miami—and they're all looking for a good club scene on weekends. Most of the Anglo clubs also reserve at least 1 night a week for Latin rhythms.

Añoranzas Taberna You've heard of *son*? Hear it here—along with salsa, cumbia, merengue, vallenato, and house music. This neighborhood Latin disco and nightclub gets going after hours with a wild strobe-lit atmosphere. If you don't know how to do it, just wait. You'll have plenty of willing teachers on hand. Open Tuesday and Friday to Sunday 8pm to 5am. 241 23rd St. (1 block west of Collins Ave.), South Beach. © 305/538-1196. No cover.

Cafe Nostalgia As the name implies, Cafe Nostalgia is dedicated to reminiscing about old Cuba. After watching a Celia Cruz film, you can dance to the hot sounds of Afro-Cuban jazz. With pictures of old and young Cuban stars smiling down on you and a live band celebrating Cuban heritage, Cafe Nostalgia sounds like a bit much, and it is. Be prepared—it's packed after midnight and dance space is mostly between the tables. Films are shown from 10pm to midnight, followed by live music. Another location, which is much ritzier, is on Miami Beach next to the Forge restaurant. Open Thursday to Sunday 9pm to 4am. 2212 SW 8th St. (Calle Ocho), Little Havana. © 305/541-2631. Cover $10.

Casa Panza (Finds) This *casa* is one of Little Havana's liveliest and most popular nightspots. Every Tuesday, Thursday, and Saturday night, Casa Panza, in the heart of Little Havana, becomes the House of Flamenco, with shows at 8 and 11pm. You can either enjoy a flamenco show or strap on your own dancing shoes and participate in the celebration. Enjoy a fantastic Spanish meal before the show, or just a glass of sangria before you start stomping. Casa Panza is a hot spot for young Latin club kids, and, occasionally, a few older folks who are so taken by the music and the scene that they've failed to realize that it's well past their bedtime. Open daily until 2am, sometimes later Tuesday and Thursday. 1620 SW 8th St. (Calle Ocho), Little Havana. © 305/643-5343. No cover.

La Covacha (Finds) This hut, located virtually in the middle of nowhere (West Miami), is the hottest Latin joint in the entire city. Sunday features the best in Latin rock, with local and international acts. But the shack is really jumping on weekend nights when the place is open until 5am. Friday is *the* night here, so much so that the owners had to place a red velvet rope out front to maintain some semblance of order. It's an amusing sight—a velvet rope guarding a shack—but once you get in, you'll understand the need for it. Do not wear silk here, as you *will* sweat. Open Monday to Wednesday 7am to 7:30pm; Thursday 7am to 2am; Friday to Saturday 7am to 5am; and Sunday 9am to 2am. 10730 NW 25th St. (at NW 107th Ave.), West Miami. © 305/594-3717. Cover $0–$10.

Mango's Tropical Café Claustrophobic types do not want to go near Mango's. Ever. One of the most popular spots on Ocean Drive, this outdoor enclave of Latin liveliness shakes with the intensity of a Richter-busting earthquake. Welcome and *bienvenido*, Mango's is *Cabaret*, Latin-style. Nightly live Brazilian and other Latin music, not to mention scantily clad male and female dancers, draw huge gawking crowds in from the sidewalk. But pay attention to the music if you can: Incognito international musicians often lose their anonymity and jam with the house band on stage. Open daily 11am to 5am. 900 Ocean Dr., South Beach. © 305/673-4422. Cover $5–$15.

THE GAY & LESBIAN SCENE

Miami and the beaches have long been host to what is called a "first-tier" gay community. Similar to the Big Apple, the Bay Area, or LaLa land, Miami has had a large alternative community since the days when Anita Bryant used her citrus power to boycott the rise in political activism in the early '70s. Well, things have changed and Miami–Dade now has a gay rights ordinance.

Newcomers intending to party in any bar, whether downtown or certainly on the beach, will want to check ahead for the schedule, as all clubs must have a gay or lesbian night to pay their rent. Though we've provided the usual cover charges for each listing below, you can generally get in for free or for a discounted rate earlier in the night.

Academy Hordes of gay men (and some women) join the Academy at Level every Friday 10pm to 5am, when the dance floor is packed with wall-to-wall hard bodies. 1235 Washington Ave., South Beach. © **305/532-1525.** Cover $20–$30.

Anthem Sunday nights (10pm–5am) at crobar cater to a gay clientele with this hyperpopular one-nighter featuring Miami's own superstar deejay Abel. 1445 Washington Ave., South Beach. © **877/CRO-SOBE** or 305/531-5027. Cover $25.

Cactus Bar & Grill Somewhere, over the causeway, there is life beyond South Beach—that is, for Miami's gay society. Housed in a large two-story space, Cactus attracts a mix of unpretentious, professional, and very attractive men and women. There's something for everyone here, whether it's the indoor pool tables, the outdoor swimming pool, or drinks that are considerably cheaper than on South Beach. Friday evening happy hours and Sunday afternoon Tea Dances are a virtual cattle call, attracting hordes of folks looking to quench their thirst at Miami's sprawling urban oasis. Daily 11am to 2am, until 3am Friday and Saturday. 2401 Biscayne Blvd., downtown. © **305/438-0662.** No cover.

Loading Zone A leather and Levi's bar known for its cruisability, pool tables, movies, and pitchers of beer. There's also an in-house leather store for the kinky shopper. Open daily 10pm to 5am. 1426 Alton Rd., South Beach. © **305/531-5623.** Cover $15–$20.

O-Zone This is the zone of choice for gay men with an aversion to South Beach's cruisy, scene-heavy vibes. It's known for a heavily Latin crowd (mixed with a few college boys from nearby University of Miami) and fantastic, outlandish drag shows on the weekends. Open daily 9pm to 5am. 6620 SW 57th Ave. (Red Rd.), South Miami. © **305/667-2888.** No cover for men on Sat; other nights $5–$10.

Score There's a reason this Lincoln Road hotbed of gay social activity is called Score. In addition to the huge pick-up scene, Score offers a multitude of bars, dance floors, lounge-like areas, and outdoor tables in case you need to come up for air. Sunday afternoon Tea Dances are legendary here. Open daily noon to 5am. 727 Lincoln Rd., South Beach. © **305/535-1111.** No cover.

1771 For those seeking liberation from the cookie-cutter mold of run-of-the-mill Saturday-night dance clubs, this place, formerly known as Salvation, is where you'll find it. Housed in an old warehouse, Salvation is spacious but always filled to capacity with shirtless, sweaty circuit boys dancing themselves into oblivion. Major DJs spin here and, at times, divas like Bette Midler (who gave a rare and ribald cabaret performance to an SRO audience) sing here. You can't blame the owners for charging $20 to get in when you see this bevy of beautiful boys. Open Saturday 10pm to 5am. 1771 West Ave., South Beach. © 305/ 673-6508. Cover $20.

Twist One of the most popular bars (and hideaways) on South Beach, this recently expanded venue (which is literally right across the street from the police station) has a casual yet lively local atmosphere. Open daily 1pm to 5am. 1057 Washington Ave., South Beach. © 305/538-9478. No cover.

LIVE MUSIC

Unfortunately, Miami's live music scene is not thriving. Instead of local bands garnering devoted fans, local DJs are more admired, skyrocketing much more easily to fame—thanks to the city's lauded dance club scene. However, there are still several places that strive to bring Miami up to speed as far as live music is concerned. You just have to look—and listen—for it a bit more carefully. The following is a list of places you can, from time to time, catch some live acts, be it a DJ or an aspiring Nirvana.

Billboard Live Affiliated with the national music industry magazine, this mammoth dance club, bar, recording studio, and live music venue is much cooler than its chain-ish name implies. Although at press time the live acts haven't necessarily been major headliners (Macy Gray was supposed to kick off a tour here, but then canceled with no reason), the acoustics in this multi-level club are exceptional. Open Friday to Sunday 10pm to 5am (depending on event). 1501 Collins Ave., South Beach. © 305/538-2251. Cover $0–$20.

Churchill's Hideaway *Finds* British expatriate Dave Daniels couldn't live in Miami without a true English-style pub, so he opened Churchill's Hideaway, the city's premier space for live rock music. Filthy and located in a rather unsavory neighborhood, Churchill's is committed to promoting and extending the lifeline of the lagging local music scene. A fun no-frills crowd hangs out here. Bring earplugs with you, as it is deafening once the music starts. Open daily 11am to 3am. 5501 NE Second Ave., Little Haiti. © 305/757-1807. Cover $0–$5.

Jazid *Finds* Smoky, sultry, and illuminated by flickering candelabras, Jazid is the kind of place where you'd expect to hear Sade's "Smooth Operator" on constant rotation. Instead, however, you'll hear live jazz (sometimes acid jazz), soul, and funk. Past surprise performers at Jazid include former Smashing Pumpkin's front man Billy Corgan. An eclectic mix of mellow folk convenes here for a much-needed respite from the surrounding Washington Avenue mayhem. Open daily 10pm to 5am. 1342 Washington Ave., South Beach. © 305/673-9372. No cover.

Tobacco Road Al Capone used to hang out here when it was a speakeasy. Now, locals flock here to see local bands perform, as well as national acts such as George Clinton and the P-Funk All-Stars, Koko Taylor, and the Radiators. Tobacco Road (the proud owner of Miami's very first liquor license) is small and gritty and meant to be that way. Escape the smoke and sweat in the backyard patio, where air is a welcome commodity. The downright cheap nightly specials, such as the $11 lobster on Tuesday, are quite good and are served until 2am. Open daily until 5am. 626 S. Miami Ave. (over the Miami Ave. Bridge near Brickell Ave.), downtown. © 305/374-1198. Cover $5 Fri–Sat.

Upstairs at the Van Dyke Café *Finds* The cafe's jazz bar, located on the second floor, resembles a classy speakeasy in which local jazz performers play to an

> **Impressions**
> There are two shifts in South Beach. There's nine to five. And then there's nine to five.
> —South Beach artist Stewart Stewart

intimate, enthusiastic crowd of mostly adults and sophisticated young things, who often huddle at the small tables until the wee hours. Open daily 7am to 2am. 846 Lincoln Rd., Miami Beach. © 305/534-3600. Cover $3–$6 for a seat; no cover at the bar.

BARS & LOUNGES

Unless mentioned, the bars listed below don't charge a cover, though most require proof that you are over 21 to enter. In general, bars in the area open sometime between 8 and 10pm and close at 2am.

Blue A very laid-back, very local scene set to a sultry soundtrack of deep soul and house music has Miami's hipsters feeling the blues. Before you whip out the St. John's Wort, dive into this so-not-trendy-it's-trendy lounge, in which the pervasive color blue will actually heighten your spirits as an eclectic haze of models, locals, and lounge lizards gather to commiserate in their dreaded trendy status. Open daily. 222 Española Way (between Washington and Collins aves.), South Beach. © 305/534-1009.

Clevelander If wet T-shirt contests and a fraternity party atmosphere are your thing, then this Ocean Drive mainstay is your kind of place. Popular with tourists and locals who like to pretend they're tourists, the Clevelander attracts a lively, sporty, adults-only crowd (the burly bouncers *will* confiscate fake IDs) who have no interest in being part of a scene but are interested in taking in the very revealing scenery. A great time to check out the Clevelander is on a weekend afternoon, when beach Barbies and Kens line the bar for a post-tanning beer or frozen cocktail. Open daily. 1020 Ocean Dr., South Beach. © 305/531-3485.

Fox's Sherron Inn *Finds* The spirit of Frank Sinatra is alive and well at this dark and smoky watering hole that dates back to 1946. Everything down to the vinyl booths and the red lights make Fox's a retro fabulous dive bar. Cheap drinks, couples cozily huddling in booths, and a seasoned staff of bartenders and barflies make Fox's the perfect place to retreat from the trenches of trendiness. Oh, and the food's actually good here, too. Open daily. 6030 S. Dixie Hwy. (at 62nd Ave.), South Miami. © 305/661-9201.

Laundry Bar The only place in Miami where it's okay to let friends drink and dry, Laundry Bar features working washers, dryers, and a fully stocked bar. On Thursdays, a DJ spins the best in house music. On Wednesdays and Fridays, a gospel diva (of the Astor Place restaurant's Gospel Brunch fame) sings live to an always packed and lively house. And although it's most popular with the gay community, Laundry Bar draws a mixed crowd. Daily happy hours (5–7pm) with two-for-one drinks allow you to save your change for the washing machines. 721 Lincoln Lane (behind Burdines off Lincoln Rd.), South Beach. © 305/531-7700. www.laundrybar.com.

Lola *Finds* Lola redefines the neighborhood bar, striking the perfect balance between chill and chic. This bar, located away from the South Beach mayhem, is a showgirl in her own right—a swank, sultry lounge where people are encouraged to come as they are, leaving the attitude at home. Attracting a mixed crowd of gay, straight, young, and old(er), Lola reinvents itself each night with DJs spinning everything from retro '80s music to hard rock and classic oldies. On

Tuesdays, the bar's most popular—and populated—night, it gets mobbed inside and outside, so they tend to keep a crowd at the ropes before letting them all in like cattle. Open Tuesday and Thursday to Sunday. 247 23rd St., South Beach. ✆ 305/695-8697.

Mac's Club Deuce Standing on its own amidst an oasis of trendiness, Mac's Club Deuce is the quintessential dive bar, with cheap drinks and a cast of characters ranging from your typical barfly to your atypical drag queen. It's got a well-stocked jukebox, friendly bartenders, and a pool table. Open daily. 222 14th St., South Beach. ✆ 305/673-9537.

Piccadilly Garden Lounge *Finds* Hardly anyone in Miami knows that this completely off-the-beaten-path Design District lounge exists, which makes it that much cooler. A young, alternative crowd (bordering on Gothic) gathers in this garden every Saturday night for what is known as Pop Life, a musical homage to the sounds of British pop and alternative music. While the dank interior resembles a stuffy old Holiday Inn lounge, the music and the crowd are very mod. Open Monday to Saturday. 35 NE 40th St., the Design District of Miami. ✆ 305/573-8221. Cover $5 Sat.

Purdy Lounge Featuring a wall of lava lamps, Purdy is not unlike your best friend's basement, featuring a pool table and a slew of board games such as Operation to keep the attention deficit disordered from getting bored. Because it's a no-nonsense bar with relatively cheap cocktails (by South Beach standards), Purdy gets away with not having a star DJ or fancy bass-heavy sound system. A CD player somehow does the trick. With no cover and no attitude, a line is inevitable, so be prepared to wait. Saturday night has become the preferred night for locals, while Friday night happy hour draws a young professional crowd on the prowl. Open daily. 1811 Purdy Ave./Sunset Harbor, South Beach. ✆ 305/531-4622.

Wet Willie's With such telling drinks as "Call a Cab," this beachfront oasis is not the place to go if you have a long drive ahead of you. A well-liked pre-and

---

Late-Night Bites

Although some dining spots in Miami stop serving at 10pm, many are open very late or even around the clock—especially on weekends. So, if it's 4am and you need a quick bite after clubbing, don't fret. There are a vast number of pizza places lining Washington Avenue in South Beach that are open past 6am. Especially good are **La Sandwicherie,** 229 14th St. (behind the Amoco station; ✆ 305/532-8934), which serves up a great late-night sandwich until 5am; and its next-door neighbor **San Loco Tacos** (235 14th St.; ✆ 305/538-3009), which slings tacos until 5am on weeknights and 6am on weekends. Another place of note for night owls is the **News Café,** 800 Ocean Dr. (✆ 305/538-6397), a trendy and well-priced cafe that has an enormous menu offering great all-day breakfasts, Middle Eastern platters, fruit bowls, or steak and potatoes—and everything is served 24 hours a day. In Coconut Grove, there's another crowded News Café, 2901 Florida Ave. (behind Mayfair; ✆ 305/774-6397), serving up the same fresh food around the clock. If your night out was at one of the Latin clubs around town, stop in at **Versailles,** 3555 SW 8th St. (✆ 305/444-0240), in Little Havana. It's not open all night, but its hours extend well past midnight—usually until 3 or 4am on weekends—to cater to gangs of revelers, young and old.

post-beach hangout, Wet Willie's inspires serious drinking. Popular with the Harley Davidson set, tourists, and beachcombers, this bar is best known for its rooftop patio (get there early if you plan to get a seat) and its half-nude bikini beauties. Open daily. 760 Ocean Dr., South Beach. © **305/532-5650.**

THE PERFORMING ARTS

Highbrows and culture vultures complain that there is a dearth of decent cultural offerings in Miami. What do locals tell them? Go back to New York! In all seriousness, however, in recent years, Miami's performing arts scene has improved greatly. The city's Broadway Series features Tony Award–winning shows (the touring versions, of course), which aren't always Broadway caliber, but they are usually pretty good and not nearly as pricey. Local arts groups such as the Miami Light Project, a not-for-profit cultural organization that presents live performances by innovative dance, music, and theater artists, have had huge success in attracting big-name artists to Miami. In addition, a burgeoning bohemian movement in Little Havana has given way to performance spaces that have become nightclubs in their own right.

THEATER

The **Actors' Playhouse,** a musical theater at the newly restored Miracle Theater at 280 Miracle Mile, Coral Gables (© **305/444-9293;** www.actors playhouse.org), is a grand 1948 Art Deco movie palace with a 600-seat main theater and a smaller theater/rehearsal hall that hosts a number of excellent musicals for children throughout the year. In addition to these two rooms, the Playhouse recently added a 300-seat children's balcony theater. Tickets run from $26 to $50.

The **Coconut Grove Playhouse,** 3500 Main Hwy., Coconut Grove (© **305/442-4000;** www.cgplayhouse.com), was also a former movie house, built in 1927 in an ornate Spanish rococo style. Today, this respected venue is known for its original and innovative staging of both international and local dramas and musicals. The house's second, more intimate Encore Room is well suited to alternative and experimental productions. Tickets run from $37 to $42.

The **Gables Stage** at the Biltmore Hotel, 1200 Anastasia Ave., Coral Gables (© **305/445-1119**), stages at least one Shakespearean play, one classic, and one contemporary piece a year. This well-regarded theater usually tries to secure the rights to a national or local premiere as well. Tickets cost $22 and $28, $10 and $17 for students and seniors.

Warhol Redux?

Miami's **Artemis Performance Network** sets the stage for the city's creative types with eclectic venues and events dedicated to and showcasing the local arts community. A network of performing artists, visual artists, musicians, presenters, educators, and administrators, Artemis is backed by the support of the Miami–Dade County Cultural Affairs Council, among others. Responsible for turning Little Havana into a bohemian hangout, Artemis sponsors most of their events at a loft-like performance space simply known as **PS 742,** 742 SW 16th Ave. in Little Havana (© **305/643-6611**), in which events such as Surreal Saturdays (first Sat of every month) feature a funky roster of spoken word, multimedia, and musical artists. Locals have compared the scene at PS 742 to that of New York City's East Village, circa 1980.

The **Jerry Herman Ring Theatre** is on the main campus of the University of Miami at 1380 Miller Dr., Coral Gables (✆ **305/284-3355**). The University's Department of Theater Arts uses this stage for advanced-student productions of comedies, dramas, and musicals. Faculty and guest actors are regularly featured, as are contemporary works by local playwrights. Performances are usually scheduled Tuesday through Saturday during the academic year. In the summer, don't miss "Summer Shorts," a selection of superb one-acts. Tickets sell for $5 to $20.

The **New Theater,** 65 Almeria Ave., Coral Gables (✆ **305/443-5909**), prides itself on showing world-renowned works from America and Europe. As the name implies, you'll find mostly contemporary plays, with a few classics thrown in for variety. Performances are staged Thursday to Sunday year-round. Tickets are $20 on weekdays, $25 weekends. If tickets are available on the day of the performance—and they usually are—students pay half price.

CLASSICAL MUSIC

In addition to a number of local orchestras and operas (see below), which regularly offer quality music and world-renowned guest artists, each year brings a slew of classical music special events and touring artists to Miami. The **Concert Association of Florida (CAF)** (✆ **305/532-3491**) produces one of the most important and longest-running series. Known for longer than a quarter of a century for its high-caliber, star-packed schedules, CAF regularly arranges the best "serious" music concerts for the city. Season after season, the schedules are punctuated by world-renowned dance companies and seasoned virtuosi like Itzhak Perlman, Andre Watts, and Kathleen Battle. Since CAF does not have its own space, performances are usually scheduled in the Miami–Dade County Auditorium or the Jackie Gleason Theater of the Performing Arts (see "Major Venues," below). The season lasts from October through April, and ticket prices range from $20 to $70.

Florida Philharmonic Orchestra South Florida's premier symphony orchestra, under the direction of James Judd, presents a full season of classical and pops programs interspersed with several children's and contemporary popular music performances. The Philharmonic performs downtown in the Gusman Center for the Performing Arts and at the Miami–Dade County Auditorium (see "Major Venues," below). 1243 University Dr., Miami. ✆ **800/226-1812** or 305/476-1234. Tickets $15–$60. When extra tickets are available, students are admitted free on day of performance.

Miami Chamber Symphony This professional orchestra is a small, subscription series orchestra that's not affiliated with any major arts organizations and is therefore an inexpensive alternative to the high-priced classical venues. Renowned international soloists perform regularly. The season runs October to May, and most concerts are held in the Gusman Concert Hall, on the University of Miami campus. 5690 N. Kendall Dr., Kendall. ✆ **305/858-3500.** Tickets $12–$30.

New World Symphony This organization, led by artistic director Michael Tilson Thomas, is a stepping-stone for gifted young musicians seeking professional careers. The orchestra specializes in ambitious, innovative, energetic performances and often features renowned guest soloists and conductors. The symphony's season lasts from October to May, during which time there are many free concerts. 541 Lincoln Rd., South Beach. ✆ **305/673-3331.** www.nws.org. Tickets free–$58. Rush tickets (remaining tickets sold 1 hr. before performance) $20. Students $10 (1 hr. before concerts: limited seating).

OPERA

Florida Grand Opera Around for over 60 years, this company regularly features singers from top houses in both America and Europe. All productions are sung in their original language and staged with projected English supertitles. Tickets become scarce when Placido Domingo or Luciano Pavarotti (who made his American debut here in 1965) come to town. The opera's season runs roughly from November to April, with five performances each week. A new multimillion-dollar headquarters for the opera is scheduled to open in mid 2004; until then, performances take place at the Miami–Dade County Auditorium and the Broward Center for the Performing Arts, about 40 minutes from downtown Miami. Box office: 1200 Coral Way, Southwest Miami. © **800/741-1010**. www.fgo.org. Tickets $19–$145. Student discounts available.

DANCE

Several local dance companies train and perform in the Greater Miami area. In addition, top traveling troupes regularly stop at the venues listed below. Keep your eyes open for special events and guest artists.

Ballet Flamenco La Rosa For a taste of local Latin flavor, see this lively troupe perform impressive flamenco and other styles of Latin dance on Miami stages. 13126 W. Dixie Hwy., North Miami. © **305/899-7729**. Tickets $25 at door, $20 in advance, $18 for students and seniors.

Miami City Ballet This artistically acclaimed and innovative company, directed by Edward Villella, features a repertoire of more than 60 ballets, many by George Balanchine, and has had more than 20 world premieres. The company moved into a new $7.5-million headquarters in January 2000—the Ophelia and Juan Jr. Roca Center at the Collins Park Cultural Center in Miami Beach. The City Ballet season runs from September to April. Ophelia and Juan Jr. Roca Center, Collins Ave. and 22nd St., South Beach. © **305/532-4880** or 305/532-7713 for box office. Tickets $17–$50.

MAJOR VENUES

After a much-needed $1-million face-lift, the **Colony Theater**, 1040 Lincoln Rd., South Beach (© **305/674-1026**), has become an architectural showpiece of the Art Deco District. This multipurpose 465-seat theater stages performances by the Miami City Ballet and the Ballet Flamenco La Rosa, as well as off-Broadway shows and other special events. At the time of your visit, however, the theater may still be closed for additional renovation and restoration.

At the **Miami–Dade County Auditorium,** West Flagler Street at 29th Avenue, Southwest Miami (© **305/547-5414**), performers gripe about the lack of space, but for patrons, this 2,430-seat auditorium is the only Miami space in which you can hear the opera—for now. A multimillion-dollar performing arts center downtown has been in the works for years (see below). For now, though, the Miami–Dade County Auditorium is home to the city's Florida Grand Opera, and it also stages productions by the Concert Association of Florida, many programs in Spanish, and a variety of other shows.

At the 1,700-seat **Gusman Center for the Performing Arts,** 174 East Flagler St., downtown Miami (© **305/372-0925**), seating is tight and so is funding, but the sound is superb. In addition to hosting the Florida Philharmonic Orchestra and the Miami Film Festival, the elegant Gusman Center features pop concerts, plays, film screenings, and special events. The auditorium was built as the Olympia Theater in 1926, and its ornate palace interior is typical of that era, complete with fancy columns, a huge pipe organ, and twinkling "stars" on the ceiling.

Not to be confused with the Gusman Center (above), the **Gusman Concert Hall,** 1314 Miller Dr. at 14th Street, Coral Gables (© **305/284-6477**), is a roomy 600-seat hall that gives a stage to the Miami Chamber Symphony and a varied program of university recitals.

The elegant **Jackie Gleason Theater of the Performing Arts (TOPA),** located in South Beach at Washington Avenue and 17th Street (© **305/673-7300**), is the home of the Miami Beach Broadway Series, which has recently presented *Rent, Phantom of the Opera,* and *Les Misérables.* This 2,705-seat hall also hosts other big-budget Broadway shows, classical music concerts, and dance performances.

At press time, the city granted a budget in excess of $200 million for its official Performing Arts Center. Planned are a 2,400-seat ballet/opera house and a 2,000-seat concert hall for the Florida Philharmonic Orchestra, Florida Grand Opera, New World Symphony, Miami City Ballet, and a major concert series. Designed by world-renowned architect Cesar Pelli, it will be the focal point of a planned Arts, Media, and Entertainment District in mid-Miami. The complex will be wrapped in limestone, slate, decorative stone, stainless steel, glass curtain walls, and tropical landscaping, and is slated to be complete in mid-2004. For more information, check out their website at www.pacfmiami.org.

5

The Keys

by Lesley Abravanel

The drive from Miami to the Keys is a slow descent into an unusual but breathtaking American ecosystem: On either side of you, for miles ahead, lies nothing but emerald waters. (On weekends, however, you will also see plenty of traffic.) Strung out across the Atlantic Ocean like loose strands of cultured pearls, more than 400 islands make up this 150-mile-long chain of the Keys.

Despite the usually calm landscape, these rocky islands can be treacherous, as a series of tropical storms, hurricanes, and tornadoes reminded residents in the summer and fall of 1998, when millions of dollars of damage was inflicted. The exposed coast has always posed dangers to those on land as well as at sea.

When Spanish explorers Juan Ponce de León and Antonio de Herrera sailed amid these craggy, dangerous rocks in 1513, they and their men dubbed the string of islands "Los Martires" (The Martyrs), because they thought the rocks looked like men suffering in the surf. It wasn't until the early 1800s that the larger islands were settled by rugged and ambitious pioneers, who amassed great wealth by salvaging cargo from ships sunk nearby. Legend has it that these shipwrecks were sometimes caused by the "wreckers," who occasionally removed navigational markers from the shallows to lure unwitting captains aground. At the height of the salvaging mania (in the 1830s), Key West boasted the highest per capita income in the country.

However, wars, fires, hurricanes, mosquitoes, and the Depression took their toll on these resilient islands in the early part of this century, causing wild swings between fortune and poverty. In 1938, the spectacular Overseas Highway (U.S. 1) was finally completed atop the ruins of Henry Flagler's railroad (which was destroyed by a hurricane in 1935, leaving only bits and pieces still found today), opening the region to tourists, who had never before been able to drive to this seabound destination.

These days, the highway connects more than 30 of the populated islands in the Keys. The hundreds of small, undeveloped islands that surround these "mainline" keys are known locally as the "backcountry" and are home to a stunning abundance of tropical and exotic animals and plants. To get to the backcountry, you must take to the water, and of course, the sea and the teeming life beneath it are the main attractions here. Countless species of brilliantly colored fish can be found swimming above the ocean's floor. The warm, shallow waters (waters are deeper and rougher on the eastern/Atlantic side of the Keys) nurture living coral that supports a complex, delicate ecosystem of plants and animals—sponges, anemones, jellyfish, crabs, rays, sharks, turtles, snails, lobsters, and thousands of types of fish.

This vibrant underwater habitat thrives on one of the only living tropical reefs in the entire North American continent. As a result, anglers, divers,

The Florida Keys

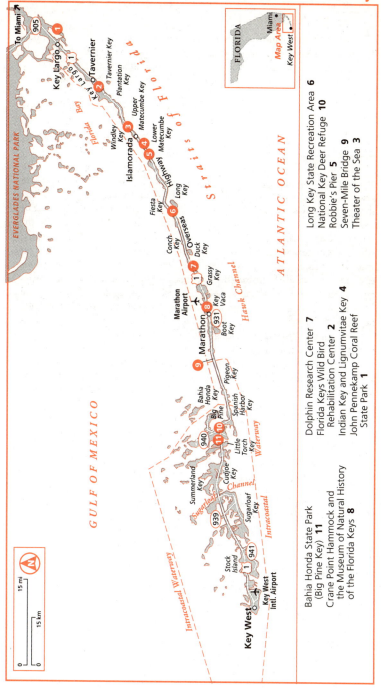

Bahia Honda State Park (Big Pine Key) **11**
Crane Point Hammock and the Museum of Natural History of the Florida Keys **8**
Dolphin Research Center **7**
Florida Keys Wild Bird Rehabilitation Center **2**
Indian Key and Lignumvitae Key **4**
John Pennekamp Coral Reef State Park **1**
Long Key State Recreation Area **6**
National Key Deer Refuge **10**
Robbie's Pier **5**
Seven-Mile Bridge **9**
Theater of the Sea **3**

> **Tips Don't Be Fooled**
> Avoid the many "Tourist Information Centers" that dot U.S. 1 as you explore the Keys. Most are private companies hired to lure visitors to specific lodgings or outfitters. You're better off sticking with the official, not-for-profit centers that we've listed below under "Essentials" in each section.

snorkelers, and water-sports enthusiasts of all kinds come to explore here. From bone fishing to spear fishing and—at appropriate times of the year—diving for lobsters, outdoor sporting opportunities abound.

Heavy traffic has taken its toll on this fragile ecoscape, but conservation efforts are underway (traffic laws are strictly enforced on Deer Key, for example, due to deer crossings). In fact, environmental efforts in the Keys exceed those in many other high-traffic visitor destinations.

Although the atmosphere throughout the Keys is that of a laid-back beach town, don't expect to find many impressive beaches here, especially after the damaging effects of the tropical storms and hurricanes in 1998. Beaches are mostly found in a few private resorts, though there are some small, sandy beaches in the Upper and Middle Keys at John Pennekamp State Park. A great exception in this area is Sombrero Beach in Marathon. In the Lower Keys, you'll find beaches at Bahia Honda State Park and in Key West.

The Keys are divided into three sections, both geographically and in this chapter. The Upper and Middle Keys are closest to the Florida mainland, so they are popular with weekend warriors who come by boat or car to fish or relax in towns like Key Largo, Islamorada, and Marathon. Further on, just beyond the impressive Seven-Mile Bridge (which actually measures only 6.4 miles), are the Lower Keys, a small, unspoiled swath of islands teeming with wildlife. Here, in the protected regions of the Lower Keys, is where you're most likely to catch sight of the area's many endangered animals—with patience, you may spot the rare eagle, egret, or Key deer. You should also keep an eye out for alligators, turtles, rabbits, and a huge variety of other birds.

Key West, the most renowned—and last—island in the Lower Keys is literally at the end of the road. The southernmost point in the continental United States (made famous by the Nobel Prize–winning Ernest Hemingway), this tiny island is the most popular destination in the Florida Keys, overrun with cruise-ship passengers and day-trippers, as well as franchises and T-shirt shops. More than 1.6 million visitors pass through each year. Still, this "Conch Republic" has a tightly knit community of permanent residents who cling fiercely to their live-and-let-live attitude—an atmosphere that has made Key West famously popular with painters, writers, and free spirits.

EXPLORING THE KEYS BY CAR

After you have gotten off the Florida Turnpike and landed on U.S. 1, which is also known as the Overseas Highway (see "Getting There," under "Essentials," below), you'll have no trouble negotiating these narrow islands, since it is the only main road connecting the Keys. The scenic, lazy drive from Miami can be very enjoyable if you have the patience to linger and explore the diverse towns and islands along the way. If you have the time, I recommend allowing at least 2 days to work your way down to Key West and 3 or more days once there.

Most of U.S. 1 is a narrow, two-lane highway, with some wider passing zones along the way. The speed limit is usually 55 miles per hour (35–45 mph on Big Pine Key and in some commercial areas). Despite the protestations of island residents, there has been talk of expanding the highway, but plans have not been finalized. Even on the narrow road, you can usually get from downtown Miami to Key Largo in just over an hour. If you're determined to drive straight through to Key West, allow at least 3½ hours. Weekend travel is another matter entirely: When the roads are jammed with travelers from the mainland, the trip could take upward of 5 to 6 hours (when there's an accident, traffic is at an absolute standstill). If at all possible, avoid driving anywhere in the Keys on Friday afternoons or Sunday evenings.

To **find an address** in the Keys, don't bother looking for building numbers; most addresses (except in Key West and parts of Marathon) are delineated by mile markers (MM), small green signs on the roadside, which announce the distance from Key West. The markers start at number 127, just south of the Florida mainland. The zero marker is in Key West, at the corner of Whitehead and Fleming streets. Addresses in this chapter are accompanied by a mile marker (MM) designation when appropriate.

1 The Upper & Middle Keys ★★: Key Largo to Marathon

58 miles SW of Miami

The Upper Keys are a popular, year-round refuge for South Floridians who take advantage of the islands' proximity to the mainland. This is the fishing and diving capital of America, and the swarms of outfitters and billboards never let you forget it.

Key Largo, once called Rock Harbor but renamed to capitalize on the success of the 1948 Humphrey Bogart film (which wasn't actually filmed there), is the largest key and is more developed than its neighbors to the south. Dozens of chain hotels, restaurants, and tourist information centers service the many water enthusiasts who come to explore the nation's first underwater state park, **John Pennekamp Coral Reef State Park,** and its adjacent marine sanctuary. **Islamorada,** the unofficial capital of the Upper Keys, offers the area's best atmosphere, food, fishing, entertainment, and lodging. It's an unofficial "party capital" for mainlanders seeking a quick tropical excursion. Here (Islamorada is actually composed of four islands), nature lovers can enjoy walking trails, historic explorations, and big-purse fishing tournaments. For a more tranquil, quieter Keys experience, any key outside of Key West and Islamorada is a better choice. **Marathon,** smack in the middle of the Florida Keys, is one of the most populated keys and is known as the heart of the Keys. It is part fishing village, part tourist center, part nature preserve. This area's highly developed infrastructure includes resort hotels, a commercial airport, and a highway that expands to four lanes.

ESSENTIALS

GETTING THERE If you are **driving** from Miami International Airport, take Le Jeune Road (NW 42nd Ave.) to Route 836 west. Follow signs to the Florida Turnpike South (about 7 miles). The turnpike extension connects with U.S. 1 in Florida City. Continue south on U.S. 1. For a scenic option, weather permitting, take Card Sound Road south of Florida City, a backcountry drive that reconnects with U.S. 1 in upper Key Largo. The view from the Card Sound Bridge is spectacular and well worth the dollar toll.

If you're coming from Florida's west coast, take Alligator Alley to the Miami exit and then turn south onto the turnpike extension. The turnpike will end in Florida City, at which time you will be dumped directly onto the one-lane road, U.S. 1, that leads to the Keys. Have plenty of quarters (at least $10 worth, round-trip) for the tolls.

You can also fly into the **Marathon airport** at 9400 Overseas Hwy. (© **305/289-6060**). **Paradise Air** (© **305/743-4222;** www.flyparadiseair.com) flies nonstop from Fort Lauderdale, and **Vintage Props and Jets** (© **800/852-0275;** www.vpj.com) flies in from Daytona Beach and Orlando.

Greyhound (© **800/231-2222;** www.greyhound.com) has three buses leaving Miami for Key West every day, which also stop in Key Largo, Tavenier, Islamorada, Marathon, Big Pine Key, Cudjoe Key, Sugarloaf, and Big Coppit on their way south. Prices range from about $13 to $32 one-way and take between an hour and 40 minutes to 4 hours and 40 minutes, depending on how far south you're going. Seats fill quickly in season, so come early. It's first come, first served.

VISITOR INFORMATION Make sure you get your information from official, not-for-profit centers. The **Key Largo Chamber of Commerce,** U.S. 1 at MM 106, Key Largo, FL 33037 (© **800/822-1088** or 305/451-1414; fax 305/451-4726; www.keylargo.org), runs an excellent facility, with free direct-dial phones and plenty of brochures. Headquartered in a handsome clapboard house, the chamber operates as an information clearinghouse for all of the Keys and is open daily from 9am to 6pm.

The **Islamorada Chamber of Commerce,** housed in an actual little red caboose, U.S. 1 at MM 82.5, P.O. Box 915, Islamorada, FL 33036 (© **800/322-5397** or 305/664-4503; fax 305/664-4289; www.islamoradachamber.com), also offers maps and literature on the Upper Keys.

You can't miss the big blue visitor center at MM 53.5, the **Greater Marathon Chamber of Commerce,** 12222 Overseas Hwy., Marathon, FL 33050 (© **800/842-9580** or 305/743-5417; fax 305/289-0183; www.floridakeysmarathon.com). Here you can receive free information on local events, festivals, shows, attractions, dining, and lodging.

WHAT TO SEE & DO
THE BEACHES
Anne's Beach (at MM 73.5, on Lower Matecumbe Key, at the southwest end of Islamorada) is really more of a picnic spot than a full-fledged beach, but die-hard suntanners still congregate on this lovely but tiny strip of coarse sand that was damaged beyond recognition during the series of storms in 1998. Plans are in place to reconstruct the boardwalk and huts, but at press time, work had not yet started.

A better choice for real beaching is **Sombrero Beach** in Marathon at the end of Sombrero Beach Road (near MM 50). This wide swath of uncluttered beachfront actually benefited from Hurricane George in September 1998, which blew in generous deposits of extra sand and was followed by a face-lift courtesy of the Monroe County Tourist Development Council. More than 90 feet of sand is dotted with palms, Australian pines, and royal poincianas as well as with barbecue grills, clean restrooms, and some brand-new tiki huts for relaxing in the shade.

THE BACKCOUNTRY

If you are interested in seeing the Keys in their natural state, before modern development, you must venture off the highway and take to the water. Two backcountry islands that offer a glimpse of the "real" Keys are **Indian Key** and **Lignumvitae Key**. Visitors come here to relax and enjoy the islands' colorful birds and lush hammocks (elevated pieces of land above a marsh).

Named for the lignum vitae ("wood of life") trees found there, **Lignumvitae Key** supports a virgin tropical forest, the kind that once thrived on most of the Upper Keys. Over the years, human settlers imported "exotic" plants and animals to the Keys, irrevocably changing the botanical makeup of many backcountry islands and threatening much of the indigenous wildlife. Over the past 25 years, however, the Florida Department of Natural Resources has successfully removed most of the exotic vegetation from this key, leaving this 280-acre site much as it existed in the 18th century. The island also holds the **Matheson House,** a historic house built in 1919 that has survived numerous hurricanes. You can go inside the house, but this is only interesting if you have a hankering for coral rock, of which the house is made. It's now a museum dedicated to the history, nature, and topography of the area. More interesting is actually seeing the area via the Botanical Gardens, which surround the house and are a state preserve. Lignumvitae Key has a visitor center at MM 88.5 (© **305/664-2540**).

Indian Key, a much smaller island on the Atlantic side of Islamorada, was occupied by Native Americans for thousands of years before European settlers arrived. The 10-acre historic site was also the original seat of Dade County before the Civil War. Interesting from an archaeological standpoint, you can see the ruins of the previous settlement and tour the lush grounds on well-marked trails, which start at Indian Key Fill, Overseas Highway, MM 79.

If you want to see both islands, plan to spend at least half a day. To get there, you can rent your own powerboat at **Robbie's Rent-A-Boat,** U.S. 1 at MM 77.5 on the bay side of Islamorada (see "Boating," later in this chapter). It's then a $1 admission fee to each island, which includes an informative hour-long guided

---

Finds   An Ancient Hammock

Crane Point Hammock, right off U.S. 1 in Marathon, is a little-known but worthwhile stop, especially for those interested in the rich botanical and archaeological history of the Keys. This privately owned 64-acre nature area is considered one of the most important historical sites in the Keys. It contains what is probably the last virgin thatch palm hammock in North America, as well as a rain-forest exhibit and an archaeological dig site with pre-Columbian and prehistoric Bahamian artifacts.

The hammock's impressive **Museum of Natural History of the Florida Keys,** 5550 Overseas Hwy. (MM 50), Marathon (© **305/743-9100**), offers simple, informative displays of the Keys' wildlife, including a walk-through replica of a coral-reef cave and life-size dioramas with tropical birds and Key deer. Kids can participate in art projects, see 6-foot-long iguanas, climb through a scaled-down pirate ship, and touch a variety of indigenous aquatic and landlubbing creatures here. The museum is open Monday through Saturday 9am to 5pm and Sunday noon to 5pm. Admission costs $7.50 for adults, $6 for those over 64, and $4 for students; it's free for children under 6.

>
> ### Cheap Thrills: What to See & Do for Free (or Almost) in the Keys
>
> - **Take in the view from Seven-Mile Bridge.** Getting weary on that road trip south? Get out and stretch your legs at Seven-Mile Bridge, between MM 40 and 47 on U.S. 1. Its apex is the highest point in the pancake-flat Keys, which makes it an excellent place to admire the watery panorama.
> - **Feed some giant fish at Robbie's Pier.** In the shallow waters off this Islamorada pier (at MM 77.5), scores of jumbo, valiant tarpon loiter, waiting for a snack or two from benevolent passersby. For $1 admission and a $2 bucket of fish, you can feed these oversize, prehistoric-looking fish, some of which can grow up to 200 pounds. Also included in the $1 entry fee is an hour-long guided tour by park rangers, whose expertise can help make sense of your beautiful surroundings.
> - **Soak up the sunset and the scene at Mallory Square.** In what has become an evening ritual, artists, acrobats, food hawkers, and animal acts gather for some end-of-the-day revelry at Mallory Square, ground zero for Key West's eccentric set. Nab a spot on the docks (at the westernmost end of Duval St.) to take it all in.
> - **Explore one man's inventive whimsy: the Sugarloaf Bat Tower.** Developer Clyde Perkey hated mosquitoes—so much so that in 1929 he built a 45-foot-high, wooden, flat-topped pyramid to lure bug-eating bats to the region. Alas, despite a pervasive bat aphrodisiac, the critters never materialized. Now empty and deserted (and devoid of any explanatory signage), the Sugarloaf Bat Tower (at MM 17) is the only human-made attraction in the Lower Keys. Admission is free.

tour by park rangers. This is a good option if you are a confident boater. However, I also recommend taking Robbie's **ferry service.** A visit to one island costs $15, $10 for kids 12 and under, which includes the $1 park admission; trips to both islands cost $25 per person. (If you have time for only one island, make it Lignumvitae.) Not only is the ferry more economical, but it's easier to enjoy the natural beauty of the islands when you aren't negotiating the shallow reefs along the way. The runabouts, which carry up to six people, depart from Robbie's Pier Thursday to Monday at 9am and 1pm for Indian Key, and at 10am and 2pm for Lignumvitae Key. In the busy season, you may need to book as early as 2 days before departure. Call © **305/664-4815** for information from the park service or © **305/664-9814** for Robbie's.

SEVEN-MILE BRIDGE

A stop at the **Seven-Mile Bridge** is a rewarding and relaxing break from the drive south along the Keys. Built in 1985 alongside the ruins of oil magnate Henry Flagler's incredible Overseas Railroad, the "new" bridge (between MM 40 and 47) is considered an architectural feat. The wide arched span, completed in 1982 at a cost of more than $45 million, is impressive, and its apex is the highest point in the Keys. The new bridge and its now-defunct neighbor provide an

- **Go wild—with the birds, that is:** The **Florida Keys Wild Bird Rehabilitation Center** (at MM 94, in Tavernier) serves as a hospital for the many native species of birds found here. Narrow wooden walkways, overhung by dense mangrove canopies, will take you past broad-winged hawks, great blue and white herons, roseate spoonbills, white ibises, cattle egrets, and a variety of pelicans. Come at feeding time (usually about 3:30pm) and see the dedicated staff feed the hundreds of those hungry beaks. This not-for-profit center doesn't charge admission but does request donations.

- **Reef madness—Snorkel in an underwater state park: John Pennekamp Coral Reef State Park** contains part of the nation's first undersea preserve, and the only living coral reef in the continental United States. To experience this park, get in the water, which is shallow enough to make the 40 species of corals and more than 650 species of fish more than accessible to divers, snorkelers, and glass-bottom-boat passengers. Mention this guide at **Hall's Dive Center & Career Institute**, U.S. 1 at MM 48.5, Marathon (© **305/743-5929**), and you'll get special discounted rates for snorkeling and diving. Park admission is $2.50 per vehicle for one occupant; for two or more, it is $4 per vehicle, plus 50¢ per passenger; $1.50 per pedestrian or bicyclist.

- **Take the Key lime challenge.** The Key lime is to Key West what chocolate is to Belgium. Wherever you go, you are bound to be tempted by the most famous Key lime concoction of all—the Key lime pie. For free samples of pies, cookies, candies, and ice creams, the **Key Lime Pie Co.** (© **305/294-6567**) has two locations for taste testing, one at 701 Caroline St., and the other at 424 Greene St.

excellent vantage point from which to view the stunning waters of the Keys. In the daytime, you may want to walk, jog, or bike along the scenic 4-mile stretch of the old bridge, or join local anglers, who catch barracuda, yellowtail, and dolphin (the fish, not the mammal) on what is known as "the longest fishing pier in the world." Parking is available on both sides of the bridge. Call © **305/289-0025** for information.

Pigeon Key, located in the middle of the Seven-Mile Bridge halfway between Key Largo and Key West, is a 5-acre island on the National Register of Historic Places. The key once served as the location of the work camp and village for the people who constructed the new bridge. Today educational and research centers on the island, open from 9am to 5pm, provide the history of the bridge and the Florida Keys to visitors. Pigeon Key is reached by foot or shuttle service from the **Pigeon Key Visitor Center** on Knight's Key at MM 47, on the ocean side (© **305/289-0025**). Parking is available at the visitor center; the shuttle runs hourly from 10am to 4pm.

VISITING WITH THE ANIMALS

Dolphin Research Center ★★★ *Kids* If you've always wanted to touch, swim, or play with dolphins, this is the place to do it. Of the three such centers in the continental United States (all located in the Keys), the Dolphin Research Center is the most organized and informative. Although some people argue that training dolphins is cruel and selfish, this is one of the most respected institutions that study and protect the mammals. Knowledgeable trainers at the Dolphin Research Center will also tell you that the dolphins need stimulation and enjoy human contact. They certainly seem to. They nuzzle and seem to smile and kiss the lucky few that get to swim with them in the daily program. The "family" of 15 dolphins swims in a 90,000-square-foot natural saltwater pool carved out of the shoreline.

If you can't get into the swim program, you can still take the interesting hour-long walking tour of the facilities or sign up for a class in hand signals, or feed the dolphins from docks. Because the Dolphin Encounter swimming program is the most popular, reservations must be made at least 1 month in advance. If you're not brave enough to swim with the dolphins or you have a child under 12 (not permitted to swim with dolphins), try the Dolphin Splash program, in which participants stand on an elevated platform from which to "meet and greet" the dolphins. A height requirement of 44 inches is enforced, and an adult must hold up children under the required height.

U.S. 1 at MM 59 (on the bay side), Marathon. © 305/289-1121. Dolphin Encounter $135. Dolphin Splash $75; free for children under 3. Call on the first day of the month to book for the following month. Educational walking tours 10am, 11am, 12:30pm, 2pm, and 3:30pm. Admission $15 adults, $12.50 seniors, $10 children 4–12; free for children under 3. Daily 9:30am–4pm.

Florida Keys Wild Bird Center

Wander through lush canopies of mangroves on narrow wooden walkways to see some of the Keys' most famous residents—the large variety of native birds, including broad-wing hawks, great blue and white herons, roseate spoonbills, white ibis, cattle egrets, and a number of pelicans. This not-for-profit center operates as a hospital for the many birds that have been injured by accident or disease. Visit at feeding time, usually about 3:30pm, when you can watch the staff fill the beaks of the hungry birds.

U.S. 1 at MM 93.6 bay side, Tavernier. © 305/852-4486. fkwbc@reefnet.com. Donations suggested. Daily 8:30am–6pm.

Robbie's Pier

One of the best and definitely one of the cheapest attractions in the Upper Keys is the famed Robbie's Pier. Here, the fierce steely tarpons, a prized catch for backcountry anglers, have been gathering for the past 20 years. You may recognize these prehistoric-looking giants that grow up to 200 pounds; many are displayed as trophies and mounted on local restaurant walls. To see them live, head to Robbie's Pier, where tens and sometimes hundreds of these behemoths circle the shallow waters waiting for you to feed them. Kayak tours promise an even closer glimpse.

U.S. 1 at MM 77.5, Islamorada. © 305/664-9814. Admission $1. Bucket of fish $2. Daily 8am–5pm. Look for the HUNGRY TARPON restaurant sign on the right after the Indian Key channel.

Theater of the Sea

Established in 1946, the Theater of the Sea is one of the world's oldest marine zoos. Recently refurbished, with newly paved walkways, landscaping, and an on-site photo service, the park's dolphin and sea lion shows are entertaining and informative, especially for children, who can also see sharks, sea turtles, and tropical fish. If you want to swim with dolphins and you haven't booked well in advance, this is the place you may be able to get into with just a few hours' or days' notice as opposed to the more rigid Dolphin Research Center (see above) in Marathon. (While the Dolphin Research Center is a legitimate, scientific establishment, this is more of a theme park attraction. That's not to say the dolphins are mistreated, but it's just not as, say, educational and professional as it is at the Dolphin Research Center.) Theater of the Sea also permits you to swim with the sea lions and stingrays. Children under 5 are not permitted to participate. There are also 4-hour adventure and snorkel cruises, $60 for adults and $35 for children, in which you can learn about the history and ecology of the marine environment.

U.S. 1 at MM 84.5, Islamorada. © 305/664-2431. www.theaterofthesea.com. Admission $17.75 adults, $11.25 children 3–12. Dolphin swim $135; sea lion swim $90; stingray swim $40 per person. Reservations mandatory. Daily 9:30am–5:45pm (ticket office closes at 4 pm).

TWO EXCEPTIONAL STATE PARKS

One of the best places to discover the diverse ecosystem of the Upper Keys is in its most famous park and preserve, **John Pennekamp Coral Reef State Park**, located on U.S. 1 at MM 102.5, in Key Largo (© **305/451-1202**). Named for a former *Miami Herald* editor and conservationist, it is the nation's first underwater park. Formed in the 1960s, Pennekamp Park represents over 100 square miles of mangrove shoreline, grass flats, and a spectacular stretch of coral reef that is part of the same reef system encompassed by nearby Biscayne National Park (see chapter 6, "The Everglades & Biscayne National Park").

Because the water is extremely shallow, the 40 species of coral and more than 650 species of fish here are particularly accessible. To experience this park, though, visitors must get in the water—you can't see the reef from the shore. A 2-hour **glass-bottom-boat tour** is the best way to see the coral reefs if you don't want to get wet. Watch for the lobsters and other sea life residing in the fairly shallow ridge walls beneath the coastal waters. But remember: These are protected waters, so you can't remove anything. **Canoeing** around the park's narrow mangrove channels and tidal creeks is also popular. You can go on your own in a rented canoe or, in winter, sign up for a tour led by a local naturalist.

Your first stop should be the **Visitors Center,** MM 102.5, Key Largo (© **305/451-6322**), which is full of educational fish tanks and a mammoth 30,000-gallon saltwater aquarium that re-creates a reef ecosystem. At the adjacent dive shop, you can rent snorkeling and diving equipment and join one of the boat trips that depart for the reef throughout the day. Snorkeling tours cost $25.95 for adults and $19.95 for children 17 and under, including equipment. Diving tours cost $41 per person, plus $29 for two tanks, a regulator, and a wet suit. Sailing and snorkeling tours are $31.95 for adults, $26.95 for children 17 and under, including equipment. Visitors can also rent canoes for $10 per hour. For experienced boaters only, four different-sized Reef boats (powerboats) rent for $27.50 to $50 per hour, with cheaper half-day and full-day rates available. A deposit of $400 or more, depending on boat size, is required. The park's boat rental is open daily from 8am to 5pm—the last boat rented is at 3pm. The center's glass-bottom-boat tours cost $18 for adults and $10 for children 11 and under. Reservations are recommended for all of the above; phone ahead for tour hours. See more vendors and activities under "Affordable Water Sports," below.

On shore, **hikers** have two short trails from which to choose: a boardwalk through the mangroves and a dirt trail through a tropical hardwood hammock. Ranger-led walks are usually scheduled daily from the end of November to April. Phone © **305/451-1202** for schedule information and reservations.

Park admission is $2.50 per vehicle for one occupant; for two or more, it is $4 per vehicle, plus 50¢ per passenger; it costs $1.50 per pedestrian or bicyclist. On busy weekend days, there's often a line of cars to get into the park. On your way into the park, ask the ranger for a map.

Further down U.S. 1 at MM 68 in Long Key, the **Long Key State Recreation Area** ★★★ (© **305/664-4815**) is one of the best places in the Middle Keys for hiking, camping, snorkeling, and canoeing. This 965-acre site is situated atop the remains of an ancient coral reef, which "suffocated" when the water level began to drop over 100,000 years ago (the water level is now 30 ft. lower than at that time). At the entrance gate, ask for a free flyer describing the local trails and wildlife. Admission to the recreation area is $3.25 per car plus 50¢ per person (except for the Layton Trail, below, which is free). It's open daily from 8am to sunset.

Three nature trails can be explored by foot or canoe here; The **Golden Orb Trail** is a 40-minute walk through the local flora, the **Layton Trail** is a 15-minute walk along the bay, and the **Long Key Canoe Trail** glides along a shallow lagoon and loops around mangroves. You can rent canoes at the trailhead for roughly $4 an hour or join one of the nature walks offered by the park on Wednesdays and Thursdays. Campsites are located along the Atlantic Ocean, and the swimming and snorkeling are top-notch here. The nearest place to rent snorkeling equipment is **Holiday Isle,** 84001 U.S. 1, Islamorada (© **800/327-7070**).

Railroad builder Henry Flagler created the Long Key Fishing Club here in 1906, and the waters surrounding the park are still popular with game fishers. See "Fishing," below, for information about local outfitters. Also, in summer, sea turtles lumber onto the protected coast to lay their eggs. It's a big event, and educational programs and tours are available through the nonprofit group **Save-a-Turtle, Inc.** (© **305/743-6056**).

AFFORDABLE WATER SPORTS

There are literally hundreds of outfitters in the Keys who will arrange all kinds of water activities, from cave dives to parasailing. If those recommended below are booked up, ask the local chamber of commerce for a list of qualified members (see "Essentials," earlier in this section).

BOATING In addition to the rental shops in the state parks, you will find dozens of outfitters along U.S. 1 offering a range of runabouts and skiffs for boaters of any experience level. **Captain Pip's,** U.S. 1 at MM 47.5, Marathon (© **800/707-1692** or 305/743-4403), rents 18- to 24-foot motorboats with 90- to 225-horsepower engines for $130 to $225 per day. Overnight accommodations are available and include a free boat rental; rates are 2-night minimum $220 to $255, weekly $1,190 to $1,890. Rooms are comfortable and charming, with ceiling fans, tile floors, and pine paneling.

Robbie's Rent-a-Boat, U.S. 1 at MM 77.5, Islamorada (© **305/664-9814**), rents 14- to 27-foot motorboats with engines ranging from 15 to 200 horsepower. Boat rentals are $70 to $205 for a half day and $90 to $295 for a full day.

CANOEING & KAYAKING We can think of no better way to explore the uninhabited, shallow backcountry on the Gulf side of the Keys than by kayak or canoe, since you can reach places big boats just can't get to with their large draft. Sometimes manatees will even cuddle up to the boats, thinking them another friendly species.

Many area hotels rent kayaks and canoes to guests, as do the outfitters listed here. **Florida Bay Outfitters,** U.S. 1 at MM 104, Key Largo (© **305/451-3018**), rents canoes and sea kayaks for use in and around John Pennekamp Coral Reef State Park for $20 to $40 for a half day and $35 to $55 for a whole day. At **Coral Reef Park Co.,** on U.S. 1 at MM 102.5, Key Largo (© **305/451-1621**),

Go Crab Hunting

Fans of stone crabs can get further acquainted with these seasonal crustaceans thanks to 3-hour tours led by **Keys Fisheries**. The tours leave from Marathon aboard 40- to 50-foot vessels and include views of fishermen as they collect crabs from traps and process their claws. The $425 tour cost includes up to six passengers and up to six pounds of fresh claws iced for travel or prepared at a dockside restaurant. Stone crab season is from October 15 to May 15. Call © **305/743-4353** or check the Web at http://www.keysfisheries.com for more information.

---

you can rent canoes and kayaks for $8 per hour, $28 for a half day; most canoes are sit-on-tops.

DIVING & SNORKELING The **Florida Keys Dive Center**, on U.S. 1 at MM 90.5, Tavernier (© **305/852-4599**), takes snorkelers and divers to the reefs of John Pennekamp Coral Reef State Park and environs every day. PADI (Professional Association of Diving Instructors) training courses are also available for the uninitiated. Tours leave at 8am and 12:30pm and cost $25 per person to snorkel (plus $8 rental fee for mask, snorkel, and fins) and $59 per person to dive (plus an extra $20 if you need to rent all the gear).

At **Hall's Dive Center & Career Institute**, U.S. 1 at MM 48.5, Marathon (© **305/743-5929**), snorkelers and divers can choose to explore Looe Key, Sombrero Reef, Delta Shoal, Content Key, or Coffins Patch. Tours are scheduled daily at 9am and 1pm. You will spend 1 hour at each of two sites per tour. If you mention this book, you will get a special discounted rate that's $5 to $10 off the regular rates of $30 per person to snorkel (additional gear is $11) and $40 per person to dive (tanks are $8.50 each).

With **SNUBA Tours of Key Largo** (© **305/451-6391**; www.pennekamp.com/sw/snuba.htm), you can dive down to 20 feet attached to a comfortable breathing apparatus that really gives you the feeling of scuba diving, without having to be certified. You can tour shallow coral reefs teeming with hundreds of colorful fish and plant life, from sea turtles to moray eels. Reservations are required; call to find out where and when to meet. A 2- to 3-hour underwater tour (typically 1–4pm) costs $75, including all equipment. If you have never dived before, you may require a 1-hour lesson in the pool, which costs an additional $45.

FISHING **Robbie's Partyboats & Charters**, on U.S. 1 at MM 84.5, Islamorada (© **305/664-8070** or 305/664-4196), located at the south end of the Holiday Isle Docks, offers day and night deep-sea and reef fishing trips aboard a 65-foot party boat. Big-game fishing charters are also available, and "splits" are arranged for solo fishers. Party-boat fishing costs $25 for a half-day morning tour (rod and reel rental $3); it's $15 extra if you want to go back out on an afternoon tour. Charters run $400 for a half day, $600 for a full day; splits begin at $65 per person. Phone for information and reservations.

Bud n' Mary's Fishing Marina, on U.S. 1 at MM 79.8, Islamorada (© **800/742-7945** or 305/664-2461; www.budnmarys.com), one of the largest marinas between Miami and Key West, is packed with sailors offering guided backcountry fishing charters. This is the place to go if you want to stalk tarpon, bonefish, and snapper. If the seas are not too rough, deep-sea and coral fishing trips can also be arranged. Charters cost $500 to $550 for a half day, $750 to $800 for a full day, and splits begin at $125 per person.

The Bounty Hunter, 15th Street at Burdine's Marina, Marathon (© **305/ 743-2446**), offers full- and half-day outings. For 28 years, Captain Brock Hook's huge sign has boasted, NO FISH, NO PAY. You're guaranteed to catch something, or your money back! Choose your prey from shark, barracuda, sailfish, or whatever else is running. Prices are $400 for a half day, $500 for three-quarters of a day, and $600 for a full day. Rates are for groups of no more than six people.

SHOPPING

On your way to the Keys, you'll find an outlet center, the **Prime Outlets at Florida City** (© **305/248-4727**), at 250 E. Palm Dr. (where the Florida Turnpike meets U.S. Hwy. 1), in Florida City. The center holds more than 60 stores, including Nike Factory Store, Bass Co. Store, Levi's, OshKosh, and Izod. Travelers can pick up a free discount coupon booklet called the Come Back Pack from the Customer Service Center. The outlet is open Monday to Saturday from 10am to 9pm, Sunday from 11am to 6pm.

The Upper and Middle Keys have no shortage of tacky tourist shops selling shells and T-shirts (the ubiquitous "beads and trinkets") and other hokey souvenirs, but for real Keys-style shopping, check out the weekend flea markets. The best, **The Key Largo Storage/Flea Market,** is held every Saturday and Sunday bay-side at MM 103.5 (© **305/451-0567**). Dozens of vendors open their stalls from 9am until 4 or 5pm, selling every imaginable sort of antiques, T-shirts, plants, shoes, books, toys, and games, as well as a hearty dose of good old-fashioned junk. Also decent is the **Grassy Key Flea Market,** at MM 60, on the ocean side. Other flea markets in the area are more unpredictable.

A mecca for fishing and sports enthusiasts, **The World Wide Sportsman** (© **305/664-4615**) at MM 81.5 is not only the largest fishing store in the Keys, but also a meeting place for anglers from all over the world. Every possible gizmo and gadget, plus hundreds of T-shirts, hats, books, and gift items are displayed in its more than 25,000 square feet. The salespeople are knowledgeable and eager to help. Travel specialists can even arrange for charter trips and backcountry tours. The store is open daily from 7am until 8:30pm.

ACCOMMODATIONS YOU CAN AFFORD

U.S. 1 is lined with chain hotels in all price ranges. In the Upper Keys, the best moderately priced option is the **Ramada Limited Resort & Casino** (© **800/ THE-KEYS** or 305/451-3939) at MM 100, off of U.S. 1 in Key Largo, which has three pools and a casino boat and is just 3 miles from John Pennekamp Coral Reef State Park. Another good option in the Upper Keys is **Islamorada Days Inn,** U.S. 1 at MM 82.5 (© **800/DAYS-INN** or 305/664-3681). In the Middle Keys, the **Wellesley Inn** at 13351 Overseas Hwy., MM 54 in Marathon (© **305/743-8550**), also offers reasonably priced ocean-side rooms.

For the best value in the Keys, plan your trip in the off-season. That doesn't necessarily mean the scorching days of summer. Try September or May for great deals; midweek specials abound year-round as well. But be sure to check that your trip doesn't coincide with a major holiday, fishing tournament, or festival.

Since the real beauty of the Keys lies mostly beyond the highways, there is no better way to see this area than by boat. Why not stay in a floating hotel? Especially if traveling with a group, houseboats can be economical. To rent a houseboat, call Ruth and Michael Sullivan at **Smilin' Island Houseboat Rentals** (MM 99.5), Key Largo (© **305/451-1930**). Rates are from $750 to $1,350 for 3 nights. Boats accommodate up to six people.

THE UPPER & MIDDLE KEYS: KEY LARGO TO MARATHON

Banana Bay Resort & Marina ★★ *Finds* *Kids*   It doesn't look like much from the sign-cluttered Overseas Highway, but when you enter the lush grounds of Banana Bay, you will realize you're in one of the most bucolic and best-run properties in the Upper Keys. Built in the early 1950s as a place for fishermen to stay during extended trips, the resort is a beachfront maze of two-story buildings hidden among banyans and palms. The rooms are moderately sized, and many have private balconies where you can enjoy your complimentary coffee and newspaper every morning. Recent additions to the hotel include a recreational activity area with horseshoe pits, a bocce court, picnic areas with barbecue grills, and a giant lawn chessboard. The hotel's kitschy restaurant serves three meals a day, indoors or poolside. This resort is family friendly, but if you're looking for an adults-only resort, there's also a Banana Bay Resort in Key West (© **305/296-6925**) that doesn't allow children.

U.S. 1 at MM 49.5, Marathon, FL 33050. © **800/BANANA-1** or 305/743-3500. Fax 305/743-2670. www.bananabay.com. 60 units. Winter $125–$250 double; off-season $85–$175 double. Rates include continental breakfast. 3- and 7-night honeymoon & wedding packages available. AE, DC, DISC, MC, V. **Amenities:** Restaurant, 3 bars; pool; tennis courts; health club; Jacuzzi; water-sports rental and excursions; charter fishing; self-service laundry. *In room:* A/C, TV, dataport, fridge, hair dryer, iron.

Conch Key Cottages ★★ *Finds* *Kids*   Here's your chance to play castaway in the Keys. Occupying its own private micro-island just off U.S. 1, Conch Key Cottages is a comfortable hideaway run by live-in owners Ron Wilson and Wayne Byrnes, who are constantly fixing and adding to their unique property. This is a place to get away from it all; the cottages aren't located close to much, except maybe one or two interesting eateries. The cabins, which were built at different times over the past 40 years, overlook their own stretch of natural, but very small, private beach. Each has a screened-in porch, cozy bedroom, bathroom, hammock, barbecue grill, and two-person kayak. Request one of the two-bedroom cottages—especially if you are traveling with the family. They are the most spacious and are well designed, practically tailor-made for couples or families. On the other side of the pool are a handful of efficiency apartments (all with fully equipped kitchens) that are similarly outfitted, but enjoy no beach frontage.

Near U.S. 1 at MM 62.3, Marathon, FL 33050. © **800/330-1577** or 305/289-1377. Fax 305/743-8207. www.conchkeycottages.com. 12 cottages. Dec 15–Sept 8 $110–$288; Sept 9–Dec 14 $74–$215. DISC, MC, V. **Amenities:** Pool; complimentary kayaks; laundry. *In room:* A/C, TV, kitchen, coffeemaker. No phone.

Faro Blanco Marine Resort ★   Spanning both sides of the Overseas Highway and all on waterfront property, this resort is a huge, two-shore marina and hotel complex. Although they're the least expensive options, you should avoid the camp-style cottages here, which are musty and in dire need of rehabilitation. Instead, the houseboats are the best choice and value. Permanently tethered (so tightly moored, you hardly move at all, even in the roughest weather) in a tranquil marina, these white rectangular boats look like floating mobile homes and are uniformly clean, fresh, and recommendable, with four hotel rooms per boat. They have colonial American-style furnishings, fully equipped kitchenettes, front and back porches, and water, water everywhere.

1996 Overseas Hwy., U.S. 1 at MM 48.5, Marathon, FL 33050. © **800/759-3276** or 305/743-9018. Fax 305/866-5235. 247 units. Winter $109–$200 houseboat. Off-season $99–$178 houseboat. AE, DISC, MC, V. **Amenities:** 4 restaurants, 2 lounges; Olympic-size pool; fully equipped dive shop; playground. *In room:* A/C, TV.

Lime Tree Bay Resort Motel   The Lime Tree Bay Resort is the only hotel in the tiny town of Layton (pop. 183). Midway between Islamorada and Marathon, the hotel is only steps from Long Key State Recreation Area. It's situated on a very pretty piece of waterfront graced with hundreds of mature palm trees and lots of other tropical foliage. Motel rooms and efficiencies have tiny bathrooms with standing showers but are clean and well maintained. Fifteen efficiencies and suites have kitchenettes.

U.S. 1 at MM 68.5 in Layton, Long Key, FL 33001. © 800/723-4519 or 305/664-4740. Fax 305/664-0750. www.limetreebayresort.com. 30 units. Winter $102–$235 double; off-season $79–$215 double. AE, DC, DISC, MC, V. **Amenities:** Restaurant; small outdoor pool; tennis court; Jacuzzi; water-sports equipment rental. *In room:* A/C, TV, dataport, kitchenette (in some units).

Ragged Edge Resort ⭐⭐ This small oceanfront property's 11 units are spread out along more than half a dozen gorgeous, grassy waterfront acres. All are immaculately clean and comfortable, and most are outfitted with full kitchens and tasteful furnishings. There's no bar, restaurant, or staff to speak of, but the retreat's affable owner, Jackie Barnes, is happy to lend you bicycles or good advice on the area's offerings. A large dock attracts boaters and a good variety of local and migratory birds.

243 Treasure Harbor Rd. (near MM 86.5), Islamorada, FL 33036. © 800/436-2023 or 305/852-5389. www.ragged-edge.com. 11 units. Winter $69–$189; off-season $49–$132. AE, MC, V. **Amenities:** Outdoor pool; free use of bikes; laundry. *In room:* A/C, kitchen (most units), fridge, coffeemaker.

SUPER-CHEAP SLEEPS

Bay Harbor Lodge ⭐ A small, simple retreat that's big on charm, the Bay Harbor Lodge is an extraordinarily welcoming place. The lodge is far from fancy, though it features new windows and paint, and the widely ranging accommodations are not created equal. The motel rooms are small and ordinary in decor, but even the least expensive is recommendable. The efficiencies are larger motel rooms with fully equipped kitchenettes. The oceanfront cottages are larger still, have full kitchens, and represent one of the best values in the Keys. The vinyl-covered furnishings and old-fashioned wallpapers won't win any design awards, but elegance isn't what the "real" Keys are about. The 1½ lush acres of grounds are planted with banana trees and have an outdoor heated pool and several small barbecue grills. A small beach is ideal for some quiet sunning and relaxation. Guests are free to use the rowboats, paddleboats, canoes, kayaks, and snorkeling equipment. Bring your own beach towels.

97702 Overseas Hwy., U.S. 1 at MM 97.7 (off the southbound lane of U.S. 1), Key Largo, FL 33037. © 800/385-0986 or 305/852-5695. www.thefloridakeys.com/bayharborlodge. 16 units. Winter $75–$165 double; $95–$165 cottage. Off-season $65–$95 double; $95–$105 cottage. MC, V. **Amenities:** Freshwater pool; water-sports equipment rental. *In room:* A/C, TV, fridge, microwave, coffeemaker, hair dryer.

Bonefish Resort Operated by the Moir family, this bare-bones accommodation is popular with anglers and boaters. Rates are extremely reasonable, considering that the price includes free use of canoes, rowboats, or paddleboats. All of the modest rooms are different; some have futons for extra guests and a potpourri of art on the wall, sent from around the world by loyal return guests. Oceanfront suites have private kitchens and decks. There's a gas grill on the property, as well as a friendly pot-bellied pig named Willie.

58070 Overseas Hwy., MM 58 (ocean side), Grassy Key, FL 33050. © 800/274-9949 or 305/743-7107. Fax 305/743-0449. www.bonefishresort.com. 14 units. Winter $59–$159 single or double; off-season $49–$99 single or double. Extra person or pet $10 a night. DISC, MC, V. **Amenities:** Jacuzzi; free use of non-motorized boats. *In room:* A/C, TV, dataport, fridge, coffeemaker.

CAMPING

One of Florida's best parks (see the "Two Exceptional State Parks" section above), **John Pennekamp Coral Reef State Park** ⭐⭐ offers 47 well-separated campsites, half of which are available by advance reservation, the rest distributed on a first-come, first-served basis. The tent sites are small but well equipped with restrooms, hot water, and showers. Two man-made beaches and a small lagoon nearby attract many large wading birds. Each site costs $24 per night without electricity, or $26 with electricity. It also costs $4 per vehicle to enter the park, plus 50¢ for each additional passenger. Call © 305/451-1202 for information and © 800/326-3521 for reservations. Reservations are held until 5pm, and the park must be notified of late arrival by phone on the check-in date. Pennekamp opens at 8am and closes around sundown. Note that the local environment provides fertile breeding grounds for insects, particularly in the late summer, so bring insect repellent or you will be sorry.

The Upper Keys' other main state park, **Long Key State Park**, is more secluded than its northern neighbor—and more popular (see the "Two Exceptional State Parks" section earlier in this chapter). All sites, costing $24 to $26 for up to four people, are located ocean-side and are surrounded by narrow rows of trees and nearby toilet and restroom facilities. It costs $3.25 per vehicle to enter the park. Reserve well in advance, especially in winter, by calling © **305/664-4815**.

GREAT DEALS ON DINING

Although not known as a culinary hot spot (though always improving), the Upper and Middle Keys do offer some excellent restaurants, most of which specialize in seafood. Often, visitors (especially those who fish) take advantage of accommodations that have kitchen facilities and cook their own meals. Some restaurants will even clean and cook your catch, for a fee.

Barracuda Grill ★★ SEAFOOD   Owned by Lance Hill and his wife, Jan, this small, casual spot serves excellent seafood, steaks, and chops, but unfortunately, it's only open for dinner. Some of the favorite dishes are the Caicos Gold Conch and Mangrove Snapper and Mango. Try the Tipsy Olives appetizer, marinated in gin or vodka, to kick-start your meal. For fans of spicy food, try the red-hot calamari. Decorated with barracuda-themed art, the restaurant also features a well-priced American wine list with lots of California vintages.

U.S. 1 at MM 49.5 (bay side), Marathon. © 305/743-3314. Main courses $10–$26. AE, MC, V. Mon–Sat 6–10pm.

Calypso's ★ SEAFOOD   The awning still bears the name of the former restaurant, Demar's, but the food here is all Todd Lollis's, an inspired young chef who looks like he might be more comfortable at a Grateful Dead concert than in a kitchen, but who turns out inventive seafood dishes in a casual and rustic waterside setting. If it's available, try the butter pecan sauce over whatever fish is freshest. Don't miss the white wine sangria, full of tangy oranges and limes and topped with a dash of cinnamon. The prices are surprisingly reasonable, but the service can be a little more laid-back than you're used to. The toughest part is finding the place. From the south, turn right at the blinking yellow lights near MM 99.5 to Ocean Bay Drive and then turn right again. Look for the blue vinyl-sided building on the left.

1 Seagate Blvd. (near MM 99.5), Key Largo. © 305/451-0600. Main courses $9–$18. MC, V. Wed–Mon 11:30am–10pm; Fri and Sat until 11pm.

Islamorada Fish Company Restaurant & Bakery ★★ SEAFOOD   The original **Islamorada Fish Company,** U.S. 1 at MM 81.5, Islamorada (© **305/664-9271**), has been selling seafood out of its roadside shack since 1948. It's still the best place to pick up a cooler of stone crab claws in season (mid-Oct to Apr). Also great are the fried-fish sandwiches, served with melted American cheese, fried onions, and coleslaw. A few hundred yards up the road you'll find the newer restaurant and bakery, which looks like an average diner but has a selection of fantastic seafood and pastas. It's also *the* place for breakfast. Locals gather for politics and gossip as well as delicious grits, oatmeal, omelets, and homemade pastries.

U.S. 1 at MM 81.6, Islamorada. © 800/258-2559 or 305/664-8363. www.islamoradafishco.com. Reservations not accepted. Main courses $8–$27; appetizers $4–$7. DISC, MC, V. Sun–Thurs 11am–9 pm; Fri-Sat 11am–10pm.

Lazy Days Oceanfront Bar and Seafood Grill ★ SEAFOOD/AMERICAN
Opened in 1992, the Lazy Days quickly became one of the most popular restaurants around, mostly because of its large portions and lively atmosphere. Dining on the oceanfront outdoor veranda is highly recommended. Meals are pricier than the casual dining room would suggest, but the food is good enough and the menu varied. Steamed clams with garlic and bell peppers make a tempting appetizer. The menu focuses on—what else?—seafood, but you can also find good pasta dishes such as linguine with littleneck clams. Most main courses come with a baked potato, vegetables, a tossed salad, and French bread, making appetizers redundant.

U.S. 1 at MM 79.9, Islamorada. © 305/664-5256. Main courses $11–$29.95. AE, DISC, MC, V. Wed–Sun 11:30am–10pm.

Lorelei Restaurant and Cabana Bar ★★ SEAFOOD/BAR FOOD
Don't resist the siren call of the enormous, sparkling roadside mermaid—you won't be dashed onto the rocks. This big old fish house and bar is a great place for a snack, a meal, or a beer. Inside, a good-value menu focuses mainly on seafood. When in season, lobsters are the way to go. For $20, you can get a good-sized tail—at least a 1-pounder—prepared any way you like. Other fare includes the standard clam chowder, fried shrimp, and doughy conch fritters. Salads and soups are hearty and satisfying. For those tired of fish, the menu also offers a few beef selections. The outside bar has live music every evening, and you can order snacks and light meals from a limited menu that is satisfying and well priced.

U.S. 1 at MM 82, Islamorada. © 305/664-4656. Main courses $12–$24. AE, DC, DISC, MC, V. Daily 7am–10:30pm. Outside bar serves breakfast 7–11am; lunch/appetizer menu 11am–9pm. Bar closes at midnight.

Time Out Barbecue ★★ BARBECUE
This barbecue joint serves up hot and hearty old-fashioned barbecue that is among the best around. According to management, the secret is in the slow cooking—more than 10 hours for the melt-in-your-mouth soft pork sandwich. Topped off with delicious, not-too-creamy coleslaw and sweet baked beans, any of the many offerings are worth a stop. You can grab a seat at the picnic table on the grassy lawn next to the Trading Post.

U.S. 1 at MM 81.5 (ocean side), Islamorada. © 305/664-8911. Sandwiches $4.25–$6; rib and chicken platters to share $7–$15. MC, V. Daily 11am–10pm.

WORTH A SPLURGE

Green Turtle Inn ★★ SEAFOOD
The Green Turtle Inn was established in 1947 as a place where anglers and travelers to and from Key West could stop for local delicacies made from sea turtles harvested in local waters. It has become the quintessential Keys eatery, with a friendly, local flavor and delicious and *different*

fare, such as turtle steaks, soups, and chowders. Alligator steak is also popular and, yes, it does taste like chicken. Campy house pianist Tina Martin has become somewhat of a local celebrity, but it's really the Turtle Chowder for which the inn has become best known. The restaurant also has a cannery so you can take some of the chowder to your friends, who won't believe how good it is until they taste it for themselves.

U.S. 1 at MM 81.5, Islamorada. ✆ 305/664-9031. Main courses $13.50–$21.95. AE, DISC, MC, V. Tues–Sun noon–10pm.

Marker 88 ✪✪✪ SEAFOOD/REGIONAL   An institution in the Upper Keys, Marker 88 has been pleasing locals and visitors for dinner since it opened in the early 1970s. Chef-owner Andre Mueller fuses tropical fruit and fish with such items as crabmeat stuffing, asparagus, tomatoes, lemons, olives, capers, and mushrooms to make the most delectable and innovative seafood dishes around. Taking full advantage of his island location, Andre offers dozens of seafood selections, including Keys lobster, Bahamas conch, Florida Bay stone crabs, Gulf Coast shrimp, and an impressive variety of fish from around the country. After you've figured out what kind of seafood to have, you can choose from a dozen styles of preparation. The Keys' standard style is meunière, which is a subtle, tasty sauce of lemon and parsley. Although everything looks tempting, don't over-order—portions are huge. The waitresses, who are pleasant enough, require a bit of patience, but the food—not to mention the spectacular Gulf views from the outdoor bar and tables—is worth it.

U.S. 1 at MM 88 (bay side), Islamorada. ✆ 305/852-9315. Reservations suggested. Main courses $14–$33. AE, DC, DISC, MC, V. Tues–Sun 5–11pm. Closed in Sept.

THE UPPER & MIDDLE KEYS AFTER DARK

Nightlife in the Upper Keys tends to start well before the sun goes down, often at noon, since most people—visitors and locals alike—are on vacation. Also, many anglers and sports-minded folk go to bed early.

Hog Heaven opened in the early 1990s, the joint venture of some young locals tired of tourist traps. Located at MM 85.3, just off the main road on the ocean side in Islamorada (✆ **305/664-9669**), it's a welcome respite from the neon-colored cocktail circuit. This whitewashed biker bar offers a waterside view and diversions that include big-screen TVs and video games. The food isn't bad, either. The atmosphere is cliquish since most patrons are regulars, so start up a game of pool or skeet to break the ice. It's open 11am to 4am daily.

No trip to the Keys is complete without a stop at the **Tiki Bar at the Holiday Isle Resort,** U.S. 1 at MM 84, Islamorada (✆ **800/327-7070** or 305/664-2321). Hundreds of revelers visit this ocean-side spot for drinks and dancing at any time of day, but the live rock music starts at 8:30pm. The thatched-roof Tiki Bar draws a high-energy but laid-back mix of thirsty people, all in pursuit of a good time. In the afternoon and early evening (when everyone is either sunburned, drunk, or just happy to be dancing to live reggae), head for **Kokomo's,** just next door. Kokomo's often closes at 7:30pm on weekends (5:30 on weekdays), so get there early. For information, call the Tiki Bar at the Holiday Isle Resort above.

Locals and tourists mingle at the outdoor cabana bar at **Lorelei** (see "Great Deals on Dining," above). Most evenings after 5pm, you'll find local bands playing on a thatched-roof stage—mainly rock-and-roll, reggae, and sometimes blues.

Woody's Saloon and Restaurant, on U.S. 1 at MM 82, Islamorada (✆ **305/664-4335**), is a lively, wacky, loud, gritty, raunchy, local legend of a place serving up mediocre pizzas and live bands almost every night. The house band, Big Dick and the Extenders, showcases a 300-pound Native American who does a lewd, rude, and crude routine of jokes and songs starting at 9pm, Tuesday through Sunday. He is a legend. There's a small cover charge most nights. Drink specials, contests, and the legendary Big Dick keep this place packed until 4am almost every night.

For a more subdued atmosphere, try the handsome stained-glass and mahogany-wood bar and club at **Zane Grey's**, on the second floor of World Wide Sportsman at MM 81.5 (© **305/664-4244**). Outside, enjoy a view of the calm waters of the bay; inside, soak up the history of some real longtime anglers. It's open from 11am to 11pm, and later on weekends. Call to find out who's playing on weekends, when there is live entertainment and no cover charge.

2 The Lower Keys ★★: Big Pine Key to Coppitt Key

128 miles SW of Miami

Unlike their neighbors to the north and south, the Lower Keys (including Big Pine, Sugarloaf, and Summerland) are devoid of rowdy spring-break crowds, boast few T-shirt and trinket shops, and have almost no late-night bars. What they do offer are the very best opportunities to enjoy the vast natural resources on land and water that make the area so rich. Stay overnight in the Lower Keys, rent a boat, and explore the reefs—it might be the most memorable part of your trip.

ESSENTIALS
GETTING THERE See "Essentials" for the Upper and Middle Keys in section 1. If you are coming from that direction, continue south on U.S. 1. You've entered the Lower Keys once you've crossed the Seven-Mile Bridge.

If instead you are driving north from the airport in Key West (see "Essentials" in section 1), simply turn left onto South Roosevelt Boulevard and go over the Stock Island Bridge, which leads directly to U.S. 1.

VISITOR INFORMATION The **Big Pine and Lower Keys Chamber of Commerce,** ocean side of U.S. 1 at MM 31 (P.O. Box 430511), Big Pine Key, FL 33043 (© **800/872-3722** or 305/872-2411; fax 305/872-0752; www.lowerkeyschamber.com), is open Monday through Friday from 9am to 5pm and Saturday from 9am to 3pm. The pleasant staff will help with anything a traveler may need. Call, write, or stop in for a comprehensive, detailed information packet.

WHAT TO SEE & DO
Once the centerpiece of the Lower Keys (these days, it's Big Pine Key) and still a great asset is **Bahia Honda State Park** ★, U.S. 1 at MM 37.5, Big Pine Key (© **305/872-2353**). Even after the violent storms of 1998, the park still possesses one of the most beautiful coastlines in South Florida. Bahia Honda (pronounced *Bah*-ya) is a great place for hiking, bird-watching, swimming, snorkeling, and fishing. The 524-acre park encompasses a wide variety of ecosystems, including coastal mangroves, beach dunes, and tropical hammocks. There are miles of trails packed with unusual plants and animals and a small white beach. Shaded seaside picnic areas are fitted with tables and grills. Although the beach is never wider than 5 feet even at low tide, this is the Lower Keys' best beach area.

True to its name (Spanish for "deep bay"), the park has relatively deep waters close to shore, and they are perfect for snorkeling and diving. Easy offshore snorkeling here gives even novices a chance to lie suspended in warm water and simply observe diverse marine life passing by. You can also head to the stunning reefs at Looe Key, where the coral and fish life are more vibrant than anywhere else in the United States. Snorkeling trips depart from Bahia Honda concessions for Looe Key National Marine Sanctuary (4 miles off-shore) twice daily from March through September and cost $25.95 for adults, $20.95 for youths 6 to 14; free for children 5 and under. Call ✆ **305/872-3210** for a schedule.

Admission to the park is $4 per vehicle (plus 50¢ per person), $1.50 per pedestrian or bicyclist, free for children 5 and under. If you are alone in a car, you'll pay only $2.50. It's open daily from 8am to sunset.

The most famous residents of the Lower Keys are the tiny Key deer. Of the estimated 300 existing in the world, two-thirds live on Big Pine Key's **National Key Deer Refuge**. To get your bearings, stop by the rangers' office at the Winn-Dixie Shopping Plaza near MM 30.5 off U.S. 1. They'll give you an informative brochure and map of the area. The refuge is open Monday through Friday from 8am to 5pm.

If the office is closed, go ahead and make your way to the **Blue Hole,** a former rock quarry now filled with the fresh water that's vital to the deer's survival. To get there, turn right at Big Pine Key's only traffic light onto Key Deer Boulevard (take the left fork immediately after the turn) and continue 1½ miles to the observation-site parking lot, on your left. The half-mile **Watson Hammock Trail,** about a third of a mile past the Blue Hole, is the refuge's only marked footpath. Try coming out to the footpath in the early morning or late evening to catch a glimpse of these gentle, dog-sized deer. There is an observation deck there from which you can watch and photograph the protected species. They are more active in cool hours and in cooler times of the year. Don't be surprised to see a lazy alligator warming itself in the sun, particularly in outlying areas around the Blue Hole. If you do see a gator, do not go near it, do not touch it, and do not provoke it. Keep your distance and if you must get a photo, use a zoom lens. Also, whatever you do, do not feed the deer—it will threaten their survival. Call the **park office** (✆ **305/872-2239**) to find out about the infrequent free tours of the refuge, scheduled throughout the year.

AFFORDABLE OUTDOOR PURSUITS

BICYCLING If you have your own bike, or your lodging offers a rental (many do), the Lower Keys are a great place to get off busy U.S. 1 to explore the beautiful back roads. On Big Pine Key, cruise along Key Deer Boulevard (at MM 30). Those with fat tires can ride into the National Key Deer Refuge.

BIRD-WATCHING Bring your birding books. A stopping point for migratory birds on the Eastern Flyway, the Lower Keys are populated with many West Indian bird species, especially during spring and fall. The small vegetated islands of the Keys are the only nesting sites in the United States for the great white heron and the white-crowned pigeon. They're also some of the very few breeding places for the reddish egret, the roseate spoonbill, the mangrove cuckoo, and the black-whiskered vireo. Look for them on Bahia Honda Key and the many uninhabited islands nearby.

BOATING Dozens of shops rent powerboats for fishing and reef exploring. Most also rent tackle, sell bait, and have charter captains available. **Bud Boats,** at the Old Wooden Bridge Fishing Camp and Marina, MM 30 in Big Pine Key (✆ **305/872-9165**), has a wide selection of well-maintained boats. Depending on the size, rentals cost between $70 and $250 for a day, between $50 and $130 for a half day. Another good option is **Jaybird's Powerboats,** U.S. 1 at MM 33,

> ### A Batty Idea
> The only man-made attraction in the Lower Keys is the **Sugarloaf Bat Tower**, off U.S. 1 at MM 17 (next to Sugarloaf Airport on the bay side). In a vain effort to battle the ubiquitous troublesome mosquitoes in the Lower Keys, developer Clyde Perkey built this odd structure to lure bug-eating bats. Despite his alluring design and a pungent bat aphrodisiac, his guests never showed. Since 1929, this wooden, flat-topped, 45-foot-high pyramid has stood empty and deserted, except for the occasional tourist who stops to wonder what it is. There is no sign or marker to commemorate this odd remnant of ingenuity. It's worth a 5-minute detour to see it. To get there, turn right at the Sugarloaf Airport sign and then right again onto the dirt road that begins just before the airport gate; the tower is about 100 yards ahead.

Big Pine Key (© **305/872-8500**). They rent for full days only. Prices start at $155 for a 19-footer.

CANOEING & KAYAKING The Overseas Highway (U.S. 1) touches on only a few dozen of the many hundreds of islands that make up the Keys. To really see the Lower Keys, rent a kayak or canoe—perfect for these shallow waters. **Reflections Kayak Nature Tours,** operating out of Parmer's Resort, on U.S. 1 at MM 28.5, Little Torch Key (© **305/872-2896**), offers fully outfitted backcountry wildlife tours with an expert guide. The expert, Mike Wedeking, a former U.S. Forest Service guide, keeps up an engaging discussion of the area's fish, sponges, coral, osprey, hawks, eagles, alligators, raccoons, and deer. The 3-hour tours cost $49 per person and include spring water, fresh fruit, granola bars, and use of binoculars. Bring a towel and sea sandals or sneakers. You can also rent a kayak here to take out on your own for $30.

FISHING A day spent fishing, either in the shallow backcountry or in the deep sea, is a great way to ensure yourself a fresh fish dinner, or you can release your catch and just appreciate the challenge. Whichever you choose, **Larry Threlkeld's Strike Zone Charters,** U.S. 1 at MM 29.5, Big Pine Key (© **305/872-9863**), is the charter service to call. Prices for guided fishing excursions start at $450 for a half day and $595 for a full day. If you have enough anglers to share the price, it isn't too steep. They may also be able to match you with other interested visitors.

HIKING You can hike throughout the flat marshy Keys, on both marked trails and meandering coastlines. The best places to trek through nature are **Bahia Honda State Park** at MM 29.5 and **National Key Deer Refuge** at MM 30 (for more information on both, see above). Bahia Honda Park has a free brochure describing an excellent self-guided tour along the Silver Palm Nature Trail. You'll traverse hammocks, mangroves, and sand dunes and cross a lagoon. The walk (less than a mile) explores a great cross-section of the natural habitat in the Lower Keys and can be done in under half an hour.

SNORKELING & DIVING Snorkelers and divers should not miss the Keys' most dramatic reefs at the **Looe Key National Marine Sanctuary.** Here, you'll see more than 150 varieties of hard and soft coral—some, centuries old—as well as every type of tropical fish, including gold and blue parrot fish, moray eels, barracudas, French angels, and tarpon. In addition to the expeditions led from

Bahia Honda Park (see above), **Looe Key Dive Center,** U.S. 1 at MM 27.5, Ramrod Key (© **305/872-2215**), offers a mind-blowing 5-hour tour aboard a 45-foot catamaran with two shallow 1-hour dives for snorkelers and scuba divers. Snorkelers pay $22.50, and divers with their own equipment pay $35. On Wednesdays and Saturdays you can do a fascinating dive to the *Adolphus Busch Sr.*, a shipwreck sunk off Looe Key in 100 feet of water, for $40. Good-quality rentals are available.

SHOPPING

Certainly not known for great shopping, the Lower Keys do happen to be home to many talented visual artists, particularly those who specialize in depicting their natural surroundings. The **Artists in Paradise Gallery,** on Big Pine Key in the Winn-Dixie Shopping Plaza, near MM 30.5, 1 block north of U.S. 1 at the traffic light (© **305/872-1828**), displays a changing selection of watercolors, oils, photos, and sculptures. This cooperative gallery displays the work of more than a dozen artists who share the task of watching the store. Hours are usually daily from 10am to 6pm.

ACCOMMODATIONS YOU CAN AFFORD

So far, there are no national hotel chains in the Lower Keys. For information on lodging in cabins or trailers at local campgrounds, see "Camping," below.

Barnacle Bed & Breakfast   Joan Cornell, the Barnacle's owner, was once an innkeeper in Vermont. Her Big Pine Key home has only four bedrooms, each with its own character. Two are located upstairs in the main house—their doors open into the home's living room, which contains a small Jacuzzi-style tub. For privacy, the remaining two rooms are best; each has its own entrance and is out of earshot of the common areas. The Cottage Room, a freestanding, peak-topped bedroom, is our favorite, outfitted with a kitchenette and pretty furnishings. The accommodations are standard, not luxurious. The property has its own private sandy beach where you can float all day on the inn's rafts, rubber boat, or kayak. Beach towels, chairs, bicycles, and coolers are available at no charge. The Barnacle is also a dedicated dive resort, where you can learn to scuba and get certified to do so.

1557 Long Beach Dr. (P.O. Box 780), Big Pine Key, FL 33043. © **800/465-9100** or 305/872-3298. Fax 305/872-3863. www.thebarnacle.net. 4 units. Winter $95–$150 single or double; off-season $85–$140 single or double. Rates include breakfast. DC, DISC, MC, V. From U.S. 1 south, turn left at the Spanish Harbor Bridge (MM 33) onto Long Beach Rd. Look left for the stone wall and signs to the house on the left. No children under 16. **Amenities:** Jacuzzi; diving instruction; free use of bikes and kayaks. *In room:* A/C, TV, fridge.

Big Pine Key Fishing Lodge *Value*   Sitting on 6 acres of lush ocean-side land, this super-affordable and well-maintained property is a favorite of campers and boaters. Most of the lodges contain full kitchenettes, and nearly all offer microwaves and refrigerators. Though you won't find a phone in your room, there are plenty of conveniently located pay phones. A large heated pool with a sun deck and lounge chairs is a plus, especially since there isn't any real beach here (a tiny swath of artificial beach suffices for determined sand lovers). The lodge also boasts an on-site marina.

In addition to the lodges, this spot also maintains 102 campsites right off the ocean, equipped with water, electricity, sewer, and satellite TV. Hurricanes George and Irene destroyed most of the trees in the camping area, so it's a good idea to bring along something that will provide you with some shade.

P.O. Box 513, MM 33, Big Pine Key, FL 33043. © **305/872-2351.** 16 units (showers only); 102 campsites. Year-round $73–$89 single or double, $89–$95 loft room for 1–4 people, $24–$31 campsites for tent or with full hookup. Discounts for stays longer than a week. Extra person $10. DISC, MC, V. **Amenities:** Heated pool; game room; laundry. *In room:* A/C, TV. Kitchenette, fridge, and microwave in some. No phone.

Deer Run Bed and Breakfast ★★ *Finds*   Located directly on the beach, Sue Abbott's small, homey, smoke-free B&B is a real find. One upstairs and two downstairs guest rooms are comfortably furnished with queen-size beds, good closets, and touch-sensitive lamps. Rattan and 1970s-style chairs and couches furnish the living room, along with 13 birds and 3 cats. Breakfast, which is served on a pretty, fenced-in porch, is cooked to order by Sue herself. The wooded area around the property is full of Key deer, which are often spotted on the beach as well. A hot tub overlooking the ocean is especially nice. Ask to use one of the bikes to explore nearby nature trails.

Long Beach Dr. (P.O. Box 431), Big Pine Key, FL 33043. © **305/872-2015.** Fax 305/872-2842. deerrunbb @aol.com. 3 units. Winter from $165 double; off-season from $95 double. Rates include full American breakfast. No credit cards. From U.S. 1 S., turn left at the Big Pine Fishing Lodge (MM 33); continue for about 2 miles. No children under 16. **Amenities:** Jacuzzi; free use of bikes. *In room:* A/C, TV.

Parmer's Resort ★★ *Kids*   Parmer's, a fixture here for more than 20 years, is well known for its charming hospitality and helpful staff. This downscale resort offers modest but comfortable cottages, each of them unique. Some are on the waterfront, many have kitchenettes, and others are just a bedroom. Room 26, a.k.a. Wahoo, a one-bedroom efficiency, is especially nice, with a small sitting area that faces the water. Room 6, a small efficiency, has a kitchenette and an especially large bathroom. The rooms have been recently updated and are consistently very clean. Many can be combined to accommodate large families. The hotel's waterfront location almost makes up for the fact that you must pay extra for maid service.

Barry Ave. (P.O. Box 430665), near MM 28.5, Little Torch Key, FL 33042. © **305/872-2157.** Fax 305/872-2014. www.parmersresort.com. 45 units. Winter $75–$220 double; from $105 efficiency. Off-season $55–$85 double; $75–$150 efficiency. Rates include continental breakfast. AE, DISC, MC, V. From U.S. 1, turn right onto Barry Ave. Resort is a half-mile down on the right. **Amenities:** Heated pool; bike rental; coin-op washers and dryers. *In room:* A/C, TV.

CAMPING

Bahia Honda State Park ★★★ (© **305/872-2353;** www.abfla.com/parks/ BahiaHonda/bahiahonda.html) offers some of the best camping in the Keys. It is as loaded with facilities and activities as it is with campers. However, don't be discouraged by its popularity—this park encompasses more than 500 acres of land, 80 campsites spread throughout three areas, and six spacious and comfortable cabin units (fitting six people each) that were reconstructed between 2000 and 2001. Cabins come complete with linens, kitchenettes, and utensils as well as a wraparound terrace, a barbecue pit, and rocking chairs. For one to four people, camping here costs about $25 per site without electricity and $26 with electricity. Depending on the season, cabin prices change: Prices range from $50 to $110. Additional people over four cost $6 each. MasterCard and Visa are accepted.

Another excellent value can be found at the **KOA Sugarloaf Key Resort** ★★, near MM 20. This ocean-side facility has 200 fully equipped sites, with water, electricity, and sewer, which rent for about $70 a night (no-hookup sites cost about $38). You can also pitch a tent on the 5 acres of lush waterfront property. This site is especially nice because of its private beaches and access to diving, snorkeling, and boating, plus its grounds are well maintained. The resort also rents travel trailers. The 22-foot Dutchman sleeps six and is equipped with eating and cooking utensils, costing about $100 a day. More luxurious trailers go for $160 a day. All major credit cards are accepted. For details, write to P.O. Box 420469, Summerland Key, FL 33042 (C) **800/562-7731** or 305/745-3549; fax 305/745-9889; www.koa.com).

GREAT DEALS ON DINING

There aren't many fine dining options in the Lower Keys, but the following restaurants are adequate choices.

Mangrove Mama's Restaurant SEAFOOD/CARIBBEAN   As the dedicated locals who come daily for happy hour will tell you, this is a true Lower Keys institution, and a dive (the restaurant is a shack that used to have a gas pump as well as a grill) in the best sense of the word. Guests share the property with some miniature horses (out back) and stray cats. You'll find a handful of simple tables, inside and out; those outside are shaded by banana trees and palm fronds. Fish is the menu's mainstay, although soups, salads, sandwiches, and omelets are also good. Grilled teriyaki chicken and club sandwiches are tasty alternatives to fish, as are meatless chef's salads and spicy barbecued babyback ribs.

U.S. 1 at MM 20, Sugarloaf Key. (C) **305/745-3030**. Main courses $10–$20; lunch $6–$9; brunch $5–$7. MC, V. Daily 11:30am–10pm (from 11am in season).

Monte's SEAFOOD   Certainly nobody goes to this restaurant/fish market for its atmosphere: Plastic place settings rest on plastic-covered picnic-style tables in a screen-enclosed dining patio. But Monte's doesn't need great atmosphere, since it has survived for more than 20 years on its very good and incredibly fresh food. The day's catch may include shark, tuna, lobsters, stone crabs, or shrimp.

U.S. 1 at MM 25, Summerland Key. (C) **305/745-3731**. Main courses $13–$17; lunch $6–$10. No credit cards. Mon–Sat 9am–10pm; Sun 10am–9pm.

SUPER-CHEAP EATS

Coco's Kitchen   CUBAN/AMERICAN   This tiny storefront has been dishing out black beans, rice, and shredded beef to fans of Cuban cuisine for more than 10 years. The owners, who are actually from Nicaragua, cook not only superior Cuban food, including Cuban-style roast pork (available on Sat), but also some local specialties, Italian food, and Caribbean food. Local specialties include fried shrimp and whole fried yellowtail. Try the daily specials, which are served with rice and beans or salad and crispy fries. Top off the huge, cheap meal with a rich caramel-soaked flan.

283 Key Deer Blvd. (in the Winn-Dixie Shopping Center), Big Pine Key. (C) **305/872-4495**. Main courses $6–$14.80; breakfast $2–$5. MC, V. Mon–Sat 7am–7:30pm. Turn right at the traffic light near MM 30.5. Stay in the left lane.

No Name Pub PUB FOOD/PIZZA   This funky old bar out in the boonies serves snacks and sandwiches until 11pm on most nights, and drinks until midnight. Pizzas are tasty—thick-crusted and super-cheesy. Try one topped with local shrimp, or consider a bowl of chili with all the fixings—hearty and cheap. Everything is served on paper plates. Locals hang out at the rustic bar, one of the Florida Keys' oldest, drinking beer and listening to a jukebox heavy with 1980s selections. The decor, if you can call it that, is basic—the walls and ceilings are plastered with thousands of autographed dollar bills.

¼ mile south of No Name Bridge on N. Watson Blvd., Big Pine Key. (C) **305/872-9115**. Pizzas $6–$18; subs $5. MC, V. 11am–11pm. Turn right at Big Pine's only traffic light (near MM 30.5) onto Key Deer Blvd. Turn right on Watson Blvd. At stop sign, turn left. Look for a small wooden sign on the left marking the spot.

A SUNDAY BRUNCH

Montego Bay SEAFOOD Known more as a drinking place than a fine-dining spot, Montego Bay does host a fine and filling Sunday brunch. With a huge room full of buffet trays of hot and cold specials like carved meats, salad, seafood, lox, bagels and cream cheese, pastas, eggs to order, and coffee drinks, the brunch is a deal at $14.95. Other days of the week, the dark, old-fashioned dining room is often half full of locals enjoying bar snacks and Caribbean fare. Stick to the basics like fish and soups for the most success.

US. 1 at MM 30.2, Big Pine Key. © 305/872-3009. Reservations recommended. Main courses $9–$19, Sun brunch buffet $14.95. AE, MC, V. Daily 10am–1am.

THE LOWER KEYS AFTER DARK

Although the mellow islands of the Lower Keys aren't exactly known for wild nightlife, there are some friendly bars and restaurants where locals and tourists gather to hang out and have a drink.

One of the most scenic is **Sandbar** (© 305/872-9989), a wide-open breezy wooden house built on slender stilts and overlooking a wide channel on Barry Avenue (near MM 28.5). It attracts an odd mix of bikers and blue-hairs daily from 11am until 10pm and is a great place to overhear local gossip and colorful metaphors. Pool tables are the main attraction, but there's also live music some nights. The drinks are reasonably priced, and the food isn't too bad, either. For another fun bar scene, see **No Name Pub,** above.

3 Key West

159 miles SW of Miami

There are two schools of thought on Key West—one argues that Key West has become way too commercial, and the other maintains that it's still a place where you can go and not worry about being prim, proper, or even well groomed. I think it's a bizarre fusion of both—a fascinating look at small-town America in which people truly live by the (off)beat of their own drum, albeit one with a Gap and Banana Republic thrown in. The locals, or "conchs" (pronounced *conks*), and the developers here have been at odds for years. This once low-key island has been thoroughly commercialized—there's a Hard Rock Cafe smack in the middle of Duval Street, and thousands of cruise-ship passengers descend on Mallory Square each day. It's definitely not the seedy town Hemingway and his cronies once called their own. Or is it?

Laid-back Key West still exists, but it's now found in different places: the backyard of a popular guesthouse, for example, or an art gallery, a secret garden, or the hip hangouts of Bahama Village. Fortunately there are plenty of these, and Key West's greatest historic charm is found just off the beaten path. Don't be afraid to explore these residential areas, as conchs are notoriously friendly. In fact, exploring the side streets always seems to yield a new discovery. Of course, there are always the calm waters of the Atlantic and the Gulf of Mexico all around.

The heart of town offers party people a good time—that is, if your idea of a good time is the smell of stale beer, loud music, and hardly-shy revelers. Here, you'll find good restaurants, fun bars, live music, rickshaw rides, and lots of shopping. Key West also supports a healthy gay community; same-sex couples walking hand in hand are the norm here. If you would prefer to avoid this scene, just look for the ubiquitous rainbow flag hanging outside of gay establishments and you'll know what to expect. For the most part, however, the scene is extremely mixed and colorful. If partying isn't your thing, then avoid Duval

Key West

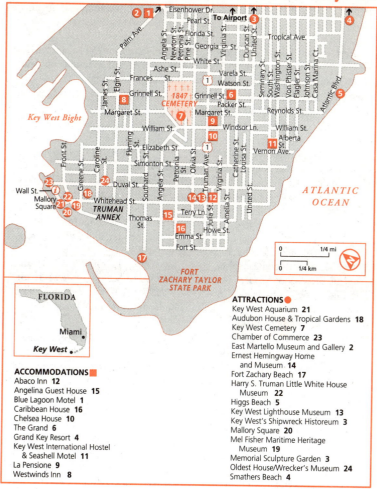

ATTRACTIONS
Key West Aquarium **21**
Audubon House & Tropical Gardens **18**
Key West Cemetery **7**
Chamber of Commerce **23**
East Martello Museum and Gallery **2**
Ernest Hemingway Home and Museum **14**
Fort Zachary Beach **17**
Harry S. Truman Little White House Museum **22**
Higgs Beach **5**
Key West Lighthouse Museum **13**
Key West's Shipwreck Historeum **3**
Mallory Square **20**
Mel Fisher Maritime Heritage Museum **19**
Memorial Sculpture Garden **3**
Oldest House/Wrecker's Museum **24**
Smathers Beach **4**

ACCOMMODATIONS
Abaco Inn **12**
Angelina Guest House **15**
Blue Lagoon Motel **1**
Caribbean House **16**
Chelsea House **10**
The Grand **6**
Grand Key Resort **4**
Key West International Hostel & Seashell Motel **11**
La Pensione **9**
Westwinds Inn **8**

Street (the Bourbon St. of South Florida) at all costs. Instead, take in the scenery at a dockside bar or ocean-side Jacuzzi. Whatever you do, don't bother with a watch or tie—this is the home of the perennial vacation.

ESSENTIALS

GETTING THERE For directions by car, see "Essentials" for the Upper and Middle Keys in section 1, and continue south on U.S. 1. When entering Key West, stay in the far-right lane onto North Roosevelt Boulevard, which becomes Truman Avenue in Old Town. Continue for a few blocks, and you will find yourself on Duval Street, in the heart of the city. If you stay to the left, you'll also reach the city center after passing the airport and the remnants of historic Houseboat Row, where a motley collection of boats made up one of Key West's most interesting neighborhoods until Hurricane George hit in 1998.

Several regional airlines fly nonstop (about 55 min.) from Miami to Key West; fares are about $120 to $300 round-trip. **American Eagle, Continental,**

Delta, and **US Airways Express** land at **Key West International Airport,** South Roosevelt Boulevard (© **305/296-5439**), on the southeastern corner of the island.

Greyhound (© **800/231-2222;** www.greyhound.com) leaves Miami for Key West every day for about $30 to $32 one-way and $57 to $60 round-trip. Seats fill up in season, so come early. The ride takes about 4½ hours.

GETTING AROUND With limited parking, narrow streets, and congested traffic, driving in Old Town Key West is more of a pain than a convenience. Unless you're staying in one of the more remote accommodations, consider trading in the car for a bicycle. The island is small and as flat as a board, which makes it easy to negotiate, especially away from the crowded downtown area. Many tourists also choose to cruise by moped, an option that can make navigating the streets risky, especially since there are no helmet laws in Key West. So be careful and spend the extra few bucks to rent a helmet; hundreds of visitors are seriously injured each year.

Rates for simple one-speed bikes start at about $8 per day (from $40 per week). Mopeds start at about $12 for 2 hours, $25 per day, and $100 per week. The best shops include **The Bicycle Center** at 523 Truman Ave. (© **305/294-4556**); the **Moped Hospital,** 601 Truman Ave. (© **305/296-3344**); and **Tropical Bicycles & Scooter Rentals** at 1300 Duval St. (© **305/294-8136**). **The Bike Shop,** 1110 Truman Ave. (© **305/294-1073**), also rents mountain bikes for $12 per day ($60 per week). A $150 deposit is required for one-speeds, and $250 for mountain bikes.

PARKING Parking in Key West's Old Town is particularly limited, but there is a well-placed **municipal parking lot** at Simonton and Angela streets, just behind the firehouse and police station. If you have brought a car, you may want to stash it here while you enjoy the very walkable downtown part of Key West.

VISITOR INFORMATION The **Florida Keys and Key West Visitors Bureau,** P.O. Box 1147, Key West, FL 33041 (© **800/FLA-KEYS;** www.keywest.com), offers a free vacation kit packed with visitor information. The **Key West Chamber of Commerce,** 402 Wall St., Key West, FL 33040 (© **800/527-8539** or 305/294-2587; www.keywestchamber.com), also offers both general and specialized information. The lobby is open daily from 8:30am to 6pm; phones are answered from 8am to 8pm. The **Key West Visitors Center** is the area's best for information on accommodations, goings-on, and restaurants; the number is © **800/LAST-KEY.** It's open weekdays from 8am to 5:30pm and weekends from 8:30am to 5pm. Gay travelers might want to call the **Key West Business Guild** (© **305/294-4603**), which represents more than 50 guesthouses and B&Bs in town, as well as many other gay-owned businesses (ask for its color brochure); or **Good Times Travel** (© **305/294-0980**), which will set up lodging and package tours on the island.

ORIENTATION A mere 2- by 4-mile island, Key West is simple to navigate, even though there is no real order to the arrangement of streets and avenues. As you enter town on U.S. 1 (also called Roosevelt Blvd.), you will see most of the moderately priced chain hotels and fast-food restaurants. The better restaurants, shops, and outfitters are crammed onto Duval Street, the main thoroughfare of Key West's Old Town. Surrounding streets contain many inns and lodges in picturesque Victorian/Bahamian homes. On the southern side of the island is the coral beach area and some of the larger resort hotels.

The area called Bahama Village has only recently become known to tourists. With several newly opened, trendy restaurants and guesthouses, this hippie-ish neighborhood, complete with street-roaming chickens and cats, is the most urban and rough you'll find in the Keys. You might see a few seedy drug dealings on street corners, but it's nothing to be overly concerned with: It looks worse than it is and resident business owners tend to keep a vigilant eye on the neighborhood. The area is actually quite funky and should be a welcome diversion from the Duvalian mainstream.

WHAT TO SEE & DO
SEEING THE SIGHTS

Before shelling out big bucks for any of the dozens of worthwhile attractions in Key West, I recommend getting an overview on either of the two comprehensive island tours, **The Conch Tour Train** or the **Old Town Trolley** (see "Organized Tours," below). There are simply too many attractions and historic houses to list. I've highlighted my favorites below but encourage you to seek out others.

Audubon House & Tropical Gardens ★★ This well-preserved home, dating from the early 19th century, stands as a prime example of early Key West architecture. Named after renowned painter and bird expert John James Audubon, who was said to have visited the house in 1832, the graceful two-story home is a peaceful retreat from the bustle of Old Town. Included in the price of admission is a self-guided audio tour that lasts about half an hour and spotlights rare Audubon prints, gorgeous antiques, historical photos, and lush tropical gardens. With voices of several characters from the house's past, the tour never gets boring—although it is at times a bit hokey. Even if you don't want to spend the time and money to explore the grounds and home, check out the impressive gift shop, which sells a variety of fine mementos at reasonable prices.

205 Whitehead St. (between Greene and Caroline sts.) © 305/294-2116. Admission $8.50 adults, $3.50 children 6–12. Daily 9:30am–5pm (last admission at 4:30pm). Discounts for students and AAA and AARP members.

Ernest Hemingway Home and Museum ★ Hemingway's particularly handsome stone Spanish Colonial house, built in 1851, was one of the first on the island to be fitted with indoor plumbing and a built-in fireplace, and it contains the first swimming pool built on Key West. The author owned the home from 1931 until his death in 1961, and he lived there with about 50 cats, whose descendants, including the famed six-toed cats, still roam the premises. It was during those years that the Nobel Prize winner wrote some of his most famous works, including *For Whom the Bell Tolls, A Farewell to Arms,* and *The Snows of Kilimanjaro.* Fans will want to take the optional half-hour tour, included in the admission, in which you'll see rooms of his house, as well as artifacts, books, and pieces of mail addressed to him. If you don't take the tour or have no literary interest in Hemingway, the admission price is really a waste of money. If you're feline phobic, beware: Cats are everywhere.

907 Whitehead St. (between Truman Ave. and Olivia St.) © 305/294-1136. Fax 305/294-2755. www.hemingwayhome.com. Admission $9 adults, $5 children. Daily 9am–5pm. Limited parking.

Harry S. Truman Little White House Museum ★★ President Harry Truman used to refer to the White House as the "Great White Jail." On temporary leave from the big house, Truman discovered the serenity of Key West and made his escape to what became known as the Little White House, which is open to the public for touring. The house is fully restored, and the exhibits document Truman's time in the Keys. Tours are every 15 minutes and last between 45 and 50 minutes.

111 Front St., Key West. ⓒ 305/294-9911. www.trumanlittlewhitehouse.com. Admission $10 adults, $5 children under 12. Daily 9am–4:30pm.

Key West Cemetery ★★★ *Finds*

This funky, picturesque cemetery is the epitome of the quirky Key West image, as irreverent as it is humorous. Many tombs are stacked several high, condominium style—the rocky soil made digging 6 feet under nearly impossible for early settlers. Headstones reflect residents' lighthearted attitudes toward life and death. I TOLD YOU I WAS SICK is one of the more famous epitaphs, as is the tongue-in-cheek widow's inscription AT LEAST I KNOW WHERE HE'S SLEEPING TONIGHT. There's a fun 1½-hour tour that's full of history and local lore, but if you want to save some money and just read the amusing inscriptions, it's free to walk through.

Entrance at the corner of Margaret and Angela sts. ⓒ 305/294-WALK for tour reservations. Free admission. Tour $18 adults, $10 kids 12 and under. Daily dawn to dusk.

East Martello Museum and Gallery

Adjacent to the airport, the East Martello Museum is located in a Civil War–era brick fort that itself is worth a visit. The museum contains a bizarre variety of exhibits that collectively do a thorough job of interpreting the city's intriguing past. Historical artifacts include model ships, a deep-sea diver's wooden air pump, a crude raft from a Cuban "boat lift," a supposedly haunted doll, a Key West–style children's playhouse from 1918, and a horse-drawn hearse. Exhibits illustrate the Keys' history of salvaging, sponging, and cigar making. After seeing the galleries, climb a steep spiral staircase to the top of a lookout tower for good views over the island and ocean. A member of the Key West Art and Historical Society, East Martello has two cousins, the Key West Museum of Art and History, 281 Front St. (ⓒ **305/295-6616**), and the Key West Lighthouse Museum, 938 Whitehead St. (ⓒ **305/294-0012**).

3501 S. Roosevelt Blvd. ⓒ 305/296-3913. Admission $6 adults, $4 seniors, $3 children 8–12; free for children 7 and under. Daily 9:30am–5pm (last admission is at 4pm).

Key West Aquarium ★★ *Kids*

The oldest attraction on the island, the Key West Aquarium is a modest but fascinating exhibit. A long hallway of eye-level displays showcase dozens of varieties of fish and crustaceans. You'll see delicate sea horses swaying in the backlit tanks. Kids can touch sea cucumbers and sea anemones in a shallow tank in the entryway. If you can, catch one of the free, guided tours, where you can witness the dramatic feeding frenzy of the sharks, tarpon, barracudas, stingrays, and turtles. Expect to spend 1 to 1½ hours here.

1 Whitehead St. (at Mallory Sq.). ⓒ 305/296-2051. www.keywestaquarium.com. Admission $9 adults, $4.50 children 4–12; free for children under 4. Tickets are good for 2 consecutive days. Look for discount coupons at local hotels, at Duval St. kiosks, and from trolley and train tours. Daily 10am–6pm. Tours at 11am, 1pm, 3pm, and 4pm.

Key West Lighthouse Museum ★

When the Key West Lighthouse opened in 1848, many locals mourned. Its bright warning to ships signaled the end of a profitable era for wreckers, the pirate salvagers who looted reef-stricken ships. The story of this and other Keys lighthouses is illustrated in a small museum that was formerly the keeper's quarters. When radar and sonar made the lighthouse obsolete, it was opened to visitors as a tourist attraction. It's worth mustering the

Going, Going, Gone: Where to Catch the Famous Key West Sunset

A tradition in Key West, the Sunset Celebration can be relaxing or overwhelming, depending on your vantage point. If you're in town, you must check out this ritual at least once. Every evening, locals and visitors gather at the docks behind Mallory Square (at the westernmost end of Whitehead St.) to celebrate the day gone by. Secure a spot on the docks early to experience the carnival of portrait artists, acrobats, food vendors, animal acts, and other performers trading on the island's bohemian image. But the carnival atmosphere isn't for everyone: In season, the crowd can be overwhelming, especially when the cruise ships are in port. Also, hold onto your bags and wallets as the tight crowds make Mallory Square at sunset prime pickpocketing territory.

A more refined choice from which to view the sunset is the Hilton's **Sunset Deck** (© **305/294-4000**), a luxurious second-floor bar on Front Street, right next door to Mallory Square. From the civilized calm of a casual bar, you can look down on the mayhem with a drink in hand.

Also near the Mallory madness is the **Ocean Key Resort's** bar. This long, open-air pier serves up drinks and decent bar food against a dramatic pink- and yellow-streaked sky. It's located at the very tip of Duval Street (© **800/328-9815** or 305/296-7701).

For the very best potent cocktails and great bar food on an outside patio or enclosed lounge, try **Pier House Resort and Caribbean Spa's Havana Docks** at 1 Duval St. (© **305/296-4600**). There's usually live music and a lively gathering of visitors. The bar is right on the water and is a prime sunset viewing spot.

---

energy to climb the 88 claustrophobic steps to the top, where you'll be rewarded with magnificent panoramic views of Key West and the ocean.

938 Whitehead St. © 305/294-0012. Admission $8 adults, $4 children 7–12; free for children 6 and under. Daily 9:30am–5pm (last admission at 4:30pm).

Key West's Shipwreck Historeum
You'll see more impressive artifacts at nearby Mel Fisher's museum (below). For those of you who can't help but look, however, this semi-morbid museum is the place to be for everything you ever wanted to know about shipwrecks and more. See movies, artifacts, and a real-life wrecker, who will be more than happy to indulge your curiosity about the wrecking industry that preoccupied the early pioneers of Key West.

1 Whitehead St. (at Mallory Sq.). © 305/292-8990. Fax 305/292-5536. Admission $8 adults, $4 children 4–12. Shows daily every half hour 9:45am–4:45pm.

Mel Fisher Maritime Heritage Museum ★★★
This museum honors local hero Mel Fisher, whose death in 1998 was mourned throughout South Florida, and who, along with a crew of other salvagers, found a multimillion-dollar treasure trove in 1985 aboard the wreck of the Spanish galleon *Nuestra Señora de Atocha*. If you're into diving, pirates, and sunken treasures, check out this small informative museum, full of doubloons, pieces of eight, emeralds, and solid-gold

bars. A 1700 English merchant slave ship, the only tangible evidence of the transatlantic slave trade, is on view on the museum's second floor. A dated but informative film tells Fisher's incredible story.

200 Greene St. © 305/294-2633. Admission $7.50 adults, $3.75 children 6–12; free for children 5 and under. Daily 9:30am–5pm. Take U.S. 1 to Whitehead St. and turn left on Greene.

Memorial Sculpture Garden Installed in 1997, this impressive sculpture garden contains a large monument to the wreckers who made Key West rich more than a century ago. Also on display are 36 bronze busts of the island's most colorful leaders and characters: There's Harry Truman, Henry Flagler, and, of course, Ernest Hemingway, all mounted on elegant coral columns.

Front St., near Mallory Sq. Free admission.

Oldest House/Wrecker's Museum Dating from 1829, this old New England Bahama House has survived pirates, hurricanes, fires, warfare, and economic ups and downs. The 1½-story home was designed by a ship's carpenter and incorporates many features from maritime architecture, including portholes and a ship's hatch designed for ventilation before the advent of air-conditioning. Especially interesting is the detached kitchen building outfitted with a brick "beehive" oven and vintage cooking utensils. Although not a must-see on the Key West tour, history and architecture buffs will appreciate the finely preserved details and the glimpse of a slower, easier time in the island's life.

322 Duval St. © 305/294-9502. Admission $5 adults, $1 children 6–12; free for children 5 and under. Daily 10am–4pm.

ORGANIZED TOURS

BY TROLLEY-BUS & TRAM Yes, it's more than a bit hokey to sit on this 60-foot tram of yellow cars, but it's worth it—at least once. The city's whole story is packed into a neat, 90-minute package on the **Conch Tour Train**, which covers the island and all its rich, raunchy history. Operating since 1958, the trains are open-air, which can make the ride uncomfortable in bad weather. The "train's" engine is a propane-powered Jeep disguised as a locomotive. Tours depart from both Mallory Square and the Welcome Center, near where U.S. 1 becomes North Roosevelt Boulevard, on the less-developed side of the island. For more information, contact the **Conch** at (© **305/294-5161**). The cost is

---

⸺ Moments A Great Escape

Many people complain that Key West's quirky, quaint panache has been lost to the vulture of capitalism, evidenced in the glut of T-shirt shops and tacky bars. But that's not entirely so. For a quiet respite, visit the **Key West Botanical Gardens,** a little-known slice of serenity tucked between the Aqueduct Authority plant and the Key West Golf Course. The 11-acre gardens—maintained by volunteers and funded by donations—contain the last hardwood hammock in Key West, plus a colorful representation of wildflowers, butterflies, and birds. A genetically cloned tree is the latest addition to the gardens. Although the gardens received a terrible blow from the storms of 1998, the calm remains within them. Admission is free here, at Botanical Garden Way and College Road in Stock Island. Follow College Road; then turn right just past Bayshore Manor. The gardens are open daily 8am until sunset.

> **Finds Parrotheads on Parade**
>
> For Jimmy Buffett fans, or Parrotheads as they're also known, there's a fabulous tour that shouldn't be missed. **Trails of Margaritaville** ★★★ (© **305/292-2040**) is an amusing 90-minute walking tour, which provides fans with an officially sanctioned peek at the stomping grounds of Buffett's carefree Key West days back in the 1970s. Decked out in full Parrothead regalia—Hawaiian shirts and parrot hats—the informative and often hilarious guides spin yarns about the musician, and Key West in general. The tour departs daily at 4pm from Captain Tony's Saloon (428 Greene St.), where Buffett used to hang out and perform, and ends at, you guessed it, Margaritaville Cafe on Duval Street. Tour tickets are $18 for adults, $15 for locals with ID, and $10 for children. Bring cash or traveler's checks; no credit cards are accepted. Reservations are required at least 2 days in advance.

$18 for adults, $9 for children 4 to 12, and free for children 3 and under. Daily departures are every half-hour from 9am to 4:30pm.

The **Old Town Trolley** ★★ is the choice in bad weather or if you are staying at one of the many hotels on its route. Humorous drivers maintain a running commentary as the enclosed tram loops around the island's streets past all the major sights. Trolleys depart from Mallory Square and other points around the island, including many area hotels. For details, call © **305/296-6688.** Tours are $18 for adults, $9 for children 4 to 12, and free for children 3 and under. Departures are daily every half hour (though not always on the half hour) from 9am to 4:45pm. Whichever you choose, these historic trivia-packed tours are well worth the price of admission.

BY AIR   Proclaimed by the mayor as "the official air force of the Conch Republic," **Island Airplane Tours** ★★★, at Key West Airport, 3469 S. Roosevelt Blvd. (© **305/294-8687**), offers windy rides in its open-cockpit 1940 Waco biplanes, which take you over the reefs and around the islands. Thrill seekers—and only they—will also enjoy a spin in the company's S2-B aerobatics airplane, which does loops, rolls, and sideways figure-eights. Company owner Fred Cabanas was "decorated" in 1991, after he spotted a Cuban airman defecting to the United States in a Russian-built MIG fighter. Sightseeing flights cost $50 to $200, depending on the duration.

BY BOAT   The pride of Key West, **Fireball** ★★★, at Zero Duval St. (© **305/296-6293;** fax 305/294-8704), is a 58-foot glass-bottom catamaran that goes on both daytime coral-reef tours (at noon, 2pm, 4pm) and evening sunset cruises. Reef trips cost $25 per person; sunset cruises (4:30pm) are $30 per person and include snacks, sodas, and a glass of champagne. Kids sail for half price.

Schooner Western Union ★★★ (© **305/292-9830**) was built in 1939 and served as a cable-repair vessel until it was designated the flagship of the city of Key West and began day, sunset, and charter sailings. Sunset sailings are especially memorable and include entertainment, cocktails, and a cannon fire. A day sail costs $30 for adults, $12 for kids under 12; a sunset sail costs $45 for adults, $12 for children under 12.

OTHER TOURS   For a lively look at Key West, try a 2-hour tour of the island's five **most famous pubs** ★★★. It starts daily at 2:30pm, lasts 1½ hours,

Literary Key West

Counting Ernest Hemingway and Tennessee Williams among your denizens would give any city the right to call itself a literary mecca. But over the years, tiny Key West has been home—or at least home away from home—to dozens of literary types who are drawn to some combination of its gentle pace, tropical atmosphere, and lighthearted mood (not to mention its lingering reputation for an oft-ribald lifestyle). Writers have long known that more than a few muses prowl the tree-laden streets of Key West.

Robert Frost first visited Key West in 1934 and wintered here for the remainder of his life. In the early 20th century, writers like John Dewey, Archibald MacLeish, John Dos Passos, Wallace Stevens, and S. J. Perelman were drawn to the island.

Even as Key West boomed and busted and boomed again, and despite the island's growing popularity with world travelers, writers continued to move to Key West or visit with such regularity that they were deemed honorary "conchs." Novelists Phil Caputo, Tom McGuane, Jim Harrison, John Hershey, Alison Lurie, and Robert Stone were among these.

Of course, one of Key West's favorite sons also earned a spot in the annals of local literary history. Famous for his good-time, tropical-laced music, Jimmy Buffett was also a surprisingly well-received novelist in the 1990s. Although Buffett now makes the infinitely ritzier Palm Beach his Florida home, his presence is still felt in virtually every corner of Key West.

But it is Nobel Prize–winner and avid outdoorsman Ernest Hemingway who is most identified with Key West. Much of the island has changed since he lived here from 1931 to 1961. Even the famous Sloppy Joe's bar, which Hemingway frequented mostly from 1933 to 1937, has changed locations. Fortunately, the Ernest Hemingway House & Museum (see above) has been lovingly preserved for visitors. But perhaps to get the best feel for what Hemingway loved most about Key West, visit the docks at Garrison Bight. It is from there that Hemingway and his many famous (and infamous) friends and contemporaries departed for Caribbean ports of call and for sport upon the sea.

Key West pays homage to its literary legacy with the annual **January Key West Literary Seminar.** For information, call © **888/293-9291** or visit www.keywestliteraryseminar.org.

costs $21, and includes four drinks. Another fun tour is the 1-mile, 90-minute **nightly ghost tour**, leaving at 8pm from the Holiday Inn La Concha, 430 Duval St. Cost is $18 for adults and $10 for children under 12. This spooky and interesting tour gives participants insight into many old island legends. The **Key West Tour Association** (© **305/294-9255**) offers both tours.

THE BEACHES

Unlike the rest of the Keys, you'll actually find a few small beaches here, although they don't compare with the state's wide natural wonders up the coast:

A narrow rocky beach is typical here. Your options include **Smathers Beach,** off South Roosevelt Boulevard west of the airport; **Higgs Beach,** along Atlantic Boulevard between White Street and Reynolds Road; and **Fort Zachary Beach,** located off the western end of Southard Boulevard.

A magnet for partying teenagers, **Smathers Beach** is Key West's largest and most overpopulated beach. Despite the number of rowdy teens, the beach is actually quite clean and it looks lovely since its renovation in the spring of 2000. If you go early enough in the morning, you may notice some people sleeping on the beach from the night before.

Higgs Beach is a favorite among Key West's gay crowds. Higgs has a playground and tennis courts and is near the minute Rest Beach, which is actually hidden by the White Street Pier.

Although there is an entrance fee ($3.75 per car, plus more for each passenger), we recommend the beach at **Fort Zachary**, since it also includes a great historical fort, a Civil War museum, and a large picnic area with tables, barbecue grills, restrooms, and showers. Plus, large trees scattered across 87 acres provide shade for those who are reluctant to bake in the sun. Hurricane George damaged the vulnerable point in 1998, but replanting of native vegetation has made it even better than before.

AFFORDABLE OUTDOOR PURSUITS

BICYCLING & MOPEDING A popular mode of transportation for locals and visitors, bikes and mopeds are available at many rental outlets in the city (see "Essentials," earlier in this section). Escape the hectic downtown scene and explore the island's scenic side streets by heading away from Duval Street toward South Roosevelt Boulevard and the beachside enclaves along the way.

DIVING & SNORKELING One of the area's largest scuba schools, **Dive Key West Inc.,** 3128 N. Roosevelt Blvd. (© **800/426-0707** or 305/296-3823; fax 305/296-0609; www.divekeywest.com), offers instruction for all levels of experience, and its dive boats take participants to scuba and snorkel sites on nearby reefs. A two-tank dive with equipment included costs $65 per person for 4 hours.

Wreck dives and night dives are two of the special offerings of **Lost Reef Adventures,** 261 Margaret St. (© **800/952-2749** or 305/296-9737). Regularly scheduled runs and private charters can be arranged; a two-tank dive costs $56 per person, and snorkeling trips cost $30 per person. Phone for departure information.

Also see **Mosquito Coast Outfitters,** under "Kayaking," below.

FISHING As any angler will tell you, there's no fishing like Keys fishing. Key West has it all: bonefish, tarpon, dolphin, tuna, grouper, cobia, and more. Sharks, too. Step aboard a small exposed skiff for an incredibly diverse day of fishing. In the morning, you can head offshore for sailfish or dolphin (the fish, not the mammal), and then by afternoon, get closer to land for a shot at tarpon, permit, grouper, or snapper. Here in Key West, you can probably pick up more

---

Tips Reel Deals

When looking for the best deals on fishing excursions, know that the bookers from the kiosks in town generally take 20% of a captain's fee in addition to an extra monthly fee. You can usually save yourself money by booking directly with a captain or going straight to one of the docks.

cobia—one of the best fighting and eating fish around—than anywhere else in the world. For a real fight, ask your skipper to go for the tarpon—the greatest fighting fish there is, famous for its dramatic "tail walk" on the water after it's hooked. Shark fishing is also popular.

When checking out charter options, you should know that the advantage of the smaller, more expensive charter boats is that you can call the shots. They'll take you where you want to go, to fish for what you want to catch. These "light tackles" are also easier to maneuver, which means you can go to backcountry spots for tarpon and bonefish, as well as out to the open sea for tuna and dolphin. Larger boats, for up to six or seven people, are cheaper and are best for kingfish, billfish, and sailfish. Consider Captain Vinnie Argiro's **Heavy Hitters Charters** (© **305/745-6665**) if you want a light-tackle experience. For a larger boat, try Captain Henry Otto's 44-foot *Sunday*, docked at the Hyatt in Key West (© **305/294-7052**). Both charge roughly $350 for a half day or $550 for a full day of fishing. This rate covers up to four people, and includes ice, bait, and tackle.

The huge commercial party boats are more for sightseeing than serious angling, though you can get lucky and get a few bites at one of the fishing holes. One especially good deal is the *Gulfstream III* (© **305/296-8494**), an all-day charter that goes out daily from 9:30am until 4pm. You'll pay $35, plus $3 for a rod and reel. It's $25 for kids under 12. This 65-foot party boat usually has at least 30 other anglers. Bring your own cooler or buy snacks on the boat. Beer and wine are allowed.

You'll find plenty of competition among the charter fishing boats in and around Mallory Square. You can negotiate a good deal at **Charter Boat Row,** 1801 N. Roosevelt Ave. (across from the Shell station), home to more than 30 charter fishing and party boats. Just show up to arrange your outing, or call **Garrison Bite Marina** (© **305/292-8167**) for details.

Serious anglers should consider the light-tackle boats that leave from **Oceanside Marina** (© **305/294-4676**) on Stock Island, at 5950 Peninsula Ave., 1½ miles off U.S. 1. It's a 20-minute drive from Old Town on the Atlantic side. There are more than 30 light-tackle guides, with boats ranging from flatbed, backcountry skiffs to 28-foot open boats. There are also a few larger charters. Call for details.

KAYAKING **Mosquito Coast Outfitters,** housed in a woodsy wine bar at 1017 Duval St. (© **305/294-7178**), operates a first-rate kayaking and snorkeling tour every day as long as the weather is mild. The tour departs at 9am sharp (returns around 3pm) and cost $45 per person. Included in the price are snacks, soft drinks, and a guided tour of the mangrove-studded islands of Sugar Key or

---

Fun Fact   Conch If You Love Key West

Ever wonder how Key West got the nickname "The Conch Republic"? In 1982, the U.S. Border Patrol set up a roadblock on U.S. 1 to search for illegal aliens and drugs. This maneuver effectively slowed passage from the Keys to the mainland and damaged the economy (albeit temporarily). In response, Key West mayor Dennis Wardlow collaborated with five businessmen and established the so-called Conch Republic, declaring Key West's independence from—and war on—the U.S. The roadblock was removed, but the moniker stuck.

Geiger Key just north of Key West. The tour is primarily for kayaking, but you will have the opportunity to get in the water for snorkeling, if you're interested.

SHOPPING

You'll find all kinds of unique gifts and souvenirs in Key West, from coconut postcards to Key lime pies. On Duval Street, **T-shirt shops** outnumber almost any other business. If you must get a wearable memento, be careful of unscrupulous salespeople. Despite efforts to curtail the practice, many shops have been known to rip off unwitting shoppers. It pays to check the prices and the exchange rate before signing any sales slips. You are entitled to a written estimate of any T-shirt work before you pay for it.

At Mallory Square is the **Clinton Street Market,** a mall of kiosks and stalls designed for the many cruise-ship passengers who never venture beyond this super-commercial zone. Amid the dreck are some delicious coffee and candy shops and some high-priced hats and shoes. There's also a free and clean restroom.

Once the main industry of Key West, cigar making is enjoying renewed success at the handful of factories that survived the slow years. Stroll through **"Cigar Alley"** (while on Green St., go 2 blocks west from Whitehead St. and you'll hit it, also known as Pirate's Alley), where you will find *viejitos* (little old men) rolling fat stogies just as they used to do in their homeland across the Florida Straits. Stop at the **Key West Cigar Factory,** at 308 Front St. (© 305/294-3470), for an excellent selection of imported and locally rolled smokes, including the famous El Hemingway. Remember, buying or selling Cuban-made cigars is illegal. Shops advertising "Cuban Cigars" are usually referring to domestic cigars made from tobacco grown from seeds that were brought from Cuba decades ago. To be fair, though, many premium cigars today are grown from Cuban seed tobacco—only it is grown in Latin America and the Caribbean, not Cuba.

If you are looking for local or Caribbean art, you will find nearly a dozen galleries and shops clustered on Duval Street between Catherine and Fleming streets. You'll also find some excellent shops scattered on the side streets. One worth seeking out is the **Haitian Art Co.,** 600 Frances St. (© **305/296-8932**), where you can browse through room upon room of original paintings from well-known and obscure Haitian artists in a range of prices from a few dollars to a few thousand. Also, check out **Cuba, Cuba!** at 814 Duval St. (© **305/295-9442**), where you'll find paintings, sculpture, and photos by Cuban artists as well as books and art from the island.

A favorite stop in the Keys is the deliciously fragrant **Key West Aloe** at 524 Front St., between Simonton and Duval streets (© **305/294-5592**). Since 1971, this shop has been selling a simple line of bath products, including lotions, shampoos, and soothing balms for those who want a reminder of the tropical breezes once they're back home. For foodies, the **Key Lime Pie Co.** (© **305/294-6567**) is so popular for its pies, cookies, and pretty much anything you can think of made with Key lime (candles, soaps, lotions), that there are two on the tiny island. One is at 701 Caroline St. and the other is at 424 Greene St. From sweet to spicy, **Peppers of Key West** (© **305/295-9333**) at 602 Greene St. is a hot sauce lover's heaven, with hundreds of variations. Grab a seat at the tasting bar and be prepared to let your taste buds sizzle.

Key West Island Bookstore (© **305/294-2904**) at 513 Fleming St. carries new, used, and rare books and specializes in fiction by residents of the Keys, including Hemingway, Tennessee Williams, Shel Silverstein, Ann Beattie,

Richard Wilbur, and John Hersey. **Flaming Maggie's** (© 305/294-3931) at 830 Fleming St. carries a wide selection of gay books. Both shops are open daily.

Also worth checking out in the newly revitalized Bahama Village section of town are the shops along Petronia Street between Thomas and Whitehead streets. Especially interesting is **Maskerville** (© 305/293-6937), which sells a variety of feather-laden artwork from masks to lampshades. Off the beaten track at 814 Fleming St. (© 305/294-7901) is the **Helio Gallery Store,** featuring locally made crafts and fine art.

For anything else, from bed linens to candlesticks to clothing, go to downtown's oldest and most renowned department store, **Fast Buck Freddie's,** 500 Duval St. (© 305/294-2007). For the same merchandise at reduced prices, try **Half Buck Freddie's,** 726 Caroline St. (© 305/294-2007), where you can shop for out-of-season bargains and "rejects" from the main store.

ACCOMMODATIONS YOU CAN AFFORD

You'll find a wide variety of places to stay in Key West, from resorts with all the amenities to seaside motels, quaint bed-and-breakfasts, and clothing-optional guesthouses. Unless you're in town during Key West's most popular holidays—Fantasy Fest (around Halloween), when Mardi Gras meets South Florida for the NC-17 set; Hemingway Days (in July), when Papa is seemingly and eerily alive and well; and Christmas and New Year's—or for a big fishing tournament (many are held Oct–Dec) or boat-racing tourney, you can almost always find a place to stay at the last minute. However, you may want to book early, especially in winter, when prime properties fill up and many require 2- or 3-night minimum stays. Prices at these times are also extremely high. Finding a decent room for under $100 a night is a real trick.

A better option is to call **Vacation Key West** (© 800/595-5397 or 305/295-9500; www.vacationkw.com), which is a wholesaler that offers discounts of 20% to 30% and is skilled at finding last-minute deals. They represent mostly larger hotels and motels but can also place visitors in guesthouses. The phones are answered weekdays from 9am to 6pm and Saturday from 11am to 2pm. The **Key West Innkeepers Association,** P.O. Box 6172, Key West, FL 33041 (© 800/492-1911 or 305/292-3600), can also help find lodging in any price range from its dozens of members and affiliates.

Gay travelers will want to call the **Key West Business Guild** (© 305/294-4603), which represents more than 50 guesthouses and B&Bs in town, as well as many other gay-owned businesses. Be advised that most gay guesthouses have a clothing-optional policy.

Abaco Inn *Value* This tidy little guesthouse is situated on a secluded lane just off Duval Street. Although there is no pool or view, the three simple but comfortable rooms are well stocked, immaculate, and charming. Each room has a sizeable private bathroom, queen bed, and twin-size Murphy bed. Once the home of a cigar maker, the house dates from the early 1900s. Now it is owned and operated by George Fontana, a friendly and knowledgeable tour guide and writer. Look for his column on local characters in the *Key West Citizen*. You can't beat the price in this super-convenient location. No smoking is allowed on the property.

415 Julia St. (between Truman Ave. and Virginia St.), Key West, FL 33040. © 800/358-6307 or 305/296-2212. Fax 305/295-0349. www.abaco-inn.com. 3 units. Winter $99–$109 double; off-season from $69 double. 4-day minimum stay in season. Additional person $15 extra. AE, DISC, MC, V. **Amenities:** Bike rental; concierge. *In room:* A/C, TV, fridge, microwave, coffeemaker, hair dryer.

Chelsea House ★
Despite its decidedly English name, the Chelsea House is "all American," a term that in Key West isn't code for "conservative." Chelsea House caters to a mixed gay/straight clientele and displays its liberal philosophy most prominently on the clothing-optional sun deck. One of only a few guesthouses in Key West that offer TVs, VCRs, private bathrooms, and kitchenettes in each guest room, Chelsea House has a large number of repeat visitors. The bathrooms and closets could be bigger, but both are adequate and serviceable. When weather permits, which is almost always, breakfast is served outside by the pool.

707 Truman Ave., Key West, FL 33040. © 800/845-8859 or 305/296-2211. Fax 305/296-4822. www.chelsea housekw.com. 20 units. Winter $135–$245 double; off-season $85–$135 double. Rates include breakfast. AE, DC, DISC, MC, V. Free parking. Children 17 and under not accepted. Pets accepted for $15 per night. **Amenities:** Outdoor pool; access to nearby health club; bike rental; concierge. *In room:* A/C, TV/VCR, kitchenette, fridge, hair dryer, iron.

The Grand ★★ *Finds*
Don't expect cabbies or locals to know about this well-kept secret, located in a modest residential section of Old Town, about 5 blocks from Duval Street. It's got almost everything you could want, including a very moderate price tag. Proprietor Elizabeth Rose goes out of her way to provide any and all services for her appreciative guests. All rooms have private bathrooms, air-conditioning, and private entrances. Room 2 on the backside of the house is the best deal; it's small, but it has a porch and the most privacy. Suites are a real steal, too. The large two-room units come with a complete kitchen. This place is undoubtedly the best bargain in town.

1116 Grinnell St. (between Virginia and Catherine sts.), Key West, FL 33040. © 888/947-2630 or 305/294-0590. Fax 305/294-0477. www.thegrandguesthouse.com. 10 units. Winter $98–$188; off-season $88–$118. Rates include continental breakfast. AE, DISC, MC, V. **Amenities:** Concierge; bike/scooter rental. *In room:* A/C, TV/VCR, fridge.

Southernmost Point Guest House ★★ *Finds* *Kids*
One of the few inns that actually welcome children and pets, this romantic and historic guesthouse is a real find. The antiseptically clean rooms are not as fancy as the house's ornate 1885 exterior, but each is unique and includes some combination of basic beds and couches and a hodgepodge of furnishings, including futon couches, high-back wicker chairs, and plenty of mismatched throw rugs. Room 5 is best; situated upstairs, it has a private porch, an ocean view, and windows that let in lots of light. Every room has fresh flowers, a refrigerator, and a full decanter of sherry. Mona Santiago, the hotel's kind, laid-back owner, provides chairs and towels that can be brought to the beach, which is just a block away. Plus, guests can help themselves to free wine as they soak in the 14-seat hot tub. Kids will enjoy the swings in the backyard and the pet rabbits.

1327 Duval St., Key West, FL 33040. © 305/294-0715. Fax 305/296-0641. www.southernmostpoint.com. 6 units. Winter $105–$250; off-season $65–$165. Rates include breakfast. AE, MC, V. Pets accepted $5 in summer, $10 in winter. **Amenities:** Garden pool; Jacuzzi; laundry. *In room:* A/C, TV/VCR, fridge, coffeemaker, hair dryer, iron.

Westwinds Inn ★
A close second to staying in your own 19th-century clapboard, tin-roofed house is this tranquil inn located just 4 blocks from Duval Street in the historic Seaport district. Lush landscaping—banana stalks, mango, and Spanish Lime trees—keeps the inn extremely private and secluded, and at times, you do feel as if you're alone. And that's not a scary thing; it's absolutely fabulous. Two pools are offset by alcoves, fountains, and the extremely well-maintained whitewashed inn, which is actually composed of five separate

houses. Rooms are Key West comfortable, with wicker furnishing and fans. All rooms are nonsmoking.

914 Eaton St., Key West, FL 33040. © **800/788-4150** or 305/296-4440. Fax 305/293-9031. www.westwindskeywest.com. 26 units. Winter $90–$150; off-season $70–$120. Rates include continental breakfast. DISC, MC, V. Children under 12 not allowed. **Amenities:** 2 pools (1 heated); bike rental; self-service laundry. *In room:* A/C (some rooms have TVs and kitchenettes).

Wicker Guesthouse ★★   Occupying six restored homes, one overlooking busy Duval Street, the Wicker offers some of the best value accommodations in Key West and has consistently been voted one of the best guesthouses here. The least expensive rooms are in the front of the complex. These have shared bathrooms and are predictably sparse, with no telephones, TVs, or even closets. The guest rooms get nicer, quieter, and more expensive the farther back on the property you go. Way back, beyond a kidney-shaped, heated swimming pool, are the guesthouse's top accommodations, each furnished with two double beds, cable TVs, and the ubiquitous wicker furnishings that give this house its name. Some have small kitchenettes. A few two-bedroom apartments are also available, a rare find in Key West guesthouses. Three connected units share a living room and stoveless kitchen, and are particularly good for families and small parties.

913 Duval St., Key West, FL 33040. © **800/880-4275** or 305/296-4275. Fax 305/294-7240. www.wickerhousekw.com. 18 units. Winter $130–$235 single or double; off-season $89–$160 single or double. $15 for extra person. Rates include continental breakfast. AE, DC, DISC, MC, V. **Amenities:** Pool; access to nearby health club; concierge; in-room massage. *In room:* AC, TV, fridge, coffeemaker, hair dryer, safe. No phones in some rooms.

SUPER-CHEAP SLEEPS

Angelina Guest House ★★   This youth hostel–type guesthouse is about the cheapest in town and conveniently located near a hot, hippie restaurant called Blue Heaven (see "Great Deals on Dining," below). It is generally safe and full of character. The rooms are all furnished differently in a modest style, recently upgraded with new decor. A gorgeous lagoon-style heated pool with waterfall and tropical landscaping was an excellent addition. Even better are the poolside hammocks—get out there early, as they go quickly! Even though the Angelina is sparse, it's a great place to crash if you are on the cheap. Many repeat guests consider "this old house" their home away from home.

302 Angela St. (at the corner of Thomas St.), Key West, FL 33040. © **888/303-4480** or 305/294-4480. Fax 305/272-0681. www.angelinaguesthouse.com. 15 units, 12 with bathroom. Winter $75–$149; off-season $49–$95. Rates include continental breakfast. DISC, MC, V. **Amenities:** Outdoor heated pool; concierge. *In room:* A/C, hair dryer, iron. Kitchen, fridge, microwave in some. No phones.

Blue Lagoon Motel   More than half of the rooms at this funky ocean-side resort rent for less than $100 year-round—an all-too-unusual occurrence in Key West, especially for full-service resorts. The rooms, furnished in heavy cedar wood, are basic and a bit run-down but still decent—along the lines of a Howard Johnson or other budget accommodation. Second-floor rooms are generally quieter. The pricier waterfront rooms aren't really worth the extra money (although some include a jet-ski ride). Guests tend to be young college-aged kids out for a wild time. Although pretty far from Old Town, the resort is convenient by scooter and car, and it is literally surrounded by jet skis, boats, parasailing, and diving fun.

3101 N. Roosevelt Blvd., Key West, FL 33040-4118. © **305/296-1043**. Fax 305/296-6499. 72 units. Winter $80–$240 double; off-season $50–$110 double. MC, V. *In room:* A/C, TV.

Caribbean House For the really budget-conscious, Key West offers a funky inn with 10 modest but brightly decorated rooms and two separate cottages. The walls behind the beds in the tiny but clean rooms have been painted with likenesses of elaborately styled headboards, and the rich turquoise and shocking pinks are reminiscent of a quaint Bahamian fish shack—appropriate to this gingerbread home's location in the largely untouristed Bahama Village. The ghetto-like neighborhood is what disturbs some visitors. Here you'll run into European backpackers, descendants of Bahamian immigrants, and local bohemians who share the streets with roosters, stray dogs, and the occasional wobbling drunk. The hospitable Jamaican hosts are happy to welcome a third guest to any room and will even provide an extra futon.

226 Petronia St., Key West, FL 33040. © **800/543-4518** or 305/296-1600. Fax 305/296-9840. www.caribbeanhousekeywest.com. 10 units. Winter and special holidays $69 single or double; off-season $49 single or double. Rates include continental breakfast. Extra person free. 1-night deposit by cashier's check required in advance. MC, V. **Amenities:** Bike/scooter rental. *In room:* A/C, TV, fridge.

Key West International Hostel & Seashell Motel This well-run, affordable hostel is a 3-minute walk to the beach and to Old Town. Very busy with European backpackers, it's a great place to meet people. The dorm rooms are dark and sparse, but clean enough. The higher-priced motel rooms are a good deal, especially those equipped with full kitchens. The common area room has been upgraded, and a two-bedroom suite has been added for those looking to upgrade a bit. Amenities include a pool table under a tiki roof, and bicycle rentals for $8 per day. There's also cheap food available for breakfast, lunch, and dinner, as well as discounted prices for snorkeling, diving, and sunset cruises.

718 South St., Key West, FL 33040. © **800/51-HOSTEL** or 305/296-5719. Fax 305/296-0672. www.keywesthostel.com. 100 units. Year-round members $19.50, nonmembers $22.50. Motel units $75–$105 in season; $55–$85 off-season. MC, V. **Amenities:** Kitchen; bike rental. *In room:* TV, fridge, coffeemaker, hair dryer. A/C in dorm rooms.

WORTH A SPLURGE

Grand Key Resort *Finds* If you don't mind staying on the quiet "other" side of the island, a 10-minute cab ride away from Duval Street, the Grand Key Resort is an excellent choice, not to mention value. An ecologically conscious resort, Grand Key has been renovated with eco-sensitive materials as well as an interior created to conserve energy, reduce waste, and preserve the area's natural resources. Rooms are clean and comfortable, with some looking out onto the spacious pool area, which is surrounded by an unsightly empty lot of mangroves and marshes. The hotel's restaurant is also very good, but for excitement, you will need to look elsewhere.

3990 S. Roosevelt Blvd., Key West, FL 33040. © **888/310-1540** or 305/293-1818. Fax 305/296-6962. www.grandkeyresort.com. 216 units. Winter $179–$489; off-season $125–$420. Rates include continental breakfast. AE, DISC, MC, V. Free parking. **Amenities:** Restaurant, tiki bar and lounge; pool; concierge; meeting rooms; limited room service. *In room:* A/C, TV, dataport, minibar, coffeemaker, hair dryer.

La Pensione ★★ This classic bed-and-breakfast, located in the 1891 home of a former cigar executive, distinguishes itself from other similar inns by its extreme attention to details. The friendly and knowledgeable staff treats the stunning home and its guests with extraordinary care. The comfortable rooms all have air-conditioning, ceiling fans, king-size beds, and private bathrooms. Many also have French doors opening onto spacious verandas. Although the rooms have no phones or televisions, the distractions of Duval Street, only steps away, should keep you adequately occupied during your visit. Breakfast, which includes made-to-order Belgian waffles, fresh fruit, and a variety of breads or muffins, can be taken on the wraparound porch or at the communal dining table.

809 Truman Ave. (between Windsor and Margaret sts.), Key West, FL 33040. © 800/893-1193 or 305/292-9923. Fax 305/296-6509. www.lapensione.com. 9 units. Winter from $178 double; off-season from $98 double. Rates include breakfast. 10% discount for readers who mention this book. AE, DC, DISC, MC, V. No children accepted. **Amenities:** Outdoor pool; access to nearby health club; bike rental. *In room:* A/C. No phones.

GREAT DEALS ON DINING

With its share of the usual drive-through fast-food franchises (mostly up on Roosevelt Blvd.), and Duval Street succumbing to the lure of a Hard Rock, you might be surprised to learn that, over the years, an upscale and high-quality dining scene has begun to thrive in Key West. Wander Old Town or the newly spruced up Bahama Village and browse menus after you have exhausted the list of my picks below.

If you don't feel like venturing out, call **We Deliver** (© 305/293-0078), a service that will bring you anything you want from any of the area's restaurants or stores for a small fee ($3–$6). We Deliver operates between 3 and 11pm. If you are staying in a condominium or efficiency, you may want to stock your refrigerator with groceries, beer, wine, and snacks from the area's oldest grocer, **Fausto's Food Palace.** Open since 1926, there are now two locations: 1105 White St. and 522 Fleming St. The Fleming Street location will deliver (© 305/294-5221 or 305/296-5663). Fausto's has a $25 delivery minimum.

Alonzo's Oyster Bar SEAFOOD   Alonzo's Oyster Bar offers good seafood in a casual setting. It's located on the ground floor of the A&B Lobster House at the end of Front Street in the marina. To start off your meal, try the steamed beer shrimp—tantalizingly fresh jumbo shrimp in a garlic, Old Bay, beer, and cayenne pepper sauce. A house specialty is white clam chili, a delicious mix of tender clams, white beans, and potatoes served with a dollop of sour cream. An excellent entree is the panfried lobster cakes, served with sweet corn, mashed potatoes, chipotle gravy, and roasted corn salsa. The staff is cheerful and informative, and the service is very good.

231 Margaret St. © 305/294-5880. Appetizers $5–$8; main courses $11–$17. MC, V. Daily 11am–11pm.

Anthony's Cafe ITALIAN DELI/ROTISSERIE   Although owned and operated by a Greek import, this rustic Italian-style trattoria is a welcome addition to an area crowded with more expensive and less delicious options. Fragrant roasted chicken and overstuffed sandwiches on fresh baked bread are the best choices. Also good are the many salads and daily specials.

1111 Duval St. (at Amelia St.). © 305/296-8899. Breakfast $2–$5; sandwiches and salads $5.50–$7 with a side; hot plates $8–$13. Cash only. Daily 8am–10pm.

Bahama Mama's Kitchen BAHAMIAN   Sit outside under an umbrella and enjoy the authentic Bahamian dishes made from recipes that have been handed down through owner Corey's family for the past 150 years. Prepared fresh daily, all dishes are created with their special "Bahamian" seasonings. Try the coconut shrimp butterflied, soaked in coconut oil, battered with egg, and then rolled in fresh shredded coconut and deep-fried. The fresh catch of the day comes blackened, broiled, or fried and is served with island plantains, shrimp hash cakes, and crab rice. The service is good, and the staff is friendly.

In the Bahama Village Market, 324 Petronia St. © 305/294-3355. Appetizers $4–$7; main courses $9–$13. MC, V. Daily 11am–10pm.

Banana Café ★★★ FRENCH
Banana Café benefits from a French country cafe look and feel. It's an upscale local eatery that's been discovered by savvy visitors on the less congested end of Duval Street and that's kept its loyal clientele with affordable prices and delightful, light preparations. Banana Café's crepes are legendary on the island for breakfast or lunch, and fresh quality ingredients and a French-themed menu bring daytime diners back for the casual yet classy tropical-influenced dinner menu. Every Thursday night, there's live jazz.

1211 Duval St. © **305/294-7227.** Main courses $4.80–$23; breakfast and lunch $2–$8.50. AE, DC, MC, V. Daily 8am–11pm.

Blue Heaven ★★ *Finds* SEAFOOD/AMERICAN/NATURAL
This little hippie-run gallery and restaurant has become the place to be in Key West—and with good reason. Be prepared to wait in line. The food here is some of the best in town, especially for breakfast. You can enjoy homemade granola, huge tropical fruit pancakes, and seafood Benedict. Dinners are just as good and run the gamut from fresh-caught fish dishes to Jamaican-style jerk chicken, curried soups, and vegetarian stews. But if you're a neat freak, don't bother. Some people are put off by the dirt floors and roaming cats and birds, but frankly, it adds to the charm. The building used to be a bordello, where Hemingway was said to hang out watching cockfights. It's still lively here, but not that lively!

305 Petronia St. © **305/296-8666.** Main courses $10–$30; lunch $6–$14; breakfast $5–$11. DISC, MC, V. Daily 8am–11:30am, noon–3pm, and 6–10:30pm; Sun brunch 8am–1pm. Closed mid-Sept to early Oct.

Mangia, Mangia ★ *Value* ITALIAN/AMERICAN
Locals appreciate that they can get good, inexpensive food here in a town filled with tourist traps. Off the beaten track, in a little corner storefront, this great Chicago-style pasta place serves some of the best Italian food in the Keys. The family-run restaurant offers superb homemade pastas of every description, as well as one of the tastiest marinara sauces around. The simple grilled chicken breast brushed with olive oil and sprinkled with pepper is another good choice, as is the Picadillo Pasta—black-bean pasta shells smothered in a Cuban-inspired sauce with meat, tomatoes, olives, capers, and spices. Check out the fantastic little outdoor patio dotted with twinkling pepper lights and lots of plants. You can relax out back with a glass of one of their excellent wines—they're said to have the largest selection in the Keys—or homemade beer while you wait for your table.

900 Southard St. (at Margaret St.). © **305/294-2469.** Reservations not accepted. Main courses $9–$15. AE, MC, V. Daily 5:30–10pm.

Pepe's *Finds* AMERICAN
This old dive has been serving good, basic food for nearly a century. Steaks and Apalachicola Bay oysters are the big draw for regulars who appreciate the rustic barroom setting and historic photos on the walls. Look for original scenes of Key West in 1909, when Pepe's first opened. If the weather is nice, choose a seat on the patio under a stunning mahogany tree. Burgers, fish sandwiches, and standard chili satisfy hearty eaters. Buttery sautéed mushrooms and rich mashed potatoes are the best comfort food in Key West. Stop by early for breakfast when you can get old-fashioned chipped beef on toast and all the usual egg dishes. In the evening, there are reasonably priced cocktails on the deck.

806 Caroline St. (between Margaret and Williams sts.). © **305/294-7192.** Main courses $13–$22; breakfast $2–$9; lunch $5–$9. DISC, MC, V. Daily 6:30am–10:30pm.

PT's Late Night ★ *Finds* AMERICAN
This place is worth knowing about not only because it's one of the only places in town serving food past 10pm, but also

because it happens to serve good food at extremely reasonable prices. PT's is more like a sports bar than a restaurant, and service can be a bit slow and brusque, but you'll enjoy their heaping plates of nachos, sizzling fajitas served with all the trimmings, and super-fresh salads—so big they can be a meal in themselves.

920 Caroline St. (at the corner of Margaret St.). © **305/296-4245.** Main courses $6.95–$14.95. DISC, MC, V. Daily 11am–4am.

Turtle Kraals Wildlife Grill ⭐ *Kids* *Finds* SOUTHWESTERN/SEAFOOD
You'll join lots of locals in this out-of-the-way converted warehouse with indoor and dockside seating that serves innovative seafood at great prices. Try the twin lobster tails stuffed with mango and crabmeat or any of the big quesadillas or fajitas. Kids will like the wildlife exhibits and the very cheesy menu. Blues bands play most nights.

213 Margaret St. (corner of Caroline St.). © **305/294-2640.** Main courses $10–$20. DISC, MC, V. Mon–Thurs 11am–10:30pm; Fri–Sat 11am–11pm; Sun noon–10:30pm. Bar closes at midnight.

SUPER-CHEAP EATS
The Deli DINER/AMERICAN In operation since 1950, this family-owned corner eatery has kept up with the times. It's really more of a diner than a deli and has a vast menu with all kinds of hearty options, from meat loaf to yellowtail snapper. The seafood options are pretty good. A daily selection of more than a dozen vegetables includes the usual diner choices of beets, corn, and coleslaw with some distinctly Caribbean additions, such as rice and beans and fried plantains. Most dinners include a choice of two vegetables and homemade biscuits or corn bread. Breakfasts are made to order and attract a loyal following of locals. The Deli also offers ice cream sundaes and gourmet coffees.

531 Truman Ave. (corner of Truman Ave. and Simonton St.). © **305/294-1464.** Full meals $7–$23; sandwiches $3–$8. DISC, MC, V. Daily 7:30am–10pm.

El Siboney Restaurant ⭐ *Value* CUBAN For good, cheap Cuban food, stop at this corner dive that looks more like a gas station than a diner. Be prepared, however, to wait like the locals for succulent roast pork, Cuban sandwiches, grilled chicken, and *ropa vieja* (a stew-like dish of beef, onion, garlic, and tomatoes), all served with heaps of rice and beans.

900 Catherine St. (at Margaret St.). © **305/296-4184.** Main courses $5–$13. No credit cards. Mon–Sat 11am–9:30pm.

WORTH A SPLURGE
Bagatelle ⭐⭐⭐ SEAFOOD/TROPICAL Reserve a seat at the elegant second-floor veranda overlooking Duval Street's mayhem. From the calm above, you may want to start your meal with the excellent herb-and-garlic stuffed whole artichoke or the sashimi-like seared tuna rolled in black peppercorns. Also recommended is a lightly creamy garlic-herb pasta topped with Gulf shrimp, Florida lobster, and mushrooms. The best chicken and beef dishes are given a tropical treatment: grilled with papaya, ginger, and soy.

115 Duval St. © **305/296-6609.** Reservations recommended. Main courses $14–$21; lunch $5–$10. AE, DISC, MC, V. Sun–Thurs 11:30am–10pm; Fri–Sat 11:30am–11pm.

La Trattoria ⭐ ITALIAN Have a true Italian feast in a relaxed atmosphere. Each dish here is prepared and presented according to old Italian tradition and is cooked to order. The antipasti are scrumptious. Try the delicious baked, breadcrumb-stuffed mushroom caps; they're firm yet tender. The stuffed eggplant with ricotta and roasted peppers is light and flavorful. Or have the seafood salad of shrimp, calamari, and mussels, which is fish-market fresh and tasty. The pasta dishes are also great: Try the penne Venezia, with mushrooms, sun-dried tomatoes, and crabmeat, or the cannelloni stuffed with veal and spinach. For dessert, don't skip the homemade tiramisu; it's light yet full-flavored. The dining room is spacious but still intimate, and the waiters are friendly and informative. Before you leave, be sure to visit Virgilio's, the restaurant's very own cocktail lounge with live jazz until 2am.

524 Duval St. © 305/296-1075. Pasta $10–$17; main courses $17–$22. AE, DC, DISC, MC, V. Daily 5:30–11pm.

Mangoes ★★★ FLORIBBEAN   This restaurant's large brick patio, shaded by overgrown banyan trees, is so alluring to passersby that it's packed almost every night of the week. Many people don't realize how pricey the meals can be here because, upon first glance, it looks like a casual Duval Street cafe, but both its prices and cuisine are a notch above casual. Spicy sausage with black beans and rice, crispy curried chicken, and local snapper with passion fruit sauce are typical among the entrees, but the Garlic and Lime Pinks—a half pound of Key West pink shrimp seasoned and grilled with a roasted garlic and Key lime glaze—are the menu's best offering by far. The Cuban Coffee Pork is definitely a different take on roast pork, rubbed with Cuban coffee and grilled with a vanilla-bean butter sauce and banana black currant chutney. Even though it is right on tourist-laden Duval Street, Mangoes enjoys a good reputation among locals and stands out from the rest of the greasy bar fare found there.

700 Duval St. (at Angela St.). © 305/292-4606. Reservations recommended for parties of 6 or more. Main courses $12–$26; pizzas $10–$13; lunch $7–$14. AE, DC, DISC, MC, V. Daily 11am–midnight; pizza until 1am.

KEY WEST AFTER DARK

Duval Street is the Bourbon Street of Florida. Amid the T-shirt shops and clothing boutiques, you'll find bar after bar serving neon-colored frozen drinks to revelers who bounce from one to the next from noon till dawn. Bands and crowds vary from night to night and season to season. Your best bet is to start at Truman Avenue and head up Duval to check them out for yourself. Cover charges are rare, except in gay clubs (see "The Gay Scene," below), so stop into a dozen and see which you like. For the most part, Key West is a late-night town, and bars and clubs are open daily until around 3 or 4am.

You'll have to stop in at **Sloppy Joe's**, 201 Duval St. (© **305/294-5717, ext. 10**), just to say you did. Scholars and drunks debate whether this is the same Sloppy Joe's that Hemingway wrote about, but there's no argument that this classic bar's turn-of-the-century wooden ceiling and cracked tile floors are Key West originals. There's live music nightly as well as a cigar room and martini bar. Just around the corner from Duval's beaten path, **Captain Tony's Saloon**, 428 Greene St. (© **305/294-1838**), is a smoky old wooden bar, about as authentic as you'll find, where old-time regulars claim Hemingway drank, caroused, and even wrote. The owner, Captain Tony Tarracino, a former controversial Key West mayor—"immortalized" in Jimmy Buffett's "Last Mango in Paradise"—has recently capitalized on the success of this once-quaint tavern by franchising the place.

Speaking of the Key West legend, **Jimmy Buffett's Margaritaville Cafe,** 500 Duval St. (© **305/292-1435**), is a worthwhile stop. Although Mr. Buffett moved to glitzy Palm Beach years ago, his name is still attracting large crowds. This kitschy restaurant/bar/gift shop features live bands every night—from rock to blues to reggae and everything in between. The touristy cafe is furnished with plenty of Buffett memorabilia, including gold records, photos, and drawings. The margaritas are high priced but tasty, but the cheeseburgers aren't worth singing about.

Durty Harry's, 208 Duval St. (© **305/296-4890**), is a large complex featuring live rock bands almost every night. You can wander to one of the many outdoor bars or head up to Upstairs at Rick's, an indoor/outdoor dance club that gets going late. For the more racy singles or couples, there is also the Red Garter, a pocket-sized strip club.

Until an arsonist put an end to the legend in 1995, the former gay club **Epoch,** 623 Duval St. (© **305/296-8521**), was the place to dance to everything from techno to house and disco to reggae. Now expanded to include seven bars, an even bigger dance floor, a huge outside deck overlooking Duval Street, and a new state-of-the-art sound system, this is a better-than-ever choice for people of any orientation who can appreciate a good time.

Wax, 422 Applerouth Lane (© **305/296-6667**), oozes a cosmopolitan ambience, looking as if it were shipped down from New York, with its blood red interior, very hip lounge atmosphere, and excellent dance music. Though it has a more elegant atmosphere than any other place on the island, Wax's patrons (it's where all the locals go to avoid tourists) dress down.

THE GAY SCENE

Key West's bohemian live-and-let live atmosphere extends to its thriving and quirky gay community. Since Tennessee Williams and before, Key West has provided the perfect backdrop to a gay scene unlike that of many large urban areas. Seamlessly blended with the prevailing culture, there is no "gay ghetto" in Key West, where alternative lifestyles are embraced and even celebrated.

In Key West, the best music and dancing can be found at the predominantly gay clubs. While many of the area's other hot spots are geared toward tourists who like to imbibe, the gay clubs are for those who want to rave, gay or not. Covers vary, but are rarely more than $10.

Two adjacent popular late-night spots are the **801 Bourbon Bar** and **One Saloon** (801 Duval St. and 514 Petronia St.; © **305/294-9349** for both), featuring great drag and lots more disco. A mostly male clientele frequents this hot spot from 9pm until 4am. Another Duval Street favorite is **Diva's,** at 711 Duval St. (© **305/292-8500**), where you might catch drag queens belting out torch songs or judges voting on the best package in the wet jockey shorts contest.

Sunday nights are fun at two local spots. **Tea by the Sea,** on the pier at the Atlantic Shores Motel (510 South St.; © **800/520-3559**), attracts a faithful following of regulars and visitors alike. The clothing-optional pool is always an attraction. Show up after 7:30pm. Better known around town as La-Te-Da, **La Terraza de Marti,** the former Key West home of Cuban exile Jose Marti, at 1125 Duval St. (© **305/296-6706**), is a great spot to gather poolside for the best martini in town—but don't bother with the food. Just upstairs from there is **The Crystal Room** (© **305/296-6706**), with a high-caliber cabaret performance featuring the popular Randy Roberts in the winter.

The Everglades & Biscayne National Park

by Lesley Abravanel

Miami has been called the "gateway to the world," with its port leading the pack in passengers heading to the Caribbean and to Latin America. But many tourists also take some time out in this area to explore Dade County's two full-fledged, federally designated national parks: Everglades National Park, a swampy, slow-moving river area filled with wild plant and animal life; and Biscayne National Park, which boasts 181,500 acres of underwater treasures.

If you're short on time and have to pick one, don't miss the Everglades, the perfect place to experience the beauty of Florida's most primitive natural resources. But for those with more flexibility, schedule a visit to Biscayne National Park as well, where you can submerge yourself in an entirely different, underwater ecosystem.

1 Everglades National Park 🌟🌟🌟

35 miles SW of Miami

For many who have never visited Everglades National Park, the place conjures up images of one big swamp swarming with ominous creatures. Contrary to popular belief, however, the Everglades really isn't a swamp at all, but one of the country's most fascinating natural resources. Imagine a shallow river of grass protected by canopies of lush mangroves and you've got the real Everglades, where primitive wildlife peacefully coexists with awestruck visitors.

For first-timers or those with dubious athletic skills, the best way to see the 'glades is probably via airboat, which actually aren't allowed in the park proper, but cut through the sawgrass on the park's outskirts, taking you past countless birds, alligators, deer, and raccoons. A walk on one of the park's many trails will provide you with a different vantage point; up-close interaction with an assortment of tame wildlife. But the absolute best way to see the 'glades is via canoe, where you can get incredibly close to nature. Whichever method you choose, I guarantee you will marvel at the sheer beauty of the Everglades. In addition to the multitude of mosquito bites (the bugs seem immune to repellent—wear long pants and cover your arms, if possible), an Everglades experience will definitely contribute to a newfound appreciation of Florida's natural (and beautiful) wonderland.

This vast and unusual ecosystem is actually a shallow, 40-mile-wide, slow-moving river. Rarely more than knee-deep, the water is the lifeblood of this wilderness, and the subtle shifts in water level dictate the life cycles of the native plants and animals. Most folks viewed the Everglades as a worthless swamp until Marjory Stoneman Douglas (who fought tirelessly to save this fragile resource

Everglades & Biscayne National Parks

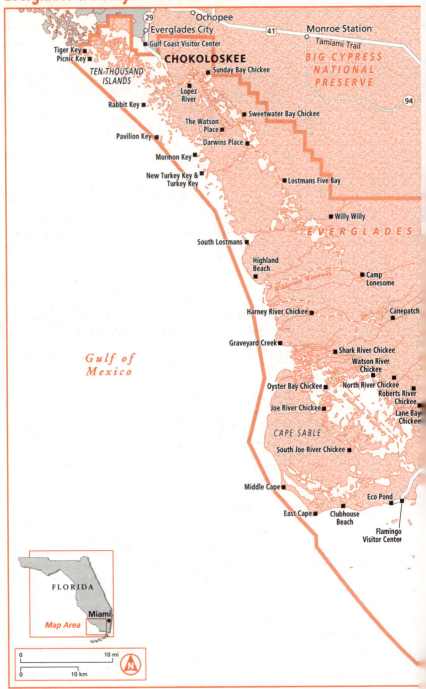

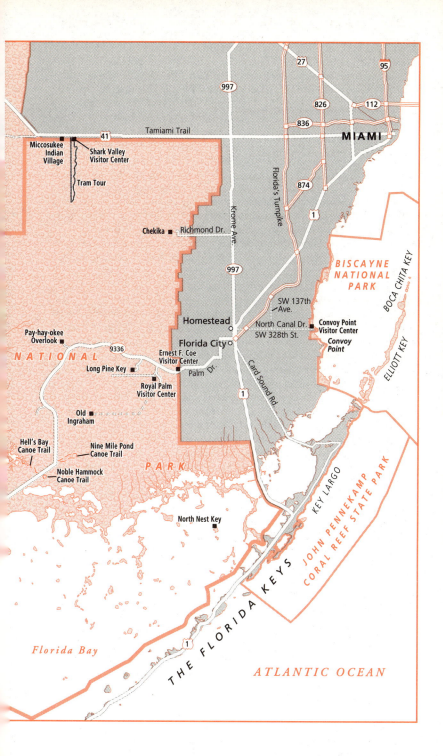

until her death in 1998 at the age of 108) focused attention on the area with her moving and insightful book *The Everglades: River of Grass,* published in 1947.

In that same year, 1.5 million acres—less than 20% of the Everglades' wilderness—were established as Everglades National Park. At that time, few lawmakers understood how neighboring ecosystems relate to each other. Consequently, the park is heavily affected by surrounding territories and is at the butt end of every environmental insult that occurs upstream in Miami. Recently, environmental activists have succeeded in persuading politicians to enact legislation to clean up the pollution that has threatened this unusual ecosystem ever since the days when heavy industry—most notably the sugar industry—first moved into the area.

> **Lazy River**
> It takes a month for 1 gallon of water to move through Everglades National Park.

While there has been a marked decrease in the indigenous wildlife here, Everglades National Park nevertheless remains one of the few places where you can see dozens of endangered species in their natural habitat, including the swallowtail butterfly, American crocodile, leatherback turtle, southern bald eagle, West Indian manatee, and Florida panther.

Take your time on the trails, and a hypnotic beauty begins to unfold. Follow the rustling of a bush, and you might see a small green tree frog or tiny brown anole lizard, with its bright-red spotted throat. Crane your neck to see around a bend and discover a delicate, brightly painted mule-ear orchid.

The slow and subtle splendor of this exotic land may not be immediately appealing to kids raised on video games and rapid-fire commercials, but they'll certainly remember the experience and thank you for it later. Meanwhile, you'll find plenty of dramatic fun around the park, such as airboat rides, alligator wrestling, and biking to keep the kids satisfied for at least a day.

In the 1800s, before the southern Everglades were designated a national park, the only inhabited piece of this wilderness was a quiet fishing village called Flamingo. Accessible only by boat and leveled every few years by hurricanes, the mosquito-infested town never grew very popular. When the 38-mile-long road from Florida City was completed in 1922, many of those who did live here fled to someplace either more or less remote. Today, Flamingo is a center for visitor activities and is the main jumping-off point for backcountry camping and exploration. It is also now home to National Park Service and concessionaire employees and their families. Some 1,400 residents still live in this small enclave in the eastern section of the park, though the local agency governing the area has recently begun a buyout program to remove them so that the area can be returned to its original state.

ESSENTIALS

GETTING THERE & ACCESS POINTS Although the Everglades may seem overwhelmingly large and unapproachable, it's easy to get to the park's two main areas—the northern section, which is accessible via Shark Valley and Everglades City, or the southern section and main entrance, accessible through the Main Visitors Center, near Homestead and Florida City.

In addition to the main entrances discussed below, you can also access the park through a central entrance at **Chekika,** which lies 6 miles west of Krome Avenue (S. R. 997) on SW 168th Street. This area was badly damaged by Hurricane Irene in October 1999, but has reopened for day use. Facilities include a picnic area and nature trails, but no visitor center or camping facilities at this time.

Northern Access **Shark Valley** is the section of the Everglades that is closest to Miami and is accessible by the Tamiami Trail, an old two-lane road that cuts across the southern part of the state along the park's northern boundary. Roadside attractions (boat rides, alligator farms, and more) along the Trail are operated by the Miccosukee Indian Village and are fun and worth a quick stop en route. Shark Valley offers a 13-mile paved road that leads to an observation tower overlooking the nucleus of the Everglades. The **Shark Valley Visitors Center** (open 8:30am–5pm in season) offers tours of the area, including an excellent tram tour, which goes deep into the park along a trail that's also terrific for biking.

Two miles west along the Tamiami Trail from Shark Valley, you'll discover the **Big Cypress National Preserve,** in which stretches of vibrant green cypress and pine trees make for a fabulous Kodak moment. If you pick up State Road 29 and head south from the Tamiami Trail, you'll hit a modified version of civilization in the form of **Everglades City** (where the Everglades meets the Gulf of Mexico) and see another entrance to the park and the **Gulf Coast Visitors Center.**

From Miami to Shark Valley: Go west on I-395 to State Road 821 south (the Florida Turnpike). Take the U.S. 41/SW 8th Street (Tamiami Trail) exit. The Shark Valley entrance is just 25 miles west. To get to Everglades City and the Gulf Coast Visitors Center, continue west on the Tamiami Trail and head south on State Road 29. Everglades City is approximately a 2½-hour drive from Miami.

Southern Access/Main Entrance Just southeast of Homestead and Florida City, off State Road 9336, you'll find the park's southern access and **Main Visitors Center** (open 24 hr.). Right inside the park, beyond the Main Visitors Center, is the **Royal Palm Visitor Center** (open 8am–4pm in season), which is the starting point for the two most popular walking trails, Gumbo Limbo and Anhinga. Thirty-eight miles from the park's southern entrance is the **Flamingo Visitors Center** (open 8:30am–5pm in season), the gateway for campers and those embarking on water trips through the park.

From Miami to the Southern entrance: Go west on I-395 to State Road 821 south (Florida Turnpike). The Turnpike will end in Florida City. Take your first right turn through the center of town (you can't miss it) and follow the signs to the park entrance on State Road 9336. Make a left when you reach the Robert Is Here fruit stand (19200 SW 344th St., between SW 197th and 202nd aves. in Homestead). The Main Visitors Center is about 1½ hours from Miami. Once there, they will guide you to the park's other visitor centers and points of interest.

VISITOR CENTERS & INFORMATION General inquiries and specific questions should be directed to **Everglades National Park Headquarters,** 40001 S.R. 9336, Homestead, FL 33034 (© **305/242-7700**). Ask for a copy of *Parks and Preserves,* a free newspaper that's filled with up-to-date information about

---

Impressions

There are no other Everglades in the world. They are, they have always been, one of the unique regions of the earth, remote, never wholly known. Nothing anywhere else is like them: their vast glittering openness, wider than the enormous visible round of the horizon, the racing free saltiness and sweetness of their massive winds, under the dazzling blue heights of space.

—Marjory Stoneman Douglas, *The Everglades: River of Grass,* 1947

goings-on in the Everglades. The office is staffed by helpful phone operators daily from 8:30am until 4:30pm. You can also try www.florida-everglades.com.

The **Ernest F. Coe Visitor Center** is located at the park headquarters' entrance, west of Homestead and Florida City, and is a great place to gather information for your trip. In addition to information on tours and boat rentals, and free brochures outlining trails, wildlife, and activities, you will also find state-of-the-art educational displays, films, and interactive exhibits. The center is open from 8am until 5pm daily.

Other visitor centers lying throughout the park are listed above under "Getting There & Access Points." For more detailed directions to each center, contact the Everglades National Park Headquarters (above).

ENTRANCE FEES, PERMITS & REGULATIONS Permits and passes can be purchased only at the main park entrance, the Chekika entrance, or the Shark Valley entrance stations (see "Getting There & Access Points," above).

Even if you are just visiting the park for an afternoon, you'll need to buy a **7-day permit,** which costs $10 per vehicle. Pedestrians and cyclists are charged $5 each and $4 at Shark Valley. For a year's worth of unlimited admissions to the Everglades, the **Everglades Park Pass** is also available for $20. U.S. citizens also have the choice of purchasing a **Golden Eagle Passport** for $65, which is valid for entrance into any U.S. national park over a 12-month period. U.S. citizens aged 62 and older can receive an even better deal with the **Golden Age Passport;** for only $10, this pass grants its holder unlimited entrance to any U.S. national park, plus it's valid for life. A **Golden Access Passport** offers the same package free to U.S. citizens with disabilities.

Additional permits are required for **campers** staying overnight either in the backcountry or in the primitive campsites. See "Accommodations You Can Afford," later in this chapter, for more information.

Saltwater fishing in the Everglades area also requires a license. Those planning on riding along with a charter captain are generally covered by the boat's vessel license; however, ask ahead of time to be sure. If you'd rather fish without a charter captain, you must obtain a standard State of Florida saltwater fishing license. These are available within Everglades National Park at **Flamingo Lodge,** 1 Flamingo Lodge Hwy., Flamingo, FL 33034 (© **800/600-3813** or 941/695-3101), or at any tackle shop or sporting goods store nearby. Nonresidents will pay $17 for a 7-day license or $7 for 3 days. Florida residents can get a fishing license good for the whole year for $14. Snook and crawfish licenses must be purchased separately at a cost of $2.

Island Hopping

Beginning at Marco Island, 20 miles south of Naples on Florida's Gulf Coast, and heading south into the Everglades, there are a whopping 10,000 islands in the fittingly named **Ten Thousand Islands** area, whose primary residents are the same red mangrove trees that can be found elsewhere throughout the Everglades. Often called "walking trees" because of their roots, mangrove tree roots arch above the ground like crouched legs. Though docking isn't allowed at many of these islands, you can pilot your boat nearby to catch a close-up glimpse of nature at play. The Flamingo Visitor Center (See "Getting There & Access Points" earlier in the chapter under "Essentials") also leads tours to the area.

Freshwater fishing licenses are available at various bait and tackle shops outside the park at the same rates as those offered inside the park. A good one nearby is **Don's Bait & Tackle,** 30710 S. Federal Hwy., in Homestead right on U.S. 1 (© **305/247-6616**). *Note:* Most of the area's freshwater fishing, limited to murky canals and artificial lakes near housing developments, is hardly worth the trouble when so much good saltwater fishing is available.

Firearms are not allowed anywhere in the park.

SEASONS There are two distinct seasons in the Everglades: high season and mosquito season. High season is also dry season and lasts from late November to May. Despite the bizarre cold and wet weather patterns that El Niño brought in 1998, most winters here are warm, sunny, and breezy—a good combination for keeping the bugs away. This is the best time to visit because low water levels attract the largest variety of wading birds and their predators.

As the dry season wanes, wildlife migrates elsewhere; by the end of May, the only living things you are sure to spot will cause you to itch. The worst, called "no-see-ums," are not even swattable. If you choose to visit during the buggy season, be vigilant in applying bug spray. Also, realize that many establishments and operators either close or curtail offerings in the summer, so always call ahead to check schedules.

RANGER PROGRAMS More than 50 ranger programs, free with admission, are offered each month during high season and give visitors an opportunity to gain an expert's perspective. Ranger-led walks and talks are offered year-round from the Royal Palm Visitor Center, west of the main entrance, and at the Flamingo and Gulf Coast visitor centers as well as the Shark Valley Information Center during the winter months (see "Getting There & Access Points," above). Park rangers tend to be helpful, well informed, and good-humored. Some programs occur regularly, such as Royal Palm Visitor Center's **Glade Glimpses,** a walking tour during which rangers point out flora and fauna and discuss issues affecting the Everglades' survival. These tours are scheduled at 12:30pm daily. The **Anhinga Ambles,** a similar program led from the Royal Palm center that takes place on the Anhinga Trail, starts at 10:30am and 3:30pm daily. Since times, programs, and locations can vary from month to month, check a schedule, available at any of the visitor centers.

SAFETY There are many dangers inherent in this vast wilderness area. *Always* let someone know your itinerary before you set out on an extended hike. It's mandatory that you file an itinerary when camping overnight in the backcountry. When you're on the water, watch for weather changes; severe thunderstorms and high winds often develop rapidly. Swimming is not recommended because of the presence of alligators, sharks, and barracudas. Watch out for the region's four indigenous poisonous snakes: diamondback and pygmy rattlesnakes, coral snakes (identifiable by their colorful rings), and water moccasins (which swim on the surface of the water). Again, bring insect repellent to ward off mosquitoes and biting flies.

First aid is available from park rangers. The nearest hospital is in Homestead, 10 miles from the park's main entrance.

EXPLORING THE PARK

Shark Valley, a 13-mile paved road through the Everglades, provides a fine introduction to the wonder of the park. Bicycling or taking a guided tram tour in the area (see "Organized Tours," below) are fantastic ways to become acquainted with the Everglades, but don't plan on spending more than a few hours here.

If you want to see a greater array of plant and animal life, make sure that you venture into the park through the main entrance, pick up a trail map, and dedicate at least a day to exploring from there. Stop first along the Anhinga and Gumbo-Limbo Trails, which start right next to one another, 3 miles from the park's main entrance. These trails provide a thorough introduction to Everglades flora and fauna and are highly recommended to first-time visitors. Each of them is a half mile round-trip.

Gumbo-Limbo Trail 🌟🌟🌟 meanders through a gorgeous shaded, jungle-like hammock of gumbo limbo trees, royal palms, ferns, orchids, air plants, and a general blanket of vegetation, though it doesn't put you in close contact with much wildlife. **Anhinga Trail** 🌟🌟, on the other hand, is one of the most popular trails in the park because of its abundance of wildlife: There's more wildlife in this area of the park than in most parts of the Everglades, especially during dry season. Alligators, lizards, turtles, river otters, herons, egrets, and other animals abound. Arrive early to spot the widest selection of exotic birds, such as the Anhinga, the trail's namesake, a large black fishing bird so accustomed to humans that many of them build their nests in plain view. Take your time—at least an hour is recommended for each trail. Both are wheelchair accessible. If you treat the trails and modern boardwalk as pathways to get through quickly, rather than destinations to experience and savor slowly, you'll miss out on the still beauty and hidden treasures that await.

If you want to get even closer to nature, a few hours in a **canoe** along any of the trails allows paddlers the chance to sense the park's fluid motion and to become a part of the ecosphere. Visitors who choose this option end up feeling more like explorers than merely observers. (See "Affordable Outdoor Activities," below.)

No matter what you choose to do here (and there are many options), we strongly recommend staying for the 7pm program at the **Long Pine Key Amphitheater** at the Long Pine Key campground (© **305/242-7700**), available during high season. This talk and slide show, given by one of the park's rangers, will give you a detailed overview of the park's history, natural resources, wildlife, and threats to its survival.

AFFORDABLE OUTDOOR ACTIVITIES

BIKING If the park isn't flooded from excess rain (which it often is, especially in spring), **Shark Valley** in Everglades National Park is South Florida's most scenic bicycle trail. Many locals haul their bikes out to the 'glades for a relaxing day of wilderness-trail riding here. You can ride the 15-mile loop with no traffic in sight. Instead, you'll share the flat paved road only with other bikers and a menagerie of wildlife. (Don't be surprised to see a gator lounging in the sun or a deer munching on some grass. Otters, turtles, alligators, and snakes are common companions in the Shark Valley area.) There are no shortcuts, so if you become tired or are unable to complete the entire 15-mile trip, turn around and return on the same road.

The relatively flat 38-mile-long, paved **Main Park Road,** originating at the Main Visitor Center (see "Getting There & Access Points," above) is also great for biking. The multitude of hardwood hammocks (dense stands of dwarfed hardwood trees) and a dwarf cypress forest make this a lovely route, all the way to the Flamingo Visitor Center. Expect to spend 2 to 3 hours here. Those who love to mountain bike, and who prefer solitude, might check out the **Southern Glades Trail,** a 14-mile-long unpaved trail opened in late 1998 that is lined with native trees and teeming with wildlife such as deer, alligators, and the occasional snake. The remote trail runs along the C-111 canal, off State Road 9336 and SW 217th Street.

Bike rentals are available at the **Flamingo Lodge, Marina and Outpost Resort** (see "Accommodations You Can Afford," below) for $17 per 24 hours, $14 per full day, $8.50 per half day (any 4-hr. period), and $3 per hour. A $50 deposit is required for each rental. Rentals can be picked up starting at 7am and the bikes have to be returned by 5pm. Bicycles are also available from **Shark Valley Tram Tours** (© 305/221-8455), at the park's Shark Valley entrance, for $4.75 per hour; rentals can be picked up anytime between 8:30am and 3pm and must be returned by 4pm.

BIRD-WATCHING More than 350 species of birds make their homes in the Everglades. Tropical birds from the Caribbean and temperate species from North America can be found here, along with exotics that have blown in from more distant regions. **Eco and Mrazek Ponds,** located near Flamingo, are two of the best places for birding, especially in early morning or late afternoon in the dry winter months. Pick up a free birding checklist from a visitor center (see "Essentials," earlier in this chapter), and ask a park ranger what's been spotted in recent days.

CANOEING Canoeing through the Everglades may be one of the most serene, surprisingly diverse adventures you'll ever have. From a canoe (where you're incredibly close to the water level), your vantage point is priceless. Canoers in the 'glades can co-exist with the gators and birds there in a way no one else can; the animals behave as if you are part of the ecosystem—a miracle that can't be experienced from an airboat.

A ranger-guided canoe tour is the best bet for first-time visitors and costs $19.95, plus a required deposit. As always, a ranger will provide an educational context for understanding your surroundings. One such tour leaves from the ranger station in Everglades City, at the Parks Docks on Chokoloskee Causeway on State Road 29, a half mile south of the traffic circle. Call **Everglades National Park Boat Tours** at © 800/445-7724 for more information. Everglades National Park's longest "trails" are designed for boat and canoe travel, and many are marked as clearly as walking trails. The **Noble Hammock Canoe Trail,** a 2-mile loop, takes 1 to 2 hours and is recommended for beginning canoers. The **Hell's Bay Canoe Trail,** a 3- to 6-mile course for hardier paddlers, takes 2 to 6 hours, depending on how far you choose to go. Both trails are located off of Main Park Road and are marked by signs. Park rangers can recommend other trails that best suit your abilities, time limitations, and interests.

You can rent a canoe at the **Flamingo Lodge, Marina and Outpost Resort** (see "Accommodations You Can Afford," below) for $40 for 24 hours, $32 per full day, $22 per half-day (any 4-hr. period), and $8 per hour. They also have family canoes that rent for $12, $30, $40, and $50, respectively. Skiffs, kayaks, and tandem kayaks are also available. The concessionaire will shuttle your party to the trailhead of your choice and pick you up afterward. Overnight canoe rentals are available for $50 to $60. During ideal weather conditions (stay away during bug season!), you can paddle right out to the Gulf and camp on the beach. However, Gulf waters at beach sites can be extremely rough, and people in small watercraft such as a canoe should exercise caution. Rental facilities are open daily from 6am to 8pm.

FISHING About one-third of Everglades National Park is open water. Freshwater fishing is popular in brackish **Nine-Mile Pond** (25 miles from the main entrance) and other spots along the Main Park Road, but because of the high mercury levels found in the Everglades, freshwater fishers are warned not to eat their catch. Before casting, check in at a visitor center, as many of the park's lakes are preserved for observation only. Fishing licenses are required; see "Essentials," earlier in this chapter.

Saltwater anglers will find snapper and sea trout plentiful. Charter boats and guides heading out to the Gulf are available at **Flamingo Lodge, Marina and Outpost Resort** (see "Accommodations You Can Afford," below). A fishing excursion for two people costs roughly $350 for a full day or $250 for a half day; a third or fourth person will be charged $25 each. Phone for information and reservations.

MOTORBOATING Motorboating around the Everglades seems like a great way to see plants and animals in remote habitats, and, indeed, is an interesting and fulfilling experience as you throttle into nature. However, environmentalists are taking stock of the damage motorboats (especially airboats) inflict on the delicate ecosystem. If you choose to motor, remember that most of the areas near land are "no wake" zones and that, for the protection of nesting birds, landing is prohibited on most of the little mangrove islands.

Motorboating is allowed only in certain areas, including Florida Bay (the freshwater inlet set off from the Gulf near Everglades City) and the Ten Thousand Islands area. In all the freshwater lakes, however, motorboats are prohibited if they're above five horsepower. There's a long list of restrictions and restricted areas, so get a copy of the park's boating rules from National Park Headquarters before setting out (see "Visitor Centers & Information" under "Essentials," above).

The Everglades' only marina—accommodating about 50 boats with electric and water hookups—is the **Flamingo Lodge, Marina and Outpost Resort** (see "Accommodations You Can Afford," below). The well-marked channel to the Flamingo is accessible to boats with a maximum 4-foot draft and is open year-round. Reservations can be made through the marina store (© **941/695-3101, ext. 304**). Skiffs with 15-horsepower motors are available for rent for $90 per day, $65 per half day (any 5-hr. period), and $22 per hour. A $125 deposit is required.

ORGANIZED TOURS
AIRBOAT TOURS Shallow-draft, fan-powered airboats were invented in the Everglades by frog hunters who were tired of poling through the brushes. Airboats cut through the sawgrass and are sort of like hydraulic boats in which, at high enough speeds, the boat actually lifts above the sawgrass and into the air. These shallow-bottom runabouts tend to inflict severe damage on the animals and plants and are not permitted in the park. Just outside the boundaries, however, you'll find a number of outfitters offering rides. If you choose to ride on one, you should consider bringing earplugs; these high-speed boats are loud, though they're also a lot of fun.

Airboat rides are offered at the **Miccosukee Indian Village,** just west of the Shark Valley entrance on U.S. 41/the Tamiami Trail (© **305/223-8380**). Native American guides will take you through the reserve's swampy brushes at high speeds and stop along the way to point out alligators, native plants, and exotic birds. The price is $7. The **Everglades Alligator Farm,** 4 miles south of Palm Drive/State Route 9336 on SW 192nd Avenue (© **305/247-2628**),

At Home in the Everglades

The Everglades offers a protective area in which an eclectic mix of mammals and reptiles can flourish. One such mammal is the endangered sea cow, or **manatee**, which typically inhabits saltwater, except during winter months when they migrate to the rivers and springs for warmth. Manatees are amorphous-looking, gray-toned creatures with no distinct shape; they can grow to 13 feet in length and 1,300 pounds. Although their size is intimidating, they are extremely timid, gentle mammals.

Also sharing space among the mangroves, and found in most bodies of water in the Everglades, are the ubiquitous **alligators**, reminiscent of half-submerged logs. We've seen an alligator baited right up to our boat by a boat captain with a chunk of raw meat. Though the alligator thankfully did not jump into the boat, it was a frightening experience akin to a 3-D movie, which you should not try to duplicate. If an alligator approaches you, *do nothing*. Use your common sense and either stand still or walk (don't run) away. Do not touch them or they will attack!

The alligator is a protected species in the state, but a designated alligator-hunting season, done on a lottery system, exists to control the population.

---

offers half-hour guided airboat tours from 9am until 6pm daily. The price, which includes admission to the park, is $14.50 for adults, $8 for children.

MOTORBOAT TOURS Both Florida Bay and backcountry tours are offered by the **Flamingo Lodge, Marina and Outpost Resort** (see "Accommodations You Can Afford," below). Florida Bay tours cruise nearby estuaries and sandbars, while six-passenger backcountry boats visit smaller sloughs. Passengers can expect to see birds and a variety of other animals. Both are available in 1½- and 2-hour versions that cost an average of $16 for adults, $8 for children, and are free for children under 6. Tours depart throughout the day, and reservations are recommended. There are also charter-fishing boats that can be booked through the resort's main reservation number (© **941/695-3101**).

TRAM TOURS At the park's Shark Valley entrance, open-air tram buses take visitors on 2-hour naturalist-led tours that delve 7½ miles into the wilderness. At the trail's midsection, passengers can disembark and climb a 65-foot observation tower that offers good views of the 'glades, though the tower on the Pa-Hay-Okee trail is better. Visitors will see plenty of wildlife and endless acres of sawgrass. Tours run November to April only, daily from 9am to 4pm, and are sometimes stalled by flooding or particularly heavy mosquito infestation. Reservations are recommended from December to March. The cost is $9.30 for adults, $5.15 for children 12 and under, and $8.25 for seniors. For further information, contact the **Shark Valley Tram Tours** at © **305/221-8455**.

SHOPPING

You won't find big malls or lots of boutiques in this area, although there is an outlet center nearby, the **Keys Factory Shops** (© **305/248-4727**), at 250 E. Palm Dr. (where the Florida Turnpike meets U.S. 1) in Florida City. More than 60 stores are found here, including Nike Factory Store, Bass Co. Store, Levi's, OshKosh B'Gosh, and Izod. You can pick up a free coupon booklet (called the

Come Back Pack) from the Customer Service Center. The outlet center is open Monday to Saturday until 9pm, Sunday until 6pm.

A necessary stop and a good place for a refreshment is one of Florida's best-known fruit stands: **Robert Is Here** (© **305/246-1592**). Robert has been selling his homegrown treats for nearly 40 years at the corner of SW 344th Street (Palm Dr.) and SW 192nd Avenue. Here, you'll find the freshest pineapples, bananas, papayas, mangos, and melons anywhere, as well as his famous shakes in unusual flavors like Key lime, coconut, orange, and cantaloupe. Exotic fruits, bottled jellies, hot sauces, and salad dressings are also available. This is a great place to pick up culinary souvenirs and sample otherwise unavailable goodies. Open daily 8am until 7pm.

Along Tamiami Trail, there are several roadside shops hawking Native American handicrafts, including one at the **Miccosukee Indian Village** (© **305/223-8380**), just west of the Shark Valley entrance. At nearly every one of these shops, you'll find the same stock of feathered dreamcatchers, stuffed alligator heads and claws, turquoise jewelry, and other trinkets. Be sure to take note of the unique, colorful, handmade Miccosukee dolls.

ACCOMMODATIONS YOU CAN AFFORD

The only lodging in the park proper is the Flamingo Lodge, a fairly priced and very recommendable option. However, there are a few hotels just outside the park that are even cheaper. A $45-million casino hotel, the **Miccosukee Resort and Convention Center,** was built adjacent to the Miccosukee bingo and gaming hall on the northern edge of the park at 500 SW 177th Ave. (at the intersection with SW 8th St.), Miami, FL 33194 (© **877/242-6464**). Rates here are $99 for a double and $135 for a suite, and all rooms sleep up to four people.

Although bugs can be a major nuisance, especially in the warmer months, camping is really the way to go in this very primitive environment, since it's the best way to fully experience South Florida's wilderness.

LODGING IN EVERGLADES NATIONAL PARK

Flamingo Lodge, Marina and Outpost Resort ★★   The Flamingo Lodge is the only lodging actually located within the boundaries of Everglades National Park. This woodsy, sprawling complex offers rooms overlooking the Florida Bay in either a two-story, simple motel or the lodge. Either option feels very much like being at summer camp, with a few more amenities. Rooms are in a standard, cookie-cutter motel style, with functional bathrooms. No luxury here, but it's nonetheless a comfort for those who'd rather not experience the great outdoors while they sleep. More interesting than the actual motel, however, are the visitors who crop up on the lawn—alligators, raccoons, and other nomadic creatures. The hotel is open year-round, although the restaurant (see the "Great Deals on Dining" section below) closes in the summer.

Note that the Flamingo Lodge is also the only full-service outfitter located within the park, offering a variety of rentals and excursions from canoes to houseboat charters (see also "Affordable Outdoor Activities," above).

1 Flamingo Lodge Hwy., Flamingo, FL 33034. © **800/600-3813** or 941/695-3101. Fax 941/695-3921. www.flamingolodge.com. 127 units. Winter from $95 double, $99–$135 cottage, $110–$145 suite. Off-season $65–$79 double, $59 cottage, $99–$110 suite. Rates for cottages or suites are for 1–4 people. Children under 18 stay free. Continental breakfast included May–Oct. AE, DC, DISC, MC. Take Florida Tpk. south to Florida City; exit on U.S. 1. at 4-way intersection, and turn right onto Palm Dr. Continue for 3 miles and turn left at Robert Is Here fruit stand. Turn right at the 3-way intersection; the park entrance is 3 miles ahead. Continue for about 38 more miles to reach lodge. **Amenities:** Waterside bar and restaurant; freshwater swimming pool; bike, canoe, and kayak rentals; marina with boat tours; boat rentals; houseboat and fishing

charters; coin-op washers and dryers. *In room:* A/C, TV in standard rooms and suites but not in cottages, kitchen in cottages and suites only.

CAMPING & HOUSEBOATING IN THE EVERGLADES

Campgrounds are available year-round in Flamingo, Chekika, and Long Pine Key. All three have drinking water, picnic tables, charcoal grills, restrooms, tent and trailer pads, and welcome RVs, though there are no electrical hookups. Flamingo has cold-water showers, Chekika has free hot showers, and Flamingo offers hot showers for $3. Private ground fires are not permitted, but supervised campfire programs are conducted during winter months. Chekika campers must register before 5pm, after which time the gates are locked and only registered campers are allowed access. Long Pine Key and Flamingo are much more popular and require advance reservations. All reservations may be made through **The National Park Reservations Service** at © **800/365-CAMP.** Campsites are $14 per night with a 14-consecutive-day stay limit, 30 days a year maximum.

Camping is also available in the **backcountry** (those remote areas accessible only by boat, foot, or canoe—basically most of the park) year-round on a first-come, first-served basis. Campers must register with park rangers and get a free permit (see "Essentials," earlier in this chapter) in person or by telephone no less than 24 hours before the start of their trip. For more information, contact the **Gulf Coast Visitor Center** (© **941/695-3311**) or the **Flamingo Visitor Center** (© **941/695-2945**), which are the only two places that give out these permits. Once you have one, camping sites cost $10 for one to six people, $20 for 7 to 12 people, and $30 for more than 13 people. Campers can use only designated campsites, which are plentiful and well marked on visitor maps.

Many backcountry sites are *chickee huts*—covered wooden platforms (with toilets) on stilts. They're accessible only by canoe and can accommodate free-standing tents (without stakes). Ground sites are located along interior bays and rivers, and beach camping is also popular. In summer especially, mosquito repellent is necessary gear.

Houseboat rentals are one of the park's best-kept secrets. Available through the **Flamingo Lodge, Marina and Outpost Resort,** motorized houseboats make it possible to explore some of the park's more remote regions without having to worry about being back by nightfall. You can choose from two different types of houseboats. The first, a 40-foot pontoon boat, sleeps six to eight people in a single large room that's separated by a central head (bathroom) and shower. There's a small galley (kitchen) that contains a refrigerator, stove, oven, and charcoal grill. Prices aren't cheap, unless you are with a good-sized group, but it might be worth a splurge for the incredible experience. It rents for between $340 and $475 for 2 nights (there is a 2-night minimum in high season).

The newer, sleeker Gibson fiberglass boats sleep six and have toilets and showers, air-conditioning, electric stoves, and a full rooftop sun deck. These rent for $575 for 2 nights (the 2-night minimum lasts all year long). With either boat, the seventh night is free when renting for a full week.

Boating experience is helpful but not mandatory, as the boats only cruise up to 6 miles per hour and are surprisingly easy to use. In-season, reservations should be made months in advance; call © **800/600-3813** or 941/695-3101.

LODGING IN EVERGLADES CITY

Since Everglades City is 35 miles southeast of Naples and 83 miles west of Miami, many people choose to explore this western entrance to Everglades National Park, located off the Tamiami Trail, on State Road 29. An annual seafood festival held the first weekend in February is a major event that draws hordes of people. Everglades City (the gateway to the Ten Thousand Islands), where the 'glades meets the Gulf of Mexico, is the closest thing you'll get to civilization in South Florida's swampy frontier, with a few tourist traps—er, shops—a restaurant, and two bed-and-breakfasts (see below).

Ivey House B&B ★★ *Finds* Housed in what used to be a recreational center for the men who built the Tamiami Trail, the Ivey House offers three types of accommodations. In the original house, there are 10 small rooms that share communal bathrooms (one each for women and men). One private cottage consists of two bedrooms, a full kitchen, a private bathroom, and a screened-in porch. The Ivey's new inn (opened in 2001) adds 17 rooms (with private bathrooms) that face a courtyard with a screened-in, shallow "conversation" pool. During the summer, however, the mosquitoes are out in full force and a trip to the pool could leave you with multiple bites, screens or not. Bring bug spray! A living room area offers guests the opportunity to mingle. Boxed lunches, stored in a cooler so you can bring them along for your Everglades excursions, are offered for $9.50 each. Note that no smoking is allowed in any of the buildings here.

107 Camellia St., Everglades City, FL 34139. © 941/695-3299. Fax 941/695-4155. www.iveyhouse.com. 28 units. Winter $60–$85 main house (older rooms); $125–$155 cottage (2-night minimum); from $100 newer rooms. Off-season $50–$70 main house; $90–$105 cottage; from $90 newer rooms. MC, V. Closed in Sept. **Amenities:** Restaurant; small pool; free use of bikes; Everglades excursions available. *In room:* A/C (all rooms), TV, fridge (inn and cottage), kitchen (cottage only).

On the Banks of the Everglades ★★★ *Finds* This very cute bed-and-breakfast is right on the money, as far as kitsch is concerned. On the Banks of the Everglades is a fabulous retreat from the lush greenery of the swampy Everglades to the even more lush greenery of money (it's located in a building that was formerly the first bank established, in 1923, in Collier County). Rooms such as the Trust Room, the Checking Department, and the Stocks and Bond Room are clean and comfortable (though bathrooms are down the hall) and are all located on the floor where banking was conducted until 1962. All other rooms, such as the Mortgage Loan Department, Savings Department, and Dividends Department, have private bathrooms. In addition to congenial and knowledgeable service, On the Banks boasts wonderful extras such as a breakfast area located in the bank's fully restored vault and original bank artifacts scattered about the premises, such as the 3,000-pound cannonball safe.

201 W. Broadway, Everglades City, FL 34139. © 888/431-1977 or 941/695-3151. Fax 941/695-3335. www.banksoftheeverglades.com. 10 units, 6 with private bathroom. $85 without bathroom; $153–$160 with bathroom. Rates include continental breakfast. AE, DISC, MC, V. Closed July–Oct. **Amenities:** Free use of bikes; Everglades excursions available. *In room:* A/C, TV.

Rod & Gun Lodge ★ This rustic, old white clapboard house has plenty of history and all kinds of activities for sports enthusiasts, including a swimming pool, bicycle rentals, tennis center, and nearby boat rentals and private fishing guides. Sitting on the banks of the sleepy Barron River, the Rod & Gun Lodge was originally built as a private residence nearly 170 years ago, but Barron Collier turned it into a cozy hunting lodge in the 1920s. President Herbert Hoover vacationed here after his 1928 election victory, and President Harry S. Truman flew in to sign Everglades National Park into existence in 1947 and stayed over as well. Other guests have included President Richard Nixon, Burt Reynolds, and Mick Jagger. The public rooms are beautifully paneled and hung with tarpon, wild boar, deer antlers, and other trophies. Guest rooms in this single-story building are unfussy but perfectly comfortable. Out by the swimming pool and riverbank, a screened veranda with ceiling fans offers a pleasant place for a libation. The excellent seafood restaurant serves breakfast, lunch, and dinner. The entire property is non-smoking.

Riverside Dr. and Broadway (P.O. Box 190), Everglades City, FL 34139. © **941/695-2101.** 17 units (some with shower only). Winter $95 single or double; off-season $75 single or double. No credit cards. Closed after July 4th for the summer. **Amenities:** Restaurant; pool; tennis courts; bicycle rentals. *In room:* A/C, TV.

LODGING NEARBY IN HOMESTEAD & FLORIDA CITY

Homestead and Florida City, two adjacent towns that were almost blown off the map by Hurricane Andrew in 1992, have come back better than before. Located about 10 miles from the park's main entrance, along U.S. 1, 35 miles south of Miami, these somewhat rural towns offer several budget lodging options, including a handful of chain hotels. The **Days Inn,** 51 S. Homestead Blvd., Homestead, FL 33030 (© **305/245-1260**), costs $89 for a double. Also, the **Hampton Inn,** 124 E. Palm Dr., Homestead, FL 33034 (© **800/426-7866** or 305/247-8833), offers double rooms for $114.

Best Western Gateway to the Keys This two-story standard motel offers contemporary style and comfort about 10 miles from the park's main entrance. A decent-sized pool and a small spa make it an especially attractive option to some. Each identical standard room has bright, tropical bedspreads and oversized picture windows. The suites offer convenient extras like a microwave, a coffeemaker, an extra sink, and a small fridge. Clean and conveniently located, the motel has as its only drawback a 3-day minimum stay in high season. You'd do best to call the local reservation line (© **305/246-5100**) instead of the toll-free number—on several occasions we've experienced that the hotel will make an exception to this rule while the central reservation line will not.

411 S. Krome Ave. (U.S. 1), Florida City, FL 33034. © **800/528-1234** or 305/246-5100. Fax 305/242-0056. www.bestwestern.com. 114 units. Winter $91–$109; off-season $71–$89. Rates include continental breakfast. During races and the very high season, there may be a 3-night minimum stay. AE, DC, DISC, MC, V. **Amenities:** Pool; spa; laundry/dry cleaning. *In room:* A/C, TV, dataport, fridge, coffeemaker, hair dryer.

Super-Cheap Sleeps

Everglades Motel This one-story hotel is probably the cheapest option you'll find in Homestead, but certainly not the greatest. There is a small swimming pool, coin laundry, and free coffee in the lobby. Though not thoroughly fluent in English, the East Indian staff is accommodating and friendly. Rooms are modest in size and decor, but could use a good scrub. Nonetheless, the place is safe, super-affordable, and perfectly fine for 1 or 2 nights. Make your local calls from here, since they are free.

605 S. Krome Ave., Homestead, FL 33030. © **305/247-4117.** 14 units. Year-round rates $29–$69. Additional person $5 extra. AE, DISC, MC, V. **Amenities:** Pool; laundry. *In room:* A/C, TV, dataport, fridge.

GREAT DEALS ON DINING
IN & AROUND THE PARK

You won't find fancy nouvelle cuisine in this suburbanized farm country, but there are plenty of fast-food chains along U.S. 1, plus a few old favorites worth a taste, which we've listed below.

Here for nearly a quarter of a century, **El Toro Taco** at 1 S. Krome Ave. (near Mowry Dr. and Campbell Dr.; © **305/245-8182**) opens daily at 9:30am and stays crowded until at least 9pm most days. The fresh grilled meats, tacos, burritos, salsas, guacamole, and stews are all mild and delicious. No matter how big your appetite, it's hard to spend more than $12 per person at this Mexican outpost. Bring your own beer or wine.

Florida's "Filet Mignon of the Ocean"

If you haven't tasted Florida stone crabs, don't bother making comparisons. No, they aren't like blue crabs, snow crabs, soft-shelled crabs, Alaskan kings, or even lobster. These meaty limbs are whiter, juicier, and sweeter than any other crustacean you've ever tasted. It was these tender morsels that James Bond devoured in *Goldfinger,* and these delicacies drew the normally reclusive Duke and Duchess of Windsor out for their only public meal in Miami when they visited in 1941.

Made famous in the 1920s by a (pricey) Miami Beach institution called Joe's Stone Crab restaurant, this popular delicacy has since been the object of cravings for locals and visitors alike. Demand is so high, in fact, that most Florida stone crab claws never make their way out of the state. Fish stores and restaurants report a brisk business in overnight shipping, but with Joe's alone serving nearly 500,000 pounds of the stuff each year, there's hardly enough to export commercially. Thankfully, stone crabs face no real threat to their survival. Unlike most commercially harvested crustaceans, these sweeties are cultivated only for their luscious claws, which actually regenerate in little over a year.

It's estimated that more than two-thirds of Florida's claws come from the waters surrounding Everglades City. So swing into town any evening during the mid-October through early-May season, and watch the trappers hauling in their catch. Most every local restaurant serves the tender flesh in-season, but you can save some money by buying direct from the fish markets. They're sold precooked and ready to crack and dunk in some tangy mustard sauce. Claws are usually graded in four categories: medium, large, jumbo, and colossal. One pound of mediums usually contains between six and eight claws; colossals can weigh nearly three-quarters of a pound each. Get the biggest claws you can afford, and ask the vendor to crack them for you.

There are several reputable vendors in town. Make a stop at **Everglades Fish Corp.,** 208 Camellia St. (© 941/695-3241). It's open every day and sells the very freshest claws, as well as some excellent smoked fish. It also takes most major credit cards. **Triad Fish Co.,** 410 School Dr. (© 941/695-2662), also sells claws at reasonable prices—along with Mrs. Hilton's famous mustard sauce. Perhaps the area's oldest purveyor is **Ernest Hamilton's,** 100 Hamilton Lane, on Chokoloskee Island (© 941/695-2771). To get there, take Fla. 29 to Chokoloskee; after the post office, turn right (across the street from JT's grocery store); go straight and look for the bright yellow building.

Warning: Bargain hunters may be lured roadside with promises of cheap claws, but if prices are less than $8 or $9 a pound, you can be sure these are the castaways from the more reputable traders. The seconds are waterlogged and less meaty than their super-fresh counterparts. You can tell the difference by feeling the weight in the palm of your hand. A good fresh claw of any size should feel solid and hefty; the second-rate ones are "light as a hawk's feather," according to one local trapper. Any visible meat should not look shriveled or as if it is shrinking away from its shell. Open one before committing to more.

Housed in a squat, one-story, windowless stone building that looks something like a medieval fort, the **Capri Restaurant,** 935 N. Krome Ave., Florida City (© 305/247-1542), has been serving hearty Italian–American fare since 1958. Great pastas and salads complement a full menu (portions are big) of meat and fish dishes. They serve lunch and dinner every day (except Sun) until 11pm.

The **Miccosukee Restaurant** (© 305/223-8380), just west of the Shark Valley entrance on the Tamiami Trail (U.S. 41), serves authentic pumpkin bread, fry bread, fish, and not-so-authentic Native American interpretations of tacos and fried chicken. It's worth a stop for brunch, lunch, or dinner.

In Everglades City, **The Oyster House** (© 941/695-2073) on Chokoloskee Causeway, Highway 29 South, is a large, but homey, seafood restaurant with modest prices, excellent service, and a fantastic view of the Ten Thousand Islands. Try their hush puppies.

Once inside the Everglades, you'll want to eat at the only restaurant within the boundaries of this huge park, **The Flamingo Restaurant** (© 941/695-3101). Located in the Flamingo Lodge (see "Accommodations You Can Afford," above), this is a very civilized and affordable restaurant. Besides the spectacular view of Florida Bay and numerous Keys from the large, airy dining room, you'll also find fresh fish that is grilled, blackened, or deep-fried. Dinner entrees come with salad or conch chowder, and steamed vegetables, black beans, and rice or baked potato. The large menu has something for everyone, including basic and very tasty sandwiches, pastas, burgers, and salads. A kids' menu offers standard choices like hot dogs, grilled cheese, or fried shrimp for less than $6. Prices are surprisingly moderate, with full meals starting at about $11 and going no higher than $22. You may need reservations for dinner, however, especially in season.

IN EVERGLADES CITY

Everglades City has no gourmet restaurants, but you can get your fill of fresh seafood at several local eateries. Since the town produces about two-thirds of Florida's crab catch, most have fresh-off-the-boat claws from mid-October through mid-May. If you are in town on a weekend, swing by the Shell station at Fla. 29 and U.S. 41 to sample another local favorite, boiled peanuts. "Goobers," as the old-timers call them, are sold in paper bags from a colorful trailer. These soggy, spicy nuts are a real treat for some.

Do stop and have a chat with the friendly Joan of **Joan's Quik Stop,** at 39395 U.S. 41, in Ochopee (© 941/695-2682). This pleasant little eatery serves a great breakfast from 9am until 5pm. A favorite is the Indian breakfast of eggs on flat bread with sautéed vegetables like zucchini, eggplant, and broccoli. Lunch specials include lots of fried seafood like gator nuggets, fritters, and shrimp. Take a free postcard and send one back when you get home. It will join the hundreds of others on the walls of this quaint and inexpensive diner. Most dishes are under $7, but be sure to have cash or traveler's checks, because no checks or credit cards are accepted.

The **Oyster House,** on Fla. 29 opposite the Everglades National Park Visitor Center (© 941/695-2073), also specializes in seafood. Main courses range from $12 to $17; sandwiches are $4.50 to $9.50. A narrow, screened front porch here is a fine place to sip a drink while watching the sun set over the Everglades. It's open daily from 11am to 9pm. On some weekends you may find live music and dancing, too.

The down-home **Oar House Restaurant,** 305 Collier Ave. (Fla. 29), in town (© 941/695-3535), offers "cooters, legs, and tails" (turtles, frogs' legs, and alligator tails) as specialties. Main courses range from $8 to $16, and sandwiches and seafood baskets run $2 to $8. It's open daily from 6am to 9pm.

2 Biscayne National Park

35 miles S of Miami, 21 miles E of Everglades National Park

With only about 500,000 visitors each year (mostly boaters and divers), the unusual Biscayne National Park is one of the least-crowded parks in the country. Perhaps that's because the park is a little more difficult than most to access—more than 95% of its 181,500 acres are underwater.

The park's significance was first formally acknowledged in 1968 when, in an unprecedented move (and against intense pressure from developers), President Lyndon B. Johnson signed a bill to conserve the barrier islands off South Florida's east coast as a national monument—a protected status that's just a rung below national park. After being twice enlarged, once in 1974 and again in 1980, the waters and land surrounding the northernmost coral reef in North America became a full-fledged national park—the largest of its kind in the country.

To be fully appreciated, Biscayne National Park should be thought of more as a preserve than as a destination. We suggest using your time here to explore underwater life, of course, but also to relax.

The park's extensive reef system is renowned among divers and snorkelers worldwide, while its small mainland mangrove shoreline and keys are best explored by boat. The park consists of 44 islands, but only a few of them are open to visitors. The most popular one is **Elliott Key,** which has campsites and a visitor center plus freshwater showers (cold water only), restrooms, trails, and a buoyed swim area. It's located about 9 miles from **Convoy Point,** the park's official headquarters on the mainland. During Columbus Day weekend on Elliott Key, there is a very popular regatta in which a lively crowd of party people gathers—sometimes in the nude—to celebrate the long weekend.

If you'd prefer to rough it a little more, the 29-acre island known as **Boca Chita Key,** once an exclusive haven for yachters, has now become a popular spot for all manner of boaters. Visitors can enjoy camping and tour the island's restored historic buildings, including the county's second-largest lighthouse and a tiny chapel.

ESSENTIALS

GETTING THERE & ACCESS POINTS **Convoy Point,** the park's mainland entrance, is located 9 miles east of Homestead. To reach the park from Miami, take the Florida Turnpike to the Tallahassee Road (SW 137th Ave.) exit. Turn left, then left again at North Canal Drive (SW 328th St.) and follow signs to the park. Another option is to rent a speedboat in Miami and cruise south for about an hour and a half. If you're coming from U.S. 1, whether you're heading north or south, turn east at North Canal Drive (SW 328th St.). The entrance is approximately 9 miles away.

Once you're inside Biscayne National Park, most of what you'll want to see is accessible only to boaters. There's a boat launch at adjacent Homestead Bayfront Park, and 66 slips on Elliott Key, available free on a first-come, first-served basis. New docks surround the small harbor off of Boca Chita as well. Both Elliott and Boca Chita keys offer overnight docking for a $15 fee. Mooring buoys abound, since it is illegal to anchor on coral. When no buoys or docks are available, boaters must anchor on sand.

Even the most experienced boaters should carry updated nautical charts of the area, which are available at Convoy Point. The waters are often murky, making the abundant reefs and sandbars difficult to detect—and there are more interesting ways to spend a day than waiting for the tide to rise.

Transportation to and from Convoy Point's visitor center and Elliot Key costs $24.95 round-trip per person and takes about an hour. This is a convenient option, ensuring that you don't get lost on some deserted island by boating there yourself. Call for a seasonal schedule (© **305/230-1100**).

VISITOR CENTERS & INFORMATION The **Convoy Point Visitor Center,** 9700 SW 328th St., Homestead, FL 33033-5634, at the park's main entrance (© **305/230-7275;** fax 305/230-1190; www.biscayne.nationalpark.com), is the natural starting point for any venture into the park without a boat. In addition to providing comprehensive information about the park, on request, rangers will show you a short video on the park, its natural surroundings, and what you may see. The center is open Monday to Friday from 8:30am to 4:30pm and Saturday and Sunday from 8:30am to 5pm.

For information on transportation, glass-bottom boat tours, canoe rentals, and snorkeling and scuba diving expeditions, contact the park concessionaire, **Biscayne National Underwater Park, Inc.,** P.O. Box 1270, Homestead, FL 33030 (© **305/230-1100;** fax 305/230-1120; captsaw@bellsouth.net). The company is open daily from 8:30am to 5pm and later in winter.

ENTRANCE FEES & PERMITS Entering Biscayne National Park is free. There is a $15 overnight docking fee at both Boca Chita Key Harbor and Elliott Key Harbor ($7.50 per night for holders of Golden Age or Golden Access Passports; see "Essentials" in section one for more information about these passes). Backcountry camping permits are free and can be picked up from the Convoy Point Visitor Center. Fishing permits are required unless you are covered by a charter boat; see "Essentials" in section one for more information. For more information on fees and permits in general, call the park ranger at © **305/230-1144.**

EXPLORING THE PARK

Since the park is primarily underwater, the only way to truly experience it is with snorkel or scuba gear. Beneath the surface of Biscayne National Park, the aquatic universe pulses with multicolored life: Bright parrotfish and angelfish, gently rocking sea fans, and coral labyrinths abound. See "Snorkeling & Scuba Diving," below, for more information.

Afterward, take a picnic out to Elliott Key and taste the crisp salt air blowing off the Atlantic. Or head to Boca Chita, an intriguing island that was once the private playground of wealthy yachters.

AFFORDABLE OUTDOOR ACTIVITIES

CANOEING & KAYAKING Biscayne National Park offers excellent canoeing, both along the coast and across the open water to nearby mangroves and artificial islands that dot the longest uninterrupted shoreline in the state of Florida. Since tides can be strong, only experienced canoeists should attempt to paddle far from shore. If you do plan to go far, first obtain a tide table from the visitor center (see "Essentials," above) and paddle with the current.

Free ranger-led canoe tours (canoes included) are scheduled every Saturday, from 9am to noon. You can also rent a canoe on your own at the park's concession stand; rates are $8 an hour or $22 for 4 hours. Kayakers will have to bring their own boats but are welcome to explore the same quiet routes. Call ✆ **305/230-1100** for reservations, information, ranger tours, and canoe rentals.

FISHING Ocean fishing is excellent year-round at Biscayne National Park; many people cast their lines right from the breakwater jetty at Convoy Point. A fishing license is required (see "Essentials" in section one of this chapter for complete information). Bait is not available in Biscayne National Park but is sold in adjacent Homestead Bayfront Park, 4 miles from the entrance. Stone crabs and Florida lobsters can be found here, but you're allowed to catch these only on the ocean side of the Keys, when they're in season. There are strict limitations on size, season, number, and method of take (including spearfishing) for both fresh- and saltwater fishing. The latest regulations are available at most marinas, at bait and tackle shops, and at the park's visitor centers. You can also contact the **Florida Game and Fresh Water Fish Commission,** Bryant Building, 620 S. Meridian St., Tallahassee, FL 32399-1600 (✆ **904/488-1960**).

HIKING & EXPLORING Since the majority of this park is underwater, hiking is not the main attraction here, but, nonetheless, there are some interesting sights and trails. At **Convoy Point,** you can walk along the 370-foot boardwalk and along the half-mile jetty that serves as a breakwater for the park's harbor. From there, you can usually see brown pelicans, little blue herons, snowy egrets, and a few exotic fish.

Elliott Key is accessible only by boat, but once you're there, you have two good trail options. True to its name, the Loop Trail makes a 1½-mile circle from the bay-side visitor center, through a hardwood hammock and mangroves, to an elevated ocean-side boardwalk. It's likely that you'll see purple and orange land crabs scurrying around the mangrove roots. Also, don't miss the Old Road trail, a 7-mile tropical hammock trail that runs the length of Elliott Key. This trail is one of the few places left in the world to see the highly endangered Schaus' swallowtail butterfly, recognizable by its black wings with diagonal yellow bands. They're usually out from late April through July.

Reopened in 1998, **Boca Chita Key** was once the playground for wealthy tycoons, and it still offers the peaceful beauty that attracted elite anglers from cold climates. Many of the historical buildings are still intact, including an ornamental lighthouse, which was never put into use. A walk around this key can be fun and interesting.

Take advantage of **ranger-led tours** of the park, which are available every Sunday at 1pm. The tour, including the boat trip, takes about 3 hours. The price is $19.95 for adults and $9.95 for children. However, call ✆ **305/230-1100** in advance if the weather is somewhat off the day you intend to go—the boats won't run in rough seas.

SNORKELING & SCUBA DIVING The clear, warm waters of Biscayne National Park are packed with colorful tropical fish that swim in the offshore reefs. The best way to see the park from underwater is to take a snorkeling or scuba diving tour operated by **Biscayne National Underwater Park, Inc.** (✆ **305/230-1100**). Snorkeling tours depart at 1:30pm daily, last about 3 hours, and cost $29.95 per person, including equipment. They also run weekend two-tank dives for certified divers. The price is $44.95 per person, including two tanks and weights. Reef dives depart on Saturdays and wall dives depart on Sundays. Make your reservations in advance. The shop is open daily from 9am to 5pm. You can also rent gear here and try a trip on your own.

SWIMMING You can swim at the protected beaches of **Elliott Key** and **Boca Chita Key,** but be aware that neither of these beaches will match the width or softness of others in South Florida. Check the water conditions before heading into the sea: the strong currents that make this a popular destination for windsurfers and sailors can be dangerous, even for strong swimmers. **Homestead Bayfront Park** is really just a marina located next to Biscayne National Park, but it does have a beach and picnic facilities as well. It's located at Convoy Point, 9698 SW 328th St., Homestead (© **305/230-3033**).

GLASS-BOTTOM BOAT TOURS

If you prefer not to dive, the best way to see the underwater life here is on a glass-bottom boat tour. **Biscayne National Underwater Park, Inc.** (© **305/230-1100**) offers daily trips to view some of the country's most beautiful coral reefs and tropical fish. Boats depart year-round from Convoy Point at 10am and stay out for about 3 hours. At $19.95 for adults, $17.95 for seniors, and $9.95 for children 12 and under, the scenic and informative tours are well worth the price. Boats carry fewer than 50 passengers; reservations are almost always necessary.

ACCOMMODATIONS YOU CAN AFFORD

Besides campsites, there are no facilities available for overnight guests to this watery park. Visitors who aren't the camping type generally come for an afternoon, on their way to the Keys, and stay overnight in nearby Homestead, where there are many national chain hotels and other affordable lodgings (see "Accommodations You Can Afford" in section 1 of this chapter).

CAMPING

Although you won't find hotels or lodges in Biscayne National Park, the area does offer some of the state's most pristine campsites. Since they are inaccessible by motor vehicle, you'll be sure to avoid the mass of RVs so prevalent in many of the state's other campgrounds. Sites are on **Elliott Key** and **Boca Chita** and can only be reached by boat. If you don't have your own, call © **305/230-1100** to arrange a drop-off from Convoy Point; transportation to and from the visitor center costs $21 per person.

Boca Chita only has saltwater toilets and no showers; Elliot Key has freshwater showers, but is otherwise no less primitive. Both areas offer picnic tables and grills. Campsites on Elliot Key cost $25.

With a backcountry permit, available free from the Convoy Point's visitor center, you can pitch your tent somewhere even more private. Ask for a map at the visitor center, and be sure to bring plenty of bug spray. Backcountry camping is allowed only on Elliot Key. Backcountry sites cost $10 a night for up to six persons staying in one or two tents.

7

The Gold Coast: Hallandale to the Palm Beaches

by Lesley Abravanel

Named not for the sun-kissed skin of the area's residents but for the gold salvaged from shipwrecks off its coastline, the Gold Coast embraces more than 60 miles of beautiful Atlantic shoreline—from the legendary strip of beaches in Fort Lauderdale to the pristine sands of Jupiter in northern Palm Beach County.

If you haven't visited the cities along Florida's southeastern coast in the last few years, you'll be amazed at how much has changed. Miles of sprawling grassland and empty lots have been replaced with luxurious resorts and high-rise condominiums. In addition to an influx of tourists, thousands of transplants, fleeing the rising population in Miami and the frigid winters up north, have arrived here and made this area their home. The resulting construction boom can be seen not only throughout the cities, but even westward, into the swampy areas of the Everglades.

Fortunately, amid all the building, much of the natural treasure of the Gold Coast remains. There are 300 miles of Intracoastal Waterway, not to mention Fort Lauderdale's Venetian-inspired canals. And the largely unspoiled splendor of the Everglades is just a few miles inland.

The most popular areas along the Gold Coast are Fort Lauderdale, Boca Raton, and Palm Beach. While Fort Lauderdale is a favored beachfront destination, Boca Raton and Palm Beach are better known for their country-club lifestyles and excellent shopping. Further north is the quietly popular Jupiter, best known for spring training at the Roger Dean Stadium and for its former resident Burt Reynolds. In between these better-traveled destinations are a few things worth stopping for, but not much. Driving north along the coastline is one of the best ways to fully appreciate what the Gold Coast is all about—it's a perspective you certainly won't find in a shopping mall.

EXPLORING THE GOLD COAST BY CAR

Like most of South Florida, the Gold Coast consists of a mainland and an adjacent strip of barrier islands. You'll have to check the maps to keep track of the many bridges that allow access to the islands where most of the tourist activity is centered. Interstate 95, which runs north-south, is the area's main highway. Farther west is the Florida Turnpike, a toll road that can be worth the expense since the speed limit is higher and it is often less congested than I-95. Also on the mainland is U.S. 1, which generally runs parallel to I-95 (to the east) and is a narrower thoroughfare mostly crowded with strip malls and seedy hotels.

I recommend taking Fla. A1A, a slow ocean-side road that connects the long, thin islands of Florida's whole east coast. Although the road is narrow, it is the most scenic and forces you into the relaxed atmosphere of these resort towns.

1 Broward County ★★: Hallandale & Hollywood to Fort Lauderdale

23 miles N of Miami

Until the 2000 presidential election fiasco, most people had never heard of Broward County. Less exposed than the highly hyped Miami, Broward County is a lot calmer and, according to some, a lot friendlier than the magic city. With more than 23 miles of beachfront and 300 miles of navigable waterways, Broward County is also a great outdoor destination. Scattered amid the shopping malls, condominiums, and tourist traps is a beautiful landscape lined with hundreds of parks, golf courses, tennis courts, and, of course, beaches.

The City of Hallandale Beach is a small, peaceful oceanfront town located just north of Dade County's Aventura. Condos are the predominant landmarks in Hallandale, which is still pretty much a retirement community, although the revamped multimillion-dollar Westin Diplomat Resort is trying to revitalize and liven up the area.

Just north of Hallandale is the more energetic, but not-yet-thriving, Hollywood. Like many other small American towns, Hollywood has been working on redeveloping its downtown area for years. Once a sleepy community wedged between Fort Lauderdale and Miami, Hollywood is now a bustling area of 1.5 million people belonging to an array of ethnic and racial identities: from white and African American, to people of Jamaican, Chinese, and Dominican descent.

A spate of redevelopment in Hollywood has made the pedestrian-friendly center along Hollywood Boulevard and Harrison Street, east of Dixie Highway, a popular destination for travelers and locals alike. Some predict the city will be South Florida's next big destination—South Beach without the attitude, traffic jams, and parking nightmares. While the prediction is a dubious one, Hollywood is definitely awakening from its long slumber. Prices are a fraction of those in other tourist areas, and a quasi-bohemian vibe is apparent in the galleries, clubs, and restaurants that dot the new "strip." Its gritty undercurrent, however, prevents it from becoming too trendy.

Fort Lauderdale, along with its well-known strip of beaches, restaurants, bars, and souvenir shops, has also undergone a major transformation. Once famous (or infamous) for the annual mayhem it hosted during spring break, this area is now attracting a more affluent, better-behaved yachting crowd. In addition to beautiful wide beaches, the city, also known as the Venice of America, has more than 300 miles of navigable waterways and innumerable canals, which permit thousands of residents to anchor boats in their backyards. Boating is not just a hobby here; it's a lifestyle. Visitors can easily get on the water, too, by renting a boat or simply hailing a moderately priced water taxi.

Huge cruise ships take advantage of Florida's deepest harbor, Port Everglades, whose name is somewhat misleading because it is not part of the Florida Everglades. The seaport is actually located on the southeastern coast of the Florida peninsula, near the Fort Lauderdale Hollywood International Airport on the outskirts of Hollywood and Dania Beach. Port Everglades is the second-busiest cruise-ship base in Florida after Miami and one of the top five in the world. For further information about cruises, consult *Frommer's Caribbean Cruises* or *Frommer's Caribbean Ports of Call.*

ESSENTIALS

GETTING THERE If you're driving from Miami, it's a straight shot north to Hollywood or Fort Lauderdale. Visitors on their way to or from Orlando should take the Florida Turnpike to Exit 53, 54, 58, or 62, depending on the location of your accommodations.

The **Fort Lauderdale/Hollywood International Airport** (© **954/359-6100**) is easy to negotiate and located just 15 minutes from both of the downtown areas it services. Most major airlines fly here; see "Getting There" in chapter 2, "Planning an Affordable Trip to Florida," for a list of carriers.

Amtrak (© **800/USA-RAIL**) stations are at 200 SW 21st Terrace (Broward Blvd. and I-95), Fort Lauderdale (© **954/587-6692**); and at 3001 Hollywood Blvd., Hollywood (© **954/921-4517**).

VISITOR INFORMATION The **Greater Fort Lauderdale Convention & Visitors Bureau,** 1850 Eller Dr., Suite 303 (off I-95 and I-595 east), Fort Lauderdale, FL 33316 (© **954/765-4466**; fax 954/765-4467; www.sunny.org), is an excellent resource for area information, in English, Spanish, and French. Call them in advance to request a free comprehensive guide covering events, accommodations, and sightseeing in Broward County. In addition, once you are in town, you can call an **information line** (© **954/527-5600**) to get easy-to-follow directions, travel advice, and assistance from multilingual operators who staff a round-the-clock help line. Also available for brochures, information, and vacation packages in Fort Lauderdale are operators at © **800/22-SUNNY.**

The **Greater Hollywood Chamber of Commerce,** 330 N. Federal Hwy. (on the corner of U.S. 1 and Taylor St.), Hollywood, FL 33020 (© **954/923-4000**; fax 954/923-8737), is open Monday through Friday from 8:30am to 5pm. Here you'll find the low-down on all of Hollywood's events, attractions, restaurants, hotels, and tours.

WHAT TO SEE & DO
THE BEACHES

Composing the southern end of the Gold Coast, Broward County is lined with the region's most popular and amenities-laden beaches, which stretch for more than 23 miles. Most do not charge for access, though all are well maintained. Here's a selection of some of the county's best from south to north.

Hollywood Beach, stretching from Sheridan Street to Georgia Street, is a major attraction in the city of Hollywood, a virtual carnival with a motley assortment of young hipsters, big families, and sunburned French Canadians, who dodge bicyclers and skaters along the rows of tacky souvenir shops, T-shirt shops, game rooms, snack bars, beer stands, hotels, and even miniature golf courses. The 3-mile-long Hollywood Beach **Broadwalk**, modeled after Atlantic City's legendary boardwalk, is Hollywood's most popular beachfront pedestrian thoroughfare, a cement promenade that's 30 feet wide and stretches along the shoreline. Despite efforts to clear out a seedy element, the area remains a haven for drunks and scammers, so keep alert. If you tire of the hectic diversity that defines Hollywood's broadwalk, enjoy the natural beauty of the beach itself, which is wide and clean. There are lifeguards, showers, restroom facilities, and public areas for picnics and parties.

The **Fort Lauderdale Beach Promenade**, along the beach stretching beside Fla. A1A from SE 17th Street to Sunrise Boulevard, underwent a $26-million renovation, and it looks fantastic. It's especially peaceful in the mornings when there's just a smattering of joggers and walkers, but even at its most crowded on the weekend, the expansive promenade provides room for everyone. Note, however, that the beach is hardly pristine; it is across the street from an uninterrupted stretch of hotels, bars, and retail outlets. Just across the road, on

Broward County Attractions & Accommodations

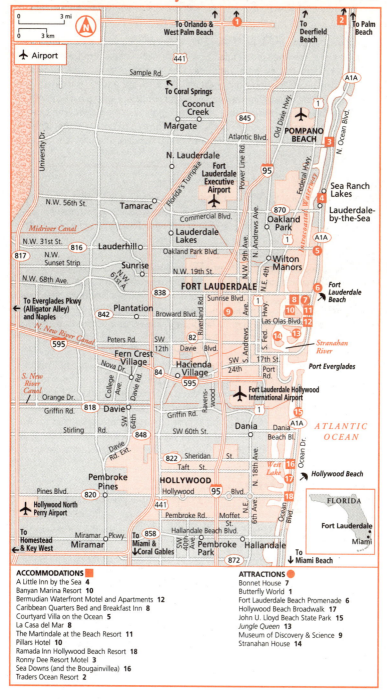

ACCOMMODATIONS
A Little Inn by the Sea 4
Banyan Marina Resort 10
Bermudian Waterfront Motel and Apartments 12
Caribbean Quarters Bed and Breakfast Inn 8
Courtyard Villa on the Ocean 5
La Casa del Mar 8
The Martindale at the Beach Resort 11
Pillars Hotel 10
Ramada Inn Hollywood Beach Resort 18
Ronny Dee Resort Motel 3
Sea Downs (and the Bougainvillea) 16
Traders Ocean Resort 2

ATTRACTIONS
Bonnet House 7
Butterfly World 1
Fort Lauderdale Beach Promenade 6
Hollywood Beach Broadwalk 17
John U. Lloyd Beach State Park 15
Jungle Queen 13
Museum of Discovery & Science 9
Stranahan House 14

> ### Moments Turtle Trail
>
> In June and July, the John U. Lloyd Beach is crawling with nature lovers, who come for the spectacular **Sea Turtle Awareness Program.** Park rangers begin the evening with a lecture and slide show while scouts search the beach for nesting loggerhead sea turtles. If a turtle is located—plenty of them usually are—a beach walk is conducted, where participants can see the turtles nesting and, sometimes, hatching their eggs. The program begins at 9pm. Call © 954/923-2833 for reservations. Comfortable walking shoes and insect repellent are recommended. The park entrance fee of $2 to $4 per carload applies.

the sand, most days you will find hard-core volleyballers, who always welcome anyone with a good spike, and an inviting ocean welcoming swimmers of any level. The unusually clear waters are under the careful watch of some of Florida's best-looking lifeguards. Freshen up afterward in any of the clean showers and restrooms conveniently located along the strip.

Pets have been banned from most of Fort Lauderdale beach in order to maintain the impressive cleanliness not commonly associated with such highly trafficked public beaches; a designated area for pets exists away from the main sunbathing areas. Also, especially on weekends, parking along the ocean-side meters is nearly impossible to find. Try biking, skating, or hitching a ride on the water taxi instead.

Dania Beach's **John U. Lloyd Beach State Park** ★★★, 6503 N. Ocean Dr., Dania (© 954/923-2833), is 251 acres of barrier island between the Atlantic Ocean and the Intracoastal Waterway, from Port Everglades in the north to Dania in the south. A $2 to $4 fee per car is charged for entrance. The natural setting here contrasts sharply with the urban development of Fort Lauderdale. Lloyd Beach, one of Broward County's most important nesting beaches for sea turtles, produces some 10,000 hatchlings a year. The park's broad, flat beach is popular for swimming and sunning. Self-guided nature trails are great for those who are too restless to sunbathe.

AFFORDABLE OUTDOOR ACTIVITIES

BOATING Often called the "yachting capital of the world," Fort Lauderdale provides ample opportunity for visitors to get out on the water, either along the Intracoastal Waterway or on the open ocean. If your hotel doesn't rent boats, try **Bill's Sunrise Watersports,** 2025 E. Sunrise Blvd., Fort Lauderdale (© 954/462-8962). They will outfit you with a variety of craft, including jet skis, 13-foot Cigarette boats, 15-foot jet boats, and 8-foot powerboats, year-round. Bill's is open daily from 9am to 6pm. Rates start at $50 per half hour for jet skis, $75 to $85 for boats (for 2 hr., with a 2-hr. minimum), and $65 for parasailing solo, or $120 for a tandem flight.

CRUISES The *Jungle Queen,* 801 Sea Breeze Blvd. (3 blocks south of Las Olas Blvd. on Fla. A1A), in the Bahia Mar Yacht Center, Fort Lauderdale (© 954/462-5596), a Mississippi River–style steamer, is one of Fort Lauderdale's best-known attractions, cruising up and down the New River. All-you-can-eat dinner cruises and 3-hour sightseeing tours take visitors past Millionaires' Row, Old Fort Lauderdale, and the new downtown. Dinner cruises depart nightly at 7pm and cost $29 for adults and $15 for children 12 and under. Sightseeing tours are scheduled daily at 10am and 2pm and cost $13.75 for adults and $8.75 for children 10 and under.

If you're interested in gambling, several casino boat companies operate day cruises out of Port Everglades and offer blackjack, slots, and poker. **Discovery Cruise Lines** (© 800/937-4477) has daily cruises to the Bahamas, where you can gamble, eat, and party for 5 to 6 hours (you have about 3 hours in the Bahamas to go to the straw market or to do even more gambling) for about $120. The price includes breakfast, lunch, and dinner, but drinks cost extra.

Sea Escape (© 800/327-2005 or 954/453-3333) also launches daily casino cruises 13 times a week. But theirs don't travel more than a few miles offshore. These trips "to nowhere" depart Monday to Thursday from 11am to 4:30pm and 7:30pm to 12:30am. The daytime party cruises offer buffet meals and full casinos for $30 to $40 a person. For an additional $20, you can rent a cabin (do not expect *Love Boat* luxe here), in which you can stretch out and relax in between hands. Keep in mind that even though the cruises don't go far from the coast, 5 or 6 hours is a long time to spend at sea, especially if the weather is rough. Evening cruises, which return at 1:30am on weekends, cost $48 and offer full buffet dinners and a Las Vegas–style show. Port charges are included, although you must pay a $3 departure tax and $2.65 passenger charge. This is one of the best deals you'll find. Sea Escape also has a new 2- and 3-night cruise option, where visitors can go to Nassau, the Bahamas, for as little as $199 per person with all meals included.

FISHING Completed in 1999 at a cost of more than $32 million, the **IGFA (International Game Fish Association) World Fishing Center** at 300 Gulf Stream Way (© 954/922-4212) in Dania Beach is an angler's paradise. While you can't do any real fishing here, one of the highlights of this museum, library, and park is the virtual reality fishing simulator, which allows visitors to reel in computer-generated catch and improve their game. Also included in the 3-acre park are displays of antique fishing gear, record catches, famous anglers, various vessels, and a wetlands lab. **IGFA headquarters** (© 954/927-2628) maintains a list of local captains and guides leading fishing excursions in the area; call and ask for the librarian. Admission is $5 for adults, $4 for children between 3 and 12, and free for children under 3. On the grounds is also **Bass**

Kids **Wild Things**

Deerfield Island Park, 1720 Deerfield Beach (on the ocean, 2 miles south of the Palm Beaches), surrounded by the Intracoastal Waterway and two canals, is an urban wilderness accessible only by boat. The heavily wooded 56-acre site includes an 8½-acre mangrove swamp and is home to the gopher tortoise, as well as squirrels, raccoons, and armadillos. Visitors can hike the park's two main trails and take advantage of picnic areas equipped with grills and tables. A small playground completes this Tom Sawyer adventure, all of which makes a great day trip for children. The park is open Wednesday through Sunday 9am to 5pm. A free boat shuttle transports visitors to the island hourly, but book early as the shuttle fills up quickly. Call © 954/360-1320 for times and reservations. The shuttle takes off from the Sullivan Park boat dock. To get there from I-95, head east on Hillsboro Boulevard past Federal Highway and then north (left) on Riverview Road to the park.

Pro Shops Outdoor World, a huge multifloor retail complex situated on a 3-acre lake.

GOLF   More than 50 golf courses in all price ranges compete for players here. For one of Broward's best municipal challenges, try the 18-holer at the **Orangebrook Golf Course** at 400 Entrada Dr. in Hollywood (© 954/967-GOLF). Built in 1937, this is one of the state's oldest courses and one of the area's best bargains. Morning and noon rates range from $21 to $33. After 2pm, you can play for less than $20, including a cart. Men must wear collared shirts to play here, and no spikes are allowed.

SCUBA DIVING   In Broward County, the best wreck dive is the *Mercedes I,* a 197-foot freighter that washed up in the backyard of a Palm Beach socialite in 1984 and was sunk for divers the following year off Pompano Beach. The artificial reef, filled with colorful sponges, spiny lobsters, and barracudas, is located 97 feet below the surface, a mile offshore between Oakland Park Boulevard and Sunrise Boulevard. Dozens of reputable dive shops line the beach. Ask at your hotel for a nearby recommendation or contact **Undersea Operations,** 401 SE 15th Ave., Pompano Beach (© 954/783-9300), which offers 2-tank diving excursions in the area for $45 per person.

SPECTATOR SPORTS   Baseball fans can get their fix at the **Fort Lauderdale Stadium,** 5301 NW 12th Ave. (© 954/938-4980), where the Baltimore Orioles play Spring Training exhibition games starting in early March; call © 954/776-1921 for tickets. General admission is $6, a spot in the grandstand $9, kids 14 and under $3, and box seats $12. During the season, the Florida Marlins play just south of Hallandale at **Pro Player Stadium** near the Dade–Broward County line. Call Ticketmaster for tickets (© 305/358-5885), which range from $2 to $40. Tickets go on sale in January.

Jai alai, a sort of Spanish-style indoor lacrosse, was introduced to Florida in 1924 and still draws big crowds, who bet on the fast-paced action. Broward's only fronton, **Dania Jai Alai,** 301 E. Dania Beach Blvd. at the intersection of Fla. A1A and U.S. 1 (© 954/920-1511 or 954/426-4330), is a great place to spend an afternoon or evening.

Wrapped around an artificial lake, **Gulfstream Park,** at U.S. 1 and Hallandale Beach Boulevard, Hallandale (© 954/454-7000), is pretty and popular. Large purses and important horse races are commonplace at this recently refurbished suburban course, and the track is often crowded. It hosts the Florida Derby each March. Call for schedules. Admission is $3 to the grandstand, and $5 to the clubhouse. From January 3 to March 15, post times are Wednesday to Monday at 1pm, and the doors open at 11am. Many weekends feature live concerts by well-known musicians.

Pompano Park Racing, 1800 SW 3rd St., Pompano Beach (© 954/972-2000), features parimutuel harness racing from October to early August. Grandstand admission is free; clubhouse admission is $2.

In the sport of ice hockey, the young **Florida Panthers** (© 954/835-7000) have already made history. In the 1994–95 season, they played in the Stanley Cup finals, and the fans love them. They play in Sunrise at the National Car Rental Center at 2555 NW 137th Way. Tickets range from $14 to $100. Call for directions and ticket information.

TENNIS   There are hundreds of courts in Broward County, and plenty are accessible to the public. Famous as the spot where Chris Evert got in her early serves, the **Jimmy Evert Tennis Center,** 701 NE 12th Ave. (off Sunrise Blvd.),

One if by Land . . . Taxi if by Sea . . .

Plan to spend at least an afternoon or evening cruising Fort Lauderdale's 300 miles of waterways the only way you can: by boat. **The Water Taxi of Fort Lauderdale (© 954/467-6677)** is one of the greatest innovations for water lovers since those cool Velcro sandals. A trusty fleet of old-port boats serves the dual purpose of transporting and entertaining visitors as they cruise through "The Venice of America."

Taxis operate on demand and also along a fairly regular route, carrying up to 48 passengers. Choose a hotel on the route, so you can be picked up at your hotel, usually within 15 minutes of calling, and then be shuttled to any of the dozens of restaurants, bars, and attractions on or near the waterfront. If you aren't sure where you want to go, ask one of the personable captains who can point out historic and fun spots along the way.

This is a great option for a day cruise with the kids. And in the evening, the water taxi is ideal for bar-hopping—no worrying about parking or choosing a designated driver. Starting daily from 10am, boats usually run until midnight and until 2am on weekends, depending on the weather. The cost is $7 per person per trip, $13 round-trip, and $15 for a full day. Children under 12 ride for half price and free on Sunday. Opt for the all-day pass; it's worth it.

Fort Lauderdale (© **954/828-5378**), has 18 clay and three hard courts (15 lighted). Her coach and father, James Evert, still teaches young players here, though he is very picky about whom he'll accept. Nonresidents of Fort Lauderdale pay $3.50 (singles) to $4.50 (doubles) per hour. Reservations are accepted after 2pm for the following day but cost an extra $3. Lights are also an extra $3 per hour and are available only for the clay courts.

At the **Marina Bay Resort,** 2175 S.R. 84, west of I-95 in Fort Lauderdale (© **954/791-7600**), visitors can play for free on any one of nine hard courts on a first-come, first-served basis. Three are lighted at night.

SEEING THE SIGHTS

Billie Swamp Safari 🐊 Billie Swamp Safari is an up close and personal view of the Seminole Indians' 2,200-acre Big Cypress Reservation. There are daily tours into reservation wetlands, hardwood hammocks, and areas where wildlife (deer, water buffalo, bison, wild hogs, ornery ostriches, rare birds, and alligators) reside. Tours are provided aboard swamp buggies, customized motorized vehicles specially designed to provide visitors with an elevated view of the frontier while comfortably riding through the wetlands and cypress heads. For the more adventurous, you may want to take a fast-moving airboat ride or trek through a nature trail. A stop at an alligator farm reeks of Disney, but the kids won't care. You can also stay overnight in a native tiki hut if you're really looking to immerse yourself in the culture.

Big Cypress Reservation, 1½-hr. drive west of Fort Lauderdale. © **800/949-6101.** Free admission. Swamp buggy tours $20 adults, $18 seniors, $10 children. Boat tours $10–$20. Daily 8am–8pm. Airboats depart every 30 min.; last ride at 4:30pm.

Bonnet House ★★★   This historic 35-acre plantation home and estate, accessible by guided tour only, will provide you with a fantastic glimpse of old South Florida. Built in 1921, the sprawling two-story waterfront home (surrounded with formal tropical gardens) is really the backdrop of a love story, which the very chatty volunteer guides will share with you if you ask. Some have actually lunched with the former resident of the house, the late Evelyn Bartlett, the wife of world-acclaimed artist Frederic Clay Bartlett. The worthwhile 1¼-hour tour brings you quirky people, whimsical artwork, lush grounds, and interesting design. Inquire about the literary walks and science workshops, which are offered regularly on the grounds.

900 N. Birch Rd. (1 block west of the ocean, south of Sunrise Blvd.), Fort Lauderdale. © **954/563-5393.** www.bonnethouse.org. Admission $9 adults, $8 seniors, $7 students under 18; free for children 6 and under. Tours Wed–Fri 10am–1:30pm; Sat–Sun 12:30–2:30pm.

Butterfly World *Kids*   One of the world's largest butterfly breeders, Butterfly World cultivates more than 150 species of these colorful and delicate insects. In the park's walk-through, screened-in laboratory, visitors can see thousands of caterpillars and watch newborn butterflies emerge from their cocoons and flutter around as they learn to fly. Depending on how interested you are in these winged beauties, you may want to allow from 1 to 2 hours to tour the gardens and the well-stocked gift shop. There's also a new, separate aviary dedicated to lorikeets (the "clowns" of the bird world, because they are quite animated and very colorful), which offers visitors the opportunity to hand-feed the birds.

Tradewinds Park S., 3600 W. Sample Rd., Coconut Creek (west of the Florida Tpk.). © **954/977-4400.** www.butterflyworld.com. Admission $13.95 adults, $8.95 children 4–12; free for children 3 and under. Mon–Sat 9am–5pm; Sun 1–5pm; last admission at 4pm. Directions: From I-95, exit at Sample Rd. and head west until you reach Tradewinds Park on the south side of Sample Rd. Enter the park and the butterfly house is inside, straight ahead, about ⅓ mile.

Museum of Discovery & Science ★★ *Kids*   This museum's high-tech, interactive approach to education proves that science can equal fun. Adults won't feel as if they're in a kiddie museum, either. During the week, school groups meander through the cavernous two-story modern building. Kids 7 and under enjoy navigating their way through the excellent explorations in the "Discovery Center." Florida Ecoscapes is particularly interesting, with a living coral reef, bees, bats, frogs, turtles, and alligators. Most weekend nights, you'll find a diverse crowd ranging from hip high-school kids to 30-somethings enjoying a rock film in the IMAX 3-D theater, which also shows short, science-related, films daily. Out front, see the 52-foot-tall "Great Gravity Clock," located in the museum's atrium, the largest kinetic-energy sculpture in the state. Call for changing exhibits.

401 SW 2nd St., Fort Lauderdale. © **954/467-6637.** www.mods.org. Museum admission (includes admission to 1 IMAX film) $13 adults, $12 seniors, $11 children 3–12. Mon–Sat 10am–5pm; Sun noon–6pm. Movie theaters stay open later. From I-95, exit on Broward Blvd. E. Continue to SW 5th Ave.; turn right, garage on right.

Stranahan House ★★★   In a town whose history is younger than many of its residents, visitors may want to take a minute to see Fort Lauderdale's very oldest standing structure and a prime example of classic "Florida Frontier" architecture. Built in 1901 by the "father of Fort Lauderdale," Frank Stranahan, this house once served as a trading post for Seminole trappers who came here to sell pelts. It's been a post office, town hall, and general store and now is a worthwhile little museum of South Florida pioneer life, containing turn-of-the-last-century

> **Finds Attention Bargain Shoppers**
> The well-known department store **Lord & Taylor** has a little-known clearance center where discounts on new clothing for women, kids, and men can be as big as 75%. If you can handle open dressing rooms, overstuffed racks, and surly sales help, it's a great find at 6820 N. University Dr. in Tamarac. Call © **954/720-1915** to find out about specials.

furnishings and historical photos of the area. It is also the site of occasional concerts and social functions. Call for details.

335 SE Sixth Ave. (Las Olas Blvd. at the New River Tunnel), Fort Lauderdale. © **954/524-4736**. www.stranahanhouse.com. Admission $5 adults, $3 students and children. Wed–Sat 10am–4pm; Sun 1–4pm. Tours are on the hour; last tour at 3pm. Accessible by water taxi.

SHOPPING

While most of the best shopping is located within Fort Lauderdale proper, there are other areas in the county also worth browsing. Dania is known as the **Antique Capital of the South,** with over a hundred dealers clustered within 1 square mile of Federal Highway, selling everything from small collectibles to fine antiques. Although many of the more upscale shops are overpriced, many of the smaller dealers offer bargains to hagglers.

For bargain mavens, there's a strip of "fashion" stores on Hallandale Beach Boulevard's **"Schmatta Row,"** east of Dixie Highway and the railroad tracks, where off-brand shoes, bags, and jewelry are sold at deep discounts. **Hollywood Boulevard** also offers some interesting shops, selling everything from Indonesian artifacts to used and rare books, leather bustiers, and handmade hats. Dozens of shops line the pedestrian-friendly strip just west of Young Circle.

You'll find most shopping in Broward County at area malls. The area's only beachfront mall, **Beach Place,** is in Fort Lauderdale on Fla. A1A just north of Las Olas Boulevard. The recipient of a $1.6-million face-lift in 2001, this 100,000-square-foot giant sports the usual chains like Sunglass Hut, Limited Express, Banana Republic, and the Gap, as well as lots of popular bars and restaurants. While it used to be all the rage with the spring break set, Beach Place is now aiming for a much more upscale clientele, adding many new higher-end stores and restaurants.

The monster of all outlet malls is **Sawgrass Mills,** 12801 W. Sunrise Blvd., Sunrise (© **800/FL-MILLS** or 954/846-2350; fax 954/846-2312). Since the most recent expansion, this behemoth (shaped like a Florida alligator) now holds more than 300 shops, kiosks, a 24-screen movie theater, and many restaurants and bars including a Hard Rock Cafe. Make sure you note which section you parked in, as it is nearly impossible to locate your car in the equally mammoth, labyrinthine parking lot. You may want to invest in a coupon booklet ($5), which entitles you to even greater discounts at many of the mall's stores and restaurants as well as area attractions. To get there, take I-95 to I-595 west to the Flamingo Road exit, turn right, and drive 2 miles to Sunrise Boulevard; you will see the large complex on the left. From the Florida Turnpike, exit Sunrise Boulevard west.

ACCOMMODATIONS YOU CAN AFFORD

The Fort Lauderdale beach has a hotel or motel on nearly every block, and they range from the run-down to the luxurious. Both the **Howard Johnson**

(© **800/327-8578** or 954/563-2451), at 700 N. Atlantic Blvd. (on Fla. A1A, south of Sunrise Blvd.), and the **Days Inn** (© **800/329-7466** or 954/462-0444), at 435 N. Atlantic Blvd. (Fla. A1A), offer clean ocean-side rooms starting at about $150.

In Hollywood, where prices are generally cheaper, the **Holiday Inn** at 101 N. Ocean Blvd. (© **954/921-0990**) operates a full-service hotel right on the ocean. With prices starting at around $110 in season and discounts for AAA members, it's a great deal. **Howard Johnson** (© **800/423-9867** or 954/925-1411) also has a good location right on the beach at 2501 N. Ocean Dr. (I-95 to Sheridan St. east to Fla. A1A south).

Extended Stay America/Crossland Economy Studios (© **800/398-7829**) has four super-clean properties in Fort Lauderdale and offers year-round rates as low as $49 a night and $159 per week. The studios are designed with business travelers in mind. Each includes free local calls, a dataport, a kitchenette, a recliner, and a well-lit desk.

Especially for rentals for a few weeks or months, call **Florida Sunbreak** (© **800/SUNBREAK**), which can locate good deals. Or call the **South Florida Hotel Network** (© **800/538-3616**) for help in finding small inns and lodges in any price range. Also, check out the annual list of small lodgings compiled by the **Fort Lauderdale Convention & Visitors Bureau** (© **954/765-4466**). It is especially helpful for those looking for privately owned, charming, and affordable lodgings.

Banyan Marina Resort ★★

These fabulous waterfront apartments, located on a beautifully landscaped residential island, may have you vowing never to stay in a hotel again. They're intimate, charming, *and* reasonably priced. Built around a stunning 75-year-old banyan tree, the Banyan Marina Resort is located directly on the active canals halfway between Fort Lauderdale's downtown and the beach. When available, you'll choose between one- and two-bedroom apartments, which have been recently renovated. All are comfortable and spacious, with French doors, full kitchens, and living rooms. The best part of staying here, besides your gracious and knowledgeable hosts, Dagmar and Peter Neufeldt, is that the convenient water taxi will find you here and take you anywhere you want to be day or night. There is a small outdoor heated pool and a marina for those with boats in tow.

111 Isle of Venice, Fort Lauderdale, FL 33301. © 954/524-4430. Fax 954/764-4870. www.banyanmarina.com. 10 units. Winter $95–$250 apt.; off-season $60–$170 apt. Weekly and monthly rates available. MC, V. Free parking. To get there from I-95, exit Broward Blvd. E.; cross U.S. 1 and turn right on SE 15th Ave. At the first traffic light (Las Olas Blvd.), turn left. Turn left at the third island (Isle of Venice). **Amenities:** Restaurant; pool. *In room:* A/C, TV, dataport, kitchen, coffeemaker, hair dryer.

Bermudian Waterfront Motel and Apartments

This formerly elegant little Spanish-style building sits right on a gorgeous bayfront spot. It's just a 2-minute walk to the ocean, and it's on the water-taxi route. The two-story 1950s building could use some repairs, but it couldn't be more private. You probably won't see your American and European fellow travelers since there is no lobby or other common area. All of the decent-sized rooms are quiet, are well-laid out, and have kitchenettes, new carpeting, and small tiled bathrooms. Some overlook the bay or a small tropical courtyard. Their hodgepodge of secondhand furniture is comfortable and functional. The managers, when they're around, can seem a bit harried. Still, for the money, this is one of the best deals here.

315 N. Birch Rd., Fort Lauderdale, FL 33304. © 954/467-0467. Fax 954/467-0467, ext. 5. www.bermudian.tropical.com. 24 units. Winter $65 single or double, $65–$110 efficiency, $90–$170 apt;

off-season $30 single or double, $30–$50 efficiency, $43–$80 apt. Weekly rates available. DISC, MC, V. Free parking. From Sunrise Blvd., head east to A1A, then south to Grenada Rd. and turn right. **Amenities:** Heated pool; shuffleboard; laundry. *In room:* A/C, TV, kitchen, coffeemaker.

La Casa Del Mar ★★ *Finds* The 10 themed rooms in this Spanish-Mediterranean B&B, situated right on the beach, are splendid, each decorated in a motif inspired by an artist (such as Monet), regional style (such as Southwestern), or star (Judy Garland). Enjoy exquisite personal service by the English- and German-speaking co-owners. A delicious, home-cooked buffet-style breakfast is served in the main house but can be enjoyed outdoors under a mango tree in the resplendent garden. The swimming pool is large for such a small accommodation and is a great place to mingle at a late afternoon wine and cheese party with the other guests, who range from young couples to savvy European travelers. Best of all, it's a deal and a pretty well-kept secret.

3003 Granada St., Fort Lauderdale, FL 33304. © 954/467-2037. Fax 954/467-7439. www.lacasadelmar.com. 10 units. Winter $110–$145; off-season $80–$100. Rates include breakfast. AE, DISC, MC, V. **Amenities:** Outdoor pool. *In room:* A/C, TV/VCR, fridge.

A Little Inn by the Sea ★ One of the most imaginatively designed inns on the Gold Coast, this little Mediterranean-style, family-run B&B is meticulously fashioned both inside and out. It's actually a pair of former motels connected by a fountain courtyard with small cafe tables. The rooms are themed with boats or birds or shells, and many come with balconies and small kitchenettes. Some rooms include a romantic mesh canopy over the bed and sofas in a tasteful sitting area. Breakfast is served in the courtyard, and guests are welcome to bring the pool furniture onto the adjacent 300-foot, palm-lined private beach.

4546 El Mar Dr., Lauderdale-by-the-Sea, FL 33308. © 954/772-2450. Fax 954/938-9354. www.alittleinn.com. 29 units. Winter $119–$199 single, double, suite; off-season $79–$159 single, double or suite. Rates include continental breakfast. Extra person $10. Children 11 and under stay free in parents' room. AE, MC, V. Free self- or valet parking. **Amenities:** Heated pool; tennis courts; bike rental; concierge. *In room:* A/C, TV, dataport, kitchenettes in some, fridge, coffeemaker, hair dryer, iron, safe.

The Martindale at the Beach Resort ★ One of the best little bargains on the strip, the Art Deco Martindale keeps getting better. You'll walk through a pretty gate into the lushly landscaped garden that frames this simple, motel-style resort, which lies a mere 300 feet from the Fort Lauderdale beach and boardwalk. Free coffee is served in the courtyard, and the herb garden is perfect for a quiet stroll. Rooms, especially the efficiencies and apartments, are spacious and pleasantly decorated and have been newly remodeled and spruced up. Plus, most have at least a small fridge. For recreation you can putt a few balls on the mini-golf course, swim in the small outdoor heated pool, or have a little barbecue with the gas grill.

3006 Bayshore Dr. (between Sunrise and Las Olas blvds.), Fort Lauderdale, FL 33304. © **800/666-1841** or 954/467-1841. Fax 954/763-8109. www.martindaleatthebeach.com. 18 units (some with shower only). Winter $75–$95 single or double, $125 1-bedroom apt., $125–$175 2-bedroom apt or penthouse for up to 4 people; off-season $50–$70 single or double, $80 1-bedroom apt; $90–$120 2-bedroom apt for up to 4 people. AE, MC, V. Free parking. **Amenities:** Heated pool; miniature golf course. *In room:* A/C, TV, safe.

Ramada Inn Hollywood Beach Resort There is nothing cozy or quaint about this sprawling 1920s beachfront hotel, but it couldn't be better located—on the ocean, halfway between Miami and Fort Lauderdale—or better priced. This eight-story building actually operates as a privately held condominium building where owners can elect to put their units on a rental program. There's no telling how rooms may be outfitted, but management does maintain certain standards—and you're always guaranteed a full kitchen. On the premises are a large outdoor pool, tiki bar, and Jacuzzi; a 4-mile boardwalk makes for a great early-morning power walk. Nearby is burgeoning downtown Hollywood, which offers restaurants, bars, and shops.

101 N. Ocean Dr. (at Fla. A1A and Hollywood Blvd.), Hollywood, FL 33019. ⓒ 954/921-0990. Fax 954/920-9480. 400 units (approx. 200 on rental program). Winter $127–$245 condo; off-season $79–$159 condo. AE, MC, V. Valet parking $9 per day. **Amenities:** Pool; Jacuzzi; laundry, tiki bar. *In room:* A/C, TV, kitchen.

Sea Downs (and the Bougainvillea) ★★
This bargain accommodation is often booked months in advance by returning guests who want to be directly on the beach without paying a fortune. The hosts of this super-clean 1950s motel, Claudia and Karl Herzog, live on the premises and keep things running smoothly. Renovations completed in 1997 have replaced bathroom fixtures, and many rooms have been redecorated here and at the Herzogs' other even less expensive property next door, the 11-unit Bougainvillea. Guests at both hotels share the Sea Downs' pool.

2900 N. Surf Rd., Hollywood, FL 33019. ⓒ 954/923-4968. Fax 954/923-8747. www.seadowns.com or www.bougainvilleahollywood.com. 12 units. Winter $80–$135 daily, $511–$875 weekly; off-season $52–$99 daily, $315–$651 weekly. No credit cards accepted. From I-95, exit Sheridan St. E. to Fla. A1A and go south.; drive a half mile to Coolidge St. and turn left. **Amenities:** Freshwater outdoor pool; concierge; laundry. *In room:* A/C, TV, dataport, kitchen, fridge, coffeemaker.

Traders Ocean Resort ★
Located directly on the beach, this recently renovated hotel is not luxurious, but its service is superb, amenities are plentiful, and its atmosphere is completely conducive to a most relaxing vacation. Rooms are large and comfortable, and many feature ocean views. An outdoor tiki bar, often with live entertainment, provides further encouragement to unwind. The hotel attracts a mostly mature crowd, but if it's a tranquil vacation you're after, Traders may make a loyal customer out of you, regardless of your age.

1600 S. Ocean Blvd., Lauderdale-by-the-Sea, FL 33062. ⓒ 800/325-5220 or 954/941-8400. Fax 954/941-1024. www.tradersresort.com. 93 units. Winter $95–$239 double; off-season $79–$139 double. AE, DC, DISC, MC, V. **Amenities:** Restaurant, lounge, tiki bar; freshwater heated outdoor pool; extensive watersports equipment/rental; shuffleboard; volleyball; concierge; massage. *In room:* A/C, TV.

SUPER-CHEAP SLEEPS

Ronny Dee Resort Motel ★
The good news is that this family-owned motel is just 100 yards from the beach and extremely affordable. The bad news is that it's located on busy Fla. A1A. Popular with European guests, this two-story yellow motel is wrapped around a central swimming pool; its guest rooms are wood-paneled (suburban style) and filled with an eclectic mix of furniture. A new coat of paint and new flooring helped to spruce up the place recently. It's clean but not overflowing with all the creature comforts of nearby chain motels.

717 S. Ocean Blvd., Pompano Beach, FL 33062. ⓒ 954/943-3020. Fax 954/783-5112. 35 units. Winter $49–$72 double; off-season $35–$41 double. AE, MC, V. From I-95, exit Atlantic Blvd. E. to Fla. A1A N. **Amenities:** Outdoor heated pool; game room. *In room:* A/C, TV, dataport, fridge.

WORTH A SPLURGE

Caribbean Quarters Bed and Breakfast Inn ★★ *Kids*
Built in 1939, this wonderful three-story bed-and-breakfast (a rarity in these parts) surrounds a lush courtyard. Caribbean-influenced, plantation-style wooden verandas dot the inn, and louvered doors open from the spacious guest quarters. Most rooms have a private bedroom and a pullout couch in the living room, accommodating up to four people. The original cypress wood floors set off the plantation-style white wicker furniture and the colorful bedspreads. All have private

bathrooms and most come with a well-stocked kitchenette, making this place especially good for long stays and families. The inn is located a half block from the beach and a number of shops and restaurants.

3012 Granada St., Fort Lauderdale, FL 33304. © 888/414-3226 or 954/523-3226. Fax 954/523-7541. www.caribbeanquarters.com. 12 units. Winter $110–$220 double; off-season $95–$175 double. Rates include continental breakfast. AE, DISC, MC, V. *In room:* A/C, TV/VCR, kitchenette or full kitchen, coffeemaker.

Courtyard Villa on the Ocean ★★ Nestled between a bunch of larger hotels, this small, eight-room historic hotel offers a romantic getaway right on the beach. It recently underwent a complete renovation, adding 19th-century antique reproduction furnishings to its charmed setting. Courtyard Villa offers spacious oceanfront efficiencies with private balconies, larger suites overlooking the pool, and full two-bedroom apartments. Rooms are plush with chenille bedspreads and carved four-poster beds; fully equipped kitchenettes are an added convenience. The tiled bathrooms have strong hot showers to wash off the beach sand. Room 8 is especially nice, with French doors that open to a private balcony overlooking the ocean. Relax in the hotel's unique heated pool/spa or on the second-floor sun deck. You can also swim off the beach to a living reef just 50 feet offshore. Scuba diving instruction is available on the premises.

4312 El Mar Dr., Lauderdale-by-the-Sea, FL 33308. © 800/291-3560 or 954/776-1164. Fax 954/491-0768. www.courtyardvilla.com. 10 units. Winter $159 double, $175 1-bedroom, $250 2-bedroom; off-season $105 double, $135 1-bedroom, $150 2-bedroom. Rates include full breakfast. AE, MC, V. Pets under 35 lb. are accepted with a $200 deposit, must be caged while outside; no pit bulls, Dobermans, or Rottweilers. **Amenities:** Outdoor heated pool; Jacuzzi; scuba instruction; free use of bikes; limited room service. *In room:* A/C, TV/VCR, kitchenette, coffeemaker, hair dryer.

AN OFF-SEASON DEAL

Pillars Hotel ★★★ *Finds* It took us a while to discover this hotel and, apparently, that's exactly the point. One of Fort Lauderdale's best-kept secrets, if not the best, Pillars Hotel transports you from the neon-hued flash and splash of Fort Lauderdale's strip to a two-story British Colonial, Caribbean-style retreat tucked away on the bustling Intracoastal Waterway. The quintessential Fort Lauderdale retreat, the Pillars is the zenith of Fort Lauderdale accommodations; though winter prices reflect that standing, you might find a good deal here in the off-season, when doubles start at $119. With just 23 rooms, you will feel as if you have the grand house all to yourself, albeit with white-tablecloth room service, an Eden-istic courtyard with free-form pool, lush landscaping, access to a water taxi, and signing privileges at nearby restaurants and spas. Rooms are luxurious and loaded with amenities such as private-label bath products, ultra-plush bedding and, if you're so inclined, a private masseuse to iron out your personal kinks. All rooms are nonsmoking.

111 N. Birch Rd., Fort Lauderdale, FL 33304. © 954/467-9639. Fax 954/763-2845. www.pillarshotel.com. 23 units. Winter $189–$259 double; off-season $119–$199 double. AE, MC, DC, DISC, V. Complimentary off-street parking. **Amenities:** Waterfront pool; preferred rates at beachfront and downtown health clubs; 24-hr. concierge; business services; 24-hr. room service; same-day laundry. *In room:* AC, TV/VCR, dataport, minibar, hair dryer, iron, safe.

GREAT DEALS ON DINING

It took a while for a more sophisticated, varied Epicurean scene to reach these shores, but Fort Lauderdale, and to some extent Hollywood, finally have several fine restaurants. Increasingly, ethnic options are joining the legions of surf-and-turferies that have dominated the area for so long. **Las Olas Boulevard** in Fort Lauderdale has so many eateries that the city has put a moratorium on the opening of new restaurants on the 2-mile-long street. Surprisingly, deals are not hard to come by either.

Aruba Beach Café CARIBBEAN   A local favorite, Aruba Beach Café is quintessential South Florida, located directly on the beach with a spectacular view of the ocean. As for the food, it's good for the proverbial "quick bite" or some drinks after beaching it all day. Enjoy safe bets like salads, pastas, and hamburgers; trying-too-hard-to-be-creative dishes such as Caribbean bamboo chicken and Pacific crab nachos may sound tasty, but they're better left on the menu. A lively, friendly atmosphere of singles, boaters, and assorted beach bums contributes to Aruba's enormous popularity. Although the restaurant stops serving food at 11pm, the bar scene is alive and well until at least 2am.

1 E. Commercial Blvd. (east of A1A), Lauderdale-by-the-Sea. © **954/776-0001.** Main courses $7.95–$15.95. AE, DC, DISC, MC, V. Mon–Fri 11am–11pm; Sat–Sun 8:30am–11pm. Bar until 2am.

Brasserie Las Olas ★   AMERICAN   This is the News Café of Fort Lauderdale, owned by the same man who spread the News and its uncomplicated cafe cuisine in Miami way back when. Located on the bottom floor of an office building and just over the bridge from the Broward County Courthouse, the Brasserie is a big power lunch spot, with high ceilings and high noise levels. Food is simple, from pizza to pasta, with some comfort food thrown in the mix. The calves' liver with caramelized onions and the balsamic marinated pork chop are excellent choices if pizza with Gorgonzola and bacon sound too simple for you. Desserts and coffees are plenty, and just like its Miami sibling, the Brasserie won't frown if you'd prefer to order a cappuccino rather than an entire meal.

333 Las Olas Blvd., Fort Lauderdale. © **954/779-7374.** Reservations for 6 or more. Main courses $8–$17. AE, DC, DISC, MC, V. Mon–Fri 11am–11pm; Sat–Sun 9am–11pm.

Conca 'D' Oro ★ Kids   ITALIAN   This family-oriented Italian restaurant is always busy. It's not that the food is so extraordinary, but that the portions are large, service is quick, and the attitude is straight from Brooklyn. The pizzas, served Neapolitan (thin crust) or Sicilian style, are large and topped with lots of cheese and a tangy tomato sauce. Don't expect more than iceberg lettuce in the salads, but do take advantage of the huge hero sandwiches and palatable house wines. If you are with a group, order one or two entrees to share. You will have leftovers. Ask for fresh mussels if they're in season (they're not always on the menu); although other appetizers are battered and fried, the young black mussels are done to perfection in a red or white sauce. Also good is the hearty lasagna, which is full of chunks of garlicky meatballs and mild sausage.

1833 Tyler St. (on Young Circle), Hollywood. © **954/927-6704.** Reservations not accepted. Pizzas $7–$12.50. Main courses $10–$28. MC, V. Mon–Thurs 11am–11pm; Fri–Sat 11am–midnight; Sun 4–11pm.

Sugar Reef ★★   FRENCH VIETNAMESE   We could go on about the restaurant's priceless, unobstructed ocean view, but the menu of Mediterranean, Caribbean, and French-Vietnamese dishes is just as outstanding. A pleasant tropical decor is bolstered by the fresh air wafting in from the Atlantic through the open windows. Seafood bouillabaisse in green curry and coconut broth and pork loin Benedict—layers of jerk-spiced pork and hollandaise sauce—are among the restaurant's most popular dishes. The restaurant puts a savory spin on duck, roasted and topped with sweet chile and papaya salsa. This is not a restaurant you'd expect to find on a beach boardwalk, which makes it all the more delightful.

600 N. Surf Rd. (on the Broadwalk just north of Hollywood Blvd.), Hollywood. © 954/922-1119. Reservations for 6 or more. Main courses $10–$24; sandwiches and salads $4–$9. AE, DISC, MC, V. Mon 4–10:30pm; Tues–Thurs 11am–10:30pm; Fri–Sun 11am–11pm (sometimes later in winter).

Sushi Blues Cafe JAPANESE   Live loud blues and jazz combine with good sushi to make an unusual pair at this slightly grungy, small storefront eatery located on Hollywood's largest traffic circle. About 12 tables and a dozen counter stools make up this relatively straightforward and unadorned sushi room. In addition to raw fish, the cafe offers some inventive specials like salmon carpaccio with caper sauce, fried soft-shell crab drizzled with a spicy sesame sauce, miso-broiled eggplant, and grilled smoked sausage with Japanese mustard. The restaurant is popular with a 20-something crowd that doesn't seem to be bothered by the fact that there are petrified rice grains on the floor. Live music packs them in on Friday and Saturday nights.

1836 S. Young Circle (east on Hollywood Blvd.), Hollywood. © 954/929-9560. Reservations recommended on weekends. Main courses $11–$20; sushi $1.75–$2.75 per piece. AE, MC, V. Mon–Thurs 6pm–midnight; Fri–Sat 6pm–2am.

Tarpon Bend ★★ *Finds* SEAFOOD/AMERICAN   This restaurant is one of the few places where the fishermen still bring the fish to the back door. The oysters from the raw bar are shucked to order and are incredible. Try the house specialty, "smoked fish dip," a king fish smoked on the premises. The steamed clambake, with half a Maine lobster, clams, potatoes, mussels, and corn on the cob, is scrumptious and served in its own pot. Also try some of the homemade side dishes. For chocolate lovers, the chocolate brownie sundae is a must. There's live entertainment Wednesday through Saturday, and a full bar.

200 SW 2nd St., Fort Lauderdale. © 954/523-3233. Reservations available for parties of 6 or more. Main courses $12–$15. AE, M, V. Mon–Thurs 11:30am–1am; Fri–Sat 11:30am–3am.

Taverna Opa ★★ *Value* GREEK   Don't get nervous if you hear plates breaking when you enter this raucous, authentic Greek taverna situated directly on the Intracoastal Waterway—it's just the restaurant's lively staff making sure your experience here is 100% Greek. Delicious *meze* (appetizers), meant to be shared by the table, make up the menu and are offered at ridiculously cheap prices. You should order a lot of them, including the large Greek salad with hunks of fresh feta cheese, moist and savory stuffed grape leaves, and grilled calamari, to get the full experience of the restaurant. When you've had enough ouzo, you may want to consider hopping up on one of the tables and dancing to the jacked-up Greek music. If not, don't worry; the waiters usually wind up on the tabletop, encouraging diners to shout the restaurant's name, "Opa!" making sure you don't forget it. You won't.

410 N. Ocean Dr., Hollywood. © 954/929-4010. Reservations accepted weekdays only. Appetizers $2.95–$10. AE, DC, DISC, MC, V. Open daily from 4pm "until the ouzo runs out."

Thai Spice ★★ THAI   This could be the best Thai in Fort Lauderdale, but you'd never guess it from the tacky decor. Regular menu items include a slightly sweet and almost buttery pad Thai with a generous serving of shrimp, chicken chunks, and scallions. Lunch specials are incredibly cheap and include all the favorites.

1514 E. Commercial Blvd. (east of I-95), Fort Lauderdale. © 954/771-4535. Fax 954/771-5678. Reservations recommended. Lunch $6.95–$9.95. Main courses $9.95–$36.95. AE, DC, DISC, MC, V. Lunch Mon–Fri 11am–3pm. Dinner Sun–Thurs 5–10pm; Fri–Sat 5–11pm.

Tuscan Today Trattoria ★★ *Finds* ITALIAN   For classic Tuscan food in a charming atmosphere, Tuscan Today is something you should not put off until tomorrow. Inspired by the peasant origins of the original trattoria, the restaurant consistently turns out outstanding pizzas and flavorful meat and fish from a customized wood-burning brick oven imported from Tuscany. A reasonable and excellent wine list provides you with a difficult choice in two affordable price ranges: $18.75 and $22.50. Artichokes steamed in white wine broth provide a flavorful balance between garlic and sun-dried tomatoes. Grilled thin-crusted pizzas are prepared as the Italians prefer them—light on sauce and cheese but heavy on flavor. For pasta lovers, the powerful but surprisingly light gnocchi with spinach is a good way to go. And if you order a meat or fish entree, be sure to try the rosemary roasted potatoes.

1161 N. Federal Hwy., Fort Lauderdale. © 954/566-1716. Reservations for 6 or more. Main courses $8.95–$14.95. AE, DC, DISC, MC, V. Sun–Thurs 11am–10pm; Fri–Sat 11am–11pm.

SUPER-CHEAP EATS

Calypso ★ CARIBBEAN   A small strip-mall restaurant, Calypso has its pulse on the beat of Caribbean cuisine, serving delicious, spicy dishes such as Jamaican jerk wings, barbecued shrimp, and smoked pork.

460 S. Cypress Rd., Pompano Beach. © 954/942-1633. Main courses $8–$15. AE, MC, V. Mon–Thurs 11am–10pm; Fri–Sat 11am–10:30pm; Sun noon–9:30pm.

Carlos & Pepe ★ MEXICAN   Tucked away in yet another strip mall, Carlos & Pepe is a restaurant that doesn't need fancy digs to convince you that its authentic homemade Mexican cuisine is worth eating. The salsa, in particular, is excellent, not the watery bottled version you find in many Mexican establishments. The food is extremely fresh and flavorful and typical of what you'd find on a Mexican menu: fajitas, burritos, quesadillas, and enchiladas. The margaritas are also quite good, but beware—they do not skimp on the tequila. A low-key local crowd tends to frequent this very casual restaurant.

1302 SE 17th St. (south of Broward Blvd.), Fort Lauderdale. © 954/467-7192. Main courses $8–$16. AE, DC, DISC, MC, V. Mon–Thurs 11:30am–11pm; Fri–Sat 11:30am–midnight; Sun noon–10pm.

Deli Den ★ *Kids* JEWISH-STYLE DELI   Catering to Broward's New York crowd for nearly 3 decades, this warehouse-sized deli serves the area's finest cheese blintzes, red cabbage soup, and matzo balls. Breakfast selections include super-thick French toast with bacon, sausage, or ham, plus dozens of egg specialties like minced lox, eggs, and onions; or corned beef hash and eggs. All baking is done on the premises. The owners are proud to say that absolutely everything else, from coleslaw to blintzes, is also homemade. Kids under 12 eat free every Monday and Thursday.

2889 Stirling Rd. (west of I-95), Hollywood. © 954/961-4070. Lunch $4.95–$6.95; main courses $9–$13; bagel sandwiches $1–$7.50. AE, MC, V. Daily 8am–10pm.

The Floridian Restaurant ★ *Value* AMERICAN/DINER   The Floridian has been filling South Florida's diner void for over 63 years, serving breakfast, lunch, and dinner, 24/7. It's especially busy on weekend mornings when locals and tourists come in for huge omelets, fresh oatmeal, sausage, and biscuits.

1410 E. Las Olas Blvd., Fort Lauderdale. © 954/463-4041. Fax 954/761-3930. Sandwiches $3–$7; breakfast combos $3.50–$8; hot platters $7–$14. No credit cards. Open daily 24 hr.

Lester's Diner ★ AMERICAN   Since 1968, Lester's Diner has been serving swarms of hungry South Floridians large portions of great greasy-spoon fare until the wee hours. Try the eggs Benedict and the 14-ounce "cup" of classic coffee, or sample one of Lester's many homemade desserts. The place serves breakfast 24 hours a day and is a Fort Lauderdale institution that attracts locals, after-club crowds, city officials, and a generally motley, friendly crew of hungry people craving no-nonsense food.

250 State Rd. 84, Fort Lauderdale. © **954/525-5641**. AE, MC, V. Main courses $5–$12. Open daily 24 hr.

WORTH A SPLURGE

Armadillo Cafe ★★★ SOUTHWESTERN   The city of Davie may be best known for farmland and rodeos, but it's also celebrated for this outstanding Southwestern restaurant, which attracts city slickers from all over South Florida. The Armadillo recently moved from its strip-mall digs to a much larger space to accommodate all the foodies who flock here in search of porcini-dusted sea bass and lobster quesadillas, among other things. At press time, a more casual offshoot, Armadillo Cafe 2.0, was slated to open, offering light meals, lunch, and dinner.

3400 S. University Dr., Davie. © **954/791-5104**. Reservations essential. AE, DC, DISC, MC, V. Main courses $16.95–$28.95. Mon–Thurs 5–10pm; Fri–Sun 5–11pm.

Cap's Place Island Restaurant ★★★ *Finds* SEAFOOD   Opened in 1928 by a bootlegger who ran in the same circles as gangster Meyer Lansky, this barge-turned-restaurant is one of South Florida's best-kept secrets. Although it's no longer a rum-running restaurant and gambling casino, its illustrious past (FDR and Winston Churchill dined here together, too) landed it a coveted spot on the National Register of Historic Places. To get there, you have to take a ferryboat, provided by the restaurant. The ride across the Intracoastal is not long and it definitely adds to the Cap's Place experience. And the food's good, too! Traditional seafood dishes such as Florida or Maine lobster, clams linguine, clams casino, and oysters Rockefeller will take you back to the days when a soprano was thought to be just an opera singer.

2765 NE 28th Court, Lighthouse Point. © **954/941-0418**. Reservations accepted. Main courses $20–$25. MC, V. Daily 5:30pm–midnight. To get to Cap's Place motor launch from I-95, exit at Copan's Rd. and go east to U.S. 1 (Federal Hwy.). At NE 24th St., turn right and follow the double lines and signs to the Lighthouse Point Yacht Basin and Marina (8 miles north of Fort Lauderdale). From there, follow a CAP'S PLACE sign pointing you to the shuttle.

Creolina's ★★ CREOLE   You'll find authentic Louisiana Creole cuisine at this small but very popular restaurant along the Riverwalk. Try the shrimp jambalaya with sausage and vegetables in a rich brown Cajun sauce served over rice, or the crawfish étouffée with crawfish tails simmered in a mellow Cajun sauce served over rice. The mashed potatoes are homemade, and the delicious fresh-squeezed lemonade is made daily. There is also a terrific New Orleans Sunday brunch. Ask to sit in sassy Rosie's section.

209 SW 2nd St., Fort Lauderdale. © **954/524-2003**. Appetizers $4–$9; main courses $13–$18. AE, MC, V. Tues–Fri 11am–2:30pm and 5–10pm; Fri–Sat 5–11pm; Sun–Mon 5–9pm.

Mark's Las Olas ★★★ NEW WORLD CUISINE   Before star chef Mark Militello hit Las Olas Boulevard, there was really no reason to dine here. However, once he opened the doors to his sleek, modern restaurant, he opened the eyes and mouths of discriminating Fort Lauderdale gourmands to his excellent new world cuisine. Grilled spiny lobster, with applewood smoked bacon-conch sauce, sweet plantain mash, and conch fritters, is possibly the best item on the menu. If the kitchen is out of it—they tend to run out quickly—everything else on the menu, from the tuna pizza to the wood-oven–roasted salmon, is delicious. Save room for a chocolate dessert—any one will do.

1032 E. Las Olas Blvd., Fort Lauderdale. © 954/463-1000. Reservations suggested. Main courses $14–$30. AE, DC, MC, V. Mon–Fri 11:30am–2:30pm; Mon–Thurs 6–10:30pm; Fri–Sat 6–11pm; Sun 6–10pm.

Sunfish Grill ★★★ SEAFOOD   Unlike its fellow contemporary seafood restaurants, the Sunfish Grill chooses to focus on fish, not fusion. Chef Anthony Sindaco doesn't want to be a star, either. He'd prefer to leave the spotlight on his fantastic fish dishes, which are possibly the freshest in town thanks to the fact that he buys his fish at local markets and often from well-known local fishermen who appear at his back door with their catches of the day. The shrimp bisque cappuccino is a deliciously rich soup served in a demitasse cup—because it's that rich. Conch fritters are purely spectacular, not full of filler. Chilean sea bass, expertly cooked with roasted fennel, saffron potatoes, and a caramelized onion broth, is wonderful, but the best item is the seared tuna resting on a bed of mushroom and oxtail ragout with garlic mashed potatoes. It's not your typical Japanese-style seared tuna; it's better. In fact, almost everything is better than most seafood restaurants at the Sunfish Grill.

2771 E. Atlantic Blvd., Pompano Beach. © 954/788-2434. Reservations accepted. Main courses $17–$28. AE, MC, V. Mon–Thurs 6–9:30pm, Fri–Sat 6–10:30pm. Closed Sun.

BROWARD COUNTY AFTER DARK

Fort Lauderdale no longer mimics the raucous antics of *Animal House* as far as nightlife and partying are concerned. It has gotten hip to the fact that an active nightlife is vital to the city's desires to distract sophisticated, savvy visitors from the magnetic lure of South Beach. And while Fort Lauderdale is no South Beach, it has vastly improved the quality of nightlife throughout the city by welcoming places that wouldn't dare host wet T-shirt and beer-chugging contests. It also lacks the South Beach attitude, which is part of the attraction.

Hollywood's nightlife seems to be in the throes of an identity crisis, touting itself as the next South Beach, while at the same time hyping its image as an attitude-free nocturnal playground. Here's the real deal: At press time, Hollywood nightlife was barely awake, with the exception of a few bars and one struggling dance club. If you're looking for a quiet night out, it's probably your best bet. But don't come too late—after midnight, the city is absolutely deserted.

For information on clubs and events, pick up a free copy of Fort Lauderdale's weekly newspaper *City Link* or the Fort Lauderdale edition of the *New Times*.

Beach Place   This outdoor shopping and entertainment complex, modeled after Coconut Grove's hugely successful Cocowalk, landed on the legendary Lauderdale "strip" with several franchised bars and restaurants. It's the beachy version of a mall and is popular with a very young set at night. The view overlooking the ocean makes it worth a stop for a drink. Hours vary depending on establishment. 17 S. Atlantic Blvd., Fort Lauderdale. © 954/760-9570. No cover charge.

Chili Pepper   David Bowie, who rarely gives concerts anymore, played here: not on South Beach, but right in the heart of downtown Fort Lauderdale. And what a coup that was. Since Bowie, there've been tons of Billboard-charting, mostly alternative musicians who have made Chili Pepper a requisite stop on touring itineraries. Open Wednesday to Saturday 10pm to 3am. 200 W. Broward Blvd., east of I-95, Fort Lauderdale. © 954/525-0094. Cover $0–$20.

Elbo Room   Formerly spring break central, the Elbo Room has actually managed to maintain its rowdy and divey reputation by serving up frequent drink specials and live bands. Open daily 10am to 2am. 241 S. Atlantic Blvd. on the corner of Las Olas Blvd. and Fla. A1A., Fort Lauderdale. © 954/463-4615. No cover.

Mai Kai *Finds* Immerse yourself in this fabulous vestige of Polynesian kitsch: hula dancers, fire-eaters, and potent (and sickly-sweet) drinks served in coconuts. The food, which draws an ambiguous line between Chinese, Polynesian, and other forms of Asian cuisine, is tasty enough but definitely overpriced. No matter, it's bound to get cold as you watch the hilarious show, which includes everything from Tahitian classics to Polynesian versions of American hits. Trippy and undeniably fun, a trip to Mai Kai is a must. *Note:* the cocktails cost almost as much as a meal. Open daily 5pm to midnight. 3599 N. Federal Hwy. (between Commercial and Oakland Park blvds.), Fort Lauderdale. © 954/563-3272. Reservations required. Shows (2 nightly) are $9.95 for adults; children 12 and under free.

Nick's With an idyllic location on Hollywood's Broadwalk, Nick's is the best place to enjoy cocktails with an unobstructed view of the ocean. Open daily 10am to 4am. 1214 N. Broadwalk, Hollywood. © 954/920-2800. No cover.

O'Hara's What used to be a mediocre jazz club has turned into a premier venue for excellent live R&B, pop, and funk music. Hours are daily 5pm to 2am. The club has 2 locations: at 1905 Hollywood Blvd., Hollywood (© 954/925-2555 or the 24-hr. Jazz & Blues Hotline © 954/524-2801); and 722 E. Las Olas Blvd., Fort Lauderdale (© 954/524-1764). No cover.

The Parrot Fort Lauderdale's most famous—and fun—dive bar, The Parrot is a local's and out-of-towner's choice for an evening of beer (16 kinds on tap), bonding, and browsing of the bar's virtual gallery of photos of almost everyone who's ever imbibed here since its opening in 1970. Hours are Sunday to Thursday 11am to 2am; Friday to Saturday 11am to 3am. 911 Sunrise Lane, Fort Lauderdale. © 954/563-1493. No cover.

The Poor House Despite its unfortunate name, the Poor House is rich in live blues music and is a good spot for a couple of drinks and conversation. Daily 8pm to 4am. 110 SW Third Ave., Fort Lauderdale. © 954/522-5145. No cover.

Riverwalk You'll find this outdoor shopping and entertainment complex in the heart of downtown Fort Lauderdale on the sleepy yet scenic New River;. As a result of its river site, it's got more charm than most such complexes. In fact, if you've got a boat, you can sail here and anchor away until you're ready to move on. A host of bars, restaurants, and shops, not to mention a high-tech virtual reality arcade, The Escape, and a multiplex cinema, are enough to keep you occupied for at least a few hours. On weekends, this place is packed. 400 SW 2nd St. (along the New River from NE Sixth Ave. to SW Sixth Ave.), Fort Lauderdale. © 954/468-1541.

Rush Street Known for the ice-cream flavors given to their martinis, from chocolate to Key lime, Rush Street is a sleek bar, with two dance floors, which attracts a young professional crowd. Try their two-for-one drink specials between 4 and 7pm. Daily 4pm to 4am. 220 SW 2nd St., Fort Lauderdale. © 954/522-6900. No cover.

Shooters This waterfront bar is quintessential Fort Lauderdale. Inside, you'll find nautical types, families, and young professionals mixed in with a good dose of sunburned tourists enjoying the live reggae, jazz, or Jimmy Buffett–style tunes with the gorgeous backdrop of the bay and marinas all around. Hours are Monday to Friday 11:30am to 2am; Saturday 11:30am to 3am; and Sunday 10am to 2am. 3033 NE 32nd Ave., Fort Lauderdale. © 954/566-2855. No cover.

Where the Boys Are: Gay Fort Lauderdale

While South Beach is a magnet for the so-called circuit boys—gay men who party on a continual, ritualistic basis—Fort Lauderdale has more of a low-key, small-town scene similar to, say, Provincetown. Here, local gay-owned and -operated bars, clubs, and restaurants are the places of choice for those who find South Beach's scene too pretentious, superficial, and drug-infested. The Fort Lauderdale neighborhood of Wilton Manors is the hub of gay life, but there is a smattering of gay establishments throughout the city.

The Copa, located at 2800 S. Federal Hwy. (east on I-595, near the airport; © 954/463-1507) is the hottest gay spot north of South Beach—the granddaddy of Fort Lauderdale's gay club scene. Patrons of **Cathode Ray** call this bar their "Cheers." It's located at 1105 E. Las Olas Blvd. (© 954/462-8611). **Georgie's Alibi** is Wilton Manors' most popular gay bar. Find it at 2266 Wilton Dr., Wilton Manors (© 954/565-2526). Two great dance clubs are the **Coliseum** (2520 S. Miami Rd.; © 954/832-0100) and **The Saint** (1000 W. S.R. 84; (© 954/525-7883).

The Velvet Lounge This lounge and dance club comes closest to the South Beach vibe with a (sometimes) chic crowd, pretty good DJs, and very little attitude. Open Tuesday, Friday, and Saturday 10pm to 3am. 2975 N. Federal Hwy. © 954/563-4331. Cover $0–$10.

2 Boca Raton ⋆⋆ & Delray Beach ⋆

26 miles S of Palm Beach, 40 miles N of Miami, 21 miles N of Fort Lauderdale

Boca Raton is one of South Florida's most expensive, well-maintained cities—home to ladies who lunch and SUV-driving yuppies. The city's name literally translates as "rat's mouth," but you'd be hard-pressed to find rodents in this area's fancy digs.

If you're looking for funky, wacky, and eclectic, look elsewhere. Boca is a luxurious resort community and, for some, the only place worth staying in South Florida. Although Jerry Seinfeld's TV parents retired to the fictional Del Boca Vista, Boca's just too pricey to be a retirement community. With minimal nightlife, entertainment in Boca is restricted to leisure sports, excellent dining, and upscale shopping. The city's residents and vacationers happily comply.

Delray Beach, named after a suburb of Detroit, grew up completely separate from its southern neighbor. This sleepy yet starting-to-awaken beachfront community was founded in 1894 by a Midwestern postmaster who sold off 5-acre lots through Michigan newspaper ads. Because of their close proximity, Boca and Delray can easily be explored together. Budget-conscious travelers would do well to eat and sleep in Delray and dip into Boca for sightseeing and beaching only. The 2-mile stretch of beach here is well maintained and crowded, but not mobbed. Delray's "downtown" area is confined to Atlantic Avenue, which is known for casual to chic restaurants, quaint shops, and art galleries. Compared to sprawling, swanky, suburban Boca, Delray is much more laid-back and a cute little beach town.

Attractions from Boca Raton to Jupiter

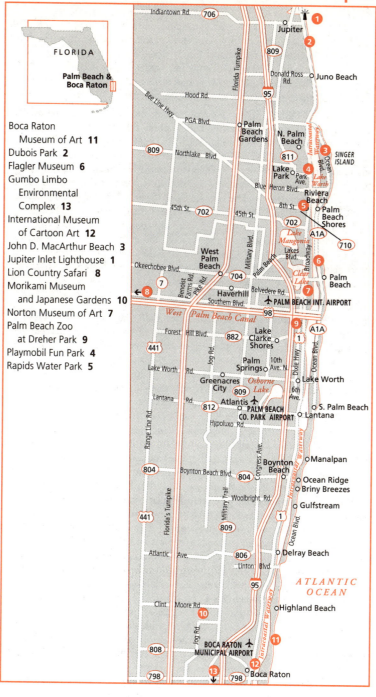

Boca Raton
  Museum of Art **11**
Dubois Park **2**
Flagler Museum **6**
Gumbo Limbo
  Environmental
  Complex **13**
International Museum
  of Cartoon Art **12**
John D. MacArthur Beach **3**
Jupiter Inlet Lighthouse **1**
Lion Country Safari **8**
Morikami Museum
  and Japanese Gardens **10**
Norton Museum of Art **7**
Palm Beach Zoo
  at Dreher Park **9**
Playmobil Fun Park **4**
Rapids Water Park **5**

ESSENTIALS

GETTING THERE Like the rest of the cities on the Gold Coast, Boca Raton and Delray are easily reached by car from I-95 or the Florida Turnpike. The Fort Lauderdale/Hollywood International Airport and the Palm Beach International Airport are each about 20 minutes away (see "Essentials" in sections 1 and 3). **Amtrak** (© **800/USA-RAIL;** www.amtrak.com) trains make stops in Delray Beach at an unattended station at 345 S. Congress Ave.

VISITOR INFORMATION We recommend contacting or stopping by the **Palm Beach County Convention and Visitors Bureau,** 1555 Palm Beach Lakes Blvd., Suite 800, West Palm Beach, FL 33401 (© **800/554-PALM** or 561/233-3000; fax 561/471-3990; www.palmbeachfl.com), since it offers information on the entire county. They're open Monday to Friday from 8:30am to 5:30pm and have excellent coupons and discounts. On weekdays from 8:30am until at least 4pm, stop by **The Greater Boca Raton Chamber of Commerce,** 1800 N. Dixie Hwy. (4 blocks north of Glades Rd.), Boca Raton, FL 33432 (© **561/395-4433;** fax 561/392-3780; www.bocaratonchamber.com), for information on attractions, accommodations, and events in the area. Also, try **The Greater Delray Beach Chamber of Commerce,** 64 SE Fifth Ave. (half a block south of Atlantic Ave. on U.S. 1), Delray Beach, FL 33483 (© **561/278-0424;** fax 561/278-0555; www.delraybeach.com).

WHAT TO SEE & DO

Thankfully, Florida had the foresight to set aside some of its most beautiful coastal areas for the public's enjoyment. Many of the area's best beaches are located in state parks and are free to pedestrians and bikers, though most do charge for parking.

Delray Beach's **Atlantic Dunes Beach**, 1600 S. Ocean Blvd., is a 7-acre developed beach with lifeguards, restrooms, changing rooms, and a family park area. Admission is free, though parking meters cost 25¢ for every 20 minutes. Boca Raton's **South Beach Park Beach**, 400 N. Ocean Blvd., offers 1,670 feet of beach, 25 acres, lifeguards, picnic areas, restrooms, and showers, including 955 feet of developed beach south of the Boca Inlet. Admission is $7 on weekdays and $9 on weekends. Both beaches are open to the public from 8am to sundown, with lifeguards on duty from 9am to 5pm.

The **Delray Beach Public Beach**, on Ocean Boulevard at the east end of Atlantic Avenue, is one of the area's most popular hangouts. Weekends especially attract a young and good-looking crowd of active locals and tourists. Regular volleyball, Frisbee, and paddleball games make for good entertainment. Refreshments, snack shops, bars, and restaurants are just across the street. Families enjoy the protection of lifeguards on the clean, wide beach, and gentle waters make it good for swimming. Restrooms and showers are available, and there's limited parking at meters along Ocean Boulevard. The beach is open from sunrise to sunset.

Spanish River Park Beach, on North Ocean Boulevard (Fla. A1A), 2 miles north of Palmetto Park Road in Boca Raton, is a huge 95-acre oceanfront park with a half-mile-long beach complete with lifeguards as well as a large grassy area, making it one of the best choices for picnicking. Facilities include picnic tables, grills, restrooms, showers, and a bilevel 40-foot observation tower. You can walk through tunnels under the highway to access nature trails that wind through fertile grasslands. Volleyball nets are ocean-side and always boast at least one serious game in play. The park is open from 8am until 8pm. Admission is $8 for vehicles on weekdays and $10 on weekends and major holidays.

Also check out Red Reef Park, discussed under "Scuba Diving & Snorkeling," below.

AFFORDABLE OUTDOOR ACTIVITIES

GOLF A great place to swing your clubs is at the **Deer Creek Golf Club,** 2801 Country Club Blvd., Deerfield Beach (© **954/421-5550**), a 300-plus-yard driving range where a large bucket of balls costs $7, and a small one costs $4.

The semiprivate, 18-hole, par-61 course at the **Boca Raton Executive Country Club,** 7601 E. Country Club Blvd. (© **561/997-9410**), is usually open to the public and is an excellent choice for those looking to improve their game in a professional setting. A driving range is on the property as well as a restaurant and a pro shop, where you can rent clubs. If you like, take lessons from a PGA pro. Greens fees are $20 per person.

The **Boca Raton Municipal Golf Course,** 8111 Golf Course Rd. (© **561/483-6100**), is the area's best public golf course. There's an 18-hole, par-72 course covering approximately 6,200 yards as well as a nine-hole, par 30 course. There's a snack bar and a pro shop where clubs can be rented. Greens fees are $11 to $14 for nine holes and $19 to $25 for 18 holes. Ask for special summer discount fees.

From May to October or November, about a dozen private courses open their greens to visitors staying in Palm Beach County hotels. This "Golf-A-Round" program is free or severely discounted (carts are additional), and reservations can be made through most major hotels. Ask at your hotel, or contact the **Palm Beach County Convention and Visitors Bureau** (© **561/471-3995**) for information on which clubs are available for play.

SCUBA DIVING & SNORKELING **Moray Bend,** a 58-foot dive spot located about three-quarters of a mile off Boca Inlet, is the area's most popular. It's home to three moray eels that are used to being fed by scuba divers. The reef is accessible by boat from **Force E Dive Center,** 877 E. Palmetto Park Rd., Boca Raton (© **561/368-0555**). Phone for dive times. Dives cost $40 to $45 per person.

Red Reef Park, 1400 N. Ocean Park Blvd. (© **561/393-7974**), a fully developed 67-acre oceanfront park in Boca Raton, has good swimming and year-round lifeguard protection. There's snorkeling for beginners around the rocks and reefs that lie just off the beach in 2 to 6 feet of water. The park also has restrooms and a small picnic area with grills and tables. Located a half mile north of Palmetto Park Road, it is open daily from 8am to 10pm. You pay only if you drive in. It's $8 per car during the week or $10 on weekends.

You can rent snorkeling equipment, including mask, fins, and snorkel, for $11 at **Force-E,** 2181 N. Federal Hwy., Boca Raton (© **561/368-0555**).

TENNIS The snazzy **Delray Beach Tennis Center,** 201 W. Atlantic Ave. (© **561/243-7360;** www.delraytennis.com), has 14 lighted clay courts and five hard courts available by the hour. Phone for rates and reservations.

The 17 public lighted hard courts at **Patch Reef Park,** 2000 NW 51st St. (© **561/997-0881;** www.ci.boca-raton.fl.us/parks/Patchreef.cfm), are available by reservation. The fee for nonresidents is $5.75 per person per hour. Courts are available Monday to Saturday from 7:30am to 10pm and Sunday from 7:30am to dusk; you can phone ahead to see if a court is available. To reach the park from I-95, exit at Yamato Road West and continue past Military Trail to the park.

SEEING THE SIGHTS

Boca Raton Museum of Art ★★ In addition to a relatively small but well-chosen permanent collection that's strongest in 19th-century European oils, the museum stages a wide variety of temporary exhibitions by local and international artists. Lectures and films are offered on a fairly regular basis, so call ahead for details.

Mizner Park, 501 Plaza Real, Boca Raton. © **561/392-2500**. www.bocamuseum.org. Admission $8 adults, $6 seniors, $4 students; children under 12 free. Additional fees may apply for special exhibits and performances. Free on Wed except during special exhibitions. Tues, Thurs, Sat 10am–5pm; Wed and Fri 10am–9pm; Sun noon–5pm. Closed Mon.

Daggerwing Nature Center ★ Kids Seen enough snowbirds? Head over to this 39-acre swampy splendor where birds of another feather reside, including herons, egrets, woodpeckers, and warblers. The park's trails come complete with a soundtrack provided by songbirds hovering above (watch your head). The park's Night Hikes will take you on a nocturnal wake-up call for owls at 6pm and is fun for kids as well as adults. Bring a flashlight.

South County Regional Park, 11200 Park Access Rd., Boca Raton. © **561/488-9953**. Free admission. Tues–Fri 1–4:30pm; Sat 9am–4:30pm. Call for tour and activity schedule.

Gumbo Limbo Environmental Complex ★★★ If manicured lawns and golf courses aren't your idea of communing with nature, then head to Gumbo Limbo. Named for an indigenous hardwood tree with continuously shedding bronze bark, the 20-acre complex protects one of the few surviving coastal hammocks, or forest islands, in South Florida. Visitors can walk through the hammock on a half-mile-long elevated boardwalk that ends at a 40-foot observation tower, from which you can see the Atlantic Ocean, the Intracoastal Waterway, and much of Boca Raton. From mid-April to September, sea turtles come ashore here to lay their eggs.

1801 N. Ocean Blvd. (on Fla. A1A between Spanish River Blvd. and Palmetto Park), Boca Raton. © **561/338-1473**. Fax 561/338-1483. Free admission. Mon–Sat 9am–4pm; Sun noon–4pm.

International Museum of Cartoon Art ★ Kids This extensive collection of cartoon art spans the decades and styles in its glitzy home in Mizner Park. In a gorgeous 52,000-square-foot gallery space, cartoon fans can see prints, frames, moving pictures, and books by some of the world's greatest cartoonists, including many by the museum's late founder, Mort Walker (of *Beetle Bailey* fame). A fantastic gift shop offers posters, books, and lots of memorabilia.

201 Plaza Real at Mizner Park, Boca Raton. © **561/391-2200**. www.cartoon.org. Donation requested. Wed–Sun 10am–5pm.

Morikami Museum and Japanese Gardens ★★★ Slip off your shoes and enter a serene Japanese garden that dates from 1905, when an entrepreneurial farmer, Jo Sakai, came to Boca Raton to build a tropical agricultural community. The Yamato Colony, as it was known, was short-lived; by the 1920s only one tenacious colonist remained: George Sukeji Morikami. But Morikami was quite successful, eventually running one of the largest pineapple plantations in the area. The 200-acre Morikami Museum and Japanese Gardens (a stroll through the garden is actually seven-eighths of a mile), which opened to the public in 1977, was Morikami's gift to Palm Beach County and the State of Florida. The park section, dedicated to the preservation of Japanese culture, is constructed to appeal to all the senses. An artificial waterfall that cascades into a koi- and carp-filled moat; a small rock garden for meditation; and a large bonsai collection that includes miniature maple, buttonwood, juniper, and Australian pine trees, are all worth contemplation. There's also a cafe with an Asian-inspired menu if you want to stay for lunch.

4000 Morikami Park Rd., Delray Beach. © 561/495-0233. www.morikami.org. $8 adults, $7 seniors, $5 children 6–18; free for members and children 5 and under. Museum Tues–Sun 10am–5pm; gardens Tues–Sat 10am–5pm. Closed major holidays.

SHOPPING

Even if you don't plan to buy anything, a trip to Boca Raton's **Mizner Park** is essential for capturing the essence of the city. Like Main Street in a small town, Mizner is the place to see and be seen, where Rolls Royces and Ferraris are parked curbside, freshly coifed women sit amidst shopping bags at outdoor cafes, and young movers and shakers make evening plans on their constantly buzzing cell phones. Beyond the human scenery, however, Mizner Park is scenic in its own right with beautiful landscaping. It's really an outdoor mall, with 45 specialty shops, seven good restaurants, and a multiplex. Each shopfront faces a grassy island with blue and green gazebos, potted plants, and garden benches. Mizner Park is located on Federal Highway (between Palmetto Park Rd. and Glades Rd.; © **561/362-0606**).

Boca's **Town Center Mall,** located on the south side of Glades Road, just west of I-95, has seven huge department stores, including the state's only Nordstrom as well as Bloomingdale's, Burdines, Lord & Taylor, and Saks Fifth Avenue. Add to that the hundreds of specialty shops, an extensive food court, and a range of other restaurants, and you have the area's most comprehensive shopping center.

A lifeless, overrated area, but good enough for a quick stroll, is the more artsy community of Delray Beach, known by many as **Pineapple Grove.** Here, along Atlantic Avenue, especially east of Swinton Avenue, you'll find a few antiques shops, clothing stores, and art galleries shaded by palm trees and colorful awnings. Pick up the "Downtown Delray Beach" map and guide at almost any of the stores on this strip, or call © **561/278-0424** for more information.

ACCOMMODATIONS YOU CAN AFFORD

A number of national chain hotels worth considering around Boca include a moderately priced **Holiday Inn Highland Beach Oceanside** at 2809 S. Ocean Blvd., on Fla. A1A, southeast of Linton Boulevard (© **800/234-6835** or 561/278-6241). Rates here are $79 to $299 for a double during winter, and $79 to $109 for a double during off-season.

Even more economical options can be found in Deerfield Beach, Boca's neighbor, south of the county line. A number of beachfront efficiencies offer great deals, even in the winter months. Try the **Panther Motel and Apartments,** at 715 S. A1A (© **954/427-0700**). This clean and convenient motel has rates starting as low as $40, although in season you may have to book for a week at a time. Weekly rates in season start at $457.

Although you won't find rows of cheap hotels as in Fort Lauderdale and Hollywood, a handful of mom-and-pop motels have survived along Fla. A1A between the towering condominiums of Delray Beach. Look along the beach just south of Atlantic Boulevard. Especially noteworthy is the pleasant little two-story, shingle-roofed **Bermuda Inn** at 64 S. Ocean Blvd. (© **561/276-5288**). Doubles here cost $115 to $135 in winter, or $85 to $110 in the off-season.

If you are looking for something more private or for longer than just a few days, you may want to call a reservations service for help. **Palm Beach Accommodations** (© **800/543-SWIM**) handles rentals for a few weeks or months.

Ocean Lodge Situated around a small heated pool and sun deck, this two-story motel is a particularly well-kept accommodation in an area of run-down or overpriced options. The large rooms offer furnishings and decor that are clean but a bit impersonal. A recent renovation that added modern Formica and floral wallpaper lifts this a notch above a basic motel. Ask for a room in the back, since the street noise can be a bit loud, especially in season. The bonus is that you are across the street from the ocean and in one of Florida's most upscale resort towns.

531 N. Ocean Blvd. (just north of Palmetto Park Rd. on Fla. A1A), Boca Raton, FL 33432. © 800/STAY-BOCA or 561/395-7772. Fax 561/395-0554. 18 units. Winter $99–$125 double; off-season $75–$99 double. AE, MC, V. **Amenities:** Pool. *In room:* A/C, TV.

Shore Edge Motel Another relic of the 1950s, this motel has been recently spiffed up with new landscaping and some redecorating and is a good choice, especially because of its location—across the street from a public beach, just north of downtown Boca Raton. It's the quintessential South Florida motel: a small, pink, single-story structure surrounding a modest swimming pool and courtyard. Although the rooms are on the small side, they're very neat and clean. The higher-priced accommodations are larger and come with full kitchens.

425 N. Ocean Blvd. (on Fla. A1A, north of Palmetto Park Rd.), Boca Raton, FL 33432. © 561/395-4491. Fax 561/347-8759. 16 units. Winter $85–$99 double; off-season $55–$65 double. AE, MC, V. **Amenities:** Pool. *In room:* A/C, TV.

SUPER-CHEAP SLEEPS

Boca Inn Owned by a pleasant East Indian family, this super-budget motel is located right on busy U.S. 1 but is set back enough from the road to make it quiet. The squat, two-story building surrounds a large pool deck with lounge furniture, vending machines, and laundry facilities. All rooms have cable TV, small refrigerators, and telephones. Many have king-size beds, too. For the price, this is a thoroughly decent place to crash just about half a mile from the beach. Next door is a fantastic Punjab restaurant and nearby is lots of shopping.

1801 N. Federal Hwy. (between Glades Rd. and 20th St.), Boca Raton, FL 33432. © 800/442-2622 or 561/395-7500. Fax 561/391-0287. 50 units. Winter $75–$95 single or double; off-season $45–$55 single or double. AE, MC, V. Take Exit 39 off 95 (Glades Rd.); turn right, then at U.S. 1 (Federal Hwy.) turn left; the inn is 3 blocks on the left. **Amenities:** Pool; laundry. *In room:* A/C, TV, fridge.

Riviera Palms Motel The Riviera Palms offers plain, simple, and relatively inexpensive accommodations just across the street from a wide, pretty beach. Behind the motel's two-story, cream-colored exterior are large rooms filled with a mixed bag of 1950s-era furnishings. The efficiencies come with full kitchens complete with dishes and flatware. There are no phones in the rooms. A large swimming pool is surrounded by a nice courtyard with sunning lounges, patio tables, barbecue grills, and shuffleboard courts.

3960 N. Ocean Blvd. (2 miles north of Atlantic Ave.), Delray Beach, FL 33483. © 561/276-3032. 34 units. Winter $60–$70 single or double, from $80 efficiency; off-season $50 single or double, from $55 efficiency. Weekly rates available. No credit cards. **Amenities:** Pool; shuffleboard courts. *In room:* A/C, TV. No phone.

AN OFF-SEASON DEAL

Delray Beach Marriott Delray Beach may be a sleepy beach town, but those looking for a bit more excitement will find it in this Marriott, which features a host of activities and amenities that may almost convince you that Delray is an exciting, lively place! The hotel, decked out in a typical, yet charming, Marriott–Florida decor, offers the best of both worlds: It's located directly across the street from the slumberous beach, but on the premises are an enormous, active outdoor pool and a lively lounge. Children under 18 stay free with an adult.

10 N. Ocean Blvd., Delray Beach, FL 33483. © **800/228-9290** or 561/274-3200. Fax 561/274-3202. 268 units. Winter $245–$269; off-season $119–$139. AE, DC, DISC, MC, V. **Amenities:** Restaurant, lounge; large outdoor pool; health club; concierge. *In room:* A/C, TV, dataport, hair dryer, coffeemaker.

GREAT DEALS ON DINING

Boca Raton, and its surrounding area, is the kind of place where you discuss dinner plans at the breakfast table. Nightlife in Boca means going out to a restaurant. But who cares? These are some of the best restaurants in South Florida.

Baja Cafe ★ *Value* MEXICAN   A jeans and T-shirt kind of place with wooden tables, Baja Cafe serves fantastic Mexican food at even better prices. It's located right by the Florida East Coast Railway tracks, so don't be surprised if you feel a little rattling. Live music and entertainment in the evening make this place a hot spot for an unpretentious crowd.

201 NW First Ave., Boca Raton. © **561/394-5449**. No reservations. Main courses $6–$10. No credit cards. Mon–Thurs 11:30am–10:30pm; Fri–Sat 11:30am–11pm; Sun 5–10pm.

Mario's of Boca ★ ITALIAN   This extremely popular, bustling Italian bistro keeps Boca's biggest mouths busy with massive portions of great homemade Italian food. The garlic rolls and the pizza are especially worth the calories. If you're really hungry, there's an all-you-can-eat buffet 7 days a week.

2200 Glades Rd. (between 19th St. and Sheridan Way), Boca Raton. © **561/392-5595**. Reservations not accepted. Main courses under $15. AE, MC, V. Mon–Thurs 11:30am–10pm; Fri–Sat 11:30am–11pm; Sun noon–9:30pm.

Splendid Blendeds ★★ *Finds* ECLECTIC   Loyal regulars would like to keep this storefront bistro a secret so that the lines won't get even longer on weekends. The draw here is fresh, uncomplicated seafood and pastas that are interesting without being overly ambitious. The Southwestern-inspired chicken Santa Cruz is tender and juicy, served with a black-bean sauce and tangy pico de gallo. Many seafood specialties, like tuna, snapper, and shrimp dishes, are slight departures from classic recipes and work most of the time. The only drawback of this otherwise superb spot, aside from the name, is the well-meaning but easily flustered staff.

432 E. Atlantic Ave., Delray. © **561/265-1035**. Reservations recommended. Main courses $10.95–$21.95; sandwiches and salads $3.50–$8.95. AE, DC, MC, V. Mon–Fri 11:30am–2:30pm; Mon–Sat 5:30–10pm. Closed Aug.

32 East ★★ NEW AMERICAN   The menu changes every day at this very popular people-watching outpost of tasty, contemporary American food, which has finally added a little hip to the Delray Beach dining scene. Delicious items have included rigatoni with braised lamb shank and oregano; thinly cut steak on roasted-garlic polenta; and grilled salmon with arugula purée and olive tapenade.

32 E. Atlantic Ave., Delray Beach. © **561/276-7868**. Reservations recommended. Main courses $10–$16. AE, DC, MC, V. Sun–Thurs 5:30–10pm; Fri–Sat 5:30–11pm. Bar until 2am.

Tom's Place ★★ *Finds* BARBECUE   There are two important factors in a successful barbecue: the cooking and the sauce. Tom and Helen Wright's no-nonsense shack wins on both counts, offering flawlessly grilled meats paired with well-spiced sauces. Beef, chicken, pork, and fish are served soul-food style, with your choice of two sides such as rice with gravy, collard greens, black-eyed peas, coleslaw, or mashed potatoes. Signed celebrity photographs decorate the walls.

7251 N. Federal Hwy., Boca Raton. © 561/997-0920. Reservations not accepted. Main courses $8–$15; sandwiches $5–$6; early-bird special $7.95. AE, MC, V. Tues–Thurs 11:30am–9:30pm; Fri 11:30am–10pm; Sat noon–10pm.

SUPER-CHEAP EATS

The Tin Muffin Cafe ★ BAKERY/SANDWICH SHOP   Popular with the downtown lunch crowd, this excellent storefront bakery keeps them lining up for big sandwiches on fresh bread, plus muffins, quiches, and good homemade soups like split pea or lentil. The curried chicken sandwich is stuffed with oversized chunks of white meat doused in a creamy curry dressing and fruit. There are a few cafe tables inside and even one outside on a tiny patio. Be warned, however, that service is forgivably slow and parking is a nightmare. Try parking a few blocks away at a meter on the street.

364 E. Palmetto Park Rd. (between Federal Hwy. and the Intracoastal Bridge), Boca Raton. © 561/392-9446. Sandwiches and salads $6.50–$10.95. No credit cards. Mon–Fri 11am–5pm; Sat 11am–4pm.

WORTH A SPLURGE

Max's Grille ★★ AMERICAN   Max's Grille is a very popular, very good option in Mizner Park, but you will inevitably wait to be seated. With a large exhibition kitchen that occupies the entire back wall of the restaurant, those lucky enough to score a table can watch as their yellowfin tuna steak or filet mignon is seared on a flaming oak grill. There's also a large selection of chicken, meat loaf, pastas, and main-course salads.

404 Plaza Real, in Mizner Park, Boca Raton. © 561/368-0080. Reservations accepted for 6 or more. Main courses $14–$26; pastas $10.95–$16.95. AE, DC, DISC, MC, V. Lunch Mon–Sat 11:30am–3pm. Dinner Mon–Thurs 5–10:30pm; Fri–Sat 5–11pm. Sun brunch/dinner 11:30am–10pm.

Zemi ★★★ NEW AMERICAN   Possibly the best privately owned restaurant to be attached to a mall, Zemi is a sleek neo-American restaurant that's a favorite with the ladies-who-lunch set, the Boca scenesters, and foodies alike. Chili-crusted shrimp with manchego cheese, roasted garlic, sun-dried tomatoes, lemon oil, and cilantro; grilled pork T-bone in a pear-ginger compote; and the marinated, grilled skirt steak with vegetable hash and crispy onions are all so good that even the size-two chic set would be happy to go up a half size for a taste.

5050 Towne Center Circle, in the Boca Center, Boca Raton. © 561/391-7177. Reservations accepted for 6 or more. Main courses $18–$28. AE, DC, DISC, MC, V. Lunch Mon–Fri 11:30am–2:30pm. Dinner Mon–Thurs and Sun 6–10 pm; Fri–Sat 6–11pm.

BOCA RATON & DELRAY AFTER DARK
THE BAR, CLUB & MUSIC SCENE

South Ocean Boulevard and Atlantic Avenue in Delray Beach are slowly but surely getting hip to nightlife—though they are still a far cry from the Fort Lauderdale "strip." In Boca Raton, Mizner Park is the nucleus of a makeshift nightlife, with restaurants masking themselves as nightclubs or, at the very least, very sceney bars. These include **Gigi's Tavern,** 346 Plaza Real, Mizner Park (© **561/368-4488**); and **Mark's Mizner Park,** 344 Plaza Real (© **561/395-0770**).

Boston's on the Beach   This is a family restaurant with a somewhat lively bar scene. It's a good choice for post-sunbathing, super-casual happy hours Monday through Friday from 4 to 8pm, or for live reggae on Monday. With two decks overlooking the ocean, Boston's is an ideal place to mellow out and take in the scenery. Daily 7am to 2am. 40 S. Ocean Blvd., Delray Beach. © 561/278-3364. No cover.

Dakotah 624 Creative cocktails such as the Kissing Cousin (Southern Comfort, Fris vodka, lime juice, and triple sec) and its own line of cigars attract a hip, young clientele to this vaguely Southwestern-style bar on the beach. Hours are Monday to Wednesday 4pm to 1am; Thursday to Saturday 4pm to 2am; Sunday 4 to 11pm. 270 E. Atlantic Ave., Delray Beach. © **561/274-6244.** No cover.

Gatsby's This always-busy bar is singles central, featuring big-screen TVs, microbrews, and martinis. Thursday-night college nights are especially popular, as are Friday happy hours. Hours are Monday to Friday 4pm to 2am; Saturday to Sunday 6pm to 4am. 5970 SW 18th St., Boca Raton. © **561/393-3900.** No cover.

Mezzanotte The Mezzanotte on South Beach's Washington Avenue used to be the place for a bacchanalian funfest. Then the place went from crazy to closed. The good times have traveled north to this Boca offshoot, where a well-tanned, glitzy crowd of young and old let their hair (or toupees) down, especially on weekends. Hours are Sunday to Thursday 5 to 10pm; Friday to Saturday 5pm to 2am. 150 E. Palmetto Park Rd., Boca Raton. © **561/361-0111.** No cover.

Radius This big, noisy techno-trance warehouse west of the highway attracts a range of big-haired girls and macho guys with gold chains. It's Boca's only attempt at a clubby nightlife and, if you don't mind dancing with a really young crowd, it can be amusing depending on your sense of humor. Call ahead to ask to be placed on the "list," so you won't have to shell out $20 or more for this nocturnal gamble. Hours are Thursday to Sunday 9pm to 5am. 7000 W. Palmetto Park Rd. (at the SW corner of Powerline Rd. in the Bank of America building), Boca Raton. © **561/392-3747.** Cover $5–$20.

THE PERFORMING ARTS

For details on upcoming events, check the Boca News or the Sun-Sentinel, or call the **Palm Beach County Cultural Council** information line at © **800/882-ARTS.** During business hours, a staffer can give details on current performances. After hours, a recorded message describes the week's events.

The **Florida Symphonic Pops,** a 70-piece professional orchestra, performs jazz, swing, rock, big band, and classical music throughout Boca Raton. For nearly 50 years, this ever-growing musical force has entertained audiences of every age. Call © **561/393-7677** for a schedule of concerts.

Boca's best theater company is the **Caldwell Theatre,** and it's worth checking out. Located in a strip shopping center at 7873 N. Federal Hwy., this equity showcase does well-known dramas, comedies, classics, off-Broadway hits, and new works throughout the year. Prices are reasonable (usually $29–$38). Full-time students with ID will be especially interested in the little-advertised "Student Rush." When available, tickets are sold for $5 to those who arrive at least an hour in advance. Call © **561/241-7432** for details.

3 Palm Beach ★★★ & West Palm Beach ★

65 miles N of Miami, 193 miles E of Tampa, 45 miles N of Fort Lauderdale

Palm Beach County encompasses cities from Boca Raton in the south to Jupiter and Tequesta in the north. But it is Palm Beach, the small island town across the Intracoastal Waterway, that has been the traditional winter home of America's aristocracy—the Kennedys, the Rockefellers, the Pulitzers, the Trumps, titled socialites, and plenty of CEOs. For a real-time perspective on what it means to put on the ritz, there is no better place than Palm Beach, where teenagers cruise around in their parents' Rolls Royces and where socialites, otherwise seen only in society publications, seem to jump out of the glossy pages and into an even glossier, glitzier real life. It's really something to be seen, despite the fact that some may consider it all over the top and, frankly, obscene. But Palm Beach is not only a city of upscale resorts and chic boutiques. In fact, Palm Beach holds some surprises, from a world-class art museum to one of the top bird-watching areas in the state.

Across the water from Palm Beach proper, or the "island" as locals call it, is downtown West Palm Beach, which is where everybody else lives. Clematis Street is the area's nightlife hub, with a great selection of bars, clubs, and restaurants. City Place is West Palm's version of Mizner Park; shops, restaurants, and other entertainment options liven up this once-dead area of West Palm. In addition to good beaching, boating, and diving, you'll find great golf and tennis throughout this area.

ESSENTIALS

GETTING THERE If you're **driving** up or down the Florida coast, you'll probably reach the Palm Beach area by way of I-95. Exit at Belvedere Road or Okeechobee Boulevard and head east to reach the most central part of Palm Beach. Visitors on their way to or from Orlando or Miami should take the Florida Turnpike, a toll road with a speed limit of 65 miles per hour. Tolls are pricey, though; you may pay upward of $9 from Orlando and $4 from Miami. If you're coming from Florida's west coast, you can take either S.R. 70, which runs north of Lake Okeechobee to Fort Pierce, or S.R. 80, which runs south of the lake to Palm Beach.

All major airlines fly to the **Palm Beach International Airport,** at Congress Avenue and Belvedere Road (© **561/471-7400).** Amtrak (© **800/USA-RAIL;** www.amtrak.com) has a terminal in West Palm Beach, at 201 S. Tamarind Ave. (© **561/832-6169).**

GETTING AROUND Although a car is almost a necessity in this area, a recently revamped public transportation system is extremely convenient for getting to some attractions in both West and Palm Beach. **Palm Tran** underwent a major expansion in late 1996, increasing service to 32 routes and more than 140 buses. The fare is $1 for adults and 50¢ for children ages 3 to 18, seniors, and riders with disabilities. Free route maps are available by calling © **561/233-4-BUS.** Information operators are available from 6am to 7pm, except Sunday.

In downtown West Palm, **free shuttles** from City Place to Clematis Street operate Monday through Friday from 9am until 4pm, with plans to expand operations to evenings and weekends too. Allegedly, the shuttles come every 5 minutes, but count on them taking longer. Look for the bubble-gum–pink minibuses throughout downtown. Call © **561/833-8873** for more details.

VISITOR INFORMATION The **Palm Beach County Convention and Visitors Bureau,** 1555 Palm Beach Lakes Blvd., Suite 204, West Palm Beach, FL 33401 (© **800/554-PALM** or 561/471-3995; www.palmbeach.com), distributes an informative brochure and will answer questions about visiting the

---

Tips Winter Advisory

Palm Beach's population swells from 20,000 in the summer to 40,000 in the winter. Book early if you plan to visit during the winter months!

The Sport of Kings

The annual ritual of the ponies is played out each season at the posh **Palm Beach Polo and Country Club.** It is one of the world's premier polo grounds and hosts some of the sport's top-rated players. Even if you're not a sports fan, you must attend a match. Although the field is actually on the mainland in an area called Wellington, rest assured that the spectators, and many of the players, are pure Palm Beach. After all, a day at the pony grounds is one of the only good reasons to leave Palm Beach proper. Don't worry, though—you need not be a Vanderbilt or a Kennedy to attend. Matches are open to the public and are surprisingly affordable.

Even if you haven't a clue to how the game is played, you can spend your time people-watching. Stargazers have spotted Prince Charles, Sylvester Stallone, Tommy Lee Jones, Bo Derek, and Ivana Trump in recent years, among others. Dozens of lesser-known royalty, and just plain old characters, keep box seats or chalets right on the grounds.

Incidentally, the point of polo is to keep the other team from getting the ball through your goal. The fast-paced game is divided into six chukkers—like an inning in baseball—each 7 minutes long. There are 3-minute breaks between chukkers except at half time, which lasts 10 minutes. The whole thing is narrated by a British chap, who sounds as though he walked off a *Monty Python* set.

Dress is casual; a navy or tweed blazer over jeans or khakis is standard for men, while neat-looking jeans or a pantsuit is the norm for women. On warmer days, shorts and, of course, a polo shirt are fine, too.

General admission is $6 to $10; box seats cost $10 to $36. Matches are held throughout the week. Schedules vary, but the big names usually compete on Sunday at 3:30pm from January to April. The fields are located at 11809 Polo Club Rd., Wellington, 10 miles west of the Forest Hill Boulevard exit of I-95. Call © **561/793-1440** for tickets and a detailed schedule of events.

Palm Beaches. Ask for a map, as well as a copy of its Arts and Attractions Calendar, a day-to-day guide to art, music, stage, and other events in the county.

WHAT TO SEE & DO
THE BEACHES

Public beaches are a rare commodity in Palm Beach. Most of the island's best beaches are fronted by private estates and are inaccessible to the general public. However, there are a few notable exceptions, including **Midtown Beach** ★★★, east of Worth Avenue, on Ocean Boulevard, between Royal Palm Way and Gulfstream Road, which boasts more than 100 feet of undeveloped beach with no admission cost. This newly widened sandy coast is now a centerpiece and a natural oasis in a town dominated by commercial glitz. There are no restrooms or concessions here, although a lifeguard is on duty until sundown. About 1½ miles north of this area, near Dunbar Street, is a popular hangout for locals, who prefer it to Midtown Beach because of the relaxed and serene atmosphere. Parking is available at meters along Fla. A1A.

At the south end of Palm Beach, there's a less popular but better-equipped beach at **Phipps Ocean Park**. On Ocean Boulevard, between the Southern Boulevard and Lake Avenue causeways, is a large and lively public beach encompassing more than 1,300 feet of groomed and guarded oceanfront. With picnic and recreation areas, as well as plenty of parking, the area is especially good for families. No admission is charged.

AFFORDABLE OUTDOOR ACTIVITIES

BIKING Rent anything from an English single-speed to a full-tilt mountain bike at the **Palm Beach Bicycle Trail Shop**, 223 Sunrise Ave. (© **561/659-4583**). The rates are $8 an hour, $20 a half day (9am–5pm), or $26 for 24 hours, and include a basket and lock (not that a lock is necessary in this fortress of a town). The most scenic route is called the **Lake Trail,** running the length of the island along the Intracoastal Waterway. On it, you'll see some of the most magnificent mansions and grounds and will enjoy the views of downtown West Palm Beach as well as some great wildlife.

GOLF Good golfing abounds in the Palm Beaches, but many of the private club courses are maintained exclusively for the use of their members. Ask at your hotel, or contact the **Palm Beach County Convention and Visitors Bureau** (© **561/471-3995**) for information on which clubs are currently available for play. In the off-season, some private courses open their greens to visitors staying in a Palm Beach County hotel. This "Golf-A-Round" program offers free greens fees (carts are additional); reservations can be made through most major hotels.

One of the state's best public courses is **Emerald Dunes Golf Course**, 2100 Emerald Dunes Dr. in West Palm Beach (© **561/687-1700**). Designed by Tom Fazio, this dramatic 7,006-yard, par-72 course was voted "One of the Best 10 You Can Play" by *Golf* magazine. It is located just off the Florida Turnpike at Okeechobee Boulevard. Bookings are taken up to 30 days ahead. Fees start at $130, including carts.

The **Palm Beach Public Golf Course,** 2345 S. Ocean Blvd. (© **561/547-0598**), a popular public 18-hole course, is a par-54. The course opens at 8am and runs on a first-come, first-served basis. Club rentals are available. Greens fees start at $20 per person.

SCUBA DIVING Year-round warm waters, barrier reefs, and plenty of wrecks make South Florida one of the world's most popular places for diving. One of the best-known artificial reefs in this area is a vintage **Rolls-Royce Silver Shadow,** which was sunk offshore in 1985. Mother Nature has taken her toll, however, and divers can no longer sit in the car, which has been ravaged by time and saltwater.

Call either of the following outfitters for gear and excursions: **Jim Abernethy's Scuba Adventures,** 2116 Avenue B, Riviera Beach (© **561/691-5808**); or **Ocean Sports Scuba Center,** 1736 S. Congress Ave., West Palm Beach (© **561/641-1144**). Abernethy's offers a two-tank dive off Palm Beach for $46 a person, and Ocean Sports charges $45 per person for a two-tank dive in the area.

TENNIS There are hundreds of tennis courts in Palm Beach County. Wherever you are staying, you are bound to be within walking distance of one. In addition to the many hotel tennis courts (see "Accommodations You Can Afford," below), you can play at **Currie Park,** 2400 N. Flagler Dr., West Palm Beach (© **561/835-7025**), a public park with three lighted hard courts. They are free and available on a first-come, first-served basis.

WATER SPORTS Call the **Seaside Activities Station,** 301 Clematis St., West Palm Beach (✆ 561/835-8922), to arrange sailboat, jet-ski, bicycle, kayak, water-ski, and parasail rentals throughout Palm Beach County.

NATURE PRESERVES & ATTRACTIONS

Lion Country Safari ★ Kids More than 1,300 animals on this 500-acre preserve are divided into their re-created indigenous regions, from the East African preserve of the Serengeti to the American West. Elephants, wildebeest, ostriches, American bison, buffalo, watusi, pink flamingos, and many other more unusual species roam the preserve. When the lions are awake, they travel freely throughout the cageless, grassy landscape. In fact, you're the one who's confined in your own car without an escort (no convertibles allowed; you can also rent a van). You're given a detailed informational pamphlet with photos and descriptions and are instructed to obey the 15-mile-per-hour speed limit—unless you see the rhinos charge (a rare occasion), in which case you're encouraged to floor it. To drive the loop takes just over an hour, though you could make a day of just watching the chimpanzees play on their secluded islands. Included in the admission price is Safari World, an amusement park with paddleboats, a carousel, miniature golf, and a nursery for baby animals born in the preserve. Picnics are encouraged, and camping is available (call for reservations). The best time to go is late afternoon right before the park closes when they herd up all the animals; plus, it's much cooler then, so the lions are more active.

Southern Blvd. W. at S.R. 80, West Palm Beach. ✆ 561/793-1084, or 561/793-9797 for camping reservations. www.lioncountrysafari.com. Admission $16.95 adults, $14.95 seniors, $12.95 children 3–9; free for children under 3. Van rental is $8 per hr. Daily 10am–5:30pm (last vehicle admitted at 4:30pm). From I-95, exit on Southern Blvd. Go west for about 18 miles.

Palm Beach Zoo at Dreher Park ★ Kids If you want animals, go to Lion Country Safari (above). Unlike big-city zoos, this intimate 23-acre park is more like a stroll than an all-day excursion. It does features about 500 animals representing more than 100 different species. A special monkey exhibit and petting zoo are favorites with kids. Stroller and wagon rentals are available.

1301 Summit Blvd. (east of I-95 between Southern and Forest Hill blvds.). ✆ 561/547-WILD. Fax 561/585-6085. www.palmbeachzoo.org. Admission $7.50 adults, $6 seniors, $5 children 3–12; children under 3 free. Daily 9am–5pm. Closed Thanksgiving.

Rapids Water Park ★ Kids It may not be on the same grand scale as the theme parks in Orlando, but Rapids is a great way to cool off on a hot day. There are 12 acres of water rides, including a children's area and miniature golf course.

6566 N. Military Trail, West Palm Beach (1 mile west of I-95 on Military between 45th St. [Exit 54] and Blue Heron Blvd. [Exit 55]). ✆ 561/842-8756. www.rapidswaterpark.com. Admission $17–$24 per person; free for ages 2 and under. Open mid-Mar to Sept. Mon–Fri 10am–5pm; Sat–Sun 10am–6pm.

SEEING THE SIGHTS

Flagler Museum ★★★ The Gilded Age is preserved in this luxurious mansion, commissioned by Standard Oil tycoon Henry Flagler as a wedding present to his third wife. *Whitehall,* also known as the "Taj Mahal of North America," is a classically columned Edwardian-style mansion containing 55 rooms, including a Louis XIV music room and art gallery, a Louis XV ballroom, and 14 guest suites outfitted with original antique European furnishings. Out back, climb aboard "The Rambler," Mr. Flagler's private, restored railroad car. Allow at least 1½ hours to tour the stunning grounds and interior. School and group tours are available, but for the most part, this is a self-guided museum.

One Whitehall Way (at Cocoanut Row and Whitehall Way), Palm Beach. © 561/655-2833. www.flagler.org. Admission $8 adults, $3 children ages 6–12. Tues–Sat 10am–5pm; Sun noon–5pm.

Norton Museum of Art ★★★

Since a 1997 expansion doubled the Norton's space, the museum has gained even more prominence in the art world. It is world famous for its prestigious permanent collection and top temporary exhibitions. The museum's major collections are divided geographically. The American galleries contain major works by Edward Hopper, Georgia O'Keeffe, and Jackson Pollock. The French collection contains Impressionist and post-Impressionist paintings by Cézanne, Degas, Gauguin, Matisse, Monet, Picasso, Pissarro, and Renoir. And the Chinese collection contains more then 200 bronzes, jades, and ceramics, as well as a collection of monumental Buddhist sculptures.

1451 S. Olive Ave., West Palm Beach. © 561/832-5196. Fax 561/659-4689. www.norton.org. Admission $6 adults, $2 ages 13–21; free for children 12 and under. Mon–Sat 10am–5pm; Sun 1–5pm. Closed Mon May–Oct and all major holidays. Take I-95 to Exit 52 (Okeechobee Blvd. E.). Travel east on Okeechobee to Dixie Hwy., then south a half mile to the Norton. Parking may be accessed through entrances on Dixie Hwy. and S. Olive Ave.

Playmobil Fun Park ★★

In a child's mind, it doesn't get any better than this. The 17,000-square-foot Playmobil Fun Park is housed in a replica castle and loaded with themed areas for imaginative play: a medieval village, a western town, a fantasy dollhouse, and more. Plus, there are two water-filled tables on which kids can play with the Playmobil boats. Tech-minded kids could get bored, but toddlers (and up to age 5 or so) will love this place. You *could* spend hours here and not spend a penny, but parents beware: Everything is available for purchase.

8031 N. Military Trail, Palm Beach Gardens. © 800/351-8697 or 561/691-9880. Fax 561/691-9517. www.playmobil.com. Admission $1. Mon–Sat 10am–6pm; Sun noon–5pm. From I-95, go north to Palm Beach Lakes Blvd., then west to Military Trail. Turn left, and the park is about a mile down on the right.

Unreal Estate

No trip to Palm Beach is complete without at least a glimpse of **Mar-A-Lago,** 1100 S. Ocean Blvd., Palm Beach, the stately residence of Donald Trump, the 21st century's answer to Jay Gatsby. In 1985, Trump purchased Mar-A-Lago, the former estate of cereal heiress Marjorie Merriweather Post, for what was considered a meager $8 million (for a fully furnished beachfront property of this stature, it was a relative bargain, actually) to the great consternation of locals, who feared that he would turn the place into a casino. Instead, Trump, who resides in a portion of the palace, opened the house to the public—for a price, of course—as a tony country club (membership fee: $100,000). Infinitely more interesting than any of Trump's other real estate acquisitions, Mar-A-Lago, Spanish for "from sea to lake," has a history that's priceless.

While there are currently no tours open to the public, you can glimpse the gorgeous manse as you cross the bridge from West Palm Beach into Palm Beach. Its website (www.pbol.com/maralago/tour.html) offers photos, a calendar of events, and more details than you'd ever care to know.

SHOPPING

No matter what your budget is, be sure to take a stroll down **Worth Avenue**, "the Rodeo Drive of the South." Between South Ocean Boulevard and Cocoanut Row, there are more than 200 boutiques, posh shops, art galleries, and upscale restaurants. The prices here make this a window-shopping-only option for the most part, but it's a terrific place to check out the local scene. If you want to fit in, dress as if you were going to an elegant luncheon and not to the mall down the street.

City Place, 222 Lakeview Ave., West Palm Beach (© 561/835-0862), is a $550-million, Mediterranean-style shopping, dining, and entertainment complex that's responsible for revitalizing what was once a lifeless downtown West Palm Beach. Among the 78 mostly-chain stores are Macy's, FAO Schwarz, Benetton (which has an in-line skating track inside), Armani Exchange, Pottery Barn, and SEE eyewear. Restaurants include a Ghiradelli ice cream shop, Legal Seafood, City Cellar Wine Bar and Grill, and Cheesecake Factory. Best of all is the Muvico Parisian, a 20-screen movie theater where you can wine and dine while watching a feature.

Elsewhere, downtown West Palm Beach has a scant amount of interesting boutiques along Clematis Street. In addition to a large and well-organized bookstore, **Clematis Street Books,** 206 Clematis (© 561/832-2302), you'll find a few used-record stores, clothing shops, and several art galleries.

The **Palm Beach Outlet Center,** 5700 Okeechobee Blvd. (3 miles west of I-95), West Palm Beach, is the most elegant outlet mall we've ever seen. Upscale clothing, luggage, and shoes are offered at bargain prices in lushly decorated surroundings. The fully enclosed mall also sports a food court.

ACCOMMODATIONS YOU CAN AFFORD

A few of the larger hotel chains operating in Palm Beach include the **Palm Beach Marriott/Fairfield Inn and Suites,** at 2870 S. Ocean Blvd. (© 800/654-2000 or 561/582-2581), which is across the street from the beach and offers doubles for a year-round rate of $70. An excellent and affordable alternative right in the middle of Palm Beach's commercial section is a condominium that operates as a hotel, too: the **Palm Beach Hotel,** at 235 Sunrise Ave. (between County Rd. and Bradley Place, across the street from the Publix supermarket; © 561/659-7794). With winter prices starting at about $105, this clean and comfortable accommodation is a great option for those looking for the rare bargain in Palm Beach.

In West Palm Beach, the chain hotels are mostly located on the main arteries close to the highways and a short drive from the activities in downtown. They include a **Best Western,** 1800 Palm Beach Lakes Blvd. (© 800/331-9569 or 561/683-8810), and, just down the road, a **Comfort Inn,** 1901 Palm Lakes Blvd. (© 800/221-2222 or 561/689-6100). The Best Western charges $95 for a double in winter and $65 in the off-season, and Comfort Inn charges $90 for a double year-round. Further south is the **Parkview Motor Lodge,** 4710 S. Dixie Hwy., just south of Southern Boulevard (© 561/833-4644). This 28-room, single-story motel is the best of the many motels along Dixie Highway (U.S. 1). With rates starting at $50 for a room with television, air-conditioning, and telephone, you can't ask for more.

For other options, try **Palm Beach Accommodations** (© 800/543-SWIM).

Beachcomber Apartment Motel ★★ It's not just the bright pink building that makes this two-story beachfront motel stand out. For more than 35 years, the

Beachcomber has been bringing sanity to pricey Palm Beach by offering a good standard of accommodation at reasonable prices. Squeezed between beachfront high-rises, the motel is located on a 300-foot private beach, adjacent to Lake Worth Beach and a short drive from Worth Avenue shops and local attractions. Every room has two double beds, large closets, and distinctive green-and-white tropical-style furnishings; some have kitchenettes. The most expensive have balconies overlooking the ocean. The bathrooms are basic, and amenities are limited.

3024 S. Ocean Blvd., Palm Beach, FL 33480. © 800/833-7122 or 561/585-4646. Fax 561/547-9438. 45 units. Winter $95–$250 double; off-season $55–$130 double. AE, DISC, MC, V. From I-95, exit 10th Ave. N. Head east to Federal Hwy. and turn right. Continue to Lake Ave. and turn left. Go over the bridge and turn right at the first traffic light. **Amenities:** Large pool; coin-operated laundry. *In room:* A/C, TV, kitchenettes in some.

Heron Cay *Value* This charming little bed-and-breakfast is minutes away from the hustle and bustle of Palm Beach but is located on its own private island. All rooms open onto a wraparound second-floor balcony. For the adventurous, there's a slide from the second floor to the large tiled mosaic pool! There's also a dock for those who want to arrive by boat. The best deals going are the two three-bedroom, two-bathroom cottages, one with its own pool. Both sleep up to eight people, making them a real steal at $210 to $250. For a little peace and quiet in an Old Florida–style home, this is the place to be. Note that at press time, Heron Cay was up for sale, either as a B&B or a private residence, so to avoid ending up on a stranger's property with your luggage, call in advance to make sure it remains a B&B.

15106 Palmwood Rd., Palm Beach Gardens, FL 33410. © 561/744-6315 or 561/744-2188. www.heron cay.com. 4 units, 2 cottages (some with shower only). Winter $115–$180 single or double, $250 cottage; off-season $95–$150 single or double, $210 cottage. Extra person $10. Cash or checks preferred. MC, V. No children allowed. Take I-95 to Donald Ross Rd. Pass Alt. A1A. Turn left on Palmwood Rd. The resort is 1 mile down on the right. **Amenities:** Pool. *In room:* A/C, TV.

Hibiscus House ★★ *Finds* Inexpensive bed-and-breakfasts are rare in Southeast Florida, making the Hibiscus House, one of the area's firsts, a true find. Located a few miles from the coast in a quiet residential neighborhood, this 1920s-era B&B is filled with handsome antiques and tapestries in luxurious fabrics. Every room has its own private terrace or balcony. The Red Room has a fabulous new bathroom with Jacuzzi. The backyard, a peaceful retreat, has been transformed into a tropical garden, complete with heated swimming pool and lounge chairs. You'll also find plenty of pretty areas to enjoy inside; one little sitting room is wrapped in glass and is stocked with playing cards and board games. *Beware:* Breakfast portions are enormous. The gourmet creations are as filling as they are beautiful. Ask for any special requests in advance; owners Raleigh Hill and Colin Rayer will be happy to oblige.

501 30th St., West Palm Beach, FL 33407. © 800/203-4927 or 561/863-5633. Fax 561/863-5633. www.hibiscushouse.com. 8 units. Winter $105–$260 double; off-season $75–$180 double. Rates include breakfast. AE, MC, V. Pets accepted. From I-95, exit onto Palm Beach Lakes Blvd. E. and continue 4 miles. Turn left onto Flagler Dr. and continue for about 20 blocks. Then turn left onto 30th St. **Amenities:** Heated pool; concierge. *In room:* A/C, TV, hair dryer.

Hotel Biba ★★ *Finds* As West Palm Beach comes into its own as far as nightlife is concerned, it was only a matter of time before a hip boutique hotel made its appearance in the historic El Cid neighborhood, located 1 mile from City Place and nightlife-heavy Clematis Street. The very cool Hotel Biba answers the call for an inexpensive, chic hotel for young hipsters. Housed in a renovated Colonial-style 1940s motor lodge, Biba has been remarkably updated on the inside by de rigueur designer Barbara Hulanicki and features a sleek and chic lobby with the requisite hip hotel bar, the Biba Bar, a gorgeously landscaped outdoor pool area with Asian gardens, and a reflection pond. Rooms are equally fabulous, with private patios, mosaic tile floors, custom-made mahogany furniture, Egyptian cotton linens, down pillows, and exquisite bathroom products. *A word of advice, however:* The hotel is not exactly soundproof; rooms may be cloistered by fence and gardens, but they are still extremely close to a major thoroughfare. Ask for one that's on the quieter Belvedere Road as opposed to those facing S. Olive Avenue.

320 Belvedere Rd., West Palm Beach, FL 33405. © 561/832-0094. Fax 561/833-7848. www.hotelbiba.com. 43 units. Year-round $79–$179 double. **Amenities:** Restaurant, lounge; outdoor pool; concierge. *In room:* A/C, TV, dataport, hair dryer.

The Hummingbird Bed and Breakfast ★

Newly renovated and in the center of not-so-bustling, but charming, downtown Lake Worth, this 1930s-era building with black and white awnings and hanging, potted plants is a throwback to the old days, but inside is hardly old or stale. Hand-laid tile floors, glass blocks, and cozy rooms with dark wood and four-poster beds are a warm and welcome distraction from the typical, tropical Florida decor ubiquitous in other hotels.

631 Lucerne Ave., Lake Worth, FL 33460. © 561/582-3224. Fax 561/540-8817. www.hummingbird hotel.com. 23 units (21 with private bathroom). Winter $35 single, $65–$95 double; off-season $29 single, $49–$85 double. Rates include breakfast in season. AE, MC, V. Take 10th Ave. exit off 95 to Dixie, turn right on Dixie to Lake Ave., turn left on Lake to K St., and turn left on K, which crosses Lucerne. **Amenities:** Laundry. *In room:* A/C, TV.

Sea Lord Hotel

A very good value on Florida's priciest island beach, this aged oceanfront hotel looks like a retirement home, circa 1950, and the dated furnishings inside concur. The rooms, however, are very clean and pleasant enough, fitted with old wooden beds and bureaus, small refrigerators, and no-frills tiled bathrooms. The best rooms are located in the five-story main building and have a patio or balcony. Many face the sand. The least desirable rooms are in the smaller south wing and have no views. The Sea Lord's exceptionally friendly employees staff the front desk 24 hours. Beach towels and lounge chairs are always available for use on the sand or at the well-maintained swimming pool. A small poolside cafe serves three American-style meals daily.

2315 S. Ocean Blvd., Palm Beach, FL 33480. © 561/582-1461. 40 units. Winter $97–$147 single or double; off-season $49–$94 single or double. Extra person $10. DISC, MC, V. **Amenities:** Cafe; heated freshwater pool. *In room:* A/C, TV, kitchens in efficiencies.

Tropical Gardens Bed & Breakfast ★★

A quaint little place, the former West Palm Beach B&B is a compact and cozy home with just four individually styled, small guest rooms. The tropically inspired interior is decorated with plenty of knickknacks, and it's a bright and clean place with lots of windows. Two of the bedrooms are located in the main house. The front room has a queen-size bed, white wicker furnishings, and a large carpet on hardwood floors. The room's bathroom is not shared, but it is a few steps down the hall (bathrobes are provided). Also in the main house is a cozy pink room with a tiny private bathroom with little counter space. Two cottage rooms located out back provide more privacy and more amenities, one with a full kitchenette. Other guests share a full kitchen in the main house. A continental breakfast is served each morning from 8:30 to 10:30am, and a glass of wine is offered each evening. The inn is entirely nonsmoking.

419 32nd St., West Palm Beach, FL 33407. © 800/736-4064 or 561/848-4064. Fax 407/842-1688. www.tropicalgardensbandb.com. 4 units. Winter $80–$125 single or double; off-season $70–$95 single or

double. Rates include large continental breakfast. Weekly rates available. AE, DC, MC, V. From I-95, take Exit 53 east (Palm Beach Lakes Blvd.) to Flagler Dr. Turn left at the stop sign (30th St.); continue to Poinsetta (1 block down); turn right. Turn left on 32nd St. **Amenities:** Pool; complimentary bikes; limited room service; dry cleaning. *In room:* A/C, TV in all, VCR, fridge, microwave in cottage rooms (kitchenette in 1).

SUPER-CHEAP SLEEPS

ParkView Motor Lodge The best of the many hotels along shabby U.S. 1, this single-story, clean, family-run spot is a real find in the Palm Beaches. There's no pool, but there are charming touches, like the colored sheets and towels in the rooms, and the bougainvillea that grows in pretty terra-cotta pots along the hallways. The nondescript rooms all have refrigerators, and the location is ideal, only 3 miles from downtown.

4710 S. Dixie Hwy., West Palm Beach, FL 33405. **561/833-4444.** Fax 561/833-4644. 28 units (some with shower only, some with tub only). Winter $82–$98 single or double; off-season $56–$70 single or double. Rates include continental breakfast. AE, DC, DISC, MC, V. Extra person $8 in winter, $5 off-season. *In room:* A/C, TV, fridge.

WORTH A SPLURGE

Palm Beach Historic Inn *Kids* Built in 1923, the Palm Beach Historic Inn is an area landmark located within walking distance of Worth Avenue, the beach, and several good restaurants. The small lobby is filled with antiques, books, and magazines, all of which add to the homey feel of this intimate bed-and-breakfast. In your room, wine, fruit, snacks, tea, and cookies ensure that you won't go hungry—never mind the excellent continental breakfast that is brought to you daily. All the rooms are on the second floor and are uniquely decorated, featuring hardwood floors, down comforters, fluffy bathrobes, and plenty of nice-smelling toiletries. Gone are the frills, floral prints, and plethora of lace that once made this inn feel like staying at your grandmother's house. What you'll find here, thanks to new innkeepers who took over in July 2001, is a casual elegance that's comfortable for everyone. A baby grand piano and guitars for the musically inclined, as well as videotapes to keep the kids entertained, have also been added. No smoking is allowed here.

365 S. County Rd., Palm Beach, FL 33480. **561/832-4009.** Fax 561/832-6255. www.palmbeach historicinn.com. 13 units. Winter $150–$325 double; off-season $95–$175 double. Rates include continental breakfast. Children stay free in parents' room. Small pets accepted. AE, MC, V. *In room:* A/C, TV/VCR, fridge, hair dryer.

OFF-SEASON BARGAINS

Heart of Palm Beach Hotel It's this hotel's location—in the heart of Palm Beach, within walking distance of Worth Avenue shopping, and just half a block from the beach—that is its greatest asset. Ongoing renovations since the 1990s have improved the patio space, as well as the rooms in the hotel's two buildings, but there's nothing particularly inspiring about this hotel's rather bland atmosphere and decor. A new exterior paint job and refurbished landscaping have improved the hotel's appearance slightly, however. Most rooms are decorated with modest but new furnishings and fittings in a colorful contemporary style; all come with a balcony or a patio. The tiled bathrooms are small, clean, and functional. Additionally, the staff is particularly outgoing and will help guests plan outings and itineraries. A clubby restaurant serves a mediocre selection of salads, sandwiches, pastas, and cocktails.

160 Royal Palm Way, Palm Beach, FL 33480. **800/523-5377** or 561/655-5600. Fax 561/832-1201. www. heartofpalmbeach.com. 88 units. Winter $209–$359 double; off-season $99–$209 double. AE, DC, MC, V. Free parking. From I-95, exit onto Okeechobee Blvd. E. and continue over the Royal Palm Bridge onto Royal Palm

Way. Pets are accepted. **Amenities:** Restaurant; heated pool; access to nearby health club; bike rental; concierge; limited room service; babysitting; laundry/dry cleaning. *In room:* A/C, TV, dataport, fridge, hair dryer.

Plaza Inn ★★   This three-story, family-run bed-and-breakfast–style inn located 1 block from the beach is as understated and luxurious as the guests it hosts. From the simple and elegant flower arrangements in the marble lobby to the well-worn period antiques haphazardly placed throughout, the Plaza Inn, whose exterior was renovated in 2001, has the look of studied nonchalance. The courtyard, with its waterfalls and pool, and the intimate piano bar are just two examples of the inn's infinite charms. A small staff is remarkably hospitable and knowledgeable about the island's inner workings. Each uniquely decorated room is dressed with quality furnishings, several with carved four-poster beds, hand-crocheted spreads, and lace curtains. The bathrooms, renovated in 2000, are lovely if quite small, and the wall-mounted air-conditioners can be noisy when they are needed in the warm months. Choose a corner room or one overlooking the small pool deck for the best light.

215 Brazilian Ave., Palm Beach, FL 33480. © **800/233-2632** or 561/832-8666. Fax 561/835-8776. www.plazainnpalmbeach.com. 48 units. Winter $225–$375 double; off-season $105–$195 double. Rates include breakfast. AE, MC, V. From I-95, exit onto Okeechobee Blvd. E. and cross the Intracoastal Waterway. Turn right onto Cocoanut Row, then left onto Brazilian Ave. Small pets permitted. **Amenities:** Restaurant, lounge; heated outdoor pool; exercise room; access to nearby health club ($15 per day); Jacuzzi; bike rental; concierge; secretarial services; limited room service; in-room massage; babysitting; laundry/dry cleaning. *In room:* A/C, TV, dataport, fridge, coffeemaker, hair dryer on request.

GREAT DEALS ON DINING

Palm Beach has some of the area's swankiest restaurants. Thanks to the development of downtown West Palm Beach, however, there is also a great selection of trendier, less expensive spots. Dress here is slightly more formal than in most other areas of Florida: Men wear blazers, and women generally put on modest dresses or chic suits when they dine out, even in the oppressively hot days of summer.

Amici ★ *Overrated* ITALIAN   This is one of those restaurants in which the scene is tastier than the cuisine. An upper-crusty Palm Beach set tends to convene here and consistently raves about what can only be considered above-average, overpriced Italian food. The best item on the entire menu is gnocchi with white truffle oil, fontina cheese, and spinach. Everything else is fairly standard: grilled sandwiches, pastas with rustic sauces, pizzas, grilled shrimp, and fish. Despite its less than stellar food, it's always crowded and very noisy.

288 S. County Rd. (at Royal Palm Way), Palm Beach. © **561/832-0201**. Reservations strongly recommended on weekends. Main courses $18–$27; pastas and pizzas $8–$19. AE, DC, MC, V. Mon–Thurs 11:30am–3pm and 5:30–10:30pm; Fri–Sat 11:30am–3pm and 5:30–11pm; Sun 5:30–10:30pm.

Montezuma ★★ MEXICAN   Up to now, 50 seats have managed to accommodate patient patrons who wait for some of the freshest burritos, tacos, mariscos, and tortillas in Palm Beach County. Try any of the huge egg platters for breakfast like Montezuma Chamulan, scrambled eggs with cheese and avocado, or a seafood omelet with shrimp, octopus, and squid. Eggs come with refried beans, chilaquiles, and fresh corn tortillas. Lunch is the most popular meal here, when you can get huge enchiladas, salads, tacos, and enormous platters of steak, chicken, or pork dishes. Also offered is authentic tongue in green sauce.

5607 S. Dixie Hwy. (between Forest Hill and Southern blvds.), West Palm Beach. © **561/586-7974**. Main courses $4–$12. AE, DC, DISC, MC, V. Weekdays 7am–10pm; weekends 7am–11pm.

SUPER-CHEAP EATS

Green's Pharmacy ★ *Value* AMERICAN   This neighborhood corner pharmacy offers one of the best meal deals in Palm Beach. Both breakfast and lunch are served coffee-shop style either at a Formica bar or at plain tables placed on a black-and-white checkerboard floor. Breakfast specials include eggs and omelets served with home fries and bacon, sausage, or corned-beef hash. At lunch, the grill serves burgers and sandwiches, as well as ice-cream sodas and milk shakes, to a loyal crowd of pastel-clad Palm Beachers.

151 N. County Rd., Palm Beach. ⓒ 561/832-0304. Fax 561/832-6502. Breakfast $2–$5; burgers and sandwiches $3–$6; soups and salads $2–$7. AE, DISC, MC, V. Mon–Sat 7am–5pm; Sun 7am–3pm.

John G's ★ AMERICAN   This coffee shop is the most popular in the county. For decades, John G's has been attracting huge breakfast crowds; lines run out the door (on weekends, all the way down the block). Stop in for some good, greasy-spoon–style food served in heaping portions right on the beachfront. This place is known for fresh and tasty fish and chips and its selection of creative omelets and grill specials.

10 S. Ocean Blvd., Lake Worth. ⓒ 561/585-9860. www.johngs.com. Reservations not accepted. Breakfast $3–$8.50; lunch $5–$14. No credit cards. Daily 7am–3pm. From the Florida Tpk., take the Lake Worth exit and head toward the ocean.

Sandwiches by the Sea SANDWICHES   Large classic subs that put Subway to great shame, healthful salads, and pita pockets for the price of a meal at McDonald's make this little narrow take-out shop a real find in pricey Palm Beach. Breakfast choices are limited to fruit salads, muffins, breads, and croissants, but lunch choices include hearty homemade soups and overstuffed sandwiches. Choose the daily special sandwich and a large drink for about $4. Fresh white meat chicken salad and tuna are favorites. Also tempting are frozen yogurt treats, brownies, and cookies. This is the place to come for picnic supplies or a super-bargain lunch to enjoy at a tiny counter.

363 S. County Rd., Palm Beach. ⓒ 561/655-7911. Salads and hoagies $4–$6. No credit cards. Mon–Sat 9am–4pm.

TooJay's DELI   This simple and predictable restaurant and take-out spot is a favorite with locals and out-of-towners who want good old-fashioned deli fare. It is so popular, in fact, that TooJay's now has more than eight locations throughout South Florida. This is no Carnegie Deli, but by South Florida deli standards, the food is excellent. All the classic sandwiches are available: hot pastrami, roast beef, turkey, chicken, chopped liver, egg salad, and more. Comfort food in the form of huge portions of stuffed cabbage, chicken pot pie, beef brisket, and sautéed onions and chicken livers is sure to satisfy.

313 Royal Poinciana Plaza (3 miles east of I-95, off Exit 52A), Palm Beach. ⓒ 561/659-7232. Reservations not accepted. Main courses $9–$13; lunch $6–$10. AE, DC, MC, V. Daily 8am–9pm.

WORTH A SPLURGE

Chuck & Harold's Cafe AMERICAN   This old standby delivers predictable American fare at somewhat inflated prices. But remember, you are paying for one of the area's best people-watching perches. Main dishes include fresh grilled or broiled fish, boiled lobster, and a small variety of straightforward homemade pasta and chicken dishes. If you happen to visit during the season for stone crabs, order them. The crab claws are steamed or chilled and served with a traditional honey-mustard sauce. Considering Chuck and Harold's status as a Waspy enclave, its surprise treat is excellent matzo ball soup!

207 Royal Poinciana Way (corner of S. County Rd.), Palm Beach. ✆ 561/659-1440. Fax 561/659-2197. Reservations recommended. Main courses $13–$28. AE, DC, DISC, MC, V. Mon–Thurs 7:30am–midnight; Fri–Sat 7:30am–1am; Sun 8am–11pm.

Rhythm Café ★ *Finds* ECLECTIC AMERICAN   This funky hole-in-the-wall is where those in the know come to eat some of West Palm Beach's most laid-back gourmet food. On the hand-written, photocopied menu (which changes daily), you'll always find a fish specialty accompanied by a hefty dose of greens and garnishes. Also reliably outstanding is the sautéed medallion of beef tenderloin, served on a bed of arugula with a tangy rosemary vinaigrette. Salads and soups are a great bargain, since portions are relatively large and the display usually spectacular. The kitschy decor of this tiny cafe comes complete with vinyl tablecloths and a changing display of paintings by local amateurs. Young, handsome waiters are attentive but not solicitous. The old drugstore where the restaurant recently relocated features an original 1950s lunch counter and stools.

3800 S. Dixie Hwy., West Palm Beach. ✆ 561/833-3406. Reservations recommended on weekends. Main courses $12–$31. AE, DISC, MC, V. Tues–Sat 6–10pm. Sun Dec–Mar 5:30–9pm. From I-95, exit east on Southern Blvd. Go 1 block north of Southern Blvd.; restaurant is on the right. Closed in Sept.

Testa's *Kids* AMERICAN   On one of the island's ritziest streets, this large, upscale diner has been serving hearty breakfasts, lunches, and dinners to a picky Palm Beach crowd since 1921. Prices aren't dirt cheap, but the selection, quality, and service make this a great choice. It's standard American fare with a number of recommendable Italian specialties thrown in, too. A full bar, huge selection of salads, pizzas, and a good-size children's menu rounds out this very equitable menu. Look for discount coupons, sunset menus from 4pm until 6pm, and happy hour specials, too.

221 Royal Poinciana Way (between Flagler and A1A), Palm Beach. ✆ 561/832-0992. Reservations recommended. Main courses $15–$30. AE, DC, DISC, MC, V. Daily 7am–11pm or midnight.

THE PALM BEACHES AFTER DARK

A decade-old project to revitalize downtown West Palm Beach has finally become a reality, with **Clematis Street** at its heart. Artist lofts, sidewalk cafes, bars, restaurants, consignment shops, and galleries dot the street from Flagler Drive to Rosemary Avenue, creating a hot spot for a night out, especially on weekends when yuppies mingle with stylish Euros and disheveled artists. Every Thursday night is a mob scene of 20- and 30-somethings who come out for "Clematis by Night." Each week features a different rock, blues, or reggae band plus an art show. Vendors sell food and drinks, and the street's bars and restaurants are packed. It is a bit raucous at times, but fun. Minors unaccompanied by their guardians are not permitted in the downtown area around Clematis Street after 10pm on weeknights and after 11pm on weekend nights.

Over the bridge, it's a completely different world. Palm Beach is much quieter and better known for its rather private society balls and estate parties, though you might stake out some of the area's livelier restaurants or upscale hotels to locate a subtle bar scene.

BARS & CLUBS
West Palm Beach

Bliss Lounge   With its techno music and VIP rooms, this West Palm club seems like it belongs in the velvet-roped world of South Beach. Hours are Tuesday to Saturday 10pm to 4am. 313 Clematis St. ✆ 561/833-1444. $7 cover. No cover before midnight.

> **Fun Fact** **Equal Gambling Rights**
> ER Bradley's is named for a legendary Palm Beach gambler and horse racer, who opened the first casino to ever allow women to gamble.

E.R. Bradley's What used to be a swank saloon on the island of Palm Beach is now a very casual, friendly indoor/outdoor bar in downtown West Palm, attracting a mixed crowd. The later-night bar scene is a real draw. If you're hungry, try the "crab bomb," Maryland lump crabmeat baked in a light cream sauce with steamed vegetables. Hours are Sunday to Wednesday 8am to 3am; Thursday to Saturday 8am to 4 am. 104 Clematis St. © 561/833-3520. No cover.

Liquid Room Former South Beach hot spot Liquid may have evaporated (and subsequently reopened by name alone, in a new space that's not nearly as haute as the original) from the scene, but this Clematis Street location, which shares the building with Bliss (located upstairs; see above), is flowing with Palm Beach club kids who revel in the fact that they finally have a chic, celebrity-saturated dance club to call their own. Hours are Thursday to Saturday 10pm to 4am. 313 Clematis St. © 561/655-2332. $10 cover.

Lost Weekend I'm not sure whether it's the local artists' displays, the pool tables, or the more than 200 beers from around the world sold here, but for some reason, many of Palm Beach's hipsters love losing themselves in this place, which is actually quite nice. Hours are Tuesday to Friday from 4:30pm. 115 S. Olive Ave. © 561/832-3452. No cover.

Monkey Club This tacky yet trendy Caribbean-inspired dance club is 7,500 square feet of wall-to-wall, well-dressed revelers. Theme nights are popular here, from ladies' nights to the classier version of the wet T-shirt contest—the Miss Hawaiian Tropic Model Search. Hours are Tuesday and Thursday 8pm to 3am; Friday to Saturday 8pm to 4am. 219 Clematis St. © 561/833-6500. Cover up to $10.

Respectable Street Café This is one of the premier live music venues in South Florida. In addition to the requisite DJs, this grungy bar features an impressive lineup of alternative music acts. The café's plain storefront exterior belies its funky high-ceilinged interior, decorated with large black booths, psychedelic wall murals, and a large checkerboard-tile dance floor. Hours are Wednesday to Saturday 9pm to 4am. 518 Clematis St. © 561/832-9999. Cover varies.

Palm Beach

Brazilian Court Bistro and Rio Bar Despite its location in the ritzy Brazilian Court Hotel's bistro, the bar here is surprisingly laid-back and unpretentious, featuring a mostly older crowd of couples and, at times, swinging singles. Open daily 7am to 10:30pm. 301 Australian Ave. © 561/655-7740. No cover.

The Leopard Lounge *Finds* *The Flintstones* meet *Dynasty* at the spotty lounge in the Chesterfield Hotel, in which the carpeting, tablecloths, and wait staff's waistcoats are all in leopard print. There's live music every night from Cole Porter to swing. The crowd's a bit older here, but younger couples and a celebrity or two often find their way here, which makes for an amusing scene. Open daily 6pm to 2am. 363 Cocoanut Row. © 561/659-5800. No cover.

Ta-boo Ta-boo is reminiscent of an upscale TGI Fridays (with food that's about on the same level)—one that caters to a well-heeled crowd—with lots of greenery, a fireplace, and a somewhat cheesy Southwestern decor. But make no mistake, Ta-boo is not about the food: This stellar after-dinner spot is where bejeweled socialites spill out of fancy cars to show off their best Swarovski and salsa. Just find somewhere else to eat first. 221 Worth Ave., Palm Beach. © **561/835-3500.** Sun–Thurs 11:30am–11pm; Fri–Sat 11:30am–1am.

THE PERFORMING ARTS

With a number of dedicated patrons and enthusiastic supporters of the arts, this area happily boasts many good venues for those craving culture. Check the *Palm Beach Post* or the *Palm Beach Daily News* for up-to-date listings and reviews.

The **Raymond F. Kravis Center for the Performing Arts,** 701 Okeechobee Blvd., West Palm Beach (© **561/832-7469**; www.kravis.org), is the area's largest and most active performance space. With a huge curved-glass facade and more than 2,500 seats in two lushly decorated indoor spaces, plus a new outdoor amphitheater, The Kravis, as it is known, stages more than 300 performances each year. Phone or check their website for a current schedule of Palm Beach's best music, dance, and theater.

4 Jupiter ★★ & Northern Palm Beach County

20 miles N of Palm Beach, 81 miles N of Miami, 60 miles N of Fort Lauderdale

While Burt Reynolds is Jupiter's hometown hero (and Celine Dion just built a sprawling manse there, too), the true stars of quaint Jupiter are the beautiful beaches. In the springtime, you can also catch a glimpse of the St. Louis Cardinals and the Montreal Expos during their spring training seasons. North Palm Beach County's other towns—Tequesta, Juno Beach, North Palm Beach, Palm Beach Gardens, and Singer Island—are inviting for tourists who want to enjoy the many outdoor activities that make this area so popular with retirees, seasonal residents, and families.

ESSENTIALS

GETTING THERE The quickest route from West Palm Beach to Jupiter is on the Florida Turnpike or the sometimes congested I-95. You can also take a slower but more scenic coastal route, U.S. 1 or Fla. A1A. Since Jupiter is so close to Palm Beach, it's easy to fly into the **Palm Beach International Airport** (© **561/471-7420**; see "Essentials," in section 3 of this chapter) and rent a car there. The drive should take less than half an hour.

VISITOR INFORMATION A **Visitor Information Center** is located between I-95 and the Florida Turnpike at 8020 Indiantown Rd. in Jupiter (© **561/575-4636**; www.jupiterfloridausa.com), and is open from 9am to 6pm daily.

WHAT TO SEE & DO
THE BEACHES

The farther north you head from populated Palm Beach, the more peaceful and pristine the coast becomes. Just a few miles north of the bustle, castles and condominiums give way to wide open space and public parkland, and dozens of recommendable spots.

John D. MacArthur Beach ★★★ is a spectacular beach that preserves the natural heritage of subtropical coastal habitat that once covered Southeast Florida. This state park has a remarkable 4,000-square-foot Nature Center with exhibits, displays, and a video interpreting the barrier island's plant and animal communities. Dominating a large portion of Singer Island, the barrier island just north of Palm Beach, this beach has lengthy frontage on both the Atlantic

Ocean and Lake Worth Cove. It's a great area for hiking, swimming, and sunning. Restrooms and showers are available. To reach the park from the mainland, cross the Intracoastal Waterway on Blue Heron Boulevard and turn north on Ocean Boulevard.

Jupiter Inlet meets the ocean at **Dubois Park** ★★, a 29-acre beach popular with families. The shallow waters and sandy shore are perfect for kids, while adults can play in the rougher swells of the lifeguarded inlet. A footbridge leads to **Ocean Beach,** an area of the park popular with windsurfers and surfers. There's a short fishing pier here and plenty of trees shading barbecue grills and picnic tables. Visitors can also explore the Dubois Pioneer Home, a small house situated atop a shell mound built by the Jaega Indians. Made of cypress wood, the home was built in 1898 by Harry Dubois, a citrus worker, as a wedding gift to his wife Susan, whose pictures are still in the house. You will see an original butter churn and pump sewing machine in the living room, and the dining room and bedroom are almost straight out of *Little House on the Prairie.* The park entrance is on Dubois Road, about a mile south of the junction of U.S. 1 and Fla. A1A.

AFFORDABLE OUTDOOR ACTIVITIES

BIKING   Rent a bike from **Raleigh Bicycles of Jupiter,** 103 U.S. 1, Unit F1 (© **561/746-0585**). Prices start at $15.50 per day and $49.50 per week. Bike enthusiasts will enjoy exploring this flat and uncluttered area. North Palm Beach has hundreds of miles of smooth, paved roads. Loggerhead Park in Juno Beach or Fla. A1A along the ocean also has great trails for beginners. You'll find many more scenic routes over the bridges and west of the highway.

CANOEING   You can rent a boat at several outlets throughout northern Palm Beach County, including **Canoe Outfitters,** 8900 W. Indiantown Rd. (west of I-95), North Jupiter (© **561/746-7053**), which provides access to one of the area's most beautiful natural waterways. Canoers start at Riverbend Park along an 8-mile stretch of Intracoastal Waterway, where the lush foliage supports dozens of exotic birds and reptiles. Keep your eyes open for the gators who love to sunbathe on the shallow shores of the river. You'll end up, exhausted, at Jonathan Dickinson Park about 5 or 6 hours later. A pamphlet describing local flora and fauna is available for $1. Trips run Wednesday to Sunday and cost $40 per person for a double canoe with guide.

CRUISES   Several sightseeing cruises offer tours of the magnificent waterways that make up northern Palm Beach County. Water taxis conduct daily narrated tours through the scenic waters. One interesting excursion that will take you past the mansions of the rich and famous and possibly past the manatees swimming off the port of Palm Beach departs from **Panama Hatties** at PGA Boulevard and the Intracoastal Waterway. Prices are $17 for adults and $9 for children under 12 for the 1½-hour ride. Call © **561/775-2628**. The *Manatee Queen*, 1065 N. Ocean Blvd. (at the Crab House), Jupiter (© **561/744-2191**), is a 40-foot catamaran with bench seating for up to 49 people. Two-hour tours of Jupiter Island depart daily at 2:30pm, passing Burt Reynolds's and Perry Como's former mansions, among other historical and natural spots of interest. Reservations are highly recommended, especially in season; call for the current schedule of offerings. Prices start at $17 for adults and $10 for children. Bring your own lunch or purchase chips and sodas at the mini–snack bar.

FISHING   Before you leave, send for an information-packed fishing kit with details on fish camps, charters, and tournament and tide schedules, distributed by the **West Palm Beach Fishing Club** (© **561/832-6780**). The cost is $10 and well worth it. Allow at least 4 weeks for delivery.

Once in town, several outfitters along U.S. 1 and Fla. A1A have vessels and equipment for rent if your hotel doesn't. One of the most complete facilities is the **Sailfish Marina & Resort,** 98 Lake Dr. (off Blue Heron Blvd.), Palm Beach Shores (© **561/844-1724**). Call for equipment, bait, guided trips, or boat rentals.

GOLF Even if you're not lucky enough to be staying at the **PGA National Resort & Spa,** 400 Avenue of the Champions, Palm Beach Gardens (© **800/633-9150**), you may still be able to play on their award-winning courses. If you or someone in your group is a member of another golf or country club, have the head pro write a note on club letterhead to Jackie Rogers at PGA to request a play date. Be sure the pro includes his PGA number and contact information. Allow at least 2 weeks for a response. Also, ask about the Golf-A-Round program, where select private clubs open to nonmembers for free or discounted rates. Contact the **Palm Beach County Convention and Visitors Bureau** (© **561/471-3995**) for details.

Plenty of other great courses dot the area, including the **Golf Club of Jupiter,** 1800 Central Blvd., Jupiter (© **561/747-6262**), where a well-respected 18-hole, par-70 course is situated on more than 6,200 yards featuring narrow fairways and

---

Moments Turtle-Watching in North Palm Beach

North Palm Beach is well known for the giant sea turtles that lay their eggs on the county's beaches from May to August. These endangered marine animals return here annually, from as far away as South America, to lay their clutch of about 115 eggs each. Nurtured by the warm sand, but targeted by birds and other predators, only about one or two babies from each nest survive to maturity.

Many environmentalists recommend that visitors take part in an organized turtle-watching program (rather than go on their own) to minimize disturbance to the turtles. The **Marinelife Center of Juno Beach** in Loggerhead Park, 14200 U.S. 1, Juno Beach (© **561/627-8280**), conducts narrative walks along a nearby beach during high breeding season (June and July). Reservations are a must. The booking list opens on May 1 and is usually full by mid-month. The center is one place in which you're likely to see live sea turtles year-round. A science museum and nature center, the small Marinelife Center is dedicated to the coastal ecology of northern Palm Beach County. Hands-on exhibits teach visitors about wetlands and beach areas, as well as offshore coral reefs and the local sea life. Visitors are encouraged to walk the center's sand-dune nature trails, all of which are marked with interpretive signs. Admission to the center is free, though donations are accepted. It's open Tuesday to Saturday from 10am to 4pm and Sunday from noon to 3pm.

The **Jupiter Beach Resort** (© **800/228-8810** or 561/746-2511; see "Accommodations You Can Afford," below) also sponsors free, guided expeditions to egg-laying sites from May to August. Phone for times and reservations.

fast greens. Fees are $55 until noon, $45 after noon, $25 after 3pm, and include a mandatory cart. The course borders I-95.

HIKING In an area that's not particularly known for extraordinary natural diversity, **Blowing Rocks Preserve** has a terrific hiking trail along a dramatic limestone outcropping. You won't find hills or scenic vistas, but you will see Florida's unique and varied tropical ecosystem. The well-marked, mile-long trail passes oceanfront dunes, coastal strands, mangrove wetlands, and a coastal hammock. The preserve, owned and managed by the Nature Conservancy, also protects an important habitat for West Indian manatees and loggerhead turtles. Free, guided tours are available Fridays and Sundays at 11am, and no reservations are necessary. Located along South Beach Drive (Fla. A1A), north of the Jupiter inlet, the preserve is about a 10-minute drive northeast of Jupiter. From U.S. 1, head east on S.R. 707 and cross the Intracoastal Waterway to the park. Admission is free, but a $3 per person donation is requested. For more information, contact the Preserve Manager, Blowing Rocks Preserve, P.O. Box 3795, Tequesta, FL 33469 (© **561/744-6668**).

SCUBA DIVING & SNORKELING Year-round warm, clear waters make northern Palm Beach County great for both diving and snorkeling. The closest coral reef is located a quarter mile from shore and can easily be reached by boat. Three popular wrecks are clustered near each other, less than a mile offshore of the Lake Worth Inlet at about 90 feet. The best wreck, however, is the 16th- or 17th-century Spanish galleon discovered by lifeguard Peter Leo just off Jupiter Beach (see the box, "Remnants of the Past," below). If your hotel doesn't offer dive trips, call the **South Florida Dive Headquarters**, 23141 Lyons Rd., Boca Raton (© **800/771-DIVE** or 561/627-9558); or **Seafari Dive and Surf**, 75 E. Indiantown Rd., Suite 603, Jupiter (© **561/747-6115**).

SPECTATOR SPORTS The **Roger Dean Stadium**, 4751 Main St. (© **561/775-1818**), hosts baseball spring training for both the St. Louis Cardinals and the Montreal Expos, along with minor-league action from Florida's state league, the Hammerheads. Tickets range in price from $6 to $18. Call for schedules and specific ticket information.

TENNIS In addition to the many hotel tennis courts (see "Accommodations You Can Afford," below), you can swing a racquet at a number of local clubs. The **Jupiter Bay Tennis Club**, 353 U.S. 1, Jupiter (© **561/744-9424**), has seven clay courts (three lighted) and charges $12 per person per day. Reservations are highly recommended.

More economical options are available at relatively well-maintained municipal courts. Call for locations and hours (© **561/966-6600**). Many are available free on a first-come, first-served basis.

Finds Remnants of the Past

Any diving outfit in Jupiter beach will take you to the spot where the remnants of a shipwreck from a 16th- or 17th-century **Spanish galleon** lie. Discovered in 1988 by Jupiter lifeguard Peter Leo, who on his morning swim came across an anchor and a cannon, the wreck has since produced 10 more cannons and over 10,000 gold and silver coins. However, should you come across more coins, you won't be able to throw them in your piggy bank—Leo owns the mining rights to the wreck.

JUPITER & NORTHERN PALM BEACH COUNTY

A HISTORIC LIGHTHOUSE

Jupiter Inlet Lighthouse Completed in 1860, this redbrick structure is the oldest extant building in Palm Beach County. Still owned and maintained by the U.S. Coast Guard, the lighthouse is now home to a small historical museum, located at its base. The Florida History Museum sponsors tours of the lighthouse, enabling visitors to explore the cramped interior, which is filled with artifacts and photographs illustrating the rich history of the area. A 15-minute video explains the various shipwrecks, Indian wars, and other events that helped shape this region. Helpful volunteers are eager to tell colorful stories to highlight the 1-hour tour.

500 S.R. 707, Jupiter. 561/747-8380. Admission $5. Sun–Wed 10am–4pm (last tour departs at 3:15pm). Children must be 4 ft. or taller to climb. No open-backed shoes.

SHOPPING

Northern Palm Beach County may not have the glitzy boutiques of Worth Avenue, but it does have an impressive indoor mall, the **Gardens of the Palm Beaches,** at 3101 PGA Blvd., where you can find large department stores including Bloomingdale's, Burdines, Macy's, and Saks Fifth Avenue, as well as more than 100 specialty shops. A large, diverse food court and fine sit-down restaurants in this 1.3-million-square-foot facility make this shopping excursion an all-day affair. Call 561/775-7750 for store information.

ACCOMMODATIONS YOU CAN AFFORD

The northern part of Palm Beach County is much more laid-back and less touristy than the rest of the Gold Coast. Here, there are relatively few fancy hotels or attractions. In addition to several **Holiday Inns** (800/325-8193), there is a reasonably priced and recently renovated **Wellesley Inn,** 34 Fisherman's Wharf (I-95, exit east on Indiantown Rd.; turn left before the bridge), in Jupiter (800/444-8888). Suites include sofa beds, refrigerators, and microwaves and cost $49.50 year-round. Although not within walking distance of the beach, the inn is located near shops and restaurants and Fla. A1A.

Baron's Landing Motel & Apartments *Value* This charming family-run inn is a perfect little beach getaway. It's not elegant, but it is cozy. The single-story motel fronting the Intracoastal Waterway is often full in winter with snowbirds, who dock their boats at the hotel's marina for weeks or months at a time. Nearly all rooms, which are situated around a small pool, have small kitchenettes. Each unit has a funky mix of used furniture, and some have pullout sofas. Bathrooms have been remodeled. Considering that you're a few blocks from some of the most expensive real estate in the country, this is a good deal. Dock rentals are available.

18125 Ocean Blvd. (Fla. A1A at the corner of Clemens St.), Jupiter, FL 33477. 561/746-8575. 8 units. Winter $75–$125 double; $1,350–$1,700 monthly. Off-season $45–$75 double; $700–$900 monthly. No credit cards. **Amenities:** Small pool. *In room:* A/C, TV, dataport, kitchenette, fridge, coffeemaker, iron.

Bon-Aire Yacht Club A great find at the southern tip of Singer Island, this small and exclusive apartment house is located just on the lake's edge where guests enjoy a marina, barbecue grill, hammocks, and comfy lounge furniture. There is also a good-size pool and hot tub. Plus, it's just 2 blocks from the ocean. Still, the best part is that all apartments have fully stocked kitchens with stoves and ranges. The best are the two-bedroom apartments, which have private sun decks. A renovation in 2001 included new furniture and remodeled kitchens.

188 Lake Dr., Palm Beach Shores, FL 33404. © **800/627-8328** or 561/844-5588. Fax 561/844-9007. www.cannonsport.com. 14 units. Winter $110 1-bedroom apt, $299 2-bedroom apt; off-season $85 1-bedroom apt, from $120 2-bedroom apt. AE, DC, DISC, MC, V. **Amenities:** Pool; Jacuzzi; water-sports equipment; fishing equipment; free shuttle to town; laundry. *In room:* A/C, TV/VCR, kitchen, fridge, coffeemaker, iron.

SUPER-CHEAP SLEEPS

Cologne Motel A modest roadside motel, the Cologne is a well-maintained one-story building with a pool but very little in the way of amenities. The small rooms were updated in 1999 with modest but bright bedspreads and curtains, and the retiled bathrooms are small but clean. The area is safe if not scenic and only about a 5-minute drive to the beach. A more direct route by foot gets you there in about 15 minutes.

220 U.S. 1, Tequesta/Jupiter, FL 33469. © **561/746-0616.** 9 units. Winter $70 double; off-season $36 double. Weekly rates available. AE, MC, V. **Amenities:** Pool. *In room:* A/C, TV, fridge. No phone.

WORTH A SPLURGE

Jupiter Beach Resort 🌟🌟 The only resort located directly on Jupiter's beach, this unpretentious retreat is popular with families and seems a world away from the more luxurious resorts just a few miles to the south. The lobby and public areas have a Caribbean motif, accented with green marble, arched doorways, and chandeliers. The simple and elegant guest rooms are furnished in a comfortable island style, and every room has a private balcony with ocean or sunset views looking out over the uncluttered beachfront. A thorough refurbishing in the mid-1990s is responsible for the resort's increasing popularity. In fact, it is so popular that it is being gradually converted into a timeshare property. Excursions to the area's top-rated golf courses are available.

5 N. A1A, Jupiter, FL 33477. © **800/228-8810** or 561/746-2511. Fax 561/747-3304. www.jupiterbeachresort.com. 153 units. Winter $170–$450 double; off-season $97–$205 double. AE, DC, DISC, MC, V. Valet parking $5. From I-95, take Exit 59A, going east to the end of Indiantown Rd. at A1A. Jupiter Beach Resort is at this intersection on the ocean. **Amenities:** Restaurant, 2 bars; pool; tennis court; exercise room; extensive water-sport equipment/rental; bike rental; children's programs; concierge; business center; limited room service; in-room massage; dry cleaning. *In room:* A/C, TV, VCR for $10, dataport, kitchenette in suites, minibar, coffeemaker, iron.

GREAT DEALS ON DINING

In addition to all the national fast-food joints that line Indiantown Road and U.S. 1, you'll find a number of touristy fish restaurants serving battered and fried everything. There are only a few really exceptional eateries in North Palm Beach and Jupiter. Try those listed below for guaranteed good food at reasonable prices.

Capt. Charlie's Reef Grill 🌟🌟 SEAFOOD/CARIBBEAN The trick here is to arrive early, ahead of the crowd of local foodies who come for the more than a dozen daily local-catch specials prepared in dozens of styles. Imaginative appetizers include Caribbean chili, a rich chunky stew filled with fresh seafood; and a tuna spring roll big enough for two. The enormous Cuban crab cake is moist and perfectly browned without tasting fried and is served with homemade mango chutney and black beans and rice. Sit at the bar to watch the hectic kitchen turn out perfect dishes on the 14-burner stove. Somehow, the pleasant waitresses keep their cool even when the place is packed. In addition to the terrific seafood, this little dive offers an extensive, affordable wine and beer selection—more than 30 of each from around the world.

12846 U.S. 1 (behind O'Brian's and French Connection), Juno Beach. © **561/624-9924.** Reservations not accepted. Main courses $9.95–$18.95. MC, V. Sun–Thurs 11:30am–9:30pm; Fri–Sat 11:30am–10pm.

Nick's Tomato Pie ★ Kids ITALIAN   A fun, family restaurant, Nick's is a popular attraction that's known to bring folks even from Miami for a piece of this pie. With a huge menu of pastas, pizzas, fish, chicken, and beef, this cheery (and noisy) spot has something for everyone. On Saturday night, you'll see lots of couples on dates and some families leaving with take-out bags left over from the impossibly generous portions. The homemade sausage is a delicious treat, served with sautéed onions and peppers. The *pollo marsala*, too, is good and authentic.

1697 W. Indiantown Rd. (1 mile east of I-95, Exit 59A), Jupiter. © 561/744-8935. Reservations accepted only for parties of 6 or more. Main courses $12–$20; pastas $10–$15. AE, DC, DISC, MC, V. Mon–Thurs and Sun 5–10pm; Fri–Sat 5–11pm.

SUPER-CHEAP EATS

Athenian Cafe ★ Finds GREEK   Peter Papadelis and his family have been running this pleasant storefront cafe for more than a decade. Tucked in the corner of a strip mall, this place is a favorite with businesspeople, who stop in for a heaping portion of rich and meaty moussaka or a flaky spinach pie made fresh by Peter himself. You could make a meal of the thick and lemony Greek soup and the large fresh antipasto. In a town replete with tourist-priced fish joints, this is a welcome alternative. Early bird specials, served until 7pm, include many Greek favorites and broiled local fish with soup or salad, rice, vegetables, pita, dessert, and coffee or tea.

In the Chasewood Shopping Center, 6350 Indiantown Rd., Suite 7, Jupiter. © 561/744-8327. Main courses $5–$16. AE, MC, V. Mon–Sat 11am–9pm; Sun 4–9pm in high season only.

Lanna Thai THAI   There are dozens of great choices at Lanna Thai, including all the old reliables like pad Thai, panang curry, pad king, and pad puck to pair with meat, chicken, or fish. This inauspicious storefront has a quaint, whitewashed dining room where only a dozen tables sit beneath latticework bedecked with fake plants. Come for the lunch specials that include spring rolls, soup, and fried rice for less than $6. The earnest service staff is always checking to make sure everything is all right—and it usually is.

4300 S. U.S. 1 (in the Bluff's Square Shopping Center, between Indian Town and Donald Ross rds.), Jupiter. © 561/694-1443. Reservations not accepted. Main courses $10; chef's specials $10–$18. MC, V. Mon–Fri 11am–3pm and 5–10pm; Sat–Sun 5–10pm.

JUPITER & NORTHERN PALM BEACH COUNTY AFTER DARK

With one notable exception, there just isn't much going on here after dark. However, **Club Safari**, 4000 PGA Blvd. (just east of I-95), in Palm Beach Garden's Marriott Hotel (© **561/622-8888**), has a hilarious Vegas-style safari-themed decor, with faux, albeit life-like, animals positioned throughout the club. The huge, sunken dance floor is surrounded by vines and lanky, potted trees. Nearby, a large Buddha statue blows steam and smoke while waving its burly arms in front of a young gyrating crowd. There is DJ music, a large video screen, and a modest cover charge on the weekends. It's open nights, Wednesday through Sunday. For more options, check your hotel or do what most people do—go to West Palm Beach.

8

The Treasure Coast: Stuart to Sebastian

by Lesley Abravanel

The area north of Palm Beach is known as the Treasure Coast for the same reason that the area from Fort Lauderdale to Palm Beach is known as the Gold Coast—it was the site of a number of shipwrecks that date back over 300 years, which led to the discovery of priceless treasures in the water (some historians believe that treasures from these sunken vessels *still* lie buried deep beneath the ocean floor).

The difference, however, is that while the Gold Coast is a bit, well, tarnished as far as development is concerned, the Treasure Coast remains, for the most part, an unspoiled, quiet natural jewel. Miles of uninterrupted beaches and aquamarine waters attract swimmers, boaters, divers, anglers, and sun worshippers who love to dip, dive, and surf. If you love the great outdoors and prefer a more understated environment than hyper-developed Miami and Fort Lauderdale, the Treasure Coast is a real find.

For hundreds of years, Florida's east coast was a popular stopover for European explorers, many of whom arrived from Spain to fill coffers with gold and silver. Rough weather and poor navigation often took a toll on their ships, but in 1715, a violent hurricane stunned the northeast coast and sank an entire fleet of Spanish ships laden with gold. Although Spanish salvagers worked for years to collect the lost treasure, much of it remained buried beneath the shifting sand. Workers hired to excavate the area in the 1950s and 1960s discovered centuries-old coins under their tractors.

Today, you can still see shipwrecks and incredible barrier reefs in St. Lucie County, which can be reached from the beaches of Fort Pierce and Hutchinson Island. On these same beaches, you'll also find an occasional treasure hunter trolling the sand with a metal detector, alongside swimmers and sunbathers who come to enjoy the stretches of beach that extend into the horizon. The sea, especially around Sebastian Inlet, is a mecca for surfers, who find some of the largest swells in the state.

Along with the pleasures of the talcum powder sands, the Treasure Coast also offers great shopping, entertainment, clubbing, sporting, and numerous other opportunities to take a reprieve from the hubbub of the rat race. Visitors to this part of South Florida should not miss the extensive array of wildlife, which includes the endangered West Indian manatee, a nesting area for loggerhead and leatherback turtles, tropical fish, alligators, deer, and exotic birds. For sports enthusiasts, there are boundless opportunities—from golf and tennis to polo, motorcar racing, the New York Mets during their spring training, and the best freshwater fishing around.

The downtown areas of the Treasure Coast have been experiencing a rebirth in the past few years, along with the influx of unprecedented numbers of new residents. Fortunately, the area's

THE TREASURE COAST: STUART TO SEBASTIAN

growth has occurred at a reasonable pace so that the neighborhoods have been able to retain their small-town feel. The result is a batch of freshly spruced-up accommodations, shops, and restaurants from Stuart to Sebastian.

For the purposes of this chapter, the Treasure Coast runs roughly from Stuart and Hobe Sound in the south to the Sebastian Inlet in the north, encompassing some of Martin, St. Lucie, and Indian River counties and all of Hutchinson Island.

ESSENTIALS

GETTING THERE Since virtually every town described in this chapter runs along a straight route, along the Atlantic Ocean, I've given all directions below.

By Plane The **Palm Beach International Airport** (called PBI; © **561/471-7420**), located about 35 miles south of Stuart, is the closest gateway to this region if you're flying. If you are traveling to the northern part of the Treasure Coast, **Melbourne International Airport,** off U.S. 1 in Melbourne (© **407/723-6227**), is less than 25 miles north of Sebastian and about 35 miles north of Vero Beach.

The best and easiest way to get from each airport into Stuart, Sebastian, and their surrounding areas is by car. Most major rental car companies are located at each airport. At PBI, you'll find **Alamo** (© 877/252-6600), **Avis** (© 800/230-4898), **Budget** (© 800/527-0700), **Dollar** (© 800/800-3665), **Hertz** (© 800/654-3131), and **National** (© 800/227-7368). At Melbourne International, you can visit **Avis** (© 321/723-7755), **Budget** (© 321/723-0284), **Hertz** (© 321/723-3414), or **National** (© 321/723-3035).

By Car If you're driving up or down the Florida coast, you'll probably reach the Treasure Coast via I-95. If you are heading to Stuart or Jensen Beach, take Exit 61 (Rte. 76/Tanner Hwy.) or 62 (Rte. 714); to Port St. Lucie or Fort Pierce, take Exit 63 or 64 (Okeechobee Rd.); to Vero Beach, take Exit 68 (S. R. 60); to Sebastian, take Exit 69 (County Rd.).

You can also take the Florida Turnpike; this toll road is the fastest (but not the most scenic) route, especially if you're coming from Orlando. If you are heading to Stuart or Jensen Beach, take Exit 133; to Fort Pierce, take Exit 152 (Okeechobee Rd.); to Port St. Lucie, take Exit 142 or 152; to Vero Beach, take Exit 193 (S. R. 60); to Sebastian, take Exit 193 to S. R. 60 east and connect to I-95 north.

If you are staying in Hutchinson Island, which runs almost the entire length of the Treasure Coast, you should check with your hotel or see the listings below to find the best route to take.

Finally, if you're coming directly from the west coast, you'll probably take State Route 70, which runs north of Lake Okeechobee to Fort Pierce, located just up the road from Stuart.

By Rail Amtrak (© **800/USA-RAIL;** www.amtrak.com) stops in West Palm Beach at 201 S. Tamarind Ave., and in Okeechobee at 801 N. Parrot Ave., off U.S. 441 north.

By Bus Greyhound buses (© **800/231-2222;** www.greyhound.com) service the area with terminals in Stuart, at 1308 S. Federal Hwy. (© **561/287-7777**); in Fort Pierce, at 7005 Okeechobee Rd. (© **561/461-3299**); and in Vero Beach, at U.S. 1 and S. R. 60 (© **561/562-6588**).

GETTING AROUND A car is a necessity in this large and rural region (see "Getting There" above, for rental companies). Although heavy traffic is not usually a problem here, on the smaller coastal roads, like A1A, expect to travel at a slow pace, usually between 25 and 40 miles per hour.

1 Stuart ★★★ & Jensen Beach

130 miles SE of Orlando, 98 miles N of Miami

Once just a stretch of pineapple plantations, the towns of Martin County, which include Stuart and Jensen Beach, still retain much of their rural character. Dotted between citrus groves and mangroves are modest homes and an occasional high-rise condominium. Although the area is definitely still seasonal (with a distinct rise in street and pedestrian traffic beginning after the Christmas holidays), the atmosphere is pure small town. Even in historic downtown Stuart, the result of a successful, ongoing restoration, expect the storefronts to be dark and the streets abandoned after 10pm.

ESSENTIALS

VISITOR INFORMATION The **Stuart/Martin County Chamber of Commerce,** 1650 S. Kanner Hwy., Stuart, FL 34994 (© **800/524-9704** or 561/287-1088; fax 561/220-3437), is the region's main source of information. The **Jensen Beach Chamber of Commerce,** 1901 NE Jensen Beach Blvd., Jensen Beach, FL 34957 (© **561/334-3444;** fax 561/334-0817), also offers visitors information about its simple beachfront town.

WHAT TO SEE & DO
BACK TO NATURE: THE BEACHES & BEYOND

BEACHES The beaches of Hutchinson Island, a long, thin barrier island, are easily accessible from Stuart. Just look for "coastal access" signs pointing the way. The island is one of the most popular beach destinations of the Treasure Coast, located just north of Palm Beach on the Atlantic Ocean. Seventy miles of excellent beaches and laid-back, old Florida ambience make for an idyllic frozen cocktail.

The best of them is **Bathtub Beach** ★★, on North Hutchinson Island. Here, the calm waters are protected by coral reefs. Pick a secluded spot on the wide stretch of beach, or enjoy the marked nature trails across the street. Facilities include showers and toilets open during the day. To reach Bathtub Beach from the northern tip of Hutchinson Island, head east on Ocean Boulevard (Stuart Causeway) and turn right onto MacArthur Boulevard. The beach is about a mile ahead on your left, just north of the Hutchinson Island Marriott Beach Resort and Marina. Parking is plentiful.

CANOEING Jonathan Dickinson State Park (see the box, "Wildlife Exploration: From Gators to Manatees to Turtles," below) is the area's most popular spot for canoeing. The route winds through a variety of botanical habitats. You'll see a variety of birds and the occasional manatee. Canoes cost $6 per hour and can be rented through the concession located in the back of the park. The concession (© **561/746-1466**) is open Monday to Friday from 9am to 5pm and Saturday and Sunday from 8am to 5pm.

FISHING Several independent charter captains operate on Hutchinson Island and Jensen Beach. One of the largest operators is the **Sailfish Marina,** 3565 SE St. Lucie Blvd. in Stuart (© **561/221-9456**), which maintains half a dozen charter boats for fishing excursions year-round. Also on-site are a bait-and-tackle shop and a knowledgeable, helpful staff. Other reputable charter operators include **Hungry Bear Adventures, Inc.,** docked at Indian River Plantation Marriott Resort, 4730-1 SE Teri Place in Stuart (© **561/283-8034;** fishing@tci.net); and **Bone Shaker Sportfishing,** 3585 SE St. Lucie Blvd. in Stuart

The Treasure Coast

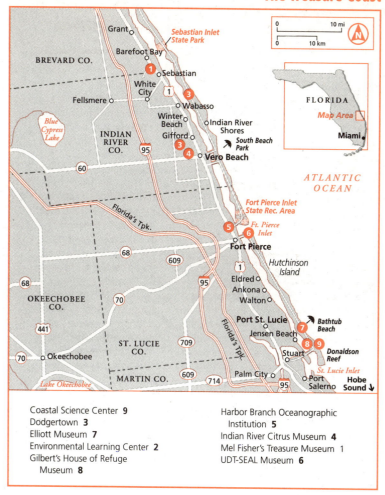

Coastal Science Center **9**
Dodgertown **3**
Elliott Museum **7**
Environmental Learning Center **2**
Gilbert's House of Refuge
  Museum **8**
Harbor Branch Oceanographic
  Institution **5**
Indian River Citrus Museum **4**
Mel Fisher's Treasure Museum **1**
UDT-SEAL Museum **6**

(© **561/286-5504**; veejay4842@aol.com). For each, a full-day outing costs roughly $750 and a half day $500 per charter.

GOLF Try the **Champions Club at Summerfield,** on U.S. 1, south of Cove Road in Stuart (© **561/283-1500**), a somewhat challenging championship course designed by Tom Fazio. This rural course, the best in the area, offers great glimpses of wildlife amid the wetlands. Winter greens fees are around $60, and carts are mandatory. Reservations are a must and are taken 4 days in advance.

SCUBA DIVING & SNORKELING Three popular artificial reefs off Hutchinson Island provide excellent scenery for both novice and experienced divers. The **USS** *Rankin* lies 7 miles east-northeast of the St. Lucie Inlet. The *Rankin* is a 459-foot ship that lays on its port side in 80 feet of water. This ship was used in World War II for troop transportation and was sunk in 1988. Deck hatches on the wreck are open and allow exploration. Inside, there are thousands of Atlantic spiny oysters, and a cannon is attached to the bow. The 58-foot-deep

Wildlife Exploration: From Gators to Manatees to Turtles

One of the most scenic areas on this stretch of the coast is **Jonathan Dickinson State Park**, 12 miles south of Stuart at 16450 S. Federal Hwy. (U.S. 1), Hobe Sound (© **561/546-2771**). The park intentionally receives less maintenance than other, more meticulously maintained parks so that it will resemble the rough-around-the-edges, wilderness environment of hundreds of years ago, before Europeans started chopping, dredging, and "improving" the area. Dozens of species of Florida's unique wildlife, including alligators and manatees, live on the park's more than 11,300 acres. Bird-watchers will also be delighted by glimpses of rare and endangered species such as the bald eagle, the Florida scrub-jay, and the Florida sandhill crane, who still call this park home. You can rent canoes from the concession stand to explore the Loxahatchee River on your own. Admission is $3.25 per car of up to eight adults. Day hikers, bikers, and walkers pay $1 each. See "Accommodations You Can Afford," below, for details on camping. The park is open from 8am until sundown.

Close to Jonathan Dickinson State Park is **Hobe Sound Wildlife Refuge**, on North Beach Road off State Route 708, at the north end of Jupiter Island (© **561/546-6141**). This is one of the best places to see sea turtles that nest on the shore in the summer months, especially in June and July. Because it's home to a large variety of other plant and animal species, the park is worth visiting at other times of year as well. Admission is $4 per car, and the preserve is open daily from sunrise to sunset. Exact times are posted at each entrance and change seasonally.

For free **turtle walks** on Hutchinson Island, call © **877/375-4386**. These walks take place from May 22 through July 22 at 9pm Fridays and Saturdays. Reservations are necessary and should be made well in advance, as walks are limited to 50 people. Reservations are accepted as of May 1.

Donaldson Reef consists of a cluster of steel tanks and barrels. It's located due east of the Gilbert's House of Refuge Museum (see below). The **Ernst Reef**, made from old tires, is a 60-foot dive located 4½ miles east-southeast of the St. Lucie inlet.

For snorkeling and scuba gear, the **Deep Six Dive Shop**, 3289 NW Federal Hwy., Jensen Beach (© **561/692-2747**), has everything you need. Snorkeling equipment rentals cost $10, and scuba equipment rents for $25, including tank, fins, and mask.

SEEING THE SIGHTS

Balloons Over Florida ★★★ *Finds* For a lofty view of Martin County's wildlife, take a hot air balloon ride above the animals' natural habitat. Two fully licensed and insured balloons and pilots will take a maximum of four people up, up, and away for about an hour, depending on wind and weather conditions. After you've landed, drink in the sights over a glass of complimentary champagne and a continental breakfast. A certificate of flight is given to each passenger as a souvenir.

Tours begin at approximately 6:30am from a takeoff point to be determined. © 561/334-9393. $150 per person, including continental breakfast and champagne.

Elliott Museum ★★ A treasure trove of wacky artifacts that really personify Americana, the Elliott Museum is a rich tribute to inventors, sports heroes, and collectors. The museum was created by the son of turn-of-the-century inventor Sterling Elliott to display the genius of the American spirit. Among the bizarre things you'll see here are displays of an apothecary, ice cream parlor, barbershop, and other old-fashioned commercial enterprises, and an authentic hand-carved miniature circus. Sports fans will appreciate the baseball memorabilia—a half-million dollars' worth—including an autographed item from every player in the Baseball Hall of Fame.

A gallery of patents and models of machines, invented by the museum's founder, Harmon Parker Elliott, and his son, provides an intriguing glimpse into the business of tinkering. Their collection of restored antique cars is also impressive. Expect to spend at least an hour seeing the highlights.

825 NE Ocean Blvd. (north of Indian River Plantation Resort), Hutchinson Island, Stuart. © 561/225-1961. Admission $6 adults, $2 children 6–13; free for children 5 and under. Daily 10am–4pm.

Florida Oceanographic Coastal Center ★★ This is a nature lover's Disney World. Opened by the South Florida Oceanographic Society in late 1994, this 44-acre site (surrounded by coastal hammock and mangroves) is its own little ecosystem and serves as an outdoor classroom, teaching visitors about the region's flora and fauna. The modest main building houses saltwater tanks and wet and dry "discovery tables" with small indigenous animals. The incredibly eager staff of volunteers encourages visitors to wander the lush, well-marked nature trails.

890 NE Ocean Blvd. (across the street from the Elliott Museum), Hutchinson Island, Stuart. © 561/225-0505. www.fosusa.org. Admission $6 adults, $3 children 3–12; free for children under 3. Mon–Sat 10am–5pm; Sun noon–4.

Gilbert's House of Refuge Museum ★ Gilbert's, the oldest structure in Martin County, dates from 1875, when it functioned as one of 10 rescue centers for shipwrecked sailors. After undergoing a thorough rehabilitation to its original condition along the rocky shores, the house now displays marine artifacts and turn-of-the-century lifesaving equipment and photographs and is worth a quick visit to get a feel for the area's early days.

301 SE MacArthur Blvd. (south of Indian River Plantation resort), Hutchinson Island, Stuart. © 561/225-1875. Admission $4 adults, $2 children 6–13; free for children 5 and under. Daily 10am–4pm.

A BOAT TOUR

The *Loxahatchee Queen* ★★★ (© 561/746-1466), a 35-foot pontoon boat in Jonathan Dickinson State Park in Hobe Sound, outside of Stuart, makes daily tours of the area's otherwise inaccessible backwater, where curious alligators, manatees, eagles, and tortoises often peek out to see who's in their yard. Try to catch the 2-hour tour, given Wednesday to Sunday as the tide permits, when it includes a stop at Trapper Nelson's home. Known as the "Wildman of Loxahatchee," Nelson lived in primitive conditions on a remote stretch of the water in a log cabin he built himself, which is preserved for visitors to see. Tours leave four times daily at 9am, 11am, 1pm, and 3pm and cost $12 for adults and $7 for children 6 to 12; it's free for children 5 and under. See the box, "Wildlife Exploration: From Gators to Manatees to Turtles," above, for more information on the park.

SHOPPING

Downtown Stuart's historic district, along Flagler Avenue between Confusion Corner and St. Lucie Avenue, offers shoppers diversity and quality in a small, old-town setting. Shops offer a range of goods: antique bric-a-brac, old lamps and fixtures, books, gourmet foods, furnishings, and souvenirs. For bargains, check out the **B & A Flea Market**, 2885 SE U.S. 1, Stuart (© **561/288-4915**), the Treasure Coast's oldest and largest flea market.

ACCOMMODATIONS YOU CAN AFFORD

One of the bigger hotel chains in this area is the **Holiday Inn**. Its recently renovated, stunning beachfront property is at 3793 NE Ocean Blvd., on Hutchinson Island in Jensen Beach (© **800/992-4747** or 561/225-3000). Rates in season range from $130 to $180. Holiday Inn also has a downtown location at 1209 S. Federal Hwy. (© **561/287-6200**). This simple two-story building on a busy main road is kept in very good shape and is convenient to Stuart's downtown historic district. Rates range from $99 to $140.

Harborfront Inn Bed & Breakfast ★★ *Finds*   A bona fide return to Old Florida, the Harborfront Inn has the advantage of being right on the river, where you can sail, kayak, and water-ski. It consists of a series of little blue-trimmed shingled cottages within walking distance of the restaurants of downtown Stuart. Each room (all with a sitting area and a private bathroom) has its own private entrance. The two best rooms are the bright Garden Suite, which has a queen-size bed, rattan furnishings, and a deck with river and garden views; and the Guest House, which has an extra-large bathroom with two sinks and can be rented with an adjoining full kitchen. An enclosed porch surrounds the inn's cozy public areas where breakfast (usually including fresh fruit from the trees that grow on the property) is served. A must-do is the in-room candlelight dinner. Smoking is not permitted here.

310 Atlanta Ave., Stuart, FL 34994. © **800/294-1703** or 561/288-7289. Fax 561/221-0474. 6 units. Winter $90–$183 double. Off-season discounts available. Rates include breakfast. DISC, MC, V. Free dockage. From I-95 take Exit 61 heading east to U.S. 1 N. Turn left on W. Ocean Blvd. and make the first right (Atlanta Ave.). Children not allowed. **Amenities:** Jacuzzi; water-sports equipment/rentals. *In room:* A/C, TV/VCR, hair dryer.

WORTH A SPLURGE

Hutchinson Inn ★★   It doesn't look like much from the road—only the tennis court is visible—but you'll soon happen upon striking white gazebos dotting thick green lawns. Located directly on the beach, the Hutchinson Inn is a quiet and charming two-story hideaway. Unfortunately, so many people know about it that it's usually booked a year in advance in high season. The refurbished rooms have rattan furnishings; sofas convert into pullout beds, and several rooms can be joined to accommodate large families. Some contain kitchens.

9750 S. Ocean Dr. (Fla. A1A), Jensen Beach, FL 34957. © **800/909-4204** or 561/229-2000. www.hutchinson inn.com. 21 units. Winter from $125 double; $165–$250 efficiency or suite. Off-season from $95 double; $125–$175 efficiency or suite. Rates include expanded continental breakfast. MC, V. From I-95 take Exit 61, heading east to Monterey; turn right and cross U.S. 1. Go to second light; turn right on E. Ocean Blvd. onto the island. Inn is about 8 miles ahead. **Amenities:** Large outdoor heated pool; tennis court; nearby water-sports equipment/rental; bike rental. *In room:* A/C, TV, kitchen in some rooms, fridge, hair dryer.

A GREAT OFF-SEASON BARGAIN

Hutchinson Island Marriott Beach Resort and Marina ★★★ *Kids*   This sprawling 200-acre compound offers many diversions for active (or not-so-active) vacationers, and families in particular. The amenities and roster of outdoor options are simply unparalleled in this area. After a $6-million renovation in 1998 and further updates in 2000 and 2001, the resort is in sparkling condition, occupying the lush grounds of a former pineapple plantation. Though oceanview units here are quite pricey, the resort offers a wonderful bargain during the off-season in the main building's deluxe rooms, which contain king beds and overlook the main road. With the beach still right around the corner and water sports, tennis, and game rooms awaiting you, this is a great value at $99 a night.

555 NE Ocean Blvd., Hutchinson Island, Stuart, FL 34996. © 800/775-5936 or 561/225-3700. Fax 561/225-0003. www.marriott.com/marriott/pbiir. 298 units. Winter $209–$399; off-season $99–$349. AE, MC, V. Pets accepted with a $50 deposit. From downtown Stuart, take E. Ocean Blvd. over 2 bridges to NE Ocean Blvd.; turn right. **Amenities:** Restaurant, coffee shop, lounge; 4 large pools; 18-hole golf course; 13 tennis courts; fitness center & spa; extensive water sports; bike rental; children's programs; game room; concierge; on-property transportation; limited room service; babysitting; laundry/dry cleaning. *In room:* A/C, TV, dataport, kitchenette, minibar, coffeemaker, hair dryer.

CAMPING

There are comfortable campsites in **Jonathan Dickinson State Park** in Hobe Sound (see the box, "Wildlife Exploration: From Gators to Manatees to Turtles," above). The River Camp area of the park offers the benefit of the nearby Loxahatchee River, while the Pine Grove site has beautiful shade trees. Along with concession areas for daytime snacks, you'll find 135 campsites equipped with showers, clean restrooms, water, optional electricity, and an open-fire pit for cooking. Overnight rates in the winter are $18 without electricity, $20 with electricity. In the summer, rates are about $14 for four people.

For a more cushy camping experience, reserve a wood-sided cabin with a furnished kitchen, a bathroom with shower, heat and air-conditioning, and an outdoor grill. Bring your own linens. Cabins rent for $65 and up a night and sleep four people comfortably, six if your group is really into togetherness. Call © **561/546-2771** Monday to Friday from 9am to 5pm, well in advance, to reserve a spot. A $50 key deposit is required.

GREAT DEALS ON DINING

Black Marlin ★ FLORIDA REGIONAL   Although it sports the look and feel of a dank English pub, the Black Marlin offers full Floridian flavor. The salmon BLT is typical of the dishes here—grilled salmon on a toasted bun topped with bacon, lettuce, tomato, and coleslaw. Designer pizzas are topped with shrimp, roasted red peppers, and the like; and main dishes, all of which are served with vegetables and potatoes, include a lobster tail with honey-mustard sauce, and a charcoal-grilled chicken breast served on radicchio with caramelized onions.

53 W. Osceola St., downtown Stuart. © **561/286-3126.** Reservations not accepted. Salads and sandwiches $4–$8; full meals $9–$24. AE, MC, V. Mon–Thurs 5–10pm; Fri–Sat 5–11pm (the bar is open later).

Conchy Joe's Seafood ★★ *Finds* SEAFOOD   Known for fresh seafood and Old Florida hospitality, Conchy Joe's enjoys an excellent reputation that's far bigger than the restaurant itself. Dining is either indoors, at red-and-white cloth-covered tables, or on a covered patio overlooking the St. Lucie River. The restaurant features a wide variety of freshly shucked shellfish and daily-catch selections that are baked, broiled, or fried. Beer is the drink of choice here, though other beverages and a full bar are available. Conchy Joe's has been the most active place in Jensen Beach since it opened in 1983. The large bar is especially popular at night and during weekday happy hours.

3945 NE Indian River Dr. (a half mile from the Jensen Beach Causeway), Jensen Beach. © **561/334-1130.** Reservations not accepted. Main courses $12–$20. AE, DISC, MC, V. Daily 11:30am–2:30pm and 5–10pm.

SUPER-CHEAP EATS

Bubba's Fish Camp ★★ *Finds* SEAFOOD/SOUTHERN   As you would imagine from its name, Bubba's is an ultra-casual spot designed to resemble an old-Florida fish camp. Don't miss the great crawfish gumbo, corn bread, catfish, creamy spinach, hush puppies, or fried green tomatoes. They have a sort of early-bird special, starting at 4pm, when you'll find bargain deals on hearty Southern classics like meat loaf, baked Virginia ham with red-eye gravy, fried chicken, and pork chops. Each includes a choice of delicious side dishes. Locals and highway travelers line up outside the screened porch to get into this rustic eatery. The wait is usually 20 minutes to half an hour, but it's worth it, especially for a very interesting look at the colorful locals and visitors.

421 S. Federal Hwy. (at south side of Roosevelt Bridge), Stuart. © **561/220-3747.** Full meals $8–$10. AE, MC, V. Daily 4–10pm and later on weekends. Call about weekend breakfasts.

Jan's Place ★ AMERICAN   The wooden rafters at Jan's are loaded with the weight of thousands of old photographs, blinking Christmas lights, fans, hanging lanterns, fishnets, and a 10-foot mural of swaying palms. The food is served in generous portions. Especially for breakfast, you'll find some fresh and delicious dishes, like the Neptune Benedict, which has large chunks of shrimp, scallops, and crab, and a very garlicky hollandaise. The seafood's from a can but tastes great. The large lunch menu is mostly dressed-up diner fare, but specials like blackened mahimahi can be spectacular.

1897 Jensen Beach Blvd., Old Jensen Beach Village. © **561/334-9598.** Breakfast $4–$9; lunch $7–$10. MC, V. Daily 7am–4pm (until 3pm on Sun) and Thurs 5:30–9:30pm.

Nature's Way Cafe ★ HEALTH FOOD   This lovely dining room has dozens of little tables, a few barstools, and some sidewalk seating, too. A sort of health-food deli, Nature's Way excels in serving quick and nutritious meals such as huge salads, vegetarian sandwiches, and frozen yogurts. Try some of the homemade baked goods. Sit outside on quaint Osceola Street or ask them to pack your lunch for you to take to the beach.

25 SW Osceola St., in the Post Office Arcade, Stuart. © **561/220-7306.** Sandwiches and salads $4–$7; juices and shakes $1–$3. No credit cards. Mon–Fri 10am–4pm; Sat 11am–3pm.

WORTH A SPLURGE

Eleven Maple Street ★★★ AMERICAN   The most highly rated restaurant in Jensen Beach, Eleven Maple Street occupies a lovely little house. Dining is both indoors and out, in any one of a series of cozy dining rooms or on a covered patio surrounded by gardens. Interesting dishes such as the wood-grilled venison or the braised Moulard duck leg with wood-grilled Oregon quail are not typically found in these parts of Florida. The restaurant also uses organically grown produce from its own garden (when available) and poultry and meats that are farm-raised and free of chemical additives.

11 Maple St., Jensen Beach. © **561/334-7714.** Reservations recommended. Main courses $17.50–$30. MC, V. Wed–Sun 6–10pm. Head east on Jensen Beach Blvd. and turn right after the railroad tracks.

Flagler Grill ★★ AMERICAN/FLORIDA REGIONAL   In the heart of historic downtown, this seemingly out-of-place Manhattan-style bistro serves up classics with a twist. The dishes are not so unusual as to alienate the conservative pink-shirted golfers who frequent the place, yet they're fresh and light enough to quench the appetites of the more adventurous. For example, you'll find Maryland jumbo lump crabmeat and rock shrimp cake served with a Key lime aioli and spicy Cajun aioli. For main courses, the grilled double-stuffed pork chop filled with pecan-apple corn-bread stuffing with cranberry orange chutney, fresh vegetables, and smashed garlic potatoes give literal meaning to the term comfort food. The menu changes every few weeks, so see what your server recommends. The desserts, too, are worth the calories.

47 SW Flagler Ave. (just before the Roosevelt Bridge), downtown Stuart. © **561/221-9517.** Reservations strongly suggested in season. Main courses $18–$28. AE, DC, DISC, MC, V. Winter daily 5–10pm; off-season Tues–Sat 5:30–9:30pm. Lounge and bar open to 11:30pm. Special sunset menu offered 5–6pm.

STUART & JENSEN BEACH AFTER DARK

The nightlife on the Treasure Coast may as well be called night*dead,* because there really isn't any! That said, Stuart and Jensen Beach are the closest you get to nightlife in the entire region, where local restaurants serve as the centers of after-dark happenings.

The bar at the **Black Marlin** (see "Great Deals on Dining," above) is popular with locals and out-of-towners alike. Plus, no list of Jensen nightlife would be complete without mention of **Conchy Joe's Seafood** (see "Great Deals on Dining," above), one of the region's most active spots. Inside, locals chug beer and watch a large-screen TV, while outside on the waterfront patio, live bands perform a few nights a week for a raucous crowd of dancers. Happy hours, weekdays from 3 to 6pm, draw large crowds with low-priced drinks and snacks (no cover).

In a strip mall just outside of downtown, you'll find pickup trucks as far as the eye can see parked outside the **Rock 'n' Horse,** 1580 S. Federal Hwy. (U.S. 1), Stuart (© **561/286-1281**). It's a real locals' country-and-western spot and the only real late-night spot in town. The cover varies.

The centerpiece of Stuart's slowly expanding cultural offerings is the newly restored **Lyric Theater,** at 59 SW Flagler Ave. (© **561/286-7827**). This beautiful 1920s-era, 600-seat theater hosts a variety of shows, readings, concerts, and films throughout the year.

2 Port St. Lucie ★ & Fort Pierce ★

7 miles N of Stuart

Worlds apart from the Gold Coast or Miami, Port St. Lucie and Fort Pierce are two sleepy Old Florida towns, a great place to experience pre-neon, pre-condomaniacal Florida. Both thrive on sportfishing; a seemingly endless row of piers juts out along the Intracoastal Waterway and the Fort Pierce Inlet for both river and ocean runs. Here visitors can also dive, snorkel, beachcomb, and sunbathe in an area that has been left untouched by the overdevelopment that has altered its neighbors to the south and north.

Most sightseeing takes place along the main beach road, A1A. Driving along Fla. A1A on Hutchinson Island, you'll discover several secluded beach clubs interspersed with 1950s-style homes, a few small inns, grungy raw bars, and a few high-rise condominiums. Much of this island is government owned and kept undeveloped for the public's enjoyment.

ESSENTIALS

VISITOR INFORMATION The **St. Lucie County Chamber of Commerce,** 2200 Virginia Ave., Fort Pierce, FL 34982 (© **561/595-9999**), is the region's main source of information. There's another branch at 1626 SE Port St. Lucie Blvd., in Port St. Lucie. Both spots are open Monday through Friday from 9am to 5pm.

WHAT TO SEE & DO
BEACHES & NATURE PRESERVES
North Hutchinson Island's beaches are the most pristine in this area. You won't find restaurants, hotels, or shopping; instead, spend your time swimming, surfing, fishing, and diving. Most of the beaches along this stretch of the Atlantic Ocean are private, but thankfully, the state has set aside some of the best areas for the public.

Fort Pierce Inlet State Recreation Area ★★★ (© **561/468-3985**) is a stunning 340-acre park with almost 4,000 feet of sandy shores that were once the training ground for the original Navy frogmen. A short nature trail leads through a canopy of live oaks, cabbage palms, sea grapes, and strangler figs. The western side of the area has swamps of red mangroves that are home to fiddler crabs, osprey, and a multitude of wading birds. **Jack Island State Preserve,** in the State Recreation Area, is popular with bird-watchers and offers hiking and nature trails. Jutting out into the Indian River, the mangrove-covered peninsula contains several marked trails, varying in distance from a half mile to over 4 miles. The trails go through mangrove forests and lead to a short observation tower.

The best beach in the recreation area, called **Jetty Park,** lies in the northern part of the State Recreation Area. Families enjoy the picnic areas and barbecue grills. There are restrooms and outdoor showers, and lifeguards look after swimmers.

The Fort Pierce Inlet State Recreation Area is located at 905 Shorewinds Dr., north of Fort Pierce Inlet. To get there from I-95, take Exit 66 east (Rte. 68) and turn left onto U.S. 1 north; in about 2 miles, you will see signs to Fla. A1A and the North Bridge Causeway. Turn right on A1A and cross over to North Hutchinson Island. Admission is $3.25 per vehicle, and the park is open daily from 8am to sunset.

SPECTATOR SPORTS & OUTDOOR PURSUITS
BASEBALL The **New York Mets** hold spring training in Port St. Lucie from late February through March at the **Thomas J. White Stadium,** 525 NW Peacock Blvd. (© **561/871-2115**). Tickets for spring training exhibition games and practices cost $10 to $15. From April through August, their farm team, the Port St. Lucie Mets, plays home games in the stadium.

FISHING The **Fort Pierce City Marina,** 1 Ave. A, Fort Pierce (© **561/464-1245**), has more than a dozen charter captains who keep their motors running for anglers anxious to catch a few. Brochures available at the marina list all the privately owned charter operators, who organize trips on an as-desired basis. The price usually starts at $150 per person for half-day tours, depending on the season.

GOLF The most notable courses in Port St. Lucie are at the **PGA Golf Club at the Reserve** at 1916 Perfect Dr. (© **561/467-1300**). The club's first of three 18-hole public golf courses opened in January 1996 and was designed by Tom Fazio; another course was designed by Pete Dye. The South Course, a classic Old Florida–style course, is set on wetlands, offering views of native wildlife, and is the most popular. The center also offers lessons for amateurs. The club is open 7am to 6pm daily. Greens fees are usually under $45; after 2pm, $25. Reserve at least 9 days in advance.

SEEING THE SIGHTS
Harbor Branch Oceanographic Institution ★★ Harbor Branch is a working nonprofit scientific institute that studies oceanic resources and welcomes

visitors on regularly scheduled tours. The first stop is the J. Seward Johnson Marine Education Center, which houses institute-built submersibles that are used to conduct marine research at depths of up to 3,000 feet. A video details current research projects, and several large aquariums simulate the environments of the Indian River Lagoon and a saltwater reef. Tourists are then shuttled by minibus to the Aqua-Culture Farming Center, a research facility containing shallow tanks growing seaweed and other oceanic plants. The 90-minute Lagoon Wildlife Tour explores the Indian River Lagoon by pontoon boat and is fascinating. The bus tour of the 600-acre campus is $10 and leaves Monday to Saturday at 10am, noon, and 2 pm. The boat tours are Monday to Saturday at 10am, 1pm, and 3 pm and cost $19 for adults, $12 for children 6 to 12.

5600 U.S. 1 N., Fort Pierce. © 800/333-4264 or 561/465-2400. www.hboi.com. Admission $10 adults, $6 children 6–12; free for children 5 and under. Mon–Fri 8am–5pm. Gift shop Mon–Sat 9am–5pm. Arrive at least 20 min. before tour.

Savannahs Recreation Area ★★★ *Finds*
A 550-acre former reservoir, Savannahs is a veritable wilderness, with botanical gardens, nature trails, campsites, a petting zoo, and scenery reminiscent of the Florida Everglades, but in a much more contained environment.

1400 E. Midway Rd., Fort Pierce. © 561/464-7855. Admission $1 per car. Daily 8am–6pm.

UDT-SEAL Museum (Underwater Demolition Team Museum)
Florida is full of unique museums, but none is more curious than the UDT-SEAL Museum, a most peculiar tribute to the secret forces of the U.S. Navy frogmen and their successors, the SEAL teams. Chronological displays trace the history of these clandestine divers and detail their most important achievements. The best exhibits are those of the intricately detailed equipment used by the navy's most elite members. Expect to spend about an hour here, depending on your level of interest.

3300 N. State Rd. A1A, Fort Pierce. © 561/595-5845. Admission $4 adults, $1.50 children 6–12; free for children 5 and under. Mon–Sat 10am–4pm; Sun noon–4pm. Closed Mon in off-season.

ACCOMMODATIONS YOU CAN AFFORD

The Port St. Lucie mainland is pretty run-down, but there are a number of inexpensive hotel options on scenic Hutchinson Island that are both charming and well priced. A great chain option in this area is the **Hampton Inn** (© 800/426-7866 or 561/460-9855), 2831 Reynolds Dr., which is relatively new and beautifully maintained. However, if you want to be closer to the water, try the **Days Inn Hutchinson Island,** 1920 Seaway Dr. (© 800/325-2525 or 561/461-8737), a small motel that sits along the Intracoastal inlet and is simple but very well kept. Another inexpensive option to consider is the **Edgewater Motel and Apartments,** 1160 Seaway Dr. (next door to and under the same ownership as the Dockside–Harborlight Inn and Resort), Fort Pierce (© 800/286-1745 or 561/468-3555). Motel rooms start at less than $60 in high season, and efficiencies are also available from $80. Guests can enjoy a private pool, shuffleboard courts, and a nearby fishing pier.

Dockside–Harborlight Inn and Resort ★
Fronting the Intracoastal Waterway, the Harborlight is a great choice for boating and fishing enthusiasts, offering 15 boat slips and two private fishing piers. The hotel itself carries on the nautical theme with pierlike wooden stairs and rope railings. Rooms are straight out of Rooms to Go, albeit with the signature nautical flair, with wood headboards and wicker. While not exactly captain's quarters, the rooms are attractive

and were thoroughly renovated in 1999. Higher-priced rooms have either waterfront balconies or small kitchenettes.

1160 Seaway Dr., South Hutchinson Island, FL 34949. © **800/286-1745** or 561/468-3555. Fax 561/489-9848. www.docksideinn.com. 64 units. Winter $65 standard rooms, $79–$130 efficiencies. Off-season $49–$89 standard rooms and efficiencies. AE, DC, DISC, MC, V. From I-95, exit at 66A east to U.S. 1 north to Seaway Dr. **Amenities:** 2 outdoor heated pools; self-service laundry. *In room:* A/C, TV, dataport, kitchenettes (in some), minibar, coffeemaker.

Kiwi Motel and Apartments *Kids* This simple and tiny one-story charmer is popular with diving, boating, and fishing clientele—many of whom come to stay for weeks or even months at a time in the little villas that are perfect for families or large groups (*hint:* call well in advance for reservations). It's one of the few accommodations in the area with two-bedroom, two-bath units. It's located directly on the inlet on Hutchinson Island, so you can fish, dock, or swim. There are also a small pool and spacious sun deck. Rooms are well-worn but clean and comfortable. Most have kitchenettes.

1240 Seaway Dr., Fort Pierce, FL 34949. © **561/461-6645**. 10 units. Year-round $40–$100 single or double. MC, V. **Amenities:** Pool. *In room:* A/C, TV, kitchenette.

Mellon Patch Inn ★★ *Finds* The Mellon Patch offers just four bright rooms in what looks like a single-family house. Each room has a large bathroom and sturdy soundproof walls, making it very quiet. The public living room is nicer than any of the small guest rooms: It's designed with a two-story vaulted ceiling, a fireplace, and lots of windows that overlook the Indian River. A gourmet breakfast that might include chocolate-chip pancakes or spinach soufflé is served here each morning. The best part is that there are free tennis courts and a public beach across the street. The inn is nonsmoking.

3601 N. Fla. A1A, North Hutchinson Island, FL 34949. © **561/461-5231**. Fax 561/464-6463. www.mellonpatchinn.com. 4 units. $85–$150 double year-round. Rates include breakfast. AE, DISC, MC, V. Children not allowed. *In room:* A/C, TV.

SUPER-CHEAP SLEEPS

Angler Motel and Apartments This tiny waterfront motel next door to the pricier Harborfront Inn is the smallest and one of the quaintest around town. It's especially popular in summer with boaters and fishers who dock at the small wooden dock out back on the Fort Pierce inlet. There is no pool but plenty of cool shade trees and bright splashes of bougainvillea. Rooms here are standard but well outfitted with fully equipped kitchenettes.

1172 Seaway Dr., Fort Pierce, FL 34949. © **561/466-0131**. 7 units. Year-round $55–$60 single or double; $350 weekly for 1-bedroom, from $1,000 monthly. 2-night minimum. Children under 12 stay free in parents' room. MC, V. *In room:* A/C, TV, kitchenette.

WORTH A SPLURGE

Villa Nina Island Inn ★★ *Finds* A more private option just down the road from the Mellon Patch is Villa Nina, in another simple but new home on 8 acres of the river's edge. Although it's more private, the silence is not nearly as heavy here as it is at the Mellon Patch. In fact, the atmosphere is rather cheery and extremely romantic. Innkeepers Nina and Glenn Rappaport live in the main house and have built homey riverfront rooms along the back, each with a private entrance, private bathroom, and either a fully equipped kitchen or a kitchenette. Enjoy breakfast poolside or delivered to your room (you may also opt out of breakfast for a $10 nightly savings). Canoes and rowboats are available for river rides, and a nearby shipwreck site makes for an excellent diving excursion. Smoking is not permitted anywhere in the inn.

3851 N. State Rd. A1A, North Hutchinson Island 34949. © and fax 772/467-8673. www.villanina.com. 5 units. Winter $115–$195; off-season $95–$165. DISC, MC, V. **Amenities:** Outdoor heated pool; canoe rental; diving and snorkel rental; bike rental; free laundry. *In room:* A/C, TV, kitchen or kitchenette, minibar (in most rooms), fridge, coffeemaker.

GREAT DEALS ON DINING

There are a number of good seafood restaurants in the Fort Pierce and St. Lucie area, but it's also easy to drive to Stuart for more diverse dining options. See section 1 of this chapter for recommendations in Stuart.

Harbortown Fish House ⭐ SEAFOOD You have to drive to the end of the harbor to reach this open-air waterfront fish house. It's a rustic place with outdoor tables overlooking the port, and you might be surprised to learn that it serves the area's best and freshest seafood. The menu is posted on white boards throughout the dining room and might include jumbo shrimp cocktail or New England clam chowder. Other dishes include angel-hair pasta with scallop- and anchovy-stuffed mushrooms, roast Muscovy duck with wild-mushroom risotto, and charcoal-grilled pepper-crusted tuna served over sautéed escarole.

1930 Harbortown Dr., Fort Pierce. © **561/466-8732.** Main courses $14–$20. AE, DISC, MC, V. Sun–Thurs 11:30am–9pm; Fri–Sat 5–10pm.

Mangrove Mattie's ⭐⭐ SEAFOOD A rustic restaurant on the Fort Pierce Inlet, Mangrove Mattie's is the best place for outdoor dining. It offers a priceless location right on the inlet, affording panoramic views of the Atlantic, and excellent fresh seafood. Weekday happy hours (4–7pm) are especially popular, thanks to the view and the free buffet.

1640 Seaway Dr., Fort Pierce. © **561/466-1044.** Reservations accepted. Main courses $11–$18. AE, DISC, MC, V. Daily 11:30am–10pm.

P.V. Martin's ⭐⭐ SEAFOOD/AMERICAN This relatively elegant eatery with an eclectic American menu is as funky as it gets in Fort Pierce. The wood floors, beamed ceilings, tiled tabletops, and rattan chairs would be nice anywhere, but here diners enjoy them as they look out through floor-to-ceiling windows onto sweeping ocean vistas. At night the room is warmed by a huge central stone fireplace, and on weekends there's live entertainment in the adjacent bar. Surf 'n' turf dinners run the gamut from crab-stuffed shrimp and grouper baked with bananas and almonds to Brie- and asparagus-stuffed chicken breast and barbecued baby back ribs. An excellent selection of appetizers includes escargots in mushroom caps and a succulent fried soft-shell crab (available in season). Be sure to try the lively Sunday champagne brunch.

5150 N. State Rd. A1A, North Hutchinson Island. © **561/569-0700.** Reservations recommended. Main courses $11–$20. AE, MC, V. Mon–Sat 5–10pm; Sun 10:30am–8pm.

Theo Thudpucker's Raw Bar and Seafood Restaurant ⭐ SEAFOOD Located in a little building by the beach and wallpapered with maps and newspapers, Thudpucker's is a straightforward chowder bar. There's not much more to the dining room than one long bar and a few simple tables. Chowder and stews, often made with sherry and half-and-half, make excellent starters or light meals. The most recommendable (and filling) dinner dishes are sautéed scallops, deviled crabs, and deep-fried Okeechobee catfish.

2025 Seaway Dr., Fort Pierce. © **561/465-1078.** Reservations not accepted. Main courses $12–$29. MC, V. Mon–Thurs 11:30am–9:30pm; Fri–Sat 11:30am–11pm; Sun 1–9:30pm.

SUPER-CHEAP EATS

Captain's Galley SEAFOOD   Anywhere else this might be just another coffee shop. But here, just over the Intracoastal Waterway at the north end of Hutchinson Island, it's a local institution. Dressed up with printed window valances and hanging plants, the Captain's Galley is busiest at breakfast, when locals catch up over eggs, toast, and home fries. Lunch specials usually include a variety of burgers and a small selection of salads and sandwiches. And dinner is for seafood, when the Galley serves up shrimp scampi, the day's fish, or land specialties like strip steak and chicken Francais.

827 N. Indian River Dr., Fort Pierce. © 561/466-8495. Reservations not accepted. Dinner $9–$12; breakfast/lunch $2–$5. DISC, MC, V. Mon–Sat 7am–2pm and 4:30–9pm; Sun 7am–12:30pm. Go north on U.S. 1 to Seaway Dr.; turn right and continue over the railroad tracks. Look for one of the only buildings on the left just before the bridge.

PORT ST. LUCIE & FORT PIERCE AFTER DARK

ArtWalk, a monthly event to showcase the downtown galleries, restaurants, and shops of Fort Pierce, takes place the second Wednesday of every month from 5 to 8pm and costs $5 per person, beginning in front of downtown's Sunrise Theater (© **561/466-3880**). All galleries are usually open to the public for this event, and they supply free beverages and cheese. The **Friday Fest Street Festival** occurs on the first Friday of every month at the Historic Downtown Riverfront in Fort Pierce and is free of charge, featuring live music and refreshments for sale.

The **St. Lucie Blues Club,** 338 Port St. Lucie Blvd. (© **561/873-1111**), features live jazz, blues, and rock music Tuesday through Sunday nights. Reservations are recommended.

3 Vero Beach & Sebastian

85 miles SE of Orlando, 130 miles N of Miami

Old Florida is thriving in these remote and tranquil villages. Vero Beach, known for its exclusive and affluent winter population, and Sebastian, known as one of the last remaining fishing villages, are located at the northern tip of the Treasure Coast region in Indian River County. These two beach towns are populated with folks who knew Miami and Fort Lauderdale in the days before massive high-rises and overcrowding. They appreciate the area's small-town feel, and that's exactly the area's appeal for visitors: a laid-back, relaxed atmosphere, friendly people, and friendlier prices.

A crowd of well-tanned surfers from all over the state descends on the region, especially the Sebastian Inlet, to catch some of the state's biggest waves. Other water-sports enthusiasts enjoy the area's fine diving and windsurfing. Anglers are also in heaven here, and in spring, baseball buffs can catch some action from the L.A. Dodgers as they train in exhibition games.

ESSENTIALS

Visitor Information   The **Indian River County Tourist Council,** 1216 21st St., Vero Beach, FL 32961 (© **561/567-3491;** fax 561/778-3181; www.verobeach.fl.us/chamber), will send visitors an incredibly detailed information packet on the entire county (which includes Vero Beach and Sebastian), with a full-color map of the area, a comprehensive listing of upcoming events, a hotel guide, and more.

WHAT TO SEE & DO
BEACHES & OUTDOOR ACTIVITIES

BEACHES You'll find plenty of free and open beachfront along the coast—most beaches are uncrowded and are open from 7am until 10pm.

South Beach Park, on South Ocean Drive, at the end of Marigold Lane, is a busy, developed, lifeguarded beach with picnic tables, restrooms, and showers. It's known as one of the best swimming beaches in Vero Beach and attracts a young crowd that plays volleyball and Frisbee in a tranquil setting. A nicely laid-out nature walk takes you into beautiful secluded trails.

At the very north tip of Wabasso Island, **Sebastian Inlet** has flat sandy beaches with lots of facilities, including kayak, paddleboat, and canoe rentals; a well-stocked surf shop; picnic tables; and a snack shop. The winds seem to stir up the surf with no jetty to stop their swells, to the delight of surfers and boarders, who get here early to catch the big waves. Campers enjoy fully equipped sites in a wooded area for $29.95 nightly. Admission to the Sebastian Inlet State Recreation Area, 9700 S. Fla. A1A, Melbourne, is $3.25 per car and $1 for those who walk or bike in.

FISHING Captain Jack Jackson works 7 days a week out of **Vero's Tackle and Sport-Shop,** 57–59 Royal Palm Point (© **561/567-6550**), taking anglers out on his 25-foot boat for private river excursions (all equipment is provided). Half-day jaunts on the Indian River cost $250 for two people (the minimum required for a charter), tackle, rigs, and everything included; $50 extra for a third person. You can either bring your own food and drinks or purchase food from the shop.

Many other charters, guides, party boats, and tackle shops operate in this area. Consult your hotel for suggestions, or call the chamber of commerce (© **561/567-3491**) for a list of local operators.

GOLF Hard-core golfers insist that of the dozens of courses in the area, only a handful are worth their plot of grass.

Set on rolling hills with uncluttered views of sand dunes and sky, the **Sandridge Golf Club** at 5300 73rd St., Vero Beach (© **561/770-5000**), offers two par-72 18-holers. The Dunes is a long course with rolling fairways, and the newer Lakes course has lots of water. Both charge $38, including a cart. Weekends cost $32 after noon. A small snack bar sells drinks and sandwiches. Reservations are recommended and are taken 2 days in advance.

Although less challenging, the **Sebastian Municipal Golf Course,** 1010 E. Airport Dr. (© **561/589-6800**), is a good 18-hole par-72. It's scenic, well maintained, and a relative bargain. Greens fees are $35.30 per player with a cart and about half that if you want to play nine holes after 1:30pm.

SURFING See Sebastian Inlet details under "Beaches," above. Also consider the beach north of the Barber Bridge (State Route 70), where waves are slightly gentler and the scene less competitive, and Wabasso Beach, Fla. A1A and County Road 510, a secluded area where lots of teenage locals congregate, especially when the weather gets rough.

TENNIS There are dozens of tennis courts around Vero Beach and Sebastian, though many of them are at hotels and resorts, which do not allow nonguests. Try **Riverside Racket Complex,** 350 Dahlia Lane, at Royal Palm Boulevard at the east end of Barber Bridge in Vero Beach (© **561/231-4787**). This popular park has 10 hard courts (six lighted) that can be rented for $3.20 per person per hour, and two racquetball courts, also with reasonable rates. Reservations are accepted up to 24 hours in advance. Nature trails are also on the premises.

SEEING THE SIGHTS

Environmental Learning Center ★★ *Kids*
The Indian River is not really a river at all, but a large brackish lagoon that's home to a greater variety of species than any other estuary in North America—it has thousands of species of plants, animals, fish, and birds, including 36 species on the endangered list. The privately funded Environmental Learning Center was created to protect the local habitat and educate visitors about the Indian River area's environment. Situated on 51 island acres, the center features a 600-foot boardwalk through the mangroves and dozens of hands-on exhibits that are geared to both children and adults. There are live touch-tanks, exhibits, and microscopes for viewing the smallest sea life up close. The best thing to do here is join one of the center's interpretive canoe trips, offered by reservation only ($10 for adults, $5 for children).

255 Live Oak Dr. (just off the 510 Causeway), Wabasso Island (a 51-acre island sitting in the middle of the Indian River Lagoon). © 561/589-5050. www.elcweb.org. Free admission. Tues–Fri 10am–4pm; Sat 9am–noon; Sun 1–4pm.

Indian River Citrus Museum
The tiny Indian River Citrus Museum exhibits artifacts relating to the history of the citrus industry, from its initial boom in the late 1800s to the present. A small grove displays several varieties. The gift shop sells clever citrus-themed gift items, along with, of course, ready-to-ship fruit.

2140 14th Ave., Vero Beach. © 561/770-2263. Admission $1 donation. Tues–Fri 10am–4pm.

McKee Botanical Garden ★★
This impressive 18-acre attraction was originally opened in 1932 and featured a virtual jungle of orchids, exotic and native trees, monkeys, and birds. After years of neglect, it was placed on the National Register of Historic Places in 1998. It underwent a top-to-bottom overhaul that was completed in February 2000, and you can now again experience the full charms of this little Eden.

350 U.S. 1, Vero Beach. © 561/794-0601. Fax 561/794-0602. www.mckeegarden.org. Admission $6 adults, $5 seniors, $3.50 children 5–12. Tues–Sat 10am–5pm; Sun noon–5pm.

McLarty Treasure Museum ★
If you're unconvinced about why this area is called the Treasure Coast, then this is a must-see. Erected on the actual site of a salvaging camp from a 1715 shipwreck, this quaint little museum is full of interesting history. It may not have the vast treasures of the nearby Mel Fisher museum (see below), but it does offer a very engaging 45-minute video describing the many aspects of treasure hunting. You'll also see household items salvaged from the Spanish fleet and dioramas of life in the 18th century.

13180 N. Fla. A1A, Sebastian Inlet State Recreation Area, Vero Beach. © 561/589-2147. Admission $1; children under 6 free. Daily 10am–4:30pm.

Mel Fisher's Treasure Museum ★★
This museum, where you can see millions of dollars of treasures from the doomed Spanish fleet that went down in 1715, is truly priceless. Although not as extensive as the Mel Fisher Maritime Heritage Museum in Key West (p. 215), this exhibit includes gold coins, bars, and Spanish artifacts that are worth a look. Also, the preservation lab shows how the goods are extricated, cleaned, and preserved.

1322 U.S. 1, Sebastian. © 561/589-9874. www.melfisher.com. Admission $5 adults, $4 seniors over 55, $1.50 children 6–12; free for children 5 and under. Mon–Sat 10am–5pm; Sun noon–5pm.

DODGERTOWN
Vero is the winter home of the **Los Angeles Dodgers** (at least for the time being; there's been talk of a move), and the town hosts the team in grand style. The

450-acre compound, Dodgertown, 3901 26th St. (© **561/569-4900**), encompasses Spring Training Camp, two golf courses, a conference center, a country club, a movie theater, a recreation room, citrus groves, and a residential community. It is a city unto its own for baseball fanatics and retirees. You can watch afternoon exhibition games during the winter (usually between mid-Feb and the end of Mar) in the comfortable 6,500-seat outdoor stadium. Even if the game sells out, you can sprawl on the lawn for just $5. The stadium has never turned away an eager fan.

Even when spring training is over, you can still catch a game; the Dodgers' farm team, the Vero Beach Dodgers, has a full season of minor-league baseball in summer.

Admission to the complex is free; tickets to games are $12 for a reserved seat. The complex is open daily from 9am to 5pm; game time is usually 1pm. From I-95, take the exit for S. R. 60 east to 43rd Avenue and turn left; continue to 26th Street and turn right.

SHOPPING

Ocean Boulevard and Cardinal Drive are Vero's two main shopping streets. Both are near the beach and are lined with specialty boutiques, including antiques and home-decorating shops.

The **Horizon Outlet Center,** at S. R. 60 and I-95, Vero Beach (© **877/GO-OUTLET** or 561/770-6171), contains more than 80 discount stores selling name-brand shoes, kitchenware, books, clothing, and more. The center is open Monday to Saturday from 9am to 8pm and Sunday from 11am to 6pm.

The **Indian River Mall,** 6200 20th St. (S. R. 60, about 5 miles east of I-95; © **561/770-6255**), is a monster mall with all the big national chains, as well as several department stores, and is open Monday through Saturday from 10am to 9pm and Sunday from noon to 6pm.

If you want to send fruit back home, the local source is **Hale Indian River Groves,** 615 Beachland Blvd. (© **800/562-4502;** www.halegroves.com), a shipper of local citrus and jams since 1947. Note that it is closed 2 to 3 months a year, usually from summer through early fall, depending on the year's crop; the season generally runs from November through Easter. There are four locations in Vero Beach.

ACCOMMODATIONS YOU CAN AFFORD

You can choose from accommodations on the mainland or on the beach. Although the beaches in many areas have eroded, leaving only narrow strips of sand, most areas offer pristine beachfronts where turtles lay eggs and sand crabs scurry around. As you might expect, the beachfront accommodations are a bit more expensive—but, I think, worth it.

There are deals to be had in the chain hotels and some lovely privately owned properties, especially on weekdays and during the off-season. Both **The Palm Court Inn,** 3244 Ocean Dr. (© **800/245-3297** or 561/231-2800), and the **Holiday Inn Oceanside,** 3384 Ocean Dr. (© **800/465-4329** or 561/231-2300), offer oceanfront rooms and suites at comparable prices (from around $80 for a standard room off-season to $185 for an oceanfront suite). The Holiday Inn may be a better choice since it offers discounts to AAA members and its restaurant and lounge directly face the ocean. The Palm Court (formerly a Days Inn) was thoroughly renovated in 1998.

Another great spot to know, especially if you are planning to fish, is **Captain Hiram's,** where there are four clean and cozy rooms available adjacent to the restaurant and overlooking the marina. Anglers flock to this popular fishing spot. Rates are between $80 and $110.

Comfortable and inexpensive chain options near the Vero Beach Outlet Center off S. R. 60 include a **Holiday Inn Express** (© **800/465-4329** or 561/567-2500), which opened in June 1998, and a slightly older **Hampton Inn** (© **800/426-7866** or 561/770-4299). Rates for both run between $70 and $80 and include breakfast and free local phone calls.

Aquarius Resort Hotel/Motel   Hotels are a rare commodity in this condo-canyon, where seeing the sky through the high-rise buildings is a trick. Finding an inexpensive one should precipitate applause—and here it is! Just near Dodgertown in Vero Beach are two surprising facilities, the Aquarius Hotel and its sister, the Aquarius Motel. The resort is on the south end of the beach and has a swimming pool, shuffleboard courts, and a barbecue. And the best part is, there are kitchenettes in each of the 28 units. The decor is nothing spectacular—modern Formica and dime-store prints—but the rooms are clean and well-maintained. Just a few yards away is one of Vero's prettiest uncrowded beaches.

3544 Ocean Dr., Vero Beach, FL 32963. © **561/231-1133.** 28 units (some with shower only). Winter $65–$115 single or double; off-season $50–$85 single or double. Extra person $5. AE, DC, DISC, MC, V. Children 11 and under stay free in parents' room. **Amenities:** Pool; shuffleboard. *In room:* A/C, TV, kitchenette.

Davis House Inn ★★   Each of the dozen rooms in this contemporary three-story B&B has a private entrance. The rooms are large and clean, although somewhat plain, and each has a king-size bed, a pullout sofa, and a small kitchenette, making the rooms popular with long-term guests. The bathrooms are equally ample and have plenty of counter space. Guests will find a large wooden deck for sunbathing and a sunny second-floor breakfast room. The inn is a bit out of the way but is within walking distance of some nearby restaurants; the beach is a 10-minute drive away.

607 Davis St., Sebastian, FL 32958. © **561/589-4114.** Fax 561/589-1722. 12 units. Winter $69–$79 double; off-season $50–$69 double. 7-night minimum in Feb. Weekly and monthly rates available. AE, DISC, MC, V. From I-95, take Exit 69, heading east to Indian River Dr., and turn left. Go 1¼ miles to Davis St.; turn left. **Amenities:** Coin-op washers and dryers. *In room:* A/C, TV.

Driftwood Resort ★★ *Finds*   Originally planned in the 1930s as a private estate by eccentric entrepreneur Waldo Sexton, the Driftwood was opened to the public after several travelers stopped by to inquire about renting a room here. Today the hotel's rooms and public areas are filled with the nautical knickknacks collected by Sexton on his travels all over the world. All of the guest rooms were renovated in 2000, and each is unique. Some feature terra-cotta–tiled floors and lighter furniture, while others have a more rustic feel with hardwoods and antiques. Two of the best rooms at the Driftwood are the Captain's Quarters, overlooking the ocean with a private staircase to the pool, and the town house located in the breezeway building, featuring a spiral staircase and living room and bedroom views of the ocean. The resort is listed on the National Register of Historic Places and, to say the least, has lots of quirky charm.

3150 Ocean Dr., Vero Beach, FL 32963. © **561/231-0550.** Fax 561/234-1981. www.thedriftwood.com. 100 units. Winter $110–$180 double; off-season $75–$130 double. AE, DISC, MC, V. **Amenities:** 2 outdoor heated pools; dry cleaning. *In room:* A/C, TV, kitchen (in most 1-bedroom and all 2-bedroom units), coffeemaker, Jacuzzi in some rooms.

Islander Inn ★   This is one of the most comfortable and welcoming inns in the area. Well located in downtown Vero Beach, this small, quaint Key West meets Old Florida–style motel is just a short walk to the beach, restaurants, and shops. Every breezy guest room has a small refrigerator, either a king-size bed or two double beds, paddle fans, wicker furniture, and vaulted ceilings, and opens onto a pretty courtyard and sparkling pool. Efficiencies have full kitchens.

3101 Ocean Dr., Vero Beach, FL 32963. © 800/952-5886 or 561/231-4431. 16 units. Winter $105–$120 double; off-season $72–$99 double. Efficiencies cost $10 extra. AE, MC, V. **Amenities:** Cafe; pool. *In room:* A/C, TV, kitchens in efficiencies, fridge.

Sea Turtle Inn & Azalea Lane Apartments This two-part property offers the best value on the beach (just 2 blocks from the ocean). The 1950s motel and an adjacent apartment building have been fully renovated and outfitted with understated but efficient furnishings. You won't find any fancy amenities (or even a phone for that matter, unless you request one), but its price and beachfront location make up for what it lacks in frills. The properties share a small pool and sun deck. Book early, especially in season, since it fills up quickly with long-term visitors.

835 Azalea Lane, Vero Beach, FL 32963. © **561/234-0788.** Fax 561/234-0717. www.vero-beach.fl.us/seaturtle. 20 units. Winter $79–$109 double; off-season $59–$89 double. Weekly and monthly rates available. MC, V. From I-95, go east on S.R. 60 (about 10 miles) to Cardinal Dr.; turn right onto Azalea Lane. **Amenities:** Small pool; bike rental; laundry. *In room:* A/C, TV, small fridge, coffeemaker. No phone.

CAMPING

The Vero Beach and Sebastian area of the Treasure Coast is popular with campers, who can choose from nearly a dozen camping locations. If you aren't camping at the scenic and very popular **Sebastian Inlet** (see "Beaches & Outdoor Activities," above), then try the **Vero Beach KOA RV Park,** 8850 U.S. 1, Wabasso (© **561/589-5665**). This 120-site campground is 2 miles from the ocean and the Intracoastal Waterway and a quarter mile from the Indian River, a big draw for fishing fanatics. There's access to running water and electricity, as well as showers, a shop, and hookups for RVs. Rates range from $20 to $24 per site, and $19 for tents. To get there, take I-95 to Exit 69 east; at U.S. 1, turn left.

GREAT DEALS ON DINING

Black Pearl Brasserie and Grill CONTINENTAL This sophisticated brasserie may seem out of place in this beachy town, but it happens to be one of Vero Beach's trendiest spots. The restaurant's small list of appetizers includes salads, chilled sweet-potato vichyssoise, crispy fried chicken fingers with mango dipping sauce, and grilled oysters with tangy barbecue sauce. Equally creative main courses are uniformly good. Don't miss their signature dish, an onion-crusted mahimahi with caramel citrus glaze. Both this original, unassuming restaurant and its newer counterpart, The **Black Pearl Riverfront,** at 4445 N. Fla. A1A (© **561/234-4426**), serve fantastically fresh and inventive food. The riverfront location is more formal and only serves dinner, starting at 5pm.

2855 Ocean Dr., Vero Beach. © **561/234-7426.** Reservations recommended. Main courses $12–$21. AE, DC, DISC, MC, V. Mon–Sun 11:30am–10pm; Sun brunch 10:30am–2pm.

Nino's Cafe ITALIAN This little beachside cafe looks like a stereotypical pizza joint, complete with fake brick walls, murals of the Italian countryside, and red-and-white checked tablecloths. The atmosphere is pure cheese and so is much of the food—pizza and parmigiana dishes are smothered in the stuff. Still, the thin crust and fresh toppings make the pizza here a cut above the rest. Entrees and pastas are also tasty.

1006 Easter Lily Lane (off Ocean Dr., next to Humiston Park), Vero Beach. © **561/231-9311.** Main courses $9–$12.95. No credit cards. Mon–Thurs 11am–9pm; Fri–Sat 11am–10pm; Sun 4–9pm.

SUPER-CHEAP EATS

Beachside Restaurant at the Palm Court Resort *Value* AMERICAN/DINER For a great big, cheap American breakfast with an ocean view, this is the place to go. You can get omelets, home fries, creamed chipped beef, corn beef hash, pancakes, Belgian waffles, and even grits. Friendly waitresses also serve lunch and dinner in the comfy wooden booths. The best dishes, like chili, fried chicken, and steaks, are hearty and delicious. No smoking.

3244 Ocean Dr., Vero Beach. © 561/234-4477. Breakfast $2–$5; full dinners from $8.95. AE, DC, DISC, MC, V. Mon–Sat 6am–9pm; Sun 6am–1:30pm.

WORTH A SPLURGE

Ocean Grill *Finds* AMERICAN The Ocean Grill attracts its faithful devotees with its traditional, rich dishes and its stunning locale, right on the ocean's edge; ask for a table along the wall of windows that open onto the sea. This huge and handsome old-timer specializes in steaks and seafood. Try stone crab claws when they are in season, or the house shrimp scampi baked in butter and herbs and served with a tangy mustard sauce, or any of the big servings of meats. We especially recommend the Cajun rib eye—the béarnaise sauce is delightfully jolting to the taste buds. Dinners are uniformly good.

1050 Sexton Plaza (by the ocean at the end of S.R. 60), Vero Beach. © 561/231-5409. Reservations accepted only for large parties. Main courses $17–$30. AE, DC, DISC, MC, V. Weekdays 11:30am–2:30pm and 5:30–10pm; weekends 5:30–10pm. Closed Thanksgiving, Superbowl Sun, and July 4.

A PRIX-FIXE STEAL

Chez Yannick FRENCH/CONTINENTAL Excellent cooking, a comprehensive wine list, and white-glove service complement the crystal and gilded decor at this French standout. On Wednesday nights during the off-season, treat yourself to a fabulous fixed-price menu, a lobster special that includes a 2-pound Maine lobster, soup, salad, and dessert for $29.95. The regular menu is tempting as well, with main courses such as beef tenderloin stuffed with Gorgonzola cheese, and sautéed soft-shell crabs. Desserts might include profiteroles with ice cream and chocolate or raspberry sauce, crème caramel, chocolate-mousse pie, or raspberry sorbet.

1605 S. Ocean Dr., Vero Beach. © 561/234-4115. Reservations recommended. Main courses $15–$30; fixed-price dinner $29 in off-season. AE, MC, V. Mon–Sat open at 6pm; closing time varies based on last reservation.

VERO BEACH & SEBASTIAN AFTER DARK

More than half the residents in this area are retirees, so it shouldn't be a surprise that even on weekends, this town retires relatively early. Hotel lounges often have live music and a good bar scene, especially in high season, and sometimes stay open as late as 1am, if you're lucky. For beachside drinks, go to the Driftwood Resort (see "Accommodations You Can Afford," above).

In Vero Beach, a mostly 30-something and younger crowd goes to **Bombay Louie's**, 398 21st St. (© **561/978-0209**), where a DJ spins dance music after 9pm from Wednesday to Saturday. Vero Beach is also known as an artsy enclave, hosting galleries such as **The Art Works**, 2855 Ocean Dr. (© **561/231-4688**), and the **Bottalico Gallery**, 3121 Ocean Dr. (© **561/231-0414**). **The Civic Arts Center** at Riverside Park is a hub of culture, including the Riverside Theatre (© **561/231-6990**), the Agnes Wahlstrom Youth Playhouse (© **561/234-8052**), and the Center for the Arts (© **561/231-0707**), known for films and an excellent lecture series.

In Sebastian, you'll find live music every weekend (and daily in season) at **Captain Hiram's,** 1606 N. Indian River Dr. (© **561/589-4345**), a salty outdoor restaurant and bar on the Intracoastal Waterway that locals and tourists love at all hours of the day and night. The feel is tacky Key West, complete with a sand floor and thatched-roof bar.

North of the inlet, head for the tried-and-true **Sebastian Beach Inn** (SBI to locals), 7035 S. Fla. A1A (© **321/728-4311**), for live music on the weekends. Jazz, blues, or sometimes rock-and-roll starts at 9pm on Friday and Saturday. On Sunday, it's old-style reggae after 2pm. The inn is open daily for drinks from 11am until anywhere from midnight to 2am.

4 A Side Trip Inland: Fishing at Lake Okeechobee
60 miles SW of West Palm Beach

Many visitors to the Treasure Coast come to fish, and they certainly get their fill of it off the miles of Atlantic shore and on the inland rivers. But if you want to fish freshwater and nothing else, head for "The Lake"—**Lake Okeechobee,** that is. The state's largest, it's chock-full of good eating fish. Only about a 1½-hour drive from the coast, it makes a great day or weekend excursion.

Okeechobee comes from the Seminole Indian word for "big water"—and big it is. The lake covers more than 467,000 acres; that's more than 730 square miles. At one time, the lake supported an enormous commercial fishing industry, but due to a commercial fishing-net ban, much of that industry has died off, leaving the rich bounty of the lake (especially bass) to the sportfishers.

As you approach the lake area, you'll notice a large levee surrounding its circumference. This was built after two major hurricanes killed hundreds of area residents and cattle. In an effort to control future flooding, the Army Corps of Engineers, which had already built a cross-state waterway, constructed a series of locks and dams. The region is now safe from the threat of floods, but the ecological results of the flood control have not been as positive. The bird and wildlife population suffered dramatically, as did the southern portion of the Everglades, which relied on the down-flow of water from the lake to replenish and clean the entire ecosystem. In early 2001, 30,000 acres of the lake's bottom caught fire due to a severe drought or, some say, arson. Drought had reduced the lake's depth to below 11 feet, provoking officials to impose water restrictions. Surprisingly, however, experts say the fire was beneficial for the lake. High water levels had previously prevented fire, which is a part of the natural cycle of the lake, and surrounding torpedo grass threatened to take over the marshes where native fish tend to swim. The fire brought with it the hope that now that the grass has been burned, the fish and the native plants will return to the lake. In early 2002, the water levels had returned to very close to normal.

ESSENTIALS
GETTING THERE From Palm Beach, take I-95 south to Southern Boulevard (U.S. 98 west) in West Palm Beach, which merges with State Route 80 and State Route 441. Follow signs for State Route 80 west through Belle Glade to South Bay. In South Bay, turn right onto U.S. 27 north, which leads directly to Clewiston.

VISITOR INFORMATION Contact the **Clewiston Chamber of Commerce,** 544 W. Sugarland Hwy., Clewiston, FL 33440 (© **863/983-7979;** www.clewiston.org), for maps, business directories, and the names of numerous fishing guides throughout the area. In addition, you might contact the **Pahokee Chamber of Commerce,** 115 E. Main St., Pahokee, FL 33476 (© **561/924-5579;** fax 561/924-8116; www.pelinet.net/pahokee); they'll send a complete package of magazines, guides, and accommodations listings.

For an excellent map and a brief history of the area, contact the **U.S. Army Corps of Engineers,** Natural Resources Office, 525 Ridgelawn Rd., Clewiston, FL 33440 (© **863/983-8101;** fax 863/983-8579). It is open weekdays from 8am to 4:30pm.

AFFORDABLE OUTDOOR PURSUITS

FISHING See the box, "Going After the Big One," below.

SKY DIVING Besides fishing, the biggest sport in Clewiston is jumping out of planes due to the area's limited air traffic and vast areas of flat undeveloped land. **Air Adventures** (© **800/533-6151** or 863/983-6151) operates a year-round program from the Airglades Airport. If you've never jumped before, you can go on a tandem dive, where you'll be attached to a "jumpmaster." For the first 60 seconds, the two of you free-fall, from about 12,500 feet. Then, a quick pull of the chute turns your rapid descent into a gentle, balletic cruise to the ground, with time to see the whole majestic lake from a privileged perspective. Dive packages start at $165; group rates start at $150.

ACCOMMODATIONS YOU CAN AFFORD

If you aren't camping (see below), book a room at the **Clewiston Inn** ★★, 108 Royal Palm Ave., Clewiston (© **800/749-4466** or 863/983-8151). Built in 1938, this Southern plantation–inspired hotel is the oldest in the Lake Okeechobee region. Its 52 rooms are simply decorated and nondescript. The lounge area sports a 1945 mural depicting the animals of the region. Double rooms start at $99 a night; suites begin at $129. All have air-conditioning and TVs.

Another choice, especially if you're here to fish, is **Roland Martin,** 920 E. Del Monte (© **800/473-6766** or 863/983-3151), the "Disney of fishing." This RV park (no tent sites) offers modest motel rooms, efficiencies, condominiums, apartments, or campsites, with two heated pools, gift and marina shops, and a restaurant. The modern complex, dotted with prefab buildings painted in white and gray, is clean and well manicured. Rooms rent for $68 and efficiencies cost $88. Condominiums are about $150 a night with a 3-night minimum. RV sites are about $25 with TV and cable hookup.

CAMPING

During the winter, campers own the Clewiston area. Campsites are jammed with regulars, who come year after year for the simple pleasures of the lake and, of course, the warm weather. Every manner of RV, from simple pop-top Volkswagens to Winnebagos to fully decked-out mobile homes, finds its way to the many campsites along the lake. Also see Roland Martin, above.

Okeechobee Landings, U.S. 27 east (© **863/983-4144**), is one of the best camping areas; it has every conceivable amenity included in the price of a site. More than 250 sites are situated around a small lake, clubhouse, snack bar, pool, Jacuzzi, horseshoe pit, shuffleboard court, and tennis court. Full hookup includes a sewage connection, which is not the case throughout the county. RV spots are sold to regulars, but there are usually some spots available for rental to one-time visitors. Rates start at $24.50 a day or $150 weekly plus tax, including hookup. Year-round rates for trailer rentals, which sleep two people, start at $32 Sunday to Thursday and from $37 Friday and Saturday.

Going After the Big One

Fishing on Lake Okeechobee is a year-round affair, though the fish tend to bite a little better in the winter, perhaps for the benefit of the many snowbirds that flock here (especially in Feb and Mar). RV camps are mobbed with fish-frenzied anglers who come down for weeks at a time for a decent catch.

You'll need a fishing license to go out with a rod and reel. It's a simple matter to apply. The chamber of commerce and most fishing shops can sign you up on the spot. The cost for non-Florida residents is $16.50 for 7 days and $31.50 for the year.

You can rent, charter, or bring your own boat to Clewiston; just be sure to schedule your trip in advance. You don't want to show up during one of the frequent fishing tournaments only to find you can't get a room, campsite, or fishing boat because hundreds of the country's most intense bass fishers are vying for the $100,000 prizes in the Redman Competition, which happens four times a year in the spring and winter.

There are, of course, more than a few marinas where you can rent or charter boats. If it's your first time on the lake, I suggest chartering a boat with a guide who can show you the lake's most fertile spots and handle your tackle while you drink a beer and get some sun. **Roland Martin,** 920 E. Del Monte (© **863/ 983-3151**), is the one-stop spot where you can find a guide, boat, tackle, rods, bait, coolers, picnic supplies, and a choice of boats. Rates, including the boat, start at $175 for a half day. A full day costs $250 and includes all necessary equipment except bait. You'll need a license for this, too, which Roland Martin also sells. They also have boat rentals: A 16-foot johnboat is $40 for a half day and $60 for a full day with a $40 deposit. A 26-foot pontoon is $125 for a full day and $85 for a half day with a $50 deposit.

Another reputable boat-rental spot is **Angler's Marina,** 910 Okeechobee Blvd. (© **800/741-3141** or 863/983-BASS). Rentals for a 14-footer start at $40 for a half day, for a maximum of four people. A full day is $60. If you want a guide, rates start at $150 (for two people) for a half day, though in the summer (June–Oct), when it's slow, you can usually get a cheaper deal.

GREAT DEALS ON DINING

If you aren't frying up your own catch for dinner, you can find a number of good eating spots in town. At the **Clewiston Inn** (see "Accommodations You Can Afford," above), you can get catfish, beef stroganoff, ham hocks, fried chicken, and liver and onions in a setting as Southern as the food. The dining room is open daily from 6am to 2pm and 5 to 9pm, and entrees cost $9 to $18. **L&L Restaurant,** 265 N. Devils Garden Rd. (© **941/983-6666**), is a good Spanish restaurant, with entrees ranging from $8 to $12. **Pinky's On the Green Pub,** Highway 80 (© **941/983-8464**), is a no-frills diner, with entrees under $8.

9

Southwest Florida

by Bill Goodwin

Thanks to a citizenry that has fought to protect both its history and its present-day environment, the southwest corner is one of the best parts of the state to discover remnants of Old Florida and enjoy the great outdoors.

Bordered on the east by the wild, wonderful Everglades and on the west by an intriguing, island-studded coast, Southwest Florida traces its nature-loving roots to inventor and amateur botanist Thomas A. Edison, who was so enamored with it that he spent his last 46 winters in Fort Myers. His friend Henry Ford liked it, too, and built his own winter home next door. The world's best tarpon fishing lured President Teddy Roosevelt and his buddies to Useppa, one of literally 10,000 islands dotting this coast. Some of the planet's best shelling helped entice the du Ponts of Delaware to Gasparilla Island, where they founded the Nantucket-like village of Boca Grande. The unspoiled beauty of Sanibel and Captiva so entranced Pulitzer Prize–winning political cartoonist J. N. "Ding" Darling that he campaigned to preserve much of those islands in their natural states. And the millionaires who built Naples enacted tough zoning laws that to this day make their town one of the most alluring in Florida.

Many well-heeled individuals still are attracted to Southwest Florida, making it one of the more expensive parts of the state to visit during the winter from mid-December to April. This is especially true of favorite enclaves of the rich and famous such as Boca Grande and Sanibel, Captiva, and Marco islands. During the off-season, however, even the most expensive resorts drop their room rates substantially, some drastically. And you can get some bargains in ritzy Naples even in winter—provided you book several months in advance. Consider visiting Southwest Florida during the "shoulder seasons" of November to mid-December and during May. The weather is warm and pleasant, rates are reduced, and most establishments that close during the slow summer season are open.

GETTING TO SOUTHWEST FLORIDA Southwest Florida International Airport, on the eastern outskirts of Fort Myers, is this region's major airport (see "Essentials" in section 1, below). From here, it's only 20 miles to Sanibel Island, 35 miles to Naples, or 46 miles to Marco Island. If you have a car, you can see the area's sights and participate in most of its activities easily from one base of operations.

EXCURSIONS TO THE EVERGLADES & KEY WEST You won't be in Southwest Florida for long before you see advertisements for excursions to the Everglades. Naples is only 36 miles from Everglades City, the "back door" to wild and wonderful Everglades National Park, so it's easy to combine a visit to the national park with your stay in Southwest Florida. See chapter 6, "The Everglades & Biscayne National Park," for full details about the Everglades.

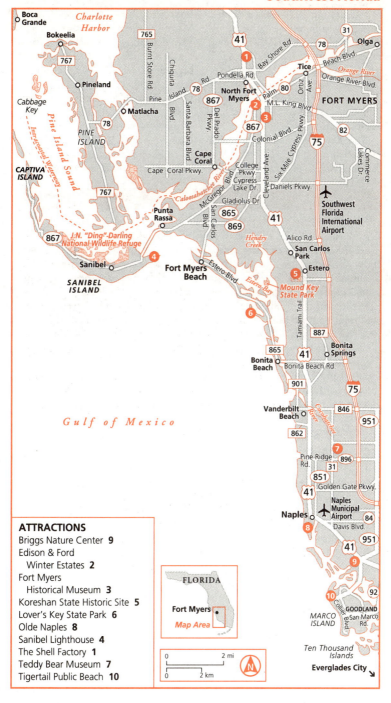

You also can easily make a day trip to Key West from here by air or sea. **Cape Air** (© 800/352-0714; www.flycapeair.com) shuttles its small planes several times a day between Key West and both Southwest Florida International Airport and Naples Municipal Airport. The same-day round-trip is about $180.

The **Key West Shuttle** (© 888/539-2628 or 239/732-7744; www.keywestshuttle.com) runs to Key West from both Fort Myers Beach and Marco Island from November through May, departing in the morning, arriving in Key West about midday, and beginning the return voyage at about 5pm. That will give you about 5 hours in Key West, so you may want to stay there overnight in order to more thoroughly explore the town. Round-trip boat fare is about $120 for adults, $80 for children 6 to 12. Contact the shuttle for schedules and reservations.

1 Fort Myers

148 miles NW of Miami, 142 miles S of Tampa, 42 miles N of Naples

It's difficult to picture this pleasant city of broad avenues along the Caloosahatchee River as a raucous cow town, but that's exactly what Fort Myers was just a few years before inventor Thomas Alva Edison came here in 1885 to regain his health after years of incessant toil and the death of his wife. Today, the city's prime attractions are the homes Edison and Henry Ford built on the banks of the Caloosahatchee. Edison planted lush tropical gardens around the two homes and royal palms in front of the properties along McGregor Boulevard, once a cow trail leading from town to the docks at Punta Rassa. Now lining McGregor Boulevard for miles, the trees give Fort Myers its nickname: The City of Palms.

Like most visitors to the area, you'll probably opt to stay near the sands at nearby Fort Myers Beach or on Sanibel or Captiva islands (see sections 2 and 3, below), but drive into Fort Myers at least to visit the Edison and Ford homes and have a riverside lunch. You also can venture inland and observe incredible numbers of wildlife in their native habitats, including those at the Babcock Ranch, largest of the surviving cattle producers and now a major game preserve.

ESSENTIALS

GETTING THERE This entire region is served by **Southwest Florida International Airport** (© 239/768-1000; www.swfia.com), on Daniels Parkway east of I-75. You can get here on **Air Canada** (© 800/776-3000), **AirTran** (© 800/247-8726), **America West** (© 800/235-9292), **American** (© 800/433-7300), **American Trans Air** (© 800/225-2995), **Continental** (© 800/525-0280), **Delta** (© 800/221-1212), **JetBlue** (© 800/538-2583), **LTU International** (© 800/888-0200), **Midwest Express** (© 800/452-2022), **Northwest/KLM** (© 800/225-2525), **Royal** (© 800/667-7692), **Spirit** (© 800/772-7117), **Sun Country** (© 800/359-5786), **United** (© 800/241-6522), and **US Airways** (© 800/428-4322).

Alamo (© 800/327-9633), **Avis** (© 800/331-1212), **Budget** (© 800/527-0700), **Dollar** (© 800/800-4000), **Enterprise** (© 800/325-8007), **Hertz** (© 800/654-3131), **National** (© 800/CAR-RENT), and **Thrifty** (© 800/367-2277) have rental cars here.

Vans and taxis are available at a booth across the street from the baggage claim. The maximum fares for one to three passengers are $26 to downtown Fort Myers, $38 to Fort Myers Beach, $40 to $47 to Sanibel Island, $60 to Captiva Island, $60 to Naples, and $75 to Marco Island. Each additional passenger pays $8.

Fort Myers

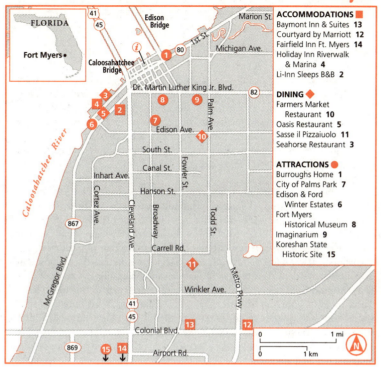

Amtrak provides bus connections between Fort Myers and its nearest station, in Tampa (✆ 800/USA-RAIL; www.amtrak.com). The Amtrak buses arrive in and depart from the **Greyhound/Trailways** bus station, 2275 Cleveland Ave. (✆ 800/231-2222; www.greyhound.com).

VISITOR INFORMATION For advance information about Fort Myers, Fort Myers Beach, and Sanibel and Captiva islands, contact the **Lee Island Coast Visitor and Convention Bureau**, 2180 W. 1st St., Suite 100, Fort Myers, FL 33901 (✆ 800/237-6444 or 239/338-3500; fax 239/334-1106; www.leeislandcoast.com).

Volunteers staff information booths in the baggage-claim areas at Southwest Florida International Airport.

Once you're here, the **Greater Fort Myers Chamber of Commerce** (✆ 800/366-3622 from outside Florida, or 239/332-3624; fax 239/332-7276; www.fortmyers.org) has a walk-in visitor center at the corner of Edwards Drive and Lee Street on the downtown waterfront. It's open Monday to Friday from 9am to 4:30pm.

There's also an information booth at the Edison and Ford Winter Estates (see "What to See & Do," below).

GETTING AROUND LeeTran (✆ 239/275-8726; www.rideleetran.com) operates public buses. System maps are available from the Greater Fort Myers Chamber of Commerce (see "Visitor Information," above). There's no public bus service to Sanibel and Captiva islands, but you can connect to the Fort Myers Beach trolleys (see "Getting Around," in section 2, below).

For a taxi, call **Yellow Cab** (© 239/332-1055), **Bluebird Taxi** (© 239/275-8294), or **Admiralty Taxi** (© 239/275-7000).

WHAT TO SEE & DO
TOURING THE ESTATES
Edison and Ford Winter Estates ★★ Thomas Edison and his second wife, Mina, brought their family to this Victorian retreat—they called it Seminole Lodge—in 1886 and wintered here until the inventor's death in 1931. Mrs. Edison gave the 14-acre estate to the city of Fort Myers in 1947, and today it's Southwest Florida's top historic attraction. In fact, it looks exactly as it did during Edison's lifetime. Costumed actors portraying the Edisons, the Fords, and their friends, such as Harvey Firestone, give "living history" accounts of how the wealthy lived in those days.

An avid amateur botanist, Edison experimented with the exotic foliage he planted in the lush tropical gardens surrounding the mansion (he turned goldenrod into rubber and used bamboo for light-bulb filaments). Some of his light bulbs dating from the 1920s still burn in the laboratory where he and his staff worked on some of his 1,093 inventions. The monstrous banyan tree that shades the laboratory was 4 feet tall when Harvey S. Firestone presented it to Edison in 1925; today it's the largest banyan in Florida. A museum displays some of Edison's inventions, as well as his unique Model-T Ford, a gift from friend Henry Ford. In 1916 Ford and his wife, Clara, built **Mangoes,** their bungalow-style house next door, so they could winter with the Edisons. Like Seminole Lodge, Mangoes is furnished as it appeared in the 1920s.

Allow an extra hour here to take a scenic ride on the river in a replica of Edison's electric boat *Reliance.*

2350 McGregor Blvd. © 239/334-3614 for a recording, or 239/334-7419. www.edison-ford-estate.com. Admission $12 adults, $6 children 6–12; free for children 5 and under. Boat rides $4 per person. Homes open Mon–Sat 9am–4pm; Sun noon–4pm (1½-hr. tours of both homes depart continuously). Boat rides Mon–Fri 9am–3pm (weather permitting). Closed Thanksgiving, Christmas Eve, and Christmas Day.

OTHER DOWNTOWN ATTRACTIONS
A good way to explore downtown Fort Myers during the winter season is on a leisurely, 2-hour guided walking tour hosted by the **Fort Myers Historical Museum,** 2300 Peck St., at Jackson Street (© **239/332-5955;** www.cityftmyers.com/attractions/historical.htm). The tours are held on Wednesday from 10am to noon and cost $5 a head. Reservations are required.

The historical museum itself is housed in the restored Spanish-style depot served by the Atlantic Coast Line from 1924 to 1971. Inside you'll see exhibits depicting the city's history from the ancient Calusa peoples and the Spanish conquistadors to the first settlers, including the remains of a P-39 Aircobra, which helps explain the town's role in training fighter pilots in World War II. Outside stands a replica of an 1800s "cracker" home and the Esperanza, the longest and one of the last of the plush Pullman private cars. Admission is $6 for adults, $5.50 for seniors, $3 for children 3 to 12, and is free for kids under 3. The museum is open Tuesday to Saturday from 9am to 4pm.

The Georgian Revival **Burroughs Home,** 2505 1st St., at Fowler Street (© **239/332-6125;** www.cityftmyers.com/attractions/burroughs.htm), was built on the banks of the Caloosahatchee River in 1901 by cattleman John Murphy and later sold to the Burroughs family. You must take a 30-minute tour; they usually are given from mid-October to mid-May, Tuesday to Friday, on the hour from 11am to 3pm and by appointment off-season, but call ahead any time of year. Admission is $6 for adults, $3 for children 3 to 12, and free for children under 3.

Rather than have the kids go stir-crazy on a rainy day, head for the **Imaginarium,** 2000 Cranford Ave., at Martin Luther King, Jr. Boulevard (© **239/ 337-3332;** www.cityftmyers.com/attractions/imaginarium.htm), a hands-on museum in the old city water plant. A host of toylike exhibits explains such basic scientific principles as gravity and the weather. Admission is $6 for adults, $5.50 for seniors, and $3 for children 3 to 12. It's open Tuesday to Saturday from 10am to 5pm and Sunday noon to 5pm. It's closed Thanksgiving and Christmas.

A NEARBY HISTORICAL ATTRACTION

Koreshan State Historic Site Worth a 15-mile drive south of downtown Fort Myers if you're into canoeing or quirky gurus, these 300 acres on the narrow Estero River were home to the Koreshan Unity Movement (pronounced Ko-*RESH*-en), a sect led by Chicagoan Cyrus Reed Teed. The Koreshans, who believed that humans lived *inside* the earth and—ahead of their time—that women should have equal rights, established a self-sufficient settlement here in 1894. You can visit their garden and several of their buildings, plus view photos from their archives. Canoeists will find marked trails winding down the slow-flowing river to **Mound Key,** an islet made of the shells discarded by the Calusa Indians (see "Canoeing & Kayaking" under "Affordable Outdoor Activities," below). There's also a picnic and camping area with 60 wooded sites for tents or RVs. For information, contact the park superintendent at P.O. Box 7, Estero, FL 33928.

U.S. 41 at Corkscrew Rd., Estero (15 miles south of downtown Fort Myers). © 239/992-0311. www.florida stateparks.org/district4/koreshan. Admission $3.25 per vehicle, $1 pedestrians or bikers; tours $1 adults, 50¢ children. Canoes $3 an hour, $15 per day. Camping, winter $16; off-season $10. Park daily 8am–sunset; settlement buildings daily 8am–5pm; 1-hr. tours Sat–Sun 1pm. From I-75, take Corkscrew Rd. (Exit 19), go 2 miles west, and cross U.S. 41 into site.

AN OLD-FASHIONED TRAIN RIDE

Train and murder-mystery aficionados will enjoy a ride on the **Seminole Gulf Railway** (© **800/736-4853** or 239/275-8487; www.semgulf.com), the original railroad that ran between Fort Myers and Naples. Today it chugs on daytime sightseeing trips and evening dinner-murder mystery excursions south to Bonita Springs and north across the river. Daytime rides cost between $8 and $12 for adults and $5 and $7 for children. The evening excursions begin at $50 per person. Call for the schedule and for reservations, which are required for the dinner trips. The trains depart Fort Myers from its Colonial Station, a small coral-colored building on Colonial Boulevard at Metro Parkway. The Bonita Springs station is on Old U.S. 41 at Pennsylvania Avenue.

AFFORDABLE OUTDOOR ACTIVITIES

CANOEING & KAYAKING The area's slow-moving rivers and quiet, island-speckled inland waters offer fine canoe and kayak ventures; you'll visit birds and manatees along the way. Two popular local venues are the winding waterways around **Pine Island** west of town and the **Estero River** south of Fort Myers. The Estero River route is an official Florida canoe trail and leads 3½ miles from U.S. 41 to Estero Bay, which is itself a state aquatic preserve. Near the mouth of the river lies **Mound Key State Archeological Site,** one of the largest Calusa shell middens. Scholars believe that this mostly artificial island dates back some 2,000 years and was the capital of the Calusa chief who ruled all of South Florida when the Spanish arrived. There's no park ranger on the key, but signs explain its history.

> ### Moments "Buggy" Rides Through a Mysterious Swamp
>
> One of the easiest and most informative ways to see Southwest Florida's abundant wildlife is on a "swamp buggy" ride with **Babcock Wilderness Adventures** ★★★, 8000 S.R. 31, Punta Gorda, about 11 miles northeast of Fort Myers (© **800/500-5583** for reservations or 239/338-6367 for information; www.babcockwilderness.com). Experienced naturalists lead 90-minute tours through the Babcock Ranch, the largest contiguous cattle operation east of the Mississippi River and home to countless birds and wildlife as well as domesticated bison and quarter horses. Alligators scurry from a bridge or lie motionless in the dark-brown waters of the mysterious Telegraph Swamp when the buggies pass overhead. Visitors dismount to visit an enclosure where southern cougars stand in for their close cousins, the rare Florida panthers (which are tan, not black).
>
> Unlike most wildlife tours in the region, this one covers five different ecosystems, from open prairie to cypress swamp. A replica of an Old Florida house built by the crew making the Sean Connery movie *Just Cause* serves as a small museum. Alligator bites are on the menu of a restaurant serving lunch. Admission is $17.95 for adults and $9.95 for children 3 to 12. The tours usually leave on the hour between 9am and 3pm from November to April, from 9am to noon from May through October. Reservations are required, so call ahead.
>
> The naturalists also lead 3-hour off-road bicycle tours. These cost $35 for adults and $30 for children. Reservations are required at least 3 days in advance.

Koreshan State Historic Site, half a mile south of the bridge at the intersection of U.S. 41 and Corkscrew Road (© **239/992-0311**), rents canoes (see "A Nearby Historical Attraction," above). Less than a mile from the site, **Estero River Tackle & Canoe Outfitters,** 20991 S. Tamiami Trail (U.S. 41), Estero, at the Estero River bridge (© **239/992-4050**; www.all-florida.com/swestero.htm), has guided historic and nature tours (call for schedule and prices) and rents canoes and kayaks at prices ranging from $18 to $30 a day. They are open daily 7am to 6pm.

In addition to its cruises mentioned below, **Tropic Star Cruises,** based at Knight's Landing marina, 16499 Porto Bello in Bokeelia on Pine Island (© **239/283-0015**; www.tropicstarcruises.com), rents kayaks and has guided tours over 18 miles of paddling trails. Rentals cost $35 a day for single seaters, $45 for doubles. Call for schedule and prices of guided tours. The company also has a ferry service to Cayo Costa State Park, where it rents kayaks (see "Nearby Island Hopping," in section 3, "Sanibel & Captiva Islands," later in this chapter).

CRUISES   **J. C. Boat Cruises** (© **239/334-7474**; www.floridatravel.com/jc cruises) presents a variety of year-round cruises on the Caloosahatchee River and its tributaries, including lunch and dinner voyages on the sternwheeler *Captain J. P.* The 3-hour Everglades Jungle Cruise is a good way to observe the area's wildlife, with lots of manatees to be seen from November to April. Once a week a full-day cruise goes all the way up the Caloosahatchee to Lake Okeechobee and back. The ticket office is at the downtown Fort Myers City Yacht Basin, Edwards Drive at Lee Street, opposite the chamber of commerce. Prices range from $14 to $75 for adults. Schedules change and advance reservations are required.

If you're headed out to Cabbage Key, Cayo Costa State Park, or Boca Grande (see "Nearby Island Hopping," in section 3, later in this chapter), **Tropic Star Cruises** (© **239/283-0015;** www.tropicstarcruises.com) offers a faster way to get there from Fort Myers than driving to Captiva Island and taking a boat from there. Tropic Star's all-day nature cruises on Pine Island Sound depart from Knight's Landing marina, 16499 Porto Bello in Bokeelia on Pine Island, daily at 9:30am. They include a stop at Cayo Costa and Cabbage Key and cost $25 for adults, $15 for kids under 12. The company also runs daily ferries to Cayo Costa State Park ($20 adults, $15 children 3–12), and to Boca Grande ($25 adults, $15 kids 3–12). The ferries take less than 30 minutes to cross the sound. Call for departure times.

Much more luxurious, the sleek, 100-foot-long yacht **Sanibel Harbour Princess** (© **239/466-2128**) goes on sunset dinner cruises from its base at Sanibel Harbour Resort & Spa, 17260 Harbour Pointe Rd., at Punta Rassa near the Sanibel Island causeway. Evening cruises start at $35 for adults, $27 for children, depending on the season. A 2-hour Sunday brunch cruise during winter costs $31.50 for adults, $20.15 for children. Call ahead for departure times and reservations.

GOLF For an excellent rundown of Southwest Florida golf courses, pick up a free copy of *Golfer's Guide,* available at the visitor information centers and many hotel lobbies, or on the Internet at www.golfersguide.com. See "The Active Vacation Planner," in chapter 2, "Planning an Affordable Trip to Florida," for information about subscribing or ordering the current edition. And don't forget that you can call **Tee Times USA** (© **800/374-8633** or 888/465-3356; www.teetimesusa.com) and book starting times at Florida courses.

Although it looks like an exclusive private enclave, the **Fort Myers Country Club,** McGregor Boulevard at Hill Avenue (© **239/936-2457**), actually is a municipal course. Designed in 1917 by Donald Ross, it's flat and uninteresting by today's standards, but it's right in town. A steak-and-seafood restaurant now occupies the fine old clubhouse. The city's other municipal course is the more challenging **Eastwood Golf Club,** on Ortiz Avenue between Colonial Boulevard and Dr. Martin Luther King, Jr. Boulevard in the eastern suburbs (© **239/275-4848**). Greens fees at both range from about $30 in summer to $55 during winter. Nonresidents must book tee times at least 24 hours in advance.

Other area courses open to the public include the Tom Fazio–designed **Gateway Golf & Country Club,** on Daniels Parkway east of the airport (© **239/561-1010**), and the two nationally acclaimed **Pelican's Nest** courses in Bonita Springs (© **239/947-4600**).

WATCHING THE BOYS OF SPRING

While many Major League Baseball teams have jumped around Florida for their **spring training,** the Boston Red Sox and the Minnesota Twins have worked out in Fort Myers for years. The **Boston Red Sox** play at the 6,500-seat City of Palms Park, at Edison Avenue and Broadway (© **877/733-7699** or 239/334-4700). The **Minnesota Twins** work out at the 7,500-seat William Hammond Stadium in the Lee County Sports Complex on Six Mile Cypress

Cheap Thrills: What to See & Do for Free (or Almost) in Southwest Florida

- **Catch the "green flash" at sunset.** Like the Tampa Bay Area to the north (see chapter 10, "The Tampa Bay Area"), Southwest Florida has mile after mile of beaches facing due west, thus providing glorious sunsets over the Gulf of Mexico and a chance to see the elusive "green flash," the moment the top of the sun dips below the horizon. The best places to watch for free are anywhere along Fort Myers Beach, at Blind Pass between Sanibel and Captiva islands, from the Naples Pier, and at the public access area on Marco Island's Crescent Beach.

- **Search for oldies but goodies at Fleamasters.** Florida has numerous flea markets where bargain hunters can browse for antiques, crafts, fashions, and fresh produce. With more than 800 busy booths, Fort Myers's weekend **Fleamasters,** 4135 Dr. Martin Luther King, Jr. Blvd. (© **239/334-7001**), is one of the biggest and best. It has snack bars and entertainment, too.

- **Canoe down a lazy river.** An official Florida canoe trail, the Estero River south of Fort Myers winds its way into Estero Bay, which is itself a state aquatic preserve. Near the mouth of the river lies Mound Key State Archeological Site, a Calusa Indian shell midden dating back some 2,000 years. **Koreshan State Historic Site,** on the river at U.S. 41 and Corkscrew Road (© **239/992-0311**), rents canoes for just $3 an hour, $15 per day.

- **Worship at a diamond.** With both the **Boston Red Sox** (© **239/334-4700**) and **Minnesota Twins** (© **800/338-9467** or 239/768-4270) holding their spring training here from mid-February through March, Fort Myers is a great place to see some of your favorite big league baseball stars get ready for the regular grind. Great seats close to the action cost $10 to $15, a bargain compared to what you'll pay when the boys of spring get back north.

- **Love nature on Lover's Key.** Possessed of one of Florida's best undeveloped beaches, the **Lover's Key State Park** south of Fort Myers Beach (© **239/463-4288**) is a great place to spend a day swimming, sunning, and shelling—a place where you'll find birds instead of condos as your neighbors. Admission is $2 for single-occupant vehicles, $4 for vehicles with two to eight occupants, and $1 for pedestrians and bicyclists. After that, the restrooms, showers, and tram ride through the mangroves to the deserted beach are free.

Parkway between Daniels and Metro parkways (© **800/338-9467** or 239/768-4270). The Twins' minor league affiliate, the **Fort Myers Miracle** (© **239/768-4210;** www.miraclebaseball.com), plays in the stadium from April through August.

Fort Myers is about an hour's drive south of Charlotte County Stadium (© **941/625-9500**), where the **Texas Rangers** hold their spring training. To get

- **Walk or ride along Wildlife Drive.** The mangrove swamps, winding waterways, and uplands of Sanibel Island's **J. N. "Ding" Darling National Wildlife Refuge** (© 239/472-1100) are great places to see alligators, raccoons, otters, and hundreds of species of birds. You can see many of the creatures from the 5-mile, one-way Wildlife Drive, which costs $5 per vehicle or $1 per pedestrian or biker. A naturalist will explain what you're seeing on a 2-hour narrated tram tour—a very good value at $10 for adults and $5 for children 12 and under.
- **Stoop for shells.** Okay, you'll have to pay a $3 toll to get here and a small fee to park your car (or lock your bike to a tree for nothing), but you can stroll Sanibel Island's world-famous shelling beaches as long as you want for free. After a few hours hunched over in the "Sanibel stoop," you're sure to go home with a prize find or two.
- **Bike on Sanibel Island.** Affluent but nature-loving Sanibel Island has one of the best networks of paved biking/blading/hiking trails in Florida. The trails end at Blind Pass, between Sanibel and Captiva, but catching a sunset here will make every pump of the pedal worth the effort. Ride your own across the 3-mile causeway from Fort Myers to the island, or rent a basic model from several Sanibel firms for $5 per hour or $15 a day.
- **Watch the millionaires from Naples Pier.** Olde Naples residents love to stroll out on their ancient pier to fish, catch a sunset, or look at Millionaires' Row, a string of magnificent mansions along the town's lovely beach. Now a state historic site, the pier is open 24 hours a day and is free, although it will cost you a few quarters to park in the nearby municipal lots.
- **Pretend you're rich on 3rd Street.** It costs not a penny to window-shop the ritzy 3rd Street district in Olde Naples. This town has industrial-strength money, but it's so Midwestern-friendly that nobody will care if you maxed out your credit cards just to get here.
- **Hunker down at happy hour.** Right on the beach and facing the glorious gulf sunsets, the chickee hut bar at **Vanderbilt Inn Naples,** a motel about 4 miles north of Olde Naples (© 800/643-8654 or 239/597-3151), cuts the price of libation during happy hour Monday to Friday from 4:30 to 8:30pm and on Saturday and Sunday from 3:30 to 7:30pm. The place really fills up on Sunday, when bands play. You can almost crawl here after a day on the undeveloped beach at Delnor-Wiggins State Park, next door.

there, take I-75 north to Exit 31 and go south on Kings Highway (Fla. 769); then make an immediate right on Veterans Boulevard (Fla. 776) to the stadium on the left.

SHOPPING

A kitschy tourist attraction, **The Shell Factory,** 5 miles north of the Caloosahatchee River bridge on U.S. 41 (© **888/4-SHELLS** or 239/995-2141;

www.shellfactory.com), not only carries one of the world's largest collections of shells, corals, sponges, and fossils, but it also has bumper boat rides, a "Waltzing Waters" light show, a gallery of African art, a food court, and two restaurants. Entire sections are devoted to shell jewelry and shell lamps, and many items here cost under $10, some under $1. The factory is open daily from 10am to 6pm.

Bargain hunters can browse more than 800 booths carrying antiques, crafts, fashions, and produce at **Fleamasters**, 4135 Dr. Martin Luther King, Jr. Blvd. (Fla. 82), 1½ miles west of 1-75 (© **239/334-7001**). There are snack bars and entertainment, too. It's open on Friday, Saturday, and Sunday from 8am to 4pm.

Anchored by Saks Fifth Avenue and Jacobson's, the Spanish-style **Bell Tower Shops,** Tamiami Trail (U.S. 41) at Daniels Parkway (© **239/489-1221**), is Fort Myers's upscale mall. You'll find most of the familiar national stores at **Edison Mall,** Cleveland Avenue (U.S. 41) at Winkler Avenue (© **239/939-5464**).

Outlet shoppers will find a large Levi's store among other major-brand shops at the **Sanibel Tanger Factory Stores,** on the way to the beaches at the junction of Summerlin Road and McGregor Boulevard (© **888/SHOP-333** or 239/454-1616). Another Levi's plus many more stores are at **Miromar Outlets,** on Corkscrew Road at I-75 in Estero (© **239/948-3766**), about halfway between Fort Myers and Naples. Both outlet malls are open Monday to Saturday from 10am to 9pm and Sunday from 11am to 6pm.

ACCOMMODATIONS YOU CAN AFFORD

As in the rest of Southern Florida, room rates here are highest, and reservations essential, during winter, from mid-December to April. Even the chain hotels and motels charge premium rates then. During the off-season, they drop by as much as 50% or more.

If you can't get a room at the properties mentioned below, the **Lee Island Coast Visitor and Convention Bureau** operates a free reservation service (© **800/733-7935**) covering many more accommodations in Fort Myers, Fort Myers Beach, and Sanibel and Captiva islands.

Most chain motels in Fort Myers are located along Cleveland Avenue (U.S. 41). Among the least expensive is the local **Motel 6** (© **800/466-8356** or 239/656-5544; fax 239/656-6276), a converted older property just across the river in North Fort Myers. South of downtown are an **Econo Lodge** (© **800/553-2666** or 239/995-0571) and a **Red Carpet Inn** (© **800/251-1962** or 239/9366-3229).

A few blocks from the Edison and Ford homes, Jim Haas's **The Li-Inn Sleeps Bed & Breakfast,** 2135 McGregor Blvd., at Clifford Street (© **239/332-2651;** fax 239/332-8922; www.cyberstreet.com/users/li-inn/li-inn.html), has five comfortable rooms, all with private bathroom, in a charming wooden house built a century ago in North Fort Myers. The building was later split in two, floated across the river, and nailed back together. Almost twice the size of the others, "Therese" is the choice unit here. Rates range from $95 to $115 in winter, $65 to $85 off-season, including full breakfast.

The 25-story, 416-unit **Ramada Inn & Suites at Amtel Marina,** 2500 Edwards Dr., at Fowler Street (© **800/833-1620** or 239/337-0300; fax 239/337-1530; www.amtelmarinahotel.com), is downtown Fort Myers's only large hotel. Rates are about $89 single or double year-round.

Many business travelers opt for the Art Deco **Quality Inn Historic District,** 2431 Cleveland Ave. (U.S. 41), at Edison Avenue (© **800/998-0466** or 239/332-3232). Its location, a 2-block walk to the Boston Red Sox training facility and a short drive to the Edison and Ford homes, is a plus for vacationers too.

Minor league hopefuls stay here during baseball spring training, so you could meet a future major-leaguer. Rooms range from $80 to $95 single or double in winter and cost $49 to $65 off-season.

All hotel bills in Southwest Florida are subject to a 9% tax.

The only campground with tent sites here is at **Koreshan State Historic Site,** on U.S. 41 in Estero (© **239/992-0311;** fax 239/992-1607), which has 60 wooded sites for tents or RVs at $16 per night during winter, $10 a night off-season. See "A Nearby Historical Attraction," above, for information about the historic site. For camping reservations call © **800/326-3521** or go to the website www.reserveamerica.com.

Courtyard by Marriott

This member of the exceptionally comfortable hotel chain designed for business travelers is situated 4 miles south of downtown and 10 miles north of the beach. The hotel surrounds a landscaped courtyard with swimming pool. The marble lobby features a fireplace and dining area serving breakfast only. The sizable rooms all have patios or balconies, sofas or easy chairs, and rich mahogany writing tables and chests of drawers.

4455 Metro Pkwy. (at the corner of Colonial Blvd.), Fort Myers, FL 33901. © **800/321-2211** or 239/275-8600. Fax 239/275-7087. 149 units. Winter $119–$179 double; off-season $80–$110 double. Weekend rates available. AE, DC, DISC, MC, V. **Amenities:** Heated outdoor pool; exercise room with Jacuzzi; coin-op washers and dryers. *In room:* A/C, TV, dataport, coffeemaker, hair dryer, iron.

SUPER-CHEAP SLEEPS

Baymont Inn & Suites

Like most members of this excellent small chain, formerly known as Budgetel Inns, this modern, four-story establishment offers good value with large, well-equipped rooms. It's centrally situated near the Courtyard by Marriott (see above) and offers an outdoor swimming pool. Entered from exterior walkways, the comfortably furnished rooms have extras like coffeemakers, desks, hair dryers, irons and boards, and free local calls. (We consider Baymont Inns the poor person's Courtyard by Marriott.) An extensive continental breakfast is served in a room off the lobby.

2717 Colonial Blvd., Fort Myers, FL 33907. © **800/301-0200** or 239/275-3500. Fax 239/275-5426. www.baymontinns.com. 123 units. Winter $120 double; off-season $80–$95 double. Rates include continental breakfast and local phone calls. AE, DC, DISC, MC, V. Pets accepted ($25 fee). **Amenities:** Outdoor pool. *In room:* A/C, TV, coffeemaker, hair dryer, iron.

Fairfield Inn Ft. Myers

About halfway between downtown and the beaches, this 1999-vintage Marriott property is within walking distance of the Bell Tower Shops and a plethora of chain restaurants. Although you'll have to do without coffeemakers or other niceties, the rooms are spacious and come with writing desks and easy chairs. A heated outdoor pool and an exercise room are the only guest facilities here.

7090 Cypress Terrace (off U.S. 41 a block south of Daniels Pkwy.), Fort Myers, FL 33907. © **800/228-2800** or 239/437-5600. Fax 239/437-5616. 104 units. Winter $79–$119 double; off-season $64 double. Rates include continental breakfast and local phone calls. AE, DC, DISC, MC, V. **Amenities:** Heated outdoor pool; exercise room; Jacuzzi. *In room:* A/C, TV.

WORTH A SPLURGE

Holiday Inn Riverwalk & Marina

This islandlike riverside hotel is a convenient base from which to explore the nearby Edison and Ford Winter Estates and other downtown attractions. The L-shaped building wraps around an attractively landscaped pool area. A riverfront building known as La Marina holds the Seahorse Restaurant (see "Great Deals on Dining," below), which has live music Friday and Saturday nights. The bands stop playing by 11pm, but you should ask for a room at the front of the property, which will be far enough removed from the action to escape most of the noise. Some of these have Jacuzzi tubs and small patios. Other units here lack both patios and balconies.

2220 W. 1st St. (at Euclid Ave.), Fort Myers, FL 33901. © **800/HOLIDAY** or 239/334-3434. Fax 239/334-3844. 145 units. Winter $139–$189 double; off-season $99–$129 double. Weekend rates available. AE, DC, DISC, MC, V. **Amenities:** Restaurant, bar; outdoor adult and children's pools; activities desk; salon with massage; limited room service; coin-op washers and dryers. *In room:* A/C, TV, fridge, coffeemaker, hair dryer, iron.

GREAT DEALS ON DINING

Some Southwest Florida restaurants adjust their hours from season to season and even from year to year, so you may want to call ahead to make sure of an establishment's business hours.

Fort Myers's main commercial strip, Cleveland Avenue (U.S. 41), has most national fast-food and family chain restaurants, especially near College Parkway. There's a branch of **Mel's Diner,** the excellent regional chain, at 4820 S. Cleveland Ave., opposite Page Field (© **239/275-7850**), offering inexpensive diner-style fare including breakfast served anytime.

Sasse il Pizzaiuolo ★★ *Finds* CONTINENTAL/ITALIAN In a small shopping strip north of the Edison Mall, Michael and Karen Gavala's informal, often noisy spot offers one of the area's most unusual and reasonably priced dining experiences. Aromas waft from Michael's wood-fired oven in the open kitchen, from which come enormous slabs of pizzalike bread (served with seasoned olive oil for dipping). The selections change daily, although you can usually count on braised lamb shank served over polenta, and veal scaloppini stuffed with prosciutto, roasted peppers, and mozzarella. It's all of a quality rarely found at these prices, and the portions are so huge that most patrons carry home doggy bags. Note that reservations are not accepted, so be prepared to wait for a table, especially on weekends.

3651 Evans Ave., in Carrell Corner shopping center (between Carrell Rd. and Winkler Ave.). © **239/278-5544**. Reservations not accepted. Main courses $8–$18. No credit cards. Tues–Fri 11:30am–1:15pm; Wed–Sat 5:30–8:15pm.

Seahorse Restaurant ★ INTERNATIONAL In the La Marina part of the Holiday Inn Riverwalk & Marina, this restaurant's sliding-glass walls opening to a riverside deck make it the most attractive place in town for taking a relaxing, alfresco lunch break while seeing the sights, or for watching the sun set over the Caloosahatchee. Best bet at lunch is the reliable fried, blackened, or grilled grouper sandwich. At dinner the cuisine switches to a mix of styles, from grilled fish and steaks to scallops in a Thai spicy green curry sauce.

At Holiday Inn Riverwalk & Marina, 2220 W. 1st St. (at Euclid Ave.) © **239/334-2727**. Reservations accepted. Main courses $10–$24; salads and sandwiches $7.50–$10; Sun brunch $15 adults, $6 children under 11. AE, DC, DISC, MC, V. Daily 7am–10pm (bar open later); Sun brunch 10am–2pm.

SUPER-CHEAP EATS

Farmers Market Restaurant ★★ *Finds* SOUTHERN Cabbage, okra, green beans, and tomatoes at the retail Farmers Market next door provide the fodder for some of the best country-style cooking in Florida at this plain and simple restaurant frequented by everyone from business executives to truck drivers. Specialties are beef and pork barbecue from the tin smokehouse out by Edison Avenue, plus other Southern favorites like country-fried steak, fried chicken livers and gizzards, and smoked ham hocks with a bowl of lima beans. Yankees can order fried chicken, roast beef, or pork chops, and they can have hash browns instead of grits with their big breakfast. No alcohol is served, nor is smoking permitted.

2736 Edison Ave. (at Cranford Ave.). ℂ 239/334-1687. Breakfast $3–$7.50; sandwiches $3–$6; meals $7.50. No credit cards. Mon–Sat 6am–8pm; Sun 6am–7pm.

Oasis Restaurant AMERICAN   A fine place for breakfast before touring the nearby Edison and Ford homes, Bonnie Grunberg and Tammie Shockey's narrow storefront spot also appeals to local professionals who don't mind sitting elbow to elbow recovering from a night at Shooters Waterfront Cafe USA (just behind this shopping center) with a "hangover" omelet chock-full of bacon, cheese, peppers, tomatoes, and onions.

In Edison-Ford Sq., 2222 McGregor Blvd. (at Euclid Ave.). ℂ 239/334-1566. Breakfast $3–$6; sandwiches, burgers, and salads $4–$6. No credit cards. Mon–Fri 8am–3pm; Sat–Sun 7am–2pm.

FORT MYERS AFTER DARK

For entertainment ideas and schedules, consult the daily *News-Press* (www.news-press.com), especially Friday's "Gulf Coasting" section. Also be on the lookout for *Happenings*, a tabloid-size entertainment guide distributed free at the visitor information offices and in some hotel lobbies. Tickets for most events are available from **Ticketmaster** (ℂ 239/334-3309).

The city's showcase performing-arts venue is the **Barbara B. Mann Performing Arts Hall**, 8099 College Pkwy., at Summerlin Road (ℂ 800/440-7469 or 239/481-4849 for tickets; www.bbmannpah.com), on the campus of Edison Community College. It features world-famous performers and Broadway plays.

Originally a downtown vaudeville playhouse, the 1908-vintage **Arcade Theater**, 2267 1st St., between Bay and Hendry streets (ℂ 239/332-6688), presents a variety of performances.

2 Fort Myers Beach ★★

13 miles S of Fort Myers, 28 miles N of Naples, 12 miles E of Sanibel Island

Often overshadowed by trendy Sanibel and Captiva islands to the north and ritzy Naples to the south, down-to-earth Fort Myers Beach, which occupies all of skinny Estero Island, offers just as much sun and sand as its affluent neighbors, both a half-hour drive away, but at more moderate prices. In fact, Fort Myers Beach is the most affordable destination in Southwest Florida.

Droves of both families and young singles flock to the busy intersection of San Carlos and Estero boulevards, an area so packed with bars, beach apparel shops, restaurants, and motels that the locals call it "Times Square." That Coney Island image certainly doesn't apply to the rest of Estero Island, where old-fashioned beach cottages, manicured condos, and quiet motels beckon couples and families in search of more sedate vacations. In fact, promoters of the southern end of the island say that they're not in Fort Myers Beach; they're on Estero Island. It's their way of distinguishing their part of town from congested Times Square.

Narrow Matanzas Pass leads into broad Estero Bay and separates the island from the mainland. While the pass is the area's largest commercial fishing port (when they say "fresh off the boat" here, they aren't kidding), the bay is an official state aquatic preserve inhabited by a host of birds as well as manatees, dolphins, and other sea life. Nature cruises go forth onto this lovely protected bay, which is dotted with islands.

A few miles south of Fort Myers Beach, a chain of pristine barrier islands includes unspoiled **Lover's Key** ★★★, a state park where a tractor-pulled tram runs through a mangrove forest to one of Florida's best beaches.

ESSENTIALS

GETTING THERE See "Essentials" in section 1, "Fort Myers," earlier in this chapter, for information about Southwest Florida International Airport, car-rental firms, and Amtrak's trains to the area.

VISITOR INFORMATION You can get advance information from the Lee Island Coast Visitor and Convention Bureau (see "Essentials," in section 1, earlier in this chapter) and from the **Fort Myers Beach Chamber of Commerce,** 17200 San Carlos Blvd., Fort Myers Beach, FL 33931 (© **800/782-9283** or 239/454-7500; fax 239/454-7910; www.fmbchamber.com), which provides free information, sells a detailed street map for $2, and operates a visitor welcome center on the mainland portion of San Carlos Boulevard just south of Summerlin Road. The chamber is open Monday to Friday from 8am to 5pm, Saturday from 10am to 5pm, and Sunday from 11am to 5pm.

GETTING AROUND Estero Island is absolutely inundated with traffic during the peak winter months, but you can get around on the **Beach Trolley,** which operates every 15 minutes daily from 7am to 9:30pm along the full length of Estero Boulevard from Bowditch Regional Park at the north end south to Lover's Key. It operates year-round. During the winter, the **Beach Park & Ride Trolley** runs daily from 6:30am to 9:30pm between Summerlin Square Shopping Center, on the mainland at Summerlin Road and San Carlos Boulevard, to Bowditch Regional Park. Rides on both trolleys cost 25¢ per person. Ask your hotel staff or call **LeeTran** (© **239/275-8726;** www.rideleetran.com) for more information.

For a cab, call **Local Motion Taxi** (© **239/463-4111**).

There are no bike paths per se here, although many folks ride along the paved shoulders of Estero Boulevard. A variety of rental bikes, scooters, and in-line skates are available at **Fun Rentals,** 1901 Estero Blvd. at Ohio Avenue (© **239/463-8844**), and **Scooters, Inc.,** 1698 Estero Blvd. at Avenue E (© **239/463-1007**). Charges start at $40 a day for one-passenger scooters, $14 a day for bikes.

WHAT TO SEE & DO
HITTING THE BEACH

A prime attraction for both beachgoers and nature lovers is the gorgeous **Lover's Key State Park**, 8700 Estero Blvd. (© **239/463-4588;** www.floridastateparks.org/district4/loverskey), on the totally preserved Lover's Key, south of Estero Island. Although the highway runs down the center of the island, access to this unspoiled beach from the parking lot is restricted to footpaths or a tractor-pulled tram through a bird-filled forest of mangroves. The beach itself is known for its multitude of shells. You'll find bathhouses with outdoor showers, and a snack shop. The park is open daily from 8am to sunset. Admission is $4 per vehicle with two to eight occupants, $2 for single-occupant vehicles, and $1 for pedestrians and bicyclists. No alcohol is allowed, nor are pets permitted on the beach or in the water (you must keep them on a leash elsewhere in the park).

A branch of Tarpon Bay Recreation on Sanibel Island (see section 3, later in this chapter), **Kayak Shack** (© **239/765-1880;** www.loverskey.net) provides kayak and canoe rentals in the park for $20 for a half day and $35 for a full day, and bicycles for $5 for a half day and $10 for a full day. Kayak Shack also offers 2- and 3-hour guided paddling tours to Mound Key and the back bays, starting at $25 (reservations are essential).

On Estero Island, **Lynn Hall Memorial Park** features a fishing pier and beach in the middle of Times Square. It has changing rooms, restrooms, and one

Fort Myers Beach

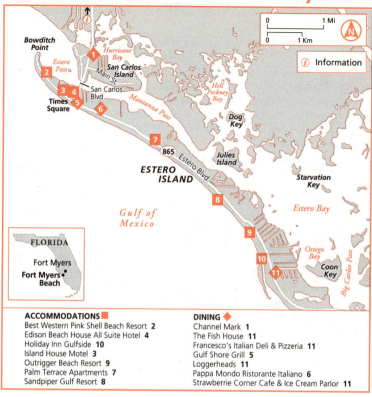

ACCOMMODATIONS
Best Western Pink Shell Beach Resort **2**
Edison Beach House All Suite Hotel **4**
Holiday Inn Gulfside **10**
Island House Motel **3**
Outrigger Beach Resort **9**
Palm Terrace Apartments **7**
Sandpiper Gulf Resort **8**

DINING
Channel Mark **1**
The Fish House **11**
Francesco's Italian Deli & Pizzeria **11**
Gulf Shore Grill **5**
Loggerheads **11**
Pappa Mondo Ristorante Italiano **6**
Strawberrie Corner Cafe & Ice Cream Parlor **11**

of the few public parking lots in the area; the meter costs 75¢ per hour, but keep it fed—there's a $32 fine if your time runs out. At the island's north end, **Bowditch Regional Park** has picnic tables, cold-water showers, and changing rooms. It has parking only for drivers with disabilities permits, but it's the turn-around point for the Beach Connection Trolley.

Several beach locations are hotbeds for parasailing, jet skis, sailboats, and other beach activities. **Times Square,** at the intersection of San Carlos Boulevard and Estero Boulevard, and the **Best Western Beach Resort,** about a quarter mile north, are popular spots on Estero's busy north end. Other hotbeds are **Diamond Head All Suite Beach Resort,** just south of Times Square, and the **Junkanoo Beach Bar** in the middle beach area (see "Fort Myers Beach After Dark," later in this chapter). Down south, activities are centered at the **Holiday Inn** and the **Outrigger Beach Resort** (see "Accommodations You Can Afford," below).

AFFORDABLE OUTDOOR ACTIVITIES
BOATING & BOAT RENTALS Powerboats are available from the **Mid Island Marina** (© 239/765-4371), the **Fort Myers Beach Marina** (© 239/463-9552), the **Fish Tale Marina** (© 239/463-3600), the **Palm Grove Marina** (© 239/463-7333), and the **Summer Winds Marina** (© 239/454-6333). **Dockside Boat Rentals** (© 239/765-4433) also rents them at the Best Western Pink Shell Beach Resort on Estero Island's northern end (see "Accommodations

You Can Afford," below). Boats cost about $125 for a half day or $200 for a full day.

CRUISES A good way to get out on the water and see some of this area's wildlife is on a nature cruise aboard the *Island Princess* (© **239/765-4433**), an open-air pontoon boat based at the Best Western Pink Shell Beach Resort marina on the north end of the island (see "Accommodations You Can Afford," below). The boat usually goes on 1½-hour nature cruises Monday through Saturday afternoons. Prices are $12.50 for adults and $7 for children. The *Island Princess* also offers bay fishing trips departing at 9am on Monday, Wednesday, Friday, and Saturday ($25 adults, $22.50 children) and shelling trips at 9am on Tuesday and Thursday ($25 adults, $12 children). Call ahead for reservations, which are required, and they will tell you what time the current afternoon nature cruises depart.

FISHING You can surf-cast, throw your line off the pier at Times Square, or venture offshore on a number of charter fishing boats here. The staff at **Getaway Marina**, 18400 San Carlos Blvd., about a half mile north of the Sky Bridge (© **239/466-3600**), is very adept at matching clients with skilled charter-boat skippers. Expect to spend about $600 a day for a full day's fishing for up to six people.

No reservations are required on "party boats" that take groups out. Operating year-round, the *Great Getaway* and *Great Getaway II* (© **239/466-3600**) sail from the Getaway Marina, about a half mile north of Sky Bridge. The *Island Lady* (© **239/482-2005**) is docked at Fisherman's Wharf, virtually under the San Carlos Island end of the Sky Bridge. Both operators depart between 8 and 9:30am; charge between $30 and $50 per person, depending on the length of the voyage; and have air-conditioned lounges with bars. Call for details and reservations.

SCUBA DIVING & SNORKELING Scuba diving is available at **Seahorse Scuba**, 15600 San Carlos Blvd. (© **239/454-3111**; www.seahorsescuba.com). Two-tank dives start at $59. In business since 1989, the company also teaches diver certification courses.

The live-aboard dive boat *Ultimate Getaway*, based at Getaway Marina, 18400 San Carlos Blvd. (© **239/466-3600**; fax 239/644-7529; www.ultimate getaway.net), makes 4-day voyages to the Dry Tortugas (70 miles west of Key West). This 100-foot vessel carries a maximum of 20 divers and is equipped with a dive platform, chase boat, and TV/VCR. Trips cost about $500 per person, including meals, beer, air, and weights, but bring your own regulator, mask, and fins. Reservations are essential.

ACCOMMODATIONS YOU CAN AFFORD

The hostelries recommended below are removed from the crowds of Times Square, but three chain motels offer comfortable accommodations right in the center of the action: **Ramada Inn** (© **800/544-4592** or 239/463-6158), **Days Inn** (© **800/544-4592** or 239/463-9759), and **Howard Johnson's Motel** (© **800/544-4592** or 239/463-9231). The mid-rise **Best Western Beach Resort** (© **800/336-4045** or 239/463-6000) is a quarter mile north, just far enough to escape the noise but still have a lively beach.

Sunstream Resorts, 6640 Estero Blvd., Fort Myers Beach, FL 33931 (© **800/ 625-4111**; fax 239/463-3060; www.sunstream.com), manages three "condominium hotels" in this area, including the plush **Casa Playa**, 510 Estero Blvd. (© **800/569-4876** or 239/765-0510; www.casaplayaresort.com), and the

Lover's Key Beach Club & Resort, 8771 Estero Blvd. (© **877/798-4879** or 239/765-1040; www.loverskey.com), both of which opened in 2000. The latter and **The Grand View Resort,** 8701 Estero Blvd. (© **239/765-4422**), are on the north end of Lover's Key. The 60 spacious apartments in the older, 16-story **Pointe Estero Island Resort,** 6640 Estero Blvd. (© **239/765-1155**), all have whirlpool bathtubs and screened balconies with gorgeous gulf or bay views. The less expensive **Santa Maria,** 7317 Estero Blvd. (© **239/765-6700**), is on the bay side of the island.

For campers, the somewhat-cramped **Red Coconut RV Resort,** 3001 Estero Blvd. (© **239/463-7200;** fax 239/463-2609; www.redcoconut.com), has sites for RVs and tents both on the gulf side of the road and right on the beach. They start at $40 a night during winter, $25 during off-season.

Island House Motel ★ *Value*

Sitting on stilts in the Old Florida fashion, but with modern furnishings, Ken and Sylvia Lachapelle's clapboard-sided Island House Motel enjoys a quiet location along a bay-side channel, directly across the boulevard from the Best Western Beach Resort and within walking distance of busy Times Square. Four of their units have screened porches; all have kitchens and ceiling fans. Ken and Sylvia maintain an open-air lounge with a small library beneath one of the units. They also provide free beach chairs and bikes. Book as early as possible for February and March. The Lachapelles also operate the three-story **Edgewater Inn,** less than a block away at 781 Estero Blvd. (same phone, fax, and website). The two one-bedroom and four two-bedroom apartments there all have screened lanais. They are available on a weekly basis during winter, for 3-day minimum stays off-season.

701 Estero Blvd., Fort Myers Beach, FL 33931. © **800/951-9975** or 239/463-9282. Fax 239/463-2080. www.edgewaterfmb.com. 5 units. Winter $119–$139 double; off-season $59–$79 double. Rates include local phone calls. Weekly rates available. MC, V. **Amenities:** Heated outdoor pool; access to nearby health club; coin-op washers and dryers. *In room:* A/C, TV, kitchen, coffeemaker, hair dryer, iron.

Outrigger Beach Resort

Well known for its **beachside tiki bar** (one of the best places for sunset-watching here), this clean, pleasant motel has been owned and operated by the same family since 1965. Their "garden efficiencies" in the original building have the feel of small cottages, with excellent ventilation through both front and rear windows and doors opening to backyard decks. Other buildings here are two-story blocks containing motel-style rooms and efficiencies, which have views of the large parking lot.

6200 Estero Blvd., Fort Myers Beach, FL 33931. © **800/749-3131** or 239/463-3131. Fax 239/463-6577. www.outriggerfmb.com. 144 units. Winter $115–$215 double; off-season $85–$185 double. AE, MC, V. **Amenities:** Restaurant (American), bar; heated outdoor pool; small exercise room; Jacuzzi; water-sports equipment rental; game room; coin-op washers and dryers; concierge-level rooms. *In room:* A/C, TV, kitchen, coffeemaker, hair dryer.

Palm Terrace Apartments ★ *Value*

Many European guests stay in these comfortable, well-maintained apartments about midway down the beach. In fact, between them, husband-and-wife owners Deborah Bowers and Peter Piazza speak fluent German and French and passable Italian. Their smaller, less-expensive units are on the ground level, with sliding-glass doors opening to a grassy yard, but even these units have cooking facilities including microwave ovens. Most units are upstairs, with screened porches or decks overlooking a courtyard with a heated swimming pool, a shuffleboard court, and a charcoal grill for barbecuing. Public access to the beach is across Estero Boulevard. There's no daily maid service, but you'll have an ample supply of clean linens.

3333 Estero Blvd., Fort Myers Beach, FL 33931. © **800/320-5783** or 239/765-5783. Fax 239/765-5783. www.palm-terrace.com. 9 units. Winter $89–$132 double; off-season $49–$81 double. 3-day minimum stay required in winter. Weekly rates available. AE, DISC, MC, V. **Amenities:** Heated outdoor pool; access to nearby health club; coin-op washers and dryers. *In room:* A/C, TV/VCR, dataport, kitchen, coffeemaker.

Sandpiper Gulf Resort The units at this quiet, family-oriented gulf-side motel all have living and sleeping areas, full kitchens, and convertible sofas, and overlook either the gulf or a courtyard. Steps lead from the pool directly to the beach. Some suites are in two- or three-story buildings arranged in a U, with the flattened ends right on the beach; others are in the Sandpiper II, a palm-fronted mid-rise with its own heated pool next door. All suites are identical, but those facing directly onto the beach are more expensive. Restaurants are nearby.

5550 Estero Blvd., Fort Myers Beach, FL 33931. © **800/584-1449** or 239/463-5721. Fax 239/765-0039. www.sandpipergulfresort.com. 63 units. Winter $152–$206 double; off-season $85–$115 double. DISC, MC, V. **Amenities:** Heated outdoor pool; Jacuzzi; water-sports equipment rental; bike rental; coin-op washers and dryers. *In room:* A/C, TV, dataport, kitchen, coffeemaker, hair dryer, iron.

WORTH A SPLURGE

Best Western Pink Shell Beach Resort Not to be confused with the nearby Best Western Beach Resort, this popular, family-oriented establishment fronts both the gulf and the Matanzas Pass from its perch on Estero's quiet northern end. It has efficiencies, suites, and one- and two-bedroom fully equipped apartments in three mid-rise, gulf-front buildings, with lovely views of Sanibel Island from screened balconies. The standard efficiencies are the least expensive units here. Sailboats and nature and sightseeing cruises pick up guests at the bay-side marina, which rents boats and bikes. The scenic Hungry Pelican Cafe, on a covered deck overlooking the channel, is a great spot for breakfast or lunch.

275 Estero Blvd., Fort Myers Beach, FL 33931. © **800/554-5454** or 239/463-6181. Fax 239/481-4947. www.pinkshell.com. 208 units. Winter $175–$449 condo or cottage; off-season $135–$309 condo or cottage. Packages and weekly rates available. AE, DC, DISC, MC, V. **Amenities:** Restaurant (American), bar; 4 heated outdoor pools; lighted tennis courts; water-sports equipment rental; bike rental; babysitting; laundry service; coin-op washers and dryers. *In room:* A/C, TV, kitchen, coffeemaker, hair dryer, iron.

Holiday Inn Gulfside Built by the shifting sands, the slowly emerging Little Estero Island (actually a peninsula) has left the surf a considerable distance from this conventional two-story motel, the center of beach activity on Estero's south end. Guests need not walk far, however, to a courtyard swimming pool, a tiki bar, and a grill serving lunches and snacks. Beachfront suites are the choice accommodation here. Otherwise, you're better off paying a little more for a room The shops and restaurants of Santini Marina Plaza are a short walk away.

6890 Estero Blvd., Fort Myers Beach, FL 33931. © **800/465-4329** or 239/463-5711. Fax 239/463-7038. www.holidayinnfmb.com. 103 units. Winter $155–$265 double; $315–$460 suite. Off-season $105–$155 double; $280 suite. AE, DC, DISC, MC, V. **Amenities:** Cafe, Grille, 2 bars; outdoor pool; 2 lighted tennis courts; water-sports equipment rental; game room; business center; shopping arcade; salon; limited room service; coin-op washers and dryers. *In room:* A/C, TV, dataport, kitchen (suites only), fridge (some rooms), coffeemaker, hair dryer, iron, safe.

AN OFF-SEASON BARGAIN

Edison Beach House All Suite Hotel No standardized list of amenities does justice to this intimate, five-story beachside inn, for when owner Larry Yax built it in 1999, he equipped every unit as if he were going to live in it. The light and airy units all have a balcony, a ceiling fan, a fully equipped kitchen (look for your complimentary bag of popcorn in the microwave oven), a writing desk stocked with office supplies, and a linen closet packed with extra towels. Most of the bathrooms have a combo washer-dryer. The freshly laundered bedspreads provided to each new guest are but one example of the premium Larry puts on cleanliness. The beachfront units have the best view, but much more romantic are the "A" suites, whose queen-size beds are almost surrounded by windows formed by a turret on one corner of the building—as in, you fall asleep and wake up to a panoramic view spanning gulf to bay.

830 Estero Blvd., Fort Myers Beach, FL 33931. © **800/399-2511** or 239/463-1530. Fax 239/765-9430. www.edisonbeachhouse.com. 24 units. Winter $225–$295 double; off-season $95–$175. AE, DC, DISC, MC, V. **Amenities:** Heated outdoor pool; laundry service. *In room:* A/C, TV, dataport, kitchen, coffeemaker, hair dryer, iron.

GREAT DEALS ON DINING

The busy area around Times Square has fast-food joints to augment several local restaurants catering to the beach crowds. The pick is the moderately priced **Beach Pierside Grill,** directly on the beach at the foot of Lynn Hall Memorial Pier (© **239/765-7800**), a lively pub with bright-blond wood trim and vivid fabric colors reminiscent of establishments in Miami's South Beach. It all opens onto a large beachside patio with dining at umbrella tables, outstanding sunsets, and live bands playing at night. The reasonably priced fare is a catchall of conch fritters, shrimp and fish baskets, burgers, and seafood main courses. They take reservations—a plus in this busy area. Food is served daily from 11am to 11pm.

Channel Mark ★★ SEAFOOD   Maryland-style crab cakes, delicately seasoned with Old Bay spice in true Maryland fashion, are enough to make this the beach's best place for seafood. Nestled by the "Little Bridge" leading onto San Carlos Island's northern end, every table here looks out on a maze of channel markers on Hurricane Bay. A dock with palms growing through it makes this a relaxing place for a waterside lunch. At night, a relaxed tropical ambience is ideal for kindling romance. The adjacent lounge offers the same menu and has live entertainment on weekends.

19001 San Carlos Blvd. (at the north end of San Carlos Island). © **239/463-9127.** Reservations recommended on major holidays; not accepted other times. Main courses $10–$21. AE, DISC, MC, V. Sun–Thurs 11am–10pm; Fri–Sat 11am–11pm.

Gulf Shore Grill SEAFOOD/AMERICAN   On the southern fringes of Times Square, this old clapboard building offers splendid views of the gulf and the beach. It began life in the 1920s as the Crescent Beach Casino and has seen various incarnations as a bathhouse, gambling casino, dance hall, and rooming house. These days, an extensive salad bar accompanies traditional Florida-style main courses, such as baked grouper imperial, grilled mahimahi, and shrimp wrapped in bacon and coated with honey. This is one of the best breakfast spots on the beach, with choices ranging from biscuits under sausage gravy to eggs served on a muffin under Alaskan crabmeat and a charon sauce. The kitchen also provides the pub fare for **The Cottage Bar,** an open-air drinking establishment next door (open daily 11am–2am).

1270 Estero Blvd. (on the beach at Ave. A). © **239/463-9951.** Reservations recommended for dinner. Main courses $13–$25; breakfast $4–$11; sandwiches and burgers $6–$13. AE, DISC, MC, V. Daily 8am–3pm and 5–10pm.

Loggerheads SEAFOOD/AMERICAN   The motto "The Local's Nest" accurately describes this friendly storefront restaurant, the best bet on the island's south end. Charter boat captains and other locals congregate around a big square bar on one side of the knotty-pine–accented dining room. The menu offers a wide range of appetizers, big salads, sandwiches, burgers, and main course options from both land and sea. Grouper prepared in a number of satisfying if not spectacular ways leads the main courses, but you can order traditionally fried, grilled, broiled, or blackened seafood plus pastas, steaks, ribs, and jerk chicken.

In Santini Marina Plaza, 7205 Estero Blvd. (at Lennel Rd.). 239/463-4644. Reservations recommended on weekends. Sandwiches and burgers $7–$8; main courses $12–$18. AE, DISC, MC, V. Sun–Thurs 11am–11pm; Fri–Sat 11am–midnight.

Pappa Mondo Ristorante Italiano ★★ Value NORTHERN ITALIAN Pasquale Riso (he's the chef) and Andrea Mazzonetto hail from Italy, and the fare they present in their attractive dining room-or out on their roadside patio—is authentic old-country cooking. They make everything from scratch—you can watch them producing pasta at a big machine behind a large picture window. Especially tasty is the ravioli, either ricotta-and-cheese topped with butter and sage sauce, or stuffed with veal and served with a light cream sauce tinged with balsamic vinegar.

1821 Estero Blvd. (at Ohio Ave.). 239/765-9660. Reservations recommended. Main courses $11–$16. AE, MC, V. Daily 3:30–10pm. Closed Christmas.

SUPER-CHEAP EATS

The Fish House SEAFOOD You'll find the beach's least-expensive outdoor dining at the dockside tables of this no-frills friendly pub. You'll also see charter boat skippers slaking their thirst at a large wooden bar occupying about half the open-air but screened dining room. Go for the fried or grilled grouper and other fish the captains have just landed. Sandwiches are available all day, including a tasty grouper version.

7225 Estero Blvd. (at Fish Tale Marina, behind Santini Marina Plaza). 239/765-6766. Sandwiches $6.50–$9; main courses $7–$20. AE, DISC, MC, V. Winter daily 11am–11pm. Off-season daily 11am–10pm. Closed Thanksgiving and Christmas.

Francesco's Italian Deli & Pizzeria ★ ITALIAN Wonderful aromas of baking pizzas, cannoli, breads, cookies, and fabulous calzones waft from this New York–style Italian deli. Order at the counter over a chiller packed with fresh deli meats, Italian sausage, and cheeses; then devour your goodies at tables inside or out on the covered walkway, or take them to the beach for a picnic. You can also take "heat and eat" meals of spaghetti, lasagna, eggplant parmigiana, manicotti, and ravioli to your hotel or condominium oven. Shelves are loaded with Italian wines, pastas, butter cookies, and anisette toast.

In Santini Marina Plaza, 7205 Estero Blvd. (at Lennel Rd.). 239/463-5634. Subs and sandwiches $5.50–$8; pizzas $12–$14; ready-to-cook meals $9–$11. No credit cards. Mon–Sat 8am–7pm.

Strawberrie Corner Cafe & Ice Cream Parlor DELI/ICE CREAM "Your Willpower Ends Here" is the motto of this bright ice-cream parlor and deli in Santini Marina Plaza. Strawberry-print wallpaper, strawberry dolls, and photos of strawberries provide the decor, and strawberry shortcake is the house specialty. In addition, the menu offers terrific homemade soups, shrimp salads, made-to-order deli sandwiches, fish and chips, and hamburgers. Each white table here is adorned with colorful fresh flowers.

In Santini Marina Plaza, 7205 Estero Blvd. 239/463-1155. Menu items $4–$7. No credit cards. Winter daily 7:30am–9:30pm. Off-season daily 11am–9:30pm. Closed Sept.

FORT MYERS BEACH AFTER DARK

To find out what's going on while you're here, pick up copies of the daily *News-Press* (www.news-press.com) and of the *Beach Bulletin* and the *Fort Myers Beach Observer,* two local tabloid newspapers. They're available at the chamber of commerce (see "Essentials," earlier in this chapter).

The area around Times Square is always active, every day during winter and on weekends off-season. In the very heart of Times Square at the foot of Lynn Hall Memorial Pier, the **Beach Pierside Grill,** 1000 Estero Blvd. (© **239/765-7800**), has live entertainment on its beachside patio. Facing due west, **Jimmy's Beach Bar,** in the Days Inn at 1130 Estero Blvd. (© **239/463-9759**), has live music nightly for the "best sunsets on the island" (actually, you can say that of all the beachside establishments here). It's not directly on the beach, but locals in the know head for the rooftop bar at **The Beached Whale,** 1249 Estero Blvd. (© **239/463-5505**), which supplies free chicken wings during nightly happy hour. Rock and reggae music is played downstairs for nighttime dancing.

Away from the crowds in the "middle beach" area, the **Junkanoo Beach Bar,** under Anthony's on the Gulf, 3040 Estero Blvd. (© **239/463-2600**), attracts a more affluent crowd for its bohemian-style parties that run from 11:30am to 1:30am daily. Live bands here specialize in reggae and other island music. The menu offers inexpensive subs, sandwiches, burgers, and pizzas, and a concessionaire rents beach cabanas and water-sports toys, making it a good place for a lively day at the beach.

On Sunday afternoons, revelers jam the docks for the famous outdoor reggae parties at **The Bridge Waterfront Restaurant,** 708 Fisherman's Wharf (© **239/765-0050**), which is under the Sky Bridge on San Carlos Island.

3 Sanibel & Captiva Islands

14 miles W of Fort Myers, 40 miles N of Naples

Sanibel and Captiva are unique in Florida. Here you will find none of the neon signs, amusement parks, and high-rise condos that clutter most beach resorts in the state. Indeed, Sanibel's main drag, Periwinkle Way, runs under a canopy of whispery pines and gnarled oaks so thick they almost obscure the small signs for chic shops and restaurants. This wooded ambience is the work of local voters, who have saved their trees and tropical foliage, limited the size and appearance of signs, and permit no building higher than the tallest palm and no WaveRunner or other noisy beach toy within 300 yards of their gorgeous, shell-strewn beaches. I've been to Sanibel many times, but it was only recently that I saw an aerial photo of the island and realized its southern shore is lined with hotels and condominiums. The foliage disguises the buildings that well.

Furthermore, more than half of the two islands is preserved in its natural state as wildlife refuges. Here you can ride, walk, bike, canoe, or kayak through the J. N. "Ding" Darling National Wildlife Refuge, one of Florida's best.

Legend says that Ponce de León named the larger of these two barrier islands "San Ybel," after Queen Isabella of Spain. Another legend claims Captiva's name comes from the infamous pirate José Gaspar's keeping captured women here. The modern era dates from 1892, when a few farmers settled on the islands. One of them, Clarence Chadwick, started an unsuccessful Key lime and copra plantation on Captiva; many of his towering coconut palms still stand, adding to that skinny island's tropical luster.

Sanibel and Captiva are among Florida's more upmarket destinations (a wag once said that having to pay $3 to get onto an island tells you something about how much you'll pay when you arrive). You can dine very well here for no more than you will pay on the mainland, but most room rates skyrocket into the stratosphere from mid-December to Easter. So either visit during the off-season, or stay in Fort Myers Beach during winter and make easy day trips to the islands.

ESSENTIALS
GETTING THERE See "Getting There" under "Essentials" in section 1 of this chapter for information about air, train, bus, and rental-car services. The Amoco station at 1015 Periwinkle Way, at Causeway Road, is the Sanibel agent for **Enterprise Rent-a-Car** (© **800/325-0007** or 239/395-3880).

VISITOR INFORMATION The **Sanibel–Captiva Islands Chamber of Commerce,** 1159 Causeway Rd., Sanibel Island, FL 33957 (© **239/472-1080;** fax 239/472-1070; www.sanibel-captiva.org), maintains a visitor center on Causeway Road as you drive onto Sanibel from Fort Myers. The chamber gives away an island guide and sells a detailed street map for $3. Other books are for sale, including comprehensive shelling guides and a helpful collection of menus from the islands' restaurants. There are phones for making hotel and condominium reservations (check the brochure racks for discounts during summer and Dec). The office is open Monday to Saturday from 9am to 7pm and Sunday from 10am to 5pm.

GETTING AROUND Neither Sanibel nor Captiva has public transportation. **No parking** is permitted on any street or road on Sanibel, and the hotels have parking only for their guests, so you'll have to stash your car in a public parking lot if you're not staying here overnight. Free beach parking is available on the Sanibel Causeway. Other municipal lots either are reserved for local residents or have a 75¢ hourly fee. Accordingly, many residents and visitors get around by bicycle (see "Affordable Ways to Enjoy the Outdoors," below).

If you need a cab, call **Sanibel Taxi** (© **239/472-4160**).

WHAT TO SEE & DO
PARKS & NATURE PRESERVES
Named for the *Des Moines Register* cartoonist who was a frequent visitor here and who started the federal Duck Stamp program, the outstanding **J. N. (Ding) Darling National Wildlife Refuge** ★★★, on Sanibel-Captiva Road, is home to alligators, raccoons, otters, and hundreds of species of birds. Occupying more than half of Sanibel Island, this 6,000-plus–acre area of mangrove swamps, winding waterways, and uplands has a 2-mile boardwalk nature trail and a 5-mile, one-way **Wildlife Drive.** The visitor center shows brief videos about the refuge's inhabitants every half hour and sells a map keyed to numbered stops along the Wildlife Drive. The best times for viewing the wildlife are early morning, late afternoon, and at low tide (tables are posted at the visitor center and are available at the chamber of commerce). Mosquitoes and "no-see-ums" (tiny, biting sand flies) are especially prevalent at dawn and dusk, so bring repellent.

Admission to the visitor center is free. The Wildlife Drive costs $5 per vehicle, $1 for hikers and bicyclists (free to holders of current federal Duck Stamps and National Park Service access passports). The visitor center is open from November to April, daily from 9am to 5pm; off-season, daily from 9am to 4pm. The center is open on federal holidays from January through May, closed on holidays the rest of the year. The Wildlife Drive is open all year, Saturday to

Sanibel & Captiva Islands

Thursday from 1 hour after sunrise to 1 hour before sunset. For more information, contact the refuge at 1 Wildlife Dr., Sanibel Island, FL 33957 (© **239/472-1100**).

You'll get a lot more from your visit to the refuge by taking a naturalist-narrated tram tour given by **Tarpon Bay Recreation,** at the north end of Tarpon Bay Road (© **239/472-8900;** www.tarponbay.com). The tours last 2 hours and cost $10 for adults, $5 for children 12 and under. Schedules are seasonal, so call ahead.

Tarpon Bay Recreation also offers a variety of guided **canoe and kayak tours,** with an emphasis on the historical, cultural, and environmental aspects of the refuge (call for the schedule and reservations, which are required). It also rents canoes, kayaks, and small boats with electric trolling motors (see "Affordable Ways to Enjoy the Outdoors," below).

A short drive from the visitor center, the nonprofit **Sanibel/Captiva Conservation Foundation,** 3333 Sanibel-Captiva Rd. (© **239/472-2329;** www.sccf.org), maintains a nature center, a native plant nursery, and 4½ miles of nature trails on 1,100 acres of wetlands along the Sanibel River. You can learn more about the islands' unusual ecosystems through environmental workshops, guided 1½-hour trail walks, beach walks, and a 2-hour natural-history boat cruise (call for seasonal schedules and reservations). Various items are for sale, including native plants and publications about the islands' birds and other wildlife. Admission is $3 for adults and is free for children 16 and under. The nature center is open November 15 to April 14, Monday to Friday from 8:30am to 4pm, Saturday 10am to 3pm; off-season, Monday to Friday 8:30am to 3pm.

Also nearby, the **Clinic for the Rehabilitation of Wildlife (C.R.O.W.)**, 3883 Sanibel-Captiva Rd. (© **239/472-3644;** www.crowclinic.org), is dedicated to the care of sick, injured, or orphaned wildlife. Tours of the facility usually take place year-round Monday to Friday at 11am and Sunday at 1pm, but call to make sure. Tours cost $3 per person.

HITTING THE BEACH: SHELLING & SEA LIFE

BEACHES Sanibel has four public beach-access areas with metered parking: the eastern point around **Sanibel Lighthouse,** which has a fishing pier; **Gulfside City Park,** at the end of Algiers Lane, off Casa Ybel Road; **Tarpon Bay Road Beach,** at the south end of Tarpon Bay Road; and **Bowman's Beach,** off Sanibel-Captiva Road. **Turner Beach,** at Blind Pass between Sanibel and Captiva, is highly popular at sunset since it faces due west; there's a small free parking lot on the Captiva side, but parking on the Sanibel side is limited to holders of local permits. All except Tarpon Bay Road Beach have restrooms. *Be forewarned:* Although nude bathing is illegal, the end of Bowman's Beach near Blind Pass often sees more than its share of bare straight and gay bodies.

Another popular beach on Captiva is at the end of Andy Rosse Lane in front of the Mucky Duck Restaurant. It's the one place here where you can rent motorized water-sports equipment (see "Affordable Ways to Enjoy the Outdoors," below), but you'll have to use the Mucky Duck's restrooms. There's limited free parking just north of here, at the end of Captiva Drive (go past the entrance to South Seas Resort to the end of the road).

SHELLING Sanibel and Captiva are famous for their seashells, and local residents and visitors alike can be seen in the "Sanibel stoop" or the "Captiva crouch" while searching for some 200 species.

Before you start scouring the beaches, visit the impressive **Bailey-Matthews Shell Museum,** 3075 Sanibel-Captiva Rd. (© **888/679-6450** or 239/395-2233; www.shellmuseum.org), the only museum in the United States devoted solely to saltwater, freshwater, and land shells (yes, snails are included). Shells from as far away as South Africa surround a 6-foot globe in the middle of the main exhibit hall, thus showing their geographic origins. A spinning wheel–shaped case identifies shells likely to wash up on Sanibel. Other exhibits are devoted to shells in tribal art, fossil shells found in Florida, medicinal qualities of various mollusks, the endangered Florida tree snail, and "sailor's Valentines"-shell craft made by natives of Barbados for sailors to bring home to their loved ones. The upstairs library attracts serious malacologists—for the uninitiated, those who study mollusks—and a shop purveys clever shell-themed gifts. The museum is open Tuesday to Sunday from 10am to 4pm; admission is $5 for adults, $3 for children 8 to 16, and free for children under 8.

Tips   Don't Take Live Shells

Florida law prohibits taking live shells from the beaches, and federal regulations prevent them from being removed from the J. N. (Ding) Darling National Wildlife Refuge.

The months from February to April, or after any storm, are the prime times of the year to look for whelks, olives, scallops, sand dollars, conch, and many other varieties. Low tide is the best time of day. The shells can be sharp, so wear Aqua Socks or old running shoes whenever you go walking on the beach.

With so many residents and visitors scouring Sanibel, you may have better luck finding that rare shell on the adjacent shoals and nearby islands, such as Upper Captiva and Cayo Costa (see "Nearby Island Hopping," later in this section). **Captiva Cruises** ★★ (© 239/472-5300; www.captivacruises.com) offers shelling trips leaving from the South Seas Resort on Captiva daily at 9am and noon. They cost $35 for adults and $17.50 for children. Reservations are required. Captiva Cruises also has popular dolphin-watching and wildlife cruises, with narration by a naturalist from the Sanibel-Captiva Conservation Foundation, daily from 4 to 5:30pm. These cost $20 for adults and $10 for kids. All of Captiva Cruises' boats are air-conditioned and have restrooms and snack bars.

At least 15 charter-boat skippers also offer to take guests on shelling expeditions to these less-explored areas. Their half-day rates are about $200 for up to four people, so get a group together. Several operate from the **'Tween Waters Inn Marina** (© 239/472-5161) on Captiva, including **Capt. Mike Fuery** (© 239/472-1015, or 239/994-7195 on his boat). Others are based at **Jensen's Twin Palms Marina,** on Captiva (© 239/472-5800), and at the **Sanibel Marina,** on North Yachtsman Drive, off Periwinkle Way east of Causeway Boulevard (© 239/472-2723). They all distribute brochures at the chamber of commerce visitor center (see "Essentials," earlier in this section) and are listed in the free tourist publications found there.

AFFORDABLE WAYS TO ENJOY THE OUTDOORS

BICYCLING, WALKING, JOGGING & IN-LINE SKATING   Paved bicycle paths follow alongside most major roads in Sanibel, including the entire length of Periwinkle Way and along Sanibel-Captiva Road to Blind Pass, making the island a paradise for cyclists, walkers, joggers, and in-line skaters. And you can walk or bike the 5-mile, one-way nature trail through the J. N. (Ding) Darling National Wildlife Refuge (see "Parks & Nature Preserves," above).

The chamber of commerce visitor center has bike maps, as do Sanibel's rental firms: **Finnimore's Cycle Shop,** 2353 Periwinkle Way (© 239/472-5577); **The Bike Rental,** 2330 Palm Ridge Rd. (© 239/472-2241); **Billy's Rentals,** 1470 Periwinkle Way (© 239/472-5248); **Boats, Bikes & Beach Stuff,** 2427 Periwinkle Way (© 239/472-8717); and **Tarpon Bay Recreation,** at the north end of Tarpon Bay Road (© 239/472-8900). On Captiva, **Jim's Bike & Skate Rentals** on Andy Rosse Lane (© 239/472-1296) rents bikes and beach equipment. Bike rates range from $3 per hour to $15 a day for basic models. Both Finnimore's and Jim's rent in-line skates as well.

There are no bike paths on Captiva, where trees alongside the narrow roads can make for dangerous riding.

BOATING & FISHING   On Sanibel, rental boats and charter-fishing excursions are available from **The Boat House** at the Sanibel Marina, on North Yachtsman Drive (© 239/472-2531), off Periwinkle Way east of Causeway Road. **Tarpon Bay Recreation,** at the north end of Tarpon Bay Road (© 239/472-8900), rents boats with electric trolling motors and tackle for fishing.

On Captiva, check with **Sweet Water Rentals** at the 'Tween Waters Inn Marina (© 239/472-6376), **Jensen's Twin Palms Marina** (© 239/472-5800), and **McCarthy's Marina** (© 239/472-5200), all on Captiva Road.

Rental boats on both islands cost about $125 for a half day, $200 for a full day. Half-day rates for charter-fishing excursions are about $300 for up to four people. The skippers leave free brochures at the chamber of commerce visitor center (see "Essentials," above), and they're listed in the free tourist publications found there.

CANOEING & KAYAKING As noted under "Parks & Nature Preserves," above, **Tarpon Bay Recreation** (© 239/472-8900; www.tarponbay.com) offers guided canoe and kayak trips in the J. N. (Ding) Darling National Wildlife Refuge. Do-it-yourselfers can rent canoes and kayaks here. They cost $20 for the first 2 hours, $5 for each additional hour. **Captiva Kayak Co./WildSide Adventures,** based at McCarthy's Marina (© **877/395-2925** or 239/395-2925; www.captivakayak.com), rents canoes and kayaks on Captiva, as does **'Tween Waters Inn Marina** (© 239/472-5161).

Naturalist, avid environmentalist, and former Sanibel mayor Mark "Bird" Westall of **Canoe Adventures** ✶✶ (© 239/472-5218; fax 239/472-6833) takes visitors on guided canoe trips through the wildlife refuge and on the Sanibel River. His excursions are timed for low tide and cost $40 for adults and $20 for children under 18. He will tailor shorter trips to accommodate children or anyone else not up to 2½ to 3 hours in a canoe. Naturalist **Brian Houston** leads kayaking trips from 'Tween Waters Inn Marina on Captiva, but make your reservations at Tarpon Bay Recreation on Sanibel (© **239/472-8900**). Brian also charges $40 per person. **Captiva Kayak Co./WildSide Adventures** (see above) offers both day and night back-bay ecology trips for $35 for adults, $25 for teenagers, $20 for children (add $10 to each price for night trips). They will customize tours, including camping on Cayo Costa (see "Nearby Island Hopping," later in this section), for advanced kayakers. Reservations are essential with all these operators.

GOLF & TENNIS For a serious splurge, golfers may view a gallery of wild animals while playing the 5,600-yard, par-70, 18-hole course at the **Dunes Golf and Tennis Club,** 949 Sandcastle Rd., Sanibel (© **239/472-2535;** www.dunes-golfsanibel.com), whose back nine runs across a wildlife preserve. Call a day in advance for seasonal greens fees and a tee time. The Dunes also has seven tennis courts. You can also play nine water-bordered holes at **Beachview Golf Club,** 1100 Par View Dr. (© **239/472-2626**). The **South Seas Resort** (see "Accommodations You Can Afford," below) has tennis courts and a nine-hole golf course, but they're for guests only.

SAILING If you want to learn how to sail, noted yachties Steve and Doris Colgate have a branch of their **Offshore Sailing School** (© **888/454-9002** or 239/472-5111, ext. 7141; www.offshore-sailing.com) at the South Seas Resort (see "Accommodations You Can Afford," below). You can either learn to sail or polish your skills here. Clinics ranging from a half day to a full week are available. The rates vary greatly by season and program, so call or check the website for current prices. When you do, ask about their popular women-only, father/son, and mother/daughter programs.

Also based on Captiva, two sailboats take guests out on the waters of Pine Island Sound: The *Adventure* (© **239/472-6300** or 239/472-4386) and the *New Moon* (© **239/395-1782**). They cost $95 per hour with a 2-hour minimum. Reservations are required.

Do-it-yourselfers can rent small sailboats from **Captiva Kayak Co./WildSide Adventures,** based at McCarthy's Marina (© **877/395-2925** or 239/395-2925;

www.captivakayak.com). Prices range from $25 to $55 an hour, depending on the size of the craft.

WATER SPORTS   Sanibel may prohibit motorized water-sports equipment on its beaches, but Captiva doesn't. **Yolo Watersports** (© **239/472-9656**) offers parasailing and WaveRunner rentals on the beach in front of the Mucky Duck Restaurant, at the gulf end of Andy Rosse Lane on Captiva.

MORE TO SEE & DO

Worth a brief stop after you've done everything else here, the **Sanibel Historical Village & Museum,** 950 Dunlop Rd. (© **239/472-4648**), includes the 1913-vintage Rutland home and the 1926 versions of Bailey's General Store (complete with Red Crown gasoline pumps), the post office, and Miss Charlotta's Tea Room. Displays highlight the islands' prehistoric Calusa tribal era, as well as old photos from pioneer days, turn-of-the-century clothing, and a variety of other memorabilia. The village and museum are open from November to May, Wednesday to Saturday from 10am to 4pm; June to mid-August, Wednesday to Saturday from 10am to 1pm. Admission is $3.

At the east end of Periwinkle Way, the **Sanibel Lighthouse** has marked the entrance to San Carlos Bay since 1884. The lightkeepers used to live in the cottages at the base of the 94-foot tower. The now-automatic lighthouse isn't open to visitors, but the grounds and beach are.

The best way to get the lay of the land and learn all about the islands' history is on a 2-hour **Sanibel Island Eco-History Trolley Tour,** staged by Adventures in Paradise (© **239/472-8443;** www.adventureinparadiseinc.com). They depart the chamber of commerce (see "Essentials," earlier in this section) Monday to Saturday at 10:30am and 1pm and cost $18 for adults, $15 for children; free for kids 3 and under. Call for reservations.

In addition to its other trips, **Captiva Cruises** (© **239/472-5300;** www.captivacruises.com) sets out daily on sunset cruises from the South Seas Resort on Captiva. These cost $17.50 for adults and $10 for children. Call for daily departure times and reservations.

SHOPPING & BROWSING

If you have no luck at beach-hunting for shells, several Sanibel shops sell thousands of them. **Sanibel Sea Shell Industries,** 905 Fitzhugh St. (© **239/472-1603**), has one of the largest collections, with more than 10,000 shells in stock. **She Sells Sea Shells** has two locations: 1157 Periwinkle Way near Causeway Road (© **239/472-6991**) and 2422 Periwinkle Way near the island's center (© **239/472-8080**). Others include **Neptune's Treasures Shell Shop,** in the Tree Tops Center, 1101 Periwinkle Way opposite the Dairy Queen (© **239/472-3132**), which also has a good collection of fossils.

For excellent window shopping, you can burn up a rainy day cruising Sanibel's numerous upscale boutiques, which carry expensive jewelry, apparel, and gifts. Many are in **Periwinkle Place** and **Tahitian Gardens,** the main shopping centers along Periwinkle Way. The larger Periwinkle Place sports mostly high-end men's and women's clothiers. Tahitian Gardens also has some excellent gift shops, including the **Audubon Nature Store** (© **239/395-2020**), which carries gifts and books with a wildlife theme, and **The Cheshire Cat** (© **239/472-3545**), offering nature toys and other unique items for kids.

More than a dozen Sanibel galleries feature original works of art, which are fun to browse; pick up a gallery guide at the chamber of commerce visitor center (see "Essentials," earlier in this chapter). On Captiva, the treehouselike **Jungle Drums,** on Andy Rosse Lane (© 239/395-2266), has the area's most unique collection of wildlife art.

Founded in 1899, **Bailey's General Store** is still going strong at the corner of Periwinkle Way and Tarpon Bay Road (© 239/472-1516), with a supermarket, deli, salad bar, hardware store, beach shop, shoe repair, and Western Union all under one roof.

Bailey's General Store is open daily from 7am to 9pm. Most other shops are open Monday to Saturday from 9am to 6pm and Sunday from noon to 5pm.

ACCOMMODATIONS YOU CAN AFFORD

Sanibel & Captiva Central Reservations, Inc. (© 800/325-1352 or 239/472-0457; fax 239/472-2178; www.sanibel-captivarent.com) and **1-800-SANIBEL** (© 800/726-4235 or 239/472-1800; fax 239/395-9690; www.1-800-sanibel.com) are reservations services that will book you into most condominiums and cottages here.

In general, Sanibel and Captiva room and condominium rates are highest during the shelling season, February to April. January is usually somewhat less expensive. But note that most rates fall drastically during the off-season. Don't hesitate to ask for a discount or special deal then. Since most properties on the islands are geared to 1-week vacations, you can also save by purchasing a package deal if you're staying for 7 nights or longer.

The islands' sole campground, the **Periwinkle Trailer Park,** 1119 Periwinkle Way, Sanibel Island (© 239/472-1433), is so popular it doesn't even advertise. No other camping is permitted on either Sanibel or Captiva.

SANIBEL ISLAND

Palm View Motel In a quiet residential area less than a block from the Holiday Inn Beach Resort and Morgan's Forest restaurant, this little property is one of Sanibel's few inexpensive motels. The best choices here are the spacious, well-ventilated one- and two-bedroom apartments, but even the smaller efficiencies have kitchens and separate living and sleeping areas. You'll have to do without a phone in your room, but you can bring your pet. There's a hot tub in the backyard.

706 Donax St., Sanibel Island, FL 33957. © 239/472-1606. Fax 239/472-1606. www.palmviewmotel.com. 5 units. Winter $145–$185 efficiency and apts. Off-season $85–$135 efficiency and apts. Weekly rates available. MC, V. Pets accepted ($10 per day). **Amenities:** Jacuzzi; bike rental; free guest laundry. *In room:* A/C, TV, kitchen, coffeemaker, hair dryer, iron. No phone.

Tarpon Tale Inn *Finds* Owners Dawn and Joe Ramsey preside over this low-slung gray building in the "Old Sanibel" neighborhood, the island's first settlement, where the ferries from Fort Myers used to dock near the lighthouse. White walls and tile floors make their comfortable units bright; French doors lead to gardens dense with seagrape, palm, and ficus trees, which provide privacy for a large outdoor hot tub. Three of their five units have separate bedrooms, while two other "deluxe studios" actually are two-bedroom suites. Continental breakfast makings are delivered the night before.

367 Periwinkle Way, Sanibel Island, FL 33957. © 239/472-0939. Fax 239/472-6202. www.tarpontale.com. 5 units (shower only). Winter $119–$210 double; off-season $79–$159 double. Rates include continental breakfast. AE, DC, DISC, MC, V. Some pets accepted ($30 fee); call first. **Amenities:** Jacuzzi; free use of bikes; coin-op washers and dryers. *In room:* A/C, TV/VCR, kitchen, coffeemaker, hair dryer and iron on request. No phone.

Worth an Off-Season Splurge

Best Western Sanibel Island Beach Resort One of only two chain properties here, this excellently managed motel boasts spacious rooms, efficiencies, and apartments whose screened balconies face either the beach or a lawn festooned with palms, pink hibiscus, orange trees, a swimming pool, tennis courts, and white Adirondack chairs for lounging. Choice units are on the beach end of the building.

3287 W. Gulf Dr. (at St. Kilda Rd.), Sanibel Island, FL 33957. © 800/645-6559 or 239/472-1700. Fax 239/472-5032. www.bwsanibel.com. 45 units. Winter $249–$465 double; off-season $135–$295 double. AE, DC, DISC, MC, V. **Amenities:** Heated outdoor pool; tennis courts; free use of bikes; coin-op washers and dryers. *In room:* A/C, TV, kitchen, coffeemaker, hair dryer, iron.

Island Inn It's difficult to get accommodations here during the peak winter season, but it's worth trying because this classic beach resort has been in business for more than a century. Its original central building houses a bright, genteel dining room, a spacious lounge, and a library brightly furnished with old-style bentwood and wicker sofas and chairs. This is the kind of place where guests dress for dinner—jackets and collared shirts required, ties recommended for men at dinner—and seating is assigned (some guests have had the same table for years). This main building looks out over a sandy, South Pacific–like yard to the gulf. Although neither charming in an Old Florida sense nor luxurious by today's standards, the cottages and motel rooms (with or without kitchens) are modern and comfortable. Most have screened porches or balconies.

3111 W. Gulf Dr., Sanibel Island, FL 33957. © 800/851-5088 or 239/472-1561. Fax 239/472-0051. www.islandinnsanibel.com. 57 units, including 9 cottages. Winter (including breakfast and dinner) $175–$425 double; off-season (no meals) $110–$215 double. AE, DISC, MC, V. **Amenities:** Restaurant (American), bar; small heated outdoor pool; tennis court; croquet area; coin-op washers and dryers. *In room:* A/C, TV, kitchen (some units), fridge, coffeemaker, hair dryer, iron.

Sundial Beach Resort *Kids* The largest resort on Sanibel, this condominium complex lacks intimacy but has lots to keep families occupied, from a palm-studded, beachside pool area to a complimentary marine biology program and a small ecology center with a touch tank. The one-, two-, and three-bedroom condominiums are housed in two- and three-story buildings (as high as they get on Sanibel) and have screened balconies overlooking the beach or tropically landscaped gardens. Among several dining options here, the award-winning **Windows on the Water** dining room offers glorious gulf views at breakfast, lunch, and dinner. Also, the master chefs put on a show as they prepare delicious steak, chicken, and seafood dishes right by your table in **Noopie's Japanese Seafood & Steakhouse,** where dinner reservations are required (© **239/395-6014**). Overlooking the pool and the gulf, the relaxing **Beaches Grill & Bar** is popular at sunset and has entertainment nightly.

1451 Middle Gulf Dr., Sanibel Island, FL 33957. © 800/237-4184 or 239/481-3636. Fax 239/481-4947. www.sundialresort.com. 275 units. Winter $209–$650 condo apt.; off-season $155–$350 condo apt. Packages available. AE, DC, DISC, MC, V. **Amenities:** 4 restaurants (Gulfshore, Japanese, and 2 American), 2 bars; 5 heated outdoor pools; 12 tennis courts; exercise room; Jacuzzi; water-sports equipment rental; bike rental; children's programs; game room; concierge; activities desk; business center; limited room service; massage; babysitting; laundry service; coin-op washers and dryers. *In room:* A/C, TV/VCR, kitchen, coffeemaker, hair dryer, iron.

CAPTIVA ISLAND
An Off-Season Deal

Captiva Island Inn Bed & Breakfast This B&B complex sits virtually surrounded by restaurants, art galleries, and boutiques along Captiva's block-long commercial street. That can make it a bit too busy for some eyes and ears, but it has its charms. Two suites in the Key West–style main building open to porches overlooking the lane, while four Dutch clapboard cottages sit out back on the fringes of a gravel parking lot (you get just enough yard here for hammocks and a gas grill). The ceiling in one cottage that once housed aviator Charles Lindbergh has clouds painted against a blue sky. It and the rest of the units have ceiling fans, kitchens, large bathrooms, queen-size sofa beds in their living rooms, cool tile floors, and designer bed linens (including down comforters for the occasional chilly night). Guests get free use of bicycles, and towels and chairs for the beach (a block away), and get a complimentary full breakfast at R.C. Otter's Island Eats across the lane.

11509 Andy Rosse Lane (P.O. Box 848), Captiva Island, FL 33924. © 800/454-9898 or 239/395-0882. Fax 239/395-0862. www.captivaislandinn.com. 7 units (some with shower only). Winter $220–$260 double; off-season $130–$150 double. Rates include full breakfast. AE, DISC, MC, V. **Amenities:** Access to nearby health club; free use of bikes. *In room:* A/C, TV, kitchen, fridge, coffeemaker.

Worth an Off-Season Splurge

South Seas Resort ★★★ *Kids* Formerly Clarence Chadwick's 330-acre copra plantation, this exclusive establishment is the premier property on these two islands. It's one of the best choices in southern Florida for serious tennis buffs, its gulf-side golf course is one of the most picturesque nine-holers anywhere, and its two marinas host scuba dive operators. The resort occupies all of Captiva's northern third, making it ideal if you want to step from your luxury house or condominium right onto 2½ miles of gorgeous beach. The resort is so spread out along the shore that a free trolley shuttles back and forth through the mangrove forests.

Most accommodations are so-called villas (actually condominium apartments), but there's a great variety of offerings, including luxury homes with private pools and their own tennis courts (many are occupied exclusively by their owners; watch for famous folks wandering about). With three bedrooms or more, some units are ideal for families or couples who want to share the cost of a vacation. The least expensive (and least inspired) units are the "Harbourside" hotel rooms at the yacht basin and marina near the island's northern tip, the jumping-off point for Captiva Cruises and Steve and Doris Colgate's Offshore Sailing School. Next up are the "Bayside Villas" and "Beachside Villas"—condominium apartments in three-story buildings near the main-gate area and its shops and restaurants. Whatever type of living space you choose, by all means inquire about package deals, which can result in significant savings for stays of 3 nights or more.

Outside the main gate, Chadwick's Shopping Center includes restaurants, high-fashion boutiques, jewelry stores, and gift shops, all open to the public, but the resort's no-cash, charge-to-your-room policy prevents gate-crashers from enjoying the resort proper.

P.O. Box 194, Captiva Island, FL 33924. © 800/554-5454 or 239/472-5111. Fax 239/481-4947. www.south-seas-resort.com. 660 units. Winter $260–$370 double; $350–$1,800 condo or house. Off-season $169–$240 double; $165–$1,300 condo or house. $8 per person per day added to room bills, 18–20% to food and bar bills, in lieu of tipping. Packages available. AE, DC, DISC, MC, V. **Amenities:** 5 restaurants (American, Italian), 2 bars; 18 heated outdoor pools; 9-hole golf course; 18 tennis courts; health club; Jacuzzis; water-sports equipment rental; bike rental; children's programs; game room; concierge; activities desk; business center; shopping arcade; salon; limited room service (7am–11pm); massage; babysitting; laundry service; coin-op washers and dryers. *In room:* A/C, TV, dataport (some units), kitchen (larger units only), coffeemaker, hair dryer, iron.

'Tween Waters Inn ★★ Wedged between the gulf beach and the bay on the narrowest part of Captiva, this venerable establishment was the regular haunt of cartoonist J. N. (Ding) Darling. Anne Morrow Lindbergh also dined often here while writing *A Gift from the Sea*. Just as Darling preserved the islands' wildlife, the 'Tween Waters has saved the cottages he stayed in. Situated in a sandy palm grove, these pink shiplap buildings have been upgraded but still capture Old Florida. Some face the gulf; others, the bay. Themed to honor their famous guests, they range in size from the bay-side honeymoon cottage with barely enough room for its king-size bed and a tiny kitchen to a three-bedroom, two-bathroom house. The spacious hotel rooms and apartments are in three modern buildings on stilts; they all have screened balconies facing the gulf or the bay. Charter captains dock at the full-service marina here.

The **Old Captiva House** restaurant appears very much as it did in Ding Darling's days (note his cartoons adorning the dining room walls), and **The Canoe and The Kayak** restaurant provides inexpensive lunches on its bay-side deck. The popular **Crow's Nest Lounge** has live entertainment and provides snacks and light evening meals from 9pm to 1am.

P.O. Box 249, Captiva Island, FL 33924. © 800/223-5865 or 239/472-5161. Fax 239/472-0249. www.tween-waters.com. 138 units. Winter $195–$250 double; $220–$560 suites; $115–$425 cottage. Off-season $160–$240 double; $215–$420 suites; $110–$335 cottage. Rates include continental breakfast. Packages available. AE, DC, MC, V. Pets accepted in some units ($15 per day). **Amenities:** 2 restaurants (regional), 2 bars; outdoor pool; 3 tennis courts; exercise room; Jacuzzi; water-sports equipment rentals; bike rentals; coin-op washers and dryers. *In room:* A/C, TV, dataport, kitchen (suites and cottages), fridge, coffeemaker, hair dryer, iron (suites only), safe.

COTTAGES

The islands have several Old Florida–style cottages that offer charming and often less expensive alternatives to hotels and condominiums. Some of the best are members of the **Sanibel-Captiva Small Inns & Cottages Association.** You can contact the association (via its website only) at www.sanibelsmallinns.com for a complete listing of properties.

Sitting between two condominium complexes off Middle Gulf Drive, **Gulf Breeze Cottages** ★★, 1081 Shell Basket Lane, Sanibel Island, FL 33957 (© **800/388-2842** or 239/472-1626; www.gbreeze.com), is a collection of clapboard cottages separated from the beach by a lawn with a covered picnic area and outdoor shower. One two-story building is divided into four efficiencies (the pick is no. 7, with a two-way view of the gulf from its big picture windows). Rates are $215 to $350 a day in winter, $115 to $230 a day off-season.

With only one monstrous mansion standing between them and a narrow bay beach near Sanibel Lighthouse, **Buttonwood Cottages** ★, 1234 Buttonwood Lane, Sanibel Island, FL 33957 (© **887/395-COTTAGE** or 239/395-9061; fax 239/395-2620; www.buttonwoodcottages.com), are less expensive options at $125 to $220 a day in winter, $75 to $160 off-season. Remodeled and equipped with many modern amenities, the five units occupy two long cottages built on stilts. Four of them have screened porches, with two overlooking a lushly tropical backyard sporting two hammocks and two hot tubs. The Lighthouse Cafe (see "Great Deals on Dining," below) is around the corner.

Barely updated since the 1950s are the 32 pink clapboard structures at **Beachview Cottages,** 3325 W. Gulf Dr., Sanibel Island, FL 33957 (© **800/860-0532** or 239/472-1202; fax 239/472-4720; www.beachviewsanibel.com). None of the cottages has a phone, and some have shower-only bathrooms. There's a heated outdoor swimming pool here. Rates are $169 to $269 a day in winter, $125 to $195 a day off-season.

On Captiva, **Jensen's On the Gulf,** P.O. Box 460, Captiva Island, FL 33924 (© **239/472-4684;** www.jensen-captiva.com), has cottages as well as homes, apartments, and studios ranging from $210 to $550 a day in winter, $140 to

$385 a day off-season. **Jensen's Twin Palm Resort & Marina,** P.O. Box 191, Captiva Island, FL 33924 (✆ **239/472-5800;** same website), on the bay side near the Andy Rosse Lane dining district, has cottages ranging from $120 to $190 a day during winter, from $105 to $130 a day off-season.

GREAT DEALS ON DINING

No restaurant can survive on these affluent islands without serving good food, so you're assured of getting a fine meal wherever you go and whatever you pay. Oddly, only five restaurants offer dining with water views: the Thistle Lodge at Casa Ybel Resort and Windows on the Water at Sundial Beach Resort (see "Accommodations You Can Afford," above); and the Mad Hatter, the Green Flash, and the Mucky Duck (see below).

SANIBEL ISLAND

The lively **Cheeburger Cheeburger,** 2413 Periwinkle Way, at Palm Ridge Road (✆ **239/472-6111**), has Sanibel's biggest and best burgers. Also, you'll find very reasonably priced pub fare at Sanibel's sports bars, such as the **Lazy Flamingo II** (see below) and the **Sanibel Grill,** 703 Tarpon Bay Rd., near Palm Ridge Road (✆ **239/472-3128**), which actually serves as the bar for the Timbers, the fine seafood restaurant next door (see below). They all have reduced-price beer and munchies during televised football games.

For picnics at Sanibel's beaches or on a canoe, the deli and bakery in **Bailey's General Store,** at Periwinkle Way and Tarpon Bay Road (✆ **239/472-1516**), carries a gourmet selection of breads, cheeses, and meats. **Huxter's Deli and Market,** 1203 Periwinkle Way, east of Donax Street (✆ **239/472-6988**), has sandwich fixings and "beach box" lunches to go.

Hungry Heron ★★ *Kids* AMERICAN   This tropically decorated eatery is Sanibel's most popular family restaurant. There's something for everyone on the huge, tabloid-size menu—from hot and cold appetizers and overstuffed "sea-wiches" to pasta and steamed shellfish. And if the 255 regular items aren't enough, there's a list of nightly specials. Seafood, steaks, and stir-fries from a sizzling skillet are popular with local residents, who bring the kids here for fun and a children's menu. An all-you-can-eat breakfast buffet on Saturday and Sunday mornings is an excellent value.

In Palm Ridge Place, 2330 Palm Ridge Rd. (at Periwinkle Way). ✆ 239/395-2300. Reservations not accepted, but call for preferred seating. Main courses $9–$18; sandwiches, burgers, snacks $6–$11; weekend breakfast buffet $9 adults, $5 children under 10. AE, DISC, MC, V. Mon–Fri 11am–9pm; Sat–Sun 7:30am–9pm (breakfast buffet to 11am Sat, to noon Sun).

Jerry's Family Restaurant AMERICAN   Retirees, young couples, affluent families, and everyone else looking for fine food at great prices head for this spotless diner-style restaurant whose big window walls look out at palms, banana trees, and other thick tropical foliage. Outstanding breakfasts are served until 4pm, and you can usually get a table quickly here—which can't be said of Sanibel's other popular eye-opening spots. The huge flaky croissants filled with scrambled eggs, cheese, and bacon, ham, or sausage are a steal at $4.25, and the freshly brewed cappuccino and espresso here are as good as Starbucks'. Served from 11am to 9:30pm, the lunch menu features hot and cold deli sandwiches (the fresh grouper's great) and lighter fare such as half a pineapple stuffed with seafood or chicken salad. Dinner sees the likes of grilled steaks, salmon with a dill sauce, shrimp sautéed with garlic butter, and chicken cordon bleu—all accompanied by a trip to the salad bar.

1700 Periwinkle Way (in Jerry's Supermarket, at Casa Ybel Rd.). ⓒ 941/472-9300. Main courses $9–$16; breakfast $3–$7; burgers and sandwiches $4–$8. DISC, MC, V. Daily 6am–9:30pm.

McT's Shrimp House & Tavern SEAFOOD

Shrimp reigns at this casual Old Florida–style establishment, where you'll see a line outside at 4pm waiting for the early bird specials served to the first 100 persons in the door. Everyone else gets to view the daily catch displayed in a chiller case, including the night's shrimp ready for the chef to prepare in one of at least a dozen ways, from steamed to fried in a coconut-and-almond batter. There are also grouper and swordfish, plus steaks and chicken for the land-minded, but stick to the shrimp here (see below for The Timbers Restaurant & Fish Market, which does a much better job of cooking fish). McT's Tavern offers an extensive choice of appetizers and light dinners.

1523 Periwinkle Way (at Fitzhugh St.). ⓒ 239/472-3161. Main courses $13–$22; early bird specials $10. AE, DC, DISC, MC, V. Shrimp House daily 4:45–10pm. McT's Tavern daily 4pm–midnight. Closed Thanksgiving and Christmas.

Sanibel Cafe ★ (Value) AMERICAN

Seashells are the theme at Lynda and Ken Boyce's pleasant cafe, whose tables are museum-like glass cases containing delicate fossilized specimens from the Miocene and Pliocene epochs. Fresh-squeezed orange and grapefruit juice, Danish Havarti omelets, and homemade muffins and biscuits highlight the breakfast menu (eggs Benedict and fruit-filled waffles are served until closing). Lunch features specialty sandwiches; shrimp, Greek, and chicken-and-grape salads made with a very light, fat-free dressing; and a limited list of main courses such as grilled or blackened chicken breast. At dinner they add homemade meat loaf, crunchy grouper, and certified Angus steaks. Fatten up on Lynda's homemade red raspberry jam, apple or cherry crisps, and terrific Key lime pie.

In the Tahitian Gardens Shops, 2007 Periwinkle Way. ⓒ 239/472-5323. Call ahead for preferred seating. Breakfast $3.50–$9; salads, sandwiches, and burgers $4.50–$13; main courses $7.50–$17. MC, V. Daily 7am–9pm.

Super-Cheap Eats

Grandma Dot's Seaside Saloon SEAFOOD

One of Sanibel's most popular lunch spots, this open-air but screened cafe on the docks of Sanibel Marina offers excellent salads (try the seafood Caesar) and fine sandwiches, plus a few main courses led by broiled grouper in a sauce of lemon, dill, butter, and white wine.

At Sanibel Marina, 634 N. Yachtsman Dr. ⓒ 239/472-8138. Reservations not accepted. Main courses $6–$23; salads and sandwiches $6–$12. MC, V. Daily 11:30am–7:30pm.

The Lazy Flamingo II (Value) SEAFOOD/PUB FARE

T-shirts and shorts or jeans are the dress code at this friendly pub that always seems packed by the young and young-at-heart, who flock here for reasonably priced food, a wide choice of beers iced down in a huge box behind the bar, and sports TVs. Some of that beer is used to steam shrimp and a finger-stinging collection of oysters, clams, and spices known as "The Pot." Best pick, however, is grouper from the charcoals, as either a main course or a sandwich. The flamingo-pink menu also has an array of sandwiches, burgers, fish platters, and very spicy "Dead Parrot Wings." Fillet your own catch, and the chef will cook it to order for you. Happy-hour prices prevail whenever football games are on the TVs. A sister institution, the **Lazy Flamingo I,** 6520–C Pine Ave., at Sanibel-Captiva Road, a quarter mile south of Blind Pass (ⓒ **239/472-5353**), has the same menu and hours.

1036 Periwinkle Way, west of Causeway Blvd. © 239/472-6939. Reservations not accepted. Main courses $11–$15; sandwiches and snacks $5–$9. Cook your catch $8. AE, DISC, MC, V. Daily 11:30am–1am.

Lighthouse Cafe ★ *Value* AMERICAN   Decorated with photos and drawings of lighthouses, this casual storefront establishment located appropriately near the Sanibel Lighthouse dishes up breakfast omelets that are meals in themselves, especially the ocean frittata containing delicately seasoned scallops, crabmeat, shrimp, broccoli, and fresh mushrooms, and crowned with an artichoke heart and creamy Alfredo sauce. Seafood Benedict is another unusual offering. Interesting sandwiches are served after 11am. Reasonably priced cafe-style dinners are served during winter only.

In Seahorse Shops, 362 Periwinkle Way (at Buttonwood Lane, east of Causeway Rd.). © 239/472-0303. Call ahead to get on waiting list. Breakfast $3.50–$7.50; sandwiches and salads $4.50–$8.50; main courses $10–$15. MC, V. Mid-Dec to Easter daily 7am–3pm and 5–9pm. Easter to mid-Dec daily 7am–3pm.

Worth a Splurge

Jacaranda SEAFOOD/PASTA/STEAKS   With live music nightly, the Patio Lounge attracts an affluent over-40 crowd to this friendly and casual restaurant named for the purple-flowered jacaranda tree. Although the Jacaranda is best known as a local gathering spot, it has received several dining awards. Fresh fish is well prepared here, or you can choose certified Angus steaks or prime rib. The linguine with a dozen littleneck clams tossed in a piquant red or white clam sauce is consistently excellent. For dessert, the gooey turtle pie—ice cream, caramel, fudge sauce, chopped nuts, and whipped cream—will send you away stuffed.

1223 Periwinkle Way (east of Donax St.). © 239/472-1771. Reservations recommended. Main courses $16–$30. AE, MC, V. Daily 5–10pm. Lounge daily 4pm–12:30am. Closed Christmas.

Mad Hatter ★★ ECLECTIC   One of Sanibel's best choices for a romantic special dinner, this gulf-front restaurant has only 12 tables, but each has a view that's perfect at sunset. The ever-changing eclectic menu features flavors from around the world, such as Thai-style peanut sauce over a seared, sesame-encrusted yellowfin tuna steak. The jumbo shrimp Wellington is a fascinating twist on the classic beef dish, and the stuffed crab served with a lobster voluté is another winner.

6467 Sanibel-Captiva Rd., at Blind Pass. © 239/472-0033. Reservations highly recommended. Main courses $25–$35. AE, MC, V. Dec 15–Jan 31 daily 5–9pm. Feb 1 to Easter Sun–Mon 5–9:30pm; Tues–Sat 11:30am–2pm and 5–9:30pm. Easter to May 31 daily 5–9:30pm. June 1–Dec 14 Mon–Sat 5–9:30pm. Closed Sept after Labor Day.

Morgan's Forest *Kids* SEAFOOD   The kids will love dining in this miniature jungle patterned after the Rainforest Cafes elsewhere. Almost hidden among all the foliage are mechanical but lifelike moving jaguars, monkeys, birds, and a huge python entangled in vines above the bar. Squawking bird sounds, strobe-lightning bolts followed by claps of thunder, and an occasional faux fog rolling across the floor add to the Amazonian ambience. The owner of Fort Myers Beach's excellent Channel Mark restaurant is in charge here, which means that your taste buds will be as entertained as well as your eyes and ears. The fine crab cakes are the pick of a menu otherwise accented with South- and Central-American seasonings. Kids can choose from a well-rounded children's menu.

1231 Middle Gulf Dr., at the Holiday Inn Beach Resort. © 239/472-3351. Main courses $14–$23. AE, DC, DISC, MC, V. Mon–Sat 7–11am and 5–10pm; Sun 7am–noon and 5–10pm.

The Timbers Restaurant & Fish Market ★★ SEAFOOD/STEAK   This casual upstairs restaurant, with bamboo railings, oversized canvas umbrellas, and paintings of tropical scenes through faux windows, consistently is Sanibel's best place for fresh fish and aged beef hot off the charcoal grill. In the fish market out front, you can view the catch and have the chef charcoal-grill or blacken it to order. The steaks, cut on the premises, are the island's best. You can order a drink from the adjoining Sanibel Grill sports bar and wait for a table outside on the shopping center's porch.

703 Tarpon Bay Rd. (between Periwinkle Way and Palm Ridge Rd.). © 239/472-3128. Main courses $15–$23; early birds get $2.50 off regular price. AE, MC, V. Winter daily 4:30–9:30pm; off-season daily 5–9:30pm.

CAPTIVA ISLAND

Big deli sandwiches and picnic fare are available at the **Captiva Island Store,** Captiva Road at Andy Rosse Lane (© **239/472-2374**), and at the gourmet-oriented **C. W.'s Market and Deli,** at the entrance to the South Seas Resort (© **239/472-5111;** see "Accommodations You Can Afford," above). The beach is a block from these stores.

The Green Flash ★ SEAFOOD   You can't miss this restaurant, which sits at the infamous "curve" where Captiva Road takes a sharp turn to the north. You won't see the real "green flash" as the sun sets here, because this modern building looks eastward across Pine Island Sound, but it does make for a nice view at lunch. And seeing the full moon turn the sound into glistening silver is worth having at least an evening drink here. The overall quality of the cuisine is very good, and the prices are very reasonable for Captiva. Start with oysters Rockefeller or shrimp bisque. Both are house specialties, as is the garlicky grouper "café de Paris" and salmon with a dill-accented béarnaise sauce.

15183 Captiva Rd. © 239/472-3337. Reservations recommended. Main courses $13–$22. AE, DC, DISC, MC, V. Daily 11:30am–3:30pm and 5:30–9:30pm (bar open 11:30am–9:30pm).

Mucky Duck ★ SEAFOOD/PUB FARE   A Captiva institution since 1976, this lively, British-style pub is the only place on either island here where you can dine right by the beach. If you don't get a real seat with this great view, the humorous staff will gladly roll a fake window over to appease you. The menu offers a selection of fresh seafood items, plus English fish and chips, steak-and-sausage pie, and a ploughman's lunch. There's a vegetarian platter. No smoking is allowed inside. You can't make a reservation, but you can order drinks, listen to live music (Mon–Sat), and bide your time at beachside picnic tables out front (come early for sunset).

Andy Rosse Lane (on the gulf). © 239/472-3434. Reservations not accepted. Lunch $5.50–$11; dinner main courses $13–$18.50. AE, DC, DISC, MC, V. Mon–Sat 11am–2:30pm and 5–9:30pm.

Super-Cheap Eats

R. C. Otter's Island Eats ★★ *Value* AMERICAN   Occupying an old clapboard-sided island cottage, this Key West–style cafe brings informality and good inexpensive food to Captiva. In contrast to the island's 15 or so formal

---

Tips **Deals on Meals**

Local restaurants often run advertisements containing discount coupons in the "Sanibel-Captiva Shopper's Guide," a free publication available at the chamber of commerce visitor center (see "Essentials," earlier in this section).

haute-cuisine restaurants, you can dine in your bare feet and not spend a fortune for an excellent breakfast, snack, lunch, or full meal. The tables are covered with wrapping paper, and rolls of paper towels substitute for napkins. The choice seats are under ceiling fans on the front porch or beneath umbrellas on the brick patio. In hot weather you can opt for the air-conditioned dining room whose walls are adorned with the works of local artists. The wide-ranging menu includes salads, hot dogs, burgers, sandwiches, stir-fries, meat loaf, country-fried steak, broiled fish, and soft-shell crabs, plus delicious nightly specials. The island's best breakfasts are equally varied, from bacon and eggs to a seafood quesadilla. Musicians perform out in the yard every day, and you could find yourself dancing on the front porch.

11506 Andy Rosse Lane. © 239/395-1142. Reservations not accepted, but call for preferred seating. Breakfast $6–$12; salads, sandwiches, burgers $6–$12; main courses $10–$20. AE, DISC, MC, V. Daily 7:30am–10pm (breakfast to 11:30am).

Worth a Splurge

The Bubble Room *Kids* SEAFOOD/STEAK The gaudy bubble-gum pink, yellow, purple, and green exterior of this amusing restaurant is only a prelude to the 1930s, 1940s, and 1950s Hollywood motif inside. The dining rooms are adorned with a collection of puppets, statues of great movie stars, toy trains, thousands of movie stills, and antique jukeboxes that play Big Band–era tunes. The menu carries on the cinematic theme: prime ribs Weismuller, Eddie Fisherman filet of fresh grouper, and Henny Young-One boneless breast of young chicken. Both adults and children (who can dine for $7 at dinner, $3.50 at lunch) are attracted to this expensive but fun establishment, where the portions are huge. For lighter appetites, the "Tiny Bubble" sampler includes a salad, a choice of appetizer, and a dessert.

15001 Captiva Rd. (at Andy Rosse Lane). © 239/472-5558. Reservations not accepted. Main courses $15–$28; lunch $6–$12. AE, DC, DISC, MC, V. Daily 11:30am–2:30pm and 5–10pm. Closed Christmas.

Captiva Sunshine Cafe ECLECTIC This friendly, open-kitchen cafe has only 12 tables—five of them inside, seven on the shopping center's porch—but the food is worth the close quarters. Everything except the bread is prepared on the premises; all of it is available for take-out. Specialties are steak, fish, and shrimp from a wood-fired grill. The portions are as big as the prices are high here; in fact, appetizers such as black beans and rice can make a meal for lighter appetites. Various desserts are offered daily; the apple crisp is a winner.

In Captiva Village Sq., Captiva Rd. at Laika Lane. © 239/472-6200. Reservations recommended. Main courses $23–$33; burgers $10. AE, MC, V. Daily 11:30am–3:30pm and 5–9pm.

SANIBEL & CAPTIVA ISLANDS AFTER DARK

You won't find glitzy nightclubs on these family-oriented islands, but night owls have some fun places to roost at the resorts and restaurants mentioned above. Here's a brief recap:

ON SANIBEL The Sundial Beach Resort's **Beaches Bar & Grill,** 1451 Middle Gulf Dr. (© **239/472-4151**), features entertainers during dinner, then live bands for dancing from 9pm on. The **Patio Lounge,** in the Jacaranda, 1223 Periwinkle Way (© **239/472-1771**), attracts an affluent crowd of middle-agers and seniors with its live music every evening. **McT's Tavern,** 1523 Periwinkle Way (© **239/472-3161**), has darts, video games, and a large-screen TV for sports fans. The **Sanibel Grill,** 703 Tarpon Bay Rd. (© **239/472-4453**), and the two **Lazy Flamingo** branches (see "Great Deals on Dining," above) are other popular sports bars.

The Pirate Players, a group of professional actors, perform Broadway dramas and comedies from November to April in Sanibel's state-of-the-art, 150-seat **J. Howard Wood Theatre,** 2200 Periwinkle Way (© **239/472-0006;** www.thewoodtheatre.com). The **Old Schoolhouse Theater,** 1905 Periwinkle Way (© **239/472-6862;** www.oldschoolhousetheater.com), complements its neighbor by offering Broadway musicals and revues from December to April. Call for the current schedule and prices.

ON CAPTIVA Local songwriters perform their works nightly at **R. C. Otter's Island Eats,** 11500 Andy Rosse Lane (© **239/395-1142**). The **Crow's Nest Lounge,** in the 'Tween Waters Inn, on Captiva Road (© **239/472-5161**), is Captiva's top nightspot for dancing. **Chadwick's Lounge,** at the entrance to the South Seas Resort (© **239/472-5111**), has a large dance floor and music from 9pm on.

NEARBY ISLAND HOPPING

Sanibel and Captiva are jumping-off points for island-hopping boat trips to barrier islands and keys teeming with ancient legends and Robinson Crusoe–style beaches. You don't have to get completely lost out there, however, because several islets have comfortable inns and restaurants. The trip across shallow Pine Island Sound is itself a sightseeing adventure, with playful dolphins surfing on the boats' wakes and a variety of cormorants, egrets, frigate birds, and (in winter) rare white pelicans flying above or lounging on sandbars between meals.

Captiva Cruises (© **239/472-5300;** www.captivacruises.com) offers daily trips, departing from the South Seas Resort on Captiva (see "Accommodations You Can Afford," above). One vessel goes daily to Cabbage Key, departing at 10:30am and returning at 3:30pm. It stops at Useppa Island going and coming Tuesday through Sunday. During the winter months, another goes to Boca Grande by way of Cayo Costa State Park, departing Tuesday through Saturday at 10:30am and returning at 4pm. These day trips cost $27.50 per adult, $15 for children to Cabbage Key or Useppa; $35 for adults, $17.50 for children to Boca Grande or Cayo Costa. Reservations are required.

From Pine Island off Fort Myers, you can take **Tropic Star Cruises'** daily ferry service (© **239/283-0015;** www.tropicstarcruises.com) to Cayo Costa (see "Affordable Outdoor Activities" in section 1).

CABBAGE KEY

You never know who's going to get off a boat at 100-acre Cabbage Key and walk unannounced into the funky **Cabbage Key Inn**, a rustic house built in 1938 by the son and daughter-in-law of mystery novelist Mary Roberts Rinehart. Ernest Hemingway liked to hang out here in the early days, and novelist John D. MacDonald was a frequent guest 30 years later. Today you could find yourself rubbing elbows at the bar with the likes of Walter Cronkite, Ted Koppel, Sean Connery, or Julia Roberts. Singer and avid yachtie Jimmy Buffett likes Cabbage Key so much that it inspired his hit song "Cheeseburger in Paradise."

A path leads from the tiny marina across a lawn dotted with coconut palms to this white clapboard house that sits atop an ancient Calusa shell mound. Guests dine in the comfort of two screened porches and seek libations in the Rineharts' library-turned-bar, its pine-paneled walls now plastered with dollar bills left by visitors. The straight-back chairs and painted wooden tables show their age, but that's part of Cabbage Key's laid-back, don't-give-a-hoot charm.

Fishing with the Bushes in Boca Grande

Former President George Bush, present President George W. Bush, Florida Governor Jeb Bush—indeed, the entire Bush clan—like to retreat to **Boca Grande** for a little rest and relaxation every now and then. And well they should, for this charming village on Gasparilla Island is a head-of-state's kind of place. The du Ponts, the Astors, the Morgans, the Vanderbilts, and other moneyed folk started coming here in the 1920s and still turn the island into a Florida version of Nantucket during their winter "social season." In addition to the warm weather, the lure was then, and still is, some of the world's best tarpon fishing. Descendants of the watermen who were here first still guide the rich and famous. They live in modest homes on streets named Dam-If-I-Know, Dam-If-I-Care, and Dam-If-I-Will. You can see their backyards full of boats and fishnets, but high hedges hide the manicured "beachfronter" mansions over by the gulf.

You can explore the little village in a few hours on foot or on a bike rented from **Island Bike 'n' Beach,** 333 Park Ave. (© **941/964-0711**). The pink-brick **Railroad Depot,** at the corner of Park Avenue and 4th Street, has been restored to the grandeur it enjoyed when the rich arrived by train. It now houses a cluster of upscale boutiques and the **Loose Caboose** restaurant and ice cream parlor (© **941/964-0440**), where movie stars have been seen satiating their sweet teeth. **Banyan Street** (actually 2nd St.) is canopied with tangled banyan trees and is one of the prettiest places for a stroll. The **Johann Fust Community Library,** at Gasparilla Road and 10th Street (© **941/964-2488**), contains the extraordinary **Du Pont Shell Collection,** gathered by Henry Francis du Pont during nearly 50 years of combing the island's beaches. At the island's south end, **Boca Grande Lighthouse Museum and Visitor's Center** (© **941/964-0060**) occupies the wood-frame lighthouse that began marking the pass into Charlotte Harbor in 1890. Exhibits explain the island's history, its tarpon fishing, and its wildlife and seashells. The white-sand beaches of **Gasparilla Island State Recreation Area** (© **941/964-0375;** www.floridastateparks.org/district4/gasparillaisland) trim the lighthouse.

Captiva Cruises (© **239/472-5300**) offers daily trips here during the winter season (see above). The fare is $35 adults, $17.50 children, and reservations are required. **Tropic Star** cruises (© **239/283-0015;** www.tropicstarcruises.com) come here daily from Pine Island off Fort Myers (see "Affordable Outdoor Activities" in section 1, above). Fares are $25 adults, $15 for children. Call for departure times.

For more information contact the **Boca Grande Area Chamber of Commerce,** 5800 Gasparilla Rd. (P.O. Box 704), Boca Grande, FL 33921 (© **941/964-0568;** fax 239/964-0620; www.bocagrandechamber.com).

In addition to the famous thick, juicy cheeseburgers so loved by Jimmy Buffett, the house specialties are fresh broiled fish and shrimp steamed in beer. Lunches range from $5 to $10; main courses at dinner, $15 to $25.

Most visitors come out here for the day, but if you want to stay overnight, the Cabbage Key Inn has six rooms and six cottages. The more expensive cottages, four of which have kitchens, are preferable to the rooms. Although the units have private bathrooms and air conditioners, they are very basic by today's standards, and some of their original 1920s furnishings have seen better days. Service for overnight guests can leave a lot to be desired, and there's no place on the islet to buy snacks or sundries. If you do decide to rough it, room rates are $89 single or double for rooms, $145 to $239 for cottages. For information or reservations, contact Cabbage Key Inn, P.O. Box 200, Pineland, FL 33945 (© **239/283-2278**; fax 239/283-1384; www.cabbage-key.com).

CAYO COSTA

You can't get any more deserted than at **Cayo Costa State Park** (pronounced *Kay*-oh *Cos*-tah), which occupies a 2,132-acre, completely unspoiled barrier island with miles of white-sand beaches, pine forests, mangrove swamps, oak-palm hammocks, and grasslands. Other than natural wildlife, the only permanent residents here are park rangers.

Day-trippers can bring their own supplies and use a picnic area with pavilions. A free tram carries visitors from the sound-side dock to the gulf beach. The state maintains 12 very basic cabins and a primitive campground on the northern end of the island near Johnson Shoals, where the shelling is spectacular. Cabins cost $20 a day, and campsites are $13 a day all year. For camping or cabin reservations call © **800/326-3521** or go to the website www.reserveamerica.com. There's running water on the island but no electricity.

The park is open daily from 8am to sundown. There's a $1-per-person honor-system admission fee for day visitors. You can rent single-seat kayaks for $35 a day, two-seaters for $45 a day; for reservations, call **Tropic Star Cruises** on Pine Island (© **239/283-0015**; www.tropicstarcruises.com). For more information contact **Cayo Costa State Park**, P.O. Box 1150, Boca Grande, FL 33921 (© **941/964-0375**; www.floridastateparks.org/district4/cayocosta). Office hours are Monday to Friday from 8am to 5pm.

UPPER (NORTH) CAPTIVA

Cut off by a pass from Captiva, its northern barrier-island sibling is occupied by the upscale resort of **North Captiva Island Club,** P.O. Box 1000, Pineland, FL 33945 (© **800/576-7343** or 239/395-1001; fax 239/472-5836; www.north-captiva.com). Despite the development, however, about 750 of the island's 1,000 acres are included in a state preserve. The club rents accommodations ranging from efficiencies to luxury homes. There's scheduled water-taxi service from **Jensen's Twin Palms Marina** on Captiva (© **239/472-5800**), or you can get here from Matson Marine on Pine Island with **Island Charters** (© **800/340-3321** or 239/283-1113). Both charge $25 per person round-trip.

USEPPA ISLAND

Useppa was a refuge of President Theodore Roosevelt and his tarpon-loving industrialist friends at the turn of the century. New York advertising magnate Barron G. Collier bought the island in 1906 and built a lovely wooden home overlooking Pine Island Sound. His mansion is now the **Collier Inn,** where day-trippers and overnight guests can partake of lunches and seafood dinners in a country-club ambience. They also can visit the **Useppa Museum,** which explains the island's history and displays 4,000-year-old Calusa artifacts. Admission is by $2 donation.

The Collier Inn is the centerpiece of the **Useppa Island Club,** an exclusive development with more than 100 luxury homes, all of the clapboard-sided, tin-roofed style of Old Florida. For information, rates (all on the modified American plan), and reservations, contact **Collier Inn & Cottages,** P.O. Box 640, Bokeelia, FL 33922 (✆ **888/735-6335** or 239/283-1061; fax 239/283-0290; www.useppa.com).

4 Naples ★★★

42 miles S of Fort Myers, 106 miles W of Miami, 185 miles S of Tampa

Because its wealthy residents are accustomed to the very best, Naples is easily Southwest Florida's most sophisticated city. Indeed, its boutiques and galleries are at least on a par with those in Palm Beach or Beverly Hills. And yet Naples has an easygoing friendliness to all comers.

Naples was born in 1886, when a group of 12 Kentuckians and Ohioans bought 8,700 acres, laid out a town, and started selling lots. They built a pier and the 16-room Naples Hotel, whose first guest was President Grover Cleveland's sister Rose. She and other notables soon built a line of beach homes known as "Millionaires' Row." Known today as Olde Naples and carefully protected by its modern residents, their original settlement retains the air of that time a century ago.

Although high-rise buildings now line the beaches north of the old town, the newer sections of Naples still have their charm, thanks to Ohio manufacturer Henry B. Watkins, Sr. In 1946, Watkins and his partners bought the old hotel and all the town's undeveloped land and laid out the Naples Plan, which created the environmentally conscious city you see today.

About 4 miles north of Olde Naples, Vanderbilt Beach has a more traditional beach resort character than the historic district. Lined with a mix of two-story, 1960s-style motels and high-rise hotels and condos, the main beach here sits like an island of development between two preserved areas—Delnor-Wiggins Pass State Recreation to the north, and a county reserve fronting the expensive Pelican Bay golf-course community to the south.

ESSENTIALS

GETTING THERE Most visitors arrive at the **Southwest Florida International Airport,** 35 miles north of Naples in Fort Myers (see "Essentials," in section 1).

Naples Municipal Airport, on North Road off Airport-Pulling Road (✆ 239/643-6875; www.flynaples.com), is served by the commuter arms of **American** (✆ 800/433-7300) and **United/US Airways** (✆ 800/428-4322), which means you'll have to change planes in Miami, Tampa, or Orlando. Taxis await all flights outside the small terminal building; and **Avis** (✆ 800/331-1212), **Budget** (✆ 800/527-0700), **Hertz** (✆ 800/654-3131), and **National** (✆ 800/CAR-RENT) have booths at the airport. **Enterprise** (✆ 800/325-8007) is in town.

VISITOR INFORMATION The most comprehensive source of information is the **Naples Area Chamber of Commerce,** which maintains a visitor center at 895 Fifth Ave. S. (at U.S. 41), Naples, FL 34102 (✆ **239/262-6141;** fax 239/435-9910; www.napleschamber.org). The center has a host of free information and phones for making hotel reservations, and it sells a detailed street map for $2. By mail, it will send you a free list of accommodations and other

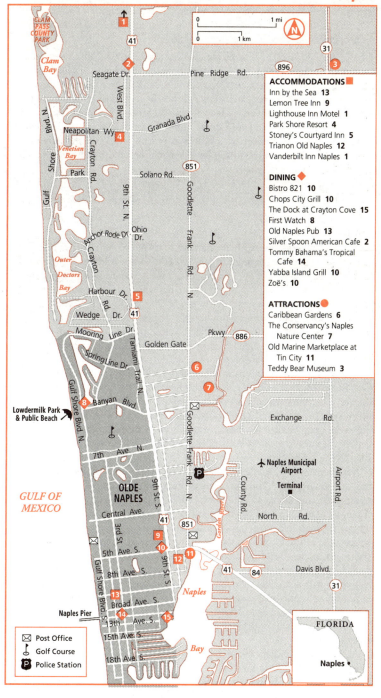

basic information, or you can order a complete Naples vacation packet for $8 ($12 to Canada and other countries) and the street map for $5. The visitor center is open Monday to Saturday from 9am to 5pm.

GETTING AROUND The **Naples Trolley** (© 239/262-7300; www.naplestrolleytours.com) clangs around 25 stops between the Naples Trolley General Store and Welcome Center, 1010 Sixth Ave. S. at 10th Street S. (2 blocks west of Tin City in Olde Naples), and Vanderbilt Beach on Monday to Saturday from 8:30am to 5:15pm and on Sunday from 10:15am to 5:15pm. Daily fares include free reboarding and are $16 for adults, $7 for children 4 to 12; free for children under 4. Schedules are available in brochure racks in the lobbies of most hotels and motels. The drivers provide narration, so the entire loop makes a good 2-hour sightseeing tour.

Call **Yellow Cab** (© 239/262-1312), **Checker Cab** (© 239/455-5555), **Maxi Taxi** (© 239/262-8977), or **Naples Taxi** (© 239/775-0505).

WHAT TO SEE & DO
HITTING THE BEACH

Unlike many Florida cities where you have to drive over to a barrier island to reach the beach, this city's beach is right in Olde Naples. And rather than being fronted by tall condominium buildings, here the mansions along Millionaires' Row form the backdrop. Access to the gorgeous white sand is at the gulf end of each avenue, although parking in the neighborhood can be precious. Try the metered lots on 12th Avenue South near the **Naples Pier,** the town's most popular beaching spot (see "Exploring Olde Naples," below), where there are restrooms and a food concession. Families gather on the beach north of the pier, while local teens congregate on the south side.

Also popular with families, lovely **Lowdermilk Park,** on Millionaires' Row at Gulf Shore Boulevard and North Banyan Boulevard, has a pavilion, restrooms, showers, a refreshment counter, professional-quality volleyball courts (the area's best players practice here), a duck pond, and picnic tables. There's metered parking, so bring quarters. A few blocks farther north is another metered parking lot with beach access beside the Naples Beach Hotel & Golf Resort, 851 Gulf Shore Blvd. N., at Golf Drive.

Nature lovers head to the Pelican Bay development north of the historic district and the popular **Clam Pass County Park** ★★ (© 239/353-0404). A free tram takes you along a 3,000-foot boardwalk winding through mangrove swamps and across a back bay to a beach of fine white sand. It's a strange sight, what with high-rise condominiums standing beyond the mangrove-bordered backwaters, but this actually is a miniature wilderness. Some 6 miles of canoe and kayak trails—with multitudes of birds and an occasional alligator—run from Clam Pass into the winding streams. The beach pavilion here has a bar, restrooms with foot showers only, picnic tables, and beach equipment rentals, including one- and two-person kayaks and 12-foot canoes. Entry is from a metered parking lot beside The Registry Resort at the end of Seagate Drive. There's a $3-per-vehicle parking fee. You can push, but not ride, bicycles on the boardwalk.

At Vanderbilt Beach, about 4 miles north of Olde Naples, the **Delnor-Wiggins Pass State Park** ★★★, at the west end of Bluebill Avenue–111th Avenue North (© 239/597-6196; www.floridastateparks.org/district4/delnor-wiggins), has been listed among America's top 10 stretches of sand. It has bathhouses, a boat ramp, and the area's best picnic facilities. A concessionaire sells hot dogs, sandwiches, and ice cream and rents beach chairs, umbrellas, kayaks, canoes, and snorkeling gear. Fish viewing is great over a small reef under 12 feet of water about 50 yards offshore. Fishing from the beach is excellent here, too. Rangers provide nature tours throughout the year, with the most interesting during the loggerhead turtle nesting season from June to October (call or check the website for the schedule).

The area is open daily from 8am to sunset. Admission is $2 per single-occupant vehicle, $4 for vehicles with two to eight occupants, and $1 for pedestrians and bikers. To get here from Olde Naples, go north on U.S. 41 about 4 miles and take a left on 111th Avenue, which turns into Bluebill Avenue before reaching the beach. Note that 111th Avenue is known as Immokalee Road east of U.S. 41.

NATURE PRESERVES

You can experience Southwest Florida's abundant natural life without leaving town at **The Conservancy's Naples Nature Center**, 14th Avenue North, east of Goodlette-Frank Road (© **239/262-0304;** www.conservancy.org), one of two preserves operated by The Conservancy of Southwest Florida (see the Briggs Nature Center under "Parks & Nature Preserves," in section 5 of this chapter). There are nature trails and an aviary with bald eagles and other birds. You can take 45-minute guided boat rides beginning at 9am, 10am, 11am, noon, 1pm, 2pm, and 3pm, weather permitting. The naturalist guides will explain the vegetation along the upper reaches of the Gordon River, and you may see some wildlife—including an occasional monkey escapee from Caribbean Gardens next door (see "Museums & Zoos," below). You can also rent canoes and kayaks and see it by yourself. An excellent nature store carries gift items. Admission fees of $7.50 for adults and $2 for children 3 to 12 (free for children under 3) include the boat rides. Canoes and kayaks cost $13 for 2 hours, $5 for each additional hour. The center is open year-round Monday to Saturday from 9am to 4:30pm. It's closed July 4, Labor Day, Thanksgiving, Christmas Eve, and Christmas Day.

The National Audubon Society operates the **Corkscrew Swamp Sanctuary,** 375 Sanctuary Rd. (© **239/348-9151;** www.audubon.org/local/sanctuary/corkscrew), 16 miles northeast of Naples off Immokalee Road (County Rd. 846). One of the state's largest private preserves, this 11,000-acre wilderness is home to countless wood storks that nest high in the cypress trees from November to April. Wading birds also are best seen in winter, when the swamp is likely to be dry (they don't nest when water levels are high). The birds congregate around pools near a boardwalk that leads 2 miles through the largest bald cypress forest with some of the oldest trees in the country. Ferns and orchids also flourish. Admission is $8 for adults, $5.50 for full-time college students, $3.50 for children 6 to 18, and free for children 5 and under. The sanctuary is open December to April, daily from 7am to 5pm; May to November, daily from 8am to 5pm. To reach the sanctuary, take Exit 17 off I-75 and go 15 miles east on Immokalee Road (County Rd. 846).

AFFORDABLE OUTDOOR ACTIVITIES

BOATING Powerboat and WaveRunner rentals are available from **Naples Watersports,** at the Old Naples Seaport, 10th Avenue South at 10th Street South in Olde Naples (© **239/435-9595**); from **Club Nautico,** at the Boat Haven Marina, 1484 E. Tamiami Trail (© **239/774-0100**), on the east bank of the Gordon River behind Kelly's Fish House; and from **Port-O-Call Marina,** also behind Kelly's Fish House (© **239/774-0479**).

CRUISES The Gordon River and Naples Bay from the U.S. 41 bridge on Fifth Avenue South to the gulf are prime territory for sightseeing, dolphin watching, and sunset cruises. The double-decked *Double Sunshine* (© 239/263-4949; www.ladybrett.com) sallies forth onto the river and bay daily from Tin City, where it has a ticket office. The 1½-hour cruises usually leave at 10am, noon, 2pm, and an hour before sunset. They cost $23 for adults, $11.50 for children under 12.

The *Sweet Liberty* (© 239/793-3525; www.sweetliberty.com), a 53-foot sailing catamaran, makes 3-hour morning shelling cruises to Keewaydin Island. The vessel then spends the afternoon on 2-hour sightseeing cruises (you'll usually see dolphins playing in the river on this one) and 2-hour sunset cruises on Naples Bay before docking at Boat Haven Marina on the east side of the Gordon River Bridge. Shelling cruises cost $35 for adults, $15 for children; sightseeing and sunset cruises cost $25 for adults, $15 for children.

For a good deal more luxury, the 83-foot *Naples Princess* (© 800/728-2970 or 239/649-2275; www.naplesprincesscruises.com) has narrated breakfast, lunch, and sunset dinner cruises from Port-O-Call Marina, on the eastern shore of the Gordon River. With extensive buffets, the sightseeing, lunch, sunset, and dinner cruises are good values at $23, $28, $28.50, and $42 per person, respectively. Call for schedules and reservations.

FISHING The locals like to fish from the **Naples Pier** (see "Exploring Olde Naples," below). The pier has tables on which to clean your catch, but watch out for the ever-present pelicans, which are master thieves. You can buy tackle and bait from the local marinas. The pier is open around the clock, and admission is free. No fishing license is required.

The least-expensive way for singles, couples, and small families to fish without paying for an entire boat is on the 45-foot *Lady Brett* (© 239/263-4949; www.ladybrett.com), which makes two daily trips from Tin City for $50 for adults, $45 for kids under 12. Rod, reel, bait, and fishing license are included, but bring your own drinks and lunch. Its sister boat, the *Captain Paul,* goes on half-day backcountry fishing trips, departing daily at 9am. These cost $45 for adults, $40 for children.

A number of charter boats are based at the marinas and outfitters mentioned under "Boating," above; call or visit them for booking information and prices.

GOLF Naples has an extraordinary number of fine golf courses for a city its size. Most are out in the suburbs, but not the flat but challenging 18 holes at the **Naples Beach Hotel & Golf Club,** 851 Gulf Shore Blvd. N. (© 239/261-2222), which are right in the middle of town. Nonguests can play here, but call ahead for a tee time.

Two of the best-known courses are at **Lely Flamingo Island Club** ★★ and the **Lely Mustang Golf Club,** both on U.S. 41 between Naples and Marco Island (© 800/388-GOLF or 239/793-2223). The Lely Flamingo course was designed by Robert Trent Jones, Sr., and its hourglass fairways and fingerlike bunkers present many challenges. Designed by Lee Trevino, the Lely Mustang course is more forgiving but still fun. Former PGA Tour player Paul Trittler has his golf school at these courses. You'll pay a price here in winter, when 18-hole fees are about $135 at Lely Flamingo and $150 at Lely Mustang, including cart and range balls, but they drop progressively after Easter to about $40 and $50, respectively, in the muggy summer months.

Boyne South, on U.S. 41 between Fla. 931 and Fla. 92 (© 239/732-5108), is another winner, with lots of wildlife inhabiting its many lakes (a 16-ft. alligator reportedly resides near the 17th hole). There are a driving range, practice facility, and restaurant; instruction is available. Wintertime fees are about $70, but in the off-season they drop to $45 or less. Tee times are taken up to 4 days in advance.

Another local favorite is the player-friendly **Hibiscus Golf Club,** a half mile east of U.S. 41 off Rattlesnake Hammock Road in East Naples (© **239/774-0088**). A pro shop and teaching professional are available. Fees are about $70 in winter, cart included, dropping to about $30 in summer.

At the intersection of Vanderbilt Beach and Airport/Pulling roads, the Greg Norman–designed 27 championship holes at the **Tiburón Golf Club**, 2620 Tiburón Dr. (© **877/WCI-PLAY** or 239/594-2040), play like a British Open course—but without the thick-thatch rough. Fees reach $200 in winter but drop as low as $70 in summer. The course is home to the **Rick Smith Golf Academy** (© **877/464-6531** or 239/ 593-1111) and The Ritz-Carlton Golf Resort.

The area has several other courses worth playing, most described in the Naples–Fort Myers edition of the *Golfer's Guide* available at the chamber of commerce visitor center (or check the magazine's website at www.golfersguide.com). On the Web, www.naplesgolf.com is a good source of information about area courses.

SCUBA DIVING Kevin Sweeney's **SCUBAdventures,** 971 Creech Rd., at Tamiami Trail (© **239/434-7477**; www.scubadventureslc.com), which also has a base on Marco Island (see "Affordable Outdoor Activities" in section 5 of this chapter), takes divers into the gulf, teaches diver-certification courses, and rents water-sports equipment. Two-tank dives range from $65 to $85.

TENNIS In Olde Naples, the city's **Cambier Park Tennis Center**, 755 Eighth Ave. S., at 9th Street South (© **239/434-4694**; www.cambiertennis.com), is one of the country's finest municipal facilities. In fact, it matches those found at many luxury resorts. Play on its 12 lighted clay courts costs $10 for 90 minutes. Book at the pro shop upstairs in the modern building, which has restrooms but no showers. The shop is open Monday to Friday from 8am to 9pm and Saturday and Sunday from 8am to 5pm.

WATER SPORTS **Good Times Rental,** 1947 Davis Blvd. (© **239/775-7529**), rents WaveRunners, Windsurfers, skim boards, snorkeling gear, and other beach equipment. Hobie Cats and Windsurfers can also be rented on the beach at the **Naples Beach Hotel & Golf Club,** 851 Gulf Shore Blvd. N. (© **239/261-2222**), and at **Clam Pass County Park,** at the end of Seagate Drive (© **239/353-0404**). See "Hitting the Beach," above, for more about Clam Pass.

EXPLORING OLDE NAPLES

Its history may go back only to 1886, but the beach skirting **Olde Naples** still has the charm of that Victorian era. The heart of the district lies south of 5th Avenue South (that's where U.S. 41 takes a 45° turn). The town docks are on the bay side, the glorious **Naples Beach** along the gulf. Laid out on a grid, the tree-lined streets run between many houses, some dating from the town's beginning, and along Millionaires' Row between Gulf Shore Boulevard and the beach. With these gorgeous homes virtually hidden in the palms and casuarinas, the Naples Beach seems a century removed from the high-rise condominiums found farther north.

The **Naples Pier,** at the gulf end of 12th Avenue South, is a focal point of the neighborhood. Built in 1888 to let steamers bring potential real-estate customers to land, the original 600-foot-long, T-shaped structure was destroyed by hurricanes and damaged by fire. Local residents have rebuilt it because they like strolling its length to catch fantastic gulf sunsets—and to get a glimpse of Millionaires' Row from the gulf side. The pier is now a state historic site. It's open 24 hours a day, but parking in the nearby lots is restricted between 11pm and 7am.

Nearby, **Palm Cottage,** 137 12th Ave. S., between 1st Street and Gordon Drive (© **239/261-8164**), was built in 1885 by one of Naples's founders, *Louisville Courier-Journal* publisher Walter Haldeman, as a winter retreat for his chief editorial writer. After World War II, its socialite owners hosted many galas attended by Hollywood stars such as Hedy Lamarr, Gary Cooper, and Robert Montgomery. One of the few remaining Southwest Florida houses built of tabby mortar (made by burning shells), Palm Cottage today is the home of the Naples Historical Society, which maintains it as a museum filled with authentic furniture, paintings, photographs, and other memorabilia. Tours are given during winter, Monday to Friday from 1 to 3:30pm. Admission is $5 for adults and free for children.

Near the Gordon River Bridge on Fifth Avenue South, the old corrugated waterfront warehouses now compose a shopping-and-dining complex known as the **Marketplace at Tin City,** which tourists throng to and local residents assiduously avoid during the winter months.

MUSEUMS & ZOOS

Caribbean Gardens ★ *Kids* A family favorite once headed by the late Colonel Larry Tetzlaff, a noted animal collector and wildlife filmmaker, this 52-acre, environmentally conscious zoo features a variety of animals and birds, including a fascinating community of monkeys living free on their own islands. You can see them on a boat safari through the spectacular tropical gardens. Kids especially will be captivated by "Safari Canyon," in which zookeepers display animals while wildlife programming appears on TV screens mounted in the rocks of a simulated canyon. Everyone gets to handle some of the animals and reptiles at the "Scales & Tails" area. The presentations are set up to keep you and the kids busy throughout the full day it will take to ingest it all. A Subway branch sells sandwiches, and there are picnic facilities on the premises.

1590 Goodlette-Frank Rd. (at Fleischmann Blvd.). © **239/262-5409.** www.caribbeangardens.com. Admission $14.95 adults, $9.95 children 4–15; free for children 3 and under. Daily 9:30am–4:30pm. Closed Easter, Thanksgiving, Christmas.

Teddy Bear Museum *Kids* Another family favorite, this entertaining museum contains 3,000-plus examples of stuffed bears from around the world. They're displayed descending from the rafters in hot-air balloons, attending board meetings, sipping afternoon tea, and even doing bear things like hibernating.

2511 Pine Ridge Rd. (at Airport-Pulling Rd.). © **800/365-2327** or 239/598-2711. www.teddymuseum.com. Admission $6 adults, $4 seniors, $2 children 4–12; free for children under 4. Tues–Sat 10am–5pm. Closed New Year's Day, July 4, Thanksgiving, Christmas.

GREAT WINDOW SHOPPING

Two blocks of **3rd Street South** ★★, at Broad Avenue, is the Rodeo Drive of Naples. This glitzy collection of jewelers, clothiers, and art galleries may be too rich for many wallets, but the window shopping here is unmatched. Be sure to pick up a free brochure from the chamber of commerce visitor center (see "Essentials," earlier in this section); it lists the merchants and has a map of the area.

Nearby, the **Fifth Avenue South** ★ shopping area, between 3rd and 9th streets South, has seen a renaissance in recent years and is now Naples's hottest dining spot. The avenue is longer and a bit less chic than 3rd Street South, with stockbrokerages and real-estate offices thrown into the mix of boutiques and antiques dealers.

Also in Olde Naples, the **Old Marine Marketplace at Tin City,** 1200 Fifth Ave. S., at the Gordon River (© **239/262-4200**), has 50 boutiques selling everything from souvenirs to avant-garde resort wear and imported statuary. There are more boutiques in the **Dockside Boardwalk,** a half block west on Sixth Avenue South.

Even the malls in Naples have their charms. The **Village at Venetian Bay,** 4200 Gulf Shore Blvd., at Park Shore Drive (© **239/261-0030**), evokes images of its Italian namesake, with 50 canal-side shops featuring high-fashion men's and women's clothiers and fine-art galleries. Ornate Mediterranean architecture and a tropical waterfall highlight the open-air **Waterside Shops at Pelican Bay,** Seagate Drive at North Tamiami Trail (U.S. 41; © **239/598-1605**), where the anchor stores are Saks Fifth Avenue and Jacobson's. There's a huge Barnes & Noble bookstore across Seagate Drive.

Discount shoppers can head to **Prime Outlets Naples,** on Fla. 951 about a mile south of U.S. 41 on the way to Marco Island (© **888/545-7196** or 239/775-8083; www.primeoutlets.com). The 43 shops are open 10am to 8pm Monday to Saturday and 11am to 6pm Sunday.

ACCOMMODATIONS YOU CAN AFFORD

Even the national chain motels in Naples tend to be of higher quality and better value than their counterparts elsewhere in Southwest Florida. Within walking distance of the historic district, the **Comfort Inn on the Bay,** 1221 Fifth Ave. S. (© **800/228-5150** or 239/649-5800), enjoys a picturesque setting on the east bank of the Gordon River. A good budget choice is the new, all-modern **Red Roof Inn,** 1925 Davis Blvd. (© **800/THE-ROOF** or 239/774-3117), also east of the river.

One of the most reasonably priced of the town's many condominium complexes, **Park Shore Resort,** 600 Neapolitan Way, Naples, FL 34103 (© **800/548-2077** or 239/263-2222; fax 239/263-0946; www.parkshorefl.com), has 156 attractive one- and two-bedroom condominiums surrounding an artificial lagoon with waterfalls cascading on its own island. Guests can walk across a bridge to the artificial island, where they can swim in the heated pool, barbecue on gas grills, or order a meal from the restaurant or a drink from the bar. There's once-a-day complimentary transport to the beach. The condominiums range from $153 to $239 in winter but drop to $89 to $119 off-season.

One of the biggest condominium-rental agents here is **Bluebill Properties,** 26201 Hickory Blvd., Bonita Springs, FL 33923 (© **800/237-2010** or 239/992-6620; www.naplesvacation.com).

Inn by the Sea 🌟 Listed in the National Register of Historic Places, this bed-and-breakfast 2 blocks from the beach in the heart of Olde Naples was built in 1937 as a boardinghouse by Alice Bowling, one of Naples's first schoolteachers and a grocer and entrepreneur to boot. The Federal-style house still has much of its original pine floors and pine or cypress ceilings and woodwork. With windows on three sides, the Sanibel on the ground floor is the lightest and airiest unit here, while the Bokeelia suite is the most romantic, with its bed set at an angle in one corner. The upstairs suites have assigned bathrooms, but you'll have to cross the hallway to get to them. Bikes, beach chairs, and towels are provided; in season, guests are served oranges from the backyard tree.

287 11th Ave. S., Naples, FL 34102. © **800/584-1268** or 239/649-4124. Fax 239/434-2842. www.innbythesea-bb.com. 5 units (3 with bathroom). Winter $149–$189 double; off-season $94–$114 double. Rates include continental breakfast. AE, DISC, MC, V. Children 10 and under not accepted. **Amenities:** Access to nearby health club; free use of bikes. *In room:* A/C, hair dryer. No phone.

Lemon Tree Inn   A real surprise on busy U.S. 41, this property just 3 blocks north of Fifth Avenue South once was a roadside motel but now brings a touch of Key West charm to Olde Naples. Corrugated tin roofs top the two lemon-colored wings, which flank a lush tropical courtyard sporting a heated pool and a gazebo, where guests congregate for complimentary continental breakfasts. The tropically accented rooms aren't spacious—their combination tub-shower bathrooms are so tiny that the wash basins are in the main living area—but they have exposed-beam ceilings hung with fans, and they are more than adequately equipped with wicker armoires serving as closets, wood dinette tables with rattan chairs, refrigerators, coffeemakers, microwave ovens, and toasters. Better choices are the larger efficiencies, which have kitchens. Some units have screened porches, while others open onto patios.

250 9th St. S. (U.S. 41), Naples, FL 34102. © **888/800-LEMON** or 941/262-1414. Fax 941/262-2638. www.ltreeinn.com. 35 units. Winter $149–$199 double; off-season $59–$79 double. Rates include continental breakfast. AE, DISC, MC, V. **Amenities:** Heated outdoor pool. *In room:* A/C, TV, kitchen (efficiencies only), fridge, coffeemaker, hair dryer.

SUPER-CHEAP SLEEPS

Lighthouse Inn Motel   A relic from decades gone by, Judy and Buzz Dugan's no-frills but spotlessly clean motel sits across the street from other more expensive gulfside properties on Vanderbilt Beach and within walking distance of The Ritz-Carlton, Naples. The efficiencies and apartments are simple, with freshly painted cinder-block walls and small kitchens. The one kitchenless room has a small fridge and coffeemaker. Most guests take advantage of weekly and monthly rates in winter, when it's heavily booked. The Dugans also operate Buzz's Lighthouse Cafe next door, a pleasant place for an inexpensive dockside breakfast, lunch, or dinner.

9140 Gulf Shore Dr. N., Naples, FL 34108. © **239/597-3345**. Fax 239/597-5541. 15 units (some with shower only). Winter $105 double; $110 efficiency; $120 apt. Off-season $49 double; $59 efficiency; $69 apt. MC, V. From Olde Naples, go 3½ miles north on U.S. 41; take a left on Vanderbilt Beach Rd. (C.R. 862). Turn right on Gulf Shore Dr. to hotel on right. **Amenities:** Restaurant (American), bar; heated outdoor pool. *In room:* A/C, TV, kitchen, fridge, coffeemaker. No phone.

Stoney's Courtyard Inn *Value*   This locally owned two-story motel is one of the better bargains in town. There's nothing fancy about Stoney's, but it is clean and comfortable, and it does indeed have a courtyard, with tropical foliage and a thatch-roof pavilion next to a heated swimming pool. The rooms facing this scene are preferable to those on the parking lot side. All open to external walkways, and most are of standard motel configuration, with two double beds and a spacious dressing area with an open closet. Restaurants are nearby on U.S. 41.

2630 N. Tamiami Trail (U.S. 41, at 28th Ave. N.), Naples, FL 34103. © **800/432-3870** or 239/261-3870. Fax 239/261-4932. 76 units. Winter $90–$105 single or double, $125 suite; off-season $45–$60 single or double, $70–$105 suite. Rates include continental breakfast. AE, DISC, MC, V. **Amenities:** Outdoor pool; exercise room; coin-op washers and dryers. *In room:* A/C, TV, safe (some units).

OFF-SEASON DEALS

Trianon Old Naples ✶   Constructed in 1998 in a quiet residential neighborhood, this elegant Mediterranean-style building with a classical European interior offers convenience and comfort without a lot of frills. The spacious rooms are equipped with Ritz-Carlton–quality furniture, including mahogany armoires, chairs, and writing desks. All have seating areas and extra-large bathrooms. Some units have balconies large enough for chairs, but others are for standing only. There's no restaurant here, but continental breakfast is served on silver in a refined lounge, where coffee and tea are available all day, and the staff will arrange for meals to be delivered from local restaurants. Champagne and port are served at a wine bar in the evenings.

955 Seventh Ave. S., Naples, FL 34102. © 877/482-5228 or 239/437-9600. Fax 239/261-0025. www.trianon.com. 58 units. Winter $160–$280 double; off-season $85–$190 double. Rates include continental breakfast. AE, DC, DISC, MC, V. **Amenities:** Heated outdoor pool; laundry service. *In room:* A/C, TV, dataport, fridge (in some units), coffeemaker, hair dryer, iron.

Vanderbilt Inn Naples ★ *Kids* Cheerful tropical decor in the accommodations and public areas sets the tempo for a casual, fun vacation at this two-story motel right on Vanderbilt Beach, where you can go parasailing and rent boats and water-sports equipment. Nature lovers can walk along the beach and into Delnor-Wiggins Pass State Park next door (see "Hitting the Beach," earlier in this section). The 16 efficiencies (with kitchens) on the ends of the building open to the beach. About half the standard motel-style rooms face a magnificently landscaped courtyard with a kidney-shaped swimming pool surrounded by a brick terrace, while the other, least expensive units open to parking lots. Although the rooms are entered from exterior walkways, their big windows are darkly tinted to provide privacy. A thatch-roof bar and full-service outdoor restaurant serve lunches and dinners by the beach and draw a crowd for sunset happy hour. Another restaurant turns lively when bands play on Friday and Saturday nights. Kids 13 and under dine free when accompanied by adults here.

11000 Gulf Shore Dr., Naples, FL 34108. © 800/643-8654 or 239/597-3151. Fax 239/597-3099. www.vanderbiltinn.com. 147 units. Winter $205–$350 double; off-season $110–$210 double. Weekly rates available. AE, DC, DISC, MC, V. From Olde Naples, go 4 miles north on U.S. 41; take a left on 111th Ave. (which becomes Bluebill Ave.) to hotel on left. **Amenities:** 2 restaurants (American), 2 bars; heated outdoor pool; Jacuzzi; water-sports equipment rental; business center; limited room service; laundry service. *In room:* A/C, TV, dataport, kitchen (efficiencies only), coffeemaker, hair dryer, iron.

GREAT DEALS ON DINING

If this is your first time here, you may opt to have a lunch or dinner at the touristy **Old Marine Marketplace at Tin City,** on the Gordon River at Fifth Avenue South, where the **Riverwalk Fish & Ale House** (© **239/262-2734**) specializes in moderately priced seafood and steaks. Like its sibling, The Dock at Crayton Cove (see below), it's a fun establishment with dockside seating.

Naples's beaches are ideal for picnics. In Olde Naples, you can get freshly baked breads and pastries, prepackaged gourmet sandwiches, and fruit plates at **Tony's Off Third,** 1300 3rd St. S. (© **239/262-7999**). **Wynn's on Fifth,** 745 Fifth Ave. S. (© **239/261-0901**), between 8th Street and Park Street South, has high-quality deli items, prepackaged sandwiches, salads, take-out meals, and gourmet pastries at very reasonable prices. Both have a few sidewalk tables and are fine places for coffee or a snack while window-shopping on Third and Fifth avenues South.

You'll find budget-priced fast-food and family-style restaurants along U.S. 41, including a branch of the inexpensive **Mel's Diner,** 3650 Tamiami Trail N. (© **239/643-9898**).

Bistro 821 ★ FUSION This noisy bistro launched the dining revitalization along Fifth Avenue South and still is an excellent choice for Mediterranean-influenced Fusion cuisine. A bench covered in bright print fabric runs down one side of this storefront to a bar and open kitchen in the rear. Although the quarters are too close for private conversations, small spotlights hanging from the ceiling romantically illuminate each table. The house specialty is rotisserie chicken, and a daily risotto leads a menu featuring penne pasta in a vodka sauce and a seasonal vegetable plate with herb couscous. There's sidewalk dining here, too.

821 Fifth Ave. S. (between 8th and 9th sts. S.). 239/261-5821. Reservations recommended. Main courses $13–$26. AE, DC, MC, V. Daily 5–10:30pm.

The Dock at Crayton Cove *Value* SEAFOOD   Located right on the City Dock, this lively pub is the best place in town for an open-air meal or a cool drink while watching the boats go back and forth across Naples Bay. The chow ranges from hearty chowders by the mug to seafood with a Floribbean flair, with Jamaican-style jerk shrimp thrown in for spice; main courses are moderately priced. Grilled seafood Caesar salad and a good selection of sandwiches, hot dogs, and other pub-style fare also appear on the menu. "Margarita madness" happy hour and a half-price raw bar (don't miss the steamed mussels with French bread for dipping the garlic sauce) run daily from 9:30 to 11:30pm. The "Great Dock Canoe Race" draws thousands on the second Saturday in May.

12th Ave. S. (at the City Dock in Olde Naples). 239/263-9940. Reservations not accepted. Main courses $11–$26; sandwiches $9–$13. AE, DISC, MC, V. Daily 11am–midnight.

Old Naples Pub *Value* AMERICAN/PUB FARE   You would never guess that the person sitting next to you at the bar here is very, very rich, so relaxed is this small, somewhat-cramped pub in the middle of the fabulous 3rd Street South shops. Diners fortunately find more room at tables on the shopping center's patio. Inside, the pine-paneled walls are hung with trophy fish, a dartboard, and old newspaper clippings about Naples. The menu features very good pub fare (and at extraordinarily inexpensive prices for Olde Naples), including homemade soups, nachos, burgers, and sandwiches ranging from charcoal-grilled bratwurst to fried grouper. Only six main courses are offered: platters with New York strip steak, grilled tuna, the catch of the day, fried grouper or clam strips, and baby back ribs. Best bets are the chicken salad with grapes and walnuts, and the burgers, steaks, and fish from the charcoal grill. You can catch live entertainment here nightly during winter, Wednesday to Saturday off-season.

255 13th Ave. S. (between 3rd and 4th Sts. S.). 239/649-8200. Main courses $11–$15; salads, sandwiches, and burgers $5–$9. AE, DISC, MC, V. Mon–Sat 11am–10pm; Sun noon–9pm.

Silver Spoon American Cafe *Value* AMERICAN/ITALIAN/SOUTHWEST   Even though this chic member of the American Cafe chain is in the swanky Waterside Shops complex, it is one of Naples's best dining bargains. It flaunts sophisticated black-and-white high-tech decor and has large window walls overlooking the mall action. Thick sandwiches are served with french fries, spicy pecan rice, or black beans. The tomato-basil soup is worth a try, and the bruschetta appetizer—served on toasted French bread—is nearly a full meal in itself. Gourmet pizzas and pasta dishes also are popular, especially with the after-theater crowds from the nearby Philharmonic Center for the Arts, and the less expensive main courses such as Cajun or herb-grilled chicken are both tasty and an excellent value. Matron shoppers love to do lunch here, so come early or be prepared for a wait.

In the Waterside Shops at Pelican Bay, 5395 N. Tamiami Trail (at Seagate Dr.). 239/591-2123. Reservations not accepted, but call ahead for preferred seating. Main courses $9.50–$15; pizza and pasta $8–$12;

soups, salads, and sandwiches $7–$9. AE, DC, DISC, MC, V. Sun–Thurs 11am–10pm; Fri–Sat 11am–11pm. From Olde Naples, go north on U.S. 41 and left on Seagate Dr. directly into shopping center. Go right at dead end to restaurant on left.

Yabba Island Grill ★★ *Value* CARIBBEAN

Naples's most reasonably priced chic restaurant, this lively joint re-creates a raucous Caribbean beachside bar in the middle of the Fifth Avenue South dining district. The chow is as lively as Yabba's pastel color scheme, with most items providing a riot of flavors from across the Caribbean. We love the St. Croix Sizzler, a terrific combination of small lobster tail, a chunk of mahimahi, and mussels over a bed of peppers, onions, and a sweet mango curry sauce. Also worthy of a repeat: the Monsoon salad consisting of grilled chicken breast, hearts of palm, candied pecans, and mushrooms under a warm bacon-and-berry vinaigrette and topped with crispy onion rings.

711 Fifth Ave. S. (between 8th St. S. and Park Ave. S.). © 239/262-5787. Reservations recommended. Main courses $10–$24; sandwiches $8–$10. AE, DISC, MC, V. Daily 4:30–11pm (bar to 2am Fri–Sat).

SUPER-CHEAP EATS

First Watch *Value* AMERICAN

Just like its siblings elsewhere in Florida, this shop is a favorite local haunt for breakfast, late brunch, or a midday meal. You may have to wait for a table, but once you're seated, a young staff will provide quick and friendly service. The menu leans heavily on healthy selections, but you can get your cholesterol from a sizzling skillet of fried eggs served over layers of potatoes, vegetables, and melted cheese. Lunch features large salads, sandwiches, and quesadillas. In addition to the dining room, there's seating at umbrella tables in the shopping center's courtyard.

In Gulf Shore Sq., 1400 Gulf Shore Blvd. (at Banyan Rd.). © 239/434-0005. Most items $3.50–$8. AE, DISC, MC, V. Daily 7am–2:30pm. Closed Christmas.

WORTH A SPLURGE

Chop's City Grill ★★ STEAKS/SEAFOOD

Wonderful aromas waft from the open kitchen at the rear of this urbane bistro. Aged, top-quality steaks and lamb chops are the house specialties, either chargrilled to perfection and served with thick onion rings and mashed potatoes, or peppered and served with a blackberry and cabernet wine sauce. Fresh fish from the grill is another good choice. Asian influences appear here, too, such as sea scallops "shocked" in a wok with Thai curry sauce and served over noodles with wild mushrooms and stir-fried vegetables.

837 Fifth Ave. S. (between 8th and 9th sts. S.). © 239/262-4677. Reservations recommended. Main courses $17–$30. AE, DC, DISC, MC, V. Daily 5:30–10pm.

Tommy Bahama's Tropical Cafe ★★ CARIBBEAN

You walk through a thatch gateway into this lively, island-style pub—an incongruous sight in the middle of the staid 3rd Street South shopping enclave. Diners gather on a large front patio under shade trees, where a musician performs, or inside, where a large back-wall mural creates a Polynesian scene. An open kitchen and service bar are on one side of the dining room, a real bar dispensing drinks on the other. In between, round-backed cane chairs and classic ceiling fans add to the exotic mood. Although the Jamaican pork, salmon St. Croix, and other Caribbean-style cuisine don't quite live up to the ambience, you'll have too much fun here to care whether or not it's gourmet—and the huge portions will satisfy any appetite. They don't appear on the dinner menu, but sandwiches are served if you ask for them (the meal-size grouper sandwich is a bargain at $10).

1220 3rd St. S. (between 12th and 13th aves. S.) © 239/643-6889. Reservations recommended. Main courses $17–$27; sandwiches $8–$14. AE, MC, V. Winter daily 11am–11pm; off-season daily 11am–10pm.

Zoë's ★★ ECLECTIC   This slightly Art Deco bistro draws a lively crowd of young professionals who preen at the big bar to one side or at a raised, English pub–style drinking table (you can dine at the table, too, which is handy if you're traveling alone since you're sure to get into conversations with your fellow guests). The eclectic menu changes every week or so to take advantage of fresh produce. Meat loaf, macaroni and cheese, and pot roast are regulars. They sound on the menu like those your mother made, but they're seasoned as lively as Zoë's patrons. If they're offered, opt for the pecan-crusted sea bass or the seared, sesame-coated yellowfin tuna served with a cucumber relish, a horseradish-tinged mayonnaise drizzle, and spicy soba noodles. Zoë's turns into a high-energy nightclub on Friday and Saturday nights.

720 Fifth Ave. S. (between 7th and 8th sts. S.) © 239/261-1221. Reservations recommended. Main courses $15–$34. AE, MC, V. Sun–Thurs 5–10pm; Fri–Sat 5–10:30pm (music and dancing Fri–Sat 11pm–2am).

NAPLES AFTER DARK

For entertainment ideas, check the *Naples Daily News* (www.naplesnews.com), especially the "Neapolitan" section in Friday's edition.

PERFORMING ARTS   Known locally as "The Phil," the impressive **Philharmonic Center for the Arts**, 5833 Pelican Bay Blvd., at West Boulevard (© **800/597-1900** or 239/597-1900; www.thephil.org), is the home of the Naples Philharmonic, but its year-round schedule is filled with cultural events, concerts by celebrated artists and internationally known orchestras, and Broadway plays and shows aimed at children and families. Call or check the website for its seasonal calendar.

A fine local theater group, the **Naples Players,** holds their winter-season performances in the new Sugden Community Theatre, 701 Fifth Ave. S. (© **239/263-7990;** www.naples.net/presents/theatre). Tickets can be hard to come by, so call well in advance.

THE CLUB & BAR SCENE   The restaurants and bistros along Fifth Avenue South are popular watering holes, especially for young single professionals who make this their "meat market" on Friday nights. Zoë's, 720 Fifth Ave. S. (© **239/261-1221;** see "Great Deals on Dining," above), turns into a high-energy nightclub Friday and Saturday from 10:30pm to 2am. Nearby, **McCabe's Irish Pub,** 699 Fifth Ave. S. (© **239/403-7170**), features traditional Irish music nightly.

In the 3rd Street South shopping area, **Old Naples Pub,** 255 13th Ave. S. (© **239/649-8200**), has live music nightly during winter, Wednesday to Saturday nights off-season. See "Great Deals on Dining," above.

The **Old Marine Marketplace at Tin City,** comprising the restored waterfront warehouses on Fifth Avenue South on the west side of the Gordon River, comes alive during the winter when visitors flock to its shops and the **Riverwalk Fish & Ale House** (© **239/262-2734**), which has live entertainment during the season.

Some hotels here have entertainment throughout the year. The beachside "chickee hut" bar at the **Naples Beach Hotel & Golf Club,** 851 Gulf Shore Blvd. N. (© **239/261-2222**), is always popular, has live entertainment many nights, and is *the* place to go on Sunday afternoon and early evening. So is the beachside bar at the **Vanderbilt Inn Naples** (© **239/597-3151;** see "Accommodations You Can Afford," above).

5 Marco Island

15 miles SE of Naples, 53 miles S of Fort Myers, 100 miles W of Miami

Captain William Collier would hardly recognize Marco Island if he were to come back from the grave today. No relation to Collier County founder Barron Collier, the captain settled his family on the north end of this largest of Florida's Ten Thousand Islands back in 1871. He traded pelts with the Native Americans, caught and smoked fish to sell to Key West and Cuba, and charged fishermen and other guests $2 a day for a room in his home. A few turn-of-the-century buildings still stand here, but Captain Collier would be shocked to come across the high-rise bridge to the island and see it now sliced by human-made canals and virtually covered by resorts, condominiums, shops, restaurants, and winter homes. These are the products of an extensive real-estate development begun in 1965, which means that Marco lacks any of the charm found in Naples and on Sanibel and Captiva islands. Much of the sales effort here was aimed at the northeastern states, so the island smacks more of New York and Massachusetts than of the laid-back Midwestern style of its neighbors.

Marco's top attractions are its crescent-shaped beach and access to the nearby waterways running through a maze of small islands, its excellent boating and fishing, and the island's proximity to thousands of acres of wildlife preserves.

ESSENTIALS

GETTING THERE See "Essentials" in sections 1 and 4 of this chapter for information about the **Southwest Florida International Airport** and the **Naples Municipal Airport,** respectively, and about Amtrak's train service and Greyhound/Trailways buses to those cities.

VISITOR INFORMATION The **Marco Island Area Chamber of Commerce,** 1102 N. Collier Blvd., Marco Island, FL 34145 (© **800/788-6272** or 239/394-7549; fax 239/394-3061; www.marcoislandchamber.org), provides free information about the island. A message board and a phone are located outside for making hotel reservations even when the office is closed. The chamber is open Monday to Friday from 9am to 5pm and Saturday from 10am to 3pm during winter.

GETTING AROUND **Marco Island Trolley Tours** (© **239/394-1600**) makes four complete loops around the island from 10am to 3:15pm Monday to Saturday. The conductors sell tickets and render an informative narration about the island's history. Daily fare is $16 for adults and $7 for children 11 and under, with free reboarding. The entire loop takes about 1 hour and 45 minutes.

Enterprise Rent-a-Car (© **800/325-8007** or 239/642-4488) has an office here. For a cab, call **A-Action Taxi** (© **239/394-4400**), **Classic Taxi** (© **239/394-1888**), or **A-Okay Taxi** (© **239/394-1113**).

Depending on the type, rental bicycles cost $5 an hour to $65 a week at **Scootertown,** 845 Bald Eagle Dr. (© **239/394-8400;** www.islandbikeshop.com), north of North Collier Boulevard near Olde Marco. Scooters cost about $50 for 24 hours.

WHAT TO SEE & DO
AFFORDABLE OUTDOOR ACTIVITIES

BEACHES The sugar-white Crescent Beach curves for 3½ miles down the entire western shore of Marco Island. Its southern 2 miles are fronted by an unending row of high-rise condominiums and hotels, but the northern 1½ miles are preserved in **Tigertail Public Beach** (© 239/642-8414). There are restrooms, cold-water outdoor showers, a children's playground, a water-sports rental concessionaire, and a snack bar. The park is at the end of Hernando Drive. It's open daily from dawn to dusk. There's no admission charge to the beach, but parking in the lot costs $3 per vehicle.

The beaches in front of the Marriott, Hilton, and Radisson resorts have parasailing, windsurfing, and other water-sports activities, all for a fee.

If you're not staying at the big resorts, Collier County maintains a $3-per-vehicle parking lot and access to the developed beach on the southern end of the island, on Swallow Avenue at South Collier Boulevard.

GOLF Naples's Lely and Boyne South golf courses are a short drive away (see "Affordable Outdoor Activities," in section 4 of this chapter). The closest public courses are the **Marco Shores Golf Club,** 1450 Mainsail Dr. (© 239/394-2581), and **Marriott's Golf Club at Marco** (© 239/353-7061), both in the marshlands off Fla. 951 north of the island. A sign at the Marriott's course ominously warns: PLEASE DON'T DISTURB THE ALLIGATORS. Fees range from about $120 in winter down to $75 in summer.

WATER SPORTS **Marco River Marina,** 951 Bald Eagle Dr. (© **239/394-2502;** www.marcoriver.com), is the center for boat rentals, fishing, and cruises. Operating from a booth on the marina's dock, **Sunshine Tours** (© **239/642-5415**) will book offshore fishing charters and arrange back-bay fishing ($47 adults, $37 kids under 10), shelling excursions to the small islands ($37 adults, $27 children under 10), sunset cruises ($30 adults, $15 children under 10), and dinner cruises ($49 per person). The back-bay fishing trips go at high tide, the shelling trips at low tide, so call for the schedule and reservations.

SCUBAdventures has a base at 845 Bald Eagle Dr. (© **239/389-7889**) in Olde Marco. Two-tank dives range from $65 to $85 depending on the distance offshore.

PARKS & NATURE PRESERVES

Operated by The Conservancy and part of the Rookery Bay National Estuarine Research Reserve, the **Briggs Nature Center**, on Shell Island Road, off Fla. 951 between U.S. 41 and Marco Island (© **239/775-8569**), has a half-mile boardwalk through a pristine example of Florida's disappearing scrublands, home to the threatened scrub jays and gopher tortoises. Rangers lead a variety of nature excursions (call for the seasonal schedule), and there is a self-guided canoe trail, with canoes for rent from Tuesday to Saturday mornings (you must return them by 1pm) at $13 for the first 2 hours, $5 for each additional hour. The center is open Monday to Saturday from 9am to 4:30pm. Admission to the boardwalk is $7.50 for adults, $3 for children 3 to 12, and is free for children under 3. For more information, contact **The Conservancy of Southwest Florida,** 1450 Merrihue Dr., Naples, FL 34102 (© **239/262-0304;** fax 239/262-0672; www.conservancy.org).

Many species of birds inhabit **Collier Seminole State Park,** 20200 E. Tamiami Trail, Naples, FL 34114 (© **239/394-3397;** www.floridastateparks.org/district4/collier-seminole), an inviting, 6,423-acre preserve on the edge of Big Cypress Swamp, 12 miles east of Marco Island on U.S. 41 (just east of Fla. 92). It offers fishing, boating, picnicking, canoeing over a 13-mile loop with a primitive campsite, observing nature along 6 miles of hiking trails (open during dry periods) and a 1-mile nature walk, and regular tent and RV camping. A "walking" dredge used to build the Tamiami Trail in the 1920s sits just inside the park entrance.

Housed in a replica of a Seminole Wars–era log fort, an interpretive center has information about the park, and there are ranger-led programs from December to April. Well worth taking, 1-hour **narrated boat tours** (✆ **239/ 642-8898**) wander through the winding waterways. They depart daily every 90 minutes from 9:30am to 3:30pm and cost $10 for adults, $7.50 for children 6 to 12, and are free for children 5 and under. Canoes can be rented for $3 per hour, $15 a day, but the park has only four primitive camping sites along the canoe trails. The park has 130 tent and RV sites laid out in circles and shaded by palms and live oaks. The campground has hot showers and a screened, open-air lounge. From December through April, sites cost $15 with electricity, $13 without. Off-season rates are $10 with electricity, $8 without. For camping reservations call ✆ **800/326-3521** or go to the website www.reserve america.com. Admission to the park is $3.25 per vehicle, $1 for pedestrians and bikers. It is open daily from 8am to sundown. You can bring your pets, but keep them on a leash.

ACCOMMODATIONS YOU CAN AFFORD

There are no chain hotels on Marco Island other than the large, high-rise **Marco Island Hilton Beach Resort,** 560 S. Collier Blvd., Marco Island, FL 34145 (✆ **800/443-4550** or 239/394-5000; fax 239/394-8410; www.marcoisland. hilton.com); the **Marco Island Marriott Resort & Golf Club,** 400 S. Collier Blvd., Marco Island, FL 34145 (✆ **800/438-4573** or 239/394-2511; fax 239/642-2628; www.marcomarriottresort.com); and the **Radisson Suite Beach Resort,** 600 S. Collier Blvd., Marco Island, FL 34145 (✆ **800/992-0651** or 239/394-4100; fax 239/394-0262; www.marcobeachresort.com). None inexpensive, they stand in a row along Crescent Beach on the island's southwestern corner.

Century 21 First Southern Trust (✆ **800/523-0069** or 239/394-7653; fax 239/394-8048; www.c21marco.com) is one of the largest agents representing rental property owners.

As elsewhere in South Florida, the high season here is from mid-December to mid-April. Rates drop precipitously in the off-season.

Collier Seminole State Park has the nearest campground with tent sites (see "Parks & Nature Preserves," above).

Boat House Motel ⭐   One of the best bargains in these parts, this comfortable little motel sits beside the Marco River in Old Marco, on the island's northern end. The rooms are in a two-story, lime-green-and-white building near a wooden dock. Here there's a small heated swimming pool with lounge furniture, picnic tables, and barbecue grills. Two rooms on the end have their own decks, and all open to tiny courtyards. Bright paint, ceiling fans, and louvered doors add a tropical ambience throughout. The one-bedroom condos next door open to the riverside dock, upon which is built a two-bedroom cottage named "The Gazebo," whose peaked roof is supported by umbrella-like spokes from a central pole. Olde Marco restaurants are a short stroll away.

1180 Edington Place, Marco Island, FL 34148. ✆ **239/642-2400.** Fax 239/642-2635. www.theboathouse motel.com. 25 units. Winter $92.50–$147.50 single or double, $107.50–$240 apt or cottage; off-season $57.50–$77.50 single or double, $75–$135 apt or cottage. MC, V. **Amenities:** Bike rentals; laundry. *In room:* A/C, TV.

GREAT DEALS ON DINING

For inexpensive fare, head for the Town Center Mall, at the corner of North Collier Boulevard and Bald Eagle Drive, where you'll find two good choices. **Susie's Diner** (© **239/642-6633**) is popular with the locals for breakfasts and especially for Susie's inexpensive full-meal lunch specials. She's open Monday to Saturday from 6:30am to 2:30pm and Sunday from 6:30am to 1pm (for breakfast only). **Breakfast Plus** (© **239/642-6900**) has eye-openers ranging from bacon and eggs to kippers to latkes. It's open daily from 7am to 2:30pm.

The island's popular sports bars also offer inexpensive pub fare to go with their multitudinous TVs. Most popular are **Rookie's Bar & Grill,** in Mission de San Marco Plaza at the corner of South Collier Boulevard and Winterberry Drive (© **239/394-6400**), and the **Crazy Flamingo,** in the Town Center Mall, North Collier Boulevard at Bald Eagle Drive (© **239/642-9600**).

Kahuna Restaurant AMERICAN   With fanciful Hawaiian themes highlighted by a small steaming volcano and a big mural of porpoises playing underwater on one wall, Kahuna is the least expensive choice here. You can sit outside on the shopping center's parking lot or inside at colored booths and round tables under ceiling fans. The burgers are some of Marco's best (there's a condiment bar with a variety of fixings). Main courses include several fried seafood selections, baked crab cakes, and charcoal-grilled tuna, but your best bet should be a nightly special such as salmon in a light dill sauce. Don't expect gourmet dining here, but the quality is good for the price.

1035 N. Collier Blvd., in Town Center Mall (at Bald Eagle Dr.). © 239/394-4300. Reservations not accepted. Breakfast $3–$8; sandwiches and burgers $3.50–$7.50; main courses $8.50–$15. MC, V. Winter daily 8:30am–9pm. Off-season daily 11:30am–9pm.

Kretch's ★★ *Value* SEAFOOD/CONTINENTAL   Noted pastry chef Bruce Kretschmer rules this shopping-center roost, Marco's best all-around restaurant. Bruce has created a sinfully rich seafood strudel by combining shrimp, crab, scallops, cheeses, cream, and broccoli in a flaky Bavarian pastry and serving it all under a lobster sauce. It's available in appetizer or main course-size portions. Cholesterol counters can choose from broiled or charcoal-grilled fish, shrimp, Florida lobster tail, steaks, or lamb chops. Bruce's popular "Mexican Friday" lunches feature delicious tacos and other inexpensive south-of-the-border selections. Sunday is home-cooking night during winter, with chicken and dumplings, Yankee pot roast, and braised lamb shanks.

527 Bald Eagle Dr. (south of N. Collier Blvd.). © 239/394-3433. Reservations recommended in winter. Main courses $14–$25. DISC, MC, V. Mon–Fri 11am–3pm and 5–9pm; Sat–Sun 5–9pm. Closed Sun off-season and Easter, July 4, Thanksgiving, Christmas Eve, and Christmas Day.

Snook Inn SEAFOOD   The choice dinner seats at this Old Florida establishment are in an enclosed dock right beside the scenic Marco River, but for lunch or libation head to the dockside Chickee Bar, a fun place anytime but especially at sunset. Live entertainment is featured out there both day and night during the winter season, nightly the rest of the year. Although seafood is the specialty, tasty steaks, chicken, burgers, and sandwiches are among the choices. Even the sandwiches come with a trip to the salad bar at dinner, making them a fine bargain. Bring a filet of that fish you caught that day and the chef will cook it for you. Call A-Okay Taxi (see "Essentials," above) for a free ride from anywhere on Marco Island.

1215 Bald Eagle Dr. (at Palm St.), Olde Marco. © 239/394-3313. Reservations not accepted. Main courses $11.50–$20.50; sandwiches $8–$10; cook-your-catch $11. AE, DC, DISC, MC, V. Daily 11am–4pm and 4:30–10pm. Closed Thanksgiving, Christmas.

WORTH A SPLURGE

Cafe de Marco ★★ SEAFOOD   Purveyor of some of the island's finest cuisine, this homey establishment at the Marco Village shops was originally constructed as housing for maids at Captain William Collier's Olde Marco Inn. The chef specializes in excellent treatments of fresh seafood, from your choice of shrimp or fresh baked fish with mushrooms, seasoned shallots, and garlic butter to his own luscious creation of seafood and vegetables combined in a lobster sauce and served over linguine. If your waistline can stand it, finish with a Cafe Puff, an almond praline ice-cream ball rolled in chocolate cookie crumbs, placed in a puff pastry shell, and served with whipped cream. Early bird specials here are a very good value. You can dine inside or on a screened patio.

244 Palm St., Olde Marco. © 239/394-6262. Reservations recommended. Main courses $16–$30; early bird specials $13. Minimum charge $13 per adult, $4.50 per child. AE, MC, V. Winter daily 5–10pm. Off-season Mon–Sat 5–10pm. Early bird specials 5–6pm.

MARCO ISLAND AFTER DARK

To find out what's going on, check the *Naples Daily News* (www.naplesnews.com), especially the "Neapolitan" section in Friday's edition and its weekly "The Marco Islander" section, available at the chamber of commerce (see "Essentials," above).

It's not after dark, but one of the biggest parties in Florida takes place every Sunday afternoon at **Stan's Idle Hour Seafood Restaurant,** on County Road 892 in Goodland (© **239/394-3041**), where owner Stan Gober—an Ernest Hemingway look-alike—plays host and fires up the barbecue grills; bands crank up country music for dancing the "Buzzard Lope"; and men compete to see who has the best legs. Stan's Goodland Mullet Festival, always the weekend before the Super Bowl, is the mother of all parties.

Marco Island's much tamer but nevertheless entertaining version is the **Snook Inn,** where bands play out in the dockside Chickee Bar.

Much more sedate are the lounges in the **Marriott and Hilton resorts** (see "Accommodations You Can Afford," above), which provide pianists every evening.

Everyone turns out for free outdoor entertainment at the **Mission San Marco Plaza** shopping center, South Collier Boulevard at Winterberry Drive, every Tuesday night year-round, and at the **Town Center Mall,** at North Collier Boulevard and Bald Eagle Drive, every Thursday night.

10

The Tampa Bay Area

by Bill Goodwin

Many families visiting Orlando's theme parks eventually drive an hour west on I-4 to another major kiddie attraction, Busch Gardens Tampa Bay. But this area shouldn't be a mere side trip from Disney World, for Florida's central west coast is an exciting—and affordable—destination unto itself.

The city of Tampa is the commercial center of Florida's west coast—the country's 11th busiest seaport and a center of banking, high-tech manufacturing, and cigar making (half a billion drugstore stogies a year). Downtown Tampa may roll up its sidewalks after dark, but you can come here during the day to see the sea life at the Florida Aquarium and stroll through the Henry B. Plant Museum, housed in an ornate, Moorish-style hotel built a century ago to lure tourists to Tampa. A short (soon to be trolley) ride will take you to Ybor (*Ee*-bore) City, the historic Cuban enclave, which is now an exciting entertainment and dining venue. And out in the suburbs, Busch Gardens may be best known for its scintillating rides, but it's also one of the world's largest zoos.

Two bridges and a causeway will whisk you westward across Old Tampa Bay to St. Petersburg, Pinellas Park, Largo, Clearwater, Dunedin, and other cities on the Pinellas Peninsula, one of Florida's most densely packed urban areas. Over here on the bayfront, lovely downtown St. Petersburg is famous for wintering seniors, a shopping and dining complex built way out on a pier, and the world's largest collection of Salvador Dalí's surrealist paintings.

Keep driving west, and you'll come to a line of barrier islands where St. Pete Beach, Treasure Island, Clearwater Beach, and other gulfside communities boast 28 miles of sunshine, surf, and white sand. Yes, they're lined with resorts and condos, but parks on each end preserve two of the nation's finest beaches. You don't have to spend a fortune to enjoy it all, for these beaches have a place to stay for everyone in all income ranges.

Drive north up the coast, and you'll go back in time at the old Greek sponge enclave of Tarpon Springs, one of Florida's most attractive small towns, and at Weeki Wachee Springs, a tourist attraction where "mermaids" have been entertaining underwater for half a century.

Heading south, I-275 will take you across the mouth of Tampa Bay to Sarasota and to another chain of barrier islands, which stretch 42 miles along the coast south of Tampa Bay. One of Florida's cultural centers, affluent Sarasota is the gateway to St. Armands and Longboat Keys, two playgrounds of the rich and famous, and to Lido and Siesta Keys, both attractive to families of more modest means. Even more reasonably priced is Anna Maria Island, off the riverfront town of Bradenton. You might say the bridge from Longboat to Anna Maria goes from one price range to another.

1 Tampa

85 miles SW of Orlando, 200 miles SW of Jacksonville, 254 miles NW of Miami, 63 miles N of Sarasota

Even if you stay at the beaches 20 miles to the west, you should consider driving into Tampa to see its sights. If you have children in tow, they may *demand* that you go into the city so they can ride the rides and see the animals at Busch Gardens. While in the city, you can educate them at the Florida Aquarium and the city's fine museums. If you don't have kids, historic Ybor City has the bay area's liveliest nightlife.

Tampa was a sleepy little port when Cuban immigrants founded Ybor City's cigar industry in the 1880s. A few years later, Henry B. Plant put Tampa on the tourist map by building a railroad into town and constructing the bulbous minarets over his garish Tampa Bay Hotel, now a museum named in his honor. During the Spanish American War, Teddy Roosevelt trained his Rough Riders here and walked the Ybor City streets with Cuban revolutionary José Marti. A land boom in the 1920s gave the city its charming, Victorian-style Hyde Park suburb, now a gentrified redoubt for the baby boomers just across the Hillsborough River from downtown.

Today's downtown skyline is the product of the 1980s and 1990s booms, when banks built skyscrapers and the city put up an expansive convention center, a performing-arts center, and the Ice Palace, a 20,000-seat bay-front arena that is home to professional hockey's Tampa Bay Lightning. It hasn't been as rapid as planned, given the recent economic recession, but the renaissance is continuing into the 21st century with redevelopment of the seaport area east of downtown. There the existing Florida Aquarium and the Garrison Seaport Center (a major home port for cruise ships bound for Mexico and the Caribbean) are being joined by office buildings, apartment complexes, and a major shopping-and-dining center known as Channelside at Garrison Seaport.

You won't want to spend your entire Florida vacation here, but all this adds up to a fast-paced, modern city on the go.

ESSENTIALS

GETTING THERE Tampa International Airport (© 813/870-8770; www.tampaairport.com), 5 miles northwest of downtown Tampa, is the major air gateway to this area (**St. Petersburg–Clearwater International Airport** has limited service; see section 2, "St. Petersburg," later in this chapter). Most major and many no-frills airlines serve Tampa International, including **Air Canada** (© 800/268-7240 in Canada, 800/776-3000 in the U.S.), **AirTran** (© 800/AIR-TRAN), **America West** (© 800/235-9292), **American** (© 800/433-7300), **British Airways** (© 800/247-9297), **Canadian Airlines International** (© 800/426-7000), **Cayman Airways** (© 800/422-9626), **Condor German Airlines** (© 800/524-6975), **Continental** (© 800/525-0280), **Delta** (© 800/221-1212), **JetBlue** (© 800/538-2583), **Lufthansa** (© 800/824-6200), **MetroJet** (© 800/428-4322), **Midway** (© 800/446-4392), **Midwest Express** (© 800/452-2022), **Northwest/KLM** (© 800/225-2525), **Southwest** (© 800/435-9792), **Spirit** (© 800/722-7117), **TWA** (© 800/221-2000), **Tango** (© 800/315-1390), **United** (© 800/241-6522), and **US Airways** (© 800/428-4322).

Alamo (© 800/327-9633), **Avis** (© 800/331-1212), **Budget** (© 800/527-0700), **Dollar** (© 800/800-4000), **Enterprise** (© 800/325-8007), **Hertz** (© 800/654-3131), **National** (© 800/CAR-RENT), and **Thrifty** (© 800/367-2277) all have rental-car operations here.

Tampa & St. Petersburg

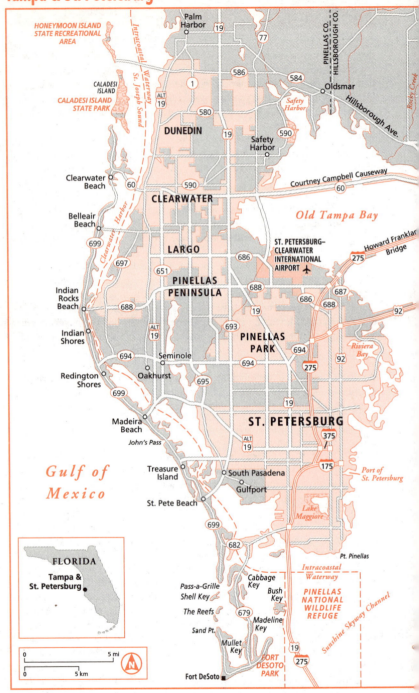

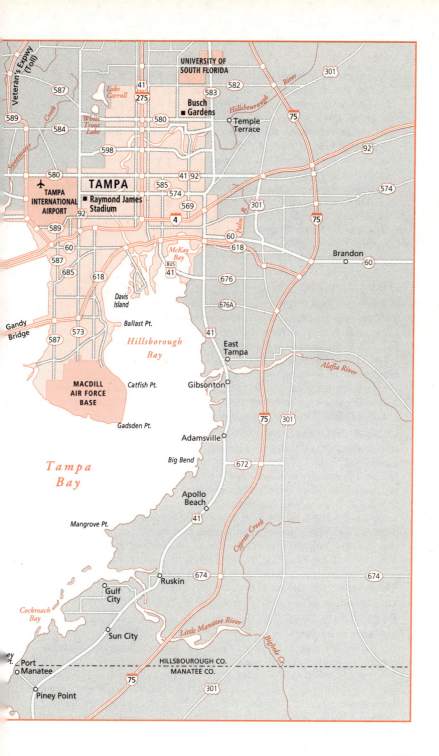

> **Tips A Money-Saving Stop for Info & Advice**
>
> Near Busch Gardens, the privately owned **Tampa Bay Visitor Information Center,** 3601 E. Busch Blvd., at N. Ednam Place (✆ **813/985-3601;** fax 813/985-7642; www.hometown.aol.com\tpabayinfoctr), offers free brochures about attractions in Tampa and sells discounted tickets to many attractions. You may be able to both save $2 a head and avoid waiting in long ticket lines at Busch Gardens by buying here. Owner Jim Boggs worked for the park for 13 years and gives expert advice about how to get the most out of your visit. He sells discounted tickets to Busch Gardens, Adventure Island, and other attractions, and he will book hotel rooms and car rentals for you, often at a discount. The center is open Monday to Saturday from 10am to 5:30pm, Sunday from 10am to 2pm. Operating as Swiss Chalet Tours, this same company also has organized excursions of the area (see "Organized Tours" later in this chapter).

The **Limo/SuperShuttle** (✆ **800/282-6817** or 727/527-1111; www.supershuttle.com) operates van services between the airport and hotels throughout the Tampa Bay area. Fares for one person range from $9 to $27 anywhere in the bay area. **Taxis** are plentiful at the airport; the ride to downtown Tampa takes about 15 minutes and costs $11 to $15.

Local **HARTline buses** stop in front of the red baggage-claim area (see "Getting Around," below), but you're much better off taking a shuttle or taxi to your hotel, where you can get your bearings before tackling the area's public buses.

Amtrak trains arrive downtown at the **Tampa Amtrak Station,** 601 Nebraska Ave. N. (✆ **800/USA-RAIL;** www.amtrak.com).

VISITOR INFORMATION   Contact the **Tampa Bay Convention and Visitors Bureau,** 400 N. Tampa St., Tampa, FL 33602-4706 (✆ **800/826-8358** or 813/342-4077; fax 813/229-6616; www.visittampabay.com), for advance information. Once you're downtown, head to the bureau's visitor information center at the corner of Ashley Drive and Madison Street (✆ **813/223-1111**). It's open Monday to Saturday from 9am to 5pm.

Operated by the Ybor City Chamber of Commerce, the **Centro Ybor Museum and Visitor Information Center,** in Centro Ybor, 1600 E. Eighth Ave. (between 16th and 17th sts. E.), Tampa, FL 33605 (✆ **877/934-3782** or 813/248-3712; fax 813/242-0398; www.ybor.org), distributes information and has exhibits about the area's history. A 7-minute video will help get you oriented. The center is open Monday to Saturday from 10am to 6pm and Sunday from noon to 6pm.

GETTING AROUND   Like most other Florida destinations, it's virtually impossible to see Tampa's major sights and enjoy the best restaurants without a car. You can get around downtown via the free **Uptown-Downtown Connector Trolley,** which runs north-south between Harbor Island and the city's North Terminal bus station on Marion Street at I-275. The trolleys run every 10 minutes from 6am to 6pm Monday to Friday. Southbound, they follow Tampa Street between Tyler and Whiting streets, and Franklin Street between Whiting Street and Harbor Island. Northbound trolleys follow Florida Avenue from the Ice Palace to Cass Street. It's operated by the Hillsborough Area Regional Transit/HARTline (✆ **813/254-HART;** www.hartline.org), the area's transportation authority, which also provides scheduled **bus service** between downtown Tampa and the suburbs. Pick up a route map at the visitor information center (see above).

The situation will get much better when the **TECO Line Street Car System,** a new but old-fashioned streetcar system, complete with overhead power lines, begins hauling passengers between downtown and Ybor City via the Ice Palace, Channelside, Garrison Seaport, and the Florida Aquarium. Plagued by delays, the system at presstime was expected to begin operating in late 2002. Check with the visitor center or call HARTline to find out if indeed it is running, and if so, its schedule and fares. In the meantime, you'll have to drive or take a taxi from downtown to Ybor City.

Taxis in Tampa don't normally cruise the streets for fares, but they do line up at public loading places, such as hotels, the performing-arts center, and bus and train depots. If you need a taxi, call **Tampa Bay Cab** (© 813/251-5555), **Yellow Cab** (© 813/253-0121), or **United Cab** (© 813/253-2424). Fares are 95¢ at flag fall, plus $1.50 for each mile.

WHAT TO SEE & DO
EXPLORING THE THEME & ANIMAL PARKS

Adventure Island *Kids* If the summer heat gets to you before one of Tampa's famous thunderstorms brings late-afternoon relief, you can take a waterlogged break at this 25-acre outdoor water theme park near Busch Gardens Tampa Bay (see below). In fact, you can frolic here even during the cooler days of spring and fall, when the water is heated. The Key West Rapids, Tampa Typhoon, Gulf Scream, and other exciting water rides will drench the teens, while other, calmer rides are geared for younger kids. There are places to picnic and sunbathe, a games arcade, a volleyball complex, and an outdoor cafe. If you forget to bring your own, a surf shop sells bathing suits, towels, and suntan lotion.

10001 Malcolm McKinley Dr. (between Busch Blvd. and Bougainvillea Ave.). © 813/987-5600. www.4adventure.com. *Note:* Admission and hours vary from year to year so call ahead, check website, or get brochure at visitor centers. Admission at least $25.95 adults, $23.95 children 3–9, plus tax; free for children 2 and under. Combination tickets with Busch Gardens Tampa Bay (1 day each) $59.95 adults, $49.95 children 3–9; free for children under 3. Parking $4. Mid-Mar to Labor Day daily 10am–5pm; Sept–Oct Fri–Sun 10am–5pm (extended hrs. in summer and on holidays). Closed Nov to late Feb. Take Exit 33 off I-275 and go east on Busch Blvd. for 2 miles. Turn left onto McKinley Dr. (N. 40th St.) and entry is on right.

Busch Gardens Tampa Bay ★★ *Kids* Although its heart-stopping thrill rides get much of the ink, this venerable theme park (it predates Disney World) ranks among the largest zoos in the country. It's a don't-miss attraction for children, who can see in person all those wild beasts they've watched on the *Animal Planet*—and they'll be closer to them here than at Disney's Animal Kingdom in Orlando (see chapter 11, "Walt Disney World & Orlando"). Several thousand animals live in naturalistic environments and help carry out the park's overall African theme. Most authentic is the 80-acre plain, strongly reminiscent of the real Serengeti of Tanzania and Kenya, upon which zebras, giraffes, and other animals actually graze. Unlike the animals on the real Serengeti, however, the grazing animals have nothing to fear from lions, hyenas, crocodiles, and other predators, which here are confined to enclosures—as are hippos and elephants.

Most of the large animals live in the Edge of Africa, the most unique of the park's eight areas, each of which has its own theme, animals, live entertainment, thrill rides, kiddie attractions, dining, and shopping. A Skyride cable car soars over the park, offering a bird's-eye view of it.

Tampa Attractions

- Adventure Island **3**
- Busch Gardens Tampa Bay **4**
- Florida Aquarium/Garrison Seaport Center **13**
- Henry B. Plant Museum **10**
- Lowry Park Zoo **5**
- MOSI (Museum of Science and Industry) **2**
- N.Y. Yankees Spring Training Complex **6**
- Raymond James Stadium **7**
- Tampa Bay Downs **1**
- Tampa Museum of Art **11**
- University of Tampa **10**
- Visitor Information Center **12**
- Ybor City Brewing Company **11**
- Ybor City State Museum **8**

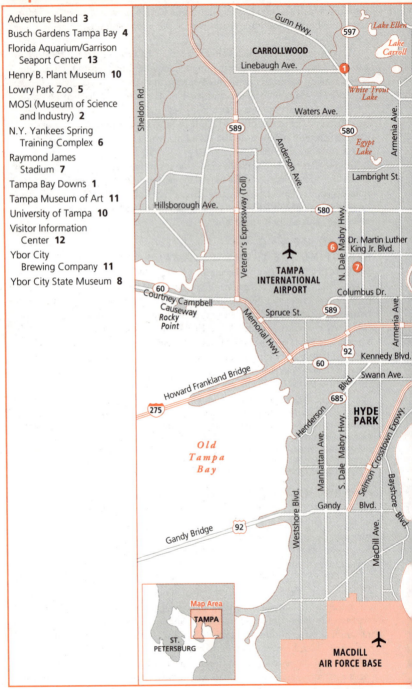

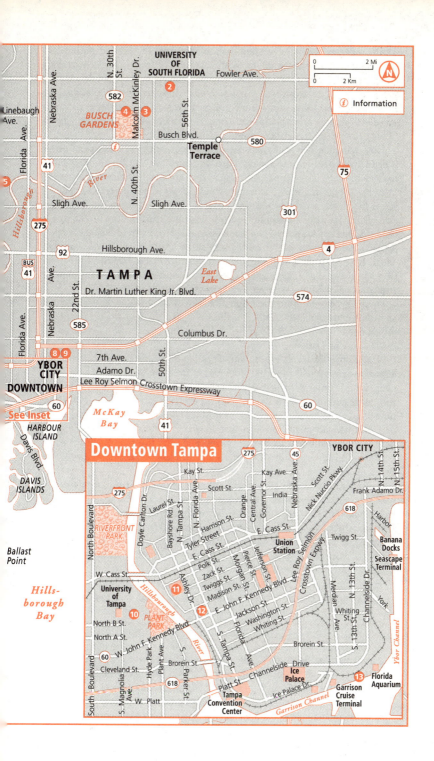

Turn left after the main gate and head to **Morocco,** a walled city with exotic architecture, craft demonstrations, a sultan's tent with snake charmers, and an exhibit featuring alligators and turtles. The Moorish-style Moroccan Palace Theater features an ice show, which many families consider to be the park's best entertainment for both adults and children. Here you can also attend a song-and-dance show in the Marrakech Theater. Overlooking it all is the Crown Colony Restaurant, the park's largest.

After watching the snake charmers, walk eastward past Anheuser-Busch's fabled Clydesdale horses to **Egypt,** where you can visit King Tut's tomb with its replicas of the real treasures and listen to comedian Martin Short narrate "Akbar's Adventure Tours," a wacky simulator that "transports" one and all across Egypt via camel, biplane, and mine car. The whole room moves on this ride, which lasts only 5 minutes—much less time than the usual wait to get inside. Adults and kids over 53 inches tall can ride Montu, the tallest and longest inverted roller coaster in the world, with seven upside-down loops. Your feet dangle loose on Montu, so make sure your shoes are tied tightly and your lunch has had time to digest. Youngsters can dig for their own ancient treasures in an attraction called King Tut's Tomb, close to this monster coaster.

From Egypt, walk onto the **Edge of Africa**, home of most of the big animals. Go immediately to the Expedition Africa Gift Shop and see if you can get on one of the park's zoologist-led wildlife tours (see the box, "How to See Busch Gardens," below).

Next stop is **Nairobi,** where you can see gorillas and chimpanzees in the Myombe Reserve. The most beautiful part of the park, this lush area replicates their natural rainforest habitat. Nairobi also has a baby animal nursery, a petting zoo, turtle and reptile displays, an elephant exhibit (alas, the magnificent creatures seem to be bored to the point of madness), and Curiosity Caverns, where bats, reptiles, and small mammals that are active in the dark are kept in cages (it's the most traditional zoolike area here). The entry to Rhino Rally, the park's new safari adventure, is at the western end of Nairobi (see the "How to See Busch Gardens" box, below).

Next, head to **The Congo**, highlighted by rare white Bengal tigers that live on Claw Island. The Congo also is home to two roller coasters: the Kumba, the largest and fastest roller coaster in the southeastern United States; and the Python, which twists and turns for 1,200 feet. You will get drenched—and refreshed on a hot day—by riding the Congo River Rapids (you're turned loose in round boats that float down the swiftly flowing "river"). There are bumper cars and kiddie rides here, too.

From The Congo, walk south into **Stanleyville,** a prototype African village with a shopping bazaar, orangutans living on an island, and the Stanleyville

---

Tips If You Need Another Day

Once you're inside Busch Gardens Tampa Bay and decide you really need more time to see the park, you can buy a **Next Day ticket** which lets you back in on the following day for about $13 per person.

Also, if you're going to Orlando, Busch Gardens Tampa Bay is included in the five-park version of the **FlexTicket,** which also gains you admission to Universal Studios Florida, SeaWorld, Islands of Adventure, and Wet 'n Wild for $169.95 for adults and $134.95 for children 3 to 9.

How to See Busch Gardens

As noted in the box, "A Money-Saving Stop for Info & Advice," above, you can save a few dollars and avoid waiting in long lines by buying your tickets to Busch Gardens Tampa Bay at the privately owned **Tampa Bay Visitor Information Center,** opposite the park at 3601 E. Busch Blvd., at North Ednam Place (© 813/985-3601; fax 813/985-7642; www.hometown.aol.com\tpabayinfoctr).

Allow at least a day to see the park. Arrive early—but try not to come when it's raining, since some rides may not operate. Bring comfortable shoes; and, remember, you will get wet on some of the rides, so wear appropriate clothing (shops near the rides sell inexpensive plastic ponchos). There are lockers throughout the park where you can stash your gear. Don't be surprised if the park's security staff asks to search your bags before they'll let you enter the main gate.

As soon as you're through the turnstiles, pick up a copy of a park map and the day's activity schedule, which tells what's showing and when at 14 entertainment venues. Then take a few minutes to carefully plan your time—it's a big park with lots to see and do. Busch Gardens continues to grow, so be on the lookout for new attractions.

Although you'll get close to Busch Garden's predators, hippos, and elephants in their glass-walled enclosures, the only way to get out on the plain among the grazers is on a tour. The best is a **VIP Animal Adventure Tour,** on which you'll roam the plains in the company of a zoologist. These 1-hour excursions cost a pricey $75 per person (in addition to the park's entry fee) and usually leave about 1:30pm daily. These tours can fill up fast, and you can't call ahead for reservations, so as soon as you enter the park go to the Expedition Africa Gift Shop, opposite the Crown Colony Restaurant in the Edge of Africa, to reserve a spot. A less attractive alternative is the 30-minute, zoologist-led **Serengeti Safari Special Tours,** in which you ride out among the grazers on the back of a flat-bed truck. These are worth an extra $30 per person regardless of age. You can make reservations for the morning tour at the Expedition Africa Gift Shop, but the midday and afternoon tours are first-come, first-served. Note that children under 5 are not allowed on either tour.

You won't have to pay extra for the **Rhino Rally,** which is included in the park's admission fee. This thrill ride uses four-wheel-drive Land Rovers like those used on photo safaris in Africa. They race each other around the edge of the plain and plunge into a river (you'll probably get wet). You won't have much time to see the animals, since the adventure lasts a whopping 7 minutes.

Theater, usually featuring shows for children. Two more water rides are here: the Tanganyika Tidal Wave (you'll come to a very damp end) and the Stanley Falls Flume (an aquatic version of a roller coaster). Serving ribs and chicken, the picnic-style Stanleyville Smokehouse has some of the best chow here.

Cheap Thrills: What to See & Do for Free (or Almost) in the Tampa Bay Area

- **Hike, bike, or blade along Bayshore Boulevard.** The best view of downtown Tampa's skyline is from Bayshore Boulevard, a broad promenade facing the city from the western side of Hillsborough Bay. Its sidewalk is the city's favorite place to stroll, bike, or in-line skate, especially at sunset when lights in the high-rise buildings begin to twinkle on the water.
- **Party for Free in Ybor City.** Weekend afternoons turn into parties with live music in the patio of **Centro Ybor** (© **813/241-4545**), the new dining-entertainment complex in midst of Tampa's historic Ybor City district. You may find yourself paying for a pitcher of sangria in one of the center's lively pubs, but the music outside is free.
- **Watch the setting sun paint the sky.** Facing due west, the St. Pete and Clearwater beaches offer glorious sunsets over the gulf. If you can afford to stay right on the beach, watch the colorful show from your balcony or patio. For the rest of us, the area's many public beaches are good vantage points, and most are free. The two with the least development to spoil the moment are Fort Desoto Park, south of St. Pete Beach, and Sand Key Park, just across the inlet from Clearwater Beach. They both close at dark, but by then, you may have seen the "green flash" just as the top of the sun hits the horizon. And don't forget the area's many beachside bars, where you can watch for the cost of a drink.
- **Take the ferry to a great beach.** You'll have to pay admission to Honeymoon Island State Recreation Area and another $7.50 for adults or $3.50 per kid to ride the ferry, but that's a small price to pay to reach **Caladesi Island State Park,** north of Clearwater (© **727/469-5942**), and one of Florida's best beaches—a lovely, relatively secluded stretch of fine soft sand edged in sea grass and palmettos. You might even see dolphins cavorting offshore, or perhaps rattlesnakes, black racers, raccoons, armadillos, or rabbits from the park's nature trail.
- **Help birds to mend.** You can visit more than 500 sea and land birds recuperating at the **Suncoast Seabird Sanctuary** in Indian Shores (© **727/391-6211**), the nation's largest wild-bird hospital. Cormorants, great white herons, birds of prey, ubiquitous brown

The next stop is **Land of the Dragons,** the most entertaining area for small children. They can spend an entire day enjoying a variety of play elements in a fairy-tale setting, plus just-for-kids rides. The area is dominated by Dumphrey, a whimsical dragon who interacts with visitors and guides children around a three-story tree house with winding stairways, tall towers, stepping stones, illuminated water geysers, and an echo chamber.

The next stop is **Bird Gardens,** the park's original core, offering rich foliage, lagoons, and a free-flight aviary for hundreds of exotic birds, including golden and American bald eagles. Be sure to see the Florida flamingos and Australian koalas.

pelicans: They're all here. Down Sarasota way, the **Pelican Man's Bird Sanctuary** (© 941/388-4444) treats more than 5,000 injured birds and other wildlife each year. Admission is free to both, but you'll want to make a donation.
- **Poke through a rustic museum dedicated to sponges.** The highlight of any stroll along the carnival-like Sponge Docks in Tarpon Springs is the rickety **Spongeorama** (© 727/943-9509), a warehouse-turned-museum dedicated to sponges and sponge divers. You can buy a wide variety of fresh-from-the-gulf sponges here and watch a 30-minute video about sponge-diving. Admission is free. The docks also have a host of inexpensive restaurants featuring authentic Greek cuisine brought here by the town's sponge-diving settlers.
- **Play great golf on the cheap.** A round of golf in southern Florida can cost $70 and up in winter, but Sarasota's municipal **Bobby Jones Golf Complex** (© 941/365-GOLF) has two 18-hole championship layouts and a nine-hole executive course. But get this: Greens fees range from just $25 to $31, including cart rental.
- **Find out what the Big Top bought.** Adults pay $8 or $9 to get in, but you'll have three "rings" to visit at the **FSU Ringling Center for the Cultural Arts** in Sarasota (© 941/359-5700, or 941/351-1660 for recorded information), which houses the phenomenal collections of circus master John Ringling. A pink Italian-Renaissance villa is filled with more than 500 years of European and American art, including one of the world's most important collections of grand 17th-century baroque paintings. The Ringlings' 30-room winter residence displays their personal mementos. And the Circus Galleries are devoted to memorabilia from The Greatest Show on Earth.
- **Hide your plastic at St. Armand's Circle.** Don't bring your credit cards, but by all means do some window-shopping on Sarasota's St. Armand's Circle, the lushly landscaped home to more than 150 international boutiques, gift shops, and galleries rivaling those in Palm Beach and on Naples's Third Avenue South. Plan to take a break at lunch, when the otherwise expensive restaurants here offer some good deals.

Next take a break at the **Hospitality House,** which offers piano entertainment and free samples of Anheuser-Busch's famous beers. You must be 21 to imbibe (there's a limit of two free mugs per seating), but soft drinks also are available.

If your stomach can take another hair-raising ride, the last stop is at **Gwazi,** the park's pair of old-fashioned wooden roller coasters named the Lion and the Tiger, which start simultaneously and whiz within a few feet of each other six times as they roar along at 50 miles per hour. Since the coasters rise to "only" 90 feet (that's low compared to the park's other thrillers), most family members can give them a go. In Gwazi's "Water Wars," participants shoot water-filled balloons at each other with big slingshots. It's a soaking way to end your visit.

You can exchange foreign currency in the park, and interpreters are available.

Note: You can get here from Orlando via shuttle buses, which pick up at area hotels between 8:00am and 10:15am for the 60-minute ride, with return trips starting at 5pm and continuing until the park closes. Round-trip fares are $5 per person. Call © 800/511-2450 for schedules and reservations.

<small>3000 E. Busch Blvd. (at McKinley Dr./N. 40th St.). © 888/800-5547 or 813/987-5283. www.busch gardens.com. *Note:* Admission and hours vary so call ahead, check website, or get brochure at visitor centers. Admission at least $49.95 adults, $40.95 children 3–9, plus tax; free for children 2 and under. Annual pass $84.95 adults, $74.95 children 3–9, plus tax. Combination season pass with Adventure Island $115. Daily 10am–6pm (extended hrs. to 7 and 8pm in summer and holidays). Parking $7. Take I-275 north of downtown to Busch Blvd. (Exit 33), and go east 2 miles. From I-75, take Fowler Ave. (Exit 54) and follow the signs west.</small>

The Florida Aquarium ★★ *Kids* See more than 5,000 aquatic animals and plants that call Florida home at this entertaining and informative aquarium. The exhibits follow a drop of water from the pristine springs of the Florida Wetlands Gallery, through a mangrove forest in the Bays and Beaches Gallery, and out onto the Coral Reefs, where an impressive 43-foot-wide, 14-foot-tall panoramic window lets you look out to schools of fish and lots of sharks and stingrays. Also worth visiting are the "Explore a Shore" playground to educate the kids, a deep-water exhibit, and a tank housing moray eels. You can also go out on the bay to look for birds and sea life on 90-minute Dolphin Quest cruises in the *Bay Spirit,* a 64-foot diesel-powered catamaran.

<small>701 Channelside Dr. © 813/273-4000. www.flaquarium.net. Admission $15 adults, $12 seniors, $10 children 5–13; free for children under 5. Dolphin Quest $18 adults, $17 seniors, $13 children 5–13; free for children under 5. Combination aquarium admission and Dolphin Quest $30 adults, $26 seniors, $20 children 5–13; free for children under 5. Parking $4. Daily 9:30am–5pm. Dolphin Quest Mon–Fri 2pm; Sat–Sun 1 and 3pm. Closed Thanksgiving, Christmas.</small>

Lowry Park Zoo *Kids* Watching 2,000-pound manatees, Komodo dragons, and rare red pandas makes this a worthwhile excursion after the kids have seen the plains of Africa at Busch Gardens. With lots of greenery, bubbling brooks, and cascading waterfalls, this 24-acre zoo displays animals in settings similar to their natural habitats. Other major exhibits include a Florida wildlife display, an Asian Domain, a Primate World, an Aquatic Center, a free-flight aviary with a birds-of-prey show, an Australian-themed children's zoo (as in kangaroos and wallabies), a hands-on Discovery Center, and an endangered-species carousel ride.

<small>1101 W. Sligh Ave. © 813/935-8552 or 813/932-0245 for recorded information. www.lowryparkzoo.com. Admission $9.50 adults, $8.50 seniors, $5.95 children 3–11; free for children 2 and under. Daily 9:30am–5pm. Closed Thanksgiving, Christmas. Take I-275 to Sligh Ave. (Exit 31) and follow the signs.</small>

VISITING THE MUSEUMS

Henry B. Plant Museum ★★ Originally built in 1891 by railroad tycoon Henry B. Plant as the 511-room Tampa Bay Hotel, this ornate building alone is worth a short trip across the river from downtown to the University of Tampa campus. Its 13 silver minarets and distinctive Moorish architecture, modeled after the Alhambra in Spain, make this National Historic Landmark a focal point of the Tampa skyline. Although the building itself is the highlight of a visit, don't skip the contents: art and furnishings from Europe and the Orient; and exhibits that explain the history of the original railroad resort, Florida's early tourist industry, and the hotel's role as a staging point for Teddy Roosevelt's Rough Riders during the Spanish–American War.

<small>401 W. Kennedy Blvd. (between Hyde Park and Magnolia aves.). © 813/254-1891. www.plantmuseum. com. Admission free; suggested donation $5 adults, $2 children 12 and under. Tues–Sat 10am–4pm; Sun</small>

noon–4pm. Closed Thanksgiving, Christmas Eve, and Christmas Day. Take Kennedy Blvd. (Fla. 60) across Hillsborough River.

MOSI (Museum of Science and Industry) *Kids*

A great place to take the kids on a rainy day, MOSI is the largest science center in the Southeast and has more than 450 interactive exhibits. You can step into the Gulf Hurricane and experience 74 mile-per-hour winds, defy the laws of gravity in the unique *Challenger* space experience, cruise the mysterious world of microbes in LifeLab, and explore the human body in The Amazing You. If your heart's up to it, you can ride a bicycle across a 98-foot-long cable suspended 30 feet in the air above the lobby (don't worry: you'll be harnessed to the bike). You can also watch stunning movies in Florida's first IMAX dome theater. Outside, trails wind through a 47-acre nature preserve with a butterfly garden.

4801 E. Fowler Ave. (at N. 50th St.). © 813/987-6300. www.mosi.org. Admission $13.95 adults, $11.95 seniors, $9.95 children 2–12; free for children under 2. Admission includes IMAX movies. Daily 9am–5pm or later. From downtown, take I-275 north and then Fowler Ave. east for 2 miles to museum on right.

Tampa Museum of Art

Located on the east bank of the Hillsborough River next to the round NationsBank building (locals facetiously call it the "Beer Can"), this fine-arts complex offers eight galleries with changing exhibits ranging from classical antiquities to contemporary Florida art. There's also a 7-acre riverfront park and sculpture garden. Call or check the website for the schedule of temporary exhibits.

600 N. Ashley Dr. (at Twiggs St.), downtown. © 813/274-8130. www.tampamuseum.com. Admission $5 adults, $4 seniors, $3 children 6–18 and students with identification cards; free for children under 6. Admission by donation Thurs 5–8pm and Sat 10am–noon. Tues–Wed and Fri–Sat 10am–5pm; Thurs 10am–8pm; Sun 1–5pm. Parking 90¢ per hour. Take I-275 to Exit 25 (Ashley Dr.).

YBOR CITY

Northeast of downtown, the city's historic Latin district takes its present name from Don Vicente Martinez Ybor (*Ee*-bore), a Spanish cigar maker who arrived here in 1886 via Cuba and Key West. Soon his and other Tampa factories were producing more than 300,000 hand-rolled stogies a day.

It may not be the cigar capital of the world anymore, but Ybor is the happening part of Tampa and it's one of the best places in Florida to buy hand-rolled cigars. It's not on a par with New Orleans's Bourbon Street, Washington's Georgetown, or New York's SoHo, but good food and great music dominate the

---

Tips Quacking Around

A fun way to tour downtown and Ybor City is with **Duck Tours of Tampa Bay** (© 813/432-3825; www.ducktoursoftampabay.com), which uses refurbished World War II amphibious "Ducks." Now equipped with bench seats under canopies, these bright yellow half-truck, half-boat vehicles pick up at the company's "Quack Shack" at Newk's Cafe, 514 Channelside Dr. opposite the Ice Palace, Wednesday through Sunday from 11am to 5pm. The narrated 1-hour, 20-minute excursions go on land through Ybor City, then on the river back to downtown. They cost $18.50 for adults, $16.50 for seniors, $9.95 for children 3 to 12, plus tax. Kids under 3 ride free. Call for the schedule and reservations, which are a good idea on weekends and holidays. The company also offers land-sea tours in St. Petersburg (see "Organized Tours" in section 2 of this chapter).

scene, especially on weekends when the streets bustle until 4am. Live-music offerings run the gamut from jazz and blues to indie rock.

At the heart of it all is **Centro Ybor**, a new dining-shopping-entertainment complex sprawling between Seventh and Eighth avenues and 16th and 17th streets (© 813/241-4545). Here you'll find a multi-screen cinema, a comedy club, several restaurants, a large open-air bar, and several mall regulars such as Victoria's Secret and American Eagle Outfitters. The Ybor City Chamber of Commerce has its visitor center here (see "Essentials," earlier in this section), as does the Ybor City State Museum its gift shop (see below).

Check with the visitor center about **walking tours** of the historic district. **Ybor City Ghost Walks** (© 813/242-4660) will take you to the spookier parts of the area beginning at 4pm Thursday and Saturday. They cost $10 per person and are by reservation only.

Even if you're not a cigar smoker, you'll enjoy a stroll through the **Ybor City State Museum**, 1818 Ninth Ave., between 18th and 19th streets (© 813/247-6323; www.ybormuseum.org), housed in the former Ferlita Bakery (1896–1973). You can take a self-guided tour around the museum to see a collection of cigar labels, cigar memorabilia, and works by local artisans. Admission is $2 per person. Depending on the availability of volunteer docents, admission includes a 15-minute guided tour of **La Casita**, a renovated cigar worker's cottage adjacent to the museum; it's furnished as it was at the turn of the last century. The museum is open daily from 9am to 5pm, but the best time to visit is between 11am and 3pm, when you can take a guided tour of La Casita. Better yet, plan to catch the cigar-rolling demonstrations Friday to Sunday from 10am to 3pm.

Housed in a 100-year-old, three-story former cigar factory, **Ybor City Brewing Company**, 2205 N. 20th St., facing Palm Avenue (© 813/242-9222), produces Ybor Gold and other brews, none with preservatives. Admission of $3 per person includes a tour of the brewery and a taste of the end result. Tours usually are given Monday to Friday at 11am, noon, and 1pm.

ORGANIZED TOURS

Swiss Chalet Tours, 3601 E. Busch Blvd. (© 813/985-3601; www.hometown.aol.com\tpabayinfoctr), opposite Busch Gardens in the privately run Tampa Bay Visitor Information Center (see the box "A Money-Saving Stop for Info & Advice," earlier in this section), operates guided bus tours of Tampa, Ybor City, and environs. The 4-hour tours of Tampa are given from 10am to 2pm daily, with a stop for lunch at the Columbia Restaurant in Ybor City. They cost $40 for adults and $35 for children. The full-day tours of both Tampa and St. Petersburg give a good overview of the two cities and the beaches; these cost $70 for adults and $65 for children. Reservations are required at least 24 hours in advance; passengers are picked up at major hotels and various other points in the Tampa/St. Petersburg area. You also can book bus tours to Orlando, Sarasota, Bradenton, and other regional destinations (call for schedules, prices, and reservations).

AFFORDABLE OUTDOOR ACTIVITIES

BIKING, IN-LINE SKATING & JOGGING Bayshore Boulevard, a 7-mile-long promenade, is famous for its sidewalk right on the shores of Hillsborough Bay and is a favorite for runners, joggers, walkers, and in-line skaters. The route goes from the western edge of downtown in a southward direction, passing stately old homes in Hyde Park, a few high-rise condominiums, retirement communities, and houses of worship, ending at Ballast Point Park. The view from the promenade across the bay to the downtown skyline is unmatched here (Bayshore Blvd. also is great for a drive).

> **Walk This Way**
> Bayshore Boulevard's 7-mile-long promenade is reputed to be the world's longest continuous sidewalk.

FISHING One of Florida's best guide services, **Light Tackle Fishing Expeditions,** 6105 Memorial Hwy., Suite 4 (© **800/972-1930** or 813/963-1930; www.leftcoastfishing.com), offers private sportfishing trips for tarpon, redfish, cobia, trout, and snook. Call for the schedule, prices, and required reservations.

GOLF Tampa has three municipal golf courses where you can play for about $30, a relative pittance when compared with fees at the privately owned courses here and elsewhere in Florida. The **Babe Zaharias Municipal Golf Course,** 11412 Forest Hills Dr., north of Lowry Park (© **813/631-4374**), is an 18-hole, par-70 course with a pro shop, putting greens, and a driving range. It's the shortest of the municipal courses, but small greens and narrow fairways present ample challenges. Water provides obstacles on 12 of the 18 holes at **Rocky Point Municipal Golf Course,** 4151 Dana Shores Dr. (© **813/673-4316**), located between the airport and the bay. It's a par-71 course with a pro shop, a practice range, and putting greens. On the Hillsborough River in north Tampa, the **Rogers Park Municipal Golf Course,** 7910 N. 30th St. (© **813/673-4396**), is an 18-hole, par-72 championship course with a lighted driving and practice range. All the courses are open daily from 7am to dusk, and lessons and club rentals are available.

Other public courses include the **Hall of Fame Golf Club,** just south of the airport at 2222 N. Westshore Blvd. (© **813/876-4913**), an 18-hole, par-72 course with a driving range; **Persimmon Hill Golf Club,** 5109 Hamey Rd. (© **813/623-6962**); **Silver Dollar Trap & Golf Club,** 17000 Patterson Rd., Odessa (© **813/920-3884**); **Westchase Golf Club,** 1307 Radcliff Dr. (© **813/854-2331**), and **University of South Florida Golf Course,** Fletcher Avenue and 46th Street (© **813/632-6893**), just north of the University of South Florida campus.

You can book starting times and get information about these and the area's other courses by calling **Tee Times USA** (© **800/374-8633;** www.teetimesusa.com).

SPECTATOR SPORTS National Football League fans can catch the **Tampa Bay Buccaneers** at the modern, 66,000-seat Raymond James Stadium, 4201 N. Dale Mabry Hwy., at Dr. Martin Luther King, Jr. Boulevard (© **813/879-2827;** www.buccaneers.com) from August through December.

The National Hockey League's **Tampa Bay Lightning** play in the Ice Palace, on Ice Palace Drive downtown, beginning in October (© **813/301-6500;** www.tampabaylightning.com).

New York Yankees fans can watch the Boys in Blue during baseball spring training from mid-February through March at Legends Field (© **813/879-2244** or 813/875-7753; www.yankees.mlb.com), opposite Raymond James Stadium (see above). This scaled-down replica of Yankee Stadium is the largest spring-training facility in Florida, with a 10,000-seat capacity. The club's minor-league team, the **Tampa Yankees** (same phone and website), plays at Legends Field from April through August. See the box, "The Boys of Spring," in chapter 2, "Planning an Affordable Trip to Florida," for more information about spring-training events.

The only oval thoroughbred race course on Florida's west coast, **Tampa Bay Downs**, 11225 Racetrack Rd., Oldsmar (© **800/200-4434** in Florida, or 813/855-4401; www.tampadowns.com), is the home of the Tampa Bay Derby. Races are held from December to May, and the track presents simulcasts year-round. Call for post times.

SHOPPING

Hyde Park and Ybor City are two areas of Tampa worth some window-shopping, perhaps sandwiched around lunch at one of their fine restaurants (see "Great Deals on Dining," later in this section).

CIGARS   Ybor City no longer is a major producer of hand-rolled cigars, but you can watch artisans making stogies at the **Gonzales y Martinez Cigar Factory**, 2025 Seventh Ave., in the Columbia Restaurant building (© **813/247-2469**). Gonzales and Martinez are recent arrivals from Cuba and don't speak English, but the staff does at the adjoining **Columbia Cigar Store** (it's best to enter here). Rollers are on duty Monday to Saturday from 10am to 6pm.

You can stock up on fine domestic and imported cigars at **El Sol**, 1728 E. Seventh Ave. (© **813/247-5554**), the city's oldest cigar store; **King Corona Cigar Factory**, 1523 E. Seventh Ave. (© **813/241-9109**); and **Metropolitan Cigars & Wine**, 2014 E. Seventh Ave. (© **813/248-3304**).

SHOPPING CENTERS   **Old Hyde Park Village**, 1507 W. Swann Ave., at South Dakota Avenue (© **813/251-3500;** www.oldhydeparkvillage.com), is a terrific alternative to cookie-cutter suburban malls. Walk around little shops in the sunshine and check out Hyde Park, one of the city's oldest and most historic neighborhoods, at the same time. The cluster of 50 upscale shops and boutiques is set in a village layout. The selection includes Williams-Sonoma, Pottery Barn, Banana Republic, Brooks Brothers, Crabtree & Evelyn, Godiva, and Anthropologie, to name a few. There's a free parking garage on South Oregon Avenue behind Jacobson's department store. Most shops are open Monday to Saturday from 10am to 7pm and Sunday from noon to 5pm.

The centerpiece of the downtown seaport renovation, the huge new mall known as **Channelside at Garrison Seaport,** on Channelside Drive between the Garrison Seaport and the Florida Aquarium (© **813/223-4250;** www.channelside.com), has stores, restaurants, a dance club, a games arcade, and a multi-screen cinema with an IMAX screen. It opened in 2001 and was still a work in progress when we went to press.

In Ybor City, the new **Centro Ybor,** on Seventh Avenue East at 16th Street (© **813/242-4660;** www.thecentroybor.com), is primarily a dining and entertainment complex, but you'll find a few national stores here such as American Eagle, Birkenstock, and Victoria's Secret.

ACCOMMODATIONS YOU CAN AFFORD

None of the hotels downtown or in the Westshore commercial area south of the airport are inexpensive, so your best bet is to stay near the theme parks. The accommodations listed below are near Busch Gardens and within short drives of Adventure Island, Lowry Park Zoo, and the Museum of Science and Industry

> **Tips Ask About Busch Garden Tickets**
> Many Tampa hotels combine tickets to major attractions like Busch Gardens in their packages, so always ask about special deals.

(MOSI). From here you can drive into downtown to visit the Florida Aquarium, the Tampa Museum of Art, the Henry B. Plant Museum, the Tampa Bay Performing Arts Center, and the dining and shopping opportunities in the Hyde Park historic district.

Staying in Ybor City will put you within walking distance of numerous restaurants and the city's hottest nightspots. The best Ybor motel option is the **Hilton Garden Inn,** 1700 E. Ninth Ave., between 17th and 18th streets (© **800/HILTONS** or 813/769-9267). This modern, four-story building stands just 2 blocks north of the heart of Ybor City's dining and entertainment district. Rates start at $99 single or double year-round.

The nearest chain motel to the theme and animal parks is **Howard Johnson Hotel Near Busch Gardens Maingate,** 4139 E. Busch Blvd. (© **800/444-5656** or 813/988-9191), an older property which was extensively renovated and reopened in 1999. It's 1½ blocks east of the main entrance. Rooms start at $69 single or double year-round. Although it's completely surrounded by a black-top parking lot and is less appealing than the nearby Red Roof Inn (see below), the **Days Inn Maingate,** 2901 E. Busch Blvd. (© **800/DAYS-INN** or 813/933-6471), is also convenient for families on a budget. There's an outdoor swimming pool, and a Denny's and a Taco Bell are both on the premises. Year-round rates range from $44 to $55 single or double.

Room rates at most hotels in Tampa vary little from season to season. This is especially true downtown, where the hotels do a brisk convention business all year. Hillsborough County adds 12% tax to your hotel room bill.

North of Tampa, **Hillsborough River State Park,** 15402 U.S. 301 N., Thonotosassa, FL 33592 (© **813/986-1020;** www.floridastateparks.org/district4/hillsboroughriver), offers 111 campsites year-round, plus fishing, canoeing, and boating. For reservations call © **800/326-3521** or go to the website www.reserveamerica.com.

Baymont Inn & Suites *Value*

Fake banana trees and a parrot cage welcome guests to the terra-cotta–floored lobby of this comfortable and convenient member of the small chain of cost-conscious but amenity-rich motels. All rooms are spacious and have ceiling fans and desks. Rooms with king beds also have recliners, business rooms sport dataport phones and extra-large desks, and the suites have refrigerators and microwave ovens. Outside, a courtyard with an unheated swimming pool has plenty of space for sunning. There's no restaurant on the premises, but plenty are within walking distance.

9202 N. 30th St. (at Busch Blvd.), Tampa, FL 33612. © **800/428-3438** or 813/930-6900. Fax 813/930-0563. www.baymontinns.com. 146 units. Winter $84–$109 double; off-season $79–$99 double. Rates include continental breakfast and local phone calls. AE, DC, DISC, MC, V. **Amenities:** Outdoor pool; game room; coin-op washers and dryers. *In room:* A/C, TV, dataport, fridge in suites, coffeemaker, hair dryer, iron.

Best Western All Suites Hotel ★★ *Kids Value*

This three-story all-suites hotel will provide you with more of a beach-style vacation than you'll find anywhere else close to the park. The product of hands-on owner John Ruzic, whimsical signs lead you around a lush tropical courtyard with a heated pool, a hot

Tampa Accommodations & Dining

ACCOMMODATIONS
Baymont Inn & Suites 4
Best Western All Suites Hotel 6
Days Inn Maingate 3
Hilton Garden Inn 14
Howard Johnson Hotel
   Near Busch Gardens
   Maingate 7
Red Roof Inn 2

DINING
Bella's Italian Cafe 10
Bern's Steak House 10
Cactus Club 10
Cafe Creole & Oyster Bar 15
Cafe Don José 9
Carmine's Restaurant & Bar 15
The Colonnade 11
Columbia 15
Four Green Fields 13
Le Bordeaux 10
Mel's Hot Dogs 8
Mise en Place 12
Ovo Cafe 15
Ristorante Francesco 2
Shells 5

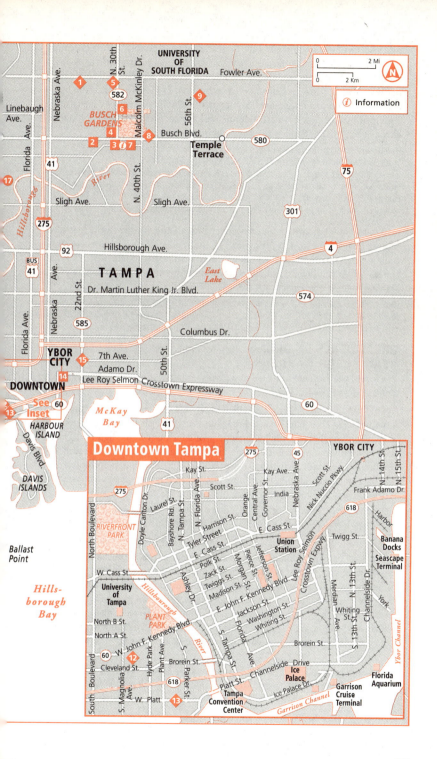

tub, and a lively, sports-oriented tiki bar. The bar can get noisy before closing at 9pm, and ground-level units are musty, so ask for an upstairs suite away from the action. Suite living rooms are well equipped and separate bedrooms have narrow screened patios or balconies. Great for kids, 11 "family suites" have bunk beds in addition to a queen-size bed for parents. Another 28 suites are especially equipped for business travelers (but are great for couples, too) with ergonomic chairs at big writing desks with speaker phones.

Near University of South Florida, behind Busch Gardens, 3001 University Center Dr. (faces N. 30th St. between Busch Blvd. and Fowler Ave.), Tampa, FL 33612. © **800/786-7446** or 813/971-8930. Fax 813/971-8935. www.thatparrotplace.com. 150 units. Winter $99–$159 suite for 2; off-season $79–$99 suite for 2. Rates include hot and cold breakfast buffet. AE, DC, DISC, MC, V. **Amenities:** Restaurant (American), bar; heated outdoor pool; access to nearby health club; Jacuzzi; game room; limited room service; laundry service; coin-op washers and dryers. *In room:* A/C, TV, dataport, fridge, coffeemaker, hair dryer, iron.

Red Roof Inn Less than a mile west of Busch Gardens, this is the best low-budget choice close to the park. Most of the rooms in the pleasant two-story building are away from the busy boulevard, but make sure to request one toward the rear of the building to avoid the road noise. Although in-room amenities are scarce, the units are spacious for the price.

2307 E. Busch Blvd. (between 22nd and 26th sts.), Tampa, FL 33612. © **800/THE-ROOF** or 813/932-0073. Fax 813/933-5689. 108 units. Winter $60–$85 double; off-season $40–$76 double. Rates include local phone calls. AE, DC, DISC, MC, V. **Amenities:** Heated outdoor pool; Jacuzzi; sauna. *In room:* A/C, TV, dataport.

GREAT DEALS ON DINING
NEAR BUSCH GARDENS

You'll find the national fast-food and family restaurants east of I-275 on Busch Boulevard and Fowler Avenue.

Cafe Don José SPANISH/AMERICAN It's not nearly on a par with Columbia in Ybor City (see below), but this Spanish-themed restaurant is among the best there is within a short drive of Busch Gardens. High-back chairs, dark wood floors, and Spanish posters and paintings set an appropriate scene for the house specialties of traditional paella (allow 30 min. for preparation) and Valencia-style rice dishes. Don José also offers non-Spanish fare such as chateaubriand and red snapper baked in parchment.

11009 N. 56th St. (in Sherwood Forest Shopping Center, ¼ mile south of Fowler Ave.). © **813/985-2392.** Main courses $13–$22. AE, DC, MC, V. Mon–Fri 11:30am–4:30pm and 5–10pm; Sat 5–10pm.

Ristorante Francesco ★ NORTHERN ITALIAN Gregarious owner Francesco "Frankie" Murchesini patrols the tables in the hottest dining spot in North Tampa (as witnessed by the photos of famous patrons adorning the walls). When not playing his harmonica to celebrate someone's birthday, Frankie's making sure everyone is enjoying his delicious *cernia portofino* (grouper in a brandy sauce with shrimp) and other Northern Italian dishes. His sister makes the pasta, which shows up in more traditional fare such as seafood over linguine *pestatore* with a choice of marinara or white wine sauce. Be sure to start with half a Caesar salad.

In La Place Village Shopping Center, 1441 E. Fletcher Ave. (between 14th and 15th sts.). © **813/971-3649.** Reservations recommended. Main courses $10–$27. AE, DC, DISC, MC. V. Mon–Fri 11:30am–2:30pm and 5:30–10pm; Sat 5:30–10pm; Sun 5–9pm.

Shells ★ *Value* SEAFOOD You'll see Shells restaurants in many parts of Florida, and with good reason, for this casual, award-winning chain consistently provides excellent value. They all have virtually identical menus, prices, and hours. Particularly good are the spicy Jack Daniel's buffalo shrimp and scallop appetizers. Main courses range from the usual fried seafood platters to pastas and charcoal-grilled shrimp, fish, steaks, and chicken.

11010 N. 30th St. (between Busch Blvd. and Fowler Ave.). © 813/977-8456. Main courses $9–$20 (most $10–$12). AE, DISC, MC, V. Sun–Thurs 11:30am–10pm; Fri–Sat 11:30am–11pm.

Super-Cheap Eats

Mel's Hot Dogs *Kids* AMERICAN   Catering to everyone from businesspeople on a lunch break to hungry families craving inexpensive all-beef hot dogs, Mel Lohn's red-and-white cottage offers everything from "bagel-dogs" to bacon/cheddar Reuben-style hot dogs. All choices except the bagel-dogs are served on a poppy-seed bun and can be ordered with french fries and a choice of coleslaw or baked beans. Even the decor is dedicated to wieners: The walls and windows are lined with hot-dog memorabilia. And just in case hot-dog mania hasn't won you over, there are a few alternative choices (chicken, beef and veggie burgers, and terrific onion rings).

4136 E. Busch Blvd., at 42nd St. © 813/985-8000. Most items under $7. No credit cards. Sun–Thurs 11am–8pm; Fri–Sat 11am–9pm.

HYDE PARK

Bella's Italian Cafe ★ *Value* ITALIAN   Creative dishes and very reasonable prices makes this sophisticated yet informal cafe one of SoHo's most popular neighborhood hangouts. Although you can order the homemade pasta under traditional Bolognese or Alfredo sauces, the stars here feature the tasty likes of blackened chicken in a creamy tomato sauce over fettuccine, or shrimp and scallops in a roasted tomato sauce over bow-tie pasta. Finish off with the house version of tiramisù. Local professionals flock to the friendly bar during two-for-one happy hours nightly from 4 to 7pm and from 11pm until closing. The open kitchen provides only appetizers, salads, pizzas and desserts after 11pm.

1413 S. Howard Ave. (at Mississippi Ave.). © 850/254-3355. Reservations not accepted. Main courses $7–$12; pizza $6.50–$8.50. AE, DC, DISC, MC, V. Mon–Tues 11:30am–11:30pm; Wed–Thurs 11:30am–12:30am; Fri 11am–1:30am; Sat 4pm–1:30am; Sun 4–11:30pm.

Cactus Club *Value* AMERICAN SOUTHWEST   You can definitely taste the freshness at this Texas roadhouse–style cantina in the middle of the Old Hyde Park shops, because all ingredients except the beans come straight from the market. My favorite dish is the "fundido"—a spicy casserole of marinated fajita-style chicken strips and sautéed vegetables topped with melted Jack cheese, with beans and rice on the side. Other offerings are more traditional: tacos, enchiladas, chili, sizzling fajitas, hickory-smoked baby back ribs, Jamaican jerk chicken, burgers, quesadillas, enchiladas (including vegetarian versions), sandwiches, and smoked chicken salad. The lively Cactus Cantina bar is another favorite neighborhood watering hole. Dine inside or outside, but get here early at lunchtime—it's usually packed.

In Old Hyde Park Village shopping complex, 1601 Snow Ave. (south of Swann Ave.). © 813/251-4089. Reservations not accepted. Main courses $6.50–14; burgers and sandwiches $7–$8. AE, DC, MC, V. Sun–Thurs 11:30am–10pm; Fri–Sat 11:30am–11pm.

The Colonnade SEAFOOD   Local couples and families have been flocking to this rough-hewn, shiplap place since 1935, primarily for the great view of Hillsborough Bay across Bayshore Boulevard. The food is a bit on the Red Lobsterish side, but the vista from the window tables more than makes up for any shortcomings in the fresh seafood: grouper prepared seven ways, crab-stuffed

> **Moments** **Dining on the Bay**
>
> One of the newest additions to Tampa's dining scene is the 180-foot long **StarShip Dining Yacht** (© **877/744-7999** or **813/223-7999**; www.starship dining.com), which makes lunch and dinner cruises from the Channelside out onto Tampa Bay. The ship's four dining rooms serve exceptional cruise fare from a kitchen overseen by executive chef Jayson Polanski, who has done stints at some of Tampa's better restaurants. A house band plays during dinner and then moves to the top deck for dancing under the stars. Lunch cruises cost $30 per person with a meal, $16 for sightseers. Dinner cruises range from $50 during the week to $60 on weekends, whether you dine onboard or not. Call for the schedule and reservations.

flounder, Maryland-style crab cakes, even wild Florida alligator as an appetizer. Prime rib, steaks, and chicken are also available.

3401 Bayshore Blvd. (at W. Julia St.). © **813/839-7558**. Reservations accepted only for large parties. Main courses $8–$20 (most $11–$15). AE, DC, DISC, MC, V. Sun–Thurs 11am–10pm; Fri–Sat 11am–11pm.

Four Green Fields IRISH/AMERICAN Just across the bridge from the downtown convention center, America's only thatched-roof Irish pub may be surrounded by palm trees instead of potato fields, but it still offers the ambience and tastes of Ireland. Staffed by genuine Irish immigrants, the large room with a square bar in the center smells of Bass and Harp ales. The Gaelic stew is predictably bland, but the salads and sandwiches are passable. The live Irish music from Thursday through Saturday nights and on Sunday afternoon draws a crowd ranging from post-college to early retirees.

205 W. Platt St. (between Parker St. and Plant Ave.). © **813/254-4444**. Reservations accepted. Main courses $9.50–$15; sandwiches $6–$7. AE, MC, V. Daily 11am–3am.

Worth a Splurge

Bern's Steak House STEAKS The exterior of this famous steak house looks like a factory. Inside, however, you'll find eight ornate dining rooms with themes like Rhône, Burgundy, and Irish Rebellion. Their atmospheres are perfect for meat lovers, for here you order and pay for expertly charcoal-grilled steaks of perfectly aged beef according to the thickness and weight (the 60-oz., 3-in.-thick Porterhouse can feed four adults). The phone book-size wine list offers more than 7,000 selections, with many available by the glass.

The big secret here, however, is that the steak sandwiches available at the bar are not mentioned on the menu. Smaller versions of the chargrilled steaks served in the dining rooms, they come with a choice of french fries or crispy onion rings. Add a salad and you have a terrific meal for about half the price of the least-expensive main course.

The surprise here is the dessert quarters upstairs, where 50 romantic booths paneled in aged California redwood can privately seat from 2 to 12 guests each. All of these little chambers are equipped with phones for placing your order and closed-circuit TVs for watching and listening to a resident pianist. The dessert menu offers almost 100 delicious selections, plus some 1,400 after-dinner drinks. It's possible to reserve a booth for dessert only, but preference is given to those who dine.

1208 S. Howard Ave. (at Marjory Ave.). © 800/282-1421 within Florida or 813/251-2421. Reservations recommended. Main courses $17–$58.50; sandwiches $9. AE, DC, DISC, MC, V. Daily 5–11pm. Closed Christmas. Valet parking $4.

Le Bordeaux ★★ TRADITIONAL FRENCH   Located in a converted home, this romantic bistro's authentic French fare is some of the region's best. French-born chef/owner Gordon Davis offers seating in the living room-style main dining room of this converted house, which was expanded to include a plant-filled conservatory. His blackboard menu changes daily, but usually features traditional French favorites such as rack of lamb, cassoulet, and magret of duck. Part of the establishment is the lounge-style Left Bank Jazz Bistro, featuring live jazz Thursday to Saturday from 9pm to 1am.

1502 S. Howard Ave. (2 blocks north of Bayshore Blvd.). © 813/254-4387. Reservations recommended. Main courses $15–$27. AE, DC, MC, V. Sun and Tues–Thurs 5:30–10pm; Fri–Sat 5–11pm.

Mise en Place ★★ ECLECTIC   Look around at all those happy, stylish people soaking up the trendy ambience, and you'll know why chef Marty Blitz and his wife, Maryann, have been among the culinary darlings of Tampa since 1986. They present the freshest of ingredients, with a creative menu that changes weekly. Main courses often include fascinating choices such as Creole-style mahimahi served with chili cheese grits and a ragout of black-eyed peas, andouille sausage, and rock shrimp.

In Grand Central Place, 442 W. Kennedy Blvd. (at S. Magnolia Ave., opposite the University of Tampa). © 813/254-5373. Reservations recommended. Main courses $16–$27; tasting menu $35. AE, DC, DISC, MC, V. Tues–Thurs 11:30am–2:30pm and 5:30–10pm; Fri 11:30am–2:30pm and 5:30–11pm; Sat 5–11pm.

YBOR CITY

Cafe Creole and Oyster Bar ★★ *Value* CREOLE/CAJUN   Resembling a turn-of-the-century railway station, this brick building dates from 1896 and was originally known as El Pasaje, the home of the Cherokee Club, a gentlemen's hotel and private club with a casino and an opulent decor with stained-glass windows, wrought-iron balconies, Spanish murals, and marble bathrooms. Today it's home to Tampa's best Creole and Cajun restaurant. Specialties include exceptionally prepared Louisiana crab cakes, oysters, blackened grouper, and jambalaya. If you're new to bayou cuisine, try the Creole sampler. Dine inside or out.

1330 Ninth Ave. (at Avenida de Republica de Cuba/14th St.). © 813/247-6283. Reservations not accepted, but call for preferred seating. Main courses $10.50–$18. AE, DC, DISC, MC, V. Mon–Thurs 11:30am–10pm; Fri 11:30am–11:30pm; Sat 5–11:30pm.

Ovo Cafe ★ INTERNATIONAL   This cafe, popular with the business set by day and the club crowd on weekend nights, features a melange of sophisticated offerings. Pierogies and pasta pillows come with taste-tempting sauces and fillings, and there are several creative salads and unusual individual-size pizzas. Strawberries or blackberries and a splash of liqueur cover the thick waffles. Portions are substantial, but be careful with your credit card here: Pricing is strictly a la carte. The big black bar dispenses a wide variety of martinis, plus some unusual liqueur drinks.

1901 E. Seventh Ave. (at 19th St.). © 813/248-6979. Reservations strongly recommended Fri–Sat. Main courses $10–$15; sandwiches $7–$8.50; pizza $8.50–$10. AE, DC, DISC, MC, V. Mon–Tues 11am–3pm; Wed–Thurs 11am–10pm; Fri–Sat 11am–1am.

Super-Cheap Eats

Carmine's Restaurant & Bar CUBAN/ITALIAN/AMERICAN   Bright blue poles hold up an ancient pressed-tin ceiling above this noisy corner cafe. It's not the cleanest joint in town, but a great variety of loyal local patrons gather here for genuine Cuban sandwiches—smoked ham, roast pork, Genoa salami, Swiss cheese, pickles, salad dressing, mustard, lettuce, and tomato on a crispy submarine roll. There's a vegetarian version, too, and the combination half-sandwich and choice of black beans and rice or a bowl of Spanish soup made with sausages, potatoes, and garbanzo beans all make a hearty meal for just $6 at lunch, $7 at dinner. Main courses are led by Cuban-style roast pork, thin-cut pork chops with mushroom sauce, spaghetti with a blue-crab tomato sauce, and a few seafood and chicken platters.

1802 E. Seventh Ave. (at 18th St.). © 813/248-3834. Reservations not accepted. Main courses $7–$17; sandwiches $4–$8. No credit cards. Mon–Tues 11am–11pm; Wed–Thurs 11am–1am; Fri–Sat 11am–3am; Sun 11am–6pm.

Worth a Splurge

Columbia ★★ SPANISH   Hide some money to have a meal at this famous restaurant, which is an attraction in itself. Dating from 1905, the hand-painted tile building occupies an entire city block in the heart of Ybor City. Both tourists and locals flock here to soak up the ambience because it's so much fun to clap along during fire-belching Spanish flamenco floor shows Monday to Saturday at 7 and 9:30pm. You may find yourself coming back for the famous Spanish bean soup and original "1905" salad. The paella à la Valenciana is outstanding, with more than a dozen ingredients from gulf grouper and gulf pink shrimp to calamari, mussels, clams, chicken, and pork. Lighter appetites can choose from a limited menu of tapas, including "Cuban caviar" (actually a spicy black bean dip). The decor throughout is graced with hand-painted tiles, wrought-iron chandeliers, dark woods, rich red fabrics, and stained-glass windows. You can breathe your own fumes in the Cigar Bar.

2117 E. Seventh Ave. (between 21st and 22nd sts.). © 813/248-4961. Reservations recommended. Main courses $14–$23. AE, DC, DISC, MC, V. Mon–Thurs 11am–10pm; Fri–Sat 11am–11pm.

TAMPA AFTER DARK

The Tampa/Hillsborough Arts Council maintains an **Artsline** (© 813/229-ARTS), a 24-hour information service providing the latest on current and upcoming cultural events. Racks in many restaurants and bars have copies of *Weekly Planet* (www.weeklyplanet.com), *Focus*, and *Accent on Tampa Bay*, three free publications detailing what's going on in the entire bay area. And you can also check the "Baylife" and "Friday Extra" sections of the *Tampa Tribune* (www.tampatrib.com) and the Thursday "Weekend" section of the *St. Petersburg Times* (www.sptimes.com). The visitor center usually has copies of the week's newspaper sections (see "Essentials," earlier in this section).

THE CLUB & MUSIC SCENE   Ybor City is Tampa's favorite nighttime venue by far. All you have to do is stroll along Seventh Avenue East between 15th and 20th streets, and you'll hear music blaring out of the clubs. The avenue is packed with people, a majority of them high-schoolers and early 20-somethings,

---

Tips Careful Where You Park

Parking can be scarce during nighttime in Ybor City, and the area has seen an occasional robbery late at night. Play it safe and use the municipal parking lots behind the shops on Eighth Avenue East or the new parking garages near Centro Ybor on Seventh Avenue East at 16th Street.

on Friday and Saturday from 9pm to 3am, but you'll also find something going on from Tuesday to Thursday and even on Sunday. The clubs change names and character frequently, so you don't need names, addresses or phone numbers; your ears will guide you along Seventh Avenue East.

The center of the action these days is **Centro Ybor,** on Seventh Avenue East at 16th Street (© **813/242-4660;** www.thecentroybor.com), the district's large new dining-and-entertainment complex. The restaurants and pubs in this family-oriented center tend to be considerably tamer than many of those along Seventh Avenue, at least on non-weekend nights. You don't have to pay to listen to live music in the center's patio on weekend afternoons.

THE PERFORMING ARTS With a prime downtown location on 9 acres along the east bank of the Hillsborough River, the huge **Tampa Bay Performing Arts Center**, 1010 N. MacInnes Place (© **800/955-1045** or 813/229-STAR; www.tampacenter.com), is the largest performing-arts venue south of the Kennedy Center in Washington, DC. Accordingly, this four-theater complex is the focal point of Tampa's performing-arts scene, presenting a wide range of Broadway plays, classical and pop concerts, operas, cabarets, improv, and special events.

A sightseeing attraction in its own right, the restored **Tampa Theatre,** 711 Franklin St. (© **813/223-8981;** www.tampatheatre.org), between Zack and Polk streets, dates from 1926 and is on the National Register of Historic Places. It presents a varied program of classic, foreign, and alternative films, as well as concerts and special events.

The 66,321-seat **Raymond James Stadium,** 4201 N. Dale Mabry Hwy. (© **813/673-4300;** www.raymondjames.com/stadium), is frequently the site of headliner concerts. The **USF Sun Dome,** 4202 E. Fowler Ave. (© **813/974-3111;** www.sundome.org), on the University of South Florida campus, hosts major concerts by touring pop stars, rock bands, jazz groups, and other contemporary artists.

Ticketmaster (© **813/287-8844**) sells tickets to most events and shows.

2 St. Petersburg

20 miles SW of Tampa, 289 miles NW of Miami, 84 miles SW of Orlando

On the western shore of the bay, St. Petersburg stands in contrast to Tampa, much like San Francisco compares to Oakland in California. While Tampa is the area's business, industrial, and shipping center, St. Petersburg was conceived and built almost a century ago primarily for tourists and wintering snowbirds. Here you'll find one of the most picturesque and pleasant downtowns of any city in Florida, with a waterfront promenade and the famous, pyramid-shaped pier offering great views across the bay, plus quality museums, interesting shops, and fine restaurants.

Away from downtown, the city pretty much consists of strip malls dividing residential neighborhoods, but plan at least to have a look around the charming bay-front area. If you don't do anything else, go out on The Pier and take a pleasant stroll along Bayshore Drive.

ESSENTIALS
GETTING THERE **Tampa International Airport,** approximately 16 miles northeast of St. Petersburg, is the prime gateway for the area (see "Essentials," in section 1 of this chapter). At presstime, only **Pan Am** (© **800/FLY-PANAM;**

www.flypanam.com) had year-round scheduled service to **St. Petersburg–Clearwater International Airport,** on Roosevelt Boulevard (Fla. 686) about 10 miles north of downtown St. Petersburg (© **727/535-7600**). The Canadian carrier **Air Transat** (© **877/872-6728;** www.airtransat.com) flies here during the winter months. **Amtrak** (© **800/USA-RAIL;** www.amtrak.com) has bus connections from its Tampa station to downtown St. Petersburg (see "Essentials," in section 1 of this chapter).

VISITOR INFORMATION   For advance information about both St. Petersburg and the St. Pete and Clearwater beaches (see section 3 of this chapter), contact the **St. Petersburg/Clearwater Area Convention & Visitors Bureau,** 14450 46th St. N., Clearwater, FL 34622 (© **800/345-6710,** or 727/464-7200 for advance hotel reservations; fax 727/464-7222; www.stpete-clearwater.com or www.FloridasBeach.com for information specific to the beaches).

Once you get here, head to the **St. Petersburg Area Chamber of Commerce,** 100 Second Ave. N. (at 1st St.), St. Petersburg, FL 33701 (© **727/821-4069;** fax 727/895-6326; www.stpete.com). Across the street from the BayWalk shopping-and-dining complex, this downtown main office and visitor center is open Monday to Friday from 8am to 5pm, Saturday 10am to 4pm, and Sunday noon to 4pm. Ask for a copy of the chamber's visitor's guide, which lists hotels, motels, condominiums, and other accommodations.

The chamber also operates the **Suncoast Welcome Center** (© **727/573-1449**), on Ulmerton Road at Exit 18 southbound off I-275 (there's no exit here for northbound traffic). The center is open daily from 9am to 5pm except New Year's Day, Easter, Thanksgiving, and Christmas.

Also downtown, there are **walk-in information centers** on the first level of The Pier and in the lobby of the Florida International Museum (see "Seeing the Top Attractions," below).

GETTING AROUND   You can see everything on the very pink **Downtown Trolleys** (© **727/571-3440**), which run out to the end of The Pier and past all of the downtown attractions every 30 minutes from 11am to 5pm daily except Thanksgiving and Christmas. Rides cost 50¢ per person.

The **Pinellas Suncoast Transit Authority/PSTA** (© **727/530-9911;** www.psta.net) operates regular bus service throughout St. Petersburg and the rest of the Pinellas Peninsula. Rides cost $1.25 for adults, 60¢ for seniors, and 75¢ for students.

If you need a cab, call **Yellow Cab** (© **727/821-7777**) or **Independent Cab** (© **727/327-3444**). Fares are $1.50 at flag fall, plus 20¢ for each seventh of a mile.

WHAT TO SEE & DO
SEEING THE TOP ATTRACTIONS

Florida Holocaust Museum   ★   This thought-provoking museum has exhibits about the Holocaust, including a boxcar used to transport human cargo to the Auschwitz death camp in Poland. Its main focus, however, is to promote tolerance and understanding in the present. It was founded by Walter P. Loebenberg, a local businessman who escaped Nazi Germany in 1939 and fought with the U.S. Army in World War II.

55 5th St. S. (between Central Ave. and First Ave. S.). © 727/820-0100. www.flholocaustmuseum.org. Admission $6 adults, $5 seniors and college students, $2 children under 18. Mon–Fri 10am–5pm; Sat–Sun noon–5pm. Closed Easter, Rosh Hashanah, Yom Kippur, Thanksgiving, and Christmas.

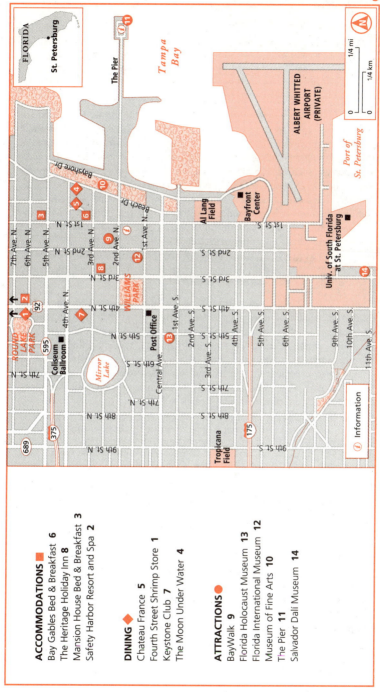

> **Fun Fact Open-Air Mail**
> St. Petersburg residents don't have to go inside to get mail out of their boxes at St. Petersburg's oft-photographed, open-air **U.S. Post Office**, at the corner of First Avenue North and 4th Street North.

Florida International Museum ★★ Housed in the former Maas Brothers Department Store, long an area landmark, this excellent museum attracted 600,000 visitors from around the world when it opened its first exhibition in 1995, and the success has continued. Its outstanding exhibit on the Cuban Missile Crisis was such a smash hit that it's now permanent—and well worth seeing even if the two temporary exhibits don't catch your fancy. On the other hand, they very well could, since the museum is associated with—and gets some of its staff on loan from—the Smithsonian Institution in Washington, DC. Call to see what's scheduled during your visit. Allow at least 3 hours to tour all three exhibitions. There's an excellent museum store here.

100 2nd St. N. (between First and Second aves. N.). © **877/535-7469** or 727/822-3693. www.floridamuseum.org. Admission to all exhibits $12 adults, $11 seniors, $6 children 6–18; free for children under 6. Mon–Sat 9am–5pm; Sun noon–5pm (last entry 4pm daily).

Museum of Fine Arts ★★ Resembling a Mediterranean villa on the waterfront, this museum houses an excellent permanent collection of European, American, pre-Columbian, and Far Eastern art, with works by such artists as Fragonard, Monet, Renoir, Cézanne, and Gauguin. Other highlights include period rooms with antiques and historical furnishings, plus a gallery of Steuben crystal, a new decorative-arts gallery, and world-class rotating exhibits. The best way to see it all is on a free, guided tour, which takes about 1 hour. Ask about classical-music performances from October to April.

255 Beach Dr. NE (at Third Ave. N.). © **727/896-2667.** www.fine-arts.org. Admission Tues–Sat $6 adults, $5 seniors, $2 students; free for children under 6. Admission free on Sun (donation suggested). Admission includes guided tour. Tues–Sat 10am–5pm; Sun 1–5pm. Winter, third Thurs of each month 10am–9pm. Guided tours Tues–Sat 11am, 1, 2, and 3pm; Sun 1 and 2pm. Closed New Year's Day, Martin Luther King, Jr. Birthday, Thanksgiving, Christmas.

The Pier ★ Walk or ride the free trolley out on The Pier and enjoy this festive waterfront dining-and-shopping complex overlooking Tampa Bay. Originally built as a railroad pier in 1889, today it's capped by a spaceship-like inverted pyramid offering five levels of shops, three restaurants, a tourist information desk, an observation deck, catwalks for fishing, boat docks, miniature golf, boat and water-sports rentals, sightseeing boats, and a food court, plus an aquarium and **Great Explorations** (© **727/821-8992;** www.greatexplorations.org), a hands-on children's museum offering a variety of exhibits—great for a rainy day or for kids who've overdosed on the sun and need to cool off indoors. Cruise boats often operate from The Pier during the winter months, and you can rent fishing gear and drop your line into the bay all year. There's valet parking at the end of the pier, or you can park on land and ride a free trolley out to the complex.

800 Second Ave. NE. © **727/821-6443.** www.stpete-pier.com. Free admission to all the public areas and decks; donations welcome at the Pier Aquarium. Great Explorations $4, $2 seniors; free for children under 3. Valet parking $6; self-parking $3. Pier Mon–Thurs 10am–9pm; Fri–Sat 10am–10pm; Sun 11am–7pm. Aquarium Mon–Sat 10am–8pm; Sun 11am–6pm. Great Explorations Mon–Sat 10am–8pm; Sun 11am–6pm. Shops and restaurant hours vary.

Salvador Dalí Museum ★★★ This starkly modern museum houses the world's most comprehensive collection of works by the renowned Spanish surrealist—and for art lovers is reason enough to visit downtown St. Petersburg. It includes oil paintings, watercolors and drawings, and more than 1,000 graphics, plus posters, photos, sculptures, objets d'art, and a 5,000-volume library on Dalí and surrealism. Reynolds Morse, an Ohio plastics engineer, and his wife, Eleanore, discovered the Catalonian artist and began collecting his works in 1943. They moved the collection here in 1980.

1000 3rd St. S. (near 11th Ave. S.). © 727/823-3767. www.salvadordalimuseum.org. Admission $10 adults, $7 seniors, $5 students; free for children 10 and under. Thurs 5–8pm 50% discount. Mon–Wed and Fri–Sat 9:30am–5:30pm; Thurs 9:30am–8pm; Sun noon–5:30pm. Closed Thanksgiving and Christmas.

Sunken Gardens Dating back to 1935, this former tourist attraction is now operated as a 7-acre botanical garden by the City of St. Petersburg. It contains a vast array of 5,000 plants, flowers, and trees; plus a butterfly aviary; a display of snakes, spiders, and scorpions; and a rain-forest information center. There's a daily wildlife show. Call for a schedule of exhibits and tours.

1825 4th St. N. (between 18th and 19th aves. NE). © 813/896-3186. www.stpete.org/sunken.htm. Admission $7 adults, $5 seniors, $3 children 3–12; free for children 2 and under. Wed–Sun 10am–4pm.

ORGANIZED TOURS

The only organized tours of St. Petersburg—and they are pretty good ones—are with **Duck Tours of Tampa Bay** (© 727/432-3825; www.ducktoursoftampabay.com), which offers 1-hour, 30-minute tours of downtown and the nearby waterways using reconditioned World War II amphibious "Ducks." The vehicles depart from The Pier daily from 11am to 5pm. The narrated tours cost $18.50 for adults, $16.50 for seniors, and $9.95 for children 3 to 12, plus tax. Kids under 3 ride free. The same company has tours of Tampa (see the box, "Quacking Around," in section 1 of this chapter).

AFFORDABLE OUTDOOR ACTIVITIES

You can get up-to-the-minute recorded information about the city's sports and recreational activities by calling the **Leisure Line** (© 727/893-7500).

BIKING, IN-LINE SKATING, & HIKING With miles of flat terrain, the St. Petersburg area is ideal for bikers, in-line skaters, and hikers. The **Pinellas Trail** is especially good, since it follows an abandoned railroad bed 47 miles from St. Petersburg north to Tarpon Springs and from there to Tampa. It crosses the bay via the old Gandy Bridge, now known as the **Friendship Trail-Bridge** (© 813/289-4400). Paralleling the new bridge, the 2.6-mile-long old structure is open to hikers, bikers, fishers, and in-line skaters, but be careful going up and down the steep center span, especially if you're on skates. The St. Pete trailhead is on 34th Street South (U.S. 19) between Eighth and Fairfield avenues south. It's packed on the weekends. Free strip maps of the trail are

---

Tips Car Smarts

You can spend a small fortune in a parking garage or by feeding the meters in St. Petersburg, or you can cut costs substantially by parking at The Pier ($3 all day) and taking The Looper, the city's trolley service, which operates between The Pier and all major downtown attractions. See "Getting Around," above.

The Crystal River Area: Mermaids & Manatees

Drive north of St. Petersburg for an hour on congested U.S. 19, and you'll come to the Crystal River area, home of the famous **Weeki Wachee Spring Water Park** (© 800/678-9335 or 352/596-2062; www.weekiwachee.com), one of Florida's original tourist attractions. "Mermaids" have been putting on acrobatic swimming shows here every day since 1947. It's a sight to see these gorgeous young women doing their dances in waters that come from one of America's most prolific freshwater springs, pouring some 170 million gallons of 72°F (22°C) water a day into the river. There's more than mermaids here; you can take a Wilderness River Cruise across the Weeki Wachee River and send the kids on the flume ride at **Buccaneer Bay,** the water-park part of the attraction. Admission is $15.95 for adults, $11.95 for children 3 to 10. Kids under 3 get in free. The spring is open daily from 10am to 3pm in winter, to 4 or 5pm in spring and fall, to 6pm in the hot summer months (call for precise times and special shows). The water park is open from March to mid-autumn, daily from 10am to 5pm. You can also rent canoes (© 352/597-0360).

From Weeki Wachee, travel 21 miles north to the **Homosassa Springs State Wildlife Park,** 4150 S. Suncoast Blvd. (U.S. 19) in Homosassa Springs (© 352/628-5343; www.dep.state.fl.us/parks/district2/homosassa springs). The highlight here is a floating observatory where visitors can watch manatees in a rehabilitation facility, as well as thousands of fresh- and saltwater fish. You'll also see deer, bears, bobcats, otters, egrets, and flamingos along unspoiled nature trails elsewhere in the

available at the St. Petersburg Area Chamber of Commerce (see "Essentials," above).

GOLF One of the nation's top 50 municipal courses, the **Mangrove Bay Golf Course** ★★, 875 62nd Ave. NE (© 727/893-7797), hugs the inlets of Old Tampa Bay and offers 18-hole, par-72 play. Facilities include a driving range; lessons and golf-club rental are also available. Fees are about $25 in winter, slightly lower off-season.

In Largo, northwest of St. Petersburg, the **Bardmoor Golf Club,** 7919 Bardmoor Blvd. (© 727/397-0483), is often the venue for major tournaments. Lakes punctuate 17 of the 18 holes on this par-72 championship course. Lessons and rental clubs are available, as is a Tom Fazio–designed practice range. Call the clubhouse for seasonal greens fees. The course is open daily from 7am to dusk.

Call **Tee Times USA** (© 800/374-8633; www.teetimesusa.com) to reserve times at these and other area courses.

If you want to take up golf or sharpen your game, TV "Golf Doctor" Joe Quinzi hosts his **Quinzi Golf Academy** (© 727/725-1999) at the Safety Harbor Resort and Spa (see "Accommodations You Can Afford," below). His school offers personalized instruction (starting at $35 for 30 min.) and clinics ($15 per person).

SAILING Both Steve and Doris Colgate's **Offshore Sailing School** (© 800/221-4326 or 941/454-1700; www.offshore-sailing.com) and the **Annapolis**

park. The park is open daily from 9am to 5:30pm (last ticket sold at 4pm). Admission is $7.95 for adults and $4.95 for children 3 to 12, plus tax, and includes a 20-minute narrated boat ride. Kids under 3 get in free.

About 7 miles north of Homosassa Springs, some 300 manatees spend the winter in Crystal River, and you can **swim or snorkel with the manatees** in the warm-water natural spring of Kings Bay. **American Pro Diving Center,** 821 SE Hwy. 19, Crystal River, FL 34429 (© **800/291-DIVE** or 352/563-0041; fax 352/563-5230; www.americanprodive.com), offers daily swimming and snorkel tours. Early mornings are the best time to see the manatees, so try to take the 6:30am departure. The trips range from about $30 to $50 per person. Call for the schedule and reservations. American Pro Diving also rents cottages on the Homosassa River.

Baseball fans won't want to miss the **Ted Williams Museum & Hitters Hall of Fame,** 2455 N. Citrus Hills Blvd., off C.R. 486 west of Hernando (© **352/527-6566;** www.twmuseum.com). Built in the shape of a baseball diamond, the museum holds the great hitter's personal memorabilia, including his two Triple Crown batting titles. It's open Tuesday to Sunday from 10am to 4pm. Admission is $9 adults and $1 for children.

For more information about the area, contact the **Citrus County Chamber of Commerce,** 28 NW Hwy. 19, Crystal River, FL 34428 (© **352/ 795-3149;** fax 352/795-4260; www.citruscountychamber.com). The chamber's visitor center is open Monday to Friday from 8:30am to 4:30pm and Saturday from 9am to 1pm.

Sailing School (© **800/638-9192** or 727/867-8102; www.annapolissailing. com) have operations here. Various courses lasting from 2 days to a week are offered. Contact the schools for prices and schedules.

SPECTATOR SPORTS St. Petersburg has always been a baseball town, and **Tropicana Field,** a 45,000-seat domed stadium alongside I-175 between 9th and 16th streets (© **727/825-3100;** www.stpete.org/dome.htm), is the home of the American League **Tampa Bay Devil Rays** (© **888/FAN-RAYS** or 727/825-3250; www.devilrays.mlb.com). The baseball season runs from April through September. Call or check the website for schedule and ticket information. The Devil Rays move outdoors to Florida Power Park at Al Lang Field, on Second Avenue South at 1st Street South, for their spring-training games from mid-February through March.

The **Philadelphia Phillies** play their spring-training season at Jack Russell Stadium, 800 Phillies Dr., in nearby Clearwater (© **727/442-8496** or 215/ 436-1000; www.phillies.mlb.com). Their minor-league affiliate, the **Clearwater Phillies** (© **727/441-8638;** www.clearwaterphillies.com), plays in the stadium from April through August. The **Toronto Blue Jays** do their spring thing at Grant Field, 373 Douglas Ave. in Dunedin (© **800/707-8269** or 813/ 733-9302; www.bluejays.mlb.com), which also is home to their minor-league affiliate, the **Dunedin Blue Jays** (© **727/733-9302;** www.dunedinbluejays. com), from April through August.

For more information on spring-training events, see the box, "The Boys of Spring," in chapter 2.

TENNIS You can learn to play or hone your game at the **Phil Green Tennis Academy** at Safety Harbor Resort and Spa (see "Accommodations You Can Afford," below).

SHOPPING

The Pier, at the end of Second Avenue Northeast (see "Seeing the Top Attractions," earlier in this section), houses more than a dozen boutiques and craft shops; but nearby **Beach Drive,** running along the waterfront, is one of the most fashionable downtown strolling and window-shopping venues. Here you'll find the **Glass Canvas Gallery,** at Fourth Avenue Northeast (© 727/821-6767; www.glasscanvasgallery.com), featuring a dazzling array of glass sculpture, tableware, art, and craft items by 250 local, national, and international artists. Also at Fourth Avenue Northeast is **P. Buckley Moss** (© 727/894-2899), a museum-grade store carrying the works of the individualistic artist best known for her portrayal of the Amish and the Mennonites. The works include paintings, graphics, figurines, and collector dolls. **Red Cloud,** between First and Second avenues (© 727/821-5824), is an oasis for Native American crafts, including jewelry, headdresses, and art.

Downtown's new commercial showplace is **BayWalk** (© 727/895-9277; www.baywalklive.com), an open-air shopping, dining, and entertainment complex bordered by 1st and 2nd streets and Second and Third avenues North. It has branches of Ann Taylor, Chico's, Sunglass Hut, and a few other mall stores, plus some small boutiques.

Central Avenue is another shopping area, featuring the **Gas Plant Antique Arcade,** between 12th and 13th streets (© 727/895-0368), the largest antiques mall on Florida's west coast, with more than 100 dealers displaying their wares. (Downtown has several antiques-and-collectibles dealers; get a list and map from the chamber of commerce.) The **Florida Craftsmen Gallery,** at 5th Street (© 727/821-7391; www.floridacraftsmen.net), is a showcase for the works of more than 150 Florida artisans and craftspeople: jewelry, ceramics, woodwork, fiber works, glassware, paper creations, and metalwork.

ACCOMMODATIONS YOU CAN AFFORD

The **St. Petersburg/Clearwater Area Convention & Visitors Bureau** (see "Essentials," earlier in this section) operates a free **reservations service** (© 800/345-6710), through which you can book rooms at most hotels and motels in both St. Petersburg and at the beaches. The bureau also publishes a brochure that lists members of its Superior Small Lodgings program; all establishments have fewer than 50 rooms and have been inspected and certified for cleanliness and value.

The hotel tax rate in Pinellas County is 11%. Room rates here vary little from season to season.

Bay Gables Bed & Breakfast You can walk to The Pier from this charming B&B with wraparound porches on all three of its stories. Built in 1901, the Key West–style house overlooks a flower-filled garden with a gazebo. The guest quarters have been furnished with ceiling fans and Victorian pieces, including a canopy bed in one room. The honeymoon suite is equipped with a large double shower, Jacuzzi, and bidet; the rest have both claw-foot tubs and modern showers in their bathrooms. Half of the rooms open onto the porches, while the rest have a separate sitting room and kitchenette.

136 Fourth Ave. NE (between Beach Dr. and 1st St. N.), St. Petersburg, FL 33701. © **800/822-8803** or 727/822-8855. Fax 727/824-7223. www.baygables.com. 10 units. $99–$135 single or double. Rates include continental breakfast. AE, DISC, MC, V. *In room:* A/C, TV, kitchenette in some, hair dryer.

The Heritage Holiday Inn No ordinary Holiday Inn, the Heritage dates from the early 1920s, and although significantly updated, it still retains the ambience of an old-fashioned hotel, with tall double-hung windows and hardwood floors that creak as you walk down the long central hallway. A sweeping veranda, French doors, and a tropical courtyard help attract an eclectic clientele, from business travelers to seniors. The furnishings include period antiques and brass beds. Some one-bedroom suites have sofa beds, two televisions, two phones, and two bathrooms.

234 Third Ave. N. (between 2nd and 3rd sts.), St. Petersburg, FL 33701. © **800/283-7829** or 727/822-4814. Fax 727/823-1644. www.sixcontinentshotels.com. 71 units. $100–$140 double. AE, DC, DISC, MC, V. **Amenities:** Restaurant (steaks), bar; heated outdoor pool; Jacuzzi; limited room service; laundry service. *In room:* A/C, TV, dataport, coffeemaker, hair dryer, iron.

Mansion House Bed & Breakfast Mirror images of each other, these two Arts-and-Crafts–style houses separated by a landscaped courtyard were built between 1901 and 1912. The comfortable living room in the main house, which has 6 of the 10 units here, opens to a sun room, off which a small screened porch provides mosquito-free lounging and the only place where guests can smoke. Both houses have upstairs front parlors with TVs, VCRs, and libraries. Tall, old-fashioned windows let lots of light into the attractive guest rooms. The pick of the litter is the "Pembroke" room, upstairs over the carriage house. It has a four-poster bed with mosquito netting, and its residents have their own whirlpool in an outdoor screened hut. The brick courtyard between the two houses (there's a heated swimming pool and Jacuzzi out there) is a popular spot for weddings, receptions, and other functions.

105 Fifth Ave. NE (at 1st St. NE), St. Petersburg, FL 33701. © **800/274-7520** or 727/821-9391. Fax 727/821-6909. www.mansionbandb.com. 10 units. $99–$220 double. Rates include full breakfast. AE, DC, DISC, MC, V. **Amenities:** Heated outdoor pool; access to nearby health club; Jacuzzi; bicycle rentals; laundry service. *In room:* A/C, TV, dataport, hair dryer.

A NEARBY SPA WITH GOOD PACKAGE DEALS

Safety Harbor Resort and Spa *Value* Hernando de Soto thought he had found Ponce de León's fabled Fountain of Youth when in 1539 he happened upon five mineral springs in what is now Safety Harbor on the western shore of Old Tampa Bay (see the "Tampa & St. Petersburg" map, earlier in this chapter). This sprawling complex of beige stucco buildings with Spanish tile roofs sits on 22 waterfront acres in the sleepy town of Safety Harbor, north of St. Petersburg. Moss-draped Safety Harbor has a charming small-town ambience, with a number of shops and restaurants just outside the spa's entrance. You may not recover your youth at this venerable spa, which has been in operation since 1926 and got a face-lift in 1998, but you will be rejuvenated with such services as massage and hydrotherapy and a full menu of fitness classes from boxing to yoga. The mineral springs enable the resort to offer acclaimed water-fitness programs, and this is also a good place to work on your games at the Quinzi Golf Academy and the Phil Green Tennis Academy (see "Affordable Outdoor Activities," earlier in this section). Given the reasonable off-season room rates and special packages available, this is one of Florida's better spa values.

105 N. Bayshore Dr., Safety Harbor, FL 34695. © 888/BEST-SPA or 727/726-1161. Fax 727/724-7749. www.safetyharborspa.com. 193 units. Winter $209–$229 double; off-season $139–$159 double. Packages available. AE, DC, DISC, MC, V. Valet parking $8; free self-parking. Pets accepted ($35-per-night charge). **Amenities:** 2 restaurants (American), bar; heated indoor and outdoor pools; golf course; 9 tennis courts; full-service spa; concierge; activities desk; car-rental desk; bicycle rentals; business center; limited room service; laundry service; coin-op washers and dryers. *In room:* A/C, TV, dataport, coffeemaker, hair dryer, iron.

GREAT DEALS ON DINING

Don't overlook the food court at **The Pier,** where the inexpensive chow is accompanied by a very rich, but quite free, view of the bay. Among The Pier's restaurants is a branch of Tampa's famous **Columbia** (© 727/822-8000). Downtown also has an offshoot of Ybor City's **Ovo Cafe,** at 515 Central Ave. (© 727/895-5515). See "Great Deals on Dining" in section 1 of this chapter for details about Columbia and Ovo Cafe.

Keystone Club ★ STEAKS/PRIME RIB Resembling an exclusive men's club, this cozy restaurant's forest green walls accented by dark wood and etched glass create an atmosphere that's reminiscent of a Manhattan-style chophouse. But women are also welcome to partake of the beef, which is king here. Specialties include roast prime rib, New York strip steak, and filet mignon. Seafood also makes an appearance, with fresh lobster and grouper at market price.

320 4th St. N. (between Third and Fourth aves. N.). © 727/822-6600. Reservations recommended. Main courses $12–$24. AE, DC, DISC, MC, V. Mon–Thurs 4:30–9pm; Fri–Sat 4:30–10pm.

The Moon Under Water ★ ASIAN/MIDDLE EASTERN/AMERICAN Tables on the veranda or sidewalk in front of this pub are a great place to take a break during your downtown stroll. The British Raj rules supreme inside the darkly paneled dining room with its slowly twirling ceiling fans and plethora of colonial artifacts, including obligatory pith helmets. Your taste buds are in for a treat here, because the bill of fare covers a number of former British outposts, including America (burgers and Philly cheese steaks), but the emphasis here is on mild, medium, or blazing-hot Indian curries—with a recommended Irish, British, or Australian beer to slake the resulting thirst. For lighter fare, consider Mideastern tabbouleh. There's live music on weekend evenings.

332 Beach Dr. NE (between Third and Fourth aves.). © 727/896-6160. Main courses $7.50–$17; sandwiches and salads $6–$8. AE, DC, DISC, MC, V. Sun–Thurs 11:30am–11pm; Fri–Sat 11:30am–midnight. Closed New Year's Day, Thanksgiving, Christmas.

SUPER-CHEAP EATS

Fourth Street Shrimp Store ★★ *Value* SEAFOOD If you're anywhere in the area, don't miss at least driving by to see the colorful, cartoon-like mural on the outside of this eclectic establishment just north of downtown. On first impression it looks like graffiti, but it's actually a gigantic drawing of people eating. Inside, it gets even better, with paraphernalia and murals on two walls making the main dining room seem like a warehouse with windows that look out on an early-19th-century seaport (one painted sailor permanently peers in to see what you're eating). You'll pass a seafood market counter when you enter, from which comes the fresh namesake shrimp, the star here. You can also pick from grouper, clam strips, catfish, or oysters fried, broiled, or steamed, all served in heaping portions. This is the best and certainly the most interesting bargain in town.

1006 4th St. N. (at 10th Ave. N.). © 727/822-0325. Main courses $5–$14; sandwiches $2.50–$7. MC, V. Daily 11am–9pm.

WORTH A SPLURGE

Chateau France ★★ CLASSICAL FRENCH   Chef Antoine Louro provides St. Petersburg's finest cuisine and most romantic setting in this charming pink Victorian house built in 1910. He specializes in French classics such as homemade paté, Dover sole meunière, filet mignon au poivre, coq au vin, orange duck, and a rich seafood bouillabaisse. Fresh baby vegetables, Gruyère cheese potatoes, and Antoine's special Eiffel Tower salad accompany all main courses. The wine list is excellent, as are the bananas flambé and crêpes Suzette.

136 Fourth Ave. N. (between Bayshore Dr. and 1st St. N.). © 727/894-7163. Reservations recommended. Main courses $20–$30. AE, DC, DISC, MC, V. Daily 5–11pm.

ST. PETERSBURG AFTER DARK

Good sources of nightlife information are the Thursday "Weekend" section of the *St. Petersburg Times* (www.sptimes.com), the "Baylife" and "Friday Extra" sections of the *Tampa Tribune* (www.tampatrib.com), and the *Weekly Planet* (www.weeklyplanet.com), a tabloid available at the visitor information offices and in many hotel and restaurant lobbies.

The heart of downtown's nighttime scene is **BayWalk** (© 727/895-9277; www.baywalklive.com), downtown's new shopping-dining-entertainment complex bordered by 1st and 2nd streets and Second and Third avenues North. A 20-screen cinema and several restaurants and bars will keep you busy.

THE CLUB & MUSIC SCENE   A historic attraction as well as an entertainment venue, the Moorish-style **Coliseum Ballroom,** 535 Fourth Ave. N. (© 727/892-5202; www.stpete.org/coliseum.htm), has been hosting dancing, big bands, boxing, and other events since 1924 (it even made an appearance in the 1985 movie *Cocoon*). Come out and watch the town's many seniors doing the jitterbug just like it was 1945 again! Call for the schedule and prices.

PERFORMING-ARTS VENUES   The **Bayfront Center,** 400 1st St. S. (© 727/892-5767, or 727/892-5700 for recorded information), houses the 8,100-seat Bayfront Arena (www.stpete.org/bayfront.htm) and the 2,000-seat Mahaffey Theater (www.stpete.org/mahaffey.htm). The schedule includes a variety of concerts, Broadway shows, big bands, ice shows, and circus performances. **Ticketmaster** (© 813/287-8844) sells tickets to most events and shows.

Tropicana Field, 1 Stadium Dr. (© 727/825-3100; www.stpete.org/dome.htm), has a capacity of 50,000 for major concerts, but it also hosts a variety of smaller events when the Devil Rays aren't playing baseball.

3 St. Pete & Clearwater Beaches ★★

If you're looking for sun and sand, you'll find plenty of both on the 28 miles of slim barrier islands that skirt the gulf shore of the Pinellas Peninsula. With some one million visitors coming here every year, don't be surprised if you have lots of company. Despite the development, you'll discover quieter neighborhoods geared to families, and this area has some of the nation's finest beaches, which are protected from development by parks and nature preserves.

There's an upside to this many tourists, for it means that the St. Pete and Clearwater beaches have a wide array of accommodations in all price ranges, making them one of Florida's most affordable destinations.

At the southern end of the strip, St. Pete Beach is the granddaddy of the area's resorts. In fact, visitors started coming here nearly a century ago, and they haven't quit. Today St. Pete Beach is heavily developed and often overcrowded during the winter season. If you like high-rises and mile-a-minute action, St. Pete Beach is for you. But even here, Pass-a-Grille, on the island's southern end, is a quiet residential enclave with eclectic shops and a fine public beach.

A more gentle lifestyle begins just to the north on 3½-mile-long Treasure Island. From there, you cross famous John's Pass to Sand Key, a 12-mile island occupied by primarily residential Madeira Beach, Redington Shores, Indian Shores, Indian Rocks Beach, and Belleair Beach. Finally the road crosses a soaring bridge to Clearwater Beach, whose silky sands attract active families and couples.

If you like your great outdoors unfettered by development, the jewels here are Fort Desoto Park, down below St. Pete Beach at the mouth of Tampa Bay, and Caladesi Island State Park, north of Clearwater Beach. They are consistently rated among America's top beaches. And Sand Key Park, looking at Clearwater Beach from the southern shores of the pass separating Clearwater Beach from Belleair Beach, is one of Florida's finest local beach parks.

ESSENTIALS

GETTING THERE See "Getting There" in section 1 of this chapter for information about getting to the beaches.

VISITOR INFORMATION See "Visitor Information," in section 2 of this chapter, for the St. Petersburg/Clearwater Area Convention & Visitors Bureau and the St. Petersburg Area Chamber of Commerce. The bureau's website at www.FloridasBeach.com has information specific to the beaches.

Once you're here, you can get beach information at the **Gulf Beaches of Tampa Bay Chamber of Commerce,** 6990 Gulf Blvd. (at 70th Ave.), St. Pete Beach, FL 33706 (© **800/944-1847** or 727/360-6957; fax 727/360-2233; www.gulfbeaches-tampabay.com). The chamber is open Monday to Friday from 9am to 5pm.

For advance information about Clearwater Beach, contact the **Clearwater Regional Chamber of Commerce,** 1130 Cleveland St., Clearwater, FL 33755 (© **727/461-0011;** fax 727/449-2889; www.clearwater.org). You can also walk into the **Clearwater Visitor Information Center,** on Causeway Boulevard in the lobby of the Clearwater Beach Marina Building (© **727/462-6531**). It's open Monday to Saturday from 9am to 5pm and Sunday from 1 to 5pm.

GETTING AROUND The **Pinellas Suncoast Transit Authority/PSTA** (© **727/530-9911**) operates a motorized trolley service along Gulf Boulevard (Fla. 699) between the Hurricane Restaurant in St. Pete Beach and the Sheraton Sand Key Resort, where it connects with Clearwater Beach's **Jolly Trolley** (© **727/445-1200**), which continues on Gulf Boulevard through Clearwater Beach. The PSTA trolley runs daily, every 20 minutes between 5am and 10pm, to midnight on Friday and Saturday. Rides cost $1, or you can buy a daily pass for $3. One-ride fares on the Jolly Trolley are 50¢ per person, 25¢ for seniors. Call the trolleys for schedules, or pick up printed copies at the Gulf Beaches of Tampa Bay Chamber of Commerce (see "Visitor Information," above).

Along the beach, the major cab company is **BATS Taxi** (© **727/367-3702**). Fares are $1.50 at flag fall, plus 20¢ for each seventh of a mile.

WHAT TO SEE & DO
HITTING THE BEACH

This entire stretch of coast is one long beach, but since hotels, condominiums, and private homes occupy much of it, you may want to sun and swim at one of

St. Pete & Clearwater Beaches

ACCOMMODATIONS
Beach Haven **11**
Belleview Biltmore Resort & Spa **24**
Best Western Beachfront Resort **7**
Best Western Sea Stone Resort **21**
Clearwater Beach Hotel **14**
Clearwater Beach International Hostel **15**
Great Heron Inn **3**
Island's End Resort **13**
Pelicanæ East & West **1**
Radisson Suite Resort on Sand Key **23**
Sheraton Sand Key Resort **22**
Sun West Beach Motel **20**
Tradewinds Sirata Beach Resort **9**

DINING
Beachside Grille **6**
Bob Heilman's Beachcomber **17**
Bobby's Bistro & Wine Bar **18**
Crabby Bill's **10**
Frenchy's Original Café **16**
Guppy's **2**
Hurricane **12**
Lobster Pot **5**
The Salt Rock Grill **4**
Seafood & Sunsets at Julie's **19**
Skidder's Restaurant **8**

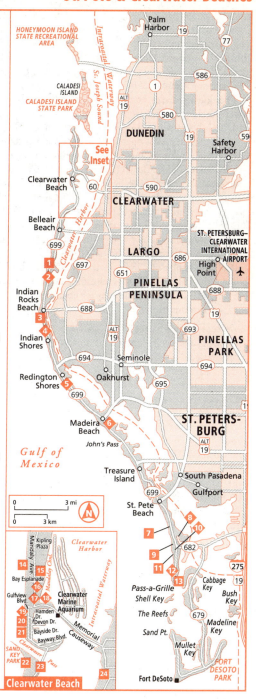

the area's public parks. The very best are described below, but there's also the fine **Pass-a-Grille Public Beach,** on the southern end of St. Pete Beach, where you can watch the boats going in and out of Pass-a-Grille Channel and slake your thirst at Hurricane restaurant (see "Great Deals on Dining," later in this section). This and all other Pinellas County public beaches have metered parking lots, so bring a supply of quarters. There are public restrooms along the beach.

The fine **Sand Key Park**, on the northern tip of Sand Key facing Clearwater Beach, sports a wide beach and gentle surf and is relatively off the beaten path in this commercial area. It's great to get out of the hotel for a morning walk or jog here. The park is open 8am to dark and has restrooms. Admission is free, but the parking lot has meters. For more information, call © 727/464-3347.

Clearwater Public Beach (also known as Pier 60) has beach volleyball, watersports rentals, lifeguards, restrooms, showers, and concessions. The swimming is excellent, and there is a fishing pier with a bait and tackle shop, plus a children's playground. Gated municipal parking lots here cost $1 per hour or $7 a day. The lots are right across the street from Clearwater Beach Marina, a prime base for boating, cruises, and other waterborne activities (see "Affordable Outdoor Activities," below). A somewhat-less-crowded spot in Clearwater Beach is at the gulf end of Bay Esplanade; the metered parking lot here is flanked by two lively beach bars: **Palm Pavilion Grill and Bar,** on the beach at 18 Bay Esplanade (© 727/446-6777), and **Frenchy's Rockaway Grill** (see "Great Deals on Dining," later in this section).

Caladesi Island State Park

Occupying a 3½-mile-long island north of Clearwater Beach, **Caladesi Island State Park** boasts one of Florida's top beaches—a lovely, relatively secluded stretch with fine soft sand edged in sea grass and palmettos. Dolphins often cavort in the waters offshore. In the park itself is a nature trail, and you might see one of the rattlesnakes, black racers, raccoons, armadillos, or rabbits that live here. A concession stand, a ranger station, and bathhouses (with restrooms and showers) are available. Caladesi Island is accessible only by ferry from **Honeymoon Island State Recreation Area,** which is connected by Causeway Boulevard (Fla. 586) to Dunedin, north of Clearwater.

You'll first have to pay the admission to Honeymoon Island: $4 per vehicle with two to eight occupants, $2 per single-occupant vehicle, $1 for pedestrians and bicyclists. Beginning daily at 10am, the ferry (© 727/734-1501) departs Honeymoon Island every hour on winter weekdays, every 30 minutes on summer weekdays, and every 30 minutes on weekends year-round. Round-trip rides cost $7.50 for adults and $3.50 for kids.

Neither Caladesi nor Honeymoon allows camping, but pets are permitted in the inland parts of Honeymoon Island and on its South Beach (bring a leash and use it at all times).

The two parks are open daily from 8am to sunset and are administered by Gulf Islands Geopark, 1 Causeway Blvd., Dunedin, FL 34698 (© 727/469-5942; www.dep.state.fl.us/parks/district4/caladesiisland and www.dep.state.fl.us/parks/district4/honeymoonisland).

To really get to know the islands, go with Linda Taylor of **It's Our Nature, Inc.** (© 727/441-2599; www.itsournature.com), on one of her guided walks of Honeymoon (usually at 9:30am Wed) and Caladesi (10am Thurs). They last about 2 hours and cost $15 for adults, $8 for children, plus park admission and ferry fare. Call for reservations, which are required, and for information about Linda's kayak tours and other guided walks.

Fort Desoto Park ★★

South of St. Pete Beach at the very mouth of Tampa Bay, **Fort Desoto Park** encompasses all of Mullet Key, set aside by Pinellas County as a 900-acre bird, animal, and plant sanctuary. Besides the stunning white-sugar sand, it is best known for a Spanish-American War–era fort, which has a museum (open daily 9am–4pm). Other diversions include great fishing from piers, large playgrounds for kids, and 4 miles of trails winding through the park for in-line skaters, bicyclists, and joggers. Park rangers conduct nature and history tours, and you can rent canoes and kayaks to explore the winding mangrove channels along the island's bay side. There are changing and restrooms.

Sitting by itself on a heavily forested island, the park's **campground** ★★ is one of Florida's most picturesque (many sites are beside the bay). It's such great camping that the 233 sites usually are sold out, especially on weekends, so it's best to reserve well in advance. But, there are a few catches: You must appear in person no more than 30 days in advance at the campground office, at 631 Chestnut St. in Clearwater, or at 150 5th St. N. in downtown St. Petersburg. You must pay when you make your reservation in cash or by traveler's check (no credit cards). You must reserve for at least 2 nights, but you can stay no more than 14 nights in any 30-day period. Sites cost $33.30 a night from January through July, $23.30 a night the rest of the year. All sites have water and electricity hookups.

Admission to the park is free. It's open daily from 8am to dusk, although campers and persons fishing from the piers can stay later. To get here, take the Pinellas Byway (50¢ toll) east from St. Pete Beach and follow Fla. 679 (35¢ toll) and the signs south to the park. For more information, contact the park at 3500 Pinellas Byway, Tierra Verde, FL 33715 (© **727/582-2267**; www.fort desoto.com).

AFFORDABLE OUTDOOR ACTIVITIES

BOATING, FISHING & OTHER WATER SPORTS   You can indulge in parasailing, boating, deep-sea fishing, wave running, sightseeing, dolphin watching, water-skiing, and just about any other waterborne diversion your heart could desire here. All you have to do is head to one of two beach locations: **Hubbard's Marina,** at John's Pass Village and Boardwalk (© **727/393-1947**; www.hubbardsmarina.com), in Madeira Beach on the southern tip of Sand Key; or **Clearwater Beach Marina,** at Coronado Drive and Causeway Boulevard (© **800/772-4479** or 727/461-3133), which is at the beach end of the causeway leading to downtown Clearwater. Agents in booths there will give you the schedules and prices (they are approximately the same at both locations), answer any questions you have, and make reservations if necessary. Go in the early morning to set up that day's activities, or in the afternoon to book the next day's.

CRUISES   The top nature cruise here is the **Sea Life Safari** ★★ (© **727/462-2628**), operated by the Clearwater Marine Aquarium (see "Attractions on Land," below). These 2½-hour "sea-life safaris" are more like field trips than pleasure cruises. Aquarium biologists go along to explain what they pull up in trawl nets (don't worry: they throw it all back). You'll see birds and other wildlife on a visit to a bird sanctuary islet. Dolphin sightings are likely, too. The cruises are well worth $14.50 for adults and $9.50 for kids 3 to 12. You can combine the cruise with aquarium admission and save $3. Call for the schedule and to reserve. Also ask about sunset nature cruises from mid-April to mid-October.

Hubbard's Sea Adventures, based at John's Pass Village and Boardwalk in Madeira Beach (© 727/398-6577), also offers a 2-hour dolphin-watching excursion daily at $12 for adults, $6 for kids under 12, but its best outings are cruises to fascinating **Egmont Key State Park** on historic Egmont Key at the mouth of Tampa Bay (www.dep.state.fl.us/parks/district4/egmontkey). This uninhabited island is the site of a lighthouse, the now-crumbling Fort Dade (built in 1900 during the Spanish-American War but abandoned long ago), and threatened gopher tortoises. Sea turtles come ashore here to nest. You can go snorkeling and shelling here, so bring your swimsuit (snorkeling gear is available). The half-day cruises leave from St. Pete Beach Tuesday through Sunday and cost $35 for adults and $25 for children.

Another popular cruise target is lovely **Shell Key,** one of Florida's last completely undeveloped barrier islands. Shell Key is great for bird-watchers, who could spot a remarkable 88 different species, including some of North America's rarest shorebirds. Hubbard's Shell Key beachcombing trips usually depart at 9am Monday through Saturday, for $20 adults and $10 for kids. You can rent beach chairs, umbrellas, snorkeling gear, and other equipment once you get there. Call to confirm the schedule and make reservations, which are recommended.

You can also get there on the **Shell Key Shuttle,** Merry Pier, on Pass-a-Grille Way at the eastern end of Eighth Avenue in southern St. Pete Beach (© 727/360-1348; www.shellkeyshuttle.com). Boats leave daily at 10am, noon, and 2pm. Prices are $12 for adults, $6 for children 12 and under. The ride takes 15 minutes, and you can return on any shuttle you wish.

The most unusual outings here are with **Captain Memo's Pirate Cruise,** at Clearwater Beach Marina (© 727/446-2587; www.captmemo.com), which sails the *Pirate's Ransom,* a reproduction of a pirate ship, on 2-hour daytime "pirate cruises," as well as sunset and evening champagne cruises. Call for prices and schedules.

Two paddle-wheel riverboats operate here: The **Show Queen** has lunch, sunset dinner, and Sunday brunch cruises from Clearwater Beach Marina (© 800/772-4479 or 727/461-3113; www.showqueen.com). The **Starlite Princess** does likewise from 3400 Pasadena Ave. S. (© 800/444-4814 or 727/462-2628; www.starlitecruises.com), at the eastern side of the Corey Causeway linking St. Pete Beach to the mainland. Call for prices, schedules, and reservations.

SCUBA DIVING You can dive on reefs and wrecks with **Dive Clearwater,** P.O. Box 3594, Clearwater, FL 33767 (© 800/875-3483 or 727/443-6731; www.diveclearwater.com), which also operates the live-aboard boat *Plunger V.* Call for the schedule and prices.

ATTRACTIONS ON LAND

Clearwater Marine Aquarium ★★ Kids
This little jewel of an aquarium on Clearwater Harbor is very low-key and friendly; it's dedicated to the rescue and rehabilitation of marine mammals and sea turtles. Exhibits include otters, sea turtles, sharks, stingrays, mangroves, and sea grass.

249 Windward Passage, Clearwater Beach. © 888/239-9414 or 727/441-1790. www.cmaquarium.org. Admission $8.75 adults, $5.25 children 3–11; free for children 2 and under. Mon–Fri 9am–5pm; Sat 9am–4pm; Sun 11am–4pm. The aquarium is off the causeway between Clearwater and Clearwater Beach; follow the signs.

John's Pass Village and Boardwalk
Casual and charming, this Old Florida fishing village on John's Pass consists of a string of simple wooden structures topped by tin roofs and connected by a 1,000-foot boardwalk. Most of the

buildings have been converted into shops, art galleries, restaurants, and saloons. The focal point is the boardwalk and marina, where many water sports are available for visitors (see "Affordable Outdoor Activities," above). If you don't go out on the water, this is a great place to have an alfresco lunch—**Sculley's** (© 727/393-7749) is the best restaurant here—and watch the boats go in and out of the pass.

12901 Gulf Blvd. (at John's Pass), Madeira Beach. © **800/944-1847** or 727/397-1511. www.johnspass.com. Free admission. Shops and activities daily 9am–6pm or later.

Suncoast Seabird Sanctuary At any one time there are usually more than 500 sea and land birds living at the sanctuary, from cormorants, white herons, and birds of prey to the ubiquitous brown pelican. The nation's largest wild-bird hospital, dedicated to the rescue, repair, recuperation, and release of sick and injured wild birds, is also here.

18328 Gulf Blvd., Indian Shores. © **727/391-6211.** www.seabirdsanctuary.org. Free admission; donations welcome. Daily 9am–dusk. Free tours Wed and Sun 2pm.

SHOPPING

John's Pass Village and Boardwalk, on John's Pass in Madeira Beach (see "Attractions on Land," above), has an unremarkable collection of beach souvenir shops, but the atmosphere makes it worth a stroll. The pick of the lot is the **Bronze Lady** (© **727/398-5994**), featuring the world's largest collection of works by the late comedian-artist Red Skelton, best known for his numerous clown paintings. The shops are open daily from 9am to 6pm or later.

If you're in the market for one-of-a-kind hand-hammered jewelry, try **Evander Preston Contemporary Jewelry,** 106 Eighth Ave., Pass-a-Grille (© **727/367-7894**), a unique gallery/workshop housed in a 75-year-old building in Pass-a-Grille's 1-block-long Eighth Avenue business district. Check out the golden miniature train with diamond headlight (it's not for sale). It's open Monday to Saturday from 10am to 5:30pm.

Among the shops in St. Pete Beach's Corey Landings Area, the town's original business strip along 75th Street east of Gulf Boulevard, **The Shell Store** (© **727/360-0586**) specializes in corals and shells, with an on-premises mini-museum illustrating how they live and grow. There's a good selection of shell home decorations, shell hobbyist supplies, shell art, planters, and jewelry. The store is open Monday to Saturday from 9:30am to 5pm.

ACCOMMODATIONS YOU CAN AFFORD

St. Pete Beach and Clearwater Beach have national chain hotels and motels of every name and description. You can also use the St. Petersburg/Clearwater Convention & Visitors Bureau's free **reservations service** (© **800/345-6710**) to book rooms at most of them. The **St. Petersburg Area Chamber of Commerce** lists a wide range of hotels, motels, condominiums, and other accommodations in its annual visitor guide (see "Essentials," in section 2 of this chapter), and it publishes a brochure listing all members of its Superior Small Lodgings program.

As is the case throughout Florida, there are more rental condominiums here than there are hotel rooms. Many of them are in high-rise buildings right on the beach. Among local rental agents, **JC Resort Management,** 17200 Gulf Blvd., North Redington Beach, FL 33708 (© **800/535-7776** or 727/397-0441; fax 727/397-8894; www.jcresort.com), has many from which to choose.

Rates are highest from January to April. Ask about special discounted packages in the summer. Any time of year, though, it's wise to make reservations early. The hotel tax in Pinellas County is 11%.

ST. PETE BEACH AREA

Beach Haven 🅚 *Value* Nestled on the beach between two high-rise condominiums, these low-slung, pink-with-white-trim structures look from the outside like the early 1950s motel they once were. But Jone and Millard Gamble, who used to own this motel and still have the charming Island's End Resort (see below), replaced the innards and installed bright tile floors, vertical blinds, pastel tropical furniture, and many modern amenities, including VCRs and refrigerators. Five of the original quarters remain motel rooms (with shower-only bathrooms), but the others are linked to make 12 one-bedroom units and one two-bedroom unit, all with kitchens. The top choice is the one-bedroom suite with sliding-glass doors opening to a tiled patio beside an outdoor heated pool. There's also a sunning deck with lounge furniture by the beach. You don't get maid service on Sunday or holidays, and the rooms and bathrooms are 1950s smallish; but every unit here is bright, airy, and comfortable.

4980 Gulf Blvd. (at 50th Ave.), St. Pete Beach, FL 33706. ⓒ 727/367-8642. Fax 727/360-8202. www.beachhavenvillas.com. 18 units (5 with shower only). Winter $90–$147 double; off-season $58–$122 double. AE, DISC, MC, V. **Amenities:** Heated outdoor pool; coin-op washers and dryers; concierge-level rooms. *In room:* A/C, TV/VCR, dataport, kitchen, fridge, coffeemaker, hair dryer, iron.

Best Western Beachfront Resort Two long, gray buildings flank a courtyard with heated swimming pool at this beachside property popular with young families. Furnished in dark woods and rich tones, most of the guest rooms have picture-window views of the courtyard. They open to wide exterior walkways, but each room has its own plastic chairs and drink table out there. About half of the units are efficiencies with kitchenettes. Jimmy B.'s beach bar is a fine place for a sunset cocktail and for evening entertainment, including beachside bonfires on Saturdays in winter.

6200 Gulf Blvd. (at 62nd Ave.), St. Pete Beach, FL 33706. ⓒ 800/544-4222 or 727/367-1902. Fax 727/367-4422. www.bestwesternstpetebeach.com. 102 units. Winter $168–$228 double; off-season $108–$168 double. Rates include continental breakfast. AE, DC, DISC, MC, V. **Amenities:** Restaurant (American), 2 bars; 2 heated outdoor pools; access to nearby health club; water-sports equipment rentals; game room; laundry service. *In room:* A/C, TV, kitchenette in some, fridge, coffeemaker, hair dryer, iron.

Island's End Resort 🅚🅚 *Value* A wonderful respite from the maddening crowd, and a great bargain to boot, this little all-cottage hideaway sits right on the southern tip of St. Pete Beach, smack-dab on Pass-a-Grille, where the Gulf of Mexico meets Tampa Bay. You can step from the six contemporary cottages right onto the beach. And since the island curves sharply here, nothing blocks your view of the emerald bay. Strong currents run through the pass, but you can safely swim in the gulf or grab a brilliant sunset at the Pass-a-Grille public beach, just one door removed. Linked to each other by boardwalks, the comfortable one- or three-bedroom cottages have dining areas, living rooms, VCRs, and fully equipped kitchens. You will love the one monstrous unit with two living rooms (one can be converted to sleeping quarters), two bathrooms (one with a whirlpool tub and separate shower), and its own private bay-side swimming pool. Maid service is on request.

1 Pass-a-Grille Way (at First Ave.), St. Pete Beach, FL 33706. ⓒ 727/360-5023. Fax 727/367-7890. www.islandsend.com. 6 units. Winter $125–$235 cottage; off-season $87–$235 cottage. Weekly rates available. Complimentary breakfast served Tues, Thurs, Sat. MC, V. **Amenities:** Coin-op washers and dryers. *In room:* A/C, TV/VCR, kitchen, coffeemaker, hair dryer, iron.

Travelodge St. Pete Beach This U-shaped beachfront complex of one- and two-story units is a favorite with no-frills, cost-conscious families traveling on package tours from Canada and the United Kingdom. All units were completely renovated in 1999. Some open to the surrounding parking lots; much more preferable are those facing a landscaped central courtyard with pool and large sunning area. On the premises is a branch of the very good and very inexpensive Shells seafood restaurant (see "Great Deals on Dining," in section 1 of this chapter). An indoor lounge and a lively beach bar offer light refreshments. The water-sports shack here offers parasailing equipment rentals and also services the Best Western Beachfront Resort next door (see above).

6300 Gulf Blvd. (at 63rd Ave.), St. Pete Beach, FL 33706. © 800/237-8918 or 727/367-2711. Fax 727/367-7068. 200 units. Winter $104–$144 double; off-season $80–$112 double. AE, DC, DISC, MC, V. **Amenities:** Restaurant (American), 2 bars; heated outdoor pool; water-sports equipment rental; game room; coin-op washers and dryers. *In room:* A/C, TV, fridge in some, coffeemaker, hair dryer, iron.

Worth an Off-Season Splurge

TradeWinds Sirata Beach Resort ★★   A ton of money was spent a few years ago to completely renovate this older property and bring it up to second-tier status here, almost on a par with its sister hotel, the TradeWinds Island Grand Resort. A yellow-and-green Old Florida–style facade now disguises the eight-story main building, which houses hotel rooms and one-bedroom suites upstairs (upper-level units have nice views) and a convention center. Some guest rooms in this two-story building face the courtyard, but the choice quarters here are its gulf-side rooms, the only units with patios or balconies opening directly onto the beach. The most spacious units are efficiencies and one-bedroom suites in two long, two-story buildings; they all have kitchenettes, but they look out primarily on parking lots.

5300 Gulf Blvd. (at 53rd Ave.), St. Pete Beach, FL 33706. © 800/237-0707 or 727562-1212. Fax 727/562-1222. www.justletgo.com. 380 units. Winter $175–$317 double; $267–$399 efficiency or suite. Off-season $145–$245 double; $198–$327 efficiency or suite. Resort amenities fee of $12 per day per unit covers most activities. AE, DC, DISC, MC, V. **Amenities:** 2 restaurants (Seafood/Steaks), 2 bars; 3 heated outdoor pools; exercise room; Jacuzzi; water-sports equipment rental; children's programs; game room; concierge; business center; limited room service; babysitting; laundry service; coin-op washers and dryers. *In room:* A/C, TV, dataport, kitchenettes in some, fridge, coffeemaker, hair dryer, iron.

INDIAN ROCKS BEACH AREA
Super-Cheap Sleeps

Great Heron Inn *Value*   A real heron named Harry patrols the beach at this family-oriented motel owned and operated by transplanted Michiganders Ralph and Teena Hickerson. It sits at the narrowest section of Indian Rocks Beach, facing the gulf on one side and its own Intracoastal Waterway dock on the other. The buildings flank a central courtyard, with a heated pool, which opens to the beach. The airy one-bedroom apartments offer modern furnishings and Berber carpets, and each has a full kitchen and dining area. There are no king- or queen-size beds here, only doubles (plus pullout sleeper sofas in the living rooms).

68 Gulf Blvd. (south of First Ave.), Indian Rocks Beach, FL 33785. © 727/595-2589. Fax 727/517-2705. www.heroninn.com. 16 units. Winter $85–$100 double; off-season $67–$75 double. Weekly and monthly rates available. AE, DISC, MC, V. Hotel is 4 blocks south of Fla. 688. **Amenities:** Coin-op washers and dryers. *In room:* A/C, TV, fax, kitchen, coffeemaker.

CLEARWATER BEACH

Best Western Sea Stone Resort   Located just across the street from the gulf in Clearwater Beach's busy south end, the Sea Stone is a six-story building of classic Key West–style architecture, containing 43 one-bedroom suites, each with a kitchenette and a living room. The living-room windows of the suites look across external walkways to the harbor. A few steps away, the older

> **Tips Cheap Bunks for the Young-at-Heart**
>
> The young and young-at-heart can find an inexpensive bed at **Clearwater Beach International Hostel,** 606 Bay Esplanade (✆ and fax **727/433-1211;** www.clearwaterbeachhostel.com), in a predominantly residential neighborhood a short walk north of the busy beach area. There's a swimming pool, communal kitchen, TV lounge with hundreds of videos to watch, canoes and other toys to borrow, and bicycles to rent. The hostel's 33 dorm beds rent for $13 a night, while four private rooms range from $34 to $57. MasterCard and Visa credit cards are accepted. Reservations are strongly advised during the winter and summer months. The hostel is affiliated with both Hostelling International and American Youth Hostels.

five-story Gulfview Wing offers 65 standard motel rooms, the least expensive choices here.

445 Hamden Dr. (at Coronado Dr.), Clearwater Beach, FL 33767. ✆ **800/444-1919,** 800/528-1234, or 727/441-1722. Fax 727/441-1680. www.seastoneresort.com. 106 units. Winter $89–$179 double; off-season $59–$115 double. AE, DC, DISC, MC, V. **Amenities:** Restaurant (American); bar; heated outdoor pool; Jacuzzi; coin-op washers and dryers. *In room:* A/C, TV, kitchenette, fridge, coffeemaker, hair dryer, iron.

Pelican—East & West *Value* Mike and Carol McGlaughlin's simple but friendly motel complex offers a choice of two settings. You'll pay more at Pelican West, but it's directly on the beachfront. Its four beachside apartments each have a living room, a bedroom, a kitchen, a patio, tub-shower combination bathrooms, and unbeatable views of the gulf. The lowest rates are at Pelican East, in a residential area 500 feet from the beach, where four apartments each have a bedroom, a separate kitchen, and shower-only bathrooms. Also over there, a motel room and one-bedroom apartment reside in a newer building sitting on stilts. You won't get any frills here, but this is a clean and comfortable choice.

108 21st Ave. (at Gulf Blvd.), Indian Rocks Beach, FL 33785. ✆ **727/595-9741.** Fax 727/596-4170. www.beachdirectory.com/pelican. 10 units (some with shower only). Winter $45–$90 double; off-season $45–$80 double. Weekly rates available. MC, V. *In room:* A/C, TV, kitchen, coffeemaker, iron.

Super-Cheap Sleeps

Sun West Beach Motel *Value* Sitting among several small motels a 2-block walk from the beach, Scott and Judy Barrows's simple one-story establishment dates from 1954, but it's well maintained, overlooks the bay, and has a fishing/boating dock and a heated bay-side pool and sun deck. All units, which face the bay, the pool, or the sun deck, were recently upgraded and have tropical-style furnishings, which make the place seem more modern than it is. The four motel rooms have small refrigerators, the 10 efficiencies have kitchens, and a few suites have separate bedrooms. The biggest and best unit is the Bayside Suite, which has vaulted ceilings, a steam room in its bathroom, and a fully equipped kitchen.

409 Hamden Dr. (at Bayside Dr.), Clearwater Beach, FL 33767. ✆ **727/442-5008.** Fax 727/461-1395. 15 units. Winter $63–$99 double, off-season $44–$70 double. MC, V. **Amenities:** Heated outdoor pool; access to nearby health club; coin-op washers and dryers. *In room:* A/C, TV, kitchen (some units), fridge, coffeemaker.

Worth a Splurge

Clearwater Beach Hotel ★ Besides the great beach location, you'll enjoy easy access to many nearby shops and restaurants from this Old Florida–style structure, built in 1986 to replace an old wooden hotel. The resort has been owned and operated by the same family since the 1950s and attracts a mixed clientele including European families. Directly on the gulf, the complex consists of the six-story main building and two contemporary motel-style wings. Some rooms have balconies, and the efficiencies in the wings have kitchenettes. Offering French cuisine, the formal dining room is romantic at sunset and offers great views of the gulf, while the nautically themed lounge has entertainment nightly. A bar provides snacks and libations beside an outdoor heated swimming pool.

500 Mandalay Ave. (at Baymont St.), Clearwater Beach, FL 33767. © 800/292-2295 or 727/441-2425. Fax 727/449-2083. www.clearwaterbeachhotel.com. 157 units. Winter $159–$269 double; off-season $115–$209 double. AE, DC, MC, V. Free valet parking. **Amenities:** Restaurant (French), outdoor bar, lounge; heated outdoor pool; access to nearby health club; concierge, limited room service; laundry service. *In room:* A/C, TV, kitchen (efficiencies only), fridge, coffeemaker.

Radisson Suite Resort on Sand Key *Kids*
You'll see the beauty of Sand Key from the suites in this boomerang-shaped, 10-story, all-suites hotel located across the boulevard from the Sheraton Sand Key Resort (see below). Although the resort sits on the bay and not the gulf, it has a large swimming pool complex next to the water, and the beach and beautiful Sand Key Park are short walks or trolley rides away. The resort has a good children's program, and the whole family will enjoy exploring the adjacent boardwalk with 25 shops and restaurants, including a branch of Tampa's excellent Columbia (see "Great Deals on Dining" in section 1 of this chapter). Each suite has a bedroom with a balcony offering water views, as well as a complete living room with a sofa bed, a wet bar, and an entertainment unit. Like the Sheraton Sand Key Resort, this Radisson does a brisk European business during the summer months, so room rates do not drop appreciably throughout the year.

1201 Gulf Blvd., Clearwater Beach, FL 33767. © 800/333-3333 or 727/596-1100. Fax 727/595-4292. www.radissonsandkey.com. 220 units. $169–$339 suite. Packages available. AE, DC, DISC, MC, V. **Amenities:** 5 restaurants (American, Spanish, Italian), 3 lounges; heated outdoor pool; golf course; exercise room; Jacuzzi; sauna; children's programs; game room; car-rental desk; business center; shopping arcade; limited room service; massage; babysitting; laundry service; coin-op washers and dryers. *In room:* A/C, TV, dataport, minibar, coffeemaker, hair dryer, iron.

Sheraton Sand Key Resort
Away from the honky-tonk of Clearwater, this nine-story Spanish-style hotel on 10 acres next to Sand Key Park is a big favorite with water-sports enthusiasts and groups. It also gets lots of European guests year-round. You'll appreciate being next to the park, since it's a 150-yard walk across the broad beach in front of the hotel to the water's edge. The moderately spacious guest rooms here all have traditional dark wood furniture and balconies or patios with views of the gulf or the bay. The exercise room here is on the top floor, rendering great workout views.

1160 Gulf Blvd., Clearwater Beach, FL 33767. © 800/325-3535 or 727/595-1611. Fax 727/596-8488. www.sheratonsandkey.com. 390 units. $135–$240 double. AE, DC, DISC, MC, V. **Amenities:** 2 restaurants (American), 2 bars; heated outdoor pool; 3 tennis courts; exercise room; Jacuzzi; sauna; water-sports equipment rental; children's programs (summer only); game room; concierge; business center; limited room service; babysitting; laundry service; concierge-level rooms. *In room:* A/C, TV, dataport, coffeemaker, hair dryer, iron.

A NEARBY HISTORIC GOLF RESORT
Belleview Biltmore Resort & Spa
The Gulf Coast's oldest operating tourist hotel, this gabled clapboard structure was built in 1896 by Henry B. Plant as the Hotel Belleview to attract customers to his Orange Belt Railroad. Sited on a bluff overlooking the bay, it's the largest occupied wooden structure in the world. Today it attracts mostly groups and serious golfers (guests can play at the adjoining Belleview Country Club, an 18-hole, par-72 championship course), but there's no denying its Victorian charm and old-fashioned

ambience—once you get past the out-of-place glass-and-steel foyer added by more recent owners. Historic tours are given daily (call for schedule and prices). The creaky hallways lead to several shops and a museum explaining the hotel's history. The hotel provides complimentary shuttle service to the country club and to Clearwater Beach.

25 Belleview Blvd., Clearwater, FL 33756. © 800/237-8947 or 727/373-3000. Fax 727/441-4173 or 727/443-6361. www.belleviewbiltmore.com. 240 units. Winter $119–$229 double; off-season $89–$199 double. AE, DC, DISC, MC, V. Valet parking $3; free self-parking. Resort is 1 mile south of downtown on Belleview Blvd., off Alt. U.S. 19. **Amenities:** Restaurant (American), 2 bars; heated indoor and outdoor pools; golf course; 4 tennis courts; health club; Jacuzzi; sauna; concierge; business center; shopping arcade; salon; limited room service; babysitting; laundry service. *In room:* A/C, TV, coffeemaker, hair dryer, iron.

GREAT DEALS ON DINING

St. Pete Beach and Clearwater Beach both have a wide selection of national chain fast-food and family restaurants along their main drags.

ST. PETE BEACH AREA

Crabby Bill's (Kids) SEAFOOD The least expensive gulf-side dining here, this member of a small local chain sits right on the beach in the heart of the hotel district. There's an open-air rooftop bar, but big glass windows enclose the large dining room. They offer fine water views from picnic tables equipped with rolls of paper towels and buckets of saltine crackers, the better to eat the blue, Alaskan, snow, and stone crabs that are the big draws here. The crustaceans fall into the moderate price category or higher, depending on the market, but most other main courses, such as fried fish or shrimp, are inexpensive—and they aren't overcooked or overbreaded. The creamy smoked fish spread is a delicious appetizer, and you'll get enough to whet the appetites of at least two persons. This is a very good place to feed the entire family.

5100 Gulf Blvd. (at 51st Ave.), St. Pete Beach. © 727/360-8858. Main courses $7.50–$20; sandwiches $4.50–$7. AE, MC, V. Mon–Thurs 11:30am–10pm; Fri–Sat 11:30am–11pm; Sun noon–10pm.

Hurricane SEAFOOD A longtime institution across the street from Pass-a-Grille Public Beach, this three-level gray Victorian building with white gingerbread trim is a great place to toast the sunset, especially at the rooftop bar. It's more beach pub than restaurant, but the grouper sandwiches are excellent, and there's always fresh fish to be fried, broiled, or blackened, and shrimp and crab to be steamed. Downstairs you can dine inside the knotty-pine paneled dining room or on the sidewalk terrace, where bathers from across Gulf Way are welcome (there's a walk-up bar for beach libation). The second-floor dining area also has seating on a wraparound veranda. You must be at least 21 years old to go up to the Hurricane Watch rooftop bar or to join the revelry when the second level turns into Stormy's Nightclub at 10pm Wednesday to Saturday.

807 Gulf Way (at Ninth Ave.), Pass-a-Grille. © 727/360-9558. Main courses $10–$18; sandwiches $7. AE, MC, V. Daily 8am–1am (breakfast Mon–Fri 8–11am; Sat–Sun 8am–noon).

Skidder's Restaurant (Kids) (Value) ITALIAN/GREEK/AMERICAN A local favorite, this inexpensive family restaurant in the hotel district offers a full range of breakfast fare plus handmade pan pizzas (available to eat here or carry out), burgers and sandwiches, big salads, gyro and souvlaki platters, and Italian-style veal, fish, and chicken dishes (Italian-style grouper is a house specialty). A children's menu features burgers and spaghetti.

5799 Gulf Blvd. (at 60th Ave.), St. Pete Beach. © 727/360-1029. Main courses $8–$16; breakfast $3–$6; sandwiches and burgers $3.50–$8; pizza $6–$16. AE, DC, DISC, MC, V. Daily 7am–11pm.

INDIAN ROCKS BEACH AREA

You'll find a bay-front edition of **Shells**, the fine and inexpensive local seafood chain, opposite the Lobster Pot on Gulf Boulevard at 178th Avenue in Redington Shores (🕾 **727/393-8990**). See "Great Deals on Dining," in section 1 of this chapter, for more information about Shells' menu and prices, which are the same at all branches.

Beachside Grille ★★ *Finds* SEAFOOD   Locals don't mind waiting for the best seafood bargains on the beach at this tiny (seven tables) place tucked into the rear of a two-store commercial building opposite the Friendly Tavern, a major landmark in Redington Shores. They are rewarded with a savory Louisiana seafood gumbo as a starter, then off-the-boat-fresh grouper or mahimahi grilled or blackened, salmon under a dill sauce, or grilled shrimp with a zesty fruit salsa. Falling-off-the-bone barbecued ribs, chargrilled steaks, and steamed shrimp and crab legs also appear on the menu. Main courses come with rice, sautéed vegetables, and a salad with owner Dan Casey's pesto salad dressing, which is so good he sells it by the bottle. Try a pitcher of the homemade white or red sangria, another local favorite. The lunch menu features hot dogs with french fries, stuffed pitas, and subs and other sandwiches.

35 182nd Ave. (at Gulf Blvd., opposite Friendly Tavern), Redington Shores. 🕾 **727/397-1865**. Reservations not accepted. Main courses $9–$15, sandwiches and burgers $5–$7.50. AE, DISC, MC, V. Daily 11am–10pm. Closed Thanksgiving and Christmas.

Guppy's ★★ SEAFOOD   Locals love this small bar and grill across from Indian Rocks Public Beach because they know they'll always get terrific chow (it's associated with the excellent Lobster Pot, below). You won't soon forget the salmon coated with potatoes and lightly fried, then baked with a creamy leek and garlic sauce; it's fattening, yes, but also a bargain at $10. Another good choice is lightly cooked tuna finished with a peppercorn sauce. The atmosphere is casual beach friendly, with a fun bar in the middle of it all. Scotty's famous upside-down apple-walnut pie topped with ice cream will require a little extra work on the weights tomorrow. You can dine outside on a patio beside the main road.

1701 Gulf Blvd. (at 17th Ave.), Indian Rocks Beach. 🕾 **727/593-2032**. Main courses $10–$18; sandwiches $6–$7. AE, DC, DISC, MC, V. Sun–Thurs 11:30am–10:30pm; Fri–Sat 11:30am–11pm.

Worth a Splurge

Lobster Pot ★★★ SEAFOOD/STEAKS   Step into this weathered-looking restaurant near the beach and experience some of the finest seafood in the area. The prices are high, but the variety of Maine lobster dishes is amazing. The lobster Américaine is flambéed in brandy with garlic, and the bouillabaisse is as authentic as any you'd find in the south of France. In addition to lobster, there's a wide selection of grouper, snapper, salmon, swordfish, shrimp, scallops, crab, Dover sole, and steaks, most prepared with elaborate sauces. The children's menu here is definitely out of the ordinary: It features half a Maine lobster and a petite filet mignon.

17814 Gulf Blvd. (at 178th Ave.), Redington Shores. 🕾 **727/391-8592**. Reservations recommended. Main courses $15.50–$39.50. AE, DC, MC, V. Daily 4:30–10pm.

The Salt Rock Grill ★★ SEAFOOD/STEAKS   Affluent professionals and other gorgeous folk pack this waterfront restaurant, making it *the* place to see and be seen on the beaches. The big urbane dining room is built on three levels, thus affording every table a view over the creeklike waterway out back. And in warm, fair weather you can dine out by the dock or slake your thirst at the lively tiki bar (bands play out here on Sat and Sun during the summer). Anything from the wood-fired grill is excellent here. Thick, aged steaks are the house specialties. You can get a good sampling with the mixed grill: small portions of filet mignon, pork tenderloin, a two-bone lamb chop, and dessert-sweet coconut shrimp. Pan-seared peppered tuna and salmon cooked on a cedar board lead the seafoods. You can avoid spending a fortune by showing up in time for the early bird specials or by ordering the meat loaf topped with mashed potatoes and onion straws ($8) or the half-pound sirloin steak ($10).

19325 Gulf Blvd. (north of 193rd Ave.), Indian Shores. © 727/593-7625. Reservations strongly advised. Main courses $9–$36 (early bird specials $8–$10). AE, DC, DISC, MC, V. Sun–Thurs 4–10pm; Fri–Sat 4–11pm (early bird specials daily 4–5:30pm). Tiki bar opens Sat–Sun 2pm.

CLEARWATER BEACH

Seafood & Sunsets at Julie's ★ *Value* SEAFOOD   A Key West–style tradition takes over Julie Nichols's place at dusk as both locals and visitors gather at sidewalk tables or in the rustic upstairs bar to toast the sunset over the beach across the street. The predominantly seafood menu features fine and very reasonably priced renditions of charcoal-broiled mahimahi with sour cream, Parmesan, and herb sauce; bacon-wrapped barbecued shrimp on a skewer; broiled, fried, or blackened fresh Florida grouper; and flounder stuffed with crabmeat. Everything is cooked to order here, so come prepared to linger over a cold drink.

351 S. Gulfview Blvd. (at 5th St.). © 727/441-2548. Main courses $10–$20; salads and sandwiches $6–$10. AE, MC, V. Daily 11am–10pm.

Super-Cheap Eats

Frenchy's Original Café SEAFOOD   Popular with locals and visitors in the know since 1981, this casual pub makes the best grouper sandwiches in the area and has all the awards to prove it. The sandwiches are fresh, thick, juicy, and delicious. The atmosphere is pure Florida casual style. There can be a wait during winter and on weekends year-round. For a similarly relaxed setting, directly on the beach, **Frenchy's Rockaway Grill,** at 7 Rockaway St. (© **727/446-4844**), has a wonderful outdoor setting, and it keeps a charcoal grill going to cook fresh fish.

41 Baymont St. © **727/446-3607.** Sandwiches and burgers $5–$7.50. AE, MC, V. Mon–Thurs 11:30am–11pm; Fri–Sat 11:30am–midnight; Sun noon–11pm.

For a Few Bucks More

Bob Heilman's Beachcomber ★ AMERICAN   In a row of restaurants, bars, and T-shirt shops, Bob and Sherri Heilman's establishment has been popular with the locals since 1948. Each dining room here is unique: large models of sailing crafts create a nautical theme in one, a pianist makes music in a second, works of art create a gallery in the third, and booths and a fireplace make for a cozy fourth. The menu presents a variety of well-prepared fresh seafood and beef, veal, and lamb selections. If you tire of fruits-of-the-sea, the "back to the farm" fried chicken—from an original 1910 Heilman family recipe—is incredible. The Beachcomber shares valet parking and an extensive wine collection with Bobby's Bistro & Wine Bar (see below).

447 Mandalay Ave. (at Papaya St.). © **727/442-4144.** Reservations recommended. Main courses $13–$29. AE, DC, DISC, MC, V. Mon–Sat 11:30am–11pm; Sun noon–10pm.

Bobby's Bistro & Wine Bar ★ AMERICAN   Son of Bob Heilman's Beachcomber, this chic bistro draws a more urbane crowd than its parent. A wine-cellar

The Sponge Capital of the World

One of Florida's most fascinating small towns and a fine day trip from Tampa, St. Petersburg, or the beaches, **Tarpon Springs** calls itself the "Sponge Capital of the World." That's because Greek immigrants from the Dodecanese Islands settled here in the late 19th century to harvest sponges, which grew in abundance offshore. By the 1930s, Tarpon Springs was producing more sponges than any other place in the world. A blight ruined the business in the 1940s, but the descendants of those early immigrants stayed on. Today they compose about a third of the population, making Tarpon Springs a center of transplanted Greek culture.

Sponges still arrive at the historic **Sponge Docks**, on Dodecanese Boulevard. With a lively, carnival-like atmosphere, the docks are a great place to spend an afternoon or early evening, poking your head into shops selling sponges and other souvenirs while Greek music comes from the dozen or so family restaurants purveying authentic Aegean cuisine. You can also venture offshore from here, because booths on the docks hawk sightseeing and fishing cruises. Make your reservations as soon as you get here; then go sightseeing ashore or grab a meal at one of the multitudinous Greek restaurants facing the dock while waiting for the next boat to shove off.

On the same boulevard, you also can visit the tin-roofed **Spongeorama** (no phone; open daily 10am–5pm), a museum dedicated to sponges and sponge divers, which sells a wide variety of sponges here (they'll ship your purchase home) and shows a 30-minute video several times a day about sponge diving. Admission is free. A scuba diver feeds sharks three times a day in the **Coral Sea Aquarium** (© **727/938-5378;** open Mon–Sat 10am–5pm, Sun noon–5pm), at the western end of the boulevard. Admission is $4.75 adults, $4 seniors, $2.75 for children 3 to 11, and free for kids under 3.

South of the docks, the **Downtown Historic District** sports turn-of-the-last-century commercial buildings along Tarpon Avenue and Pinellas Avenue (Alt. U.S. 19). On Tarpon Avenue west of Pinellas Avenue, you'll come to the Victorian homes overlooking **Spring Bayou.** This creekside area makes for a delightfully picturesque stroll.

The **Tarpon Springs Chamber of Commerce,** 11 E. Orange St., Tarpon Springs, FL 34689 (© **727/937-6109;** fax 727/937-2879; www.tarponsprings.com), has an information office on Dodecanese Boulevard at the Sponge Docks, which is open Tuesday to Sunday from 10:30am to 4:30pm.

To get to Tarpon Springs from Tampa or St. Petersburg, take U.S. 19 north and turn left on Tarpon Avenue (C.R. 582). From Clearwater Beach, take Alt. U.S. 19 north through Dunedin. The center of the historic downtown district is at the intersection of Pinellas Avenue (Alt. U.S. 19) and Tarpon Avenue. To reach the Sponge Docks, go 10 blocks north on Pinellas Avenue and turn left at Pappas' Restaurant onto Dodecanese Boulevard.

theme is amply justified by the real thing: a walk-in closet with several thousand bottles kept at a constant 55°F. Walk through and pick your vintage, then listen to jazz while you dine inside at tall, bar-height tables or outside on a covered patio. The chef specializes in gourmet pizzas on homemade focaccia crust (as a tasty appetizer), plus charcoal-grilled veal chops, filet mignon, fresh fish, and monstrous pork chops with caramelized Granny Smith apples and a Mount Vernon mustard sauce. Everything's served a la carte here, so watch your credit card. On the other hand, there's an affordable sandwich menu featuring the likes of bronzed grouper and chicken with a spicy Jack cheese.

447 Mandalay Ave. (at Papaya St., behind Bob Heilman's Beachcomber). © 727/446-9463. Reservations recommended. Main courses $8–$22; sandwiches and pizzas $6–$10. AE, DC, DISC, MC, V. Sun–Thurs 5–11pm; Fri–Sat 5pm–midnight, bar later.

THE BEACHES AFTER DARK

If you haven't already found it during your sightseeing and shopping excursions, the restored fishing community of **John's Pass Village and Boardwalk,** on Gulf Boulevard at John's Pass in Madeira Beach, has plenty of restaurants, bars, and shops to keep you occupied after the sun sets. Elsewhere, the nightlife scene at the beach revolves around rocking bars that pump out the music until 2am.

Down south in Pass-a-Grille is the popular, always-lively lounge at **Hurricane,** on Gulf Way at Ninth Avenue opposite the public beach (see "Great Deals on Dining," above).

On Treasure Island, **Beach Nutts,** on West Gulf Boulevard at 96th Avenue (© 727/367-7427), is perched atop a stilt foundation, like a wooden beach cottage, on the Gulf of Mexico. The music ranges from Top 40 to reggae and rock. Up on the northern tip of Treasure Island, **Gators on the Pass** (© 727/367-8951) claims to have the world's longest waterfront bar, with a huge deck overlooking the waters of John's Pass. The complex also includes a no-smoking sports bar and a three-story tower with a top-level observation deck for panoramic views of the Gulf of Mexico. There's live music, from acoustic and blues to rock, most nights.

In Clearwater Beach, the **Palm Pavilion Grill & Bar,** on the beach at 18 Bay Esplanade (© 727/446-6777), has live music Tuesday through Sunday nights during winter, on weekends off-season. Nearby, **Frenchy's Rockaway Grill,** at 7 Rockaway St. (© 727/446-4844), is another popular hangout.

If you're into laughs, **Coconuts Comedy Club,** at the Howard Johnson motel, Gulf Boulevard at 61st Avenue in St. Pete Beach (© 727/360-5653), has an ever-changing program of live stand-up funny men and women. Call for the schedule, performers, and prices.

For a more highbrow evening, go to the Clearwater mainland and the 2,200-seat **Ruth Eckerd Hall,** 1111 McMullen-Booth Rd. (© 727/791-7400; www.rutheckerdhall.com), which hosts a varied program of Broadway shows, ballet, drama, symphonic works, popular music, jazz, and country music.

4 Sarasota & Bradenton

52 miles S of Tampa, 150 miles SW of Orlando, 225 miles NW of Miami

Far enough away from Tampa Bay to have an identity very much its own, **Sarasota** is one of Florida's cultural centers. In fact, many retirees spend their winters here because there's so much to keep them entertained and stimulated, including the very fine Asolo Center for the Performing Arts and the Van Wezel

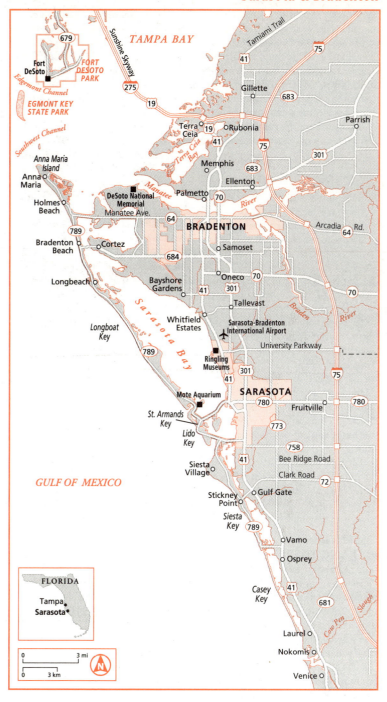

Performing Arts Hall. Like affluent Naples down in Southwest Florida, it also has an extensive array of first-class resorts, restaurants, and upscale boutiques.

Sarasota's most famous resident was circus legend John Ringling, who came here in the 1920s, built a palatial bay-front mansion known as Ca'd'Zan, acquired extensive real-estate holdings, and erected a magnificent museum to house his world-class collection of baroque paintings. He also built a causeway out to 35 miles of gloriously white beaches fringing a chain of narrow barrier islands stretching south from the entrance to Tampa Bay.

Shielded from the gulf by **Lido Key,** which has a string of affordable hotels attractive to family vacationers, **St. Armands Key** sports one of Florida's ritziest shopping and dining districts. To the south, **Siesta Key** is a residential enclave popular with artisans and writers but also home to Siesta Village, this area's funky, laid-back, and often noisy beach hangout. And **Longboat Key** is one of Florida's wealthiest and most expensive islands. The resorts and restaurants on Longboat Key are too expensive to be included in this book, even as a splurge, but you should drive along Gulf of Mexico Drive, the island's main drag, just to see what a whole lot of money can do.

> **Fun Fact Soto's Sara**
> Legend has it that Sarasota was named after the explorer Hernando de Soto's daughter, Sara—hence, Sara-sota.

Sarasota is only 10 miles south of **Bradenton,** a predominantly working-class town which visitors often overlook as they speed south on their way to Sarasota and beyond. Off Bradenton, **Anna Maria Island** claims 7½ miles of those white-sand beaches—but no glitzy resorts, just casual island getaways. Anna Maria Island's communities—Bradenton Beach, Holmes Beach, and Anna Maria—are popular with family vacationers and seniors, offering a variety of public beaches, fishing piers, bungalows, low-rise motels, and a terrific bed-and-breakfast. You can have a very relaxing beach vacation on Anna Maria without the bustle and out-of-sight prices found across the bridge on Sarasota's Longboat Key.

Sarasota and Bradenton share an airport, which sits astride their mutual boundary halfway between the two downtowns. Accordingly, you can stay in either town and easily explore the other—an important consideration for budget travelers, since accommodation on Anna Maria Island off Bradenton is less expensive than on Sarasota's keys.

ESSENTIALS

GETTING THERE You probably will get a less expensive airfare by flying into **Tampa International Airport,** an hour's drive north of Sarasota (see "Essentials," in section 1 of this chapter), and you could save even more since Tampa's rental-car agencies usually offer some of the best deals in Florida. If you don't rent a car, **Sarasota-Tampa Express** (© **800/326-2800** or 941/727-1344) provides bus connections for $22 per adult or $11 per child. Call in advance for the schedule and pickup locations.

If you decide to fly directly here, **Sarasota–Bradenton International Airport** (© **941/359-2770;** www.srq-airport.com), north of downtown Sarasota off University Parkway between U.S. 41 and U.S. 301, is served by **American Trans Air** (© 800/225-2995), **American** (© 800/433-7300), **Canada 3000** (© 800/993-4378), **Continental** (© 800/525-0280), **Delta** (© 800/221-1212), **Northwest/KLM** (© 800/225-2525), and **US Airways** (© 800/428-4322).

Alamo (© 800/327-9633), **Avis** (© 800/331-1212), **Budget** (© 800/527-0700), **Dollar** (© 800/800-4000), **Enterprise** (© 800/325-8007), **Hertz** (© 800/654-3131), and **National** (© 800/CAR-RENT) have car rentals here.

Diplomat Taxi (© 941/355-5155) has a monopoly on service from the airport to hotels in Sarasota and Bradenton. Look for the cabs at the west end of the terminal outside baggage claim. Fares range from about $10 to downtown Sarasota to $35 to Longboat Key or Anna Maria Island.

Amtrak has bus connections here from its Tampa station (© **800/USA-RAIL;** www.amtrak.com).

VISITOR INFORMATION Contact the **Sarasota Convention and Visitors Bureau,** 655 N. Tamiami Trail (U.S. 41), Sarasota, FL 34236 (© **800/522-9799** or 941/957-1877; fax 941/951-2956; www.sarasotafl.org). The bureau and its helpful visitor center are in a blue pagoda-shaped building on Tamiami Trail (U.S. 41) at 6th Street. They're open Monday to Saturday from 9am to 5pm and Sunday from 11am to 3pm; closed holidays.

You can get a packet of advance information about Bradenton and surrounding Manatee County from the **Greater Bradenton Area Convention and Visitors Bureau,** P.O. Box 1000, Bradenton, FL 34206 (© **800/4-MANATEE** or 941/729-9177; fax 941/729-1820; www.floridaislandbeaches.org).

If you're driving from the north via I-75, get off at U.S. 301 (Exit 43) and head west to the **Manatee County Tourist Information Center** (© **941/729-7040**), where volunteers are on hand to answer your questions and sell you excellent road maps for less than you'll pay elsewhere. It's open daily from 8:30am to 5pm except Easter Sunday, Thanksgiving, the day after Thanksgiving, and Christmas Day. The office has an information kiosk at **Prime Outlets,** across I-75, which is open Monday to Saturday 10am to 6pm and Sunday 11am to 6pm.

GETTING AROUND Operated by the Sarasota County Area Transit, or SCAT (© **941/316-1234;** www.co.sarasota.fl.us/public_works_scat/scat.asp), the **Sarasota Trolley** runs every 20 minutes from 9am to 5pm Monday to Friday, less frequently on Saturday. The Scenic Loop Trolley operates from Island Park, Bayfront at Ringling Boulevard, through downtown Sarasota, north to the FSU Ringling Center for the Cultural Arts, and out to St. Armands and Lido keys (but not to Siesta or Longboat keys). The Main Street Trolley goes from Island Park through downtown and eastward along Main Street. Fares are $1 on the Scenic Loop, 25¢ on the Main Street line, or you can buy a daily pass to both lines for $2. SCAT also operates regularly scheduled bus service. The Sarasota Convention and Visitors Bureau distributes route maps (see "Visitor Information," above).

Manatee County Area Transit, known locally as **Manatee CAT** (© **941/749-7116**), operates scheduled public bus service throughout the Bradenton and Anna Maria area.

Sarasota taxi companies include **Diplomat Taxi** (© 941/355-5155), **Green Cab Taxi** (© 941/922-6666), and **Yellow Cab of Sarasota** (© 941/955-3341). In Bradenton call **Bruce's Taxi** (© 941/755-6070), **Checker Cab** (© 941/751-3181), or **Yellow Cab** (© 941/748-4800).

WHAT TO SEE & DO
HITTING THE BEACH
Many of the area's 40-plus miles of beaches are occupied by hotels and condominium complexes, but there are excellent public beaches here, all of them with

restrooms. The area's most popular is **Siesta Key Public Beach,** with a picnic area, a 700-car parking lot, crowds of families, and quartz sand reminiscent of the blazingly white beaches in Northwest Florida. There's also beach access (but no public restrooms) at **Siesta Village,** which has a plethora of casual restaurants and pubs with outdoor seating (see "Great Deals on Dining," later in this section). More secluded and quiet is **Turtle Beach,** at Siesta Key's south end. It has shelters, boat ramps, picnic tables, and volleyball nets.

After you've driven the length of Longboat Key and admired the luxurious homes and condominiums blocking access to the beach, take a right off St. Armands Circle onto Lido Key and **North Lido Beach.** The south end of the island is occupied by **South Lido Beach Park,** with plenty of shade making it a good spot for picnics and walks.

On Anna Maria Island the largest and best is **Coquina Beach,** which occupies the southern mile of the island below Bradenton Beach. It has both gulf and bay sides, is sheltered by whispering Australian pines, and has a nature trail and large parking lots. **Cortez Beach** is in Bradenton Beach, just north of Coquina Beach. In the island's center, **Manatee County Public Beach** is at Gulf Drive. **Holmes Beach** is at the west end of Manatee Avenue (Fla. 64). **Anna Maria Bayfront Park** is on Bay Boulevard at the northwest end of the island, fronting both the bay and the Gulf of Mexico.

AFFORDABLE OUTDOOR ACTIVITIES

BICYCLING & IN-LINE SKATING The flat terrain makes for good in-line skating and for fine if not challenging bike riding. You can bike and skate from downtown Sarasota to Lido and Longboat keys, since paved walkways/bike paths run alongside the John Ringling Causeway and then up Longboat Key. **Siesta Sports Rentals,** 6551 Midnight Pass Rd., in the Southbridge Mall just south of Stickney Point Bridge on Siesta Key (© **941/346-1797;** www.siesta sportsrentals.com), rents bikes of various sizes, including stroller attachments for kids, plus motor scooters, in-line skates, kayaks, and beach chairs and umbrellas. Bike rentals range from about $14 a day to $50 a week, while scooters go for $15 an hour, $50 a day, or $175 a week. The shop is open daily 9am to 5pm.

On Anna Maria, **Island Rental Service,** 3214 E. Bay Dr. (© **800/248-8797** or 941/778-1472), next to Shells Restaurant in Holmes Beach; and **Neumann's Island Beach Store,** 427 Pine Ave., at Tarpon Street in Anna Maria (© **941/ 778-3316**), both rent bikes and various beach equipment. Island Rental Service will deliver.

BOAT RENTALS **All Watersports,** in the Boatyard Shopping Village, on the mainland end of Stickney Point Bridge (© **941/921-2754**), rents personal watercraft such as jet skis, speedboats, runabouts, and bowriders. At the island end of the bridge, **C. B.'s Saltwater Outfitters,** 1249 Stickney Point Rd. (© **941/349-4400**), and **Siesta Key Boat Rentals,** 1265 Old Stickney Point Rd. (© **941/349-8880**), both rent runabouts, pontoon boats, and other craft. Bait and tackle are available at the marinas.

On Anna Maria Island, you can rent boats from **Bradenton Beach Marina,** 402 Church Ave. (© **941/778-2288**); **Captain's Marina,** 5501 Marina Dr., Holmes Beach (© **941/778-1977**); and **Five O'Clock Marina,** 412 Pine Ave., Anna Maria (© **941/778-5577**). On northern Longboat Key, **Cannons Marina,** 6040 Gulf of Mexico Dr. (© **941/383-1311**), also rents boats. Several deep-sea–fishing charter boats are based at these marinas.

CRUISES The area's best nature cruises go forth from Mote Aquarium (see "Exploring the Area," below).

You can head over to Marina Jack's Marina, U.S. 41 at Island Park Circle, for 2-hour dolphin-watching, sightseeing, and sunset cruises around Sarasota's waterways aboard the 65-foot, two-deck *Le Barge* (© **941/366-6116;** www.lebargetropicalcruises.com). The dolphin-watching cruises run Tuesday, Thursday, and Saturday at 11am, while the other trips operate Tuesday through Sunday, with the sightseeing cruise at 2pm. Departure of the sunset cruises (with live music) changes with the time of sunset. The cruises cost $15 adults and $10 for kids under 13. Snacks and libations are available for an extra charge, but credit cards are not accepted. Call for reservations.

That paddle wheeler you see going up and down the bay is the *Seafood Shack Showboat*, operated by the Seafood Shack restaurant, 4110 127th St. W., in Cortez (© **800/299-5048** or 941/794-5048). It has afternoon cruises to Sarasota Bay, Tampa Bay, and as far away as the Sunshine Skyway. Prices are $15 for adults, $13.50 for seniors, and $7.50 for children 4 to 11. The *Showboat* goes to a different destination each day, and its schedule is seasonal, so call a day ahead for the schedule. Reservations are not accepted.

FISHING Charter fishing boats dock at most marinas here. Check out www.sarasotaboating.com for a list. In downtown Sarasota, the **Flying Fish Fleet,** at Marina Jack's Marina, U.S. 41 at Island Park Circle (© **941/366-3373;** www.flyingfishfleet.com), offers party-boat charter fishing excursions, with bait and tackle furnished. Prices for half-day trips are about $30 adults, $25 seniors, $20 for kids 4 to 12. All-day voyages cost about $45, $40, and $35, respectively. Call for the schedule. Charter boats also line up along the dock here.

In the old fishing village of Cortez, at the east end of the Cortez Bridge opposite Bradenton Beach, you can go deep-sea fishing with the **Cortez Fleet,** 4330 127th St. W. (© **941/794-1223**). Party-boat deep-sea fishing voyages range from 4 to 9 hours, with prices starting at $28 for adults, $25 for seniors, and $14 for children. Call for the schedules, which can change from day to day.

You also can fish for free from **Anna Maria City Pier,** on the north end of Anna Maria Island; and at the **Bradenton Beach City Pier,** at Cortez Road.

GOLF The **Bobby Jones Golf Complex** ★, 1000 Circus Blvd. (© **941/365-GOLF**), is Sarasota's only municipal facility, but it has two 18-hole championship layouts—the American (par-71) and British (par-72) courses—and the nine-hole Gillespie executive course (par-30). Tee times are assigned 3 days in advance. Greens fees range from $25 to $35, including cart rental.

The semi-private **Rolling Green Golf Club,** 4501 Tuttle Ave. (© **941/355-6620**), is an 18-hole, par-72 course. Facilities include a driving range, rental clubs, and lessons. Tee times are assigned 2 days in advance. Prices, including cart, are about $50 in winter, $30 off-season. Also semi-private, the **Sarasota Golf Club,** 7820 N. Leewynn Dr. (© **941/371-2431**), is an 18-hole, par-72 course. Facilities include a driving range, lessons, club rentals, a restaurant, a lounge, and a golf shop. Fees, including cart, are about $45 in winter, $30 off-season.

If you have reciprocal privileges, **University Park Country Club,** west of I-75 on University Parkway (© **941/359-9999**), is Sarasota's only nationally ranked course.

In Bradenton, locals prefer the county's 18-hole, par-72 **Buffalo Creek Golf Course,** on the north side of the river at 8100 Erie Rd. in Palmetto (© **941/776-2611**). At well over 7,000 yards, it's the longest in the area, and lots of water and alligators will keep you entertained. Wintertime greens fees are about $35 with cart, $25 without. They drop to about $30 and $20, respectively, during summer. You'll pay the same at **Manatee County Golf Course,** 5290 66th St. W. (© **941/792-6773**), an 18-hole, par-72 course on the southern rim of the city. Both county courses require that tee times be set up at least 2 days in advance. Also open to the public, the city's **River Run Golf Links,** 1801 27th St. E. (© **941/747-6331**), set beside the Braden River, is an 18-hole, par-70 course with lots of water in its layout. Winter fees here are about $26 with cart, $17 walking. They're about $16 riding, $8 walking in summer. A 2-day advance notice is required for tee times here too.

Bradenton is home to the well-known **David Leadbetter Golf Academy,** 1414 69th Ave., at U.S. 41 (© **800/424-3542** or 941/739-2483; www.leadbetter.com), a part of the Nick Bollettieri Sports Academy (see "Tennis," below). Presided over by one of golf's leading instructors, this facility offers practice tee instruction, video analysis, and scoring strategy, as well as general tuition. Call for current rates.

KAYAKING Based at Mote Aquarium (see "Exploring the Area," below), **Sarasota Bay Explorers** ★★ (© **941/388-4200**; www.sarasotabayexplorers.com), uses a 38-foot pontoon boat to ferry both novice and experienced kayakers and their craft to a marine sanctuary, where everyone paddles through tunnels formed by mangroves. The paddling is easy and the waters are shallow. Experienced naturalists serve as guides. Wear swimsuits and tennis shoes or rubber-soled booties, and bring a towel and lunch. The 3-hour trips cost $50 for adults, $40 for children 5 to 17, and is free for kids under 5 (seats are provided for the youngsters). Reservations are required.

SAILING "Rag-haulers" will enjoy a leisurely cruise on the waters of both Sarasota Bay and the Gulf of Mexico aboard the 41-foot, 12-passenger sailboat ***Enterprise,*** docked at Marina Jack's Marina, U.S. 41 at Island Park Circle (© **888/232-7763** or 941/951-1833; www.sarasotaboating.com/sailingcharters.html). Cruises range from 2 hours for $35 per person to 4 hours for $55 a head, while sunset cruises cost $35 per person. Departure times vary, and reservations are required. **Siesta Key Sailing,** 1219 Southport Dr. (© **941/346-7245**; www.siestakeysailing.com), charges the same for similar cruises in a 42-foot Morgan Outlander sloop. Reservations are essential.

You can also get to historic Egmont Key, 3 miles off the northern end of Anna Maria Island at the mouth of Tampa Bay (see "Cruises," under "Affordable Outdoor Activities," in section 3 of this chapter, for more information), on a 30-foot sloop-rigged sailboat with **Spice Sailing Charters** (© **941/778-3240**), based at the Galati Yacht Basin on Bay Boulevard on northern Anna Maria Island. The company also has sunset cruises. Call for schedule, prices, and reservations, which are required.

SPECTATOR SPORTS **Ed Smith Stadium,** 2700 12th St., at Tuttle Avenue, east of downtown (© **941/954-4464**), is the winter home of the **Cincinnati Reds** (© **941/955-6501**; www.cincinnatireds.com), who hold spring training here in February and March. From April to August, the stadium is home to the **Sarasota Red Sox** (© **941/365-4460, ext. 2300**; www.sarasox.com), a Class A minor-league affiliate of the Boston Red Sox.

The **Pittsburgh Pirates** (© **941/748-4610**; www.pirateball.com) do their February-through-March spring training at 6,562-seat McKechnie Field, 9th Street West and 17th Avenue West, south of downtown Bradenton.

For more information on spring-training events, see the box, "The Boys of Spring," in chapter 2.

The **Sarasota Polo Club,** 8201 Polo Club Lane, Sarasota (© **941/359-0000**), at Lakewood Ranch, a planned community midway between Sarasota and Bradenton, is the site of weekly polo matches from November through March, on Sunday afternoons. General admission is $6, or free for children under 13. Call for the schedule of matches.

TENNIS   The **Nick Bollettieri Sports Academy,** 5500 34th St. W. in Bradenton (© **800/872-6425** or 941/755-1000; www.bollettieri.com), is one of the world's largest tennis training facilities, with more than 70 championship courts and a pro shop. It's open year-round, and reservations are required for all activities. You must be a student at the academy to play here; call for current programs and prices.

WATER SPORTS   You'll find water-sports activities in front of the major hotels out on the keys (see "Accommodations You Can Afford," later in this section). **Siesta Sports Rentals,** 6551 Midnight Pass Rd. on Siesta Key (© **813/346-1797**; www.siestasportsrentals.com), rents kayaks and sailboats, plus beach chairs and umbrellas. You can soar above the bay with **Siesta Parasail,** based at C. B.'s Saltwater Outfitters at the western end of the Stickney Point Bridge (© **877/591-0925** or 941/349-1900; www.siestaparasail.com).

EXPLORING THE AREA
In Sarasota

Art Center Sarasota   In addition to the marvelous John and Mable Ringling Museum of Art (see below), Sarasota is home to more than 40 art galleries and exhibition spaces, all open to the public year-round. A convenient artistic starting point is this downtown community art center, next to the Sarasota Convention and Visitors Bureau. It contains three galleries and a small sculpture garden, presenting the area's largest display of art by national and local artists, from paintings and pottery to sculpture, cartoons, jewelry, and enamelware. There are also art demonstrations and special events.

707 N. Tamiami Trail (at 6th St.). © 941/365-2032. Admission free ($2 suggested donation). Tues–Sat 10am–4pm; Sun noon–4pm.

FSU Ringling Center for the Cultural Arts ★★★   By far the top attraction here, this 60-acre site is where showman John Ringling and his wife, Mable, collected art and built houses on a grand scale. Now under the aegis of Florida State University, **The John and Mable Ringling Museum of Art** is the state's official art museum. It's filled with more than 500 years of European and American art, including one of the world's most important collections of grand 17th-century baroque paintings. The old-master collection includes five world-renowned tapestry cartoons by Peter Paul Rubens and his studio. The museum also contains collections of decorative arts and traveling exhibits.

Built in 1925 and modeled after a Venetian palace, the Ringlings' 30-room winter residence **Ca'd'Zan** ("House of John" in the Venetian dialect) has been closed recently for a substantial restoration; even if it has not reopened, a visit to the museums should be on your Sarasota agenda. An 8,000-square-foot terrace leads down to the dock at which Mable Ringling moored her Venetian gondola.

The **Ringling Museum of the Circus** is devoted to circus memorabilia including parade wagons, calliopes, costumes, and colorful posters.

The grounds also include a classical courtyard, a rose garden, a museum shop, and the historic **Asolo Theater,** a 19th-century Italian court playhouse, which the Ringlings moved here in the 1950s. It's now the centerpiece of the Florida State University Center for the Performing Arts. You'll need most of a day to see it all.

5401 Bay Shore Rd. at N. Tamiami Trail (U.S. 41). © 941/359-5700 or 941/351-1660 for recorded information. www.ringling.org. Admission $10 adults, $9 seniors, $5 out-of-state students; free for Florida students and all children 12 and under. Daily 10am–5:30pm. Closed New Year's Day, Thanksgiving, Christmas. From downtown, take U.S. 41 north to University Pkwy. and follow signs to museum.

Marie Selby Botanical Gardens   A must-see for serious plant lovers, this peaceful retreat on the bay just south of downtown is said to be the only botanical garden in the world specializing in the preservation, study, and research of epiphytes; that is, "air plants" such as orchids. It's home to more than 20,000 exotic plants, including more than 6,000 orchids, as well as a bamboo pavilion, a butterfly and hummingbird garden, a medicinal plant garden, a waterfall garden, a cactus and succulent garden, a fernery, a hibiscus garden, a palm grove, two tropical food gardens, and a native shore-plant community. Selby's home and the Payne Mansion (both on the National Registry) are also located here.

811 S. Palm Ave. (south of U.S. 41). © 941/366-5731. www.selby.org. Admission $10 adults, $5 children 6–11; free for children 5 and under accompanied by an adult. Daily 10am–5pm. Closed Christmas.

Sarasota Classic Car Museum   There's more to this museum than its 90-plus classic and "muscle" autos, from Rolls-Royces and Pierce Arrows to the four cars used personally by circus czar John Ringling. Also here are more than 1,200 antique music boxes and several of Thomas Edison's early phonographs, including a 1909 diamond-tipped needle model. Check out the Penny Arcade with antique games (with original prices), and grab a cone at the ice-cream and sandwich shop. In operation since 1953, this is now a nonprofit museum dedicated to preserving antique automobiles.

5500 N. Tamiami Trail (at University Pkwy.). © 941/355-6228. www.sarasotacarmuseum.org. Admission $8.50 adults, $7.65 seniors, $5.75 children 13–17, $4 children 6–12; free for children under 6. Daily 9am–6pm. Take U.S. 41 north of downtown; museum is 2 blocks west of the airport.

Sarasota Jungle Gardens *Kids*   If you don't mind black Asian leopards, squirrel monkeys, and other animals going stir-crazy in cages, you and the kids should enjoy this commercial park's lush tropical vegetation, cool jungle trails, tropical plants, alligators and other reptiles, and exotic waterfowl including a resident flock of pink flamingoes. Children like the petting zoo, pony rides, and bird and animal shows, too (call for a show schedule).

3701 Bay Shore Rd. © 941/355-5305. www.sarasotajunglegardens.com. Admission $10 adults, $9 seniors, $6 children 3–12; free for children 2 and under. Daily 9am–5pm. Closed Christmas. From downtown, take U.S. 41 north to Myrtle St., turn left, and go 2 blocks.

> *Tips* **How to See the Ringling Museums**
>
> It's best to visit the FSU Ringling Center for the Cultural Arts on a weekday when you can take guided tours. Call ahead or check at the information desk as soon as you arrive for tour times. You can take the art museum tour in the morning and tour the circus museum in the afternoon, or vice versa. In between you can explore the gardens and have lunch at The Banyan Cafe.

On St. Armands Key

Mote Aquarium ★★ *Kids* Kids get to touch cool stuff like a stingray (minus the stinger, of course) and watch sharks in the shark tank at this excellent aquarium. Part of the noted Mote Marine Laboratory complex, it is more broad-based than Tampa's Florida Aquarium, which concentrates primarily on local sea life. The kids won't believe all the seahorse babies that come from the dad's pouch (one of Mother Nature's strange-but-true surprises), and they surely will gawk at a 35-foot-long deceased giant squid (it was 45 feet long when alive). They can see manatees in the Marine Mammal Center, a block's walk from the aquarium. There are also many research-in-progress exhibits. Start by watching the aquarium's 12-minute film on the feeding habits of sharks; then allow at least 90 minutes to take in everything on land. Add another 2 hours to take a narrated sea-life encounter cruise with **The Sarasota Bay Explorers** (② **727/388-4200;** www.sarasotabayexplorers.com). These fun and informative cruises visit a deserted island, and the guides throw out nets and bring up sea life for inspection. It's a good idea to make reservations for the cruise a day in advance. This company has unusual kayaking adventures too (see "Affordable Outdoor Activities," above).

1600 Ken Thompson Pkwy. (on City Island). ② **800/691-MOTE** or 941/388-2541. www.mote.org. Admission $12 adults, $8 children 4–12; free for children under 4. Nature cruises $24 adults, $20 children 4–12; free for kids under 4. Combination aquarium-cruise tickets $30 adults, $25 children. Daily 10am–5pm. Nature cruises daily 11am, 1:30pm, and 4pm. From St. Armands Circle, go north toward Longboat Key; turn right just before the Lido-Longboat bridge.

Pelican Man's Bird Sanctuary Next to the Mote Aquarium (see above), this sanctuary and rehabilitation center treats more than 5,000 injured birds and other wildlife each year. It is home to more than 50 species of birds. Allow about 30 minutes to see it all, a few more to check out the gift shop with many bird-oriented items for sale.

1708 Ken Thompson Pkwy. ② 941/388-4444. www.pelicanman.org. Admission $4 adults; free for children 18 and under. Daily 10am–5pm.

In & Near Bradenton

DeSoto National Memorial Nestled on the Manatee River west of downtown, this park attracts history buffs by re-creating the look and atmosphere of the period when Spanish explorer Hernando de Soto landed here in 1539. It includes a restoration of de Soto's original campsite and a scenic half-mile nature trail that circles a mangrove jungle and leads to the ruins of one of the first settlements in the area. Start by watching a 21-minute film about de Soto in America. From December to March, park employees dress in 16th-century costumes and portray the way the early settlers lived, including demonstrations of cooking and the firing of an arquebus, one of the world's earliest firearms.

DeSoto Memorial Hwy. (north end of 75th St. W.). ② **941/792-0458.** www.nps.gov/deso. Free admission. Daily 9am–5pm. Take Manatee Ave. (Fla. 64) west to 75th St. W. and turn right; follow the road to its end and the entrance to the park.

Gamble Plantation Situated northeast of downtown Bradenton, this is the oldest structure on the southwestern coast of Florida, and a fine example of an antebellum plantation home. Built over a 6-year period in the late 1840s by Major Robert Gamble, it was constructed primarily of "tabby mortar" (a mixture of oyster shells, sand, molasses, and water), with 10 rooms, verandas on three sides, 18 exterior columns, and eight fireplaces. Maintained as a state historic site, it includes a fine collection of 19th-century furnishings. Entrance to

Milky White Stallions

Horse lovers are drawn to the famous **Lipizzaner Stallions,** who do their spectacular leaps at the Ottomar Herrmann training grounds, 32755 Singletary Rd., Myakka City (© **941/322-1501**), from late December through March (they tour the country the rest of the year). Members of a now-rare breed, the parents of these milky white stallions were brought here from Austria in the 1960s by Colonel Ottomar Herrmann. Their *haute école* performances are straight from Vienna's famous Spanish Riding School. Call for a schedule and directions. Admission is by donation.

---

the house is by tour only, although you can explore the grounds on your own. The Prime Outlets Ellenton is a 5-minute drive from here via U.S. 301, so you can combine a plantation visit with some bargain hunting (see "Great Window & Discount Shopping," below).

3708 Patten Ave. (U.S. 301), Ellenton. © 941/723-4536. www.dep.state.fl.us/parks/district4/gamble plantation. Free admission. Tours $4 adults, $2 children 6–12; free for children under 6. Thurs–Mon 9am–4:30pm; 30-min. guided house tour 9:30 and 10:30am, and 1, 2, 3, and 4pm. Take U.S. 301 north of downtown to Ellenton; the site is on the left just east of Ellenton-Gillette Rd. (Fla. 683).

South Florida Museum and Parker Manatee Aquarium *Kids* If you haven't seen manatees in the wild, the star at this downtown complex is "Snooty," the oldest manatee born in captivity (1948) and Manatee County's official mascot. Snooty and his pal "Mo" live in the **Parker Manatee Aquarium.** The South Florida Museum tells the story of Florida's history, from prehistoric times to the present, including a Native American collection with life-size dioramas and a Spanish courtyard containing replicas of 16th-century buildings. (Fire recently damaged the museum's Bishop Planetarium, which is now closed.)

201 10th St. W. (on the riverfront, at Barcarrota Blvd.). © 941/746-4131. www.southfloridamuseum.org. Admission $7.50 adults, $6 seniors, $4 children 5–12; free for children 4 and under. Jan–Apr and July Mon–Sat 10am–5pm; Sun noon–5pm. Rest of year Tues–Sat 10am–5pm; Sun noon–5pm. Closed New Year's Day, Thanksgiving, and Christmas. From U.S. 41, take Manatee Ave. west to 10th St. W. and turn right.

A NEARBY STATE PARK WITH A WILD & SCENIC RIVER

About 20 miles southeast of Sarasota, the **Myakka River State Park**, on Fla. 72 about 9 miles east of I-75, is Florida's largest, covering more than 35,000 acres flanking 14 miles of the Myakka River, one of two official Wild and Scenic Rivers in the state. It's an outstanding wildlife sanctuary and breeding ground, home to hundreds of species of plants and animals, including alligators. There are 39 miles of backcountry trails and boardwalks, including one snaking high up in the treetops, giving great views over the surrounding wetlands, prairies, and dense woodlands. The park is open daily from 8am to sunset. Admission is $4 per car with two to eight occupants, $2 for car with driver, or $1 per pedestrian or bicyclist. You can stay out here in a campground or in five log cabins built by the Civilian Conservation Corps during the Great Depression (they now have air-conditioners, electric stoves, refrigerators, and hot-water showers). Campsites cost $13 a night from May to November, $16 from December to April (plus $2 for electricity year-round). Cabins rent for $55 a night year-round. For camping reservations call © **800/326-3521** or go to the website www.reserveamerica.com. For more information about the park, contact the headquarters at 13207 S.R. 72, Sarasota, FL 34241 (© **941/361-6511;** www.dep.state.fl.us/parks/district4/myakkariver).

The best and certainly easiest ways to see the park are on 1-hour-long nature "safaris" by boat or tram with **Myakka Wildlife & Nature Tours** (© **941/ 365-0100**). The boat tours onto Myakka Lake are in the world's largest airboat, while on land, the tram tours take you into the wilderness where other vehicles aren't allowed. Either excursion costs $8 for adults, $4 for children 6 to 12, and is free for kids 5 and under. Call for the schedules, which change seasonally. Reservations are not accepted, so buy your tickets at the camp store as soon as you arrive.

GREAT WINDOW & DISCOUNT SHOPPING

Visitors come from all over the world to shop at **St. Armands Circle**, on St. Armands Key. Wander around this outdoor circle of more than 150 international boutiques, gift shops, galleries, restaurants, and nightspots, all surrounded by lush landscaping, patios, and antiques. Pick up a map at the Sarasota Convention and Visitors Bureau (see "Essentials," earlier in this section). Many shops here are comparable to those in Palm Beach and on Naples's Third Avenue South, so check your credit-card limits—or resort to some great window-shopping.

For great discount shopping, head out to **Prime Outlets Ellenton,** on U.S. 301 at Exit 43 off I-75 in Ellenton (© **941/723-1150**), about a 15-minute drive northeast of downtown Bradenton (turn left at the first stoplight east of I-75). This sprawling, Spanish-style outdoor center has more than 100 factory and outlet stores. They are open Monday to Saturday from 10am to 9pm and Sunday from 11am to 6pm.

ACCOMMODATIONS YOU CAN AFFORD

Most visitors stay out at the beaches, but cost-conscious travelers will find some good deals on the mainland, such as the **Best Western Midtown,** 1425 S. Tamiami Trail (U.S. 41), at Prospect Street (© **800/722-8527** or 941/955-9841; fax 941/954-8948; www.bwmidtown.com). This older but well-maintained motel is 2 miles in either direction from the main causeways leading to the keys. Winter rates are $119 for a double room, dropping to $79 off-season.

In addition, you'll find the **Comfort Inn** (© **800/228-5150** or 941/355-7091), **Days Inn Airport** (© **800/329-7466** or 941/355-9271), and **Hampton Inn** (© **800/336-9335** or 941/351-7734) standing side by side on Tamiami Trail (U.S. 41) just south of the airport and near the Ringling Museums and the Asolo Center for the Performing Arts. All are of recent vintage and thoroughly modern. A **Courtyard by Marriott** (© **800/321-2211** or 941/355-3337) and the **Sleep Inn** (© **800/627-5447** or 941/359-8558) are nearby on University Parkway opposite the airport. The **Wellesley Inn & Suites,** 1803 N. Tamiami Trail (U.S. 41, at 18th St.; © **800/444-8888** or 941/366-5128), is the closest chain motel to downtown.

The annual visitors' guides published by the Sarasota Convention and Visitors Bureau and the Bradenton Area Convention and Visitors Bureau (see "Essentials," earlier in this section) are good starting points for finding other

Tips Car Smarts

Parking on or near St. Armands Circle can be scarce as hen's teeth, and if you can find a spot, on-street parking is limited to 3 hours. Your best bets are the free, unrestricted lots on Adams Drive at Monroe and Madison drives.

options such as condos and cottages. Among the rental agencies requiring stays of less than a month are **Argus Property Management,** 1200 Siesta Bayside, Sarasota, FL 34242 (C 800/237-2252 or 941/346-3499; fax 941/349-6156; www.argusmgmt.com); and **Florida Vacation Accommodations,** 4030 Gulf of Mexico Dr., Longboat Key, FL 34228 (C 800/237-9505 or 941/383-9505; fax 941/383-1830; www.vacationinfl.com).

The Bradenton Area Convention and Visitors Bureau operates a free **reservation service** (C 800/4-MANATEE). The bureau also publishes a list of Superior Small Lodgings, clean and comfortable properties with no more than 50 rooms (see "Tips on Accommodations" in chapter 2, "Planning an Affordable Trip to Florida").

The high season here is from January to April. Rates are usually higher along the beaches at all times, so bargain hunters should stick to the downtown area and commute to the beach—or stay on Anna Maria Island. The hotel tax here is 9%.

ON LIDO KEY
Worth a Splurge

Half Moon Beach Club   Near the south end of Lido, this two-story Art Deco–style hotel is right on the beach and less than half a block from South Lido Beach Park. The front of the building forms a circle around a small but very attractive courtyard with a heated pool and sunning area. From there, guests take a hallway through a motel-style block of spacious rooms to the beach, where they can rent cabanas and order drinks to be delivered from the bar inside. All units have balconies or patios, some have kitchenettes with microwave ovens, but only the four beachfront rooms have gulf views.

2050 Ben Franklin Dr. (at Taft Dr.), Sarasota, FL 34236. C **800/358-3245** or 941/388-3694. Fax 941/388-1938. www.halfmoon-lidokey.com. 85 units. Winter $144–$274 double; off-season $124–$194 double. AE, DC, DISC, MC, V. **Amenities:** Restaurant (American); bar; heated outdoor pool; water-sports equipment rental; bike rental; limited room service; coin-op washers and dryers. *In room:* A/C, TV, dataport, kitchen, fridge, coffeemaker, hair dryer, iron.

Holiday Inn Lido Beach   Conveniently located at the north end of Lido, this modern seven-story hotel is within walking distance of St. Armands Circle. Unfortunately, the beach across the street (you'll have to dodge the traffic) isn't the best stretch of sand here. The motel-style bedrooms have balconies that face the gulf or the bay, and the rooftop restaurant and lounge offer panoramic views of the Gulf of Mexico.

233 Ben Franklin Dr. (at Thoreau Dr.), Sarasota, FL 34236. C **800/HOLIDAY** or 941/388-5555. Fax 941/388-4321. 135 units. Winter $180–$210 double; off-season $129–$210 double. AE, DC, MC, V. **Amenities:** Restaurant (American), 2 bars; heated outdoor pool; access to nearby health club; exercise room; water-sports equipment rental; bike rental; limited room service; babysitting; laundry service; coin-op washers and dryers; concierge-level rooms. *In room:* A/C, TV, dataport, fridge, coffeemaker, hair dryer, iron.

ON SIESTA KEY

Captiva Beach Resort *Value*   Owners Robert and Jane Ispaso have substantially upgraded and improved this older property in the Stickney Point business district, about half a block from the beach on a narrow, closely packed circle populated by other small motels. Every one of the comfortable, sparkling-clean units here has some form of cooking facility, and some have separate living rooms with sleeper sofas. These are older buildings, so you'll find window air-conditioners mounted through the walls, and shower-only bathrooms in some units. It's very popular with longer-term guests during winter. You'll get fresh towels daily but maid service only once a week. This and the circle's other motels share a common pool area, and guests get complimentary use of beach towels, chairs, and umbrellas. Several restaurants are a short walk away.

6772 Sara Sea Circle, Siesta Key, FL 34242. © **800/349-4131** or 941/349-4131. Fax 941/349-8141. www.captivabeachresort.com. 20 units (some with shower only). Winter $130–$245; off-season $85–$180. Weekly and monthly rates available. AE, DISC, MC, V. **Amenities:** Heated outdoor pool; coin-op washers and dryers. *In room:* A/C, TV, kitchen, coffeemaker, hair dryer.

ON ANNA MARIA ISLAND

Anna Maria's lone chain motel is the moderately priced **Econo Lodge Surfside**, 2502 Gulf Dr. N. (at 25th St. N.), Bradenton Beach, FL 34217 (© **800/55-ECONO** or 941/778-6671; fax 941/778-0360). This clean and well-maintained beachfront facility has 18 suites and 36 spacious rooms in its main three-story building, plus 18 rooms in another building on the beach and five more across the street (the latter are the least expensive).

The Beach Inn ★ Jo and Frank Davis, owners of the Harrington House (see below), have turned this two-story beachfront motel into a couples-oriented inn. The property has two buildings, one on the beach, the other to the rear facing a tropical courtyard. Beachfront rooms have fireplaces, raised Jacuzzi tubs, bar areas, small microwaves, king-size beds, and either upstairs balconies or downstairs spacious decks separated from the gulf by sea oats. The less expensive units in the rear building are less well equipped; they have two double beds. Bungalows and apartments in other buildings are available, too. There's no restaurant here, but guests receive complimentary continental breakfast.

101 66th St., Holmes Beach, FL 34217. © **800/823-2247** or 941/778-9597. Fax 941/778-8303. www.thebeachinn.com. 14 units (shower only). Winter $149–$209 double; off-season $99–$209 double. Rates include continental breakfast. MC, V. **Amenities:** Jacuzzi; coin-op washers and dryers. *In room:* A/C, TV, fridge, coffeemaker, hair dryer, iron.

Bungalow Beach Resort ★★ If you want an Old Florida–style bungalow by the beach, owners Bert and Gayle Luper have them at this romantic little complex. In fact, white-sand walkways join the beach to these bright and airy clapboard cottages, built in the 1930s and 1940s but considerably spiffed up in recent years with hardwood floors, bright tropical furniture, and ceiling fans. Ranging in size from efficiencies to three bedrooms, they all have cooking facilities and a deck or porch. A few have single-person whirlpool bathtubs. The five choice cottages open directly to the beach; the largest has a whirlpool bathtub with a steam maker, a full gourmet kitchen, and a deck. Three others are grouped around an outdoor swimming pool. There is no restaurant on the grounds, but several are within walking distance. No smoking is allowed in the units here.

2000 Gulf Dr. N. (between 17th and 22nd aves.), Bradenton Beach, FL 34217. © **800/779-3601** or 941/778-3600. Fax 941/778-1764. www.bungalowbeach.com. 15 units (some with shower only). Winter $134–$314 double; off-season $84–$254 double. AE, MC, V. **Amenities:** Heated outdoor pool; Jacuzzi; coin-op washers and dryers; concierge-level rooms. *In room:* A/C, TV, kitchen, coffeemaker, hair dryer.

Rod & Reel Motel Sitting beside the Rod & Reel Fishing Pier on Anna Maria Island's northeastern end, this basic but clean and well-maintained motel opens to a sandy beach with a great view of the Skyway Bridge across Tampa Bay. The one-story, L-shaped structure flanks a courtyard with barbecue grills and a large thatch-roof cabana for shady picnics. The two best rooms open directly to the beach, but four others have views across the courtyard to the bay. The units are smallish (as are their 1950s-vintage bathrooms), but they are bright and airy, and sport kitchenettes. You can walk out on the pier and have breakfast, lunch, or dinner at the Rod & Reel Pier Restaurant & Snack Bar (see "Great Deals on Dining," below).

877 N. Shore Dr. (P.O. Box 1939; at Allamanda St.), Anna Maria, FL 34216. ⓒ 941/778-2780. www.rodandreelmotel.com. 10 units (shower only). Winter $84–$119; off-season $60–$89. Minimum 1-week rental Feb–Apr. AE, DISC, MC, V. *In room:* A/C, TV, kitchen, coffeemaker, hair dryer.

Tropic Isle Inn *Value* Owners Bill and Heather Romberger have worked marvels in renovating and upgrading this older motel, across Gulf Drive from its own narrow strip of beach. They installed a high wall along the roadside, behind which you'll find a lushly landscaped courtyard surrounding a big tin-roof gazebo for lounging in the shade and a pool and brick patio for swimming and sunning. Most guest units open to the courtyard, and all have their own balconies or brick patios behind white fences. Three of the bright and airy units are standard motel rooms. The others are apartments with one or two bedrooms and living areas with kitchens. Restaurants are within walking distance. No smoking is allowed in the rooms.

2103 Gulf Dr. N. (at 22nd St.), Bradenton Beach, FL 34217. ⓒ 800/883-4092 or 941/778-1237. Fax 941/778-7821. www.annamariaisland.com. 15 units (some with shower only). Winter $119–$275; off-season $89–$235. Rates include evening reception. Weekly rates available. Minimum 3-night stay Feb–Apr. AE, DISC, MC, V. **Amenities:** Heated outdoor pool; free washers and dryers. *In room:* A/C, TV, dataport, kitchen, coffeemaker.

Worth a Splurge
Harrington House ★★ Flowers will be awaiting when you arrive at Jo and Frank Davis's exceptional bed-and-breakfast. In a tree-shaded setting on the beach overlooking the gulf, this three-story coquina-and-rock house was built in 1925 and exudes an Old Florida ambience. The eight bedrooms are individually decorated with antique, wicker, or rattan furnishings. Some units have four-poster or brass beds, Jacuzzis, fireplaces, and French doors leading to balconies overlooking the gulf. In addition to the bedrooms in the main house, four rooms are available in the adjacent Spangler Beach House, a remodeled 1940s captain's home, and four more are in the nearby Huth House, a beachside residence. Three units in the latter open to an expansive covered lanai facing the beach through a row of Australian pines. All guests enjoy use of the main house's high-ceilinged living room with fireplace, beachside pool, patio, and complimentary use of bicycles, kayaks, and other sports equipment. No smoking is allowed inside here.

5626 Gulf Dr. (at 58th St.), Holmes Beach, FL 34217. ⓒ 888/828-5566 or 941/778-5444. Fax 941/778-0527. www.harringtonhouse.com. 14 units. Winter $189–$329 double; off-season $149–$289. Rates include full breakfast. MC, V. No children under 12 allowed. **Amenities:** Heated outdoor pool; complimentary use of sports equipment. *In room:* A/C, TV, hair dryer.

GREAT DEALS ON DINING
DOWNTOWN SARASOTA
Downtown's best breakfast spot is the local branch of **First Watch,** 1395 Main St., at Central and Pineapple avenues (ⓒ **941/954-1395**). Like its siblings in Naples (see "Great Deals on Dining" in section 4 of chapter 9, "Southwest Florida") and elsewhere, First Watch offers a wide variety of inexpensive breakfast and lunch fare. It's open daily from 7:30am to 2:30pm. If the wait's too long, walk south along Central Avenue; this block has several coffeehouses and cafes with sidewalk seating.

There's an inexpensive **Shells** seafood restaurant at 7253 S. Tamiami Trail (U.S. 41), south of downtown in the vicinity of Sarasota Square Mall (ⓒ **941/924-2568**). See "Great Deals on Dining," in section 1 of this chapter, for details about this inexpensive chain. You'll also find most of the national chain fast-food and family restaurants nearby along U.S. 41.

Marina Jack SEAFOOD/CONTINENTAL   Overlooking the waterfront with a wraparound 270° view of Sarasota Bay and Siesta and Lido keys, this establishment has spectacular water vistas and a carefree "on vacation" attitude, especially on the open-air raw bar deck, which often is packed all afternoon on weekends and at sunset every day. The food is good but not the best in town, so come here for a relaxing, fun time. You may have to wait for a table or barstool down on the deck, but be sure to make reservations if you want to have a meal in the upstairs dining room. Fresh local seafood is the star both upstairs and down—grilled grouper is your best bet. The downstairs lounge and raw bar also serves sandwiches and burgers.

In Island Park, Bayfront at Central Ave. © **941/365-4232.** Reservations recommended in dining room. Dining room main courses $15–$30. Deck main courses $14–$17; sandwiches and salads $8–$11. AE, DISC, MC, V. Daily 11:30am–2am. Closed Christmas.

Patrick's AMERICAN/PUB FARE   With a semicircular facade, this upscale, polished-oak and brass-rail sports bar offers wide-windowed views of downtown's main intersection. The menu offers very good pub fare: steaks and chops, burgers, seafood, pastas, small pizzas, salads, sandwiches, and omelets. Other entrees include broiled salmon with dill-hollandaise sauce, sesame chicken, and veal done three ways—piccata, Française, or marsala. There's a good happy hour here Monday to Friday between 5 and 7pm.

1400 Main St. (at Pineapple Ave. and Main St.). © **941/952-1170.** Main courses $14–$21; sandwiches and burgers $7–$9. AE, DC, DISC, MC, V. Daily 11am–midnight; Sun brunch 11am–3pm. Closed Christmas.

Yoder's *Value* AMISH/AMERICAN   Just 3 miles east of downtown Sarasota is an award-winning, value eatery operated by an Amish family (Sarasota and Bradenton have sizable Amish communities and several other Amish restaurants). Evoking the Pennsylvania Dutch country, the simple dining room displays handcrafts, photos, and paintings celebrating the Amish way. The menu emphasizes plain, made-from-scratch cooking such as home-style meat loaf, baked and Southern fried chicken, country-smoked ham, and fried filet of flounder. Burgers, salads, soups, and sandwiches are also available. Leave room for Mrs. Yoder's traditional shoo-fly and other homemade pies, one of the biggest draws here. There's neither alcohol nor smoking here.

3434 Bahia Vista St. (west of Beneva Rd.). © **941/955-7771.** Main courses $6–$12; breakfast $2–$6; sandwiches and burgers $3–$6. No credit cards (ATM machine on premises). Mon–Sat 6am–8pm.

Worth a Splurge

Bijou Cafe INTERNATIONAL   Chef Jean-Pierre Knaggs prepares award-winning cuisines from around the world in his cafe in the heart of the theater district. Although the more casual Michael's on East (see below) bistro draws a hefty after-theater crowd, this is the best place to dine within walking distance of the downtown entertainment venues. Jean-Pierre artfully presents the likes of prime veal Louisville (with crushed pecans and bourbon-pear sauce), pan-seared crab cakes served under a remoulade and over a bed of fresh greens, and gently simmered lamb shanks with rosemary and garlic. His outstanding wine list has won accolades from *Wine Spectator* magazine.

1287 1st St. (at Pineapple Ave.). © **941/366-8111.** Reservations recommended. Main courses $15–$30. AE, DC, MC, V. Mon–Sat 11:30am–2pm and 5–10pm; Sun 5–10pm. Closed Sun June–Dec. Free valet parking nightly in winter, on weekends off-season.

Michael's on East ★★ CREATIVE INTERNATIONAL   At the rear of the Midtown Plaza shopping center on U.S. 41 south of downtown, Michael Klauber's chic bistro is one of the top places here for fine dining and is the locals' favorite after-theater haunt. Huge cut-glass walls create three intimate dining areas, one a piano bar for pre- or after-dinner drinks. Prepared with fresh ingredients and a creative flair, the offerings here will tempt your taste buds. House specialties are the slightly spicy Louisiana-style crab cakes; pan-seared Chilean sea bass with couscous and artichoke hearts in a thyme-accented tomato coulis; and grilled duck breast with napa cabbage, sweet potato, and smoked bacon in an apple-cider reduction.

1212 East Ave. S. (between Bahia and Prospect sts.). © 941/366-0007. Reservations recommended. Main courses $19–$36. AE, DC, DISC, MC, V. Winter Mon–Fri 11:30am–2pm; Sat 5:30–10pm; Sun 6–10pm. Off-season Mon–Fri 11:30am–2pm; Mon–Sat 6–10pm. Complimentary valet parking.

IN SOUTHSIDE VILLAGE

Sarasota's hottest dining spot is **Southside Village,** centered on South Osprey Avenue between Hyde Park and Hillview streets, about 15 blocks south of downtown. Here you'll find several hip restaurants, including Fred's and Pacific Rim (see below). The village landmark is **Morton's Gourmet Market** ★, 1924 S. Osprey Ave. (© **941/955-9856**), which offers a multitude of deli items, specialty sandwiches, a ton of fresh salads, freshly baked pastries and desserts, and cooked meals dispensed from a cafeteria-style steam table. You dine picnic-fashion on sidewalk tables outside. Most ready-to-go items cost less than $7. It's open Monday to Saturday 8am to 8pm and Sunday 10am to 5pm.

Fred's ★ INTERNATIONAL   Directly across the avenue from Morton's Gourmet Market, Fred's is one of the city's biggest gathering places for single professionals, especially on Friday night. They have plenty of space to spread out in several dining rooms and bars, all accented with dark wood and etched glass. The fare, although often second on everyone's mind, consists of well-seasoned pizzas and main courses such as pan-seared tuna with Japanese noodles in a basil and lemongrass broth. There's even old-fashioned chicken pot pie and an open-face meat-loaf sandwich with a wild mushroom ragout to clearly set it apart from your mother's. You can sample selections from the extensive wine list in a cigar-bar–style tasting room, then buy a bottle at the adjoining liquor store.

1917 S. Osprey Ave. (between Hyde Park and Hillview sts.). © 941/364-5811. Main courses $10–$28; pizza $8–$10. AE, DC, DISC, MC, V. Mon–Thurs 11am–10pm; Fri–Sat 11am–11:30pm; Sun 11am–9pm.

Pacific Rim ★ *Value* JAPANESE/THAI   Sarasotans love this chic and very casual restaurant for exceptional cuisine at economical prices. Japanese influence is felt at the authentic sushi bar along one side of the dining room, while Thai spices make a strong impact on the regular menu. We found the chargrilled shrimp with Thai curry and coconut milk sauce especially tasty, as was the combination of chicken and vegetables stir-fried in the wok. Here you can select your meat and vegetables separately from the sauce and the chefs will combine them on the grill, in the wok, or in the bowl (as in rice dishes).

In Hillview Centre, 1859 Hillview St. (between Osprey Ave. and Laurent Place). © 941/330-8071. Main courses $7.50–$15. AE, DISC, MC, V. Mon–Thurs 11:30am–2pm and 5–9pm; Fri 11:30am–2pm and 5–10pm; Sat 5–10pm.

ON ST. ARMANDS KEY

Plan to spend at least one evening at St. Armands Circle. The nighttime scene here is like a fair, with locals and visitors alike strolling around the circle, poking

> **Tips** **Chocoholic Heaven**
>
> Instead of ordering dessert after your meal on St. Armands Circle, wander on over to **Kilwin's**, 312 John Ringling Blvd. (© **941/388-3200**), for some gourmet chocolate, Mackinac Island fudge, or ice cream or yogurt in a homemade waffle cone. It's open Sunday to Thursday until 10:30pm and Friday and Saturday until 11pm.

their heads into a few stores, which stay open after dark, and window-shopping the others. It's fun and safe, so come early and plan to stay late. See "Great Window & Discount Shopping," above, for parking tips.

There's a branch of Tampa's famous **Columbia** (see "Great Deals on Dining" in section 1 of this chapter) on St. Armands Circle between John Ringling Boulevard and John Ringling Parkway (© **941/388-3987**). The Spanish food is excellent, there's outdoor seating, and the Patio Lounge is one of the liveliest spots here for evening entertainment from Thursday to Sunday.

Like its sibling in Naples (see "Great Deals on Dining" in section 4 of chapter 9), the local edition of **Tommy Bahama's Tropical Cafe,** 300 John Ringling Blvd. (© **941/388-2888**), draws a lively crowd of young professionals to its moderately priced seafood. It's upstairs over Tommy Bahama's clothing store.

Super-Cheap Eats

Blue Dolphin Cafe *Value* AMERICAN/DINER   On the John Ringling Boulevard spoke of St. Armands Circle, Jill and Rob Ball's informal diner is this affluent area's best inexpensive place to have breakfast, and they are a font of free information, too. They serve standard breakfast fare as well as fresh crab or lobster Benedict, fresh raspberry pancakes, and pecan-peach waffles. Lunchtime highlights are homemade soups and grouper sandwiches. You can order breakfast anytime. The Blue Dolphin is open for dinner on Friday nights during the winter season, offering the likes of flaky-crust chicken pot pie, slow-roasted prime rib, and spicy crab cakes.

470 John Ringling Blvd. (1 block off St. Armands Circle). © **941/388-3566.** Breakfast $4.50–$10; sandwiches, burgers, salads $5–$10. AE, DC, DISC, MC, V. Daily 7am–3pm.

Hungry Fox AMERICAN   This upstairs restaurant is the only place on St. Armands Circle offering three relatively inexpensive meals a day year-round. It's not much to look at inside, with marble-look tables and plastic lawn chairs, so wait for a table out on the veranda, especially next to the railing where you can oversee all the action down below. Breakfast, which is served until noon, offers everything from lox and bagels to Virginia ham and eggs. Sandwiches and salads appear at lunch, followed by steaks, chicken, pastas, and spicy jambalaya for dinner. Most items are good value for the price, but stay away from anything cooked in the deep fryer.

419 St. Armands Circle (above Cha Cha Coconuts). © **941/388-2222.** Main courses $11–$17; sandwiches, burgers, salads $4.50–$9; breakfast $4.50–$10. AE, DISC, MC, V. Mon–Sat 8am–9pm; Sun 8am–2:30pm.

Worth a Splurge

Cafe l'Europe ★★ CONTINENTAL   As its name implies, a European atmosphere prevails at this consistently excellent restaurant, the best place on the circle for fine dining. You can ask for a table out on the sidewalk, but brick walls and arches, dark woods, brass fixtures, pink linens, and hanging plants all lend an elegant ambience indoors. The menu offers selections ranging from a bouillabaisse in a piquant pepper broth to a veal tenderloin glazed with balsamic vinegar and served with a rich blackberry and port wine sauce. There's a wide choice of wines by the glass here.

431 St. Armands Circle (at John Ringling Blvd.). ⓒ 941/388-4415. Reservations recommended. Main courses $18–$36. AE, DC, DISC, MC, V. Daily 11am–3:30pm and 5–10pm.

Hemingway's FLORIDIAN/CARIBBEAN For a casual spot with an eclectic Floribbean menu and a large bar with a friendly, laid-back Key West ambience, take the elevator or climb the winding stairs to this second-floor hideaway. Hemingway's is a charming and comfortable combination of good food and Old Florida tradition. You can dine inside or on one of two second-floor balconies.

325 John Ringling Blvd. (a half block off St. Armands Circle). ⓒ 941/388-3948. Reservations recommended on weekends. Main courses $16–$22. AE, DC, DISC, MC, V. Sun–Thurs 11:30am–10pm; Fri–Sat 11:30am–11pm.

SIESTA KEY

Ocean Boulevard, which runs through **Siesta Village,** the area's funky, laid-back beach hangout, is virtually lined with restaurants and pubs, including Blasé Café (see below). Most have outdoor seating and bars, which attract the beach crowd during the day. At night rock-and-roll bands draw teenagers and college students to this lively scene.

Turtles AMERICAN With tropical overtones and breathtaking water vistas across from Turtle Beach, this informal restaurant on Little Sarasota Bay has tables both indoors and on an outside deck. Unique seafood offerings include snapper New Orleans and potato-encrusted mahimahi. You can't go wrong ordering grouper grilled, broiled, blackened, or fried. There's also a selection of pastas on the menu. The economical early bird specials offer several choices ranging from a medium-sized portion of mahimahi to spicy Szechwan shrimp.

8875 Midnight Pass Rd. (at Turtle Beach Rd.). ⓒ 941/346-2207. Call for preferred seating. Main courses $11–$19; salads and sandwiches $7–$15; early bird specials $9–$11. AE, DISC, MC, V. Mon–Sat 11:30am–9:30pm; Sun 10am–9pm. Early bird specials daily 4–6pm.

Super-Cheap Eats

Blasé Café *Finds* INTERNATIONAL One of Florida's most unusual restaurants, Ralph and Cindy Cole's super-casual establishment has tables indoors and a few under the cover of the Village Corner shopping center's walkway, but most are alfresco, on a wooden deck built around a palm tree in the center's asphalt parking lot. Never mind the cars pulling in and out virtually next to your chair: Ralph's food is so good that it draws droves of locals, who don't mind waiting for an umbrella table. This is the Siesta Key's best breakfast spot, offering Italian- and Louisiana-flavored frittatas as well as plain old bacon-and-eggs. Lunch sees burgers, big salads, and platters such as chicken Alfredo and Florentine crepes with shrimp. At night, Ralph puts forth the likes of pan-seared sushi-quality yellowfin tuna with tangy wasabi and pickled ginger. You can while away the rest of the evening in the wine bar, where the Coles have installed the original bar from the Don Cesar Beach Resort & Spa in St. Pete Beach. There's live music in there on weekends.

In Village Corner, 5263 Ocean Blvd. (at Calle Miramar), Siesta Village. ⓒ 941/349-9822. Reservations recommended. Main courses $11–$22; breakfast $5–$9; lunch $5–$9. MC, V. Mon–Thurs 8:30am–9:30pm; Fri–Sat 8:30am–10pm. Closed Mon June–Nov.

ON LONGBOAT KEY

Moore's Stone Crab SEAFOOD   Located in Longbeach, the old fishing village on the north end of Longboat Key, this popular bay-front restaurant began in 1967 as an offshoot of a family seafood business established 40 years earlier. From the outside, in fact, it still looks a little like a packing house, but the view of the bay dotted with mangrove islands makes a fine complement to stone crabs fresh from the family's own traps from October 15 to May 15. Otherwise, the menu offers an incredibly large variety of seafood, most of it fried or broiled. Sandwiches and salads are served all day.

800 Broadway (at Bayside Dr.). © **941/383-1748.** Main courses $9–$23; sandwiches and salads $7–$13. AE, DISC, MC, V. Winter daily 11:30am–9:30pm. Off-season Mon–Fri 4:30–9:30pm; Sat–Sun 11:30am–9:30pm.

ON ANNA MARIA ISLAND

The Beachhouse ⭐ AMERICAN   This large, lively place sits right on Bradenton Beach with a huge open deck and a covered pavilion facing out to the gulf. Even inside, wide windows let in the view. Owned by Ed Chiles, son of the late U.S. senator and Florida governor Lawton Chiles, the Beachhouse offers daily fresh fish, including the signature beechnut grouper (with nutty crust in citrus-butter sauce). There's also a good variety of fare, including seafood salads and pastas, crab cakes, fish and chips, and broiled steaks. Local musicians play on the patio most evenings.

200 Gulf Dr. N. (at Cortez Rd.), Bradenton Beach. © **941/779-2222.** Reservations not accepted, but call for preferred seating. Main courses $11–$18; sandwiches $6–$10. AE, DC, DISC, MC, V. Daily 11:30am–10pm.

Rotten Ralph's SEAFOOD/ENGLISH   On the north end of the island overlooking Bimini Bay, this casual pub has both indoor and outdoor seating right by the boats docked in the Anna Maria Yacht Basin. You can join the fishermen for breakfast here. Later in the day you can order pots of two dozen steamed oysters, clams, or crabs, or many other seafood choices from fried clam strips to sautéed scallops. Most fall in the moderate category, but you can eat all the British-style fish and chips (the house specialty) you can hold for $8. Other choices include baby back ribs and Anna Maria chicken (marinated and grilled with a honey-mustard sauce).

902 S. Bay Blvd., Anna Maria. © **941/778-3953.** Reservations not accepted. Main courses $8–$17 (all-you-can-eat fish-and-chips $8); sandwiches and burgers $6–$9; breakfast $3.50–$8. AE, DC, DISC, MC, V. Daily 7am–9pm. From Gulf Dr., turn toward the bay on Pine Ave.; take right at dead-end to the end of Bay Blvd.

Sandbar ⭐ SEAFOOD   Sitting on the site of the former Pavilion, built in 1913 when people from Tampa and St. Pete took the ferry here, this popular restaurant is perched right on the beach overlooking the gulf. The air-conditioned, knotty-pine dining room offers several traditional as well as innovative preparations of seafood (crab cakes with a Creole mustard sauce, for example). The real action here is under the umbrellas on the lively beachside deck, where appetizers, sandwiches, salads, and platters are served all day and night. Live music makes a party on the deck Monday to Friday nights and on Saturday and Sunday beginning at 1pm. The inside bar is one of the few we've seen in Florida with no sports TVs.

100 Spring Ave. (east of Gulf Dr.), Anna Maria. © **941/778-0444.** Reservations not accepted; call ahead to get on waiting list. Main courses $13–$19; salads and sandwiches $6–$10. AE, DC, DISC, MC, V. Daily 11:30am–10pm.

Super-Cheap Eats

Duffy's Tavern *Finds* PUB FARE   This little ramshackle pub, right off Manatee County Public Beach, serves icy cold beer and the island's hottest hamburgers. It looks like a dive from the outside, but you'll find everyone from state senators to construction workers at the bar and the tavern's few tables. License plates and baseball caps are nailed to every inch of the ceiling over the screened porch. Other than burgers, the menu is limited to sandwiches, navy bean soup, hot dogs, and chili. There's no table service, so order at the bar.

3901 Gulf Dr. (at Manatee Ave.), Holmes Beach. © 941/778-2501. Burgers and sandwiches $2.50–$4. No credit cards. Mon and Wed–Sat 11am–7pm; Sun noon–7pm. Closed 3 weeks in June and 3 weeks in Sept.

Gulf Drive Café ★★ *Value* AMERICAN   Locals flock to this bright gulf-side cafe for one of the best bargains on any beach in Florida. With big windows, bentwood cafe chairs with colorful cushions, and lots of hanging plants and ceiling fans, the coral and green dining room opens to a beachside patio with tables shaded by a trellis (the wait is worth it). The breakfast fare is led by sweet Belgian waffles, which are available all day. You can also order salads, sandwiches, and burgers anytime here, with quiche du jour, Mediterranean seafood pasta, and regular seafood platters joining the show at 4pm.

900 Gulf Dr. N. (at 9th St.), Bradenton Beach. © 941/778-1919. Reservations not accepted. Main courses $7–$14; breakfast $3–$6; sandwiches and burgers $4.50–$6. DISC, MC, V. Daily 7am–9:30pm.

Rod & Reel Pier Restaurant & Snack Bar SEAFOOD   Sitting out on the Rod & Reel Pier at the north end of the island, this little no-frills fish camp enjoys a million-dollar view of Tampa Bay, including Egmont Key and the Skyway Bridge on the horizon. The chow is mostly fried or grilled seafood—fish, shrimp, scallops, forgettable crab cakes, and a piled-high combination platter of all of the above. The lone exception, a tasty Mexican-style grouper (sautéed with peppers, onions, and salsa) is by far the best dish here. They will cook your catch, provided you snag it from the pier.

875 N. Shore Dr., Anna Maria. © 941/778-1885. Reservations not accepted. Main courses $10–$14; breakfast $2.50–$6; sandwiches $3–$7. AE, DISC, MC, V. Daily 8am–10pm. Closed Thanksgiving and Christmas. From Gulf Dr., turn toward the bay on Pine Ave. and take a left at the dead-end onto Bay Blvd. Go right on N. Shore Dr. to pier.

SARASOTA & BRADENTON AFTER DARK

The cultural capital of Florida's west coast, Sarasota is home to a host of performing arts, especially during the winter season. To get the latest update on what's happening any time of year, call the city's 24-hour **Artsline** (© **941/365-ARTS**). Also check the "Ticket" section in Friday's *Herald-Tribune* (www.news coast.com), the local daily newspaper; the Sarasota Convention and Visitors Bureau usually has copies (see "Essentials," earlier in this section).

THE PERFORMING ARTS   Located at the FSU Ringling Center for the Cultural Arts (see "Exploring the Area," earlier in this section), the Florida State University Center for the Performing Arts, 5555 N. Tamiami Trail (U.S. 41; © **800/361-8388** or 941/351-8000; www.asolo.org), presents the winter-through-spring **Asolo Theatre Festival**. This annual program of ballet and Broadway-style musicals and drama is one of the state's finest. The festival is held in three venues: the Asolo Theatre, a 19th-century Italian court playhouse moved here from Asolo, Italy, in the 1950s by the Ringlings; the 487-seat Harold E. and Ethel M. Mertz Theatre, originally constructed in Scotland in 1900 and transferred piece by piece to Sarasota in 1987; and the 161-seat Asolo

Conservatory Theatre, later added for experimental and alternative offerings. The complex is under the direction of Florida State University (FSU).

Sarasota's other prime venue is the lavender, seashell-shaped **Van Wezel Performing Arts Hall**, 777 N. Tamiami Trail (U.S. 41), at 9th Street (© **800/826-9303** or 941/953-3366; www.vanwezel.org). Recently renovated, it offers excellent visual and acoustic conditions and a wide range of year-round programming, including touring Broadway shows and visiting orchestras and dance troupes. Both it and the FSU Center host performances by the **Florida West Coast Symphony** (© **941/953-4252;** www.fwcs.org), the **Jazz Club of Sarasota** (© **941/366-1552** or 941/316-9207; www.jazzclubsarasota.com), the **Sarasota Pops** (© **941/795-7677**), and the **Sarasota Ballet** (© **800/361-8388** or 941/351-8000; www.sarasotaballet.org).

Downtown Sarasota's theater district is home to the **Florida Studio Theatre,** 1241 N. Palm Ave., at Cocoanut Avenue (© **941/366-9796;** www.fst2000.org), which has contemporary performances from December to August, including a New Play Festival in May. Built in 1926 as the Edwards Theater, **The Opera House,** 61 N. Pineapple Ave., between Main and 1st streets (© **941/953-7030;** www.sarasotaopera.org), presents classical operas (in their original languages) as well as highbrow concerts. Next door to The Opera House, the **Golden Apple Dinner Theatre,** 25 N. Pineapple Ave. (© **941/366-5454**), presents cocktails, dinner, and a professional Broadway-style show year-round. The professional, nonequity **Theatre Works,** 1247 1st St., at Cocoanut Avenue (© **941/952-9170**), presents musical revues and other works all year.

THE CLUB & MUSIC SCENE You can find plenty of music to dance to on the mainland at **Sarasota Quay,** the downtown waterfront dining-shopping-entertainment complex on Tamiami Trail (U.S. 41) a block north of John Ringling Causeway. Just walk around this brick building and your ears will take you to the action. The laser sound-and-light crowd gathers at **In Extremis** (© **941/954-2008**), where a high-energy deejay spins Top 40 tunes for 20-somethings. Michael's Mediterranean Grill (© **941/951-2467**) turns into **Anthony's After Dark** rocking disco at 10:30pm. An older but still energetic crowd dances to contemporary jazz at the **Downunder Jazz Bar** (© **941/951-2467**).

Over on St. Armands Circle, the Patio Lounge in **Columbia** restaurant (© **941/388-3987**) is one of the liveliest spots along the beach strip, featuring live, high-energy dance music Tuesday to Sunday evenings. And on Siesta Key, the pubs and restaurants along Ocean Boulevard in Siesta Village have noisy rock-and-roll bands entertaining a mostly young crowd, but you can retire to the pleasant confines of the wine bar at **Blasé Café** (© **941/349-9822**) for live jazz. See "Great Deals on Dining," above, for more about these two restaurants.

The action on Anna Maria is at beach restaurants and pubs. Live bands lend a party atmosphere to the gulf-side deck at the **Sandbar** restaurant every night and from 1pm on weekends (see "Great Deals on Dining," above). **D. Coy Ducks Bar & Grille,** in the Island Shopping Center at Marina Drive and 54th Street in Holmes Beach (© **941/778-5888**), has a varied program of live Dixieland bands, jazz pianists, and guitarists.

11

Walt Disney World & Orlando

by Jim and Cynthia Tunstall

Welcome to Walt Disney World (WDW) and Orlando, where cash registers almost always sing happy songs (and they're not harmonizing over nickel-and-dime sales).

Before Disney's 1971 arrival, Gatorland was the biggest tourist show in town, and its tickets cost a seemingly meager $5. Even in the early 1980s, a family of four could get into the Magic Kingdom for under $100, eat at one of Orlando's finer restaurants for $30, and spend the night at Disney's Contemporary or Polynesian resorts for $90.

Today, the same 24-hour visit costs more than double what it did 2 decades ago. Yes, WDW is a world of dreams, but dreams aren't cheap anymore. The same resort rooms begin at $234 and $299, respectively; it's nearly $200 to get two adults and two kids into a theme park; and you need a search and rescue team to find a spot where dinner for four is $50.

Well, we're the team.

Our job is to help you find a better deal than other tourists but have as much fun or more. We're going to show you where to discover bargains and discounts but still be chin deep in the action. And trust us: There's enough action to make your head spin.

Uncle Walt's world now encompasses four major theme parks and a dozen smaller attractions, two entertainment districts, tens of thousands of hotel rooms, scores of restaurants, and a pair of cruise ships. Universal Orlando and SeaWorld add four theme parks. Universal also has its own nightclub district, CityWalk. And Orlando and Lake Buena Vista have 80 or more smaller attractions, a landslide of eateries, and enough rooms to boost the city's total to 111,000 in 2002 (with about 5,000 added each year).

Disney has built such a lead over the wanna-bes that, despite growth, Universal and SeaWorld have joined Wet 'n Wild and Busch Gardens in Tampa to offer special packages and discounts. Their **FlexTickets** let you visit up to five parks for a flat price. (See "Passes & Coupons That Save Your Orlan-Dough," below.)

Again, our job is showing the way. We've done it all—the good, the bad, and the bland—so you won't have to make the same mistakes. Over the years, the two of us have explored the parks, dined at the restaurants, and snooped inside the hotels, so we can give you the inside track on America's No. 1 landing zone for the young and young at heart. We won't even mention the bad and, if an attraction, lodging, or restaurant is only worth your time under certain circumstances, we'll tell you. So, all you need to do is a little advance planning.

And you really must ***plan ahead!*** The number of attractions begging for your time and the hyper-commercial atmosphere can put a serious dent in your wallet and stamina. Once here, it's easy to get overwhelmed by the urge to do everything in the World and then some. Even if you have 2 weeks, it won't be long enough to hit everything.

Orlando/Walt Disney World Area

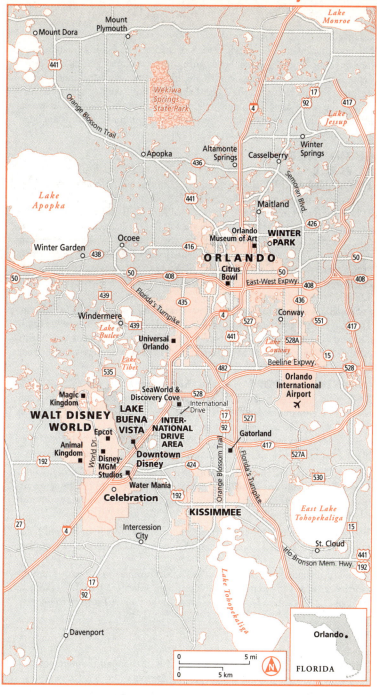

1 Orientation

WHEN SHOULD I GO?

Orlando's busiest seasons are whenever kids are out of school: weekends, early June to Labor Day, mid-December to early January, and spring break. The experience is more enjoyable when crowds are thin and the weather is moderate, so the best times to go are the week after Labor Day until the day before Thanksgiving, the week after Thanksgiving until mid-December, and the 6 weeks before and after spring vacation. The worst time is summer: Crowds are huge and the days are hot and humid.

GETTING THERE
BY PLANE

THE MAJOR AIRLINES There are 35 scheduled airlines and as many charter services that fly into Orlando. **Delta** (© 800/221-1212; www.delta.com) has 25% of the flights into Orlando International Airport. It offers service from 200 cities. Other carriers include **Air Canada** (© 888/247-2262; www.aircanada.ca), **America West** (© 800/235-9292; www.americawest.com), **American** (© 800/433-7300; www.aa.com), **British Airways** (© 800/247-9297; www.british-airways.com), **Continental** (© 800/525-0280; www.continental.com), **Northwest** (© 800/225-2525; www.nwa.com), and **US Airways** (© 800/428-4322; www.usairways.com).

Several so-called no-frills airlines—low fares but no amenities—fly to Orlando. The biggest is **Southwest Airlines** (© 800/435-9792; www.southwest.com). The best fares are usually offered November to January. If you book your flights early, 7-, 14- and 21-day advance reservations can provide savings with the major airlines.

ORLANDO'S AIRPORT Orlando International Airport (© 407/825-2001; www.state.fl.us/goaa) has direct or nonstop service from 60 U.S. cities and two dozen international destinations. It serves more than 30 million passengers in a typical year. It's a thoroughly modern and user-friendly facility with restaurants, shops, a 446-room on-premises Hyatt Regency Hotel, and centrally located information kiosks. All major car-rental companies are located at or near the airport.

Airport Transportation The airport is 25 miles from Walt Disney World. **Mears Transportation** (© 407/423-5566) shuttles people to and from the airport. The vans run 24 hours a day, departing every 15 to 25 minutes. Round-trip fares are $23 to $27 for adults and $16 to $19 for children 4 to 11.

BY CAR Orlando is 436 miles from Atlanta; 1,312 miles from Boston; 1,120 miles from Chicago; 1,170 miles from Dallas; and 1,088 miles from New York City.

From Atlanta, take I-75 south to the Florida Turnpike to I-4 west. From the Northeast, take I-95 south to I-4 west. From Chicago, take I-65 south to Nashville, I-24 south to I-75, then go south to the Florida Turnpike to I-4 west.

> **Fun Fact** **Name Game**
>
> Universal may be suffering an identity crisis. It changed the name of its umbrella company to Universal Studios Escape when local operations expanded beyond a single theme park. But critics thought that was confusing, so now it's Universal Orlando and that name seems to fit.

ORIENTATION

From Dallas, take I-20 east to I-49, then south to I-10, east to I-75, and south to the Florida Turnpike to I-4 west.

If you're an **American Automobile Association (AAA)** call ✆ **800/222-4357** or your local office for maps and directions. Some other clubs provide similar services.

BY TRAIN **Amtrak** trains (✆ **800/872-7245;** www.amtrak.com) pull into stations in downtown Orlando (23 miles from Walt Disney World), Kissimmee (15 miles from Disney), and Winter Park (10 miles north of downtown). Sanford (23 miles northeast of downtown Orlando) is the terminal point for **Amtrak's Auto Train,** which allows you the convenience of bringing your car without having to drive it all the way. It travels between Lorton, Virginia (about a 4-hr. drive from New York) and Sanford.

You can get train discounts if you book far in advance. There may be travel restrictions, mostly around holidays. Traveling into Orlando instead of Winter Park, about 10 miles away, will save you some money. Amtrak also offers money-saving packages—including hotel accommodations (some at WDW resorts), car rentals, tours, and more—with your train fare. For information, call ✆ **800/321-8684.**

BY BUS **Greyhound** buses (✆ **800/231-2222;** www.greyhound.com) stop in terminals at 555 N. Magruder Blvd. (John Young Pkwy.), a few miles west of downtown Orlando (✆ **407/292-3422**), and 16 E. Dakin Ave. in Kissimmee, 14 miles from Walt Disney World (✆ **407/847-3911**). From Orlando you can call a **Mears shuttle van** (✆ **407/423-5566**), which will cost $14 one-way per person to a Disney-area hotel, $10 for children 4 to 11. A **taxi** to the Disney-area hotels costs about $45.

PACKAGE TOURS

The diversity of package tours to Orlando is staggering. But savings can be significant if you're willing to do the research. Your best bet is to visit a large travel agency, grab brochures from several companies, and compare them at home to find the best package for your trip. You should also obtain the **Walt Disney World Vacations** brochure or video by writing or calling Walt Disney World, Box 10000, Lake Buena Vista, FL 32830-1000 (✆ **407/934-7639**). The number to call to book a **WDW package,** ✆ **800/828-0228,** is free;

> **Tips** **Picking a Package**
> A great website, www.vacationpackager.com, allows you to shop and compare dozens of vacation packages at once. It could save you time and money.

you can also book online at www.disneyworld.com. Some packages are tied into a season and others are themed to a special vacation, such as golf or a honeymoon.

While it's not as complete as Disney's menu, **Universal Orlando** is offering more packages since the opening of its Islands of Adventure theme park, the CityWalk entertainment district, and the Portofino Bay and Hard Rock hotels. The menu includes resort stays, VIP access to the parks, and discounts to other non-Disney attractions. Call ✆ **888/322-5537** or visit **www.universalorlando.com** on the Internet.

SeaWorld doesn't have hotels or many restaurants, but you can book packages with it and its partners (✆ **800/423-8368;** www.seaworld.com).

American Express is the official card of Walt Disney World, and **American Express Travel** (✆ **800/732-1991;** http://travel.americanexpress.com/travel)

lets card holders book reservations at Disney resorts and get perks, such as discounts on merchandise, dinner shows, and certain Disney-related tours.

Some airlines offer packages, too. Try any of the following to get specific information: **Delta Airlines** (© 800/872-7786; www.deltavacations.com); **Continental Airlines Vacations** (© 800/301-3800; www.coolvacations.com); and **American Airlines Vacations** (© 800/321-2121; www.aa.com).

Touraine Travel (© 800/967-5583; www.tourainetravel.com) also offers a wide variety of tour packages to Disney and Disney properties, as well as Universal Orlando, SeaWorld, and beyond.

Golfers should try **Golf Getaways** (© 800/800-4028; www.golfgetaways.com) or **Golfpac Vacations** (© 800/327-0878; www.golfpacinc). Both of these offer play-and-stay packages.

VISITOR INFORMATION

As soon as you decide to go to Orlando, write or call the **Orlando/Orange County Convention & Visitors Bureau,** 8723 International Dr., Suite 101, Orlando, FL 32819 (© **407/363-5872**). The bureau can answer questions and send maps and brochures, such as the *Official Visitors Guide, African-American Visitors Guide, Area Guide* to restaurants, *Official Accommodations Guide,* and *Discover the Unexpected Orlando!* The free packet should land in about 3 weeks and include the "Magicard," which is good for up to $500 in discounts on rooms, car rentals, attractions, and more. If you don't require a human voice, you can order by calling © 800/643-9492 or 800/551-0181.

> **Value More for Less**
>
> Get a leg up on those paying full price. Don't overlook additional discounts that might be available if you belong to a credit union, labor union, club or association, AAA, or AARP.

For general information about **Walt Disney World**—including vacation brochures and videos—write or call Walt Disney World, Box 10000, Lake Buena Vista, FL 32830-1000 (© **407/934-7639**).

For information about **Universal Studios Florida, CityWalk,** and **Islands of Adventure,** call © 800/837-2273 or 407/363-8000, or write to **Universal Orlando,** 1000 Universal Studios Plaza, Orlando, FL 32819.

You can also contact the **Kissimmee–St. Cloud Convention & Visitors Bureau,** 1925 E. Irlo Bronson Memorial Hwy. (U.S. 192), Kissimmee, FL 34744, or P.O. Box 422007, Kissimmee, FL 34742-2007 (© **800/327-9159**). Its packet has maps, brochures, coupon books, and the *Kissimmee–St. Cloud Vacation Guide,* which details accommodations and attractions.

ONLINE SOURCES

If you have Internet access, you can get a ton of information on WDW at **www.disneyworld.com**. It has regularly updated information, maps including individual theme parks, and much, much more.

Information on Universal is at **www.universalorlando.com**, and you'll find SeaWorld information at **www.seaworld.com**. Both have maps and a basic description of rides, shows, and ticket information, though neither is as complete as Disney's.

The city's newspaper, the *Orlando Sentinel*, offers entertainment information at **www.orlandosentinel.com**. Another good site, **www.go2orlando.com**, includes tips on accommodations, restaurants, and discounts.

> **Tips Look Both Ways**
> We don't recommend foot travel anywhere in Orlando, but occasionally you'll have to walk across a parking lot or street. *Be careful.* Orlando is among the most dangerous cities in the country for pedestrians, according to a Washington, DC–based research group. Wide roads designed to move traffic quickly and a shortage of sidewalks, streetlights, and crosswalks are to blame.

The Orlando/Orange County Convention & Visitors Bureau (**www.orlandoinfo.com**) and Kissimmee–St. Cloud Convention & Visitors Bureau (**www.floridakiss.com**) also have sites filled with information on accommodations, restaurants, theme parks, smaller attractions, and other things to see and do.

Finally, the state has limited Orlando information at **www.flausa.com**.

CITY LAYOUT

Orlando's major highway is Interstate 4, or as the locals call it, **I-4**, which runs diagonally across Florida from Tampa to Daytona Beach. Exits from I-4 take you to Disney World, SeaWorld, International Drive, Universal Orlando, Kissimmee, Lake Buena Vista, downtown Orlando, and Winter Park. *Note:* I-4 is a highly congested road. It's best to use it during non-peak hours, when the locals aren't rushing to and from work. Most exits are well-marked, but construction is common in this region, and exit numbers often change. Keep this in mind so you don't end up lost and confused.

The **Florida Turnpike** crosses I-4 and links with I-75 to the north. **U.S. 192**, a major east-west artery, reaches from Kissimmee (along a major motel strip) to U.S. 27, crossing I-4 near the Walt Disney World entrance road. Farther north, a toll road called the **BeeLine Expressway** (Fla. 528) goes east from I-4 past Orlando International Airport to Kennedy Space Center. The **East-West Expressway** (also known as Fla. 408) is a toll road that can be helpful in bypassing traffic outside the main tourist areas.

Walt Disney World is bounded roughly by I-4 and Fla. 535 to the east (the latter also goes north), World Drive (the WDW entrance road) to the west, and U.S. 192 to the south. Epcot Center Drive and Buena Vista Drive cut across the complex in a more or less east-west direction; the two roads cross at Bonnet Creek Parkway. Despite an excellent highway system and explicit signs, it's relatively easy to get lost here—we do at least once every trip! Again, pay attention and drive carefully. Don't panic or pull across several lanes of traffic to make an exit once on Disney property. All roads lead where you're going—eventually.

Note: When calling or writing to Mickey, ask for a *Walt Disney World Transportation Guide Map*. It can save a lot of headaches.

NEIGHBORHOODS IN BRIEF

WALT DISNEY WORLD The empire's big and little parks, resorts, restaurants, shops, and assorted trimmings are scattered across 30,500 acres. The surprising thing to some folks: WDW isn't in Orlando. It's southwest of the city, off I-4 on west U.S. 192.

LAKE BUENA VISTA This is Disney's next-door neighbor. It's where you'll find "official" (though not Disney-owned) hotels. It's close to Downtown Disney and Pleasure Island. This charming area has manicured lawns, tree-lined thoroughfares, and free transportation from some resorts throughout the realm, though it may take a while to get where you're going.

CELEBRATION Imagine living in a Disney world 365 days a year. This 4,900-acre town eventually will have thousands of residents living in pricey gingerbread homes. Celebration's downtown area, however, is designed for tourists and has shops, restaurants, and theaters.

DOWNTOWN DISNEY This is more a Disney *doo-wa-diddy* than an actual neighborhood, and, simply put, it's what WDW has taken to calling its two nighttime entertainment areas, Pleasure Island and Downtown Disney West Side, as well as its shopping complex, Downtown Disney Marketplace. Just so you understand, we consider this area a part of Lake Buena Vista.

KISSIMMEE This once-sleepy city is closer to WDW than Orlando. It's a short drive from Mickey and more of a bargain, but some folks find it a tad on the tacky side, with a lot of budget motels and every fast-food joint known to civilization. The town centers on U.S. 192/Irlo Bronson Memorial Highway.

INTERNATIONAL DRIVE AREA (Fla. 536) Can you say tourist mecca? Known as **I-Drive**, it extends 7 to 10 miles north of the Disney parks between Fla. 535 and the Florida Turnpike. It has everything from bungee jumping and ice-skating to dozens of theme restaurants and T-shirt shops. It also has numerous hotels (upscale ones on its southern end); it's home to the Orange County Convention Center; and it offers easy access to SeaWorld and Universal Orlando. The northern end is so packed that crossing the street is an adventure, so *be careful.*

DOWNTOWN ORLANDO Take I-4 east to reach this burgeoning Sunbelt metropolis northeast of Walt Disney World. It includes the Orlando Science Center; hundreds of clubs, shops, and restaurants; and dozens of antiques shops that line "Antique Row" on Orange Avenue near Lake Ivanhoe.

WINTER PARK Just north of downtown Orlando, Winter Park is the place many of central Florida's old-money families call home. It has a collection of upscale shops and restaurants along Park Avenue and original cobblestone streets. It's a bit too far north for hotels if you're spending much time at the Disney parks.

GETTING AROUND

BY CAR If you're not driving to Orlando, you'll need to decide if a rental car is worth the money. If you're going to stay immersed in everything Disney, or you're planting yourself on International Drive, you'll probably do just as well without one. If you're staying at a Disney property, the only inconveniences in not having a car are the slow service of the Disney Transportation System (see below), and the fact that being car-less gives you little hope of escaping Goofy (and his somewhat higher restaurant prices) if you so desire. We think of this as being a POD—Prisoner of Disney.

In general, if you're going to spend all of your time at Disney and you're laid-back enough to go with the flow of traffic within the transportation network, there's no sense in renting a car that will sit in the parking lot between trips to the airport.

But if you're on an extended stay—more than a week—you'll probably want to rent a car for at least a day or two to venture beyond the tourist areas. It will give you a chance to discover downtown Orlando, visit museums, or see Kennedy Space Center.

All major rental companies have operations in Orlando and maintain desks at Orlando International Airport. Some of the handy numbers: **Alamo** (ⓒ 800/327-9633), **Avis** (ⓒ 800/331-1212), **Budget** (ⓒ 800/527-0700), **Dollar** (ⓒ 800/800-4000), **Enterprise** (ⓒ 800/325-8007), **Hertz** (ⓒ 800/654-3131), **National** (ⓒ 800/227-7368), and **Thrifty** (ⓒ 800/367-2277).

BY BUS Stops for the **Lynx** bus system (ⓒ **407/841-2279**; www.golynx.com) are marked with a "paw" print. It will get you to Disney, Universal, and I-Drive ($1 adults, 25¢ kids 8–18), but it's generally not tourist-friendly.

The **Mears Transportation Group** (ⓒ **407/423-5566**) operates buses to all major attractions, including Cypress Gardens, Kennedy Space Center, Disney, Universal Orlando, SeaWorld, and Busch Gardens in Tampa, among others. Call for details.

BY I-RIDE TROLLEY If you're staying or visiting the International Drive area, the **I-Ride Trolley** is a group of shuttle buses running from one end of I-Drive to the other with stops every 2 blocks. The trolley (ⓒ **407/354-5656**; www.iridetrolley.com) runs every 15 minutes, 7am to midnight (75¢ adults, 25¢ seniors, kids under 12 free). Due to I-Drive's high volume of traffic, this is the best way to get around if you're staying on this strip.

BY SHUTTLE Disney resorts and "official" hotels have their own transportation system running within WDW (see below). Disney hostelries offer transportation to other area attractions as well, but there's a charge. Almost all area hotels and motels also offer transportation to WDW and other theme parks. Some are free; others average $10 to $14 a day, which means if you're traveling with a family, you could almost certainly rent a car for the same price.

BY DISNEY TRANSPORATION SYSTEM If you plan to stay at a WDW resort and will spend most of your time at Disney attractions, this thorough and free network runs throughout the Disney complex, including the "official" hotels. But don't be in a hurry. You may have to catch a bus, switch to the monorail, and then hop on a ferry. The least expensive properties, the All-Star resorts, are the farthest from most parks. Wait times between buses can be considerable, and since most make a complete loop, it may take 2 hours to get where you want to be. During peak hours in the busiest seasons, you may have trouble getting a seat on the next bus, so keep that in mind if you're traveling with seniors or travelers with disabilities. Also, if you're hauling kids and strollers, consider the frustration factor of loading and unloading strollers and kiddie paraphernalia. *But*, this does save you the car rental fee and (if you aren't a resort guest) the $6 daily parking at the parks. Plus, if your party wants to split up, you can take separate transports.

 FAST FACTS: Walt Disney World & Orlando

Babysitters Many Orlando hotels, including all of Disney's resorts, offer babysitting services, and several have good child-care facilities with counselor-supervised activity programs on the premises. Babysitting rates usually run $12 TO $15 per hour for the first child and $1 per additional child, per hour.

Doctors & Dentists There are basic first-aid centers in all the major parks. If you need a referral from your room, use **Ask-A-Nurse**. It's a free service open to everyone (call ✆ **407/870-1700**). There's also a 24-hour, toll-free number for the **Poison Control Center,** ✆ **800/282-3171**. Disney offers in-room medical service 24 hours a day at ✆ **407/238-2000. Doctors on Call Service** (✆ **407/399-3627**) makes house and room calls in most of the Orlando area. **Centra-Care** lists several walk-in clinics in the Yellow Pages, including ones on International Drive (✆ **407/370-4881**) and at Lake Buena Vista near Disney (✆ **407/934-2273**). **Dental Referral Service** ((✆ **888/343-3440**) can tell you the nearest dentist who meets your needs. Phones are staffed daily from 5:30am to 6pm. Check the Yellow Pages for 24-hour emergency services.

Emergencies Dial ✆ **911** to contact the police or fire department, or to call an ambulance. Always call 911 in case of a serious medical emergency or accident. For less urgent requests, call ✆ **800/647-9284,** a number sponsored by the **Florida Tourism Industry Marketing Corporation,** the state tourism promotion board. With operators speaking more than 100 languages, it provides general directions, help with lost travel papers, and airline confirmations.

Hospitals **Sand Lake Hospital,** 9400 Turkey Lake Rd. (✆ **407/351-8550**), is 2 miles south of Sand Lake Road. From the WDW area, take I-4 east to the Sand Lake Road exit and make a left on Turkey Lake Road. The hospital is 2 miles up on your right. **Celebration Health** (✆ **407/303-4000**) is located in the town of Celebration. From I-4, take the U.S. 192 exit. At the first traffic light, turn right onto Celebration Avenue. At the first stop sign, take another right.

Kennels All the major theme parks offer animal-boarding facilities, which usually cost $5 to $6 for the day. WDW's kennels are at Fort Wilderness, Epcot, the Magic Kingdom, Disney–MGM Studios, and Animal Kingdom. Disney offers overnight boarding ($9–$11), too. *Note:* When booking a motel, ask if pets are welcome.

Lost Children Every theme park has a designated spot for parents to be reunited with lost children (or spouses). Take a minute to find it when you enter any park and instruct your children to ask park personnel to take them there if they're lost. Point out what park personnel look like. *Young children should have name tags that include their parents' names, the name of the hotel where they're staying, and a contact number back home.*

Parking Unless you're staying at an affiliated resort, all of the major parks charge $6 to $7 a day for cars, light trucks, and vans.

Pharmacies Walgreen's drugstore, 1003 W. Vine St. (Hwy. 192), just east of Bermuda Avenue (✆ **407/847-5252**), has a 24-hour pharmacy. The Eckerd drugstore at 12125 Apopka-Vineland Rd. (✆ **407/238-9333**) is open until 7pm.

Photography Skip any offer in the parks. Many convenience and discount stores, such as Walgreen's, Eckerd, Kmart, and Target, sell film and slides at reasonable prices and offer next-day processing. If you're locked into a Disney resort, buy before you come and get it developed on your return home. If you're an avid photographer, this can save you a ton of money.

> *Post Office* The main post office in Lake Buena Vista is at 12541 Hwy. 535, in the Crossroads Shopping Center (✆ 800/275-8777). It's open Monday through Friday from 9am to 4pm, Saturday from 9am to noon.
>
> *Taxes* Florida's 6% sales tax is charged on all goods except most grocery store items and medicines. Additionally, hotels in Orlando add another 5% for a total of 11%; in Kissimmee, the total is 12%.
>
> *Telephone* Because of its growth, Orlando has changed its calling procedures. If you're making a *local* call in Orlando's 407 area code, you must dial the area code followed by the number you wish to call, for a total of 10 digits, even if you're calling across the street.
>
> *Weather* Call ✆ 321/255-0212 for the local weather forecast.

2 Accommodations You Can Afford, In & Around the Parks

Psst! Beat the crowds. Reserve your room as early as you can—the minute you pick dates for your trip if possible. The average hotel rack rate for the metro area is $90 to $95 and increasing 5% to 10% a year. In some cases (but not at Disney properties), rates are lower in July, August, and September, though many places only have a few discounted rooms, and they go fast. The rates are higher in January, February, and March. And Orlando is a year-round destination thanks to tourists and the convention trade, so many hotels and motels don't offer much of a discount season. Also, make sure to factor the **11% or 12% hotel tax** into your budget.

HOW TO SAVE MONEY BY STAYING WITH MICKEY Many people assume that motels outside the Disney parks will cost less than stays on WDW premises, where the lowest rack rates are $77 to $124 at the All-Star resorts. Unless you are going in low season and the motel you choose charges for shuttle transportation to the parks—many charge $10 to $14 per person per day—that assumption is valid. Disney resort rates are usually 20% to 30% higher than the rates for comparable hotels and resorts outside of Mickeyville. That said, you can save money on transportation, parking, and tickets if you stay on the property, and you will gain the convenience of being in the center of the action.

Disney-owned hostelries and "official" hotels offer complimentary transportation to and from WDW parks and other areas. In general, however, the lower the room rate, the farther you are from the theme parks and the longer it takes to travel. You'll have to weigh time against cost to determine whether to rent a car. If you do rent a car, keep in mind that resort guests get free parking at the theme parks, so you'll save yourself $6 to $7 per day.

In or out of this World, if you book your hotel as part of a package (details below), you'll likely enjoy savings. Ask about special discounts for students, government employees, senior citizens, military, AAA, AARP, and corporate clients. Also, the **Disney Club** (it replaced the Magic Kingdom Club Gold Card) is a membership program that provides a 10% to 30% discount at WDW resorts, on packages and meals in the parks, and on some rental cars. It costs $40 the first year and $30 thereafter. The club also has a member's website (**www.disneyclub.com**). Call ✆ 800/654-6347 for more information.

Walt Disney World

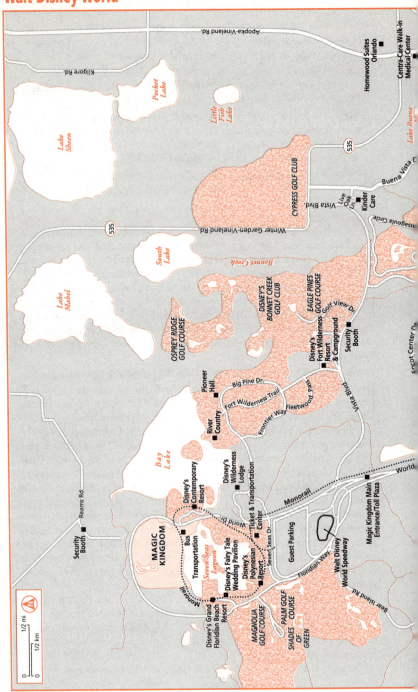

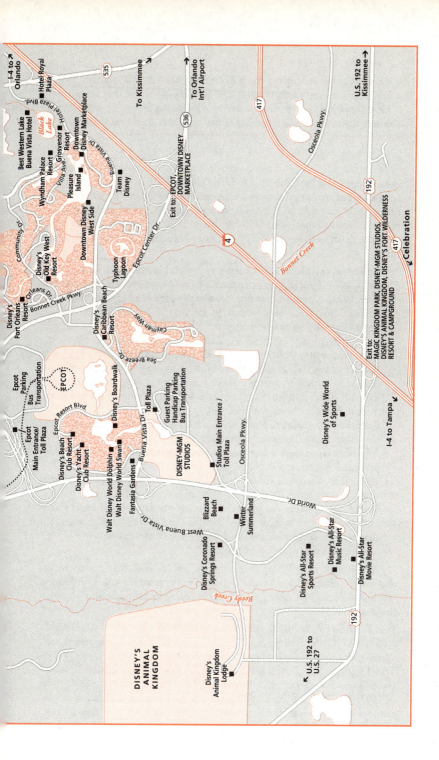

> **Tips** **Tight Squeeze**
>
> An average hotel or motel room in Orlando has 350 to 400 square feet and beds for four, hardly a castle, but most travelers find that adequate for a short stay. We've made a special note in the listings of properties where the rooms are substantially larger or smaller than that average.

There are 17 Disney-owned properties (hotels, resorts, villas, wilderness homes, and campsites) and nine privately owned "official" hotels. All within (and a few out of) our price range are described in the following pages. In addition to their proximity to the parks, there are a number of advantages to staying at a Disney property or "official" hotel. Even the budget choices offer extensive resort facilities. All WDW resorts and official hotels have these benefits:

- **Unlimited complimentary transportation** via bus, monorail, ferry, and/or water taxi to/from all four parks from 2 hours before opening until 2 hours after closing. Unlimited free rides are also provided to and from Downtown Disney, Typhoon Lagoon, Pleasure Island, Fort Wilderness, and other Disney resorts. This helps save money and also guarantees admission to all the parks, even during peak times when the parking lots sometimes fill. Note, however, that the Disney transportation system can be *excruciatingly slow*. Sometimes you have to take a ferry to catch a bus to get on the monorail to reach your hotel. The system makes a circuit, but may not necessarily take the most direct path for you. It can take an hour or more to get to a place that's right across the lagoon from you.
- **Reduced-price children's menus** in almost all restaurants, and character breakfasts and/or dinners at most resorts.
- A **guest-services desk** where you can purchase tickets to all WDW theme parks and attractions and obtain general information.
- The ability to purchase reduced-price **Ultimate Parkhopper passes** for the length of your stay. The passes can offer some significant savings.
- **Use of**—and in some cases, free transport to—the **Disney golf courses** and preferred tee times at them (these can be booked up to 30 days in advance).
- **Access to most recreational facilities** at other Disney resorts.
- **Service by the Mears airport shuttle.**

Additional perks at Disney-owned hotels, resorts, villas, and campgrounds (but not at "official" hotels) include charge privileges throughout Walt Disney World and dining and show reservations (including Epcot restaurants) through the hotel.

WALT DISNEY WORLD TRAVEL COMPANY & WDW CENTRAL RESERVATIONS To reserve a room or package at Disney hotels, resorts, and villas; "official" hotels; and Fort Wilderness homes and campsites, call **WDW Travel Company** at © **800/828-0228.** You also can contact **Central Reservations Operations** (CRO), P.O. Box 10000, Lake Buena Vista, FL 32830-1000 (© **407/934-7639**). If you have Internet access, or your local library does, you can save money by surfing the website to check out room rates and options. Click on "Resorts" at **www.disneyworld.com** to explore your options. (Click on "Reservations" to actually make reservations.)

The CRO will recommend accommodations that will suit your needs on price, location, and facilities. It can also give you information about various park ticket options and reservations for dinner shows and character breakfasts.

When you call the CRO, be sure to inquire about package plans, which include meals, tickets, recreation, and other features. The right package can save you money and time, and is helpful in computing the cost of your vacation in advance. Be sure to ask if any special discounts are being offered at the time of your trip. *Note:* If you don't ask, many Disney reservationists "forget" to tell you about specials.

THE DISNEY RESORTS

Disney's Caribbean Beach Resort

The Caribbean Beach isn't as bargain basement as the All-Star resorts but offers good value for families who don't need a lot of frills or amenities. Set amidst 200 acres, the rooms are grouped in five Caribbean villages around a duck-filled lake. When booking, ask for a recently refurbished room. Even then, your party had better be into togetherness—the bathrooms are tight. The main swimming pool replicates a Spanish-style Caribbean fort, complete with water slide, kiddie pool, and whirlpool. There are other pools on property and lakefront white-sand beaches in each village. A 1.4-mile promenade is a good place to jog or walk around the lake. The closest park is Disney–MGM Studios.

900 Cayman Way (off Buena Vista Dr.; P.O. Box 10000), Lake Buena Vista, FL 32830-1000. © 407/934-7639 or 407/934-3400. Fax 407/934-3288. www.disneyworld.com. 2,112 units. $133–$219 double. Extra person $15. Children 17 and under stay free in parents' room. AE, DC, DISC, MC, V. Free parking. Pets $9 a night. Take I-4 to the Hwy. 536/Epcot Center Dr. exit and follow signs. **Amenities:** Restaurant (American), grill, lounge; large heated outdoor pool; 6 smaller pools in the villages; kids' pool; Jacuzzi; water-sports equipment; arcade; WDW Transportation System; transportation to non-Disney parks for a fee; limited room service; babysitting; guest laundry; nonsmoking rooms. *In room:* A/C, TV, fridge ($10 a night), hair dryer, iron, safe.

Disney's Coronado Springs Resort

Here's another clone of the Disney moderate-price class. Were it not for exterior gingerbread and inside-the-room decor, it would be hard to tell one from the other. The American Southwestern theme here carries through four- and five-story hacienda-style buildings with terra-cotta tile roofs and shaded courtyards. As with most Disney properties, it has an above-par pool, in this case inspired by a Mayan temple. Rooms are smallish, suitable for four people who get along; don't expect to fit more than one into the bathroom at a time. Those nearest the central public area, pool, and lobby tend to be noisier. The nearest park is Animal Kingdom, but the Coronado is at the southwest corner of WDW and is therefore a good distance from a lot of the other action.

1000 Buena Vista Dr., near All-Star Resorts and Blizzard Beach, Lake Buena Vista, FL 32830. © 407/934-7639 or 407/939-1000. Fax 407/939-1001. www.disneyworld.com. 1,967 units. $133–$219 double; $278–$1,050 suites. Extra person $15. Children 17 and under free with parent. AE, DC, DISC, MC, V. Free parking. Pets $9 a night. Take I-4 to the Hwy. 536/Epcot Center Dr. exit and follow the signs. **Amenities:** Restaurant (Mexican), grill/food court, 2 lounges; 4 heated outdoor pools; kids' pool; health club; Jacuzzi; sauna;

Tips Sink Space

Although Disney's resort rooms have notoriously cramped bathrooms, they all sport double sinks, usually set in a small dressing area outside the bathroom. So while you may bang your shin on the shower, at least you won't have to wait in line to brush your teeth.

water-sports equipment; 2 arcades; WDW Transportation System; transportation to non-Disney parks for a fee; business center; salon; limited room service; massage; babysitting; guest laundry; nonsmoking rooms. *In room:* A/C, TV, dataport, fridge ($10 a night), hair dryer, iron, safe.

Disney's Fort Wilderness Resort & Campground Pines, cypress trees, and fish-filled lakes and streams surround this woodsy 780-acre camping resort. The biggest knock is that it's quite far from Epcot, Disney–MGM Studios, and Animal Kingdom. But it's close to the Magic Kingdom, and if you're a true outdoors type, you'll enjoy the break from some of the Mickey madness. There are 784 campsites for RVs, pull-behind campers, and tents (110/220-volt outlets, grills, and comfort stations with showers and restrooms). Guests can ride horses and attend nightly campfire programs.

Some sites are open to pets—at a cost of $3 per site, not per pet—which is cheaper than using the WDW overnight kennel, where you pay $9 per pet. The 408 wilderness cabins (actually trailers) are large enough for six people once you pull down the Murphy beds, and they also have kitchens.

3520 N. Fort Wilderness Trail (P.O. Box 10000), Lake Buena Vista, FL 32830-1000. **407/934-7639** or 407/824-2900. Fax 407/824-3508. www.disneyworld.com. 784 campsites, 408 wilderness cabins. Campsite $34–$80 double; wilderness cabin $224–$314 double. Extra person $2 for campsite, $5 for cabin. Children 17 and under free with parent. AE, DC, DISC, MC, V. Free parking. Take I-4 to the Hwy. 536/Epcot Center Dr. exit and follow the signs. **Amenities:** 2 restaurants (American), grill, lounge; 2 heated outdoor pools; kids' pool; 2 lighted tennis courts; water-sports equipment; outdoor activities (fishing, horseback and hay rides, campfires); 2 game rooms; WDW Transportation System; transportation to non-Disney parks for a fee; babysitting; guest laundry; nonsmoking homes. *In room:* A/C, TV, VCR (cabins only), kitchens, fridge, coffeemaker, outdoor grill, hair dryer (cabins only).

SUPER-CHEAP SLEEPS

Disney's All-Star Movie Resort Kids love the larger-than-life themes at the All-Star resorts, but adults usually cringe at the visual overload. Giant cartoon characters such as Buzz Lightyear adorn this one and help hide a 21st-century rendition of a 1950s Holiday Inn. The rooms are spartan and very small—the bathrooms are even worse. Like its two siblings, the All-Star Movie Resort is buried in WDW's southwest corner to avoid frightening the higher-paying guests.

1991 W. Buena Vista Dr., Lake Buena Vista, FL 32830-1000. **407/934-7639** or 407/939-7000. Fax 407/939-7111. www.disneyworld.com. 1,900 units. $77–$124 double. Extra person $10. Children 17 and under stay free with parent. AE, DC, DISC, MC, V. Free parking. Pets $9 a night. Take I-4 east to Exit 25B. Follow signs to WDW, then to resort. **Amenities:** Food court, lounge; 2 heated outdoor pools; kids' pool; arcade; WDW Transportation System; transportation to non-Disney parks for a fee; limited room service; babysitting; guest laundry; nonsmoking rooms. *In room:* A/C, TV, dataport, fridge ($10 a night), safe.

Disney's All-Star Music Resort *Value* Giant trombones and musical themes from jazz to calypso can't hide the fact that this is a clone of the All-Star Movie

---

Tips Coming Soon . . . Maybe

The **Pop Century Resort** was to open in early 2002, but the weakened economy indefinitely delayed its debut. Disney says the delay is temporary and when the resort does open, it will add 5,760 rooms to the inexpensive ($77–$124) menu. Like the All-Star resorts, Pop Century will have themes, in this case decade-long capsules of the 20th century. These would be in two half-century categories: The Legendary Years (1900s–1940s) and The Classic Years (1950s–1990s).

> ### Tips Enjoying the Parks Without Getting Fleeced
>
> It's easy to get seduced by the smiley-faced goodwill of the theme-park fantasylands—and soon you believe that 10 bucks for a hamburger (*without trimmings*) is a fair price. But a level head, advance planning, and open ear (heed our advice) will help you maximize park experiences without the usual wallet drain.
>
> 1. **Bring bottled water and snacks** with you to the parks, more so if you're traveling with small fry. You can't bring coolers inside (who wants to lug one around, anyway?), but you can carry a light lunch in a backpack and save a bundle, considering that bottled water runs $2.50, a smoked turkey drumstick is nearly $5, and a counter-service lunch costs $6 to $9 per person. You'll get away with a fraction of that by picking up a carry-in lunch and water at a grocery.
> 2. Continuing that thought, **eat bigger and better early in the day.** As frequent and thrifty park visitors, we've learned to make it through the day on a slim budget when finances insist. If you have wheels, look for steakhouses and other places pitching buffet breakfasts ($3–$7) on billboards and in hotel handouts. Then, go light at noon in the parks and let your budget determine your evening meal.
> 3. Before coming here, **buy cheap rain ponchos** for everyone. All major parks include water rides and, trust us, it's miserable to walk around wet all day, even in summer. They'll also come in handy during summer storms, which arrive quickly and violently. Something you can buy at home for $2 costs $6 in the parks. You can find the same kind of savings on **camera gear and film.**
> 4. **Drink up.** Some Disney resorts offer "bottomless" refills that allow you unlimited drinks at the hotel food courts. It's worth the cost, especially if you consume a lot of coffee or soda.

Resort. The combination of rock-bottom rates and extensive facilities at All-Star resorts may be attractive to families, but you better appreciate closeness—the rooms are tight and the tiny bathrooms may have you singing the blues. They're OK for single adults, couples traveling with one kid, or larger families using the room for one purpose only: sleep. The perks? They're at least $50 a night cheaper than other Disney resorts. The closest off-site activities are the Winter Summerland Miniature Golf Course, Blizzard Beach, and Animal Kingdom.

1801 W. Buena Vista Dr. (at World Dr. and Osceola Pkwy.; P.O. Box 10000), Lake Buena Vista, FL 32830-1000. © **407/934-7639** or 407/939-6000. Fax 407/939-7222. www.disneyworld.com. 1,920 units. $77–$124 double. Extra person $10. Children 17 and under stay free with parent. AE, DC, DISC, MC, V. Free parking. Pets $9 a night. Take I-4 to the Hwy. 536/Epcot Center Dr. exit and follow the signs. **Amenities:** Food court, lounge; 2 heated outdoor pools; kids' pool; arcade; WDW Transportation System; transportation to non-Disney parks for a fee; limited room service; babysitting; guest laundry; nonsmoking rooms. *In room:* A/C, TV, dataport, fridge ($10 a night), safe.

Disney's All-Star Sports Resort *Value* Yogi Berra said it best: "It's déjà vu all over again." It's a different theme, but the same routine. Rooms are the same size and equipped with the same micro-bathrooms as the All-Stars above. This resort's buildings sport football, baseball, basketball, tennis, and surfing motifs.

1701 W. Buena Vista Dr. (at World Dr. and Osceola Pkwy.; P.O. Box 10000), Lake Buena Vista, FL 32830-1000. © 407/934-7639 or 407/939-5000. Fax 407/939-7333. www.disneyworld.com. 1,920 units. $77–$124 double. Extra person $10. Children 17 and under stay free with parent. AE, DC, DISC, MC, V. Free parking. Pets $9 a night. Take I-4 to the Hwy. 536/Epcot Center Dr. exit and follow the signs. **Amenities:** Food court, lounge; 2 heated outdoor pools; kids' pool; arcade; WDW Transportation System; transportation to non-Disney parks for a fee; limited room service; babysitting; guest laundry; nonsmoking rooms. *In room:* A/C, TV, dataport, fridge ($10 a night), safe.

AN "OFFICIAL" HOTEL AT LAKE BUENA VISTA

Properties designated "official" Walt Disney World hotels are located on and around Hotel Plaza Boulevard. Guests enjoy some privileges that you get at WDW properties, most notably free bus transportation to Disney parks and other areas. Location is a another perk—these places are near WDW parks, within walking distance of Disney Village Marketplace, and are on a tree-line boulevard that's fun to stroll.

One difference between "official" hotels and actual Disney resorts is that the former have less relentless themes; decide for yourself if that's a plus or a minus.

Best Western Lake Buena Vista Hotel *Value*   This 12-acre lakefront hotel has nicer rooms and public areas than you might find in others within the chain. Rooms are in an 18-story tower, and all of them come with balconies. The views improve from the eighth floor up, and those guests on the west side have a better chance of seeing something Disney. Toppers, the hotel's 18th-floor lounge, offers an excellent view of the Magic Kingdom's fireworks. Accommodations in this category are usually a step above the "moderates" inside WDW. You can reserve an oversized room (20% larger) or one with a view of WDW fireworks for $10 more a night.

2000 Hotel Plaza Blvd. (between Buena Vista Dr. and Apopka-Vineland Rd./Hwy. 535), Lake Buena Vista, FL 32830. © 800/348-3765 or 407/828-2424. Fax 407/828-8933. www.downtowndisneyhotels.com or www.orlandoresorthotel.com. 325 units. $99–$159 for 4 persons; $199–$319 suites. 5th person $15. AE, DC, DISC, MC, V. Free parking. From I-4, take the Hwy. 535/Apopka–Vineland Rd. exit north to Hotel Plaza Blvd. and go left. It's the first hotel on the right. **Amenities:** Restaurant (American), grill; heated outdoor pool; kids' pool; guest-services desks; complimentary bus service to WDW parks; transportation for a fee to other parks; limited room service; guest laundry; nonsmoking rooms. *In room:* A/C, TV w/pay movies, Nintendo, coffeemaker, hair dryer, iron, safe.

LAKE BUENA VISTA AREA HOTELS

The hotels in this section are within a few minutes' drive of WDW parks. They offer the location but not the privileges of staying at an "official" hotel.

SUPER-CHEAP SLEEPS

Comfort Inn Lake Buena Vista   This is an ideally located and attractively landscaped property, with two small artificial lakes amid manicured lawns and lush greenery. It offers free transport to WDW parks, which are 2½ miles away. The rooms are very clean. The Boardwalk Buffet serves reasonably priced meals at breakfast and dinner; kids 11 and under eat free, seniors 50 and older get a 20% discount.

8442 Palm Pkwy. (between Hwy. 535 and I-4), Lake Buena Vista, FL 32830. © 800/999-7300 or 407/996-7300. Fax 407/996-7301. www.comfortinnorlando.com. 640 units. $49–$99 for up to 4 people. AE, DC, DISC, MC, V. Free parking. Pets are permitted. From I-4 east, take the northernmost Disney exit; turn north on 535, then right at 2nd light onto Palm Pkwy. **Amenities:** Restaurant (American), deli, lounge; 2 outdoor pools; video arcade; playground; guest services desk; free transportation to Disney; transportation for a fee to other parks; guest laundry. *In room:* A/C, TV, mini-fridge, microwave, coffeemaker, safe.

Orlando Days Inn Lake Buena Vista
This Days Inn offers free transportation to nearby Walt Disney parks, a restaurant that serves breakfast and dinner (kids 12 and under eat free with accompanying adults), and an outdoor pool. Rooms have pullout sofas and some are accessible for travelers with disabilities. It's not particularly fancy, but it's clean and, if you come in the off-season, you can save a bundle over what other visitors are paying. As an added bonus, it's only 1 mile from the Wizard of Disney.

12799 Apopka–Vineland Rd. (at I-4 and Hwy. 535), Lake Buena Vista, FL 32836. © **800/224-5058**, 800/329-7466 or 407/239-4441. Fax 407/239-0325. www.daysinnorlando.com. 203 units. $52–$210. Children 17 and under stay free in parents' room. AE, DC, DISC, MC, V. Free self-parking. Pets are permitted. From I-4 east, take the northernmost Disney exit; turn north on 535. **Amenities:** Restaurant (American), lounge; heated outdoor pool; video arcade; guest services desk; free transportation to Disney parks; transportation for a fee to others. *In room:* A/C, TV.

WORTH A SPLURGE

Holiday Inn Family Suites Resort ★★ *Finds*
This all-suite property opened in July 1999 and does a fantastic job of catering to a diverse clientele. Families appreciate the two-bedroom Kid Suites that feature a second semi-private bedroom equipped with bunk beds and changing themes (from Disney to Coke to the comics). In the Classic Suites, the semi-private bedroom has a queen-size bed. Others cater to honeymooners and romantics (Sweet Heart Suites with a heart-shaped tub) and movie buffs (Cinema Suites with a 60-in. big-screen TV and DVD players). All suites have small kitchenettes. The resort, voted in 2001 as best Holiday Inn property in North America, has themed activity nights (movies, magic, variety shows, and more). *Note:* If you are child-free, ask to stay in the West Track Courtyard section, which is much quieter.

14500 Continental Gateway (off Hwy. 536), Lake Buena Vista, FL 32821. © **877/387-5437** or 407/387-5437. Fax 407/387-1489. www.hifamilysuites.com; 800 units. $109–$169 Kid Suite; $109–$169 Classic Suite; $129–$189 Cinema Suite; $129–$189 Sweet Heart Suite. AE, DC, DISC, MC, V. Free self-parking. From I-4, take the Hwy. 536/International Dr. exit east 1 mile to the resort. **Amenities:** Restaurant (American), lounge, general store, several fast-food counters; large lap pool, family swimming pool; fitness center; 2 Jacuzzis; 3 outdoor Ping-Pong tables; 2 shuffleboard courts; game room; mini-golf course; complimentary recreation center for ages 4–12; kids' library; tour desk; free transportation to Disney parks; transportation for a fee to other parks; coin-op washers and dryers. *In room:* A/C, TV w/pay movies and VCR (some with Nintendo), dataport, microwave, fridge, coffeemaker, hair dryer, iron, safe.

Homewood Suites Orlando ★
These moderately priced family suites are less than 2 miles from Disney and are a good choice for travelers wanting a little home-style comfort and the chance to perform do-it-yourself stuff in the kitchen. The hotel is relatively new—it was built in 1998—so everything is in good shape. The two-bedroom suites sleep up to six. A social hour (hors d'oeuvres, beer, and wine) is held Monday through Thursday. A free shuttle is provided to the Lake Buena Vista Factory Stores.

8200 Palm Pkwy. (off S. Apopka–Vineland Rd./Hwy. 535), Orlando, FL 32836. © **800/225-5466** or 407/465-8200. Fax 407/465-0200. www.homewood-suites.com. $109–$259 double. Extra person $15. Children 17 and under stay free in parents' room. Rates include continental breakfast. AE, DC, DISC, MC, V. Free self-parking. From I-4, take the Hwy. 535/Apopka–Vineland Rd. exit east to Palm Pkwy., then go right a quarter-mile to hotel. **Amenities:** Mini-grocery; outdoor heated pool; exercise room; Jacuzzi; concierge; car-rental desk; free shuttles to Disney parks, transportation to non-Disney parks for a fee; business center; babysitting; guest laundry, valet; nonsmoking rooms. *In room:* A/C, TV/VCR w/pay movies, dataport, kitchen, fridge, microwave, coffeemaker, hair dryer, iron.

ON U.S. 192/KISSIMMEE AREA
This very eclectic stretch of highway is dotted with fast-food eateries and tourist traps. It's hardly what you'd call scenic, but it has a lot of inexpensive

> **Tips** **Youth Hostel**
>
> Hostelling International, 4840 W. Irlo Bronson Memorial Hwy./U.S. 192; Kissimmee, FL 34746 (© **800/909-4776** for reservations or 407/396-8282; fax 407/396-9311; www.hiorlando.org or www.hiayh.org), has a nice site on Lake Cecille, about 5 miles east of Walt Disney World. Rooms are $16 to $20 (MC, V) per night including linens. All have bathrooms, air-conditioning, and a maximum of six beds. There are also 20 private rooms. The property has a lakefront pool, kitchen, lockers, laundry, Internet access, picnic area with grills, and complimentary paddleboats.

accommodations that are within 1 to 8 miles of the Disney parks. All the hostelries listed below are clean and well run. There are also two branches of the budget **Motel 6** (© **800/466-8356;** www.motel6.com) in Kissimmee on U.S. 192. One branch is at 5731 W. Irlo Bronson Memorial Hwy. (© **407/396-6333**); the other, at 7455 W. Irlo Bronson Memorial Hwy. (© **407/396-6422**), is a tad nicer. They have pools, cable TV, a tolerance for small pets, and blue-light special rates ($36–$56).

A system of highway markers has been erected along Irlo Bronson Highway to help motorists better find their way. These towers by the side of the road are aptly dubbed "Marker" along with a number. For example, a property may be located between Marker 5 and Marker 6. We've included those designations where appropriate.

SUPER-CHEAP SLEEPS

Days Inn Offering good value for your hotel dollar, this Days Inn offers clean, standard motel rooms. The best bets are the efficiencies with fully equipped kitchenettes. There are also rooms with Jacuzzi, refrigerator, and microwave oven. Free coffee, juice, and doughnuts are in the lobby each morning.

4104 W. Irlo Bronson Memorial Hwy. (U.S. 192, at Hoagland Blvd. N. or Marker 15), Kissimmee, FL 34741. © **800/647-0010** or 407/846-4714. Fax 407/932-2699. www.daysinn192.com. 226 units. $29–$79 room for up to 4, depending on season; $49–$99 for deluxe with kitchen. Rates may be higher during major events. AE, DC, DISC, MC, V. Free parking. From I-4, take the U.S. 192/Irlo Bronson Memorial Hwy. exit, then turn right; the hotel is 6 miles on right. **Amenities:** 2 heated outdoor pools; video arcade; guest services desk; free transportation to Disney parks; transportation for a fee to others; guest laundry. *In room:* A/C, TV, safe.

Days Inn Eastgate This two-story, pink stucco Days Inn forms an attractively landscaped courtyard around a large swimming pool. Families will appreciate the picnic tables and a play area on the lawn. The rooms are nicely decorated. Some have fridges and microwaves. There's a restaurant where kids eat free.

5245 W. Irlo Bronson Memorial Hwy. (U.S. 192, between Poinciana and Polynesian Isle blvds., near Marker 12), Kissimmee, FL 34746. © **800/423-3864** or 407/396-7700. Fax 407/396-0293. www.daysinneastgate.com. 200 units. $39–$89 for up to 4. Rates may be higher during major events. AE, DC, DISC, MC, V. Free parking. From I-4, take the U.S. 192/Irlo Bronson Memorial Hwy. exit; it's about 3.5 miles on 192. **Amenities:** Restaurant (American), lounge; heated outdoor pool; video arcade; guest services desk; free transportation to Disney parks; transportation for a fee to others; guest laundry. *In room:* A/C, TV.

Econo Lodge Maingate Resort This property is set well back from the highway, a blessing compared to many other properties along U.S. 192, and it comes with bargain rates for those on a budget. A new lobby has been added to the hotel, which has good service and is reasonably clean.

7514 W. Irlo Bronson Memorial Hwy. (U.S. 192), Kissimmee, FL 34756. ✆ **800/365-6935** or 407/390-9063. Fax 407/390-1226. www.enjoyfloridahotels.com/econolodge. 445 units. $30–$110. AE, DC, DISC, MC, V. Free parking. From I-4, take the U.S. 192/Irlo Bronson Memorial Hwy. exit; go west 2.2 miles. Hotel is on the left past the 2nd traffic light (Reedy Creek Blvd.). **Amenities:** Restaurant (American), lounge; heated outdoor pool; video arcade; guest services desk; car rental desk; free transportation to Disney parks; transportation for a fee to others; limited room service; guest laundry. *In room:* A/C, TV, safe.

Hampton Inn Maingate West Just 4½ years old, this inn hasn't been around long enough to earn the battle scars usually found on U.S. 192 accommodations. While it's more expensive than some of its competitors, it's also much more modern and upbeat. The inn is located 1½ miles west of the WDW entrance road.

3000 Maingate Lane, Kissimmee, FL. 34747. ✆ **877/428-4782** or 407/396-6300. Fax 407/396-8989. www.hamptoninnmaingatewest.com/. 118 units. $69–$119 double. Extra person $10. Rates include continental breakfast. Children 17 and under stay free in parents' room. AE, DC, DISC, MC, V. Free self-parking. From I-4, take Exit 25A onto U.S. 192 west; go 3 miles, then turn right on Maingate Lane (across the street from Celebration). **Amenities:** Outdoor heated pool; guest services desk; free shuttle to Disney parks, transportation to non-Disney parks for a fee; nonsmoking rooms. *In room:* A/C, TV, dataport, coffeemaker, iron.

Howard Johnson Inn Maingate East Like most motels fronting U.S. 192, this HoJo offers traffic congestion and noise, but it's only 2 miles from Disney. Rooms are typical of the chain—basic, but a fraction nicer than those in the Econo Lodge, above. One kid under 12 eats free with each paying adult. Efficiencies and suites with full kitchens are available.

6051 W. Irlo Bronson Memorial Hwy. (U.S. 192), Kissimmee, FL 34747. ✆ **800/288-4678** or 407/396-1748. Fax 407/649-8642. www.hojomge.com. 567 units. $75–$105 double; efficiencies $10 more, suites $20 more. Extra person $10. Children 18 and under stay free in parents' room. AE, DC, DISC, MC, V. Free self-parking. From I-4, take the U.S. 192 exit east 1 mile. Motel is on left. Pets are permitted. **Amenities:** Restaurant (American); 2 outdoor heated pools, kids' pool; Jacuzzi; arcade; guest services desk; free bus to Disney parks, transportation to non-Disney parks for a fee; guest laundry; nonsmoking rooms. *In room:* A/C, TV w/pay movies & Nintendo, dataport, safe.

Larson Inn Family Suites ⭐ With a water park next door, a playground, poolside picnic tables, barbecue grills, and a Shoney's restaurant, Larson's is a good choice for families. There are efficiency units available with fully equipped kitchenettes. Rates include a free newspaper and coffee served in the lobby each morning. A supermarket is just a few minutes away by car.

6075 W. Irlo Bronson Memorial Hwy. (U.S. 192, east of I-4 between Markers 8 and 9), Kissimmee, FL 34747. ✆ **800/327-9074** or 407/396-6100. Fax 407/396-6965. www.larsoninnfamilysuites.com. 128 units. $49–$109 double (to $125 in season). Children under 18 free with parents. AE, DC, DISC, MC, V. Free parking. Pets are permitted. Take I-4 to U.S. 192 exit; it's on left, across from old-fashioned water tower at the Celebration entrance and behind Water Mania. **Amenities:** Restaurant (American); heated outdoor pool; Jacuzzi; video arcade; guest services desk; transportation for a fee to all parks; guest laundry. *In room:* A/C, TV, fridge, microwave, safe.

Quality Inn Maingate West Overlooking a lake, this inn's standard rooms are small but clean and comfortable. There are 20 efficiencies with a microwave, refrigerator, two-plate burner, and utensils. It's ideal for young singles or young couples looking for a bargain.

7785 W. Irlo Bronson Memorial Hwy. (between Markers 5 and 6), Kissimmee, FL 34747. ✆ **800/634-5525** or 407/396-1828. Fax 407/396-1305. www.qualityinnorlando.com. 200 units. $43–$110 double. Children 18 and under stay free in parents' room. Rates include continental breakfast. AE, DC, DISC, MC, V. Free parking. From I-4, take the U.S. 192/Irlo Bronson exit; go west on US 192 2½ miles. **Amenities:** Restaurant (American); heated outdoor pool; video arcade; guest services desk; free transportation to Disney parks; transportation for a fee to others; guest laundry. *In room:* A/C, TV, dataport, coffeemaker.

So You Didn't Book a Room ...

If you're looking for a basic room, you can try these chain hotels and motels. They're all moderate or inexpensive in price and located in the budget motel corridors of Kissimmee/U.S. 192 or International Drive. While we can't vouch for them personally, their brand names generally mean reliability.

In Kissimmee:

- **Best Western Eastgate,** 5565 W. Irlo Bronson Memorial Hwy., Kissimmee (✆ **407/396-0707**).
- **Best Western Kissimmee,** 2261 E. Irlo Bronson Memorial Hwy., Kissimmee (✆ **407/846-2221**).
- **Comfort Suites Maingate Hotel,** 7888 W. Irlo Bronson Memorial Hwy., Kissimmee (✆ **407/390-9888**).
- **Comfort Suites Resort Maingate East,** 2775 Florida Plaza Blvd., Kissimmee (✆ **407/397-7848**).
- **Days Inn East of the Magic Kingdom,** 5840 W. Irlo Bronson Memorial Hwy., Kissimmee (✆ **407/396-7969**).
- **Days Inn Maingate–West,** 7980 W. Irlo Bronson Memorial Hwy., Kissimmee (✆ **407/997-1000**).
- **DoubleTree Maingate,** 4787 W. Irlo Bronson Memorial Hwy., Kissimmee (✆ **407/397-0555**).
- **Howard Johnson Maingate West,** 8660 W. Irlo Bronson Memorial Hwy., Kissimmee (✆ **407/396-4500**).
- **Quality Suites Maingate East,** 5876 W. Irlo Bronson Memorial Hwy., Kissimmee (✆ **407/396-8040**).

In the International Drive Area:

- **Days Inn Convention Center/SeaWorld,** 9990 International Dr., Orlando (✆ **407/352-8700**).
- **Days Inn East of Universal Studios,** 5827 Caravan Court, Orlando (✆ **407/351-3800**).
- **Days Inn International Drive,** 7200 International Dr., Orlando (✆ **407/351-1200**).
- **Holiday Inn Express International Drive,** 6323 International Dr., Orlando (✆ **407/351-4430**).
- **Sheraton Studio City Hotel,** 5905 International Dr., Orlando (✆ **407/351-2100**).
- **Travelodge International Drive,** 5859 American Way, Orlando (✆ **407/345-8880**).

You also can try **Central Reservation Service** (✆ **407/740-6442;** www.reservation-services.com) and **Discount Hotels of America** (✆ **407/294-9600;** www.discounthotelsamerica.com).

Ramada Disney Eastgate *Value* If you're looking for a peer in quality to the HoJo (above), this Ramada is it. Built in 1983 and remodeled in 1998, it's a cut cleaner than many of the chain's standard motels, but no fancier. Standard rooms sleep four but are somewhat cramped; all have balconies. One child eats free for each paying adult. The inn is 4 miles from Disney.

5150 W. Irlo Bronson Memorial Hwy. (U.S. 192), Kissimmee, FL 34746. © **888/298-2054** or 407/396-1111. Fax 407/396-1607. www.ramada.com. 402 units. $59–$129 double. Extra person $10. Children 17 and under stay free in parents' room. AE, DC, DISC, MC, V. Free self-parking. From I-4, take the U.S. 192 exit east 2½ miles to the motel. **Amenities:** Restaurant (American), lounge; outdoor heated pool, kids' pool; Jacuzzi; arcade; car-rental desk; free shuttles to Disney parks, transportation to non-Disney parks for a fee; limited room service; guest laundry, valet; nonsmoking rooms. *In room:* A/C, TV w/pay movies & Nintendo, dataport, coffeemaker, hair dryer, iron, safe.

WORTH A SPLURGE

Clarion Maingate ★ This plain, brown five-story brick building belies a pleasant, tropical theme in the lobby and rooms. All rooms have two double beds or one king-size bed and a small table and chair. There's a plain but serviceable recreation area adorned with a few palm trees lining the pool and a boardwalk overlooking a lake. It's 1.5 miles from Disney.

7675 Irlo Bronson Memorial Hwy (near Marker 5)., Kissimmee, FL 34747. © **800/568-3352** or 407/396-4000. Fax 407/396-0714. www.clariondisney.com. 198 units. $79–$139. AE, DC, DISC, MC, V. Free parking. From I-4 take the U.S. 192/Irlo Bronson exit and go west about 2 miles. **Amenities:** Restaurant (Seafood), lounge; kids' pool; exercise room; Jacuzzi; video arcade; free transportation to Disney parks; transportation for a fee to others; guest laundry. *In room:* A/C, TV, dataport, coffeemaker, hair dryer, iron, safe.

Holiday Inn Nikki Bird Resort ★ Here's another family-friendly inn with a roaming mascot (Nikki Bird) and a dedication to kids. The hotel renovated its rooms in 1997 and is in good shape. It features standard units as well as Kid Suites that have a separate area for youngsters. Suite themes vary. Kids under 12 eat free at a breakfast buffet next door; they also get entertainment, including puppet shows, songs, and games.

7300 W. Irlo Bronson Memorial Hwy. (U.S. 192), Kissimmee, FL 34747. © **800/206-2747** or 407/396-7300. Fax 407/396-7555. www.holidayinnsofcentralflorida.com. 530 units. $89–$139 for up to 4. AE, DC, DISC, MC, V. Free self-parking. Take I-4 to the U.S. 192 exit; go west. It's 1.5 miles past the Disney entrance on the left. **Amenities:** Restaurant (American), grill, lounge; outdoor heated pool, kids' pool; 3 lighted tennis courts; exercise room; Jacuzzi; kids' club; concierge; free shuttle to Disney parks, transportation to non-Disney parks for a fee; guest laundry, valet. *In room:* A/C, TV w/pay movies, dataport, fridge, coffeemaker, hair dryer, iron.

INTERNATIONAL DRIVE AREA
SUPER-CHEAP SLEEPS

Fairfield Inn International Drive ★ *Value* If you're looking for I-Drive's best value, it's hard to beat the Fairfield. This one combines a quiet location off the main drag, down-to-earth rates, and a clean, modern motel in one package. The rooms are very comfortable and there are a number of restaurants within walking distance of the hotel.

8342 Jamaican Court (off International Dr. between the Bee Line Expressway and Sand Lake Rd.), Orlando, FL 32819. © **800/228-2800** or 407/363-1944. Fax 407/363-1944. www.fairfieldinn.com. 135 units. $69–$89 for up to 4. AE, DC, DISC, MC, V. Free self-parking. From I-4, take the Sand Lake Rd./Hwy. 482 exit east 1 block, turn right on I-Drive, then right on Jamaican Court. **Amenities:** Outdoor heated pool; guest services desk; transportation for a fee to the parks; guest laundry, valet; nonsmoking rooms. *In room:* A/C, TV w/pay movies, dataport, safe.

Quality Inn Plaza The rooms at this property—across from the Pointe Orlando shopping plaza—are spread through five-, six-, and seven-story buildings. The biggest advantage in staying here is proximity to I-Drive nightlife, restaurants, and shops. The Semi-Suites have a microwave and refrigerator. The Executive rooms offer the same features as the Semi-Suites, a king bed upon request, and some additional amenities. Kids under 12 eat free.

9000 International Dr., Orlando, FL 32819. © **800/999-8585** or 407/996-8585. Fax 407/996-6839. www.qualityinn-orlando.com. 1,020 units. $59–$99 for up to 4. AE, DC, DISC, MC, V. Free self-parking. Pets $10 a night. From I-4, take the Sand Lake Rd./Hwy. 482 exit. Turn east at bottom of ramp. Turn at first intersection, International Dr. The property is 1 mile on the right. **Amenities:** Restaurant (American), deli, lounge; 3 outdoor heated pools; 2 arcades; guest services desk; transportation for a fee to all theme parks; limited room service; guest laundry; valet; nonsmoking rooms. *In room:* A/C, TV w/pay movies, coffeemaker, safe.

WORTH A SPLURGE

La Quinta Inn & Suites Convention Center ★   Opened in 1998, this is one of a handful of upscale, moderately priced motels on Universal Boulevard, which runs parallel to (but isn't as congested as) International Drive. The hotel is aimed at business travelers, but this is Orlando, so families traveling with kids are welcomed with open arms. King rooms come with a fridge and microwave. There are a limited number of two-room suites offering separate living and sleeping areas.

8504 Universal Blvd., Orlando, FL 32819. © **800/531-5900** or 407/345-1365. Fax 407/345-5586. www.laquinta.com. 185 units. $89–$139 double. Extra person $10. Rates include continental breakfast. Children 18 and under stay free in parents' room. AE, DC, DISC, MC, V. Free self-parking. Take I-4 to the Sand Lake Rd./Hwy. 482 exit, go east toward Universal, then right. **Amenities:** Outdoor heated pool; exercise room; Jacuzzi; transportation for a fee to all theme parks; guest laundry; nonsmoking rooms. *In room:* A/C, TV w/pay movies & Nintendo, dataport, coffeemaker, hair dryer, iron.

3 Great Deals on Dining, In & Around the Parks

Because many Orlando visitors spend most of their time in the Walt Disney World area, we've focused on the best and most reasonably priced choices throughout that vast empire. Also listed are some worthwhile places beyond the realm, including some at CityWalk, the dining and entertainment district at Universal Orlando.

There are plenty of other places to eat in Orlando. International Drive and U.S. 192 (Irlo Bronson Memorial Hwy.) are packed with a variety of budget restaurants. Parents find that just about every restaurant in town offers a low-priced children's menu and usually provides some kind of kid's activity as well. The downside of restaurants that cater to kids is that they're noisy; if you're looking for a quiet meal, head for restaurants listed as "Worth a Splurge."

HOW TO ARRANGE PRIORITY SEATING AT WALT DISNEY WORLD RESTAURANTS

Priority seating is similar to a reservation. It means you get the next table available when you arrive at a restaurant, but a table isn't kept empty pending your arrival. You can arrange priority seating up to 60 days in advance at almost all full-service Magic Kingdom, Epcot, Disney–MGM Studios, and Animal Kingdom restaurants, as well as those at Disney resorts and Downtown Disney. The same goes for character meals and shows. Just call © **407/939-3463.**

Since the priority-seating phone number was instituted in 1994, it has become much more difficult to obtain a table by just showing up; we *strongly* advise you to avoid disappointment by calling ahead. Remember—guests at Disney resorts and "official" hotels can make reservations through guest-services or concierge desks.

If you don't reserve in advance, you can try to reserve a table in the parks:

At Epcot: Make reservations at the WorldKey interactive terminals at Guest Relations in Innoventions East, at WorldKey Information Service Satellites on the main concourse to World Showcase, at Germany in World Showcase, or at the restaurants.

At the Magic Kingdom, Disney–MGM Studios, & Animal Kingdom: Reserve at the restaurants or via the telephones noted in the guide maps you get when you enter.

TIPS ON WALT DISNEY WORLD RESTAURANTS

- All park restaurants are **nonsmoking.**
- Magic Kingdom restaurants don't serve alcohol, but those at Animal Kingdom, Epcot, and Disney–MGM Studios do.
- Sit-down restaurants in WDW take American Express, Diners Club, Discover, MasterCard, Visa, and the Disney Card.
- Unless otherwise noted, *restaurants in the parks require park admission.* Unless you're using WDW transportation, there's also a $6 parking fee.
- Nearly all WDW restaurants with sit-down or counter service offer children's menus with items ranging from $4 to $6.

Keep in mind that theme-park eateries as a general rule are about 25% more expensive than comparable places in the "outside" world. The prices that follow are for entrees only; other courses, drinks, and tax are extra.

Also see the listings for dinner shows in "Walt Disney World & Orlando After Dark," later in this chapter. For online information, go to **www.disneyworld.com.**

INSIDE THE WDW THEME PARKS

With few exceptions, you won't find Disney's park restaurants winning accolades from *Food & Wine* or *Bon Appétit.* The food at most of them is on par with the food at Universal Orlando—filling and palatable, but overpriced for the quality. The following list includes the Magic Kingdom, Epcot, Disney–MGM Studios, and Animal Kingdom. Get information on all Disney restaurants by calling © **407/939-3463** or visiting **www.disneyworld.com.**

EPCOT

Though an ethnic meal at one of the World Showcase pavilions is a traditional part of the Epcot experience, we again stress that most of the major restaurants are expensive, especially for the value received. In the listings that follow, we're going to give you a taste of Epcot's better restaurants, along with information on some lower-priced walk-in eateries throughout the park.

World Showcase

The restaurants below are arranged geographically, beginning at the Canada pavilion and moving counterclockwise around World Showcase Lagoon.

Value **Bargain Buffets**

We won't list them all, but International Drive and U.S. 192/Irlo Bronson Memorial Highway have billboards peddling all-you-can-eat breakfast buffets for $4 to $6. This is a good way to fill up early and go easy on lunch, especially on days spent in the parks, where food is overpriced. Buffets are served by **Golden Corral,** 8033 International Dr. (© **407/352-6606**); **Ponderosa Steak House,** 6362 International Dr. (© **407/352-9343**), and 7598 U.S. 192 W. (© **407/396-7721**); and **Sizzler Restaurant,** 9142 International Dr. (© **407/351-5369**), and 7602 U.S. 192 W. (© **407/397-0997**).

CANADA **Le Cellier Steakhouse** has a castlelike ambience accentuated by vaulted stone arches. Red-meat main events (all Midwest, corn-fed) include the usual range of cuts—filet, porterhouse, prime rib, sirloin, and so on. Wash down your meal with a Canadian wine or choose from a selection of Canadian beers. Lunch runs $9 to $18; dinner is $15 to $26.

UNITED KINGDOM The Tudor-beamed **Rose & Crown** is a cozy pub suggestive of Victorian England. Visitors from the U.K. flock to this spot, where folk music and sometimes-saucy servers entertain you as you feast on a short but joyfully traditional menu including steak-and-mushroom pie and fish and chips. The outdoor dining area overlooks the lagoon and is a good place to see the IllumiNations fireworks display. Lunch is $10 to $14; dinner is $13.75 to $21.

MOROCCO Of all the Epcot restaurants, **Marrakesh** exemplifies the spirit of the park, yet a lot of guests don't know it's there or ignore it because they're worried that the menu is too exotic. Expect belly dancers to entertain while you feast on options like marinated beef shish kabob, braised chicken with green olives, and a medley of seafood, chicken, and lamb. Most entrees come with the national dish, couscous (steamed semolina with veggies and, sometimes, other embellishments). The palatial restaurant—with hand-set mosaic tiles, latticed shutters, and a ceiling painted in elaborate Moorish motifs—represents 12 centuries of Arabic design. Lunch costs $12 to $17.50; dinner is $17 to $26.

JAPAN If you've been to any of the Japanese steakhouse chains, you know the drill at **Teppanyaki:** Diners sit around grill tables while white-hatted chefs rapidly dice, slice, stir-fry, and sometimes launch the food onto your plate with amazing skill. Unfortunately, the culinary acrobatics here are better than the cuisine. Lunch is $9 to $21; dinner is $16.50 to $31. The adjoining **Yakitori House** is a bamboo-roofed cafeteria that serves casual fare for under $10.

ITALY Patterned after Alfredo De Lelio's celebrated ristorante in Rome, **L'Originale Alfredo di Roma** is Epcot's most popular restaurant. Nevertheless, critics say its pasta is overpriced and its servers are carefree. It's hard to take issue with the former when one meatless-pasta dish tops the $20 mark—the celebrated fettuccine. On the meatier side of the menu, a smallish veal chop is served with a Chianti-and-truffle sauce, mushrooms, asparagus, and roasted potatoes. There's an extensive Italian wine list. If you want a quieter setting, ask for a seat on the veranda. Lunch costs $10 to $26; dinner runs $17 to $38.

GERMANY The **Biergarten** simulates a Bavarian village at Oktoberfest. Unfortunately, the festive atmosphere hardly makes up for the bland food. The all-you-can-eat buffet is filled with traditional Bavarian fare (assorted sausages, chicken schnitzel, sauerbraten, spaetzle with gravy, sauerkraut, and a large assortment of trimmings). The lunch buffet is $14 for adults, $6 for kids 3 to 11; dinner is $19 for adults, $8 for children. At **Sommerfest,** a cafeteria, you can purchase bratwurst sandwiches with sauerkraut. All items are under $8.

CHINA When it comes to decor, **Nine Dragons** shines with carved rosewood furnishings and a dragon-motif ceiling. Some windows overlook the lagoon outside. The food, alas, doesn't match its surroundings. Main courses feature Mandarin, Cantonese, and Szechuan cuisine, but portions are small. You can order Chinese or California wines with your meal. Lunch runs $9.50 to $19; dinners go for $12.50 to $30. If you want something lighter, the open-air **Lotus Blossom Café** sells egg rolls, pork fried rice, and stir-fried chicken and vegetables served over noodles ($4.50–$6.50).

> **Tips** **Best Protein Snack in the Parks**
>
> For our money, you can't beat the smoked turkey drumsticks sold in WDW parks for under $5. How popular are they? Last year, Disney guests gobble-gobbled 1.6 million of them.

NORWAY **Akershus** is a re-created 14th-century castle where you can sample a 40-item smorgasbord of *smavarmt* (hot) and *koldtbord* (cold) dishes. The reasonably good entrees usually include such dishes as venison stew, stuffed pork, gravlax, smoked mackerel, and mustard herring. Norwegian beer and Aquavit complement a list of French and California wines. The lunch buffet costs $11.95 for adults, $5.25 for children 4 to 9; the dinner buffet is $18.50 for adults, $7.95 for kids. The **Kringla Bakeri og Kafe** has open-face sandwiches, sugar-sprinkled waffles, and fresh-baked Norwegian pastries. All items cost under $8.

MEXICO It's always night at the **San Angel Inn**, where candlelit tables set the mood, and the menu delivers reasonably authentic food. One top seller is the *mole poblano* (chicken brought to life with more than 20 spices, carrots, and a hint of chocolate). Another favorite: *filete motuleno* (grilled beef tenderloin served over black beans, melted cheese, pepper strips, and fried plantains). Lunch is $9 to $17; dinners are $17 to $22. The **Cantina de San Angel,** a cafeteria with outdoor seating at umbrella tables overlooking the lagoon, offers tacos, burritos, and other items under $8.

Future World
THE LAND PAVILION **Sunshine Season Food Fair** won't impress gourmets, but its diversity—there are six counter-service eateries inside—and prices make it ideal. There's a sandwich shop (subs and more); a barbecue joint (ribs, chicken, pork); a potato place (with stir-fry, chili, and veggies); and a pasta counter (fettuccine, vegetable lasagna, and chicken Alfredo). There's also a small bakery and ice cream stand. Most items are $5 to $9.

THE MAGIC KINGDOM
The full-service restaurants in the Magic Kingdom, like those in most theme parks, are almost ridiculously expensive. They charge as much as $8 to $10—even for burgers and sandwiches. Fortunately, there are dozens of fast-food places, almost all of them with pleasant outdoor tables. *Remember:* No alcoholic beverages are served in Magic Kingdom restaurants.

TOMORROWLAND The major restaurant here is **Cosmic Ray's Starlight Cafe,** which is enormous. The low-budget, high-fat menu includes chicken, chicken, and more chicken (whole or half rotisserie, dark meat, white meat, fried or grilled). It's typical theme-park on-the-fly cuisine. Bring plenty of antacid. *Note:* Most items are under $7; a whole rotisserie chicken is $16.

Another possibility is **The Lunching Pad at Rockettower Plaza** (smoked turkey legs and other snacks, mostly under $6), which is near the entrance to the Tomorrowland Transit Authority.

FANTASYLAND **Cinderella's Royal Table** in Cinderella Castle is the headliner. Servers treat you like a lord or lady while fetching entrees like spice-crusted salmon, a New York strip, or roasted chicken. Lunch costs $11 to $16; dinner sells for $20 to $26.

The **Pinocchio Village Haus,** a large cafeteria, has a charming alpine-castle/storybook-themed interior and outdoor seating at umbrella tables, some overlooking the fountains. Items such as burgers and smoked turkey subs are under $10. Lighter options can be found at **Mrs. Potts' Cupboard** (soft-serve ice cream, sundaes), the **Enchanted Grove** (lemonade slushes, strawberry swirls), and **Scuttle's Landing** (snow cones, beverages).

LIBERTY SQUARE   The **Columbia Harbor House,** a pleasant cafeteria, offers clam chowder, fried fish, and chicken strips for under $10.

The Liberty Tree Tavern's colonial decor and mood are fun, but the food (including the evening character buffet) is basic. Expect roast turkey, flank steak, and ham. Lunch is $10.75 to $17; the buffet is $21 for adults, $10 for kids 3 to 11.

The Diamond Horseshoe Saloon Revue has sandwiches, salads, and snacks for under $10. Although the food is basic, you can eat while watching the show (later in this chapter).

FRONTIERLAND   The **Pecos Bill Cafe,** a large cafeteria adjacent to Adventureland, has a rustic interior with stone fireplace. The fare (all under $10) consists of burgers, hot dogs, salads, sandwiches, root-beer floats, and beverages.

Aunt Polly's Landing on Tom Sawyer's Island, reached via a short raft trip, has outdoor tables on a porch overlooking the water. It provides a respite from the park's hyperactivity. The light fare includes ham-and-cheese sandwiches, picnic lunches, and soft drinks (under $9). It's open for lunch only.

ADVENTURELAND   The major eats joint is **El Pirata y El Perico,** a cafeteria with covered seating on a Mexican-style Saltillo-tile patio. The menu includes nachos, tacos, and taco salads. Everything is under $8.

Juices, frozen yogurt, and iced cappuccino are available from the **Sunshine Tree Terrace,** a thatch-roof structure with outdoor seating at umbrella tables.

DISNEY–MGM STUDIOS

There are more than a dozen eateries in this Hollywood-themed park, but the food quality and value are pretty poor.

The **50's Prime Time Café** lets you watch black-and-white TV sets showing "My Little Margie" while servers threaten to withhold dessert if you don't eat all your food. Although the desserts are good, the meat loaf and pot roast don't deliver. Meals cost $13 to $18.50 at lunch and dinner.

The safest things at **Mama Melrose's Ristorante Italiano** are the wood-fired flat breads (grilled pepperoni, portobello mushroom, and four cheese). The

---

Tips   Special Tastes

Looking for kosher food? Worried WDW can't entertain your vegetarian taste buds? Disney usually can handle those diets and other special ones (people who need fat-free or sugar-free meals, folks who have allergies or a lactose intolerance, for instance) as long as guests give Disney advance notice—usually no more than 24 hours. You can do that when you make priority-seating arrangements (© **407/939-3463** or, if you're staying at a Disney resort, at its guest services desk). If you're not staying at WDW, call © **407/824-2222**. That said, the price will be high for less than haute cuisine.

menu is fleshed out with so-so Italian pretenders—chicken marsala, cioppino, and others. Lunch is $12 to $18; dinner is $15 to $18.

The **Sci-Fi Dine-In Theater Restaurant** is the 50's Prime Time Café with a sci-fi spin. You watch newsreels, cartoons, and "B" horror flicks that help you forget the so-so beef, pork, poultry, tuna, and pasta. Lunches set you back $10 to $16.50; dinners are $15 to $18.50.

If you must eat at Disney–MGM, we recommend you stick to one of the following counter-service options, all of which sell items for under $8 or $10:

- **Toy Story Pizza Planet,** located in the Muppets Courtyard, offers what the name implies along with salads, espresso, and cappuccino.
- **Rosie's All-American Café,** located on Sunset Boulevard near the Rock 'n' Roller Coaster, sells burgers including veggie burgers, cold sandwiches, soups, and salads.
- The **ABC Commissary,** on Commissary Lane, has burgers, chicken, and wraps.
- **Catalina Eddie's,** next to Rosie's, serves pizza and salads.

ANIMAL KINGDOM

Most restaurants in this park are eat-on-the-go, counter-style places where most items are under $10. These include **Tusker House** in Africa (grilled chicken salad in a sourdough-bread bowl; rotisserie or fried chicken; and a chicken, ham, and Swiss cheese sandwich) and **Pizzafari** near the Tree of Life.

The kingdom's main sit-down restaurant is the **Rainforest Cafe** (© 407/938-9100; www.rainforestcafe.com). The food tends to be tasty and sometimes creative, but the cafe, like other Disney restaurants, charges more than it should. Dishes include a turkey pita with fried onions, romaine, and tomatoes. The mixed grill has ribs, steak on skewers, barbecued chicken, and peppered shrimp. Lunch and dinner run $10 to $40.

AT DISNEY RESORTS

Maya Grill AMERICAN/CAJUN   Some call it "Nuevo Latino." But it's nothing fancier than steaks, chicken, shellfish, and other seafood items raised an octave by Southwestern-style spices. The atmosphere, though, is more than a notch higher than that of the food courts, and in the morning, breakfast arrives with the same kind of warm-you-up flavor.

1000 Buena Vista Dr. (in Disney's Coronado Springs Resorts). © 407/934-7639 for priority seating. Main courses and breakfast items under $9; dinner $9–$18. AE, DC, DISC, MC, V. Daily 7–11:30am and 5–10pm.

SUPER-CHEAP EATS

Intermission Food Court INTERNATIONAL   This cheerful food court, adorned with music paraphernalia and memorabilia, has stations ranging from baked goods and pizza to subs. You can get a barbecued beef, chicken, or pork dinner for under $13. Wine and beer are available, and kids can head to a video arcade while Mom and Dad linger over coffee. All-you-can-eat buffet breakfasts cost under $10 for those 9 and older and under $7 for those under 9.

The **End Zone Food Court** at the adjoining All-Star Sports Resort (© 407/939-5000) and the **World Premiere Food Court** at the All-Star Movie Resort (© 407/939-7000) have similar menus and prices.

1801 W. Buena Vista Dr. (at Disney's All-Star Music Resort, at World Dr. and Osceola Pkwy.). © 407/939-6000. Reservations not accepted. Most items under $10. AE, DC, DISC, MC, V. Daily 7am–11pm (bakery opens at 6am; pizza served to midnight).

Market Street Old Port Royale Food Court AMERICAN This place has all of the usual food-court offerings (rotisserie chicken, sandwiches, pizza, salads, cookies, cakes, pies, ice cream cones, and sundaes). Kids will enjoy the large video-game arcade on the premises and a room where Disney movies and cartoons are aired.

900 Cayman Way (at Disney's Caribbean Beach Resort, off Buena Vista Dr.). © **407/934-3400.** Reservations not accepted. Most items under $10. AE, DC, DISC, MC, V. Daily 7am–11pm (bakery opens at 6am; pizza served to midnight).

WORTH A SPLURGE

Cape May Café CLAMBAKE BUFFET As a rule, all-you-can-eat marine feasts tend to promise more than they deliver, and this is no exception. Yes, there's an honest seafood selection (clams, mussels, baked fish, and microscopic peel-and-eat shrimp). But seafood served buffet style—allowed to sit out where it collects all sorts of airborne bacteria—isn't an ideal meal in our book, especially inland. If you're still inclined, the nautically themed restaurant has a full bar and it's said that enough alcohol kills any germ. If you're inclined but not willing to take the risk, the buffet also has chicken, ribs, and flank steak. Cape May Café also offers a character breakfast (see below).

1800 Epcot Resorts Blvd., at Disney's Beach Club Resort. © **407/939-3463.** www.disneyworld.com. Priority seating. Buffet $22 adults at dinner, $10 children 3–11. AE, DC, DISC, MC, V. Daily 5:30–9:30pm. Free self- and valet parking.

'Ohana ✦ PACIFIC RIM Its star is earned on the fun front, but the decibel level will turn some off. As your luau is being prepared over an 18-foot-wide fire pit, the staff keeps you busy with coconut races, hula lessons, and other shenanigans. The feed bag includes salad, fruit, fresh-baked focaccia bread, turkey, shrimp, pork loin, and steak, plus dessert. A full bar offers tropical drinks, including non-alcoholic ones for kids, and there's a limited selection of wines.

1600 Seven Seas Dr., at Disney's Polynesian Resort. © **407/939-3463** or 407/824-2000. www.disneyworld.com. Priority seating is strongly encouraged. $21 adults, $10 children 3–11. AE, DC, DISC, MC, V. Daily 7:30–11am and 5–10pm. Free self- and valet parking.

AT DOWNTOWN DISNEY
SUPER-CHEAP EATS

Planet Hollywood AMERICAN Some folks come for a first look, but most diners are fans who flock here for the scenery (including a planetarium-like ceiling and Peter O'Toole's *Lawrence of Arabia* duds). The compulsion is much like that of Hard Rock Cafe fans who go for the tunes. The Planet's servers can cop an attitude and the food is blasé. If you must, you'll find the usual suspects: wings, pot stickers, sandwiches, big burgers, ribs, fajitas, pizzas, pasta, and questionable steaks. Lines can get long during special events and in peak season.

1506 Buena Vista Dr., at Pleasure Island (look for the big globe). © **407/827-7827.** www.planethollywood.com. Limited priority seating. Main courses $8–$20 (most under $15). AE, DC, DISC, MC, V. Daily 11am–1am. Free self-parking.

Rainforest Cafe ✦ CALIFORNIA Don't arrive starving. Waits average 2 hours if you fail to call ahead for priority seating, although even then you'll wait longer than at Animal Kingdom's Rainforest Cafe (see above). The menu can be tasty and creative, though somewhat overpriced. Fun dishes include Mojo Bones (pork ribs), Rumble in the Jungle Turkey Pita, and Mixed Grill (ribs, steak skewers, chicken breast, and peppered shrimp). There's a good selection of beer and wine. The tables are very close together, so those with physical disabilities may find it difficult to maneuver here.

Downtown Disney Marketplace; near the smoking volcano. © 407/827-8500. www.rainforest.com. Priority seating. Main courses $11–$40 at lunch and dinner (most under $25). AE, DISC, MC, V. Sun–Thurs 10:30am–11pm, Fri–Sat 10:30am–midnight. Free self-parking.

MEALS WITH DISNEY CHARACTERS

Dining with costumed characters is a treat for almost any Disney fan, but it's a special treat for those under 10. Some of their favorite cartoon characters show up to greet them, sign autographs, pose for family photos, and interact. These aren't low-turnout events, so make reservations as far in advance as possible. It's best to make reservations when you book your room.

The prices for character meals are much the same, no matter where you're dining. Breakfast (most serve it) runs $14 to $16 for adults and $8 to $10 for children 3 to 11; those that serve dinner charge $19 to $22 for adults, $9 to $13 for kids. The prices vary a bit, though, from location to location.

To make reservations for WDW character meals call © **407/939-3463**. American Express, Diners Club, Discover, MasterCard, Visa, and the Disney Card are accepted at all character meals. For Internet information, go to **www.disneyworld.com**.

Note: We strongly recommend against promising children they will meet a specific character at a meal. If you have your heart set on meeting a certain character, call to confirm his or her appearance when making your priority seating arrangement.

Character meals are offered at **Cape May Café** (in Disney's Beach Club Resort), **Chef Mickey's** (at Disney's Contemporary Resort), **Cinderella's Royal Table** (in Cinderella Castle, Magic Kingdom), **Crystal Palace Buffet** (at Crystal Palace, Magic Kingdom), **Donald's Prehistoric Breakfastosaurus** (in Dinoland U.S.A., Animal Kingdom), **Garden Grill** (in The Land Pavilion at Epcot), **Hollywood & Vine Character Dining** (at Hollywood & Vine, in Disney–MGM Studios), **Liberty Tree Tavern** (in Liberty Square, in the Magic Kingdom), **'Ohana** (at Disney's Polynesian Resort), and **1900 Park Fare** (at Disney's Grand Floridian Resort & Spa).

UNIVERSAL ORLANDO

Universal stormed onto the restaurant scene with the mid-1999 opening of its dining and club venue, CityWalk, located between and in front of its two parks, Universal Studios Florida and Islands of Adventure (© **407/363-8000**; www.citywalk.com).

Note: Parking will cost you $7 before 6pm at the following restaurants.

Jimmy Buffett's Margaritaville CARIBBEAN As soon as the parrotheads have enough to drink (no later than 4pm on weekends), the noise makes it futile to try conversation, but most folks come to Margaritaville to sing and get stupid, not to gab. Despite the cheeseburgers in paradise (yes, they're on the menu at $7.95), Jimmy's reasonably tasty victuals lean toward the Caribbean side, including jerk chicken and a Cuban meat loaf survival sandwich that's a cheeseburger of another kind. If you don't yearn for margaritas, there's a long list of domestic and imported beer.

1000 Universal Studios Plaza, in CityWalk. © 407/224-2155. www.universalorlando.com. Reservations not accepted. Main courses $8–$19. AE, DISC, MC, V. Daily 11:30am–midnight. Parking $7 (free after 6pm). From I-4, take the Kirkman Rd./Hwy. 435 exit and follow the signs to Universal.

> **Tips** **Saving with Take-out**
>
> Even if you don't rent an efficiency or kitchenette, you can save some on your meal budget by getting take-out. In addition to places like delis, pizza joints, and fast-food restaurants, a number of Orlando-area supermarkets sell ready-to-eat meals. Some of the more notable ones are Publix, Winn-Dixie, Albertson's, and Gooding's. You can find them in the Yellow Pages under "Grocers."

SUPER-CHEAP EATS

Bob Marley—A Tribute to Freedom CARIBBEAN   Part club and part restaurant, Marley's is a replica of the late reggae singer's home in Kingston, complete with tile roof and green-shuttered windows. There's live reggae nightly. The menu has nothing but modestly priced Jamaican fare, including a jerk snapper sandwich on coca bread with yucca fries, a tomato-based fish chowder, and grouper fingers lightly breaded, fried, and topped with red and green peppers. Of course, most folks don't leave without sipping at least one Red Stripe—Jamaica's national beer.

1000 Universal Studios Plaza, in CityWalk. © 407/224-2262. www.universalorlando.com. Reservations not accepted. Main courses $6–$9. AE, DISC, MC, V. Daily 4pm–2am. Parking $7 (free after 6pm). From I-4, take the Kirkman Rd./Hwy. 435 exit and follow the signs to Universal.

Pastamore Ristorante SOUTHERN ITALIAN   This family-style restaurant greets you with display cases brimming with mozzarella and other goodies on the menu. The antipasto primo is a meal unto itself. It includes bruschetta, eggplant caponata, melon with prosciutto, grilled portobello mushrooms, Italian cold cuts, olives, plum tomatoes, mozzarella, and more. The menu also has traditional features such as veal marsala, chicken piccata, shrimp scampi, fettuccine Alfredo, lasagna, and pizza. An open kitchen allows diners a view of the chefs at work. You can also eat in a cafe where lighter fare—breakfast and sandwiches—is served from 8am to 2am.

1000 Universal Studios Plaza, in CityWalk. © 407/363-8000. www.universalorlando.com. Reservations accepted. Main courses $7–$18. AE, DISC, MC, V. Daily 5pm–midnight. Parking $7 (free after 6pm). From I-4, take the Kirkman Rd./Hwy. 435 exit and follow the signs to Universal.

WORTH A SPLURGE

Emeril's NEW ORLEANS   It's next to impossible to get short-term reservations for dinner (less than 6–8 weeks in advance) unless your stars are aligned or you're willing to come at the opening or closing bell and take your chances with no-shows. But most who get in say the dynamic, Creole-inspired cuisine is worth the struggle. Best bets are andouille-crusted redfish (a moist white fish with roasted pecan-vegetable relish and meunière sauce) and the quail (yes, they *are* little) stuffed with Louisiana oyster dressing and served with a ragout of vegetables and cornmeal-crusted oysters. If you want some *vino* with your meal, no problem; the back half of the building is a glass-walled, 12,000-bottle, above-ground cellar. Prices are high enough that Emeril can afford tons of legroom between tables. If you want a show, we recommend one of eight counter seats where you can watch chefs working their magic, but to get one, reservations are required *excruciatingly* early.

Note: Lunch costs about half what you'll spend on dinner, and the menu and portions are almost the same. It's also easier to get a midday reservation and the dress code is more casual—jackets are recommended for gents at dinner.

6000 Universal Studios Blvd., in CityWalk. © 407/224-2424. www.universalorlando.com or www.emerils.com/restaurants/orlando. Reservations necessary. Main courses $17–$26 at lunch; $18–$42 at dinner. Daily 11:30am–2:30pm and 5:30–10pm (until 11pm Fri–Sat). AE, DISC, MC, V. Parking $7 (free after 6pm). From I-4, take the Kirkman Rd./Hwy. 435 exit and follow the signs to Universal.

IN THE LAKE BUENA VISTA AREA

There are a number of good choices in this area, which is outside Disney but adjacent to its theme parks.

Pebbles ★★ *Finds* CALIFORNIA   If you want to dine like a gourmet without paying a heavy price, here's your meal ticket. Pebbles is a local chain that has earned a reputation for great food, a sexy though small wine list, and creative appetizers. When they're available, the chèvre-coated lamb chops are worth fighting for. Like many of the entrees, they come with three-cheese mashed potatoes and zucchini wedges. The twin Brie filet mignons are almost as tempting (they come with morel sauce). There's also roast duck in a glaze of strawberries, pistachios, and Triple Sec. Pebbles is popular among a crowd ranging from young yuppies to aging baby boomers.

Note: Pebbles also has locations downtown: 17 W. Church St. (© **407/839-0892**); in Longwood, 2110 W. Hwy. 434 (© **407/774-7111**); and in Winter Park, 2516 Aloma Ave. (© **407/678-7001**).

12551 Apopka-Vineland Rd., in the Crossroads Shopping Center. © **407/827-1111**. www.pebblesworldwide.com. Reservations not accepted. Main courses $10–$21. AE, DC, DISC, MC, V. Sun–Thurs noon–11pm, Fri–Sat 11am–11pm. Free self-parking. Take the I-4 Hwy. 535/Apopka-Vineland Rd. exit north to the Crossroads Shopping Center on the right.

SUPER-CHEAP EATS

Chili's Grill & Bar SOUTHWESTERN   This Texas-based chain has always been a good choice for family dining, especially this branch, where children's books and toys are provided for youngsters. Adults, on the other hand, might appreciate the bar area, where sports are aired on four TV monitors and drinks are priced two-for-one during a daily 11am-to-7pm happy hour.

Chili is a specialty, of course, including a half-pound chili cheeseburger served with home fries. Other possibilities include battered, farm-raised catfish with fries and corn on the cob, steak or chicken fajitas, grilled baby-back ribs, and salads. Save room for dessert: a chocolate brownie topped with vanilla ice cream and hot fudge. Several low-fat items are specified on the menu.

12172 Apopka–Vineland Rd. (just north of Hwy. 535/Palm Pkwy.). © **407/239-6688**. www.chilis.com. Reservations not accepted, but you can call when you leave your hotel to get on a waiting list. Main courses $7.25–$18. AE, DC, DISC, MC, V. Sun–Thurs 11am–midnight, Fri–Sat 11am–1am.

Romano's Macaroni Grill ★ NORTHERN ITALIAN   Though it's part of a multi-state chain, Romano's has the down-to-earth cheerfulness of a mom-and-pop joint. The menu is decorated with thin-crust pizzas made in a wood-burning oven and topped with such items as barbecued chicken. The grilled chicken portobello (simmering between smoked mozzarella and spinach orzo pasta) is worth the visit. Equally good is an entree of grilled salmon with a teriyaki glaze, also with spinach orzo pasta. Premium wines come by the glass.

12148 Apopka–Vineland Rd. (just north of County Rd. 535/Palm Pkwy.). © **407/239-6676**. www.macaronigrill.com. Main courses $6–$9 at lunch; $8–$19 at dinner (most under $12). AE, DC, DISC, MC, V. Sun–Thurs

11:30am–10pm, Fri–Sat 11:30am–11pm. Free self-parking. Take the I-4 Hwy. 535/Apopka-Vineland Rd. exit north and continue straight when Hwy. 535 goes to the right. Romano's is about 2 blocks on the left.

INTERNATIONAL DRIVE & VICINITY

International Drive has one of the area's larger collections of fast-food joints, but the midsection and southern third also have some of this region's better restaurants. I-Drive is 10 minutes by auto from the Walt Disney World parks.

B-Line Diner AMERICAN   Come to have fun in a chrome-plated '50s-style diner where you can sink into upholstered booths or belly up to the counter on a stool. It can get noisy, partly due to a pretty exuberant wait staff. The 'round-the-clock menu features comfort foods such as chicken pot pie that's up to what mom made; a ham and cheese sandwich on a baguette; and roast pork with grilled apples, sun-dried cherry stuffing, and brandy-honey sauce. The portions are hearty, but so are the prices for diner fare. There's a full bar for those needing a mind-altering experience that falls short of the kind the late Timothy Leary provided.

9801 International Dr., in the Peabody Orlando. © 407/345-4460. www.peabody-orlando.com. Reservations not accepted. Main courses $4–$14 at breakfast; $7–$17 at lunch; $9–$26 (most under $17) at dinner. AE, DC, DISC, MC, V. Daily 24 hrs. Free self- and validated valet parking. From I-4 take the Sand Lake Rd./Hwy. 528 exit east to International Dr., then south. Hotel is on the left across from the Convention Center.

Bahama Breeze *Value* CARIBBEAN   This chain with spunk uses traditional Caribbean food as a base for creative items, such as moist and tasty "fish in a bag" (strips of mahimahi in a parchment pillow flavored with carrots, sweet peppers, mushrooms, celery, and spices) and a B+ *paella* (rice with shrimp, fish, mussels, chicken, and sausage). It's loud and always crowded, so arrive early and bring patience. The restaurant doesn't accept reservations, and during prime time—6 to 8pm—the wait can be up to 2 hours. You can pass the time watching the chefs work in the open kitchen, but the tropical drinks and 50 brands of beer make the time move faster.

8849 International Dr. © 407/248-2499. www.bahamabreeze.com. Reservations not accepted. Main courses $9–$25 full orders; $7–$14 half orders; $8–$12 sandwiches and salads. AE, MC, V. Sun–Thurs 4pm–1am, Fri–Sat 4pm–1:30am. Free self-parking. From I-4 take the Sand Lake Rd./Hwy. 528 exit east to International Dr., then south. It's on the left, 2 blocks past Cafe Tu Tu Tango (below).

Siam Orchid *Finds* THAI   Owners Tim and Krissnee Martsching grow chilies, mint, cilantro, lemongrass, wild lime, and other ingredients in their garden, and the quality of their entrees is consistently high. Pad Thai (soft rice noodles tossed with ground pork, minced garlic, shrimp, crab claws, crabmeat, crushed peanuts, and bean sprouts in a tongue-twanging sweet sauce) is one of our favorites. Curries such as Royal Thai (chicken chunks, potato, and onion in a yellow curry sauce) are another crowd pleaser. The split-level dining room seats diners in cushioned booths and banquettes and bamboo chairs; some tables overlook a lake. Siam Orchid serves sake, plum wine, and Thai beers from a full bar.

7575 Universal Dr. (between Sand Lake Rd. and Carrier Dr.). © 407/351-0821. Reservations recommended. Main courses $11–$21. AE, DC, DISC, MC, V. Mon–Fri 11am–2pm, daily 5–11pm. Free self-parking. From I-4 take the Sand Lake Rd./Hwy. 528 exit east to Universal, then go north to the restaurant (on the left).

SUPER-CHEAP EATS

Cafe Tu Tu Tango INTERNATIONAL/TAPAS   This zany restaurant is a welcome respite from Orlando's predictable "chain gang." An ongoing performance/art experience takes place while you dine and might consist of an elegantly dressed couple doing the tango past your table, a belly dancer, a magician, or artists creating pottery, paintings, and jewelry. You can munch on any of dozens of tapas or appetizer-size mini-meals. One of our favorites is the Cajun egg rolls filled with blackened chicken, corn, and cheddar and goat cheeses, served with chunky tomato salsa and Creole mustard. Sampling can get to be quite expensive, but the larger your party, the more dishes you can sample without going bust (usually two or three per person does the trick). Wine is available by the glass or bottle.

8625 International Dr. (just west of the Mercado). ✆ 407/248-2222. www.cafetututango.com. Reservations not required. Tapas (small plates) $4–$10. AE, DC, DISC, MC, V. Sun–Thurs 11:30am–11pm, Fri–Sat 11:30am–midnight. Free self-parking. From I-4 take the Sand Lake Rd./Hwy. 528 exit east to International Dr., then south. It's on the left.

Max's Café AMERICAN   Located in the town of Celebration, its Art-Deco decor is a re-creation of yesterday's "blue-plate special" joints that served stick-to-your-ribs, comfort favorites, such as roast turkey with cornbread stuffing and mashed 'taters. You get your money's worth in sandwiches (try the Havana or portobello melt) and meals such as honey-glazed ribs, roast pork, and Dijon-crusted chicken, all of which come in hearty helpings. The meat loaf may be better than Mom's (with all due respect).

701 Front St., Celebration. ✆ 321/566-1144. www.maxsrestaurants.com. Main courses $7–$12. AE, DC, DISC, MC, V. Daily 8am–9pm. Free self-parking.

WORTH A SPLURGE

Capriccio NORTHERN ITALIAN   Like its upscale Peabody sister, Dux, Capriccio virtually ensures something different from visit to visit, as its menu changes seasonally. The entrees might include bucatini tossed with chunks of mesquite-grilled chicken and mushrooms in a slightly garlicky herbed white-wine/pesto sauce; or pan-seared tuna with braised fennel and radicchio served with lentil flan and a buttery citrus sauce. Chefs in the exhibition kitchen also make pizzas and fresh breads in mesquite-burning ovens. There's an extensive wine list. The warm decor and the large amounts of natural wood in the dining room give the restaurant a somewhat refined atmosphere.

Capriccio also serves a champagne Sunday brunch (leg of lamb, prime rib, you-peel shrimp, smoked salmon, mussels, crepes, eggs Benedict, omelets, and unlimited champagne). The restaurant is smoke-free, a fact that is unusual outside of the Disney restaurants.

9801 International Dr., in the Peabody Orlando. ✆ 407/345-4540. www.peabody-orlando.com. Reservations recommended. Main courses $18–$38 (most pizza and pasta dishes priced below $15); Sun champagne brunch buffet $33 adults, $15 children 5–12. AE, DC, DISC, MC, V. Tues–Sun 6–11pm; Sun brunch 11am–2pm. Free self- and validated valet parking. From I-4 take the Sand Lake Rd./Hwy. 528 exit east to International Dr., then south. Hotel is on the left across from the Convention Center.

ELSEWHERE IN ORLANDO

Rolando's *Finds* CUBAN   Big portions and authentic cuisine are the main draws at this mom-and-pop eatery. Our favorites include *arroz con pollo* (chicken with yellow rice), *ropa vieja* (shredded beef), and, if you call a day in advance, *paella* (fish and shellfish served on a bed of rice). Entrees come with yucca or plantains. There's a very limited beer and wine list.

870 E. Hwy. 436/Semoran Blvd., in Casselberry. ✆ 407/767-9677. Reservations accepted. Main courses $4–$6 at lunch; $8–$18 at dinner. AE, DC, DISC, MC, V. Mon–Fri 11am–9:30pm, Sat noon–10pm, Sun noon–8:30pm. Free self-parking. Take I-4 take the Hwy. 408/East–West Expressway exit, head east, and make a left on Hwy. 436.

SUPER-CHEAP EATS

Bubbaloo's Bodacious BBQ ★ *Value* BARBECUE   This spot serves some of the best barbecue in Florida. Go for the full pork platter that comes with a heaping helping of pork and all the fixin's. The uninitiated should stay away from the "Killer" sauce, which produces a tongue buzz that's likely to last for hours; you might even taste-test the mild sauce before moving up to the hot.

1471 Lee Rd., Winter Park (about 5 min. from downtown Orlando). ✆ 407/628-1212. Reservations not accepted. Main courses $5–$15. AE, MC, V. Mon–Thurs 10am–9pm, Fri–Sat 10am–10:30pm. Free self-parking. Take the I-4 Lee Rd. exit and follow your nose; Bubbaloo's is on the left next to a dry cleaner.

Little Saigon ★ *Finds* VIETNAMESE   Asian immigrants created the demand for this great little eatery that's yet to be discovered by tourists. Try the summer rolls—a soft wrap filled with rice, shrimp, and pork served with a delicious peanut sauce. Head next for the grilled pork and egg over rice and noodles or barbecued beef with fried egg and rice. The numbered menu isn't translated well, but your server or the manager can help.

1106 E. Colonial Dr./Hwy. 50 (near downtown Orlando). ✆ 407/423-8539. Reservations not accepted. Main courses under $5 at lunch; $5–$8 at dinner. AE, DISC, MC, V. Daily 10am–9pm. Free self-parking. Take the Colonial Dr./Hwy. 50 exit off I-4 and head east. Turn right on Thornton Ave. The parking lot is immediately to the left.

WORTH A SPLURGE

Le Provence ★ NEW FRENCH   This upscale local favorite serves dishes that feature duck, veal, lobster, scallops, and tuna. If you're in the mood for creative seafood, try the snapper stuffed with shrimp mousse, then wrapped in phyllo with smoked tomato compote and braised cabbage. Wow! Duck lovers can drool over a combo plate: breast meat grilled in a subtle citrus marinade and a leg with natural juices and pineapple salsa. Few restaurants in town offer rabbit, and none do it better than Le Provence, where the loin is stuffed with paé and vegetables and served in cognac sauce. There are eight fixed-price menus that range from three to six courses. You can enjoy a martini or an after-dinner drink and a cigar next door at Monaco's, which also serves lunch.

Note: In addition to the valet parking noted below, early birds have a shot at a small amount of metered street parking.

50 E. Pine St., in downtown Orlando. ✆ 407/843-1320. www.cenfla.com/res/leprovence. Reservations recommended. Main courses $7–$10 at lunch; $18–$34 at dinner (most under $25); $28–$58 prix fixe. AE, DC, MC, V. Mon–Fri 11:30am–2pm and 5:30–9:30pm, Sat 5:30–10:30pm. Valet parking $6. From I-4 take the Anderson St. exit east to Church St., then left/north on Court Ave. It's near the corner of Court and Pine.

4 Tips for Visiting Walt Disney World Attractions

No wonder they call it a world. Walt Disney World encompasses the Magic Kingdom; Epcot; Disney–MGM Studios; Animal Kingdom; Pleasure Island; Downtown Disney West Side; Downtown Disney Marketplace; two water parks (Typhoon Lagoon and Blizzard Beach); scores of restaurants; and 17 Disney-owned resorts.

PLANNING YOUR TRIP

Planning is essential. Unless you're staying for considerably more than a week, you won't have time to experience all of the rides, shows, attractions, and recreational options. You'll only wear yourself to a frazzle trying—it's better to follow a relaxed itinerary, including leisurely meals, than to make a marathon.

INFORMATION   Call or write **Walt Disney World**, P.O. Box 10000, Lake Buena Vista, FL 32830-1000 (✆ **407/934-7639**), for a copy of the very

> **Tips Smoking Alert**
> Disney long has prohibited smoking in shops, attractions, restaurants, ride lines, and other areas. All WDW parks stopped selling cigarettes in 1999, and in 2000 smokers were allowed to light up only in designated areas.

informative *Walt Disney World Vacations,* an invaluable planning aid. Once you've arrived in town, guest-services, concierge, or front desks in area hotels—especially Disney properties and "official" hotels—have **up-to-the-minute information** about what's going on in the parks. If your hotel doesn't have this information, call ✆ **407/824-4321.**

There are also **information locations** in each park—at City Hall in the Magic Kingdom, at Innoventions East near the World Key terminals in Epcot, and at Guest Relations in Disney–MGM Studios and Animal Kingdom.

There's plenty of park info on the Web at **www.disneyworld.com, www.orlandosentinel.com,** and **www.orlandoinfo.com.**

BUYING TICKETS IN ADVANCE   You can purchase multiday passes (see details below) before your trip by calling ✆ **407/934-7639.** Allow 21 days for processing your request and include $2 for postage and handling. Of course, you can purchase tickets at any of the parks, but why stand in an avoidable line? *Note:* One-day tickets can't be purchased this way.

ARRIVE EARLY   Get to the parks 30 to 45 minutes before the opening bell, thus avoiding a traffic jam entering them and a long line at the gate. Early arrival also lets you experience one or two major attractions before long lines form at them. In high season, the parking lots sometimes fill and you may have to wait to get in. The longest lines in all parks are between 11am and 4pm.

ESSENTIALS

PARKING   Parking costs $6 for cars, light trucks, and vans; $7 for RVs. Folks with disabilities can park in special lots; call ✆ **407/824-4321.** Don't forget to write down where you parked; it's easy to get lost after a long day.

STROLLERS/WHEELCHAIRS   Single strollers and wheelchairs rent for $7 including a $1 deposit; electric carts are $30 plus a $10 deposit.

WHEN YOU ARRIVE   Grab a park guide map! It not only tells you where the fun is but lists the daily entertainment schedule. If you want to see certain shows or parades, arrive early to get a good seat. Use this guide and the map to come up with a game plan on where to eat, what to ride, and what to see during your stay.

BEST TIMES TO VISIT   There isn't a real off-season, but crowds are usually thinner mid-January through March and mid-September until the week before Thanksgiving. The busiest days at all of the theme parks are generally Saturdays and Sundays, when the locals visit. Beyond that, Monday, Thursday, and Saturday are pretty frantic in the Magic Kingdom; Tuesday and Friday are hectic at Epcot; Sunday and Wednesday are crazy at Disney–MGM Studios; and Monday, Tuesday, and Wednesday are a zoo at Animal Kingdom. Major holidays attract throngs: Christmas through New Year's is a frenzied time.

Note: Summer is the worst time: Crowds + heat + humidity = theme-park hell.

> ### Value Passes & Coupons That Save Your Orlan-Dough
>
> - **It's Not Just Disney Anymore.** Universal Orlando, SeaWorld, and Wet 'n Wild have joined to fight Disney's multipark pass system. The **FlexTicket** lets you see the "other-than-Disney" parks with these passes, which counter Disney's Park Hopper tickets. With the **FlexTicket,** you pay one price to visit any of the participating parks during a 14-day period. A four-park pass to Universal Studios Florida, Islands of Adventure, Wet 'n Wild, and SeaWorld is $169.95 for adults and $134.95 for children 3 to 9. A five-park pass, which adds Busch Gardens in Tampa, is $202.95 for adults and $164.95 for kids. The **FlexTicket** can be ordered through Universal (© **407/363-8000**; www.universalorlando.com); SeaWorld (© **407/351-3600**; www.seaworld.com); or Wet 'n Wild (© **800/992-9453** or 407/351-9453; www.wetnwild.com).
>
> - **Extra! Extra! Local Newspaper Saves You Money.** There's no shortage of golf courses in the Orlando area; the best way to find a good deal is to look in the sports section of the *Orlando Sentinel* for discount coupons and otherwise unadvertised specials. The **Friday** "Calendar" section of the *Sentinel* often includes two-for-one dinner special coupons or other entertainment discounts. It also lists cultural events and concerts around Central Florida, some of which are free or have a nominal admission charge.
>
> - **More Coupons.** Hotel lobbies, restaurants, newspaper racks, and some of the attractions have other free newspapers and brochures that are filled with discounts or two-for-one specials on meals, tickets, rooms, and souvenirs.

OPERATING HOURS Park hours vary and are influenced by special events and the economy. So call ahead or go to **www.disneyworld.com** to check. Generally, expect Animal Kingdom to be open 8 or 9am to 5 or 6pm; Epcot to be open 10am to 9pm; and Magic Kingdom and Disney–MGM to be open 9am to 5 or 6pm. All may open or close earlier or later.

Typhoon Lagoon and **Blizzard Beach** are open 10am to 5pm most of the year, 9am to 8pm in summer. Both have extended hours during holidays and close part of the winter.

TICKETS There are several options, from 1-day to multiday tickets. The best choices are 4- and 5-day passes. Some don't save you money—they may even cost more—but they add the flexibility of moving from park to park and returning on the same or multiple days. The following don't include **6% sales tax** unless noted. *Note:* Price hikes are frequent occurrences, so call (© **407/824-4321**) or visit WDW's website (**www.disneyworld.com**) for up-to-the-minute fees.

1-day/1-park tickets, for admission to the Magic Kingdom, Epcot, Animal Kingdom, or Disney–MGM, are $48 for adults, $38 for children 3 to 9. (Ouch!)

4-Day Park Hopper Passes provide unlimited admission to the Magic Kingdom, Epcot, Animal Kingdom, and Disney–MGM Studios. Adults pay $192; children 3 to 9 pay $152.

5-Day Park Hopper Plus Passes include your choice of two admissions to Typhoon Lagoon, River Country, Blizzard Beach, Pleasure Island, or Disney's Wide World of Sports. They sell for $247 for adults and $197 for children 3 to 9. Passes for 6 and 7 days are available, too.

1-day ticket to Typhoon Lagoon or Blizzard Beach is $29.95 for adults, $24 for children 3 to 11. **1-day ticket to River Country** is $15.95 for adults, $12.50 for children 3 to 11.

1-day ticket to Pleasure Island is $21 including tax. Since this is primarily an 18-and-over entertainment complex, there's no bargain price for children.

If you're staying at a WDW resort, you're eligible for a money-saving **Ultimate Park Hopper,** priced according to the length of your stay.

If you're planning an extended stay or going to visit Walt Disney World more than once during the year, **annual passes** ($349 for adults, $297 for children) are another option.

5 The Magic Kingdom

The Magic Kingdom offers 40 attractions plus shops and restaurants in a 107-acre package. Its centerpiece and symbol, Cinderella Castle, forms the hub of a wheel whose spokes reach to **seven themed "lands."**

From the parking lot, you have to walk or take a tram, then a ferry or monorail to the entrance. While rides are short, the wait isn't during peak periods. In this park's case, arrive an hour early because it takes 35 to 45 minutes to reach the action.

Upon entering the park, get a Magic Kingdom guide map. It shows every shop, restaurant, and attraction. Consult its entertainment schedule to see

---

Tips FASTPASS

Don't want to stand in line as long as the other guests, yet not flush enough to hire a stand-in? Disney parks use a reservation system whereby you go to the primo rides, feed your theme-park ticket into a small ticket-taker machine, and get an assigned time to return. When you reappear at the appointed time, you get into a short line and climb aboard. Here's the drill:

Hang onto your ticket stub when you enter, and head to the hottest ride on your dance card. If it's a FASTPASS attraction (they're noted in the guide map you get when you enter) and there's a line, feed your stub into the waist-level ticket taker. Retrieve your stub and the FASTPASS stub that comes with it. Look at the two times stamped on the FASTPASS. Come back during that 1-hour window and you can enter the ride with almost no wait. In the interim, go to another attraction or show.

Note: Early in the day, your window may begin 40 minutes after you feed the FASTPASS machine, but later in the day it may be hours. Initially, Disney allowed you to do this on only one ride at a time, but now you can get a pass for a second attraction 2 hours after your first assigned time.

what's cooking today. There are parades, musical extravaganzas, fireworks, band concerts, barbershop quartets, character appearances, and more.

If you have questions, **City Hall,** on your left as you enter, is an information center and, like Toontown Fair, a great place to meet costumed characters.

MAIN STREET, USA
The gateway to the Kingdom, Main Street is designed to resemble a turn-of-the-20th-century American street (okay, so it leads to a 13th-century European castle). Don't dawdle on Main Street when you enter the park; leave it for the end of the day when you're heading back to your hotel.

Walt Disney World Railroad   You can board an authentic 1928 steam-powered train for a 15-minute trip clockwise around the perimeter of the park. It's a good way to save shoe leather *if* you're headed from one of its three stations—the park entrance, Frontierland, and Mickey's Toontown Fair—to another, or if you just want to got for a ride with shorter lines.

ADVENTURELAND
Cross a bridge and stroll through an exotic jungle of foliage, thatched roofs, and totems. Amid dense vines and stands of bamboo, drums are beating and swashbuckling adventures are taking place.

Jungle Cruise   In 10 minutes, you sail through an African veldt in the Congo, an Amazon rain forest, the Nile in Egypt, and several other sets. Dozens of animatronic creatures inhabit the hanging vines, cascading waterfalls, and tropical foliage. On the shore, there's a temple guarded by snakes and a Buddha. Most boat captains keep up an amusing patter.

Magic Carpets of Aladdin ★   The first major ride added to Adventureland since 1971 delights wee ones and some older kids. Its 16 four-passenger carpets circle a giant genie's bottle while camels spit water at riders. The fiberglass carpets spin and move up, down, forward, and back.

Pirates of the Caribbean ★   It may be politically incorrect, but these pirates chase "wenches" as your boat passes audio-animatronic figures including "yo-ho-hoing" pirates who raid a Caribbean town. After a lot of looting and boozing, the pirates pass out. This ride might be scary for kids under 5.

FRONTIERLAND
From Adventureland, step into the wild and woolly past of the American frontier! The landscape is straight out of the Wild West, with log cabins and rustic saloons.

Big Thunder Mountain Railroad ★★   This low-key roller coaster has tight turns and dark descents rather than sudden, steep drops. It's situated in a 200-foot-high, red-stone mountain with 2,780 feet of track winding through caves and canyons. Your runaway train careens through the ribs of a dinosaur, under a thundering waterfall, past geysers and bubbling mud pots, and over a bottomless volcanic pool. It's tailor-made for kids and grownups who want a thrill but aren't quite up to tackling the big coasters. *Note:* You must be 40 inches or taller to ride.

Country Bear Jamboree ★★   The Jamboree is a hoot. It's a 15-minute show featuring audio-animatronic bears belting out rollicking country tunes and crooning plaintive love songs. Trixie, decked out in a satiny skirt, laments lost love in "Tears Will Be the Chaser for Your Wine." Teddi Barra descends from the ceiling in a swing to perform "Heart We Did All That We Could." Big Al moans "Blood in the Saddle," which makes everyone laugh.

Splash Mountain ★★★   Based on Disney's 1946 film *Song of the South*, Splash Mountain takes you flume-style past 26 colorful scenes that include swamps, bayous, caves, and waterfalls. Riders are caught in the schemes of Brer Fox and Brer Bear as they chase the ever-wily Brer Rabbit. Your hollow-log vehicle twists, turns, and splashes, sometimes plummeting in darkness as the ride leads to a 45°, 52-foot-long, 40 mile-per-hour splashdown in a briar-filled pond. *Note:* You must be at least 40 inches tall to ride.

Tom Sawyer Island   Board Huck Finn's raft for a short ride to this island. Kids love exploring Injun Joe's cave, a windmill, and an old mine. There's also a rickety swing, barrel bridges, and sit-downs for weary parents.

LIBERTY SQUARE

This zone depicts 18th-century America. Thirteen lanterns, symbolizing the colonies, hang from the Liberty Tree, an immense live oak. And you might encounter a fife-and-drum corps on the cobblestone streets.

Hall of Presidents ★★   Every American president is represented by a lifelike audio-animatronic figure. If you look closely, you'll see them fidget and whisper. The show begins with a film, then the curtain rises on America's leaders and, as each comes into the spotlight, he nods or waves with presidential dignity. Lincoln rises and speaks, occasionally referring to his notes. Each president's costume reflects his period's fashion, fabrics, and tailoring techniques.

Haunted Mansion ★★   Once inside, darkness, spooky music, howling, and screams enhance the ambience. The slow-motion ride has bizarre scenes: a ghostly banquet and ball, a graveyard band, a suit of armor that comes alive, luminous spiders, a talking head in a crystal ball, and weird flying objects. At the end, a ghost joins your car. It's more amusing than terrifying. And though the ride has changed little over the years and may be stale for some, it has long lines and a cult following.

The Diamond Horseshoe Saloon Revue & Medicine Show   Enjoy Dr. Bill U. Later's turn-of-the-20th-century Wild West revue. Jingles plays honky-tonk and Miss Lucille L'Amour and her dance-hall girls do a spirited cancan—all with lots of humor and audience participation. There are several shows daily.

FANTASYLAND

The attractions in this happy land are themed after classics such as *Snow White*, *Peter Pan*, and *Dumbo*. If your kids are 8 and under, you may want to make this and Mickey's Toontown your primary stops in the Magic Kingdom.

Cinderella Castle ★   There's not a lot to do, but its status as the Magic Kingdom's 185-foot icon makes it a must. The namesake character appears sometimes, and Cinderella's Royal Table restaurant is inside.

Cinderella's Golden Carousel ★★   This beauty was constructed by Italian carvers in 1917 and refurbished by Disney artists, who added 18 hand-painted scenes from *Cinderella* on a wooden canopy above the horses. The carousel organ plays Disney classics such as "When You Wish Upon a Star."

Dumbo the Flying Elephant ★ *Kids*   Here's a very tame kid's ride, in which the cars that are Dumbo clones go around in a circle, gently rising and dipping. If you can stand the lines, it's very exciting for wee ones and their parents.

It's a Small World ★   If you don't know the song, you will by the end of the ride. It'll crawl into your mind like a brain-eating mite, playing continually as you sail "around the world." Built for the 1964 New York World's Fair, this transplanted ride takes you to countries inhabited by appropriately costumed animatronic dolls singing, incessantly, "It's a small world after all," in tiny doll-like voices remarkably similar to how yours would sound if you sucked on a helium balloon. Every adult ought to pay his or her dues and ride it at least once.

Legend of the Lion King 🎭   This is a good stage show based on Disney's motion-picture musical and combines animation, movie footage, sophisticated puppetry, and high-tech special effects. Whoopi Goldberg and Cheech Marin are among the actors lending voices to the continuous show. It's a fun and entertaining opportunity to rest your feet.

Mad Tea Party *Overrated*   This is a traditional amusement park ride à la Disney, with an Alice in Wonderland theme. Riders sit in big pastel-hued teacups on saucers that careen around a circular platform while tilting and spinning. This can be a pretty nauseating ride if you spin your steering-like wheel enough.

The Many Adventures of Winnie the Pooh   The Many Adventures of Winnie the Pooh features the cute-and-cuddly little fellow along with pals Eyeore, Piglet, and Tigger. You board a golden honey pot and ride through a storybook version of the Hundred-Acre Woods, keeping an eye out for Heffulumps, Woozles, and Blustery Days.

Peter Pan's Flight   Riding in airborne versions of Captain Hook's ship, riders take a flight over nighttime London to Never-Never Land. There, you encounter mermaids, a ticking crocodile, the Lost Boys, Princess Tiger Lilly, Tinker Bell, Hook, and Smee. It's fun the first time (from a '70s perspective anyway).

Snow White's Scary Adventures   Snow White now appears in pleasant scenes, such as at the wishing well and riding off to live happily ever after. The colors and story line are bright, but it still could be scary for kids under 5.

MICKEY'S TOONTOWN FAIR

Where's Mickey? This 2-acre site is a great place for small children to find him and his cronies. Toontown offers a chance to meet Disney characters, including Mickey, Minnie, Donald, and Goofy. There's also a small collection of cottages and candy-striped tents like those at long-gone county fairs.

The Barnstormer at Goofy's Wiseacre Farm 🎭🎭   This mini-roller coaster likely inspired Woody Woodpecker's Nuthouse Coaster at Universal Studios Florida (later in this chapter). It looks and feels like a crop duster that flies off-course and through Goofy's barn. The ride has very little in the dip-and-drop department but a bit of zip on the spin-and-spiral front. (It even gets squeals from adults). The 60-second ride has a 35-inch height minimum.

Mickey's & Minnie's Country Houses 🎭   These separate cottages offer a lot of visual fun and some marginal interactive areas for youngsters. Mickey's place features garden and garage playgrounds. Minnie's lets kids play in her kitchen, where popcorn goes wild in a microwave and the utensils play melodies.

Donald's Boat (S.S. *Miss Daisy*) 🎭   The *Miss Daisy* offers a lot of interactive fun, and the "waters" around it feature fountains of water snakes and other wet fun things that earn squeals of joy (and relief on hot days).

TOMORROWLAND

In 1994, WDW folks decided Tomorrowland (originally designed in the 1970s) was beginning to look like "Yesteryear," so it was revamped to add a more futuristic feel.

THE MAGIC KINGDOM 497

> **Tips Swap Meet**
>
> Many attractions at Walt Disney World offer a Ride-Share program for parents traveling with small children. One parent rides while the other stays with the kids; then the adults switch places without having to stand in line again. Notify a cast member if you wish to participate.

The ExtraTERRORestrial Alien Encounter ★★★ *Star Wars* director George Lucas earned a tidy payday when he added his space-age vision to this attraction, in which a corporation sells transporter services to Earthlings like you. But things go wrong when it tries to transport its CEO and instead an ugly alien lands in your backyard. This carries a legitimate child warning: It's dark, scary, and confining (a shoulder plate locks you in). Special effects include the alien's breath on your neck and a mist of its slime. *Note:* Minimum height is 44 inches.

Astro Orbiter *Overrated* This ride is like those in kiddie carnivals everywhere: Its "rockets" are on arms attached to "the center of the galaxy" and they move up and down. It's tame and lame. Skip it unless you can breeze right through.

Buzz Lightyear's Space Ranger Spin ★ Join Buzz and try to save the universe while flying your cruiser through a world you'll recognize from the original *Toy Story* movie. Kids enjoy using the dashboard-mounted laser cannons as they spin through the sky (filled with gigantic toys instead of stars). If they're good shots, they can set off sight and sound gags with their lasers.

Space Mountain ★ This cosmic coaster usually has *long* lines (if you don't use FASTPASS), even though it's years past its prime. Once aboard a rocket, you'll climb and dive through the inky, starlit blackness of outer space. The hairpin turns and plunges make it seem as if you're going at breakneck speed, but your car doesn't go any faster than 28 miles per hour. If you like dark or semi-dark thrill rides, you'll be much happier with Rock 'n' Roller Coaster at Disney–MGM Studios. *Note:* Riders must be at least 44 inches tall.

The Timekeeper At the time this was written, Disney had closed, then reopened on a *very* limited basis this multimedia show. It's hosted by a robot/mad scientist (Robin Williams) and his assistant, 9-EYE, a flying, camera-headed 'droid that moonlights as a time-machine test pilot. In this jet-speed escapade, the audience hears Mozart as a young prodigy playing for French royalty, watches da Vinci work, and floats in a hot-air balloon over Red Square.

Tomorrowland Indy Speedway Younger kids love this ride, especially if their adult companion lets them drive (without a big person, there's a 52-inch height minimum for driving a lap), but teens and other fast starters hate it. The cars go only 7 miles per hour and are loosely locked into lanes.

Walt Disney's Carousel of Progress *Overrated* Here's another *now-you-see-it, now-you-don't* attraction open on a very limited basis—*if, by the time this book goes to press, at all.* It was "updated" a few years ago, but it still comes up way short in terms of wow power or keeping abreast of progress. That said, it's one of the few surviving things actually designed by Uncle Walt.

PARADES, FIREWORKS & MORE

For up-to-the-moment information, see the entertainment schedule given in the park guide map that you get when entering the park.

Fantasy in the Sky Fireworks ★★★   This is one of the most explosive displays in Orlando. Disney has pyrotechnics down to an art form, and this is clearly the best way to end your day in the Magic Kingdom. The fireworks go off nightly during peak periods, but only on selected nights the rest of the year.

SpectroMagic ★★ *Moments*   This after-dark display returned in 2001 for a second engagement at WDW, replacing the **Main Street Electrical Parade.** The 20-minute production features fiber optics, holographic images, old-fashioned twinkling lights, and a soundtrack of classic Disney tunes. The parade runs on a *very limited basis.*

6 Epcot

What's an Epcot? It's an acronym for Experimental Prototype Community of Tomorrow, and it was Walt Disney's dream for a huge planned community. Instead, after his death, it opened as a theme park in 1982.

Epcot is huge. The 260-acre park has two sections, **Future World** and **World Showcase.** It's so large that hiking World Showcase from tip to tip (1.3 miles) can be exhausting. That's why some folks say Epcot really stands for "Every Person Comes Out Tired." Depending on how long you intend to linger at each of the 11 countries in World Showcase, this park can be seen in 1 day, but it's better over 2. Conserve your energy by taking launches across the lagoon from the edge of Future World to Germany or Morocco. Double-deckers circle World Showcase, making stops at Norway, Italy, France, and Canada.

FUTURE WORLD

Future World is centered on Epcot's icon, a giant geosphere known as Spaceship Earth (or "that big golf ball"). Major corporations sponsor its 10 themed areas, and the focus is on discovery, scientific achievements, and tomorrow's technologies in areas running from energy to undersea exploration. Here are the headliners:

Innoventions ★   House of Innoventions in **Innoventions East** heralds a smart house equipped with a refrigerator that can make your grocery list, a picture frame that can send photos to other smart frames, and a commode outfitted with a seat warmer, an automatic lid opener, and a sprayer and dryer that eliminate the need for toilet paper. The exhibits in **Innoventions West** are led by Video Games of Tomorrow, in which Sega showcases games at nearly three dozen game stations.

Imagination ★★   The fountains are magical—they fire "water snakes" that arch into the air and dare kids to avoid their "bite." The 3-D **Honey I Shrunk the Audience** ★★ show shrinks you, then terrorizes you with giant mice, a cat, and a 5-year-old who gives you a sound shaking. **Journey into Your Imagination** ★ was recently renovated and welcomes back an old park favorite—Figment the dinosaur.

The Land ★   The largest of Future World's pavilions looks at our relationships with food and nature. **Living with the Land** ★ is a 13-minute boat ride through a rain forest, an African desert, and the windswept American plains. **Circle of Life** ★★ blends spectacular live-action footage with animation in a 15-minute, 70mm motion picture based on *The Lion King* that delivers a cautionary environmental message. In **Food Rocks** ★, audio-animatronic mock rock-performers deliver an entertaining message about nutrition.

The Living Seas ★ This pavilion's 5.7-million-gallon saltwater aquarium has a coral reef and more than 4,000 sea creatures, such as sharks, barracudas, parrot fish, rays, and dolphins. A 2½-minute multimedia preshow about today's ocean technology is followed by a 7-minute film on the formation of the earth and seas as a means to support life. After the films, you enter "hydrolators" for a rapid "descent" to the simulated ocean floor, where you get close-up views through acrylic windows of the denizens in a natural coral-reef habitat.

Spaceship Earth *Overrated* This large, silvery geosphere is Epcot's icon, but all that awaits inside is a 15-minute yawn of a show/ride that takes you through the history of communications. During the Renaissance, you may notice that several beings look an awful lot like Barbie's dream date, Ken. Sharp-eyed riders may also notice at least two "exit" lights peeking through the heavens, once near the very end of the ride. *Tip:* Skip it.

Test Track ★★ Test Track is a long-time-coming marvel that combines GM engineering and Disney imagineering. The line can be more than an hour long, so consider FASTPASS. The preride area (that's theme-park talk for the last part of the line) has a number of exhibits from GM's proving grounds. Once you're in your six-passenger convertible, the 5-minute ride follows what looks like a real highway and includes a brake test, climb, and tight S-curves. There's also a 12-second burst of speed that reaches 65 miles per hour on the straightaway. *Note:* Riders must be at least 40 inches tall.

Universe of Energy ★ Sponsored by Exxon, the main event is a 32-minute ride, **Ellen's Energy Adventure,** that features comedian Ellen DeGeneres as an energy expert tutored by Bill Nye the Science Guy to be a "Jeopardy!" contestant. In the process, you learn about energy resources from the dinosaurs to tomorrow, while Ellen becomes a game-show champ.

Wonders of Life ★★ Housed in a vast geodesic dome fronted by a 75-foot-tall replica of a DNA strand, this pavilion offers some of Future World's most engaging shows and attractions. The ***Making of Me*** is a captivating 15-minute motion picture combining live action (starring Martin Short) with animation and spectacular in-utero photography to create the sweetest introduction imaginable to the facts of life. (If your kids are under 10, this show may prompt certain questions about reproduction.) In **Body Wars,** you're reduced to the size of a cell in order to join a medical rescue inside the immune system of a human body. The motion simulator takes you on a wild ride through gale-force winds in the lungs and pounding heart chambers. This one isn't a smart choice for those prone to motion sickness or who generally prefer to be stirred rather than shaken. *Note:* Riders must be at least 40 inches tall. In the hilarious, multimedia **Cranium Command** ★★, you tag along with Buzzy, an audio-animatronic brain-pilot-in-training charged with a seemingly impossible task—controlling

---

Tips Coming Soon

Epcot is working with Compaq and NASA on a new out-of-this-world attraction called **Mission: Space**. Located in the former Horizons pavilion, its headliner will be a motion simulator like those used by astronauts training for missions. (Think g-force and weightlessness.) The $150 million exhibit, scheduled to open in 2003, will include interactive games and programs about space exploration.

the brain of a typical 12-year-old boy. Charles Grodin, Jon Lovitz, Bobcat Goldthwaite, George Wendt, Kevin Nealon, and Dana Carvey play the boy's body parts as he encounters preadolescent traumas such as meeting a girl and having a run-in with the principal.

WORLD SHOWCASE

This community of 11 miniaturized nations surrounds a 40-acre lagoon at the park's south end. All of these "countries" have indigenous architecture, landscaping, restaurants, and shops. The nations' cultural facets are explored in art exhibits, dance or other live performances, and innovative films. The employees in each pavilion are natives of that country. The World Showcase opens at noon daily, so there's time for Future World forays if you arrive earlier.

U.S.A.—The American Adventure ★   Housed in a Georgian-style structure, this 29-minute dramatization of U.S. history uses video, rousing music, and a cast of audio-animatronic figures, including narrators Mark Twain and Ben Franklin. You'll see Jefferson writing the Declaration of Independence, Matthew Brady photographing a family being divided by the Civil War, the stock market crash of 1929, the attack on Pearl Harbor, and the *Eagle* heading for the moon.

Canada ★★   The architecture ranges from a mansard-roofed replica of Ottawa's 19th-century, French-style Château Laurier (here called Hôtel du Canada) to a British-influenced stone building modeled after a famous landmark near Niagara Falls. Don't miss the stunning floral displays. But the highlight is **O Canada!** ★★, a dazzling, 18-minute, 360° CircleVision film that shows Canada's scenic splendor, from a dogsled race to the thundering flight of thousands of snow geese.

China ★   Bounded by a serpentine wall that wanders its perimeter, the China pavilion is entered via a triple-arched ceremonial gate inspired by the Temple of Heaven in Beijing, a summer retreat for Chinese emperors. Passing through the gate, you'll see a half-size replica of this ornately embellished red-and-gold circular temple, built in 1420 during the Ming dynasty. Gardens simulate those in Suzhou, with miniature waterfalls, fragrant lotus ponds, bamboo groves, corkscrew willows, and weeping mulberry trees. **Wonders of China** ★★ is a 20-minute, 360° CircleVision film that explores 6,000 years of dynastic and communist rule and the breathtaking diversity of the Chinese landscape. It includes scenes of the Great Wall (begun 24 centuries ago!), a performance by the Beijing Opera, the Forbidden City in Beijing, rice terraces of Hunan Province, the Gobi Desert, and tropical rain forests of Hainan Island. Visitors will also find a bustling Chinese marketplace offering an array of native merchandise.

France ★   This pavilion focuses on La Belle Epoque, a period from 1870 to 1910 in which French art, literature, and architecture flourished. It's entered via a replica of the Pont des Arts footbridge over the "Seine" and leads to a park filled with sycamores, Bradford pear trees, flowering crape myrtles, and a $^{1}/_{10}$-scale model of the Eiffel Tower constructed from Gustave Eiffel's original blueprints. The piéce de résistance here is ***Impressions de France*** ★★. Shown in a palatial sit-down theater á la Fontainebleau, this 18-minute film is a scenic journey through diverse French landscapes that's enhanced by the music of French composers and shown on a vast, 200°wraparound screen.

Germany   Enclosed by castle walls and towers, this festive pavilion is centered on a cobblestone square with pots of colorful flowers girding a fountain statue of St. George and the Dragon. The adjacent clock tower has glockenspiel figures that herald each hour with quaint melodies. The pavilion's **Biergarten** was inspired by medieval Rothenberg and features a year-round Oktoberfest. Sixteenth-century facades replicate a merchant's hall in the Black Forest and the town hall in Römerberg Square. The two main activities here are shopping and eating, and you'll find more than enough German specialties—from bratwurst to Hummel figurines—to indulge in.

Note: Model-train enthusiasts and kids enjoy the exquisitely detailed miniature version of a small **Bavarian town** ⊕, complete with working train station.

Italy One of the prettiest World Showcase pavilions, Italy lures visitors over an arched stone footbridge to a replica of Venice's intricately ornamented pink-and-white Doge's Palace. Other highlights include an 83-foot-tall bell tower, Venetian bridges, and a central piazza enclosing a version of Bernini's Neptune Fountain. A garden wall suggests a backdrop of provincial countryside, and Mediterranean citrus, olive trees, cypresses, and pines frame a formal garden. Gondolas are moored on the lagoon. You can shop for Italian specialties such as Murano glass.

Japan ⊕★ A flaming red *torii* (gate of honor) leads the way to the Goju No To pagoda, inspired by a shrine built at Nara in A.D. 700. In a traditional Japanese garden, cedars, yews, bamboos, willows, and flowering shrubs frame pebbled footpaths, rustic bridges, waterfalls, rock landscaping, and a pond of koi. The Yakitori House is modeled after the 16th-century Katsura Imperial Villa in Kyoto, considered the crowning achievement of Japanese architecture. Another highlight is the moated **White Heron Castle,** a replica of the Shirasagi-Jo, a 17th-century fortress overlooking the city of Himeji. Artisans often give craft demonstrations in the pavilion's courtyard, and you'll also find a department store stocked with native goods. The drums of **Matsuriza** ⊕★—one of the best performances in the World Showcase—entertain guests daily.

Mexico ⊕ You'll hear marimbas and mariachi bands (including **Mariachi Cobre**) as you approach this festive showcase, fronted by a towering Mayan pyramid modeled on the Aztec temple of Quetzalcoatl (God of Life) and surrounded by dense Yucatán jungle landscaping. Upon entering the pavilion, you'll find yourself in a museum of pre-Columbian art and artifacts. Down a ramp, **El Rio del Tiempo** (River of Time) ⊕ offers an 8-minute cruise through Mexico's past and present. Passengers get a close-up look at a Mayan pyramid.

Morocco ⊕★ Note the imperfections in the mosaic tile in the Koutoubia Minaret, the prayer tower of a 12th-century mosque in Marrakech. They were put there intentionally in accordance with the belief that only Allah is perfect. The **Medina** (old city), entered via a replica of an arched gateway in Fez, leads to Fez House (a traditional Moroccan home) and the narrow, winding streets of the *souk,* a bustling marketplace where all manner of authentic handcrafted merchandise is on display. The Medina's rectangular courtyard centers on a replica of the ornately tiled Najjarine Fountain in Fez, the setting for musical entertainment.

Treasures of Morocco is a daily, 35-minute guided tour (noon–7pm) that highlights this country's culture, architecture, and history.

Norway ⊕ This pavilion is centered on a picturesque cobblestone courtyard. A *stavekirke* (stave church), styled after the 13th-century Gol Church of Hallingdal, features changing exhibits. A replica of Oslo's 14th-century **Akershus Castle,** next to a cascading woodland waterfall, is the setting for the pavilion's featured restaurant.

Maelstrom ⭐, a ride in a dragon-headed Viking vessel, traverses fjords before trolls cast a spell on you. The boat crashes through a gorge and spins into the North Sea, where you're hit by a storm (don't worry—this is relatively calm). Then passengers disembark at a 10th-century Viking village to view the 70mm film *Norway,* which documents a thousand years of Norwegian history.

United Kingdom The U.K. pavilion takes you to Merry Olde England through **Britannia Square,** a formal London-style park complete with a copper-roofed gazebo bandstand, a stereotypical red phone booth, and a statue of the Bard. Four centuries of architecture are represented along quaint cobblestone streets, complete with a traditional British pub. A formal garden with low box hedges in geometric patterns, flagstone paths, and a stone fountain replicates the landscaping of 16th- and 17th-century palaces.

Don't miss **The British Invasion** ⭐⭐, a group that impersonates the Beatles daily except Sundays, and pub pianist Pam Brody (Tues, Thurs, Fri, and Sun).

IllumiNations ⭐⭐⭐ *Moments* Little has changed since Epcot's millennium version ended January 1, 2001. This grand nightcap continues to be a blend of fireworks, lasers, and fountains in a display that's signature Disney. The show is worth the crowds that flock to the parking lot when it's over. *Tip:* Stake your claim to the best viewing areas a half hour before show time (listed in your entertainment schedule). The ones near Showcase Plaza have a head start for the exits. The Rose & Crown Pub in the U.K. pavilion, above, offers a great view.

7 Disney–MGM Studios

You'll probably spy the Tower of Terror and the Earful Tower—a water tower outfitted with gigantic mouse ears—before you enter this park, which Disney bills as "the Hollywood that never was and always will be." Once inside, you'll find pulse-quickening rides such as the **Rock 'n' Roller Coaster** and movie- and TV-themed shows such as **Who Wants to Be a Millionaire—Play It!** On Hollywood and Sunset boulevards, Art Deco movie sets remember the golden age of Hollywood. New York Street is lined with miniature renditions of Gotham's landmarks and typical characters, including peddlers hawking knock-off watches. This 110-acre park has some of the best street performing anywhere.

ATTRACTIONS & SHOWS

Beauty and the Beast Live on Stage ⭐ Producers adapted this 30-minute, live show from the same-name movie. Musical highlights from the show include the rousing "Be Our Guest" opening number and the poignant title song featured in the romantic waltz-scene finale. A highlight is "The Mob Song" scene in a dark forest. The sets and costumes are lavish, and the production numbers are pretty spectacular. Arrive early to get a good seat.

Disney–MGM Studios Backlot Tour ⭐ This 35-minute tram tour takes you behind the scenes for a look at the vehicles, props, costumes, sets, and special effects used in movies and TV shows. But the real fun begins once you reach **Catastrophe Canyon,** where an earthquake causes canyon walls to rumble. A raging oil fire, massive explosions, torrents of rain, and flash floods threaten you and other riders before you're taken behind the scenes to see how filmmakers use special effects to make such disasters.

The Great Movie Ride Film footage and 50 audio-animatronic replicas of movie stars re-create some of the most famous scenes in films on this 22-minute train ride. Many grown-ups enjoy it for two reasons: You get to sit down, and you relive magic moments from the 1930s to the present. You'll see the classic airport farewell scene by Bergman and Bogart in *Casablanca;* Brando bellowing "Stellaaaaa"; and Gene Kelly singin' in the rain. Kids may be bored until they get to Sigourney Weaver fending off slimy alien foes. The action is enhanced by special effects, and outlaws hijack your tram.

Hunchback of Notre Dame: A Musical Adventure   This rollicking stage show brings the animated feature's main characters to life, mainly in costumes but sometimes in puppets. Dozens of performers tell the story of Quasimodo, an orphan banished to a church bell tower. Show up 30 minutes early to ensure a good seat during the summer and holiday seasons.

Indiana Jones Epic Stunt Spectacular   Peek into the world of movie stunts in this 30-minute show that re-creates major scenes from the Indiana Jones films. The show opens on an elaborate Mayan temple backdrop. Indy crashes the party on a rope and, as he searches with a torch for the golden idol, he encounters several booby traps. The set is dismantled to reveal a colorful market where the action includes a sword fight, bullwhip maneuvers, gunfire, and a truck bursting into flame. An explosive finale takes place in a desert scenario. Theme music and an entertaining narrative enhance the show, which helps explain how elaborate stunts are pulled off. *Tip:* Arrive early and sit near the stage for your shot at being picked as an audience participant. *You get to wear a turban.* Alas, this is a job for adults only.

Jim Henson's Muppet*Vision 3D   Kermit and Miss Piggy star in this must-see film that marries Jim Henson's puppets with Disney audio-animatronics, special effects, 70mm film, and 3-D technology. Wow! It's the best of the 3-D films at Disney, and the in-your-face action includes flying Muppets, cannonballs, wind, fiber-optic fireworks, bubble showers, and even an actual spray of water. Kermit is the host, Miss Piggy sings, and Statler and Waldorf critique the action (which includes numerous mishaps and disasters) from a balcony.

The Magic of Disney Animation   You'll see Disney characters come alive at the stroke of a brush or pencil as you tour glass-walled animation studios. Walter Cronkite and Robin Williams explain what's going on via video monitors and star in an 8-minute Peter Pan–themed film about the basics of animation. It's painstaking work: To produce an 80-minute movie, the animation team must do more than 1 million drawings of characters and scenery! Original cels (paintings or drawings on celluloid sheets) from famous Disney movies and some of the many Oscars won by Disney artists are on display. The 35-minute tour also includes a selection of magical moments from Disney's classic films.

Playhouse Disney—Live on Stage!   *Kids*   Younger audiences (2–5) love this 20-minute show where they meet characters from Bear in the Big Blue House, The Book of Pooh, and others. It encourages preschoolers to dance, sing, and play along with the cast. It happens several times a day. Check your show schedule.

Rock 'n' Roller Coaster   *Moments*   Want the best thrill ride WDW has to offer? Then tackle this fast-and-furious coaster. You sit in a 24-passenger "stretch limo" customized with 120 speakers that blare Aerosmith at 32,000 watts as you blast from 0 to 60 miles per hour in 2.8 seconds, then fly into the first gut-tightening inversion at 5Gs. It's a real launch (sometimes of lunch) followed by a wild ride through a make-believe California freeway system in the semi-darkness. The ride lasts 3 minutes, 12 seconds, about the running time of Aerosmith's hit "Sweet Emotion." *Note:* Riders must be at least 48 inches tall.

Sounds Dangerous Starring Drew Carey Drew provides laughs while dual audio technology provides some hair-raising effects during this 12-minute show at ABC Sound Studios. You'll feel like you're right in the middle of the action of a TV pilot that features undercover police work and plenty of amusing mishaps. Even when the picture disappears and the theater is plunged into darkness, you continue on a chase that shows off 3-D sound effects.

Star Tours Cutting-edge when it opened, this galactic journey based on the original *Star Wars* trilogy (George Lucas collaborated on the ride) is now a couple of rungs below the latest technology, but is still a ton of fun. You board a 40-seat "spacecraft" for an interstellar journey that greets you with sudden drops, crashes, and oncoming laser blasts as it careens out of control. *Note:* Riders must be at least 40 inches tall.

The Twilight Zone Tower of Terror ★★★ *Moments* Disney continues to fine-tune this ride into a true stomach-lifter. As legend has it, during a violent storm on Halloween night 1939, lightning struck the Hollywood Tower Hotel, causing an entire wing and an elevator full of people to disappear. And you're about to meet them as you star in a special episode of *The Twilight Zone*. En route to this formerly grand hotel, guests walk past overgrown landscaping and faded signs that once pointed the way to stables and tennis courts; the vines over the entrance trellis are dead, and the hotel is a crumbling ruin. Eerie corridors lead to a dimly lit library, where you can hear a storm raging outside. After various spooky adventures, the ride ends in a dramatic climax: a terrifying, 13-story free-fall. For some this is the best thrill anywhere in Disney. At 199 feet, it's surely the tallest ride in WDW, and it's a grade above Dr. Doom's Fearfall at Islands of Adventure (later in this chapter). *Note:* You must be at least 40 inches tall to ride.

Voyage of the Little Mermaid ★ Hazy lighting creates an underwater effect in a reef-walled theater and helps set the mood for a charming musical show that combines live performers with puppets, film clips, and more. Sebastian sings the movie's theme, "Under the Sea"; Ariel shares her dream of becoming human in "Part of Your World"; and Ursula, the tentacled one, belts out "Poor Unfortunate Soul." The 17-minute show is a great place to rest and sing along.

Who Wants to Be a Millionaire—Play It! ★ Contestants can't win $1 million, but they can win points used to buy prizes ranging from collectible pins to a leather jacket or a trip to New York to meet Regis Philbin. Based on Disney-owned ABC TV's game show, the theme-park version features lifelines (such as asking the audience or calling a stranger on two phones set up in the park). Contestants get a shot at up to 15 multiple-choice questions in the climb to the top. Games run continuously in the 600-seat studio. Audience members play along on keypads. The fastest to answer qualifying questions become contestants.

Tips **Front-Row Seat**

Make a priority seating reservation for the Hollywood Brown Derby, Mama Melrose's Ristorante Italiano, or Hollywood & Vine and, when you do, ask for the Fantasmic! package (no extra charge). After dinner you'll get preferred seating at the show.

AN EVENING EXTRAVAGANZA

Fantasmic! ★★★ *Moments* This end-of-the-day visual feast features laser lights, fireworks, shooting comets, great balls of fire, and the Magic Mickey. The 25-minute show includes 50 performers, a giant dragon, a king cobra, and one million gallons of water, just about all of which are orchestrated by a sorcerer mouse who looks more than remotely familiar. You'll recognize characters from Disney movie classics such as *Fantasia, Pinocchio, Snow White and the Seven Dwarfs, The Little Mermaid,* and *The Lion King.* You'll also shudder at the villainy of Jafar, Cruella De Vil, and Maleficent in the battle of good vs. evil. In peak seasons there are two shows nightly. Check your schedule for time. *Tip:* The ample amphitheater holds 9,000 souls, so be prepared to wait to get in, or come late and try your luck at last-minute seating.

8 Animal Kingdom

Disney's fourth major park combines animals, elaborate landscapes, and a handful of rides. The centerpiece of the 500-plus-acre park is the 145-foot tall **Tree of Life.** It's an intricately carved free-form representation of animals, handcrafted by a team of artists over the period of a year. The $800 million, lushly landscaped park opened in 1998, and the final "land," Asia, opened in 1999. If the animals are cooperative, you can have an up-close encounter that you aren't likely to find anywhere else.

Animal Kingdom ranks with Tampa's Busch Gardens (see chapter 10, "The Tampa Bay Area") as one of the top two critter parks in Florida. Animal Kingdom is a 500-acre park for animals, a conservation venue as much as an attraction. It's easy for most of the animals to escape your eyes here. Busch (335 acres) has fewer places for hide-and-seek, so it's easier to see them there if you want to make the 3-hour round-trip (there's a $5 shuttle service, ✆ **800/221-1339**). Animal Kingdom wins the battle of the shows with **Tarzan Rocks!** and **Festival of the Lion King,** but Busch wins hands-down the battle of the thrill rides with five roller coasters.

Animal Kingdom is divided into five "regions": **Safari Village,** a shopping/entertainment area; **Africa,** the main animal-viewing area, which is dedicated to the wildlife in Africa today; **Dinoland U.S.A.,** focusing on issues of extinction; and **Camp Minnie-Mickey,** a kid zone equivalent of Mickey's Toontown in the Magic Kingdom. **Asia,** the most recent to open, has a raft ride called **Kali River Rapids** and the **Maharajah Jungle Trek.** The latter has a series of wildlife exhibits including Bengal tigers and giant fruit bats in an elaborate series of buildings that resemble the ruins of an ancient city.

But enough of an appetizer. Let's get better acquainted.

THE OASIS

This painstakingly designed entrance to the park is landscaped with streams, grottoes, and waterfalls, setting the tone for other areas. It's also your first chance to see critters such as iguanas, wallabies, tiny deer, anteaters, sloths, tree kangaroos, otters, and macaws that frequent the thick foliage. There are no rides in this area, and many guests miss seeing the animals in their rush to get to the heart of the park.

SAFARI VILLAGE

Like Cinderella Castle in the Magic Kingdom, the 14-story **Tree of Life** ★★ is the park's central landmark. WDW artisans built the tree, which has 8,000 limbs, 103,000 leaves, and 325 mammals, reptiles, amphibians, bugs, birds,

> **Tips** **Stay Tuned**
>
> Dinoland U.S.A. is scheduled to get a new ride, **Primeval Whirl,** a carnival-style twin roller coaster with spinning, rider-controlled cars. The small coaster debuted in summer 2002.

Mickeys, and dinosaurs in its trunk, limbs, and roots. Teams of artisans worked for a year creating its sculptures, and it's worth a walk around its roots, especially on the way to see It's Tough to Be a Bug (below).

It's Tough to Be a Bug! ★★ Take the path through the Tree of Life's 50-foot base, grab your 3-D specs, and settle into a sometimes creepy-crawly seat. Based on the film *A Bug's Life*, the special effects in this multimedia adventure are pretty impressive. This isn't a good one for very young kids (it's dark and loud) or bug haters, but for others it's a fun, sometimes-poignant look at life from a smaller perspective. Once you put on your bug-eye glasses, all of your senses will be awakened by the stars, which include ants, beetles, spiders, and, sigh, a stink bug.

Discovery Island Trails The trails offer a leisurely stroll through the root system of the Tree of Life and a chance to see real, not-so-rare critters, such as otters, flamingos, tamarinds, lemurs, tortoises, ducks, storks, and cockatoos.

DINOLAND U.S.A.

Enter by passing under "Olden Gate Bridge," a 40-foot-tall Brachiosaurus reassembled from excavated fossils. Speaking of which, until late summer 1999, this land had three paleontologists working on the very real skeleton of "Sue," a monstrously big Tyrannosaurus Rex unearthed in the Black Hills of South Dakota in 1990. They worked here mainly because Disney helped pay for the project. Alas, Sue has moved on, but Disney has a replica made from a mold of her 67-million-year-old bones.

The Boneyard ★ *Kids* Kids love the chance to slip, slither, slide, and slink through this giant playground where they can discover the real-looking remains of triceratops, T-rex, and other vanished giants. It's also a great place for parents to take a break from the pavement pounding that goes into a day in the park.

Dinosaur Formerly called Countdown to Extinction, this ride hurls you through darkness in CTX Rover "time machines" that pass an array of snarling (though somewhat hokey) dinosaurs. Young children may find the dinos and darkness a bit frightening. Stay away if you have heart problems or are prone to dizziness or motion sickness. *Note:* You must be 40 inches or taller to climb aboard.

Tarzan Rocks! ★ Phil Collins's soundtrack and a cast of 27 very live performers (tumblers, dancers, and in-line skating daredevils) put on quite a show during this 28-minute production. The costumes and music are spectacular, second in Animal Kingdom only to Festival of the Lion King (below). Our only criticisms: The story line is pretty thin, and Tarzan didn't appear for 14 minutes. The show is held in the 1,500-seat Theater in the Wild.

TriceraTop Spin This is a mini-thrill for youngsters that will bore adults and teenagers. Cars that look like cartoon dinosaurs are attached to arms that circle a hub while moving up and down and all around.

CAMP MINNIE-MICKEY

Join your favorite Disney characters "on vacation" in Camp Minnie-Mickey, an entire land that re-creates a kid-friendly Adirondack resort.

Character Greeting Trails ★ *Moments*   This is a must-do for people traveling with children. A variety of Disney characters, from Winnie the Pooh and Pocahontas to Timon and Baloo, have separate trails where you can meet and mingle. Mickey, Minnie, Goofy, and Pluto also make appearances.

Festival of the Lion King ★★★ *Finds*   Almost everyone in the audience comes alive when the music starts in this rousing, 28-minute show—the best in Animal Kingdom and one of the top three shows in Walt Disney World. The several-times-per-day extravaganza celebrates nature's diversity with a talented, colorfully attired cast of singers, dancers, and life-size critters that lead the way to an inspiring sing-along that gets the entire audience caught up in the fun. Based loosely on the animated movie, this stage show combines the pageantry of a parade with a tribal celebration. Make sure to arrive at least 20 minutes early.

AFRICA

Enter through the town of Harambe, a run-down representation of an African coastal village poised on the edge of the 21st century. The whitewashed structures, built of coral stone and thatched with reeds by craftspeople brought over from Africa, surround a central marketplace rich with local wares and colors.

Kilimanjaro Safaris ★★★   Animal Kingdom doesn't have many rides, so calling this the best may sound like a qualified endorsement. But the animals make it a winner as long as your timing is right. They're scarce at midday most times of year (in cooler months you may get lucky), so *ride this one as close to the park's opening or closing as you can.* Your vehicle is a very large truck that takes you through a simulated African landscape. These days, you might see black rhinos, hippos, antelopes, crocodiles, wildebeests, zebras, and lions that, if your timing is good, might offer a half-hearted roar toward some gazelles that are safely out of reach. There's even a little drama as you and your mates help catch some dastardly poachers.

Pangani Forest Exploration Trail ★★ *Moments*   Hippos, tapirs, ever-active mole rats, and some other critters often are on the trail for your viewing, but the real prize is getting a look at the gorillas. One area houses a family including a 500-pound silverback; the other has five bachelors. They're not always cooperative, especially in hot weather when they tend to spend most of the day in shady areas out of view. Those who come early, stay late, are patient, or make return visits can be rewarded with a close look at some special creatures.

Rafiki's Planet Watch *Overrated*   Board an open-sided train near Pangani Forest Exploration Trail for the trip to the back edge of the park, which has three attractions. **Conservation Station** offers a behind-the-scenes look at how Disney cares for animals. You'll pass nurseries and veterinarian stations. But these facilities need to be staffed to be interesting, and that's not always the case. **Habitat Habit!** is a trail with small animals such as cotton-top tamarins. The **Affection Section's** petting zoo has goats and potbelly pigs.

ASIA

Disney's Imagineers have outdone themselves in creating the mythical kingdom of **Anandapur.** The intricately painted artwork at the front is appealing, and it also helps make the lines seem to move a little faster.

Flights of Wonder *Overrated* This bird show is a low-key break from the madness and has a few laughs, but it's not much different from the other bird shows you'll find throughout Florida.

Kali River Rapids ★★ Here's a darn good raft ride—slightly better, we think, than Congo River Rapids at Busch Gardens in Tampa (see chapter 10, "The Tampa Bay Area") but not quite as good as Popeye & Bluto's Bilge-Rat Barges at Islands of Adventure (p. 519). Its churning water mimics real rapids, and some optical illusions will have you wondering if you're about to drop over the falls. You *will* get wet. The lines are long, but keep your head up and enjoy some of the marvelous art overhead and on the beautiful murals. *Note:* There's a 38-inch height minimum.

Maharajah Jungle Trek ★ With this exhibit, Disney keeps its promise to provide up-close views of animals. If you don't show up in the midday heat, you may see Bengal tigers through thick glass barriers, while nothing but air divides you from dozens of giant fruit bats (wing spans up to 6 ft.) in another habitat. Guides are on hand to answer questions, and you can also check a brochure that lists the animals you may spot; it's available on your right as you enter.

9 Other Walt Disney World Attractions

WATER PARKS

Disney has three excellent water parks to choose from. **Typhoon Lagoon** and **Blizzard Beach** are $29.95 for adults, $24 for kids 3 to 9. Hours are generally from 10am to 5pm with extended hours during holidays and summer.

As this book went to press, Disney's third park, River Country, was facing an uncertain future. Normally closed from Labor Day into March for refurbishment, a WDW insider said the park could be closed longer or even entirely because it doesn't have the popularity of Typhoon Lagoon or Blizzard Beach. If it does reopen, it's uncertain whether ticket prices (normally $15.95 for adults, $12.50 for kids 3–9) would remain the same. For more information, call © **407/824-4321** or visit **www.disneyworld.com**.

TYPHOON LAGOON ★★★

A storm-stranded fishing boat—the *Miss Tilly*—sits atop 95-foot-high Mount Mayday and overlooks this Disney water park. Every few minutes the boat blows its stack, shooting a 50-foot geyser into the air. It has several other attractions.

Castaway Creek's rafts and inner tubes glide along a 2,100-foot-long river that circles most of the park and includes a rain forest, caves, and grottoes. At **Water Works,** jets of water spew from shipwrecked boats.

Ketchakiddie Creek is for 2- to 5-year-old guests. An innovative water playground, it has bubbling fountains to frolic in, mini-water slides, a pint-sized "white-water" tubing run, spouting whales and squirting seals, rubbery crocodiles to climb on, grottoes to explore, and waterfalls to loll under.

> *Tips* **Closed for the Winter**
>
> All Disney water parks are refurbished annually. That means if you're traveling in fall or winter, it' likely one park will be closed temporarily. So if the water parks are on your itinerary, ask in advance about closings.

> **Tips Water Park Dos & Don'ts**
>
> 1. Go in the afternoons, about 2pm, even in summer, if you can stand the heat that long and want to avoid crowds. The early birds usually are gone by then.
> 2. Go early in the week when most of the week-long guests are filling the lines at the theme parks.
> 3. Kids can get lost just as easily at a water park as at the other parks, and the consequences can be worse. All Disney parks have lifeguards, usually wearing bright red suits, but, to be safe, ask and make yourself the first line of safety.
> 4. Women should remember to wear a **one-piece bathing suit**. By the same token, all bathers should remember **the "wedgie" rule** on the more extreme rides, such as Summit Plummet (at Blizzard Beach, below). What's the "wedgie" rule? It's a principle of physics that says you may start out wearing baggies and end up in a thong.
> 5. Use a waterproof sunscreen and drink plenty of fluids. Despite all that water, it's easy to get dehydrated in summer.

At **Shark Reef,** guests get free equipment and instructions for a 15-minute swim through this very small snorkeling area that includes a simulated reef populated by parrotfish, rays, and small sharks.

Typhoon Lagoon, the park's 2.75 million-gallon wave pool, launches **big breakers** every 90 seconds. A foghorn warns you when, in case you want to head for cover. Young children can wade in the lagoon's more peaceful tidal pools—**Blustery Bay** or **Whitecap Cove.** There's also a 2½-hour **surfing program** (pre-park opening Tues and Fri $125, minimum age 8; © **407/939-7529**).

Humunga Kowabunga consists of three 214-foot Mount Mayday slides that propel you down the mountain on a serpentine route through waterfalls and bat caves and past nautical wreckage before depositing you into a bubbling catch pool. *Note:* You must be 48 inches or taller to ride this. **White-Water Rides** at Mount Mayday is the setting for three white-water rafting adventures—**Keelhaul Falls, Mayday Falls,** and **Gangplank Falls**—all offering steep drops coursing through caves and passing lush scenery.

For more information, call © **407/560-4141** or go online to **www.disneyworld.com.**

BLIZZARD BEACH

Disney's newest water park is a 66-acre "ski resort" in the midst of a tropical lagoon centering on the 90-foot Mount Gushmore.

Its 2,900-foot-long **Cross Country Creek** is a lazy tube run, but watch out for the cave where you'll get splashed with melting ice. **Runoff Rapids** offers another tube job. This one lets you careen down one of three twisting, turning runs through semi—darkness.

Ski-Patrol Training Camp, designed for preteens, features a rope swing, a T-bar hanging over the water, the wet and slippery **Mogul Mania** slide, and an ice-floe walk along slippery floating icebergs.

Snow Stormers has three flumes descending from the top of Mount Gushmore, following a switchback course through slalom-type gates.

Summit Plummet ★★ is one of the most breath-defying adventures in any water park. Read every speed, motion, vertical-dip, wedgie, and hold-onto-your-breast-plate warning before hopping on. This starts slow, with a lift ride to the 120-foot summit. But it finishes as the world's fastest body slide—a test of your courage and swimsuit—that virtually goes straight down and has you moving sans vehicle at 60 miles per hour into the catch pool. *Note:* It has a 48-inch height minimum.

Teamboat Springs is this World's longest white-water raft ride, twisting down a 1,200-foot series of rushing waterfalls.

Tike's Peak is a kiddie version of Mount Gushmore. It has short water slides, animals to climb aboard, a snow castle, a squirting ice pond, and a fountain play area for young guests.

For more information, call ✆ **407/560-3400,** or surf over to **www.disneyworld.com**.

OTHER ATTRACTIONS
FANTASIA GARDENS & WINTER SUMMERLAND

Fantasia Gardens Miniature Golf ★★, located off Buena Vista Drive across from Disney–MGM Studios, offers two 18-hole miniature courses drawing inspiration from the Walt Disney classic cartoon of the same name. You'll find hippos, ostriches, and alligators on the **Fantasia Gardens** course, where the Sorcerer's Apprentice presides over the final hole. It's a good bet for beginners and kids. Seasoned minigolfers probably will prefer **Fantasia Fairways,** which is a scaled-down golf course complete with sand traps, water hazards, tricky putting greens, and holes ranging from 40 to 75 feet.

Santa Claus and his elves provide the theme for **Winter Summerland** ★★, which has two 18-hole miniature golf courses across from Blizzard Beach on Buena Vista Drive. The **Winter** course takes you from an ice castle to a snowman to the North Pole. The **Summer** course is pure Florida, from sandcastles to surfboards to a visit with Santa on the "Winternet."

Tickets at both venues are $9.75 for adults and $7.80 for children 3 to 9. Both are open from 10am to 10pm daily. For information about Fantasia Gardens, call ✆ **407/560-8760.** For information about Winter Summerland, call ✆ **407/560-3000.** You can find both on the Internet at **www.disneyworld.com**.

DISNEY'S WIDE WORLD OF SPORTS ★

This 200-acre complex has a 7,500-seat baseball stadium, 10 other baseball and softball fields, six basketball courts, a dozen lighted tennis courts, a track-and-field complex, a golf driving range, and six sand volleyball courts.

Organized programs and events include:

- The **NFL Experience.** Ten drills test your running, punting, passing, and receiving skills. You can dodge cardboard defenders and run pass patterns while a machine shoots you passes. Depending on your stamina and the size of the crowds, the experience lasts 45 minutes to several hours. It's included in general admission (below).
- The **Atlanta Braves** play 18 spring-training games beginning in early March. Tickets cost $11.50 and $19.50. For tickets call ✆ **407/839-3900.**

DisneyQuest

The reaction to DisneyQuest's virtual video arcade ★★★ is usually the same, whether it's from kids who are just reaching the video-game age, teens who are firmly hooked, or adults who never outgrew Pong. Almost everyone leaves saying, "Awesome!"

This five-level arcade has everything from nearly old-fashioned pinball to virtual games and rides. Here's a sampling:

- **Aladdin's Magic Carpet Ride** puts you astride a motorcycle-like seat while you fly through the 3-D Cave of Wonders.
- **Invasion: An Extraterrestrial Alien Encounter** finds you trying to save colonists from intergalactic bad guys. One member of your group flies the module as the other three fire an array of weapons at the uglies.
- **Pirates of the Caribbean: Battle for Buccaneer Gold** outfits you and three mates in 3-D helmets so you can battle pirate ships virtual reality–style. One of you plays captain, steering the ship, while the others use cannons to blast the black hearts into oblivion.
- **Songmaker** lets you step into a phone booth–size recording studio to make your own CD (it costs $10 extra to buy it).
- Try the **Mighty Ducks Pinball Slam** if you're a pinball fan. It's an interactive, life-size game in which you ride platforms and use body English to score points.
- If you have an inventive mind, stop in **The Create Zone** ★★, where Bill Nye the Science-Turned-Roller-Coaster Guy helps you create the ultimate loop-and-dipster, which you then can ride in a lifelike simulator.

Note: Heavy crowds after 1pm can cut into your fun time.

DisneyQuest (✆ 407/828-4600; www.disneyworld.com) is located in Downtown Disney West Side. The admission ($29 for adults, $23 for children 3–9) gives you unlimited play from 11:30am to 11pm.

- The **NFL, NBA, NCAA, PGA,** and **Harlem Globetrotters** also host events, sometimes annually and sometimes more frequently, at the complex. Admission varies by event.

General admission is $8.70 for adults and $6.70 for kids 3 to 9. Disney's Wide World of Sports is open daily, 10am to 5pm. It's on Victory Way, just north of U.S. 192 (west of I-4). For information, call ✆ **407/828-3267** or 407/939-1500.

RICHARD PETTY DRIVING EXPERIENCE ★

Epcot's Test Track is for sissies. Here's the real thing: The Petty team gives you a chance to drive a 600-horsepower, Winston-Cup car. How real is it? Expect to sign a two-page waiver that features words like *dangerous* and *calculated risk* before you climb in. At one end of the spectrum, you can ride shotgun for a couple of laps at 145 miles per hour ($90). At the other, spend from 3 hours to 2 days learning how to drive this machine yourself and race fellow daredevils in

8 to 30 laps of excitement ($350–$1,200). *Note:* You must be 18 years old to do this. Hours and seasons vary. For reservations, call ⓒ **800/237-3889.**

10 Universal Orlando

Universal Orlando is the No. 1 contender to Walt Disney World in the ongoing, "anything-you-can-do-we-can-do-better," knock-down, drag-out battle between the Magic Mickster and the Orlando area's wanna-bes. But make no mistake—Universal is a distant second when it comes to numbers. Walt Disney World leads in theme parks (4 to 2) and smaller attractions (10 to 1). It has a 2-to-1 edge in nightclub venues, a larger lead in restaurants, and when it comes to accommodations, Disney has an insurmountable lead.

Still, Universal is trying, and it's unquestionably the champion at entertaining teenagers and the older members of the thrill-ride crowd.

In addition to its original park, **Universal Studios Florida,** it has added a nighttime entertainment complex, **CityWalk;** a second theme park, **Islands of Adventure;** and the Portofino Bay and Hard Rock hotels (both have rates well out of the range of this guide). A third hotel, the Royal Pacific, opened just as this book was going to press. Universal also has plans to expand onto all or some of 2,000 neighboring acres. While its lips are sealed, there are plans for many more hotel rooms, a golf course, and 300 acres of additional rides and attractions.

PLANNING YOUR TRIP

You can get information before you leave home by calling **Universal Orlando Guest Relations** at ⓒ **800/711-0080,** 800/837-2273, or 407/363-8000. Ask about travel packages as well as theme-park information. Universal sometimes offers a promotion that adds a second day free or at a deeply discounted price. You can also write to Guest Relations, 1000 Universal Studios Plaza, Orlando, FL 32819-7601.

ONLINE Find information about Universal at **www.universalorlando.com**. Orlando's daily newspaper, the *Orlando Sentinel,* also produces Orlando Sentinel Online at **www.orlandosentinel.com**. Additionally, there's a lot of information about the parks, hotels, restaurants, and more at **www.orlandoinfo.com**.

ESSENTIALS

GETTING TO UNIVERSAL ORLANDO Universal Orlando is a half mile north of I-4 off the Kirkman Road/Highway 435 exit. There may be construction in the area, so follow the signs directing you to the park.

PARKING If you park in the multilevel garage, make a note of the row and theme in your area to help you find your car later. Parking costs $8 for cars, light trucks, and vans. Valet parking is available for $14.

STROLLERS/WHEELCHAIRS Single strollers rent for $7; it's $12 for a double. Regular wheelchairs can be rented for $7; electric wheelchairs are $30. Wheelchair rentals require a credit-card imprint, driver's license, or $50 as a deposit.

BEST TIMES TO VISIT As with Walt Disney World, there's really no off-season for Universal, but the week after Labor Day until mid-December (excluding Thanksgiving week) and January to April are known for smaller crowds, cooler weather, and less humid air. The summer months, when the masses throng to the parks, are the worst time for crowds and hot, sticky, humid days.

Universal Orlando

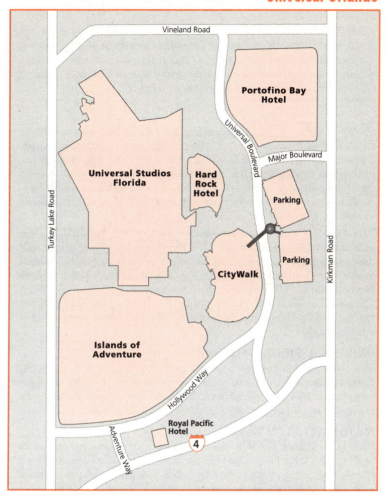

During the cooler months, you also won't have to worry about daily summer electrical storms. You should also avoid spring-break months unless you're a breaker.

It's best to visit the Universal parks near the end of the week, on a Thursday or Friday. The pace is somewhat fast Monday to Wednesday, with the heaviest crowds on weekends and during summer and holidays.

OPERATING HOURS The parks are open 365 days a year, generally from 9am to 6pm, though often later, especially in summer and around holidays, when they're sometimes open until 9pm. Also, during Halloween Horror Nights at Universal Studios Florida, that park closes around 5pm, reopens at 7pm (with a new admission), and remains open until at least midnight. The best bet is to call before you go so that you're not caught by surprise.

TICKET PRICES A 1-day ticket costs $49.95 (plus 6% sales tax) for adults, $40.95 for children 3 to 9. A 2-day, two-park unlimited-access Escape Pass is

> **Value   Money Saver**
> You can save 10% off your purchase at any Universal Orlando gift shop or meal by showing your AAA (American Automobile Association) card. This discount isn't available at food and merchandise carts or on tobacco, candy, film, collectibles, and sundry items.

$94.95 for adults, $81.95 for children 3 to 9; a 3-day, two-park pass is $109.95 for adults, $96.95 for children 3 to 9. All multiday passes let you move between Universal Studios Florida and Islands of Adventure. *Multiday passes also get you free access to the CityWalk clubs at night.* Since the parks are within walking distance of each other, you won't lose much time jockeying back and forth. Nevertheless, it's a long walk for tykes and people with limited mobility, so consider a stroller or wheelchair.

THE FLEXTICKET   The cheapest way to see Universal, SeaWorld, *and* Wet 'n Wild is with one of these passes. With FlexTicket, you pay one price to visit the participating parks during a 14-day period. A four-park pass to Universal Studios Florida, Islands of Adventure, Wet 'n Wild, and SeaWorld is $169.95 for adults and $134.95 for children 3 to 9. A five-park pass, which adds Busch Gardens in Tampa, is $202.95 for adults and $164.95 for kids. The **FlexTicket** can be ordered through Universal (© **407/363-8000;** www.universal orlando.com).

UNIVERSAL STUDIOS FLORIDA

This is the original and our favorite Universal park. Even with fast-paced, grown-up rides such as Terminator and Back to the Future, it's still a ton of fun for kids, plus it's a working movie and TV studio, so occasionally there's some live filming in the park or more often at the Nickelodeon soundstages.

MAJOR ATTRACTIONS

Back to the Future: The Ride   Blast through the space-time continuum in a flight simulator built to look like the movie's famous DeLorean car. You'll blaze a trail through volcanic tunnels, collide with glaciers, thunder through caves and canyons, and briefly get swallowed by a dinosaur in a multisensory adventure. You twist, turn, dip, and dive—all the while feeling like you're really flying. This is similar to but *more intense* than Body Wars at Epcot (p. 499). *Note:* It's bumpy and might not be a good idea if you're prone to dizziness or motion sickness. Riders must be at least 40 inches tall.

Beetlejuice's Rock 'n' Roll Graveyard Revue   Dracula, Wolfman, Frankenstein, and Beetlejuice stage a rock musical with loud and lively pyrotechnic special effects and MTV-style choreography. It's loud and lively enough to scare some small children—and aggravate some older adults. It also carries Universal's PG-13 rating, meaning it may not be suitable for some preteens.

A Day in the Park with Barney *Kids*   Set in a theater-in-the-round, this 25-minute musical stars the Purple One, Baby Bop, and BJ. It uses song, dance, and interactive play to deliver an environmental message. This could be the highlight of the day for preschoolers. However, for many adults, it can have serious, brain-eating effects. The adjacent playground has chimes to ring, tree houses to explore, and lots to intrigue little visitors.

Earthquake—The Big One 🌟 Not long after you climb on a BART train in San Francisco, there's an earthquake that's 8.3 on the Richter scale! As you sit helplessly trapped, concrete slabs collapse around you, a propane truck bursts into flames, a runaway train hurtles your way, and the station floods (65,000 gallons of water cascade down the steps).

E.T. Adventure 🌟 Soar with E.T. on a mission to save his ailing planet, passing through the forest and into space aboard a bicycle. You'll also meet some new characters that Steven Spielberg created for the ride, including Botanicus, Tickli Moot Moot, Horn Flowers, and Tympani Tremblies.

The Funtastic World of Hanna-Barbera 🌟 *Kids* This spaceship/motion-simulator offers a surprisingly wild ride as pilot Yogi Bear tries to save Elroy Jetson from Dick Dastardly. Its brain-scrambling motion is similar to Back to the Future (above), although this one's a bit tamer. At press time, it was likely that Universal would close this ride in favor of one based on the movie *Jimmy Neutron: Boy Genius*. *Note:* There's a 40-inch height minimum.

Jaws 🌟 As your boat heads into a 7-acre, five-million-gallon lagoon, a dorsal fin cuts across the surface. Then, what goes with the fin—a 3-ton, 32-foot-long, mechanical great white shark—attacks. The wall of flame that surrounds your boat truly causes you to feel the heat in this $45 million attraction. *Note:* The effects of this ride are more spectacular after dark.

Kongfrontation King Kong is back and everyone must evacuate The Big Apple, so it's all aboard a tram. Police helicopters hover overhead, putting you directly in the line of fire; then the tram malfunctions; and, of course, you encounter Kong—40 feet tall and 12,000 pounds. He belches banana breath into your face and dangles you over the East River. The big ape executes 46 movements, including simulated noogies on top of your tram. *Note:* Insiders say Kong may soon be replaced by an indoor roller coaster based on the movie *The Scorpion King*.

Men in Black Alien Attack 🌟🌟🌟 Board a six-passenger cruiser, buzz the streets of New York, and use your "zapper" to splatter up to 120 bug-eyed targets. You have to contend with return fire and light, noise, and clouds of liquid nitrogen (a.k.a. fog) that can spin you out of control. Your laser tag-style gun fires infrared bullets. The 4-minute ride relies on 360° spins rather than speed for its thrill factor. At the end, a giant roach (30 ft. tall with 8-ft. fangs and 20-ft. claws) swallows you. Fortunately, it explodes. Unfortunately, the blast douses you with bug guts (okay, it's only warm water) as you blast your way out. *Note:* Guests must be at least 42 inches tall for this $70 million ride.

Nickelodeon Studios 🌟 You'll tour the sound stages where Nick shows are produced. You'll also view concept pilots, visit the kitchen where Gak and green slime are made, and try new Sega video games. This 45-minute behind-the-scenes walking tour is a fun escape from the hustle of the midway. A child volunteer gets slimed, but it's only green applesauce or a reasonable facsimile.

Terminator 2: 3-D Battle Across Time 🌟🌟🌟 *Finds* James Cameron, who directed the movie, supervised this $60 million production, which features Arnie and other original cast members (on film). It combines three huge screens with technical effects and live action on stage, including a custom-built Harley and six 8-foot-tall cyberbots. *Note:* The crisp 3-D effects are among the best in any Orlando park, but Universal has given this show a PG-13 rating, too.

Twister . . . Ride It Out ★ Two million cubic feet of air per minute (that's enough to fill four full-size blimps) create an ominous funnel cloud, five stories tall. And the roar of a freight train, at rock-concert level, fills the theater as cars, trucks, and a cow fly by while the audience watches just 20 feet away. It's the windy version of *Earthquake* and packs quite a wallop. *Note:* This ride has Universal's PG-13 rating, so it may not be suitable for preteens.

The Wild, Wild, Wild West Stunt Show ★ Actors demonstrate falls, gun and whip fights, dynamite explosions, and other Wild West staples in this 18-minute show that's a real hit with Far East visitors, who are intrigued by America's Wild West. *Warning:* Heed the splash zone or you will get very wet.

Woody Woodpecker's Nuthouse Coaster ★★ This kiddie coaster will thrill some moms and dads, too. Although only 30 feet at its peak, it offers quick, banked turns. The ride lasts only about 60 seconds and waits can be 30 minutes or more, but few kids will want to miss the experience. It's much like The Barnstormer at Goofy's Wiseacre Farm in the Magic Kingdom (p. 496). *Note:* The coaster has a 36-inch height minimum.

ADDITIONAL ATTRACTIONS
The Boneyard is an oft-changing area where you can see props used in a number of Universal movies. **Alfred Hitchcock: The Art of Making Movies** is a tribute to the "master of suspense." At press time, Universal was planning to close this attraction in favor of *Shrek and Donkey's Scary-Tale Adventure*, a 4-D fractured fairytale based on the hit movie *Shrek*. The **Gory, Gruesome & Grotesque Horror Make-up Show** offers behind-the-scenes looks at transformation scenes from such movies as *The Fly* and *The Exorcist* (shows from 11am).

Universal Cuisine

The best restaurants here are just outside the main gates at CityWalk, Universal's restaurant and nightclub venue. But there are more than a dozen places to eat inside the park. Here are our favorites:

Best Sit-Down Meal: Lombard's Landing has a hearty fried clam basket, as well as lobster, steak, pasta, and burgers ($11–$30). It's located across from Earthquake.

Best Counter Service: Universal Studios' Classic Monsters Cafe is one of the newer park eateries. It serves salads, pizza, pasta, and rotisserie chicken ($6–$11). It's off Seventh Avenue near the Boneyard.

Best Place for Hungry Families: Similar to a mall food court, the **International Food and Film Festival** offers a variety of food in one location. With options ranging from stir-fry to fajitas, it's a place where a family can split up and still eat under one roof. There are kid's meals for under $4 at most locations. The food is far from gourmet but a cut above regular fast food ($6–$11). It's located near the back of Animal Planet Live and the entrance to Back to the Future.

Best Snack: The floats ($3–$5) at **Brody's Ice Cream Shop** are just the thing to refresh you on a hot summer afternoon. Brody's is located near the Wild, Wild, Wild West Stunt Show.

> **Tips** **Some Practical Advice for Island Adventurers**
>
> 1. **The Shorter They Are** Nine of the 14 major rides at Islands of Adventure have height restrictions. Dueling Dragons and the Incredible Hulk Coaster, for instance, deny access to anyone under 54 inches. For those who want to ride but come with kids, there's a baby or child swap at all of the major attractions, allowing one parent to ride while the other watches the tykes. But sitting in a waiting room isn't much fun for the little ones. So take your child's height into consideration before coming to the park or at least some of the islands.
> 2. **Cruising the Islands** If you hauled your stroller with you on your vacation, bring it with you to the park. It's a very long walk from your car, through the massive parking garage and the nighttime entertainment district, CityWalk, before you get to the fun. Carrying a young child and the accompanying paraphernalia, even with a series of moving sidewalks, can make the long trek seem even longer—especially at the end of the day.
> 3. **The Faint of Heart** Even if you don't have children, make sure you consider all of the ride restrictions. Expectant mothers, guests prone to motion sickness, and those with heart, neck, or back trouble will be discouraged—with good reason—from riding most primo attractions. There's still plenty to see and do, but without the roller coasters, Islands of Adventure isn't so special.
> 4. **Beat the Heat** Several rides require that you wait outside without any cover to protect you from the sizzling Florida sun, so bring some bottled water with you for the long waits (a 50¢ free-world bottle costs $2.50 if you buy it here) or take a sip or two from the fountains placed in the waiting areas. Also, beer, wine, and liquor are more available at the Universal parks than the Disney ones, but booze, roller coasters, and hot weather can make for a messy mix.
> 5. **Cash in on Your Card** You can save 10% on your purchases at any gift shop or on a meal in Islands of Adventure by showing your AAA (American Automobile Association) card. This discount isn't available at food or merchandise carts. And tobacco, candy, film, collectibles, and sundry items aren't included.

Lucy, A Tribute is a remembrance of America's queen of comedy, and the **Blues Brothers** launch their foot-stomping revue five times a day.

Back at Woody Woodpecker's KidZone, **Fievel's Playland** is a playground with a house to climb and a water slide for small fry. **Curious George Goes to Town** has water- and ball-shooting cannons, while **Animal Planet Live!** is a 20-minute multi-media show with critters as its stars.

ISLANDS OF ADVENTURE

Universal's second park opened in 1999 with a collection of fast, fun rides. At 110 acres, it's the same size as the original park, but it seems packed with more to do. Roller coasters roar above pedestrian walkways, water rides careen through the center of the park, and themed eateries are camouflaged to match their surroundings.

This $1-billion park is divided into six areas: the **Port of Entry,** where you'll find a collection of shops and eateries, and the themed sections—**Seuss Landing, Toon Lagoon, Jurassic Park, Marvel Super Hero Island,** and **The Lost Continent.** This park has loads of thrill rides and some play areas for the kids. The trade-off is few—read, two—shows and stage productions.

PORT OF ENTRY
This park gateway has five shops, four restaurants, and the **Island Skipper Tours,** which ferries passengers to **Jurassic Park.**

SEUSS LANDING
The main attractions here are aimed at youngsters. But anyone who loved the good Doctor as a child will enjoy some nostalgic fun on the rides, and those who aren't familiar with his work will enjoy the visuals—Seussian art is like Dalí for kids.

The Cat in the Hat ★★   Seuss fans recognize the giant candy-striped hat looming over the entrance to this ride, and probably the chaotic journey. Comparable to, but a lot spunkier than It's a Small World at WDW, The Cat in the Hat puts you in a spinning couch that travels through 18 scenes from the famous book, retelling the tale of a day gone very much awry. You'll meet characters such as Thing 1 and Thing 2. Kids must be 48 inches or taller to go alone, and pop-up characters may scare the very young.

One Fish, Two Fish, Red Fish, Blue Fish ★   This kiddie charmer is similar to the Dumbo ride at WDW (including the ridiculously long lines). Here, your controls let you move your funky fish up or down 15 feet as you spin around on an arm attached to a hub. Watch out for "squirt posts," which spray unsuspecting riders who don't follow the rhyme (and some who do).

Caro-Seuss-El ★★★ *Moments*   Forget tradition. Try a not-so-normal carousel that gives you a chance to ride whimsical characters from Dr. Seuss, including Cowfish, elephant birds, and Mulligatawnies. They move up and down as well as in and out. Pull the reins to make their eyes blink or heads bob as you twirl through the riot of color surrounding the ride. There is a rocking-chariot platform and wheelchair-loading system, too.

If I Ran the Zoo ★★   This 19-station interactive play land features flying water snakes and a chance to tickle the toes of a Seussian animal. Kids can also spin wheels, explore caves, fire water cannons, climb, slide, and otherwise burn off excited energy that most adults can't remember ever having.

MARVEL SUPER HERO ISLAND
Thrill junkies love the twisting, turning, stomach-churning rides on this island filled with building-tall murals of Marvel Super Heroes.

The Amazing Adventures of Spider-Man ★★★ *Moments*   The original web master stars in this ride that combines 3-D action and special effects. Passengers squeal as their 12-passenger cars twist and spin, plunge and soar through a comic-book universe. There's a simulated 400-foot drop that feels an awful lot like the real thing. *Note:* Expectant mothers or those with heart, neck, or back problems shouldn't get on. Those who ride must be at least 40 inches tall.

Doctor Doom's Fearfall 🌶 Look! Up in the sky! It's a bird, it's a plane . . . uh, it's you falling 150 feet, if you're courageous enough to climb aboard. The screams that can be heard far from the ride's entrance add to the anticipation. You're blasted to the top, with feet dangling, and dropped in intervals, leaving your stomach at several levels. The fall isn't quite up to the Tower of Terror's at Disney–MGM Studios, but it's still frightful. *Note:* Expectant mothers or those with heart, neck, or back problems shouldn't ride. Minimum height is 52 inches.

Incredible Hulk Coaster ★★★ *Moments* Expect a ride that launches you from a dark tunnel and hurtles you into the lower ozone while accelerating from 0 to 40 miles per hour in 2 seconds. While that's only two-thirds the speed of Rock 'n' Roller Coaster at Disney–MGM Studios, the Hulk has more action. You spin upside down 128 feet from the ground, feel weightless, and careen through the center of the park. Coaster-lovers will be pleased to know that this ride, which lasts 2 minutes and 15 seconds, includes seven inversions and two deep drops. The 32-passenger coasters glow green at night (riders who ignore all the warnings occasionally turn green as well). *Note:* Expectant mothers or those with heart, neck, or back problems shouldn't ride. Riders must be at least 54 inches tall.

Storm Force Accelatron You and the X-Men's super-heroine, Storm, try to defeat the evil Magneto by converting human energy into electrical forces. To do that, you need to spin faster and faster. In addition to some upset stomachs, the spiraling creates a thunderstorm of sound and light that gives Storm all the power she needs to blast Magneto into the ever-after (or until the next riders arrive). *Note:* This ride is sometimes closed during off-peak periods.

TOON LAGOON
More than 150 life-size sculpted cartoon images let you know you've entered the land of the Sunday funnies.

Dudley Do-Right's Ripsaw Falls ★★ Dudley's staid red hat can be deceiving: The ride that lies under it has a lot more speed and drop than onlookers think. Six-passenger logs launch you into a 75-foot dip at 50 miles per hour. You *will* get wet on this ride. *Note:* Once again, expectant mothers or folks with heart, neck, or back problems should go elsewhere. Riders must be 44 inches or taller.

Me Ship, The Olive 🌶 *Kids* This three-story boat is family-friendly from bow to stern. Kids can toot whistles, clang bells, or play the organ. Sweet Pea's Playpen is fun for young guests. Adults and kids 6 and up love Cargo Crane, which lets you drench riders on Popeye & Bluto's Bilge-Rat Barges (see below).

Popeye & Bluto's Bilge-Rat Barges ★★★ This ride's rafts are similar to the ones on Kali River Rapids at WDW's Animal Kingdom (earlier in this chapter), but they're faster and bouncier. Adding to the fun, you'll be squirted by water cannons fired from Me Ship, The Olive (above). The rafts bump, churn, and dip 14 feet at one point, as you travel a *c-c-cold* white-water course. You will get *s-s-soaked!* Again, expectant mothers or people with heart, neck, or back problems shouldn't get in line. Riders must be at least 42 inches tall.

Toon Trolley Beach Bash Beetle Bailey and other favorites from the Sunday comics will have you rockin' and rollin' in the streets as they sing and make you laugh during this several-times-a-day, surfing-safari-and-limbo show.

Dining at Islands of Adventure

There are a number of stands where you can get a quick bite to eat and a handful of full-service restaurants. The park's creators have taken some extra care to tie in restaurant offerings with the theme. The **Green Eggs and Ham Cafe** may be one of the few places on earth where you'd be willing to eat tinted huevos. (The green eggs get their color from a variety of spices, not food dye.) There are dozens of sit-down restaurants, eateries, and snack carts. To save money, look for the kiddie menus, offering a children's meal and a small beverage for $5. Also consider combo meals, which usually offer a slight price break. **Thunder Falls Terrace** in Jurassic Park, for instance, offers a rib-and-chicken combo as well as other options in the $8 to $12 range.

Here are some of our other favorites at Islands:

- **Best Sit-Down Restaurant** At **Mythos** in the Lost Continent, choose from occasionally changing selections such as jerk grouper, lobster-stuffed potato, pepper-painted salmon with lemon couscous, or pan-fried crab cakes with lobster sauce and basil. This is a grown-up dining affair, best suited for older children and adults ($10–$21; 11:30am–3:30pm daily).

- **Best Atmosphere for Adults** The **Enchanted Oak Tavern (and Alchemy Bar),** also in the Lost Continent, has a cavelike interior, which from the outside looks like a mammoth tree, and is brightened by an azure blue skylight with a celestial theme. The tables and chairs are thick planks, and the servers are clad in "wench wear." Try the chicken/rib combo with waffle fries for $13. The menu offers 45 types of beer.

- **Best Atmosphere for Kids** The fun never stops under the big top at **Circus McGurkus Cafe Stoo-pendous** in Seuss Landing, where animated trapeze artists swing from the ceiling. Kids' meals, including a souvenir cup, are $6. The adult menu features fried chicken, lasagna, spaghetti, and pizza. Try the fried chicken platter for $8 or the lasagna for $7.

- **Best Vegetarian Fare** **Fire-Eater's Grill,** located in the Lost Continent, is a fast-food stand that offers a tasty veggie falafel for $5. You can also get a tossed salad for $2.79.

- **Best Diversity** **Comic Strip Café,** located in Toon Lagoon, is a four-in-one counter service–style eatery offering burgers, Chinese food, Mexican food, and pizza and pasta ($6–$8).

JURASSIC PARK

All the basics and some of the high-tech wizardry from Stephen Spielberg's wildly successful films are incorporated in this lushly landscaped tropical locale, which includes a replica of the visitor center from the movie. Expect long lines at the River Adventure.

Camp Jurassic ★★ *Kids*   This play area has everything from lava pits with dino bones to a rain forest. Watch out for the spitters that lurk in dark caves. The multilevel play area has plenty of places for kids to crawl, explore, and spend energy. But keep an eye on young ones: It's easy to get confused in the caverns.

Jurassic Park Discovery Center ★ Here's an amusing, educational pit stop that offers life-size dinosaur replicas and interactive games. The sequencer lets you combine your DNA with a dinosaur's. "Beasaur" allows you to see and hear as "they" did. The highlight is watching a velociraptor "hatch" in the lab. Because there are a limited number of interactive stations, this can consume a lot of time on busy days.

Jurassic Park River Adventure ★★★ After you enjoy a leisurely raft tour along a faux river, things get dicey. A T-Rex thinks you look like a tasty morsel, and spitters launch "venom" your way. The only way out: an 85-foot plunge in your log-style life raft. It's steep and quick enough to lift your fanny out of the seat. (Spielberg designed it, but on a test run insisted on getting out before the drop.) Expect to get wet. *Note:* Expectant mothers or those with heart, neck, or back problems shouldn't ride. Guests must be at least 42 inches tall.

Pteranodon Flyers ★ *Kids* The ride's metal frames and simple seats are flimsy, the landing is bumpy, and you'll swing from side to side 25 feet up, which makes some riders queasy. But you will get a great bird's-eye view of the park. Unlike some sky rides, this one lets your feet dangle from the two-seat flyer and there's only a restraining belt between you and the ground. *That said, it's a kids' ride*—single passengers must be between 36 and 56 inches tall; adults can climb aboard only when accompanying someone that size. *Note:* Two passengers launch every 30 to 45 seconds, so this ride can consume an hour of your day even in the off-season.

Triceratops Discovery Trail Meet a "living" dinosaur and learn from its "trainers" about the care and feeding of a 24-foot-long, 10-foot-high Triceratops. It responds to touch, and its movements include realistic blinks, breathing, and flinches. *Note:* This exhibit is at least seasonally closed.

THE LOST CONTINENT

Although it mixed its millennia—ancient Greece with medieval forest—Universal has done a good job creating a foreboding mood in this section of the park, where the entrance is marked by menacing stone griffins.

Dueling Dragons ★★★ *Moments* Designers created two roller coasters that roar at each other. Coaster crazies love the intertwined set of leg-dangling racers that climb to 125 feet, invert five times, and three times come within 12 inches of each other as the dragons test your bravery and bowels. There's a special (yes, longer!) line for the front seat. *Note:* Expectant moms or those with heart, neck, or back problems shouldn't ride. Riders must be at least 54 inches tall.

Eighth Voyage of Sindbad *Overrated* The mythical sailor is the star of a stunt show that includes six water explosions and 50 pyrotechnic effects, including a 10-foot circle of flames. It's pretty corny and doesn't come close to the Indiana Jones stunt show at Disney–MGM Studios.

The Flying Unicorn ★★ The Unicorn is a small roller coaster that travels through a mythical forest. It's like Woody Woodpecker's Nuthouse Coaster at Universal Studios Florida (p. 516) and The Barnstormer at Goofy's Wiseacre Farm in the Magic Kingdom (p. 496). That means a fast, corkscrew run sure to earn squeals but probably not at the risk of losing lunch.

The Mystic Fountain ★ *Finds* Those who notice it have fun at this "smart" fountain, which especially delights kids. It can "see," "hear," and talk, leading to a lot of kibitzing with those who stand before it and take the time to kibitz back.

Poseidon's Fury ★   The park's best show (given the lack of competition, that's something of a back-handed compliment) has changed a couple of times, but it still revolves around a battle between the evil Poseidon, god of the sea, and Zeus, king of the gods. Speaking of revolving, you'll pass through a small room that has a 42-foot vortex where 17,500 gallons of water swirl around you, barrel-roll style, and see the gods hurl fireballs at each other.

11 SeaWorld

A 200-acre marine-life park, **SeaWorld** (🕿 407/351-3600; www.seaworld.com) explores the deep in a format that combines conservation awareness with entertainment. While that's what Disney is attempting at Animal Kingdom, the message here is subtle and a more inherent part of the experience.

Shamu, a killer whale, is the star of the park, which also has several other orcas, including some babies. The pace is much more laid-back than at Universal or Disney and it's a good way to take a day off from trudging through the frenzied parks. Though **Journey to Atlantis** and **Kraken** are pretty high-tech, SeaWorld can't compete with the wonders of Walt's World or Universal. But those parks don't let you discover the crushed-velvet texture of a stingray or the song of the sea lions.

SeaWorld opened a second park, Discovery Cove, in summer 2000. While it's the most expensive park ticket anywhere in Florida, the 30-acre playground offers a chance to swim with a real dolphin, among other options (see "Discovery Cove: A Dolphin Encounter," later in this section).

PLANNING YOUR VISIT

Get information before you leave by writing to **SeaWorld Guest Services** at 7007 SeaWorld Dr., Orlando, FL 32801, or call 🕿 **800/327-2424** or 407/351-3600.

Online   SeaWorld information is available at **www.seaworld.com**. The *Orlando Sentinel* newspaper produces *Orlando Sentinel Online* at **www.orlandosentinel.com**. You can get a ton of information from the Orlando/Orange County Convention & Visitors Bureau website, **www.orlandoinfo.com**.

ESSENTIALS

GETTING TO SEAWORLD   Going south from Orlando, take the Sand Lake Road exit off I-4 and follow the signs.

BEST TIMES TO VISIT   Since this is a mostly outdoor, water-related park, keep in mind that Florida can get a tad nippy in January and February. SeaWorld has smaller crowds from January through April.

Weekends, Thursday, and Friday are busy days at this park. Monday through Wednesday are usually better days to visit because tourists coming for a week go to Disney and Universal early in their stays, saving SeaWorld for the end, if at all.

> **Tips VIP Privileges**
>
> SeaWorld's guided **Adventure Express** tour gets you front-of-the-line access to Kraken, Journey to Atlantis, and Wild Arctic, plus reserved seating for shows, a personal introduction to a penguin, a chance to feed dolphins and stingrays, and lunch. It costs $65 for adults and $60 for kids 3 to 9, plus park admission (🕿 800/406-2244).

OPERATING HOURS The park is usually open 9am to at least 6pm, and later during summer and holidays when there are additional shows at night.

STROLLERS/WHEELCHAIRS Dolphin-shaped single strollers rent for $7; it's $12 for a double. Regular wheelchairs are available for $7; electric chairs are $30, with a $25 deposit.

TICKET PRICES A **1-day ticket** costs $49.95 for ages 10 and over, $40.95 for children 3 to 9, plus 6% sales tax. **Parking** is $7.

THE FLEXTICKET The most economical way to see SeaWorld, the Universal parks, and Wet 'n Wild is with a **FlexTicket.** It lets you pay one price to visit any of the parks in a 14-day period. A four-park pass to Universal Studios Florida, Islands of Adventure, Wet 'n Wild, and SeaWorld is $169.95 for adults and $134.95 for children 3 to 9. A five-park pass, which adds Busch Gardens in Tampa, is $202.95 for adults and $164.95 for kids (see chapter 10), is $197 for adults and $158 for kids. You can order it from SeaWorld (© **407/351-3600;** www.seaworld.com).

TOURS Since it has few thrill rides, SeaWorld has few restrictions, but you may want to check out the special tour programs offered through the education department. SeaWorld lives up to its reputation for making education fun. There are three 1-hour options: **Polar Expedition Tour** (touch a penguin), **Predators** (touch a shark), and **To the Rescue** (see manatees and sea turtles). All cost $8 for adults and $7 for children, plus park admission. Call © **800/406-2244** or 407/351-3600 for information.

MAJOR ATTRACTIONS

Clyde & Seamore Take Pirate Island ⭐ A lovable sea lion and otter, with a supporting cast of walruses and harbor seals, appear in this fishy comedy with a swashbuckling conservation theme. It's corny, but fun.

Intensity Water-Ski Show ⭐⭐⭐ *Moments* Arguably, this is an unrivaled ski show that has evolved over more than 15 years. It's a not-to-be-missed, hyper-competition involving some of the most skilled athletes on water. The 20-person team includes world-class skiers, wake-boarders, and stunt men and women from across the United States performing nonstop aquabatics.

Journey to Atlantis ⭐⭐ Taking a cue from Disney's imagineers, SeaWorld created a story to go with its $30 million water coaster. But what really matters is the drop—a wild plunge from an altitude of 60 feet, with luge-like curves and a shorter drop added for good measure. *Note:* Riders must be at least 46 inches tall and pregnant women as well as folks with heart, neck, or back problems should find something else to do.

Key West at SeaWorld This attraction includes three naturalistic animal habitats: **Stingray Lagoon,** where visitors enjoy hands-on encounters with harmless Southern diamond and cownose rays; **Dolphin Cove,** a habitat for bottlenose dolphins that interact with visitors; and **Sea Turtle Point,** home to threatened and endangered turtles. *Warning:* The dolphins here will readily approach you, provided you offer the right incentive—smelt. You easily can blow $10 or $20 feeding these loveable beggars.

Key West Dolphin Fest Atlantic bottlenose dolphins perform flips and high jumps, twirl, swim on their backs, and give rides to trainers. The tricks are impressive, but it's like any other dolphin show. If you go, see this before Shamu. He puts these little mammals to shame.

> **Tips Shuttle Service**
> SeaWorld and Busch Gardens in Tampa, both owned by Anheuser-Busch, have a shuttle service that offers $5 round-trip tickets to get you from Orlando to Tampa and back. The 1½- to 2-hour one-way shuttle runs daily and has five pick-up locations in Orlando, including at Universal and on I-Drive (© **800/221-1339**). The schedule allows about 7 hours at Busch Gardens.

Kraken ★★★ SeaWorld's deepest venture into thrill rides starts slow but ends with speed. Named for a mythological sea beast, the ride's floor-less, open-sided, 32-passenger trains plant you on a pedestal high above the track. You climb 151 feet, fall 144 feet, hit 65 miles per hour, go underground three times (spraying bystanders with water), and make seven loops during a 4,177-foot-long course. It may be the longest 3 minutes and 39 seconds of your life. *Note:* Kraken has a 54-inch height minimum.

Manatees: The Last Generation? ★ Underwater viewing stations, innovative cinema techniques, and interactive displays combine for a tribute to these gentle marine mammals. While this isn't as good as seeing them in the wild, it's as close as most folks get, and it's a much roomier habitat than the tight quarters their kin have at The Living Seas in Epcot (p. 499).

Penguin Encounter *Overrated* Sadly, this is a very superficial encounter that transports you by moving sidewalk through Arctic and Antarctic displays. You'll get a glimpse of penguins as they preen, socialize, and swim at bullet speed in their 22° habitat. You'll also see puffins and murres in a similar, separate area.

Shamu's Happy Harbor ★ *Kids* This 3-acre play area has a four-story net tower with a 35-foot-high crow's nest, water cannons, remote-controlled vehicles, nine slides, a submarine, and a water maze. Most kids love it.

The Shamu Adventure ★★★ *Moments* Everyone comes to SeaWorld to see the big guy and his friends—the stars of this well-choreographed show. The whales (up to 25 ft. and 10,000 lb.) really dive into their work. When you hear the warning that Hurricane Shamu is approaching, it's time for those sitting in the first 14 rows to hightail it. Those who don't are drenched with *icy water* as the orcas race around the pool, creating a huge wave that rolls over the edge and into the audience. Veteran animal handler Jack Hanna also makes a video appearance on the big overhead monitors.

Terrors of the Deep Remember Shark Encounter? SeaWorld has added other species—220 in all. Pools out front have small sharks and rays (feeding isn't allowed). The interior aquariums have big eels, poisonous lionfish, menacing barracudas, and bug-eyed pufferfish. *Note:* This isn't a tour for the claustrophobic—you walk through a tube, beneath millions of gallons of water.

Wild Arctic ★ Enveloping guests in the beauty, exhilaration, and danger of a polar expedition, Wild Arctic combines a high-definition adventure film with flight-simulator technology to display breathtaking Arctic panoramas. After a hazardous flight over the frozen north, visitors emerge into an exhibit where you can see a playful polar bear or two, beautiful beluga whales, and walruses performing aquatic ballets. Kids and those prone to motion sickness may find the ride bumpy. There's a separate line if you want to skip the flight.

ADDITIONAL ATTRACTIONS

Other features at SeaWorld include **Pacific Point Preserve,** a 2½-acre natural setting that duplicates the rocky home of California sea lions and harbor seals. **Tropical Rain Forest,** a bamboo and banyan-tree habitat, is the home of cockatoos and other birds. At the 5½-acre **Anheuser-Busch Hospitality Center,** indulge in free samples of Anheuser-Busch beers and then stroll through the stables to watch the famous Budweiser Clydesdale horses being groomed.

DISCOVERY COVE: A DOLPHIN ENCOUNTER

Anheuser-Busch spent $100 million building SeaWorld's sister park, which debuted in 2000. That's 10 times less than Universal's Islands of Adventure(above), but the admission is as much as four times higher. There are two options: Pay $219 per person ($229 beginning March 1, 2003) plus 6% sales tax (ages 6 and up only) if you want to swim with a dolphin; $119 ($129 starting March 1) if you can skip that luxury.

The **dolphin encounter** ✯✯✯ stars an amazing group of 28 of these mammals. They do tricks and take guests on brief but thrilling rides. The experience lasts 90 minutes, 35 to 40 minutes of which is spent in the lagoon with a dolphin. The rest is used as a classroom on these remarkable mammals.

Here's what you get for your money, with or without the dolphin encounter:

- A limit of *no more than 1,000 other guests a day.* (The average daily attendance at Disney's Magic Kingdom is 41,000.)
- Lunch (fajitas, salmon, stir-fry, pesto chicken pasta, salad, or sandwich), a towel, locker, and snorkeling gear. Souvenir photos are $17 a pop.
- Other 9am-to-5:30pm activities including a chance to swim near (but on the other side of Plexiglas from) **barracudas and black-tip sharks.** There are no barriers, however, between you and the gentle rays and brightly colored tropical fish in the 1.3-million-gallon coral reef. The 3,300-foot-long Tropical River is a great place to swim or float in a mild current—it goes through a cave, two waterfalls, and a 100-foot-long, 30-foot-high aviary where you can take a stroll, becoming a human perch. There also are beaches for tanning.
- Seven days of **unlimited admission** to SeaWorld (park admission normally costs $49.95 a day for adults, $40.95 for children 3–9).

Get more information on Discovery Cove by calling ✆ **877/434-7268** or go to **www.discoverycove.com**. If you want to try it, make a reservation as far in advance as possible. Despite the price, it reaches its capacity almost every day.

12 Other Area Attractions

We've covered the monster parks. Now we're going to explore some of the best smaller attractions. Many of these require less than a day (or a fortune) to see, so we'll note how much time and money to budget. **Add 6% sales tax** to the prices below unless otherwise noted.

IN KISSIMMEE

Kissimmee's tourist strip is 10 to 15 minutes west of Disney.

Florida Splendid China   Crowds are reasonably small at this 76-acre attraction, partly due to a lack of publicity but mainly because it lacks the pizzazz of the big parks. Highlights include replicas of China's 4,200-mile Great Wall, the Forbidden City's 9,999-room Imperial Palace, and the Mongolian mausoleum of Genghis Khan. The Mysterious Kingdom of the Orient is a 90-minute dance-and-acrobatic show held nightly except Monday in the Golden Peacock Theater. (Separate tickets are $16.) Allow 4 to 5 hours to tour the park.

3000 Splendid China Blvd. (off Irlo Bronson Memorial Hwy./U.S. 192). © **800/244-6226** or 407/396-7111. www.floridasplendidchina.com. Admission $28.88 adults, $18.18 children 5–12 including tax. Daily from 9:30am; closing hours vary seasonally (call ahead). Free parking. From I-4 take the U.S. 192 west exit and turn left at the Florida Splendid China dragons.

Flying Tigers Warbird Restoration Museum This is a working restoration facility and museum that allows visitors to see, smell, and touch the history many have only heard or read about. With B-17 Flying Fortress (among many others) restoration projects underway year round, as well as dozens of flyable WWII and vintage airplanes on exhibit and memorabilia and armament displays, you'll like it here if you're a fan of vintage flying machines and their restoration. Admission includes a guided tour. The museum also has a restoration school and available daily flights in an authentic WWII Warbird for an extra charge.

231 N. Hoagland Blvd. (south of U.S. 192). © 407/933-1942. www.warbirdmuseum.com. Admission $9 adults (plus tax), $8 seniors 60 and over and children 8–12 (plus tax). Free for children 7 and under. Mon–Sat 9am–5:30pm; Sun 9am–5pm. Free parking. Take U.S. 192 east of Disney to Kissimmee, then turn right (south) on Hoagland.

Gatorland Founded in 1949 with only a handful of alligators living in huts and pens, Gatorland now houses thousands of alligators and crocodiles on its 70-acre spread. There are three shows. **Gator Wrestlin'** uses the old "put-them-to-sleep" trick, but it's more of an environmental awareness program. **The Gator Jumparoo** is a crowd-pleaser in which one of these big reptiles lunges 4 or 5 feet out of the water to snatch a dead chicken from a trainer's hand. And **Jungle Crocs** is a showcase of toothy carnivores. Plan to spend 4 to 5 hours here.

14501 S. Orange Blossom Trail (U.S. 441; between Osceola Pkwy. and Hunter's Creek Blvd.). © **800/ 393-5297** or 407/855-5496. www.gatorland.com. Admission $17.95 adults, $8.50 children 3–12 including tax. Open daily at 9am; closing times vary. Free parking. From I-4 take the Osceola Pkwy. exit east to U.S. 17/92/441 and go left/north. Gatorland is 1½ miles on the right.

Water Mania You can boogie board or body surf in the continuous-wave pools, float lazily along an 850-foot-long river, enjoy a white-water tube run on **Riptide,** and spiral down the **Twin Tornadoes** water slide. If you dare, ride the **Abyss,** an enclosed tube slide that corkscrews through 380 feet of darkness, exiting into a splash pool. There's a water playground for kids, a miniature golf course, and a picnic area, too. Allow 4 to 5 hours here.

6073 W. Irlo Bronson Memorial Hwy./U.S. 192 (just east of I-4). © **800/527-3092** or 407/396-2626. www.watermania-florida.com. Admission $17 ages 3–adult. Mar–Oct daily 10am–5pm. Parking $5. From I-4 take U.S. 192 east about a half mile.

INTERNATIONAL DRIVE

Like Kissimmee attractions, these are a 10- to 15-minute drive from the Disney area and 5 to 10 minutes from Universal Orlando.

Peabody Ducks *Moments* One of the best shows in town is short and sweet, but, more importantly—*free.* The Peabody Orlando's five mallards march into the lobby each morning, accompanied by John Philip Sousa's "King Cotton March" and their own red-coated duck master. They spend the day splashing in a marble fountain. Then, in the afternoon, they march back to the elevator and up to their fourth-floor "penthouse." Donald Duck never had it this good. Allow 1 hour.

9801 International Dr. (between the Bee Line Expressway and Sand Lake Rd.). © **800/732-2639** or 407/352-4000. Free admission. Daily at 11am and 5pm. Free self-parking, valet parking $8. From I-4, take the Sand Lake Rd./Hwy. 528 exit east to International Dr., then south. Hotel is on the left across from the Convention Center.

Ripley's Believe It or Not! Odditorium *Overrated*

Do you crave weird science? The oddities here include a two-headed kitten, a three-quarter–scale model of a 1907 Rolls Royce made of one million matchsticks, and a Tibetan flute created from human bones. Allow 2 hours.

8201 International Dr. (1½ blocks south of Sand Lake Rd.). © **800/998-4418** or 407/363-4418. www.ripleys.com/orlando2.htm. Admission $15 adults, $13 seniors, $10 children 4–12. Daily 9am–1am. Free parking. From I-4, exit onto Sand Lake Rd. and then turn right on International Dr.

Titanic—Ship of Dreams *Overrated*

Didn't get enough with the movie? This exhibit has some 200 artifacts (a deck chair, life jacket, etc.), movie memorabilia, actors, and a replica of the great ship's grand staircase. Allow 1 or 2 hours.

8445 International Dr. (3 blocks south of Sand Lake Rd.). © **407/248-1166**. www.titanicshipofdreams.com. Admission $17 adults, $13 children 6–12. Daily 10am–9pm. Free parking. Take I-4 to the Sand Lake Rd./Hwy. 528 exit and turn left on International Dr.; go three-quarters of a mile. It's in the Mercado.

Wet 'n Wild ★★

Orlando's favorite non-Disney water park offers 25 acres of fun including: **Fuji Flyer,** a six-story, four-passenger toboggan run through 450 feet of banked curves; **The Surge,** one of the longest (580 ft. of curves) and fastest multipassenger tube rides in the Southeast; and **Black Hole,** a two-person, spaceship-style raft that makes a 500-foot, twisting, turning voyage through darkness (all three require that kids 36 to 48 in. tall be accompanied by an adult). You also can ride **Raging Rapids,** a simulated white-water run with a waterfall plunge; **Blue Niagara,** a 300-foot-long, six-story loop-and-dipster that also has a plunge (48-in. height minimum); **Knee Ski,** a cable-operated kneeboarding course that's open in warm-weather months only (56-in. height minimum); and **Mach 5,** a trio of twisting, turning flumes. The park also has a large kids' area with mini-versions of the big rides. Plan on a full day here.

In addition to the admission prices below, Wet 'n Wild is part of the multi-day **FlexTicket package** that includes admission to Universal Orlando (which owns this attraction), SeaWorld, and Busch Gardens in Tampa. You pay one price to visit any of them during a 14-day period. A four-park pass to Universal Studios Florida, Islands of Adventure, Wet 'n Wild, and SeaWorld is $169.95 for adults and $134.95 for children 3 to 9. A five-park pass, which adds Busch Gardens in Tampa, is $202.95 for adults and $164.95 for kids.

6200 International Dr. (at Universal Blvd.). © **800/992-9453** or 407/351-9453. www.wetnwild.com. Admission $31 adults, $25 children 3–9. Hours vary seasonally, weather permitting. You can rent tubes ($4), towels ($2), and lockers ($5); all require a $2 deposit. Parking is $6 for cars, light trucks, and vans. From I-4, take the Universal Orlando exit and follow the signs.

ORLANDO

These attractions are in close proximity to each other, making for a pleasant day's excursion. Loch Haven Park is about 35 minutes by car from the Disney area. You probably can incorporate some Winter Park sights into the same day.

Harry P. Leu Gardens *Value*

This 50-acre garden offers a respite from theme-park razzle-dazzle. Paths lead through camphors, oaks, palms, cicadas, and camellias—the latter represented by one of the world's largest collections, 50 species and 2,000 plants that bloom October through March. There's also an extensive rose garden. Orlando businessman Harry P. Leu, who donated his 49-acre estate to the city in the 1960s, created the gardens. There are free 20-minute tours of his house, built in 1888. It takes about 2 hours to see everything.

1920 N. Forest Ave. (between Nebraska St. and Corrine Dr.). © 407/246-2620. www.ci.orlando.fl.us/departments/leu_gardens/. Admission $4 adults, $1 children grades K–12. Daily 9am–5pm, later in summer and during holidays; museum tours 10am–3:30pm (closed during July). Free parking. Take I-4 to the Princeton St. exit and go east, then right on Mills Ave. and left on Virginia Dr. Look for the gardens on your left, just after you go around a curve.

Orlando Museum of Art This local heavyweight handles some of the most prestigious traveling exhibits in the nation. It hosts special exhibits throughout the year, but even if you miss one it's worth a stop to see the rotating permanent collection of 19th- and 20th-century American art, pre-Columbian art dating from 1200 B.C. to A.D. 1500, and African art. Allow 2 to 3 hours.

2416 N. Mills Ave. (in Loch Haven Park). © 407/896-4231. www.omart.org. Admission $6 adults, $5 seniors and students, $3 children 4–11. Tues–Sat 10am–5pm, Sun noon–5pm. Free parking. Take the I-4 Princeton St. exit east and follow signs to Loch Haven Park.

Orlando Science Center Finds The four-story center has 10 exhibit halls that explore everything from swamps to the plains of Mars. One of the big attractions is the **Dr. Phillips CineDome,** a 310-seat theater that presents films, planetarium shows, and laser light displays. **KidsTown** has a pint-size park and construction site. **Science City** includes a power plant, and **123 Math Avenue** uses puzzles and other things to make learning fun. Allow 3 to 4 hours.

777 E. Princeton St. (between Orange and Mills aves., in Loch Haven Park). © 888/672-4386 or 407/514-2000. www.osc.org. Basic admission (exhibits only) $9.50 adults, $8.50 seniors 55 and older, $6.75 children 3–11; additional prices for CineDome film and planetarium show. Tues–Thurs 9am–5pm, Fri–Sat 9am–9pm, Sun noon–5pm. Parking available in a garage across the street for $3.50. Take the I-4 Princeton St. exit east and cross Orange Ave.

ELSEWHERE IN CENTRAL FLORIDA

Audubon of Florida—National Center for Birds of Prey Finds In addition to being a rehabilitation center—one of the biggest and most successful in the Southeast—this is a great place to get to know rehabilitated winged wonders that roost here and earn their keep by entertaining the relatively few visitors who come. You can get a close look at hams like Elvis, the blue suede shoe-wearing American kestrel; Daisy the polka dancing barn owl; and Trouble, an eagle born with a misaligned beak. *Note:* The center reopened in spring 2002 after a $2 million, 4-year expansion. Allow 2 hours.

1101 Audubon Way, Maitland. © 407/644-0190. www.adoptabird.org/. Recommended donation $5 adults, $4 children 3–12. Tues–Sun 10am–4pm. From Orlando, go north on I-4 to Lee Rd., turn right/east, and at the first light (Wymore Rd.) go left, then right/east at the next light (Kennedy Blvd.). Continue a half mile to East Ave., turn left, and go to the stop sign at Audubon Way. Turn left, and the center is on the right.

Charles Hosmer Morse Museum of American Art Value Louis Comfort Tiffany left a fingerprint on this museum, which has 40 vibrantly colored windows and 21 paintings of his. There are also non-Tiffany windows by Frank Lloyd Wright, paintings by John Singer Sargent and Maxfield Parrish, and photographs by Tiffany and other 19th-century artists. Allow 2 hours.

445 Park Ave. N. © 407/645-5311. www.inusa.com/tour/fl/orlando/morse.htm. Admission $3 adults, $1 children 12–17. Tues–Sat 9:30am–4pm, Sun 1–4pm. Take I-4 to Fairbanks Ave., exit east to Park Ave., and go left for 4 traffic lights.

A SIDE TRIP TO CYPRESS GARDENS

Cypress Gardens ★★ FDR was in his first term when this foundation tourist attraction opened in 1936. Water-ski shows and flowers are still its bread and butter, but a lot has changed over the years.

At **Carousel Cove,** kids ride ponies and an ornate carousel. **Cypress Junction** is outfitted with a model railroad that travels 1,100 feet of track with up to 20 trains, visiting miniature places such as New Orleans and Mount Rushmore. You can rise 153 feet in **Island in the Sky** for a panoramic vista of the gardens and a beautiful chain of Central Florida lakes. And **Do You Know Your Animals?** features a show-and-tell with coatimundis, ring-tailed lemurs, muntjac deer, colorful macaws, and a 15-foot albino python affectionately called Banana Boy.

On the water, the **Greatest American Ski Team** keeps a legendary tradition going strong with standards such as ramp jumping, the aqua-maid ballet line, human pyramid, flag line, and slapstick comedy. Shows change, but they usually combine yesterday with modern magic acts. On the frozen-water front, **Moscow on Ice** presents *Skate the States,* a tribute to some of the U.S.A.'s finest.

Wings of Wonder is a conservatory with 1,000 brilliant butterflies in a Victorian-style, free-flight aviary. The **Birdwalk Aviary** has 40 to 50 hand-raised lories and lorikeets that welcome visitors by landing on their shoulders.

Allow a full day to see Cypress Gardens.

2641 S. Lake Summit Dr. (Hwy. 540 at Cypress Gardens Blvd., 40 miles southwest of Disney World), Winter Haven. © 800/282-2123 or 863/324-2111. www.cypressgardens.com. Admission $35 (plus 6% tax) adults, $20 children 6–17. Daily 9:30am–5pm, later during some periods. Parking $6. Take I-4 west to U.S. 27 south, and proceed west to Hwy. 540.

COST CUTTERS

While everyone else is emptying their wallets in theme parks, here are some great places to dodge crowds and save money.

Cornell Fine Arts Museum ★ This showplace has 6,000 works on display, making it one of Florida's most distinguished and comprehensive art collections. There also are lectures and gallery tours. The museum gets a limited number of traveling exhibits as well.

East end of Holt Ave., Winter Park (located on Rollins College campus). © 407/646-2526. www.rollins.edu/cfam. Free admission. Tues–Fri 10am–5pm, Sat–Sun 1–5pm. Take I-4 to the Fairbanks Ave. exit, go east to Park, turn right, then turn left on Holt.

Eatonville and the Zora Neale Hurston National Museum of Fine Arts ★ America's oldest black municipality is located just north of Orlando. It's the birthplace of Hurston—a too-little heralded, African-American author. There's an annual festival in January honoring her and her work. A small gallery on the site has periodically changing exhibits of art and other work, and there's a map for a walking tour of the community, established in 1887. Make sure to call in advance.

227 E. Kennedy Blvd., Eatonville. © 407/647-3307. www.cs.ucf.edu/~zora. $3 donation suggested. Mon–Fri 9am–4pm. Take I-4 to the Lee Rd. exit, then left on Wymore, then right on Kennedy. It's a quarter mile on the left.

Lake Eola Park ★ This quiet hideaway in downtown Orlando has the city's skyline as a backdrop. The lake has a cascading fountain that features a 12-minute, lighted show at dark. The park has a .9-mile walking and jogging path, a playground, and paddleboats for rent ($7 per half hour). FunnyEola features comedy acts the second Tuesday of each month at 7:30pm. There are a variety

Hot Links: Orlando's Top Golf Courses

Disney operates five 18-hole, par-72 golf courses and one 9-hole, par-36 walking course. The rates are $105 to $170 per 18-hole round for resort guests ($5 more if you're not staying at a WDW property). For tee times and information, call ✆ **407/824-2270** up to 7 days in advance (up to 30 days for guests of the Disney resort and official properties). Call ✆ **407/934-7639** about golf packages.

Beyond Mickey's shadow, **Golfpac** (✆ **800/327-0878** or **407/260-2288**; www.golfpacinc.com) is an organization that packages golf with accommodations and arranges tee times at more than 40 Orlando-area courses. **Tee Times USA** (✆ **800/465-3356**; www.teetimesusa.com) and **Florida Golfing** (✆ **866/833-2663**; www.floridagolfing.com) are two others offering package information and course reservations.

---

of other performances, most of which are free (call for details). The Shakespeare Festival (Apr to early May) is $5 to $30 nightly (✆ **407/893-4600**).

Washington St. and Rosalind Ave., Orlando. ✆ **407/246-2827**. Free admission. Daily during daylight hours. Take I-4 to Anderson St., exit right, turn left at the 4th light (Rosalind). The amphitheater is on the right.

13 Outdoor Activities & Spectator Sports

There are plenty of recreational options. The Disney facilities described here are open to everyone, no matter where you're staying. For further information about WDW recreational facilities, call ✆ **407/939-7529**.

BICYCLING Bike rentals (singles, multi-speeds, tandems, and bikes with training wheels or baby seats) are available from the **Bike Barn** (✆ **407/824-2742**) at Fort Wilderness Resort and Campground. Rates are $7.55 per hour, $20.75 per day. Fort Wilderness offers good bike trails.

BOATING With a ton of man-made waterways, WDW owns a navy of pleasure boats. **Capt. Jack's** at Downtown Disney rents Water Sprites, canopy boats, and 20-foot pontoon boats ($22–$35 per half hour). For information call ✆ **407/828-2204**.

FISHING Disney has a variety of fishing excursions, but true anglers won't find them a challenge. The excursions can be arranged 2 to 90 days in advance by calling ✆ **407/824-2621**. The cost is $160 to $185 for up to five people for 2 hours. Bait is extra. Outside Disney, **A Pro Bass Guide Service** offers guided trips along some of central Florida's most picturesque rivers and lakes. Hotel pickup is available (✆ **800/771-9676** or 407/877-9676; www.probassguideservice.com). The cost is $225 for two people per half day, $325 for a full day.

HAYRIDES Wagons depart **Pioneer Hall** at Disney's Fort Wilderness at 7 and 9:30pm for 45-minute old-fashioned hayrides with singing, jokes, and games. The cost is $8 for adults, $4 for children ages 3 to 10. An adult must accompany children under 12. No reservations; it's first-come, first-served. Call ✆ **407/824-2832**.

HORSEBACK RIDING **Disney's Fort Wilderness** offers 45-minute guided trail rides daily. The cost is $30.20 per person. Children must be at least 9. Maximum weight limit is 250 pounds. For information call ✆ **407/824-2832**.

The **Villas of Grand Cypress' Equestrian Center** offers 45-minute walk-trot trail rides for $45. A 30-minute private lesson is $55; a 1-hour lesson is $100. Call ⓒ **407/239-4700** and ask for the equestrian center.

JOGGING The **Yacht** and **Beach Club** resorts share a 2-mile trail; the **Disney Institute** has a 3.4-mile course, with 32 exercise stations; the **Caribbean Beach Resort's** 1.4-mile promenade circles a lake; and **Fort Wilderness's** tree-shaded 2.3-mile path has exercise stations about every quarter mile. Pick up a jogging trail map at any Disney property's guest-services desk.

SWIMMING The **YMCA Aquatic Center** has a full fitness center, racquetball courts, and an indoor Olympic-size pool. Admission is $10 per person, $25 for families. It's at 8422 International Dr. For information call ⓒ **407/363-1911**.

TENNIS There are 22 lighted tennis courts throughout Disney properties. Most are free. If you're willing to pay, courts can be reserved at Disney's **Contemporary** and **Grand Floridian** resorts by calling ⓒ **407/824-2270**. Both charge $18 per hour. Lessons are also available.

SPECTATOR SPORTS Central Florida has a number of venues for inactive sportsters.

Arena Football The **Orlando Predators** play from April until August. Game tickets ($7.50–$40) are often available the day of the game at the **TD Waterhouse Centre,** 600 W. Amelia St., between I-4 and Parramore Avenue (ⓒ **407/447-7337**).

Baseball The **Atlanta Braves** play 18 spring-training games at Disney's Wide World of Sports beginning in early March. Tickets are $11.50 to $19.50. Call ⓒ **407/839-3900** for more information. From April to September, the **Orlando Rays,** the Tampa Bay Devil Rays' Class AA Southern League affiliate, play their 70 home games at the same complex. Tickets through **Ticketmaster** (ⓒ **407/839-3900**) sell for $5 to $8.

Basketball The **TD Waterhouse Centre,** 600 W. Amelia St., between I-4 and Parramore Avenue, is the home of the **Orlando Magic,** which plays 41 of its games here from October to April. Call ⓒ **407/896-2442** or check out www.nba.com/magic. Single-game tickets are $25 to $175. On the women's side, the WNBA's **Orlando Miracle** has a 16-game home stand beginning in early June on the same court. Tickets are $8 to $34. Call ⓒ **407/916-9622** or surf over to **www.wnba.com/miracle/**.

> **Value A Disney Bargain?**
>
> From pink Cadillacs to 4-foot beer steins, tons of wacky treasures are regularly put on the auction block at Walt Disney World. And these little-known, surplus-property auctions are the best bargain in Disney.
>
> In addition to cast-offs from the parks and resorts, routine items are available, from well-worn lawn mowers to never-used stainless-steel pots. If you're looking for a unique piece of Disney, the auctions are held four to six times a year—always on a Thursday, when Disney workers get paid. You might even run into furniture from Miss Piggy's dressing room. Call ⓒ **407/824-6878** for information, dates, and directions.

14 Shopping

There's no shortage of tourist areas on International Drive and the Kissimmee strip, featuring 3-for-$10 T-shirt shacks, and the parks are filled with shops selling overpriced goods. *Best bet:* Steer clear of all tourist shops except for must-have souvenirs.

On International Drive, look for **Pointe Orlando** (✆ **407/248-2838**), a complex with three dozen stores including FAO Schwarz and Banana Republic. Also on International Drive, **Festival Bay** (✆ **407/345-1311**) has a 20-screen theater, a Bass Pro Shop, a skateboard park, and several restaurants.

There are several factory outlets, but their publicized discounts of 25% to 75% are often a mirage. You can avoid being taken by knowing suggested retail prices, so you can decide whether you're making a killing. **Belz Factory Outlet World,** 5401 W. Oak Ridge Rd. (at the north end of International Dr.; ✆ **407/354-0126;** www.belz.com), and **Orlando Premium Outlets,** 8200 Vineland Ave. (✆ **407/238-7787;** www.PremiumOutlets.com), are two of the better ones.

Florida Mall, 8001 S. Orange Blossom Trail (✆ **407/851-6255;** www.shop simon.com), which offers Saks, Dillards, and 200 more stores; and **Mall at Millennia,** scheduled to open in October 2002 near Universal Orlando (Bloomingdale's, Macy's, Neiman Marcus, Tiffany's), are the best of the malls.

Old-stuff buffs love **Antique Row** on Orange Avenue in downtown Orlando. This collection of shops is about as far away as you can get from the manufactured fun of Disney. Headliners include **Flo's Attic** (✆ **407/895-1800**), which sells traditional antiques. **Wildlife Gallery** (✆ **407/898-4544**) has pricey, original works of wildlife art, including sculptures. And the **Fly Fisherman** (✆ **407/898-1989**) sells—no surprise here—fly-fishing gear. Sometimes, you can spot people taking casting lessons in the park across the street.

15 Walt Disney World & Orlando After Dark

After a day in the parks, the last thing we're looking for is after-hours entertainment, so we tip our hats to those of you with the stamina to party into the night.

This is mainly a kids' destination, so most of the evening shows and entertainment at WDW parks are geared toward families. Still, there are a lot of adult things to do at the parks and in downtown Orlando. Universal's food-and-entertainment complex, **CityWalk,** continues to develop. WDW's nighttime options include **Pleasure Island** and **Downtown Disney West Side.** And the real downtown, as in Orlando, is 25 miles up the road and has its own bars, clubs, and restaurants. (*Note:* Church Street Station is one major player missing from the downtown mix. It folded in 2001.)

Check the "Calendar" section of Friday's *Orlando Sentinel* for up-to-the-minute details on local clubs, visiting performers, concerts, and events. It has hundreds of listings, many of which can be found at **www.orlando sentinel.com**. The *Orlando Weekly* is a free magazine circulated in red boxes throughout Central Florida. It highlights the more offbeat and often more of-the-minute performances. You can find it online at **www.orlandoweekly.com**.

WALT DISNEY WORLD DINNER SHOWS

These fall into the worth-a-splurge class due to price, perhaps reserved for a day when you cut back by stuffing yourself at one of those cheap breakfast buffets and avoiding the theme parks in favor of a free or inexpensive daylight activity.

Hoop-Dee-Doo Musical Revue *Moments* As WDW's most popular show, Hoop-Dee-Doo requires priority-seating reservations as early as possible. The reward: You can feast on an all-you-can-eat barbecue (fried chicken, smoked ribs, salad, corn on the cob, baked beans, freshly baked bread, strawberry shortcake, and coffee, tea, beer, sangria, or soda). While you stuff yourself silly, performers in 1890s garb lead you in a foot-stomping, hand-clapping high-energy show that includes jokes you haven't heard since second grade. Show times are 5pm, 7:15pm, and 9:30pm daily. 3520 N. Fort Wilderness Trail (at WDW's Fort Wilderness Resort and Campground). © **407/939-3463**. www.disneyworld.com. Reservations required. Adults $47.80, kids 3–11 $24.80, including tax and gratuity. Free parking.

Polynesian Luau Dinner Show *Moments* Almost as popular as the Hoop-Dee-Doo, the luau presents a delightful 2-hour show that's a favorite among kids. They're invited on stage as part of an evening that includes hyperactive entertainers from New Zealand, Hawaii, and Tahiti, who perform hula, warrior, ceremonial, and fire dances on a flower-filled stage. Arrive early for a preshow featuring crafts (lei making, hula lessons, and more). The all-you-can-eat meal includes island fruits, roasted chicken and pork, fried rice, vegetables, potatoes, tropical ice-cream sundaes, coffee, tea, beer, wine, and soda. Show times are 5:15 and 8pm Tuesday through Saturday. 1600 Seven Seas Dr. (at Disney's Polynesian Resort). © **407/939-3463**. www.disneyworld.com. Reservations required. Adults $47.80, kids 3–11 $24.80, including tax and gratuity. Free parking.

ENTERTAINMENT COMPLEXES
PLEASURE ISLAND

This 6-acre complex has nightclubs, restaurants, shops, and movie theaters where during the day you can enjoy for free whatever's open. At night, for a single admission price ($21 including tax; © **407/934-7781**), you can go club hopping and rock into the wee hours every night of the week. The mood is festive, especially at midnight, when the New Year's Eve party gets started. The clubs open at 7pm and generally stay open until 2am; the shops open at 11am and close at 2am. The complex is open daily and there's plenty of free self-parking. *Note:* At night, this is primarily an adult venue. Here's the lineup:

Adventurers Club The most unique of Pleasure Island's clubs, Adventurers occupies a multistory building chock-full of artifacts like 1940s aviation photos, hunting trophies, shrunken heads, Buddhas, and a mounted "yakoose"—a half yak, half moose that occasionally speaks, whether you've been drinking or not. In the Mask Room, the 100 or so masks move their eyes, jeer, and make bizarre pronouncements. Improv comedy takes place throughout the evening in the salon. We could easily hang out here all night, sipping potent tropical drinks in the library or the bar, where elephant-foot bar stools rise and sink mysteriously.

BET Soundstage This club grooves with traditional R&B and the rhyme of hip-hop. If you like the BET Cable Network, you'll love it. Boogie on an expansive dance floor or kick back on the terrace. The club sometimes has concerts for a separate charge. Call © **407/934-7666**.

Mannequins Dance Palace Housed in a vast dance hall with a small-town movie-house facade, Mannequins is supposed to be a converted mannequin warehouse (remember, you're still in Disney World). This high-energy club has a big, rotating dance floor, and its popularity makes it one of the toughest nightspots to get into. It offers three levels of bars and hangout space that are festooned with elaborately costumed mannequins and moving scenery suspended from the overhead rigging. A DJ plays contemporary tunes filtered through speakers that could wake the dead, and there are high-tech lighting effects. You must be 21 to get in, and they're *very* serious about it.

The Pleasure Island Jazz Company   This big, barnlike club features contemporary and traditional live jazz. Most performers are locals, but about once a month there's a big name, such as Kenny Rankin or Maynard Ferguson.

Rock 'n' Roll Beach Club   Live bands play classic rock from the 1960s through the 1990s. There are bars on all three floors. The first level has a dance floor; the others offer arcade-style games, pizza, and more.

Motion   Pleasure Island's newest dance club features Top 40 tunes and alternative rock. This club replaced the Wildhorse Saloon.

DISNEY'S WEST SIDE

This area of Downtown Disney clubs and restaurants is located next to Pleasure Island.

Bongo's Cuban Café   *Overrated*   Created by Cuban-American singer Gloria Estefan and her husband, Emilio, the cafe is Disney's version of old Havana. There are mosaic bar stools shaped like bongo drums and a Desi Arnaz lookalike might show up to sing a few tunes. There's no dance floor to speak of, but you could cha-cha on an upstairs patio that overlooks the rest of West Side. It's a great place to sit back and enjoy the view while basking in the Latin rhythms. But the food is lacking. Daily 11am to 2am. Downtown Disney West Side. © 407/828-0999. www.bongoscubancafe.com. No reservations. No cover charge. Free parking.

House of Blues   Past performers have included Jethro Tull, Quiet Riot, Duran Duran, and others. The three-tier, barn-like building may be a little difficult for those with disabilities to maneuver in, but there really isn't a bad seat in the house. The atmosphere is dark, perfect for the oft-featured bluesy sounds that raise the rafters. The dance floor is big enough to boogie on without doing the bump with a stranger. You can dine in the adjoining restaurant ($9–$24) on baby-back ribs, blackened chicken, jambalaya, Orleans-style shrimp, and Cajun meat loaf. There's also a Sunday gospel brunch. Downtown Disney West Side. © 407/934-2583. www.hob.com. Cover charges vary by event/artist. Free parking.

CITYWALK

Located between Islands of Adventure and Universal Studios Florida, this 30-acre club-and-restaurant district (© **407/363-8000;** www.citywalk.com) is five times larger than Pleasure Island. Alcohol is prominently featured, so an adult should accompany all children and free-flowing peers.

You can walk the district for free or visit individual clubs for the cover charges in the following listings. CityWalk also offers two **party passes.** A pass to all clubs costs $7.95 plus tax. For $11.95 plus tax, you can add a movie at Universal Cineplex (© **407/354-5998**) to the basic club access. *Note:* Daytime parking in the Universal Orlando garages costs $7, but parking is free after 6pm.

Bob Marley—A Tribute to Freedom   This hybrid bar/restaurant has a party atmosphere that makes the food more appealing as the night wears on. The clapboard building is said to be a replica of Marley's home in Kingston. Jamaican food—meat patties, jerk red snapper, and, of course, the brew of champions, Red Stripe—is served amid portraits of the original Rastamon. If you try an Extreme Measure, have a designated driver. Reggae bands, local and national,

Moments Not Your Ordinary Circus

Cirque du Soleil, the famous no-animals circus, is located in Downtown Disney West Side. At times, it seems as if all 64 performers are onstage simultaneously, especially during the intricately choreographed trampoline routine. Trapeze artists, high-wire walkers, an airborne gymnast, a posing strongman, mimes, and two zany clowns cement a show called **La Nouba** ★★★ (it means "live it up") into a five-star performance.

But, in a world of pricey attractions, this is one of the pricier. The 90-minute show costs $67 for adults and $39 for children 3 to 9 (plus 6% tax). Shows are at 6 and 9pm, Wednesday through Sunday, though times and days rotate and there's sometimes a matinee. Call © **407/939-7600** or check out **www.cirquedusoleil.com**.

---

perform on a microdot-sized stage. Hours are Sunday to Friday 4pm to 2am; Saturday 2pm to 2am. © 407/224-2262. Cover charge $4.25 after 8pm, more on special nights.

CityJazz The cover includes the **Downbeat Jazz Hall of Fame** (which has memorabilia from Louie Armstrong and other greats) as well as the **Thelonious Monk Institute of Jazz,** a performance venue that's also the site of jazz workshops. The two-story, 10,500-square-foot building has more than 500 pieces of memorabilia representing Dixieland, swing, bebop, and jazz. For the food, look for tapas, sushi, and more. Hours are Sunday through Thursday 8:30pm to 1am; Friday to Saturday 8:30pm to 2am. © 407/224-2189. Cover charge $3.25 (more for special events).

the groove This club is Universal's answer to Mannequins at Pleasure Island, though it's not as popular and, therefore, has less of a waiting list. There's a high-tech sound system that will blow your hair back and a spacious dance floor in a room gleaming with chrome. A DJ plays tunes most nights, featuring the latest in hip-hop, jazz-fusion, techno, and alternative music. Bands occasionally play the house, too. The decor touches five entertainment eras, reaching from vaudeville to the millennium. Each area has a unique design, bar, and specialty drink to fit its ambience. Hours are Sunday through Wednesday 9pm to 2am; Thursday through Saturday 9pm to 3am. © 407/363-8000. Cover charge $5.25. Must be 21 to get in.

Hard Rock Cafe/Hard Rock Live The cafe side is the chain's standard—a theme restaurant with memorabilia and other tributes to rock's greats. The difference is that this one has the first concert hall with the Hard Rock name on the door. Call ahead to find out what acts are featured. Tickets for big-name performers sell fast. Cafe daily 11am to midnight. © 407/351-7625. www.hardrock.com. No cover in the cafe; concerts $6–$150.

Jimmy Buffett's Margaritaville Music from the maestro drifts through the building, and live tunes are performed on a small stage inside later in the evening. A Buffett sound-alike also strums on the back porch. Inside, there are three themed bars: The Volcano erupts margarita mix; the Land Shark has fins hanging from the ceiling; and the 12 Volt, is, well, a little electrifying—we'll leave it at that. If you opt for dinner among the palm trees, go for the true Key West experience. Early in the day that means a cheeseburger (in paradise, of course); later, it's one of several kinds of fish (pompano, sea bass, dolphin). Daily 11:30am to 2am. ⓒ **407/224-2155.** Cover $4.75 after 10pm.

Latin Quarter This two-level restaurant/nightclub offers you a chance to absorb the salsa-and-samba culture and cuisine of 21 Latin nations. If you don't know how to move your hips, there's a dance instructor to lend a hand. The music ranges from merengue to Latin rock. The sound system is loud enough to blow you into the next county, but before that happens you can leave on your own to peruse a Latin American art gallery. Open 11am to 2am. ⓒ **407/363-5922.** Cover charge $5–$10 Thurs–Sat after 10pm.

Motown Cafe Orlando Try finger food and sandwiches ($8–$15.50), or just enjoy the canned music of Motown greats like Smoky Robinson and the Supremes. A live band frequently plays. Open Sunday to Thursday 11:30am to 11pm, Friday to Saturday 11am to 2am. ⓒ **407/363-8000.** www.motown.com. Cover charge $5.25 after 9pm Mon–Thurs, Fri–Sat.

Pat O'Brien's *Overrated* Just like the French Quarter, which is home to the original Patty O's, drinking, drinking, and more drinking are the highlights here. Enjoy dueling Baby Grands and a flame-throwing fountain while you suck down the drink of the Big Easy, a Hurricane. There's a limited menu of sandwiches and treats like jambalaya and shrimp Creole ($6–$12). Daily 4pm to 2am. ⓒ **407/363-8000.** Cover charge $2.25 after 9pm.

DOWNTOWN ORLANDO

There are dozens of clubs and restaurants along Orange Avenue, the main street in downtown Orlando. A free bus called **Lymmo** runs in a designated lane that connects many of the nighttime spots, but Lymmo stops running about 11pm.

Cairo One of the newer arrivals downtown, this popular dance club has bars on three levels, lots of 1970s retro clothes, and kids trying to look older than their age. Reggae arrives on weekends. Hours are Friday to Sunday 10pm to 3am. 22 S. Magnolia Ave. (1 block off Orange Ave.), Orlando. ⓒ **407/422-3595.** www.cairo-nightclub.com. Cover charge $5–$10. Free street parking.

Cricketers Arms Pub Regardless of whether you're British or just a fun lover, this pub is a place to party. As the name implies, cricket (as well as soccer) matches are shown on the telly. Live blues and soft-rock bands are featured, too, mainly on weekends. The revelry offers a good excuse to try a pint or two of any of 17 imports. The menu offers steak-and-ale pie and bangers and mash, among others ($6–$12). Daily 11am to 2am. 8445 International Dr. ⓒ **407/354-0686.** No cover for music; $10 for soccer. Free parking.

8 Seconds *Finds* Sure, there's a bar and dance floor inside, but what's outside really sets this place apart. A rodeo pen next to the parking lot features "Buckin' Bull Nights" with live bull riding. Rising country stars occasionally hold concerts here. Open Friday to Saturday 8pm to 2am. 100 W. Livingston Ave. ⓒ **407/839-4800** or 407/843-5775. www.8-seconds.com. Cover charge $5 for 21 and older; $7 for 18–21. Parking in city lot $3.

Howl at the Moon Saloon Your best bet is to hit this joint on a full moon—even if you're too shy to cock your head back and *howllll* with the best of them when the club's dueling pianos march through classic rock tunes from the 1950s to the 1990s. Daily 6pm to 2am. 55 W. Church St. ⓒ **407/841-9118.** www.howlatthemoon.com. Cover charge Wed–Sat $2–$4. Metered-lot parking runs about $1 an hour.

> **Value Money Saver**
> Orlando's Official Visitor Center has a program called "OTIX!" that offers half-price tickets to 90 cultural activities, such as theater performances, the ballet, operas, and symphonies. In most cases, tickets are for same-day performances. You can call © 407/363-5872 for information, but you have to go to the center at 8723 International Dr. (4 blocks south of Lake Rd.) to get the tickets.

Sak Comedy Lab Locals perform at this 200-seat club that has 8 to 10 performances weekly (usually Tues, Thurs, and Sat). Favorites include the Duel of Fools, where two teams face off in improvised scenes based on suggestions from the audience, and Lab Rats, where students play in improv formats. Shows usually at 8 and 10pm, plus midnight on Saturday. 380 W. Amelia St. © 407/648-0001. www.sak.com. Admission $5–$13. Parking $5.

THE PERFORMING ARTS
While Disney occasionally hosts classical music acts, you'll have to go into Orlando for a taste of the traditional arts.

CONCERT HALLS & AUDITORIUMS
The city continues to dream of getting financing for a multimillion-dollar world-class performing arts center. While you're holding your breath, there are two existing entertainment facilities, both of which fall under the wand of Orlando Centroplex. The **Florida Citrus Bowl** is at 1610 W. Church St., at Tampa Street; and the **TD Waterhouse Centre** is at 401 W. Livingston St., between I-4 and Parramore Avenue (© **407/849-2020;** www.orlandocentroplex.com).

THEATER
Orlando–UCF Shakespeare Festival *Finds* The company is known for placing traditional plays in contemporary settings and offers special programs throughout the year, such as *Shakespeare Unplugged,* a reading series. Performances are held in three venues: The Ken and Trisha Margeson Theater, which has 300 seats wrapped around three sides of the stage; the Marilyn and Sig Goldman Theater, an intimate 120-seater; and the Lake Eola Amphitheater, where the 936 seats give a view of Shakespeare under the stars. Tickets are $10 to $35 and sell pretty fast, so call ahead for reservations. 812 E. Rollins St. © 407/447-1700. www.shakespearefest.org. Free parking for indoor season; metered parking in fall.

OPERA
Orlando Opera Company Local professionals, joined by guest artists from around the country, perform a repertoire of traditional fare. Standards include *Carmen, Macbeth,* and the *Marriage of Figaro,* among others. Shows held during the October-to-May season seldom sell out. Tickets start at $20. Performances are staged at the Bob Carr Performing Arts Centre. 401 W. Livingston St. © 800/336-7372 or 407/426-1700. www.orlandoopera.org.

DANCE
Southern Ballet Theatre Traditional shows such as *The Nutcracker* use guest artists to augment local talent. There has been a resurgence of interest in

the ballet in recent years, but performances rarely sell out. The season runs from October to May. Tickets start at around $15. Performances feature the Orlando Philharmonic Orchestra (see below) and are at the Bob Carr Performing Arts Centre. 401 W. Livingston St. © **407/426-1739** for information, © **407/839-3900** to get tickets via Ticketmaster. www.southernballet.org.

CLASSICAL MUSIC

Orlando Philharmonic Orchestra   The orchestra offers a varied schedule of classics and pop-influenced concerts throughout the year at the Bob Carr Performing Arts Centre. The musicians also accompany the Southern Ballet (see above). Tickets begin at $20. 401 W. Livingston St. © **407/896-6700**. www.orlandophil.org.

12

Northeast Florida

by Bill Goodwin

Northeast Florida traces its history to 1513, when the Spaniard Juan Ponce de León, who later undertook a Quixotic quest for the Fountain of Youth, sighted this coast, landed somewhere between present-day Jacksonville and Cape Canaveral, and named it "La Florida." In 1565, the Spanish established a colony at St. Augustine, making it the country's oldest permanent settlement.

If they were to come back to life, those early colonists would feel right at home in St. Augustine, where the streets of the restored Old City look like they did in Spanish times. For us modern mortals, St. Augustine offers a rich look back to when the settlers struggled to establish a life in a new, unfamiliar, and often hostile world.

But they would surely be astonished at what they would see elsewhere in Northeast Florida.

To the south, their eyes would pop open with disbelief at today's "Space Coast," where rockets blast off from the Kennedy Space Center at Cape Canaveral. Nearby in Cocoa Beach, they would see another peculiar curiosity: surfers. And in Daytona Beach, they would hear the deafening roar of the stock cars and motorbikes that make "The World's Most Famous Beach" the "World Center of Racing."

Heading north along the coast, they would come to the rich folks' haven of Ponte Vedra Beach, where golf definitely takes precedence over manual labor. And they would marvel at sprawling Jacksonville, Florida's largest metropolis and a thriving example of today's New South.

Up on the Georgia border, they'd cross a bridge to Amelia Island, where exclusive resorts take full advantage of 13 miles of beautiful beaches. Amelia's Victorian-era town, Fernandina Beach, would seem modern to them; to us, it's a quaint and historic retreat.

Despite its ritzy enclaves, Northeast Florida is one of the most attractive parts of the state for budget-minded travelers. Granted, it's not as warm in winter up here as in the southern parts of Florida, but that translates into much less expensive hotel room rates.

1 Cocoa Beach, Cape Canaveral & the Kennedy Space Center ★

46 miles SE of Orlando, 186 miles N of Miami, 65 miles S of Daytona

Today's "Space Coast" around Cape Canaveral was once a sleepy place where city dwellers escaped the crowds from the exploding urban centers of Miami and Jacksonville. But then came the NASA space program. Today the region accommodates its own crowds, especially hordes of tourists who come to visit the Kennedy Space Center and enjoy 72 miles of beaches, plus fishing, surfing, golfing, and tennis.

Thanks to NASA, this also is a prime destination for nature lovers. The space agency originally took over much more land than it needed to launch rockets.

Rather than sell off the unused portions, it turned them over to the Cape Canaveral National Seashore and the Merritt Island National Wildlife Refuge, which have preserved them in their pristine natural states.

A handful of the major Caribbean-bound cruise ships depart from the manmade Port Canaveral. The south side of the port is lined with seafood restaurants and marinas, which serve as home base for the area's deep-sea charter- and group-fishing boats.

ESSENTIALS
GETTING THERE   The nearest airport is **Melbourne International Airport** (© **321/723-6227**; www.mlbair.com), 22 miles south of Cocoa Beach, which is served by **Continental** (© **800/525-0280**) and **Delta** (© **800/221-1212**). **Orlando International Airport,** about 35 miles to the west, is a much larger hub with many more flight options and generally less expensive fares (see "Orientation" in chapter 11, "Walt Disney World & Orlando"). It's an easy 45-minute drive from the Orlando airport to the beaches via the Beeline Expressway (Fla. 528)—it can take almost that long from the Melbourne airport. **Comfort Travel** (© **800/567-6139** or **407/799-0442**) or the **Cocoa Beach Shuttle** (© **407/784-3831**) will take you from Orlando to the beaches for about $20 per person.

VISITOR INFORMATION   For information about the area, contact the **Florida Space Coast Office of Tourism,** 8810 Astronaut Blvd., Suite 102, Cape Canaveral, FL 32920 (© **800/872-1969** or 321/868-1126; fax 321/868-1139; www.space-coast.com). The office is in the Sheldon Cove building, on Fla. A1A a block north of Central Boulevard, and is open Monday to Friday from 8am to 5pm.

The office operates an information booth at the John F. Kennedy Space Center Visitor Complex (see below).

GETTING AROUND   A car is essential in this area, so rent one at the airport. The **Space Coast Area Transit** (© **321/633-1878**; www.ridescat.com) operates buses, but routes tend to be circuitous and therefore extremely time-consuming.

WHAT TO SEE & DO
SEEING THE ASTRONAUT ATTRACTIONS
In addition to the two attractions below, Brevard College's **Astronaut Memorial Planetarium and Observatory,** 1519 Clearlake Rd., Cocoa Beach (© **321/634-3732**), south of Fla. 528, has its own International Hall of Space Explorers, but its big attractions are sound and light shows in the planetarium. Call for a schedule of events and prices.

Astronaut Hall of Fame *Kids*   Children will enjoy a playful visit to this hands-on museum at the mainland end of NASA Causeway (Fla. 405). In addition to honoring space voyagers, the museum has artifacts from the space program and several interactive exhibits. A flight simulator and a G-Force Trainer will subject you to four times the pull of gravity, and the "3-D 360" will flip you around 360°. Most kids eat this stuff up; adults need a relatively strong stomach! A tamer moon walk uses swings to let you experience a degree of weightlessness, and a Mars mission ride will take you on a simulated trip to the red planet. That full-size replica of a space shuttle you see by the highway actually holds a theater with a multimedia presentation. The rooftop observation deck is a grand place to watch a shuttle launch if you can't get into the Kennedy Space Center (see below).

Northeast Florida

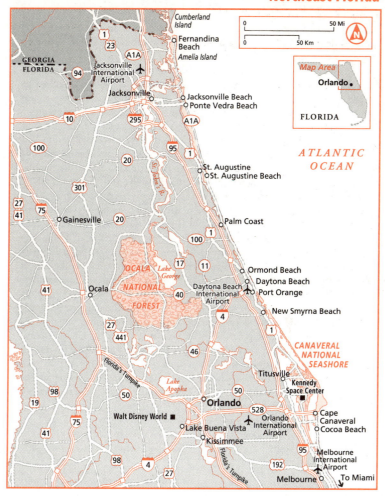

You can park your kids here for a week in the museum's **Space Camp** (✆ 800/63-SPACE; www.spacecamp.com). They will come home trained to be junior astronauts; you will have had a quiet stay at the beach. The camp costs $700 per child in winter and $800 in summer.

6225 Vectorspace Blvd., Titusville. ✆ 321/269-6100. www.astronauthalloffame.com. Admission $13.95 adults, $12.95 seniors, $9.95 children 6–12; free for kids under 6. Daily 9am–5pm.

John F. Kennedy Space Center ★★★   Whether you're a space buff or not, you'll appreciate the sheer grandeur of the facilities and technological achievements displayed at NASA's primary space launch facility. Astronauts departed Earth at this site in 1969 en route to the most famous "small step" in history— humankind's first voyage to the moon—and today space shuttles regularly lift off on their missions in orbit.

Since all roads other than Fla. 405 and Fla. 3 are closed to the public in the space center, you must begin your visit at the **Kennedy Space Center Visitor**

Complex. A bit like a themed amusement park, this privately operated complex has been undergoing an ambitious $130 million renovation and expansion, so don't blame us if they have changed their tours and exhibits. Call beforehand to see what's happening on the day you plan to be here, and arrive early to plan your visit. You'll need at least 2 hours to see the highlights on the bus tour through the space center, up to 5 hours if you linger at the stops along the way, a full day to see and do everything here. Buy a copy of the Official Tour Book; it's easier to use than the rental cassette tapes, and you can take it home as a colorful souvenir.

The visitor complex has real NASA rockets and the actual Mercury Mission Control Room from the 1960s. Exhibits look at early space exploration and where it's going in the new millennium. There are space-related hands-on activities aimed at kids, a daily "Encounter" with a real astronaut, several dining venues, and a shop selling a variety of space memorabilia and souvenirs. IMAX movies shown on 5½-story-high screens are informative and entertaining.

While you could spend your entire day at the visitor complex, you must take a **KSC Tour** to see the actual space center where rockets and shuttles are prepared and launched. Plan to take the bus tour early in your visit. Be sure to hit the restrooms before boarding the bus—there's only one out on the tour. The buses depart every 10 minutes, and you can reboard as you wish. They stop at the LC-39 Observation Gantry, with a dramatic 360° view over launchpads where space shuttles blast off; the International Space Station Center, where scientists and engineers prepare additions to the space station now in orbit; and the impressive Apollo/Saturn V Center, which includes artifacts, photos, interactive exhibits, and the 363-foot-tall Saturn V, the most powerful rocket ever launched by the United States.

It's worth the extra cost to take the **NASA Up Close** tour. These 90-minute excursions are better than the regular bus tours since they are narrated by program experts and go to the space shuttle launchpads, the shuttle landing facility, the massive Vehicle Assembly Building (where shuttles are prepared for launch), and other places normally restricted to NASA personnel. They generally take you along the same route the astronauts follow on launch days.

Only 25 persons are allowed on board the NASA Up Close tour, and the last bus leaves 4 hours before closing, so call ahead for departure times and reservations.

Tips Out to Launch

The best places to watch space shuttles taking off from the **Kennedy Space Center** for free are the causeways leading to the islands, and on U.S. 1 as it skirts the waterfront in Titusville. The **Holiday Inn Riverside Kennedy Space Center**, on Washington Avenue (U.S. 1) in Titusville (© 800/HOLIDAY or 321/269-2121; www.holidayinnksc.com), has a clear view of the launchpads across the Indian River. Of course, the absolutely best place to watch is at the Kennedy Space Center itself. You'll have to pay for a ticket, but it's well worth it. Call © 321/867-4636 or check NASA's official website (www.ksc.nasa.gov) for a schedule of upcoming takeoffs. You can buy launch tickets at the Kennedy Space Center Visitor Complex (© 321/449-4444) or online at www.ksctickets.com. If you can't get into the space center, another good spot for pay-viewing is on the rooftop observation deck of the **Astronaut Hall of Fame** (© 321/269-6100; www.astronauthalloffame.com).

Cape Canaveral

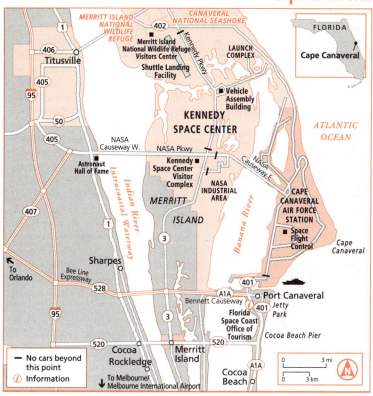

NASA Pkwy. (Fla. 405), 6 miles east of Titusville, a half mile west of Fla. 3. © **321/449-4444** for general information, 321/449-4444 for guided bus tours and launch reservations. www.kennedyspacecenter.com. Admission $26 adults, $16 children 3–11. Annual passes $44 adults, $28 children 3–11. Add $20 per person for NASA Up Close guided tour. Audio tours $5 per person. All tours and movies free for children under 3. Daily 9am–5:30pm. Shuttle bus tours daily 9:45am–2:15pm. Closed Christmas and some launch days.

BEACHES & WILDLIFE REFUGES

To the north of the Kennedy Space Center, **Canaveral National Seashore** is a protected 13-mile stretch of barrier-island beach backed by cabbage palms, sea grapes, palmettos, marshes, and Mosquito Lagoon. This is a great area for watching herons, egrets, ibis, willets, sanderlings, turnstones, terns, and other birds. You might also glimpse dolphins and manatees in Mosquito Lagoon. Canoeists can paddle along a marked trail through the marshes of Shipyard Island, and you can go backcountry camping from November through April (permits required).

The main **visitor center** is at 7611 S. Atlantic Ave., New Smyrna Beach, FL 32169 (© **321/867-4077** or 321/867-0677 for recorded information). The center actually is on Apollo Beach at the north end of the island. The southern access gate is 8 miles east of Titusville on Fla. 402, just east of Fla. 3. A paved road leads from there to undeveloped **Playalinda Beach**, one of Florida's most beautiful. It's now officially illegal, but nude sunbathing has long been a tradition here (at least for those willing to walk a few miles to the more deserted areas). The beach has toilets but no running water or other amenities, so bring everything you will need. The seashore is open daily from 6am to 8pm during daylight saving time, daily 6am to 6pm during standard time. Admission fees are $5 per motor vehicle, $1 for pedestrians or bicyclists. National Park Service passports are accepted. Backcountry camping permits cost $10 for up to six persons and must be obtained from the New Smyrna Beach visitor center (see above). For advance information, contact the seashore headquarters at 308 Julia St., Titusville, FL 32796 (© **321/867-4077** or 321/267-1110; www.nps.gov/cana).

Its neighbor to the south and west is the 140,000-acre **Merritt Island National Wildlife Refuge**, home to hundreds of species of shorebirds, waterfowl, reptiles, alligators, and mammals, many of them endangered. Stop and pick up a map and other information at the visitor center, on Fla. 402 about 4 miles east of Titusville (it's on the way to Playalinda Beach). The center has a quarter-mile-long boardwalk along the edge of the marsh and has displays showing the animals you may see here. You can see them from the 6-mile-long Black Point Wildlife Drive or one of the nature trails through the hammocks and marshes. The visitor center is open Monday to Friday from 8:30am to 4:30pm, Saturday and Sunday from 9am to 5pm (closed Sun Apr–Oct). Admission is free. For more information and a schedule of interpretive programs, contact the refuge at P.O. Box 6504, Titusville, FL 32782 (© **321/861-0667**; http://merrittisland.fws.gov/ or www.nbbd.com/godo/minwr/).

Note: Those parts of the national seashore and the wildlife refuge near the Kennedy Space Center close 3 days before a shuttle launch and usually reopen the day after a launch.

Other beach areas here include **Lori Wilson Park,** on Atlantic Avenue at Antigua Drive in Cocoa Beach (© **321/868-1123**), a fine municipal facility that preserves a stretch of beach backed by a forest of live oaks. It's home to a small but interesting nature center, and it has restrooms by the beach. The park is open daily from sunrise to sunset; the nature center, Monday to Friday from 1 to 4pm.

The beach at **Cocoa Beach Pier,** on Meade Avenue east of Fla. A1A (© **321/783-7549**), is a popular spot, especially with surfers, who consider this the East Coast's surfing capital. The rustic pier was built in 1962 and has 842 feet of fishing, shopping, and food and drinks overlooking a wide, sandy beach (see "Great Deals on Dining," later in this section). This is not a public park, so there are no restrooms other than in the restaurants on the pier.

The privately owned **Jetty Park,** 400 E. Jetty Rd. (© **321/783-7111**; fax 321/783-5005; www.portcanaveral.org/floridafun/recreation.htm), at the south entry to Port Canaveral, has lifeguards, a fishing pier with bait shop, a children's playground, a volleyball court, a horseshoe pitch, picnic tables, a snack bar, a grocery store, restrooms and changing facilities, and the area's only campground. From here you can watch the big cruise ships as they enter and leave the port's narrow passage. The park is open daily from 7am to 10pm, and the pier is open 24 hours for fishing. Admission is $3 per car, $7 for RVs. The 150 tent and RV campsites (some of them shady, most with hookups) cost $17 to $26 a night, depending on location and time of year. No pets are allowed.

AFFORDABLE OUTDOOR ACTIVITIES

ECOTOURS Funday Discovery Tours (© **321/725-0796**; www.fundaytours.com) offers a variety of day trips, including backcountry kayaking, airboat and swamp buggy rides, dolphin-watching cruises, bird-watching expeditions,

> ### Lookin' Like a Surfer
>
> Billboards hundreds of miles away from Cocoa Beach will lure you to the **Ron Jon Surf Shop**, at 4151 N. Atlantic Ave. (© **321/799-8888**). It's a 24-hour-a-day Hollywood version of Art Deco gone wild with tropical colors, lights, and towering sand sculptures of famous surfers. Most of the stock doesn't live up to the hype: mainly souvenirs of every description and equipment and clothing to make you look like a surfer—most at relatively high prices. The shop also rents beach bikes, boogie boards, surfboards, scuba-diving gear, and in-line skates by the hour, day, or week, and offers scuba lessons. They even have a cafe—well, a fast-food burger joint, anyway.

and personalized tours of the Kennedy Space Center and Merritt Island National Wildlife Refuge. Reservations are required, so call, check the website, or pick up a list of trips from the visitor center (see "Essentials," above).

FISHING Head to Port Canaveral for catches like snapper and grouper. **Jetty Park** (© **321/783-7111**), at the south entry to the port, has a fishing pier equipped with a bait shop (see "Beaches & Wildlife Refuges," above). The south bank of the port is lined with charter boats, and you can go deep-sea fishing on the *Miss Cape Canaveral* (© **321/783-5274** or 321/648-2211 in Orlando; www.misscape.com), one of the party boats based here. All-day voyages departing daily at 8am cost $60 for adults, $50 for seniors, $30 for students 11 to 17, and $30 for kids 6 to 10, including breakfast, lunch, soft drinks, gear, and bait.

GOLF You can read about Northeast Florida's best courses in the free *Golfer's Guide*, available at the tourist information offices and in many hotel lobbies. See "The Active Vacation Planner" in chapter 2, "Planning an Affordable Trip to Florida," for information about ordering copies.

In Cocoa Beach, the municipal **Cocoa Beach Country Club**, 500 Tom Warringer Blvd. (© **321/868-3351**), has 27 holes of championship golf and 10 lighted tennis courts set on acres of natural woodland, rivers, and lakes. Greens fees are about $40 in winter, dropping to about $35 in summer, including cart.

On Merritt Island south of the Kennedy Space Center, **The Savannahs at Sykes Creek**, 3915 Savannahs Trail (© **321/455-1377**), has 18 holes over 6,636 yards bordered by hardwood forests, lakes, and savannahs inhabited by a host of wildlife. You'll have to hit over a lake to reach the seventh hole. Fees with cart are about $35 in winter, less in summer.

The best nearby course is the Gary Player–designed **Baytree National Golf Club**, 8010 N. Wickham Rd., a half mile east of I-95 in Melbourne (© **321/259-9060**), where challenging marshy holes are flanked by towering palms. This par-72 course has 7,043 yards with a unique red-shale waste area. Fees are about $90 in winter, dropping to about $50 in summer, including cart.

SURFING Rip through some occasionally awesome waves at the **Cocoa Beach Pier** area or down south at **Sebastian Inlet**. Get outfitted at Ron Jon Surf Shop (see the box, "Lookin' Like a Surfer" above) and learn how with the store's **Cocoa Beach Surfing School**, 150 E. Columbia Lane (© **321/452-0854**; www.ronjons.com/surfschool). They offer equipment and lessons for beginners or pros at area beaches. Private lessons start at $45 for a 1-hour session; semi-private lessons begin at $40 for 1 hour. Be sure to bring along a towel, flip-flops, sunscreen, and a lot of nerve.

ACCOMMODATIONS YOU CAN AFFORD

The hotels listed below are all in Cocoa Beach, the closest resort to the Kennedy Space Center, about a 30-minute drive to the north. Closest to the space center and Port Canaveral is the **Radisson Resort at the Port,** 8701 Astronaut Blvd. (Fla. A1A) in Cape Canaveral (© **800/333-3333** or 321/784-0000; fax 321/784-3737). It isn't on the beach, but you can relax in a lushly landscaped courtyard with a waterfall cascading over fake rocks into an outdoor heated pool. This comfortable, well-equipped hotel caters to business travelers and passengers waiting to board cruise ships departing nearby Port Canaveral. Rates range from $129 to $159 for a single or double room year-round.

The newest chain motels in Cocoa Beach are the **Hampton Inn Cocoa Beach,** 3425 Atlantic Blvd. (© **877/492-3224** or 321/799-4099; www.hamptoninncocoabeach.com), and **Courtyard by Marriott,** 3435 Atlantic Blvd. (© **800/321-2211** or 321/784-4800). Opened in 2000 and 2001, respectively, they stand side-by-side and have access to the beach via a pathway through a condominium complex.

The **Florida Space Coast Office of Tourism** (see "Essentials," earlier in this section) publishes a booklet of the area's Superior Small Lodgings. See "Tips on Accommodations" in chapter 2 for information about this excellent program.

The area has a plethora of rental condominiums and cottages. **King Rentals Inc.,** 102 W. Central Blvd., Cape Canaveral, FL 32920 (© **888/295-0934** or 321/784-5046; www.kingrentals.com), has a wide selection in its inventory.

Given the proximity of Orlando, the generally warm weather all year, and business travelers visiting the space complex, there is little if any seasonal fluctuation in room rates here. They are highest weekends, holidays, and during special events, such as space-shuttle launches. You'll also pay a 4% hotel tax on top of the Florida sales tax here.

Tent and RV camping are available at **Jetty Park** in Port Canaveral (see "Beaches & Wildlife Refuges," above).

Cocoa Beach Hilton

Instead of balconies or patios from which you can enjoy the fresh air and view down the shore, the rooms at this seven-story Hilton have smallish, sealed-shut windows, and only 16 of them actually face the beach. That and other architectural features make it seem more like a downtown commercial hotel transplanted to a beachside location. Nevertheless, it's one of the few upscale beachfront properties here. No doubt you will run into a crew of name-tagged conventioneers, since it's especially popular with groups. Despite their lack of fresh air, the rooms are spacious and comfortable.

1550 N. Atlantic Ave., Cocoa Beach, FL 32931. © **800/HILTONS** or 321/799-0003. Fax 321/799-0344. 296 units. $79–$179 double. AE, DC, DISC, MC, V. **Amenities:** Restaurant (American), 2 bars; heated outdoor pool; exercise room; game room; water-sports equipment rentals; business center; limited room service; laundry service; coin-op washers and dryers; concierge-level rooms. *In room:* A/C, TV, dataport, coffeemaker, hair dryer, iron.

DoubleTree Hotel Cocoa Beach Oceanfront

This six-story hotel was extensively remodeled and upgraded in 1998, and although not as upscale as the Cocoa Beach Hilton (see above), it's the pick of the full-service beachside hotels here. All rooms have balconies with ocean views. Oceanfront units also have easy chairs, and 10 suites have living rooms with sleeper sofas and separate bedrooms. A charming dining room facing the beach serves decent Mediterranean fare and opens to a bilevel brick patio with water cascading between two heated swimming pools. Conference facilities draw groups.

2080 N. Atlantic Ave., Cocoa Beach, FL 32931. © **800/552-3224** or 321/783-9222. Fax 321/799-3234. www.cocoabeachdoubletree.com. 148 units. $125–$179 double; $185–$275 suite. AE, DC, DISC, MC, V.

Amenities: Restaurant (Mediterranean), bar; 2 heated outdoor pools; exercise room; game room; limited room service; laundry service; coin-op washers and dryers; concierge-level rooms. *In room:* A/C, TV, dataport, coffeemaker, hair dryer, iron.

Econo Lodge of Cocoa Beach *Value*

About half of the spacious rooms at this Econo Lodge—more charming than most members of this budget-priced chain—face a tropical courtyard with a V-shaped swimming pool by which stands a sign bearing the names of the seven original astronauts who built and owned this motel in its original incarnation as the Cape Colony Inn. It was the center of activities in those 1960s days, with helicopters bringing in the likes of anchorman Walter Cronkite and that genie herself, actress Barbara Eden. Today a variety of comfortable and clean units here include standard motel rooms and four suites with living rooms and kitchenettes. Amenities vary greatly, so tell the reservation clerk which features you require. Regardless of amenities, rooms facing the courtyard are preferable to those fronting the surrounding parking lots. For drinks, try the indoor sports bar or the poolside tiki hut.

1275 N. Atlantic Ave. (Fla. A1A, at Holiday Lane), Cocoa Beach, FL 32931. © 800/553-2666 or 321/783-2252. Fax 321/783-4485. 128 units. $45–$105 double. AE, DC, DISC, MC, V. Pets accepted, no fee. **Amenities:** Restaurant (Chinese), 2 bars; heated outdoor pool; coin-op washers and dryers. *In room:* A/C, TV, kitchen (suites only), fridge, coffeemaker.

Holiday Inn Cocoa Beach Oceanfront Resort *Kids*

Set on 30 beachside acres, this sprawling, family-oriented complex offers a wide variety of spacious hotel rooms, efficiencies, and apartments. A few suites even come equipped with bunk beds and Nintendo games for the kids. Most are in 1960s-style motel buildings flanking a long central courtyard with tropical foliage surrounding tennis courts. Only those rooms directly facing the beach or pool have patios or balconies; the rest are entered from exterior corridors. A convention center draws groups here.

1300 N. Atlantic Ave. (Fla. A1A, at Holiday Lane), Cocoa Beach, FL 32931. © 800/206-2747 or 321/783-2271. Fax 321/783-8878. www.holidayinnsofcentralflorida.com. 500 units. $69–$159 double. AE, DC, DISC, MC, V. **Amenities:** 2 restaurants (American), 2 bars; heated outdoor pool; 2 tennis courts; exercise room; Jacuzzi; water-sports equipment rentals; game room; concierge; limited room service; laundry service; coin-op washers and dryers. *In room:* A/C, TV, dataport, coffeemaker, hair dryer, iron.

WORTH A SPLURGE

The Inn at Cocoa Beach ★★

Despite having 50 units, an intimate bed-and-breakfast ambience prevails at this seaside inn, far and away the most romantic place to stay here (the reason it draws so many couples). The inn began as a beachfront motel but underwent a transformation under current owner Karen Simpler, a skilled interior decorator. She has furnished each unit with an elegant mix of pine, tropical, and French country pieces. Rooms in the three- and four-story buildings are much more spacious and have better sea views from their balconies than the "standard" units in the original two-story motel wing (all but six units here have balconies or patios). The older units open to a courtyard with a swimming pool tucked behind the dunes. Highest on the romance scale are two rooms with Jacuzzi tubs, double showers, and easy chairs facing gas fireplaces. Guests are served a deluxe continental breakfast in a room opening to a beachside lawn, where they are also treated to evening wine-and-cheese socials.

4300 Ocean Blvd., Cocoa Beach, FL 32932. © 800/343-5307 or 321/799-3460. Fax 321/784-8632. www.theinnatcocoabeach.com. 50 units. $145–$295 double. Rates include continental breakfast. AE, DISC, MC, V. No children under 12 accepted. **Amenities:** Bar (guests only); heated outdoor pool; sauna; massage; laundry service. *In room:* A/C, TV, dataport.

Cheap Thrills: What to See & Do for Free (or Almost) in Northeast Florida

- **Watch a space shuttle blast off from Cape Canaveral.** Although you'll have to pay to get in, the best place to watch the space shuttles blasting off from Cape Canaveral is at the Kennedy Space Center itself (© 321/449-4444). On the other hand, it costs not a cent to watch from the causeways leading to the islands, and on U.S. 1 as it skirts the waterfront in Titusville. Call © 321/867-4636 or check NASA's official website (www.ksc.nasa.gov) for a schedule of upcoming take-offs. You can buy launch tickets at the Kennedy Space Center Visitor Complex or online at www.ksctickets.com.

- **Contemplate skinny dipping at Playalinda Beach.** It isn't legal anymore, but you'll feel like stripping it all off on beautiful and deserted **Playalinda Beach,** in the Canaveral National Seashore (© 321/267-1110), a protected 13-mile stretch of barrier-island beach backed by cabbage palms, sea grapes, palmettos, marshes, and Mosquito Lagoon. The $5 per vehicle, $1 per pedestrian or cyclist admission is a small price to pay to visit this wild beach. The seashore and the adjacent **Merritt Island National Wildlife Refuge** (© 321/861-0667) also are great places to see herons, egrets, ibises, and other birds, plus giant sea turtles nesting from May to August.

- **Vroom around Daytona International Speedway.** You can't really drive your own race car around Daytona Beach's world center of racing, but the next best thing is the action-packed IMAX film *Daytona USA* (© 386/947-6800). You'll think you're in the winner's seat of the Daytona 500. You also can participate in a pit stop on a NASCAR Winston Cup stock car, see the actual winning car still covered in track dust, talk via video with favorite competitors, and play radio or television announcer by calling the finish of a race. Compared to admissions to other Florida theme parks, Daytona USA charges a reasonable $16 for adults, $13 for seniors, and $8 for children 6 to 12. Kids 5 and under get in free.

GREAT DEALS ON DINING

On the **Cocoa Beach Pier,** at the beach end of Meade Avenue, you'll get a fine view down the coast to accompany the seafood offerings at **Atlantic Ocean Grill** (© 321/783-7549) and the mediocre pub fare at adjacent **Marlins Good Times Bar & Grill** (same phone). The restaurants may not justify spending an entire evening on the pier, but their outdoor, tin-roofed **Boardwalk Tiki Bar** ✯, where live music plays most nights, is a prime spot to have a cold one while watching the surfers or a sunset.

Cocoa Beach has fast-food outlets along Fla. A1A and Fla. 520, a profusion of bars serving bar snacks, Chinese restaurants, and barbecue joints.

Bernard's Surf/Fischer's Seafood Bar & Grill ✯ SEAFOOD/STEAKS Photos on the walls testify that many astronauts—and Russian cosmonauts, too—come to these adjoining establishments to celebrate their landings. It all started as Bernard's Surf, which has been serving standard steak-and-seafood fare

- **Relive the past in America's oldest city.** Older than either Jamestown or Plymouth Rock, St. Augustine's restored Spanish Quarter offers a look back to America's very beginnings. You'll have to pay a few dollars to enter sites such as the nation's oldest store and oldest jail, but you can freely stroll these narrow streets for hours, poking your head into antiques shops, peering into lush yards surrounding ancient buildings, and watching the boats out on the Matanzas River. Or for $15 adults, $5 children, you can ride around town all day on a trolley, train, or horse-drawn carriage.
- **Stroll along a lazy river.** City leaders have developed appealing, park-like commercial complexes on the banks of the broad, slow-moving St. Johns River. On the north stands **Jacksonville Landing (© 904/353-1188)**, a 6-acre dining/shopping/entertainment center with a small maritime museum, more than 65 shops, about half a dozen full-service restaurants, and an inexpensive food court with indoor and outdoor seating overlooking the river. The Landing is the scene of special events such as arts festivals and free outdoor rock, blues, country, and jazz concerts. On the opposite shore, you can stroll along the 1.2-mile wooden zigzag boardwalk of the Southbank Riverwalk.
- **Visit a new breed of national park.** Jacksonville's Timucuan Ecological and Historic Preserve is not your usual national park. For one thing, it's a vast, intriguing system of sites on both sides of the St. Johns River. And for another, admission is free. The prime attraction is the **Fort Caroline National Memorial (© 904/641-7155)**, the site of a 16th-century French Huguenot settlement wiped out by the Spanish who landed at St. Augustine. On the north side of the river, the **Zephaniah Kingsley Plantation (© 904/251-3537)** was an early 19th-century manse owned by Zephaniah Kingsley, a white man who married a Senegalese woman he once owned and then moved his family to Haiti to escape racism at home. You can make a donation, but admission to the park is free.

in a nautically dressed setting since 1948. Bernard's offers house specials such as filet mignon served with sautéed mushrooms and béarnaise sauce, but your best bets are chargrilled fish supplied by the Fischer family's own boats. The fresh seafood also finds its way into Fischer's Seafood Bar & Grill, a friendly, *Cheers*-like lounge popular with the locals. Fischer's menu features fried combo platters, shrimp and crab claw meat sautéed in herb butter, and mussels with a wine sauce over pasta, to mention a few worthy selections. Fischer's also provides sandwiches, burgers, and other pub fare, and it has the same 25¢ happy-hour oysters and spicy wings as a branch of **Rusty's Seafood & Oyster Bar** (see below), also part of this complex.

2 S. Atlantic Ave. (at Minuteman Causeway Rd.), Cocoa Beach. © 321/783-2401. Reservations recommended in Bernard's, not accepted in Fischer's. Bernard's main courses $14–$35. Fischer's main courses $9–$16; sandwiches and salads $4–$8. AE, DC, DISC, MC, V. Bernard's Mon–Thurs 4–10pm; Fri–Sat 4–11pm. Fischer's Mon–Thurs 11am–10pm; Fri–Sat 11am–11pm. Closed Christmas.

Rusty's Seafood & Oyster Bar (Value) SEAFOOD This lively sports bar beside Port Canaveral's man-made harbor offers inexpensive chow ranging from very spicy seafood gumbo to a pot of seafood that will give two people their fill of steamed oysters, clams, shrimp, crab legs, potatoes, and corn on the cob. Raw or steamed fresh oysters and clams from the raw bar are first-rate and a very good value, as is a lunch buffet on weekdays. Seating is available indoors or out, but the inside tables have the best view of fishing boats and cruise liners going in and out of the port. Daily happy hours from 3 to 6pm see beers drafted at 59¢ a mug, and tons of raw or steamed oysters and spicy Buffalo wings go for 25¢ each. It's a busy and sometimes noisy joint, especially on weekend afternoons, but the clientele tends to be somewhat older and better behaved than at some other pubs along the banks of Port Canaveral. There's another **Rusty's** in the Bernard's Surf/Fischer's Seafood Bar & Grill restaurant complex in Cocoa Beach (see above). It has the same menu.

628 Glen Cheek Dr. (south side of the harbor), Port Canaveral. © 321/783-2033. Main courses $7–$18; sandwiches and salads $4–$6; lunch buffet $6. AE, DC, DISC, MC, V. Sun–Thurs 11am–11:30pm; Fri–Sat 11am–12:30am (lunch buffet Mon–Fri 11am–2pm).

WORTH A SPLURGE

The Mango Tree ★★ CONTINENTAL Gourmet seafood, pastas, and chicken are served in a plantation-home atmosphere with elegant furnishings in this stucco house, the finest dining venue here. Goldfish ponds inside and a waterfall splashing into a Japanese koi pond out in the lush tropical gardens provide pleasing backdrops. Start with finely seasoned Indian River crab cakes, then go on to the chef's expert spin on fresh tuna filets, roast Long Island duckling, tournedos with peppercorn mushroom sauce, and other excellent dishes drawing their inspiration from the continent.

118 N. Atlantic Ave. (Fla. A1A, between N. 1st and N. 2nd sts.), Cocoa Beach. © 321/799-0513. Reservations recommended. Main courses $15–$39. AE, MC, V. Tues–Sun 6–10pm.

THE SPACE COAST AFTER DARK

For a rundown of current performances and exhibits, call the **Brevard Cultural Alliance's Arts Line** (© 321/690-6819). For live music, walk out on the **Cocoa Beach Pier,** on Meade Avenue at the beach, where **Oh Shuck's Seafood Bar & Grill** (© 321/783-7549), **Marlins Good Times Bar & Grill** (© 321/783-7549), and the alfresco **Boardwalk Tiki Bar** ★ (see "Great Deals on Dining," above) have bands on weekends, more often during the summer season. The tiki bar is ideal for hanging out over a cold beer all afternoon and evening.

2 Daytona Beach ★★

54 miles NE of Orlando, 251 miles N of Miami, 78 miles S of Jacksonville

Daytona Beach is a town with many personalities. It is at once the "World's Most Famous Beach," the "World Center of Racing," a mecca for motorcyclists and spring breakers, and an affordable summer beach vacation spot. It has been a destination for racing enthusiasts since the early 1900s when "horseless carriages" raced on the hard-packed sand beach. One thing is for sure: Daytonans still love their cars. Recent debate over the environmental impact of unrestricted driving on the beach caused an uproar from citizens who couldn't imagine it any other way. As it worked out, they can still drive on the sand, but not in areas where sea turtles are nesting, or on a 1-mile stretch between International Speedway Boulevard (U.S. 92) and Seabreeze Avenue, the busiest part of the beach where scantily clad bathers nest.

Daytona Beach

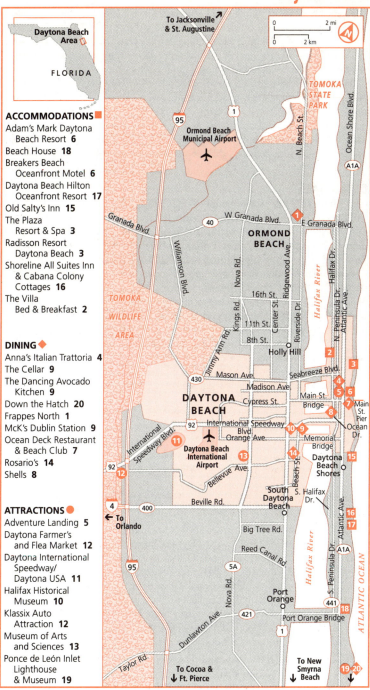

ACCOMMODATIONS
Adam's Mark Daytona Beach Resort **6**
Beach House **18**
Breakers Beach Oceanfront Motel **6**
Daytona Beach Hilton Oceanfront Resort **17**
Old Salty's Inn **15**
The Plaza Resort & Spa **3**
Radisson Resort Daytona Beach **3**
Shoreline All Suites Inn & Cabana Colony Cottages **16**
The Villa Bed & Breakfast **2**

DINING
Anna's Italian Trattoria **4**
The Cellar **9**
The Dancing Avocado Kitchen **9**
Down the Hatch **20**
Frappes North **1**
McK's Dublin Station **9**
Ocean Deck Restaurant & Beach Club **7**
Rosario's **14**
Shells **8**

ATTRACTIONS
Adventure Landing **5**
Daytona Farmer's and Flea Market **12**
Daytona International Speedway/ Daytona USA **11**
Halifax Historical Museum **10**
Klassix Auto Attraction **12**
Museum of Arts and Sciences **13**
Ponce de León Inlet Lighthouse & Museum **19**

551

Today, hundreds of thousands of race enthusiasts come to the home of the National Association for Stock Car Auto Racing (NASCAR) for the Daytona 500, the Pepsi 400, and other races throughout the year. The Speedway is home to DAYTONA USA, a state-of-the-art motor-sports entertainment attraction worth a visit even by non-racing fans.

But you don't have to be a car aficionado to enjoy Daytona. It has 23 miles of sandy beach, surprisingly good museums, and an active nightlife. Be sure to check the "Florida Calendar of Events" in chapter 2 to know when the town belongs to college students during spring break, hundreds of thousands of leather-clad motorcycle buffs during Bike Week, or racing enthusiasts for big competitions. You can't find a hotel room, drive the highways, or enjoy a peaceful vacation when they're in town.

ESSENTIALS

GETTING THERE **Continental** (© 800/525-0280; www.continental.com) and **Delta** (© 800/221-1212; www.delta.com) fly into the small, pleasant, and calm **Daytona Beach International Airport** (© 386/428-8030; http://fly daytonafirst.com), 4 miles inland from the beach on International Speedway Boulevard (U.S. 92), but you usually can find less expensive fares to **Orlando International Airport,** about an hour's drive away (see "Orientation" in chapter 11). **Daytona-Orlando Transit Service (DOTS)** (© **800/231-1965** or 386/257-5411; www.dots-daytonabeach.com) provides van transportation to or from Orlando International Airport. Fares are about $27 for adults one-way, $49 round-trip; children 11 and under are charged half. The service brings passengers to the company's terminal at 1034 N. Nova Rd., between 3rd and 4th streets, or to beach hotels for an additional fee.

There are no shuttles at the Daytona airport, so you'll have to take a taxi. The ride from the airport to most beach hotels via **Yellow Cab Co.** (© **386/255-5555**) costs between $7 and $15.

Alamo (© 800/327-9633), **Avis** (© 800/331-1212), **Budget** (© 800/527-0700), **Dollar** (© 800/800-4000), **Hertz** (© 800/654-3131), and **National** (© 800/CAR-RENT) have booths at the Daytona airport. **Enterprise** (© 800/325-8007) is in town. If it suits you, why not rent a Harley? This is Daytona, after all. Contact **Daytona Harley-Davidson** (© 386/253-2453; www.daytona hd.com).

Amtrak (© **800/USA-RAIL;** www.amtrak.com) trains stop at Deland, about 15 miles southwest of Daytona Beach, with connecting bus service from Deland to the beach.

VISITOR INFORMATION The **Daytona Beach Area Convention & Visitors Bureau,** 126 E. Orange Ave. (P.O. Box 910), Daytona Beach, FL 32115 (© **800/854-1234** or 386/255-0415; fax 386/255-5478; www.daytonabeach. com), can help you with information on attractions, accommodations, dining, and events. The office is on the mainland just west of the Memorial Bridge. The information area of the lobby is open daily from 9am to 5pm. The bureau also maintains a branch at DAYTONA USA, 1801 W. International Speedway Blvd. (open daily 9am–7pm), and a kiosk at the airport.

GETTING AROUND Although Daytona is primarily a driver's town, VOTRAN, Volusia County's public transit system (© **386/761-7700;** http:// votran.org), runs a **free shuttle** around the Main Street Pier/Ocean Walk Village area and a pay **trolley** along Atlantic Avenue on the beach, Monday to Saturday from noon to midnight. Trolley fares are $1 for adults, 50¢ for seniors and children 6 to 17, and free for kids under 6 riding with an adult. VOTRAN also runs **buses** throughout downtown and the beaches.

For a taxi, call **Yellow Cab** (© **386/255-5555**) or **Southern Komfort Cab** (© **386/252-2222**).

Over at the beach, **Scooters & Cycles,** 2020 S. Atlantic Ave. (Fla. A1A; © **386/253-4131**), rents both.

WHAT TO SEE & DO
A VISIT TO THE WORLD CENTER OF RACING

Daytona International Speedway/DAYTONA USA   You don't have to be a racing fan to enjoy a visit to the **Daytona International Speedway,** 4 miles west of the beach. Opened in 1959 with the first Daytona 500, this 480-acre complex is the keynote of the city's fame. The track presents about nine weekends of major racing events annually, featuring stock cars, sports cars, motorcycles, and go-karts, and is used for automobile and motorbike testing and other events nearly every other day of the year. Its grandstands can accommodate more than 150,000 fans. Big events sell out months in advance (tickets to the Daytona 500 in Feb can be gone a year ahead of time), so get your tickets and hotel reservations as early as possible.

Start your visit at the **World Center of Racing Visitors Center,** in the NASCAR office complex at the east end of the speedway. Admission to the center is free, and you can walk out and see the track during non-race days (there's a small admission to the track during qualifying races leading up to the main events). Entertaining 25-minute guided tram tours of the facility (garage area, pit road, and so on) depart from the visitor center and are well worth taking.

The visitor center houses a large souvenir shop, a snack bar, and the phenomenally popular **DAYTONA USA,** a 60,000-square-foot, state-of-the-art interactive motor-sports entertainment attraction. Here you can learn about the history, color, and excitement of stock car, go-kart, and motorcycle racing in Daytona. In Daytona Dream Laps, one of its newest "rides," you get the feel of what it's like to zoom around the track in a Daytona 500 race from a 32-seat motion simulator. If that doesn't get your stomach churning, hop inside your own 80-percent scale NASCAR car in Acceleration Alley, buckle up, and roar up to 200 mph in a spectacular simulator that combines motion, video, projection, and sound for the ultimate virtual reality-like racing experience. On the milder side, you can participate in a pit stop on a NASCAR Winston Cup stock car, see the actual winning Daytona 500 car still covered in track dust, talk via video with favorite competitors, and play radio or television announcer by calling the finish of a race. An action-packed IMAX film will put you in the winner's seat of a Daytona 500 race.

To really experience what it's like, you can actually make three laps (for $99) around the track in a stock car from May to October with the **Richard Petty Driving Experience Ride-Along Program** (© **800/BE-PETTY;** www.1800 bepetty.com). Neither you nor racing legend Petty does the driving—other

---

> **Tips Driving on the Beach**
>
> You can drive and park directly on sections of the sand along 18 miles of the beach during daylight hours and at low tide (Hurricane Floyd and other recent storms have greatly reduced the beach's width). Watch for signs warning of sea turtles nesting. There's a $5 per vehicle access fee.

professionals will be at the wheel—but you'll see just how fast an average 115 miles per hour speed really is.

Allow at least 3½ hours and definitely bring your video camera.

Write to the Daytona International Speedway at P.O. Box 2801, Daytona Beach, FL 32120-2801, for more information.

1801 W. International Speedway Blvd. (U.S. 92, at Bill France Blvd.). © **386/253-RACE** for race tickets, 386/253-7223 for information or 386/947-6800 for DAYTONA USA. www.daytonaintlspeedway.com and www.daytonausa.com. Speedway admission free except on race days; tram rides $7. DAYTONA USA admission $16 adults, $13 seniors, $8 children 6–12. Combination DAYTONA USA–tram tour $20 adults, $17 seniors, $14 children 6–12. Tram rides and DAYTONA USA admission free for children under 6. Speedway daily 9am–7pm; trams depart every 30 min. 9:30am–5pm except during races and special events. DAYTONA USA daily 9am to 7pm (later during race events). Closed Christmas.

HITTING THE WORLD'S MOST FAMOUS BEACH

The beautiful and hard-packed beach here runs for 24 miles along a skinny peninsula separated from the mainland by the Halifax River. The bustling hub of activity is at the end of Main Street, near the Adam's Mark Daytona Beach Resort. Here you'll find the **Main Street Pier,** which was the longest wooden pier on the East Coast until Hurricane Floyd washed away about a third of its 1,006 feet in 1999. Out here you'll find a restaurant, a bar, a bait shop, beach-toy concessions, a chairlift running its entire length, and views from the 180-foot-tall Space Needle. Admission as far out as the restaurant and bar is free (at about a third of the way, this is far enough for a good view down the beach), but you'll have to pay $1 to walk out beyond there, more if you fish (see "Affordable Outdoor Activities," below). Beginning at the pier, the city's famous ocean-side **Boardwalk** is lined with restaurants, bars, and T-shirt shops, as are the 4 blocks of Main Street nearest the beach. The city's Ocean Walk Village redevelopment project begins here and runs several blocks north.

There's another busy beach area at the end of **Seabreeze Boulevard,** which has a multitude of restaurants, bars, and shops.

Couples seeking greater privacy usually prefer the northern or southern extremities of the beach. Especially peaceful is **Ponce Inlet** at the very southern tip of the peninsula, where there is precious little commerce or traffic to disturb the silence.

AFFORDABLE OUTDOOR ACTIVITIES

CRUISES Take a leisurely cruise on the Halifax River aboard the 14-passenger, 25-foot *Fancy,* a replica of an 1890s-style fantail launch. It's operated by **A tiny Cruise Line River Excursions,** 425 S. Beach St., at Halifax Harbor Marina (© **386/226-2343**). Captain Jim regales passengers with river lore and points out dolphins (which are more commonly spotted in the mornings), manatees, herons, diving cormorants, pelicans, egrets, osprey, oyster beds, and other natural phenomena during his 2-hour midday cruise. In the afternoon you can see the man-made estates along the river. Cruises range from $9.50 to $15 for adults, $6 to $8 for children 4 to 12, and are free for children 3 and under. Weather permitting, the midday cruises depart year-round (with a brief hiatus during the holidays), Monday through Saturday at 11:30am. The 1-hour tour of riverfront homes is at 2pm and of historic downtown at 3:30pm; there are no Monday cruises in winter months. Call for reservations. Romantic sunset cruises are also available.

FISHING The easiest and least expensive way to fish offshore for marlin, sailfish, king mackerel, grouper, red snapper, and more is with the **Critter Fleet,**

4950 S. Peninsula Dr., just past the lighthouse in Ponce Inlet (✆ **800/338-0850** or 386/767-7676; www.critterfleet.com), which operates two party boats. One goes on all-day trips (about $55 adults, $35 kids under 12), while the other makes morning and afternoon voyages (about $35 adults, $25 kids under 12). The fares include rod, reel, and bait. Call for schedules and reservations.

Deep-sea charter fishing boats are available from the Critter Fleet and from **Sea Love Marina,** 4884 Front St., Ponce Inlet (✆ **386/767-3406** or 407/293-2050 in Orlando).

Save the cost of a boat and fish with the locals from the **Main Street Pier,** at the ocean end of Main Street near the Adam's Mark (✆ **386/253-1212**). Admission for fishers is $3.50 for adults, $2 for kids under 12. Bait and fishing gear are available, and no license is required.

GOLF   More than 25 courses await you within 30 minutes of the beach, and most hotels can arrange starting times for you. **Golf Daytona Beach,** 126 E. Orange Ave., Daytona Beach, FL 32114 (✆ **800/881-7065** or 386/239-7065; fax 386/239-0064; www.golf-daytona.com), publishes an annual brochure describing the major courses. It's available at the tourist information offices (see "Essentials," above).

Two of the nation's top-rated links for women golfers are at the **LPGA International** ★★, 1000 Championship Dr. (✆ **386/274-5742**; www.lpgainternational.com). They are the Champions course designed by Rees Jones, and the Legends course designed by Arthur Hills. Both boast 18 outstanding holes. LPGA International is a center for professional and amateur women golfers (workshops and teaching programs), and the pro shop carries a great selection of ladies' equipment and clothing. Greens fees with a cart are usually about $75, less in summer. You do not have to be female to play here.

A Lloyd Clifton–designed course, the centrally located 18-hole, par-72 **Indigo Lakes Golf Course,** 2620 W. International Speedway Blvd. (✆ **386/254-3607**; www.indigolakesgolf.com), has flat fairways and large bunkered Bermuda greens. Fees here are about $55 in winter, including a cart, less in summer.

The semi-private South Course at **Pelican Bay Country Club,** 550 Sea Duck Dr. (✆ **386/788-6494**; www.pelicanbaygolfclub.com), is one of the area's favorites, with fast greens to test your putting skills. Fees are about $40 with cart in winter, less in summer (no walking allowed). The North Course here is for members only.

The city's prime municipal course is the **Daytona Beach Country Club,** 600 Wilder Blvd. (✆ **386/258-3119**), which has 36 holes. Winter fees here are about $20 to walk, $30 to share a cart. They drop $3 in summer.

HELICOPTER RIDES   Take a helicopter ride around the Daytona area to see the city from a different point of view. **Air Florida** (✆ **386/257-6993**; www.airfloridahelicopters.com) offers rides starting at $20, leaving from the pier and across from the Daytona Farmer's and Flea Market (see below).

HORSEBACK RIDING   **Shenandoah Stables,** 1759 Tomoka Farms Rd., off U.S. 92 (✆ **386/257-1444**), offers daily trail rides and lessons. Call for prices and schedules.

SPECTATOR SPORTS   The **Daytona Cubs** (✆ **386/872-2827**; www.daytonacubs.com), a Class A minor-league affiliate of the Chicago Cubs, play baseball from April through August at Jackie Robinson Ballpark, on City Island downtown. A game here is a treat, since the park has been restored to its classic

> **Tips** **Browsing for a Bargain**
>
> You never know what you'll find at the **Daytona Farmer's and Flea Market,** on Tomoka Farms Road at the junction of I-95 and U.S. 92, a mile west of the Speedway (© **386/252-1999**; www.daytonafleamarket.com). This huge market has 1,000 covered outdoor booths plus 100 antiques and collectibles vendors in an air-conditioned building. Most of the booths feature new (though not necessarily first rate) wares along the lines of socks, sunglasses, luggage, handbags, jewelry, and the like. It's open year-round Friday through Sunday from 8am to 5pm. Admission and parking are free.

1914 style by the designers of Baltimore's Camden Yards and Cleveland's Jacobs Field.

WATER SPORTS Water-sports equipment, as well as bicycles, beach buggies, and mopeds, can be rented along the Boardwalk, at the ocean end of Main Street (see "Hitting the World's Most Famous Beach," above), and in front of major beachfront hotels. For jet-ski rentals, contact **Daytona High Performance—MBI,** 925 Sickler Dr., at the Seabreeze Bridge (© **386/257-5276**).

AN AMUSEMENT PARK

Part of the Ocean Walk Village redevelopment project, **Adventure Landing,** 601 Earl St., west of Atlantic Avenue (© **386/258-0071;** www.adventure landing.com), is a multifaceted amusement center offering indoor and outdoor activities to keep you and especially the kids entertained—and thoroughly wet. You enter a cacophony of deafening noise and music in a huge electronic games arcade. Outside there are pools, slides, and waterfalls, plus go-kart rides and a 27-hole minigolf course. Admission is free to the games area, but water-park entry costs about $20 for anyone over 48 inches tall, $17 for anyone shorter, and free for kids under 3. Ask about a discounted "night splasher" (4–8pm) pass. Adventure Landing is open during summer daily 10am to midnight.

MUSEUMS & ATTRACTIONS

Halifax Historical Museum ★ Located on Beach Street, Daytona's original riverfront commercial district on the mainland side of the Halifax River (see "Shopping," below), this local history museum is worth a look just for the 1912 neoclassical architectural details of its home, a former bank (you can still see the old vault). A mural of Old Florida wildlife graces one wall, the stained-glass ceiling reflects the sunlight, and across the room an old gold-metal teller's window still stands. The Halifax's eclectic and interesting collection includes Native American artifacts, more than 10,000 historic photographs, possessions of past residents (such as a ball gown worn at Lincoln's inauguration), and, of course, model cars. A noteworthy race exhibit opens annually in mid-January as a stage-setter for Race Week.

252 S. Beach St. (just north of Orange Ave.). © 386/255-6976. www.halifaxhistorical.org. Admission $4 adults; $1 children 11 and under; free Sat for children. Tues–Sat 10am–4pm.

Klassix Auto Attraction True aficionados of the car will enjoy a visit to this attraction, which showcases Corvettes—a model from every year since 1953—and historic vehicles from every motor sport. The rest of us will head to the original "Batmobile" from the 1960s *Batman* TV series, the car from *The Flintstones* series, the "Dragula" owned by the Munsters, and the "Greased Lightning" from the movie *Grease*. A 1950s-style soda shop and gift shop are on the premises.

2909 W. International Speedway Blvd., at Tomoka Farms Rd., just west of I-95. © 386/252-3800. Admission $8.50 adults, $4.25 children 7–12; free for children under 7. Daily 9am–6pm.

Marine Science Center (Kids)
This new (opened in June 2002) center has interior displays (with exhibits on mangroves, mosquitoes, marine mammal bones, shells, artificial reefs, dune habitats, and pollution solutions), a 5,000 gallon aquarium, as well as educational programs and activities. Though the exhibit area is rather small, there's more than enough information for a child to digest at one time. Perhaps the most interesting part of the center is the space reserved for the rehabilitation of endangered and threatened sea turtles (once they're "cured," the healthy turtles are set back into nature). You can watch them in any of 7 turtle tanks—look for the ones who need life jackets to stay afloat!

100 Lighthouse Dr., Ponce Inlet. © 386/304-5545. www.marinesciencecenter.com. $3 adults, $1 children 5–12, free for children under 5. Tues–Sat 10am–4pm; Sun noon–4pm; closed Mondays. See directions for Ponce de León Inlet Lighthouse & Museum (below).

Museum of Arts and Sciences
An exceptional institution for a town Daytona's size, this museum is best known for its Cuban Museum, with paintings acquired in 1956, when Cuban dictator Fulgencio Batista donated his private collection to the city. Among them is a portrait of Eva ("Evita") Perón, said to be the only existing painting completed while she was alive (it hangs near the lobby, not in the Cuban Museum). The Dow Gallery displays Smithsonian-quality examples of American decorative arts, and the Bouchelle Study Center for the Decorative Arts contains both American and European masterpieces. Other rooms worth visiting include the Schulte Gallery of Chinese Art; Africa: Life and Ritual, with the largest collection of Ashante gold ornaments (these are stunning) in the United States; and the Prehistory of Florida gallery, with the skeleton of a 13-foot-tall, 130,000-year-old giant ground sloth. A recent addition is the unique collection of the late Chapman S. Root, a Daytona philanthropist and a founder of the Coca-Cola empire; among the Root memorabilia is the mold for the original Coke bottle as well as many other changing exhibitions (the collection is very large). The Root family's two private railroad cars also are on display. The planetarium presents 30-minute shows of what the night sky will look like on the date of your visit. Even though this is a first-class art museum, except for the skeleton and the model railroads, children are apt to be bored here.

1040 Museum Blvd. (off Nova Rd./Fla. 5A between International Speedway Blvd. and Bellevue Ave.). © 386/255-0285. www.moas.org. Museum $7 adults, $2 children and students with ID; free for children 5 and under. Planetarium shows $3 adults, $2 children and students. Tues–Fri 9am–4pm; Sat–Sun noon–5pm. Planetarium shows Tues–Fri 2pm; Sat–Sun 1 and 3pm. Closed Thanksgiving, Christmas Eve, Christmas Day. Take International Speedway Blvd. west, make a left on Nova Rd. (Fla. 5A), and look for a sign on your right.

Ponce de León Inlet Lighthouse & Museum
This National Historic Landmark is well worth a stop even if you're not a lighthouse enthusiast. The 175-foot brick-and-granite structure is the second-tallest lighthouse in the United States, second only to the beacon at Cape Hatteras, North Carolina. Built in the 1880s, the lighthouse and the graceful Victorian brick buildings surrounding it have been restored (it's one of the only light stations in the United States to have all its original buildings still standing). There are no guided tours, but you can walk through the 12 areas which feature different exhibits (lighthouse lenses, historical artifacts, and a film of early car racing on the nearby beach) and around the tugboat *F. D. Russell*, now sitting high-and-dry in the

sand. Use common sense if you climb the 203 steps to the top of the lighthouse; it's a grinding ascent, but the view from up there is spectacular.

4931 S. Peninsula Dr., Ponce Inlet. ⓒ 386/761-1821. www.ponceinlet.org. Admission $5 adults, $1.50 children under 12. Memorial Day–Labor Day daily 10am–8pm; rest of year daily 10am–4pm. Follow Atlantic Ave. south, make a right on Beach St., and follow the signs.

SHOPPING

On the mainland, Daytona Beach's main riverside drag, **Beach Street,** is one of the few areas in town where people actually stroll. The street is wide and inviting, with palms down its median and decorative wrought-iron archways and fancy brickwork overlooking a branch of the Halifax River that separates downtown from City Island, home of municipal offices and the lovingly restored Jackie Robinson Ballpark (see "Spectator Sports," above). Today, Beach Street between Bay Street and Orange Avenue offers antiques and collectibles shops, art galleries, clothiers, a magic shop, the local historical museum (see "Museums," above), and several good cafes. 154 S. Beach St. is the home of the **Angell & Phelps Chocolate Factory** (ⓒ **800/969-2634**), which has been making candy for more than 75 years. Come here to watch the goodies being made (and get a free sample!) or just to buy some of the handmade treats.

You "Hog" riders will find several shops to your liking along Beach Street north of International Speedway Boulevard, including the **Harley Davidson Store,** 290 Beach St., at Dr. Mary McLeod Bethune Boulevard (ⓒ **386/253-2453**), a 20,000-square-foot retail outlet and diner serving breakfast and lunch. It's one of the nation's largest dealerships. In addition to hundreds of gleaming new and used Hogs, you'll find as much fringed leather as you've ever seen in one place.

ACCOMMODATIONS YOU CAN AFFORD

Room rates here are among the most affordable in Florida. Some properties have as many as 20 rate periods during the year, but generally they are somewhat higher from the day after Christmas all the way to Labor Day. They skyrocket during major events at the Speedway, during bikers' gatherings and during spring college break (see "Florida Calendar of Events," in chapter 2), when local hotels fill to the bursting point. Even if you can find a room then, there's often a minimum-stay requirement.

Hundreds of hotels and motels line Atlantic Avenue along the beach, many of them family owned and operated. The Daytona Beach Area Convention & Visitors Bureau (see "Essentials," earlier in this section) distributes a brochure that lists **Superior Small Lodgings** for the Daytona Beach area. None of these properties has more than 75 rooms, and all have been inspected for cleanliness, quality, comfort, privacy, and safety. All of the small motels listed below are members.

In addition, thousands of rental condominiums line the beaches here. One of the largest rental agents is **Peck Realty,** 2340 S. Atlantic Ave., Daytona Beach Shores, FL 32118 (ⓒ **800/44-PECK** or 386/257-5000; www.peckrealty.com).

If you're going to the races and don't care about staying on the beach, some upper-floor rooms at the new **Hilton Garden Inn Daytona Beach Airport,** 189 Midway Ave. (ⓒ **877/944-4001** or 386/944-4000), actually overlook the international speedway track. Unlike most members of Hilton's Garden Inn chain, this one has a restaurant.

In addition to the 6% state sales tax, Volusia County levies a 4% tax on hotel bills.

Adam's Mark Daytona Beach Resort ★
Already Daytona's largest beachfront hotel, the Adam's Mark recently added another 310 units as part of the city's Ocean Walk Village development plans. With extensive on-site meeting facilities and the city's Ocean Center convention complex across the street, that means lots of big groups staying here. It's also in the middle of the beach action, right on the city's Boardwalk and a block north of the busy Main Street Pier (see "Hitting the World's Most Famous Beach," earlier in this section). One of Daytona's best-equipped properties, it's designed so that every room has an ocean view.

100 N. Atlantic Ave. (Fla. A1A, between Earl St. and Auditorium Blvd.), Daytona Beach, FL 32118. © 800/444-ADAM or 386/254-8200. Fax 386/253-0275. www.adamsmark.com. 746 units. $105–$165 double. AE, DC, DISC, MC, V. Valet parking $8; free self-parking. **Amenities:** 3 restaurants (American), 3 bars; heated outdoor pool; exercise room; Jacuzzis; sauna; water-sports equipment rentals; bike rental; game room; concierge; limited room service; massage; babysitting; laundry service; coin-op washers and dryers; concierge-level rooms. *In room:* A/C, TV, dataport, coffeemaker, hair dryer, iron.

Beach House
You'll know as soon as you see its nicely landscaped exterior that owners Patrick and Barbara Welsh care about this place. And inside, the furnishings and appointments are excellent for a property in this price range. The accommodations have front lawns with umbrella tables overlooking the ocean, and all but two have full kitchens. There are barbecue grills and a heated swimming pool.

3221 S. Atlantic Ave. (at El Portal Ave., a half mile north of Dunlawton Ave.), Daytona Beach, FL 32118. © 800/647-3448 or 904/788-7107. Fax 904/760-3672. 11 units. $29–$89 single or double; $70–$120 oceanview suite. Weekly rates available. AE, DISC, MC, V. **Amenities:** Outdoor pool; water-sports equipment rentals; coin-op washers and dryers. *In room:* A/C, TV, kitchen (9 units), coffeemaker, safe.

Breakers Beach Oceanfront Motel
This is a friendly, just-folks kind of place, where guests (many of them repeat visitors) socialize with each other and affable owners Tom and Virginia Brown. The location at the boardwalk and the Main Street Pier is right in the middle of the action here, so don't expect a quiet vacation like you'll get farther south in Daytona Beach Shores. The rooms aren't fancy, but they're clean and well maintained. Especially desirable are the oceanfront efficiencies with full kitchens, though all rooms have small refrigerators. Facilities include a picnic area with barbecue grills, a heated swimming pool, and coin-op laundry.

27 S. Ocean Ave. (between Harvey and Main sts.), Daytona Beach, FL 32118. © 800/441-8459 or 386/252-0863. Fax 386/238-1247. www.breakersbeach.com. 21 units. $50–$129 single or double. Weekly and monthly rates available. AE, DC, DISC, MC, V. **Amenities:** Heated outdoor pool; coin-op washers and dryers. *In room:* A/C, TV, kitchen, coffeemaker.

Daytona Beach Hilton Oceanfront Resort ★★
Far enough south to escape the maddening crowds at Main Street, the Hilton is among the best choices here. It welcomes you in an elegant terra-cotta–tiled lobby with comfortable seating areas, a fountain, and potted palms. The large guest rooms are grouped in pairs and can be joined to form a suite; only one of each pair has a balcony. Oceanfront rooms are preferable, but all have sea and/or river views. A few also have kitchenettes. The surprisingly good Blue Water lobby restaurant is one of Daytona's most beautiful; patio dining is an option.

2637 S. Atlantic Ave. (Fla. A1A, between Florida Shores Blvd. and Richard's Lane), Daytona Beach, FL 32118. © 800/525-7350 or 386/767-7350. Fax 386/760-3651. 214 units. $116–$359 double. AE, DC, DISC, MC, V. **Amenities:** Restaurant (American), bar; heated outdoor pool; Jacuzzi; exercise room; water-sports equipment rentals; game room; salon; limited room service; babysitting; laundry service; coin-op washers and dryers; concierge-level rooms. *In room:* A/C, TV, dataport, kitchenette (in some), coffeemaker, hair dryer, iron.

Old Salty's Inn ⭐ The most unusual of the many mom-and-pop beachside motels here, Old Salty's is a lush tropical enclave carrying out a *Gilligan's Island* theme, with old motors, rotting boats, lifesavers, and a Jeep lying about, and the TV series' main characters depicted in big murals painted on the buildings. The two-story wings flank a courtyard festooned with palms and banana trees (you can pick a banana for breakfast). Facing this vista, the bright rooms have microwaves, refrigerators, and front-and-back windows to let in good ventilation. The choice units have picture windows overlooking the beach. There are gas grills and rocking chairs under a gazebo out by a heated beachside swimming pool.

1921 S. Atlantic Ave. (Fla. A1A, at Flamingo Ave.), Daytona Beach Shores, FL 32118. © **800/417-1466** or 386/252-8090. Fax 386/947-9980. www.oldsaltys.com. 19 units. $53–$121 double. AE, DISC, MC, V. **Amenities:** Heated outdoor pool; free use of bikes; coin-op washers and dryers. *In room:* A/C, TV, kitchen, fridge, coffeemaker, hair dryer, iron.

The Plaza Resort & Spa ⭐⭐ Remodeled to the tune of $26 million (the original 7-story hotel was built in the early 20th century) in 2000, these elegant adjoining seven- and 13-story buildings now hold some of Daytona Beach's best rooms (in a much more tasteful atmosphere than many of the neighboring hotels)—provided you don't need a large bathroom. The choice units are the corner suites, which have sitting areas and two balconies overlooking the Atlantic; some even have a Jacuzzi. All units have balconies and microwave ovens (an on-premises convenience store sells frozen dinners). The renovations also saw the opening of the full-service **Ocean Waters Spa** ⭐⭐ (© **386/267-1660;** www.oceanwatersspa.com), Daytona's only such facility. There are 16 treatment rooms and a soothing menu of facials, massages, and wraps.

600 N. Atlantic Ave. (at Seabreeze Ave.), Daytona Beach, FL 32118. © **800/767-4471** or 386/255-4471. Fax 386/253-7543. www.plazaresortandspa.com. 323 units. $69 doubles; up to $449 suites. AE, DC, DISC, MC, V. **Amenities:** Restaurant (Seafood/Sushi), bar; heated outdoor pool; exercise room; spa; Jacuzzi; water-sports equipment rentals; game room; business center; limited room service; massage; babysitting; laundry service; coin-op washers and dryers; concierge-level rooms. *In room:* A/C, TV, dataport, fridge, coffeemaker, hair dryer, iron.

Radisson Resort Daytona Beach ⭐ This 11-story, all-modern Radisson sits beachside a half mile north of the Main Street Pier and around the corner from restaurants and bars on Seabreeze Boulevard. The rooms here are among the most spacious on the beach and have angled balconies facing the beach (your neighbor's air conditioner exhausts onto your balcony, however, which can create noise and heat when you're sitting out there). About a third have small additional rooms with wet bars with microwaves and refrigerators.

640 N. Atlantic Ave. (Fla. A1A, between Seabreeze and Glenview blvds.), Daytona Beach, FL 32118. © **800/355-1721** or 386/239-9800. Fax 386/253-0735. www.daytonaradisson.com. 206 units. $99–$169 double. AE, DC, DISC, MC, V. **Amenities:** Restaurant (American), bar; heated outdoor pool; exercise room; water-sports equipment rentals; limited room service; babysitting; coin-op washers and dryers; concierge-level rooms. *In room:* A/C, TV, dataport, fridge (in some), coffeemaker, hair dryer, iron.

Shoreline All Suites Inn & Cabana Colony Cottages ⭐ *Value* The Shoreline All Suites Inn, built in 1954 but substantially modernized, features one- and two-bedroom suites that occupy two buildings separated by a walkway leading to the beach. Most have small bathrooms with scant vanity space and—shall we say—intimate shower stalls. Every unit has a full kitchen, plus there are barbecue grills on the premises. For a change of scenery, consider the fine little cottage complex at the Shoreline's sister property, the **Cabana Colony Cottages** ⭐. All 12 of the cottages were built in 1927 but have been upgraded by owner-managers

Frank and Barbara Molnar. They aren't much bigger than a motel room with a kitchen, but they're light and airy, and are attractively furnished with white wicker pieces. The cottages share a heated beachside swimming pool with the Shoreline.

2435 S. Atlantic Ave. (Fla. A1A, at Dundee Rd.), Daytona Beach Shores, FL 32118. © **800/293-0653** or 386/252-1692. Fax 386/239-7068. www.daytonashoreline.com. 32 units (shower only), including 12 cottages. $59–$139 suites and cottages. Rates include continental breakfast. Golf packages available. AE, DISC, MC, V. **Amenities:** Heated outdoor pool; coin-op washers and dryers. *In room:* A/C, TV/VCR, kitchen, coffeemaker.

The Villa Bed & Breakfast You'll think you're in Iberia upon entering this Spanish mansion's great room with its fireplace, baby grand piano, terra-cotta floors, and walls hung with Mediterranean paintings. Also downstairs are a sun room equipped with a TV and VCR, a formal dining room, and a breakfast nook where guests gather at their leisure to start the day. The lush backyard surrounds a swimming pool and covered, four-person Jacuzzi. Upstairs, the nautically themed Christopher Columbus room has a vaulted ceiling and a small balcony overlooking the pool. The largest quarters here is the King Carlos suite, the original master bedroom with a four-poster bed, entertainment system, refrigerator, rooftop deck, dressing area, and bathroom equipped with a four-head shower. The Queen Isabella room has a portrait of the queen over a queen-size bed, and the Marco Polo room has Chinese black lacquer furniture and Oriental rugs evoking the great explorer's adventures. Owner Jim Camp's friendly black lab Andy keeps an eye on things, but he accepts neither your pets nor your children. The beach is 4 blocks away; the river, 1 block.

801 N. Peninsula Dr. (at Riverview Blvd.), Daytona Beach, FL 32118. © **904/248-2020.** Fax same as phone. www.thevillabb.com. 4 units. $85–$190 single or double. Rates include continental breakfast. AE, MC, V. *In room:* A/C, TV.

GREAT DEALS ON DINING

Don't come to Daytona Beach specifically for fine dining. The town has a few interesting restaurants, but none is likely to leave an indelible memory. A profusion of fast-food joints line the major thoroughfares, especially along Atlantic Avenue on the beach and along International Speedway Boulevard (U.S. 92) near the racetrack. Restaurants come and go in the Beach Street district on the mainland, and along Main Street and Seabreeze Boulevard on the beach. A casual restaurant serves burgers and chicken wings and lots of suds out on the Main Street Pier.

AT THE BEACHES

The local **Shells** seafood restaurant is on the beach at 200 S. Atlantic Ave. (© **904/258-0007**), a block north of International Raceway Boulevard. See "Great Deals on Dining" in section 1 of chapter 10, "The Tampa Bay Area," for details about this inexpensive chain.

Anna's Italian Trattoria SOUTHERN ITALIAN Originally from Sicily, the Triani family makes all the pastas at their simple yet comfortable trattoria, which offers more formal dining than Rosario's equally good *ristorante* on the mainland (see below). The star here isn't the pasta, however; it's risotto alla Anna, an Italian version of Spanish paella. Portions are hearty; main courses come with soup or salad and a side dish of angel-hair pasta or a vegetable, and a bit of between-courses sorbet will cleanse the palate. There's a good selection of Italian wines to complement your meal. Everything is cooked to order, so be patient.

304 Seabreeze Blvd. (at Peninsula Dr.). © 386/239-9624. Reservations recommended. Main courses $10–$17. AE, DISC, MC, V. Tues–Sun 5–10pm. Closed 1 week in June.

Down the Hatch ★ *Value* SEAFOOD   Occupying a 1940s fish camp on the Halifax River, Down the Hatch serves up big portions of fresh fish and seafood (note its shrimp boat docked outside). Inexpensive burgers and sandwiches are available, too, and you can start your day here with a Belgian waffle, French toast, or a country-style breakfast while taking in the scenic views of boats and shorebirds through the big picture windows—you might even see dolphins frolicking. At night, arrive early to catch the sunset over the river, and also to beat the crowd at this very popular place. In summer, light fare is served outside on an awninged wooden deck.

4894 Front St., Ponce Inlet. © 386/761-4831. Call ahead for priority seating. Main courses $9–$25 (most $10–$16); breakfast $2–$5; burgers and sandwiches $3–$6.50; early bird menu (served 11am–5pm) $6–$8. AE, MC, V. Daily 7am–10pm. Closed 1st week in Dec. Take Atlantic Ave. south, make a right on Beach St., and follow the signs.

Ocean Deck Restaurant & Beach Club *Value* SEAFOOD/PUB FARE   Known by spring-breakers, bikers, and other beachgoers as Daytona's best "beach pub" since 1940, the Ocean Deck also is the best restaurant in the busy area around the Main Street Pier. Opening to the sand and surf, the downstairs reggae bar is as sweaty, noisy, and packed as ever (a band plays down there nightly from 9pm until 2:30am). The upstairs dining room can be noisy, too, but both you and the kids can come here for some good food, reasonable prices, and great ocean views. You can choose from a wide range of seafood, chicken, sandwiches, and the best burgers on the beach, but don't pass up the mahimahi, first broiled with peppery Jamaican spices and then finished off on a grill, a bargain at $9. There's valet parking after dark, or you can park free at the lot behind the Ocean Deck's Reggae Republic surf shop, a block away on Atlantic Avenue.

127 S. Ocean Ave. (at Kemp St.). © 386/253-5224. Main courses $8–$16; salads and sandwiches $5–$8. AE, DISC, MC, V. Daily 11am–2am (bar to 3am).

ON THE MAINLAND

Rosario's ★★ SOUTHERN ITALIAN/TUSCAN   A Victorian boardinghouse with lace curtains on high windows makes an incongruous setting for Chef Rosario Vinci's lively Italian restaurant. Originally from Florence, Italy, gregarious Rosario offers pastas with the familiar Bolognese and marinara sauces, but his nightly specials are much more intriguing, drawing inspiration from ancient Tuscan recipes. If the mixed grill of squirrel, pheasant, rabbit, and quail in a hunter's sauce doesn't appeal, you can always opt for Rosario's trusty grouper Livornese. There's music in the cozy bar Thursday through Saturday nights.

In Live Oak Inn, 448 S. Beach St. (at Loomis Ave.). © 386/258-6066. Reservations recommended. Main courses $12–$21. MC, V. Tues–Sat 5–10pm.

Super-Cheap Eats

The Cellar AMERICAN   An excellent place for a ladies' lunch, this tea room occupies the basement of a Victorian home built in 1907 as President Warren G. Harding's winter home (he spent election eve here in 1920) and now is listed in the National Register of Historic Places. It couldn't be more charming, with low ceilings, back-lit reproduction Tiffany windows, fresh flowers everywhere, linen tablecloths and napkins, and china teacups. If you can play the piano, help yourself to the baby grand. A wide-ranging lunch menu offers the likes of the house signature chicken salad as a platter or croissant sandwich, quiche du jour, crab cake sandwich, vegetarian lasagna, or chicken pot pie. In the warm months, there's outdoor seating at umbrella tables on a covered garden patio.

220 Magnolia Ave. (between Palmetto and Ridgewood aves.). © 386/258-0011. Soups, salads, sandwiches $6–$9. AE, DISC, MC, V. Mon–Fri 11am–3pm.

The Dancing Avocado Kitchen ⭐ VEGETARIAN   A healthy place to start your day, or have lunch while touring downtown, this storefront establishment purveys a number of vegetarian omelets, burritos, salads, personal-size pizzas, and hot and cold sandwiches such as an avocado Reuben. A few chicken and turkey items are on the menu, but the only red-meat selection is a hamburger. You can dine outside or inside the store with vegetable drawings on its brick walls and ceiling fans suspended from black rafters. No smoking.

110 S. Beach St. (between Magnolia St. and International Speedway Blvd.). © 386/947-2022. Breakfast $2–$4.50; sandwiches, salads, pizzas $4–$7. AE, DC, DISC, MC, V. Mon–Sat 8am–4pm.

McK's Dublin Station AMERICAN/IRISH   Worth knowing about because it serves food after midnight, this upscale Irish tavern has a highly eclectic menu. The pub fare includes club sandwiches, burgers, a tasty mahimahi wrap, and a few main courses of steaks, fish, and chicken. The food isn't exceptional, but it's perfectly acceptable after a few Bass ales. The service is sometimes rushed, but usually pleasant.

218 S. Beach St. (between Magnolia St. and Ivy Lane). © 386/238-3321. Reservations not accepted. Main courses $6–$13; salads and sandwiches $5–$7. AE, MC, V. Mon–Wed 11am–9pm; Thurs–Sat 11am–10pm (bar open later).

Worth a Splurge

Frappes North ⭐⭐ CREATIVE AMERICAN/FUSION   It's worth the 6-mile drive north to Bobby and Meryl Frappier's sophisticated, hip establishment, at which they provide this area's most entertaining cuisine. Several chic dining rooms—one has beams extending like spokes from a central pole—set the stage for an inventive, ever-changing "Menu of the Moment" fusing a multitude of styles. Ingredients are always fresh, and the herbs come from the restaurant's garden. Outstandingly presented with wonton strips and a multi-hued rice cake, our Southeast Asian–style pompano in a piquant peanut sauce was a memorable dish. Bobby and Meryl always have at least one vegetarian (though not necessarily nondairy) main course. Lunch is a steal here, with dinner-size main courses at a fraction of the dinnertime price. The restaurant is in a storefront on the mainland stretch of Granada Boulevard, Ormand Beach's main drag.

123 W. Granada Blvd. (Fla. 40; between Ridgewood Ave. and Washington St.), Ormand Beach. © 386/615-4888. Reservations recommended. Main courses $15–$25. AE, MC, V. Mon–Thurs 11:30am–2:30pm and 5–9pm; Fri 11:30am–2:30pm and 5–10pm; Sat 5–10pm. From the beaches, drive 4 miles north on Fla. A1A to left on Granada Blvd. (Fla. 40); cross Halifax River to restaurant on right.

DAYTONA BEACH AFTER DARK

Check the Daytona Beach *News-Journal* (www.n-jcenter.com) Friday edition for its weekly "Go-Do" and the Sunday paper for the "Master Calendar" section, both listing present and upcoming events. Other good sources are *Happenings Magazine* and *Backstage Pass Magazine,* two tabloids available at the visitor center (see "Essentials," earlier in this section) and in many hotel lobbies.

THE PERFORMING ARTS   The city-operated **Peabody Auditorium,** 600 Auditorium Blvd., between Noble Street and Wild Olive Avenue (© **386/255-1314**), is Daytona's major venue for serious performances, including concerts by the local Symphony Society (© **386/253-2901**). Professional actors perform Broadway musicals during winter and summer at the **Seaside Music Theater,** 176 N. Beach St., downtown (© **800/854-5592** or 386/252-6200; www.seasidemusictheater.org).

Under the city auspices, the **Oceanfront Bandshell** (© **386/258-3169**), on the boardwalk next to the Adam's Mark Hotel, hosts a series of free big-name concerts every Sunday night from early June to Labor Day. It's also the scene of raucous spring-break concerts.

THE CLUB & BAR SCENE In addition to the following, the sophisticated **Clocktower Lounge** at the Adam's Mark (see "Accommodations You Can Afford," earlier in this section) is worth a visit.

Main Street and **Seabreeze Boulevard** on the beach are happening areas where dozens of bars (and a few topless shows) cater to leather-clad bikers.

A popular beachfront bar for more than 40 years, the **Ocean Deck Restaurant & Beach Club,** 127 S. Ocean Ave. (© **386/253-5224;** see "Great Deals on Dining," above), is packed with a mix of locals and tourists, young and old, who come for live music and cheap drinks. Reggae or ska bands play after 9:30pm. There's valet parking after dark, or leave your vehicle at Ocean Deck's Reggae Republic surf shop on Atlantic Avenue.

3 St. Augustine: America's First City

105 miles NE of Orlando, 302 miles N of Miami, 39 miles S of Jacksonville

With its 17th-century fort, old city gates, horse-drawn carriages clip-clopping along narrow streets, historic buildings, and reconstructed 18th-century Spanish Quarter, St. Augustine seems more like a picturesque European village than a modern American city. This is, after all, the oldest permanent European settlement in the United States (no, it wasn't Jamestown in 1607 or the Pilgrims at Plymouth Rock in 1620). A group of French Huguenots settled in 1562 near the mouth of the St. Johns River, in present-day Jacksonville. Three years later, a Spanish force under Pedro Menéndez de Avilés arrived on the scene, wiped out the Huguenot men (de Avilés spared their women and children), and established a settlement on the harbor he named "St. Augustín."

The colony survived a succession of attacks by pirates, Indians, and the British over the next 2 centuries. The Treaty of Paris ending the French and Indian War ceded the town to Britain in 1763, but the British gave it back 20 years later. The United States took control when it acquired Florida from Spain in 1821.

Tourism is St. Augustine's main industry these days; but despite the daily invasion (with good reason—there are a plethora of interesting attractions), it's an exceptionally charming town, with good restaurants, an active nightlife, and shopping bargains. Give yourself 2 days here just to see the highlights, longer to savor this historic gem: St. Augustine is one of those places that actually lives up to most of the sickly sweet and sentimental promotional literature written about it.

ESSENTIALS

GETTING THERE The Daytona Beach airport is about an hour's drive south of St. Augustine, but services are more frequent—and fares usually lower—at Jacksonville's international airport, about the same distance north. Likewise with Amtrak's train station in Jacksonville. See "Essentials," in sections 2 and 4 of this chapter, for details.

St. Augustine

ACCOMMODATIONS
Bayfront Westcott House Bed & Breakfast Inn **28**
Best Western Spanish Quarter Inn **8**
Carriage Way Bed and Breakfast **13**
Casa Monica Hotel **23**
Kenwood Inn **27**
Monterey Inn **14**
Pirate Haus Inn & Hostel **19**
Ponce de León Hotel, Golf & Conference Resort **1**
Victorian House **26**

DINING
A1A Ale Works **20**
The Bunnery Bakery & Café **16**
Gypsy Cab Co. **17**
La Parisienne **15**
Raintree **6**
The Spanish Bakery **11**

ATTRACTIONS
Authentic Old Jail **3**
Castillo de San Marcos National Monument **9**
Colonial Spanish Quarter **12**
Florida Heritage Museum at the Authentic Old Jail **3**
Fountain of Youth Archaeological Park **4**
Government House Museum **22**
Lightner Museum **24**
Mission of Nombre de Dios **5**
Old St. Augustine Village Museum **29**
Ripley's Believe It Or Not! Museum **7**
Spanish Military Hospital **21**
St. Augustine Alligator Farm and Zoological Park **18**
St. Augustine Lighthouse & Museum **18**
The Oldest House **30**
The Oldest Wooden Schoolhouse in the USA **10**
The Oldest Store Museum **25**
World Golf Village **2**

565

VISITOR INFORMATION Before you go, contact the **St. Augustine, Ponte Vedra & The Beaches Visitors and Convention Bureau,** 88 Riberia St., Suite 400, St. Augustine, FL 32084 (© **800/OLD-CITY** or 904/829-1711; fax 904/829-6149; www.visitoldcity.com), and request the *Visitor's Guide,* detailing attractions, events, restaurants, accommodations, shopping, and more.

Your first stop upon arrival should be the **St. Augustine Visitor Information Center,** 10 Castillo Dr., at San Marco Avenue, opposite the Castillo de San Marcos National Monument (© **904/825-1000**). There are numerous ways to see the city, depending on your interest and time, and this is a good place to make your plans. Before setting out, everyone can pay $1 to watch "Struggle to Survive," a 42-minute video about the town's difficult first 14 years (history buffs will enjoy it; otherwise, it's a good way to kill an hour on a rainy day). A free 22-minute orientation video is more helpful in planning your visit. Once you've made a plan, you can buy tickets for sightseeing trains and trolleys, which include discount admissions to the attractions (see "Getting Around," below). The center is open daily from 8:30am to 5:30pm.

GETTING AROUND Once you've parked at the visitor center, you can walk or take one of the sightseeing trolleys, trains, or horse-drawn carriages around the historic district. The trolleys and trains follow 7-mile routes, stopping at the visitor center and at or near most attractions between 8:30am and 5pm daily. You can get off at any stop, visit the attraction, and step aboard the next vehicle that comes along. Several vehicles make continuous circuits along the route throughout the day; you won't ever have to wait more than 15 or 20 minutes. If you don't get off at any attractions, it takes about 1 hour and 10 minutes to complete the tour. They don't all go to the same sights, so speak with their agents at the visitor center in order to pick the right one for you. You can buy tickets there or from the drivers. The companies also sell **discounted tickets** to some attractions.

St. Augustine Historical Tours (© **800/397-4071** or 904/829-3800) operates the green-and-white, open-air buses (and enclosed buses when it rains, a definite advantage). You can park your car at the headquarters (the Authentic Old Jail and the Florida Heritage Museum at the Authentic Old Jail, which are also stops on the tour). The bus tours cost $15 for adults, $5 for kids 6 to 12, and are free for kids under 6. They also run twice-nightly (7 and 8:30pm) "Ghosts & Gravestones" tours that are theatrical and mildly amusing/interesting ($16 adults, $6 kids).

St. Augustine Sightseeing Trains (© **800/226-6545** or 904/829-6545; www.redtrains.com) covers all the main sites except the Authentic Old Jail and the Florida Heritage Museum at the Authentic Old Jail, but its red open-air trains are small enough to go down more of the narrow historic-district streets. $12 for adults, $5 for kids 6 to 12, and are free for kids under 6, and tickets are good for 3 consecutive days. The company also sells package tickets for your convenience.

> *Tips* **Where to Park in "St. Aug"**
>
> On-street parking is nonexistent in St. Augustine's historic district, and a number of metered parking lots are difficult to find and often full. Your best bet is to park in the lots behind the visitor information center on Castillo Drive. The $3 fee is good for 2 consecutive days, so you may leave it and return later. Most of the top historic attractions are within walking distance of the center.

You may also want to see the sights from the back of a horse-drawn carriage. **Colee's Carriage Tours** (© 904/829-2818) has been showing people around town since 1877. The carriages line up on Avenida Menendez south of Castillo de San Marcos National Monument. Slow-paced, entertainingly narrated 1-hour rides past major landmarks and attractions are offered from 8am to midnight. Private tours and hotel and restaurant pickups are available. Carriage tours cost $15 for adults, $5 for kids 6 to 12, and are free for kids under 6.

For more-personalized tours, call **Tour St. Augustine** (© 800/797-3778 or 904/825-0087), which offers guided walking tours around the historical area. Tours range from $10 per person for 1 hour.

You can search for the old spirits with the nightly **Ghost Tours of St. Augustine** ★★ (© 888/461-1009 or 904/461-1009; www.ghosttoursofstaugustine.com), in which guides in period dress lead you through the historic district or the St. Augustine Lighthouse; tickets are $8 per person, and free for children under 6. They also have 1-hour ghost cruises on the river in a 72-foot tall-mast schooner. They cost $28 per person including soft drinks and snacks. Call for the schedule and reservations.

The Sunshine Bus Company (© 904/823-4816) runs two public bus routes Monday to Saturday from 6am to 7pm. The north-south line runs between the St. Augustine Airport on U.S. 1 and the historic district via San Marco Avenue and the Greyhound bus terminal on Malaga Street. Rides cost $1 per person. Call for the exact schedule.

For a taxi, call **Yellow Cab** (© 904/824-6888).

Open daily 10am to 6pm, **Solano Cycle,** 61 San Marco Ave., at Locust Avenue (© 904/825-6766), 2 blocks north of the visitor center, rents bicycles, mopeds, and scooters. Bikes cost $12 a day; scooters and mopeds, $30 to $40 a day.

WHAT TO SEE & DO
SEEING THE TOP HISTORIC ATTRACTIONS

St. George Street from King Street north to the Old City Gate (at Orange St.) is the heart of the historic district. Lined with a plethora of restaurants and boutiques selling everything from T-shirts to antiques, these 4 blocks get the lion's share of the town's tourists. You'll have much less company as you poke around the narrow streets of the primarily residential neighborhood south of King Street.

Unless noted in the listings below, the town's attractions do not have guided tours, but most do have docents on hand to answer questions.

Be sure to drive through the parking lot of the Howard Johnson Express Inn, at 137 San Marco Ave., to see a gorgeous and stately Live Oak tree ★★ that is at least 600 years old and then continue east to Magnolia Avenue ★★, which is a spectacularly beautiful street with a lovely canopy of old magnolia trees.

Castillo de San Marcos National Monument ★★   One of the two best attractions here, America's oldest and best-preserved masonry fortification took 23 years (1672–1695) to build. It is stellar in design, with a double drawbridge entrance (the only way in or out) over a 40-foot dry moat. Diamond-shaped bastions in each corner, which enabled cannons to set up a deadly crossfire, contained domed sentry towers. The seemingly indestructible Castillo was never captured in battle, and its coquina (limestone made from broken sea shells and corals) walls did not crumble when pounded by enemy artillery or violent storms throughout more than 300 years. Today, the old bombproof storerooms surrounding the central plaza house exhibits documenting the history of the fort, a national monument since 1924. You can also tour the vaulted powder magazine, a dank prison cell (supposedly haunted), the chapel, and guard rooms. Then, climb the stairs to get a great view of the Mantanzas Bay. A self-guided tour map and brochure are provided at the ticket booth. If available, the 20- to 30-minute ranger talks are well worth attending. There are popular torchlight tours of the fort in winter (call for schedule).

If you like forts, you should also check out **Fort Mantanzas,** built on an island in the 1740s to warn St. Augustine of enemy attacks from the south (which were out of reach of the Castillo de San Marcos). For more information, call © **904/471-0116** or visit www.nps.gov/foma/. The monument is open daily from 8:30am to 5:30pm, and both admission to the fort and the ferry ride to the island are free, though donations are accepted.

1 E. Castillo Dr. (at San Marco Ave.). © **904/829-6506.** www.nps.gov/casa. Admission $5 adults, $2 children 6–16; free for children under 6 with an adult. Fort daily 8:45am–4:45pm; grounds daily 5:30am–midnight.

Colonial Spanish Quarter and Spanish Quarter Museum ★★
The city's colonial architecture and landscape have been re-created in this 2-square-block history park, which interprets St. Augustine's history circa 1750. Once inside the museum, you can take a 20-minute guided tour of the **DeMesa-Sanchez House** (ca. 1740–60), the only authentic colonial-era structure in the compound (the others are reproductions). Elsewhere, interpreters (as craftsmen, storekeepers, and more) in 18th-century attire are on hand to help you envision the life of early inhabitants. If you have to make a choice of one or the other, the Old St. Augustine Village Museum (see below) covers more history.

33 St. George St. (between Cuna and Orange sts.). © **904/825-6830.** Admission $6.50 adults, $5.50 seniors, $4 students 6–18, $13 per family; free for children 5 and under. Daily 9am– 5:30pm (last entry at 4:30pm).

Government House Museum
This museum is neither as informative nor as entertaining as the Old St. Augustine Village Museum (see below) or the Colonial Spanish Quarter (see above), but a walk through it will give you a quick overview of the Old City's history. Spanish coins, pottery, and other items unearthed during archaeological digs are the most fascinating exhibits.

48 King St. (at St. George St.). © **904/825-5079.** www.historicstaugustine.com. Admission $2.50 adults, $2 seniors, $1 children. Daily 9am–5pm.

Lightner Museum ★★
Henry Flagler's opulent Spanish Renaissance–style Alcazar Hotel, built in 1889, closed during the Depression and stayed vacant until Chicago publishing magnate Otto C. Lightner bought the building in 1948 to house his vast collection of Victoriana. The building is an attraction in itself and makes a gorgeous museum, centering on an open palm courtyard with an arched stone bridge spanning a fish pond. The first floor houses a Victorian village, with shop fronts representing emporia selling period wares. A Victorian Science and Industry Room displays shells, rocks, minerals, and Native American artifacts in beautiful turn-of-the-20th-century cases. Other exhibits include stuffed birds, an Egyptian mummy, steam-engine models, and amazing examples of Victorian glassblowing. Plan to spend about 90 minutes exploring it all, and be sure to be here at 11am or 2pm, when a room of automated musical instruments erupts in concerts of period music. The imposing building across King Street was Henry Flagler's opulent rival resort, the Ponce de León Hotel. It now houses **Flagler College,** which runs tours from May through August of its magnificent Tiffany stained glass windows, Spanish-Renaissance architecture, and gold-leafed Maynard murals. ($4 adults, $1 kids under 12; call © **904/823-3378**

> **Fun Fact** **Columbus's Crewman**
> Juan Ponce de León, the conquistador who discovered Florida in 1513 in a futile attempt to find the Fountain of Youth, first came to the New World from Spain on one of Columbus's voyages.

or visit www.flagler.edu/news_events/tours.html for more information.). Across Cordova Street stands another competitor of the day, the 1888-vintage Casa Monica Hotel (see "Accommodations You Can Afford," later in this section).

75 King St. (at Granada St.). © 904/824-2874. www.lightnermuseum.org. Admission $6 adults, $2 college students with ID and children 12–18; free for children 11 and under. Daily 9am–5pm (last tour 4pm).

Old St. Augustine Village Museum ★★
Operated by Daytona Beach's excellent Museum of Arts and Sciences (see p. 557), this museum brings to life each period of the city's history, from Spanish colonial times to the late 19th century. The buildings here (an entire block of 10 restored homes—built between 1790 and 1910—plus formal gardens) are original (and on their original building sites), the oldest of which was built in 1790 and owned (for a year in the early 19th century) by Achille Murat, Napoleon's exiled nephew (original letters from the French emperor are among the many fascinating exhibits). Many of the houses have varying exhibits inside, though since this museum is a work in progress, some are also closed, temporarily, until refurbishments are complete. The reconstructed Star General Store sells preserves and other Victorian-era goods. You'll need 2 hours to see it all, including the 30-minute guided tour. Admission is good all day, so if you miss the start of a tour, you can leave and come back.

250 St. George St. (entry on Bridge St. between St. George and Cordova sts.). © 904/823-9722. www.old-staug-village.com. Admission $7 adults, $6 seniors, $5 children under 12. Daily 9am–5pm. Guided tours on the hour 10am–4pm.

The Oldest House ★★
Archaeological surveys indicate that a dwelling stood on this site as early as the beginning of the 17th century. What you see today, called the Gonzáles-Alvarez House (named for two of its prominent owners), evolved from a two-room coquina dwelling built between 1702 and 1727. The rooms are furnished to evoke various historical eras. Admission also entitles you to explore the adjacent **Manucy Museum of St. Augustine History,** where artifacts, maps, and photographs document the town's history from its origins through the Flagler era a century ago. Both are owned and operated by the St. Augustine Historical Society. Allow about 30 minutes.

14 St. Francis St. (at Charlotte St.). © 904/824-2872. www.oldcity.com/oldhouse. Admission $5 adults, $4.50 seniors 55 and over, $3 students, $12 families; free for children under 6. Daily 9am–5pm; tours depart every half hour (last tour at 4:30pm).

The Oldest Store Museum ★★
The C&F Hamblen General Store was St. Augustine's one-stop shopping center from 1835 to 1960, and the museum on its premises today replicates the emporium at the turn of the century. On display are more than 100,000 items sold here in that era, many of them gleaned from the store's attic. They include high-button shoes, butter churns, spinning wheels, 1890s bathing suits, barrels of dill pickles (you can purchase one), and medicines that were 90% alcohol. Some 19th-century brand-name products shown here are still available today, among them Hershey's chocolate, Coca-Cola, Ivory soap, and Campbell's soups. It all makes for about 30 minutes of fascinating browsing.

4 Artillery Lane (between St. George and Aviles sts. behind Trinity Episcopal Church). © 904/829-9729. www.oldcity.com/oldstore. Admission $5 adults, $4.50 seniors over 60, $1.50 children 6–12; free for children 5 and under. Mon–Sat 10am–4pm; Sun noon–4pm.

The Oldest Wooden Schoolhouse in the U.S.A. ★ Kids
One of three structures here dating from the Spanish colonial period of more than 2 centuries ago, this red-cedar and cypress structure is held together by wooden pegs and handmade nails, its hand-wrought beams still intact. The last class was held here in 1864. Today, the old-time classroom is re-created using cheesy animated pupils and teacher, complete with a dunce and a below-stairs "dungeon" for unruly children. Today's kids may not approve of those stern disciplinary methods, but they will count their lucky stars they weren't in school back then.

14 St. George St. (between Orange and Cuna sts.). © 888/OLD-SCHL or 904/824-0192. www.oldestschoolhouse.com. Admission $2.75 adults, $2.25 seniors 55 and over, $1.75 children 6–12; free for children 5 and under. Daily 9am–5pm (later during summer).

Spanish Military Hospital
This clapboard building is a reconstruction of part of a hospital that stood here during the second Spanish colonial period from 1784 to 1821. A 20-minute guided tour will show you what the apothecary, the administrative offices, the patients' ward, and the herbarium probably looked like in 1791. The ward and a collection of actual surgical instruments of the period will enhance your appreciation of modern medicine.

3 Aviles St. (south of King St.). © 904/825-6830. Admission $2.50 adults, $2 seniors, $1.50 children. Mon–Sat 10am–5pm; Sun noon–5pm.

MORE HISTORIC ATTRACTIONS

Authentic Old Jail
This compact prison, a mile north of the visitor center, may be authentic, but it is not particularly historic. It was built in 1890 and served as the county jail until 1953. The sheriff and his wife raised their children upstairs and used the same kitchen facilities to prepare the inmates' meals and their own. Among the "regular" cells, you can also see a maximum-security cell where murderers and horse thieves were confined; a cell housing prisoners condemned to hang (they could see the gallows being constructed from their window); and a grim solitary-confinement cell—with no windows or mattress. A restaurant serves inexpensive lunch fare.

167 San Marco Ave. (at Williams St.). © 904/829-3800. Admission $5 adults, $4 children 6–12; free for children 5 and under. Daily 8:30am–5pm.

Florida Heritage Museum at the Authentic Old Jail
After you've seen the Authentic Old Jail, you can spend another 30 minutes wandering through this commercial museum documenting 400 years of Florida's past, focusing on the colorful life of Henry Flagler, the Civil War, and the Seminole Wars. Highlights are an extraordinary collection of toys and dolls, mostly from the 1870s to the 1920s; and a replica of a Spanish galleon filled with weapons, pottery, and treasures complementing display cases filled with actual gold, silver, and jewelry recovered by treasure hunters. A typical wattle-and-daub hut of a Timucuan Indian in a forest setting illustrates the lifestyle of St. Augustine's first residents.

167 San Marco Ave. (at Williams St.). © 904/829-3800. Admission $5 adults, $4 children 6–12; free for children 5 and under. Admission free with purchase of Old Town Trolley Tour. Daily 8:30am–5pm.

Fountain of Youth Archaeological Park *Overrated*
Never mind that Juan Ponce de León never did find the Fountain of Youth, this 25-acre archaeological park bills itself as North America's first historic site. Smithsonian Institution archaeological digs have established that a Timucuan Indian village existed on

ST. AUGUSTINE: AMERICA'S FIRST CITY

this site some 1,000 years ago, but there's no evidence that Ponce de León visited here during his 1513 voyage of discovery. You can wander around the not-so-interesting grounds yourself, but you'll learn more on a 45-minute guided tour or a planetarium show about 16th-century celestial navigation. *Be warned:* this place could be a secondary dictionary definition for the phrase tourist trap (not to mention the water from the fountain smells and tastes *awful*). Nevertheless, the grounds are lovely and the non-fountain exhibits are ok, which is good, because people feel the need to come here, even though they know it's basically a waste of time.

11 Magnolia Ave. (at Williams St.). © 800/356-8222 or 904/829-3168. Admission $5.75 adults, $4.75 seniors, $2.75 children 6–12, free for children 5 and under. Daily 9am–5pm.

Mission of Nombre de Dios   This serene setting overlooking the Intracoastal Waterway is believed to be the site of the first permanent mission in the United States, founded in 1565. The mission is a popular destination of religious pilgrimages. Whatever your beliefs, it's a beautiful tree-shaded spot, ideal for quiet meditation.

27 Ocean Ave. (east of San Marco Ave.). © 904/824-2809. Free admission; donations appreciated. Daily 8am–5:30pm.

Old Florida Museum ★★ *Kids*   This mostly outdoors museum gives you the chance to experience historic Florida, with many hands-on activities (shelling and grinding corn, pumping water, writing with a quill pen, and so on) that kids will enjoy (as will their parents). Showcasing daily living activities, everyday objects (games, weapons, tools, and more), and recreational pastimes, the museum is able to demonstrate how 3 different eras of people in the area—the native Timucuan Indians, Colonial Spaniards, and American Pioneers—lived, worked, and played during the 16th through early-20th centuries.

254-D San Marco Ave. © 800/813-3208 or 904/824-8874. www.oldfloridamuseum.com. Adults $5, kids $3. Daily 10am–5pm.

St. Augustine Lighthouse & Museum ★   This 165-foot-tall structure, Florida's first official lighthouse, was built in 1875 (with a signature black and white spiral stripe and red lantern) to replace the old Spanish lighthouse that had stood at the inlet since 1565. Sitting in a shady grove of live oaks, the lightkeeper's Victorian cottage was destroyed by fire in 1970 but was meticulously restored to its Victorian splendor. Also new is a Victorian-style visitor center that houses a museum explaining the history of both the lighthouse and the area. You should be in good physical condition and not pregnant to climb the 219 steps to the top of the lighthouse, where you can see 19 nautical miles on a clear day. Children must be at least 7 yr. old and 4 ft. tall to make the ascent.

81 Lighthouse Ave. (off Fla. A1A east of the Bridge of Lions). © 904/829-0745. www.stauglight.com. Admission to museum and tower $6.50 adults, $5.50 seniors, $4 children 7–11; free for kids under 7 and all active duty and retired military personnel. Daily 9am–6pm. Closed Easter, Thanksgiving, Christmas Eve, and Christmas Day. Follow Fla. A1A south across Bridge of Lions; take last left before turnoff to Anastasia State Park.

OTHER ENTERTAINING ATTRACTIONS

Ripley's Believe It or Not! Museum *Kids*   This is the original Ripley's museum, housed in an architecturally interesting converted 1887 Moorish Revival residence—complete with battlements, massive chimneys, and rose windows. Like the Ripley's in a dozen other U.S. cities, the exhibits run the gamut, from a Haitian voodoo doll owned by Papa Doc Duvalier to letters carved on a pencil with a chain saw by Ray "Wild Mountain Man" Murphy.

19 San Marco Ave. (at Castillo Dr.). © 904/824-1606. www.staugustine-ripleys.com. Admission $9.95 adults, $7.95 seniors, $5.95 children 5–12; free for children 4 and under. June 8–Labor Day daily 9am–9pm; day after Labor Day to June 7 9am–7pm.

St. Augustine Alligator Farm and Zoological Park ★★ *Kids*

You can't leave Florida without seeing at least one real live gator, and there are more than 2,700 gators and crocodiles—including some rare white gators—on display at this century-old attraction. In fact, it houses the world's only complete collection of every species (22) of crocodilians, a category that includes alligators, crocodiles, caimans, and gavials. Other creatures living here include geckos, prehensile-tailed skinks, lizards, snakes, tortoises, monkeys, and exotic birds. There are ponds and marshes filled with a variety of ducks, geese, swans, herons, egrets, ibises, wood storks, and other native wading birds as well as a petting zoo with pygmy goats, potbellied pigs, miniature horses, mouflon sheep, and deer. Entertaining (and educational) 20-minute alligator and reptile shows take place hourly throughout the day, and spring through fall you can often see narrated feedings. There's also a taxidermied (and famous) giant crocodile from New Guinea named Gomek on display. Allow at least 2 hours to tour the extensive and well-maintained facilities.

999 Anastasia Blvd. (Fla. A1A), east of Bridge of Lions at Old Quarry Rd. © 904/824-3337. www.alligatorfarm.com. Admission $14.25 adults, $8.50 children 3–10; free for children under 3. Daily 9am–5pm; summer hours 9am–6pm.

HITTING THE BEACH

There are several places to find sand and sea: in **Vilano Beach,** on the north side of St. Augustine Inlet; and in **St. Augustine Beach,** on the south side (the inlet dumps the Matanzas and North rivers into the Atlantic). Be aware, however, that erosion has almost swallowed the beach from the inlet as far south as Old Beach Road in St. Augustine Beach. The U.S. Army Corps of Engineers is reclaiming the sand, but in the meantime hotels and homes here have rock seawalls instead of sand bordering the sea.

Erosion has made a less noticeable impact on the beautiful **Anastasia State Park** ★★, on Anastasia Boulevard (Fla. A1A) across the Bridge of Lions and just past the Alligator Farm, where the 4 miles of beach (on which you can drive and park) are still backed by picturesque dunes. On its river side, the area faces a lagoon flanked by tidal marshes. Available here are shaded picnic areas with grills, nature trails, restrooms, and concessionaires offering windsurfing, sailing, and canoeing (on a saltwater lagoon). If you bring your own equipment, you can cast your line from the surf for bluefish, pompano, whiting, sea trout, redfish, and flounder (a license is required for out-of-state residents). In summer, you can rent chairs, beach umbrellas, and surfboards. There's good bird-watching here, too, especially in spring and fall; pick up a brochure at the entrance. The 139 wooded campsites are in high demand all year. They have picnic tables, grills, and electricity. Admission to the park is $3.25 per vehicle and $1 for bicyclists and pedestrians. Campsites cost $16 per night plus $2 for

---

Tips Parking at the Beach

All St. Augustine municipal beaches charge a fee of $3 per car at official access points from Memorial Day to Labor Day; the rest of the year you can park free. There are no lifeguards on duty and no toilet facilities on the municipal beaches any time of the year.

Where Golf Is King

Passionate golf fans can easily spend a day at the **World Golf Hall of Fame** (© 904/940-4123), a state-of-the-art museum honoring professional golf, its great players, and the sport's famous supporters (including comedian Bob Hope and singer Dinah Shore). It's the centerpiece of **World Golf Village,** a complex of hotels, shops, offices, and 18-hole golf courses (see "Affordable Outdoor Activities," below). There's an IMAX screen next door.

Museum admission is $10 adults, $9 seniors and students, $6 children 5 to 12. IMAX movie tickets range from $7 to $10 adults, $6 to $9 seniors and students, $5 to $8 children 3 to 12. Combination tickets to the museum and one IMAX movie cost $15 for adults, $13 seniors and students, $10 children 5 to 12. Throw in a round on the putting green and you'll pay $21 for adults, $18 seniors and students, and $14 children 5 to 12. Admission and movies are free for children under 5. The museum is open daily from 10am to 6pm (IMAX movies to 8pm on Fri and Sat).

You don't have to play the real courses, because the village is built around a lake with a "challenge hole" sitting out in the middle, 132 feet from the shoreline. You can hit balls at it or play a round on the nearby putting course. The Walkway of Champions (whose signatures appear in pavement stones) circles the lake and passes a shopping complex whose main tenant is the two-story **Tour Stop** (© **904/940-0422**), a purveyor of pricey apparel and equipment.

You can stay at the luxurious **World Golf Village Renaissance Resort,** 500 S. Legacy Trail, St. Augustine, FL 32092 (© **800/228-9290** or 904/940-8000; www.worldgolfrenaissance.com).

The village is at Exit 95A off I-95. For more information, contact World Golf Village, 21 World Golf Place, St. Augustine, FL 32092 (© **904/940-4000**; www.wgv.com).

---

electricity. For camping reservations call © **800/326-3521** or go to the website www.reserveamerica.com. The day-use area is open daily from 8am to sunset. You can bring your pets. For more information contact Anastasia State Park, 1340A Fla. A1A S., St. Augustine, FL 32084 (© **904/461-2033**; www.myflorida.com/communities/learn/stateparks/district3/anastasia).

AFFORDABLE OUTDOOR ACTIVITIES

For additional outdoor options, contact the St. Augustine, Ponte Vedra & The Beaches Visitors and Convention Bureau (see "Essentials," earlier in this section) and ask them to send you a copy of their *Outdoor Recreation Guide.*

CRUISES The Usina family has been running **St. Augustine Scenic Cruises** (© **800/542-8316** or 904/824-1806; www.scenic-cruise.com) on Matanzas Bay since the turn of the century. They offer 75-minute narrated tours aboard the double-decker *Victory III,* departing from the Municipal Marina just south of the Bridge of Lions. You can sometimes spot dolphins, brown pelicans, cormorants, and kingfishers. Snacks, soft drinks, beer, and wine are sold on board. Departures normally are at 11am and at 1, 2:45, and 4:30pm daily except Christmas, with an additional tour at 6:15pm from April 1 to May 21 and Labor Day to

October 15; May 22 to Labor Day there are two additional tours, at 6:45 and 8:30pm. Call ahead—schedules can change during inclement weather. Fares are $10.50 adults, $8.50 seniors, $7 juniors ages 13 to 18, $5 children 4 to 12, and free for children under 4. If you're driving, allow extra time to find a parking space on the street.

You can also take the free ferry to Fort Mantanzas on Rattlesnake Island. There are often dolphins in the water as you make the trip, and the fort is interesting if you have the time. Ferries take off from 8635 Highway A1A, South (follow A1A south out of St. Augustine for about 15 miles). Call © **904/ 471-0116** or visit www.nps.gov/foma/ for more information.

FISHING   You can fish to your heart's content at **Anastasia State Park** (see "Hitting the Beach," above). You can also cast your line off **St. Johns County Fishing Pier,** on the north end of St. Augustine Beach (© **904/461-0119**). The pier is open 24 hours daily and has a bait shop with rental equipment open from 6am to 10pm. Admission is $2 ($1 children under 2) for fishing, 50¢ per person for sightseeing.

For full-day, half-day, and overnight **deep-sea fishing** excursions (for snapper, grouper, porgy, amberjack, sea bass, and other species), contact the **Sea Love Marina,** 250 Vilano Rd. (Fla. A1A north), at the eastern end of the Vilano Beach Bridge (© **904/824-3328;** www.sealovefishing.com). Full-day trips on the party boat *Sea Love II* cost about $50; half-day trips, $35. No license is required, and rod, reel, bait, and tackle are supplied. Bring your own food and drink.

GOLF   The area's best golf resorts are in Ponte Vedra Beach about a half-hour's drive north on Fla. A1A, closer to Jacksonville than St. Augustine (see "Accommodations You Can Afford" in section 4 of this chapter for details).

At World Golf Village, 12 miles north of St. Augustine at Exit 98A off I-95 (see the box, "Where Golf is King," above), **The Slammer & The Squire** and **The King & The Bear** (© **904/940-6088;** www.wgv.com) together offer 36 holes amid a wildlife preserve. Locals say they're not as challenging as their greens fees, about $100 in summer, $165 in winter, including cart. For those not schooled in golf history, the "Slammer" is in honor of Sam Sneed; the "Squire" is for Gene Sarazen; the "King" is Arnold Palmer; and the "Bear" is Jack Nicklaus. Palmer and Nicklaus actually collaborated in designing their course.

There are only a few courses in St. Augustine, including a rather flat 18 at the **Ponce de León Hotel, Golf & Conference Resort** (see "Accommodations You Can Afford," below) and the **St. Augustine Shores Golf Club,** 707 Shores Blvd., off U.S. 1 (© **904/794-4653**). The latter is a par-70 course featuring 18 holes, lots of water, a lighted driving range and putting green, and a restaurant and lounge. Greens fees usually are under $30, including cart.

SAILING   You can spend 3 to 4 hours under sail with Captain Paul Kulik on board his *Voyager* (© **904/347-7183;** www.villavoyager.com), a 22-foot-wide trimaran, which departs the Municipal Marina next to the Bridge of Lions. The cruises cost $35 per person, including lunch, soft drinks, and beer. The boat can carry a maximum of six guests, so call for reservations and a schedule.

WATER SPORTS   Jet skis and surfing and windsurfing equipment can be rented at **Surf Station,** 1020 Anastasia Blvd. (Fla. A1A), a block south of the Alligator Farm (© **904/471-9463**); at **Raging Water Sports,** at the Conch House Marina Resort, 57 Comares Ave. (© **904/829-5001**), which is off Anastasia Avenue (Fla. A1A) halfway between the Bridge of Lions and the Alligator

Farm; and at **Watersports of St. Augustine,** at Sea Love Marina, 250 Vilano Rd. (Fla. A1A north), at the eastern end of the Vilano Beach Bridge (✆ **904/823-8963**).

GOOD WINDOW-SHOPPING

The winding streets of the historic district are home to dozens of **antiques stores** and **art galleries** stocked full of original paintings, sculptures, bric-a-brac, fine furnishings, china, and other treasures. Brick-lined **Aviles Street,** 1 block from the river, has an especially good mix of shops for browsing, as does **St. George Street** south of the visitor center and the Uptown area on **San Marco Avenue** a few blocks north of the center. The **Alcazar Courtyard Shops** at the Lightner Museum (✆ **904/824-2874**) has a good selection of antiques shops (see "Seeing the Top Historic Attractions," earlier in this section). The visitor center has complete lists of art galleries and antiques shops; or you can contact the **Antique Dealers Association of St. Augustine,** 60 Cuna St., St. Augustine, FL 32084 (no phone), and **Art Galleries of Saint Augustine** (✆ **904/829-0065** or 904/825-4577).

Experience chocolate heaven at **Whetstone Chocolates,** 2 Coke Rd. (Fla. 312), between U.S. 1 and the Mickler O'Connell Bridge (✆ **904/825-1700**). Free tours of the store and factory usually take place Monday to Saturday from 10am to 5:30pm, but call to make sure of the factory's schedule. Whetstone has a retail outlet at 42 St. George St. in the historic district.

Outlet shoppers will find plenty of good hunting 7 miles northwest of downtown on Fla. 16 at I-95 in the **St. Augustine Outlet Mall** (✆ **904/825-1555**), on the west side of I-95; and in the enclosed, air-conditioned **Belz Factory Outlet World** (✆ **904/826-1311;** www.belz.com), on the east side of the Interstate. Stores in both malls are open Monday to Saturday 9am to 9pm and Sunday 10am to 6pm.

ACCOMMODATIONS YOU CAN AFFORD

There are plenty of moderate and inexpensive motels and hotels here. Most convenient to the historic district is the 40-room **Best Western Spanish Quarter Inn,** 6 Castillo Dr. (✆ **800/528-1234** or 904/824-4457; fax 904/829-8330), directly across the street from the visitor center. It's completely surrounded by an asphalt parking lot but does have a swimming pool and hot tub.

The best of the budget-priced chain motels near the historic district, the **Super 8,** 3552 N. Ponce de León Blvd., between Rambla and Fairbanks streets (✆ **800/800-8000** or 904/824-6399; fax 904/823-8687), has attractively landscaped grounds with a palm-fringed lawn surrounding a swimming pool. The upstairs units with peaked beamed ceilings are especially appealing.

In addition to those listed below, St. Augustine has more than two dozen bed-and-breakfasts in restored historic homes. They all provide free parking, complimentary breakfast, 24-hour refreshments, and plenty of atmosphere (the St. Francis Inn has a spectacular walled courtyard), but most accept neither young children nor guests who smoke (check before booking). Those listed below are in the historic district. For more choices, contact **St. Augustine Historic Inns,** P.O. Box 5268, St. Augustine, FL 33085-5268 (no phone; www.staugustineinns.com), for descriptions of its member properties.

Although we have concentrated on hotels and bed-and-breakfasts in or near the Old City, St. Augustine Beach, approximately 5 miles southeast of the historic district, has several chain motels, all on A1A Beach Boulevard (Fla. A1A).

Value A Swashbuckling Hostel

International travelers on the cheap congregate at the **Pirate Haus Inn & Hostel,** 32 Treasury St., at Charlotte Street (© **904/808-1999;** www.piratehaus.com), smack in the middle of the historic district. Done up in a pirate theme, this Spanish-style building has a communal kitchen, living room, and rooftop terrace. Affiliated with both Hostelling International and American Youth Hostels, the inn has five private units (three with their own bathrooms) equipped with either a queen or double bed plus one or two bunk beds. Two other units have dormitory-style bunk beds. Rooms cost $36 to $56 a night (higher on holiday weekends), while dorm beds go for $13 a night. MasterCard and Visa credit cards are accepted. Reservations are advised, especially on weekends.

Three are on the beach side of the highway: the **Hampton Inn St. Augustine Beach** (© **800/426-7866** or 904/471-4000; fax 904/471-4888), the **Holiday Inn Beachside** (© **800/626-7263** or 904/471-2555; fax 904/461-8450), and the **Howard Johnson Resort Hotel** (© **800/752-4037** or 904/471-2575; fax 904/471-1247). But note that erosion has removed the beach at the Hampton Inn and Howard Johnson (see "Hitting the Beach," above). A **Hilton Garden Inn** (© **800/HILTONS** or 904/471-5559; fax 904/471-7146) and an inexpensive **Econo Lodge** (© **800/446-6900** or 904/471-2330) are on the western side of A1A.

Almost all accommodations increase their prices on weekends when the town is most crowded with visitors. St. Johns County charges a 9% tax on hotel bills.

Bayfront Westcott House Bed & Breakfast Inn Overlooking Matanzas Bay, this two-story, wood-frame house offers rare opportunities for an uncluttered view from the porch, the second-story veranda, and a shady courtyard. The rooms—some with bay windows, two-person whirlpool tubs, and working fireplaces—are exquisitely furnished and immaculate. Yours might have authentic Victorian furnishings and a brass bed made up with a white quilt and lace dust ruffle.

146 Avenida Menendez (between Bridge and Francis sts.), St. Augustine, FL 32084. © **800/513-9814** or 904/824-4301. Fax 904/824-4301. www.westcotthouse.com. 9 units. $95–$250 double. Rates include full breakfast. AE, DISC, MC, V. **Amenities:** Access to nearby health club; Jacuzzi; free bicycles; massage. *In room:* A/C, TV, hair dryer.

Carriage Way Bed and Breakfast Value   Primarily occupying an 1883 Victorian wood-frame house fronted by roses and hibiscus, this bed-and-breakfast isn't fancy or formal, but it is comfortable, relaxed, and a good value. Rooms in the main house are furnished with simple antique reproductions, including many four-poster beds. One room even retains its original fireplace. A console TV, books, magazines, and games are provided in a homey parlor. For more privacy, two more rooms are down the street in "The Cottage," a one-story clapboard house built in 1885. It has its own living room and kitchen, and both the Miranda and the Ashton rooms have claw-foot bathtubs. Miranda also sports a two-person Jacuzzi, and Ashton has its own small back porch.

70 Cuna St. (between Cordova and Spanish sts.), St. Augustine, FL 32084. © **800/908-9832** or 904/829-2467. Fax 904/826-1461. www.carriageway.com. 11 units. $85–$190 double. Rates include full breakfast. AE, DISC, MC, V. **Amenities:** Free use of bikes. *In room:* A/C, dataport.

Kenwood Inn Mark and Kerianne Constant's inn is unusual because of its relatively large outdoor space, which includes a swimming pool, a lushly landscaped sun deck, and a secluded garden courtyard (complete with a fish pond and neat flower bed under a sprawling pecan tree). Their Victorian wood-frame house with graceful verandas has served as a boardinghouse or inn since the late 19th century. Everything from the carpeting to the linens to the china is first-class. Rooms are larger and more private than most other accommodations in converted single-family homes. Some rooms have neither televisions nor telephones.

38 Marine St. (at Bridge St.), St. Augustine, FL 32084. © **800/824-8151** or 904/824-2116. Fax 904/824-1689. www.oldcity.com/kenwood. 14 units. $95–$175 double; bridal suite $225. Rates include continental breakfast. DISC, MC, V. **Amenities:** Outdoor pool; free use of bikes. *In room:* A/C, TV (in some), fax, dataport, kitchen, minibar, fridge, coffeemaker, hair dryer, iron. No phone in some.

Monterey Inn *Value* For the price, you can't find a better choice than this modest, wrought iron-trimmed motel overlooking the Matanzas Bay and close to the attractions and nightlife of the Old City. Three generations of the Six family have run this simple two-story motel, and they keep the 1960s building and grounds always clean and functional. Rooms are not especially spacious, but they are comfortable.

16 Avenida Menendez (between Cuna and Hypolita sts.), St. Augustine, FL 32084. © **904/824-4482.** Fax 904/829-8854. www.themontereyinn.com. 59 units. $49–$99 double. AE, DC, DISC, MC, V. **Amenities:** Heated outdoor pool. *In room:* A/C, TV, dataport, hair dryer.

Ponce de León Hotel, Golf & Conference Resort Located 2½ miles north of the historic district, this 400-acre complex, until recently known as the Radisson Ponce de León Golf & Conference Resort, primarily appeals to golfers, who can play a round on its Donald Ross–designed par-72 course before heading off to see the sights. Although it's been in business since Henry Flagler built a resort here in 1916, today's establishment is a modern motel. Rooms are in one- and two-story buildings spread out in a virtual forest of palms, magnolias, centuries-old live oaks, and clumps of sawgrass, with a large swimming pool in the center. The units all have balconies or patios. Minisuites are good for families, with trellises separating small sitting rooms from sleeping areas. The Fairway Grill, with its big window walls overlooking the golf course and the marshes beyond, offers breakfast, lunch, and dinner. On weekend evenings you can join conferences unwinding in the lounge for live entertainment in a cozy bar overlooking the greens. Other activities include a putting green; volleyball, shuffleboard, croquet, boccie ball, and basketball courts; and a horseshoe pitch.

4000 U.S. Hwy. 1 N., St. Augustine, FL 32095. © **800/228-2821** or 904/824-2821. Fax 904/824-8254. www.theponce.com. 193 units. $69–$149 double. Golf, family, and other packages available. AE, DC, DISC, MC, V. **Amenities:** Restaurant (American), bar; heated outdoor pool; golf course; 6 tennis courts; varied sports facilities; Jacuzzi; limited room service; laundry service. *In room:* A/C, TV, dataport, coffeemaker, hair dryer, iron.

Victorian House *Kids* Ken and Marcia Cerotzke's bed-and-breakfast occupies an 1897-vintage Victorian residence, complete with wraparound porch, and an adjoining old store, now dubbed the "Carriage House." The latter is divided into four units, one of which has a kitchenette. It's also unusual in that children are welcome to stay in the Carriage House units, all of which have TVs and private entrances. Kids are not welcome to stay in the main house, whose rooms lack TVs. Country Victorian antiques adorn all units here, but none of the units has a telephone.

11 Cadiz St. (between Aviles and Charlotte sts.), St. Augustine, FL 32084. © 877/703-0742 or 904/824-5214. Fax 904/824-7990. www.victorianhouse-inn.com. 8 units. $90–$175 double. Rates include full breakfast. AE, DISC, MC, V. **Amenities:** Free bikes. *In room:* A/C, TV (4 units), kitchen (1 unit). No phone.

WORTH A SPLURGE

Casa Monica Hotel ★★ This hotel was built in 1888 as a luxury hotel by Bostonian and YMCA founder Franklin W. Smith. (Unfortunately, Smith never really opened it, since the furniture he'd purchased for the hotel never made it to St. Augustine, thanks to Henry Flagler who owned the railroad the furniture was to be shipped on as well as the neighboring—and thus competitor—hotel. In a bind and losing too much money, Smith finally sold the hotel to Flagler, for 25 cents on the dollar for what he originally spent, and the furniture mysteriously appeared almost immediately!) This Spanish-Moorish-style building (look for the atmospheric, arched, old-time carriage entrance near the present garage) was also used as the St. Johns County Courthouse from the 1960s until 1997.

Now totally restored, it's easily the best hotel here, with top-notch rooms and services. Most of the lovely guest quarters are spacious and fully modern hotel rooms, with Iberian-style armoires, wrought-iron headboards, and tapestry drapes. "Premium" rooms have sitting areas with sofas and easy chairs. All units have big bathrooms equipped with high-end toiletries and either a huge walk-in shower or a combination tub-shower. Much more interesting are the "signature suites" installed in the building's two tile-topped towers and fortresslike central turret. Each of these one- to four-bedroom units is unique. One in the turret has a half-round living room with gun-port windows overlooking the historic district, while a three-story town-house model in one of the towers has a huge whirlpool bathroom on its top floor. The 95 Cordova restaurant, which serves regional fare, has an excellent wine list, great service, and is beautifully decorated. However, though a lot of people swear the food served there is the best in the city, we couldn't find much to our taste. A player piano provides music in the adjoining bar. Guests here can pay $15 a day to use the swimming pools, restaurants, and other facilities at an exclusive oceanfront club in Ponte Vedra Beach.

95 Cordova St. (at King St.), St. Augustine, FL 32084. © 800/648-1888 or 904/827-1888. Fax 904/819-6065. www.casamonica.com. 138 units. $149–$239 double. Packages available. AE, DC, DISC, MC, V. Valet parking $8; limited free self-parking 2 blocks from hotel. **Amenities:** Restaurant (American, with several additional influences), marketplace, bar; heated (and cooled) outdoor pool; access to nearby health club; exercise room; Jacuzzi; bike rental; children's programs; concierge; business center; limited room service; babysitting; coin-op washers and dryers. *In room:* A/C, TV, dataport (high-speed access), fridge, coffeemaker, hair dryer, iron.

GREAT DEALS ON DINING

In a town with as much tourist traffic as St. Augustine, there are, of course, a fair number of "tourist trap" restaurants. But on the whole, the food in St. Augustine, even at the popular eateries, is fairly priced and of good quality.

The historic district has a branch of Tampa's famous **Columbia** restaurant at 98 St. George St., at Hypolita Street (© **904/824-3341**). Like the original (see "Great Deals on Dining" in section 1 of chapter 10), this one sports Spanish architecture, including intricate tilework and courtyards with fountains.

A1A Ale Works ★ SEAFOOD You can't miss this two-story Victorian-style building on the waterfront opposite the Bridge of Lions. One of the city's most popular watering holes, the noisy downstairs bar offers nightly entertainment, which sometimes filters upstairs into the restaurant. Despite the noise potential, the kitchen turns out a surprisingly good blend of new-world Floribbean,

Cuban, Caribbean, and Latino styles, in a nice setting with big windows and outside balcony seating overlooking the river and Bridge of Lions. Most of the seafood is very fresh, and the sauces are made to order. The spicy ahi stick appetizer (sushi grade tuna, pickled ginger, and sesame seeds wrapped in a wonton skin, cooked rare, served over Caribbean slaw and topped with a wasabi and siracha aioli) is as good as it gets, and you shouldn't leave without trying it. Don't overlook the nightly specials, either, especially the fresh fish. The house brew ranges from a very light lager to a nonalcoholic root beer.

1 King St. (at Avenida Menendez). © 904/829-2977. Call for preferred seating. Main courses $12–$20; sandwiches $7–$9. AE, DC, DISC, MC, V. Sun–Thurs 11am–10:30pm; Fri–Sat 11am–11pm. Late-night menu served downstairs.

Gypsy Cab Co. ★★ *Value* NEW AMERICAN Billing itself as a temple of "urban cuisine," owner-chef Ned Pollack's high-energy establishment, with gaudy purple neon stripes outside and bright, art-filled dining rooms inside, offers the town's most interesting culinary experience. Ned's creative menu changes daily, although a hearty black-bean soup is a constant winner. We had expertly cooked shrimp with artichokes sautéed with scallions, mushrooms, and julienned carrots and served with a pleasantly peppered white wine and butter sauce—a delightful combination of flavors. Grouper in a tomato basil sauce, strip steak under a peppercorn sauce, and Cayman Island–style pork were among the other offerings. The house salad dressing is so good they sell it by the bottle. Also worshipped here during autumn: Beaujolais nouveau, by the glass or bottle. Lunch is served in the Gypsy Bar & Grill next door, which has live music Tuesday and Wednesday nights and serves as a comedy club from Thursday to Saturday evenings (© **904/808-1305**).

828 Anastasia Blvd. (Fla. A1A, at Ingram St., east of Bridge of Lions). © **904/824-8244.** Reservations not accepted. Main courses $12–$20. AE, DC, DISC, MC, V. Mon–Thurs 11am–4pm and 4:30–10pm; Fri–Sat 11am–4pm and 4:30–11pm; Sun 10:30am–4pm and 4:30–10pm.

SUPER-CHEAP EATS

The Bunnery Bakery & Café ★ *Value* BAKERY/DELI Alluring aromas waft from this bakery and cafe in the heart of the historic district. It's lovely to come here for breakfast before you start your rounds, or for a fresh pastry and hot cup of latte, cappuccino, or espresso anytime you need a break from sightseeing. At lunch, plop yourself into one of the colorful booths and indulge in soup, salads, burgers, panini, or a croissant stuffed with walnut-and-pineapple chicken salad. Order at the counter; the staff will call your number when it's ready.

121 St. George St. (between Treasury and Hypolita sts.). © **904/829-6166.** Breakfast $3–$7; sandwiches and salads $3.50–$7.50. No credit cards. Daily 8am–6pm. Closed New Year's Day, Easter, Thanksgiving, Christmas Eve, Christmas.

The Spanish Bakery COLONIAL Occupying a reconstructed 17th-century kitchen building, this little family-operated establishment bakes almond, lemon, and cinnamon cookies, using recipes from the Spanish colonial period, when a lack of refrigeration limited the use of milk and eggs. A couple of these crunchy morsels, eaten at the picnic tables outside, make a fine snack while you're touring the historic district. Or you can have lunch here, choosing from daily specials such as spicy Spanish-style chili over rice.

Rear of 42½ St. George St. (between Cuna and Orange sts.). © **904/471-3046.** Reservations not accepted. Lunch specials $5; cookies and rolls 40¢–50¢ each. No credit cards. Daily 9:30am–3pm. Closed Thanksgiving and Christmas.

WORTH A SPLURGE

La Parisienne ★★ CONTEMPORARY FRENCH   Despite its name, this lovely dining room evokes the French countryside, with a rough-hewn beamed pine ceiling, lace-curtained windows, and ladder-back chairs. Changing seasonally, the menu always features fresh seafood, and in fall you'll see venison and quail. If they're offered, begin with pan-seared sea scallops in a citrus sauce; then go on to steak au poivre with a Cognac cream sauce, roast rack of lamb Provençal, or the day's treatment of fresh local fish. A fixed-price, five-course menu offers a choice of meat or seafood appetizers and main courses plus cheeses and dessert. The weekend brunch menu offers beignets, eggs Benedict, and scrambled eggs with smoked salmon.

60 Hypolita St. (between Spanish and Cordova sts.). © 904/829-0055. Reservations recommended. Main courses $19–$28; 5-course prix fixe menu $58. AE, DISC, MC, V. Tues–Fri 5–9pm; Sat–Sun 11am–3pm and 5–9pm.

Raintree ★ INTERNATIONAL   Even if you don't have a full meal at this romantic 1879 Victorian house (about half a mile north of the historic district), the tempting variety of hot crepes and an exemplary crème brûlée is worth a visit. Sweetness works its way onto the main menu, too, starting with fruit salsa with the blue-crab cake appetizer and progressing to the likes of cashew-encrusted pork tenderloin mignonettes with a champagne and frothed blackberry butter sauce. More traditional main courses include beef Wellington and rack of New Zealand lamb. It's all very good, though not as exciting as at Gypsy Cab Co. or as expertly prepared as at La Parisienne (see above). The list of more than 300 vintages has won *Wine Spectator* awards.

102 San Marco Ave. (at Bernard St.). © 904/824-7211. Reservations recommended. Main courses $15–$23; dessert bar $5.50. AE, DC, MC, V. Sun–Thurs 6–9:30pm; Fri–Sat 6–10pm. Courtesy car provides transportation from/to downtown hotels.

ST. AUGUSTINE AFTER DARK

Especially on weekends, the Old Town is full of strollers and partyers making the rounds to the dozens of active bars, clubs, and restaurants. For up-to-date details on what's happening in town, check the local daily, the *St. Augustine Record* (www.staugustine.com), or the irreverent *Folio Weekly* (www.folioweekly.com).

The best-looking crowd in town can be found at the **A1A Ale Works** (see "Great Deals on Dining," above). Twenty-something hipsters and middle-age partyers mingle at this handsome New Orleans–style microbrewery and restaurant. Thursday through Saturday nights, downstairs at the bar, on a crowded window-front stage, you'll find live music, often light rock and R&B tunes.

Ann O'Malley's, 23 Orange St., near the Old City Gate (© 904/825-4040), is an Irish pub, open day and night until 1am. Besides the selection of ales, stouts, and drafts, this is one of the only spots in town where you can grab a late-night bite.

Also popular with locals, **Mill Top Tavern,** 19½ St. George St., at the Fort (© 904/829-2329), is a warm and rustic tavern housed in a 19th-century mill building (the waterwheel is still outside). Weather permitting, it's an open-air space. There's music every day from 1pm until 1am.

Scarlett O'Hara's, 70 Hypolita St., at Cordova Street (© 904/824-6535), boasts a catacomb of cozy rooms with working fireplaces. The rambling, 19th-century wood-frame house is the setting for live rock, jazz, and R&B bands nightly. Sporting events are aired on a large-screen TV.

Across the river, the **Gypsy Bar & Grill,** part of the Gypsy Cab Co. restaurant, 828 Anastasia Blvd. (✆ **904/824-8244**), has live music Tuesday and Wednesday nights, then transforms itself into a comedy club Thursday to Saturday evenings (✆ **904/808-1305**).

You can also take one of the many ghost tours that are offered nightly.

4 Jacksonville

36 miles S of Georgia, 134 miles NE of Orlando, 340 miles N of Miami

Once infamous for its smelly paper mills, the sprawling metropolis of Jacksonville—residents call it "Jax," from its airport abbreviation—is now one of the South's insurance and banking capitals. Development was rampant throughout Duval County during the 1990s, with hotels, restaurants, attractions, and clubs springing up, especially in suburban areas near the interstate highways. Nevertheless, there are shady older neighborhoods to explore, 20 miles of Atlantic Ocean beaches upon which to sun and swim, many championship golf courses to play, and an abundance of beautiful and historic national and state parks to roam.

Spanning the broad, curving St. Johns River, downtown Jacksonville is a vibrant center of activity during weekdays and on weekend afternoons and evenings, when many locals return to the restaurants and bars of the Jacksonville Landing and Southbank Riverwalk, two dining-and-entertainment complexes facing each other across the river. Like Baltimore's Inner Harbor, the two centers have helped to revitalize downtown.

ESSENTIALS

GETTING THERE **Jacksonville International Airport,** on the city's north side about 12 miles from downtown (✆ **904/741-2000;** www.jaxairports.org), is served by **Air Canada** (✆ 888/247-2262), **AirTran** (✆ 800/AIR-TRAN), **American** (✆ 800/433-7300), **Continental** (✆ 800/525-0280), **Delta** (✆ 800/221-1212), **Midway** (✆ 800/446-4392), **Northwest** (✆ 800/225-2525), **Southwest** (✆ 800/435-9792), **United** (✆ 800/241-6522), and **Metro Jet** and **US Airways** (✆ 800/428-4372).

You can get visitor information about Jacksonville, St. Augustine, and Amelia Island at the **First Coast Welcome Center,** on the lower level by the baggage area (✆ **904/741-4902**). It's open daily from 9am to 9pm.

Alamo (✆ 800/327-9633), **Avis** (✆ 800/331-1212), **Budget** (✆ 800/527-0700), **Dollar** (✆ 800/800-4000), **Enterprise** (✆ 800/325-8007), **Hertz** (✆ 800/654-3131), and **National** (✆ 800/CAR-RENT) have rental-car booths at the airport.

Gator City Taxi (✆ **904/741-0008** at the airport or 904/355-TAXI elsewhere) provides cab service. Fares for up to four persons are about $20 to downtown, $38 to $45 to beach hotels, $55 to $65 to St. Augustine, and $40 to Amelia Island. **Express Shuttle** (✆ **904/353-8880** or 904/355-2583) provides

---

Fun Fact Once a Cow Town

Although Jacksonville claims to be the capital of Florida's historic "First Coast," the city dates its beginnings from an early-1800s settlement named Cowford, because cattle crossed the St. Johns River here. It changed its name in 1822 to honor General Andrew Jackson, who had forced Spain to cede Florida to the United States 2 years earlier.

> *Fun Fact* **Escaping Intolerance**
> Zephaniah Kingsley, the white man who from 1817 to 1829 owned the plantation that is now part of the Timucuan Ecological and Historic Preserve, held some seemingly contradictory views on race. Although he owned more than 200 slaves, he believed that "the coloured race were superior to us, physically and morally." He married a Senegalese woman—one of his former slaves—and in 1837 moved his mixed-race family to what is now the Dominican Republic to escape what he called the "spirit of intolerant injustice" in Florida.

van service to and from hotels and resorts throughout the area. Per-person fares are about $17 to downtown Jacksonville, $22 to $28 to the beaches, $57 to $67 to St. Augustine, and $35 to Amelia Island.

There's an **Amtrak** station in Jacksonville at 3570 Clifford Lane, off U.S. 1, just north of 45th Street (© **800/USA-RAIL;** www.amtrak.com).

VISITOR INFORMATION Contact the **Jacksonville and the Beaches Convention & Visitors Bureau,** 201 E. Adams St., Jacksonville, FL 32202 (© **800/733-2668** or 904/798-9111; fax 904/789-9103; www.jaxcvb.com), for maps, brochures, calendars, and advice. The bureau is open Monday to Friday from 8am to 5pm. It operates information booths at the airport (see above) and in the upstairs food court of **Jacksonville Landing** (see "Exploring the Area," below). The latter is open Monday to Saturday from 10am to 7pm and Sunday 12:30 to 5:30pm. The bureau also has a walk-in information office in **Jacksonville Beach** at 403 Beach Blvd., between 3rd and 4th Sts. (© **904/242-0024**), which is open Monday to Saturday from 10am to 6pm.

GETTING AROUND You can get around downtown Jacksonville via the **Skyway,** an elevated and completely automated train that runs down Hogan Street from the Florida Community College Jacksonville campus through downtown and across the river via the Acosta/Fla. 13 bridge to the Southbank Riverwalk. The Skyway operates Monday to Friday from 6am to 11pm, Saturday from 10am to 11pm, and Sunday only for special events. Skyway rides cost 35¢. **The Trolley** connects with the Skyway and runs east-west through downtown, primarily along Bay Street. It's free and operates Monday to Friday from 6:30am to 7pm. Get maps and schedules from the convention and visitors bureau or at the visitor information booth at Jacksonville Landing (see above). Both are operated by the **Jacksonville Transportation Authority** (© **904/630-3100;** www.ridejta.net), which also provides local bus service.

Otherwise, you're better off having a car if you want to explore this vast area. You can hail a **taxi** downtown if you spot one, although it is usually best to call **Gator City Taxi** (© **904/355-8294**) or **Yellow Cab** (© **904/260-1111**) for a pickup. Fares are $1.25 when the flag drops, and 25¢ for each fifth of a mile thereafter.

Out at the beaches, the **St. Johns River Ferry** (© **904/241-9969**) shuttles vehicles across the river between Mayport, an Old Florida fishing village on the south side, and Fort George on the north shore. The boats depart Mayport on the hour and the half-hour Monday to Friday from 6am to 10pm, weekends from 6:20am to 10pm. One-way fare is $2.75 per two-axle private vehicle, 50¢ for pedestrians and bicyclists. Even if you have to wait 30 minutes for the next

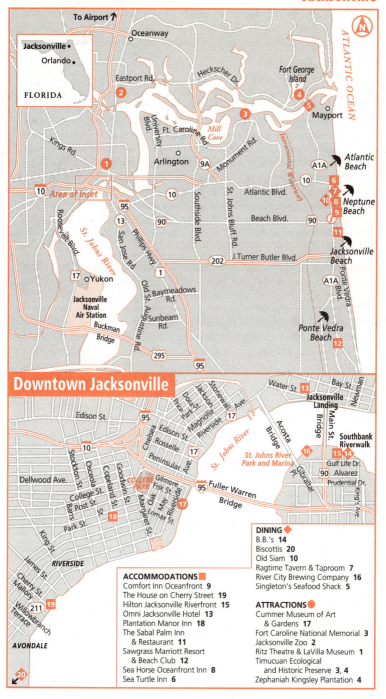

ferry, the 5-minute ride greatly shortens the trip between the Jacksonville beaches and Amelia Island. We always stop for lunch at Singleton's Seafood Shack in Mayport (see "Great Deals on Dining," later in this section).

WHAT TO SEE & DO
EXPLORING THE AREA

Cummer Museum of Art & Gardens ★★   Built on the grounds of a private Tudor mansion, this modestly sized but outstanding museum is worth a visit for anyone who appreciates the visual arts. The permanent collection encompasses works from 2000 B.C. to the present. It's especially rich in American impressionist paintings and includes an impressive collection of 18th-century porcelain and 18th-century and early-19th-century Japanese netsuke ivory carvings. Don't miss the stunning Italian and English gardens set on the scenic St. Johns River. The museum hosts temporary and traveling exhibits and sponsors a multitude of activities during the year, so call to see what's on tap.

829 Riverside Ave. (between Post and Fisk sts.). © 904/356-6857. www.cummer.org. Admission $6 adults, $4 seniors over 65 and military, $3 students, $1 children under 5; free Tues after 4pm. Tues and Thurs 10am–9pm; Wed and Fri–Sat 10am–5pm; Sun noon–5pm.

The Jacksonville Landing   Resembling New York City's South Street Seaport, Boston's Faneuil Hall, and Baltimore's Inner Harbor, this glass-and-steel complex on the north bank of the river serves as the focus of downtown activity. There are more than 65 stores here, but shopping is secondary to dining and entertainment. You can choose from about half a dozen full-service restaurants, plus an inexpensive food court with indoor and outdoor seating overlooking the river. The Landing is the scene of numerous special events, ranging from arts festivals to baseball-card shows, and outdoor rock, blues, country, and jazz concerts on weekends. Call or check the website to find out what's going on during your stay.

2 Independent Dr. (between Main and Pearl sts.), on the St. Johns River. © 904/353-1188. www.jacksonvillelanding.com. Free admission. Mon–Thurs 10am–8pm; Fri–Sat 10am–9pm; Sun noon–5:30pm; bars and restaurants open later. From I-95, take Exit 107 downtown to Main St., go over the Blue Bridge, and turn left at Bay St. Then go 2 blocks and make a left on Laura St., which dead-ends at the Landing. Park on east side of complex.

Jacksonville Zoo ★ (Kids)   Between downtown and the airport, this environmentally sensitive zoo is well on its way to becoming one of the country's best. While the zoo's new Wild Florida area presents local fauna including black bears, red wolves, Florida panthers, and alligators, the main exhibits feature an extensive and growing collection of lions, rhinos, elephants, antelopes, Nile crocodiles, cheetahs, monkeys, western lowland gorillas, and other African wildlife. You'll enter the 73-acre park through the authentic thatched roof built in 1995 by 24 Zulu craftsmen. Whether you go on foot or by tram, allow at least 2 hours to tour this vast and lush zoo. When you arrive, ask about current animal shows and special events. Strollers and wheelchairs are available for rent.

8605 Zoo Pkwy. © 904/757-4462 or 904/757-4463. www.jaxzoo.org. Admission $8 adults, $6.50 seniors, $5 children 3–12; free for children under 3. Daily 9am–5pm. Closed Thanksgiving and Christmas. Take I-95 north to Heckscher Dr. (Exit 124A) and follow the signs.

Ritz Theatre & LaVilla Museum   From 1921 to 1971, the Ritz Theatre was the center of cultural life in LaVilla, an African-American neighborhood so vibrant that it was known as the Harlem of the South. Many entertainers played the Ritz before moving on to the Apollo Theater in the real Harlem. Most of

LaVilla's small, clapboard "shotgun" houses (so called because you could fire a shotgun through the central hallway and not hit anything) have been torn down in anticipation of urban renewal, but the Ritz has been rebuilt and is once again a center of the city's cultural life. Only the northwest corner of the building, including the Ritz sign, is original, but the new 426-seat theater captures the spirit of vaudevillian times. Off the lobby, LaVilla Museum recounts local African-American history and exhibits the works of black artists.

829 N. Davis St. (between State and Union sts.). © 904/632-5555. Admission $4 adults, $2 seniors and children 18 and under. Tues–Fri 10am–6pm; Sat 10am–2pm; Sun 2–5pm. From downtown take Main St. north, turn left (west) on State St. to theater and museum at Davis St.

Southbank Riverwalk   Bordering the St. Johns River directly opposite the Jacksonville Landing (see above), this 1.2-mile wooden zigzag boardwalk is usually filled with joggers, tourists, folks sitting on benches, and lovers walking hand-in-hand, all of them watching the riverboats, the shorebirds, and downtown's skyline reflected on the water. At 200 feet in diameter, the **Friendship Fountain** near the west end is the nation's largest self-contained fountain; it's especially beautiful at night when illuminated by 265 colored lights. Nearby you'll pass military memorials, a small museum dedicated to the city's history, and the **Museum of Science & History of Jacksonville (MOSH)**, at Museum Circle and San Marco Boulevard (© **904/396-MOSH**; www.themosh.org). The latter is an interactive children's museum focusing on science and the history of Northeast Florida. One of its stars is an Allosaurus dinosaur skeleton. It also has a small planetarium, whose shows are included in admission to the museum. The Riverwalk is the scene of special MOSH programs, seafood fests, parties, parades, and arts-and-crafts festivals.

On the south bank of the St. Johns River, flanking Main St. Bridge between San Marco Blvd. and Ferry St. © 904/396-4900. Free admission. MOSH $6 adults, $4.50 seniors, $4 children 3–12; free for children under 3. Riverwalk open 24 hrs. daily. MOSH Mon–Fri 10am–5pm; Sat 10am–6pm; Sun 1–6pm. Take I-95 north to Prudential Dr. exit, make a right, and follow signs.

THE TIMUCUAN ECOLOGICAL & HISTORIC PRESERVE: AN UNUSUAL BREED OF NATIONAL PARK

Named after the American Indians who inhabited Central and North Florida some 1,000 years before European settlers arrived, the **Timucuan Ecological and Historic Preserve** offers visitors an opportunity to explore untouched wilderness, historical buildings, and informative exhibits on the area's natural history. Unusual for a national park, this 46,000-acre preserve hasn't been hacked off from the rest of the community and drawn within arbitrary boundaries. The result is a vast, intriguing system of sites joined by rural roads alongside tumble-down fish camps, trailer parks, strip malls, condominiums, and stately old homes.

Admission to all park facilities is free (donations accepted). The visitor centers at Fort Caroline National Memorial and Zephaniah Kingsley Plantation are open daily from 9am to 5pm except New Year's Day, Thanksgiving, and Christmas. The Theodore Roosevelt natural area is open daily from 7am to 5pm during eastern standard time, daily from 7am to 8pm during daylight saving time, and is closed at Christmas.

South of the River

The preserve's prime attractions are 14 miles northeast of downtown on the south bank of the St. Johns River. Your starting point is the **Fort Caroline National Memorial**, 12713 Ft. Caroline Rd. (© **904/641-7155**; www.nps.gov/timu), which serves as the preserve's visitor center. This was the site of the 16th-century French Huguenot settlement that was wiped out by the Spanish who landed at St. Augustine. This two-thirds-size replica shows you what the original was like. You can see archaeological artifacts and two very well produced half-hour videos highlighting the area.

The fort sits at the northwestern edge of the 600-acre **Theodore Roosevelt Area,** a beautiful woodland and marshland rich in history and undisturbed since the Civil War. On a 2-mile hike along a centuries-old park trail, you'll see a wide variety of birds, wildflowers, and maritime hammock forest. Bring binoculars if you have them, since such birds as the endangered wood storks, great and snowy egrets, ospreys, hawks, and painted buntings make their home here in spring and summer. On the ground, you might catch sight of a gray fox or raccoon. You may also want to bring a blanket and picnic basket to spread out under the ancient oak trees that shade the banks of the wide and winding St. Johns River. After the trail crosses Hammock Creek, you're in ancient Timucuan country, where their ancestors lived as far back as 500 B.C. Farther along is the site of a cabin in the wilderness that belonged to the reclusive brothers Willie and Saxon Browne, who lived without the modern conveniences of indoor plumbing or electricity until the last brother's death in 1960.

If you're here on a weekend, take the fascinating 1½-hour guided tours of the fort and Theodore Roosevelt Area, offered every Saturday and Sunday (when weather and staffing permit). Call the fort for details and schedules.

The **Ribault Monument,** on St. Johns Bluff about a half mile east of the fort, was erected in 1924 to commemorate the arrival in 1562 of French Huguenot Jean Ribault, who died defending Fort Caroline from the Spanish. It's worth a stop for the dramatic view of the area.

To get here from downtown, take Atlantic Boulevard (Fla. 10) east, make a left on Monument Road, and turn right on Fort Caroline Road; the Theodore Roosevelt Area is entered from Mt. Pleasant Road, about 1 mile southeast of the fort; look for the trailhead parking sign, and follow the narrow dirt road to the parking lot.

North of the River

On the north side of the river, history buffs also will appreciate the **Zephaniah Kingsley Plantation**, at 11676 Palmetto Ave. on Fort George Island (© **904/ 251-3537**). A winding 2½-mile dirt road runs under a canopy of dense foliage to the remains of this 19th-century plantation. The National Park Service maintains the well-preserved two-story clapboard residence, kitchen house, barn/carriage house, and remnants of 23 slave cabins built of "tabby mortar"—oyster shell and sand. Exhibits in the main house and kitchen focus on slavery as it existed in the rice-growing areas of Northern Florida, Georgia, and South Carolina. You can see it all on your own, but 40-minute ranger-guided tours are the best way. They usually are given at 1pm Monday to Friday, 1 and 3pm on weekends, but call to confirm. Allot some extra time to explore the grounds. A well-stocked book and gift shop will keep you even longer. The plantation is open daily from 9am to 5pm except Christmas.

To get here from I-95, take Heckscher Drive (Fla. 105) east and follow the signs. From Fort Caroline, take Fla. 9A north over the St. Johns River to Heckscher Drive east. The plantation is about 12 miles east of Fla. 9A, on the left. From the beaches, take Fla. A1A to the St. Johns River Ferry, and ride it from Mayport to Fort George; the road is half a mile east of the ferry landing.

HITTING THE BEACH

You can fish, swim, snorkel, sail, sunbathe, or stroll on the sand dunes (at least Mar–Nov, since winter can get downright chilly here). All of these activities are just a 20- to 30-minute drive east of downtown at Jacksonville's four beach communities.

Atlantic Boulevard (Fla. 10) will take you to **Atlantic Beach** and **Neptune Beach.** The boulevard divides the two towns, and where it meets the ocean you'll come to **Town Center,** a quaint community with a number of shops, restaurants, pubs, the Sea Horse Oceanfront Inn, and the Sea Turtle Inn (see "Accommodations You Can Afford," below). You won't need your car to hit the beach, shop, dine, or imbibe here.

Beach Boulevard (U.S. 90) dead-ends at **Jacksonville Beach,** where'll you find beach concessions, rental shops, and a fishing pier. This is also the most popular local surfing beach.

To the south, the freeway-grade J. Turner Butler Boulevard (Fla. 202) leads from I-95 to the boundary between Jacksonville Beach and Ponte Vedra Beach. A right turn there will take you to **Ponte Vedra Beach** (pronounced here as Ponti *Vee*-dra*)*. This ritzy, golf-oriented enclave is worth exploring just to see its mansions and championship links. The Sawgrass Marriott Resort & Beach Club is a fine place to stay if you're into golf and can afford a splurge (see "Accommodations You Can Afford," below).

AFFORDABLE OUTDOOR ACTIVITIES

CRUISES Jacksonville River Cruises (© 800/711-3470 or 904/396-2333; www.rivercruise.com) operates sightseeing, dinner, and dancing cruises on the stern-wheel paddleboats *The Lady St. Johns* and *The Annabelle Lee*. They usually dock at the Radisson Riverwalk Hotel on the Southbank Riverwalk. Prices range from $22 to $45. Schedules vary greatly by season and whether or not the boat has been reserved for private parties, so call or check the website.

FISHING The least expensive way to fish for red snapper, grouper, sea bass, small sharks, amberjack, and more, 15 to 30 miles offshore in the Atlantic Ocean, is aboard the ***King Neptune,*** a 65-foot air-conditioned deep-sea party boat. The full-day trips depart at 7:30am daily from Monty's Marina, 4378 Ocean St. (Fla. A1A), half a mile south of the Mayport Ferry landing (© **904/ 246-7575**), and return at 4:30pm. The price is $50 per person, including all bait and tackle. You don't need a license, but reservations are required.

GOLF The Jacksonville area offers a great variety of golf courses, some of which are ranked among the top in the country. In Ponte Vedra Beach, the Sawgrass Marriott Resort & Beach Club sits on the most famous course, the **TPC at Sawgrass** ★★★, home of The Players championship in March. Ranked among the nation's top courses, its island hole is one of the most photographed in the world. Nearby are the Ocean and Lagoon courses at the **Ponte Vedra Inn & Club,** 200 Ponte Vedra Blvd. (off Fla. A1A; © **800/234-7462** or 904/285-1111). See "Accommodations You Can Afford," below, for information about the Marriott.

Top courses open to the public include the **Golf Club of Jacksonville,** at 10440 Tournament Lane (© **904/779-0800**), which is managed by the PGA Tour. It's a great bargain, with greens fees ranging from $30 to $40. The semi-private **Cimarrone,** at 2690 Cimarrone Blvd. (© **904/287-2000**), is a fast and watery course with greens fees ranging from $30 to $50.

On your way out to the beach, the semi-private **Windsor Parke Golf Club,** at 4747 Hodges Blvd., at Turner Butler Boulevard (© **904/223-GOLF**), is one of the most challenging and scenic courses in Jacksonville. Designed by Arthur Hill, the 6,740 yards of green are surrounded by towering pines and lots of water. Fees are usually less than $45 and include a cart, even on the weekends. Nonmembers should call 4 or 5 days in advance for tee times.

Be on the lookout for the free *Golfer's Guide* in visitor centers and hotel lobbies (see "The Active Vacation Planner," in chapter 2, for information about ordering copies).

HORSEBACK RIDING For a scenic ride along the sand and dunes, call **Sawgrass Stables,** 23900 Marsh Landing Pkwy., off Fla. A1A in Ponte Vedra Beach (© **904/285-3791**). Call for rates and reservations. Lessons are also available.

SPECTATOR SPORTS The 73,000-seat **Alltel Stadium,** 1 Stadium Place, at East Duval and Haines streets (© **904/630-3901** for information, or 904/353-3309 to charge tickets), hosts the annual Florida-Georgia football game every October, and other college football games September to December. It also is the home field of the National Football League's **Jacksonville Jaguars** (© **800/618-8005** or 904/633-2000 for ticket information; www.jaguars.com). One of the stadium's biggest draws is the **Toyota Gator Bowl,** usually on New Year's Day (see "Florida Calendar of Events," in chapter 2).

Adjacent to the stadium, the 10,600-seat **Jacksonville Veterans Memorial Coliseum,** 1145 E. Adams St. (© **904/630-3900** for information, or 904/353-3309 to charge tickets), hosts National Hockey League exhibition games, college basketball games, ice-skating exhibitions, wrestling matches, and various family shows.

SHOPPING & BROWSING

Jacksonville offers plenty of shopping opportunities, including an upscale mall, **The Avenues Mall,** south of town at 10300 Southside Blvd., as well as a number of flea markets, including the **Beach Boulevard Flea and Farmer's Market,** on Beach Boulevard (Fla. 90; © **904/645-5961**). More than 600 vendors show up daily from 9am to 5pm to sell their wares in a partially covered facility.

San Marco Square, at San Marco and Atlantic boulevards, south of the river, is a quaint shopping district in the middle of a stunning residential area. Shops in meticulously refashioned Mediterranean-revival buildings sell antiques and home furnishings, as well as clothing, books, and records.

Another worthwhile neighborhood to explore is the **Avondale/Riverside** historic district southwest of downtown on St. Johns Avenue between Talbot Avenue and Boone Park, on the north bank of the river. More than 60 boutiques, antiques stores, art galleries, and cafes line the wide, tree-lined avenue. The stores here tend to be expensive, but a shrewd eye might catch a bargain.

Nearby, the younger set hangs out at **Five Points,** on Park Street at Avondale Avenue, where used-record stores, vintage clothiers, coffee shops, and funky art galleries stay open late.

Like St. Augustine, Jacksonville is a mecca for chocoholics, particularly **Peterbrooke Chocolatier Production Center,** 1470 San Marco Blvd., on San Marco Square (© **904/398-4812**). If you've never tried chocolate-covered popcorn or pretzels, this is the place. It's open Monday to Friday from 10am to 5pm. Peterbrooke also has a retail shop on St. Johns Avenue in Avondale.

ACCOMMODATIONS YOU CAN AFFORD

If you'll be in Jax on a weekend, the big downtown commercial hotels such as the monstrous **Adams Mark Jacksonville,** next to The Jacksonville Landing (© **800/444-ADAM** or 904/633-9095; fax 904/633-9988; www.adamsmark.com); the **Omni Jacksonville Hotel,** a block west of The Jacksonville Landing (© **800/THE-OMNI** or 904/355-OMNI; fax 904/791-4809; www.omnihotels.com); and the **Hilton Jacksonville Riverfront,** on the Southbank Riverwalk (© **800/HILTONS** or 904/398-8800; fax 904/398-9170; www.jacksonvillehilton.com) all reduce their rates substantially on Friday and Saturday nights.

In addition to the Hilton Jacksonville Riverfront, the Southbank Riverwalk is home to the **Radisson Riverwalk Hotel** (© **800/333-3333** or 904/396-5100), the **Hampton Inn Central** (© **800/HAMPTON** or 904/396-7770), and the all-suites **Extended Stay American Downtown** (© **800/EXT-STAY** or 904/396-1777; www.extendedstay.com).

Beach accommodations are slightly less expensive in the cold months from December through March.

For a complete list of lodgings, contact the Jacksonville and the Beaches Convention & Visitors Bureau (see "Essentials," earlier in this section).

IN JACKSONVILLE

The House on Cherry Street ⭐   This colonial-style, wood-frame house, on the St. Johns River in the Riverside neighborhood, is ideal for a romantic B&B vacation. French doors open to a delightful screened-in back porch furnished with rocking chairs; it overlooks an expanse of tree-shaded lawn (where guests play croquet) leading to the river (where they play with kayaks and canoes). You might select the Rose or the Duck room, both with canopied four-poster beds and river views. Ducks are rather a theme here, with hundreds of antique decoys on display. All accommodations offer adjacent sitting rooms and ceiling fans and are supplied with fresh flowers, books, and magazines. No smoking is permitted inside.

1844 Cherry St. (on the St. Johns River), Jacksonville, FL 32205. © **904/384-1999.** Fax 904/384-5013. houseoncherry@compuserve.com. 4 units. $85–$115 double. Rates include full breakfast. AE, MC, V. No small children accepted. **Amenities:** Free use of bikes, canoes, kayaks. *In room:* A/C, TV, hair dryer. No phone.

Worth a Splurge

Plantation Manor Inn ⭐   The setting for many weddings and special events, this three-story plantation-style bed-and-breakfast in the historic Riverside district is 2 blocks from the river, 10 minutes from downtown, and a short drive to Avondale's shopping and dining. Its homey interior, outfitted with a mix of thrift-store antiques, features glossy pine floors and gorgeous cypress paneling, wainscoting, and carved moldings. Breakfast, including freshly baked muffins and breads, is served in a lovely dining room with a working fireplace. When the sun is shining, take the morning meal on a brick patio, a delightful setting with ivy-covered walls, flower beds, and garden furnishings under the shade of a massive oak tree. The patio also contains a lap pool and whirlpool spa. On the second floor you can enjoy a big wraparound porch with seating amid potted geraniums, hibiscus, and bougainvillea.

1630 Copeland St. (between Oak and Park sts.), Jacksonville, FL 32204. © **904/384-4630.** Fax 904/387-0960. www.plantationmanorinn.com. 9 units (8 with shower only). $145–$175 double. Rates include full breakfast. AE, DC, MC, V. **Amenities:** Outdoor pool; Jacuzzi. *In room:* A/C, TV, hair dryer.

AT THE BEACHES

A dozen modest hotels line Jacksonville Beach's 1st Street, along the Atlantic Ocean. The **Comfort Inn Oceanfront,** 1515 N. 1st St., 2 blocks east of Fla. A1A (C **800/654-8776** or 904/241-2311; fax 904/249-3830; www.comfortinn jaxbeach.com), is one of the better values. Its rooms all have balconies or screened patios, and guests can enjoy a large pool with four rock waterfalls and a palm-fringed sun deck, a secluded grotto whirlpool, an exercise room, a gift/sundries shop, and a multi-court sand volleyball park.

The Sabal Palm Inn & Restaurant Bed-and-breakfast lovers will find a comfortable and charming home in this Victorian-era house set on a residential street just half a block from the beach. Bay windows shed plenty of light in the first-floor formal parlor and dining room, occupied by a French restaurant serving breakfast to house guests and lunch and dinner to all comers. One apartment-size unit, complete with kitchen, runs the entire length of the house on the first floor. Two other guest units are at the top of a central stairway, from which a door leads to a porch with a fine view of the Jacksonville Fishing Pier. Two more guest units are upstairs. One is a suite with a monstrous bathroom with both shower stall and claw-foot tub, and its own stairway to the backyard. The other apartment-size suite contains a kitchen. Beside the house is a small swimming pool with a sun deck.

115 Fifth Ave. S. (between 1st and 2nd sts.), Jacksonville Beach, FL 32250. C **877/725-6466** or 904/241-4545. Fax 904/241-2407. 5 units. $75–$110 double. Rates include full breakfast. AE, DISC, MC, V. **Amenities:** Restaurant (French); outdoor pool; free bicycles; limited room service; laundry service. *In room:* A/C, TV, dataport, kitchen (2 units), fridge, coffeemaker, hair dryer, iron.

Sea Horse Oceanfront Inn *Value* One of the anchors of quaint Town Center, this older but well-run beachfront motel offers clean, spacious rooms with ocean views from balconies or patios. Families will appreciate the six units here with kitchenettes, not to mention a big beachfront lawn with a pool, shuffleboard, picnic tables, and a barbecue grill. And young couples will enjoy proximity to some of Jacksonville's top night spots. If you have a large family or group, consider the vast and lovely third-floor penthouse—it has a big living room and dining area, a full kitchen, and a separate bedroom as well as sofa beds and a huge balcony furnished with a dining table and chaise lounges. A coffee shop adjoins the motel, and Town Center's restaurants and bars are across the street.

120 Atlantic Blvd. (at beach end of Atlantic Blvd.), Neptune Beach, FL 32266. C **800/881-2330** or 904/246-2175. Fax 904/246-4256. www.seahorseresort.com. 38 units. $89–$129 double; $200–$225 penthouse suite for up to 6. AE, DC, DISC, MC, V. **Amenities:** Bar; heated outdoor pool. *In room:* A/C, TV, dataport, kitchen (6 units).

Sea Turtle Inn Completely gutted and restored in 1999 and 2000, this elegant, eight-story beachfront hotel is much more upscale than the Seahorse Oceanfront Inn, which it faces across Atlantic Boulevard (despite their shouting-distance proximity, one technically is in Atlantic Beach; the other, in Neptune Beach). The guest units are spacious except for their faux-marble—but somewhat cramped—bathrooms. Choice units on the beachfront have balconies, but the majority of rooms don't face the beach nor do they have balconies. Plantains Restaurant is a fine spot for an alfresco beachside meal, and it has live music on weekends. There's a lounge in the restaurant and a summertime tiki bar beside the swimming pool by the beach.

1 Ocean Blvd. (at beach end of Atlantic Blvd.), Atlantic Beach, FL 32233. C **800/874-6000** or 904/249-7402. Fax 904/247-1517. www.seaturtle.com. 193 units. $119–$209 double. AE, DC, DISC, MC, V. **Amenities:**

Restaurant (American), 2 bars; outdoor pool; access to nearby health club; water-sports equipment rentals; limited room service; babysitting; laundry service, coin-op washers and dryers. *In room:* A/C, TV, fax, dataport, minibar, fridge, coffeemaker, hair dryer, iron.

Worth a Splurge

Sawgrass Marriott Resort & Beach Club ★★   One of the nation's largest golf resorts, this duffer's paradise is virtually surrounded by 99 holes, including the Pete Dye–designed **TPC at Sawgrass** ★★★, home of the annual Players Championship in March. In fact, this course has appeared on every critic's "best of" list since it opened in 1980. Overlooking the TPC's picturesque 13th hole, the seven-story hotel sits beside one of the lakes that make the course so challenging. The view augments the gourmet fusion cuisine served in the Augustine Grille, the hotel's signature restaurant. The guest rooms in the hotel are comfortable but of modest size. Best for families are the fully equipped one- and two-bedroom "villa suites" (condominium apartments) on or near a golf course, which offer large furnished patios or balconies. Especially luxurious are the one- to three-bedroom beachfront units, which sport huge kitchens, living rooms with working fireplaces, full dining rooms, and large, screened wooden decks. A complimentary shuttle takes guests to the ocean-side Cabana Beach Club for snacks and meals. The children's program here is overseen by Jacksonville's branch of the renowned Mayo Clinic.

1000 PGA Tour Blvd. (off Fla. A1A between U.S. 210 and J. Turner Butler Blvd.), Ponte Vedra Beach, FL 32082. © **800/457-GOLF**, 800/228-9290, or 904/285-7777. Fax 904/285-0906. www.sawgrassmarriott.com. 508 units. $109–$125 double; $159–$199 suites and villas. Add $15 per night per unit for resort amenities fee. Golf packages available. AE, DC, DISC, MC, V. Valet parking $12; free self-parking. **Amenities:** 7 restaurants (Fusion/American), 4 bars; 3 outdoor pools (2 heated); 5 golf courses; 17 tennis courts; 2 health clubs; Jacuzzi; water-sports equipment rentals; bike rental; children's programs; game room; concierge; activities desk; business center; limited room service; babysitting; laundry service; coin-op washers and dryers; concierge-level rooms. *In room:* A/C, TV, dataport, kitchen (condos only), minibar, coffeemaker, hair dryer, iron.

GREAT DEALS ON DINING

The convention and visitor bureau's annual guide (see "Essentials," earlier in this section) contains a complete list of restaurants. For more choices, check listings in the "Shorelines" and "Go" sections of Friday's *Florida-Times-Union* (www.jacksonville.com) and in *Folio Weekly* (www.folioweekly.com), the free local alternative paper available at restaurants, hotels, and nightspots all over town.

IN DOWNTOWN JACKSONVILLE

Southbank Riverwalk is the city's up-and-coming mecca for eating out. B.B.'s and the River City Brewing Company, both reviewed below, are here, and you can splurge big-time at the super-expensive riverfront branches of **Ruth's Chris Steakhouse,** in the Hilton Jacksonville Riverfront, 1201 Riverplace Blvd. (© **904/396-6200**); **Morton's of Chicago,** 1510 Riverplace Blvd. (© **904/399-3933**); and **The Chart House,** in the Radisson Riverwalk Hotel, 1515 Prudential Dr. (© **904/398-3353**). Also on the very high end, the **Wine Cellar,** 1314 Prudential Dr. (© **904/398-8989**), offers fine continental fare and has a wine list to justify its name.

You will find a plethora of good cafes and restaurants in which to take breaks from your shopping excursions to the San Marco Square and Avondale neighborhoods.

Don't forget that on the north side of the river, **The Jacksonville Landing** has several full-service restaurants and an inexpensive food court with outdoor seating (see "Exploring the Area," earlier in this section).

B.B.'s ★★ ECLECTIC   A block south of the Southbank Riverwalk, this bistro son of Biscottis (see below) is one of the city's hottest restaurants. You'll find local yuppies congregating at the big marble-top bar on one side of the sometimes noisy Art Deco dining room, especially during weekday "wine-downs" featuring beer and wine specials and discounted appetizers (the mozzarella bruschetta is a big hit both here and at Biscottis), from 4 to 7pm. There's a small but inventive selection of sandwiches, salads, and individual-size pizzas available all day. Featuring local seafood, the nightly main-course specials run the gamut from roasted sea bass with citrus couscous to seared scallops with lemongrass-scented rice, sun-dried tomatoes, and lobster butter. Save room for the famous desserts, available for inspection in the chiller case located near the open kitchen. Saturday brunch sees the likes of yummy Benedict-style crab cakes and flaming bananas Foster.

1019 Hendricks Ave. (between Prudential Dr. and Home St.). © **904/306-0100.** Call for priority seating. Main courses $12–$22; sandwiches and salads $5–$8; pizzas $6–$8. AE, DC, DISC, MC, V. Mon–Thurs 11am–10:30pm; Fri 11am–midnight; Sat 10am–midnight (Sat brunch 10am–2pm).

Biscottis ★★ *Value* ECLECTIC   This brick-walled little gem in the trendy Avondale neighborhood might have come out of New York's East Village. A young and hip wait staff is pleasant and well informed. You can start your day here with a pastry and a cup of joe. For lunch and dinner, daily specials like pan-seared tuna or pork loin are always fresh and beautifully presented. The huge and inventive salads are especially good: Try the Asian version with chicken breast, orange slices, roasted peppers, and creamy sesame dressing. Pizzas, too, are served with wonderfully exotic and delicious toppings—ever try guacamole and black beans on your slice? And by all means don't leave without sampling the wonderful desserts. On warm days choose a tiny sidewalk table for great people-watching. If the wait's too long here, several other choices ranging from a neighborhood diner to expensive haute cuisine line these 2 blocks of St. Johns Avenue in Avondale.

3556 St. Johns Ave. (between Talbot and Ingleside aves. in Avondale). © **904/387-2060.** Main courses $9–$17; sandwiches and salads $5–$8; pizzas $7–$8.50. AE, DC, DISC, MC, V. Tues–Thurs 7am–10pm; Fri 7am–midnight; Sat 8am–midnight; Sun 8am–3pm.

River City Brewing Company ★★ NEW AMERICAN/LOUISIANA   Occupying a prime location on the Southbank Riverwalk, this gorgeous restaurant and microbrewery is a good choice for lunch or dinner with dramatic waterfront and skyline views. For an even better vantage point, sit outside on the enormous covered deck. The quality of the cuisine very nearly lives up to the vista, especially the "hanging" coconut shrimp served with a sweet Mandarin orange sauce. For a main course, try the Cajun chicken linguine with mushrooms and ham in a spicy cream sauce, or pretzel-encrusted mahimahi with a mustard cream sauce. While you can easily drop a bundle in the main dining room, you can devise an inexpensive, simpler meal in the Brew Haus, a large sports bar that opens to the big covered deck and the riverbank. Bands play on the deck weekend evenings. Sunday brunch brings incredible buffets with decadent desserts.

835 Museum Circle (on Southbank Riverwalk). © **904/398-2299.** Main courses $15–$18; sandwiches and salads $5–$11. Sun brunch buffet $20 adults, $15 seniors, $12 children 3–12. AE, DC, DISC, MC, V. Dining room Sun–Thurs 11am–3pm and 5–10pm; Fri–Sat 11am–3pm and 5–11pm; Sun 10:30am–2:30pm and 5–10pm. Pub and deck (light fare) Sun–Thurs 3–10pm (bar to midnight); Fri–Sat 3–11pm (bar to 2am). Closed Christmas. Valet parking available on weekends.

AT THE BEACHES

In addition to the Ragtime Tavern & Taproom (see below), you'll have several dining (and drinking) choices in the brick storefronts of Town Center, the old-time beach village at the end of Atlantic Boulevard. Among the best is the oceanfront **Plantains,** in the Sea Turtle Inn (see "Accommodations You Can Afford," above).

Old Siam ★★ THAI   The best of several Thai restaurants here, this sophisticated little cafe serves fine cuisine and a good selection of wines to match the fare's spicy yet subtle flavors. The signature dish is a seafood special: shrimp, sea scallops, mussels, squid, and crab claws in a red chili sauce accented with sweet basil. The "number 3" spice level (out of 6) touches your tongue but does not overwhelm the other seasonings. Standard favorites like Pad Thai are light and perfectly balanced with sweet and slightly sour fish sauce.

1716 N. 3rd St. (Fla. A1A, in Holiday Plaza shopping center, between 16th and 17th aves. N.), Jacksonville Beach. © 904/247-7763. Main courses $10–$23. AE, DISC, MC, V. Mon–Thurs 5–10pm; Fri–Sat 5–11pm; Sun 5–9:30pm.

Ragtime Tavern & Taproom ★★ SEAFOOD/CAJUN   In the heart of Town Center, this lively sister of St. Augustine's A1A Ale Works offers six hand-crafted brews, including a refreshing pilsner known as Dolphin's Breath. You can imbibe at one of two bars on either end of the building. In between, a rabbit warren of dining rooms provides fine enough fare to keep it filled with local professionals right through the cool winter months. A variety of appetizers includes conch fritters and coconut shrimp. For a main course, you can select from seared sesame-coated yellowfin tuna (the best dish here if you like rare fish) or several other treatments of fish, shrimp, chicken, and pastas. Save room for some New Orleans–style beignets for dessert. Also from the Big Easy, po'boy sandwiches are served at all hours. Good local bands make music here Thursday through Sunday evenings.

207 Atlantic Blvd. (at First Ave.), Atlantic Beach. © 904/241-7877. Call to get on waiting list. Main courses $11.50–$22; sandwiches and salads $6–$8. AE, DC, DISC, MC, V. Sun–Thurs 11am–10:30pm; Fri–Sat 11am–11pm (bar open later).

Super-Cheap Eats

Singleton's Seafood Shack ★★ *Value* SEAFOOD   This rustic fish camp has been serving every imaginable kind of fresh-off-the-boat seafood since 1969. And rustic it is, constructed primarily of unpainted, well-weathered plywood nailed to two-by-fours. Unlike most other fish camps that tend to overwork the deep fryer, the fried standbys like conch fritters, shrimp, clam strips, oysters, and squid actually retain their seafood taste! In fact, the fried shrimp are among the best we've had anywhere. Singleton's also offers other preparations such as blackened mahimahi and Cajun shrimp. Best bets at lunch are the fried shrimp or oyster po'boy sandwiches covered in crispy onion rings. At dinner your Styrofoam plate will come stacked with a choice of side items like black beans and rice, marvelous horseradishy coleslaw, fries, and hush puppies. You can also choose from a selection of chicken.

4728 Ocean St. (Fla. A1A, at St. Johns River Ferry landing), Mayport. © 904/246-4442. Main courses $11–$18; sandwiches $2–$7. AE, DISC, MC, V. Sun–Thurs 10am–9pm; Fri–Sat 10am–10pm.

JACKSONVILLE AFTER DARK

In addition to the spots recommended below, check the listings in the "Shorelines" and "Go" sections of Friday's *Florida Times-Union* (www.jacksonville.com) and *Folio Weekly* (www.folioweekly.com), the free local alternative paper, available at restaurants, at hotels, and all over town. Another source is www.jaxevents.com.

THE PERFORMING ARTS   With the 73,000-seat **Alltell Stadium,** at East Duval and Haines streets (© 904/630-3900); the 10,600-seat **Jacksonville**

Veterans Memorial Coliseum, 1145 E. Adams St. (© **904/630-3900** for information or 904/353-3309 to charge tickets); the 3,200-seat **Florida Times-Union Center for the Performing Arts,** 300 Water St., between Hogan and Pearl streets (© **904/630-3900**); and the revitalized **Ritz Theatre** (© **904/632-5555;** see "Exploring the Area," earlier in this section), Jacksonville has plenty of seats for concerts, touring Broadway shows, dance companies, and big-name performers. Call or check the sources above for what's playing.

THE BAR SCENE You will find several libation options downtown at **Jacksonville Landing** (see "Exploring the Area," above), including a lively waterfront **Hooters** (© **904/356-5400**), plus free outdoor rock, blues, country, and jazz concerts every Friday and Saturday night except during winter. There's also live music on weekends across the river at the **River City Brewing Company** (see "Great Deals on Dining," above).

Out at Town Center, at the ocean end of Atlantic Boulevard, one of several popular spots is **Ragtime Tavern & Taproom** (see "Great Deals on Dining," above), where local groups play live jazz and blues Wednesday to Sunday nights. Weekends, especially, the place is really jumping and the crowd is young, but it's lively rather than rowdy. Across the street is the **Sun Dog Diner,** at 207 Atlantic Blvd. (© **904/241-8221**), with nightly acoustic music and decent diner food. If these don't fit your mood, there are more nightspots in Town Center.

5 Amelia Island ★★

32 miles NE of Jacksonville, 192 miles NE of Orlando, 372 miles N of Miami

With 13 beautiful miles of beach and a quaint Victorian town, Amelia Island is a charming getaway about a 45-minute drive northeast of downtown Jacksonville. Overall, this skinny barrier island, 18 miles long by 3 miles wide, has more in common with the Low Country of Georgia (across Cumberland Sound from here) and South Carolina than with other resort areas in Florida. In fact, it's more like St. Simons Island in Georgia or Hilton Head Island in South Carolina.

Amelia itself has five distinct personalities. First is its southern end, an expensive and exclusive real-estate development built in a forest of twisted, moss-laden live oaks. Here you will find world-class tennis and golfing at two of Florida's most luxurious resorts. Second is modest **American Beach,** founded in the 1930s so that African Americans would have access to the ocean in this then-segregated part of the country. Today it's a modest, predominantly black community tucked away among all that south-end wealth. Third is the island's middle, a traditional beach community with a mix of affordable motels, cottages, condominiums, and a seaside inn. Fourth is the historic bay-side town of **Fernandina Beach** ★★★, which boasts a 50-square-block area of gorgeous Victorian, Queen Anne, and Italianate homes listed in the National Register of Historic Places. And fifth is lovely **Fort Clinch State Park,** which keeps developers from turning the island's northern end into more ritzy resorts.

The town of Fernandina Beach dates from the post–Civil War period, when Union soldiers who had occupied Fort Clinch began returning to the island. In the late 19th century Amelia's timber, phosphate, and naval-stores industries boomed. Back then, the town was an active seaport, with 14 foreign consuls in residence. Even earlier, a railroad went from here 155 miles across Florida to Cedar Key; it was part of a planned worldwide trade network cut short by the Civil War. You'll see (and occasionally smell) the paper mills that still stand near the small seaport here. The island experienced another economic explosion in

Amelia Island

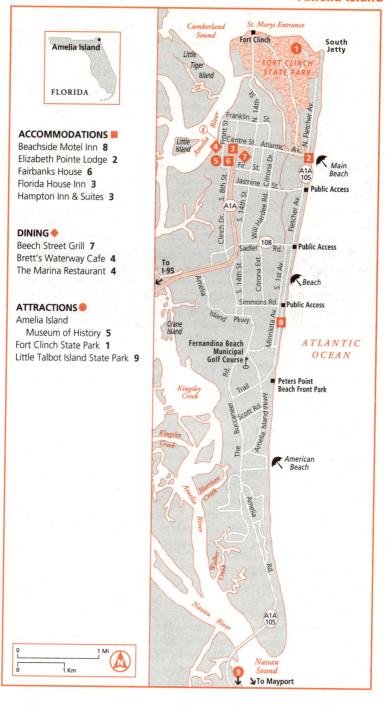

the 1970s and 1980s, when real-estate developers built the condominiums, the cottages, and the two big resorts on the island's southern end. In recent years, Fernandina Beach has seen another big boom, this time in bed-and-breakfast establishments.

ESSENTIALS
GETTING THERE The island is served by **Jacksonville International Airport** (see "Essentials" in section 4 of this chapter). Skirting the Atlantic in places, the scenic drive here from downtown Jacksonville is via Fla. A1A and the St. Johns River Ferry. The fast, four-lane way is via I-95 north and the Buccaneer Trail (Fla. A1A) east.

VISITOR INFORMATION For advance information, contact the **Amelia Island–Fernandina Beach–Yulee Chamber of Commerce,** 102 Centre St. (P.O. Box 472), Fernandina Beach, FL 32035 (© **800/2-AMELIA** or 904/ 277-0717; fax 904/261-6997; www.ameliaisland.org). The chamber's visitor information center, in the old train station at the bay end of Centre Street, is open Monday to Friday from 9am to 5pm and Saturday from 9am to 2pm.

GETTING AROUND There's no public transportation on this 13-mile-long island, so you'll need a vehicle. An informative and entertaining way to tour the historic district is on a 30-minute ride with **Old Towne Carriage Company** (© **904/277-1555**), whose horse-drawn carriages leave from the waterfront on Centre Street between 6:30 and 9pm. Advance reservations are essential. Rides cost $15 for adults, $7.50 for kids under 13, with a minimum of $55 per ride. The carriage company closes for 2 months during the winter when the horses are put out to pasture.

Another excellent way to see the town is on a walking tour sponsored by the Amelia Island Museum of History (see "An Old Jail Turned Historic Museum," below).

WHAT TO SEE & DO
HITTING THE BEACH
Thanks to a reclamation project, the widest beaches here are at the exclusive enclave on the island's southern third. Even if you aren't staying at one of the swanky resorts, you can enjoy this section at **Peters Point Beach Front Park,** on Fla. A1A north of the Ritz-Carlton. The park has picnic shelters and restrooms.

North of the resort, the beach has public access points with free parking every quarter mile or so. The center of activity is **Main Beach,** at the ocean end of Atlantic Avenue (Fla. A1A), with good swimming, restrooms, picnic shelters, showers, a food concession, and a playground. There's lots of free parking, and this area is popular with families.

The beach at **Fort Clinch State Park**, which wraps around the island's heavily forested northern end, is backed by rolling dunes and is filled with shells and driftwood. A jetty and a pier jutting into Cumberland Sound are popular with anglers. There are showers and changing rooms at the pier. Elsewhere in the park, you might see an alligator—and certainly some of the 170 species of birds who live here—by hiking the Willow Pond nature trail. Rangers lead nature tours on the trail, usually beginning at 10:30am on Saturday. There also are 6 miles of off-road bike trails here. You also can visit the remarkably well-preserved **Fort Clinch.** Construction began in 1847 on the northern tip of the island and was still underway when Union troops occupied it in 1862. The fort was abandoned shortly after the Civil War, except for a brief reactivation in 1898 during the

Spanish-American War. Reenactors gather the first full weekend of each month to re-create how the Union soldiers lived in the fort in 1864. Rangers are on duty at the fort year-round, and they lead candlelight tours on Friday and Saturday evenings during summer, beginning about an hour after sunset. The candlelight tours cost $3 per person. You can arrange guided tours at other times for an extra fee. The park entrance is on Atlantic Avenue near the beach. Entrance fees are $3.25 per vehicle with up to eight occupants, $1 for pedestrians and bicyclists. Admission to the fort costs $2 and is free for children under 5. The park is open daily 8am to sunset; the fort, daily 9am to 5pm. For a current schedule of tours and events, contact the park at 2601 Atlantic Ave., Fernandina Beach, FL 32034 (© 904/277-7274; www.dep.state.fl.us/parks/district2/fortclinch).

The park has 62 **campsites,** some behind the dunes at the beach (no shade out there), most in a forest along the sound side. They cost $20.65 per night with electricity, $18.55 without, including tax. Pets cost an extra $2 a night. You can reserve a site up to 11 months in advance (a very good idea in summer) by calling © **800/326-3521** or going to the website www.reserveamerica.com.

Pets on leashes are allowed on all the island's public beaches and in Fort Clinch State Park.

AFFORDABLE OUTDOOR PURSUITS

BOATING, FISHING, SAILING & KAYAKING The **Amelia Island Charter Boat Association,** at Tiger Point Marina on 14th Street north of the historic district (© **800/229-1682** or 904/261-2870), can help arrange deep-sea fishing charters, party-boat excursions, and dolphin-watching and sightseeing cruises. Other charter boats dock at Fernandina Harbor Marina, downtown at the foot of Centre Street.

Voyager Adventures, based at Fernandina Harbor Marina, 3977 First Ave. (© **904/321-1244;** fax 904/321-2505; www.voyageradventures.com), has several cruises aboard the *Voyager,* a 100-foot replica of a 19th-century gaff-rigged packet schooner. A prime destination is Cumberland Island, across the sound in Georgia (the late John F. Kennedy, Jr. was married over there without a single member of the paparazzi present). The half-day trips cost $35 for adults and $16 for kids under 12. Also based at the marina, **Windward Sailing School** (© **904/261-9125;** www.windwardsailing.com) will teach you to skipper your boat. Call these companies for details and reservations.

You have to be careful in the currents, but the backwaters here are great for kayaking, whether you're a beginner or a pro. Ray and Jody Hetchka of **Kayak Amelia** ★★ (© **888/30-KAYAK** or 904/321-0697; www.kayakamelia.com) have beginner- and advanced-level trips on the back bays, creeks, and marshes. Half-day trips go for about $50 per person, all-day $95. Call in advance for reservations, which are required, and they will schedule a pick-up.

GOLF Two of Florida's better courses are at **Amelia Island Plantation** (© **800/874-6878** or 904/261-6161) and **The Ritz-Carlton Amelia Island** (© **800/241-3333** or 904/277-1100), but they usually are reserved for guests of these two luxury resorts. The rest of us can play the new 18-hole **Royal Amelia Golf Links,** 4477 Amelia Rd. (© **904/491-8500;** www.royalamelia.com), or the older and less expensive 27-hole **Fernandina Municipal Golf Course,** 2800 Bill Melton Rd. (© **904/277-7370).**

HORSEBACK RIDING You can go riding on the beach with **Kelly Seahorse Ranch** (© **904/491-5166**), near Little Talbot Island State Park. Rides cost $35 per person, and reservations are required. There are pony rides for kids, too. The ranch is open daily from 10am to dark.

AN OLD JAIL TURNED HISTORIC MUSEUM
Amelia Island Museum of History ★   Housed in the Nassau County jail built of brick in 1878, this award-winning local museum explains Amelia Island's fascinating history, from Timucuan Indian times through its possession by France, Spain, Great Britain, the United States, and the Confederacy (the island changed flags eight times). Only an upstairs photo gallery is open for casual inspection, so plan to take the 1-hour, 15-minute docent-led tour.

The museum also offers excellent **walking tours** of historic Centre Street on Thursday and Friday from September through June. These depart at 3pm from the chamber of commerce (see "Essentials," above) and cost $8 for adults, $3 for students. You can't make a reservation; just show up. Longer tours of the entire 50-square-block historic district can be arranged with 24-hour notice; these cost $10 per person, with a minimum of four persons required.

233 S. 3rd St. (between Beech and Cedar sts.). © 904/261-7378. www.ameliaislandmuseumofhistory.org. Admission by donation. Tours $4 adults, $2 students. Mon–Fri 10am–5pm; Sat 10am–4pm. Tours Mon–Sat 11am and 2pm.

SHOPPING
Stroll down **Centre Street** in downtown Fernandina Beach, with its vintage storefronts and charming boutiques. Quality antiques stores, consignment shops, and bookstores line the wide boulevard ending at the marina. Be sure to poke your head into the **Island Art Association Gallery,** 205 Centre St. (© **904/261-7020**), a co-op exhibiting works by local artists.

On the south end of the island on Fla. A1A, **Palmetto Walk,** under a canopy of live oaks, and the **Village Shops,** at the entrance to Amelia Plantation, are other good shopping bets.

The chamber of commerce has complete lists and descriptions of the island's many upscale stores (see "Essentials," above).

ACCOMMODATIONS YOU CAN AFFORD
More than two dozen of the town's charming Victorian and Queen Anne houses have been restored and turned into B&Bs, and apparently they all stay busy, at least on weekends. Industry veteran David Caples, who holds seminars nationwide for wanna-be innkeepers, is based here at the Elizabeth Pointe Lodge (see below). For a complete list, contact the chamber of commerce (see "Essentials," above) or contact the **Amelia Island Bed & Breakfast Association** (© **888/ 277-0218;** www.ameliaislandinns.com). You can tour all the B&Bs during an island-wide open house the first weekend in December.

A number of agencies will book vacation properties ranging from affordable cottages to magnificent mansions. Contact **Amelia Island Lodging Systems,** 584 S. Fletcher Ave., Fernandina Beach, FL 32034 (© **800/872-8531** or 904/261-4148; fax 904/261-9200; www.amelialodgings.com), which even has two lighthouse replicas for rent. Or try **Lodging Resources, Inc.,** at the Elizabeth Pointe Lodge, 98 S. Fletcher Ave., Fernandina Beach, FL 32034 (© **904/ 277-4851;** fax 904/277-4851), which also has a lighthouse in its inventory.

There's a regular **Hampton Inn** (© **800/HAMPTON** or 904/321-1111) on Sadler Road a block from the beach. It's less expensive and a lot less charming than the Hampton Inn & Suites in the historic district (see below).

Your best **camping** option here is **Fort Clinch State Park** (see "Hitting the Beach," above).

Beachside Motel Inn *Value* This family-run property—the only motel beside the beach here—is clean and well maintained. The white-and-blue, two-story, 1970s stucco building sits on a beautiful stretch of public but uncluttered beach. The rooms, many with ocean views, are spacious and furnished with standard motel furnishings. Many long-term visitors return each season to stay in the efficiencies, which have fully equipped kitchens. An outdoor pool is surrounded by lounge chairs and a spacious deck that overlooks the ocean. The hotel is convenient to lots of sports activities and restaurants.

3172 S. Fletcher Ave. (Fla. A1A, south of Simmons Rd.), Fernandina Beach, FL 32034. © 904/261-4236. www.beachsidemotel.com. 20 units. $65–$129 double; $89–$169 efficiency. Rates include continental breakfast. Weekly discounts available. AE, DISC, MC, V. **Amenities:** Outdoor pool. *In room:* A/C, TV, kitchen (efficiencies only).

Florida House Inn ★ *Value* Built near a railroad in 1857, this clapboard Victorian building is Florida's oldest operating hotel. Ulysses S. Grant stayed here, as did Cuban revolutionary José Marti; and the Rockefellers and Carnegies broke bread at the boardinghouse-style dining room that still provides family-style, all-you-can-eat traditional Southern fare. You can rock away on the two gingerbread-trimmed front verandas (Grant made a speech from the upstairs porch) or on a back porch overlooking a brick courtyard shaded by a huge oak tree. The 11 rooms in the original building, all up to modern standards, are loaded with antiques. Most have working fireplaces, and some have claw-foot tubs. Four rooms are in a wing added in 1998; one of these has log-cabin walls, and the others are done country-style. All have fireplaces and whirlpool tubs.

20 S. 3rd St. (between Centre and Ash sts.), Fernandina Beach, FL 32034. © 800/258-3301 or 904/261-3300. Fax 904/277-3831. www.floridahouse.com. 15 units. $79–$179 double. Rates include full breakfast. AE, DISC, MC, V. Pet dogs accepted ($10 nightly fee). **Amenities:** Restaurant (Southern), bar; coin-op washers and dryers. *In room:* A/C, TV, coffeemaker, hair dryer, iron.

Hampton Inn & Suites ★★ When plans were announced a few years ago to build this four-story hotel in the center of the historic district, they created quite a stir among preservationists. But the all-woman hotel firm of Miriam Taylor & Co. put those fears to rest by designing one of the most unusual Hampton Inns I've ever seen. Although there's only one building, the exterior looks like a row of different structures, all in the styles and sherbet hues of the Victorian storefronts lining Centre Street. Above a curving staircase rising in the two-story Victorian-style lobby, quadrants of an unusual ceiling clock have been painted to represent the 4 centuries of Fernandina Beach's history. Wooden floors taken from an old Jacksonville church, slatted door panels evocative of 19th-century sailing schooners, and many other touches add to the Victorian ambience. About half of the guest rooms are near the top of the romance scale: king beds, gas-burning fireplaces, two-person whirlpool tubs. (If honeymooning in a Hampton Inn has never crossed your mind, you haven't seen the luxurious, two-room bridal suite here.) The standard suites are large enough for families, and the other standard rooms are adequately equipped for business travelers, making this a good choice for everyone. About a third of the units have balconies. Those higher up on the west side have fine views over the river and marshes. The only drawback: Trains slowly rumble by on the west side a few times a day.

19 S. 2nd St. (between Centre and Ash sts.), Fernandina Beach, FL 32034. © 800/HAMPTON or 904/491-4911. Fax 904/491-4910. 122 units. $114–$179 double. Rates include extensive breakfast buffet. AE, DC, DISC, MC, V. **Amenities:** Outdoor pool; exercise room; Jacuzzi; business center; babysitting; laundry service; coin-op washers and dryers. *In room:* A/C, TV, dataport, fridge, coffeemaker, hair dryer, iron.

WORTH A SPLURGE

Elizabeth Pointe Lodge ★★   You'd swear that this three-story, Nantucket-style shingled beauty, sitting right on the beach, was a lovingly maintained Victorian home—but you'd be wrong. Built in 1991 by B&B gurus David and Susan Caples, it has big-paned windows that look out from the comfy library (with stone fireplace) and dining room to an expansive front porch and the surf beyond. Antiques and reproductions, handmade quilts, and other touches lend the 20 rooms in the main building a turn-of-the-century cottage ambience. They all have oversize bathtubs. Four other rooms are in the Harris Lodge next door, and the two-bedroom, two-bathroom Miller Cottage is also available.

98 S. Fletcher Ave. (just south of Atlantic Ave.), Fernandina Beach, FL 32034. © **800/772-3459** or 904/277-4851. Fax 904/277-6500. www.elizabethpointelodge.com. 24 units, 1 cottage. $160–$240 double; $270 cottage. Rates include buffet breakfast and evening social hour. Packages available. AE, DISC, MC, V. **Amenities:** Restaurant (American), bar; access to nearby health club; Jacuzzi; water-sports equipment rental; bike rental; 24-hr. room service; laundry service. *In room:* A/C, TV, dataport, hair dryer, iron.

Fairbanks House ★   Having all the amenities and almost as much privacy as a first-class hotel in a superbly refurbished 1885 Italianate home, the Fairbanks House is a top B&B choice in the historic district. Many rooms and all the cottages offer private entrances for guests who prefer not to walk through the main house. Room no. 3, in the back of the house on the main floor, is one of the finest rooms, with a private entrance, a large sitting room, a plush king-size bed, period antiques, porcelain, oil paintings, and fresh flowers. Occupying the entire top floor, the two-bedroom Tower Suite has plenty of room to spread out, plus 360° views and its own whirlpool tub. Five other units here have whirlpool tubs. Note that Fairbanks is the only B&B on the island with a swimming pool. No smoking indoors or out is allowed.

227 S. 7th St. (between Beech and Cedar sts.), Fernandina Beach, Amelia Island, FL 32034. © **800/261-4838** or 904/277-0500. Fax 904/277-3103. www.fairbankshouse.com. 9 units, 3 detached cottages. $160–$275 double; $210 cottage. Rates include full breakfast. Packages available. AE, DISC, MC, V. **Amenities:** Heated outdoor pool. *In room:* A/C, TV, dataport, kitchen (cottage only), minibar, fridge, coffeemaker, hair dryer, iron.

GREAT DEALS ON DINING

You'll find several restaurants, pubs, and snack shops along Centre Street, between the bay and 8th Street (Fla. A1A), in Fernandina Beach's old town. And don't forget the **Florida House Inn** (see "Accommodations You Can Afford," above), which serves boardinghouse-style, all-you-can-eat lunches and dinners Tuesday to Saturday from 11:30am to 2:30pm ($7 per person) and from 5:30 to 9pm ($12 per person).

The Marina Restaurant *Value* AMERICAN   Occupying a brick store built in the 1880s, this quintessential small-town restaurant has been feeding Low Country fare to the locals since 1965. Granted, a lot of the seafood here is fried and broiled, but you can order crab-stuffed shrimp or flounder as well as grouper topped with scallops and a garlicky wine sauce. Budgeteers love the $10-and-under list of Southern favorites such as country-fried steak, breaded veal cutlet, grilled pork chops, and fried chicken. Meat loaf with a tomato and basil gravy, stuffed bell peppers with a Greek-style tomato sauce, and other lunchtime specials come with three fresh country-style vegetables, which are themselves worth the price of the meal. Hearty breakfasts feature eggs, omelets, French toast, and hotcakes.

101 Centre St. (at Front St.), Fernandina Beach. © **904/261-5310**. Main courses $8–$19; breakfast $2–$6; sandwiches $5–$9. DC, MC, V. Daily 7–10am and 11:30am–9pm.

WORTH A SPLURGE

Beech Street Grill ★★ REGIONAL/NEW AMERICAN   Almost on a par with The Grill in the Ritz-Carlton, the Beech Street Grill pleases all palates with a rich menu of fish, chicken, and meat choices, including seasonal game dishes like roasted venison loin in a black currant sauce with sweet potato and onion hash. Nightly fish specialties are always exceptional (some can be pricier than printed menu options). A Parmesan-encrusted red snapper with a mustard basil sauce is superb. Seared tuna is always perfect, too. The dense and tasty crab cakes and the chewy steamed dumplings are great choices for starters, as is the huge mixed-green salad with mustard-basil vinaigrette, toasted pecans, and blue cheese. Housed in a century-old landmark home and in a newer wing to one side, five dining rooms offer large tables in a lively atmosphere. Attentive and knowledgeable waiters serve the showy plates with efficiency and grace. The upstairs features a pianist.

801 Beech St. (at 8th St./Fla. A1A), Fernandina Beach. © 904/277-3662. Reservations strongly recommended. Main courses $19.50–$27.50. AE, DC, DISC, MC, V. Daily 6–10pm.

Brett's Waterway Cafe SEAFOOD/STEAKS   You'll pay for the view, but this friendly waterfront cafe at the foot of Centre Street is the only place in town to dine while watching the boats coming and going on the river—and to sip a drink while watching the sun set over the marshes between here and the mainland. In fine weather you can grab a table outside by the docks. One of the best dishes is shrimp broiled with a sun-dried tomato cream sauce. The nightly fresh fish specials are well prepared, and there are steaks and chops, some of them tossed with fresh oysters. At lunch, try the bacon, lettuce, and fried-green-tomato sandwich.

1 S. Front St. (at Centre St., on the water), Fernandina Beach. © 904/261-2660. Main courses $15–$26. AE, MC, V. Mon–Sat 11:30am–2:30pm and 5:30–9:30pm; Sun 5:30–9:30pm.

AMELIA ISLAND AFTER DARK

This romantic island goes to bed early. If you tire of the lounges in the island's resorts, check out the **Palace Saloon,** 117 Centre St., at 2nd Street (© **904/ 261-6320**). It claims to be Florida's oldest watering hole (open since 1878). Complete with a pressed-tin ceiling and a 40-foot-long mahogany bar, it once hosted the Carnegies and the du Ponts. Some nights you'll find live local blues or rock. It's open daily from 11am until the last drunk crawls home.

Another popular local watering hole, **O'Kane's Irish Pub & Eatery,** 318 Centre St., at 4th Street (© **904/261-1000**), has live music until midnight Monday to Thursday, until 1:30am on weekends.

13

Northwest Florida: The Panhandle

by Bill Goodwin

If you like beaches, you'll love Florida's northwestern Panhandle. Thanks to quartz washed down from the Appalachian Mountains, the beaches here along the Gulf of Mexico consist of dazzlingly white sand that is so talcum-like it actually squeaks when you walk across it. And walk across it you can, for some 100 miles of these incomparable sands are protected in state parks and the gorgeous Gulf Islands National Seashore.

Pensacola, Fort Walton Beach, Destin, and Panama City Beach have long been summertime beach meccas for families, couples, and singles from the adjoining states of Alabama and Georgia. Their demand for inexpensive lodging and meals make prices here among the most reasonable in the state, and their tastes put Southern specialties like turnip greens and cheese grits on many menus. And thanks to the Panhandle's proximity to their home states, this entire area has the languid charm of the Deep South.

But there's more to the northwestern Panhandle than beaches and Southern charm. Championship catches of grouper, amberjack, snapper, mackerel, cobia, sailfish, wahoo, tuna, and blue marlin have made Destin one of the world's fishing capitals. In the interior near Pensacola, the Blackwater, Shoal, and Yellow rivers teem with bass, bream, catfish, and largemouth bass, and also offer some of Florida's best canoeing and kayaking adventures.

The area also is steeped in history. Rivaling St. Augustine as Florida's oldest town, picturesque Pensacola carefully preserves a heritage derived from Spanish, French, English, and American conquest. Famous for its oysters, Apalachicola saw the invention of the air conditioner, a moment of great historical note in Florida. And Tallahassee, seat of state government since 1824, has a host of 19th-century buildings and homes, including the Old State Capitol.

EXPLORING NORTHWEST FLORIDA BY CAR

Both I-10 and U.S. 98 link Tallahassee and Pensacola, some 200 miles apart. The fastest route is I-10, but all you'll see is a huge pine forest divided by two strips of concrete. Plan to take U.S. 98, a scenic excursion in itself. Although it can be traffic-clogged in the beach towns during summer, U.S. 98 has some beautiful stretches out in the country, particularly as it literally skirts the bay east of Apalachicola and the gulf west of Port St. Joe. It's also lovely along skinny Okaloosa Island and across the high-rise bridge between Fort Walton Beach and Destin. From the bridge, you'll see the brilliant color of the gulf and immediately understand why they call this the Emerald Coast.

The Panhandle

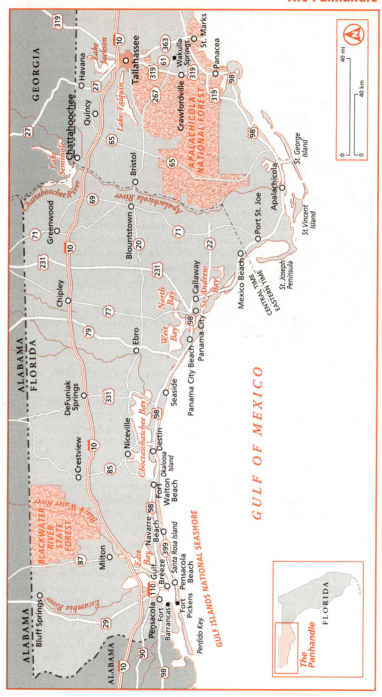

1 Pensacola ★★

191 miles W of Tallahassee, 354 miles W of Jacksonville

Native Americans left pottery shards and artifacts in the coastal dunes here centuries before Tristan de Luna arrived with a band of Spanish colonists in 1559. Although his settlement lasted only 2 years, modern Pensacolans claim that de Luna made their town the oldest in North America. Pensacola actually dates its permanence from a Spanish colony established here in 1698, however, so St. Augustine wins this friendly feud, having been permanently settled in 1565.

France, Great Britain, the United States, and the Confederacy subsequently captured (and in one case recaptured) this strategically important deep-water port. They left Pensacola with a charming blend of Old Spanish brickwork, colonial French balconies reminiscent of New Orleans, magnificent Victorian mansions built by British and American lumber barons, and its motto, "City of Five Flags."

West of town, the magnificent National Museum of Naval Aviation at the U.S. Naval Air Station celebrates the storied past of navy and marine corps pilots who trained at Pensacola. Based here, the Blue Angels demonstrate the high-tech present with thrilling exhibitions of precision flying in the navy's fastest fighters.

Also on the Naval Station, historic Fort Barrancas looks across the bay to Perdido Key and Santa Rosa Island, which reach out like narrow pincers to form the harbor. Out there, powdery white-sand beaches beckon sun-and-surf lovers to their spectacular gulf shores, which include Pensacola Beach, a small family-oriented resort, and most of Florida's share of Gulf Islands National Seashore, home of historic Fort Pickens.

ESSENTIALS

GETTING THERE **Pensacola Regional Airport** (© 850/436-5005; www.flypensacola.com), on 12th Avenue at Airport Road, is served by **AirTran** (© 800/AIR-TRAN), **Continental** (© 800/525-0280), **Delta** (© 800/221-1212), **Northwest** (© 800/225-2525), and **US Airways** (© 800/428-4322).

Alamo (© 800/327-9633), **Avis** (© 800/331-1212), **Budget** (© 800/527-0700), **Dollar** (© 800/800-4000), **Enterprise** (© 800/325-8007), **Hertz** (© 800/654-3131), and **National** (© 800/CAR-RENT) have rental-car operations here.

Taxis wait outside the modern terminal. Fares are approximately $11 to downtown, $15 to Gulf Breeze, and $20 to Pensacola Beach.

The **Amtrak** transcontinental *Sunset Limited* stops in Pensacola at 980 E. Heinberg St. (© 800/USA-RAIL; www.amtrak.com).

VISITOR INFORMATION The **Pensacola Visitor Information Center,** 1401 E. Gregory St., Pensacola, FL 32501 (© **800/874-1234** or 850/434-1234; fax 850/432-8211; www.visitpensacola.com), gives away helpful information about the Greater Pensacola area, including maps of self-guided tours of the historic districts, and sells a detailed street map of the area. The office is at the mainland end of the Pensacola Bay Bridge and is open daily from 8am to 5pm (until 4pm Sat and Sun Oct–Mar).

For information specific to the beach, contact the **Pensacola Beach Chamber of Commerce,** 735 Pensacola Beach Blvd. (P.O. Box 1174), Pensacola Beach, FL 32561 (© **800/635-4803** or 850/932-1500; fax 850/932-1551; www.visitpensacolabeach.com). The chamber's offices and visitor center are on the right as you drive onto Santa Rosa Island across the Bob Sikes Bridge. They're open daily from 9am to 5pm.

Pensacola

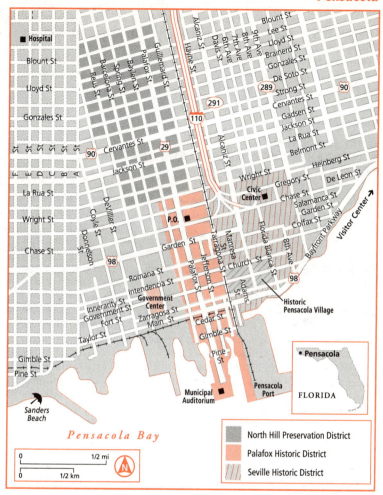

GETTING AROUND To see the historic sights in town, park at the Pensacola visitor center (see above) and take the **Five Flags Trolley** (✆ 850/436-9383). The one-way East Bay (Blue) Line runs Monday to Friday from 9am to 4pm between the visitor center and downtown. The Palafox (Red) Line runs Monday to Friday from 7am to 6pm north-south along Palafox Street between the waterfront and North Hill Preservation District. Both pass through Historic Pensacola Village. The 25¢ fare includes a transfer between the two lines. The visitor center has free route maps.

A free **Tiki Trolley** operates along the full length of Pensacola Beach from Memorial Day weekend through Labor Day weekend, Friday and Saturday from 10am to 3am, Sunday from 10am to 10pm.

Both trolleys are operated by **Escambia County Area Transit System (ECAT)** (✆ **850/595-3228;** www.ecat.pensacola.com), which also runs public buses around town Monday to Saturday—but not to the beach. Call for schedules.

If you need a cab, call **Airport Express Taxi** (© 850/572-5555), **Crosstown Cab** (© 850/456-TAXI), **Pensacola Red & Gold Taxi** (© 850/505-0025), or **Yellow Cab** (© 850/433-3333). Fares are $1.50 at flag fall, plus $1.40 a mile.

You can rent bicycles and scooters from **Floats-N-Spokes,** 500 Quietwater Beach Rd. (© 850/934-RIDE), in Pensacola Beach. Bike fees range from $5 an hour to $15 a day. Scooters go for $30 an hour to $90 a day.

TIME Pensacola is in the **central time zone,** 1 hour behind Miami, Orlando, and Tallahassee.

WHAT TO SEE & DO
HITTING THE BEACH: GULF ISLANDS NATIONAL SEASHORE

Stretching eastward 47 miles, from the entrance to Pensacola Bay to Fort Walton Beach, skinny Santa Rosa Island is home to the resorts, condominiums, cottages, restaurants, and shops of **Pensacola Beach,** the area's prime vacation spot. This relatively small and low-key resort began life a century ago as the site of a beach pavilion, or "casino" as such facilities were called back then; and the heart of town—at the intersection of Pensacola Beach Boulevard, Via de Luna, and Fort Pickens Road—is still known as **Casino Beach.** This lively area at the base of the town's water tank sports restaurants, snack bars, a games arcade for kids, a minigolf course, public restrooms, walk-up beach bars with live bands blaring away, an indoor sports bar, and an outdoor concert pavilion with summertime entertainment. And the shops, restaurants, and bars of **Quietwater Boardwalk** are just across the road on the bay side of the island. If you want an active beach vacation, it's all here in one compact zone.

One reason Pensacola Beach is so small is that most of Santa Rosa Island is included in the **Gulf Islands National Seashore** ★★★. Jumping from island to island from Mississippi to Florida, this magnificent preserve includes mile after mile of undeveloped white-sand beach and rolling dunes covered with sea grass and sea oats. Established in 1971, the national seashore is a protected environment for more than 280 species of birds.

The most interesting part of the seashore is at **Fort Pickens** ★★★ (© 850/934-2635), on the western end of Santa Rosa Island, about 7 miles west of Pensacola Beach. Built in the 1830s to team with Fort Barrancas in guarding Pensacola's harbor entrance, this huge brick structure saw combat during the Civil War, but it's best known as the prison home of Apache medicine man Geronimo from 1886 to 1888. The visitor center has a small museum featuring displays about Geronimo, coastal defenses, and the seashore's ecology. Plan to be here at 2pm, when rangers lead 1-hour guided tours of the fort (the schedule can change, so call the fort to make sure). Seven-day admission permits to the Fort Pickens area are $8 per vehicle, $3 per pedestrian or bicyclist, free for holders of National Park Service passports. The fort and museum are open March through October daily from 9:30am to 5pm, November through February daily from 8:30am to 4pm. Both are closed on Christmas.

The Fort Pickens area has 200 **campsites** (135 with electricity) in a pine forest on the bay side of Santa Rosa Island. Nature trails lead from the camp through Blackbird Marsh and to the beach. A small store sells provisions. Sites cost $15 a night without power, $20 a night with it, and you have to pay the admission fee to the Fort Pickens area. Golden Age and Golden Access cardholders get a 50% discount. Call © 800/365-2267 for reservations (enter code

Florida's Canoe Capital

About 20 miles northeast of Pensacola via U.S. 90 is the little town of **Milton,** the official "Canoe Capital of Florida" (by an act of the state legislature, no less). It's a well-earned title, because the nearby Blackwater River, Coldwater River, Sweetwater Creek, and Juniper Creek are all perfect for canoeing, kayaking, tubing, rafting, and paddleboating.

The Blackwater is considered one of the world's purest sand-bottom rivers. It has remained a primordial, backwoods beauty, thanks chiefly to Florida's largest state forest (183,000 acres of oak, pine, and juniper) and **Blackwater River State Park**, 7720 Deaton Bridge Rd., Holt, FL 32564 (© **850/983-5363**; www.floridastateparks.org/district1/blackwater), where you can closely observe plant life and wildlife along nature trails. The park has facilities for fishing, picnicking, and camping. Admission is $2 per day per vehicle, $1 for pedestrians or bicyclists. Campsites cost $8 per night per person ($10 with electricity), plus $2 per pet with tags and vaccination papers. For camping reservations call © **800/326-3521** or go to the website www.reserveamerica.com.

Adventures Unlimited, Route 6, Box 283, Milton, FL 32570 (© **800/239-6864** or 850/623-6197; fax 850/626-3124; www.adventuresunlimited.com), is a year-round resort offering day and overnight canoeing, kayaking, and rafting expeditions on the local rivers. Special arrangements are made for novices. Canoe trips start at $16 per person, kayaking adventures from $22. Inner tubes start at $6. Campsites cost $15 a night, $20 with electricity. The resort also has 14 cottages on the Coldwater River ($39–$129 a night), and bed-and-breakfast accommodations at the Wolfe Creek Old School House Inn (eight rooms, all with bathrooms, $79–$109 double). Two-night minimum stays are required, 3 nights on holidays. Call for the trips schedule and reservations for trips, accommodations, and camping.

Blackwater Canoe Rental, 10274 Pond Rd., Milton, FL 32570 (© **800/967-6789** or 850/623-0235; www.blackwatercanoe.com), also rents canoes, kayaks, floats, tubes, and camping equipment. It has day trips by canoe or kayak, or inner tubes ranging from $9 to $19 per person and overnight camping excursions by canoe and kayak ranging from $19 to $28 per person. Tents, sleeping bags, and coolers are available for rent.

GUL), or 850/934-2621 for recorded information. You can make reservations up to 5 months in advance.

The national seashore's headquarters are in the 1,378-acre **Naval Live Oaks Area,** on U.S. 98, a mile east of Gulf Breeze (© **850/934-2600**). This former federal tree plantation is a place of primitive beauty, with nature trails leading through the oaks and pines to picnic areas and a beach. Pick up a map at the headquarters building, which has a small museum and a gorgeous view through the pines to Santa Rosa Sound. Picnic areas and trails are open from 8am to sunset all year except Christmas. Admission is free. The visitor center is open daily from 8am to 5:30pm.

The national seashore also maintains historic **Fort Barrancas** 🌟🌟 on the U.S. Naval Air Station west of town. See the box, "Pensacola's Other Fort," below, for details.

For more information, contact the **Gulf Islands National Seashore**, 1801 Gulf Breeze Pkwy., Gulf Breeze, FL 32561 (© **850/934-2600;** www.nps.gov/guis).

AFFORDABLE OUTDOOR ACTIVITIES

FISHING Red snapper, grouper, mackerel, tuna, and billfish are abundant offshore all along the Panhandle. Easiest way to drop a line into the gulf is off the new **Pensacola Beach Gulf Fishing Pier,** on Fort Pickens Road in Pensacola Beach (© **850/934-7200;** www.fishpensacolabeachpier.com). At 1,471 feet, it's the longest fishing pier on the gulf coast. The pier is open 24 hours a day year-round. Fees to fish are $6.50 per day for adults, $5.50 seniors, $3.50 for children 6 to 12. Bait and equipment cost extra. Observers can watch for $1 per person.

Fishing-charter services are offered at Pensacola Beach by the *Chulamar* (© 850/434-6971), *Lively One* (© 850/932-5071), *Boss Lady* (© 850/932-0305 or 850/477-4033), *Entertainer* (© 850/932-0305), *Exodus* (© 850/626-2545 or 850/932-0305), and *Lady Kady* (© 850/932-2065 or 850/932-0305). Expect to pay between $350 and $750 for one to four passengers, depending on the length of the trip. You may be able to save by driving to Destin, where party boats charge less per person (see " Great Golf & Other Affordable Outdoor Activities," in section 2 of this chapter). Sightseeing and evening cruises here go for about $50 per person.

GOLF The Pensacola area has its share of Northwest Florida's numerous championship golf courses. Look for free copies of *Gulf Coast Tee Time* (www.teetimeweb.com), an annual directory describing all of them, at the visitor information offices and in many hotel lobbies (see "The Active Vacation Planner," in chapter 2, for information about ordering copies). Reasonably priced golf packages can be arranged through many local hotels and motels.

Among this region's best courses is **Marcus Pointe,** on Marcus Pointe Boulevard off North W Street (© **800/362-7287** or 850/484-9770), which has hosted the Nike Tour, the American Amateur Classic, and the Pensacola Open. *Golf Digest* magazine has described this wide-ranging, 18-hole course as a "great value," and it is: Greens fees with cart are about $40 to $50, depending on the season.

The Moors, on Avalon Boulevard north of I-10 (© **800/727-1010** or 850/995-4653), also has greeted the Nike Tour and is home to the Emerald Coast Classic, a PGA Seniors event. Pot bunkers here make you think you're playing in Scotland. Greens fees are about $30 without cart. The Moors also has a lodge with eight luxury rooms.

Others worth considering are **Lost Key Golf Club,** on Perdido Key (© **850/492-1300**), one of the area's more difficult courses; **Scenic Hills,** on U.S. 90 northwest of town (© **850/476-9611**), whose rolling fairways are unique for this mostly flat area; the 36-hole **Tiger Point,** 1255 Country Club Rd. east of Gulf Breeze by Santa Rosa Sound (© **850/932-1330**), overlooking the water (the fifth-hole green of the East Course actually sits all by itself on an island); **Hidden Creek,** 3070 PGA Blvd., in Navarre between Gulf Breeze and Fort Walton Beach (© **850/939-4604**); **Creekside Golf Course,** 2355 W. Michigan Ave. (© **850/944-7969**); and **Osceola Municipal Golf Course,** 300 Tonawanda, off Mobile Highway (© **850/456-2761**).

In addition, **The Sportsman Golf Resort,** 1 Doug Ford Dr. (© 850/492-1223; www.sportsmanresort.com), on the mainland north of Perdido Key, has accommodations available for visiting golfers. It was the home of the PGA Pensacola Open from 1978 to 1987, when it was known as the Perdido Bay Golf Resort. Greens fees range from $55 to $65 here.

WATER SPORTS   Visibility in the waters around Pensacola can range from 30 to 50 feet deep inshore to 100 feet deep 25 miles offshore. Although the bottom is sandy and it's too far north for coral, the battleship USS *Massachusetts,* submerged in 30 feet of water 3 miles offshore, is one of some 35 artificial reefs where you can spot loggerhead turtles and other creatures. There are also good snorkeling sites just off the beach; get a map from the Gulf Islands National Seashore (see "Hitting the Beach," above).

Scuba Shack, 711 S. Palafox St. (© 850/433-4319), is Pensacola's oldest dive shop, offering sales, rentals, classes, and diving and fishing charters on the *Wet Dream,* moored behind the office. **Divers Den,** 512 N. Ninth Ave. (© 850/438-0650; www.diversden.com), also offers trips, equipment rental, and PADI instruction. **Gulf Breeze Dive Pros,** 297B Gulf Breeze Pkwy. (U.S. 98), in Gulf Breeze (© 850/934-8845), offers rentals, all levels of instruction, and diving excursions on the 30-foot *Easy Dive.* The ***Chulamar,*** at Pensacola Beach (© 850/434-6977), and the *Lo-Baby,* in Gulf Breeze (© 850/934-5285), both make arrangements for diving excursions.

Key Sailing Center, 500 Quietwater Beach Rd., on the Quietwater Beach Boardwalk (© 850/932-5550; www.keysailing.com), and **Radical Rides,** 444 Pensacola Beach Blvd., near the Bob Sikes Bridge (© 850/934-9743), rent Hobie Cats, pontoon boats, WaveRunners, jet skis, and windsurfing boards.

EXPLORING HISTORIC PENSACOLA

In addition to Historic Pensacola Village in the **Seville Historic District** (see below), the city has two other preservation areas worth a stroll. The Pensacola Visitor Information Center provides free walking-tour maps (see "Essentials," earlier in this section).

Running up Palafox Street from the water to Wright Street, the **Palafox Historic District** is also the downtown business district. Beautiful Spanish Renaissance- and Mediterranean-style buildings stand from the early days, including the ornate Saenger Theatre. In 1821 General Andrew Jackson formally accepted Florida into the United States during a ceremony in Plaza Ferdinand VII, now a National Historic Landmark. His statue commemorates the event.

The Palafox district is home to the **Pensacola Historical Museum;** the **Pensacola Museum of Art,** in the old city jail; and the **T. T. Wentworth Jr. Florida State Museum** (see below).

Another entry in the National Register of Historic Places, the **North Hill Preservation District** covers the 50 square blocks north of the Palafox Historic District bounded by Wright, Blount, Palafox, and Reus streets. Descendants of Spanish nobility, timber barons, British merchants, French Creoles, buccaneers, and Civil War soldiers still live in some of the more than 500 homes. They are not open to the public but are a bonanza for anyone interested in architecture. In 1863 Union troops erected a fort in Lee Square, at Palafox and Gadsden streets. It later was dedicated to the Confederacy, complete with a 50-foot-high obelisk and sculpture based on John Elder's painting *After Appomattox.*

Adjacent to the Historic Pensacola Village, the city's **Vietnam Memorial,** on Bayfront Parkway at Ninth Avenue, is known as the "Wall South," since it is a three-quarters–size replica of the national Vietnam Veterans Memorial in Washington, DC. Look for the "Huey" helicopter atop the wall.

Civil War Soldiers Museum ⭐ Founded by Dr. Norman Haines, Jr., a local physician who grew up discovering Civil War relics in Sharpsburg, Maryland, this storefront museum in the heart of the Palafox Street business district emphasizes how ordinary soldiers lived during that bloody conflict. The doctor's collection of military medical equipment and treatment methods is especially informative. A 23-minute video tells of Pensacola's role during the Civil War. The museum's bookstore carries more than 600 titles about the war.

108 S. Palafox St. (south of Romana St.). © 850/469-1900. www.cwmuseum.org. Admission $5 adults, $2.50 children 6–12; free for children 5 and under. Tues–Sat 10am–4:30pm. Closed New Year's Day, Thanksgiving, Christmas Eve, Christmas.

Historic Pensacola Village ⭐⭐ Bounded by Government, Taragona, Adams, and Alcanz streets, this original part of Pensacola resembles a shady English colonial town—albeit with Spanish street names—complete with town green and **Christ Church,** built in 1832 and resembling Bruton Parish in Williamsburg, Virginia. Some of Florida's oldest homes, now owned and preserved by the state, are here, and the village has charming boutiques and interesting restaurants. During summer, costumed characters go about their daily chores and demonstrate old crafts, and University of Florida archaeologists unearth the old Spanish commanding officer's compound at Zaragosa and Tarragona streets. Among the landmarks you'll visit are the **Museum of Industry,** the **Museum of Commerce,** the French Creole–style **Charles Lavalle House,** the elegant **Victorian Dorr House,** the French Colonial–Creole **Quina House,** and **St. Michael's Cemetery** (land was deeded by the king of Spain). Another fascinating site is the **Julee Cottage Black History Museum** ⭐⭐, 204 E. Zaragosa St. Built around 1790, this small house was owned by Julee Panton, a freed slave who ran her own business, invested in real estate, and loaned money to slaves so they could buy their freedom. Today the museum recalls her life and deeds. Start your tour by buying tickets at **Tivoli House,** 205 E. Zaragosa St., just east of Tarragona Street, where you can get free maps and brochures. Try to take one of the 90-minute guided walking tours of the village, which will take you through Christ Church and other buildings not otherwise open to the public.

Admission to the village includes the **T. T. Wentworth Jr. Florida State Museum,** 330 S. Jefferson St. (© **850/595-5989**) at Church Street downtown, a classic yellow brick building housing exhibits of Western Florida's history and a special hands-on Discovery Museum for children.

205 E. Zaragosa St. (east of Tarragona St.). © 850/595-5985. www.historicpensacola.org. Admission $6 adults, $5 seniors, $2.50 children 4–16; free for children 3 and under. Mon–Fri 10am–4pm; 60-min. guided tours 11am and 1pm. Closed New Year's Day, Thanksgiving, Christmas Eve, Christmas, and all other state holidays.

National Museum of Naval Aviation ⭐⭐⭐ The U.S. Navy and Marine Corps have trained at the sprawling U.S. Naval Air Station since they began flying airplanes early in this century. Celebrating their heroics, this truly remarkable museum has more than 100 aircraft dating from the 1920s to the space age. There's even a torpedo bomber flown by former President George Bush during World War II. Both children and adults can sit at the controls of a jet trainer, and the mock-ups of aircraft carrier conning towers and hangar decks are realistic. You can almost feel the tug of gravity while watching the Blue Angels and other naval aviators soaring about the skies in the stunning *Magic of Flight,* one of two IMAX films shown at the museum. If the movie doesn't get your stomach

Pensacola's Other Fort

Standing on Taylor Road near the National Museum of Naval Aviation, **Fort Barrancas** ★★ (© 850/455-5167) is definitely worth a visit while you're at the naval station. This imposing brick structure sits on a bluff overlooking the deep-water pass into Pensacola Bay. The Spanish built the water battery in 1797. Linked to it by a tunnel, the incredibly intricate brickwork of the fort's upper section was constructed by American troops between 1839 and 1844. Entry is by means of a drawbridge across a dry moat, and an interior scarp gallery goes all the way around the inside of the fort. Meticulously restored and operated by the National Park Service as part of Gulf Islands National Seashore, the fort is open from March through October, daily from 9:30am to 4:45pm; November through February, daily from 8:30am to 3:45pm. Ranger-led, 1-hour guided tours are well worth taking. The schedule changes seasonally, so call for the latest information. Admission and the tours are free.

The **Pensacola Lighthouse** (© 850/455-2354), opposite the museum entrance on Radford Boulevard, has guided ships to the harbor entrance since 1825. Except for occasional guided tours (call the lighthouse or the Pensacola visitor centers for a schedule), the lighthouse is not open to the public, but you can drive right up to it. The nearby **Lighthouse Point Restaurant** (© 850/452-3251) offers bountiful, all-you-can-eat luncheon buffets and magnificent bay views for about $6; it's open Monday to Friday from 10:30am to 2pm, and reservations are not required.

---

churning, then a 15-minute ride in the museum's flight motion simulator will. Using high-tech video and real motion, it simulates a high-speed, low-level mission in the navy's F-18 Hornet jet fighter. All guides are retired naval and marine corps aviators, which adds a personal touch to the hour-long museum tours. Allow at least half a day here, and save 20 minutes for a Flight Line bus tour of more than 40 aircraft parked outside the museum's restoration hangar.

Radford Blvd., U.S. Naval Air Station. © 850/452-3604. www.naval-air.org. Free admission. IMAX movies $6.25 adults; $5.75 seniors, military, and children 6–13; free for children under 6. Add $3 for second movie. Flight motion simulator rides $3.50 per person. Daily 9am–5pm. Guided tours daily at 9:30am, 11am, 1pm, and 2:30pm. Flight Line bus tours daily every 30 min. 10am–noon and 1–4pm. IMAX movies on the hour daily 10am–4pm. Flight motion simulator every 15 minutes 9am–4:45pm. Closed New Year's Day, Thanksgiving, Christmas. Enter naval station either at the Main Gate at the south end of Navy Blvd. (Fla. 295) or at the Back Gate on Blue Angel Pkwy. (Fla. 173) and follow the signs. No passes are required.

Pensacola Historical Museum To learn more about Pensacola's diverse, five-flag history, spend a few minutes at this local museum in the Arbona Building, a commercial structure built about 1882. An archaeological dig of the Spanish commanding officer's compound across Zaragosa Street has a boardwalk with explanatory signposts. The museum is operated by the Pensacola Historical Society, which has a resource center and library at 117 E. Government St. (© **850/434-5455**).

115 E. Zaragosa St. (between Tarragona and Jefferson sts.). © 850/433-1559. www.pensacolahistory.org. Admission $1. Mon–Sat 10am–4:30pm.

Pensacola Museum of Art Housed in what was the city jail from 1906 to 1954, this museum showcases a fine collection of European and American decorative glass, some African tribal art, and minor works by Salvador Dalí, John Marin, Thomas Hart Benton, Lynda Benglis, Milton Avery, and Alexander Calder, among others.

407 S. Jefferson St. (at Main St.). © 850/432-6247. Admission free on Tues; other days $2 adults, $1 students and active-duty military, free for children under 6. Tues–Fri 10am–5pm; Sat 10am–4pm.

A NEARBY ZOO

The Zoo *Kids* Situated in a 50-acre forest 15 miles east of Pensacola, this environmentally sensitive zoo has more than 700 exotic animals—including tigers, lions, rhinos, and low-land gorillas—living in landscaped habitats. Japanese gardens, a giraffe-feeding tower, and a petting farm make for a fun visit. A Safari Line train chugs through a 30-acre wildlife preserve with free-ranging herds, and youngsters also will love riding the wild animals instead of horses on a merry-go-round.

5701 Gulf Breeze Pkwy., Gulf Breeze (U.S. 98). © 850/932-2229. www.the-zoo.com. Admission $9.95 adults, $8.95 seniors, $6.95 children 3–11; children 2 and under free. Train rides $3 per person. Carousel rides $1 per person. Apr–Oct daily 9am–5pm; Nov–Mar daily 9am–4pm. Closed day before Thanksgiving, Thanksgiving, Christmas Eve, and Christmas.

SHOPPING

Sightseeing and shopping can be combined in Pensacola's **Palafox and Seville Historic Districts,** where many shops are housed in renovated centuries-old buildings. The **Quayside Art Gallery,** on Plaza Ferdinand at the corner of Zaragosa and Jefferson streets (© 850/438-2363; www.quaysidegallery.com), is the largest cooperative gallery in the Southeast. More than 100 artists display their works here, and the friendly staff will direct you to other nearby galleries.

North T Street between West Cervantes Street and West Fairfield Drive has so many antiques dealers and small flea markets that it's known as **Antique Alley.** Other dealers have booths in the **Ninth Avenue Antique Mall,** 380 N. Ninth Ave. between Gregory and Strong streets (© 850/438-3961). Get a complete list of local antiques dealers from the Pensacola Visitor Information Center (see "Essentials," earlier in this section).

Browsers will enjoy poking through the 400 dealer spaces covering 45 acres at the **Flea Market,** on U.S. 98, opposite The Zoo, 15 miles east of Pensacola (© **850/934-1971**). It's open on Saturday and Sunday from 9am to 5pm. Admission is free.

ACCOMMODATIONS YOU CAN AFFORD

The Pensacola Visitor Information Center (see "Essentials," earlier in this section) publishes a complete list of rental condominiums and cottages. Among the leading rental agents are **Gulf Coast Accommodations,** 400 Quietwater Beach Rd., Box 12, Pensacola Beach, FL 32561 (© **800/239-4334** or 850/932-9788; fax 850/932-3449; www.innisfree.com/gca); and **Tristan Realty,** P.O. Box 1611, Gulf Breeze, FL 32562 (© **800/445-9931** or 850/932-7363; fax 850/932-8361; www.tristanrealty.com).

The **Fort Pickens Area** of Gulf Islands National Seashore is your best bet here for camping (see "Hitting the Beach," earlier in this section).

Escambia County adds 11.5% tax to all hotel and campground bills.

Bear in mind when making your reservations that Pensacola Beach is at least a 15-minute drive from downtown Pensacola.

DOWNTOWN PENSACOLA

Several of the town's Victorian homes have been turned into luxurious bed-and-breakfasts. Among the best is **Springhill Guesthouse,** 903 N. Spring St. (© **800/475-1956** or 850/438-6887; www.pcola.gulf.net/~guesthouse), whose wraparound porch faces the extraordinary Hopkins' Boarding House across the street (see "Great Deals on Dining," below). Room rates range from $79 to $99.

The University Mall complex at I-10 and Davis Highway, about 5 miles north of downtown, is inconvenient to the beaches, but it has a host of chain motels, including a relatively inexpensive **Fairfield Inn by Marriott,** 7325 N. Davis Hwy. (© **800/331-3131** or 850/484-8001). Even less expensive, the **Motel 6-North** (© **800/466-8356** or 850/476-5386) is within walking distance of the Marriott on the north side of I-10. There's an ample supply of inexpensive restaurants on Plantation Road and in the adjacent mall.

Another good if more expensive bet is the 1998-vintage **Hampton Inn Airport,** 2187 Airport Blvd. (© **800/HAMPTON** or 850/478-1123; fax 850/478-8519). This area is not as congested as that around University Mall. The inn runs a free shuttle to nearby Cordova Mall and its adjacent chain restaurants.

Crowne Plaza Pensacola Grand Hotel Opposite the Civic Center in the Seville Historic District near the southern end of I-110, this unique hotel has turned the historic L&N Railroad Depot into a grand lobby with bar, restaurants, lounges, meeting rooms, and cozy library. You'll see such turn-of-the-century accoutrements as an ornate railroad clock, original oak stair rails, imported marble, ceramic mosaic tile floors, and old-fashioned carved furniture. An unimpressive 15-story glass-and-steel tower behind the depot holds the rooms and suites, which are popular primarily with business travelers and groups.

200 E. Gregory St. (at Alcanz St.), Pensacola, FL 32501. © **800/348-3336** or 850/433-3336. Fax 850/432-7572. www.pensacolagrandhotel.com. 212 units. $110–$135 double; $250–$408 suite. AE, DC, DISC, MC, V. **Amenities:** Restaurant (American); bar; outdoor pool; exercise room; business center; limited room service; laundry service; concierge-level rooms. *In room:* A/C, TV, dataport, fridge (suites only), coffeemaker, hair dryer, iron.

New World Inn Near the scenic bay and in the historic district, this urban version of a comfortable country inn is part of a meeting facility known as New World Landing. From the colonial-style lobby, a grand staircase leads to high-ceilinged and spacious rooms and suites artistically decorated with antiques. The rooms depict aspects of Pensacola's rich history: four of them flaunt Spanish decor, four are très chic French style, four portray Early Americana, and four focus on Olde England.

> **Tips When Room Rates Are Lowest**
>
> Room rates at all Panhandle beaches are highest from mid-May to mid-August, and premiums are charged at Easter, Memorial Day, July 4, and Labor Day. Hotel or motel reservations are essential during these periods. There's another high-priced peak in March, when thousands of raucous college students invade during spring break. Economical times to visit are April (except Easter) and September—the weather is warm, most establishments are open, and room rates are significantly lower than during summer. The least expensive rates occur during winter, but many attractions and some restaurants may be closed then.

600 S. Palafox St. (at Pine St.), Pensacola, FL 32501. © **850/432-4111.** Fax 850/432-6836. www.newworldlanding.com. 16 units. $85–$105 double; $120 suite. Rates include continental breakfast. AE, MC, V. **Amenities:** Access to nearby health club; laundry service. *In room:* A/C, TV, dataport.

Seville Inn   Best thing about this dated two-story motel is its location at the edge of the Seville Historic District, across the street from the Civic Center and about 4 blocks from Palafox Street and the Saenger Theatre. It has two outdoor swimming pools open during the warm months; one is covered so you can swim even on rainy days. Local phone calls are free, and guests get passes to the nearby Seville Quarter entertainment complex (see "Pensacola After Dark," below). You can save a few dollars off the room rate by picking up a discount coupon at the Pensacola visitor center (see "Essentials," earlier in this section).

223 E. Garden St. (between Alcaniz and Manresa sts.), Pensacola, FL 32501. © **800/277-7275** or 850/433-8331. Fax 850/432-6849. 120 units. Summer $69–$84 single or double; off-season $39–$69 single or double. Rates include continental breakfast. AE, DC, DISC, MC, V. **Amenities:** Restaurant (regional); bar; 2 outdoor pools; exercise room; Jacuzzi; sauna; bike rentals; business center; coin-op washers and dryers. *In room:* A/C, TV, fridge, iron.

PENSACOLA BEACH

Best Western Resort Pensacola Beach   This casual motel on the gulf front is notable for bright, clean, and extra-spacious accommodations, complete with refrigerators, coffeemakers, microwaves, and wet bars. Outside corridors lead to all rooms. Although none has its own balcony or patio, units facing the beach have great views; the less expensive "inland" rooms don't. Two swimming pools and a children's playground are on the beach. Chan's Market Cafe (see "Great Deals on Dining," below) sits in the parking lot.

16 Via de Luna Dr., Pensacola Beach, FL 32561. © **800/934-3301** or 850/934-3300. Fax 850/934-4366. www.pensacolabeach.com/bestwestern. 123 units. Summer $149–$189 double; off-season $79–$149 double. Rates include continental breakfast. Golf packages available. AE, DC, DISC, MC, V. **Amenities:** 2 outdoor pools; water-sports equipment rentals; game room. *In room:* A/C, TV, dataport, fridge, coffeemaker, hair dryer, iron.

Clarion Suites Resort & Convention Center   This most unusual of Pensacola Beach's resorts resembles a village of tin-roofed, pastel-sided cottages. The attractively decorated accommodations are one-bedroom suites that can accommodate four people. The best units are those directly facing the beach. They have balconies or patios, while the others do not.

20 Via de Luna Dr., Pensacola Beach, FL 32561. © **800/874-5303** or 850/932-4300. Fax 850/934-9112. www.clarionsuitesresort.com. 86 units. Summer $127–$178 up to 4 persons. Off-season $84–$140 up to 4 persons. Rates include continental breakfast. AE, DC, DISC, MC, V. **Amenities:** Heated outdoor pool; water-sports equipment rentals; coin-op washers and dryers. *In room:* A/C, TV, dataport, kitchen, coffeemaker, hair dryer, iron.

The Dunes   This eight-story beachfront tower has spacious rooms, all with gorgeous gulf or bay vistas. All rooms have a gulf-facing balcony, and the penthouse suites have their own whirlpool tubs. The extra-large suites can accommodate small families. The Dunes has a restaurant and bar (both with lovely views of the gulf), so you don't have to go out for lunch or dinner unless you want to. There's a jogging trail, a bike path, and an undeveloped dune preserve next door.

333 Fort Pickens Rd., Pensacola Beach, FL 32561. © **800/83-DUNES** or 850/932-3536. Fax 850/932-7088. www.theduneshotel.com. 76 units. Summer $115–$175 double; $295–$345 suite. Off-season $85–$115 double; $255–$305 suite. Packages available. AE, DISC, MC, V. **Amenities:** Restaurant (American); bar; heated outdoor pool; access to nearby health club; water-sports equipment rentals; limited room service; laundry service. *In room:* A/C, TV, dataport, coffeemaker, hair dryer, iron.

Hampton Inn Pensacola Beach ⭐ This pastel, four-story hotel sits right by the gulf next to the action on Casino Beach. The bright lobby opens to a wooden sun deck with beachside swimming pools on either side (one is heated). Half the oversize rooms have balconies overlooking the gulf; these are more expensive than rooms on the bay side, which have nice views but no outside sitting areas.

2 Via de Luna, Pensacola Beach, FL 32561. © **800/320-8118** or 850/932-6800. Fax 850/932-6833. www.hamptonbeachresort.com. 181 units. Summer $149–$189 double; off-season $89–$149 double. Rates include continental breakfast and local phone calls. AE, DC, DISC, MC, V. **Amenities:** Bar; 2 outdoor pools; access to nearby health club; exercise room; water-sports equipment rentals; laundry service, coin-op washers and dryers. In room: A/C, TV, dataport, fridge, coffeemaker, hair dryer, iron.

Holiday Inn Express Pensacola Beach Another property that received a face-lift following a 1998 hurricane, this nine-story hotel boasts terrific views from its brightly furnished upper-floor rooms. It's one of the oldest hotels in the area, which means the rooms aren't as large as those at other new properties such as the Hampton Inn; there's adequate space for a king-size bed, but rooms with two double beds are relatively cramped. They all have private balconies, however, with the most expensive rooms facing directly onto the gulf.

165 Fort Pickens Rd., Pensacola Beach, FL 32561. © **800/465-4329** or 850/932-5361. Fax 850/932-7121. www.pensacolabeach.com/holiday. 150 units. Summer $120–$150 double; off-season $70–$140 double. Rates include continental breakfast. AE, DC, DISC, MC, V. **Amenities:** Heated outdoor pool; coin-op washers and dryers. In room: A/C, TV, dataport, coffeemaker, hair dryer, iron.

Super-Cheap Sleeps

Five Flags Inn (Value) Sitting between the Holiday Inn Express and The Dunes, this basic but friendly motel looks like a jail from the road, but don't be fooled. Big picture windows look from the rooms out to the swimming pool (heated Mar–Oct) and to the gorgeous white-sand beach, which comes right up to the property. Although the accommodations are small, the rates are a bargain for clean, gulf-front rooms.

299 Fort Pickens Rd., Pensacola Beach, FL 32561. © **850/932-3586**. Fax 850/934-0257. www.fiveflagsinn.com. 49 units. Summer $95 double; off-season $55–$75 double. AE, DC, DISC, MC, V. **Amenities:** Heated outdoor pool. In room: A/C, TV, hair dryer, iron.

GREAT DEALS ON DINING
PENSACOLA

Hopkins' Boarding House ⭐⭐⭐ (Value) SOUTHERN There's a delicious peek into the past when you dine at this extraordinary Victorian boardinghouse in the heart of the North Hill Preservation District. Outside, ancient trees shade a wraparound porch with old-fashioned rocking chairs in which to await the next available place at the large dining tables inside. It's all-you-can-eat family-style, so you could be seated next to the mayor or a mechanic, since everyone in town dines here. Platters are piled high with staples of down-home Southern cooking: black-eyed peas, collard greens, and other seasonal vegetables from nearby farms. Tuesday is famous as Fried Chicken Day, and you're likely to be served fried fish on Friday. You Yankees should sample the piping-hot grits accompanying each bountiful breakfast (slop on some butter to give them taste). In true boardinghouse fashion, you'll bus your own dishes and pay on the way out. No alcoholic beverages are served, but the "already-sweet" iced tea is great.

900 N. Spring St. (at Strong St.). © **850/438-3979**. Breakfast $3.50–$8; lunch and dinner $8. No credit cards. Tues–Sun 7–9:30am and 11:15am–2pm; Tues and Fri 5:15–7:30pm.

Marina Oyster Barn ⭐ (Value) SEAFOOD Exuding the ambience of the quickly vanishing Old Florida fish camps, this plain but clean restaurant at the

Johnson-Rooks Marina is to seafood what the Hopkins' Boarding House is to grits. It has been a local favorite since 1969, for both its view and its down-home–style seafood. Freshly shucked oysters, served raw, steamed, fried, or Rockefeller, are the main feature; but the seafood salad here is also first-rate, and the fish, shrimp, and oysters are breaded with cornmeal in true Southern fashion. The daily luncheon specials give you a light meal at a bargain price. No smoking.

505 Bayou Blvd. (on Bayou Texar). © 850/433-0511. Main courses $4–$12; sandwiches $2.50–$5.50; lunch specials $3.75–$6.50. AE, DISC, MC, V. Tues–Sat 11am–9pm (lunch specials 11am–2pm). Go east on Cervantes St. (U.S. 90) across the Bayou Texar Bridge, then take first left on Stanley Ave. and turn left again to the end of Strong St.

McGuire's Irish Pub STEAKS/SEAFOOD Every day is St. Patrick's Day at this lively and popular Irish pub, complete with corned beef and cabbage, Irish stew, and other such Dublin delicacies. Super-size steaks are the best offerings here, however, as are hickory-smoked ribs and chicken. You can also order seafood, including a hearty bouillabaisse with shrimp, red snapper, clams, mussels, and oysters. Big burgers come with a choice of more than 20 toppings, from smoked Gouda cheese to sautéed Vidalia onions. You can watch your ale being brewed in copper kettles and dine in a cellarlike room with 8,000 bottles of wine on display. More than 125,000 dollar bills line the bar's walls and ceilings. Live music is offered most nights.

600 E. Gregory St. (between 11th and 12th aves.). © 850/433-6789. Main courses $16–$25; snacks, burgers, and sandwiches $8–$12. AE, DC, DISC, MC, V. Daily 11am–2:30am.

Worth a Splurge

Jamie's TRADITIONAL FRENCH Occupying a restored Victorian home in Historic Pensacola Village, the town's classiest and most romantic restaurant enhances the dining experience with an Art Deco ambience augmented by glowing fireplaces, gleaming antiques, and subdued background music. The excellent fare is traditional French. Roast leg of lamb and tournedos of beef are good choices from the regular menu, but don't overlook the seafood specials.

424 E. Zaragosa St. (between Alcanz and Florida Blanca). © 850/434-2911. Reservations recommended at both lunch and dinner. Main courses $19–$28. AE, DISC, MC, V. Mon–Sat 11:30am–2pm and 5:30–9:30pm.

Skopelos on the Bay SEAFOOD/STEAKS/GREEK Perched on a bluff overlooking the bay, this family-owned restaurant has been famous hereabouts since 1959 for its great views and creative seafood dishes, such as the scamp Cervantes (scamp is a deepwater fish with white, flaky meat). Other seafood selections range from broiled scallops to Mediterranean-style grouper prepared with a sauce of tomato and roasted eggplant. The menu also features charcoal-grilled steaks and chicken and roast leg of lamb. Befitting the owner's Greek heritage, roast lamb is served with moussaka, dolmades, titopita, and spanakopita. In warm weather opt for an outside table with a bay view.

670 Scenic Hwy. (U.S. 90 east, at E. Cervantes St.). © 850/432-6565. Reservations recommended. Main courses $15–$27. AE, DISC, MC, V. Tues–Thurs and Sat 5–10:30pm; Fri 11:30am–2:30pm and 5–10:30pm.

PENSACOLA BEACH

Chan's Market Cafe *Value* AMERICAN The aroma of pastries in the oven permeates this pleasant little cafe and bakery, which shares quarters with a liquor store in the parking lot of the Best Western Pensacola Beach. It's the best place on the beach for a breakfast of freshly baked croissants or bagels. Lunches and dinners feature economical specials such as meat loaf, barbecued chicken, pot roast, and grilled fish, all served with a choice of Southern-style veggies. Or you can order a heaping sandwich on one of Chan's large flaky croissants.

16 Via de Luna. © 850/932-8454. Breakfast/lunch/snacks $3–$7; meals $5–$10. AE, DISC, MC, V. Daily 7am–9pm.

Flounder's Chowder House ★ SEAFOOD   Inside, this restaurant radiates piousness, with decor featuring stained-glass windows from an old New York convent and confessional-booth walls from a New Orleans church. Outside on the sandy beach by the bay is a totally different story, however, for in summer this is one of the most popular reggae bars here (see "Pensacola After Dark," below). The food is pretty good, with steamed Maine lobster and chargrilled tuna, grouper, and mahimahi leading the list. If you're lucky, a big smoker grill outside will be producing more fish and some exceptional ribs. Burgers, salads, and sandwiches are offered all day. A glass of champagne accompanies a sumptuous bay-side Sunday brunch.

800 Quietwater Beach Rd. (at Via de Luna and Fort Pickens Rds.). © 850/932-2003. Reservations not accepted. Main courses $15–$21; burgers and sandwiches $8–$10. AE, DC, DISC, MC, V. Sun–Thurs 11am–midnight (to 11pm in winter); Fri–Sat 11am–2am (to 11pm in winter).

PENSACOLA AFTER DARK

For what's going on, pick up the daily *Pensacola News Journal* (www.pensacola newsjournal.com), especially its Friday entertainment section. Another good source is the *Pensacola Downtown Crowd* (www.burchellpublishing.com/ downtown.asp), a free publication available at the Pensacola Visitor Information Center (see "Essentials," earlier in this section).

THE PERFORMING ARTS   Pensacola has a surprisingly sophisticated array of entertainment choices for such a relatively small city. For a schedule of upcoming events, get a copy of *Vision,* a bimonthly newsletter published by the Arts Council of Northwest Florida (© 850/432-9906; www.artsnwfl.org). Also pick up "Sneak Preview," a calendar of events at the Pensacola Civic Center and the Saenger Theater. Both publications are available at the Pensacola Visitor Information Center (see "Essentials," earlier in this section). Tickets for all major performances can be purchased from **Ticketmaster** (© 800/488-5252 or 850/433-6311; www.ticketmaster.com).

The highlight venue here is the ornate **Saenger Theatre** ★, 118 S. Palafox St., near Romano Street (© 850/444-7686; www.saengertheatre.com), a painstakingly restored masterpiece of Spanish baroque architecture that the locals call the Grande Dame of Palafox. The variety of presentations includes the local opera company and symphony orchestra, Broadway musicals, and touring performers. The 10,000-seat **Pensacola Civic Center,** 201 E. Gregory St., at Alcanz Street (© **850/432-0800;** www.pensacolaciviccenter.com), hosts a variety of concerts, exhibitions, and conventions. Call ahead for the current schedule.

THE CLUB & BAR SCENE   Pensacola's downtown nighttime entertainment center is **Seville Quarter,** 130 E. Government St., at Jefferson Street (© 850/ 434-6211; www.rosies.com), in the Seville Historic District. This restored antique brick complex with New Orleans–style wrought-iron balconies is actually a collection of pubs and restaurants whose names capture the ambience: Rosie O'Grady's Goodtime Emporium, Lili Marlene's Aviator's Pub, Apple Annie's Courtyard, End o' the Alley Bar, Phineas Phogg's Balloon Works (a dance hall, not a balloon shop), and Fast Eddie's Billiard Parlor (which has electronic games, too). The pubs all serve up libations, food, and live entertainment

> ### Finds The Last Great Road House
>
> Sitting precisely on the Florida–Alabama state line on Perdido Key, about 15 miles west of downtown Pensacola, the **Flora-Bama Lounge,** 17401 Perdido Key Dr. (© **850/492-0611;** www.florabama.com), is almost a shrine to country music. Billing itself as the "Last Great American Road House," this slapped-together gulf-side pub is famous for its special jam sessions from noon until way past midnight on Saturday and Sunday. Flora-Bama is the prime sponsor and a key venue for the Frank Brown International Songwriters' Festival during the first week of November. If you've never attended an Interstate Mullet Toss, catch the fun here during the last weekend of April. The raw oyster bar is popular all the time. Granted, the joint can get a bit rough from time to time, but you won't soon forget the great gulf views while sipping a cold one at the Deck Bar. The Flora-Bama is open daily from 8:30am to 2:30am.

from Dixieland jazz to country and western. Get a monthly calendar at the information booth next to Rosie O'Grady's. The complex is open daily from 11am to 2am.

Every night is party time at **McGuire's Irish Pub & Brewery,** the city's popular Irish pub, brewery, and eatery (see "Great Deals on Dining," above). Irish bands appear nightly during summer, on Saturday and Sunday the rest of the year.

Nightlife at the beach centers around **Quietwater Boardwalk,** Via de Luna at Fort Pickens Road (no phone), a shopping/dining complex on Santa Rosa Sound. With the lively beach and reggae bar at **Flounder's Chowder House** (see "Great Deals on Dining," above) just a few steps away, it's easy to barhop until you find a band and crowd to your liking. Across Via de Luna at Casino Beach is **The Dock,** (© **850/934-3316**), which has beachside live bands nightly during summer, on weekends off-season. You can catch all the games here at **Sidelines Sports Bar & Restaurant** (© **850/934-3660**).

2 Destin ★★ & Fort Walton Beach ★

40 miles E of Pensacola, 160 miles W of Tallahassee

Sitting on a round harbor off East Pass, which lets broad and beautiful Choctawhatchee Bay flow into the Gulf of Mexico, Destin is justly famous for its fishing fleet, the largest in the state. It's also Northwest Florida's fastest-growing and most upscale vacation destination, with a multitude of high-rise condominiums, the huge Sandestin luxury resort, several excellent golf courses, and some of Northwest Florida's best restaurants and lively nightspots. By and large, Destin attracts a more affluent crowd than does Fort Walton Beach, its more down-to-earth neighbor.

Although Fort Walton Beach has its own gorgeous strip of white sand over on Okaloosa Island, it is a "real" city whose economy is supported less by tourism than by sprawling Eglin Air Force Base. Covering more than 700 square miles, Eglin is the world's largest air base and is home to the U.S. Air Force's Armament Museum and the 33rd Tactical Fighter Wing, the "Top Guns" of Operation Desert Storm in 1991.

To the east of Destin, development is picking up steam along the beaches of southern Walton County. Still, this picturesque area has mostly cottages nestled among rolling sand dunes covered with sea oats. Here you'll find Grayton Beach State Park, which sports one of America's finest beaches, and the quaint village of **Seaside** 🌟🌟, which served as the set for Jim Carrey's movie *The Truman Show*. Seaside was built on a lovely stretch of beach in the 1980s—but with Victorian architecture that makes it look a century older. The village's gulf-side honeymoon cottages make for one of Florida's most romantic retreats; and the village has interesting shops and art galleries, a stamp-sized post office, and a resident population of artists, writers, and other creative folks, who permit only their own cars in their relatively expensive little enclave. The rest of us have to park beside Country Road 30A and explore the village on foot or by bicycle.

ESSENTIALS

GETTING THERE Flights arriving at and departing from **Okaloosa Regional Airport** (ⓒ **850/651-7160;** www.co.okaloosa.fl.us/airport.html) actually use the enormous strips at Eglin Air Force Base. The terminal is on Fla. 85 north of Fort Walton Beach and is served by **Delta** (ⓒ 800/221-1212), **Northwest/KLM** (ⓒ 800/225-2525), and **US Airways** (ⓒ 800/428-4322).

Avis (ⓒ 800/331-1212), **Budget** (ⓒ 800/527-0700), **Hertz** (ⓒ 800/654-3131), and **National** (ⓒ 800/CAR-RENT) have rental cars at the airport, and **Enterprise** (ⓒ 800/325-8007) is in town.

Top Class Shuttle Service (ⓒ **888/SHUTTLE** or 850/830-7229) and **Airport Shuttle Service** (ⓒ **850/897-5238**) provide van transportation to and from the airport. Fares are based on a zone system: $12 to $15 to Fort Walton Beach, $25 to Destin, and $32 to $35 to Sandestin and southern Walton County.

The *Sunset Limited* transcontinental service on **Amtrak** (ⓒ **800/USA-RAIL;** www.amtrak.com) stops at Crestview, 26 miles north of Fort Walton Beach.

VISITOR INFORMATION For advance information about both Fort Walton Beach and Destin, contact the **Emerald Coast Convention and Visitors Bureau,** P.O. Box 609, Fort Walton Beach, FL 32549 (ⓒ **800/322-3319** or 850/651-7131; fax 850/651-7149; www.destin-fwb.com). The bureau shares quarters with the **Okaloosa County Visitors Welcome Center** in a tin-roofed, beachside building on Miracle Strip Parkway (U.S. 98) on Okaloosa Island at the eastern edge of Fort Walton Beach. Stop there for brochures, maps, and other information. The welcome center is open Monday to Friday from 8am to 5pm and Saturday and Sunday from 10am to 4pm.

The **Destin Area Chamber of Commerce,** 4484 Legendary Dr., Destin, FL 32541 (ⓒ **850/837-6241;** fax 850/654-5612; www.destinchamber.com), gives away brochures and sells maps of the area. The chamber resides in an office complex at the entry to Regatta Bay Golf & Country Club, on U.S. 98 a half mile east of the Mid-Bay Bridge. It's open Monday to Friday from 9am to 5pm and is closed holidays.

For information about the beaches of South Walton, contact the **South Walton Tourist Development Council,** P.O. Box 1248, Santa Rosa Beach, FL 32459 (ⓒ **800/822-6877** or 850/267-1216; fax 850/267-3943; www.beachesofsouthwalton.com). Its **visitor center** is at the intersection of U.S. 98 and U.S. 331 in Santa Rosa Beach (ⓒ **850/267-3511**). Open daily 8:30am to 5:30pm.

> **Tips How to Find a Street Address**
>
> Don't worry about getting lost, since most of what you'll want to see and do in Destin and Fort Walton Beach is either on, or no more than a few blocks from, U.S. 98, the area's main east-west drag. Finding a street address is another matter, however, for even many local residents don't fully comprehend the post office's bizarre naming and numbering system along U.S. 98.
>
> In Fort Walton Beach, U.S. 98 is known as the "Miracle Strip Parkway," with "southwest" and "southeast" addresses on the mainland and "east" addresses on Okaloosa Island.
>
> In Destin, U.S. 98 is officially known as "Highway 98 East" from the Destin Bridge east to Airport Road, and street numbers get progressively higher as you head east from the bridge. East of Airport Road, however, the post office calls U.S. 98 the "Emerald Coast Parkway"—although locals still say a place is on "98 East." The highway also is known as the Emerald Coast Parkway in Walton County, but the street-numbering system changes completely once you pass the county line.
>
> Adding to the confusion in Destin, "Old Highway 98 East" is a short spur from Airport Road to the western side of Henderson Beach State Park, and "Scenic Highway 98 East" parallels the real U.S. 98 along the beach from the eastern side of Henderson Beach to Sandestin.
>
> In other words, call and ask for directions if you're not sure how to find an establishment here.

GETTING AROUND   The Okaloosa County Tourist Development Authority (© **850/651-7131**) operates a free **Island Shuttle** trolley during the summer months along the entire length of Santa Rosa Boulevard on Okaloosa Island. The two trolleys run every 30 minutes Sunday to Thursday from 7am and 10pm, Friday and Saturday from 7am to 1am. They also connect the island to the Uptown Bus station, on Eglin Parkway NE on the Fort Walton Beach mainland.

For a cab in Fort Walton Beach, call **Charter Taxis** (© 850/863-5466), **Checker Cab** (© 850/244-4491), **Crosstown Taxi** (© 850/244-7303), **JC's Cab** (© 850/865-0578), **Veterans Cab Co.** (© 850/243-1403), or **Yellow Cab** (© 850/244-3600). In Destin, call **Destin Taxi** (© 850/654-5700). Fares are based on a zone system rather than meters, with a $4 minimum. Trips within Fort Walton Beach or Destin should range from $4 to $8.

TIME   The area is in the central time zone, an hour behind Miami, Orlando, and Tallahassee.

WHAT TO SEE & DO
HITTING THE GREAT WHITE BEACH
DESTIN   Like an oasis in the middle of Destin's rapid development, the 208-acre **Henderson Beach State Park**, east of Destin Harbor on U.S. 98, allows easy access to swimming, sunning, surf fishing, picnicking, and seabird watching along its 1½ miles of beach. There are restrooms, outdoor showers, and surf chairs for persons with disabilities. The area is open daily from 8am to sunset. Admission is $2 per vehicle, $1 for pedestrians and cyclists. Several good restaurants are just outside the park's western boundary. The park also has 30 campsites in a wooded setting. They cost $16 per night, plus $2 for electricity,

and can be reserved up to 11 months in advance. Pets on leashes are allowed in the park, including the beach and campground. For camping reservations call © 800/326-3521 or go to the website www.reserveamerica.com. For more information, contact the park at 1700 Emerald Coast Pkwy., Destin, FL 32541 (© 850/837-7550; www.floridastateparks.org/district1/hendersonbeach).

The **James W. Lee Park,** between Destin and Sandestin on Scenic Highway 98, has a long white-sand beach overlooked by covered picnic tables, restrooms, an ice-cream parlor, and a moderately priced seafood restaurant.

FORT WALTON BEACH Do your loafing on the white sands of **Okaloosa Island,** joined to the mainland by the high-rise Brooks Bridge over Santa Rosa Sound. Most resort hotels and amusement parks are grouped around the Gulfarium marine park on U.S. 98 east of the bridge. Here you'll find **The Boardwalk,** a collection of tin-roofed beachside buildings that have a games arcade for the kids, a saloon for adults, covered picnic areas, a summertime snack bar, and a seafood restaurant. Just to the east, you can use the restrooms, cold-water showers, and other free facilities at **Beasley Park** ★, home of the Okaloosa County Visitor Welcome Center.

Across U.S. 98, the **Okaloosa Area, Gulf Islands National Seashore** has picnic areas and sailboats for rent on Choctawhatchee Bay, plus access to the gulf. Admission to this part of the national seashore is free.

SOUTHERN WALTON COUNTY Sporting the finest stretch of white sand on the gulf, **Grayton Beach State Park** ★★★, on County Road 30A, also has 356 acres of pine forests surrounding scenic Western Lake. There's a boat ramp and a campground with electric hookups on the lake. Get a leaflet at the main gate for a self-guided tour of the nature trail. Pets are not allowed anywhere in the recreation area. The area is open daily from 8am to sunset. Admission is $3.25 per vehicle with up to eight occupants, $1 per pedestrian or bicyclist. Campsites cost $14 from March to September, $8 from October to February. Add $2 for electricity. For camping reservations call © 800/326-3521 or go to the website www.reserveamerica.com. For information contact the park at 357 Main Park Rd., Santa Rosa Beach, FL 32459 (© 850/231-4210; www.florida stateparks.org/district1/graytonbeach).

Seaside has free public parking along County Road 30A and is a good spot for a day at the beach, a stroll or bike ride around the quaint village, and a tasty meal at one of its restaurants.

GREAT GOLF & OTHER AFFORDABLE OUTDOOR ACTIVITIES

BOATING & BOAT RENTALS Pontoon boats are highly popular for use on the back bays and on Sunday-afternoon floating parties in East Pass. Several companies rent them, including **Best Boat Rentals** (© 850/664-7872) on Okaloosa Island in Fort Walton Beach, and **Adventure Pontoon Rentals** (© 850/837-3041), **B&J Boat Rentals** (© 850/243-4488), **East Pass Watersports** (© 850/654-4253), and **Premier Powerboat Rentals** (© 850/837-7755), all on Destin Harbor. Expect to pay about $70 for a half day, $120 for all day. Premier Powerboat Rentals also has speedboats for rent.

CRUISES The *Emerald Magic* (© 888/654-1685 or 850/837-1293; www.moodysinc.com) and the *Southern Star* (© 888/424-7217 or 850/837-7741; www.dolphin-sstar.com) have daily dolphin and sunset cruises from June through August, by arrangement the rest of the year. The *Emerald Magic* is operated by Moody's, on U.S. 98 at Destin Harbor (see "Fishing," below), while

Cheap Thrills: What to See & Do for Free (or Almost) in Northwest Florida

- **Hit a powdery beach.** Admission is free to most of 100-plus miles of powdery, snow-white beaches that make this area special. A few bucks will let you into the **Gulf Islands National Seashore** at Pensacola, the **Henderson Beach** and **Grayton Beach** parks at Destin, the **St. Andrews State Park** at Panama City Beach, and the **St. George Island State Park** near Apalachicola. You won't soon forget the time you spend on these protected sands and dunes, all consistently ranked among the nation's finest beaches.

- **Stroll through Florida's second oldest town.** You'll have to pay to go into its homes and museums, but you can walk the streets of **Historic Pensacola Village** (© 850/444-8905) for free. Built in 1823, the village boasts some of Florida's oldest homes, along with charming boutiques and interesting restaurants. During summer, costumed characters go about their daily chores and demonstrate old crafts, and archaeologists unearth the old Spanish commanding officer's compound.

- **Visit the Blue Angels and Top Guns.** Next to the Smithsonian Institution's National Air and Space Museum in Washington, D.C., the best places to see our nation's war planes on display are at the **National Museum of Naval Aviation** in Pensacola (© 850/452-3604) and at the **U.S. Air Force Armament Museum** in Fort Walton Beach (© 850/882-4062). Admission to both is free. The IMAX films shown at the naval museum will make you believe you're flying in a Blue Angel's cockpit (there's a charge for the films). Near the Pensacola museum and also free, historic **Fort Barrancas** (© 850/934-2600) dates from 1797, when the Spanish built its water battery. The incredibly intricate brickwork of the upper section was laid by American troops between 1839 and 1844.

- **Get away from it all on Shell Island.** The round-trip boat fare costs $9.50 for adults, $5.50 for kids 11 and under, but the ride over to Shell Island, off Panama City Beach (© 850/233-5140), will take to you to an uninhabited natural preserve that's great for shelling, swimming, suntanning, or just relaxing. Bring chairs, beach gear, coolers, food, and beverages. The boat shuttles from April to October between the island and St. Andrews State Recreation Area.

- **Celebrate the air conditioner.** Without air-conditioning, Florida would be an uncomfortable place to live or visit during its hot, humid summers. In the late 1800s, Doctor John Gorrie of Apalachicola invented a cooling machine to keep his malaria patients comfortable. It was a moment of great note in Florida's history, duly celebrated by his hometown's **John Gorrie State Museum** (© 850/653-9347). For $1,

the *Southern Star* docks in Destin at the Harbor Walk Marina, behind the Lucky Snapper Restaurant. The *Emerald Magic* charges $15 for adults, $7.50 for kids 3 to 12. The *Southern Star* costs $2 more for adults, 50¢ less for children.

you can see a working replica of his device, the prototype of the air-conditioning units that make Florida summers bearable today.
- **Look down on the capital and out to the gulf.** State legislators meet in Tallahassee's $43-million skyscraper **New Capitol Building** (© 850/487-1902) from March to May, but you can take the elevators to the 22nd-floor observatory any day and look down over all of the capital—and on a clear day, all the way to the Gulf of Mexico, some 20 miles away. Also free are guided tours of the building and the Old Capitol, directly in front of the skyscraper. With its majestic dome, the old building has been restored to its original 19th-century beauty and has an eight-room exhibit portraying Florida's political history.
- **Learn about black history and art.** Florida A&M University in Tallahassee is one of the country's leading all-black colleges, and it's a wonderful place to learn about African-American history and see some of that community's major works of art. Housed in a columned library built by Andrew Carnegie in 1908, the **Black Archives Research Center and Museum** (© 850/561-2603) displays one of the nation's most extensive collections of African-American artifacts and historical materials, while **The Florida A&M University Art Gallery** (© 850/599-3161) focuses on works by African-American artists, with a wide variety of paintings, sculptures, and more. Admission is free to both.
- **Take in the camellias and azaleas at Maclay State Gardens.** It'll cost a few bucks to get through the gate, but you won't find many places as naturally magnificent in springtime as Maclay State Gardens, on the northeastern outskirts of Tallahassee (© 850/487-4556). The more than 300 acres here feature more than 200 varieties of flowers, with 28 acres devoted exclusively to azaleas and camellias. This floral wonderland surrounds the beautifully restored 1923 home of New York financier Alfred B. Maclay and his wife, Louise. The blooming season is January to April, with the peak about mid-March. The park also offers nature trails, canoe rentals, boating, picnicking, swimming, and fishing.
- **See where Johnny Weissmuller played Tarzan.** Wakulla Springs, 15 miles south of Tallahassee, is so jungly that some of the 1930s Tarzan movies starring Johnny Weissmuller were filmed here. Today they are within the 2,860 acres of **Edward W. Ball Wakulla Springs State Park** (© 850/922-3632), which means you'll have to pay a few dollars to get in. You can also pay $4.50 for adults, half price for children, to take glass-bottom-boat sightseeing and wildlife-observation tours. You can swim in the lake formed by the springs, but watch for alligators!

FISHING Billing itself as the "World's Luckiest Fishing Village," Destin has Florida's largest charter-boat fleet, with more than 140 vessels based at the marinas lining the north shore of Destin Harbor, on U.S. 98 east of the Destin

Bridge. Arranging a trip is as easy as walking along the Destin Harbor waterfront, where you will find the booking booths of several agents, such as **Boardwalk Fishing Charters** (© 800/242-2824 or 850/837-2343; www.harborwalkfishing.com), **Pelican Charters** (© 850/837-2343), **Harbor Cove Charters** (© 850/837-2222), and **Fishermen's Charter Service** (© 850/654-4665). Rates for private charters range from about $400 to $900 per boat, depending on length of voyage.

A less expensive way to try your luck is on a larger group-oriented party boat such as those operated by **Moody's**, at 194 U.S. 98 east on Destin Harbor (© 888/654-1685 or 850/837-1293; www.moodysinc.com). Moody's charges $35 per person ($30 off-season) for its half-day runs (morning is the best time to fish). Children 8 to 12 and nonfishing sightseers are charged half price. Other party boats are the *Destin Princess* (© 888/837-5088 or 850/837-5088), *Emmanuel* (© 850/837-6313), *Lady Eventhia* (© 850/837-6212), and three craft operated by **Olin Marler's Deep Sea Fishing Fleet** (© 850/837-7095), all based at Destin Harbor.

You don't have to go to sea to fish from the catwalk of the 3,000-foot **Destin Bridge** over East Pass. The marinas and bait shops at Destin Harbor can provide gear, bait, information, and a fishing license. In Fort Walton Beach, you can cast a line off **Okaloosa Island Fishing Pier**, 1030 Miracle Strip Pkwy. E. (U.S. 98; © 850/244-1023). The pier is open 24 hours a day. Adults pay $6.50 to fish, children $3.50. Observers pay $1. Bait and equipment rentals are available.

GOLF The area takes great pride in having more than 250 holes of golf. For advance information on all area courses, contact the **Emerald Coast Golf Association**, P.O. Box 304, Destin, FL 32540 (© 850/654-7086). Also look for *Gulf Coast Tee Time,* the free annual directory published in Pensacola (see "Affordable Outdoor Activities" in section 1 of this chapter). It's available on the Web at www.teetimeweb.com. And be sure to inquire whether your choice of accommodations here offers golf packages, which can represent significant savings.

On the mainland, nonresidents are welcome to play at the city-owned **Fort Walton Beach Golf Club**, on Lewis Turner Boulevard (County Rd. 189) north of town (© 850/862-3314 or 850/862-0933; www.fwb.org/golf/index.htm). The club has two 18-hole courses—the **Pines** (© 850/833-9529) and the **Oaks** (© 850/833-9530)—plus a pro shop. Greens fees at both courses are about $30 year-round, including a cart.

In Destin, scenic **Indian Bayou Golf and Country Club**, off Airport Road (© 850/837-6191), has three nine-hole courses with large greens and wide fairways. They look easy, but watch out for water hazards and strategically placed hidden bunkers! Greens fees, including cart, are about $60.

In southern Walton County, **Sandestin Golf and Beach Resort** on U.S. 98 East (© 850/267-8211 for tee times) is the largest facility here (see "Accommodations You Can Afford," below). Its 63 holes are spread over three outstanding championship courses. The Baytowne and Links courses overlook Choctawhatchee Bay. Fees for 18 holes are about $70 for resort guests, $90 for nonguests.

Some of the 27 championship holes at **Emerald Bay Golf Club**, 2 miles east of the Mid-Bay Bridge on U.S. 98 (© 850/837-5197; www.emeraldbaydestin.com), run along Choctawhatchee Bay; the water adds both beauty and challenges to the otherwise wide and forgiving fairways. Greens fees are about $75 with cart.

In southern Walton County, the semi-private **Santa Rosa Golf & Beach Club,** off County Road 30A in Dune Allen Beach (© 850/267-2229; www.santarosaclub.com), offers a challenging 18-hole course through tall pines looking out to vistas of the gulf. The club has a pro shop, a beachside restaurant, a lounge, and tennis courts. The **Seascape Resort & Conference Center,** 100 Seascape Dr. (© 850/837-9181), off County Road 30A, features a Joe Lee–designed 18-hole course winding through woods and around lakes, with a premium placed on accuracy rather than power. The center also has tennis courts, accommodations, a restaurant, a bar, and a pro shop. Fees at both resorts are about $65 in summer, $50 off-season.

In Niceville, a 20-minute drive north via the Mid-Bay Bridge, nonguests may play golf (four nine-hole courses) or tennis (21 courts) at the **Bluewater Bay Resort** (© 850/897-3613; www.bwbresort.com), which also has condominiums for rent. Greens fees are about $55 for 18 holes. Add $15 for a cart.

Call ahead for reservations and current fees at all these clubs, and ask about afternoon and early-evening specials.

SAILING Sailing South (© 850/837-7245; www.sailingsouth.com), on U.S. 98 at Destin Harbor, has half-day cruises aboard the 72-foot schooner *Daniel Webster Clements*. The 1½-hour morning cruise goes in search of dolphins to watch and costs $15 adults, $12 for kids under 12. The 2½-hour afternoon cruises stop for swimming and snorkeling virtually under the Destin Bridge; these cost $35 adults, $18 for kids under 12. It also offers sunset cruises and 3-day voyages. The 54-foot schooner *Nathaniel Bowditch* (© 850/650-8787; www.bowditchsailing.com) will take you on half-day shelling excursions, while the *Blackbeard* (© 850/837-2793; www.blackbeardsailing.com) concentrates on dolphin-watching cruises.

SCUBA DIVING & SNORKELING At least a dozen dive shops are located along the beaches. Considered one of the best, **Scuba Tech Diving Charters** has two locations in Destin: at 301 U.S. 98 E. (© 850/837-2822; www.scubatechnwfl.com); and at 10004 U.S. 98 E. (© 850/837-1933), about a half mile west of the Sandestin Beach Resort.

WATER SPORTS Hobie Cats, WaveRunners, jet boats, jet skis, and parasailing are available all along the beach. The largest selection of operators, including **Boogies** (© 850/654-4497), is at the marinas just east of the Destin Bridge, behind Hooter's and Fat Tuesday's pubs. **Paradise Water Sports** (© 850/664-7872) rents equipment and offers parasailing rides at seven locations along U.S. 98 in both Destin and Fort Walton Beach.

EXPLORING THE AREA

Eden Gardens State Park Evoking images from *Gone With the Wind,* the garden's magnificent 1895 Greek Revival–style Wesley Mansion has been lovingly restored and richly furnished. It stands overlooking scenic Choctawhatchee Bay and is surrounded by immense moss-draped oak trees and the Eden Gardens, resplendent with camellias, azaleas, and other typical Southern flowers. Your visit won't be complete without a guided tour of the house, so avoid coming here on a Tuesday or Wednesday. Picnicking is allowed on the plantation grounds.

181 Eden Gardens Rd. (off County Rd. 395), Point Washington. © 850/231-4214. www.floridastateparks.org/district1/edengardens. Grounds and gardens $2 per vehicle; mansion tours $1.50 adults, 50¢ children 12 and under. Gardens and grounds daily 8am–sunset; 45-min. mansion tours on the hour Thurs–Mon 9am–4pm.

Florida's Gulfarium (Kids) One of the nation's original marine parks features ongoing 25-minute shows with dolphins, California sea lions, Peruvian penguins, loggerhead turtles, sharks, stingrays, moray eels, and alligators. There are fascinating exhibits, including "The Living Sea," with special windows for viewing undersea life. During one of the shows, a scuba diver explains the sea life while swimming amongst the various creatures.

1010 Miracle Strip Pkwy. (U.S. 98) on Okaloosa Island. © 850/244-5169. www.gulfarium.com. Admission $16 adults, $14 seniors, $10 children 4–11; free for children 3 and under. Mid-May to Labor Day daily 9am–6pm (park closes 8pm). Sept to mid-May daily 9am–4pm (park closes 6pm).

Indian Temple Mound and Museum This ceremonial mound, one of the largest ever discovered, dates from A.D. 1200. The museum showcases part of its collection of more than 6,000 ceramic artifacts from southeastern American Indian tribes, the nation's largest such collection. Exhibits depict the lifestyles of the four tribes that lived in the Choctawhatchee Bay region for 12,000 years.

139 Miracle Strip Pkwy. SE, on the mainland. © 850/833-9595. www.fwb.org/html/fwbmuseum01.htm. Park free. Museum $2 adults, $1 children 6–17; free for children 5 and under. Park daily dawn–dusk. Museum Sept–May Mon–Fri 11am–4pm, Sat 9am–4pm; June–Aug Mon–Sat 9am–4:30pm, Sun 12:30–4:30pm.

U.S. Air Force Armament Museum ★★ Although this fascinating museum is not on a par with Pensacola's National Museum of Naval Aviation, you'll love it if you're into war planes. Located on the world's largest air force base, it traces military developments from World War II through the Korean and Vietnam wars to Operation Desert Storm. On display are reconnaissance, fighter, and bomber planes, including the SR-71 Blackbird spy plane.

100 Museum Dr., off Eglin Pkwy. (Fla. 85) at Eglin Air Force Base, 5 miles north of downtown. © 850/882-4062. Free admission. Daily 9:30am–4:30pm. Closed federal holidays.

GREAT OUTLET SHOPPING

The third-largest "designer" outlet mall in the United States, **Silver Sands Factory Stores,** on U.S. 98 between Destin and Sandestin (© **800/510-6255** or 850/864-9780; www.silversandsfactorystores.com), has the upscale likes of Anne Klein, Donna Karan, J. Crew, Brooks Brothers, Hartmann luggage, Coach leather, Bose electronics, and so on. Shops are open Monday to Saturday from 10am to 9pm (to 7pm Jan and Feb), Sunday from 10am to 6pm (noon–6pm Jan and Feb). The fine food court here, **Morgan's Market** (© **850/654-3320**), serves a varied menu. There are electronic games for kids and a sports bar for adults.

Over at the Sandestin Beach Resort on U.S. 98, you can window-shop in **The Market at Sandestin,** where boutiques purvey expensive clothing, gifts, and Godiva chocolates.

ACCOMMODATIONS YOU CAN AFFORD

The area has a vast supply of condominiums and cottages for rent. One good-value example is Venus by the Sea, listed below. The tourist information offices (see "Essentials," earlier in this section) will provide lists of others for rent. The largest rental agent is **Abbott Realty Services,** 3500 Emerald Coast Pkwy., Destin, FL 32541 (© **800/336-4853** or 850/837-4853; fax 850/654-2937; www.abbott-resorts.com). It publishes a magazine-sized annual brochure picturing and describing its many properties throughout the area.

There are several commercial campgrounds here, but the best camping is at **Henderson Beach State Park** in Destin and at **Grayton Beach State Park** in south Walton County (see "Hitting the Great White Beach," earlier in this section).

State and local governments add 9% to all hotel and campground bills.

DESTIN

A former Comfort Inn, the local **Motel 6 Destin**, 405 U.S. 98 E. (© **800/466-8356** or 850/837-0007; fax 850/837-5325; www.motel6.com), sitting across the highway from the harbor, has rooms that are generally larger than those at many other members of this cut-rate chain. There's an outdoor swimming pool on the premises.

Best Western SummerPlace Inn Located across U.S. 98 from the Hampton Inn Destin (see below), this four-story, Spanish-motif building offers innlike rooms and suites decorated with wildlife prints. A few suites have hot tubs in their living rooms (you won't get those at the Hampton Inn). The more expensive gulf-side units have balconies (those facing the bay do not). Larger units have microwave ovens and refrigerators. Doors open from an indoor pool, a whirlpool, and an exercise room to an outdoor pool. You'll have to negotiate your way across busy U.S. 98 to reach the gulf.

14047 Emerald Coast Pkwy. (U.S. 98, at Airport Rd.), Destin, FL 32541. © **888/BEACH-99** or 850/650-8003. Fax 850/650-8004. 72 units. Summer $115–$175; off-season $45–$99. Rates include continental breakfast and local telephone calls. AE, DISC, MC, V. **Amenities:** Indoor and outdoor pools; exercise room; Jacuzzi; business center; coin-op washers and dryers. *In room:* A/C, TV, dataport, fridge (in some), coffeemaker, hair dryer.

Hampton Inn Destin This pink, two-story building sits at the junction of the new and old U.S. 98s, about 200 yards west of Henderson Beach State Park and near a covey of restaurants just outside the recreation area and another bunch of them across U.S. 98. There's beach a short walk away on the old highway, which means you don't have to fight the traffic on U.S. 98 to reach the gulf. External corridors lead to the standard motel-style rooms and the suites with two rooms and kitchenettes. A gazebo-like sitting area offers shade next to a heated outdoor pool and hot tub.

1625 Hwy. 98 E. (at Old Hwy. 98 and Airport Rd.), Destin, FL 32541. © **800/HAMPTON** or 850/654-2677. Fax 850/654-0745. www.hamptoninndestin.com. 104 units. Summer $129–$149 double; $160–$180 suite. Off-season $69–$89 double; $99 suite. Rates include continental breakfast. AE, DC, DISC, MC, V. **Amenities:** Heated outdoor pool; Jacuzzi; coin-op washers and dryers. *In room:* A/C, TV, dataport, kitchenette (suites only), fridge, coffeemaker, hair dryer, iron.

Holiday Inn of Destin *Kids* Many guest rooms in this family-friendly gulf-front resort are in a round high-rise building, but get one facing south or east because a tall condominium next door blocks southwest-facing units from enjoying the spectacular gulf views from their balconies. Better yet, request a room in the older, four-story building, where the rooms are more spacious and many open directly onto the beach. Others open to walkways in an enclosed "Holidome" sporting a comfortable mezzanine lounge with indoor pool and billiard and Foosball tables (plenty here to keep the kids occupied).

1020 Hwy. 98 E. (P.O. Box 577), Destin, FL 32541. © **877/837-6181** or 850/837-6181. Fax 850/837-1523. www.holidayinndestin.com. 233 units. Summer $145–$220 double; off-season $75–$125 double. AE, DC, DISC, MC, V. **Amenities:** Restaurant (American); bar; 3 heated pools (1 indoor, 1 children's); exercise room; Jacuzzi; sauna; children's programs; game room; babysitting; laundry service; coin-op washers and dryers. *In room:* A/C, TV, dataport, fridge, coffeemaker, hair dryer, iron, safe.

Worth a Splurge for Hopeless Romantics

Henderson Park Inn ★★ At the end of Old U.S. 98 on the undeveloped eastern edge of Henderson Beach State Park, this shingle-sided, Cape Hatteras–style bed-and-breakfast is the area's most romantic get-away-from-it-all escape without screaming kids (no children are accepted, nor pets). Individually decorated in a Victorian theme, the rooms have high ceilings, fireplaces, Queen Anne furniture, and gulf views from private balconies. Most have Jacuzzis, and some have canopy beds. The main building (16 rooms are in a separate shingle-sided structure next door) sports a beachside veranda complete with old-fashioned rocking chairs in which to sit and admire the glorious sunsets. Guests are treated to a Southern-style buffet breakfast and to beer and wine at the nightly before-dinner social hour in the wonderful Veranda Restaurant (reservations recommended), which opens to the wraparound porch of the main building. Guests are provided with complimentary beach umbrellas and chairs.

2700 Scenic Hwy. 98 E. (P.O. Box 30), Destin, FL 32541. © **800/336-4853** or 850/837-4853. Fax 850/654-0405. www.hendersonparkinn.com. 35 units. Summer $189–$334 double; off-season $95–$189 double. Rates include full breakfast and evening cocktails. Packages and weekly rates available. AE, DISC, MC, V. No children or pets accepted. **Amenities:** Restaurant (American), bar; heated outdoor pool; Jacuzzi; limited room service; laundry service. *In room:* A/C, TV, dataport, fridge, coffeemaker, hair dryer, iron.

Worth a Splurge for Golf & Tennis Players

Sandestin Golf and Beach Resort ★★   Known until recently as The Resort at Sandestin, this luxurious real-estate development is one of Florida's biggest sports-oriented resorts. It sprawls over 2,300 acres complete with a spectacular beach 5 miles west of Destin, plus a marina. It's notable for its 81 holes of championship golf and its tennis clinic (both with instruction available), plus a fully equipped sports spa and health center. An array of handsomely decorated accommodations overlooks the Gulf or Choctawhatchee Bay, the golf fairways, lagoons, or a nature preserve. The hotel rooms and suites are in the Bayside Inn. They all have kitchenettes and balconies, but you'd be wise to opt for one of the much more spacious junior suites or one-, two-, and three-bedroom condominium apartments, which are in high- and mid-rise buildings either on the gulf or along the manicured fairways. The privately owned condominiums are individually decorated and come with full kitchen and patio or balcony, and many have washers and dryers. Most amenities are a short walk or bike or free tram ride away, and a tunnel runs under U.S. 98 to connect Sandestin's gulf and bay areas. Among the relatively limited on-site dining options is the romantic **Elephant Walk** (© **850/267-4800**), located on the gulf; it serves up different, gourmet-quality choices for dinner every evening.

9300 Emerald Coast Pkwy. W. (U.S. 98), Destin, FL 32541. © **800/277-0800** or 850/267-8000 in the U.S., or 800/933-7846 in Canada. Fax 850/267-8222. www.sandestin.com. 175 units, 620 condo apts. Summer $155–$210 double; $210–$560 condo apt. Off-season $85–$190 double; $105–$395 condo apt. Packages and weekly/monthly rates available. Rates include health club, bicycle, boogie board, canoe, and kayak use; 1-hr. tennis daily; discounts on other amenities. AE, DC, DISC, MC, V. **Amenities:** 3 restaurants (American), 3 bars; 9 heated outdoor pools; 4 golf courses; 18 tennis courts; spa; Jacuzzis; water-sports equipment rentals; children's programs; game room; concierge; shopping arcade; salon; limited room service (hotel only); massage; babysitting; laundry service; coin-op washers and dryers. *In room:* A/C, TV, dataport, kitchen, coffeemaker, hair dryer, iron.

Worth a Splurge for Families with Children

Hilton Sandestin Beach & Golf Resort ★★ *Kids*   This all-suites beachside resort, housed in two adjacent towers, is the top full-service hotel here. It's nicely situated on the grounds of Sandestin Golf and Beach Resort (see above) and shares its golf and tennis facilities. The elegant Elephant Walk restaurant is next door. "Executive suites" in one wing are equipped primarily for business travelers and conventioneers (lots of meeting space here), while the spacious "junior suites" in the old wing are geared to families, with a special area for children's

DESTIN & FORT WALTON BEACH

> **Moments** **Romance Beside the Gulf**
>
> It will demand a serious splurge, but there are few places to stay in Florida more romantic than a honeymoon cottage by the gulf in the quaint village of Seaside. If you have to ask the price, you probably can't stay in one of them, but if you can ante up the dough, contact the **Seaside Cottage Rental Agency,** P.O. Box 4730, Seaside, FL 32459 (© **800/277-8696** or 850/231-1320; fax 850/231-2293; www.seasidefl.com).

bunk beds. Mom can send the kids off to a supervised summertime program (including movies) while pampering herself at the full-service spa.

4000 Sandestin Blvd. S., Destin, FL 32541. © **800/445-8667** or 850/267-9500. Fax 850/267-3076. www.sandestinresort.hilton.com. 598 suites. Summer $250–$395 suite; off-season $150–$335 suite. Golf and tennis packages available. AE, DC, DISC, MC, V. **Amenities:** 2 restaurants (American), 2 bars; indoor and outdoor pools; golf course; tennis courts; health club, spa; Jacuzzi; water-sports equipment rentals; children's programs; game room; concierge; activities desk; car-rental desk; business center; shopping arcade; salon; 24-hr. room service; massage; babysitting; laundry service; coin-op washers and dryers; concierge-level rooms. In room: A/C, TV, dataport, minibar, coffeemaker, hair dryer, iron.

FORT WALTON BEACH

The managers of Venus by the Sea (see below) also run the new **Sea Crest Condominiums,** located next door at 895 Santa Rosa Blvd. (© **800/476-1885** or 850/301-9600; fax 850/301-9205; www.seacrestcondos.com). The 112 units in this seven-story building aren't as spacious as those in Venus, but they're considerably more luxurious, and those on the higher floors have great views toward the west. The complex has indoor and outdoor pools (actually one pool; you can swim under a glass partition between them), and it sits next to a county park with a boardwalk leading over the dunes to the beach.

Among other chain motels here is the new **Hampton Inn Ft. Walton Beach,** 1112 Santa Rosa Blvd. (© **800/HAMPTON** or 850/301-0906; www.hampton innfwb.com). It's adjacent to the Radisson Beach Resort and shares its facilities (see below).

Four Points By Sheraton *Kids*
This beachfront resort sports spacious rooms decorated with vivid, tropical colors. The older, motel-style wings here surround a lush tropical courtyard with a whirlpool, heated swimming pool, and bar. With their balconies overlooking the beach, the choice units are in a newer, seven-story gulf-side building with a second swimming pool and bar. Some rooms have kitchenettes. A summertime children's program helps make this a good if not perfect family choice.

1325 E. Miracle Strip Pkwy. (U.S. 98), Fort Walton Beach, FL 32548. © **800/874-8104** or 850/243-8116. Fax 850/244-3064. www.sheraton4pts.com. 216 units. Summer $115–$245 double; off-season $76–$175 double. Rates include full breakfast. AE, DC, DISC, MC, V. **Amenities:** 2 restaurants (American), bar; 2 heated outdoor pools; exercise room; Jacuzzi; water-sports equipment rentals; children's programs; game room; limited room service; babysitting; laundry service; coin-op washers and dryers. In room: A/C, TV, dataport, fridge, coffeemaker, hair dryer, iron.

Radisson Beach Resort
A glass-enclosed elevator at this resort climbs through a soaring, six-story lean-to atrium lobby to rooms offering spectacular gulf views from their standing-room-only balconies. Beach lovers are more likely to appreciate the units in an older two-story motel building that have sitting-room patios or balconies facing the gulf. Other units in the older building open to a lush courtyard surrounding a pool. In the atrium, a tropically adorned cafe

serves breakfast, lunch, and dinner, and a bar has nightly entertainment during summer.

1110 Santa Rosa Blvd. (at U.S. 98), Fort Walton Beach, FL 32548. © 800/333-3333 or 850/243-9181. Fax 850/664-7652. www.radissonresort.com. 287 units. Summer $129–$189 double; off-season $89–$129 double. Packages available. AE, DC, DISC, MC, V. **Amenities:** Restaurant (American), 2 bars; 3 outdoor pools (1 children's); 2 lighted tennis courts; exercise room; water-sports equipment rentals; limited room service; babysitting; laundry service. *In room:* A/C, TV, dataport, coffeemaker, hair dryer, iron.

Ramada Plaza Beach Resort This big resort boasts the prettiest outdoor areas in northwest Florida, with waterfalls cascading over lofty rocks and a romantic grotto bar, all surrounded by thick tropical foliage. Although there is another swimming pool, a large sun deck, and a bar out by the beach, this gorgeous courtyard would have even more charm if it weren't cut off from the gulf by a six-story block of hotel rooms. The guest rooms and the one-bedroom suites in this beachfront building are the best here, with gulf or courtyard views from balconies or patios. The least expensive units, in the adjacent building, overlook a parking lot. On-site dining options include a barbecue shack out in the tropical forest. The Boardwalk beach pavilion and restaurants are next door. There's also a cozy lobby lounge with sports TVs.

1500 E. Miracle Strip Pkwy. (U.S. 98), Fort Walton Beach, FL 32548. © 800/874-8962 or 850/243-9161. Fax 850/243-2391. www.ramadafwb.com. 335 units. Summer $120–$185 double; $280–$350 suite. Off-season $70–$140 double; $160–$270 suite. AE, DC, DISC, MC, V. **Amenities:** 3 restaurants (American), 3 bars; 2 outdoor pools (1 heated); exercise room; Jacuzzi; water-sports equipment rentals; children's programs; game room; limited room service; coin-op washers and dryers. *In room:* A/C, TV, dataport, fridge, coffeemaker, hair dryer, iron.

Venus by the Sea *Value* Offering considerably more space than a hotel would at these rates, this pleasant, three-story enclave on western Okaloosa Island was built in the 1970s and has been immaculately maintained ever since. Each of the one-, two-, and three-bedroom units has a long living/dining/kitchen room, with a rear door leading to a balcony or to a patio opening to a grassy courtyard. The beach is a short walk across the dunes, and you can stroll along the undeveloped beach at an Eglin Air Force Base auxiliary facility about 200 yards away. The same management also operates the new and much more luxurious **Sea Crest Condominiums** next door (see above), and guests here can use the indoor-outdoor pool there.

885 Santa Rosa Blvd., Fort Walton Beach, FL 32548. © 800/476-1885 or 850/301-9600. Fax 850/301-9205. www.venuscondos.com. 45 units. Summer $110–$180 apt.; off-season $50–$135 apt. Weekly and monthly rates available. Ask for off-season specials. MC, V. **Amenities:** Outdoor pool; tennis court; coin-op washers and dryers. *In room:* A/C, TV/VCR, kitchen, coffeemaker, iron.

Super-Cheap Sleeps

Marina Motel This family-operated, self-described "fisherman's motel" may be pedestrian-looking, but it has clean, comfortable rooms and apartments directly across U.S. 98 from the magnificent public beach at Beasley Park. A low-slung, brick-fronted motel block holds most of the rooms. Other units are in two-story stucco structures near a marina whose 560-foot pier is home to charter-fishing boats. Two one-bedroom apartments at the end of the complex overlook the marina and bay. All units here have refrigerators and microwaves; 16 have full kitchens. If traffic is too busy to cross U.S. 98 to the beach (there are no nearby overpasses or traffic lights), you can sun at the motel's little bayside beach or take a dip in its roadside pool.

1345 E. Miracle Strip Pkwy. (U.S. 98), Fort Walton Beach, FL 32548. © 800/237-7021 or 850/244-1129. Fax 850/243-6063. www.marinamotel.net. 38 units. Summer $67–$87 double; $115–$125 apt. Off-season

$39–$63 double; $65–$92 apt. AE, DC, DISC, MC, V. **Amenities:** Outdoor pool; coin-op washers and dryers. *In room:* A/C, TV, kitchen (efficiencies and apts only), fridge, coffeemaker, iron.

GREAT DEALS ON DINING

Except for the strip on Okaloosa Island, a plethora of national fast-food and family chain restaurants line U.S. 98.

DESTIN

If you didn't catch a fish to be grilled at Fisherman's Wharf (see below), you buy one to brag about from **Sexton's Seafood,** 602 Hwy. 98 E., opposite Destin Harbor (© 805/837-3040). It's the best market here.

A good budget choice here is **Morgan's Market** (© 850/654-3320), the food court at Silver Sands Factory Outlets (see "Great Outlet Shopping," above).

AJ's Seafood & Oyster Bar SEAFOOD   Jimmy Buffett tunes set the tone at this fun, tiki-topped establishment on the picturesque Destin Harbor docks, where fishing boats unload their daily catches right into the kitchen. Obviously, the best items here are grilled or fried fish, but raw or steamed Apalachicola oysters also lead the bill of fare. You can sample a bit of everything with a "run of the kitchen" seafood patter. AJ's is most famous for its topside Club Bimini, a "meet bar" featuring reggae music and limbo contests every summer evening (you may want to have dinner elsewhere if you're not in the partying mood). At lunch, picnic tables on the covered dock make a fine venue with a view across the harbor.

116 Hwy. 98 E., Destin Harbor. © 850/837-1913. Main courses $12–$19; sandwiches and salads $6–$8. AE, DISC, MC, V. Apr–Sept Sun–Thurs 11am–10pm; Fri–Sat 11am–midnight (bar until 4am). Off-season daily 11am–9pm.

Back Porch ★ SEAFOOD   This cedar-shingled seafood shack offers glorious beach and gulf views from its long porch. The popular, casual restaurant originated charcoal-grilled amberjack, which you'll now see on menus throughout Florida. Other fish and seafood, as well as chicken and juicy hamburgers, also come from the coals. Monthly specials feature crab, lobster, and seasonal fish. Come early, order a rum-laden Key Lime Freeze, and enjoy the sunset. The Back Porch sits with a number of other restaurants near the western boundary of the Henderson Beach State Park.

1740 Old Hwy. 98 E. © 850/837-2022. Main courses $12–$20; sandwiches, burgers, and pastas $6.50–$8.50. AE, DC, DISC, MC, V. Apr–Sept daily 11am–11pm. Off-season daily 11am–10pm. From U.S. 98, turn toward the beach at the Hampton Inn.

Ciao Bella Pizza *Finds* PIZZA/SOUTHERN ITALIAN   This urbane little parlor offers more than just very good 12-inch pizzas; chef Gugliemo Ianni also whips up excellent salads and pastas, which he displays on a cafeteria-style steam table, just like they do in his native Italy. Afterwards enjoy some creamy gelato.

29 Hwy. 98 (in Harborwalk Center near Destin Bridge). © 850/654-9815. Main courses $8–$11; pizza $8–$17. AE, DISC, MC, V. Mon–Sat noon–10pm; Sun 3–10pm.

Fisherman's Wharf Seafood House SEAFOOD   Have that fish you caught filleted, bring it here, and the chef will chargrill it at this atmospheric restaurant next to a charter fleet marina (the restaurant hosts most of Destin's fishing competitions). If you had no luck, and didn't stop by Sexton's Seafood on the way here to buy a few filets (see above), you can select from the restaurant's fresh-off-the-boat catch for grilling, broiling, frying, or blackening. Charcoal grilling is the house specialty—my triggerfish filet was white and flaky but still moist. All main courses include a trip to the salad bar, rice pilaf, baked potato, or roasted vegetables. Although this building dates from 1996, it evokes an Old Florida fish camp, with rough-hewn wood walls and double-hung windows looking out to a large harborside deck, a venue during the warmer months for two bars, an oyster bar, live music, and great sunsets.

210D Hwy. 98 E., Destin Harbor. © 850/654-4766. Main courses $11–$18; sandwiches and burgers $7–$9; cook-your-catch $6 lunch, $8 dinner. AE, DC, DISC, MC, V. Summer daily 11am–11pm (deck bar open later). Off-season daily 11am–9pm.

Harry T's Boat House *Kids* AMERICAN   To honor the memory of trapeze artist "Flying Harry T" Baben, his family opened this lively spot on the ground floor of Destin Harbor's tallest building. Standing guard is the stuffed Stretch, Harry's beloved giraffe. Other decor includes circus memorabilia and relics from the luxury cruise ship *Thracia,* which sank off the Emerald Coast in 1927; Harry T was presented with the ship's salvaged furnishings and fixtures for personally leading the heroic rescue of its 2,000 passengers. The tabloid-style menu offers traditional seafood, steaks, chicken, and pasta dishes. Kids eat for 99¢ until 7pm and at Sunday brunch. Watch for clowns and other children's entertainment at least 1 night a week. Both the dining room and the downstairs lounge (with live entertainment Fri and Sat nights) enjoy harbor views.

320 U.S. 98 E., Destin Harbor. © 850/654-4800. Main courses $10.50–$20; sandwiches and salads $10–$12. AE, DISC, MC, V. Summer Mon–Sat 11am–2am; Sun 10am–2am. Off-season Mon–Sat 11am–11pm; Sun 10am–11pm. Bar open later. Sun brunch year-round 10am–3pm.

McGuire's Irish Pub & Brewery STEAKS/SEAFOOD   Like Pensacola's original McGuire's (see "Great Deals on Dining" in section 1 of this chapter), this younger sibling sports thousands of dollar bills stuck on the ceilings and walls, plus Notre Dame football schedules, a prominent logo of the Boston Celtics, and other memorabilia recalling Irish American lore. This is Destin's most popular hangout, and local professionals congregate at the big oak bar in the center of the dining room, especially when live entertainment starts at 9pm Tuesday to Sunday. You can opt for a table on either side of the bar or up on a rooftop deck. Dining here is almost secondary to the see-and-be-seen scene, although the tender chargrilled steaks and giant hamburgers are worthy antidotes to a big appetite.

33 Hwy. 98 E., Destin Harbor (in Harborwalk Center near Destin Bridge). © 850/650-0000. Main courses $16–$25; snacks, burgers, and sandwiches $8–$12. AE, DC, DISC, MC, V. Mon–Sat 11am–2am; Sun 11am–1am.

Super-Cheap Eats

Callahan's Island Restaurant & Deli *Value* AMERICAN/DELI   The best place in the area for picnic fare, this family-operated deli offers burgers, excellent Reubens, and other made-to-order sandwiches, pastas, and nightly specials such as charcoal-grilled chicken and grilled pork chops. A long refrigerator case across the rear holds a variety of top-grade cheeses, deli meats, steaks, and chops (choose your own cut, and the chef will chargrill it to order). Tables and booths are set up garden fashion, adding an outdoorsy ambience to this pleasant storefront establishment. Locals like to do lunch here. Breakfast is served only on Saturday morning.

950 Gulf Shore Dr. (2 blocks south of U.S. 98). © 850/837-6328. Main courses $8–$16; sandwiches, burgers, and salads $3.50–$6.50. DISC, MC, V. Mon–Fri 10am–9pm; Sat 8am–9pm.

Donut Hole SOUTHERN   Available around the clock, breakfasts at this popular spot highlight eggs Benedict, hot fluffy biscuits under sausage gravy, Belgian waffles, and freshly baked doughnuts. Lunch sees fresh deli sandwiches, half-pound burgers, and big salads. The rough-hewn building has booths and counter seating. Be prepared to wait on the deck, especially on weekends. Daily specials such as half a Southern-fried chicken with three country-style vegetables and dessert are a bargain. There's another Donut Hole, open daily from 6am to 10pm, on U.S. 98 East in southern Walton County 2½ miles east of the Sandestin Beach Resort (C **850/267-3239**).

635 U.S. 98 E., Destin. C **850/837-8824**. Breakfast $4–$7.50; sandwiches, salads, and burgers $4.50–$6.50; main courses $6.50–$8. No credit cards. Daily 24 hr. Closed 2 weeks before Christmas.

Worth a Splurge

Criolla's ★★★ Value INTERNATIONAL One of Florida's finest restaurants, Johnny Earles's charming establishment derives its name from the archaic word *criollo,* signifying persons of pure Spanish descent born in the New World. The attractive decor, combining New Orleans with the Caribbean, features potted palms, whirling ceiling fans, and tropical island paintings. The menus change seasonally, but many fish dishes carry the wonderful aroma of smoke from a wood-fired grill (the bacon-wrapped swordfish is always a winner). Be sure to ask about a special four-course, fixed-price dinner, which draws inspiration from such warm spots as the Caribbean, Central America, and Tahiti. It's also worth asking in advance about special events featuring visiting chefs and spotlighting excellent vineyards (the wine cellar here has won awards).

170 E. Scenic Hwy. 30A, a quarter mile east of County Rd. 283, Grayton Beach. C **850/267-1267**. Reservations recommended. Main courses $19–$31. AE, DISC, MC, V. Jan–Feb and Oct–Dec Tues–Sat 5:30–10pm; Mar–Apr and Sept Mon–Sat 5:30–10pm; May–Aug daily 5:30–10pm.

Harbor Docks SEAFOOD/JAPANESE The harbor views are spectacular from indoors or outdoors at this casual, somewhat-rustic establishment. You can order your fill of fried fish, but specialties such as the daily catch sautéed with artichoke hearts are far more enjoyable. Asian influences include a sushi bar and hibachi table, which are open for dinner, and a few Thai specialties which grace the lunch menu. Except during winter, hearty fishermen's breakfasts are cooked by the owners of the Silver Sands, a popular local haunt that burned down several years ago. The bar here is popular with charter-boat skippers, and frequent live entertainment keeps the action going on the outdoor deck at night.

538 U.S. 98 E., Destin Harbor. C **850/837-2506**. Reservations accepted only for hibachi table. Main courses $16–$23; sushi $4.50–$8. AE, DC, DISC, MC, V. Feb–Oct daily 5:30am–10:30am and 11am–11pm. Nov–Jan daily 11am–11pm. Sushi bar daily 5–10pm.

Marina Cafe ★★ NEW AMERICAN Destin's finest restaurant provides a classy atmosphere with soft candlelight, subdued music, and walls of glass overlooking the harbor. The changing menu always offers nouveau preparations of seafood. Pizzas are topped with the likes of spicy cayenne rock shrimp, roasted corn, and onion marmalade, and pastas might feature fusilli with roast chicken, sun-dried tomatoes, goat cheese, broccoli, pine nuts, and an herb and balsamic vinegar broth. Any main course will be an exciting combination of flavors, too. If it's offered, try the grouper coated with crab and horseradish and served with herb-roasted potatoes and wild-mushroom parsnip and asparagus ragout. Enjoy the outdoor deck for drinks and appetizers.

404 Hwy. 98 E., Destin Harbor. C **850/837-7960**. Reservations recommended. Main courses $17–$29; pizza and pasta $9–$17. AE, DC, DISC, MC, V. Daily 5–11pm. Closed first 3 weeks in Jan.

A Friendly Pub with a Great Happy Hour

Buster's Oyster Bar and Seafood Restaurant SEAFOOD Shingles, plants, and wood make this local favorite seem not at all like a shopping-center sports bar, 1 mile west of Sandestin Golf and Beach Resort and across U.S. 98 from Silver Sands Factory Outlets. Buster claims that more than five million oysters have been shucked here, and with good reason, since they go for $1.59 a *dozen* during his daily 5 to 6pm happy hour. Another winner here is spicy gumbo, which has won recent cook-off competitions. The colorful, tabloid-style menu also offers the likes of "a toasted sea spider sandwich" (soft-shell crab). Fried, broiled, steamed, or blackened fish and seafood dinners are prepared to order. Kids have their own menu.

125 Poinciana Blvd. (in Delchamps Plaza, U.S. 98 at Scenic Hwy. 98). © 850/837-4399. Main courses $10–$22; sandwiches and burgers $7–$10. AE, DC, DISC, MC, V. Apr–Oct daily 11am–22pm; Nov–Mar 11am–10pm.

FORT WALTON BEACH

Caffè Italia NORTHERN ITALIAN Nada Eckhardt is from Croatia, but she met her American husband, Jim, while working at a restaurant named Caffè Italia in northern Italy. The Eckhardts duplicated that establishment in this 1925 Sears & Roebuck mail-order house tucked away on the waterfront. You can dine on the patio with a view of the sound through sprawling live oak trees (one table is set romantically under its own gazebo), or dine inside, where Nada has installed floral tablecloths and photos from the old country. A limited but fine menu includes excellent pizzas; pasta dishes such as tortellini with tomatoes, chicken, and peas in Alfredo sauce; northern Italian risotto with either asparagus or smoked salmon; and meat and seafood dishes to fit the season. Don't expect to make a full meal by ordering only a pasta here, because meals are served in the authentic Italian fashion, with a small portion of pasta preceding the seafood or meat course. On the other hand, you can quickly fill up on the seasoned, pizza-dough breadsticks served with olive oil for dipping. The cappuccino here is absolutely first-rate, as are the genuine Italian desserts.

189 Brooks St., on the mainland in the block west of Brooks Bridge. © 850/664-0035. Reservations recommended. Main courses $15–$18; pizza and pasta $8–$13. AE, DC, DISC, MC, V. Sun and Tues–Fri 11am–10pm; Sat 5–11pm. Closed Thanksgiving and Christmas.

Pandora's Restaurant & Lounge STEAKS/PRIME RIB/SEAFOOD The front part of this unusual restaurant is a beached yacht now housing the main-deck lounge. Below is a beam-ceilinged dining room aglow with lights from copper chandeliers. Try for the private Bob Hope booth, where you can dine below two of the great comedian's golf clubs (he used to come here to raise money for a local Air Force widow's home). Anything from the charcoal grill is excellent, including the wonderful bacon-wrapped scallops offered as an appetizer. Several varieties of freshly caught fish are among the main-course choices, but steaks and prime rib keep the locals coming back for more. The tender beef is cut on the premises and grilled to perfection. The delicious breads and pies are homemade. Live entertainment and dancing are an added attraction in the lounge Wednesday to Saturday, as are free snacks during happy hour from 5 to 7pm weekdays. There's another Pandora's in Grayton Beach at the corner of Fla. 283 and County Road 30A (© **850/231-4102**).

1120B Santa Rosa Blvd. © 850/244-8669. Reservations recommended. Main courses $12–$25. AE, DISC, MC, V. Sun–Thurs 5–10pm; Fri–Sat 5–10:30pm.

Staff's Seafood Restaurant SEAFOOD/STEAKS Considered the first Emerald Coast restaurant, Staff's started as a hotel in 1913 and moved to this barnlike building in 1931. Among the display of memorabilia are an old-fashioned phonograph lamp and a 1914 cash register. Staff's tangy seafood gumbo has gained fame for this casual, historic restaurant. One of the most popular main dishes is the "seafood skillet," sizzling with broiled grouper, shrimp, scallops, and crabmeat drenched in butter and sprinkled with cheese. All main courses are served with heaping baskets of hot, home-baked wheat bread from a secret 70-year-old recipe, a salad, and dessert. A pianist plays at dinner year-round.

24 SW Miracle Strip Pkwy. (U.S. 98), on the mainland. © 850/243-3526. Main courses $13–$30. AE, DISC, MC, V. Summer daily 5–11pm. Off-season Mon–Thurs 5–9pm; Fri–Sat 5–10pm.

Super-Cheap Eats

Big City Coffeehouse and Cafe COFFEE/PASTRIES/DELI   For a caffeine fix, an inexpensive breakfast or lunch, or afternoon tea, head to Tina and Jim Ivanchukov's bright yellow-and-purple cafe on the mainland near the Brooks Bridge. In addition to offering gourmet coffees, the owners make great salads such as herb-roasted chicken with apples, walnuts, and tarragon dressing (sold by the pound), and sandwiches served on homemade focaccia bread.

201 Miracle Strip Pkwy. SE (U.S. 98). © 850/664-0664. Sandwiches and salads $5.50–$8.50. MC, V. Mon–Fri 7am–7pm; Sat–Sun 8am–5pm.

SEASIDE

Several cafes and sandwich shops in Seaside's gulf-side shopping complex offer inexpensive snacks to beachgoers.

Worth a Splurge

Bud and Alley's   SEAFOOD/STEAKS/MEDITERRANEAN   Set among the gulf-side dunes, Seaside's first restaurant is still number one. The freshest seafood can be selected from seasonal menus featuring an innovative selection of Basque, Italian, Louisianan, and Floridian dishes prepared by owners and accomplished chefs Scott Witcoski and Dave Raushkolb. You can dine indoors or out, on the screened porch, or under an open-air gazebo where you'll hear the waves splashing against the white sands. The roof deck, open in season, serves appetizers and light meals and is a fabulous spot from which to watch the sun set on the Gulf of Mexico. Jazz is usually in the spotlight on weekends. On New Year's Eve, everyone in town and from miles around celebrates at Bud and Alley's. Call ahead to see whether a noted guest chef is cooking or a special wine-tasting dinner is scheduled. No smoking.

County Rd. 30A, in the beachside shops. © 850/231-5900. Reservations recommended. Main courses $19–$27; lunch $7.50–$14. MC, V. Apr–Sept Sun–Thurs 11:30am–3pm and 5:30–9:30pm; Fri–Sat 11:30am–3pm and 5:30–10pm. Oct–Mar Sun–Thurs 5:30–9pm; Fri–Sat 5:30–9:30pm.

DESTIN & FORT WALTON BEACH AFTER DARK

Most resorts spotlight live entertainment during the summer season, including the Radisson Beach Resort and the Ramada Plaza Beach Resort in Fort Walton Beach, and the Hilton Sandestin Beach & Golf Resort and Sandestin Golf and Beach Resort in southern Walton County (see "Accommodations You Can Afford," earlier in this section). It's a good idea to inquire ahead to make sure what's scheduled, especially during the slow season from October through February.

For other ideas and listings of what's happening, pick up a copy of the weekly *Walton Sun* newspaper.

DESTIN   Several Destin restaurants offer entertainment nightly during summer, on weekends off-season. The dockside **AJ's Club Bimini,** 116 U.S. 98 E. (© **850/837-1913**), has live reggae under a big thatch-roofed deck. A somewhat older, if not more sober, crowd gathers for entertainment at the big harborside deck at **Fisherman's Wharf,** on U.S. 98 East (© **850/654-4766**); at **The Deck,** on U.S. 98 East at the Harbor Docks restaurant, overlooking the harbor

(© 850/837-2506); and at **Harry T's Boat House** (© 850/654-6555), also on the harbor. For Irish tunes nightly year-round there's **McGuire's Irish Pub & Brewery** (© 850/650-0000), in the Harborwalk Shops on U.S. 98 just east of the Destin Bridge. See "Great Deals on Dining," above, for details about the restaurants. The **Grande Isle Sky Bar,** above Grazti Italian Restaurant, 1771 Old Hwy. 98 (© 850/837-7475), draws the after-dinner crowd from the Back Porch and other adjacent restaurants.

Twenty-somethings are attracted to the dance club, rowdy saloon, Jimmy Buffett–style reggae bar, and sports TV and billiards parlor all under one roof at the acclaimed **Nightown,** 140 Palmetto St. (© 850/837-6448; www.nightown.com), near the harbor on the inland side of U.S. 98 East. One admission covers it all. Nearby, **Hogs Breath Destin,** 541 Hwy. 98 E. (© 850/837-5991), is another lively pub with bands playing beach music.

Out toward Sandestin, **Fudrucker's Beachside Bar & Grill,** 20001 Hwy. 98 E. (© 850/654-4200), opposite the Henderson Beach State Park, offers double the fun with two summertime stages. There's another Fudrucker's at 108 Santa Rosa Blvd. on Okaloosa Island in Fort Walton Beach (© 850/243-3833).

FORT WALTON BEACH Country music and dancing fans will find a home at the **Seagull,** on Miracle Strip Parkway (U.S. 98) opposite the Gulfarium (© 850/243-3413). The generations of air force pilots who have hung out here call it the "Dirty Gull." Its main rival for the country set is the **High Tide Oyster Bar,** at Okaloosa Island off the Brooks Bridge (© 850/244-2624).

3 Panama City Beach

100 miles E of Pensacola, 100 miles SW of Tallahassee

Panama City Beach has long been known as the "Redneck Riviera," since it's a summertime mecca for millions of low- and moderate-income vacationers from nearby Southern states. It still has a seemingly unending strip of bars, amusement parks, and old-fashioned motels. But this lively and crowded destination now also has luxury resorts and condominiums to go along with its 22 miles of white-sand beach, golf courses, fishing, boating, and fresh seafood.

Panama City Beach is also the most seasonal resort in Northwest Florida, as many restaurants, attractions, and even some hotels close between October and spring break in March. Spring break is a big deal here; MTV even sets up shop in Panama City Beach for its annual beach-party broadcasts.

ESSENTIALS

GETTING THERE The commuter arms of **Delta** (© 800/221-1212), **Northwest/KLM** (© 800/225-2525), and **US Airways** (© 800/428-4322) fly into **Panama City/Bay County International Airport** (© 850/763-6751; www.pcairport.com) on Lisenby Avenue, north of St. Andrews Boulevard, in Panama City.

Alamo (© 800/327-9633), **Avis** (© 800/331-1212), **Budget** (© 800/527-0700), **Enterprise** (© 800/325-8007), **Hertz** (© 800/654-3131), and **National** (© 800/CAR-RENT) have rental-cars here.

Taxi fares to the beach range from about $12 to $25.

The *Sunset Limited* transcontinental service on **Amtrak** (© 800/USA-RAIL; www.amtrak.com) stops at Chipley, 45 miles north of Panama City.

VISITOR INFORMATION For advance information, contact the **Panama City Beach Convention & Visitors Bureau,** P.O. Box 9473, Panama City

Beach, FL 32417 (✆ **800/PC-BEACH** in the U.S., 800/553-1330 in Canada, or 850/233-6503; fax 850/233-5072; www.800pcbeach.com). It operates a visitor information center in the city hall complex, 17001 Panama City Beach Pkwy. (U.S. 98), at Fla. 79. The center is open daily from 8am to 5pm and is closed New Year's Day, Thanksgiving, and Christmas.

GETTING AROUND A **trolley** (✆ **850/769-0557**) runs five times a day Monday to Friday year-round along Thomas Drive and on Front Beach Road as far west as Fla. 79. Rides cost 50¢. Call for the schedule.

For a taxi, call **Yellow Cab** (✆ **800/763-0211** or 850/763-4691) or **AAA Taxi** (✆ **850/785-0533**). Fares at the beach are $2.50 for the first two-fifths of a mile plus 25¢ a mile thereafter, or $5 to $10 for rides within Panama City Beach.

Classic Rentals, 13226 Front Beach Rd. (✆ **850/235-1519**), rents bicycles, scooters, and motorcycles. Call for prices and reservations.

TIME The Panama City area is in the central time zone, 1 hour behind Miami, Orlando, and Tallahassee.

WHAT TO SEE & DO
HITTING THE BEACH: ST. ANDREWS STATE PARK

A nearly unbroken strand of fine white sand fronts all 22 miles of Panama City Beach, but the highlight for many here is **St. Andrews State Park** ✯✯✯, at the east end of the beach. With more than 1,000 acres of dazzling white sand and dunes, this preserved wilderness demonstrates what the area looked like before motels and condominiums lined the beach. Lacy, golden sea oats sway in the refreshing gulf breezes, and fragrant rosemary grows wild. Picnic areas are on both the gulf beach and the Grand Lagoon. Restrooms and open-air showers are available for beachgoers. For anglers, there are jetties and a boat ramp. A nature trail reveals wading birds and perhaps an alligator or two. And drive carefully here, for the area is home to foxes, coyotes, and a herd of deer. On display is a historic turpentine still formerly used by lumbermen to make turpentine and rosin, both important for caulking the old wooden ships.

The park's 176 RV and tent **campsites** are among the state's most beautiful, especially the 40 situated in a pine forest right on the shores of Grand Lagoon. They are very popular, so reservations are highly recommended—and absolutely essential in summer (call ✆ **800/326-3521** or go to the website www.reserveamerica.com). Sites cost $17 to $23 from March through September. They drop to $10 to $14 from October to February.

Park admission is $4 per car with two to eight occupants, $2 for single-occupant vehicles, and $1 for pedestrians and cyclists. The area is open daily from 8am to sunset. Pets are not allowed in the park. For more information or for camping reservations, contact the park at 4607 State Park Lane, Panama City, FL 32408 (✆ **850/233-5140;** www.floridastateparks.org/district1/standrews).

A few hundred yards across an inlet from St. Andrews State Park sits pristine **Shell Island** ✯✯, a 7½-mile-long, 1-mile-wide barrier island that's accessible only by boat. This uninhabited natural preserve is great for shelling and also fun for swimming, suntanning, or just relaxing. Visitors can bring chairs, beach gear, coolers, food, and beverages. The best way to get there is on the park's **Shell Island Shuttle** (✆ **800/227-0132** or 850/233-5140; www.shellisland shuttle.com), which runs every 30 minutes daily from 9am to 5pm in summer, weekends from 10am to 3pm in spring and fall. Fares are $9.50 for adults, $5.50 for children 11 and under, plus admission fees to the state recreation area (see above). A special snorkeling package costs $17.95, including shuttle ride and equipment. Kayak rentals cost $35 a day for a single-seat boat, $45 for a double-seater.

Several cruise boats go to Shell Island, including the glass-bottom *Captain Anderson III,* which cruises there from Captain Anderson's Marina, 5500 N. Lagoon Dr., at Thomas Drive (© 850/234-3435). It charges $10 for anyone over age 12, $8 for kids. The *Glass Bottom Boat* (© 850/234-8944) stops at Shell Island as part of its "sea school" trips from Treasure Island Marina, 3605 Thomas Dr. at Grand Lagoon (see "Cruises" under " Affordable Outdoor Activities," below).

AFFORDABLE OUTDOOR ACTIVITIES

BOATING A variety of rental boats are available at the marinas near the Thomas Drive bridge over Grand Lagoon. These include the **Captain Davis Queen Fleet,** based at Captain Anderson's Marina, 5500 N. Lagoon Dr. (© 800/874-2415, or 850/234-3435 from nearby states); **the Panama City Boat Yard,** 5323 N. Lagoon Dr. (© 850/234-3386); the **Passport Marina,** 5325 N. Lagoon Dr. (© 850/234-5609); the **Port Lagoon Yacht Basin,** 5201 N. Lagoon Dr. (© 850/234-0142); the **Pirates Cove Marina,** 3901 Thomas Dr. (© 850/234-3839); and the **Treasure Island Marina,** 3605 Thomas Dr. (© 850/234-6533).

Many resorts and hotels provide beach toys for their guests' use. WaveRunners, jet boats, inflatables, and other equipment can be rented from **Panama City Beach Sports** (© 850/234-0067), **Raging Rentals** (© 850/234-6775), and **Lagoon Rentals** (© 850/234-7245).

CRUISES You'll have your choice of numerous cruises here, from sailing to visiting the dolphins aboard noisy jet skis. The visitor information center (see "Essentials," above) has information about them all—and discount coupons for many.

One of the most comprehensive outings here is aboard the *Glass Bottom Boat,* based at Treasure Island Marina, 3605 Thomas Dr., at Grand Lagoon (© 850/234-8944). Its 3-hour, narrated "sea school" cruise includes underwater viewing, dolphin-watching, bird feeding, and a 1-hour stop for swimming at Shell Island. Along the way, the crew picks up and rebaits a crab trap and explains the creatures brought up in a shrimp net. The boat has a snack bar and an air-conditioned cabin. The trips cost about $15 for adults and $8 for children. Call for cruise times and reservations.

Children get a kick out of the make-believe swashbucklers on the *Sea Dragon* (© 850/234-7400; www.piratecruise.net), an 80-foot-long replica of a pirate ship that goes on 2-hour cruises from its dock next to the Treasure Ship on Thomas Drive at Grand Lagoon. The trips cost $16, $13 for seniors, $12 for children 3 to 12, and are free for children under 3. Call for seasonal schedules and reservations.

FISHING The least expensive way to try your luck fishing is with **Captain Anderson's Deep Sea Fishing,** at Captain Anderson's Marina on Thomas Drive at Grand Lagoon (© 800/874-2415 or 850/234-5940). The captain's party-boat trips last from 5 to 12 hours, with prices ranging from about $30 to $50 per person, including bait and tackle. Observers can go along for half price.

More expensive are the charter-fishing boats that depart daily from March to November from the marinas mentioned in "Boating," above.

You won't get seasick casting your line from the **M. B. Miller County Pier,** 12213 Front Beach Rd. (✆ **850/233-3039**), or the **Dan Russell Municipal Pier,** 16101 Front Beach Rd. (✆ **850/233-5080**).

GOLF Marriott's Bay Point Resort Village, 4200 Marriott Dr., off Jan Cooley Road (✆ **850/234-3307;** www.baypointgolf.com), offers 36 holes of championship play, including the Bruce Devlin–designed **Lagoon Legends** ★★ course, rated one of the country's most difficult. Both it and the Club Meadows course have clubhouses, putting greens, driving ranges, clinics, and private instruction. Greens fees with cart range from about $50 in summer to $80 in winter, depending on the month and day of the week. See "Accommodations You Can Afford," below.

The **Edgewater Beach Resort,** 11212 U.S. 98A (✆ **850/235-4044**), also has a nine-hole resort course, and its guests have access to **The Hombre,** 120 Coyote Pass, 3 miles west of the Hathaway Bridge off Panama City Beach Parkway/U.S. 98 (✆ **850/234-3573**), a par-72 championship course that is home to the Nike Panama City Beach Classic. Fifteen of its 18 holes have water hazards (the unforgiving seventh hole sits on an island). Greens fees are about $65 in summer, $60 in winter, including cart.

The course at the semi-private **Holiday Golf Club,** 100 Fairway Blvd. (✆ **850/234-1800**), sports lake-line fairways and elevated greens. Greens fees with cart are about $45 in summer, $35 in winter. You can play at night on a lighted nine-hole, par-29 executive course.

The least expensive place to play here is the flat and forgiving **Signal Hill,** 9516 N. Thomas Dr. (✆ **850/234-3218**), where you'll pay about $20 to walk 18 holes in summer, $15 in winter. Add about $10 per person for a cart.

SCUBA DIVING & SNORKELING Although the area is too far north for extensive coral formations, more than 50 artificial reefs and shipwrecks in the Gulf waters off Panama City attract a wide variety of sea life. The largest local operator is **Hydrospace Dive Shop,** 6422 W. Hwy. 98 (✆ **850/234-3036;** www.hydrospace.com). Others include **Panama City Dive Center,** 4823 Thomas Dr. (✆ **850/235-3390;** www.pcdivecenter.com); **Emerald Coast Divers,** 5121 Thomas Dr. (✆ **800/945-DIVE** or 850/233-3355); **West End Dive Center,** 17320 Panama City Beach Pkwy. (✆ **850/235-7873**); and **Pete's Scuba Center,** 9007 Front Beach Rd. (✆ **800/401-DIVE** or 850/230-8006). These companies lead dives, teach courses, and take snorkelers to the grass flats off Shell Island.

EXPLORING THE AREA

Gulf World Marine Park *Kids* This landscaped tropical garden and marine showcase features shows with talented dolphins, sea lions, penguins, and more. Not to be upstaged, parrots perform daily, too. Sea turtles, alligators, and other critters also call Gulf World home. Scuba demonstrations, shark feedings, and underwater shows keep the crowds entertained. Allow about 3½ hours to see it all, including the shows.

15412 Front Beach Rd. (at Hill Ave.), Panama City Beach. ✆ 850/234-5271. www.gulfworldmarinepark.com. Admission $19.40 adults, $13.40 children 5–11; free for children under 5. Summer daily 9am–4pm; off-season daily 9am–2pm.

Museum of Man in the Sea Owned by the Institute of Diving, this small museum exhibits relics from the first days of scuba diving, historical displays of the underwater world dating from 1500, and treasures recovered from sunken ships, including Spanish treasure galleons. Hands-on exhibits explain water and air pressure, light refraction, and why diving bells work. Both kids and adults can climb through a submarine and see live sea animals in a pool. Videos and aquariums explain the sea life found in St. Andrew Bay.

17314 Panama City Beach Pkwy. (at Heather Dr., west of Fla. 79), Panama City Beach. © 850/235-4101. Admission $5 adults, $2.50 children 6–16; free for children 5 and under. Daily 9am–5pm. Closed New Year's Day, Thanksgiving, and Christmas.

ZooWorld Zoological & Botanical Park *Kids* Sitting in a pine forest, this educational and entertaining zoo is an active participant in the Species Survival Plan, which helps protect endangered species by employing specific breeding and housing programs. Among the 350 guests here are orangutans and other primates, lions, tigers, leopards, and alligators and other reptiles. Also included are a walk-through aviary, a bat exhibit, and a petting zoo.

9008 Front Beach Rd. (near Moylan Dr.), Panama City Beach. © 850/230-1243. Admission $10.95 adults, $8.95 seniors, $6.95 children 3–11; free for children under 3. Daily 9am–5:30pm (to 4:30pm in winter).

AMUSEMENT PARKS

An exciting, 105-foot-high roller coaster is just one of the 30 rides at the **Miracle Strip Amusement Park,** 12000 Front Beach Rd., at Alf Coleman Road (© **850/234-5810;** www.miraclestrippark.com). Little ones will love the traditional carousel. Nine acres of fun include nonstop live entertainment and tons of junk food. Adjoining is **Shipwreck Island Water Park** (© **850/234-0368;** www.shipwreckisland.com), which offers a variety of water amusements, including the 1,600-foot-long winding Lazy River for tubing and a daring 35-mile-per-hour Speed Slide. The Tad Pole Hole is exclusively for young kids. Lounge chairs, umbrellas, and inner tubes are free, and lifeguards are on duty. Admission to either park is less than $20, and combination tickets are available. Both are open weekends from mid-March until Memorial Day weekend, then daily through mid-August, and weekends from then through Labor Day weekend. Hours and prices change from year to year, so call for the latest.

SHOPPING

An attraction in itself is the main branch of **Alvin's Island Tropical Department Store,** 12010 Front Beach Rd. (© **850/234-3048**), opposite the James I. Lark, Sr. Visitors Information Center. It not only sells a wide range of beach gear and apparel, but also has cages containing colorful parrots, tanks with small sharks, and an enclosure with alligators. The sharks are fed at 11am daily; the gators get theirs at 4pm (the older ones are too lethargic to eat during the cool winter months).

ACCOMMODATIONS YOU CAN AFFORD

There are scores of motels along the beach here, ranging from small mom-and-pop operations to sizable members of national chains. The annual guide distributed by the Panama City Beach Convention & Visitors Bureau has a complete list (see "Essentials," earlier in this section).

The most modern of the chain motels are the recently renovated **Howard Johnson Resort Hotel,** 9400 S. Thomas Dr. (© **800/654-2000** or 850/234-6521), and the **Four Points by Sheraton,** 9600 S. Thomas Dr. (© **888/625-5144** or 850/234-6511), both part of the redeveloped Boardwalk Beach Resort area, a center of beach action.

Panama City Beach also abounds with condominium complexes, such as the Edgewater Beach Resort listed below. Among the many rental agents are **Arvida Realty Services,** 726 Thomas Dr., Panama City Beach, FL 32408

(⌒ **800/621-2462** or 850/235-4075; fax 850/233-2833; www.panamabeach rentals.com); and **Condo World,** 8815A Thomas Dr. (P.O. Box 9456), Panama City Beach, FL 32408 (⌒ **800/232-6636** or 850/234-5564; fax 850/233-6725; www.condoworld.net).

The best camping is at the lovely sites in **St. Andrews State Park,** one of this area's major attractions (see "Hitting the Beach: St. Andrews State Park," above).

Rates at even the most expensive properties here drop precipitously during winter, when the town rolls up the sidewalks. Bay County adds 3.5% tax to all hotel and campground bills, bringing the total add-on tax to 9.5%.

Beachcomber by the Sea ✶ Watercolors by local artist Paul Brent grace every unit in this eight-story all-suites resort, built and opened in 1998 at the junction of Front Beach Road and Fla. 79. They also have balconies overlooking a gulf-side swimming pool and hot tub bordered by a concrete deck accented by palm trees. The well-equipped suites come in two sizes. The larger editions have living rooms with sleeper sofas, bedrooms with either king-size or two double beds, and their own phones and TVs. Bathrooms and kitchenettes separate the living rooms and bedrooms. The suites are similar to those at the Flamingo Motel & Tower (see below), except that here they have air conditioners in both living rooms and bedrooms. The smaller units are more like motel rooms, but they have microwaves. Two of the smaller units also have whirlpool tubs. There's no restaurant here but several are nearby, and complimentary continental breakfast is available in the lobby each morning. Spring-breakers are not welcome.

17101 Front Beach Rd., Panama City Beach, FL 32413. ⌒ **888/886-8916** or 850/233-3600. Fax 850/233-3622. www.beachcomberbythesea.com. 96 units. Summer $99–$229; off-season $99–$129. Rates include continental breakfast. Packages available. AE, DISC, MC, V. **Amenities:** Heated outdoor pool; access to nearby health club; Jacuzzi; game room; coin-op washers and dryers. *In room:* A/C, TV, dataport, kitchen and fridge in some, coffeemaker, hair dryer, iron.

Flamingo Motel & Tower ✶ *Value* Reggie, Rebecca, and Dana Lancaster take great pride in the gorgeous tropical garden surrounding a heated swimming pool and a large sun deck overlooking the gulf at their well-maintained motel. The brightly decorated rooms have either full kitchens or refrigerators and microwave ovens. They can sleep two to six people, some in separate bedrooms. Kitchenette rooms in a two-story motel block across the road are less appealing but will accommodate six to eight. Budget-conscious families can opt for lower-priced rooms, accommodating two to four. Next door, the seven-story Flamingo Tower contains 49 suites, all sporting living rooms with sofa beds and dining tables; bedrooms with ceiling fans and their own TVs; kitchens; and balconies overlooking the gulf and a beachside swimming pool and hot tub. These suites have air-conditioning units in their living rooms but not in their bedrooms (the ceiling fans will come in handy during the hot, humid summer months). The Dan Russell fishing pier is only half a mile away, and Gulf World Marine Park and Shuckums Oyster Pub & Seafood Grill are virtually across the road (see "Exploring the Area," above, and "Great Deals on Dining," below). College spring-breakers not welcome.

15525 Front Beach Rd., Panama City Beach, FL 32413. ⌒ **800/828-0400** or 850/234-2232. Fax 850/234-1292. www.flamingomotel.com. 117 units (some with shower only). Summer $79–$139; off-season $39–$99. AE, DISC, MC, V. **Amenities:** 2 heated outdoor pools; access to nearby health club; Jacuzzi; water-sports equipment rental; coin-op washers and dryers. *In room:* A/C, TV, kitchen in some, fridge, coffeemaker.

Georgian Terrace Located right on the beach, this two-level motel offers clean, cozy apartments with knotty-pine paneling. Opening to the beach, all units have full kitchens and private, enclosed sun porches. Some units have desktop computers with high-speed Internet connections, and the "home theater" suite comes equipped with a 54-inch TV and a surround-sound system. A greenhouse-enclosed heated pool area with lush tropical plantings and attractive lounge chairs makes this place a good pick off-season. There's a rare stretch of undeveloped beach almost next door. The mother-son team of Karen and Wes Grant make sure that everyone feels at home here.

14415 Front Beach Rd., Panama City Beach, FL 32413. © 888/882-2144 or 850/234-2144. Fax 850/234-8413. www.georgianterrace.com. 28 units. Summer $89–$149 double; off-season $39–$89 double. MC, V. **Amenities:** Heated indoor pool. *In room:* A/C, TV, dataport, kitchen, coffeemaker.

Sunset Inn This very well maintained establishment, off Thomas Drive between Chicksaw and Snapper streets near the east end of the beach, is right on the gulf but away from the crowds. The spacious beachside motel rooms accommodate families in one- and two-bedroom apartments with kitchens, while across the street stands a block of refurbished efficiencies and a new building with tropically furnished one- and two-bedroom condominiums. The condominiums are the most expensive units here, but the units with patios or balconies right on the beach will better suit sun-and-sand lovers.

8109 Surf Dr., Panama City Beach, FL 32408. © 850/234-7370. Fax 850/234-7370, ext. 303. www.poteau.com/sunset/suninn.htm. 62 units (some with shower only). Summer $65–$155 double; off-season $50–$125 double. Weekly and monthly rates available. AE, DISC, MC, V. **Amenities:** Heated outdoor pool; coin-op washers and dryers. *In room:* A/C, TV, kitchen, fridge, coffeemaker.

WORTH A SPLURGE

Edgewater Beach Resort One of the Panhandle's largest condominium resorts, this sports-oriented facility enjoys a beautiful beachfront location and 110 tropically landscaped acres. Units in five gulf-side towers enjoy commanding views of the emerald gulf and gorgeous sunsets from their private balconies. A pedestrian overpass leads across Front Beach Road to low-rise apartments and townhomes fringing ponds and the fairways of the resort's own nine-hole golf course. A daytime shuttle runs around the resort to swimming pools, whirlpools, tennis center, and golf course (guests also get privileges at the 18-hole Hombre Golf Club, a quarter mile north). The Shoppes at Edgewater restaurants are across the road.

11212 Front Beach Rd. (P.O. Box 9850), Panama City Beach, FL 32407. © 800/874-8686 or 850/235-4044. Fax 850/235-6899. www.edgewaterbeachresort.com. 500 units. Summer $150–$400 condo; off-season $70–$175 condo. $5 per day per unit amenities fee. Weekly rates and maid service available. AE, DC, DISC, MC, V. **Amenities:** 2 restaurants (American), 2 bars; 11 heated outdoor pools; 9-hole golf course; 11 tennis courts; health club; Jacuzzi; water-sports equipment rentals; children's programs; concierge; car-rental desk; limited room service; babysitting; coin-op washers and dryers. *In room:* A/C, TV, dataport, kitchen, coffeemaker, hair dryer, iron.

Holiday Inn SunSpree Resort One building removed from the Edgewater Beach Resort and across the road from the Shoppes at Edgewater, this 15-story establishment is the top full-service gulf-front hotel here. It's designed in an arch, with all rooms having balconies looking directly down on the beach, where a heated, foot-shaped swimming pool and wooden sun deck are separated from the beach by a row of palms and Polynesian torches, which are lighted at night. The hotel has won architectural awards for its dramatic lobby with a waterfall and the Fountain of Wishes (coins go to charity). The attractive, spacious guest rooms feature full-size ice-making refrigerators, microwave ovens, and two spacious vanity areas with their own lavatory sinks.

11127 Front Beach Rd., Panama City Beach, FL 32407. © 800/633-0266 or 850/234-1111. Fax 850/235-1907. www.holidayinnsunspree.com. 342 units. Summer $185–$225 double; off-season $75–$129 double. AE, DC, DISC, MC, V. **Amenities:** 2 restaurants (American), 2 bars; heated outdoor pool; exercise room; Jacuzzi; water-sports equipment rentals; game room; concierge; limited room service; babysitting; laundry service; concierge-level rooms. *In room:* A/C, TV, dataport, fridge, coffeemaker, hair dryer, iron, safe.

A SPLURGE FOR GOLFERS

Marriott's Bay Point Resort Village ★★ *Value* Not only is this luxurious vacation miniworld ranked among the nation's top golf and tennis resorts, it's an extraordinarily good value for Florida, as well. Although guests pay extra for most activities, its room rates are among the top steals in the state. They would be higher if the property were beside the gulf; instead, it's the centerpiece of a manicured real-estate development sprawling over 1,100 acres on a peninsula bordered by St. Andrew Bay and the Grand Lagoon. Situated beside the lagoon, the luxurious, vivid-coral stucco hotel is surrounded by gardens, palm trees, oaks, and magnolias. From the glamorous three-story lobby, window walls look out to scenic water views and two swimming pools (one in its own glass-enclosed building). Furnished in dark woods, the Marriottesque rooms are spacious and luxurious, and all have balconies or patios. The highlights for duffers are the Lagoon Legends and the Club Meadows golf courses (see " Affordable Outdoor Activities," earlier in this section). Water sports here are at Grand Lagoon beach, reached by the hotel's long pier. There's a free shuttle to the gulf beaches.

4200 Marriott Dr., Panama City Beach, FL 32408. © 800/874-7505 or 850/236-6000. Fax 850/236-6158. www.marriottbaypoint.com. 356 units. Summer $119–$209 double; off-season $109–$169 double. Packages available. AE, DC, DISC, MC, V. From Thomas Dr., take Magnolia Beach Rd. and bear right on Dellwood Rd. to resort complex. **Amenities:** 2 restaurants (American), 2 bars; 3 heated outdoor pools, 1 indoor pool; 2 golf courses; 4 tennis courts; health club; Jacuzzi; water-sports equipment rental; bike rental; concierge; business center; limited room service; massage; babysitting; laundry service; coin-op washers and dryers; concierge-level rooms. *In room:* A/C, TV, dataport, fridge, coffeemaker, hair dryer, iron.

GREAT DEALS ON DINING

Except for fast-food joints, there aren't many national-chain family restaurants in Panama City Beach (you'll find those along 15th and 23rd sts. over in Panama City). There is one local chain worth a meal: the **Montego Bay Seafood Houses,** which offer a wide range of munchies, sandwiches, burgers, and seafood main courses, most in the inexpensive category. Branches are at the "curve" on Thomas Drive (© **850/234-8687**); at the intersection of Thomas Drive and Middle and Front Beach roads (© **850/236-3585**); and in the Shoppes at Edgewater, Front Beach Drive at Beckrich Road (© **850/233-6033**).

Pay attention to the restaurant hours here, for some places are closed during the winter months. Even if they're open, many will close early when business is slow.

Billy's Steamed Seafood Restaurant *Value* SEAFOOD More a lively raw bar than a restaurant, Billy and Eloise Poole's casual spot has been serving the best crabs in town since 1982. These are hard-shell blue crabs prepared Maryland style: steamed with spicy Old Bay Seasoning. Unlike crab houses in Baltimore, however, Billy and Eloise remove the crab's top shell, clean out the "mustard" (intestines), and cut the crabs in two for you; all you have to do is "pick" the meat. Don't worry, they'll show you. Other steamed morsels include shrimp (also with spicy seasoning), oysters, crabs, and lobster served with corn on the cob and garlic bread. Order anything from the briny deep here, but pass over other items.

> **Fun Fact** **"We shuck 'em, you suck 'em"**
>
> That's the motto at **Shuckums Oyster Pub & Seafood Grill,** 15614 Front Beach Rd. at Powell Adams Drive (© 850/235-3214). Comedian Martin Short made this noisy, lively, and smoky pub famous when he tried unsuccessfully to shuck oysters at its bar during the making of an MTV spring-break special. The original bar where Short tried to shuck is virtually papered over with dollar bills signed by old and young patrons who have been flocking here since 1967. The obvious specialty is fresh Apalachicola oysters, served raw, steamed, or baked with a variety of toppings. Otherwise, the menu consists of pub fare and mediocre seafood main courses. Shuckums is open daily during the summer from 11am to 2am. It closes during the off-season at 9pm during the week, at midnight on weekends.

3000 Thomas Dr. (between Grand Lagoon and Magnolia Beach Rd.). © 850/235-2349. Main courses $5.50–$16; sandwiches $2.50–$5.50. AE, DISC, MC, V. Daily 11am–9pm.

Cajun Inn LOUISIANA CAJUN   This lively, family-owned restaurant with high-backed wooden booths brings the Big Easy to the gulf. Offerings include jambalaya, seafood étouffée, peppered shrimp or crawfish, and Cajun-style blackened fish. Po' boy sandwiches stuffed with fried oysters or shrimp are a specialty. You won't get gourmet New Orleans cuisine at these prices, but your tongue will have plenty of spice to savor. Dine inside or outside. There's live music on weekends.

817 Azalea Ave. (near Front Beach Rd./Middle Beach Rd. intersection). © 850/233-0403. Main courses $12–$17; sandwiches $6–$11. AE, DC, DISC, MC, V. Daily 11am–10pm.

Captain Anderson's Restaurant & Waterfront Seafood Market SEAFOOD   Since 1953 this famous restaurant has been attracting early diners who come to watch the fishing fleet unload the catch of the day at the busy marina on Grand Lagoon. It's so popular, in fact, that you may have to wait 2 hours for a table during the peak summer months; three bars are there to help you pass the time. The Captain's menu is noted for grilled local fish, crabmeat-stuffed jumbo shrimp, and a heaped-high seafood platter. The food isn't as interesting as at Hamilton's Seafood Restaurant & Lounge across the road (see below), but the local atmosphere makes it worth a visit while you're here.

5551 N. Lagoon Dr. (at Thomas Dr.). © 850/234-2225. Main courses $11–$35. AE, DC, DISC, MC, V. Summer Mon–Sat 4–10pm. Off-season Mon–Sat 4:30–10pm. Closed Nov–Jan.

Hamilton's Seafood Restaurant & Lounge ★ SEAFOOD   Proprietor Steve Stevens continues in the tradition of his noted Mississippi-born, restaurateur father. The attractive blond-wood and knotty-pine restaurant lies on Grand Lagoon. The baked oysters Hamilton appetizer—a rich combination of oysters, shrimp, and crabmeat—may leave you too full for a main course. Several other dishes are unique to Hamilton's, such as spicy snapper étouffée and a Greek-accented shrimp Cristo. Mesquite-grilled fish and steaks are also house specialties, and vegetarians can order a coal-fired vegetable kebab served over angel-hair pasta. The Lagoon Saloon makes the wait for a table go by quickly, and you can select from an extensive selection of well-chosen California and French wines.

5711 N. Lagoon Dr. (at Thomas Dr.). © 850/234-1255. Main courses $13–$22. AE, DISC, MC, V. Summer daily 4–10pm. Off-season Mon–Thurs 5–9pm; Fri–Sat 5–9:30pm. Closed 1 week in Jan.

WORTH A SPLURGE

Boar's Head Restaurant ⊀ STEAKS/SEAFOOD   An institution since 1978, this shingle-roofed establishment appears from the road to be a South Seas resort. Inside, its impressive beamed ceiling, stone walls, and fireplaces create a warm, almost English tavern atmosphere suited to the house specialties: tender, marbled prime rib of beef and perfectly cooked steaks. Beef eaters don't have the Boar's Head to themselves, however, because the coals are also used to give a charred flavor to salmon, grouper, and yellowfin tuna. Other cooking styles are offered, too, including a combination of lobster, shrimp, and scallops in a cream sauce over angel-hair pasta. And venison, quail, and other game dishes find their way here during winter. An extensive wine list has won awards, and a cozy tavern to one side has live music, usually Wednesday to Saturday evenings.

17290 Front Beach Rd. (just west of Fla. 79). © 850/234-6628. Main courses $16–$27. AE, DC, DISC, MC, V. Summer daily 4:30–10pm. Off-season Sun–Thurs 4:30–9pm; Fri–Sat 4:30–10pm.

A SPLURGE FOR ROMANTICS

Canopies ⊀⊀ SEAFOOD/STEAKS   This area's most elegant restaurant and purveyor of its finest cuisine occupies a 1910-vintage gray clapboard house with a magnificent view of St. Andrew Bay. Dining is outside on the patio or on an enclosed veranda, and the dark, cozy bar in the old living room invites before- or after-dinner drinks. The menu changes monthly but always offers the consistently excellent creamy she-crab soup under a flaky croissant dome. Other selections could include sushi-quality yellowfin tuna in a sherry-soy sauce served over a haystack of leeks; a "trio" of tuna, salmon, and grouper with a citrus butter sauce served with a mandarin orange salsa and Vidalia-onion mashed potatoes; and sautéed grouper with lump crabmeat in a sherry-butter sauce. Forget the crab cakes. Landlubbers can partake of award-winning beef, veal, lamb, pork, and game dishes. White chocolate mousse is among several wonderful sweet endings.

4423 W. Hwy. 98, Panama City (1 mile east of Hathaway Bridge on U.S. 98). © 850/872-8444. Reservations recommended. Main courses $18–$26; early-bird specials $11. AE, DC, DISC, MC, V. Daily 5–10pm. Early-bird specials 5–6pm.

SPECIAL DINING EXPERIENCES

You've got to see the **Treasure Ship,** at Treasure Island Marina, 3605 S. Thomas Dr. at Grand Lagoon (© 850/234-8881; http://thetreasureship.com), to believe it. This amazing 2 acres of ship space claims to be the world's largest land-based Spanish galleon and a reputed replica of the three-masted sailing ships that carried loot from the New World to Spain in the 16th and 17th centuries. You can get anything from an ice-cream cone to peel-it-yourself shrimp to a sophisticated dinner in the restaurant and bar here, which are open daily at 4:30pm; closed during the winter months.

Lady Anderson **dinner-dance cruises** are a romantic evening escape; they're available from March through October. This modern, three-deck ship boards at Captain Anderson's Marina, 5550 N. Lagoon Dr. (© **800/360-0510** or 850/234-5940; www.ladyanderson.com), Monday to Saturday evenings, with the cruises lasting from 7 to 10pm. Buffet dinners are featured, followed by live music for dancing Monday, Wednesday, Friday, and Saturday nights; gospel music on Tuesday and Thursday. Dinner-dance tickets cost $39.50 for adults, $37.50 for seniors, $22.50 for children 6 to 11, $14.50 for children 2 to 5. Gospel music cruises go for $34.50 for adults, $33 for seniors, $22.50 for children 6 to 11, $14.50 for children 2 to 5. Tips are included. Summertime reservations should be made well in advance.

PANAMA CITY & PANAMA CITY BEACH AFTER DARK

THE PERFORMING ARTS The Rader family and a cast of 20 perform year-round in the **Ocean Opry Show,** 8400 Front Beach Rd., Panama City Beach (© 850/234-5464; www.theoceanoprymusicshow.com), the area's answer to the Grand Ole Opry. There's a show every night at 8pm during the summer, less frequently off-season. Popcorn, hot dogs, and soft drinks are available. Admission is about $20 for adults, half price for children. Prices jump to $30 or more when stars like Kitty Welles, B. J. Thomas, and the Wilkensons are in town, usually during winter. The box office opens at 9am Monday to Saturday, and reservations are recommended but not required.

THE CLUB & BAR SCENE The **Breakers,** 12627 Front Beach Rd. (© 850/234-6060), is the area's premier supper club, with unsurpassed gulf views and music for dining and dancing. You'll swear The King has risen from the grave as "Elvis Presley" and other impersonators of **Clutch Rock 'n' Roll Cafe** perform here. The show is worth the $10 to $15 per person cover charge. The beachfront **Harpoon Harry's Waterfront Cafe** is part of the same complex.

Romantic lounges with live entertainment are at the **Treasure Ship,** 3605 S. Thomas Dr. (© 850/234-8881), where comedian-hypnotist Mike Harvey performs during summer in the top-floor Captain's Quarters; and at the **Boar's Head,** 17290 Front Beach Rd. (© 850/234-6628). See "Great Deals on Dining," above, for more information.

The 20-something crowd likes to boogie all night at beach clubs such as **Schooners,** 5121 Gulf Dr. (© 850/235-9074), where every table has a gulf view; **Spinnaker's,** on the beach at 8795 Thomas Dr. (© 850/234-7882); **Club La Vella,** a bikini-contest kind of place and one of Florida's largest nightclubs, also on the beach at 8813 Thomas Dr. (© 850/234-3866); and **Sharkey's on the Gulf,** 15201 Front Beach Rd. (© 850/235-2420). The clubs often stay open until 4am in summer while their bands play on. **Pineapple Willie's Lounge,** beachside at 9900 S. Thomas Dr. (© 850/235-0928), is open from 11am until 2am, serving ribs basted with Jack Daniels and spotlighting live entertainment during summer and a host of sports TVs all year.

4 Apalachicola ★★★

65 miles E of Panama City, 80 miles W of Tallahassee

Sometimes called Florida's Last Frontier, **Apalachicola** makes a fascinating day trip from Panama City Beach or Tallahassee, as well as a destination in its own right. The long, gorgeous beaches on **St. George Island,** 7 miles from town, are among the nation's best. Justifiably famous for Apalachicola oysters, the bays and estuaries are great for fishing and boating. And if you love nature, the area also is rich in wildlife preserves.

The charming little town of Apalachicola (pop. 2,600) was a major seaport during autumns from 1827 to 1861, when plantations in Alabama and Georgia shipped tons of cotton down the Apalachicola River to the gulf. The town had a racetrack, an opera house, and a civic center that hosted balls, socials, and gambling. The population shrank during the mosquito-infested summer months, however, when yellow fever and malaria epidemics struck. It was during one of these outbreaks that Dr. John Gorrie of Apalachicola tried to develop a method of cooling his patients' rooms. In doing so, he invented the forerunner of the air conditioner, a device that made Florida tourism possible and life a whole lot more bearable for locals.

Apalachicola has traditionally made its living primarily from the gulf and the lagoonlike bay protected by a chain of offshore barrier islands. Today this area produces the bulk of Florida's oyster crop, and shrimping and fishing are major industries. The town also has been discovered by a number of urban expatriates, who have moved here, restored old homes, and opened interesting antiques and gift shops (there aren't many towns this size where you can buy Crabtree & Evelyn products).

ESSENTIALS
GETTING THERE The nearest airport is 65 miles to the west at Panama City Beach (see "Essentials," in section 3 of this chapter). From there you'll have to rent a car or take an expensive taxi ride. The Tallahassee airport is about 85 miles to the northeast (see "Essentials," in section 5 of this chapter). **Croom's Transportation** (C **888/653-8132**) has airport shuttle service between Tallahassee and Apalachicola. Call for fares and schedule.

The scenic way to drive here is via the gulf-hugging U.S. 98 from Panama City Beach, or via U.S. 319 and U.S. 98 from Tallahassee. From I-10, take Exit 21 at Marianna, then follow Fla. 71 south to Port St. Joe, and take U.S. 98 east to Apalachicola.

VISITOR INFORMATION The **Apalachicola Bay Chamber of Commerce,** 99 Market St., Apalachicola, FL 32320 (C **850/653-9419**; fax 850/653-8219; www.baynavigator.com), supplies information about the area from its office on Market Street (U.S. 98) between Avenue D and Avenue E. The chamber is open Monday to Friday from 9:30am to 5pm.

TIME The town is in the eastern time zone, like Orlando, Miami, and Tallahassee (it's 1 hr. ahead of Panama City Beach and the rest of the Panhandle). Many shops are closed on Wednesday afternoon, when Apalachicolans go fishing.

WHAT TO SEE & DO
BEACHES, PARKS & WILDLIFE REFUGES
Some experts consider the 9 miles of beaches in **St. George Island State Park** to be among America's best. This pristine nature preserve occupies the eastern end of St. George Island, about 15 miles east of Apalachicola. A 4-mile-long paved road leads through the dunes to picnic areas, restrooms, showers, and a boat launch. An unpaved trail leads another 5 miles to the island's eastern end, but be careful: It's easy to get stuck in the soft sand even in a four-wheel-drive sports utility vehicle. From a hiking trail leading from the campground out a narrow peninsula on the bay side, you can see countless terns, snowy plovers, black skimmers, and other birds. Entry costs $2 for a vehicle with one occupant, $4 for vehicles with up to eight occupants, and $1 for pedestrians and bicyclists. Campsites cost $15 from February through August, $8 from September through January. Add $2 for electricity. Primitive camping (take everything with you, including water) costs $3 a night per adult, $2 for children. The park is open daily from 8am to sunset. Pets are allowed. For more information, contact the park at 1900 E. Gulf Beach Dr., St. George Island, FL 32328 (C **850/927-2111**; www.floridastateparks.org/district1/stgeorge).

Except for hiking and mountain-biking trails, there are no facilities whatsoever at the **St. Vincent National Wildlife Refuge,** southwest of Apalachicola. This 12,358-acre barrier island has been left in its natural state by the U.S. Fish and Wildlife Service, but visitors are welcome to walk through its pine forests, marshlands, ponds, dunes, and beaches. In addition to native species like bald eagles and alligators, the island is home to a small herd of sambar deer from Southeast Asia. Red wolves are bred here for reestablishment in other wildlife areas. Access is by boat only. **St. Vincents Island Shuttle Service** (© 850/229-1065; www.stvincentisland.com), at Indian Pass, 21 miles west of Apalachicola via U.S. 98 and County Roads 30A and 30B, will take you to the island in a pontoon boat. If you bring your bike, they'll drop you on one end of the island and pick you up later at the other. Call for prices and reservations, which are required.

The refuge headquarters, at the north end of Market Street in town, has exhibits of wetland flora and fauna. It's open Monday to Friday from 8am to 4:30pm. Admission is free. For more information, contact the refuge at P.O. Box 447, Apalachicola, FL 32329 (© 850/653-8808).

The huge **Apalachicola National Forest** begins a few miles northeast of town. It has a host of facilities, including canoeing and mountain-bike trails. See "Side Trips from Tallahassee," in section 5 of this chapter, for details.

AFFORDABLE OUTDOOR ACTIVITIES

CRUISES Jeanni McMillan of **Journeys of St. George Island** (© 850/927-3259; www.sgislandjourneys.com) takes guests on narrated nature cruises to the barrier islands and on canoe and kayak trips in the creeks and streams of the Apalachicola River basin. She also has night hikes with blue-crab netting, shelling excursions, and fishing and scalloping trips, plus excursions tailored exclusively for children. Prices range from $25 to $75 per person. Reservations are required, so call her to find out what she's offering when you'll be in town. Jeanni also rents canoes, kayaks, sailboats, and sailboards.

An easier way to see the marshes, swamps, and shallow-water rivers is via a nature cruise with **EcoVentures, Inc.** (© 850/653-2593; www.apalachicolatours.com). It uses the *Osprey,* a 40-foot, all-weather boat that can carry up to 32 passengers. Fares are $20 adults, $10 for children under 16. Call for the schedule and reservations.

You can go afternoon or sunset sailing on the bay for hours on Captain Jerry Weber's 40-foot sloop ***Wind Catcher*** (© 850/653-3881). The 2½-hour voyages cost $35 for adults, $20 for children under 16, including snacks and soft drinks. Reservations are essential.

FISHING You can't go oystering, but fishing is excellent in these waters, where trout, redfish, flounder, tarpon, shark, drum, and other fish abound. The chamber of commerce (see "Essentials," above) can help arrange charters on the local boats, many of which dock at the Rainbow Inn on Water Street. For guides, contact **Robinson Brothers Guide Service** (© 850/670-8896; fax 850/653-3118; www.flaredfish.com) or **Boss Guide Services** (© 850/653-8139).

EXPLORING THE TOWN

Start your visit by picking up a map and a self-guided tour brochure from the chamber of commerce (see "Essentials," above), and then stroll around Apalachicola's waterfront, business district, and Victorian-era homes.

Along Water Street, several tin warehouses evoke the town's seafaring days of the late 1800s, as does the 1840s-era **Sponge Exchange** at Commerce Street and Avenue E. A highlight of the residential area, centered around Gorrie Square at Avenue D and 6th Street, is the Greek Revival–style **Trinity Episcopal Church,** built in New York and shipped here in 1837. At the water end of 6th Street, Battery Park has a children's playground. A number of excellent **art galleries and gift shops** are grouped on Market Street, Avenue D, and Commerce Street.

The showpiece at the **John Gorrie Museum State Park**, Avenue D at 6th Street (© 850/653-9347; www.floridastateparks.org/district1/johngorrie), is a display replica of Doctor Gorrie's cooling machine, a prototype of today's air conditioner. It really does work. The park is open Thursday to Monday from 9am to 5pm; closed New Year's Day, Thanksgiving, and Christmas. Admission is $1 and is free for children 6 and under.

The **Estuarine Walk,** at the north end of Market Street on the grounds of the Apalachicola National Estuarine Research Reserve (© **850/653-8063**), contains aquariums full of fish and turtles and displays of various other estuarine life. It's open Monday to Friday from 8am to 5pm. Admission is free.

ACCOMMODATIONS YOU CAN AFFORD

Built in 1997, the 42-room **Best Western Apalach Inn,** 249 Hwy. 98 W. (© **800/528-1234** or 850/658-9131; fax 850/653-9136; www.apalachicola.com/bestwestern), a mile west of downtown, is the only national chain hotel here.

Apalachicola River Inn

The town's only waterfront accommodation, this two-story motel's rough-hewn exterior timbers make it look like one of the neighboring warehouses. Recently spiffed up, units in the main building all have views across a marina to Apalachicola Bay. Those on the second floor are larger and have their own balconies, making them preferable to the smaller downstairs units, whose doors open directly onto the marina's boardwalk. Two rooms and a two-bedroom apartment in a building next door have whirlpool tubs. Facing the river, Caroline's Restaurant serves breakfast, lunch, and seafood dinners (it's a bit pricey at dinner but a fine spot for an alfresco, dockside lunch). The Roseate Spoonbill Lounge, over the restaurant, is *the* local watering hole, with a grand view and music on an outdoor deck on weekends.

123 Water St., Apalachicola, FL 32320. © **850/653-8139**. Fax 850/653-2018. www.apalachicolariverinn.com. 26 units (some with shower only). $85–$95 double; $110–$160 suite. AE, DC, DISC, MC, V. Pets accepted in smoking rooms ($10 nightly fee). **Amenities:** Restaurant (American), bar. *In room:* A/C, TV.

Coombs House Inn

The most luxurious accommodation here, this large bed-and-breakfast occupies two Victorian homes. The main house was built in 1905 by a lumber baron, and it shows: Polished black cypress paneling lines the entire central hallway and grand parlor. Each of the 10 guest rooms in the main house is tastefully decorated, with lots of Victorian reproductions. Outstanding is the Coombs Suite, with bay windows, sofa, four-poster bed, and its own whirlpool. The "Love Bungalow" has its own private entrance. Less grand but still impressive are eight rooms in another restored Victorian, known as the "Coombs House East," half a block away. One of these rooms has a whirlpool tub and bidet, and there's an apartment in the carriage house over there. One room in each house is equipped for guests with disabilities. A major truck route, U.S. 98, runs along the north side of both houses; request a south room to escape the periodic road noise. Guests are treated to complimentary wine receptions on weekends.

80 6th St., Apalachicola, FL 32320. © **850/653-9199**. Fax 850/653-2785. www.coombshouseinn.com. 18 units. $89–$225 double. Rates include full breakfast. DISC, MC, V. **Amenities:** Access to nearby health club; free use of bikes. *In room:* A/C, TV, dataport, fridge (3 units), hair dryer.

Gibson Inn

Built in 1907 as a seaman's hotel and gorgeously restored in 1985, this cupola-topped inn is such a brilliant example of Victorian architecture that it's listed on the National Register of Historic Inns. No two guest rooms are alike (some still have the original sinks in the sleeping areas), but all are richly furnished with period reproductions. Nonguests are welcome to wander upstairs and peek into unoccupied rooms (whose doors are left open). Reservations are advised during summer and spring and fall weekends, and as much as 5 years ahead for the seafood festival in November. Grab a drink from the bar and relax in one of the high-back rockers on the old-fashioned veranda. The dining room serves excellent seafood and is open to all comers, so don't expect this to be private like a bed-and-breakfast; instead, you'll find yourself in a reborn, absolutely charming turn-of-the-century hotel.

51 Ave. C, Apalachicola, FL 32320. © **850/653-2191.** Fax 850/653-3521. www.gibsoninn.com. 30 units. $85–$100 double; $100–$130 suite. AE, MC, V. **Amenities:** Restaurant (American), bar. *In room:* A/C, TV.

SUPER-CHEAP SLEEPS

Rancho Inn On the western edge of the historic district, this older, Spanish-style motel has been spiffed up by owners Mark and Mary Lynn Rodgers, who keep it clean and well maintained. Although simple when compared to the more expensive properties here, the rooms are spacious and comfortable, and all have microwave ovens and fridges. Restaurants are within walking distance.

240 Hwy. 98 W., Apalachicola, FL 32320. © **850/653-9435.** Fax 850/653-9180. www.ranchoinn.com. 32 units. $50–$150 double. AE, DISC, MC, V. Pets accepted ($6 fee). **Amenities:** Outdoor pool; bicycle rental. *In room:* A/C, TV, dataport, fridge, coffeemaker.

GREAT DEALS ON DINING

Townsfolk still plop down on the round stools at the marble-topped counter to order Coca-Colas and milk shakes at the **Old Time Soda Fountain & Luncheonette,** 93 Market St. (© **850/653-2006**). This 1950s relic was once the town drugstore. It's open Monday to Saturday from 10am to 5pm.

The Boss Oyster ★ SEAFOOD   You've heard about the aphrodisiac properties of Apalachicola oysters. Well, you can see if those properties are real at this rustic, dockside eatery, whose motto is "Shut Up and Shuck." In fact, this is one of the best places in Florida to try the bivalves raw, steamed, or under a dozen toppings ranging from capers to crabmeat. They'll even steam three dozen of them and let you do the shucking. Steamed shrimp also are offered, as are delicious po' boy sandwiches. Most main courses come from the fryer, so consider this joint a great local experience, not fine dining. Sit at picnic tables inside, on a screened porch, or out on the dock.

125 Water St. (between Aves. C and D). © **850/653-9364.** Main courses $17–$22; oysters $4.50–$13.50; sandwiches and baskets $7–$10. AE, DC, DISC, MC, V. Apr–Sept Sun–Thurs 11:30am–10pm; Fri–Sat 11:30am–11pm. Oct–Mar Sun–Thurs 11:30am–9pm; Fri–Sat 11:30am–10pm.

Chef Eddie's Magnolia Grill ★★★ CONTINENTAL/CAJUN   One of the top places to dine in Northwest Florida, Boston-bred chef-owner Eddie Cass's pleasant restaurant offers nightly specials ranging from classic French rack of lamb and beef Wellington to fresh local seafood with New Orleans–style sauces. You will long remember Eddie's mahimahi Pontchartrain, with cream and artichoke hearts. The dry-aged, oak-grilled New York sirloin steak stuffed with roasted oysters, peppers, and artichoke hearts and served with a merlot bordelaise sauce is another memorable feast. Start with a bowl of spicy seafood gumbo, a consistent hit during the Florida Seafood Festival. No smoking inside.

99 11th St. (between Aves. E and F). © **850/653-8000.** Reservations recommended. Main courses $12–$24. MC, V. Mon–Sat 6–9:30pm.

The Owl Cafe ★★ SEAFOOD   Ensconced on the first floor of a two-story clapboard commercial building in the heart of downtown, this sophisticated restaurant ranks only behind Chef Eddie's Magnolia Grill as having the best cuisine in town. Go for the nightly fresh seafood specials or opt for the terrific grouper with garlic, capers, and artichokes. Now paneled in rich wood, the walls are adorned with the works of noted local photographer Richard Bickel.

15 Ave. D (at Commerce St.). © 850/653-9888. Reservations recommended. Main courses $12–$25. MC, V. Mon–Sat 11:30am–3pm and 5:30–10pm.

Tamara's Cafe Floridita FLORIBBEAN/LATIN AMERICAN Tamara Saurez's storefront cafe offers a change of pace. Before settling in Apalachicola, Tamara was a TV producer in Venezuela, and her black bean soup comes directly from the old country. Otherwise, you'll find Latino spices accentuating Floribbean fare, such as a creamy jalapeño sauce putting a little fire into pecan-encrusted grouper, and homemade mango chutney sweetening grouper stuffed with crabmeat. Her paella is a winner, too.

17 Ave. E (at Commerce St.). © 850/653-4111. Reservations recommended. Main courses $12–$22. MC, V. Tues 5–10pm; Wed–Sat 11:30am–2:30pm and 5–11pm.

APALACHICOLA AFTER DARK

Nocturnal diversions are scarce in this small town, but you can catch summer-stock performances of plays like "Same Time Next Year" in the lovingly restored, 1912-vintage **Dixie Theatre,** 21 Ave. D (© **850/653-3200**). Tickets range from $2 to $12.

Locals like to have their after-work drinks in the fine old bar at the **Gibson Inn** and then hit the **Roseate Spoonbill Lounge,** in the Apalachicola River Inn (see "Accommodations You Can Afford," above), where bands play on weekend evenings.

5 Tallahassee

163 miles W of Jacksonville, 191 miles E of Pensacola, 250 miles NW of Orlando

Tallahassee was selected as Florida's capital in 1823 because it was halfway between St. Augustine and Pensacola, then the state's major cities. That location puts it almost in Georgia; in fact, Tallahassee has more in common with Macon than with Miami. There's as much Old South ambience here as anywhere else you're likely to visit in Florida. You'll find lovingly restored 19th-century homes and buildings, including the 1845 Old Capitol. They all sit among so many towering pines and sprawling live oaks that you'll think you're in an enormous forest. The trees form virtual tunnels along Tallahassee's five official Canopy Roads, which are lined with historic plantations, ancient Native American settlement sites and mounds, gorgeous gardens, quiet parks with picnic areas, and beautiful lakes and streams. And the nearby Apalachicola National Forest is a virtual gold mine of outdoor pursuits.

While tradition and history are important here, you'll also find the modern era, beginning with the New Capitol Building towering 22 stories over downtown. Usually sleepy Tallahassee takes on a very lively persona when the legislature is in session and when the powerful football teams of Florida State University and Florida A&M University take to the gridiron.

If you're inclined to give your credit cards a workout, the nearby town of Havana is Florida's antiquing capital.

ESSENTIALS

GETTING THERE Tallahassee Regional Airport (© **850/891-7802;** http://talgov.com/citytlh/aviation), 10 miles southwest of downtown on

Southeast Capital Circle, is served by **AirTran** (© 800/AIR-TRAN), **Delta** (© 800/221-1212), **Northwest/KLM** (© 800/225-2525), and **US Airways** (© 800/428-4322).

Alamo (© 800/327-9633), **Avis** (© 800/331-1212), **Budget** (© 800/527-0700), **Dollar** (© 800/800-4000), **Enterprise** (© 800/325-8007), **Hertz** (© 800/654-3131), **National** (© 800/CAR-RENT), and **Thrifty** (© 800/367-2277) have rental cars here.

You can take a taxi to downtown for about $12.50.

Amtrak's transcontinental train, the *Sunset Limited*, stops in Tallahassee at 918½ Railroad Ave. (© **800/USA-RAIL**).

VISITOR INFORMATION For information in advance, contact the **Tallahassee Area Convention and Visitors Bureau**, 200 W. College Ave. (P.O. Box 1369), Tallahassee, FL 32302 (© **800/628-2866** or 850/413-9200; fax 850/487-4621; www.seetallahassee.com). The bureau's excellent quarterly visitor's guide has descriptions (including hours and admission fees) of just about everything going on here.

Your first stop in town should be the **Tallahassee Area Visitor Information Center**, 106 E. Jefferson St. across from the capitol (© **850/413-9200**). Come here for free street and public-transportation maps, brochures, and pamphlets outlining tours of the historic districts and the Canopy Roads. The center is open Monday to Friday 8am to 5pm and Saturday 9am to noon.

For statewide information, a **Florida Welcome Center** is in the west foyer of the New Capitol Building.

GETTING AROUND Operated by TALTRAN, the city's public transportation agency (© **850/891-5200**; www.state.fl.us/citytlh/taltran), the free **Old Town Trolley** is the best way to see the sights of historic downtown Tallahassee. You can get on or off at any point between Adams Street Commons, at the corner of Jefferson and Adams streets, and the Governor's Mansion. The trolley runs Monday to Friday every 20 minutes between 7am and 6:30pm.

TALTRAN also provides city bus service from its downtown terminal at Tennessee and Adams streets. Both the ticket booth there and the Tallahassee Area Visitor Information Center have route maps and schedules.

For taxi service, call **Yellow Cab** (© **850/580-8080**) or **City Taxi** (© **850/562-4222**). Fares are $1.60 at flag fall, plus $1.50 per mile.

TIME Tallahassee is in the eastern time zone, like Orlando, Miami, and Apalachicola. It's 1 hour ahead of the rest of the Panhandle.

WHAT TO SEE & DO
TOURING THE CAPITOL COMPLEX

Florida's capitol complex, on South Monroe Street at Apalachee Parkway, dominates the downtown area and should be your first stop after the Tallahassee Area visitor center, just across Jefferson Street.

The **New Capitol Building** (© **850/488-6167**), a $43-million skyscraper, was built in 1977 to replace the 1845-vintage Old Capitol. State legislators meet here from March to May. The chambers of the house and the senate have public viewing galleries. For a spectacular view, take the elevators to the 22nd-floor **observatory**, where on a clear day you can see all the way to the Gulf of Mexico. You can also view works by Florida artists while up here. The New Capitol is open Monday to Friday from 8am to 5pm.

Directly in front of the skyscraper is the strikingly white **Old Capitol** (© **850/487-1902**). With its majestic dome, this "Pearl of Capitol Hill" has been

Downtown Tallahassee

restored to its original beauty. An eight-room exhibit portrays Florida's political history. Turn-of-the-century furnishings, cotton gins, and other artifacts are also of interest. The Old Capitol is open Monday to Friday from 9am to 4:30pm, Saturday from 10am to 4:30pm, and Sunday and holidays from noon to 4:30pm. Admission is free to both the old and the new capitols.

Across Monroe Street from the Old Capitol are the twin granite towers of the **Vietnam Veterans Memorial,** honoring Florida's Vietnam vets. Next to it, facing Apalachee Parkway, the **Union Bank Museum** (© 850/487-3803) is housed in Florida's oldest-surviving bank building. For a while, it was the Freedman's Savings and Trust Company, which served emancipated slaves. It's worth a brief visit. Admission is free. It's open Monday to Friday 9am to 4pm.

The Old Town Trolley will take you to the lovely Georgian-style **Governor's Mansion,** north of the capitol at Adams and Brevard streets (© 850/488-4661). Enhanced by a portico patterned after Andrew Jackson's columned antebellum home, the Hermitage, and surrounded by giant magnolia trees and landscaped lawns, the mansion is furnished with 18th- and 19th-century antiques and collectibles. Tours are given when the legislature is in session from March to May. Call for schedules and reservations.

Located adjacent to the Governor's Mansion, **The Grove** was home to Ellen Call Long, known as "The Tallahassee Girl," the first child born after Tallahassee was settled.

EXPLORING THE HISTORIC DISTRICTS
Although modern buildings have made inroads in the downtown area, Tallahassee makes an ongoing effort to preserve many of its historic homes and buildings.

Many of them are concentrated in three historic districts within an easy walk north of the capitol complex. The information center in the New Capitol (see "Essentials," above) distributes free brochures of walking tours that cover the three areas. Taken together, the tours are about 4 miles long and should take half a day. Most interesting is the Park Avenue District, 3 blocks north of the capitol complex, which you can see in about 1 hour.

Tours With A Southern Accent (© 850/513-1000) offers 2-hour walking and van tours of downtown for $20 per person, free for children under 5. Call a day in advance for schedules and reservations.

ADAMS STREET COMMONS This block-long winding brick and landscaped area along Adams Street between Jefferson Street and College Avenue, on the north side of the capitol complex, retains an old-fashioned town-square atmosphere. Restored buildings include the Governor's Club, a 1900s Masonic lodge, and Gallie's Hall, where Florida's first five African-American college students received their Florida A&M University diplomas in 1892. Restaurants, shops, and Gallie Alley are also here. Adams Street crosses Park Avenue 3 blocks north of the capitol complex. This is a good place for lunch at one of several cafes that cater to downtown office workers.

PARK AVENUE HISTORIC DISTRICT The 7 blocks of Park Avenue between Martin Luther King, Jr. Boulevard and North Meridian Street are a lovely promenade of beautiful trees, gardens, and outstanding old mansions. This broad avenue with a shady median strip lined with moss-bearded live oaks was originally named 200 Foot Street and then McCarty Street, but was later renamed Park Avenue to satisfy a snobbish Anglophile society matron who didn't want an Irish name imprinted on her son's wedding invitations.

Several Park Avenue historic homes are open to the public, including the **Knott House Museum,** at Calhoun Street (see "Museums, Galleries & Archaeological Sites," below). **The Columns,** at Duval Street, was built in the 1830s and is the city's oldest surviving building (it's the home of the Tallahassee Chamber of Commerce). **The Walker Library,** between Monroe and Calhoun streets, was one of Florida's first libraries, dating from 1903 (it's home to Springtime Tallahassee, which sponsors the city's top special event). Just north of Park Avenue on Gadsden Street, the **Meginnis-Monroe House** contains the Lemoyne Art Gallery (see "Museums, Galleries & Archaeological Sites," below).

At Martin Luther King, Jr. Boulevard, the **adjacent Old City Cemetery** and **Episcopal Cemetery** contain the graves of Prince Achille Murat, Napoleon's nephew, and Princess Catherine Murat, his wife and George Washington's grand-niece. Also buried here are two governors and numerous Confederate and Union soldiers who died at the Battle of Natural Bridge during the Civil War. The cemeteries are important to African-American history since a number of slaves and the first black Florida A&M graduates are interred here. The visitor information center in the New Capitol has a cemetery walking-tour brochure.

CALHOUN STREET HISTORIC DISTRICT Affectionately called "Gold Dust Street" in the old days, the 3 blocks of Calhoun Street between Tennessee and Georgia streets, and running east on Virginia Street to Leon High School, sport elaborate homes built by prominent citizens between 1830 and 1880. A highlight here is the **Brokaw-McDougall House,** in front of Leon High School at the eastern end of Virginia Street, which was built in 1856.

MUSEUMS, GALLERIES & ARCHAEOLOGICAL SITES

Black Archives Research Center and Museum
Housed in the columned library built by Andrew Carnegie in 1908, and located on the grounds of the Florida Agricultural and Mechanical University (FAMU), this fascinating research center and museum displays one of the nation's most extensive collections of African-American artifacts, as well as such treasures as a 500-piece Ethiopian cross collection. The archives contain one of the world's largest collections on African-American history. Visitors here can listen to tapes of gospel music and of elderly people reminiscing about the past. FAMU was founded in 1887, primarily as a black institution. Today it's acclaimed for its business, engineering, and pharmacy schools.

Martin Luther King, Jr. Blvd. and Gamble St., on the Florida A&M University campus. © 850/599-3020. www.famu.edu. Free admission. Mon–Fri 9am–4pm. Closed major holidays. Parking lot next to building.

Florida State University Museum of Fine Arts
A permanent, 3,000-piece collection here features 16th-century Dutch paintings, 20th-century American paintings, Japanese prints, pre-Columbian artifacts, and much more. Touring exhibits are displayed every few weeks.

250 Fine Arts Building, Copeland and Call sts. (on the FSU campus). © 850/644-6836. www.fsu.edu/. Free admission. Sept–Apr Mon–Fri 9am–4pm; Sat–Sun 1–4pm. May–July Mon–Fri 9am–4pm. Closed Aug.

> **Fun Fact Where Slaves Were Welcome**
>
> Built in 1838, **The First Presbyterian Church,** on Park Avenue at Adams Street, is the city's oldest church and remains an important African-American historic site since slaves were welcome to worship here without their masters' consent.

Foster Tanner Art Center The focus in this gallery is on works by local, national, and international African-American artists, with a wide variety of paintings, sculptures, and more.

Florida A&M University (between Osceola and Gamble sts., off Martin Luther King, Jr. Blvd.). © 850/599-3161. www.famu.edu. Free admission. Mon–Fri 9am–5pm.

Knott House Museum ("The House That Rhymes") ★ Adorned by a columned portico, this stately mansion was constructed in 1843, probably by a free black builder named George Proctor. Florida's first reading of the Emancipation Proclamation took place here in 1865. In 1928 it was purchased by politician William Knott, whose wife Louella wrote eccentric rhymes about the house and its elegant Victorian furnishings, including the nation's largest collection of 19th-century gilt-framed mirrors, and about social, economic, and political events of the era. Attached by satin ribbons to tables, chairs, and lamps, her poems are the museum's most unusual feature. The house is in the Park Avenue Historic District and is listed in the National Register of Historic Places. It's preserved as it looked in 1928, when the Knott family left it and all of its contents to the city (it's now administered by the Florida Museum of History). The museum gift shop carries Victorian greeting cards, paper dolls, tin toy replicas, reprints of historic newspapers, and other nostalgic items.

301 E. Park Ave. (at Calhoun St.). © 850/922-2459. http://dhr.dos.state.fl.us/museum/m_sites.html. Free admission. Wed–Fri 1–4pm; Sat 10am–4pm. 1-hr. tours depart on the hour.

Lemoyne Art Gallery ★ This restored 1852 antebellum home is listed on the National Register of Historic Places and is a lovely setting for fine art. Known as the **Meginnis-Monroe House,** the gallery itself is named in honor of Jacques LeMoyne, a member of a French expedition to Florida in 1564. Commissioned to depict the natives' dwellings and map the sea coast, LeMoyne was the first European artist known to have visited North America. Exhibits here include permanent displays by local artists, traveling exhibits, sculpture, pottery, and photography—everything from the traditional to the avant-garde. The gardens, with an old-fashioned gazebo, are spectacular during the Christmas holiday season. Programs of classical music are combined with visual arts during the year; check in advance for the current schedule.

125 N. Gadsden St. (between Park Ave. and Call St.). © 850/222-8800. www.lemoyne.org. Admission $1; free for children 12 and under. Tues–Sat 10am–5pm; Sun 1–5pm. Closed holidays.

Mission San Luís de Apalachee ★★ A Spanish Franciscan mission named San Luís was set up in 1656 on this hilltop, already a principal village of the Apalachee Indians. From then until 1704, it served as the capital of a chain of Spanish missions in Northwest Florida. The mission complex included a tribal council house, a Franciscan church, a Spanish fort, and residential areas. Based on extensive archaeological and historical research, the council house and the 10-by-50-foot thatch-roofed mission church have been reconstructed. They are both open to the public. Interpretive markers are located across the 60-acre site, and self-guided tour brochures are available at the visitor center. Call for a schedule of ranger-led guided tours on weekends.

2021 Mission Rd. (between W. Tennessee and Tharpe sts.). © 850/487-3711. http://dhr.dos.state.fl.us/bar/san_luis/. Admission free. Tues–Sun 10am–4pm. Closed Thanksgiving, Christmas. From downtown, take Tennessee St. (U.S. 90) west to entrance on right past Ocala St.

Museum of Florida History ★ An 11-foot-tall mastodon greets you at the official state history museum, where you look back 12,000 years to the first

> **Moments Traveling the Canopy Roads**
>
> Graced by canopies of live oaks draped with Spanish moss, the St. Augustine, Miccousukee, Meridian, Old Bainbridge, and Centerville roads are the five official Canopy Roads leading out of Tallahassee. Driving is slow on these winding, two-lane country roads (the locals only reluctantly are turning some limited sections of them into four-lane highways); some of them are canopied for as much as 20 miles. Take along a picnic lunch, since there are few places to buy a meal along these tranquil byways.
>
> If you have time for only one, take **Old Bainbridge Road,** which leads to the Lake Jackson Mounds State Archaeological Site in the northwest suburbs and then on to Havana, Florida's antiquing capital (see "Shopping for Antiques & Homemade Sausage," below).
>
> The visitor information center in the New Capitol provides a useful driving guide map of the Canopy Roads and Leon County's country lanes (see "Essentials," earlier in this section).

Native Americans to live in Florida (mastodons were very much alive back then). Ancient artifacts from Native American tribes are exhibited, plus such relics from Florida's past as a reconstructed steamboat and treasures from 16th- and 17th-century sunken Spanish galleons. Inquire about guided tours and special exhibits. There's an interesting museum gift shop. Visitor parking is available in the garage around the corner on St. Augustine Street between Bronough and Duvall streets.

Lower level of R. A. Gray Building, 500 S. Bronough St. (at Pensacola St.). © **850/248-6400.** http://dhr.dos.state.fl.us/museum/. Admission free (suggested donation $3 adults, $1 children). Mon–Fri 9am–4:30pm; Sat 10am–4:30pm; Sun and holidays noon–4:30pm. Closed Thanksgiving and Christmas.

A PARK & GARDENS

Maclay State Gardens ★★ In 1923 New York financier Alfred B. Maclay and his wife, Louise, began planting the floral wonderland that surrounded their winter home on Lake Hall, on Tallahassee's northeastern outskirts. After her husband's death in 1944, Louise continued his dream of an ornamental garden to delight the public. In 1953 the land was bequeathed to the state of Florida. The more than 300 acres of flowers feature at least 200 varieties; 28 acres are devoted exclusively to azaleas and camellias. The extensive parkland surrounding the house and gardens offers nature trails, canoe rentals, boating, picnicking, swimming, and fishing. The high blooming season is January to April, with the peak about mid-March. Beyond the house and gardens, the state park also includes Lake Overstreet, around which wind 5½ miles of hiking, biking, and horseback-riding trails, making this a major venue for outdoor activities.

3540 Thomasville Rd. (U.S. 319, north of I-10). © **850/487-4556.** www.floridastateparks.org/district1/maclaygardens. Admission to park $3.25 per vehicle with up to 8 passengers, $1 for pedestrians and cyclists. May–Dec admission to gardens free; Jan–Apr $3 adults, $1.50 children under 12. Gardens daily 8am–sunset. Maclay House daily 9am–5pm Jan–April; closed May–Dec.

AFFORDABLE OUTDOOR ACTIVITIES

BIKING & IN-LINE SKATING   The 16-mile **Tallahassee–St. Marks Historic Railroad Trail State Park** (© **850/922-6007;** www.floridastateparks.org/district1/stmarkstrail) is the city's most popular bike route. Constructed with the financial assistance of wealthy Panhandle cotton-plantation owners and merchants, this was Florida's oldest railroad, functioning from 1837 to 1984.

Cotton and other products were transported to St. Marks for shipment to other cities. In recent years the tracks were removed and 16 miles of the historic trail were improved for joggers, hikers, bicyclists, and horseback riders. A paved parking lot is at the north entrance, on Woodville Highway (Fla. 363) just south of Southeast Capital Circle. See "Side Trips from Tallahassee," later in this section, for more about what you can see in the St. Marks area.

At presstime the park was in the process of negotiating a contract for a bike-rental concessionaire to be located at the north end of the trail. Call the park for more information.

The **Apalachicola National Forest** also has extensive mountain biking trails (see "Side Trips from Tallahassee," later in this section), and there are 5½ miles of trails at **Maclay State Gardens** (see "A Parks & Gardens," above).

GOLF Play golf at outstanding Hilaman Park, 2737 Blair Stone Rd., where the **Hilaman Park Municipal Golf Course** features 18 holes (par-72), a driving range, racquetball and squash courts, and a swimming pool. Rental equipment is available at the club, and there's a restaurant too (© 850/891-3935 for information and fees). Compared with most courses in Florida, greens fees are a steal: about $25 on weekdays, $30 on weekends, including cart (they're about $13 and $17, respectively, if you walk). The park also includes the recently renovated **Jake Gaither Municipal Golf Course,** at Bragg and Pasco streets (© 850/891-3942), with a nine-hole, par-35 fairway and a pro shop. Call for fees.

The leading golf course is at the **Killearn Country Club and Inn** (© 800/476-4101 or 850/893-2186), which once hosted the Sprint Classic. Moss-draped oaks enhance the beautiful 27-hole championship course, which is for members with reciprocal privileges only.

SPECTATOR SPORTS Tallahassee succumbs to football frenzy whenever the perennially powerful Seminoles of **Florida State University** (FSU) take to the gridiron. Call © 850/644-1830 (www.seminoles.com) well in advance for tickets. Even when the Seminoles play on the road, everything except Tallahassee's many sports bars comes to a stop while fans watch the games on TV.

The **Florida A&M University** (FAMU) Rattlers are cheered on by the school's high-stepping, world-famous Marching 100 Band. Call © 850/599-3230 or check www.famu.edu/athletics for FAMU schedules and tickets.

Both FSU and FAMU have seasonal basketball, baseball, tennis, and track schedules. Call the numbers above for information.

SHOPPING FOR ANTIQUES & HOMEMADE SAUSAGE

Antiques hounds flock to the little village of **Havana**, 12 miles northwest of I-10 on U.S. 27. Havana used to make its living from shade-grown tobacco, and when that industry went into decline in the 1960s, the town went with it. Things turned around 20 years later, however, when Havana began opening art galleries and antiques, handcrafts, and collectibles shops. Today these are housed in lovingly restored, turn-of-the-century brick buildings along Havana's commercial streets. Just drive into town on Main Street (U.S. 27), turn left on

---

Fun Fact **Semi-Tough: The Prequel**

Burt Reynolds played defensive back for Florida State University's football team in 1957 and is still an avid 'Noles booster.

Seventh Avenue, find a parking place, and start browsing. You'll have plenty of company on weekends.

Bradley's Country Store, about 8 miles north of I-10 on Centerville Road (© **850/893-1647;** www.bradleyscountrystore.com), sells more than 80,000 pounds a year of homemade sausage, both over the counter and from mail orders. You can also buy coarse-ground grits, country-milled cornmeal, hogshead cheese, liver pudding, cracklings, and specially cured hams. This friendly store, which is on the National Register of Historic Places, is also a sightseeing attraction with self-guided tours. It's open Monday to Friday from 8am to 6pm and Saturday from 8am to 5pm.

ACCOMMODATIONS YOU CAN AFFORD

There is no high or low season here, but every hotel and motel for miles around is completely booked during FSU and FAMU football weekends from September to November, and again at graduation in May. Reserve well in advance or you may have to stay 60 miles or more from the city. For the schedules, call FSU or FAMU (see "Spectator Sports," above).

Most hotels are concentrated in three areas: downtown Tallahassee, north of downtown along North Monroe Street at Exit 29 off I-10, and along Apalachee Parkway east of downtown.

North Monroe Street at I-10 has most of the national chain motels catering to the highway traffic.

Tax on all hotel and campground bills is 10% in Leon County.

Cabot Lodge North *Value* A clapboard plantation-style house with a tin roof and a partially screened wraparound porch provides Southern country charm to distinguish this friendly motel from its nearby competitors. Guests can relax in straight-back rockers on the porch or on comfy sofas and easy chairs by a fireplace in the living room. Although the guest rooms in the two-story motel buildings out back don't hold up their end of the atmosphere factor, they're still quite satisfactory at these rates, and they give quick access to the outdoor swimming pool. Guests can enjoy a complimentary continental breakfast buffet and evening cocktails.

2735 N. Monroe St., Tallahassee, FL 32303. © **800/223-1964** or 850/386-8880. Fax 850/386-4254. www.cabotlodge.com. 160 units. $66–$80 double. Rates include continental breakfast, evening reception, and local phone calls. AE, DC, DISC, MC, V. **Amenities:** Outdoor pool; access to nearby health club; laundry service. *In room:* A/C, TV, dataport, hair dryer (king-size bedrooms only).

Courtyard by Marriott Just a mile east of the Old Capitol, this comfortable member of the business-traveler–oriented chain encloses a landscaped courtyard with a swimming pool and gazebo. About half of the rooms face the courtyard; the others face parking lots. They are a bit cramped for families but ideal for singles and couples. The marble-floored lobby features a lounge with fireplace, honor bar, and dining area open for a breakfast buffet only. Several chain restaurants are within walking distance or a short drive away. The Parkway Shopping Center is also across the road.

1018 Apalachee Pkwy., Tallahassee, FL 32301. © **800/321-2211** or 850/222-8822. Fax 850/561-0354. 154 units. Mon–Thurs $120 double; Fri–Sun $70 double. AE, DC, DISC, MC, V. **Amenities:** Restaurant (breakfast only), bar; heated outdoor pool; exercise room; Jacuzzi; laundry service, coin-op washers and dryers. *In room:* A/C, TV, dataport, coffeemaker, hair dryer, iron.

DoubleTree Hotel Most of the media covering the Bush–Gore 2000 election case before the Florida Supreme Court stayed at this 16-story hotel, one of the tallest buildings in town. The best things about it are the location, just 2 blocks north of the Capitol Building at Park Avenue, and the views from the spacious

> **Fun Fact Count Them Out**
> Demand for hotel rooms during Florida State University football weekends is so great that the high-powered lawyers representing former Vice President Gore and then Texas Governor George W. Bush had to vacate their rooms when the University of Florida Gators came to play the 'Noles during the 2000 election dispute.

rooms, especially those on the upper floors. It's usually booked solid by politicians and lobbyists during legislative sessions from March through May.

101 S. Adams St., Tallahassee, FL 32301. © **800/222-TREE** or 850/224-5000. Fax 850/513-9516. 243 units. $89–$159 double. AE, DC, DISC, MC, V. **Amenities:** Restaurant (American); bar; outdoor pool; exercise room; limited room service; laundry service; concierge-level rooms. *In room:* A/C, TV, dataport, coffeemaker, hair dryer, iron.

Quality Inn & Suites *Value* In contrast to most Quality Inns, there's real charm here. In fact, an almost English country-inn atmosphere prevails in the classy, marble-lined lobby and spacious guest rooms, which are furnished with sofas and reclining wing chairs. A complimentary continental breakfast is served in a lounge with views of the inn's swimming pool, and guests can partake of a free wine bar Monday to Thursday evenings. A nearby restaurant will deliver food, and several fast-food and family-style restaurants are within a short walk.

2020 Apalachee Pkwy., Tallahassee, FL 32301. © **800/228-5151** or 850/877-4437. Fax 850/878-9964. www.qualityinn.com. 100 units. $79 double; $99 suite. Rates include full breakfast, evening drinks, and local phone calls. AE, DC, DISC, MC, V. **Amenities:** Outdoor pool; access to nearby health club; Jacuzzi; business center; limited room service; laundry service. *In room:* A/C, TV, dataport, fridge, coffeemaker, hair dryer, iron, safe.

WORTH A DEMOCRATIC SPLURGE

Governors Inn ★★ Vice President Gore's election lawyers got to this richly furnished inn just half a block north of the Old Capitol in the Adams Street Commons historic district ahead of the Bush team in 2000. The building was once a livery stable, and part of its original architecture has been preserved, including the impressive beams. The guest rooms are distinctive, with four-poster beds, black-oak writing desks, rock-maple armoires, and antique accoutrements. Of the suites, each one named for a Florida governor, one has a whirlpool bathtub; another has a loft bedroom with wood-burning fireplace. Complimentary continental breakfast and afternoon cocktails are presented in the pine-paneled Florida Room, and a restaurant across the street provides limited room service.

209 S. Adams St., Tallahassee, FL 32301. © **800/342-7717** in Florida, or 850/681-6855. Fax 850/222-3105. 40 units. $129–$149 double; $159–$229 suite. Rates include continental breakfast and evening cocktails. AE, DC, DISC, MC, V. **Amenities:** Access to nearby health club; limited room service; laundry service. *In room:* A/C, TV, dataport.

WORTH A REPUBLICAN SPLURGE

Radisson Hotel Tallahassee President George W. Bush's legal team stayed at this seven-story hotel about a half mile north of the capitol complex. The innlike lobby with reproduction antiques strikes an elegant ambience, but the regular guest rooms are rather small (this hotel was built in the 1950s as a college dormitory), and air-conditioning units eat up about a third of each unit's window. The spacious suites are much better choices; they are equipped with four-poster beds, whirlpool bathtubs, and wet bars. The pleasant Plantation Dining Room is open daily for breakfast, lunch, and dinner, and the lobby lounge provides libation.

415 N. Monroe St. (at Virginia St.), Tallahassee, FL 32301. © 800/333-3333 or 850/224-6000. Fax 850/222-0335. 119 units. $111 double; $150–$197 suite. Weekend rates available. AE, DC, DISC, MC, V. **Amenities:** Restaurant (American), bar; exercise room; sauna; limited room service; laundry service; concierge-level rooms. *In room:* A/C, TV, dataport, coffeemaker, hair dryer, iron.

GREAT DEALS ON DINING

Numerous budget-priced fast-food and family chain restaurants lie along Apalachee Parkway and North Monroe Street. For inexpensive seafood, the local **Shells** is at 2136 N. Monroe St., at Universal Drive (© **850/385-2774**). See "Great Deals on Dining," in section 1 of chapter 10, "The Tampa Bay Area," for details about the Shells chain.

Anthony's ★ SOUTHERN ITALIAN   Locals come to see and be seen at Dick Anthony's elegantly relaxed trattoria, which supplies them with the city's best Italian cuisine. Among his specialties is *pesce Venezia*, spinach fettuccine tossed in a cream sauce with scallops, crabmeat, and fish. Chicken piccata and chicken San Marino are also favorites, and Dick's thick, juicy steaks are always popular with beef eaters. A wall-size wine cupboard features choices from Italy and the United States by the bottle or glass. Espresso pie leads the dessert menu.

1950 Thomasville Rd., at Bradford Rd. in the Betton Place Shops. © 850/224-1447. Reservations recommended. Main courses $12–$21. AE, DC, DISC, MC, V. Daily 5–9pm.

Bahn Thai THAI/CANTONESE   Lamoi (Sue) Snyder and progeny have been serving the spicy cuisine of her native Thailand at this storefront since 1979. In deference to local Southerners, who may never have sampled anything spicier than cheese grits, much of her menu is devoted to mild Cantonese-style Chinese dishes. More adventurous diners, however, flock here to order such authentic tongue-burners as *yon voon-sen*, a combination of shrimp, chicken, bean threads, onions, lemongrass, ground peanuts, and the obligatory chili peppers. Sue's specialty is her deliciously sweet, slightly gingered version of Penang curry. You can ask her to turn down the heat in her other Thai dishes. Come at lunch and sample it all from the all-you-can-eat buffet, a real bargain.

1319 S. Monroe St. (between Oakland Ave. and Harrison St.). © 850/224-4765. Main courses $6–$15. Lunch buffet $6.50. DISC, MC, V. Mon–Thurs 11am–2:30pm and 5–10pm; Fri 11am–2:30pm and 5–10:30pm; Sat 5–10:30pm.

Barnacle Bill's Seafood Restaurant SEAFOOD   There's always plenty of action at this noisy, very casual spot, a favorite of the journalists and talking heads who covered the Gore–Bush election contest. Freshly shucked Apalachicola oysters are the stars at the enormous tile-topped raw bar in the middle of the room, but the menu offers a mélange of seafood to please the palates of the singles, couples, and families who flock here. The cooking is simple and usually done by Florida State University students working part-time jobs. Best bets are charcoal-grilled mahimahi, tuna, amberjack, and grouper. For a smoked sensation, try the mahimahi and amberjack cured on the premises. During summer, guests can sit at outdoor tables under a lean-to tent. A downstairs bar serves the regular seafood items plus sushi, deli sandwiches, and salads.

1830 N. Monroe St. (north of Tharpe St.). © 850/385-8734. Main courses $8–$17 (most $10–$12); sandwiches and salads $5–$9. AE, DC, DISC, MC, V. Sun–Thurs 11am–11pm; Fri–Sat 11am–midnight.

Food Glorious Food ★★ *Value* AMERICAN/INTERNATIONAL   Very unusual and very healthy sandwiches, salads, and pastas make Susan Turner's deli/cafe one of the town's favorite lunch and early-dinner spots. Items displayed in a cold case change daily but always include gazpacho, a variety of gourmet salads, inventive sandwiches, a daily quiche, and plenty of tempting pastries and cookies. Main courses feature the likes of pineapple jerk chicken, Cuban chicken, and several pastas. You can get your selection to go or dine at a few tables inside or, in good weather, on the outside courtyard.

In Betton Place Shops, 1950 Thomasville Rd. at Bradford Rd. © 850/224-9974. Reservations not accepted. Main courses $9–$20; sandwiches and salads $5.50–$11. AE, DC, MC, V. Mon–Thurs 11am–8pm; Fri–Sat 11am–9pm (table service 11am–3pm). Closed July 4, Thanksgiving, Christmas.

Kool Beanz Cafe ECLECTIC   The coolest cafe in town, this noisy emporium of trendy cooking draws lots of patrons in their late 20s and early 30s who appreciate exciting blends of flavors. The joint is dimly lit but painted in bright pastels from the Caribbean. You'll find many island-style items on the constantly changing menu, including Jamaican jerk grouper served with black beans, rice, and a sweet tropical fruit relish. You may want to get here early because more inventive items like the seared but rare tuna crusted with spice and served with a terrific roasted peanut sauce will sell out early, as will the curried lamb shank and the pork tenderloin marinated with orange molasses.

921 Thomasville Rd. (at Williams St.). © 850/224-2466. Main courses $12–$16. AE, DISC, MC, V. Mon–Fri 11am–2:30pm and 5:30–10pm; Sat 5:30–10pm.

WORTH A SPLURGE

Chez Pierre TRADITIONAL FRENCH   You become an instant Francophile in Florida at this chic restaurant in a beautifully restored 1920s brick home. French-born chef Eric Favier and his American wife and partner, Karen Cooley, offer traditional French cuisine either inside the house—where the walls are adorned with changing, for-sale works by local artists—or outside on a large deck nearly shaded by live oaks draped with Spanish moss. Opening to the deck, a bistro-style bar provides a light-fare menu between lunch and dinner. Eric offers daily specials to take advantage of fresh produce. Among his winners are rack of lamb, a version of Provençal-style ratatouille, and crab cakes with a luscious mustard and thyme demi-glacé. French table wines are moderately priced, and California house wines are also served. Live music regularly accompanies dining. No smoking except on the front porch, where stogies and brandy can be enjoyed while lounging in wicker chairs. Book as early as possible for Bastille Day (July 14), which sees a grand fete here.

1215 Thomasville Rd. (at Sixth Ave.). © 850/222-0936. Reservations recommended. Main courses $15–$23. AE, DC, DISC, MC, V. Mon–Sat 11am–10pm; Sun 11am–9pm.

TALLAHASSEE AFTER DARK

Check the "Limelight" section of Friday's *Tallahassee Democrat* (www.tallahasseedemocrat.com) for weekend entertainment listings.

As a college town, Tallahassee has numerous pubs and nightclubs with live dance music, not to mention a multitude of sports bars. Pick up a copy of ***Break*** and other entertainment tabloids at **Barnacle Bill's Seafood Emporium** or other entertainment venues.

The major performing-arts venue is the **Tallahassee–Leon County Civic Center,** 505 W. Pensacola St. (© **800/322-3602** or 850/222-0400; www.tlccc.org), which features a Broadway series, concerts, and sporting events including Florida State University (FSU) collegiate basketball games. Special concerts are presented by the **Tallahassee Symphony Orchestra** (www.tsolive.org) at FSU Ruby Diamond Auditorium, College Avenue and Copeland Street (© **850/ 224-0462**). **The FSU Mainstage/School of Theatre,** Fine Arts Building, Call and Copeland streets (© 850/644-6500; www.fsu.org), presents excellent productions from classic dramas to comedies.

SIDE TRIPS FROM TALLAHASSEE

The following excursions generally are on the way to Apalachicola, so if you're headed that way, plan to make a detour or two.

WAKULLA SPRINGS ★★

The world's largest and deepest freshwater spring is 15 miles south of Tallahassee in the 2,860-acre **Edward W. Ball Wakulla Springs State Park** ★★, on Fla. 267 just east of its junction with Fla. 61. Edward Ball, a financier who administered the du Pont estate, turned the springs and the moss-draped surrounding forest into a preservation area. Divers have mapped an underwater cave system extending more than 6,000 feet back from the spring's mouth. Wakulla has been known to dispense an amazing 14,325 gallons of water per second at certain times. Mastodon bones, including those of Herman, now in Tallahassee's Museum of Florida History, were found in the caves. The 1930s *Tarzan* movies starring Johnny Weissmuller were filmed here.

A free 10-minute orientation movie is offered at the park's theater at the waterfront. You can hike or bike along the nature trails, and swimming is allowed, but only in designated areas. It's important to observe swimming rules since alligators are present.

If the spring water is clear enough, 30-minute glass-bottom-boat sightseeing trips depart daily, every 45 minutes from 9:45am to 5pm during daylight saving time, 9:15am to 4:30pm the rest of the year. Even if the water is murky, you're likely to see alligators, birds, and other wildlife on 30-minute riverboat cruises, which operate during these same hours. Either boat ride costs $4.50 for adults, half price for children under 13.

Entrance fees to the park are $3.25 per vehicle with up to eight passengers, $1 for pedestrians and bicyclists. The park is open daily from 8am to dusk.

For more information, contact the park at 550 Wakulla Springs Dr., Wakulla Springs, FL 32305 (© 850/224-5950; fax 850/561-7251; www.floridastateparks.org/district1/wakullasprings).

Accommodations You Can Afford

Wakulla Springs Lodge On the shore of Wakulla Springs, this dated but charming lodge is distinctive for its magnificent Spanish architecture and ornate old-world furnishings, such as rare Spanish tiles, black-granite tables, marble floors, and ceiling beams painted with Florida scenes by a German artist (supposedly Kaiser Wilhelm's court painter). The guest rooms are simple by today's

---

> **Tips** **A Ramshackle Riverside Lunch**
>
> Tallahasseeans love to drive or bike down to St. Marks and have a waterside lunch at **Posey's Oyster Bar**, at the end of Fla. 363 (© 850/925-6172). Some nighttime patrons at this ramshackle wooden restaurant and bar can get rowdy, especially when country-and-western bands are playing on weekends, but it's a fine place for freshly shucked oysters or smoked mullet during the day, which will cost no more than $10. Be sure to walk all the way through the dining rooms to the bar beside the St. Marks River. Posey's opens daily at 11am.

standards (you'll get a marble bathroom and phone but no TV). By all means ask for a room at the front so you'll have a lake view. You don't have to be a lodge guest to enjoy the warm, smoky ambience of the great lobby with its huge stone fireplace and arched windows looking onto the springs, or to enjoy reasonably priced meals featuring Southern cuisine in the lovely Ball Room (reservations recommended). The fountain provides snacks and sandwiches (there's a 60-ft.-long marble drugstore-style counter for old-fashioned ice-cream sodas).

550 Wakulla Park Dr., Wakulla Springs, FL 32305. © 850/224-5950. Fax 850/561-7251. 27 units. $79–$99 double. AE, DISC, MC, V. **Amenities:** Restaurant (Southern). *In room:* A/C.

THE ST. MARKS AREA

Rich history lives in the area around the little village of **St. Marks,** 18 miles south of the capital at the end of both Fla. 363 and the Tallahassee–St. Marks Historic Railroad Trail State Park (see "Affordable Outdoor Activities," earlier in this section).

After marching overland from Tampa Bay in 1528, the Spanish conquistador Panfilo de Narvaez and 300 men arrived at this strategic point at the confluence of the St. Marks and Wakulla rivers near the Gulf of Mexico. Since their only avenue back to Spain was by sea, they built and launched the first ships made by Europeans in the New World. Some 11 years later, Hernando de Soto and his 600 men arrived here after following Narvaez's route from Tampa. They marked the harbor entrance by hanging banners in the trees, then moved inland. Two wooden forts were built here, one in 1679 and one in 1718, and a stone version was begun in 1739. The fort shifted among Spanish, British, and Native American hands until General Andrew Jackson took it away from the Spanish in 1819.

Parts of the old Spanish bastion wall and Confederate earthworks built during the Civil War are in the **San Marcos de Apalache Historic State Park,** reached by turning right at the end of Fla. 363 in St. Marks and following the paved road. A museum built on the foundation of the old marine hospital holds exhibits and artifacts covering the area's history. The site is open Thursday to Monday from 9am to 5pm; closed New Year's Day, Thanksgiving, and Christmas. Admission to the site is free; admission to the museum costs $1 and is free for children 6 and under. For more information, contact the site at 1022 DeSoto Park Dr., Tallahassee, FL 32301 (© **850/925-6216** or 850/922-6007; www.floridastateparks.org/district1/sanmarcos).

De Soto's men marked the harbor entrance in what is now the **St. Marks Lighthouse and National Wildlife Refuge**, P.O. Box 68, St. Marks, FL 32355 (© **850/925-6121**). Operated by the U.S. Fish and Wildlife Service, this 65,000-acre preserve occupies much of the coast from the Aucilla River east of St. Marks to the Ochlockonee River west of Panacea and is home to more species of birds than anyplace else in Florida except the Everglades. The visitor center is 3½ miles south of U.S. 98 on Lighthouse Road (Fla. 59); turn south off U.S. 98 at Newport, about 2 miles east of St. Marks. Stop at the center for self-guided tour maps of the roads and extensive hiking trails, some of them built atop levees running through the marshland.

The 80-foot-tall **St. Marks Lighthouse,** 8 miles south of the visitor center, was built in 1842 of limestone blocks 4 feet thick at the base. The nearby beach is a popular crabbing spot.

Admission to the refuge is $4 per vehicle, $1 for pedestrians and bicyclists (federal Duck Stamps and National Park Service passports accepted). The refuge is open daily from sunrise to sunset; the visitor center, Monday to Friday from

8am to 4pm and Saturday and Sunday from 10am to 5pm (closed all federal holidays). Contact the refuge for information about seasonal tours and hunting.

In 1865, during the final weeks of the Civil War, Federal troops landed at the lighthouse and launched a surprise attack on Tallahassee. The Confederates quickly assembled an impromptu army of wounded soldiers, old men, and boys as young as 14. This ragtag bunch fought the Federal regulars for 5 days at what is now the **Natural Bridge Battlefield State Historic Site.** Surprisingly, the old men and boys won. As a result, Tallahassee remained the only Confederate state capital east of the Mississippi never to fall into Yankee hands. The historic site is on County Road 2192, 6 miles east of Woodville on the St. Marks River, halfway between Tallahassee and St. Marks. Follow the signs from Fla. 363 and go to the end of the pavement. It's open daily from 8am to sunset and admission is free. For more information, contact the San Marcos de Apalache State Historic Site (see above) or check www.floridastateparks.org/district1/naturalbridge.

APALACHICOLA NATIONAL FOREST

The largest of Florida's three national forests, this huge preserve encompasses 600,000 acres stretching from Tallahassee's outskirts southward to the Gulf Coast and westward some 70 miles to the Apalachicola River. Included are a variety of woodlands, rivers, streams, lakes, and caves populated by a host of wildlife. There are picnic facilities with sheltered tables and grills, canoe and mountain-bike trails, campgrounds with tent and RV sites, and a number of other facilities, some of them especially designed for visitors with disabilities.

The **Leon Sinks Area** is closest to Tallahassee, 5½ miles south of Southeast Capital Circle on U.S. 319 near the Leon–Wakulla County line. Nature trails and boardwalks lead from one sinkhole (a lake formed when water erodes the underlying limestone) to another. The trails are open daily from 8am to 8pm.

A necessary stop before heading into this wilderness is the **Wakulla Area Ranger District,** 57 Taft Dr., Crawfordville, FL 32327 (© **850/926-3561;** fax 850/926-1904; www.southernregion.fs.fed.us/florida/forests/apalachicola.htm), which provides information about the forest and its facilities and sells topographical and canoe trail maps. The station is off U.S. 319 about 20 miles south of Tallahassee and 2 miles north of Crawfordville. It's open Monday to Thursday from 8am to 4:30pm and Friday from 8am to 4pm.

Appendix: Useful Toll-Free Numbers & Websites

AIRLINES

Aer Lingus
☎ 800/474-7424 in the U.S.
☎ 01/886-8888 in Ireland
www.aerlingus.com

Air Canada
☎ 888/247-2262
www.aircanada.ca

Air New Zealand
☎ 800/262-1234
   or -2468 in the U.S.
☎ 800/663-5494 in Canada
☎ 0800/737-767 in New Zealand
www.airnewzealand.com

Airtran Airlines
☎ 800/247-8726
www.airtran.com

Alaska Airlines
☎ 800/426-0333
www.alaskaair.com

American Airlines
☎ 800/433-7300
www.aa.com

American Trans Air
☎ 800/225-2995
www.ata.com

America West Airlines
☎ 800/235-9292
www.americawest.com

British Airways
☎ 800/247-9297
☎ 0345/222-111 or
   0845/77-333-77 in Britain
www.british-airways.com

Continental Airlines
☎ 800/525-0280
www.continental.com

Delta Air Lines
☎ 800/221-1212
www.delta.com

Frontier Airlines
☎ 800/432-1359
www.frontierairlines.com

Hawaiian Airlines
☎ 800/367-5320
www.hawaiianair.com

Jet Blue Airlines
☎ 800/538-2583
www.jetblue.com

Midwest Express
☎ 800/452-2022
www.midwestexpress.com

Northwest Airlines
☎ 800/225-2525
www.nwa.com

Qantas
☎ 800/227-4500 in the U.S.
☎ 612/9691-3636 in Australia
www.qantas.com

Southwest Airlines
☎ 800/435-9792
www.southwest.com

United Airlines
☎ 800/241-6522
www.united.com

US Airways
☎ 800/428-4322
www.usairways.com

Virgin Atlantic Airways
☎ 800/862-8621 in Continental U.S.
☎ 0293/747-747 in Britain
www.virgin-atlantic.com

CAR-RENTAL AGENCIES

Alamo
✆ 800/327-9633
www.goalamo.com

Avis
✆ 800/331-1212 in Continental U.S.
✆ 800/TRY-AVIS in Canada
www.avis.com

Budget
✆ 800/527-0700
https://rent.drivebudget.com

Dollar
✆ 800/800-4000
www.dollar.com

Enterprise
✆ 800/325-8007
www.enterprise.com

Hertz
✆ 800/654-3131
www.hertz.com
www.kemwel.com

National
✆ 800/CAR-RENT
www.nationalcar.com

Payless
✆ 800/PAYLESS
www.paylesscarrental.com

Rent-A-Wreck
✆ 800/535-1391
www.rentawreck.com

Thrifty
✆ 800/367-2277
www.thrifty.com

MAJOR HOTEL & MOTEL CHAINS

Baymont Inns & Suites
✆ 800/301-0200
www.baymontinns.com

Best Western International
✆ 800/528-1234
www.bestwestern.com

Clarion Hotels
✆ 800/CLARION
www.clarionhotel.com or
www.hotelchoice.com

Comfort Inns
✆ 800/228-5150
www.hotelchoice.com

Courtyard by Marriott
✆ 800/321-2211
www.courtyard.com or
www.marriott.com

Days Inn
✆ 800/325-2525
www.daysinn.com

Doubletree Hotels
✆ 800/222-TREE
www.doubletree.com

Econo Lodges
✆ 800/55-ECONO
www.hotelchoice.com

Fairfield Inn by Marriott
✆ 800/228-2800
www.marriott.com

Hampton Inn
✆ 800/HAMPTON
www.hampton-inn.com

Hilton Hotels
✆ 800/HILTONS
www.hilton.com

Holiday Inn
✆ 800/HOLIDAY
www.basshotels.com

Howard Johnson
✆ 800/654-2000
www.hojo.com

Hyatt Hotels & Resorts
✆ 800/228-9000
www.hyatt.com

Inter-Continental Hotels & Resorts
✆ 888/567-8725
www.interconti.com

ITT Sheraton
✆ 800/325-3535
www.starwood.com

Knights Inn
℡ 800/843-5644
www.knghtsinn.com

La Quinta Motor Inns
℡ 800/531-5900
www.laquinta.com

Marriott Hotels
℡ 800/228-9290
www.marriott.com

Motel 6
℡ 800/4-MOTEL6
www.motel6.com

Quality Inns
℡ 800/228-5151
www.hotelchoice.com

Radisson Hotels International
℡ 800/333-3333
www.radisson.com

Ramada Inns
℡ 800/2-RAMADA
www.ramada.com

Red Carpet Inns
℡ 800/251-1962
www.reservahost.com

Red Roof Inns
℡ 800/843-7663
www.redroof.com

Residence Inn by Marriott
℡ 800/331-3131
www.marriott.com

Rodeway Inns
℡ 800/228-2000
www.hotelchoice.com

Sheraton Hotels & Resorts
℡ 800/325-3535
www.sheraton.com

Sleep Inn
℡ 800/753-3746
www.sleepinn.com

Super 8 Motels
℡ 800/800-8000
www.super8.com

Travelodge
℡ 800/255-3050
www.travelodge.com

Westin Hotels & Resorts
℡ 800/937-8461
www.westin.com

Wyndham Hotels and Resorts
℡ 800/822-4200
www.wyndham.com

Index

A
AAA (American Automobile Association), 87
Accommodations, 76–78
   best, 18–25
   money-saving tips, 41–42, 77–78
Active vacations, 70–76
Actors' Playhouse (Coral Gables), 182
Adams Street Commons (Tallahassee), 654
Adventure Express tour (SeaWorld), 522
Adventure Island (Tampa), 389
Adventureland (WDW), 494
   restaurants, 482
Adventure Landing (Daytona Beach), 556
Adventurers Club (WDW), 533
Adventure trips, best, 11–12
Africa (WDW), 507
African Americans, 9, 51
   Amelia Island, 594
   Julee Cottage Black History Museum (Pensacola), 610
   Northwest Florida attractions, 623
   Ritz Theatre & LaVilla Museum (Jacksonville), 584–585
   Tallahassee, 654–656
Airboat tours, the Everglades, 240–241
Airfares
   for foreign visitors, 85
   money-saving tips, 37, 40, 63–66
Airlines, 61–62, 69, 85, 86
Airplane tours, Key West, 217
Air travel
   money-saving tips, 37, 40
   security measures, 62

Akershus Castle (WDW), 501
Alfred Hitchcock: The Art of Making Movies (Universal Orlando), 516
Alligators, 14, 238, 240, 241, 259, 260, 306, 307, 332, 335, 348, 392, 440, 442, 444, 510, 526, 544, 572, 584, 626, 639, 640, 663
Alltel Stadium (Jacksonville), 588, 593
Amazing Adventures of Spider-Man (Universal Orlando), 518
Amelia Earhart Park (Hialeah), 153
Amelia Island, 10, 594–601
   accommodations, 598–600
   beaches, 596–597
   nightlife, 601
   outdoor activities, 597–598
   restaurants, 600–601
   shopping, 598
Amelia Island Museum of History, 598
American Airlines Arena (Miami), 165
American Beach (Amelia Island), 594
American Express, Miami, 100
American Sandsculpting Festival (Fort Myers Beach), 55
Anandapur (WDW), 507
Anastasia State Park, 572
Anheuser-Busch Hospitality Center (SeaWorld), 525
Anhinga Trail, 238
Animal Kingdom (WDW)
   attractions, 505–508
   restaurants, 483
Animal parks and attractions
   Florida's Gulfarium, 626
   Gulf World Marine Park (Panama City Beach), 639

   Hobe Sound Wildlife Refuge, 306
   Homosassa Springs State Wildlife Park, 414
   Miami, 155–157
   Palm Beach, 285
   Sarasota, 442
   SeaWorld, 522–525
   Tampa, 389, 392–396
   Upper and Middle Keys, 193–195
Animal Planet Live! (Universal Orlando), 517
Anna Maria Bayfront Park, 438
Anna Maria Island, 7, 436, 438–440, 446, 447, 453
Anne's Beach (Lower Matecumbe Key), 190
Antiques and collectibles
   Dania, 261
   Miami, 168
   Orlando, 532
   Pensacola, 612
   St. Augustine, 575
Apalachicola, 646–651
Apalachicola National Forest, 648, 658, 665
Aquariums
   Clearwater Marine Aquarium, 424
   Florida Aquarium (Tampa), 13, 396
   Key West Aquarium, 13, 214
   Living Seas (WDW), 499
   Miami Seaquarium (Key Biscayne), 12, 156
   Mote Aquarium (St. Armands Key), 443
   Parker Manatee Aquarium (Bradenton), 444
Arcade Theater (Fort Myers), 339
Art Center Sarasota, 441
Art Deco District (South Beach), 147–148

INDEX

Art Deco Weekend (South Beach), 49
Artemis Performance Network (Miami), 182
Art Miami, 49
ArtWalk (Fort Pierce), 316
Asia (WDW), 507–508
Asolo Theatre (Sarasota), 442, 454–455
Asolo Theatre Festival (Sarasota), 454
Astronaut Hall of Fame (Titusville), 540–542
Astronaut Memorial Planetarium and Observatory (Cocoa Beach), 540
Astro Orbiter (WDW), 497
Atlanta Braves, 53, 510, 531
Atlantic Beach (Jacksonville), 587
Atlantic Dunes Beach (Delray Beach), 274
ATMs (automated-teller machines), 47, 84
Audubon House & Tropical Gardens (Key West), 213
Audubon of Florida—National Center for Birds of Prey (Maitland), 528
Authentic Old Jail (St. Augustine), 570
Aventura, 95
shopping, 167, 170
Avondale/Riverside historic district, 588

Back to the Future: The Ride (Universal Orlando), 514
Bahia Honda State Park, 204, 206, 208
Bailey-Matthews Shell Museum (Sanibel Island), 350
Bal Harbour, 95. *See also* Miami Beach
Bal Harbour Beach, 146
Ballet Flamenco La Rosa (North Miami), 184
Balloons Over Florida (Martin County), 306–307
Baltimore Orioles, 53
Barbara B. Mann Performing Arts Hall (Fort Myers), 339
Barnstormer at Goofy's Wiseacre Farm (WDW), 496
Bars, best, 33–35

Baseball, 7, 53
Daytona Beach, 555–556
Fort Lauderdale, 258
Fort Myers, 333–335
Miami, 165
Orlando, 531
Port St. Lucie, 312
Tampa, 399–400
Ted Williams Museum & Hitters Hall of Fame (near Hernando), 415
Vero Beach, 318–319
Basketball
Miami, 165
Orlando, 531
Bass Museum of Art (Miami), 1, 149
Bathtub Beach (North Hutchinson Island), 304
Bayfront Center (St. Petersburg), 419
Bay Hill Invitational (Orlando), 51
Bayshore Boulevard (Tampa), 9, 394
Bayside Marketplace (downtown Miami), 170
BayWalk (St. Petersburg), 419
Beaches
Amelia Island, 594, 596–597
Anastasia State Park, 572–573
Anne's Beach (Lower Matecumbe Key), 190
Atlantic Beach (Jacksonville), 587
Atlantic Dunes Beach (Delray Beach), 274
Bal Harbour Beach, 146
Bathtub Beach (North Hutchinson Island), 304
best, 4–6, 10
Boca Raton and Delray Beach, 274
Bowman's Beach (Sanibel), 350
Broward County, 254, 256
Caladesi Island State Park, 5, 394, 422
Canaveral National Seashore, 5, 18, 72, 543–544, 548
Cayo Costa State Park (off Captiva Island), 5, 17, 72, 332, 333, 363, 365
Clam Pass County Park, 368

Clearwater Public Beach (Pier 60), 422
Cocoa Beach Pier, 544
Crandon Park Beach (Key Biscayne), 4, 146
Crescent Beach (Marco Island), 379–380
Daytona Beach, 553, 554
Delnor-Wiggins Pass State Park, 368–369
Destin, 620–621
85th Street Beach (Miami Beach), 146
Fort Clinch State Park (Amelia Island), 596–597
Fort Lauderdale, 254, 256
Fort Myers Beach, 340–341
Fort Pierce, 312
Fort Walton Beach, 621
Fort Zachary Beach (Key West), 219
Gasparilla Island State Recreation Area, 364
Grayton Beach State Park, 621
Gulf Islands National Seashore, 5–6, 10, 26, 46, 602, 606–608, 611, 612, 621, 622
Gulfside City Park (Sanibel), 350
Haulover Beach (Miami), 146
Henderson Beach State Park, 620–621
Higgs Beach (Key West), 219
Hobie Beach (Miami), 146
Hollywood Beach, 254
Jacksonville, 587
Jetty Park (Cape Canaveral), 544
Jetty Park (Fort Pierce Inlet), 312
John D. MacArthur Beach, 295–296
John U. Lloyd Beach State Park, 256
Key West, 218–219
Lori Wilson Park, 544
Lover's Key State Park (Fort Myers Beach), 5, 17, 334, 339, 340, 343
Lowdermilk Park (Naples), 368
Lummus Park Beach (South Beach), 4–5, 146
Lynn Hall Memorial Park, 340–341

Main Beach (Amelia Island), 596
Marco Island, 379–380
Matheson Hammock Park Beach (South Miami), 4, 146, 157
Miami, 141–146
Miami Beach, 141, 144–145
Midtown Beach (Palm Beach), 283
Naples Beach, 5, 368–369, 371
Naples Pier, 368
Neptune Beach (Jacksonville), 587
northern Palm Beach County, 295–296
Northwest Florida, 7, 622
Palm Beach, 283–284
Pass-a-Grille Public Beach, 422
Peters Point Beach Front Park (Amelia Island), 596
Phipps Ocean Park (Palm Beach), 284
Playalinda Beach, 543–544, 548
Ponte Vedra Beach (Jacksonville), 587
St. Andrews State Park, 6, 10, 26, 72, 622, 637, 641
St. Augustine, 572–573
Sanibel and Captiva islands, 350
Sarasota area, 437–438
Seaside, 621
Sebastian Inlet (North Hutchinson Island), 5, 317, 321, 545
Smathers Beach (Key West), 219
Sombrero Beach (Marathon), 190
South Beach Park Beach (Boca Raton), 274
Southern Walton County, 621
Tampa Bay area, 394
Tarpon Bay Road Beach (Sanibel), 350
Tigertail Public Beach (Marco Island), 380
Turner Beach (Sanibel), 350
Upper and Middle Keys, 190
Vero Beach and Sebastian, 317
Vilano Beach (St. Augustine), 572

Beasley Park, 621
Beauty and the Beast Live on Stage (WDW), 502
Beetlejuice's Rock 'n' Roll Graveyard Revue, 514
Belz Factory Outlet World (St. Augustine), 575
BET Soundstage (WDW), 533
Bicycling, 70–71
Everglades National Park, 238–239
Jupiter, 296
Key West, 219
Lower Keys, 205
Miami, 99, 160
Art Deco Biking Tour, 148
Orlando, 530
Palm Beach, 284
St. Petersburg, 413–414
Sanibel Island, 335, 351
Sarasota area, 438
Tallahassee, 657–658
Tampa, 394, 398–399
Biga Bakery (Coral Gables), 169
Big Cypress Reservation, 259
Big Pine Key, 204–210
Big Thunder Mountain Railroad (WDW), 494
Biketoberfest (Daytona), 54
Bike Week (Daytona Beach), 50
Bill Baggs Cape Florida State Recreation Area, 8, 153
Billie Swamp Safari (Big Cypress Reservation), 259
Billy Bowlegs Festival (Fort Walton Beach), 52
Birds and bird watching, 71
Audubon of Florida—National Center for Birds of Prey (Maitland), 528
Corkscrew Swamp Sanctuary, 369
the Everglades, 239
Florida Keys Wild Bird Rehabilitation Center (Tavernier), 193, 194
Lower Keys, 205
Marco Island, 380–381
Merritt Island National Wildlife Refuge, 544
Pelican Man's Bird Sanctuary (St. Armands Key), 443
Sanibel Island, 12

Shell Key, 424
Suncoast Seabird Sanctuary (Indian Shores), 425
Biscayne Corridor (Miami), 96
Biscayne National Park, 248–251
Black Archives Research Center and Museum, 623, 655
Black College Reunion (Daytona Beach), 51
Blackwater River State Park, 12, 607
Blizzard Beach (WDW), 509–510
Blowing Rocks Preserve, 298
Blue Angels, 54, 55
Blue Hole, 205
Blues Brothers (Universal Orlando), 517
Boardwalk, The (Okaloosa Island), 621
Boating and boat rentals, 71. See also Canoeing; Kayaking
Amelia Island, 597
Broward County, 256
Clearwater Beach/St. Pete Beach area, 423
Destin/Fort Walton Beach, 621
the Everglades, 240
houseboat rentals, 243
Fort Myers Beach, 341–342
Islamorada, 191–192
Lower Keys, 205–206
Miami, 160
Naples, 369
Panama City Beach, 638
Sanibel and Captiva islands, 351–352
Sarasota area, 438
special events, 50, 54, 56
Upper and Middle Keys, 196
Walt Disney World, 530
Boat tours and cruises. See also Glass-bottom boat tours
Apalachicola, 648
Broward County, 256–257
casino cruises out of Port Everglades, 257
Cayo Costa, 365
Clearwater Beach/St. Pete Beach area, 423–424
Daytona Beach, 554

Boat tours and cruises *(cont.)*
  Destin/Fort Walton Beach, 621–622
  the Everglades, 241
  Fort Myers, 332–333
  Fort Myers Beach, 342
  Gasparilla Island, 364
  Jacksonville, 587
  John Pennekamp Coral Reef State Park, 195
  Jonathan Dickinson State Park, 307
  Key West, 217
  Marco Island, 381
  Miami, 157–158
  Naples, 370
  northern Palm Beach County, 296
  Panama City Beach, 638
  St. Armands Key, 443
  St. Augustine, 573–574
  Sanibel and Captiva islands, 351, 353, 363
  Sarasota area, 439
  Shell Island, 622, 638
  Tampa, 406
  Ybor City, 397
Bob Marley—A Tribute to Freedom (Orlando), 534–535
Boca Chita Key, 248, 250, 251
Boca Grande, 364
Boca Grande Lighthouse Museum and Visitor's Center, 364
Boca Raton, 272–281
  accommodations, 277–278
  nightlife, 280–281
  outdoor activities, 275
  restaurants, 279–280
  shopping, 277
  sights and attractions, 276
Boca Raton Museum of Art, 276
Body Wars (WDW), 499
Boneyard, The (Universal Orlando), 516
Boneyard, The (WDW), 506
Bongo's Cuban Café (WDW), 534
Bonnet House (Fort Lauderdale), 260
Bookstores
  Key West, 221–222
  Miami, 168
Boston Red Sox, 53, 333, 334
Botanical Garden, McKee (Vero Beach), 318
Botanical Garden, Miami Beach, 154
Botanical Gardens, Key West, 216
Botanical Gardens, Marie Selby (Sarasota), 442
Bowditch Regional Park, 341
Bowman's Beach (Sanibel), 350
Bradenton, 436, 437, 439–441, 443
Bradenton Beach, 438, 439, 447, 448, 453, 454
Briggs Nature Center (Marco Island), 18, 380
Britannia Square (WDW), 502
British Invasion (WDW), 502
British Night Watch & Grand Illumination Ceremony (St. Augustine), 56
Brokaw-McDougall House (Tallahassee), 655
Broward County, 253–272
  accommodations, 261–265
  beaches, 254, 256
  nightlife, 270
  outdoor activities, 256–259
  restaurants, 265–270
  shopping, 261
  spectator sports, 258
  traveling to, 253–254
  visitor information, 254
Buccaneer Bay (near St. Petersburg), 414
Bucket shops, 65
Burroughs Home (Fort Myers), 330–331
Burr's Berry Farms (Goulds), 161
Busch Gardens Tampa Bay, 13, 389, 392–396
  accommodations, 401
  restaurants near, 404–405
  shuttle service, 524
Bus travel, 86
Butterfly World (Coconut Creek), 260
Buzz Lightyear's Space Ranger Spin (WDW), 497

Cabbage Key, 363–365
Ca'd'Zan (Sarasota), 441
Caladesi Island State Park, 5, 394, 422
Caldwell Theatre (Boca Raton), 281
Calendar of events, 48–56

Calhoun Street Historic District (Tallahassee), 655
Calle Ocho Festival (Miami), 51
Caloosahatchee River, 328, 332–333
Camping, 72
  Anastasia State Park, 572–573
  best, 25
  Biscayne National Park, 251
  Boca Chita Key, 25
  Clewiston area, 324
  Collier Seminole State Park, 25
  Destin/Fort Walton Beach, 626–627
  Everglades National Park, 25, 243
  Fort Clinch State Park (Amelia Island), 597
  Fort DeSoto Park, 25, 423
  Fort Pickens (Pensacola), 606–607
  Henderson Beach State Park, 620–621
  Jonathan Dickinson State Park, 309
  Koreshan State Historic Site, 25
  Lower Keys, 208–209
  Myakka River State Park, 444
  St. Andrews State Park, 637
  Upper and Middle Keys, 200–201
  Vero Beach and Sebastian area, 321
Camp Jurassic (Universal Orlando), 520–521
Camp Minnie-Mickey (WDW), 507
Canada (WDW), 500
  restaurant, 480
Canaveral National Seashore, 5, 18, 72, 543–544, 548
Canoeing, 11, 72–73
  Biscayne National Park, 249–250
  Blackwater River State Park, 12
  the Everglades, 238, 239
  Fort Myers, 331–332
  John Pennekamp Coral Reef State Park, 195

INDEX

Jonathan Dickinson State Park, 304
Lower Keys, 206
Milton, 607
Naples, 369
northern Palm Beach County, 296
Sanibel and Captiva islands, 12, 352
Upper and Middle Keys, 196–197
Cape Canaveral, 539–540, 543, 545, 546, 548. *See also* Canaveral National Seashore; Kennedy Space Center
Captiva Island, 347–366. *See also* Sanibel and Captiva islands
Caribbean Gardens (Naples), 13, 372
Caro-Seuss-El (Universal Orlando), 518
Carousel of Progress, Walt Disney's (WDW), 497
Car racing, 51, 52
Daytona Beach, 49–50, 548
Car rentals, 69–70
money-saving tips, 40–41
Carry-on baggage restrictions, 63
Car travel, 66, 69–70, 87
safety tips for foreign visitors, 84–85
Casino Beach (Pensacola), 606
Casinos, cruises out of Port Everglades, 257
Castaway Creek (WDW), 508
Castillo de San Marcos National Monument (St. Augustine), 567–568
Catastrophe Canyon (WDW), 502
Cat in the Hat (Universal Orlando), 518
Cayo Costa State Park (off Captiva Island), 5, 17, 72, 332, 333, 363, 365
Celebration, 462
Centro Ybor (Ybor City), 394, 398, 400, 409
Channelside at Garrison Seaport (Tampa), 400
Character Greeting Trails (WDW), 507
Charles Hosmer Morse Museum of American Art (Winter Park), 528
China (WDW), 500
restaurant, 480

Christ Church (Pensacola), 610
Cigars
Key West, 221
Miami, 168–169
Ybor City (Tampa), 398, 400
Cincinnati Reds, 53, 440
Cinderella Castle (WDW), 495
Cinderella's Golden Carousel (WDW), 495
Circle of Life (WDW), 498
Cirque du Soleil (Downtown Disney), 535
Citrus Bowl Parade (Orlando), 56
CityJazz (Orlando), 535
CityWalk (Orlando), 534–536
Civic Arts Center (Vero Beach), 322
Civil War Soldiers Museum (Pensacola), 610
Clam Pass County Park, 368
Classical music
in Miami, 183
Orlando, 538
Clearwater/Clearwater Beach, 7, 419–425, 427–434
accommodations, 427–429
nightlife, 434
outdoor activities, 423–424
restaurants, 432, 434
sights and attractions, 424–425
transportation, 420
visitor information, 420
Clearwater Jazz Holiday, 54
Clearwater Marine Aquarium, 424
Clearwater Phillies, 415
Clearwater Public Beach (Pier 60), 422
Cleveland Indians, 53
Clewiston, 323–325
Climate, 47–48
Clyde & Seamore Take Pirate Island (SeaWorld), 523
Cocoa Beach, 539, 540, 544–550
Cocoa Beach Pier, 544
Coconut Grove, 97
accommodations, 116–117
restaurants, 136–138
shopping, 167, 168, 170
sights and activities, 145, 151–154
sports and outdoor activities, 160

Coconut Grove Arts Festival, 50
Coconut Grove Goombay Festival (Miami), 52
Coconut Grove Playhouse, 182
Coconuts Dolphin Tournament (Key Largo), 52
CocoWalk (Coconut Grove), 170
Collier Seminole State Park, 12, 25, 380, 381
Colonial Spanish Quarter (St. Augustine), 568
Colony Theater (South Beach), 184
Columbus Day Regatta (Miami), 54
Concert Association of Florida (CAF) (Miami), 183
Conservancy of Southwest Florida
Briggs Nature Center, 380
Naples Nature Center, 369
Consolidators, 65
Convoy Point (Biscayne National Park), 248–250
Coquina Beach, 438
Coral Gables, 97
accommodations, 117–118
nightlife, 182, 183, 185
restaurants, 138–141
shopping, 167–169, 172
sights and attractions, 151, 155, 159
sports and outdoor activities, 160, 162
tours, 159
Coral Sea Aquarium (Tarpon Springs), 433
Corkscrew Swamp Sanctuary (Naples), 17–18, 369
Cornell Fine Arts Museum (Orlando), 9, 529
Cortez Beach, 438
Country Bear Jamboree (WDW), 494
Coupons, 37
Crab tours (Marathon), 197
Crandon Park Beach (Key Biscayne), 4, 146
Crane Point Hammock (Marathon), 191
Cranium Command (WDW), 499–500
Credit and charge cards, 47, 84

Crescent Beach (Marco Island), 379
Cross Country Creek (WDW), 509
Cruises. See Boat tours and cruises
Crystal River area, 414–415
Cummer Museum of Art & Gardens (Jacksonville), 584
Curious George Goes to Town (Universal Orlando), 517
Customs regulations, 81–82
Cypress Gardens, 529

Daggerwing Nature Center (Boca Raton), 276
Dalí, Salvador, Museum (St. Petersburg), 413
Dance companies
　Miami, 184
　Orlando, 537–538
Dania/Dania Beach, 256, 258, 261
Day in the Park with Barney, A (Universal Orlando), 514–515
Daytona 500, 49–50
Daytona Beach, 7, 550–564
　accommodations, 558–561
　beaches, 553, 554
　museums and attractions, 556–558
　nightlife, 563–564
　restaurants, 561–563
　shopping, 558
　special events, 49–52, 54
　sports and outdoor activities, 554–556
　transportation, 552–553
　traveling to, 552
　visitor information, 552
Daytona Cubs, 555–556
Daytona Farmer's and Flea Market, 556
Daytona International Speedway/DAYTONA USA, 14, 553
Deerfield Beach, 257, 275, 277
Deerfield Island Park, 257
Delano Hotel (South Beach), 145
Delnor-Wiggins Pass State Park, 368–369
Delray Beach, 272, 274, 275–281
　sights and attractions, 276–277

DeMesa-Sanchez House (St. Augustine), 568
Design District (Miami), 96
DeSoto National Memorial (Bradenton), 443
Destin, 12, 52, 54, 618–636
　accommodations, 626–629
　finding addresses in, 620
　nightlife, 635–636
　outdoor activities, 621–625
　restaurants, 631–634
　time zone, 620
　transportation, 620
　traveling to, 619
　visitor information, 619
Detroit Tigers, 53
Diamond Horseshoe Saloon Revue & Medicine Show (WDW), 495
Diaspora Vibe Art Gallery (Miami), 149–150
Dinoland U.S.A. (WDW), 506
Dinosaur (WDW), 506
Disabilities, travelers with, 58
Discounts. See Money-saving tips
Discovery Cove, 525
Discovery Island Trails (WDW), 506
Disney–MGM Studios (WDW), 14
　attractions and shows, 502–505
　restaurants, 482–483
Disney–MGM Studios Backlot Tour (WDW), 502
DisneyQuest (WDW), 511
Dixie Theatre (Apalachicola), 651
Doctor Doom's Fearfall (Universal Orlando), 519
Dolphin Cove (SeaWorld), 523
Dolphin Research Center (Marathon), 11, 193–194
Dolphins, 5, 12, 73, 194, 339, 363, 370, 422, 522, 523, 543, 554, 574, 625, 626
　swimming with, 11, 156, 193, 194–195
Donald's Boat (S.S. Miss Daisy) (WDW), 496
Donaldson Reef, 306
Downtown Disney (WDW), 462
　nightlife, 534
　restaurants, 484–485

Driver's licenses, foreign, 81
Dubois Park, 296
Duck Tours of Tampa Bay, 397
Dudley Do-Right's Ripsaw Falls (Universal Orlando), 519
Dueling Dragons (Universal Orlando), 521
Dumbo the Flying Elephant (WDW), 495
Dunedin Blue Jays, 415
Du Pont Shell Collection (Boca Grande), 364

Earthquake—The Big One (Universal Orlando), 515
Earthwatch Institute, 73
East Martello Museum and Gallery (Key West), 214
Eatonville, 9, 529
Eco-adventures, 73
Ecotours, Cape Canaveral, 544–545
Eden Gardens State Park, 625
Edison, Thomas Alva, 13
Edison and Ford Winter Estates (Fort Myers), 56, 330
Edison Pageant of Light (Fort Myers), 49
Ed Smith Stadium (Sarasota), 440
Edward W. Ball Wakulla Springs State Park, 11, 623, 663
Eighth Voyage of Sindbad (Universal Orlando), 521
85th Street Beach (Miami Beach), 146
Electricity, 87
Ellen's Energy Adventure (WDW), 499
Ellenton, 443–445
Elliott Key, 248–251
Elliott Museum (Stuart), 307
Embassies and consulates, 87–88
Emergencies, 88
Entry requirements for foreign visitors, 80–81
Environmental Learning Center (Wabasso Island), 318
Epcot (WDW)
　attractions, 498–502
　restaurants, 479–481

INDEX

Epcot International Flower & Garden Festival (WDW), 51
Epcot International Food & Wine Festival (Orlando), 55
Epicure (Miami Beach), 145, 169
Epiphany Celebration (Tarpon Springs), 48
Episcopal Cemetery (Tallahassee), 655
Ernst Reef, 306
Escorted tours, 68–69
Estefan Enterprises (Miami Beach), 150
Estero Island. *See* Fort Myers Beach
Estero River, 331, 334
Estuarine Walk (Apalachicola), 649
E.T. Adventure (Universal Orlando), 515
E-tickets (electronic tickets), 65
Everglades Alligator Farm, 240
Everglades City
  accommodations, 243–245
  restaurants, 247–248
Everglades National Park, 11, 17, 45, 231–248
  accommodations in and near, 242–245
  camping, 25
  entrance fees, permits, and regulations, 236–237
  exploring, 237–238
  organized tours, 240–241
  outdoor activities, 238–239
  ranger programs, 237
  restaurants in and around, 245–248
  safety, 237
  seasons, 237
  shopping, 241–242
  sports and outdoor activities, 71, 72
  traveling to, 234–235
  visitor centers and information, 235–236
Everglades Seafood Festival (Florida City), 49
Expedia, 64
ExtraTERRORestrial Alien Encounter (WDW), 497

Fairchild Tropical Garden (South Miami), 154
Falls Shopping Center (Kendall), 171
Families with children
  best attractions for, 12–14
  information and resources, 61
  Sanibel and Captiva islands, 349
Fantasia Fairways (WDW), 510
Fantasia Gardens Miniature Golf (WDW), 510
Fantasmic! (WDW), 505
Fantasy Fest (Key West), 55
Fantasy in the Sky Fireworks (WDW), 498
Fantasyland (WDW), 495–496
  restaurants, 481–482
Fashions (clothing), Miami, 169, 172
FASTPASS (WDW), 493
FedEx Orange Bowl Classic (Miami), 48
Fernandina Beach (Amelia Island), 10, 594
Festival of States (St. Petersburg), 51
Festival of the Lion King (WDW), 507
Fiesta of Five Flags (Pensacola), 52
Fievel's Playland (Universal Orlando), 517
Film Festival, Miami, 49
Fishing, 73–74
  Apalachicola, 648
  Biscayne National Park, 250
  Boca Grande, 364
  Broward County, 257–258
  Cape Canaveral, 545
  Clearwater Beach/St. Pete Beach area, 423
  Daytona Beach, 554–555
  Destin/Fort Walton Beach, 12, 623–624
  the Everglades, 236–237, 239–240
  Fort Myers Beach, 342
  Fort Pierce, 312
  Hutchinson Island and Jensen Beach, 304–305
  Jacksonville, 587
  Key West, 219–220
  Lake Okeechobee, 323, 325
  Lower Keys, 206
  Miami, 160–162
  Naples, 370
  northern Palm Beach County, 296–297
  Orlando, 530
  Panama City Beach, 638–639
  Pensacola, 608
  St. Augustine, 574
  Sanibel and Captiva islands, 351–352
  Sarasota area, 439
  Tampa, 399
  Upper and Middle Keys, 197–198
  Vero Beach and Sebastian, 317
Fla. A1A, 8, 252
Flagler College (St. Augustine), 568–569
Flagler Museum (Palm Beach), 285–286
Flea markets
  Daytona, 556
  Fort Myers, 32, 334, 336
  Jacksonville, 588
  Pensacola, 612
  Stuart, 308
  Upper and Middle Keys, 198
FlexTicket (Orlando attractions), 392, 492, 514, 523, 527
Flights of Wonder (WDW), 508
Florida A&M University (Tallahassee), 623
Florida A&M University Art Gallery (Tallahassee), 623
Florida A&M University Rattlers, 658
Florida Aquarium (Tampa), 13, 396
Florida City, accommodations, 245
Florida Citrus Bowl (Orlando), 537
Florida Grand Opera (Miami), 184
Florida Heritage Museum at the Authentic Old Jail (St. Augustine), 570
Florida Holocaust Museum (St. Petersburg), 410
Florida International Museum (St. Petersburg), 412
Florida Keys Wild Bird Rehabilitation Center (Tavernier), 193, 194

Florida Marlins (North Miami Beach), 53, 165
Florida Oceanographic Coastal Center (Stuart), 307
Florida Panthers, 165–166, 258
Florida Philharmonic Orchestra (Miami), 183
Florida Seafood Festival (Apalachicola), 55
Florida's Gulfarium, 626
Florida Splendid China (Kissimmee), 525–526
Florida Springfest (Pensacola), 52
Florida State Fair (Tampa), 50
Florida State University Museum of Fine Arts (Tallahassee), 655
Florida State University (FSU) Seminoles, 658
Florida Studio Theatre (Sarasota), 455
Florida Symphonic Pops (Boca Raton), 281
Florida Times-Union Center for the Performing Arts (Jacksonville), 594
Flying Tigers Warbird Restoration Museum (Kissimmee), 526
Flying Unicorn (Universal Orlando), 521
Food (cuisine)
    picking your own produce, 161
    shopping for
        Miami, 169
        Robert Is Here, 242
        Vero Beach, 319
    Spanish menu items, 135
    special events, 49, 51, 54, 55
Food Rocks (WDW), 498
Football, 48
    Miami, 165
    Tampa, 399
Ford, Henry, 13
Foreign visitors, 80–90
Fort Barrancas (Pensacola), 608, 611
Fort Caroline National Memorial (Jacksonville), 549, 585–586
Fort Clinch (Amelia Island), 596–597
    State Park, 594, 596

Fort DeSoto Park, 394, 420, 423
Fort Lauderdale, 253
    accommodations, 261–265
    boating, 256
    gay and lesbian travelers, 272
    nightlife, 270–272
    shopping, 261
    special events, 52, 56
    tennis, 258–259
    traveling to, 254
    visitor information, 254
Fort Lauderdale Beach Promenade, 254, 256
Fort Lauderdale Stadium, 258
Fort Myers, 328–339
    accommodations, 336–338
    nightlife, 339
    restaurants, 338–339
    shopping, 335–336
    sights and attractions, 330–335
    transportation, 329–330
    traveling to, 328–329
    visitor information, 329
Fort Myers Beach, 6, 339–347
Fort Myers Historical Museum, 330
Fort Myers Miracle, 334
Fort Pickens (Pensacola), 606
Fort Pierce, 311–316
Fort Pierce Inlet State Recreation Area, 312
Fort Walton Beach, 618–622, 624, 625, 629–630, 634–636
    accommodations, 629–631
    beaches, 621
    nightlife, 636
    restaurants, 634–635
Fort Zachary Beach (Key West), 219
Foster Tanner Art Center (Tallahassee), 656
Fountain of Youth Archaeological Park (St. Augustine), 570–571
France (WDW), 500
Frank Brown International Songwriters' Festival (Pensacola), 55

Freedom Tower (Miami), 1, 153
Friday Fest Street Festival (Fort Pierce), 316
Friendship Fountain (Jacksonville), 585
Friendship Trail-Bridge (St. Petersburg), 413
Frommers.com, 62
Frontierland (WDW), 482, 494
FSU Ringling Center for the Cultural Arts (Sarasota), 9, 395, 441, 442
Funtastic World of Hanna-Barbera (Universal Orlando), 515
Future World (WDW), 498–500
    restaurant, 481

G

Gables Stage (Coral Gables), 182
Gamble Plantation (Ellenton), 443–444
Gambling, cruises out of Port Everglades, 257
Gardner's Market (South Miami), 169
Gasoline, 88
Gasparilla Island, 364
Gasparilla Island State Recreation Area, 364
Gasparilla Pirate Fest (Tampa), 49
Gator Bowl, Toyota (Jacksonville), 48, 588
Gatorland (Kissimmee), 526
Gay and lesbian travelers
    Fort Lauderdale, 272
    information and resources, 58–60
    Key West, 230
    Miami, 50, 55, 178–179
    Orlando, 52
Gay Weekend (Orlando), 52
Germany (WDW), 500–501
    restaurant, 480
Gilbert's House of Refuge Museum, 307
Glass-bottom boat tours
    Biscayne National Park, 251
    John Pennekamp Coral Reef State Park, 195
    Key West, 217
    Panama City Beach, 638

INDEX

Gold Coast, 45, 252–301
  exploring by car, 252
  what's new in, 1–2
Golden Apple Dinner Theatre (Sarasota), 455
Golden Orb Trail, 196
Golf, 74–75
  Amelia Island, 597
  best courses, 15–17
  Boca Raton, 15, 275
  Bradenton, 16
  Broward County, 258
  Clearwater, 429
  Cocoa Beach, 16–17
  Daytona Beach, 17, 555
  Destin/Fort Walton Beach, 624–625
  Fort Myers, 16, 333
  Hollywood, 15–16
  Jacksonville, 587–588
  Marco Island, 380
  Miami, 15, 162–163
  miniature, at Walt Disney World, 510
  Naples, 370–371
  Northeast Florida, 545
  northern Palm Beach County, 297–298
  Orlando, 16, 530
  package tours, 67
  Palm Beach, 15, 284
  Panama City Beach, 639
  Pensacola, 17, 608–609
  Port St. Lucie, 312
  St. Augustine, 573, 574
  St. Petersburg, 16, 414
  Sanibel and Captiva islands, 352
  Sarasota, 16, 395, 439–440
  Southwest Florida, 333
  Stuart, 305
  Tallahassee, 658
  Tampa, 16, 399
  tournaments, 49, 51
  Vero Beach and Sebastian, 317
  West Palm Beach, 15
Goodland Mullet Festival (Marco Island), 49
Gory, Gruesome & Grotesque Horror Make-up Show (Universal Orlando), 516
Government House Museum (St. Augustine), 568
Governor's Mansion (Tallahassee), 654
Grand Prix of Miami (Homestead), 51
Grayton Beach State Park, 621

Great Explorations (St. Petersburg), 412
Great Florida Birding Trail, 71
Great Movie Ride (WDW), 502–503
"Green flash" at sunset, 8, 334
Groove, the, 535
Guavaween, 55
Gulf Islands National Seashore, 5–6, 10, 26, 46, 602, 606–608, 611, 612, 621, 622
Gulfside City Park (Sanibel), 350
Gulfstream Park (Hallandale), 145, 165, 258
Gulf World Marine Park (Panama City Beach), 639
Gumbo Limbo Environmental Complex (Boca Raton), 276
Gumbo-Limbo Trail, 238
Gusman Center for the Performing Arts (Miami), 184–185
Gusman Concert Hall (Coral Gables), 185

Hale Indian River Groves (Vero Beach), 319
Halifax Historical Museum (Daytona Beach), 556
Hallandale, 253
Hall of Presidents (WDW), 495
Halloween, 54, 55
Harbor Branch Oceanographic Institution (Fort Pierce), 312–313
Hard Rock Cafe/Hard Rock Live (Orlando), 535
Harry P. Leu Gardens (Orlando), 18, 527–528
Harry S. Truman Little White House Museum (Key West), 213–214
Haulover Park Beach, 146, 162
Haunted Mansion (WDW), 495
Havana, 658–659
Hayrides, Walt Disney World, 530
Health insurance, for foreign visitors, 82–83
Helicopter rides, Daytona Beach, 555

Hell's Bay Canoe Trail, 239
Hemingway, Ernest, 188, 218, 363
  Home and Museum (Key West), 213
Henderson Beach State Park, 620–621
Henry B. Plant Museum (Tampa), 396–397
Hialeah Park, 165
Higgs Beach (Key West), 219
Hiking, 74
  Biscayne National Park, 250
  John Pennekamp Coral Reef State Park, 195
  Long Key State Recreation Area, 196
  Lower Keys, 206
  northern Palm Beach County, 298
  St. Petersburg, 413–414
  Tampa, 394
Historic Pensacola Village, 10, 610, 622
HIV-positive visitors, 81
Hobe Sound Wildlife Refuge, 306
Hobie Beach (Miami), 146
Holidays, 88
Hollywood, 6, 253
  accommodations, 262–264
  traveling to, 254
  visitor information, 254
Hollywood Beach, 254
Holmes Beach, 438
Holocaust Memorial (South Beach), 149
Homestead, accommodations, 245
Homestead Bayfront Park, 251
Homosassa Springs State Wildlife Park, 414
Honey I Shrunk the Audience (WDW), 498
Honeymoon Island State Recreation Area, 394, 422
Hoop-Dee-Doo Musical Revue (Orlando), 533
Horizon Outlet Center (Vero Beach), 319
Horseback riding
  Amelia Island, 597–598
  Daytona Beach, 555
  Jacksonville, 588
  Orlando/Walt Disney World, 530–531

INDEX

Horse racing
 Gulfstream Park (Hallandale), 165, 258
 Hialeah Park, 165
 Miami area, 165
 Tampa, 400
Hot-air ballooning, Martin County, 306–307
Houseboating, the Everglades, 243
House of Blues (WDW), 534
Houston Astros, 53
Humunga Kowabunga (WDW), 509
Hunchback of Notre Dame: A Musical Adventure (WDW), 503
Hutchinson Island, 304–309

Ice hockey, 165–166, 258
 Tampa, 399
If I Ran the Zoo (Universal Orlando), 518
IllumiNations (WDW), 502
Imaginarium (Fort Myers), 331
Imagination (WDW), 498
Immigration and customs clearance, 85–86
Incredible Hulk Coaster (Universal Orlando), 519
Indiana Jones Epic Stunt Spectacular (WDW), 503
Indian Key, 191
Indian River Citrus Museum (Vero Beach), 318
Indian River Mall (Vero Beach), 319
Indian Rocks Beach, 427, 428, 431
Indian Shores, 425, 432
Indian Temple Mound and Museum (Destin), 626
In-line skating, 70–71
 Miami, 163
 St. Petersburg, 413–414
 Sanibel Island, 351
 Sarasota area, 438
 Tallahassee, 657–658
 Tampa, 394, 398–399
Innoventions (WDW), 498
Insurance, 56–57
 car rental, 70
 for foreign visitors, 82–83
Intensity Water-Ski Show, 523
International Drive area (I-Drive), 462
 accommodations, 477–478
 attractions, 526–527
 restaurants, 488–489

International Museum of Cartoon Art (Boca Raton), 276
International visitors, 80–90
Islamorada, 189
 accommodations, 198–200
 nightlife, 203
 restaurants, 201–203
 sights and attractions, 192, 194–195
 visitor information, 190
Islands of Adventure (Universal Orlando), 517–522
 restaurants, 520
Isle of Eight Flags Shrimp Festival (Amelia Island), 51
Italy (WDW), 501
 restaurant, 480
It's a Small World (WDW), 495–496
It's Tough to Be a Bug! (WDW), 506

Jackie Gleason Theater of the Performing Arts (TOPA) (South Beach), 185
Jack Island State Preserve, 312
Jacksonville, 581–594
 accommodations, 589–591
 beaches, 587
 nightlife, 593–594
 outdoor activities, 587–588
 restaurants, 591–593
 shopping and browsing, 549, 588
 sights and attractions, 584–586
 spectator sports, 588
 transportation, 582, 584
 traveling to, 581–582
 visitor information, 582
Jacksonville Beach, 587
Jacksonville Jaguars, 588
Jacksonville Landing, 549, 584
Jacksonville Veterans Memorial Coliseum, 588, 593–594
Jacksonville Zoo, 584
Jai alai
 Broward County, 258
 Miami, 166
James W. Lee Park, 621
Japan (WDW)
 attractions, 501
 restaurants, 480

Jaws (Universal Orlando), 515
Jensen Beach, 304, 306, 308–311
Jerry Herman Ring Theatre (Coral Gables), 183
Jet-skiing, Miami, 160
Jetty Park (Port Canaveral), 312, 544, 545
Jim Henson's Muppet*Vision 3D (WDW), 503
Jimmy Buffett's Margaritaville (Orlando), 535–536
Jimmy Buffett's Margaritaville Cafe (Key West), 229–230
J. N. "Ding" Darling National Wildlife Refuge (Sanibel Island), 8, 17, 335, 348
Jogging
 Orlando, 531
 Sanibel Island, 351
John and Mable Ringling Museum of Art (Sarasota), 441
John D. MacArthur Beach, 295–296
John F. Kennedy Space Center (Cape Canaveral), 10, 14, 541–543
John Gorrie Museum State Park (Apalachicola), 649
John Gorrie State Museum, 622
John Pennekamp Coral Reef State Park, 193, 195
John's Pass Village and Boardwalk (Madeira Beach), 424, 425, 434
John U. Lloyd Beach State Park, 256
Jonathan Dickinson State Park, 11, 304, 306, 309
Journey into Your Imagination (WDW), 498
Journey to Atlantis (SeaWorld), 523
Julee Cottage Black History Museum (Pensacola), 610
Jungle Cruise (WDW), 494
Jupiter, 295–301
Jupiter Inlet Lighthouse, 299
Jurassic Park (Universal Orlando), 520–521
Jurassic Park Discovery Center (Universal Orlando), 521
Jurassic Park River Adventure (Universal Orlando), 521

INDEX

Kali River Rapids (WDW), 508
Kampong, The (Coconut Grove), 154
Kansas City Royals, 53
Kayaking, 72–73
   Amelia Island, 597
   Biscayne National Park, 249–250
   Captiva Island, 56
   Fort Myers, 331–332
   Key West, 220–221
   Lower Keys, 206
   Miami, 163
   Naples, 369
   Sanibel and Captiva islands, 12, 352
   Sarasota area, 440
   Shell Island, 638
   Upper and Middle Keys, 196–197
Kendall, 171
Kennedy Space Center (Cape Canaveral), 10, 14, 541–543
Ketchakiddie Creek (WDW), 508
Key Biscayne, 95–96, 145
   accommodations, 113–114
   restaurants, 134–135
   sights and attractions, 153, 154, 156–157
   sports and outdoor activities, 160, 162–164
Key Largo, 189
   accommodations, 198, 200
   restaurant, 201
   shopping, 198
   sights and activities, 195–197
   visitor information, 190
Key lime pie, 193, 221
Keys, the, 44, 186–230. *See also* Key West; Lower Keys; Upper and Middle Keys
   exploring by car, 188–189
   free and almost-free sights and activities, 192–193
Keys Factory Shops (Florida City), 241–242
Key West, 210–230
   accommodations, 222–226
   beaches, 218–219
   gay and lesbian travelers, 230
   nightlife, 229–230
   orientation, 212–213
   parking, 212
   restaurants, 226–229
   shopping, 221–222
   sights and attractions, 213–218
      literary attractions, 218
   special events, 48–50, 55
   sports and outdoor activities, 71
   sunset watching, 215
   tours, 213, 216–218
   transportation, 212
   traveling to, 211–212
   visitor information, 212
Key West Aquarium, 13, 214
Key West at SeaWorld 523
Key West Botanical Gardens, 216
Key West Cemetery, 214
Key West Dolphin Fest (SeaWorld), 523
Key West Lighthouse Museum (Key West), 214–215
Key West Literary Seminar, 48–49
Key West's Shipwreck Historeum, 215
Kilimanjaro Safaris (WDW), 507
Kingsley, Zephaniah, 582
   Plantation (Jacksonville), 586
Kissimmee, 462
   attractions, 525–526
Klassix Auto Attraction (Daytona Beach), 556–557
Knaus Berry Farm (the Redlands), 161
Knott House Museum (Tallahassee), 656
Kongfrontation (Universal Orlando), 515
Koreshan State Historic Site (near Fort Myers), 25, 331, 332, 334,
Kraken (SeaWorld), 524

La Casita (Ybor City), 398
Lake Buena Vista, 461–462
   accommodations, 472–473
   restaurants, 487–488
Lake Eola Park (Orlando), 9–10, 529–530
Lake Trail (Palm Beach), 284
Land, The (WDW), 498
   restaurant, 481
Lapidus, Morris, 150
Latin Quarter (Orlando), 536
Lauderdale-by-the-Sea, accommodations, 263–265
LaVilla Museum (Jacksonville), 584–585
Layton Trail, 196
Legal aid, 88–89
Legend of the Lion King (WDW), 496
Lemoyne Art Gallery (Tallahassee), 656
Liberty Square (WDW), 495
   restaurants, 482
Lido Key, 436, 438, 446
Lightner Museum (St. Augustine), 568
Lignumvitae Key, 191
Lion Country Safari (West Palm Beach), 285
Lipizzaner Stallions (Myakka City), 444
Liquor laws, 79
Little Havana (Miami), 7
   brief description of, 96–97
   nightlife, 177, 181, 182
   restaurants, 133–134
   shopping, 167, 169, 172
   sights and activities, 144
Living Seas (WDW), 499
Living with the Land (WDW), 498
Longboat Key, 436, 453
Long Key, 199–200
Long Key Canoe Trail, 196
Long Key State Park, 201
Long Key State Recreation Area, 196
Looe Key National Marine Sanctuary, 206
Lori Wilson Park, 544
Los Angeles Dodgers, 53, 318–319
Lost Continent (Universal Orlando), 521–522
Lover's Key State Park (Fort Myers Beach), 5, 17, 334, 339, 340, 343
Lowdermilk Park (Naples), 368
Lowe Art Museum (Coral Gables), 151
Lower Keys, 6, 204–210
Lower Keys Underwater Music Fest (Looe Key), 52, 54
Lowry Park Zoo (Tampa), 396
Lucy, A Tribute (Universal Orlando), 517
Lummus Park Beach (South Beach), 4–5, 146
Lynn Hall Memorial Park, 340–341
Lyric Theater (Stuart), 311

INDEX

McKee Botanical Garden (Vero Beach), 318
McLarty Treasure Museum (Vero Beach), 318
Maclay State Gardens (Tallahassee), 623, 657, 658
Madeira Beach, 423–425, 434
Mad Tea Party (WDW), 496
Maelstrom (WDW), 502
Magic Carpets of Aladdin (WDW), 494
Magic Kingdom (WDW), 14, 493–498
  restaurants, 481–482
Magic of Disney Animation (WDW), 503
Maharajah Jungle Trek (WDW), 508
Mail and post offices, 89
Main Beach (Amelia Island), 596
Main Street, USA (WDW), 494
Main Street Electrical Parade (WDW), 498
Main Street Pier (Daytona Beach), 554
Mallory Square (Key West), 192
Malls and shopping centers
  Boca Raton, 277
  Jacksonville, 588
  Miami, 170–171
  Orlando, 532
  St. Augustine, 575
  Tampa, 400
  Vero Beach, 319
Manatee County Public Beach, 438
Manatees, 73, 76, 241, 298, 304, 306, 307, 331, 332, 339, 396, 414–415, 443, 444, 524, 554
  Parker Manatee Aquarium (Bradenton), 444
Manatees: The Last Generation? (SeaWorld), 524
Mannequins Dance Palace (WDW), 533–534
Manucy Museum of St. Augustine History, 569
Many Adventures of Winnie the Pooh (WDW), 496
Mar-A-Lago (Palm Beach), 286
Marathon, 189, 190
  accommodations, 198, 199
  restaurant, 201

sights and activities, 190, 191, 193, 194
visitor information, 190
watersports, 196, 197
Marco Island, 12, 379–383
Mardi Gras at Universal Studios, 50
Marie Selby Botanical Gardens (Sarasota), 442
Marinelife Center of Juno Beach, 297
Marine Science Center (Daytona Beach), 557
Marjory Stoneman Douglas Biscayne Nature Center (Key Biscayne), 154–155
Marvel Super Hero Island (Universal Orlando), 518–519
Matheson Hammock Park Beach (South Miami), 4, 146, 157
Matheson House (Lignumvitae Key), 191
Maximo Gomez Park (Miami), 144
Mayfest (Destin), 52
Medical insurance, for foreign visitors, 82–83
Medical requirements for entry, 81
Meginnis-Monroe House (Tallahassee), 656
Mel Fisher Maritime Heritage Museum (Key West), 13, 215–216
Mel Fisher's Treasure Museum (Sebastian), 318
Memorial Sculpture Garden (Key West), 216
Men in Black Alien Attack (Universal Orlando), 515
Mermaid Sculpture (Miami Beach), 150
Merritt Island National Wildlife Refuge (Cape Canaveral), 18, 544, 548
Me Ship, The Olive (Universal Orlando), 519
Mexico (WDW)
  attractions, 501
  restaurants, 481
Miami, 44, 91–185
  accommodations, 102–119
  animal parks, 155–157
  area codes, 100
  arriving in, 91–92
  bars and lounges, 180–182
  beaches, 141–146
  business hours, 100

car rentals, 98–99
club and music scene, 172–180
curfew, 100
dance clubs, 172–176
doctors and dentists, 100
downtown, 144
  accommodations, 114, 116
  brief description of, 96
  nightlife, 1, 173, 175, 176, 178, 179, 183, 184
  restaurants, 130–133
  shopping, 167–170
driving rules, 99
emergencies, 100
finding addresses in, 94
free and almost-free sights and activities, 144–145
gay and lesbian travelers, 55, 178–179
Latin clubs, 176–178
laundry/dry cleaning, 101
layout of, 94
live music scene, 179–180
lost property, 101
neighborhoods, 94–97
newspapers and magazines, 101
nightlife and entertainment, 1, 172–185
  tips on, 174
parking, 99
parks and gardens, 153–155
performing arts, 182–185
pharmacies, 101
post offices, 101
radio, 102
restaurants, 1, 119–141
  late-night, 181
restrooms, 102
safety, 102
shopping, 166–172
sights and activities, 1, 141–159
  cruises and organized tours, 157–159
  for kids, 157
special events, 48–52, 54, 55
spectator sports, 164–166
sports and outdoor activities, 160–164
street maps, 94
taxes, 102
taxis, 99

theater, 182–183
time zone, 102
transportation, 97–99
visitor information, 93–94
weather conditions and forecasts, 102
what's new in, 1
Miami Art Museum at the Miami–Dade Cultural Center, 151
Miami Beach
accommodations, 110–113
beaches, 141, 144–145
brief description of, 44, 95
gay and lesbian travelers, 50
nightlife, 177, 180, 184, 185
Post Office, 150
restaurants, 127–129
Second Thursdays: Miami Beach Arts Night, 159
shopping, 169, 171, 172
special events, 50
sports and outdoor activities, 160–164
Miami Beach Botanical Garden, 154
Miami Beach Cultural Park, 1, 148
Miami Bookfair International, 55
Miami Chamber Symphony (Kendall), 183
Miami City Ballet, 184
Miami–Dade County Auditorium, 184
Miami Dolphins, 165
Miami Film Festival, 49
Miami Heat, 165
Miami International Airport (MIA), 91–92
accommodations near, 118–119
Miami International Boat Show, 50
Miami Metrozoo, 12–13, 155
Miami Museum of Science (Coconut Grove), 151–152
Miami Seaquarium (Key Biscayne), 12, 156
Miccosukee Indian Village, 240, 242, 247
Mickey's & Minnie's Country Houses (WDW), 496
Mickey's Not-So-Scary Halloween Party (WDW), 54
Mickey's Toontown Fair (WDW), 496
Middle Keys, 6

Midtown Beach (Palm Beach), 283
Milton, 607
Minnesota Twins, 53, 333–334
Miracle Mile (Coral Gables), 167, 168
Miracle Strip Amusement Park (Panama City Beach), 640
Mission: Space (WDW), 499
Mission of Nombre de Dios (St. Augustine), 571
Mission San Luís de Apalachee (Tallahassee), 656
Mizner Park (Boca Raton), 277
Mogul Mania, 509
Money matters, 47
for foreign visitors, 83–84
Money-saving tips, 36–43
accommodations, 41–42, 77–78
airfares, 63–66
air travel, 37, 40
car rentals, 40–41
nightlife, 44
restaurants, 42–43
$70-a-day premise, 36
sightseeing and activities, 43
theme parks, 43–44
Monkey Jungle (South Miami), 156
Montreal Expos, 53, 298
Mopeding, Key West, 219
Morikami Museum and Japanese Gardens (Delray Beach), 276
Morocco (WDW), 501
restaurant, 480
MOSH (Museum of Science & History of Jacksonville), 585
MOSI (Museum of Science and Industry) (Tampa), 14, 397
Mote Aquarium (St. Armands Key), 443
Motion (WDW), 534
Motown Cafe Orlando, 536
Mound Key (Fort Myers), 11–12, 331
Mound Key State Archeological Site, 331
Museum of Arts and Sciences (Daytona Beach), 557

Museum of Contemporary Art (MOCA) (North Miami), 152
Museum of Discovery & Science (Fort Lauderdale), 260
Museum of Fine Arts (St. Petersburg), 412
Museum of Florida History (Tallahassee), 656–657
Museum of Man in the Sea (Panama City Beach), 639–640
Museum of Natural History of the Florida Keys (Marathon), 191
Museum of Science & History of Jacksonville (MOSH), 585
Museum of Science and Industry (MOSI) (Tampa), 14
Music festivals, 52, 54, 55
Music stores, Miami, 171–172
Myakka River State Park, 444–445
Mystic Fountain (Universal Orlando), 521

Naples, 6–9, 366–378
accommodations, 373–375
nightlife, 378
restaurants, 375–378
sights and attractions, 368–372
transportation, 368
traveling to, 366
visitor information, 366, 368
window shopping, 372–373
Naples Beach, 5, 371
Naples Pier, 335, 368, 370, 371–372
Naples Players, 378
National Hurricane Center (Miami), 159
National Key Deer Refuge (Big Pine Key), 17, 205, 206
National Museum of Naval Aviation (Pensacola), 11, 610–611, 622
Natural Bridge Battlefield State Historic Site, 665
Nature Conservancy, 73
Naval Live Oaks Area, 607
Neptune Beach (Jacksonville), 587

New Capitol Building (Tallahassee), 623, 652
Newspapers and magazines, 79, 89
New Theater (Coral Gables), 183
New World Symphony (South Beach), 183
New York Mets, 53, 312
New York Yankees, 53, 399–400
NFL Experience (WDW), 510
Nickelodeon Studios (Universal Orlando), 515
Nightlife, 44
best, 33–35
Noble Hammock Canoe Trail, 239
North (Upper) Captiva, 365
Northeast Florida, 46, 539–601
free and almost-free sights and activities, 548–549
North Hill Preservation District (Pensacola), 609
North Lido Beach, 438
North Miami
nightlife, 176, 184
shopping, 168, 172
sights and attractions, 152, 155
North Miami Beach, 95
nightlife, 173, 176
restaurants, 129–130
shopping, 170–172
North Palm Beach County, 295–301
Northwest Florida, 46, 602–665
exploring by car, 602
free and almost-free sights and activities, 622–623
Norton Museum of Art (West Palm Beach), 286
Norway (WDW)
attractions, 501–502
restaurants, 481

Oasis, The (WDW), 505
O Canada! (WDW), 500
Ocean Beach (Jupiter), 296
Ocean Drive (South Beach), 144
Oceanfront Bandshell (Daytona Beach), 564
Oceanic Society, 73
Ocean Opry Show (Panama City Beach), 646
Okaloosa Area, Gulf Islands National Seashore, 621

Okaloosa Island, 621
Okeechobee, Lake, 6, 323–325
Old Bainbridge Road (Tallahassee), 657
Old Capitol (Tallahassee), 652, 654
Olde Naples, 335, 371–372
Oldest House (St. Augustine), 569
Oldest House/Wrecker's Museum (Key West), 216
Oldest Store Museum (St. Augustine), 569–570
Oldest Wooden Schoolhouse in the U.S.A. (St. Augustine), 570
Old Florida Museum (St. Augustine), 571
Old Hyde Park Village (Tampa), 400
Old St. Augustine Village Museum, 569
Oleta River State Recreation Area (North Miami), 155
One Fish, Two Fish, Red Fish, Blue Fish (Universal Orlando), 518
Opera
Miami, 184
Orlando, 537
Opera House (Sarasota), 455
Orange Bowl Classic, FedEx, 48
Orbitz, 64
Orlando, 45–46, 456–538. See also Walt Disney World; and specific neighborhoods and theme parks
accommodations, 465–478
attractions, 527–528
babysitters, 463
doctors and dentists, 463–464
downtown, 462
emergencies, 464
gay and lesbian travelers, 52
hospitals, 464
kennels, 464
layout of, 461
neighborhoods, 461–463
nightlife and entertainment, 532–538
outdoor activities, 530–531
package tours, 459–460
pharmacies, 464
photography, 464

post office, 465
restaurants, 478–490
seasons, 458
shopping, 532
special events, 50–52, 54, 55
transportation, 462–463
traveling to, 458–459
visitor information, 460–461
weather forecasts, 465
Orlando International Airport, 458
Orlando International Fringe Festival, 51
Orlando Magic, 531
Orlando Miracle, 531
Orlando Museum of Art, 528
Orlando Opera Company, 537
Orlando Philharmonic Orchestra, 538
Orlando Predators, 531
Orlando Rays, 531
Orlando Science Center, 528
Orlando–UCF Shakespeare Festival, 537
Outback Bowl (Tampa), 48

Pacific Point Preserve (SeaWorld), 525
Package tours, 67–68
Palafox Historic District (Pensacola), 609
Palm Beach, 8, 281–295. See also West Palm Beach
accommodations, 287–291
beaches, 283–284
outdoor activities, 284–285
restaurants, 291–293
shopping, 287
sights and attractions, 285–286
transportation, 282
traveling to, 282
visitor information, 282–283
Palm Beach Polo and Country Club, 283
Palm Beach Zoo at Dreher Park, 285
Palm Cottage (Naples), 372
Panama City Beach, 636–646
Pangani Forest Exploration Trail, 507
Parasailing, 196, 256, 285, 341, 353, 380, 423, 441, 625
Park Avenue Historic District (Tallahassee), 654–655

INDEX 683

Parker Manatee Aquarium (Bradenton), 444
Parrot Jungle and Gardens (Southern Miami–Dade County), 156
Pass-a-Grille Public Beach, 422
Passports, 80–81
Pat O'Brien's (Orlando), 536
Peabody Auditorium (Daytona Beach), 563–564
Peabody Ducks (International Drive), 526–527
Pelican Man's Bird Sanctuary (Sarasota), 395, 443
Penguin Encounter, 524
Pensacola, 10–11, 604–618
    accommodations, 612–615
    historic attractions, 609–612
    nightlife, 617–618
    outdoor activities, 608–609
    restaurants, 615–617
    sights and activities, 606–612, 622
    special events, 52, 54, 55
    time zone, 606
    transportation, 605–606
    traveling to, 604
    visitor information, 604
Pensacola Beach, 606
Pensacola Historical Museum, 611
Pensacola Lighthouse, 611
Pensacola Museum of Art, 612
Pepsi 400 (Daytona), 52
Peter Pan's Flight (WDW), 496
Peters Point Beach Front Park (Amelia Island), 596
Petrol, 88
Pets, 72
Petty, Richard, Driving Experience (WDW), 511–512
Petty, Richard, Driving Experience Ride-Along Program (Daytona Beach), 553–554
Philadelphia Phillies, 53, 415
Philharmonic Center for the Arts (Naples), 378
Phipps Ocean Park (Palm Beach), 284
Pier, The (St. Petersburg), 412, 416
Pigeon Key, 193
Pineapple Grove (Boca Raton), 277
Pine Island, 331
Pinellas Trail, 71, 413
Pirates of the Caribbean (WDW), 494
Pittsburgh Pirates, 53, 440
Plant, Henry B., Museum (Tampa), 396–397
Playalinda Beach, 543–544, 548
Playhouse Disney—Live on Stage! (WDW), 503
Playmobil Fun Park (Palm Beach), 13, 286
Pleasure Island (WDW), 533
Pleasure Island Jazz Company (WDW), 534
Polynesian Luau Dinner Show (Orlando), 533
Pompano Beach, 258, 264, 268, 270
Pompano Park Racing, 258
Ponce de León Inlet Lighthouse & Museum (Daytona Beach), 554, 557–558
Ponte Vedra Beach (Jacksonville), 587
Popeye & Bluto's Bilge-Rat Barges (Universal Orlando), 519
Port of Entry (Universal Orlando), 518
Port St. Lucie, 311–316
Poseidon's Fury (Universal Orlando), 522
Priceline, 64
Prime Outlets at Florida City, 198
Primeval Whirl (WDW), 506
Pro Player Stadium (North Miami Beach), 165
Pteranodon Flyers (Universal Orlando), 521

Qixo, 64
Quietwater Boardwalk (Pensacola), 606

Rafiki's Planet Watch (WDW), 507
Rapids Water Park (West Palm Beach), 285
Raymond F. Kravis Center for the Performing Arts (West Palm Beach), 295
Raymond James Stadium (Tampa), 409
Rental properties, 78
Restaurants
    best, 26–33
    money-saving tips, 42–43
Restrooms, 90
Ribault Monument (Jacksonville), 586
Richard Petty Driving Experience (WDW), 511–512
Richard Petty Driving Experience Ride-Along Program (Daytona Beach), 553–554
Rickenbacker Causeway (Key Biscayne), 160
Ringling Museum of the Circus (Sarasota), 441
Ripley's Believe It or Not! Museum (St. Augustine), 571–572
Ripley's Believe It or Not! Odditorium (International Drive), 527
Ritz Theatre & LaVilla Museum (Jacksonville), 584–585, 594
Robbie's Pier (Islamorada), 192, 194
Rock 'n' Roll Beach Club (WDW), 534
Rock 'n' Roller Coaster (WDW), 503–504
Roger Dean Stadium (Jupiter), 298
Rubell Family Art Collection (Miami), 152
Runoff Rapids (WDW), 509
Ruth Eckerd Hall (Clearwater), 434

Saenger Theatre (Pensacola), 617
Safari Village (WDW), 505–506
Safety, 79
    for foreign visitors, 84–85
Sailing (yachting), 71
    Amelia Island, 597
    Destin/Fort Walton Beach, 625
    Miami, 163
    Pensacola, 609
    St. Augustine, 574
    St. Petersburg, 414–415
    Sanibel and Captiva islands, 352–353
    Sarasota area, 440
St. Andrews State Park, 6, 10, 26, 72, 622, 637, 641
St. Armand's Circle (Sarasota), 395
St. Armands Key, 436, 443, 445, 450–452

St. Augustine, 10, 549, 564–581
   accommodations, 575–578
   beaches, 572–573
   nightlife, 580–581
   outdoor activities, 573–575
   restaurants, 578–580
   sights and attractions, 567–572
   special events, 52, 56
   transportation, 566–567
   traveling to, 564
   visitor information, 566
   window-shopping, 575

St. Augustine Alligator Farm and Zoological Park, 572
St. Augustine Beach, 572
St. Augustine Lighthouse & Museum, 571
St. Augustine Outlet Mall, 575
St. George Island State Park, 72, 646, 647
St. Louis Cardinals, 53, 298
St. Marks, 664–665
St. Marks Lighthouse and National Wildlife Refuge, 18, 664–665
St. Pete Beach, 7, 419–420, 422
   accommodations, 425–427
   nightlife, 434
   restaurants, 430
   transportation, 420
   visitor information, 420

St. Petersburg, 409–419
   accommodations, 416–418
   nightlife, 419
   organized tours, 413
   outdoor activities, 413–416
   restaurants, 418–419
   shopping, 416
   sights and attractions, 410–413
   spectator sports, 415–416
   transportation, 410
   traveling to, 409–410
   visitor information, 410

St. Vincent National Wildlife Refuge (Apalachicola), 18, 647–648
Salvador Dalí Museum (St. Petersburg), 413
Sand Key, 420, 429
Sand Key Park, 394, 420, 422
Sanibel and Captiva islands, 8, 347–366
   accommodations, 354–358
   beaches, 350
   free and almost-free sights and activities, 335
   nearby island hopping, 363–366
   nightlife, 362–363
   parks and nature preserves, 348–350
   restaurants, 358–362
   shopping and browsing, 353–354
   sights and attractions, 348–353
   special events, 50, 56
   tours, 349, 351, 352
   transportation, 348
   traveling to, 348
   visitor information, 348

Sanibel Historical Village & Museum, 353
Sanibel Lighthouse, 350, 353
Sanibel Shell Fair, 50
San Marcos de Apalache Historic State Park, 664
San Marco Square (Jacksonville), 588
Santa Rosa Island, 606
Sarasota, 434–455
   accommodations, 445–448
   nightlife, 454–455
   restaurants, 448–454
   shopping, 445
   sights and attractions, 441–443
   spectator sports, 440–441
   transportation, 437
   traveling to, 436–437
   visitor information, 437

Sarasota Classic Car Museum, 442
Sarasota Jungle Gardens, 442
Sarasota Polo Club, 441
Sarasota Red Sox, 440
Savannahs Recreation Area (Fort Pierce), 313
Sawgrass Mills (Sunrise), 171, 261
Scuba diving, 75–76
   Biscayne National Park, 250
   Boca Raton, 275
   Broward County, 258
   Clearwater, 424
   Destin/Fort Walton Beach, 625
   Fort Myers Beach, 342
   Hutchinson Island, 305–306
   Key West, 219
   Lower Keys, 206–207
   Marco Island, 380
   Miami, 163
   Naples, 371
   northern Palm Beach County, 298
   Palm Beach, 284
   Panama City Beach, 639
   Pensacola, 609
   Upper and Middle Keys, 197

Sea Grass Adventures (Key Biscayne), 156–157
Seaside, 619, 621, 635
Seaside Music Theater (Daytona Beach), 564
Seasons, 36, 47
Sea Turtle Point (SeaWorld), 523
Sea turtles, 194, 196, 197, 256, 276, 297, 306, 424, 523, 548, 550, 553, 557, 639
SeaWorld (Orlando), 14, 459, 522–525
Sebastian, 316–323
Sebastian Inlet (North Hutchinson Island), 5, 317, 321, 545
Security measures, air travel, 62
Seminole Gulf Railway, 331
Seniors, 60
Seuss Landing (Universal Orlando), 518
Seven-Mile Bridge, 192–193
Seville Historic District (Pensacola), 609, 612, 617–618
Shamu Adventure (SeaWorld), 524
Shamu's Happy Harbor (SeaWorld), 524
Shark Reef (WDW), 509
Shark Valley (Everglades National Park), 160, 235, 237–238
Shell Air & Sea Show (Fort Lauderdale), 52
Shelling
   in Sanibel and Captiva islands, 8, 335, 350–351
Shell Island, 622, 637–638
Shell Key, 424
Shipwreck Historeum, Key West's, 215
Shipwreck Island Water Park (Panama City Beach), 640
Shops at Sunset Place (South Miami), 171
Sierra Club, 73

INDEX

Siesta Key, 436, 446–447, 452
Siesta Key Public Beach, 438
Siesta Village, 438
Sightseeing and activities, money-saving tips, 43
Silver Sands Factory Stores (between Destin and Sandestin), 626
Ski-Patrol Training Camp (WDW), 509
Sky diving, 324
Smathers Beach (Key West), 219
Snorkeling, 75–76
   Biscayne National Park, 250
   Boca Raton, 275
   Destin/Fort Walton Beach, 625
   Fort Myers Beach, 342
   Hutchinson Island, 305–306
   John Pennekamp Coral Reef State Park, 193
   Key West, 219
   Lower Keys, 206–207
   with manatees (near Homosassa Springs), 415
   Miami, 163
   northern Palm Beach County, 298
   Panama City Beach, 639
   Pensacola, 609
   Shell Island, 638
   Upper and Middle Keys, 197
Snow Stormers (WDW), 510
Snow White's Scary Adventures (WDW), 496
Sombrero Beach (Marathon), 190
Sounds Dangerous Starring Drew Carey (WDW), 504
Southbank Riverwalk (Jacksonville), 585
South Beach (Miami), 94–95
   accommodations, 104–110
   Art Deco District, 147–150
   nightlife, 174–185
   restaurants, 119–127
   shopping, 167–170
   sports and outdoor activities, 160, 163, 164
South Beach Park Beach (Boca Raton), 274, 317
Southern Ballet Theatre (Orlando), 537–538
Southern Glades Trail (Everglades National Park), 238–239

Southern Miami-Dade County, 97
Southern Walton County, 621
South Florida Museum (Bradenton), 444
South Lido Beach Park, 438
South Miami
   nightlife, 178, 180
   restaurants, 141
   shopping, 169, 171
   sights and attractions, 151, 154–156
Southwest Florida, 45, 326–383
   excursions to the Everglades and Key West, 326, 328
   free and almost-free sights and activities, 334–335
   traveling to, 326
   what's new in, 2
Space Mountain (WDW), 497
Spaceship Earth (WDW), 499
Space Transit Planetarium (Coconut Grove), 151–152
Spanish Military Hospital (St. Augustine), 570
Spanish Monastery Cloisters (North Miami Beach), 152
Spanish Night Watch Ceremony (St. Augustine), 52
Spanish Quarter (St. Augustine), 10, 56, 549, 564, 568
Spanish River Park Beach (Boca Raton), 274
SpectroMagic (WDW), 498
Speedweeks (Daytona), 49
Splash Mountain (WDW), 495
Sponge Docks (Tarpon Springs), 433
Sponge Exchange (Apalachicola), 648
Spongeorama (Tarpon Springs), 9, 395, 433
Spring Bayou (St. Pete Beach), 433
Spring Break, 50
Springtime Tallahassee, 51
Star Tours, 504
Stingray Lagoon (SeaWorld), 523
Stone crabs, 246
Storm Force Accelatron (Universal Orlando), 519
Stranahan House (Fort Lauderdale), 260–261
Streets of Mayfair (Coconut Grove), 170–171

Stuart, 304–311
Sugarloaf Bat Tower, 192, 206
Sugarloaf Key, 208, 209
Summit Plummet (WDW), 510
Suncoast Seabird Sanctuary (Indian Shores), 394–395, 425
Sunfest (West Palm Beach), 51
Sunken Gardens (St. Petersburg), 413
Sunny Isles, 95. See also Miami Beach
Surfing
   Cocoa Beach, 545
   Labor Day Pro-Am Surfing Festival (Cocoa Beach), 54
   Sebastian, 317
   Typhoon Lagoon (WDW), 509
Surfside, 95. See also Miami Beach
Swamp buggy rides, 332, 544
Swimming. See also Beaches
   Biscayne National Park, 251
   with manatees (near Homosassa Springs), 415
   Miami, 164
   Orlando, 531

Tallahassee, 651–665
   accommodations, 659–661
   historic districts, 654–655
   nightlife, 662–663
   outdoor activities, 657–658
   restaurants, 661–662
   shopping, 658–659
   side trips from, 663–665
   sights and attractions, 652–657
   spectator sports, 658
   transportation, 652
   traveling to, 651–652
   visitor information, 652
Tallahassee–Leon County Civic Center, 662
Tampa, 385–409
   accommodations, 400–404
   nightlife, 408–409
   organized tours, 398
   outdoor activities, 398–399
   restaurants, 404–408
   shopping, 400
   special events, 49, 50, 55

686 INDEX

Tampa (cont.)
   transportation, 388–389
   traveling to, 385, 388
   visitor information, 388
Tampa Bay area, 2, 45, 384–455
   free and almost-free sights and activities, 394–395
Tampa Bay Buccaneers, 399
Tampa Bay Devil Rays (St. Petersburg), 53, 415
Tampa Bay Downs, 400
Tampa Bay Lightning, 399
Tampa Bay Performing Arts Center, 409
Tampa Bay Visitor Information Center, 388
Tampa Museum of Art, 397
Tampa Theatre, 409
Tampa Yankees, 400
Tarpon Bay Road Beach (Sanibel), 350
Tarpon Springs, 433
Tarzan Rocks! (WDW), 506
Taxes, 79
TD Waterhouse Centre (Orlando), 537
Teamboat Springs (WDW), 510
Teddy Bear Museum (Naples), 13, 372
Ted Williams Museum & Hitters Hall of Fame (near Hernando), 415
Telephones, 89–90
Temperatures, average, 48
Tennis, 76
   Boca Raton/Delray Beach, 275
   Bradenton, 441
   Broward County, 258–259
   Miami, 164
   Naples, 371
   northern Palm Beach County, 298
   package tours, 67
   Palm Beach, 284
   St. Petersburg, 416
   Sanibel and Captiva islands, 352
   Vero Beach and Sebastian, 317
   Walt Disney World, 531
Ten Thousand Islands area, 236
Terminator 2: 3-D Battle Across Time (Universal Orlando), 515–516
Terrors of the Deep (SeaWorld), 524

Test Track (WDW), 499
Texas Rangers, 53, 334–335
Theater
   Daytona Beach, 564
   Miami, 182–183
   Orlando, 537
   Tampa, 409
Theater of the Sea (Islamorada), 194–195
Theatre Works (Sarasota), 455
Theft of wallet or credit cards, 47
Thelonious Monk Institute of Jazz (Orlando), 535
Theme parks, money-saving tips, 43–44
Theodore Roosevelt Area (Jacksonville), 586
Thomas J. White Stadium (Port St. Lucie), 312
Tigertail Public Beach (Marco Island), 380
Tike's Peak (WDW), 510
Timekeeper (WDW), 497
Time zones, 90
Timucuan Ecological and Historic Preserve (Jacksonville), 10, 549, 582, 585–586
Tipping, 90
Titanic—Ship of Dreams (International Drive), 527
Toilets, public, 90
Tomorrowland (WDW), 496–498
   restaurants, 481
Tomorrowland Indy Speedway (WDW), 497
Tom Sawyer Island (WDW), 495
Toon Lagoon (Universal Orlando), 519
Toon Trolley Beach Bash (Universal Orlando), 519
TOPA (Jackie Gleason Theater of the Performing Arts) (South Beach), 185
Toronto Blue Jays, 53, 415
Tours
   escorted, 68–69
   package, 67–68
Town Center (Jacksonville), 587
Town Center Mall (Boca Raton), 277
Toyota Gator Bowl (Jacksonville), 48, 588
Trails of Margaritaville (Key West), 217
Train travel, 66–67, 70, 86

Transportation, 69–70
   for foreign visitors, 86–87
Traveler's checks, 83–84
Travel insurance, 56–57
Travelocity, 64
Treasure Coast, 45, 302–325
   transportation, 303
   traveling to, 303
Treasure Island, 420, 434
Tree of Life (WDW), 505
Triceratops Discovery Trail (Universal Orlando), 521
TriceraTop Spin (WDW), 506
Trinity Episcopal Church (Apalachicola), 648
Tropical Rain Forest (SeaWorld), 525
Tropicana Field (St. Petersburg), 415, 419
Truman, Harry S., Little White House Museum (Key West), 213–214
T. T. Wentworth Jr. Florida State Museum (Pensacola), 610
Turner Beach (Sanibel), 350
Turtle Beach, 438
Turtles, sea, 194, 196, 197, 256, 276, 297, 306, 424, 523, 548, 550, 553, 557, 639
Twilight Zone Tower of Terror (WDW), 504
Twister . . . Ride It Out (Universal Orlando), 516
Typhoon Lagoon (WDW), 508–509

UDT-SEAL Museum (Underwater Demolition Team Museum) (Fort Pierce), 313
Union Bank Museum (Tallahassee), 654
United Kingdom (WDW)
   attractions, 502
   restaurant, 480
Universal Orlando, 14, 459, 512–522
   best times to visit, 512–513
   CityWalk, 534–536
   operating hours, 513
   parking, 512
   planning your trip, 512
   restaurants, 485–487, 516
   strollers/wheelchairs, 512
   ticket prices, 513–514

INDEX 687

traveling to, 512
visitor information, 460
Universal Studios (Orlando), 50
Universal Studios Florida, 514–517
Universe of Energy (WDW), 499
Upper and Middle Keys, 189–204
   accommodations, 198–201
   camping, 200–201
   nightlife, 203–204
   restaurants, 201–203
   shopping, 198
   sights and activities, 190–196
   traveling to, 189–190
   visitor information, 190
   water sports, 196–198
Upper (North) Captiva, 365
U.S. 192/Kissimmee area, accommodations, 473–477
U.S. Air Force Armament Museum (near Destin), 11, 622, 626
U.S.A.—The American Adventure (WDW), 500
Useppa Island, 365–366
USF Sun Dome (Tampa), 409

Van Wezel Performing Arts Hall (Sarasota), 455
Vero Beach, 316–323
Versace Mansion (South Beach), 150
Vietnam Memorial (Pensacola), 609–610
Vietnam Veterans Memorial (Tallahassee), 654
Vilano Beach (St. Augustine), 572
Virginia Key, 145
Visas, 80–81
Visitor information, 46
Vizcaya Museum and Gardens (Coconut Grove), 152–153
Voyage of the Little Mermaid (WDW), 504

Wabasso Island, 317, 318
Wakulla Springs, 11, 623, 663–664
Walt Disney's Carousel of Progress (WDW), 497
Walt Disney World (WDW), 45–46, 456–512. *See also* Orlando; *and specific theme parks, areas, rides, and attractions*
   accommodations, 465, 468–472
   auctions, 531
   best times to visit, 491
   layout of, 461
   money-saving tips, 471
   nightlife and entertainment, 532–538
   operating hours, 492
   parades and fireworks, 497–498
   parking, 491
   passes and coupons, 492
   resorts, 469–472
   restaurants at, 483–484
   restaurants, 478–485
     with Disney characters, 485
     Disney–MGM Studios, 482–483
     Disney resorts, 483–484
     EPCOT, 479–481
     Magic Kingdom, 481–482
     priority seating (reservations), 478–479
     tips on, 479
   Ride-Share program, 497
   special events, 51, 52, 54–56
   sports and outdoor activities, 530–531
   strollers/wheelchairs, 491
   tickets, 492–493
   tips for visiting attractions, 490–493
   transportation, 463
   visitor information, 460, 490–491
   water parks, 508–510
   what's new in, 2–3
Walt Disney World Festival of the Masters, 55
Walt Disney World Railroad, 494
Water and Dolphin Exploration Program (WADE) (Miami), 156
Water Mania (Kissimmee), 526

Water sports
   Clearwater Beach/St. Pete Beach area, 423
   Daytona Beach, 556
   Destin/Fort Walton Beach, 625
   the Keys, 196
   Marco Island, 380
   Naples, 371
   Palm Beach County, 285
   Pensacola, 609
   St. Augustine, 574–575
   Sanibel and Captiva islands, 353
   Sarasota area, 441
Water Works (WDW), 508
Watson Hammock Trail, 205
Websites, travel-planning and booking, 64
Weeki Wachee Spring Water Park (near St. Petersburg), 414
Weissmuller, Johnny, 11, 623, 663
West Miami, 162, 171, 177
   accommodations near, 118–119
   restaurants, 141
West Palm, outdoor activities, 284–285
West Palm Beach, 282
   accommodations, 287–290
   nightlife, 293–295
   restaurants, 291–293
   shopping, 287
   sights and attractions, 285, 286
Wet 'n Wild (International Drive), 527
White Party Week (Miami), 55
White-Water Rides (WDW), 509
Who Wants to Be a Millionaire—Play It! (WDW), 504
Wide World of Sports (WDW), 510–511
Wild, Wild, Wild West Stunt Show (Universal Orlando), 516
Wild Arctic (SeaWorld), 524
Wildlife Drive (Sanibel-Captiva), 8, 335, 348–349
Williams, Ted, Museum & Hitters Hall of Fame (near Hernando), 415
Williams, Tennessee, 218
Windsurfing
   Miami, 164
   Naples, 371

Winterfest Boat Parade (Fort Lauderdale), 56
Winter Park, 462
Winter Party (Miami Beach), 50
Winter Summerland (WDW), 510
Wolfsonian–Florida International University (South Beach), 149
Wonders of China (WDW), 500
Wonders of Life (WDW), 499
Woody Woodpecker's Nuthouse Coaster (Universal Orlando), 516
World Chess Hall of Fame and Sidney Samole Chess Museum (South Miami), 151
World Golf Hall of Fame (St. Augustine), 573
World Golf Village (St. Augustine), 573
World Showcase (WDW), 498, 500–502
  restaurants, 479–481
World's Richest Tarpon Tournament (Boca Grande), 52

Ybor City, 384, 394
  accommodations, 401
  restaurants, 407–408
  sights and attractions, 397–398
  visitor information, 388
Ybor City Brewing Company, 398
Ybor City State Museum (Tampa), 398

Zephaniah Kingsley Plantation (Jacksonville), 549, 586

Zoos
  Caribbean Gardens (Naples), 372
  Jacksonville, 584
  Lowry Park Zoo (Tampa), 396
  Palm Beach Zoo at Dreher Park, 285
  Panama City Beach, 640
  Pensacola, 612
  St. Augustine Alligator Farm and Zoological Park, 572
ZooWorld Zoological & Botanical Park (Panama City Beach), 14, 640
Zora Neale Hurston Festival of the Arts and Humanities (Eatonville), 49
Zora Neale Hurston National Museum of Fine Arts (Eatonville), 9, 529